EAST AND WEST
OF SUEZ

EAST AND WEST
OF SUEZ

The Suez Canal in History

1854–1956

BY

D. A. FARNIE

CLARENDON PRESS · OXFORD

1969

Oxford University Press, Ely House, London W. 1

GLASGOW   NEW YORK   TORONTO   MELBOURNE   WELLINGTON
CAPE TOWN   SALISBURY   IBADAN   NAIROBI   LUSAKA   ADDIS ABABA
BOMBAY   CALCUTTA   MADRAS   KARACHI   LAHORE   DACCA
KUALA LUMPUR   SINGAPORE   HONG KONG   TOKYO

PRINTED IN GREAT BRITAIN
AT THE UNIVERSITY PRINTING HOUSE, CAMBRIDGE
(BROOKE CRUTCHLEY, UNIVERSITY PRINTER)

ACKNOWLEDGEMENTS

Any study of the history of the Suez Canal must make use of the work of other historians of the subject. This particular study has had the advantage of having a large number of forerunners. I would therefore like to acknowledge my own debt to all those scholars whose work I have used and, among the illustrious dead, to the engineer Voisin Bey who wrote the history of the Canal as well as building it. The Compagnie Financière de Suez permitted me to consult their Bulletin, *Le Canal de Suez*, in their London offices but are not responsible for any personal opinion expressed in the following pages.

For help in my research I am indebted to three Librarians, Harold Smith, John Perry and Dr. F. W. Ratcliffe as well as to the staff of the Central Library, Manchester. In the analysis of statistics I have been willingly aided by Professor K. S. Lomax. For permitting me to consult off-prints of their published work I am grateful to Professors J. P. C. Roach, R. L. Tignor and C. L. Robertson as well as to Dr. Giulio Cervani. I have been helped in other ways by Professors M. Arkin, C. F. Beckingham, K. A. Ballhatchet and M. F. Cunliffe as well as by Dr. W. H. Chaloner, Dr. J. R. Harris, Dr. J. R. Western, and Mr. Frank Stoakes.

CONTENTS

Contents

LIST OF GRAPHS

LIST OF STATISTICAL TABLES

LIST OF MAPS

PART 1

THE CANAL OF THE TWO SEAS
1854-1869

I

THE CONFLICT OF EAST AND WEST

OUT of the dream-world of Europe in the 1830s one dream crystallized into reality. The dream was the union of East and West, the reality was the Suez Canal. Suez became a half-way house on the overland route to India from the 1830s and a gate between two worlds from the 1880s: thenceforward it remained a focus of the world-conquering economic ethos of Europe. The relationship between East and West maintained the pattern inherited from the preceding 2400 years, one of conflict more than of co-operation. The first great clash between the two worlds, the war of the Persians against the Greeks, had inspired Herodotus to create the idea of an East–West antithesis and to project that antithesis backwards in time as far as the siege of Troy.[1] Thereafter the Greeks, the Romans and the Crusaders had sought from their bases in the West to extend their dominion over all the known world but had each failed to subdue the East:

> The East bowed low before the blast,
> In patient deep disdain;
> She let the legions thunder past,
> Then plunged in thought again.[2]

The Mediterranean was the theatre of those successive contests and remained divided after the fall of Rome. It was not fully reunited by the spread of Islam under either the Arabs or the Turks. The Ottoman expansion however advanced the frontier of Asia to the Balkans while the expansion of Europe into the Atlantic after the voyage of da Gama created a new dividing-line between East and West at the Cape of Good Hope. The economic conquest of the coastlands of Asia was begun by the Portuguese and the Dutch and completed during the commercial revolution of the mid-eighteenth century[3] through the export of opium by the English East India Company from Bengal to China in exchange for tea and porcelain. France failed under Dupleix to establish an empire in India but began the cultural conquest of Asia through Anquetil-Duperron's translation in 1771 of the *Zend-Avesta*, the first work to be independent of both the Biblical and classical traditions of Oriental scholarship.[4]

---

[1] A. J. Toynbee, *A Study of History* (London, Oxford University Press, 1954), viii. 708–710, '"Asia" and "Europe": Facts and Fantasies'.

[2] Matthew Arnold, 'Obermann Once More' (1867).

[3] H. Furber, *John Company at Work. A Study of European Expansion in India in the Late Eighteenth Century* (Cambridge, Harvard University Press, 1948), 161–2.

[4] R. Schwab, *La Renaissance Orientale* (Paris, Payot, 1950), 25, 176.

The cultural expansion of France reached its climax during the Revolutionary Wars. Bonaparte's Egyptian expedition of 1798 was intended as the French response to the British occupation of the Cape in 1795 and was directed against India, the keystone of the British Empire since the revolt of the American colonies. It destroyed French trade throughout the Levant but shattered the power of the Mamelukes, the great military élite of Islam. J. M. Lepère made the first survey of the isthmus of Suez in 1799 in accordance with Bonaparte's instructions to secure the free and exclusive use of the Red Sea to the French Republic. The publication in 1809 of Lepère's memorandum on communication between the Indian Ocean and the Mediterranean diffused his erroneous estimate of a difference in level between the two seas at Suez and Pelusium of $32\frac{1}{2}$ feet. The idea of a canal between the two seas thus emerged as a French military weapon against the Indian Empire of England, which in reply invaded Egypt in 1800 and in 1807. The successive onslaughts by the infidel on a Moslem community provoked a widespread Islamic reaction, encouraging the Wahhabi capture of Mecca in 1803, the Fulani Jihad in the Western Sudan in 1804 and the rise of the Senussi in Tripoli as well as the accession of Mehemet Ali to the pashalik of Egypt in 1805. The English occupation of Malta was intended to discourage any similar expedition in the future and established British control over the route between the western and eastern basins of the Mediterranean.

After the defeat of Asia on the field of battle its culture was first fully revealed to Europe by the Romantic movement which called in the conservative civilizations of the East to counterbalance the revolutionary spirit abroad in the West. The Romantics found their highest ideals in the Orient and recognized India as the motherland of humanity and Sanskrit as the language of the gods. H. T. Colebrook became 'the founder and father of true Sanskrit scholarship in Europe',[1] surveying the whole field of Sanskrit grammar, literature, and philosophy. Friedrich Schlegel first revealed in 1808 the close connexion between Sanskrit and the languages of Europe. Bopp analysed in 1816 the relations of Sanskrit to Latin, Greek and Persian. The newly discovered unity of the 'Indo-European' languages (1813) and of the 'Indo-Germanic' peoples (1823) seemed increasingly more fundamental than the religious division between the Christian and non-Christian worlds. The postwar generation found a new spiritual home in the world of the East with its monuments, its magic and its mystery. Thus Goethe, shaken in his intense sympathy for France by her defeat at Leipzig, buried himself in 1813 in the history and poetry of Persia. Burckhardt rediscovered Petra in 1813. Hester Stanhope settled in voluntary exile on Mount Lebanon in 1814. After Mehemet Ali's destruction of the first Wahhabi state, G. F. Sadleir became the first European ever to cross Arabia, in 1819, 'like a bale of goods' as the Arabs

---

[1] F. M. Müller, *Biographical Essays* (London, Longmans, 1884), 229, 'Colebrooke (1765–1837)'.

remembered.[1] The 'Orientalism' which Byron named in 1811 centred around Stambul and Thebes rather than Arabia. In Egypt the inscriptions of Abu Simbel were discovered by Salt in 1817. The Egyptian style of massive construction was introduced into architecture in P. F. Robinson's Egyptian Hall (1812), into painting in John Martin's 'The Fall of Babylon' (1819), and into civil engineering in I. K. Brunel's design of 1830 for the Clifton Suspension Bridge. Champollion's letter which was read to the Academy of Inscriptions in 1822 crowned the labour of fourteen years and the dream of a lifetime. It began the decipherment of hieroglyphics after the successive discovery of the keys to Sanskrit in 1785, to Pahlevi in 1793, and to cuneiform in 1803. Thus it opened up the recorded past of ancient Egypt, founded the science of Egyptology, and added a new province to the cultural empire of France.

The revelation of the East to the West coincided with the reversal of the traditional balance of commerce between the developed economies of Asia and the thitherto less-developed economies of Europe. After England established its exclusive control over the Cape route between 1805 and 1810 it abolished the East India Company's monopoly of the Indian trade in 1813. In the same confident spirit 'Caliph' Hastings as Governor-General ceased to acknowledge the titular supremacy of the Mogul Emperor and made him from 1818–19 the puppet of the British instead of that of the Mahrattas. The opening of the Indian trade to the outports encouraged John Gladstone to send the first vessel from Liverpool to Calcutta in 1814. The Indian market was thenceforward flooded with the cotton textiles of Lancashire, reversing the traditional balance of the textile trade in favour of England and encouraging Paisley to manufacture imitation Kashmir shawls on a large scale by 1820. Bengal sharply increased its exports of indigo to England from 1815. India also increased its exports of raw cotton from 1814 so that they even surpassed the volume of imports from America into England in 1818 and 1819. The establishment of British power over Bengal encouraged a demand for English education among the Brahmins of Calcutta from 1816, the foundation of the first steam cotton-spinning mill in Calcutta in 1817, and the publication of the first successful Bengali periodical in 1818. The East India Company sanctioned with reluctance the consecration of the first Anglican bishop of Calcutta in 1814 and the establishment of the first Baptist mission in the sacred city of Benares in 1816, which provoked the warning of the Abbé Dubois that the conversion of the Hindus as a nation was impossible to any sect of Christianity. Those innovations took place in a community which remained as quiet as gunpowder, convinced by its Brahmins that India was the only land wherein a holy life could be lived and that it was forbidden to Indians to pollute themselves by crossing the black water. The first Brahmin ever to cross the sea reached Liverpool in 1831 after a voyage of 144 days and thirty

[1] D. G. Hogarth, *The Penetration of Arabia. A Record of the Development of Western Knowledge Concerning the Arabian Peninsula* (London, Lawrence, 1904), 107.

years as a social outcaste for his efforts to reform the Hindu faith on a mono-
theistic basis. Ram Mohun Roy was the reply of Asia to Vasco da Gama: his
voyage linked together East and West and 'the two great branches of the
Aryan race, after they had been separated so long that they had lost all recollection of their common origin, of their common language, of their common
faith'.[1]

[1] F. M. Müller, *Biographical Essays* (London, Longmans, 1884), 12, 'Râjah Râmmohun
Roy, 1774–1833'.

2

THE EXPANSION OF THE PENINSULAR AND ORIENTAL STEAM NAVIGATION COMPANY, 1835-1854

THE Suez Canal was the product of the closer relations between Europe and Asia which were facilitated from the 1830s by the use of the over-land route to India via Egypt and the Red Sea. That steam-route emerged as the Anglo-Indian response to the stimulus of the reform move-ment in contemporary England. The Cape route to India offered equal facilities to both Bombay and Calcutta whereas the Red Sea route promised to benefit Bombay at the expense of Calcutta, whose Steam Committee of 1823 therefore preferred to support steam navigation via the Cape. The voyage of the s.s. *Enterprize* in 1825 proved a comparative failure because it covered the 13,700 miles from Falmouth to Calcutta in 114 days against the 70 days desired and the 108 days averaged by East Indiamen between 1824 and 1832. Calcutta's jealousy of Bombay inspired the Government to reject proposals made by the Governor of Bombay in 1823 and 1826 to establish steam communication via the Red Sea. Mountstuart Elphinstone became the first Governor of Bombay to return to England via the Red Sea in 1827, travelling via Kosseir so as to avoid the strong northerly winds which, fun-nelled by the great mountains on both sides of the Gulf of Suez, hindered navigation to Suez during nine months of the year.

The hindrances to the steam navigation of the Red Sea and the Arabian Sea, especially at the height of the south-west monsoon between June and September, increased interest in the alternative route via the Euphrates and the Syrian desert, a route which was favoured by the cultural pre-eminence of Persia in Mogul India and by the commerce carried on by the Parsis between the Persian Gulf and India. The wars of Russia with Persia in 1826–8 and with Turkey in 1828–9 established Russian control of the Caspian Sea and encouraged General Paskiewitch to plan to push southwards from the Caucasus to the Euphrates and to plant the standard of the Tsar on the Persian Gulf, compelling the British Government in self-defence to develop a shorter route to India which would strengthen the British position on the Euphrates against Russia. Ellenborough at the Board of Control became the greatest supporter in England of speedier communication with India but recommended on 28 July 1829 the adoption of the Red Sea route to the East India Company.[1] 'I want to bring India as near England as I can, to know

---

[1] Earl of Ellenborough, *A Political Diary 1828–1830* (edited by Lord Charles Colchester, 1881), ii. 77.

everything every man in India does, as soon as steam navigation can inform me.'[1] The East India Company's memorandum of 10 November, drawn up by Thomas Love Peacock, favoured the navigation of the Persian Gulf in order to anticipate the Russians: 'They will do everything in Asia that is worth the doing and that we leave undone.'[2] Ellenborough nevertheless expressed to Wellington on 21 December his decided preference for the Red Sea over the Euphrates route and was even encouraged, by Mehemet Ali's apparent understanding with France to conquer Algiers, to dream of annexing Egypt from India.[3] His influence encouraged the Government of Bombay to send the s.s. *Hugh Lindsay* from Bombay to Suez in 34 days (20 March– 22 April 1830). That pioneer steam navigation of the Red Sea was handicapped by the same high fuel consumption which harassed the pioneer steam voyages around the Cape, but enabled letters to reach London on 31 May in 72 days. Ellenborough estimated the time could be reduced by 14 days because ten days had been lost in coaling at Aden and Jedda.[4] The directors of the Company in London resented Ellenborough's innovations, complained that the Governor of Bombay had no important intelligence to communicate and so drove Ellenborough to despair of their political capacity.[5] Lord Clare became in 1831 the first Governor of Bombay to reach India by the new Red Sea steam route. Captain John Wilson, the first steam navigator of the Red Sea and the pioneer of the first long-distance steam-route,[6] established by his seven round voyages from Bombay to Suez between 1830 and 1835 the practicability of steam navigation during the north-east monsoon of October– January, though not during the head winds and heavy seas of the south-west monsoon of June–August. Lieutenant-Commander Robert Moresby spent four and a half years (1829–34) in surveying the Red Sea and the Gulf of Suez, demarcated their dangers and reduced them to the practical proportions of the map-maker and hydrographer.[7] Thomas Waghorn had been an advocate of the Cape route between 1827 and 1831 but turned his energies to the improvement of the Egyptian route after 1832 when steam navigation interests in England began to press for a Government subsidy for the carriage of the India mails by private enterprise.

The development of the overland route through Egypt and the French conquest of Algeria from 1830 inaugurated a century of expansion by the

---

[1] A. H. Imlah, *Lord Ellenborough* (Cambridge, Harvard University Press, 1939), 23, 49–50, 18 September 1829.

[2] Wellington, *Despatches, Correspondence and Memoranda* (London, Murray, 1877), vi. 343, T. L. Peacock, 'Memorandum respecting the Application of Steam Navigation to the Internal and External Communications of India, November 10, 1829'. C. van Doren, *The Life of Thomas Love Peacock* (London, Dent, 1911), 214–16, 218–21.

[3] *A Political Diary*, ii. 176, 26 January 1830.

[4] Ibid., 261, 2 June 1830.

[5] Ibid., 262, 5 June 1830.

[6] J. H. Wilson, *Facts Connected with the Origin and Progress of Steam Communication between India and England* (London, Johnson, 1850), 4, 131.

[7] J. Douglas, *Bombay and Western India* (London, Low, 1893), ii. 335.

Liberal monarchies of the West at the expense of the community of Islam. France gained compensation in North Africa for the colonial empire in America and India lost to England in 1763 and visualized the Mediterranean as a Roman unity under the modern heirs of the Romans. She extended her ambitions to Egypt whose Pasha gave her in 1830 the Luxor obelisk, which was transported to France in 1833 and erected in the Place de la Concorde in 1836. Mehemet Ali employed French experts to modernize his armies, disliked the British efforts to open up communication through Egypt and determined to expand his power at the expense of the Sultan. His invasion of Syria in 1831 brought under a single administration the provinces on both sides of the isthmus of Suez. The Mediterranean System of the Saint-Simonian Michel Chevalier[1] envisaged the unification of the river basins surrounding the inland sea through railways, rivers, banks and schools to the benefit of the ports of Cadiz, Barcelona, Marseilles, Taranto, Venice, Odessa and Constantinople. Thereby he hoped to make the Mediterranean a medium of reconciliation instead of a theatre of conflict between East and West. He made France the centre of the projected railway-network of his new Roman empire. For the Levant he proposed the construction of a Nile Valley Railway and a Scutari–Bagdad–Basra Railway as well as the cutting of the isthmuses of Suez and Panama in order to bring Europe and America to Asia. Prosper Enfantin, the Supreme Head of the Saint-Simonian Religion, aroused the hostility of the French State which broke up his fellowship and sent him to prison for seven months. During his imprisonment Enfantin developed the idea of an isthmian canal as a means of restoring the unity of his community and regaining public support by the achievement of 'the greatest industrial and political task of this century'.

> Our mission is to create
> Between antique Egypt and ancient Judaea,
> One of the new highways of Europe
> Leading to India and China,
> Later we will also construct the other one
> At Panama.
> Thus we will place one foot on the Nile,
> The other upon Jerusalem.
> Our right hand will reach out towards Mecca
> Our left hand will cover Rome
> And will rest upon Paris.
>
> Suez
> Is the centre of our life of labour,
> There we shall perform the act
> Which the world awaits

[1] *Œuvres de Saint-Simon et d'Enfantin. Notices Historiques* (Paris, Dentu, 1866), vi. 78, M. Chevalier, 'Exposition du Système de la Méditerranée, 5 Février 1832', a reference I owe to Mr. B. M. Ratcliffe.

In order to proclaim that we are
Male.[1]

Thus Enfantin blended the new technology with the Romantic vision of Asia as the earth-mother and of India as the eternal feminine. The union of Egypt and Syria in 1832 inspired Mehemet Ali to promise Palmerston in 1833 to open 'the canal of Suez', so as to facilitate communication between England and India[2] and reduce British opposition to his aspirations to full independence. Enfantin arrived in Egypt in 1833 with a band of engineers on his isthmian crusade and urged Mehemet Ali for five months to sanction a canal. The Pasha rejected the idea on 30 January 1834, being fully engaged by his duel with Constantinople. He preferred the idea of a Nile Barrage for summer irrigation to such a canal as much as he preferred the idea of a Cairo–Damascus Railway to that of a Cairo–Suez Railway. He diverted the Saint-Simonians to work on the Nile Barrage until 1838.

The idea of an isthmian canal was popularized by the Saint-Simonians as a long-term process of expansion began in 1833–7 in the trade of the Mediterranean and of Asia, especially in the ports of Marseilles, Trieste, Piraeus, Alexandria, Bombay, Singapore, Batavia, Canton and Sydney. In Asia the end of the East India Company's monopoly of trade with China in 1833 stimulated a boom in the exports of Bombay, close to the opium areas of Malwa, in the shipment of opium to China, and in the imports of Canton. The influx of new British firms to Canton inspired the large private firm, which had been established in 1782 and renamed Jardine Matheson & Co. in 1832, to make fresh efforts to re-establish its monopoly of the private trade of Canton: to that end it developed the trade of the East China coast and the use of the fast opium clipper.[3] Trade was encouraged by the English vision of India as a new Baltic and by the development of the consignment system in the export of piece-goods from Glasgow. In the Dutch East Indies the spread of the culture-system replaced taxes in money by a tribute in produce, especially coffee and sugar, and was imitated in the production of indigo in Bengal. The great expansion of European commerce and civilization which began in the 1830s seems to have stemmed primarily from the religious revival of the decade. The associated campaign against the slave-trade facilitated the 'natural and unrestricted growth of legitimate commerce' which was carried on under alien protection by European rather than by Arab merchants. The increase in private mercantile activity in Asia encouraged the foundation of chambers of commerce in Calcutta and Canton in 1834, in Bombay and Madras in 1836, in Singapore in 1837, in Colombo and Adelaide in 1839. In

---

[1] *Œuvres de Saint-Simon et d'Enfantin*, ix. 57, Enfantin à E. Barrault, 8 Août 1833. H. R. d'Allemagne, *Prosper Enfantin et les Grandes Entreprises du XIXe siècle* (Paris, Gründ, 1935), 359, Enfantin à Fleury, 28 Août 1833.

[2] C. W. Crawley, 'Anglo-Russian Relations, 1815–1840', *Cambridge Historical Journal* (1929), 56, Light to Palmerston, 6 January 1833.

[3] M. Greenberg, *British Trade and the Opening of China 1800–42* (Cambridge University Press, 1951), 137, 185.

the Mediterranean a great expansion of trade began fifteen years after the extinction of the independence of the three great commercial republics of Genoa, Venice and Ragusa at the Congress of Vienna. That revival took place under the influence of Levantine merchants who carried on with un-rivalled capacity the oldest mercantile tradition in the world:

'It takes the wits of–4 Turks to overreach one Frank.

2 Franks to cheat one Greek.

2 Greeks to cheat one Jew.

6 Jews to cheat one Armenian.'[1]

The diversion of Greek enterprise into trade and shipping after the failure of the attempt in the 1820s to establish an Ottoman Empire of the Greeks gave the greatest single stimulus to the revival of Mediterranean trade. The development of cotton cultivation for export in the Nile Delta encouraged the rise of Alexandria and the establishment from 1835 of its European quarter around the Frank Square. The creation of such new European quarters eroded the traditional Arab–Moslem association of the quarter and the guild, which was further weakened by the competition of English piece-goods under the Anglo-Turkish Treaty of Commerce of 1838. The efflorescence of Levantine enterprise attracted British ships to the Danube in 1834 as well as British firms to Aleppo in 1835.

The crushing victories of Mehemet Ali's son and general, Ibrahim, over the armies of the Sultan opened the road to Constantinople and alarmed Palmerston for the security of the route to India. 'Turkey is as good an occupier of the road to India as an active Arabian sovereign would be.'[2] The British Cabinet's preoccupation with Belgium, Portugal and Parliamentary Reform forced the Sultan to call on Russia for aid against his rebellious vassal. The increase in Russian influence at Constantinople compelled Palmerston to establish as official British policy from 1833 support for the independence and integrity of the Ottoman Empire. The Levant crisis of 1833, followed by the establishment of Russia's new Caucasian frontier in 1834, inspired the appointment on 3 June 1834 of a Select Committee on Steam Navigation to India, which concerned itself more with the Euphrates than with the Red Sea route and least of all with the Cape route because England's auxiliary fleet of fifty East Indiamen had been auctioned after the end of the Company's monopoly in 1833 and not replaced. The Committee recognized that the development of a Euphrates route would check the influence of France as well as Russia and recommended a steam survey of the rivers of Mesopotamia together with the immediate establishment of the Red Sea route on a regular basis as a joint enterprise between Government and Company. Bartle Frere secured special permission to travel to India via Egypt and became the first

[1] R. Curzon, *Visits to the Monasteries of the Levant* (London, Murray, 1850, third edition, omitted from first edition of 1849), 52.

[2] H. L. Bulwer, *The Life of Henry John Temple, Viscount Palmerston* (London, Bentley, 1870), ii. 145, Palmerston to W. Temple, 21 March 1833.

cadet of the Company to reach India by that route in 1834. Under Ellen-borough at the Board of Control the monthly India mails were diverted from the Cape to the Red Sea route in 1835, being carried by vessels of the Company to Suez and by Admiralty packets from Alexandria. The use of the same service for mercantile correspondence and bills, private correspondence and newspapers stimulated the improvement of the overland route through Egypt. Waghorn organized camel caravans across the desert in 1835 to halve the price of coal at Suez which would otherwise have remained wholly dependent on the transport of coal around the Cape. He also undertook from 1836 the carriage of letters inscribed 'Care of Mr. Waghorn'. Raven and Hill, the pro-prietors of the British Hotel in Cairo began from 1836 to transport travellers, luggage and merchandise from Cairo to Suez: they built a hotel at Suez and five rest-stations in the desert with the residual funds of the Bombay Steam Committee which had been established in 1833. From Cairo the Nile was used for 120 miles and then the Mahmoudieh Canal, excavated in 1819, for the remaining 48 miles to Alexandria. The development of the Egyptian route enhanced English influence in India, which had begun to grow under Corn-wallis in the 1790s. From the 1830s that influence increased through Ben-tinck's social reforms of 'Hindooism' (1829), the advent of women and missionaries, the development of hill-stations and the centralization of legis-lative power in India under the Act of 1833. The Asiatic period of European culture (1771–1835) ended in 1835 with the first issue of coinage in the name of the East India Company instead of in that of the Mogul Emperor and with the extension of Government patronage to English education in India despite the protest of the directors of the Company. Thus English began to replace Persian as under the Mogul Empire Persian had replaced Sanskrit. The new route enabled the overland mail to reach Calcutta in two months from London for the first time on 9 August 1836. It stimulated the application of auxiliary steam to sailing vessels bound for India, an innovation which proved so useful in crossing the doldrums of the Atlantic that by 1836 ships reached Bombay via the Cape in 75 days[1] or 32 per cent less time than the 110 days averaged in 1824–32. The division of interest in the new route between the Admiralty, the Company and private enterprise prevented its most effective use and provoked mercantile pressure for the transfer of the whole service to private hands as the corollary to the victorious campaign of 1829–33 by the outports against the Company. The route accelerated communication with China only indirectly so that Jardine's heard 129 days later (5 June–12 October 1837) of its loss of over £110,000 in the commercial crisis of 1837,[2] which might have been moderated by the earlier establishment of the route.[3] In 1837 the East India Company placed two powerful new steamers on the Bombay–Suez

---

[1] Hansard, *Commons Debates*, 10 August 1836, 1061, J. C. Hobhouse.
[2] Greenberg, 169.
[3] *James Finlay & Company Limited Manufacturers and East India Merchants—1750–1950* (Glasgow, Jackson, 1951), 191, Kirkman Finlay to A. S. Finlay, 26 May 1837.

route in its concern at the establishment of Russian relations with Afghanistan, the growing threat of a Persian attack on Herat with the support of Russia, and the failure of its Euphrates expedition. Thereby it made its service regular even during the four months of the south-west monsoon. That new service exacerbated Calcutta's jealousy of Bombay which was able to celebrate the accession of Queen Victoria while Calcutta was still toasting William IV at a birthday dinner. The Company limited expenditure on its steamers to a minimum so that they remained very uncomfortable and could not carry the homeward mail with perfect regularity.[1]

The low efficiency of the marine steam-engine and the strength of the south-west monsoon increased the need for a half-way house for coaling and led to the occupation from Bombay in 1834–5 of the island of Socotra which proved unsuitable because of its high surf and endemic malaria. The occupation of the 'noble harbours' of Aden was recommended in 1837,[2] ordered by the Secret Committee of the Company in London on 30 May 1838,[3] and accomplished in three hours on 16 January 1839 by Moslem sepoys against fierce Arab resistance. That half-way house between Bombay and Suez was the first territorial acquisition on the Red Sea route and the first coaling-station annexed to any empire. Aden became essentially a coaling-port, centred around Steamer Point two miles west of the old Crater Town. It was supplied by coal imported round the Cape, defended against six tribal assaults in 1839–41 and maintained at the cost of a large annual deficit to the Company.[4] The annexation of 'the eye of the Yemen' disturbed both Mehemet Ali and France, whose Consul-General in Egypt had hoped that England would be readier to recognize the independence of Egypt in consequence of the new steam route. In reply Mehemet Ali claimed Basra as well as Bahrein as districts of his province of Nejd and completed in 1839 a semaphore telegraph between Cairo and Suez, in order to give warning of any English descent on Suez. France despatched three missions to Abyssinia in 1839, a Lazarist mission, a military mission and a naval mission, followed by a mercantile expedition in 1840. Thus France began its quest for a compensatory site in the Red Sea and for an empire in Abyssinia as a counterbalance to British India.[5]

The East India Company decided in 1838 to convert its navy from sail to steam and from wood to iron. It sent three of its new iron steamers, Peacock's 'iron chickens',[6] to Basra in 1838 to discourage Egyptian activity in the Shatt el Arab. The development of the overland route made possible a fourth wave of Western expansion in Asia, encouraged the adoption of a forward policy in 1839 in the Levant, in Afghanistan and in Canton and broke down the traditional Turkish policy of excluding Christian nations from trade in the

---

[1] *The Times*, 29 October 1838, 4 iii.
[2] T. E. Marston, *Britain's Imperial Role in the Red Sea Area 1800–1878* (Hamden, Connecticut, Shoe String Press, 1961), 53, Captain J. Mackenzie to Foreign Office, 6 January 1837.
[3] Marston, 68. [4] Ibid., 108.
[5] Ibid., 126–35. [6] Doren, 219.

Red Sea. Passing through foreign seas and lands the new route was liable to 'vexations, interruptions, tolls, extortions and insults' unlike the Cape route which was 'at once comprehensive, safe, bold, truly English'.[1] The creation of that imperial route required the consent of the Pasha of Egypt and the Government of France: the Convention of 1839 for the transit of the India mails across France first divided those mails into express and sea mails. Its vulnerability was revealed in the Levant crisis of 1840 when a second clash between Mehemet Ali and his suzerain ranged England in opposition to both France and Egypt. The crisis in Western Asia coincided with one in Eastern Asia. The China War was begun not by Auckland as Governor-General of India but by Ellenborough who, at the Board of Control for the third time, ordered four regiments and twenty ships to conquer China.[2] The East India Company ordered in 1839 six new iron steamers for operations in China and enlisted in the service of its new marine technology the cooperation of the Parsi shipbuilders of Bombay, who travelled to England for the first time in 1838 via the Cape and in 1839 via the overland route. Ardaseer Cursetjee had begun to study the theory and practice of the steam engine from 1830 in an easy transition from the worship of fire to the study of steam-power and had pioneered the introduction of gas-light to Bombay in 1835. He reached England via Suez in 81 days (13 September–2 December 1839)[3] and was elected in 1840 an Associate Member of the Institution of Civil Engineers. He returned to India in 1840 as the Chief Engineer and Inspector of Machinery at the Bombay Steam Factory and Foundry of the East India Company for the repair of steamships, so becoming the first Indian to be placed in charge of Europeans. The *Nemesis* was built in profound secrecy by Lairds of Birkenhead as a heavily-armed merchant steamer, with a draught of 6 feet for the navigation of the Chinese rivers, and became the first iron steamer ever to round the Cape en route to Macao, which it reached in eight months (28 March–25 November 1840) from Portsmouth.[4] The demand for rapid communication with the East during the China War encouraged *The Times* to organize an extra-ordinary express service between Alexandria and London via Paris,[5] and Murray to publish in London the first newspaper based on the regular receipt of information via the new route.[6] The war also stimulated the organization of an accelerated service of East India mails by private enterprise with the approval of the Foreign Office, the Treasury, and the Admiralty.

On 3 July 1840 the Peninsular and Oriental Steam Navigation Company

[1] F. Scheer, *The Cape of Good Hope versus Egypt* (London, Steill, 1839), 13, 16.

[2] W. C. Costin, *Great Britain and China 1833–1860* (Oxford, Clarendon Press, 1937), 79.

[3] Ardaseer Cursetjee, *Diary of an Overland Journey from Bombay to England, and of a Year's Residence in Great Britain* (London, Henington, 1840).

[4] W. Bernard, *Narrative of the Voyages and Services of the Nemesis from 1840 to 1843...* (London, Colburn, 1844), i. 173.

[5] *The History of The Times* (London, The Times, 1939), ii, *1841–1884*, 68–91, 'Speeding up the News'.

[6] *The Indian News and Chronicle of Eastern Affairs*, 11 June 1840, 4, published by Alexander Elder Murray monthly on the day after the arrival of the Overland Mail.

announced the beginning of a monthly service to Alexandria from 1 September.[1] That company was an eastern extension of the Peninsular Steam Navigation Company founded in 1835. In turn the Peninsular Company was an Iberian extension of the City of Dublin Steam Packet Company, which had been founded in 1824 by Captain Richard Bourne (1770–1851)[2] for the transport of cattle from Dublin to Liverpool. The London agents of the City of Dublin Company were Willcox and Anderson, who had established a sail service to the Iberian Peninsula by 1822 and had tried in vain to form a company for steam navigation to the peninsula. Bourne successfully formed in 1835 the Peninsular Steam Navigation Company, supplying five of its original six ships together with its capital and its first secretary. That company was formed as one aspect of a combined diplomatic, military, naval and financial effort to support the Braganza-Coburg dynasty in Portugal and the Spanish Bourbon dynasty in Spain and to maintain the tradition of Wellington's victories, enshrined in Colonel William Napier's *History of the War in the Peninsula*, which went through three editions between 1828 and 1835. The high dynastic interests which the company served enabled it to secure the first ocean steam mail contract in history in 1837 and to make Gibraltar a coaling station as well as a smuggling centre. The Peninsular Company was a product of the Anglo-French entente extended into the Quadruple Alliance of 1834 in opposition to the Austro-Russian entente of 1833: the Peninsular and Oriental Company was a product of the Quadruple Alliance formed by England, Russia, Austria and Prussia in 1840 against France and Egypt in order to prevent the overthrow of the Sultan by his vassal and to reduce the ambitions of the French-supported Pasha within the bounds of the Nile valley.

The Levant crisis shattered the Anglo-French entente and became a duel between Palmerston and Thiers. Deprived of the opportunity of a military career by the outbreak of peace in 1815, Thiers had become a civilian Napoleon, so hypnotized by his study of the military history of the Revolutionary Wars and by the memory of the Egyptian Expedition of 1798 that he assimilated Egypt to the sacred soil of France. His bellicose policy was opposed in a hostile Chamber on 11 January 1840 by Lamartine who contrasted the 3,000 colonists in Algeria with the 75,000,000 subjects of British India, the richest and vastest empire ever conquered by any state. 'Egypt is Suez, Suez is India; India is England. England must be annihilated before France can dominate Egypt.'[3] The rupture of the liberal alliance first made England into 'perfidious Albion' in French eyes and ushered in a generation of almost unbroken Anglo-French hostility. For his part Mehemet Ali accused England of desiring to occupy Egypt in order to make it into a station on the road to

---

[1] *The Times*, 3 July 1840, 1i, 6i.

[2] W. O'Byrne, *A Naval Biographical Dictionary* (London, Murray, 1849), 103.

[3] J. Charles-Roux, *L'Isthme et le Canal de Suez. Historique. État Actuel* (Paris, Hachette, 1901), i. 180.

India. He therefore fortified Alexandria and made plans to fortify Suez. He yielded to British pressure and evacuated his troops from Arabia but provoked a rising in the Yemen in a bid to drive the infidel from Aden. In that crisis the Peninsular and Oriental Company signed the mail contract of 26 August 1840 which stipulated for the arming of its vessels when necessary with guns of the largest calibre. The *Oriental* which left Southampton on 1 September thus formed part of the Navy's new steam reserve and could be rapidly converted into the most formidable war steamer in the world.[1] The pioneer vessel of the new service was detained at Malta for three days after the British bombardment of Beirut and arrived at Alexandria on 19 September, when the British Consul sought an assurance from the Pasha that the India mails would be safe. Mehemet Ali hesitated and then said 'the mails may pass for this time'.[2] The British capture of Acre on 4 November compelled Ibrahim to evacuate Syria and Palestine and made the English as unpopular in Egypt as in 1807, although all the English merchants in Alexandria condemned Palmerston's policy of coercion. Mehemet Ali relented of his threat of 19 September and gave first verbal assurances and then written assurances on 5 November that the mails might pass without hindrance. Waghorn nevertheless became involved in a constant struggle with the Egyptian authorities to maintain the coach service which he had just organized for passengers between Cairo and Suez. The loss of Syria precipitated a reaction against Europe in Egypt after twenty years of Europeanization. Mehemet Ali abandoned his efforts to develop his army and industry in order to concentrate on agriculture and irrigation, especially through the Nile Barrage (1842–7) of Mougel Bey. He became seriously disturbed by the steady growth of traffic along the overland route and refused to sanction a Cairo–Suez Railway. He also refused to allow the East India Company to build coal depots at Cairo or Suez or to build a Suez Hotel.

The Peninsular and Oriental Steam Navigation Company was incorporated by Royal Charter on 31 December 1840. Its capital of £1,000,000 and its directors were largely supplied by the Proprietors of the City of Dublin Steam Packet Company, especially Bourne. Its Managers remained the Scots free-traders Willcox and Anderson, although its Charter, its Court of Directors and its Proprietors were modelled on those of the East India Company. It served as a marine extension of the London–Southampton Railway which had been authorized in 1834 and was completed in 1840. Its new direct service to Alexandria replaced the Admiralty's packet service with its changes at Gibraltar and Malta. Thereby it extended the company's track from 1,300 to 2,951 nautical miles and encouraged the voyage in 1841 of the first merchant vessel to carry passengers and mail direct from Suez to Calcutta. The P. & O. retained the Anglo-Irish motto of its predecessor, *Quis Separabit?*, and its house-flag, which quartered the blue and white of the Braganza above the red and yellow of the Spanish Bourbon.

[1] *The Times*, 2 September 1840, 5 ii.
[2] Ibid., 3 October 1840, 4 i; 5 October, 6 ii; 14 October, 4 vi.

The British victory in the Levant was followed by one in China, where the island of Chusan commanding access to the Yangtze was captured in accordance with Jardine's recommendation to Palmerston.[1] The news reached London five months later.[2] The destruction by the *Nemesis* of a Chinese squadron of eleven war junks on 7 January 1841 provoked immediate imitation of the steamship by the 'ingenious and indefatigable' Chinese[3] and facilitated the acquisition of the island of Hong Kong as a southern counterpart to Chusan. Elliot's recommendation to British shipping to proceed to Hong Kong rather than to Canton aroused the opposition of Jardine's,[4] which wished to maintain its base in Canton and persuaded Palmerston to supersede Elliot. The official notice of his recall was published in the local press five days before Elliot received it on 29 July 1841. Elliot's successor, Sir Henry Pottinger, arrived in Macao on 10 August via the overland route in the record time from Falmouth of 67 days as compared to the voyage-time via the Cape of 117 days (13 June–8 October 1841) of Harry Parkes and that of 164 days (20 December 1841–2 June 1842) of Colin Campbell. The recall of Elliot first revealed the new power of control given to the central authority over its local representatives by the acceleration of communications. It was followed by Peel's recall of Auckland after the rising of Kabul against the British. Pottinger exceeded his explicit instructions by retaining Hong Kong as a future 'vast Emporium of Commerce and wealth',[5] making the island the first British acquisition whose Governor arrived by the new steam route. The British success in China was reinforced by simultaneous advances in Borneo and Basra. James Brooke became in 1841 Raja of Sarawak, which formed the last link in the chain of maritime stations between the Cape and Canton. T. K. Lynch, who had established a merchant firm in Bagdad in 1831 and steam navigation on the lower Tigris in 1840, established direct communication via the Cape between Basra and London in 1841.

The news of the Treaty of Nanking signed by Pottinger on 29 August 1842 reached London eighty-four days later,[6] was greeted with incredulity in the City because of the speed of its transit and caused a panic in the China trade. That treaty was the first of the 'unequal treaties' which reduced China from its position as the 'central nation' to that of an equal in the family of nations and so made in Chinese eyes inferior powers the equals of a superior power. The treaty opened the South China coast as far as Shanghai to treaty trade, which thenceforward began to replace the traditional tributary trade. It was followed by the first naval surveys of the coast of China from 1842–3 and began a century of effort by Europe to open China to the outside world. It

---

[1] Greenberg, 213.
[2] *The Times*, 8 December 1840, 4, with news from Macao of 4 August of the capture of Chusan on 5 July.   [3] Bernard, i. 281; ii. 226.
[4] Costin, 46. J. K. Fairbank, *Trade and Diplomacy on the China Coast. The Opening of the Treaty Ports 1842–1854* (Cambridge, Harvard University Press, 1953), 82–3.
[5] Costin, 99, Pottinger to Aberdeen, 3 May 1842.
[6] *The Times*, 21 November 1842, 5.

confirmed England in her possession of Hong Kong, a harbour without soil and without history which proved the finest in Eastern Asia. That island became a main centre of the opium trade which had precipitated the war. It was therefore placed by Peel on 15 December 1842 in direct dependence on the Crown rather than upon the East India Company.

The P. & O. secured the contract to carry the mail from Suez to Galle, Madras and Calcutta and sent its first steamer around the Cape in 1842, the *Hindostan* reaching Calcutta in ninety-one days. Thus the P. & O. inaugurated the comprehensive line of communication between Suez and Calcutta, which had been the seat of the supreme Government of the Company since 1833 and supplied most of the commerce, correspondence and passengers from India. It extended its Anglo-Irish imperial connexion to the Anglo-Indian world, raised its track mileage from 3,000 to 8,200 and trebled its mail subsidy, which was paid at treble the Cunard rate. The East India Company continued to employ its slower steamers on the less profitable Suez–Bombay service and began to build a 1,170-mile road between Bombay and Calcutta in 1842. The P. & O. was compelled to accept the uneconomic necessity of two separate fleets divided by the Alexandria–Suez overland route. Its Manager, Arthur Anderson, persuaded Mehemet Ali in 1841 to reduce transit dues from 3 to $\frac{1}{2}$ per cent and to permit the introduction of steam-tugs on the Mahmoudieh Canal as well as steamboats on the Nile, so facing Waghorn with keen specialized competition on the water-route between Alexandria and Cairo. After Linant de Bellefonds proposed in 1840 a direct isthmian canal rather than the indirect Alexandria–Suez Canal of his first project of 1833 Anderson submitted memorials in 1841 to both Palmerston and Mehemet Ali in favour of a canal between Suez and Pelusium.[1] After the P. & O. brought its maiden Indian mails to England in February 1843 and secured substantial support from East India merchants,[2] Anderson urged a collective demand by the Powers on Mehemet Ali for the construction of such 'a running salt river—a Bosphorus on a smaller scale'.[3] The Pasha's unrelenting opposition compelled the P. & O. to adapt its operations to the isthmian barrier. Its eastern fleet was manned by lascars able to bear the heat of the Red Sea and was fuelled by coal carried round the Cape by sail to depots at Suez, Aden and Galle. Its home fleet was manned by English seamen and operated over relatively short distances at high speeds. Despite the high speeds and dangerous seas the P. & O. lost no great proportion of its vessels and singularly few lives.

The Anglo-French crisis of 1840 provoked France in 1841 to withdraw its special facilities for the couriers of *The Times*, to consider a steam link from Marseilles to Bourbon and Madagascar via Alexandria and Suez, and to favour an isthmian canal as a French counterpart to the British monopoly of the

[1] J. Tagher, 'Mohammed Ali et les Anglais à Suez', *Cahiers d'Histoire Égyptienne* (1950), 484.

[2] *The Times*, 20 September 1843, 5 iv.

[3] E. Clarkson, 'The Suez Navigable Canal', *Foreign and Colonial Quarterly Review* (October 1843), 622.

overland route as well as a means to restore French prestige in Egypt. Mehemet Ali would no more tolerate a French canal than an English canal and was determined to avoid the fate of China. He therefore compelled the European boats and vessels on the Nile and Mahmoudieh Canal to replace their national flags by the Egyptian flag in September 1841.[1] He was unmoved by the flattery of the P. & O. which in 1842 named its first iron steamer the *Pacha*. He encouraged the formation of the Egyptian Transit Company, which bought Hill's interests in June 1842 and secured a monopoly of the transit service in 1843 after the Pasha revoked his concession to the P. & O.[2] Samuel Shepheard who had aided Hill since 1841 took over the management of the British Hotel in Cairo from 1844 and made it into a European oasis in an Oriental city, the metropolitan counterpart of the Suez Hotel built in 1844–5 by Mehemet Ali. Thenceforward Suez began to grow at the expense of Kosseir.

The last Governor-General to use the Cape route was Ellenborough, who reached Calcutta in 115 days (6 November 1841–28 February 1842). His annexation of Sind was ostensibly intended to prevent the establishment of a French base and brought the East India Company out of monsoon Asia into desert Asia, which formed a broad cultural unity from Karachi to Cairo. That annexation inspired William Pare's proposal in 1842 for a Calais–Constantinople–Calcutta Railway which would link England to 'Young Egypt' and replace the steamboats projected for the Euphrates in 1835–7 by a steam railway. It also encouraged English efforts to develop Trieste in 1842 and Venice in 1843 as alternative terminals to Marseilles for the overland route across Europe. The French scheme for piercing the isthmus of Suez was revived in 1843 but was countered by the English proposal for a railway and enabled Mehemet Ali to avoid both by playing off France against England.

The development of the overland route increased rather than reduced traffic by the Cape route because trade could not stand the cost of transhipment except in the most valuable of commodities. The growth of mercantile communication via Egypt was thus accompanied by the expansion of trade using the Cape route as well as by the development of the trade of the Cape itself. The rise of the production of wool, which was first shipped to London in 1830, gave the Cape its first staple export and especially benefited the Eastern Province and Port Elizabeth, where the first British settlers had landed in 1820. St. Helena acquired a garrison in 1836 and a naval squadron in 1839 after the East India Company ceased to carry on trade. The annexation of Natal in 1843 counterbalanced that of Aden in 1839. The overland route remained a high-cost route used mainly by mail and by passengers. The time of the London–Bombay mail was reduced from sixty-six days in 1838 to thirty-nine days in 1840. Mail was carried faster outward than homeward, faster in summer than in winter and faster on land than on sea. The new

---

[1] M. Sabry, *L'Empire Égyptien sous Mohamed-Ali et la Question d'Orient (1811–1849)* (Paris Geuthner, 1930), 562.

[2] Clarkson, 627. *The Times*, 22 November 1842, 3 v.

facilities for mail produced a large expansion in its quantity. Passengers also reduced the time of their journey from four months via the Cape to forty days. Young cadets willingly paid double the fare charged by Smith, Green or Wigram for the Cape voyage to undergo the ordeal of the Red Sea voyage because their period of service dated from their arrival in India. Anglo-Indians in general used the overland route more for their homeward than for their outward voyage because the return voyage via the Cape was hindered by contrary winds so that Macaulay required six months to return from India in 1838 against the four months of his outward voyage in 1834. They preferred to use the Red Sea route in winter rather than in summer when the heat of land and sea combined to make the passage the worst in the world because a tail-wind compelled ships to travel with their own hot air, without the compensation of any cool breeze from the land. Troops continued to reach India via the Cape as the overland route was not a military route.

London benefited more than Calcutta by the new route[1] because England rather than India was the fountain-land of change. Ellenborough's military style of administration forced Peel to conclude that the English press would constantly discuss Indian questions and that the House of Commons would make India increasingly a subject of debate, extend its influence over Indian administration and disturb the relations of the Government with the directors of the East India Company, the Secret Committee and the local governments of India.[2] The acceleration of communication enhanced the power of the Company's Court of Directors and enabled officers to lobby directors for patronage, which had become more important than ever since the abolition of the Company's trading privileges in 1833. Thus it created a crisis in the relations between the Home and Indian Governments as well as between the dual governments established in London by the India Act of 1784. Ellenborough himself was sacrificed to the new power of rapid communication with London which he as President of the Board of Control had done more than anyone to develop. On 24 April 1844 he was recalled by unanimous vote of the Court of Directors in their first exercise of that power since 1784 and in defiance of the Cabinet. Ellenborough returned after twenty-nine months in India to deplore the establishment of the overland route as 'in one important respect one of the worst things that ever happened for our Indian Empire' because it exposed the Indian Government to 'all the little personal and party considerations of men at Home, ignorant, or only half-informed'.[3] The appointment of his brother-in-law, Hardinge, as his successor was a victory for the Cabinet over the Company because the new Governor-General was authorized to continue the policies of his predecessor. Hardinge became the first Governor-General to travel to India via the overland route, being advised by Aberdeen on 6 June 1844 to recommend Mehemet Ali to build a Cairo–

---

[1] J. H. Stocqueler, 'Calcutta as it is', *Asiatic Journal* (May–October 1843), 524.
[2] C. S. Parker, *Sir Robert Peel* (London, Murray, 1899), iii. 6–7, Peel to Ellenborough, 6 June 1843.   [3] Imlah, *Ellenborough*, 195, 204, Ellenborough to Napier, 17 September 1845.

Suez Railway at his own expense. English public life gained what India lost because most Governors-General after 1836 resumed public life after leaving India, following the example set by Auckland and Ellenborough and, before them, by only Cornwallis and Wellesley.[1]

The increased flow of Anglo-Indians on leave to England increased the strain on the Company's furlough regulations as well as on club accommodation in London. The Oriental Club, founded in 1824, modified its rules in 1843 to admit visiting members and opened a Strangers' Room in 1844. The East India United Service Club was founded in 1847 on the model of the United Service Club of Calcutta and drew military officers away from the Oriental Club. The neighbouring East India and Sports' Club was established in 1849 for civil servants. For travellers by the new route publishers produced guides and handbooks from 1841.[2] The information conveyed by the overland mail was distributed through special magazines and newspapers both in England and Asia. W. H. Allen published the *Asiatic Journal* from January 1841 immediately after the arrival of each mail instead of at the end of each month, and began the publication of *The Indian Mail* from 9 May 1843 on the arrival of each monthly overland mail. In the ports of Asia press summaries and special newspapers began in 1844 with the *Monthly Overland Circular* of Thacker & Co. of Calcutta and in 1845 with the *Overland Colombo Observer*, which was imitated in Bombay, Singapore and Hong Kong. Overland fashions spread the influence of England at the expense of that of India, replacing Nankin china by Spode or Wedgwood and the palanquin by the coach.[3] Thus a growing demand emerged among Anglo-Indians for Parisian fashions, for three-decker novels, for the pipe in place of the hookah and for the 'India pale ale' of the London brewers. The spread of English education among the Bengalis proved more important in the long run than the stimulus to trade. Dwarkanath Tagore (1794–1846), the first Hindu magistrate, followed R. M. Roy's example and became in 1842 'the first Hindu gentleman travelling by the overland route'.[4] After Hardinge opened public employment to English-educated Indians by his despatch of 10 October 1844, the first Hindu students travelled with Tagore by the overland route in 1845 to study medicine in England. The growing influence of Protestant Christianity upon Hinduism was reflected in the Brahma Samaj, which was founded in 1845 as an association of Hindu monotheists and in 1850, under the inspiration of Tagore's son, rejected the Vedas as a basis of faith.

The development of the overland route also increased English contacts

[1] Ibid., 232.

[2] G. Parbury, *Hand Book for India and Egypt* (London, Allen, 1841, 1842). T. Waghorn, *Overland Guide to India, by Three Routes to Egypt* (London, Richardson, 1844). J. H. Stocqueler, *The Hand-Book of India, A Guide to the Stranger and Traveller, and a Companion to the Resident* (London, Allen, 1844). D. L. Richardson, *The Anglo-Indian Passage, Homeward and Outward; or, a Card for the Overland Traveller* (London, Madden, 1845).

[3] W. H. Russell, *My Diary in India in the Year 1858–9* (London, Routledge, 1860), ii. 187–8.

[4] K. C. Mitra, *Memoir of Dwarkanath Tagore* (Calcutta, Thacker, 1870), 85.

with Egypt, which became the greater because the English travelled more than the French and their journey through Egypt often included a leisurely pilgrimage to the temples of Thebes. The English prejudice against the long sea voyage to Alexandria was overcome by the example of American travellers, by the lure of the colour, warmth and light of Egypt, by the rash of travel-books on the Levant appearing between 1837 and 1842[1] and by the cruises of the P. & O. from 1844. The liberation of Greece and the religious revival of the 1830s combined to popularize an eclectic pilgrimage to Athens, Gizeh and Jerusalem and to afford a new refuge from the English winter. The Cairo–Suez journey became under the influence of 'Newmania' an alternative to the sea-route via Jaffa because it made possible a journey through the desert of the Exodus to Mount Sinai and thence via Gaza to Jerusalem or via Akaba to Petra. Travellers could also enjoy on the Nile all the pleasures of an ocean cruise without its dangers. The growth of tourist-traffic gave Egypt an invisible export of increasing value, limited by the shortness of the winter season of navigation on the Nile and by Cairo's continental climate. European influence spread inland from Alexandria to Cairo, where the European colony established a literary and philosophical society in the Egyptian Society in 1835 and provided a market for coaches and coach-makers by 1840. With the spread of Levantine influence and Greek trade, drunkenness and usury increased in Moslem Egypt. The romantic appeal of the Orient was extended in the mind of the West from the Stambul of Byron to the 'baked Orient' of Flaubert and especially to 'these wild sons of freedom',[2] the Beduin Arabs. From the time of the Levant crisis of 1840 Ellenborough's hope of the annexation of Egypt was shared by travellers, scholars, sailors and soldiers[3] while the clergy hungered for the Holy Land.

The economic expansion of 1842–5 centred around railway-construction in Europe and the China trade in Asia. In that boom the P. & O. gained a share in the bimonthly mail which was begun to Bombay in January 1845. It also extended its service from Galle to Singapore and Hong Kong. The *Lady Mary Wood* brought the London mail of forty-one days beforehand to Hong Kong on 1 August 1845 and so placed London in regular contact with its new naval base in fifty-four days instead of eighty-nine days. By extending its service from India to China the P. & O. immediately began to encroach on the opium

---

[1] J. L. Stephens, *Incidents of Travel in Egypt, Arabia Petraea and the Holy Land By an American* (New York, Harper, 1837). R. M. Milnes, *Palm Leaves* (London, Moxon, 1844), xiii, xxix. J. M. Carré, *Voyageurs et Écrivains Français en Égypte* (Le Caire, 1932), ii. 37.

[2] E. Warburton, *The Crescent and the Cross; or Romance and Realities of Eastern Travel* (London, Colburn, 1845), ii. 251.

[3] E. Warburton, i. 385; ii. 43–7. A. W. Kinglake, *Eothen* (1844), ch. xx, 'The Sphinx'. J. Tagher, 'Mohammed Ali et les Anglais à Suez', *Cahiers d'Histoire Égyptienne*, (1950), 487 quoting *Bombay Courier*, 23 June 1846. E. Napier, *The Life and Correspondence of Admiral Sir Charles Napier* (London, Hurst, 1862), ii. 140, Napier to Hodges, 6 February 1841. F. S. Rodkey *The Turco-Egyptian Question...1832–1841* (University of Illinois Press, 1921), 232, 236. B. L. Tuchman, *Bible and Sword. England and Palestine from the Bronze Age to Balfour* (New York University Press, 1956), 136–9.

and silk trades as well as on the sphere of the sailing-ship. It used Galle from 1845 to tranship the mails for Singapore and Hong Kong. It also used the Straits of Malacca rather than the Straits of Sunda, making Penang into a port of call. By making Singapore its half-way house between India and China it facilitated the extension of the overland route to Batavia and enabled the Dutch Government from 1845 to send a warship to Singapore to pick up mail and passengers for Java. From 1846 the channel of the Torres Strait was explored to determine its feasibility for a steamship service from Singapore to Sydney. The successful extension of the P. & O.'s services across half the world was symbolized by the launching in 1846 of its last vessel with an Irish name, the *Erin*, and in 1847 of its first vessels with Chinese and Turkish names, the *Pekin* and the *Sultan*. The signatories to the Treaty of Nanking were commemorated in the *Pottinger* (1846), the first vessel of the P. & O. to be named after an individual, and in the *Keying*, the first Chinese junk to sail westwards around the Cape in 1847, bringing the sacred earth and rice of China into the Thames on 27 March 1848. The expansion of the China trade brought into the English language 'crown colony' in 1845, 'consular city' in 1847 and 'pidgin-English' in 1850. Into the newly opened northern ports it brought the Cantonese, the indispensable commercial allies of the British and the creators of the new lingua franca of commerce. It encouraged the prolongation in 1845 of Pare's idea for a Calais–Calcutta Railway into one for an Atlas Railway to Peking. China provided not only tea and silk in exchange for opium but also the tea plants which Robert Fortune secured in 1845 and introduced into North-West India in 1851. The departure of Yung Wing (1828–1911) from Canton in 1847 for education in the U.S.A. was a private rather than a public response to the impact of the West on China. Yung Wing graduated in 1854 at Yale College while his companion, Wong Foon, graduated at the University of Edinburgh in 1855 and so became the first Chinese doctor trained in the West. Thus the Cantonese followed the Bengalis to school in the West.

As Anglo-French friction reached its height the French began to make use of the overland route from 1845[1] with the cooperation of the P. & O., which arranged to supply coal to French vessels at Aden. A rival overland service to that of the P. & O. was developed in 1845 by the Austrian Lloyd, which had been founded in 1836 and established a bimonthly service between Trieste and Alexandria (10–16 July 1845) after the P. & O. began a competitive service to Constantinople in 1844. The overland route from Trieste to Ostend, developed by Baron Bruck, the Austrian Minister of Commerce, to renew the association between Vienna and Brussels, was used by Waghorn to bring news from Bombay to London in $29\frac{1}{2}$ days.[2] Ostend gained the cross-Channel service to Dover begun by the Belgian Government in 1846 and was recommended

[1] Marston, 138–9.
[2] *The Times*, 6 November 1845, 5 ii; 30 December 1845, 5 ii. *The New Quarterly Review; or Home Foreign and Colonial Journal* (July 1846), 167–82, 'Overland Route to India—Report Presented to the Shareholders of the Great Luxembourg Company'. J. K. Sidebottom, *The Overland Mail* (London, Allen, 1948), 100–5. *The History of The Times* (London, 1939), ii. 72–4.

as the terminus for a route to Genoa in 1847 but failed to deprive Boulogne of the India mails. Thus Trieste failed to capture the India mails from Marseilles so that the Ionian Islands remained eccentric to the overland route.

The Austrian Lloyd became interested in the idea of a study society which was proposed in 1845 by Enfantin and Dufour-Feronce, a merchant of Leipzig, on the basis of Linant de Bellefonds' plan of 1841 for 'a new Bosphorus' between East and West as superior to a mere canal.[1] Enfantin had revived his interest in an isthmian canal in 1837, 1840 and 1842 and had become General Manager of the Paris–Lyons Railway sanctioned in 1845. He established the Suez Canal Study Society on 30 November 1846 as a preliminary to a construction-company, with German, English and French 'nations' in the medieval tradition but without the fourth Egyptian group envisaged in 1845.[2] Louis-Philippe himself was won over to the cause of Suez,[3] together with the Austrian Government, Vienna, Trieste, Venice, Lyons and Marseilles. Effective cooperation was however hindered by national rivalries because Dufour-Feronce and Bruck both aspired, in opposition to Enfantin, to make Trieste the seat of the society and Negrelli its engineer. Palmerston also opposed the idea of a canal as costly and impracticable unlike the railway which he directed the British Consul in Alexandria on 8 February 1847 to urge on Mehemet Ali. The ageing Pasha had improved the overland route in 1846 by building post-stations of solid stone in the desert and by doubling the number of relays. He also replaced the Egyptian Transit Company in 1846 by the Transit Administration as a branch of the Government Administration under an Egyptian. He took over the steamers of the P. & O. on the Nile from 1 February 1847. He thereby brought the Transit under full Egyptian control, eliminated British influence and averted the creation of any enclave of alien administration. He opposed a railway as much as an Alexandria–Suez Canal or a Pelusium–Suez Canal and sought to prevent the growth of British influence in the Red Sea at the expense of Egypt. Thus he secured the rights of administration of the ports of Suakin and Massawa from the Porte in 1846. The fortification of Aden from 1846 by Hardinge and the establishment of a British consulate at Massawa in 1847[4] stimulated a French survey of the Somali coast and Socotra in 1847. The idea of an isthmian canal was also opposed by Waghorn and the British merchants in Alexandria, who were determined that any canal should pass through Alexandria to their benefit or should not be made.[5] Mehemet Ali opposed the idea of a direct canal and declared that he would himself construct a Suez Canal if it were necessary, control the navigation and collect the dues. The Study Society financed A. P. Bourdaloue's survey of the isthmus in 1847, which was one of two surveys of the direct route in addition to three made of the indirect route

[1] H. R. d'Allemagne, *Prosper Enfantin*, 87–90.   [2] Allemagne, 89–90.
[3] Allemagne, 93, Enfantin à Lambert, 9 Décembre 1846.   [4] Marston, 179.
[5] R. Georgi and A. Dufour-Feronce, *Urkunden zur Geschichte des Suezkanals* (Leipzig, Weicher, 1913), 99, Dufour-Feronce an Negrelli, 1 Dezember 1847.

between 1846 and 1849. Bourdaloue first established the true relative levels of the Mediterranean and Red Sea, revealed the error of Lepère's estimate of a difference of $32\frac{1}{2}$ feet between the levels of the two seas and so destroyed the tidal basis of all previous canal projects, including that of Linant. The economic crisis of 1847 prevented the launching of a construction-company on the Paris Bourse. The revolutions of 1848 caused the virtual abandonment of many schemes, including that for a Suez Canal, and left only Enfantin hoping that the revolutions would inspire Europe to undertake 'the peaceful conquest of the Orient'.[1] Those revolutions nevertheless contributed indirectly to the realization of the scheme in so far as they liberated Lesseps from his consular career.

Ferdinand de Lesseps stemmed from a Basque family of the frontier city of Bayonne. His family had supplied the French State since 1740 with some of its most loyal consuls. His father had paid a heavy price for his devotion to the regime of Napoleon: after twenty-three years of service he had been ruined financially by the first Restoration Government and condemned to be a consul in exile by the second Restoration Government. Ferdinand was born in Versailles but grew up in Italy and spent only three of the twenty-five years from 1825 to 1849 in France itself, becoming as deeply imbued as his father with the idea of his duty to France and to his family. As a vice-consul from 1832 to 1837 in Egypt, where he appeared 'a Parisian dandy in the desert',[2] he had been concerned with trade more than with foreign policy, studying Lepère's memoir and Linant's first project of 1833 and learning from Waghorn's perseverance in improving the overland route. The revolution of 1848 transported Lesseps suddenly from the consular to the diplomatic service in the very high rank of Minister Plenipotentiary in a body officered by aristocrats, royalists and Catholics and served by jurists, archivists and ecclesiastics. Lesseps could not be a Legitimist but was an Orleanist, a liberal, a member of the National Guard and a mason.[3] He was sent by the French Republic in 1849 to Rome on a special mission, which was intended to placate the Republican Assembly and gain time for reinforcements to reach the Legitimist General Oudinot and his Mediterranean Expeditionary Force outside the city. Louis Napoleon and Thiers ranked Rome as second only to Paris in the mind of France, were determined to maintain French prestige in Italy against Austria and would not permit a Roman Republic to displace the Pope because Louis Napoleon needed the Catholic army, clergy and peasantry in order to fulfil his own historic destiny. Lesseps failed to understand the real purpose or the limitations of his mission[4] and assumed himself to be the agent of the

---

[1] Georgi, 118, Enfantin à Negrelli, 23 Août 1848.

[2] Prince Puckler-Muskau, *Egypt under Mehemet Ali* (London, Colburn, 1845), i. 172.

[3] G. Douin, *Histoire du Règne du Khédive Ismail* (Roma, 1936), ii. 97.

[4] B. d'Harcourt, *Diplomatie et Diplomats. Les Quatre Ministères de M. Drouyn de Lhuys* (Paris, Plon, 1882), 28–56, Expédition de Rome en 1849. L. M. Floridian, *Les Coulisses du Panama* (Paris, Savine, 1891), 7–85. R. M. Johnston, *The Roman Theocracy and the Republic 1846–1849* (London, Macmillan, 1901), 282.

Assembly rather than of the Foreign Office. He so far exceeded his instructions as to recognize Mazzini's Republic and was abruptly recalled on the election of a new Catholic and conservative Assembly in France. The troops of the French Republic then destroyed the Roman Republic, the dream of a whole generation of Liberals and all possibility of a Republic of Italy. French bayonets restored the papal monarchy and permitted it to grant an amnesty with so many generic exceptions that it became more like a proscription. Arthur Hugh Clough, who spent four months in Rome during the siege, condemned both France for her intervention and England for her non-intervention, mourning the triumph of reaction in the verses he wrote in 1849:

> Say not the struggle naught availeth,
> The labour and the wounds are vain,
> The enemy faints not, nor faileth
> And as things have been they remain...

Lesseps had defied the traditions of French diplomacy as well as the faith which united throne and altar. The new Foreign Minister, Tocqueville, the son and brother of Legitimists, disapproved of such diplomats dragged from obscurity and engaged in the support of foreign republicans.[1] He therefore placed Lesseps on trial before the monarchical institution of the Council of State in a symbolic demonstration of France's determination to repudiate the revolutionary parties of Europe. The Council of State duly condemned Lesseps, ending his career abruptly after twenty-four years of distinguished and honourable service. Lesseps was immediately retired without pay or pension although he lacked the private means of an aristocrat. He deeply resented the political necessity for his repudiation and condemnation. His discharge from the service left a stain on his honour which his Spanish ancestry made him hold dearer than life itself. He still felt the memory of his humiliation keenly in 1886.[2] During his enforced retirement for five years in Berri his jet-black hair turned white and he developed a fixed interest in the canalization of the isthmus of Suez. Tocqueville himself was dismissed, like Oudinot, when he had served the ends of Louis Napoleon. His achievement was to liberate Lesseps for a wider sphere of action, for the cause of France in the service of mankind. Thus in the Roman Expedition of 1849 may be found the origins of the *Souvenirs* of de Tocqueville and the Suez Canal of de Lesseps.

Such a canal threatened to subvert the interests vested in the overland route by Marseilles, Alexandria and, above all, the P. & O., which had ended the first phase of its expansion from Biscay to Bengal. Both its Managers were returned to the House of Commons in 1847, Willcox by Southampton and Anderson by Orkney. In 1849 it erected extensive offices in Leadenhall Street, the home of the East India House, together with a substantial office and store-

---

[1] Le Comte de Tocqueville, *Souvenirs de Alexis de Tocqueville* (Paris, Levy, 1893), 360.
[2] F. de Lesseps, *Recollections of Forty Years* (London, Chapman 1887), i. 1–118, 'The Mission to Rome'.

building at Suez in acceptance of the isthmian barrier. The best natural harbour in the Red Sea thus began to attract European enterprise. Henry Levicke, who had been the first English acting vice-consul at Suez since 1839, became in 1846 the first European to take up permanent residence at Suez,[1] which gained a British Post Office in 1847. The P. & O. supported the promoters of the East India Railway in their five-year campaign (1844–9) for a guarantee of interest from the Government and the East India Company. Its branch service, begun in 1849, from Hong Kong to Shanghai brought the P. & O. into the opium trade in competition with Jardine's.[2] It built all its paddle-wheel mail-boats of timber until 1845 because the war-minded Admiralty would not permit the use of iron in their construction. From 1851 it adopted the screw propeller for its eastern service, so pioneering the use of the screw in the mail service, but retained the paddle for the Mediterranean.

The monopoly which the P. & O. enjoyed was largely non-economic in origin, being based not on its competition with sail or on its carriage of emigrants but on its successive contracts from the G.P.O. since 1837, its acceptance of Admiralty specifications from 1840, its Charter of 1840 from the Crown, its concessions from the Government of Egypt from 1841, and, above all, the protective barrier of the isthmus of Suez to which it fully reconciled and adapted itself. The existence of that isthmus made the Red Sea a dead end for shipping and a very expensive route but prevented competition by the steamships which were increasing in the trade of the Mediterranean during the 1850s. The isthmus brought into fleeting contact the outward-bound and the homeward-bound streams of passengers so that Suez became the great divide between East and West and 'the door of a new world'.[3] The mail contract served as an unofficial Navigation Law and supplied England with an auxiliary steam navy and the P. & O. with great security, immense prestige and a heavy subsidy. The P. & O. failed to incur the expected deficit[4] but found both mail and passenger traffic so far to exceed expectations that it could specialize in their carriage rather than in that of cargo. Its success encouraged R. M. Stephenson, promoter of the East India Railway, to project in 1850 a Constantinople–Lahore Railway via Trebizond, Tehran and Herat. Because it charged higher proportionate fares than the steamship companies of the competitive Atlantic route and inherited the haughtiness of the East India Company it early attracted criticism: 'The Peninsular and Oriental Company, like all great monopolies, is a model of meanness.'[5] The P. & O. nevertheless opened horizons narrowed in England by the economic crisis of 1847 and gave free scope to 'that spirit of enterprise so peculiar to the English, to journey eastward in quest of a livelihood, so difficult to be obtained in their

[1] F. Boase, *Modern English Biography* (1897, 1965), ii. 406.
[2] Fairbank, 362–5.
[3] J. A. de Gobineau, *Trois Ans en Asie* (*de 1855 à 1858*) (Paris, Grasset, 1859, 1923), i. 42.
[4] J. H. Stocqueler, *The Overland Companion* (London, Allen, 1850), 8.
[5] Bayard Taylor, *A Visit to India, China, and Japan, in the Year 1853* (New York, Putnam, 1855), 14. *The Times*, 18 January 1857, 9 v.

own country'.[1] The overland route became a familiar institution to a far wider public than the Anglo-Indians who used it through the medium of the guide-book, the travel-book, the engraving,[2] the biography[3] and the exhibition.[4] That route was perfected by the great enterprise of the P. & O. which survived a Select Committee on the Contract Packet Service in 1850 and a Select Committee on Steam Communication with India in 1851. The competition of the Eastern Steam Navigation Company, formed in 1851 to establish a service to Sydney via Alexandria and Suez, stimulated the P. & O. to inaugurate a new Australian mail service from Singapore to Sydney with the *Chusan*, which arrived in eighty days (15 May–3 August 1852) via the Cape. That service brought the mail to Sydney in twenty-eight days from Singapore and in seventy-three days from London.

Abbas Pasha carried on during his vice-royalty (1848–54) the anti-European reaction begun in 1840, restraining the development of commerce to the benefit of the fellahin. He ordered the Cairo–Suez Road to be macadamized in 1849 but resisted for three years Palmerston's pressure for the construction of an Alexandria–Suez Railway in order to preserve a diplomatic weapon against the Canal project. He only succumbed through his need for British support against a Turkish bid to deprive him of capital jurisdiction. The contract of 12 July 1851[5] was negotiated by Nubar Bey and signed by Robert Stephenson, who had built Egyptian towers for his Britannia Bridge (1846–50) across the Menai Straits. That contract granted what Mehemet Ali had always refused and was regarded as a triumph for British influence. The railway however was to extend only from Alexandria to Cairo and was to begin two miles from the P. & O. pier at Alexandria in token of Egypt's independence of the overland route.

The British success was sufficient to encourage Lesseps to approach Abbas through S. W. Ruyssenaers, the new Consul-General of the Netherlands in Egypt, for a canal concession in the year of Anglo-French tension which followed Louis Napoleon's *coup d'état* in December 1851. That request was refused by both Abbas and the Porte in the upsurge of anti-Western feeling at Constantinople in October 1852, fourteen years after the Anglo-Turkish Treaty of Commerce of 1838 and the humiliating defeats by Ibrahim in 1839. The Ottoman resurgence was a reaction to the Catholic, Orthodox and Protestant renaissances of the century as well as an expression of a dark foreboding of the four hundredth anniversary of the capture of Constantinople in 1853.

---

[1] A. Hervey, *Ten Years in India; or, The Life of a Young Officer* (London, Shoberl, 1850), i. v.

[2] D. Roberts and G. Croly, *The Holy Land* (London, Moon, 1849), iii. pl. 35, 36. D. Roberts, *Egypt and Nubia* (London, Moon, 1846), i. 3–4.

[3] *The Times*, 9 January 1850, 4 vi; 15 January, 4 vi, Waghorn's obituary.

[4] *The Times*, 30 March 1850, 1 iii. Overland Mail to India, a moving diorama prepared by T. Grieve, W. Telbin and J. Absolom and opened on Easter Monday, 1 April 1850. It inspired Charles d'Albert to compose his galop, 'The Overland Mail', in 1850.

[5] L. Wiener, *L'Égypte et ses Chemins de Fer* (Bruxelles, Weissenbruch, 1932), 64–71, 641–4.

After two centuries of disintegration the central power of the Empire began to reassert itself at the expense of the provinces.

Egypt's interests were opposed to an isthmian canal since she enjoyed unrivalled access to both the Red Sea and the Mediterranean as well as the protection afforded by the isthmian barrier to both of her coastlines. The isthmus also made Egypt the inevitable entrepôt for all trade between East and West using the Red Sea. An isthmian canal would replace that highly profitable transhipment trade by a purely transit traffic. It would also increase alien traffic through a land whose civilization was unrelated to that of any other Mediterranean land, hostile to the customs of all other nations, and incompatible with the sea, maritime navigation and foreign trade.[1] Egypt employed her merchant marine in the local and coasting trade rather than in long-distance traffic and focused her life inward to an almost unparalleled extent. That life centred around the Nile which replaced rain in her agricultural economy. 'The sea' of the fellahin remained the centre of equilibrium in that society and the great source of unity through its single valley, delta, port and capital city. The annual flood remained the central event of the year and distinguished the summer of Egypt sharply from that of the parched lands of the Mediterranean. Its silt made ploughing as unnecessary as crop-rotation for the production of harvests of unparalleled abundance of temperate as well as tropical crops in both summer and winter. The greatest river of the Mediterranean world ranked inevitably as the supreme god of its land. Its service justified the absolute power of a State which was unchecked either by free cities or by a feudal nobility and incapable of comprehending a political philosophy of the separation of the powers any more than a political economy of *laissez-faire*. Its sediment brought down and deposited in its Delta over the aeons had helped to divide the Mediterranean from the Red Sea. Its waters had filled all previous canals to the Red Sea since the time of the Pharaohs. Its interests and its worship could only suffer by the diversion of energy and reverence to an isthmian canal.

The proposal for such a canal was opposed by English as well as Egyptian interests. Thus Palmerston closely questioned one returning traveller in 1851 about the Canal and became very angry, declaring 'It shall not be made, it cannot be made, it will not be made; but if it were made, there would be a war between France and England for the possession of Egypt'.[2] Palmerston's influence over public opinion became so great after his Don Pacifico speech and the death of Wellington that his opposition to the Canal sufficed to determine British policy towards the project throughout his lifetime.[3] That opposition was no personal whim stemming from ignorance, short-sightedness or frivolity. Nor was it based on technical, economic or financial grounds or even on

[1] A. Smith, *The Wealth of Nations*, ed. E. Cannan (London, Methuen, 1904, 1950), i. 347.
[2] M. E. Grant Duff, *Notes From a Diary, 1886–1888* (Murray, 1900), i. 81, 20 March 1887, quoting George Melly, author of *Khartoum and the Blue and White Niles* (London, 1851).
[3] H. C. F. Bell, *Lord Palmerston* (London, Longmans, 1936), ii. 355–61.

the distaste of a Whig aristocrat for the new economic civilization of the Manchester School. The project was not a mere question of money, as Lesseps affirmed,[1] nor a mere question of economics, as Nassau Senior implied in suggesting that opposition was unnecessary if the canal were impracticable and would be ineffectual if the canal were practicable. The real grounds of Palmerston's opposition lay in his view of the long-term interests of Britain rather than of her short-term interests. Those interests were political and strategic rather than economic, comprising the defence of the gains made in two centuries of war with France and especially of Palmerston's own great achievement in the settlement of 1841 which had prevented France from replacing Turkey as the suzerain of Egypt. Palmerston was well aware that the importance of the isthmus was that it was closed and thereby provided an excellent natural bulwark for the protection of India as well as a serviceable military road between Turkey and Egypt. Primarily he wished to preserve the Ottoman Empire as an impregnable barrier against Russia so as to offset the more favourable opportunities of Russia for overland expansion towards India. He wished in particular to prevent the excavation of a wide, deep and defensible military trench such as would be created between Egypt and the Syrian provinces of the empire even if the canal were never completed and would permit the fortification of Egypt's eastern frontier just as the Nile Barrage would permit the defensive inundation of the whole Delta. He opposed the construction of a French canal and any associated French colonization of the isthmus as fiercely as he opposed the establishment of a French protectorate over Egypt in his determination to prevent the emergence of an Egyptian Question through the creation of a second Bosporus. He also wished to preserve the strategic value of Gibraltar, Malta and the Ionian Islands and to prevent the extension of French influence from the Levant into the Red Sea and the Indian Ocean. He recognized that French warships from Toulon could operate on interior lines of communication through such a highway and reach India in five weeks against the ten weeks taken by British warships from Portsmouth via the Cape. He therefore feared that on the outbreak of war France might seize such a canal, close it to England, send its navy into the Indian Ocean, capture Aden as well as Mauritius and permanently destroy the insularity of India. Thus he saw the canal as a naval rather than as a commercial route and as another lance in the hand of France to pierce the armour of England. As weapons against the wooden walls of her hereditary foe France had already developed the shell gun and the steam navy, which supplied mechanical compensation for her lack of sailors and so facilitated the navigation of the Channel as to cause the invasion scares of 1844 and 1852.[2] Under Napoleon Lepère had undertaken the first military survey of the

---

[1] F. de Lesseps, *Lettres, Journal et Documents pour servir à l'Histoire du Canal de Suez* (Paris, Didier, 1875), i. 22.

[2] C. J. Bartlett, *Great Britain and Sea Power, 1815–1853* (Oxford, Clarendon Press, 1963), 148–95, 286–93.

isthmus: under Napoleon III Lesseps proposed a canal suitable for the passage of the largest line of battle ships at a time when few merchant ships equalled the size of the smallest line of battle ships. In his determination to maintain British naval supremacy against such a challenge Palmerston enjoyed the full support of Cobden as well as of the country. As France became once more the greatest military power in the world, Palmerston increasingly remembered the French Wars and especially the Egyptian Expedition of 1798. The most numerous bourgeoisie in Europe had been militarized during those wars and profoundly humiliated first at Waterloo and then at Beirut in 1840. France had improved her armies faster than any other power since 1830 as well as training the armies of Mehemet Ali and Ranjit Singh for operations on the flanks of British power. Palmerston was therefore determined to oppose any new Egyptian expedition, although he did not believe that Lesseps would overcome the natural obstacles to the construction of a canal. He sought only to preserve for England her quasi-monopoly of the Cape route and to improve the overland route, which offered the advantage of rapid communication but preserved the isthmian barrier. He desired nothing more than the right of overland transit through Egypt and concluded that a canal could only divert interest from the railway. His fundamental conservatism compelled him to oppose any change in the balance of power in the Levant which would compel Britain to take out territorial guarantees for the security of her world empire, to annex Egypt and thereby to assume the heaviest of liabilities in foreign policy.

3

THE CREATION OF
THE SUEZ CANAL COMPANY, 1854–1858

THE Crimean War encouraged Lesseps to propose a Suez Canal but thwarted its construction. In that war the Ottoman Empire, responding to the triple Christian renaissance of the century, brought the rival empires of Catholic France and Protestant England into reluctant conflict with that of Orthodox Russia. In England the war encouraged a militant and militarist revulsion against the 'bagman's millennium' apparently ushered in by the repeal of the Corn Laws. The reign of the free trade ethos from 1846 to 1853 ended when the army was transformed in popular consciousness from an instrument of tyranny into a defender of liberty. Thenceforward free trade ceased to be a gospel for the total regeneration of society and became restricted to a purely economic creed. Religious and ecclesiastical in origin, the war appeared incomprehensible to the rational and liberal mind of the day which could understand more clearly its economic consequences.

The elimination of Russia as a source of supply encouraged the production of jute and linseed in India as well as of wool in Australia and South Africa. The great distance separating England and France from their chosen theatre of war created a great demand for shipping and stimulated the building of ships, especially of iron screw steamers. The rise in coal prices encouraged John Elder to develop the coal-saving compound-engine in 1854: the search for new sources of supply of coal and oil led ultimately to the production of oil in Wallachia from 1856 and in Pennsylvania from 1859. The transport of troops and supplies brought great prosperity to the half-way house of Malta as well as to the Mediterranean ports in general. Freight rates which had begun to rise in 1852 rose even more sharply to the benefit of all shipping firms, including the Messageries Impériales founded in 1852. The temporary diversion of shipping from the Cape route weakened English interest in South Africa, where the Convention of Bloemfontein of 1854 enshrined the British retreat from beyond the Vaal and undermined the security of the English colonists settled on the coast two generations earlier.

The rise in freight-rates created a demand for shorter routes and encouraged a renewal of interest in the Suez Canal by Enfantin and Dufour-Feronce after a lull of five years. Enfantin suggested to Bruck that the Canal might solve the Eastern Question by opening new outlets to the south to Russia and enabling her to become a maritime power.[1] Dufour-Feronce

---

[1] R. Georgi and A. Dufour-Feronce, *Urkunden zur Geschichte des Suezkanals* (1913), 147, Enfantin à Bruck, 28 Novembre 1853.

conceived of the Canal as a work of peace worthy of the Emperor Napoleon, Queen Victoria and the Emperor Francis Joseph,[1] who had been drawn together by their common hostility to Russia. Lesseps hoped that the Anglo-French alliance would create good relations between the two powers in Egypt as well as in the Crimea and would thus neutralize English opposition to a French-inspired Canal. In Berri on 15 September 1854 he heard the news of the succession of his friend Mohammed Said to the pashalik of Egypt on the assassination of Abbas in a drunken stupor during the night of 10–11 July 1854. Lesseps' domestic ties had been reduced by the death within the preceding year of his mother, his wife and his son and he was eager to realize his great idea so as to restore the prestige he had lost in the eyes of France in 1849. He arrived in Alexandria on 7 November and with the help of Ruyssenaers persuaded Said on 15 November to grant him a concession to form a financial company to pierce the isthmus by the direct route from Suez to Pelusium.[2] On 30 November Said signed the concession which Mehemet Ali, Abbas and the Porte had thitherto refused to grant. The concession was the more generous because it excluded Egyptian ships from any special privilege in their use of the projected waterway and exacted no payment from Lesseps in return for the grant of the right to benefit Europe at the expense of Egypt. Since Lesseps sought to make a name for himself rather than money[3] he did not wish to share the glory of his great enterprise and was compelled to exclude Enfantin, who confidently expected to form the financial company with Lesseps and Isaac Pereira, founder in 1852 of the Crédit Mobilier and of the Messageries. Lesseps had secured an 'exclusive' concession without the diplomatic support of the French Government and thenceforth preferred the patronage of 'my Viceroy' to that of 'my Emperor'.

Said, the fourth and youngest son of Mehemet Ali, had been sent on board ship at the age of thirteen to be brought up at sea as the personal representative of the Pasha's interest in his new post-Navarino navy and as the future patron of that navy. Said, however, grew up to hate the navy and to adore the army in the tradition of the French bourgeoisie as 'one of the greatest and most efficient schools of civilization'.[4] His affection for the army far exceeded that of his father. He ended the purchase of exemption from conscription and conscribed all orders of society, including Copts, Beduin and the sons of village sheikhs, one of whom, Ahmed Arabi, he promoted from the rank of lieutenant in 1857 to that of lieutenant-colonel in 1860. He first promoted fellahin to the rank of officer and encouraged poets to compose national anthems for the army. He travelled around Egypt with an army of several thousand as a retinue and spent four to five hours of each day in drilling his troops in person, especially his favourite Nubians.[5] Educated in the harem

---

[1] Georgi-Dufour, 150, Dufour-Feronce à Arlès-Dufour, 7 Septembre 1854.
[2] F. de Lesseps, *Lettres*, i. 18.   [3] Ibid., i. 109, Lesseps à Mme. Delamalle, 22 Janvier 1855.
[4] J. B. Saint-Hilaire, *Egypt and the Great Suez Canal* (London, Bentley, 1857), 117.
[5] N. W. Senior, *Conversations and Journals in Egypt and Malta* (London, Low, 1882), ii. 180. D. M. Wallace, *Egypt and the Egyptian Question* (London, Macmillan, 1883), 267.

and intensely status-conscious from his childhood Said was gnawed by an acute sense of Egypt's inferiority to Europe, especially to France. He thus became the first ruler of his dynasty to resign to the foreign consuls the government of their communities through the consular courts consolidated in 1857. He first opened the internal commerce of the land to foreigners. He permitted himself to bask in the flattery of Europeans and even to suffer intimidation by their consuls.[1] Mehemet Ali had never allowed any of his European servants to exert political influence or even to enter his presence. Said was too bold to use counsellors like his father and allowed himself to be persuaded that the land of the Nile could be 'improved' and rescued from 'misgovernment'. He permitted Europeans to use him for their ends and so nearly fulfilled his father's prophecy that the dynasty would survive him no longer than ten years.[2] Said identified the Suez Canal with the cause of Egyptian independence of Constantinople as well as with his own aspirations to immortal fame, which Lesseps deftly fostered. He hoped to gain thereby the support of public opinion in Europe,[3] and especially of the French imperial family since Lesseps was the first cousin once removed of the new Empress Eugénie. He expected that the Canal would separate Egypt physically from Turkey and that he would be independent of the Sultan before its completion. To that end he financed the preparatory studies undertaken by Lesseps between 1854 and 1858 and soon believed that he himself had conceived the idea of the Canal.

In the 1850s the diversion of the energies of Europe from political into economic channels after the failure of the revolutions of 1848 produced a great expansion in European economic and political power. Under the influence of the discovery of gold in California and Australia prices began to rise again after their long depression from 1814 to 1849. The commerce of Marseilles, Trieste, Alexandria, Khartoum, Zanzibar, Aden, Bombay, Calcutta, Singapore, Hong Kong, Shanghai, Sydney, Melbourne and Adelaide enjoyed unprecedented expansion. The cultivation of wool expanded in South Africa, like that of sugar in Natal, indigo in Bengal and coffee in Ceylon. The gold boom in Australia produced a great expansion in shipping to Australia, the establishment of new records for the voyage by sail to Melbourne and the construction of giant steam liners to challenge the sailing packets on the Cape route. The branch line established by the P. & O. from Singapore in 1852 brought the mail to Australia in seventy-three days overland, against ninety-two days via the Cape.[4] The antipodean colonies, however, found the overland route expensive, inconvenient, uncomfortable and undemocratic because the P. & O. excluded second-class passengers and charged single men more than double the fare by sail. They preferred clipper ships to carry their immigrants,

---

[1] Senior, i. 181; ii. 139–40. E. de Léon, *The Khedive's Egypt* (London, Low, 1877), 105.
[2] Senior, ii. 171.   [3] Ibid., i. 205; ii. 310.
[4] G. F. Train, *An American Merchant in Europe, Asia, and Australia* (New York, Putnam, 1857), 481.

their gold and their cargo,[1] making the route so unprofitable for the P. & O. that it was pleased to end its branch service in 1855 under the pressure of the war demands from the Crimea. The discovery of gold in California stimulated American expansion to the Pacific coast and the commerce of the Pacific Ocean. In that expansion Americans made their first use of the overland route from 1851, when Bayard Taylor reached India through Egypt. Thus American contacts with Egypt were extended after the appointment of the first American Consul-General in 1848 and the arrival at Alexandria in 1851 of the first direct cargoes of American produce in American ships.[2] American clippers captured the China tea trade and fostered the belief that the U.S.A. would inherit the wealth of the Indies as well as the dominion of the seas through its transcontinental railroads and trans-Pacific steamships.

Hong Kong and Shanghai, which had not developed greatly during the 1840s, began a sustained expansion under the influence of the Tai-Ping Rebellion.[3] That peasant rebellion against the Manchu, the mandarin and the foreigner began a decade after the Western barbarians had humiliated dynasty, kingdom and people in the Opium War. The first revolution in Chinese history began in the hills of Kwangsi near Canton and became the herald of a century of revolution in the Middle Kingdom. The flight of refugee capital and enterprise from the Heavenly Kingdom of the Great Peace to the protection of the consular cities stimulated their take-off into economic growth. In Hong Kong the Tai-Ping district became the heart of the city of Victoria, where industries were established to supply the needs of the rapidly growing Chinese population and shipping expanded to carry the rising tide of Chinese emigration from 1854. The demand for small European vessels for purchase or charter by the local Chinese was created by the paralysis of the imperial revenue service and the increase in piracy and smuggling and fostered by Bowring's ordinances of 1855 and 1856 at the expense of imperial authority. The revolt of the nine southern provinces diverted not only their taxes from Peking to Nanking but also the shipments of northern tea from Canton. Green teas were diverted with silks to Shanghai, whose tea exports eclipsed those from Canton in 1852 and made the fortune of Yung Wing. The destruction of the silk-weaving looms of Nanking during the greatest civil war in history forced raw silk on to the export market through Shanghai in 1852–3 and encouraged its shipment at very high freights via the overland route for the first time in 1855. Black teas were diverted from Canton to Foochow, which was the closest port to the Bohea Hills and was reluctantly opened to foreign trade in 1853. Shanghai's new foreign settlement attracted native merchants, much hoarded capital from the old Chinese city and silver shipments from Europe, which were diverted from the Cape to the overland route from 1853

[1] Ibid., 477.

[2] D. R. Serpell, 'American Consular Activities in Egypt, 1849–1863', *Journal of Modern History* (September 1938), 344–63.

[3] W. C. Costin, *Great Britain and China 1833–1860* (1937), 159–80. J. K. Fairbank, *Trade and Diplomacy on the China Coast 1842–1854* (1953), 311–28, 371–461.

and minted into Shanghai taels from 1856. That settlement established municipal and land regulations, a Municipal Council and its own administration of the Imperial Maritime Customs in 1854, so securing liberties denied to Hong Kong as a crown colony. From 1855 Hong Kong and Shanghai were linked together by foreign steamship services, pioneered by the American firm of Russell & Co. From 1856 Hong Kong was freed from dependence on the supply of rice from Canton by Bowring's Treaty of 1856 with Mongkut of Siam, who became the first ruler of Asia to conclude from the development of closer European relations between India and China that reform was essential for self-preservation.

In India Dalhousie realized Ellenborough's military ideal of a governor-general. His eight years of conquest and consolidation added to the Company's empire the Punjab in 1849, Lower Burma with Rangoon in 1852 and Oudh, the last independent Moslem state, in 1856. From Europe Dalhousie introduced steam railways, the electric telegraph and uniform postage. He considered them to be the three great engines of social improvement and used them to unify and centralize government at the expense of the aristocracy. The Crimean War slowed down the building of railways in India but accelerated the construction of the telegraph network, bringing the intelligence contained in the mail of 23 September 1854 from Bombay over 1,600 miles to Calcutta on the same day. Thenceforward the period of communication with England was reduced by the ten days thitherto taken by the post from Bombay to Calcutta or from thirty-five to twenty-six days. Bombay became the telegraph terminus of India while Galle fulfilled a similar function for Eastern Asia. The construction of an Indo-European telegraph was first proposed in 1855 by James Reuter.[1] From 1854 uniform postage rates were introduced between India and England as well as throughout India. The coordination of postal and telegraph services was accompanied by the revision of the Company's Furlough Rules in 1854, when the distinction drawn in 1796 between leave to England and leave 'within Indian limits' was abolished so that conditions west and east of the Cape were equalized. That change reduced the number of officers taking leave to Australia and the Cape but increased the number travelling to Europe. The Anglo-Indian career became increasingly more English than Indian through the substitution of short and frequent furloughs for a single visit of three years to Europe in a long life of expatriation, which had broken up the family as remorselessly as the slaveocracy of the American South.[2] Thus the P. & O. became an instrument of social salvation. From 1853 it carried the mails to Calcutta and Hong Kong twice per month instead of once per month and benefited by the naval survey of the Straits of Malacca undertaken from 1852. By the contract of 7 July 1854 it secured the Aden–Bombay service, which the East India Company ceased to

---

[1] M. N. Das, *Studies in the Economic and Social Development of Modern India: 1848–1856* (Calcutta, Mukhopadhyay, 1959), 152, 'The Introduction of the Electric Telegraph'.

[2] Thackeray, *The Newcomes* (1855), ch. v.

maintain, and so gained a virtual monopoly of British communications with the East. Thenceforward the basic pattern of the P. & O.'s Asiatic services was complete, as a mail-carrier between England and India, an opium-carrier between India and China[1] and the heir-apparent of the East India Company. During the 1850s it expanded more rapidly than any other trading corporation to become the largest and most successful steamship company in the world,[2] although Bourne died before he had recouped the preliminary losses sustained in its foundation.[3] It paid an average dividend of 9 per cent between 1840 and 1856 while building up substantial reserves. Its profits enabled Arthur Anderson to found in 1853 the Union Steam Ship Company which began an independent steam service to the Cape in 1857. It made Suez, Aden and Bombay into main bases and benefited especially by the rediscovery in 1855 of the water-storage tanks of Aden and by the extension in 1855 of the East India Railway from Calcutta to the coal mines of Raniganj. Its success inspired attempts to perfect steam communication on land, to link Bombay by rail to Calcutta and so to benefit by Dalhousie's annexation of West Berar in 1853 and Nagpur in 1854, which brought the finest cotton tracts in India under British administration so that it thenceforward extended almost without interruption from Calcutta to Bombay.[4]

The economic possibilities of Westernization were first revealed to Asia by the Parsis of Bombay, who had expanded during the Persian Renaissance of the eighteenth century but were threatened by the replacement of Persian by English as the language of government service in 1835. They responded ably to that challenge and travelled to England via the Cape from 1838 and via the overland route from 1839. They adopted English ideas of technical progress, education and social reform and even founded the Oriental Cricket Club in 1848. In the economic boom of the 1850s they became the greatest entrepreneurs in India and the founders of banks, factories, joint-stock companies and railways. The first Indian cotton-spinning mill was established in 1854 by Cowasjee Davar.[5] The first Indian merchant house in London, Cama & Co., was established in 1855 by the Cama brothers and Dadabhai Nairoji. The Parsis became the favoured servants of the British in India, the great beneficiaries by British rule and the model intermediaries for the anticipated regeneration of the East through the diffusion of the economic gospel of their rulers. Their example inspired the visit of the first Gujerati to England in 1856 and they supplied in Nairoji the first Professor of Gujerati to University College, London, in 1856. They accepted European merchants however only as the teachers of new techniques and then reduced them to bankruptcy by their competition. In Bombay their competition drove the British merchant

---

[1] Train, 87, 104.   [2] Ibid., 256.

[3] *Illustrated London News*, 1 November 1851, 539i.

[4] R. J. Moore, *Sir Charles Wood's Indian Policy, 1853–66* (Manchester University Press, 1966), 163.

[5] S. D. Mehta, *The Cotton Mills of India, 1854 to 1954* (Bombay, The Textile Association, 1954), 3–27, 'The Pioneers'.

houses out of existence and reduced British commerce to complete subjection. The Parsis remained the constant middlemen between the English manufacturer and the Hindu consumer: they imported to their shops in Aden cotton textiles from Switzerland and Germany as well as from England. Thus their commercial capacity and long time-horizon enabled them to profit by the development of trade between Europe and Asia and to diffuse its benefits far more widely than they were in Europe.[1]

The economic expansion of the decade increased both the traffic of the Cape route and the pressure for a Suez Canal. The immediate execution of Lesseps' scheme was frustrated by British opposition and by the improvement of the overland route necessitated by the Crimean War. Two cavalry regiments of 1,600 men and 1,400 horses were brought in 1855 from India through Egypt to the Crimea. The first use of the overland route by British military forces was accomplished with considerable inconvenience, difficulty and expense: the profits of the victualling contract consolidated the fortune of Samuel Shepheard of Cairo and enabled him to buy Eathorpe Hall in Warwickshire in 1858. The route remained an imperfect combination of different forms of transport since the railway to Cairo was still under construction and that to Suez was unsanctioned. The disorganization of the trade of Asia Minor by the war also encouraged the first proposal in 1854 for a railway from Suedia on the Mediterranean to the Euphrates.[2] Lesseps' project encouraged a counter-proposal for a long self-excavating canal from Akaba to Haifa via the 'dried up strait' of the Wadi Araba and the Dead Sea.[3] Said yielded to the pressure of the Porte and England and sanctioned in May 1855 the extension of the railway from Cairo to Suez, so compensating England for the grant of the canal concession to Lesseps. The Crimean alliance consolidated the basic pattern of the overland route, enabled Marseilles to retain the India mails, especially after the completion in 1854 of the Paris–Lyons–Mediterranean Railway, and frustrated Bruck's hopes to transfer them to Trieste. The P. & O. helped to finance the construction of the Alexandria–Cairo Railway which was opened on 1 January 1856. The first railway in Africa transferred from the river route the most troublesome section of the overland route and encouraged the Arabs to accept steam locomotion by rail as rapidly as the Indians.[4] It extended British interests in Egypt, together with the electric telegraph concession of 1854,[5] but left the P. & O. still handicapped by the lack of a graving-dock at Suez and of lighthouses in the Red Sea.

Lesseps' success in securing 'exclusive power' to form a canal company

[1] J. A. de Gobineau, *Trois Ans en Asie (de 1855 à 1858)*, ii. 228.

[2] W. Bamforth, 'British Interests in the Tigris-Euphrates Valley: 1856–1888' (M.A. Thesis, University of London, 1948), 40–1.

[3] W. Allen, *The Dead Sea, A New Route to India* (London, Longman, 1855), i. 338–61, 'The Dead Sea Canal'.

[4] M. Oliphant, *Memoir of the Life of Lawrence Oliphant* (Edinburgh, Blackwood, 1891), i. 199, 9 May 1857.

[5] N. W. Senior, *Conversations and Journals in Egypt and Malta* (1882), ii. 173.

ended his relations with Enfantin and so deprived him of the contacts of the Saint-Simonians with the Emperor Napoleon, the French Foreign Office and the bankers and railway contractors of Paris. Those excluded interests encouraged the projection of rival canal schemes designed to make Alexandria their terminal port.[1] Lesseps does not seem to have visited the isthmus before 1854 but spent three weeks (23 December 1854–15 January 1855) with the Pasha's engineers, Mougel and Linant, in a survey of the ground. The preliminary report of those two engineers was presented to Said on 20 March, proposing a lock canal to be built in six years by 20,000 fellahin and 30 steam dredgers. That project was then revised by an International Scientific Commission appointed by Lesseps under the presidency of the Dutch hydraulic engineer, F. W. Conrad (1800–70). Negrelli, the only member of the Study Society of 1846 invited to join the Commission, then paid his first visit to Egypt. The commission in its report of 2 January 1856[2] doubled the maximum size of vessel for which the canal was designed from 1,500 to 3,000 tons and increased the depth from 21 to 26 feet and the bottom width to 144 feet so as to enable two such vessels to pass each other. It also suppressed the locks and so removed the clearest sign of the Egyptian nature of the canal. It shifted the southern exit $1\frac{1}{2}$ miles to the east of Suez and the Mediterranean exit 18 miles to the west of Pelusium, so that it was sited not where the route across the isthmus was the shortest but where the sea approach to the coast was the deepest, amid the shallows created by the eastward drift of the Nile deposits. It recommended the direct route between the Red Sea and the Mediterranean as outlined by Negrelli.[3] The indirect route was favoured by the Saint-Simonians, their banker-allies and the mercantile communities of Alexandria because it would eliminate the construction of a rival port on the Mediterranean and preserve Alexandria's monopoly of trade and shipping. Such a route would however have cut through the Delta rather than through the isthmus and would have made the canal the obvious property of the Pasha. It would have maximized the impact of the Nile upon the canal and of the canal upon the Nile. The direct route was shorter and cheaper because it could use the most easterly of the frontier-lagoons of the Delta in Lake Menzaleh and Lake Ballah as well as the natural depressions of the isthmus in Lake Timsah and the Bitter Lakes. Thus it would require the minimum excavation for 62 of the 100 miles of its course and would only have to cut through the three ridges of Guisr, Serapeum, and Chalouf. Above all, the direct route was the only one acceptable to Said Pasha who would permit no intrusion of infidel shipping into his naval base at Alexandria.

[1] J. J. Baude, 'De l'Isthme de Suez et du Canal Maritime', *Revue des Deux Mondes*, 15 Mars 1855. P. Talabot, 'Le Canal des Deux Mers d'Alexandrie à Suez', *Revue des Deux Mondes*, 15 Mai 1855. A. & E. Barrault, 'Le Canal de Suez et la Question du Trace', *Revue des Deux Mondes*, 1 Janvier 1856.

[2] F. de Lesseps, *Percement de l'Isthme de Suez* (Paris, Plon, 1856), iii, 'Rapport et Projet de la Commission Internationale'.

[3] A. Sammarco, *Suez Storia e Problemi* (Milano, Garzanti, 1943), 157.

Three days after the commission made its report Said granted the Concession of 5 January 1856 which superseded the concession of 1854. The new concession granted substantial privileges to the Company which Lesseps was empowered to form in return for the allocation of 15 per cent of the profits to Egypt. For the specific purpose of creating and operating a maritime canal it granted to the Company for 99 years from the opening of the Canal the usufruct but not the property in the land it ceded in the isthmus. It stipulated that Lesseps was to be President of the Company for ten years from the opening of the Canal. It also excluded, at the request of Lesseps, a clause suggested by Linant and Mougel stipulating for the reduction of the Company's tariff when its dividend exceeded 20 per cent. The new concession first provided for a renewal for further periods of ninety-nine years at the discretion of the Government of Egypt in return for the increase in its share of the Company's profits by 5 per cent for every such extension, up to a maximum of 35 per cent for a 500-year concession. It also limited tolls to a maximum of ten francs per ton of capacity and declared the Canal a neutral passage for merchant vessels but imposed no international obligation thereby on Egypt. It omitted the provision made in 1854 for the establishment of fortifications by the Government at its own expense, in order to frustrate the determination of the Porte to occupy such forts with mixed Turco-Egyptian garrisons. The new concession was opposed by almost all the princes of the ruling family, especially Ismail, by most of the ministers of state and by the higher civil servants who thought Said was delivering Egypt 'bound hand and foot to Lesseps and his party'.[1] The merchants of Alexandria found it equally distasteful and were not appeased by the stipulation inserted by Lesseps that the Company was to have its seat at Alexandria. Thenceforward they vented all their spite against the impossible canal of Lesseps with its impossible port on the Mediterranean. Their views were shared by England which remained consistently hostile.

Throughout 1855 British opposition to the project had been maintained at the secret level of diplomacy in Cairo and Constantinople, although it was questioned for the first time in the Cabinet.[2] Lesseps visited London and Constantinople in a vain bid to secure a firman which would permit the construction works to begin. He proposed on 28 February 1856 the submission to the peace conference at Paris of a clause similar to that included in the new concession providing for the neutrality of the canal and to that included in the Clayton-Bulwer Treaty of 1850 for the neutrality of any isthmian canal built through Central America. Such a guarantee by the powers would have facilitated the flotation of his Company but was supported only by the pariah-power of Austria: it was opposed by England and was not supported by France.

---

[1] M. Kassim, 'The History of the Suez Canal Concession, 1854–1866' (M.A. Thesis, University of London, 1924), 80 note.

[2] Duchess of Argyll, *George Douglas Eighth Duke of Argyll K.G., K.T. (1823–1900)* (London, Murray, 1906), i. 568–9, 20 August 1855.

The Porte was not indifferent but was firmly opposed to the idea of such a canal which would link Egypt directly to Europe, earn revenue for its Pasha, encourage his aspirations to independence and hinder the free movement of Turkish forces overland to the Nile. Turkey had no wish to see Egypt converted by France into a new Algeria. As the greatest Moslem power her interests were opposed to the admission of European warships through her territory, and especially to their entry into the Red Sea, the maritime route to the Holy Places. Above all, the Sultan was opposed to the Canal as an engine of 'progress' since his power was absolute, aristocratic and sacerdotal. The empire had been strengthened more by the defeat of Russia during the war than by the loans secured from 1855 under the guarantee of the governments of France and England. The power of Constantinople over the provincial administrations so increased as to call forth the first Arab cry for 'independence' in 1858. Procrastination, the greatest resource and the highest art of Turkish diplomacy, prevented the grant of the firman to Lesseps more effectively than any outright refusal.

For her part France abstained from direct support of the venture before 1859 since Napoleon III wished Lesseps to undertake all the necessary preparations before committing himself on the principle and hoped that his diplomatic neutrality might induce a corresponding British neutrality towards the scheme. Napoleon was influenced by the hostility of the Saint-Simonians and the French Foreign Office to Lesseps, by his pathological fear of England and by his fixed resolve to avoid any breach in the fragile Anglo-French entente, which he deemed his best guarantee against the fate suffered by his uncle. The end of the war enabled Napoleon to end his pose as the defender of the Ottoman Empire and to establish an entente with Russia against Austria. Russia was humiliated by the war as the monarchies of Western Europe had been by the revolutions of 1848. The Treaty of Paris ended Russian control over the mouth of the Danube, placed the navigation of the river under an international commission and 'neutralized' the Black Sea, forbidding Russia to maintain warships thereon. Russian influence in Europe was reduced to its pre-1721 level, provoking a reaction in the form of the internal reforms of the 1860s, the rise of Pan-Slav sentiment and the extension of Russian power in Central Asia as well as in the Far East, where Vladivostock was founded in 1860. In the Levant Russia shifted from religious to economic expansion: the Russian Steam Navigation and Commercial Company was founded in 1856 and began services to Constantinople in 1857, to Jaffa in 1858 and to Alexandria in 1859.[1]

The grant of the second concession revived British opposition to the project.[2] Palmerston was more determined than ever to preserve the isthmian

[1] W. E. Mosse, 'Russia and the Levant, 1856–1862: Grand Duke Constantine Nicolaevich and the Russian Steam Navigation Company', *Journal of Modern History* (March 1954), 42–5.
[2] H. Reeve, 'The Suez Canal', *Edinburgh Review* (January 1856), 235–67.

barrier against France because of the improvement of the overland route by the railway. That route came into use by the first batch of 'competition wallahs' en route to India in 1856. On 28 January 1856 Canning became the first Governor-General to disembark at Bombay instead of Calcutta while Dalhousie became the first Governor-General whose notice to quit was transmitted by telegraph over 1,600 miles in three hours.[1] The success of the P. & O. inspired R. M. Stephenson, the chairman of the East India Railway, to visualize in 1856 'The World's Highway' linking London to Calcutta in twelve days by railway and steamship via the northern route through Trebizond, Basra and Karachi. The canal project inspired W. P. Andrew in 1856 to form the Euphrates Valley Railway Company for the construction of a desert railway from Seleucia to Bagdad and Basra as an extension of his Scinde Railway from Karachi, the nucleus of a London–Lahore line and the parent of the European and Indian Junction Telegraph Company Limited registered on 13 August 1856. That railway company was launched as an English rival to the French Suez Canal and proposed to link London to Karachi in $14\frac{1}{2}$ days. It would have created a wholly uneconomic military road to the East and could not divert attention from the overland route through Egypt. 'The Isthmus of the Old World is the cynosure of British policy.'[2] Its formation aroused the hostility of Bombay against its potential competitor in Karachi and encouraged the East India Railway to agree in November 1856 to build a branch line to link up with the Great Indian Peninsular Railway from Bombay at Jubbulpore.[3]

Lesseps founded his own journal[4] with the financial help of Said in order to win public opinion to his cause. Palmerston had a naval survey made of the Gulf of Pelusium in 1856 as he began to realize the inflexibility of Lesseps' resolution. He warned Said after he had agreed to supply the labour needed by the Company that he would end as 'Viceroy of M. de Lesseps, or a French Préfet, or possibly a companion in captivity of Abd-el-Kadr'.[5] Said was undaunted and began the construction in January–June 1857 of a fresh-water canal from Cairo to Timsah as the essential preliminary to a maritime canal. The occupation of Perim on 14 February 1857 established British control over the entrance to the Red Sea and brought into the open British hostility to the Franco-Russian entente as much as to an isthmian canal. France was debarred to her considerable irritation from converting Perim into a Cronstadt. Lesseps replied by appointing Negrelli on 14 March as Director-General of Works and arranged to pay a second visit to England. W. P. Andrew was encouraged

[1] M. N. Das, *Studies in the Economic and Social Development of Modern India: 1848–1856* (1959), 159.

[2] R. H. Patterson, 'Speculations on the Future', *Blackwood's Edinburgh Magazine* (June 1856), 742.

[3] R. J. Moore, *Sir Charles Wood's Indian Policy, 1853–66* (Manchester University Press, 1966), 134.

[4] *L'Isthme de Suez. Journal de l'Union des Deux Mers* (25 Juin 1856).

[5] P. Guedalla, *Palmerston* (London, Benn, 1926), 386, 489, Palmerston to Clarendon, 18 December 1856.

to seek Government support for his desert railway and asked on 26 March whether the Government would object to the amalgamation of the Euphrates Valley Railway Company with the Suez Canal Company.[1] Lesseps arrived in England armed with the calculations first made in 1857 by Gressier and Dupin of the exact savings in distance which his canal would achieve. He held twenty-two meetings in eighteen cities in forty-five days between 24 April and 24 June and lavishly distributed the book by his English secretary[2] to the merchants attending his meetings.

The immensity of his project aroused great expectations, which were more economic than mystical in the practical climate of opinion following 1848. The Canal was expected to open new sources of supply rather than new markets, despite the prophecy of Urquhart: 'The opening of this passage would be equivalent to the acquisition of a second India.'[3] Easy access to the markets of Europe would stimulate cattle-breeding in Abyssinia, horse-breeding in Arabia, corn-cultivation in the Yemen[4] and rice-cultivation in Mesopotamia, pearl-fishing in the Persian Gulf and whale-fishing in the South Seas.[5] The establishment of direct contact with the raw silk market of China would revive the French silk industry from its depression after the silkworm epidemic of 1853–4. The new route would also open up the Indian Ocean to the fishermen of the Mediterranean. Above all, it would transfer the carrying trade of Asia from England to France. It would enlarge the entrepôt trade, especially in Eastern produce, of Mauritius, Aden, Suez, Marseilles, Lyons, Trieste and Leipzig.[6] 'The Mediterranean will become the queen of commerce and navigation, the great route of nations and of their commerce.'[7] Thus the prosperity of the Middle Ages would be restored by another crusade which would be one of philanthropy, civilization and Christianity for the general good.[8] 'It will enable European intelligence, industry and civilization to bear more unreservedly, more energetically, more extensively upon the vast regions and the millions of men that are yet to be reclaimed from a state of semi-barbarism.'[9] Egypt in particular would benefit by the construction of the fresh-water canal in association with the maritime canal and by the reclamation of a fertile plain from the desert. The internal port on Lake Timsah would become a Venice of the desert and 'another Alexandria',[10] an Egyptian Calcutta where river shipping would meet ocean shipping in a great entrepôt for the exchange of

[1] Bamforth, 45.

[2] C. L. Kenney, *The Gates of the East: Ten Chapters on the Isthmus of Suez Canal* (London, Ward, 1857). J. B. Saint-Hilaire, *Egypt and the Great Suez Canal* (London, Bentley, 1857).

[3] D. Urquhart, *Progress of Russia in the West, North and South...* (London, Trübner, 1853), 423, 'The Canal of Suez'.

[4] F. de Lesseps, *Lettres* (1881), v. 69.

[5] Kenney, 43.

[6] Georgi-Dufour, 182, Arlès-Dufour à Dufour-Feronce, 27 Septembre 1856.

[7] F. de Lesseps, *Lettres* (1875), i. 357.

[8] *De Bow's Review* (December 1856), 644, 'The Suez Canal—Its Effects on Commerce'.

[9] Kenney, 46. F. W. Conrad, *Reizen naar de Landengte van Suez* (Hague, Nijhoff, 1859), 192.

[10] F. de Lesseps, *Lettres* (1875), i. 278, 30 Octobre 1855, Lesseps to *The Times*.

eastern and western produce. Egypt would become once more the highway of nations in constant contact with the current of a superior civilization.[1] 'The canalisation of the Isthmus of Suez is the keystone in the arch of prosperity of modern Egypt.'[2] The construction of the Canal would thus produce a major advance in civilization and would transfer the trade and industry of North-West Europe to the Mediterranean. 'If enthusiasts and poets are to be believed, an insurmountable Great Wall of China exists between India and Europe which the Suez Company is going to pierce in order that countless populations may fall into one another's arms through the breach and make immense advances in civilization.'[3] Gobineau doubted whether Europe could civilize Asia with its millennial misgovernment and prosperity, concluding that 'Asia is a very tempting meal which poisons those who eat it'.[4]

The commercial possibilities of the route were in fact limited by its unsuitability for sail shipping, to whose requirements the Canal was nevertheless designed. The postwar depression of freights also made the Canal less necessary as a means of saving distance and time. In France sceptics deduced that such a canal would benefit Greek shipping rather than French, would harm the eastern trade of Marseilles and would ruin that of Bordeaux. In England the merchants who heard Lesseps speak gave him their 'approval' and their 'good wishes' but neither their belief nor their effective support. Lesseps recruited as his English agent D. A. Lange, a Dutch-born civil engineer and merchant who gave up his mercantile career in the crisis of 1857 to follow Lesseps. The Lord Mayor of London refused even to preside over a London meeting.[5] Cobden declined to respond to Lesseps' Cobdenite slogan, *Aperire terram gentibus*. Lesseps' propaganda tour of 1857 occasioned the first question ever asked about the Canal in the House of Commons.[6] Palmerston then dismissed the project as a technical impossibility, a financial and commercial folly and a political menace both to Great Britain and to the Ottoman Empire: he termed Lesseps a charlatan and ranked his idea 'among the many bubble schemes that from time to time have been palmed upon gullible capitalists'.[7] The question was however approached in terms of reason rather than of rhetoric by the Netherlands, which appointed on 10 July a State Commission under the chairman of the Dutch Trading Company to examine the significance of the Canal to the Netherlands and her colonies.

The Indian Mutiny then plunged the British Empire into a crisis which revealed England's incapacity to hold India by Indian forces and the inadequacy of England's communications with India. The Mutiny was the

---

[1] J. B. Saint-Hilaire, *Egypt and the Great Suez Canal* (1857), 118.
[2] Kenney, 49.
[3] F. de Coninck, *Le Canal de Suez et le Gouvernement Ottoman* (Le Havre, Lemale, 1863), 22.
[4] J. A. de Gobineau, *Trois Ans en Asie (de 1855 à 1858)*, ii. 233.
[5] D. A. Lange, *Lord Palmerston and the Isthmus of Suez Canal* (London, Richardson, 1857), 14–15.
[6] Hansard, *Commons Debates*, 7 July 1857, H. Berkeley.
[7] Ibid., 1044.

greatest of the indigenous rebellions which spread across Africa and Asia in the years 1855–60, encouraged by the loss of British prestige in the Crimean War. It was less a revolt of the East India Company's mercenary troops than a profoundly conservative revulsion of almost all the orders of Indian society against the Westernization which had proceeded apace under Dalhousie. The insubordination of the sepoys merely expressed India's aversion to the foreigner but dominated the military interpretation of the revolt diffused by the Anglo-Irish school of Christian-military administration of the Punjab.[1] The revolt was a combined servile war and Jacquerie, a war of religion, race and revenge[2] directed against European officers, educated Bengalis, Eurasians and their barracks, police-stations, railway-stations and telegraph offices. That upheaval encouraged the emergence in or around 1858 of the idea of 'Western civilization'[3] as a civilization which was neither Christian, Frankish nor European, neither English, Scots nor British but simply Western rather than Eastern. The British Government did not understand the true magnitude of the crisis and was cut off from India by a delay of three months in inter-communication. Thus the news of the mutiny at Meerut on 10 May reached England in thirty days, that of the massacre at Delhi in forty days and that of the Cawnpore massacre in fifty days.[4] Although the Government had the power of a dictatorship after the general election of 1857 the help it sent was too little, too late and too slow, since reinforcements required three months to reach India via the Cape. Palmerston opposed the use of the overland route in order to avoid creating a precedent for its use by France and so seemed to confirm the rebels' proclamation that the Pasha and the Sultan had prohibited England's use of the Egyptian transit. Delhi was consequently relieved by troops from the Punjab without the help of a single soldier from England while Lucknow was relieved by troops from Ceylon, the Cape, Mauritius and Persia. Only from 15 July did a steady flow of troopships leave England and they were all sailing ships until 25 July.[5] Palmerston refused on 14 August a Government subsidy for the construction of the Euphrates Valley Railway. He decided to send reinforcements through Egypt only on 30 August,[6] under the strong pressure of the East India Company and the Duke of Cambridge, Commander-in-Chief from 1857. The necessary permission was granted to the Company by the British Government on 19 September and by the Sultan on 5 October, enabling the first detachments to reach Bombay in 16 days

[1] T. R. Metcalf, *The Aftermath of Revolt. India, 1857–1870* (Princeton University Press, 1965), 75–80.

[2] W. H. Russell, *My Diary in India in the Year 1858–9* (London, Routledge, 1860), i. 164, 146.

[3] W. C. Costin, *Great Britain and China 1833–1860* (1937), 245, 305, 14 January 1858. Dosabhoy Framji, *The Parsees* (23 July 1858), x. *The Times*, 16 November 1858, 7 v, Stratford Canning, 'Western civilization is knocking hard at the gates of the Levant'. E. Douwes Dekker, *Max Havelaar* (Amsterdam, Ruyter, 1860), 61.

[4] *The Times*, 8 June 1857; 27 June 1857; 15 August 1857.

[5] *Saturday Review*, 28 November 1857, 483–4, 'Steam v. Sails'.

[6] G. Douglas and G. D. Ramsay, *The Panmure Papers* (London, Hodder, 1908), 419–20, Duke of Cambridge to Lord Panmure, 29 August 1857.

(1–17 October) from Malta and to reach Calcutta in six weeks (11 November–22 December) from Plymouth. Of the 40,000 troops sent out from England to India only 5,500 or 13·5 per cent travelled through Egypt while the rest sailed via the Cape in 80 days by steamship or in 110 days by sail. The delay in the arrival of the reinforcements compelled Canning reluctantly to accept the offer of Gurkha troops.[1] Colin Campbell reached Calcutta in 32 days (12 July–13 August 1857) from London but had to wait three long months for his troops and so wasted the cool weather before he began the reconquest of Oudh on 2 March 1858. The news of the evacuation of Lucknow on 24 November had reached England in 45 days; the news of its final reduction on 19 March 1858 arrived in 26 days.[2] The military unification of India by the telegraph strengthened the demand for instant telegraphic communication between England and India, creating a new rivalry between the Red Sea and Euphrates routes as well as between the possible termini of Bombay and Karachi.[3]

The East India Company suppressed the Mutiny with unparalleled vigour in its determination either to rule or to disappear from history, dooming itself by its very success. In the new military ethos generated by the Crimean War the hostility of the Crown, the aristocracy and the Duke of Cambridge to the Company's private army combined with Palmerston's hatred of the dual government of the Company and his determination to conceal the inefficiency of his own administration to destroy the oldest joint stock company in England.[4] The organization and aspirations of 'the greatest and most famous corporation the world ever saw'[5] were inherited by the P. & O. and by the Chartered Bank of India, which began business in Calcutta, Bombay and Shanghai in 1858 and in Hong Kong in 1859. Neither firm was burdened by Government directors or by a Board of Control. In England the home government of India was consolidated while the unchanged forms of local government in India were used to make the greatest series of reforms yet known. Those reforms were inspired by England's determination to establish its power on a solid basis and to perpetuate the empire established by Clive, whose first memorial in England was unveiled at his birthplace in Shrewsbury in 1860. Those reforms ended the democratic despotism of Dalhousie and preserved the princely states as friendly bastions of British power. They profited by the defeat and disarming ot the population to assimilate the administration of India to that of England. The separate existence of the Indian Navy was ended after 250 years (1613–1863) and its functions were transferred to the

---

[1] M. Maclagan, *'Clemency' Canning...1856–1862* (London, Macmillan, 1962), 155, Canning to Colin Campbell, 18 November 1857.

[2] *Manchester Guardian*, 7 January 1858, 3 ii; *The Times*, 14 April 1858, 9 iv.

[3] *The Times*, 17 July 1857, 11 iii.

[4] *Saturday Review*, 9 January 1858, 31, 'The Middle Classes and the Abolition of the East India Company'.

[5] Ibid., 20 February 1858, 180, 'The Chancellor of the Exchequer on the East India Company'.

Royal Navy. The existence of a separate European Army in India was ended. The use of the overland route for troop transport to India was considered in 1858[1] and approved in 1863, together with the construction of permanent barracks for all British troops in India. The new Indian Army was recruited from the loyal North-West rather than from the disloyal North-East.

The victory of British power demonstrated to India the superiority of Europe and entrenched a feeling of inferiority among Indians. The Hindu élites of Bengal became increasingly disposed to accept English culture and education as a model. They assimilated the language, literature, drama, poetry, press and novels of England. They made the visit to England part of their education and ranked the English university degree above the Indian degree. Bankim Chandra Chatterji, the first Indian to graduate as a B.A. of Calcutta University in 1858, was at once appointed a deputy-magistrate. Camruddin Tyabji, the first Indian to visit England for a professional education, was admitted as a solicitor in 1858. Dadabhai Nairoji became president of the London Zoroastrian Society established in 1861, the first Indian student society in London. Ram Prasad Roy, the son of R. M. Roy, became the first Indian judge appointed to the High Court of Calcutta in 1862. The Government preferred to appoint Indians to judicial rather than to administrative posts as the Royal Navy preferred engineers below decks rather than on the bridge: the first Indian barristers were Man Mohun Ghose, admitted in 1866, and Badruddin Tyabji, admitted in 1867. The success of Satyendranath Tagore in passing the Indian Civil Service examination in 1863 set in motion a flow of 'England-going Bengalees', such as Womesh Chunder Bonnerjee who in 1865 founded the London Indian Society with Nairoji. The journey to Europe became thenceforward a new form of pilgrimage which produced England-returned officials and barristers as well as the less successful who failed in examinations or probationary service. The first Indians to acquire country estates in England were Dulip Singh, the exiled son of Ranjit Singh, who bought Elveden in Suffolk in 1863, and David S. Sassoon, who bought Ashley Park in Surrey in 1867.

The shift of British power into the heartland of Moslem India was crowned by the transfer of the whole Government from Calcutta to the hill-station of Simla in the summer of 1866 at the behest of Lawrence, the only Governor-General of the fifteen between 1836 and 1899 who was trained in India. That move so increased the efficiency of administration that for the first time all the arrears of work in all the offices could be cleared. It ushered in the golden age of Anglo-Indian official society and made Simla the model for other little Englands in the hills of the other presidencies. It removed, however, for half of every year the Governor-General and the Government from the indigenous society of the plains and the public opinion of the Presidency towns to a Versailles in the hills. It also served to divorce the princes of India from their own subjects and their traditional way of life. The education of the sons

---

[1] *Select Committee on East India (Transport of Troops)* (382 of 1 July 1858, iii).

of princes by English tutors began with the arrival in 1866 of C. E. Macnaghten. The influence of Protestant Christianity on Hinduism increased to
a maximum in the two decades following the Mutiny through the Brahma
Samaj. Keshub Chandra Sen, who became a Brahmo in the year of the
Mutiny, extended the Samaj from religious to social revolt. As a preacher he
represented the establishment of the British Empire in India as providential
for the regeneration of India but stressed to his audience of Hindu gentlemen
and students the Asiatic origins of Christianity against the European distrust
of Orientalism. 'I rejoice, yea, I am proud that I am an Asiatic. And was not
Jesus Christ an Asiatic? (Deafening Applause).'[1] Bengali consciousness was
thus not submerged beneath the rising tide of English influence but inherited
an interest in public questions as an integral part of English culture. The
failure of India's first bid for independence nevertheless diverted indigenous
energies into economic activity and increased the trade between England and
India carried by sail around the Cape.

After the final departure of Stratford Canning, Lesseps paid a third visit
to Constantinople but found it impossible to weaken the Anglo-Turkish
entente built up by Canning during sixteen years, although he offered the
Sultan a share of one-third in the 15 per cent of the profits allotted to the
Government of Egypt with an advance of £400,000 thereon before the start
of construction.[2] One month after Lesseps arrived in Constantinople Orsini
tried on 14 January 1858 to assassinate Napoleon III with bombs made by
Joseph Taylor in Birmingham. That act detonated an explosion of ferocious
anti-English sentiment in France and a corresponding outburst of anti-French
sentiment in England, which overthrew the Palmerston Ministry for truckling
to France. The new Derby Ministry did not alter in any way the unswerving
opposition of the Government, the Foreign Office and the political nation to
the Suez Canal, which Disraeli as Chancellor of the Exchequer dismissed as
'a most futile idea—totally impossible to be carried out'.[3] The crisis brought
England and France to the verge of war, created grave anxiety in the money
markets of Europe and made the prospect of raising £8,000,000 for the Suez
Canal more remote than ever. It united French and English in mutual opposition and precipitated a naval scare after France ordered its first four ironclads
in March 1858. In April 1858 Lesseps decided to capitalize on French irritation with the 'insolence and selfishness'[4] shown by England in her opposition
to the Canal and to float the Canal Company without the firman of the Sultan.[5]
He accordingly left Constantinople after five months on 19 May. On 1 June

---

[1] K. C. Sen, *Jesus Christ: Europe and Asia. Being the Substance of a Lecture delivered extem-
pore in the Theatre of the Calcutta Medical College by Kesub Chunder Sen, Esq., on Saturday,
5th May 1866* (London, Snow, 1866), 24.

[2] Georgi-Dufour, 191–2, Lesseps à Aali Pascha, 15 Janvier 1858.

[3] Hansard, *Commons Debates*, 26 March 1858, 849, Disraeli.

[4] N. W. Senior, *Conversations with M. Thiers, M. Guizot...* (London, Hurst, 1878), ii.
186, Thiers to Senior, 18 April 1858.

[5] G. Edgar-Bonnet, *Ferdinand de Lesseps* (Paris, Plon, 1951), i. 305.

the motion of the Radical Roebuck in favour of 'the greatest physical work ever undertaken since man was upon the face of the earth'[1] was defeated after a debate of five hours by a crushing vote of 290 against 62 cast by Radicals, Liberals and Peelites. 'It is the greatest bubble which was ever imposed upon the credulity and simplicity of the people of this country.'[2] Robert Stephenson lent the weight of his unrivalled authority to support Palmerston in the Commons and repeated his condemnation in the technical press two days after France had inaugurated its Cherbourg fortress, only seventy knots distant from the Portsmouth base of the new Channel Squadron. 'Nothing can be effected, even by the most unlimited expenditure of time, and life, and money, beyond the formation of a stagnant ditch between two almost tideless seas, unapproachable by large ships under any circumstances and only capable of being used by small vessels when the prevalent winds permit their exit and their entrance.'[3] That judgement was based on Bourdaloue's survey of 1847, which had given Stephenson an excuse to withdraw from the Study Society of 1846. It was refuted by Conrad and Negrelli, who showed that all the canals of the Netherlands were ditches without current but nevertheless eminently navigable.[4] English opinion was influenced profoundly by Stephenson's view of the Canal because he was the son of the inventor of the *Rocket* and of railway locomotion, the builder of the Alexandria–Cairo Railway and 'the most eminent engineer of this or any other country'.[5] The English mind retained a powerful impression that the Canal could not be practicable, that it would have been constructed long ago by English engineers if it had been, and that even if it were practicable it would be used only by the steamships which France was fast developing. English shipowners were thus encouraged to regard the whole project as a mirage.

The Suez Canal Company was floated in Paris between 5 November and 20 November 1858 without either the firman of the Porte or the sanction of Said. Its flotation was opposed by the French financial press and was unsupported by any great cosmopolitan banker. F. E. Erlanger had accompanied Lesseps on his first visit to the isthmus at the close of 1854,[6] while Baron James de Rothschild had toasted Lesseps at a banquet in Vienna in 1857.[7] Lesseps failed however to secure their support any more than that of the Crédit Mobilier of the Pereiras. He had offended 'the vultures and lynxes of the money-markets'[8] by his creation of a company-journal[9] and by his campaign for the support of the small investor. Since he thought their general

[1] Hansard, *Commons Debates*, 1 June 1858, 1366, Roebuck.
[2] Ibid., 1380, Palmerston.
[3] *The Engineer*, 6 August 1858, 94–5.
[4] Ibid., 8 October 1858, 278, F. W. Conrad, 'The Isthmus of Suez Canal'.
[5] *Manchester Guardian*, 3 June 1858, 2 iv.
[6] J. Ganiage, *Les Origines du Protectorat Français en Tunisie* (Paris, Presses Universitaires de France, 1959), 209 note.
[7] *L'Isthme de Suez*, 25 Novembre 1857, 490.
[8] F. de Lesseps, *Lettres* (1875), i. 58, 14 Décembre 1854; i. 109, 22 Janvier 1855.
[9] Georgi-Dufour, 157, Dufour an Negrelli, 28 Juni 1856.

attitude too autocratic and their commission of 5 per cent too high for their services he secured neither their capital nor their connexions. On 20 November Lesseps was left with 117,000 shares or 29 per cent of the 400,000 which were unsubscribed. He nevertheless appointed on 22 November a works committee of seven with himself as chairman, having broken off relations with Linant. He persuaded Revoltella, who was a banker of Trieste, a friend of Bruck and a vice-president of the Canal Company, to sign a convention on 30 November subscribing to 50,000 shares on behalf of Austria.[1] When Revoltella repudiated that convention Lesseps attributed an additional 114,000 shares to Said, who had insisted that the French shares should not much exceed one-half of the whole.[2] Said's allotment of shares which had risen from 30,000 in 1856 to 64,000 in 1857 thereby rose to 177,642. Lesseps was thus able formally to constitute the Universal Company of the Suez Maritime Canal on 20 December, when he held the first meeting of his board of directors.

The attribution of 45 per cent of the shares to Said raised the number of shares subscribed in countries bordering on the Mediterranean, including Russia and Portugal, to 396,324 or to 99·7 per cent of the total. In France 21,229 shareholders subscribed to 207,111 shares or to 51·78 per cent of the total.[3] Three-quarters of those shares were subscribed by small investors and one-quarter by large investors with 100 shares or more each. Of the eighty-six departments of France the four which centred around Paris, Marseilles, Lyons and Bordeaux subscribed to 62 per cent of the 207,111 shares. The investors represented French society from its summit to its centre, excluding the Republican lower orders of the great cities but including the Orleanist bourgeoisie, the Bonapartist peasantry and shopkeepers and even the Legitimist nobility, who followed the lead given by the Comte de Chambord. Landowners and merchants were powerfully reinforced by members of the great professions of State, by lawyers, magistrates, officials, soldiers, clergy and engineers. Those investors were united less by the desire for profits than by the pride of a great nation which had once more been wounded by perfidious Albion. The launching of the Canal Company would fling down the gauntlet of defiance to the hereditary enemy and secure revenge for the humiliation of Waterloo, the bombardment of 'our Beirut' in 1840,[4] the overthrow of the Orleans monarchy as well as of the Second Republic, the loss of French lives in the Crimea in English interests, and the offensive toleration extended by England to conspirators against 'imperialism' in France. It would also improve a property whose reversion had been virtually assured to France by Bonaparte, Champollion, the French officers of Mehemet Ali, the French popularizers of Egyptology in the 1840s and Mariette, who was appointed Curator of Egyptian Monuments in 1858 by Said under the influence of

---

[1] G. Cervani, *Il 'Voyage en Égypte' (1861–1862) di Pasquale Revoltella* (Trieste, A.L.U.T., 1962), 224.

[2] F. de Lesseps, *Recollections* (1887), ii. 120.

[3] F. de Lesseps, *Lettres* (1875), ii. 389, 393, 397, 404.

[4] F. S. Rodkey, *The Turco-Egyptian Question...1832–1841*, 187.

Lesseps and Napoleon. Thus France would reaffirm its mission to reclaim Egypt for civilization and thereby its claims to the valley of the Nile, to which it believed itself as much entitled as to the left bank of the Rhine. The imperial aspirations of France were recognized in the selection of Jomard Bey as the first of the three Honorary Presidents of the Company and of the Duke of Albuféra as one of the three Vice-Presidents. E. F. Jomard (1777–1862) had accompanied Bonaparte to Egypt in 1798, had defended the cause of Mehemet Ali in 1840[1] and had foretold in 1855 a circumnavigation of the earth by steamship in thirty-eight days: he was President of the Imperial Geographical Society, a member of the Institute and Dean of the Academy of Sciences. Albuféra, another Imperialist, was the son of Napoleon's Marshal Suchet as well as the son-in-law of the Prussian banker Schickler and served as Lesseps' deputy in Paris as Ruyssenaers did in Egypt. The Emperor's cousin, Prince Jerome Napoleon, became the Protector of the Company since Lesseps could secure neither the Emperor nor the Empress as an official patron. Thus the Company was created as an unofficial agent of the Imperialist cause and as a medium for the extension of French influence in the Levant.

Such powerful French support probably discouraged subscriptions by other countries. Lesseps in his superb optimism had entitled his company 'Universal', had printed its shares in Turkish, German, Italian, English and French and had established 71 agencies abroad in addition to the 153 in France. He had also reserved 20 per cent of the shares for English subscribers and 5 per cent for subscribers in the U.S.A. In accordance with the statutory provision for the representation on the board of directors of the principal nationalities interested in the enterprise, he appointed ten of the thirty-eight directors, or over one-quarter, from countries outside France, three from Italy, two from the Netherlands and one each from Spain, Portugal, Russia and the U.S.A. Foreign subscribers however numbered only 2,265 to 15,198 shares or to 3·8 per cent of the total.[2] Even that limited number was subscribed through Lesseps' own personal connexions. Lesseps himself profited by his Spanish ancestry and his consular service in Barcelona between 1840 and 1848 to secure subscriptions to 4,161 shares in Spain, which thereby became the second largest subscriber after France. Lesseps' younger brother, Jules, helped to place 1,714 shares in Tunis, where he had been consul between 1827 and 1832 and a merchant since 1833. Jules was the Bey's chargé d'affaires in Paris from 1847 to 1882 and his usual intermediary with French financiers.[3]

French sponsorship of the Company precluded subscriptions by the English in their 'innate pride and insular ignorance'[4] and their fixed belief that the scheme was a bubble-enterprise, if not a deliberate French plot to subvert

---

[1] F. Charles-Roux, *Edmé-François Jomard et la Réforme de l'Égypte en 1839* (Le Caire, Institut Français d'Archéologie Orientale, 1955).

[2] F. de Lesseps, *Lettres* (1877), iii. 2.

[3] Ganiage, 355.   [4] F. de Lesseps, *Lettres* (1875), ii. 346

England's control of the Cape route and establish French control over the road to India. 'The South Sea bubble is reproduced in the Red Sea one... The whole affair is a downright robbery of simple and deluded folks, as not one marvedi will ever be got out of the toll gates of an impossible canal.'[1] England's calm assumption that her abstention would discourage investment by other nations in a new Darien scheme was justified by Austria, which did not wish to offend her best ally against Russia. Austria had rewarded Russia for saving the Habsburg Empire in 1849 by her malevolent neutrality during the Crimean War and thenceforward dreaded Russian revenge so much that she preferred the Euphrates Valley Railway to the Suez Canal as a barrier against Russia. She had ended her support of Lesseps from August 1857 after Palmerston's renewed expression of his hostility. She resented Lesseps' continued employment of Negrelli, whom the Imperial Government had dismissed in 1855 for his pro-Italian sympathies after Sardinia's entry into the Crimean War. She was most alarmed by the ententes which were intended to destroy Habsburg hegemony in Italy and were concluded with Russia at Warsaw and with Sardinia at Plombières by France, under the influence of Orsini's explosive reminder to Napoleon III of his revolutionary mission. Jerome Bonaparte, the Protector of the Company, was most objectionable to Austria as a republican, a mason and an anti-clerical friend of Italian unity. He had served as Napoleon's secret agent in the conclusion of the Franco-Russian entente and also became the symbol of the Franco-Sardinian alliance by his marriage to the daughter of Victor Emmanuel II, which was arranged at Plombières. The anti-Austrian shift of French policy prevented Revoltella from disposing of his 50,000 shares and frustrated all his efforts to publicize the Canal, which included the exhibition of a symbolic sculpture of 'The Piercing of the Isthmus of Suez' by Pietro Magni in Trieste on 24 February 1859.[2] Vienna's abstention discouraged subscriptions in Trieste, Lombardy-Venetia, the Italian duchies, the Papal States, Naples and Bremen, rendering fruitless Lesseps' Germanic publicity.[3] The Hanseatic ports did not relish the prospect of losing their entrepôt trade to the Mediterranean. Genoa distrusted a project supported by both Sardinia and Marseilles. Spanish participation reduced Portuguese while Dutch participation reduced Belgian. Within the Netherlands the transit port of Rotterdam supported what the national port of Amsterdam opposed. The report of the Netherlands State Commission delivered on 11 January 1859 expressed Amsterdam's hostility but studied the project in economic rather than in political terms. It concluded that the Canal would benefit steamships at the expense of the sailing ship, would save a steamship 13 days of the $53\frac{1}{2}$-day voyage to Batavia and would therefore encourage the rise of Mediterranean shipping to the disadvantage of the Netherlands.

The Company was termed 'Universal' because of its intended function and

---

[1] *The Globe*, 30 November 1858, 2 v.   [2] Cervani, 68.
[3] F. Szarvady, *Der Suezkanal* (Leipzig, Brockhaus, 1859). F. W. Conrad, *Reizen naar de Landengte van Suez* (Hague, Nijhoff, 1859).

because of Lesseps' distrust of the State since 1849. Its nationality was left in obscurity for the first eight years of its existence. No specific statement of its nationality was made in 1858,[1] although it was a private profit-making company governed by private law: it was not an international company in origin, in law or even in function. It was said to be constituted with the approval of the Egyptian Government as a joint-stock company but with the very distinctive privilege of being governed by the principles common to joint-stock companies approved by the French Government and with its legal domicile at its administrative headquarters in Paris. The Imperial Decree of 7 May 1859 was issued under the French Code of Commerce of 1807 at the request which Lesseps made to the Minister of Commerce on 26 December 1858: it conferred on the Company a legal existence in France as a foreign company, enabling it to exercise all its rights in relation to third parties in accordance with the laws of the empire. Thus Lesseps sought to make the Company a quasi-state in a legal Alsatia between Egypt and France.

The enlistment of the capital of small shareholders in the Company confirmed Lesseps' breach of 1855 with Enfantin, the Saint-Simonians and high finance. Those shareholders were intended to pay within twelve months on each £20 share £8,[2] which was, however, reduced to £4. The statutes of the Company strictly limited the rights of the shareholders. They were debarred from bringing a civil suit against the Company but had to accept the arbitration procedure of the French Code of Commerce which had been abrogated in 1856. They could not bring a general suit against the Company except through the medium of the General Assembly, whose membership excluded most shareholders by limiting it to those with twenty-five shares. Thus a democracy of investors created an oligarchical company under a benevolent autocrat who could tolerate no associates. Lesseps separated himself in succession from Enfantin, Saint-Hilaire and Linant but recruited experts in finance, administration and jurisprudence for the service of the Company. The thirty-eight directors included the chief founders and shareholders while founders' shares were allotted to 166 contributors of money, advice or influence, with the maximum being held by Lesseps, Ruyssenaers, Linant and Mougel. The board included eight diplomats and politicians, eight merchants, seven landowners and six bankers but no engineers, shipowners or naval officers. It also included Lesseps' brother Jules, his brother-in-law Victor Delamalle, his cousins De Lagau and Champetier de Ribes and his uncle Adrien Corbin de Mangoux, who together helped to make the Company appear almost like a family-firm during the first phase of its existence. Egypt was represented by no director but by a commissioner, the first of whom was F. W. Conrad. The function of the board of directors was to confirm decisions taken by the executive committee, which was an emanation of Lesseps and held its first meeting on 17 December 1858, three days before

---

[1] J. Charles-Roux, *L'Isthme et le Canal de Suez* (1901), i. 281.
[2] F. de Lesseps, *Lettres*, i. 103; iii. 107.

the first meeting of the board. Thus Lesseps sought to ensure a monopoly of the power and the glory of his great enterprise. His greatest difficulty after the death of Negrelli was the shortage of capital caused by the underestimation of costs inevitable with a pioneer work and by the comparative failure of the initial flotation. His greatest gift was the ability to inspire his shareholders and his employees with confidence in himself and in his dream. As a true merchant of hope he minimized obstacles, magnified achievements and always exuded optimism. The Company was nevertheless compelled to rely on financial help from the Government of Egypt, to raise revenue in all possible ways, to develop its financial techniques and operations and so to allot financial considerations priority over all others. Thus from its foundation the Suez Canal Company became a financial company rather than a construction company and dependent on Egypt for capital as well as for labour and water.

4

THE CONSTRUCTION OF THE CANAL, 1859-1869

THE Company was compelled to begin and to complete the construction works as soon as possible because it had to pay a statutory 5 per cent interest to its shareholders during the anticipated six years of construction. Thus it repaid part of its working capital in token of the rich harvest which was yet to come. Its task was to excavate 125,000,000 cubic yards in order to pierce a maritime canal through the desert of the isthmus. The obstacles which it faced were magnified by opponents to include the storms and quicksands of the Gulf of Pelusium, the absence of any Mediterranean port, the alluvial drift from the mouth of the Nile, the liquid mud of Lake Menzaleh, the drift sands and solid rock of the isthmus, the simoon of the desert, the constant absorption of water by the insatiable sand of the bed and the evaporation of water from the extensive surface of the Bitter Lakes. Those obstacles compelled the Company to learn by experience so that the least excavation was done in the early years and the most in the last two years. The greatest hindrances were the lack of water and labour in the isthmus. The essential preliminary to the construction of a maritime canal thus became the extension of a fresh-water canal from the Nile. Moslem Egypt moreover lacked both a labour market and its associated poor law. The few wants of its peasantry were satisfied in abundance by the Nile which they served. Those wants could not be enhanced because the fear of the evil eye restrained the peasantry from competitive expenditure. The fellahin were more deeply attached to their land than even the French peasantry and could not be tempted by any wage to leave their household without its head, least of all to venture into the desert in the service of the infidel.

The first contract for the construction of the Canal and its harbours was signed on 14 February 1859 with Alphonse Hardon whose construction of railway-stations in France had made him a millionaire. The works began on 25 April 1859 when the Egyptian flag was hoisted on a surf-beaten sand-bank between the Mediterranean and Lake Menzaleh, 37 miles east of Damietta and $7\frac{1}{2}$ miles east of the old fort of Ghemil. Lesseps placed the earth excavated by European and Egyptian in a bag decorated with the colours of Imperial France. The new 'Port Said' thus came into existence as a European town and a construction-camp with a single row of barrack-huts from the Crimea planted on piles on an open beach, a lighthouse inaugurated on 20 May 1859 and a landing-jetty. The work of construction was begun in the absence of Said and without either the sanction of the Porte, the encouragement of the French Ambassador at Constantinople, the support of the French Consul in Egypt or the approval of Britain.[1] The crisis in Anglo-French relations which had arisen in 1858 became acute after England's Austrian ally went to war with Sardinia and France for the defence of Lombardy. England replied to the launching of the first French ironclad, *La Gloire*, by ordering on 11 May 1859 the first English sea-going ironclad, *Warrior*, and by launching the anti-French Volunteer Movement of May 1859. England and Austria also combined with the Porte and the Pasha to oppose the unauthorized construction of 'the French Canal'. Chérif Pasha, Said's chief minister, ordered on 9 June the immediate cessation of the works, so precipitating a crisis in the relations between Egypt and the Company.

The twenty Egyptian workmen at Port Said went on strike on 8 July. The new port was cut off from Damietta so that the Company was compelled to hire its own vessels, to distil its own water, to bake its own bread and to catch its own fish. Nevertheless it began to found camps on defensible sites in the interior of the isthmus at Toussoum in July, at Geneifa in August and at Kantara in September. The crisis of 1859 compelled Lesseps to give up hope of Austrian subscriptions to 50,000 shares in the Company, and his Works Committee to modify fundamentally on 16–17 August the 1856 plan for the Canal. The construction of an inland harbour on Lake Timsah was abandoned, the bottom width was halved from 144 to 72 feet, the curves were raised in number from 10 to 24, the cube of total excavation was reduced by 5 per cent to 120,000,000 cubic yards and the estimates of cost were reduced by 15 per cent. The reduction in the width of the Canal was intended to save as much excavation as possible in the three deep cuttings but transformed the plan from a two-way into a one-way channel: thereby it more than halved the value of the Canal and imposed a structural limit which the Company never eliminated.

In England the crisis encouraged the proposal of such rival schemes as a ship-railway to carry sailing ships at 20 m.p.h. across the isthmus,[2] an Ascalon–Akaba Canal and a Nile Valley Railway. In France Napoleon III became more confident after the success of the French army against Austria in Lombardy: he ordered on 13 October a naval mission to the Red Sea and on 19 October the maintenance of the rights of the Canal Company. Lesseps led a deputation of his directors to the Emperor on 23 October and secured from him the first definite promise of support for his enterprise. He then postponed his first meeting of shareholders for six months and appealed on 7 November for support against the British Government to the kings and princes of Europe, securing favourable replies from Austria, Russia and Italy. D. A. Lange felt compelled to resign on 12 November from his prospective seat on the board whilst remaining Lesseps' agent in England. Delane concluded that England

---

[1] *The Times*, 26 May 1859, 8 iii.
[2] J. Brunlees and E. B. Webb, *Proposed Ship-Railway Across the Isthmus of Suez* (London, Reed, 3 August 1859).

would hold her place in the world quite independently of the isthmus of Suez, just as she had survived the loss of the American colonies. 'If, however, contrary to all probabilities, the project should be actually realized, we can only say that the Canal will be so far a British canal that it will be traversed by British ships, devoted to British traffic and maintained by British tolls.'[1] Another English observer agreed that the Canal was in economic terms as practicable as steam balloons to the moon[2] and could conceal only an Imperialist plot to place the overland route to India under the control of a French company, French forts, French police and French zouaves disguised as workmen.[3] It could also protect the Pasha of Egypt against his sovereign by a military trench[4] which might become an Egyptian Dardanelles or Gibraltar. Such fears encouraged W. P. Andrew to revive the idea of a Euphrates Valley Railway in December 1859 and the British Government to maintain an unflinching opposition to the use of conscript labour in the construction of the Canal.

British interests seemed to be more directly threatened by the Canal because of the simultaneous improvement of the overland route under the stimulus of the wars in India and China. The completion of the Cairo–Suez Railway on 7 December 1858 linked Alexandria by 204 miles of rail to Suez. That triumph for British over French imperial communications emphasized that the traffic across the isthmus was an exclusively British interest.[5] The new desert railway eliminated the four-horse vans introduced by Waghorn in 1840 and provided 'the last link of the chain of locomotion by steam from London Bridge through 180 degrees of longitude east'.[6] The triumph of Suez over Kosseir was consolidated by Said's foundation in 1857 of the Medjidieh Steam Navigation Company, which began a steam service to Jedda in 1858. That first indigenous steam service in the Red Sea carried the Mahmal for the first time by steam to Jedda in 1861.

The Egyptian section of the overland route which had begun as a leisurely pilgrimage was transformed from 1858 into a brief and brisk transit, during which travellers were largely insulated from the life of the land through which they passed. Thus young cadets en route to India incurred censure for their systematic outrages on the indigenous population and their Moslem faith.[7] To benefit by the railway a new Anglo-Egyptian Postal Convention was concluded in 1858 by Trollope and Nubar, Director of the Transit since 1857. That Convention reduced the time of transit for mails to 24 hours against the strong opposition of the P. & O., which was the greatest paymaster on the railway

[1] *The Times*, 16 December 1859, 8 ii–iii.
[2] *Saturday Review*, 24 December 1859, 763–4, 'The Suez Canal'.
[3] F. de Lesseps, *Lettres* (1879), iv. 461.
[4] *The Times*, 20 December 1859, 6 iv.
[5] *The Times*, 7 April 1858, 8 iii–iv.
[6] G. F. Dassi, *Notes on Sueis* (Naples, 1860), 8.
[7] *The Times*, 23 April 1860, 6 iii, 'The English in Egypt'. Hansard, *Commons Debates*, 27 April 1860, 221, 249–50, 455, Mildmay.

and feared competition as a result of acceleration.[1] Trollope left Egypt with a very strong bias against 'M. Lesseps and his Suez Canal' and in favour of steam navigation by land through Egypt.[2] The G.P.O. was encouraged by the new Convention to introduce sea-sorting on the Southampton mail-boat from 1858, to seek tenders in 1858 for a new service from Suez to Australia and to oppose the Pacific mail service favoured by the Admiralty and by New Zealand. The P. & O. survived the competition of all rival companies, to which it denied repair facilities at Suez. Its *Salsette*, which left Sydney on 12 February 1859 for Suez, began a service via Mauritius and encouraged Lesseps to hope that Port Louis would become the entrepôt of the Indian Ocean and the great port of call for mailboats from the Cape as well as from Australia.[3] The first attempt to lay an Indo-European telegraph by the Red Sea route was undertaken by L. & F. Gisborne who had laid the electric telegraph from Alexandria to Suez in 1856 and had registered the Red Sea and India Telegraph Company Limited on 2 August 1858. Unlike the Euphrates Valley Railway, that company secured a guarantee of interest from Ellenborough who was President of the Board of Control for a third time. The first Suez–Aden cable was laid in 1859 and extended to Bombay in March 1860. The cable was too hastily laid to survive the coral and the heat of the Red Sea: it proved as unsuccessful as the first Atlantic cable, so diverting interest to the Constantinople–Bagdad telegraph, completed in December 1860, as the basis for an extension to India. The overland route remained a rail and steamship route used by Indians as well as by Anglo-Indians, for whom its familiar hazards were demarcated in a new series of railway guides[4] and romanticized in a successful comedy.[5]

Work began again on the Canal after eight months on the return of the Egyptian workmen from mid-November 1859. Camps were established at Timsah in November, at El Firdan and Serapeum in December and at El Guisr in August 1860. Each camp had a well, an oven and an Arab village: if it were large enough it had a church and a hospital. The construction of piers was begun at Port Said from April 1860 in order to create an outer port on the model of Venice. Small bucket-dredgers, built in Lyons and Brussels and reassembled at Port Said, began work in June 1860 but proved only 19 per cent as efficient as expected. The Company moved its offices from Cairo and Alexandria to Damietta but failed to secure the fishing rights of Lake Menzaleh which would have reduced the villages of the lake to feudal dependence.

The Turkish request of 4 January 1860 to England and France for guarantees

---

[1] A. Trollope, *An Autobiography* (Edinburgh, Blackwood, 1883), i. 155–6, 165–7.
[2] A. Trollope, *The West Indies and the Spanish Main* (London, Chapman, 1859), 338.
[3] F. de Lesseps, *Lettres* (1875), ii. 336.
[4] *Bradshaw's Railway . . . Through Route and Overland Guide to India, Egypt and China* (London, Adams, 1857). *Bradshaw's Hand-Book to the Bengal Presidency* (London, Adams, 1860), which was followed by similar guides to Bombay in 1861 and to Madras in 1864.
[5] T. Taylor, *The Overland Route* (Theatre Royal, Haymarket, April 1860).

for the security of the Empire and of Egypt against any threat created by the Canal was supported by the massacre of the Maronite clients of France in Syria. The resulting French expedition of 1860 to Syria was intended to lay the foundations of a new French empire in Western Asia at the expense of Turkey and with the acquiescence of Russia. To that end an Arab state was to be created under Abd el Kadr of Damascus while a Jewish state was to stretch along the Mediterranean coast from Suez to Smyrna, so encouraging the revival from 1860 of Jewish national consciousness under French patronage.[1] Thus the Sultan would be discouraged and debarred from maintaining his opposition to the Canal. Said was attracted by the prospect of independence from the Sultan and did not enforce his ultimatum of 1859 to the Company. Instead he raised his army from 10,000 to 64,000 and subscribed by the Convention of 6 August 1860[2] to 177,642 shares in the Canal Company valued at £3,520,000. In payment of the first call of £604,000 Said issued at the suggestion of Lesseps three-year 10 per cent Treasury bonds to circumvent the need for the Sultan's sanction to a foreign loan. Those bonds, together with the £1,100,000 borrowed by Said on 17 July 1860 from C. Lafitte et Cie and the Comptoir d'Escompte of Paris[3] created the nucleus of an Egyptian Debt and attracted Levantine financiers to offer Said their services in raising a loan. Support for the Canal was also extended by the French Academy's offer of a prize for a poem on the subject, which was won in 1861 by Henri de Bornier's *L'Isthme de Suez*.

The Syrian expedition failed in its state-building aims but encouraged Lesseps to seek Maronites from Beirut as worker-colonists[4] and succeeded in securing the consent of the Porte on 12 February 1861 to the preparatory works on the Canal. François Philippe Voisin arrived in January 1861 to succeed Mougel as Chief Engineer of the Company. A preliminary channel was then begun by manual labour through Lake Menzaleh. It was built by the robust fishermen of the lake who extracted 424,000 cubic yards of semi-liquid mud, squeezed it dry, spread it in successive thin layers to bake in the sun and so created a solid dyke with no other tools than their hands. That channel became the precursor of the projected Canal, a proof of its possibility and a pledge of its achievement. It opened a route southward for the dredgers which then widened and deepened it. The Porte's consent made possible the employment of conscript labour which remained on an unofficial basis in deference to English susceptibilities. The first monthly levy of 5,000 was expected from February 1861: its first contingent of 2,500 arrived at the beginning of March. After the fast of Ramadan recruitment by Hardon's agents went ahead through

[1] M. Emérit, 'La Crise Syrienne et l'Expansion Économique Française en 1860', *Revue Historique* (Avril 1952), 217, 220. B. L. Tuchman, *Bible and Sword. England and Palestine from the Bronze Age to Balfour* (1956), 146–7.

[2] F. de Lesseps, *Lettres*, iii (1877), 381–2, 391–2; iv (1879), 99, 133–4, 190. Hansard, *Commons Debates*, 23 August 1860, Danby Seymour.

[3] M. Sabry, *L'Empire Égyptien sous Ismail* (Paris, Geuthner, 1933), 63, 90.

[4] Sabry, 262, 23 January 1861.

the 2,500 villages of Egypt, which were each asked for two men, while Lesseps visited Palestine (21 March–7 April 1861) to recruit labour for 'a work announced in the Bible and in the Koran'.[1] That conscript labour was employed on the construction of the Sweet Water Canal to Timsah as well as on the preliminary channel which reached Kantara in June 1861. Lesseps profited by Said's hatred of the new Sultan, Abdul Aziz, and secured the doubling of the monthly contingent to 10,000.[2] A second parallel channel was then begun, so opening up an independent passage for light traffic and permitting dredgers to work without interruption in the first channel. By the end of 1861 the preliminary channel had been extended 38½ miles south to El Firdan and 1,330,000 cubic yards had been excavated, mostly by dry excavation.

The boom of the 1860s hindered the execution of the Canal works by draining off labour. Economic expansion was powerfully stimulated by the second China War and by the Civil War in the U.S.A. The Merchants' War of 1856–60 followed the growing use of the British flag as a flag of protection by Chinese vessels and the Chinese arrest of the *Arrow* which seems to have been as closely associated with Jardine's as Governor Bowring, whose son had been a partner since Bowring became Governor of Hong Kong in 1854. The Treaty of Tientsin in 1858 gave legal recognition to the opium trade and opened the great rivers of China to foreign trade as well as the Forbidden City to Western legations. It increased interest in Japan, which was opened to foreign trade in 1859 and linked thenceforward by a P. & O. service to Shanghai. The Treaty of Peking in 1860 ended the twenty-five years of struggle to remould the basis of relations between Europe and China. It ceded Kowloon to Hong Kong and legalized Chinese emigration in English interests as well as the propagation and practice of the Catholic faith in French interests. The war produced a great boom in Hong Kong and encouraged Shanghai to aspire to become a free city of Asia on the Hanseatic model. It also encouraged the beginning of shipping services to China and Japan by the Ben Line in 1859, by T. & J. Brocklebank in 1860 and by the Shire Line in 1861. The opening of three ports on the Yangtze and the elimination of Chinese junks from the river below Nanking by the Tai-Ping Rebellion created new opportunities for foreign steamship enterprise and led to the foundation in 1862 of the Shanghai Steam Navigation Company with the American firm of Russell & Co. as its Managing Agents. The great inland tea market of Hankow was first reached by ocean steamer in 1861, by the river steamers of the Shanghai Steam Navigation Company in 1862 and by ocean sailing vessel in 1863, giving Chinese merchants freedom of choice between the two markets of Hankow and Shanghai.

The opening of the lower Yangtze stimulated the expansion of Shanghai and completed the diversion begun in 1854 of traffic from Central China away from the overland routes to Canton to the river and coastal route via Shanghai.

---

[1] F. de Lesseps, *Lettres* (1879), iv. 32.
[2] Ibid., iv. 82, Lesseps à Beauval, 7 Juin 1861.

From 1863 Shanghai became a terminus of the European coasting trade in Chinese produce and was linked to Hong Kong by the Shanghai Steam Navigation Company. Its population, trade and revenue expanded faster than those of Hong Kong in the 1860s when it became the main centre of European trade in China, benefiting by the opening of Japan to the east and of the Yangtze to the west as well as by the expansion of Japanese silk production into the void left by the disruption in 1860–4 of the Chinese industry. Shanghai with its deep-water outport of Woosung lay on the mainland while the offshore island of Hong Kong was cut off from direct contact with China by the barrier of Canton. Shanghai became the great centre of commerce for all the basin of the Yangtze, which was navigable for half its length of 3,200 miles from the Eastern Sea to Tibet. The Yangtze had become more than ever the main artery of the empire after the shift of the course of the Hwang Ho to the north of Shantung in 1852. Thus Shanghai enjoyed direct access to the 100,000,000 inhabitants of the most fertile, productive and populous half of the empire: it could collect tea and silk for export from the richest silk-growing districts and channel imports of opium inland along the routes by which the tea travelled for export. As the most northerly ice-free port on the coast of China it served as the centre for transhipment between coastal navigation to the north and south as well as between coastal and river navigation. As the Yangtze basin was the heart and focus of Chinese civilization Shanghai replaced Canton from 1863 onwards as the great source of innovations from the outside world in the self-strengthening movement of the decade. The expansion of the China trade was also reflected in a corresponding growth of Singapore, in its shift from the orbit of India into that of China and in the five proposals made between 1857 and 1863 to pierce the Malay Peninsula by an isthmian canal.

In India a sustained expansion of economic activity followed the suppression of the Mutiny. The large-scale investment of British capital was encouraged by the abolition of the East India Company, the introduction of joint-stock legislation from 1858, the rise of the managing-agency[1] and the establishment of the supremacy of the agent over his board of directors. The resumption of railway construction from 1858 and 1859 helped to develop agricultural production for export, because all the main railway lines led to the ports and British administration had extended over all the fertile valleys of the peninsula, leaving the jungle and the desert to the princes. In the agricultural boom of the 1860s the last export of Indian manufactured cottons took place while the provinces developed the cultivation for export of the new staples of jute in Bengal, tea in Assam, rice in Burma, coffee in Ceylon and cotton in Bombay. The plantation form of production was extended from the maligned crop of indigo to tea. The prodigious financial success of the Assam Tea Company, established in 1839, and the Jorehaut Tea Company, established in 1859,

[1] S. D. Mehta, *The Cotton Mills of India 1854 to 1954* (1954), 49. Kwang-Ching Liu, *Anglo-American Steamship Rivalry in China, 1862–1874* (Harvard University Press, 1962), 31.

encouraged a mania in Bengal for tea companies and the reduction of the import duties on tea in England in 1864 and 1867. The export of jute from Bengal gave Liverpool compensation for the Cotton Famine and encouraged the building of jute clippers in iron. The rice trade from Bangkok and Rangoon was developed by R. C. Rickmers of Bremen and the teak trade of Burma by the Bombay-Burma Trading Corporation established in 1864. The Calcutta and Burmah Steam Navigation Company, established in 1856 after the Second Burma War by William Mackinnon, founder of the Bengal merchant-house of Mackinnon, Mackenzie & Co. in 1847, renamed itself in 1863 the British India Steam Navigation Company. It extended its operations to the Persian Gulf in 1862 in association with the Euphrates and Tigris Steam Navigation Co. Ltd., which had been established in 1861 by T. K. Lynch of Bagdad. Its affiliated Netherlands-India Steam Navigation Company Limited secured the Batavia–Singapore mail contract in 1862 and was registered in the Netherlands in 1865. In Java the reform of the culture-system in the interests of private enterprise more than of 'the coffee and sugar machines, called "Natives"'[1] was undertaken from 1862. The great cotton boom in Bombay expressed its faith in the pro-Southern press of London and in the power of the South to resist the North. That boom tapped the most important single industry of the presidency, ended India's exports of cotton to China and first gave Bombay a staple export to England. The replacement of American by Indian cotton in the mills of Lancashire increased the shipment of bullion and specie through Egypt to India and stimulated the advance of the railways from 1863 into the heart of the cotton country. It also attracted J. N. Tata in 1864 to England and inspired him on his return to begin from 1869 the manufacture of cotton goods, so laying the foundation of a Parsi industrial empire. The cotton boom also kept freights high to the benefit of sail, which profited by the emergence of another staple of world trade. The Cape route thus came into increasing use by bulk cargo while expensive cargo was carried by the overland route.

The expansion of French ambitions in Asia restored to France its mission to regenerate the East, brought the overland route into use by French troops from 1859–60 and increased French interests in Egypt. Debarred from expansion in the Lebanon and incited by British expansion in Burma as well as by the prostration of China by the Tai-Ping Rebellion, France forced open the port of Saigon to international trade in 1860. Thereby she established control of the Cochinese rice-granary of Annam at the same time as she developed her interests in Abyssinia, Zanzibar, Arabia and Persia. The law of 3 July 1861 authorized a new mail service by the Messageries Impériales between Suez and Saigon. Marc Fraissinet's purchase of Obock on 11 March 1862 gave France its first foothold on the Somali coast and a Cayenne in the Red Sea. The Messageries secured from Egypt what it had always refused to the P. & O.,

---

[1] 'Multatuli' (E. D. Dekker), *Max Havelaar, or the Coffee Auctions of the Dutch Trading Company* (Edinburgh, Edmonston, 1868), 353.

the construction of a dry dock at Suez under the contract of 11 April 1862 with Auguste and Elzear Dussaud and the construction in 1862–3 of the first three lighthouses in the Red Sea. The *Impératrice* opened the new mail service from Suez and brought the London mails of 18 October 1862 to Singapore thirty-five days later on 21 November.[1] The extension of the service of the Messageries to Hong Kong on 1 January 1863 ended the monopoly enjoyed by the P. & O. since 1845. The new French mail service devalued Madagascar as a port of call but benefited Singapore and Suez, which gained the imposing premises of the Messageries in 1863 and a French Hospital in 1863–4. The Messageries helped to transfer the raw silk market from London to Lyons and reduced England's re-exports of raw silk from their peak in 1862 as well as the tribute paid by France to England for imports from the East. It even drove the P. & O. out of the specie market in 1865. Its new service however consolidated the pattern of the overland route to the disadvantage of the Canal.

The P. & O. responded to the challenge of competition by ending its service to the Iberian Peninsula in 1862, using the Mediterranean thenceforward solely as a through-route to Alexandria. It built its first vessel with compound engines in 1861 and its last paddle-steamer in 1864, when it began a large programme of rebuilding after failing either to secure the Government contract for troop-transport or to prevent renewed complaints of its high-priced inefficiency. It competed with the Messageries in creating a southern extension to the main overland route to the East. In 1864 both the P. & O. and the Messageries began branch services from Aden via the Seychelles to Mauritius, where they linked up with a new service begun by the Union Line from Cape Town. Port Louis so gained compensation for the loss of the P. & O. Australian service to Galle in 1861 while Cape Town gained the object of five years' agitation. The Egyptian overland route reached its maximum extension in 1864, with Galle as the junction for the services from Calcutta, China and Sydney and with Aden as the junction for the lines from Bombay and Mauritius.

The growth of shipping stimulated the foundation of dock companies such as the Tanjong Pagar Dock Co. Ltd. in Singapore in 1863 and the Hong Kong and Whampoa Dock Co. Ltd., established in 1865 by Jardine's and the P. & O. The expansion of the 1860s was especially marked in the ports of Marseilles, Beirut, Alexandria, Suez, Bombay, Karachi, Galle, Calcutta, Rangoon, Singapore, Hong Kong, Shanghai and Yokohama, the obscure village chosen by Japan as its Canton. As Asia recognized the supremacy of Europe by sending to London the first embassies from Japan in 1862 and from China in 1866, Europe was swept by a new wave of Oriental influence through the renewed foundation from 1860 of chairs of Sanskrit, the historical romances of Meadows Taylor, 'the Scott of India', the poetry of Edward Fitzgerald and Matthew Arnold, the leading articles of Edwin Arnold in the *Daily Telegraph* from 1862, the music of Bizet from 1863 and the painting of Whistler from 1864. Flaubert

[1] W. Makepeace, *One Hundred Years of Singapore* (London, Murray, 1921), ii. 110.

projected from 1862 a novel on the modern Orient which would portray the intermingling of two worlds, the barbarization of the civilized European, and the civilization of the Oriental.[1] Egypt in particular assumed a growing role in the thought-world of the West as a cradle of civilization comparable to Greece, the source of the Phoenician alphabet deciphered in 1859 by the Vicomte Jacques de Rougé, an irrefutable proof of the specificity of race and the polygenesis of mankind[2] and the exact geographical centre of the earth.[3]

Such economic expansion encouraged Said after his first visit to the isthmus (6–8 December 1861) to issue written orders to his governors to raise the monthly levy of labour from 10,000 to 15,000 in December and to 25,000 in January 1862,[4] so replacing the unofficial levy by the official corvée and swamping European labour by Egyptian. Said also sent 5,000 demobilized soldiers from Upper Egypt to El Guisr and Ismail Bey in February 1862 to maintain order in the isthmus after the ex-soldiers deserted on a large scale. He graciously allowed his conscribed fellahin to accomplish their daily quota by night during the severe daytime fast of Ramadan in 1862. The Sweet Water Canal brought the fresh water of the Nile to Nefischa[5] to the west of Timsah on 23 January 1862 and was opened by a formal celebration on 2 February. The town of Timsah or 'Lessepsville' was founded on 27 April as a planned city with stone houses along the avenues around three squares, Lesseps' chalet off the central Place Champollion, an Arab village to the east and a Greek village to the west. The Sweet Water Canal was followed by the first telegraph line to the isthmus in 1862, after the landing of the Malta cable at Alexandria in 1861. That canal was used with caution by Nile river-boats from 1862 but made possible the renewal of settlement in the Wadi Tumilat from Zagazig to Tel el Kebir, which were linked by a carriage-road from 1861. The Company bought a 28,000-acre estate in the Wadi Tumilat in 1861, appointed Jules Guichard as its manager and so became the landlord of fellahin and beduin. In a year Guichard doubled both the population of the valley and its production of Sea Island cotton, under the influence of the wartime boom in cotton. Thus the Company encouraged the extension of the margin of cultivation towards Egypt's desert-frontier. At Port Said buildings were laid on concrete foundations from 1862 and masonry cemeteries were created aboveground because the presence of salt water in the subsoil made burial impossible. Its Arab village had suffered from the erosion of the eastern beach and was transferred from the east to the west of the port from April 1862.

The labour contingents reached their maximum number of 23,318 in the

---

[1] E. and J. de Goncourt, *Journal des Goncourt* (Paris, Charpentier, 1891), ii. 23–4, 29 Mars 1862.

[2] J. C. Nott and G. R. Gliddon, *Types of Mankind: or, Ethnological Researches* (Philadelphia, Lippincott, 1854), 141–79, 210–45, 667–88. A. Maury, J. C. Nott and G. R. Gliddon, *Indigenous Races of the Earth; or, New Chapters of Ethnological Enquiry* (London, Trübner, 1857), 100–24, 321–3.

[3] C. P. Smyth, *Our Inheritance in the Great Pyramid* (London, Strachan, 1864), 374–6, 383.

[4] F. de Lesseps, *Lettres* (1879), iv. 110.

[5] Voisin Bey, *Le Canal de Suez*, iv (1904), 339–57.

month of April 1862 and were especially employed on the deep cutting through El Guisr,[1] which formed the backbone of the isthmus and stretched for eight miles at an average height of 33 feet above sea-level. Their sustained manual labour made possible the ceremonial admission on 18 November 1862 of the waters of the Mediterranean to Lake Timsah amid the strains of the Egyptian anthem, although Said did not occupy the new kiosk built for him by the Company. The corvée proved wasteful because of the monthly turn-over of the contingents but it supplied the labour of born navigators, men who worked like oxen, lived on an onion a day and ventilated their resentment only in song.[2] The Company paid its conscript labourers double the customary wages to perform double their customary daily task. At first it supplied provisions but then allowed the workmen to bring their own.[3] The wages were swallowed up by the high cost of food, whose price was raised by transport costs, the cotton boom in the Delta and the enterprise of Greek shopkeepers from 1862. Wage-rates were still fixed too low and the wages were paid short in money and in rations, so causing many desertions. The high cost of living in the isthmus was further increased because the Company discouraged the use of small currency.[4] The selected labour-force excluded the very young and the very old but was harassed by disease because of the high concentration of labour, the mixture of labourers and the absence of social organization in the isthmus. The Company published no full statistics of mortality and thus could not check the spread of rumours of high mortality.[5] It bore no costs of transport for its labourers, despite the great distances and poor communications. In order to employ 20,000 per month its works absorbed, including those in transit, 26,000 or 3·6 per cent of a rural male labour force of 720,000.[6] The Company's demands thus diverted the fellah from his primary duty in life, the cultivation of the soil and the payment of the land-tax, at a time when the cotton boom in the Delta created a growing strain on the available supply of labour.

The admission of the Company's shares, 40 per cent paid-up, to the Paris Bourse on 19 May 1862 after three and a half years ended any doubts about the regularity of the constitution of the Company in 1858 and committed the Company thenceforward to the defence of its market quotation. At the annual meeting of the shareholders on 22 May 1862 Lesseps raised the forecast of the shipping tonnage expected to use the Canal from the 3,000,000 of 1854 to 4,000,000. His officials nevertheless turned English travellers back from the Canal works down to 1862.[7] The first English notable to tour the works was

[1] *Illustrated London News*, 31 January 1863, 125, 130; 14 February 1863, 176.
[2] N. W. Senior, *Conversations and Journals in Egypt and Malta* (1882), ii. 133.
[3] G. P. Badger, *A Visit to the Isthmus of Suez Canal Works* (London, Smith, 1862), 67.
[4] O. Ritt, *Histoire de l'Isthme de Suez* (Paris, Hachette, 1869), 247.
[5] J. Steele, *The Suez Canal: its Present and Future* (London, Simpkin, 1872), 16. D. M. Wallace, *Egypt and the Egyptian Question* (London, Macmillan, 1883), 268–9, 310–11. E. Dicey, *The Story of the Khedivate* (London, Rivingtons, 1902), 36.
[6] Ritt, 286. H. Vierne, 'Les Intérêts de la Compagnie du Canal de Suez et ceux du Gouvernement Égyptien', *Revue Contemporaine*, Janvier 1864, 340–1.
[7] Hansard, *Lords Debates*, 6 May 1861, 1555, Lord Carnarvon.

Bulwer, the Ambassador to Constantinople, on 18–19 December 1862. He concluded that the Company were sovereigns in the isthmus and persuaded Said not to double the contingents. He urged on Lord John Russell on 3 January 1863 that England should defend the yellow sands of Egypt from French invasion almost like the white cliffs of Albion: he suggested the improvement of the Alexandria–Suez Railway as a counterpoise to French influence in the isthmus. His report was less important than that made at Said's request by John Hawkshaw, President of the Institution of Civil Engineers, and published on 5 February 1863.[1] Hawkshaw showed that, by 1 December 1862, 7,484,800 cubic yards had been excavated between Port Said and Timsah and £1,984,000 had been spent. Thus 6 per cent of the reduced total cube had been removed instead of the half expected in 1858 with the expenditure of 25 per cent of the Company's initial capital, since unit-costs were at least six-fold those estimated in 1855. Hawkshaw doubled the 1859 estimate of cost of £5,000,000 but clearly established that the scheme of 'the great projector'[2] was not an engineering impossibility and so refuted Stephenson. His report was followed by the Company's termination of Hardon's contract on 14 February and by the beginning of a reappraisal of the venture in the English political mind.[3]

On the death of Said at the age of forty-one the Company's shares slid down by 3·2 per cent (17–19 January 1863) and the labour contingents were held up until Lesseps secured a confidential interview with the new Pasha on 24 January. Ismail had been educated in Paris and was more captivated by French civilization than Said had been but was less dependent on intermediaries and never fell under the spell of Lesseps.[4] He lacked the belief in Islam which Said had retained and was as scared of cholera as Mehemet Ali had been. Haunted by fear from childhood he became 'a throned Ishmaelite'[5] who paid eight visits to Constantinople between 1863 and 1873 but none at all to Mecca. He allowed the standing of the Egyptian Haj to decline at Mecca and Egypt's status in the community of Islam to deteriorate. Without the will-power to become an unbeliever Ismail believed in 'Progress' and 'Civilization', which he identified with Europe and with economic development rather than with the legal reforms undertaken in contemporary Tunis and Constantinople. He spoke of himself as a man of the nineteenth century and decorated the walls of his palaces with Arabic inscriptions from Smiles' *Self-Help*. He had a mania for public works and for racing,[6] loving building as much as Abbas and movement as much as Said. As the richest and most

[1] *L'Isthme de Suez*, 15 Juin 1863. *The Engineer*, 31 July and 7 August 1863, 60–1, 67, 75–6.

[2] B. Oliveira, *A Few Observations upon the Works of the Isthmus of Suez Canal* (London, Harrison, 1863), 18.

[3] *Saturday Review*, 1 August 1863, 150–1, 'The Suez Canal'. *The Economist*, 8 August 1863, 870–1, 'The Suez Canal'.

[4] E. de Léon, *The Khedive's Egypt* (London, Low, 1877), 165.

[5] (C. F. M. Bell), *Khedives and Pashas* (London, Low, 1884), 23.

[6] E. Dicey, *The Story of the Khedivate*, 68. F. Petrie, *Seventy Years in Archaeology* (London, Low, 1931), 40.

progressive landlord in the country he regarded Egypt as his estate, his subjects as taxpayers and Western techniques as the best means to increase their taxable capacity. He also sought to enlarge their number through the military conquest of peoples less technically advanced and to make himself 'as rich as the Rothschilds'.[1] As the first Oriental autocrat fully to accept Western techniques,[2] save for Mongkut of Siam, he sought to buy from the Sultan the freedoms which Mehemet Ali had failed to win by force of arms.

Lesseps was compelled to readjust his plans to take account of the will of the new Pasha and especially of his professed hostility to the corvée in the isthmus. Timsah was renamed Ismailia on 4 March in his honour and became the headquarters of the Company in succession to Damietta. It did not become a workshop centre as planned but became the centre of communications in the isthmus and eclipsed Toussoum, which had been the first camp in the vicinity. It became the site in 1863 of the Ismailia Waterworks, a planned garden-city and more of a French community than any other settlement. By the Convention of 20 March Ismail accepted 177,642 shares in the Canal Company to the intense annoyance of the British Government. By the Convention of 30 March with the Alexandria bankers, E. Dervieu and H. Oppenheim,[3] the Company disposed of its £252,800 of Treasury bonds at a profit of 55 per cent and so raised its shares by 9 per cent (7–11 April 1863). Those conventions were followed by the severe crisis of 1863 in relations between the Company and Ismail.

The Porte and Ismail were both determined to withdraw forced labour from the Canal works and the Company's rights to the lands along the Sweet Water Canal. Ismail was especially concerned to prevent the creation of an Arab principality under Abd el Kadr, who had visited the Canal works in 1863 en route to Mecca and on his return had become a mason at Alexandria in 1864. Lesseps offered Abd el Kadr the estate of Bir Abu Ballah by Lake Timsah[4] as a winter residence and as compensation for his dream of Arab empire in Syria which had crumbled after the departure of the French expedition in 1861. In return he was expected to colonize an area west of the Canal thirty times the size of his estate, so creating an isthmian complement to Napoleon III's 'Arab kingdom' of Algeria. Ismail was strengthened in his opposition by Britain which began the ostentatious extension of its harbour at Malta in 1863. The surrender of the Ionian Isles to Greece provoked Disraeli's protest against the removal of one link in 'a chain of Mediterranean garrisons, which secured our Indian empire'.[5] The necessary policy for England was outlined in the spirit of Palmerston by Robert Gascoyne-Cecil, who was fascinated by the new power of locomotion: 'As the greatest of commercial Powers, she can

---

[1] Wallace, 342–3.

[2] W. B. Jerrold, *Egypt under Ismail-Pacha* (London, Tinsley, 1879), 174.

[3] F. de Lesseps, *Lettres* (1879), iv. 298–300.

[4] J. Guichard, 'Colonisation de l'Isthme de Suez, 1861–1866', *Nouvelle Revue*, 1 Février 1882, 242. Charles-Roux, ii. 143. Sabry, 289–90.

[5] Hansard, *Commons Debates*, 5 February 1863, 95, Disraeli.

never suffer the highway of nations to fall into hands that may close it. The Sound, the Bosphorus and the Straits of Gibraltar, the Isthmus of Suez, and the Isthmus of Darien, must never be subject to the will of a first-rate Power.'[1]

The Porte's Note of 6 April 1863 expressed its hostility to the French colonization of the isthmus and reduced the value of the Company's shares by 9 per cent (5–11 May). The contingents declined in number from July. The Porte's Note of 1 August reaffirmed its opposition to the enterprise. Nubar, newly-created the first Christian Pasha in Egypt, was despatched by Ismail to Paris in order to by-pass Lesseps and appeal directly to the Imperial Government. There Nubar enlisted the support of French lawyers, politicians, and journalists against the French shareholders of the Company. The report made on 16 January 1864 by Émile Ollivier of the Liberal Opposition favoured Ismail's claims against the Company. Prince Jerome's public defence of the Company against England at a banquet to 1600 on 11 February left the Paris Bourse unaffected but won the approval of the Cobdenite *Morning Star*, whose editor was the brother-in-law of Bright: 'As regards the Suez Canal project, Prince Napoleon is perfectly right in supposing that any English Government which attempted to drag England into a war about the Suez Canal would fall beneath the contempt and ridicule of the English people... No English Minister, be he ever so old, has any notion of setting on a war directly or indirectly to interfere with the Suez Canal.'[2]

Ismail's acceptance of imperial arbitration[3] was welcomed by an outburst of Imperialist sentiment among the shareholders at their annual meeting on 1 March 1864 but offended the Porte and compelled Nubar to sign a compromise on 21 April with Lesseps. The decision of the arbiter of Europe was embodied in the award of 6 July 1864 which allotted the Company compensation for the withdrawal of its labour, its land and the Sweet Water Canal and for the loss of the revenues expected therefrom. The Company had first claimed £3,750,000, then £4,250,000 and finally £5,160,000[4] but accepted the award of £3,360,000 to be paid over sixteen years. It had also claimed compensation first for 133,000 hectares of land and then for 573,700 hectares but accepted compensation for 60,000 hectares, which was all that the Sweet Water Canal would be able to irrigate. The compensation was, however, generously based on the future improved value of the desert lands rather than on their negligible current value. That award was a political rather than a judicial decision and the greatest legal victory in the history of the Company. The compensation was lamented in the isthmus as inadequate[5] but was

---

[1] R. Gascoyne-Cecil, 'The Danish Duchies', *Quarterly Review* (January 1864), 284.

[2] *Morning Star*, 16 February 1864, 4v.

[3] G. Douin, *Histoire du Règne du Khédive Ismail* (1933), i. 91–2.

[4] F. de Lesseps, *Lettres* (1879), iv. 493; iv. 384, 22 Janvier 1864; iv. 470–1, 15 Mars 1864. M. Sabry, 280–1.

[5] W. von Tegethoff, 'Der Canal üeber den Isthmus von Suez', *Oesterreichische Revue* (März 1866), 107.

treble the amount expected by Ismail, who revealed great irritation with France, the Emperor and the Company. Nubar's campaign in Paris had cost £160,000[1] and compelled Ismail to dispose of 1,040 of his shares in the Canal Company at a par value of £20,000. Ismail refused to receive Lesseps, dismissed the fifteen French officers in his service and replaced Conrad as the Egyptian Commissioner with the Company by Émile Ollivier from 5 April 1865. He also made the isthmus into a province and appointed Ismail Bey as its first Governor in 1864. He ordered Abd el Kadr to leave Egypt and made plans to link the isthmus to Cairo by a new Sweet Water Canal and a railway. In the summer of 1865 he cut off the supply of Nile water to the Wadi estate of the Company, ruining the crops and envenoming relations between the Company and its tenant-farmers. He also followed Said's example in confiding his first public loan to the Anglo-German house of Oppenheim in 1864 and raised no objection to the beginning of English troop transport through Egypt to India. Nubar sought to regain favour by recommending the establishment of an international court in Egypt to judge all claims against the Government, so renewing the campaign for judicial reform.

The withdrawal of the contingents of forced labour during May 1864 after three years and three months compelled the Company to increase its European employees and its wage-rates, to introduce cost-accounting from 1865 and to mechanize its operations as far as possible. The delay to the works was estimated first at one year but became the two years necessary for the construction of machinery. The contingents had nevertheless excavated 18,500,000 cubic yards, or 15 per cent of the reduced cube of excavation. By executing the most difficult and arduous part of the works they made possible the triumph of European machinery and labour. They had pierced the plateau of El Guisr, removing 5,200,000 cubic yards or 46 per cent of the total 12,000,000 cubic yards and opening up the heart of the isthmus. They had completed a second channel to El Firdan by 15 July 1863, so creating an independent passage for traffic to El Guisr and outlining the basic width of the Canal by two channels separated by a wide causeway. They completed the extension of the Sweet Water Canal from Timsah fifty-six miles south to Suez, where it was inaugurated by Ruyssenaers on 29 December 1863. The arrival of the blessed Nile deprived the Wells of Moses of their monopoly of the local water supply and made water cheap and plentiful at Suez for the first time in history, suggesting to true Moslems that such wonder-working Europeans must also be children of Allah. That canal enabled Suez to grow rapidly in population, commerce and agriculture, to capture the pilgrim trade of Kosseir from 1864, and to aspire to become 'the Marseilles of the Red Sea'.[2] It also gave Suez an advantage over Port Said, to which water was first brought by pipe-line from Ismailia on 10 April 1864.

The Company divided the work of excavation into four sections and

---

[1] M. Sabry, 311.
[2] C. Leconte, *Promenade dans l'Isthme de Suez* (Paris, Chaix, 1864), 113.

concluded four large contracts, with Alphonse Couvreux on 1 October 1863 for the El Guisr cutting, with Dussaud Brothers on 20 October 1863 for the harbour moles of Port Said, with William Aiton of Glasgow on 13 January 1864 for the thirty-seven miles from Port Said to El Guisr and with Borel & Lavalley on 26 March 1864 for the whole of the fifty-four miles from El Guisr to the Red Sea. The main contract was that of Aiton since all the others were dependent on its execution. Aiton had successfully dredged most of the Clyde but was almost ruined by the high cost of dredging the ooze of Lake Menzaleh and surrendered his contract to Borel & Lavalley on 12 December 1864 after the English credit crisis of 1864. Thus the Company entrusted ninety miles to a single great contractor and so began to revert to its original approach. By the end of 1864 15,580,000 cubic yards had been excavated, or 13 per cent of the total cube, by the expenditure of 37·6 per cent of the Company's original capital. Machinery thenceforward proved increasingly important. Trough dredgers had been first introduced in 1862 with troughs of 30–45 feet in length as a new means of carrying the spoil and proved successful beyond all expectation and far more productive than the small dredger. The mechanical excavator of Couvreux was a land-based chain-bucket dredger which used an endless chain of buckets revolving around an iron frame to scoop up earth like a carpenter's plane and load it directly into wagons on the upper bank. Patented in 1860, it first came into use from March 1865 at the El Guisr cutting, which thenceforward was undertaken at maximum speed by the greatest labour-saving device developed on the Canal. At Port Said the first sea-going hopper barges ordered by Aiton from Scotland were delivered from April 1865 for the removal of spoil dredged from the harbour. Dussaud Brothers had completed the jetties of Cherbourg in 1858, of Algiers in 1860 and of Marseilles in 1863. At Port Said they used the rubble-mound method of construction because harbour sand was abundant for the local manufacture of concrete blocks with imported hydraulic lime. Their first concrete block of twenty-two tons was sunk into place on the harbour mole on 9 August 1865.

In November 1865 the attack began on the second elevation of the isthmus at Chalouf, a prolongation of the plateau of Geneifa, using the inclined plane as well as Piedmontese miners from the Mont Cenis Tunnel. Work was temporarily interrupted by the epidemic of cholera which broke out at Suez on 21 May and at Alexandria on 2 June. The disease was carried from the Delta by refugees fleeing to the disease-free isthmus and broke out at Ismailia on 24 June and at Port Said on 29 June. The epidemic caused a panic flight of workers led by the Greeks, reducing the labour force from 6,000 to 3,000. It impelled Ismail to leave Egypt and Lesseps to return from France to the isthmus as befitted 'the father of our great family'.[1] It afflicted Ismailia more severely than Port Said or Suez,[2] killing 6 per cent of the population of 4,000, including the only grandson of Lesseps and the wife of Voisin, before its

---

[1] O. Ritt, *Histoire de l'Isthme de Suez* (1869), 224.
[2] Voisin Bey, *Le Canal de Suez* (1906), vi. i, 379–82.

ravages ceased in August. The opening of the new locks on the Sweet Water Canal at Ismailia on 15 August 1865, the Emperor's birthday, enabled 300 tons of coal to pass on twelve barges from Port Said to Suez (13–26 August) by means of the preliminary channel in the northern half of the isthmus and the Sweet Water Canal in the southern half. The returning workmen then helped to raise the population of the isthmus from 10,000 in 1865 to 18,000 in 1866.

Lesseps had meanwhile maintained his efforts to persuade Ismail to accept the arbitration award of 1864, because the number of his shareholders had increased from 20,000 in 1858 to 40,000 in 1864[1] and so swelled the French interests in 'the greatest and most fruitful enterprise of the century',[2] 'the most stupendous work of modern ages'.[3] To rally support outside France Lesseps invited 120 chambers of commerce to send delegates to visit the works. Eighty-four delegates, mainly French and Italian, observed in mid-April 1865 an activity partly factitious,[4] picknicked by day and banqueted by night. Lesseps himself was portrayed as the presiding deity of the Suez Canal in Manzotti's ballet *Excelsior*.[5] The Canal Company began to issue its own five-franc silver tokens from 1865 for use in the stores of C. & A. Bazin. To counteract the growth of French influence Bulwer recommended on 10 March 1865 that a British warship should be stationed at Suez and that British warehouses and hospitals should be established in the isthmus.[6] British opposition to the Canal was however restrained by the failure of British policy in Denmark and Poland, by the death of Palmerston and by the free-trade reaction provoked by the victory of the protectionist North in the American Civil War.

The Egyptian reply to the Imperial Arbitration of 1864 was contained in the Conventions of 30 January, 19 February and 22 February 1866, which were the first conventions concluded between the Company and the Government. The Convention of 22 February 1866 removed any doubts about the Company's legal status and nationality after it had been subjected to taxation as a foreign company in France in 1865. That convention established Egyptian jurisdiction over the Company and the Egyptian nationality of the Company,[7] despite the protests of Lesseps. 'It puts the fate, the interests, the existence of the Company in the present and in the future, unconditionally at the discretion and beneath the despotism of all succeeding Egyptian governments...

[1] F. de Lesseps, *Lettres* (1879), iv. 439; (1881), v. 216.

[2] Ibid. (1881), v. 58, 9 Novembre 1864.

[3] T. K. Lynch, *A Visit to the Suez Canal* (London, Day, 1866), 71–2, 12–19 November 1864.

[4] Voisin Bey, vi. i, 365–6.

[5] L. Manzotti, *Excelsior* (Milano, Ricordi, 1865). Hansard, *Commons Debates*, 16 March 1865, 1760, D. Griffith.

[6] K. Bell, 'British Policy Towards the Construction of the Suez Canal, 1859–1865', *Transactions of the Royal Historical Society* (1965), 131.

[7] *L'Isthme de Suez*, 15–18 Avril 1866, 118. G. Douin, *Histoire du Règne du Khédive Ismail* (1933), i. 180–1.

In a word, Article VII makes the Universal Suez Company an Egyptian fellah unconditionally liable to taxation and forced labour at the will of any pasha or viceroy.'[1] In return for that sacrifice which made the Company a supporter of judicial reform in Egypt, Ismail accepted the 1864 Award and the Porte granted on 17 March 1866 the long-desired firman sanctioning the construction of 'the great work', despite the abandonment of its proposals of 1863 to secure a European guarantee of the security of the Canal and to restrict its navigation to merchant-vessels. Thus Ismail insured himself against any repetition of the arbitration of 1864 and compelled the Company to abandon all objects other than the creation and operation of a maritime canal. He had prevented the establishment of a French fief in the isthmus and had deprived the Company of control over its own water-supply. He established a customs post in 1866 at Port Said, which was entered by the vessels of Marc Fraissinet on 27 January 1866 and of the Russian Steam Navigation and Commercial Company on 28 January. Port Said held its first regatta in April 1866 and became the largest workshop in the world,[2] its population rising from 5,000 in 1864 to 8,000 in 1867. Ismail countered the growth of French influence in Suez by signing the contract of 1 January 1867 with Dussaud Brothers, the builders of the dry dock at Suez (1862–6), for the construction of an Egyptian deep-water harbour at the new Port Ibrahim. He also appointed an Egyptian in 1867 as Inspector of the Suez Canal. His experience with the Canal Company impressed the Chinese Government with the danger from enterprises with foreign capital.[3]

The imperial and economic expansion of the 1860s fostered the demand for speedier communication between Europe and Asia which was supplied by cable, steamship, clipper and railway. The completion of the Indo-European telegraph via Fao and Gwadur to Karachi on 27 January 1865 first established cable communication with India, enabled London to receive its first through telegram from Karachi on 1 March 1865 and stimulated efforts to improve the overland route by the use of the developing Italian railways.[4] The voyage of Alfred Holt's *Cleator* in 1865 pioneered the regular use of the steamship on the Cape route to China and provoked the greatest race ever sailed by the tea clippers in 1866. The economic crisis of 1866 shook the structure of European trade and finance throughout the ports of Asia, where it benefited the new enterprises of the Hong-Kong & Shanghai Banking Corporation, established in 1864, and Butterfield & Swire, established in 1867. The Hong Kong Bank successfully opposed the attempt of the London banks to reduce the usance

---

[1] F. de Lesseps, *Lettres* (1881), v. 213–14, Lesseps to Drouyn de Lhuys, 17 Octobre 1865. Article vii became Article xvi of the final Convention.

[2] A. Roussin, 'L'Isthme de Suez et les Travaux du Canal Maritime', *Revue des Deux Mondes*, 15 Juillet 1867, 392.

[3] M. C. Wright, *The Last Stand of Chinese Conservatism . . . 1862–1874* (Stanford University Press, 1957), 280, Alcock to Foreign Office, 1 January 1868.

[4] H. W. Tyler, 'Routes of Communication with India', *Journal of the Royal United Service Institution*, 2 March 1866, 285–6.

of bills on China from six to four months' sight and opened branches in Calcutta in 1867 and Bombay in 1869. The completion of the Atlantic telegraph encouraged efforts after the crisis to girdle the globe, and especially to span the Pacific, by steam navigation. The Panama, New Zealand & Australian Royal Mail Company, a subsidiary of the Royal Mail Steam Packet Company, began the longest steam service in the world from Panama to Sydney in 1866. That company carried Dilke on his journey around *Greater Britain* in 1867 to the most distant of the colonies from Suez, opened a rival steam route to the Pacific and compelled the P. & O. to launch its first vessel with an Australian name in 1866. The Pacific Mail Steam Ship Company began a service in 1867 from San Francisco to Hong Kong as a harbinger of the Pacific Railroad and carried the influence of the Re-United States into Asia, which was buttressed by its conclusion of the Burlingame Treaty with China on a reciprocal basis. The P. & O. followed the example of the Messageries in 1866 and extended its service to Yokohama in 1867, thereby linking India for the first time to Japan. The two new services spanning the north and south of the Pacific Ocean encouraged Louis Simonin to calculate in 1867 that a trip around the world could be made by rail and steamship in eighty-six days. The direct steam route from Valparaiso to Liverpool through the Straits of Magellan pioneered by the Pacific Steam Navigation Company in 1868 became the complement to the steam services maintained around the Cape to China by Holt & Robertson.

The P. & O. declared no dividend in 1867 and suffered a vigorous attack on its monopoly at home as well as abroad. The Treasury under a Conservative administration even solicited in a spirit of 'Free Trade gone mad'[1] the competition of the Messageries as a weapon against the P. & O. The justest tribute to that 'great national undertaking' was penned in November 1867 when it was most in need of protection: 'The importance of this enterprise of a private company to the interests of the mother-country, and her eastern dependencies, it would be difficult to overrate. It has given a character of solidity and compactness to the British empire in the Eastern world, which enables us to contemplate its expansion without any feeling of apprehension. It has linked the most distant countries of the east with the European world, and for the first time after the lapse of more than twenty centuries, given full effect to the views of Alexander the Great when he founded Alexandria, and destined it to be the highway between Europe and Asia. It has covered the Red Sea with steamers, and converted it into an English lake. It has given a political importance to the land of the Pharaohs, which constrains England to consider the maintenance of its independence, even at the hazard of war, an indispensable article of national policy. The empire of India belongs to the nearest European power, and it is the enterprise of this Company which has conferred

---

[1] Hansard, *Commons Debates*, 1 August 1867, 669, R. W. Crawford. *Saturday Review*, 3 August 1867, 145, 'The Peninsular and Oriental Company'; 24 August 1867, 251, 'Eastern Postal Contracts'.

the advantage of this position on England. Our base of operations in Asia is the sea, but while transports were four or five months going round the Cape, our interests were always exposed to adverse contingencies. It is the spirited exertions of this Company which have brought the ports of India within four weeks' reach of the resources of England, and completed our ascendancy in the east.'[1]

Under the new P. & O. contract, grudgingly approved in a thin House on 29 November 1867, Bombay did not replace Aden or Galle as the great junction-point of the P. & O. but gained an increase in the number of its annual mails from 24 to 52, together with a sea-sorting service on the voyage between Suez and Bombay. From 1868 Bombay received its mail in the contract time of 24 days, Calcutta in that of 29 days and Madras in that of 30 days. The P. & O. remained the reserve navy of the Indian Empire with its annual subsidy increased by 74 per cent from £230,000 to £400,000. The overland route made a great gain from the Cape route when the regular transit of British troops through Egypt began in the 1867–8 season. That service was not undertaken by private enterprise but by the Government which rejected tenders by the British India Line in 1862 and the P. & O. in 1863. Five large new screw-steamers were built as Government transports and operated by the Admiralty for the Secretary of State for India as 'a quiet little marine of his own on the other side of the world'.[2] Two of the transports operated between Plymouth and Alexandria while three operated between Suez and Bombay, which thenceforward became the sole trooping-port of India. The sailing troopships were transferred to the expanding emigrant trade to Australia and New Zealand. St. Helena suffered most by the transfer of trooping to the overland route. Mauritius was afflicted at the same time by an epidemic of cholera which ended the services to the island by the P. & O. in 1866 and by the Union Line in 1867. England became able to maintain a European army double the pre-Mutiny size in India by trebling the number of annual reliefs. The replacement of a cheap Indian army by an expensive European army was essential to protect England against sepoy disloyalty and the Russian advance in Central Asia. It made India more than ever before the great training-school of the British Army and 'an English barracks in the Oriental seas from which we may draw any number of troops without paying for them'.[3] The young sailor-advocate of sea-power and empire, J. C. R. Colomb, even recommended the emergency use of the overland route to send out sailors in two months to man a steam-reserve fleet for the defence of the coast of India from Bombay as 'the Portsmouth of the East'.[4]

[1] J. C. Marshman, *The History of India from the Earliest Period to the Close of Lord Dalhousie's Administration* (London, Longmans, 1867), iii. 62.

[2] Hansard, *Commons Debates*, 30 June 1865, 1023, A. S. Ayrton.

[3] Ibid., 28 November 1867, 406, Viscount Cranborne.

[4] J. C. R. Colomb, *The Protection of our Commerce and Distribution of Our Naval Forces Considered* (London, Harrison, May 1867), 23. J. C. R. Colomb, 'The Distribution of our War Forces' (15 January 1869), *Journal of the Royal United Service Institution* (1871), 271.

The Austro-Prussian War of 1866, which occasioned Colomb's counsel, transferred Venice from Austria to Italy, sealed the Prusso-Italian entente through the completion of the Brenner Railway in 1867, drew France and Austria together in an anti-Prussian entente and delayed the completion of the Mont Cenis Railway Tunnel between France and Italy. As a temporary expedient the Mont Cenis Summit Railway was constructed (1866–8) with J. B. Fell's central rail and cog-wheel. That railway was first crossed by a locomotive on 25 August 1867 and was opened to the public on 15 June 1868. It made possible the use of the Italian railway to Brindisi as a supplementary route to that via Marseilles[1] and created a new port of embarkation for Egypt. It compelled the French Government systematically to obstruct the French rail link to Italy in the interests of Marseilles, which had lost the newly united market of Italy to Genoa. It also encouraged the competition with the P. & O. of the Adriatic and Oriental Steam Navigation Company, founded in 1864 by Charles Palmer of Newcastle with an Italian subsidy for a service from Venice and Brindisi to Alexandria. The first viceroy-elect to use the Brindisi route to India was Mayo, who also visited the Canal works on 27–9 November 1868 when he passed through Egypt.[2] The new rail-route encouraged proposals for a Channel Tunnel and for a Euphrates Valley Railway[3] in the hope further to accelerate the passage to India.

The Canal Company itself entered into competition with the Egyptian section of the overland route by introducing from 2 August 1866 a transit service across the isthmus under Guichard, using the preliminary channel as far as Ismailia and thence the Sweet Water Canal to Suez. That transit service was undertaken at competitive rates, specified in the Company's Circular of 1 May 1867 to the Chambers of Commerce of Europe and America, and reduced coal prices at Suez in competition with the railway. The new route was used by the 80-ton brig *Primo* of the Austrian Lloyd (11–16 March 1867) which brought back sulphur from the mines at Gemsa on the Red Sea and became the first cargo-ship to cross the isthmus. The Austrian Lloyd also began the bulk carriage of Indian cotton via the overland route from 1867 in cooperation with the Bombay and Bengal Steamship Company which had been established in 1863. Port Said gained a French Post Office on 16 June 1867 and was first visited by the Messageries on 18 June. The expansion of the trade of the Mediterranean encouraged Trieste, Fiume and Barcelona to begin harbour works from 1868, followed by Venice in 1869, while Bordeaux considered a Biscay–Mediterranean Ship Canal as a complement to the Suez Canal.[4] The expansion of cosmopolitan 'Bult Said', 'a rapidly-increasing

---

[1] *Illustrated London News*, 23 January 1869, 94 ii, 'The New Overland Route and the Mont Cenis Railway'.

[2] *The Times*, 29 December 1868, 4 i–ii, 'The Viceroy of India and the Suez Canal'.

[3] *The Engineer*, 19 March 1869, 202, 'From London to Bombay'. *The Spectator*, 10 July 1869, 811–12, 'The Proposed Backstair to the Continent'; 31 July 1869, 895–6, 'The Heroic Remedies for Channel Sea-Sickness'.

[4] *The Engineer*, 14 May 1869, 346.

Venice'[1] like to 'a slice of great Nijni fair',[2] brought the Egyptian Customs into conflict with the Canal Company and the local merchants, who both hoped to make Port Said a free port. That hope inspired four French merchants to lead fifty Europeans on 24 August 1868 to seize their merchandise from the Port Said Customs, so precipitating another crisis between the Company and the Government. The new Cairo–Suez Railway which was completed by forced labour in four months as Ismail's reply to the Company's transit service benefited the Government as well as the P. & O. when it was opened on 8 September 1868. Its route followed that of the Sweet Water Canal via Ismailia and possessed superior traffic-potential to the desert-railway of 1858 as well as better gradients and access to water. Its competition ended the Company's branch transit service between Zagazig and Ismailia and captured the pilgrim traffic from the Company's transit service. Thenceforward Cairo and Suez were placed within three hours of Ismailia, which became more than ever the communications-hub of Egypt's new frontier-march. The west bank of the Canal secured a virtual monopoly of communications within the isthmus. The Government's victory over the Company was sealed by its ban upon the Company's issue of postage-stamps and its short-lived postal service (18 April–30 September 1868).[3]

The expansion of European trade in Asia produced widespread efforts to introduce steam navigation on the rivers of Asia from 1867, especially in the Yangtze boom of 1867–8. Attempts were even made from 1868 to reach India from Hankow so as to create an Irrawaddy–Yangtze axis from Rangoon as far as Shanghai. At the same time the voyage around the Cape was accelerated under the spur of the tea-clippers and the steamships, the s.s. *Ajax* of Holt reaching London in 75 days (19 June–2 September 1867) from Foochow. Shaw & Maxton's *Titania* sailed from Gravesend to Hong Kong in 83 days (14 October–6 January 1867). Donald Currie's *Tantallon Castle* reached Calcutta in 80 days and returned to England in 78 days on 3 November 1868.[4] The *Thermopylae* reached Melbourne from Gravesend in 63 days (7 November 1868–9 January 1869), the fastest passage ever made. Thus the sailing ship responded superbly to the new challenge of steam on the long ocean-routes.

The economic crisis of 1866 produced a collapse in the price of the Company's shares by 39 per cent from 360 francs on 1 June to the low-point of 220 francs on 23 June. That crisis compelled the Company to adopt on 19 July new profiles for the Canal which reduced the cube of excavation from 120,000,000 to 97,000,000 cubic yards,[5] extended a subterranean shelf throughout the whole course of the Canal and provided for the construction of passing-stations from 1867. The Universal Exhibition of 1867 at Paris marked a stage

[1] *The Times*, 27 March 1868, 5 v, The Duke of St. Albans, 29 February.

[2] J. MacGregor, *The Rob Roy on the Jordan, Nile, Red Sea and Gennesareth &c.* (London, Murray, 1869), 2, 28 October 1868.

[3] J. Boulad, 'Le Service Postal dans l'Isthme de Suez...de 1859 à 1869', *Bulletin, Société d'Études Historiques et Géographiques de l'Isthme de Suez* (1947), 69–73.

[4] *The Times*, 6 November 1868, 6 ii.　　　　[5] *Engineering*, 24 July 1868, 84 i.

in the spread of Oriental influence in Europe, especially through its Egyptian Pavilion. The Exhibition was used by the Canal Company to display models of the machines of Borel & Lavalley, to publicize its hopes as well as its achievements and so to prepare for the flotation of a loan necessitated by the near-exhaustion of its capital. To that end Lesseps foretold on 1 August 1867 the completion of the Canal by 1 October 1869.[1] He became the only recipient of a gold medal at the hands of Napoleon III to win the applause of a vast assembly for the prize-giving in the Hall of Industry.[2] He commissioned another book to enlist English support for 'this great victory of peace'.[3] The loan was issued (26–30 September 1867) at the same time as the Crédit Mobilier, Luxemburg and Mentana crises and proved a failure, reducing share prices by 23 per cent (16 September–2 October). 'The shares of the Suez Canal are offered to us with the persistence with which the Sibylline Books were laid before the old Roman King.'[4] The Company was rescued from its plight by the Imperial Government which gave as powerful help as it had in the crisis of 1859 and authorized a lottery loan. The additional attraction of a lottery ensured the success of the loan when it was reissued (6–9 July 1868), raising £4,000,000 at a nominal interest rate of 5 per cent but at a real interest rate of 8½ per cent.

Thenceforth the works of the Canal went forward without interruption. The trough-dredger was improved by Lavalley and came into increasing use. The trough deposited spoil directly on the bank without intermediary barges, cranes, boxes or wagons. The trough was lengthened from 115 feet in 1865 to 164 feet in June 1866 with the support of a barge, and to 197 feet in September 1866.[5] Up to that maximum length it became increasingly efficient in the disposal and distribution of spoil. During 1866 it was introduced into one northern section of the works after another. It could be moved however only with great difficulty and could not be used in deep cuttings. The smaller dredgers were more mobile and encouraged Lavalley and Voisin to develop the ancillary elevator for the disposal of spoil from November 1866. The elevator was the last important machine to come into operation on the Canal works and the least efficient, because it was purely a distributor rather than an excavator. Essentially it was an inclined tramway on a gigantic cantilever which carried boxes of spoil from a barge upwards along an endless chain for deposit on the top of the bank in those cuttings where neither excavator, trough or crane could function because of the rock or the height. It began work in the Ballah section from February 1867 and at El Guisr from September 1868.

The elimination of the causeway between the two channels began in 1866,

[1] *L'Isthme de Suez*, 1–3 Août 1867, 251. *The Times*, 27 September 1867, 5 ii.

[2] C. C. Coffin, *Our New Way Round the World* (Boston, Fields, 1869), 62.

[3] W. F. V. Fitzgerald, *The Suez Canal, The Eastern Question and Abyssinia* (London, Longmans, 1867), 25.

[4] *The Times*, 10 October 1867, 6 v.

[5] Voisin Bey, *Le Canal de Suez* (1904), v. 470–5.

so creating a wide navigable channel. The waters of the Mediterranean were first admitted on 12 December 1866 through El Guisr into Lake Timsah, which so became a lake of salt rather than of fresh water. At the limestone plateau of Serapeum, which was on the same level as the Sweet Water Canal to Suez, that canal was tapped during the successive high Niles of 1865, 1866 and 1867 in order to turn three large depressions into artificial lakes of fresh water. Within those lakes dredgers worked from January 1867, dredging their way down from a height of 33 feet above sea-level and so replacing dry excavation by dredging. They disposed of their spoil with the help of side-emptying lighters introduced from December 1866 and were reinforced by trough dredgers which arrived via the preliminary channel from April 1867. Lake Timsah held its first regatta on 12 May 1867 and admitted its first dredger on 20 June and its first lighter with base-valves on 2 July for the discharge of dredgings from El Guisr. By 15 August 1867 the lake had reached the level of the Mediterranean, in 8 months rather than the $4\frac{1}{2}$ anticipated. At El Guisr Couvreux made rapid progress during 1866 and 1867 and completed his contract by 31 January 1868, having perfected his mechanical excavator in the process. By the end of 1867, 44,000,000 cubic yards or 45 per cent of the new cube of excavation had been removed at 71 per cent of the total cost. By 15 February 1868, 49,000,000 cubic yards or 49·5 per cent of the cube of excavation had been removed, leaving only half to be excavated at steeply falling unit-costs as the Company at last reaped the advantages of its large-scale overhead investment in mastering the techniques necessary to conquer the desert.

The Abyssinian War of 1868 was an engineering rather than a military campaign, commanded by an engineer and organized from Bombay. It benefited the P. & O. and brought a war-time boom to the Red Sea, especially to Aden and Suez. Suez became a supply base, a mule depot and a hospital camp, gaining the Victoria Military Hospital for use in conjunction with the new trooping service to Bombay. The Canal works were denuded of workmen who became muleteers at higher pay. The Company benefited by the surplus of mules at the victorious close of the campaign, using them on its inclined planes. The war ended the British consulate at Massawa but strengthened the demand for a Red Sea cable to India and encouraged the incorporation of three cable companies, the Indo-European Telegraph Company Ltd. on 8 April 1868, the Anglo-Mediterranean Telegraph Company Ltd. on 18 May 1868 and the British Indian Submarine Telegraph Company Ltd. on 28 January 1869, so ushering in the cable company boom of 1868–9. For Britain the Red Sea remained a through-route rather than a base of empire. Italy, however, was inspired to consider the establishment of a penal colony at Assab and France to purchase in 1868 Sheikh Said on the south-west promontory of Arabia pointing at Perim and forty miles from Assab. Ismail began to extend his own empire in the south after the cession of Suakin and Massawa in 1865 and the destruction of the Abyssinian threat to the Sudan.

The trough-dredger was brought to Suez on 20 January 1867 along the Sweet Water Canal but found the clay of the Suez Plain recalcitrant and was abandoned in favour of dry excavation. For that task the inclined plane was introduced into the Suez Plain from 4 March 1868 and facilitated the disposal of spoil as well as it had in dynastic Egypt. At Port Said the west mole was completed on 10 September 1868 to a length of $1\frac{3}{4}$ miles, which was exceeded only by that of the breakwaters of Holyhead, Cherbourg and Marseilles. That mole provided the protection essential for the new harbour but destroyed the equilibrium of the coastline and led to the accumulation of a sandbank fifty times as fast as had been expected,[1] the formation of an inner submarine beach and the enforced displacement eastward in 1868 of the access canal to the maritime canal. The sandbank accumulated more rapidly at first than later and more rapidly after than before the Nile floods. On 31 January 1869 the less important east mole was completed, having required only 40 per cent as much concrete as the longer west mole. Together those moles created a harbour where few experts had thought it possible and where no materials existed for its construction. The area of the outer port enclosed by the two moles was trebled at no extra cost by a far-sighted decision in 1865. The moles had been reduced by 27 per cent in length from that intended in 1859: thus they reached out to a depth of only 28 feet instead of to the recommended 32 feet and did not afford complete protection from the prevalent north-east wind.

By 15 December 1868, 69,000,000 cubic yards or 70 per cent of the cube of excavation of 'this enormous cut'[2] had been extracted. Faced by the impending completion of the great Salt Water Canal English opinion reluctantly abandoned its Palmerstonian belief in its impossibility and proclaimed that it would be a financial failure even if it could be successfully maintained.[3] 'A hole in the sand is an excellent place for sinking capital.'[4] Ismail was impressed by the magnitude of the Company's achievement on his first visit to the isthmus (14–18 March 1869), when he was received with jubilation by the Arabs of Port Said. For that visit the Serapeum barrages were cut (12–16 March), releasing an unexpectedly destructive avalanche of fresh water into the Toussoum trench.[5] Ismail then gave the signal on 18 March for the admission of the Mediterranean to the Bitter Lakes, whose area was tenfold that of Lake Timsah. 'The conception of M. de Lesseps is raised out of the limbo of possibilities.'[6] Thereafter Ismail came to the financial rescue of the Company after Lesseps abandoned on 22 April his claim to exemption from customs duties on the import of machinery.[7] The Convention of 23 April 1869[8]

[1] A. Cialdi, *Port-Said. A M. Ferdinand de Lesseps* (Rome, Les Beaux-Arts, 1868), 16, 20.
[2] J. MacGregor, *The Rob Roy on the Jordan* (1869), 12.
[3] *The Times*, 18 February 1869, 4i–iii, 9iv–v, John Fowler.
[4] J. MacGregor, 3.   [5] O. Ritt, 440–1.
[6] W. H. Russell, *A Diary in the East during the Tour of the Prince and Princess of Wales* (London, Routledge, 1869), 442, 26 March 1869.
[7] G. Douin, *Histoire du Règne du Khédive Ismail*, ii. 152.
[8] *The Times*, 20 May 1869, 6i; *The Economist*, 22 May 1869, 597i.

arranged for a joint commission of the Common Domain and surrendered the interest on Ismail's shares for twenty-five years. The Company then capitalized the expectations of profit on those shares by the issue on 13 August of delegations, which raised £1,200,000 in immediate funds but committed the Company to the payment of maximum dividends for each of the next twenty-five years. Ismail also ordered the construction of four lighthouses on the Mediterranean coast between Rosetta and Port Said for the guidance of shipping approaching the Canal. Thus he sacrificed his own financial interests but enabled the Canal to be completed and provided for the security of navigation along the new route.

5

THE CEREMONY OF INAUGURATION, 1869

IN May 1869 Ismail visited Europe in order to pursue his dream of full
sovereignty over an Egypt identified with Europe. That visit infuriated the
Sultan, from whom Ismail had extorted the title of Khedive in 1867.
Abdul Aziz was disturbed because Ismail had raised £28,000,000 in foreign
loans between 1864 and 1868, so committing 23 per cent of the revenues of
Egypt to the service of that debt. Ismail had also ordered three ironclad
frigates and had apparently revived the great aspiration of his fathers to the
throne of the Golden Horn. He invited to the opening ceremony all the Moslem princes of Asia and Africa as well as all the Christian princes of Europe
and America but not the Sultan, whose presence would have deprived Ismail
of the opportunity to play host to his fellow-monarchs. The resulting Turco-
Egyptian conflict of June–December 1869[1] centred around the supreme issue
of status in a hierarchical society.

By 15 July 1869, 90,000,000 cubic yards or 91 per cent of the cube of excavation had been extracted. The fixing of the date for the opening of the Canal
for 17 November 1869[2] raised the Company's shares 23 per cent above par
to 615 francs by 1 August and created a sensation in England. It stopped
sailing shipowners from buying new vessels and gave a marked impetus to
enterprise in steam shipping, especially in Marseilles, Trieste, Genoa, Odessa,
Barcelona and Amsterdam. In Liverpool, where shipowners suffered particular depression, T. H. Ismay formed the Oceanic Steam Navigation Company on 6 September 1869 with steamships only, probably for the Australian
rather than for the Atlantic trade, and ordered his pioneer steamship *Oceanic*
with a 10:1 ratio of length to beam suitable primarily for the Suez Canal. The
final filling of the Canal took place almost unnoticed,[3] although it provided
the subject of the last chapter in the first history of the isthmus.[4] On 15 August
the barrage at the Suez end was cut and the restless waters of the Red Sea
stormed through the gap with torrential violence into the 22-mile dry cutting
which reached through the Suez Plain and the Chalouf cutting to the Bitter
Lakes, causing £40,000 of damage, the suspension of dredging for fifteen
days and a consequent delay in the completion of the works. On the pay-day
of 16 August several thousand armed workmen surrounded the Company
offices to prevent any attempt to decamp without settling accounts and so
necessitated the protection of the Company by Egyptian troops and artillery.

[1] G. Douin, *Histoire du Règne du Khédive Ismail*, ii. 309–742. A. Sammarco, *Le Règne du
Khédive Ismail de 1863 à 1875* (Le Caire, 1937), 169–89.
[2] *The Times*, 26 June 1869, 6 ii; 19 July 5 v. *The Economist*, 26 June, 749 ii.
[3] *The Times*, 21 September 1869, 5 i.
[4] O. Ritt, *Histoire de l'Isthme de Suez* (Paris, Hachette, 1869), 476–9.

Lesseps made the first direct and continuous passage from sea to sea in fifteen hours on 28 September,[1] while Jules Verne sent the *Nautilus* through an inclined Arabian tunnel beneath the isthmus in twenty minutes and praised Lesseps as 'one of the men that honour a nation more than the greatest captains'.[2] The union of the two seas on the surface as well as beneath the earth[3] began the rapid dissolution of the salt crust of the Bitter Lakes whose 100,000 acres were filled by 24 October, in seven rather than in the ten months anticipated. Thus the Bitter Lakes were filled faster and Lake Timsah slower than had been expected. The absence of current between the two ends of the Canal proved the accuracy of Bourdaloue's survey of 1847. The tidal influence of the Red Sea extended only as far as the Bitter Lakes which became thenceforward the great reservoir of the waterway and the regulator of the sea-level at either end. The Canal became a northward prolongation of the Red Sea, renewing the slow fusion of the marine fauna of the Atlantic and Indo-Pacific Oceans across the saline barrier of the Bitter Lakes. The creation of large surfaces of evaporation increased the rainfall in the isthmus but did not produce any local extension of the area of cultivation nor influence its climate in the same degree as the vast water-surface of the Delta.[4]

The Company issued its Navigation Regulations on 17 August for ships with a maximum draught of $24\frac{1}{2}$ feet. After the *Louise et Marie* of C. & A. Bazin of Marseilles arrived from Suez and Aden at Port Said on 9 October the departure of nine vessels for the new route was advertised between 16 October[5] and 10 November, seven of them belonging to three English shipowners. Donald R. MacGregor of Leith advertised the *Leith* for Bombay and the *William Miller* for Hong Kong, T. &. W. Smith of Newcastle the *Blue Cross* as the first steamer of a Calcutta line, and Gellatly, Hankey Sewell & Co. of London the *Tszru* for Japan.[6] To service the expected steamships two French coaling firms opened at Port Said, Bazin on 2 July and Hippolyte Worms of Bordeaux on 5 November. The isthmus, which had been a construction camp with a population in May 1869 of 22,800 Europeans and 19,600 Arabs, began to prepare for its transformation into a highway of commerce.

Voisin carried the works to their triumphant conclusion as well as serving the Company as its Principal Agent in Egypt from 1867. He earned the highest of reputations in civil engineering by his nine years of service in the isthmus. Borel and Lavalley were no ordinary contractors but were both graduates of the École Polytechnique. They had appeared first in 1864 but had successfully

[1] *The Times*, 30 September 1869, 10i.
[2] J. Verne, *Vingt Mille Lieues sous les Mers* (Paris, Hetzel, 1873), 244, 254.
[3] E. Suess, *The Face of the Earth* (Oxford, Clarendon Press, 1904), i. 377.
[4] T. Login, 'The Suez Canal, Egyptian Agriculture and Egyptian Cotton', *Manchester Guardian*, 1 January 1870, 6i. W. G. Black, 'The Meteorology and Climate of Suez before and after the Opening of the Canal', *Journal of the Manchester Geographical Society* (1888), 249–55.
[5] *The Times*, 16 October 1869, 1iv, 'Steam to Bombay through the Suez Canal' (*Leith*).
[6] Ibid., 20 October, 1v; 3 November, 2i; 10 November, 2i.

adapted their techniques to the conditions of the isthmus and had devised machinery rivalling English machinery in its ingenuity. They perfected the construction of the most powerful bucket-dredgers ever built as Couvreux perfected that of the small-bucket mechanical excavator. They had signed their ninth contract with the Company on 30 October 1868 and raised their share of the work from one-third to three-quarters. They gave employment to 20,000 men and excavated 74,000,000 cubic yards along ninety miles of the Canal, the greatest task ever allotted to a single contractor.[1] They ordered cranes, large dredgers, troughs and elevators from the Société des Forges et Chantiers de la Méditerranée, which had been established in Toulon in 1855 and built the fleet of the Messageries Impériales as well as Ismail's ironclads. Their dredgers and barges were supplied by Ernest Gouin et Cie, which had been established for locomotive-construction at Batignolles near Paris in 1846 and thereby undertook its first colonial enterprise.[2] Paul Borel died on 17 October 1869 under the pressure of the work while Alexandre Lavalley, who had been manager for Gouin from 1846 to 1863, gave his name to two steamships, one belonging to Ismay of Liverpool and one launched by Gouin at Nantes on 18 February 1870.

As an engineering achievement the Canal derived its grandeur from the sheer mass of the material excavated even more than from the technical skill with which obstacles had been overcome. 99,400,000 cubic yards had been excavated to create 'a mighty river'[3] 24 feet deep and 98 miles long. 50,000,000 cubic yards of the total had been dredged, including 31,000,000 by trough-dredgers, 13,000,000 by dredgers with barges and 6,000,000 by dredgers with elevators.[4] Three new ports had been created at Port Said, Port Ibrahim and Ismailia. The achievement was not complete. No harbour had been built on Lake Timsah, while the works at Port Ibrahim were more like river than marine breakwaters. The surface-width of 328 feet was deceptive because it concealed a wave-eroding submarine shelf. The bottom width of 72 feet was half the width laid down in 1856 as the absolute minimum so that the channel was equivalent to a one-way railway and required passing-stations. The curves in its course numbered eighteen and reduced the magnificent arrow-straight section from Port Said southwards to Ballah from 40 miles to 26 miles in length.[5] Above all, the depth was reduced from 24 feet to 17 feet by two beds of rock discovered at Serapeum in late October 1869.

The time taken for the construction of that restricted channel was double the six years estimated in 1856, while Lesseps himself emphasized that the eleven years of construction had been preceded by five years of meditation and five years of investigation.[6] The total costs were £18,144,000 or 108 per

[1] Voisin Bey, *Le Canal de Suez* (1904), v. 408.
[2] J. Ganiage, *Les Origines du Protectorat Français en Tunisie (1861–1881)* (1959), 468 note. Voisin Bey, *Le Canal de Suez* (1904), v. 442–3.
[3] *Daily News*, 9 November 1869, 5 ii–iii, 'A Voyage on the Suez Canal', 27 October 1869.
[4] Voisin Bey, v. 465.   [5] Ibid., iv. 123–6, 131–2.
[6] F. de Lesseps, *Lettres* (1881), v. 360, 10 Avril 1870.

cent in excess of the 1856 estimate. Those costs included £11,652,000 for construction, with costs per cubic yard treble the estimates of 1856.[1] Costs were increased by the replacement of cheap local labour by expensive machinery and European labour, by the local manufacture of the concrete blocks for the moles of Port Said, by the rock-facing of the African bank through Lake Menzaleh and, most of all, by the lack of comparative studies inevitable with a pioneer work. Costs were also raised by the British and Turkish opposition to the project, by the excessive centralization of the Canal Company, by its employment of the black-sheep sons of the French aristocracy in sinecures[2] and by its continuous payment of the 5 per cent statutory interest to shareholders. Thus interest payments, estimated at 12·8 per cent, formed 19·7 per cent of total costs while administrative expenses, estimated at 2·5 per cent, formed 5 per cent thereof. France and Egypt together supplied 91·7 per cent of the total capital. France supplied £8,182,000 or 45·09 per cent in its shares, the 1867 loan and the 1869 delegations. Egypt supplied £8,460,000,[3] or 46·62 per cent, through its shares and the compensation under the 1864 award. Its investment in the Canal formed 5·3 per cent of Ismail's total expenditure between 1863 and 1874.

The inauguration ceremonies of 16–20 November took place under the eye of the painter rather than of the photographer and were described to the public of Europe in accounts transmitted by sea-mail rather than by telegraph. Ismail was disappointed in his hope that the ceremonies would enhance his status in relation to the Sultan by associating him with the crowned heads of Europe. Respect for the Sultan restricted attendance at the ceremony to princes and was most openly displayed by England and Russia, which were represented by their ambassadors to Constantinople. Only one of the eighteen reigning sovereigns of Europe attended the ceremonies in person, the Emperor of Austria, whereas three sovereigns had attended the Paris Exhibition in 1867. Francis Joseph attended only to ensure that no Prussian prince enjoyed precedence over an Austrian prince. His name was given by a grateful Canal Company to a quay at Port Said and to an avenue in Ismailia. The Empress Eugénie reigned supreme in the absence of both the Empress Elizabeth of Austria and the Crown Princess Victoria of Prussia. She fostered the Franco-Austrian entente against Prussia which she had supported since 1863, shunning the Crown Prince of Prussia in favour of the Emperor of Austria. The Crown Prince was accompanied by the son and heir of the Grand-Duke of Hesse-Darmstadt, which was moving from the Austrian into the Prussian orbit. He displayed his own lack of confidence in the Austrian Chancellor Beust who was the architect of the Ausgleich, the opponent of German unification and the aspirant to a war of revenge against Prussia: he preferred to

[1] *The Engineer*, 10 December 1869, 375 ii.
[2] G. Ebers, *Durch Gosen zum Sinai* (Leipzig, Engelmann, 1872), 26.
[3] Excluding the cost of the graving dock and the breakwaters at Port Ibrahim, the lighthouses on the Mediterranean coast and the inauguration ceremonies.

spend his time with the Magyar Andrassy, who assured him of the monarchy's desire for peace. Thus he sought to undermine the triple entente which Napoleon was trying to form with Austria and Russia against Prussia.

'The greatest drama ever witnessed or enacted in Egypt'[1] began on 16 November at Port Said where on the beach to the west of the mole and in front of the Eugénie Quay three pavilions had been erected, with that of Ismail's guests overshadowing both those devoted to Islam and Christendom.[2] Ismail's special request that the Moslem, Catholic and Greek Orthodox creeds should be given equal status in the ceremony did not satisfy the priests who showed only hate and scorn for each other.[3] The blessing of the Canal was undertaken by the representatives of each creed in succession, beginning with Sheikh Ibrahim el Sakka (1797–1881) of El Azhar:[4] 'Allah! Bestow thy benediction upon Europe, who, as Thou seest, has come among us today. Bestow thy benediction upon the enterprise which promises to enrich our poor nation. Bestow thy benediction upon our master and father Ismail, who has presided over these great labours. Bestow thy benediction upon all peoples. And we prostrate ourselves at thy feet, O Allah!'[5] The festivities at Port Said took place amid the indifference of the local Arabs[6] but were counterbalanced at Ismail's express wish by the Arab festivities at Ismailia.

A fleet of 130 merchant vessels assembled at Port Said for the opening ceremony. Most were warships or yachts while merchant vessels were in a minority, except in one case. Italy was represented by six trading steamers but not by a single warship, ambassador or consul-general, because its fleet had left Alexandria on the news of the sudden illness of King Victor Emmanuel. The Company had promised a depth of 26 feet and admission to vessels of 24½ feet but confessed at the last moment that vessels over 18 feet could not pass through. At 8.30 a.m. on 18 November a fleet of forty-six vessels led by the imperial *Aigle* and 3 Austrian vessels began to enter the waterway.[7] The fleet included 5 Egyptian, 6 Italian, 7 Austrian, 9 French and 10 English vessels, 10 corvettes, 11 yachts and 21 steamers. At Ismailia the *Aigle* was met by 3 Egyptian gunboats from Suez and frantic cheers of 'Vive la France! Vive l'Impératrice! Vive Lesseps!' Thus the union of the seas was celebrated as an achievement of Imperial France. The next day the *Péluse* of the

---

[1] H. M. Stanley, *My Early Travels and Adventures in Africa and Asia* (London, Low, 1895) ii. 50.

[2] G. Nicole, *Inauguration du Canal de Suez. Voyage des Souverains* (Paris, Didier, 1869), pl. 8, facing p. 13, reproduces Riou's water-colour 'La Tribune des Souverains'.

[3] A. Russel, *Egypt: The Opening of the Great Canal* (Edinburgh, The 'Scotsman', 1869), 63.

[4] Kindly identified for me by Professor C. F. Beckingham and Mr. David Cowan of the School of Oriental and African Studies, London.

[5] *Putnam's Monthly Magazine*, March 1870, 334, 'Our Trip to Egypt as Guests of the Viceroy'.

[6] A. Lang, *Life, Letters and Diaries of Sir Stafford Northcote* (Edinburgh, Blackwood, 1891), i. 354, 16 November 1869.

[7] M. Fontane, *Voyage Pittoresque à travers l'Isthme de Suez. Aquarelles d'après Nature par Riou* (Paris, Dupont, 1870), Aquarelle no. xxiii, 84–5, 'Passage à El Guisr des navires venant de Port Said'.

Messageries, with twelve directors of the Canal Company and their guests on board and a draught of 17 feet, ran aground on the gypsum bed at Serapeum. Only five other ships ran fully aground either through bad steering or through eagerness to pass through quickly, in the absence of any pilots or convoy, although many ships grounded slightly over and over again, especially in the curves following the first straight stretch. Suez was first reached on 20 November not by the *Aigle* but by J. L. Ashbury's racing yacht *Cambria* which had been the sixteenth vessel to leave Port Said. Suez celebrated the completion of the first journey by water across Africa and appeared that evening like 'a New Paris of Egypt'.[1] The southern half of the Canal, the last undertaken and rumoured to be the most imperfect, proved to be the most advanced in workmanship and the easiest to navigate, although it also suffered the heaviest erosion from the tremendous scour created by the paddle-steamers. 'It is as easy sailing through the Canal as going through the Pool.'[2] Surveyors found only 5 per cent of their soundings under 24 feet while 73·5 per cent gave 27 feet and over. The frigates which had remained in Port Said then tested the capacity of the new waterway for naval use.

The creation of the Canal had been an achievement of French enterprise and French diplomacy even more than of French capital. France supplied among its 300 guests the most brilliant representatives of civilization and the most literate of publicists. In Paris the Comédie Française staged Henri de Bornier's cantata of 1861 *L'Isthme de Suez* on 17 November to provide the capital with a brief distraction after the disasters of Sadowa, Queretaro and Mentana. France was less impressed by the opening of the Canal than by the rise of Prussia and by the appointment of a liberal administration under Ollivier. The ceremonies could have given proof of the French capacity for organization. Unfortunately the arrangements for the reception of the guests broke down because Ismail and Nubar could not be ubiquitous, co-ordination proved ineffective between the Government and the Company and the number of guests increased unexpectedly from 600 to 1,600, producing such disorganization, overcrowding, discomfort and malversation as to frustrate the Khedive's good intentions and his lavish expenditure. The disorder culminated at Ismailia on 18 November[3] in the ball attended by 3,000 men and 200 ladies. Ismail's intended select assembly of monarchs and enlightened minds degenerated into a trampling plebeian herd, 'a rough kind of democratic fete...a great excursion train from Europe to Africa'.[4] The celebrations did not improve relations between Europeans and Egyptians, who at Ismailia found each other beyond comprehension or tolerance. They weakened rather than strengthened the moral authority of the Christian West in Asia.[5] They

---

[1] *Manchester Guardian*, 7 December 1869, 5 vi.

[2] E. Dicey, *The Morning Land* (London, Macmillan, 1870), ii. 163.

[3] *The Standard*, 9 December 1869, 5 iii, G. A. Henty.

[4] T. W. Reid, *The Life, Letters and Friendships of Richard Monckton Milnes, First Lord Houghton* (London, Cassell, 1890), ii. 210, 214, 22 November 1869.

[5] *The Spectator*, 27 November 1869, 1389, 'The Egyptian Carmagnole'.

cost Ismail £1,410,000[1] and the approval of the Old Turks. They served as a political festival of commerce which foreshadowed the neo-mercantilism of the 1870s and improved the quotation of Egyptian stocks in the money-markets of Europe. A commercial congress, the first international congress ever to meet in Egypt and designed by Nubar to further the cause of judicial reform, held its last session in Ismailia on 18 November. It recommended from Cairo on 24 November the international recognition of the neutrality of the Canal, the unification of tonnage-measurement and the exemption of coal from Canal dues as well as judicial reform in Egypt. Neutralization was favoured by Austria, Prussia, England and Italy but was opposed by France and Russia[2] and remained an aspiration.

The intellectual élite failed to produce a single worthy memorial of the occasion among the 245 books, articles and pamphlets published on the subject of the Canal in 1869–70. Lesseps himself left no account of the ceremony. The newspaper correspondents W. H. Russell, H. M. Stanley, G. A. Henty,[3] Gautier and Zola published no books. Fromentin never wrote the work he hoped to produce as a sequel to his studies of the Sahara and the Sahel. Charles Blanc brought to the critical attention of France not the Canal but the Islamic art of Egypt.[4] The account of Eça de Queiroz, the Portuguese Flaubert, was published only in 1957.[5] Ibsen contrasted the mighty engineering of the Canal with the pettiness of life in Norway but was more impressed by the Nile than by the Canal. He was fascinated by the spectacle of a dead culture and forced to conclude that it could never really have been alive. 'The stay in Egypt has been the most interesting and instructive period in my life.'[6] He required seven years to absorb that experience before hurling his dramatic thunderbolts at the conventions of society. The Khedive's Hymn but not *Aida* was first officially played at the opening ceremonies. Verdi twice refused to compose an opera for the occasion and only accepted the commission on 2 June 1870, a year after Mariette had provided the scenario. Egyptology and tourism were both popularized by the ceremony,[7] which attracted at least seven Egyptologists as well as Thomas Cook. The construction of the Canal had destroyed many ancient ruins in the isthmus and engulfed two miles of the 'Canal of the Pharaohs' near Chalouf. Nevertheless it enabled the greatest geologist of the century to make observations and even excavations at Chalouf.[8] Above all, it inspired Brugsch to suggest in

---

[1] T. W. Reid, *Lord Houghton*, 211. A. M. Hamza, *The Public Debt of Egypt, 1854–1876* (Cairo Government Press, 1944), 173 note.

[2] *Appleton's Annual Cyclopedia*, 1869, 238–9, Egypt.

[3] *The Times*, 30 November, 7 December, 11 December 1869, W. H. Russell. *The Standard*, 30 November, 7 December, 9 December, G. A. Henty. *The Scotsman*, 1, 6, 7 and 14 December, A. Russel. *Daily Telegraph*, 30 November, 7 December, E. Dicey.

[4] C. Blanc, *Voyage de la Haute Égypte* (Paris, Renouard, 1876).

[5] Eça de Queiroz, 'Von Port Said nach Suez', *Aufbau* (Januar 1957), 92–103.

[6] H. Koht, *The Life of Ibsen* (London, Allen, 1931), ii. 77.

[7] A. F. F. Mariette, *Itinéraire des Invités aux Fêtes d'Inauguration du Canal de Suez* (Paris, Vieweg, 1869).　　　[8] E. Suess, *The Face of the Earth* (1904), i. 376–86.

1874[1] the Pelusium route for the Exodus in preference to the traditional southerly routes via Timsah or Suez.

The dispute between Turkey and Egypt reached its climax immediately after the ceremonies, from which Ismail had eliminated the inauguration of a trilingual memorial modelled on the Rosetta Stone with a reference to the 'renowned government of the illustrious Padishah Abdul Aziz'.[2] Ismail so resented England's support of Turkey that he prevented the unveiling of a bust to Waghorn at Suez[3] and the firing of any salute by Egyptian warships to the *Psyché* on the completion of its voyage through the Canal with the British ambassador on board. The firman of 26 November 1869 forbade the Khedive to raise foreign loans without the prior approval of the Sultan and strictly curtailed the administrative autonomy of Egypt. Ismail did not consent to publish that firman without a struggle. He undertook extensive military preparations. He massed his army on the Mediterranean coast because the Canal, as Palmerston had feared, supplied effective protection to the most exposed flank of Egypt and barred the traditional route for the invasion of Africa from Asia by a great wall of water spanned by neither bridges nor tunnels. He replaced his French military mission by twenty American officers. Lacking the support of any great power he was nevertheless compelled to capitulate on 8 December. Thus the ceremony brought him to the nadir rather than to the zenith of his power. He duly surrendered his ironclads to the Sultan but thenceforward increased his floating rather than his funded debt, sought to undermine the Turkish position in Africa and Arabia[4] and established an entente with Russia from March 1870 against their common foe. England relied more than ever on Constantinople rather than on Cairo.

For England the successful completion of 'the grandest enterprise which has been achieved in Egypt since the days of the Pharaohs'[5] was a national humiliation. 'The Queen of England has opened the Holborn Viaduct, and the Empress of the French is going to open the Suez Canal.'[6] Neither the Company nor the Khedive spared the feelings of the English. The decorations at Port Said everywhere studiously excluded the British colours.[7] Every vessel in the harbour was dressed with flags unlike the vessels of the Mediterranean Fleet anchored outside. Two of the English ironclads had run aground on 14 November on a new sandbank not shown on their charts while trying to enter the harbour without a pilot: refloated on the next day they remained outside because they were deemed too deep to enter even the outer harbour. Thus they demonstrated the incapacity of the Canal to admit the largest

[1] *The Times*, 28 April 1874, 12 ii, Egyptian Notes.
[2] *The Engineer*, 10 December 1869, 385.
[3] H. Stephan, 'Der Suezkanal und seine Eröffnung', *Unsere Zeit* (1870), 118.
[4] *The Times*, 17 January 1870, 10 iii. G. Douin, *Histoire du Règne du Khédive Ismail*, ii. 493, 558.
[5] *Daily Telegraph*, 26 August 1869, 4 v, Edwin Arnold.
[6] *Saturday Review*, 13 November 1869, 636.
[7] F. Arrow, *A Fortnight in Egypt at the Opening of the Suez Canal* (London, Smith, 1869), 14.

ironclads. The P. & O. failed to display a just appreciation of the potentialities of the new highway. It did not inform the Government of Egypt or the Canal Company that it intended to send a ship through on the opening day. Consequently the *Delta*, its most beautiful paddle-steamer with a draught of 18 feet, had no place assigned to it on 17 November, waited at Port Said until 18 November and then entered the Canal as the forty-fifth of forty-six vessels. It arrived at Lake Timsah on 19 November, the day after the great ball. The three sceptical directors of the P. & O. which it carried then decided to return to Port Said instead of continuing to Suez. Thus they limited their experience to the worst section of the Canal and left the P. & O. unrepresented at the final triumphal entry into the Gulf of Suez.[1]

Many of the English guests revealed a similar lack of hope or belief in the Canal. The nine English engineers however were favourably impressed. Hawkshaw agreed with the extremely favourable verdict returned by experienced sailors.[2] *The Engineer* bestowed restrained praise on the Canal as 'the greatest engineering work ever executed, since the opening of the Manchester and Birmingham Railway'.[3] The English deputation included at least ten Manchester men and, led by the Mayor of Manchester, presented on 23 November an address of thanks to Ismail, who replied in Arabic rather than in his customary French. Admiral Milne, commander of the Mediterranean Station, cabled the Admiralty from Suez on 20 November 'Canal is a great success', and from Malta on 3 December '19 feet through Canal'. C. R. M. Talbot tested the capacity of the channel when used by a single vessel rather than by a fleet and returned from Suez in his steam-yacht *Lynx* in 10 hours, against the 48 hours of his southward transit. The Duke of Sutherland, a great railway enthusiast and the largest landowner in Britain, agreed with Stafford Northcote that 'the Canal is truly wonderful'[4] and became the first Englishman to conceive the idea of purchasing it. E. T. Gourley of Sunderland, the only English shipowner present, cabled to London on 20 November to freight two 2,000-ton ships for Bombay via the Canal.[5] The P. & O. announced on 22 November a reduction in the first-class passenger fare to Bombay. A serious fall in freight rates by sailing-vessel via the Cape to India and China occurred during November 1869 because 'the success of the Suez Canal means the revolution of half the maritime Trade of the world'.[6] 'The stupendous Canal' gave its name to the Suez Quadrille[7] as well as to the s.s. *Suez* built at Sunderland by R. M. Hudson. It provided a new subject for the lantern slides manufactured by the Stereoscopic Company.[8]

[1] *Manchester Guardian*, 7 December 1869, 5 vi. A Russel, *Egypt: The Opening of the Great Canal* (1869), 91.   [2] Russel, 87.
[3] *The Engineer*, 26 November 1869, 351 ii.
[4] A. Lang, *Sir Stafford Northcote* (1891), i. 356, 17 November 1869.
[5] E. Dicey, *The Morning Land* (1870), ii. 163. *Le Canal de Suez*, 1 Janvier 1870, 13.
[6] *Mitchell's Maritime Register*, 20 November 1869, 1486 i–ii; 27 November, 1516 i.
[7] *Illustrated London News*, 27 November 1869, 538 iii.
[8] *The Times*, 18 December 1869, 1 vi.

Its creator received the congratulations of the Foreign Secretary on 27 November but not the medal of the Royal Geographical Society for 1869, which was awarded to Mary Somerville. Ruskin used the French success to condemn the machine civilization of England in his address at the Royal Artillery Institution, Woolwich, on 14 December 1869. 'On the Baltic and the Nile your power is already departed. By machinery you would advance to discovery; by machinery you would carry your commerce; you would be engineers instead of sailors; and instantly in the North seas you are beaten among the ice, and before the very Gods of Nile, beaten among the sand.'[1]

Alfred Holt recognized that England's second-rate appearance at the ceremony was deserved but thought that England would benefit by the Canal more than all the nations of the earth put together. He was justified by the first departures on 9 December of the *Leith* and the *Blue Cross* for the new route as well as by the laying of the Red Sea cable to Bombay by private enterprise. The Admiralty issued a Notice to Navigators on 10 December[2] embodying the information on the Canal supplied by Captain G. S. Nares. Childers, the First Lord of the Admiralty, ordered the Director of Engineering Works, Andrew Clarke, on 30 December to undertake a survey of the Canal's capacity for use by troopships. The interest aroused by the new Suez route spread to all of the routes to India. Thus Rathbone Brothers of Liverpool announced on 10 December a Calcutta-direct line of screw-steamers via the Cape modelled on Holt's line to China and the Magellan service of the Pacific Steam Navigation Company. Proposals were also made to improve the railway route to India via Brindisi by the construction of a Channel Tunnel,[3] a Channel Ferry[4] and a Euphrates Valley Railway. Support for such a railway was sought by George Jenkinson from the Turkish ambassador in London on 16 February 1870 and from the Foreign Secretary on 18 March but was refused by the Cabinet on 9 April. Such a venture would have been as uneconomic as a Panama Canal[5] in reply to the Suez Canal. Merchants and shipowners agreed with the Government and prepared to reap the benefit of the French achievement.

The opening ceremony was attended and applauded by at least a dozen Americans.[6] Another American, Zerah Colburn, placed the enterprise in clear technological perspective. 'The present year, moving forward slowly amidst the stagnation of depressed trade and the absence of engineering activity, has, nevertheless, witnessed the achievement of the two greatest constructive works that have ever been undertaken—the Pacific Railroad and the Suez Canal.'[7]

[1] Ruskin, *The Crown of Wild Olive. Four Lectures on Industry and War* (4th edition. London, Smith, 1873), 171, 'The Future of England'.

[2] *Proceedings of the Royal Geographical Society*, xiv, 13 December 1869, 75–8.

[3] *The Times*, 27 August 1869, 6 ii. *The Engineer*, 27 August 1869, 140, 144.

[4] *Engineering*, 11 March 1870, 168. E. Leigh, *Plan for Conveying Railway Trains Across the Straits of Dover* (Manchester, Ireland, April 1870).

[5] *Once a Week*, 1 January 1870, 494.

[6] *New York Times*, 18 November 1869, 4 v; 20 December, 1.

[7] *Engineering*, 26 November 1869, 353 i.

Colburn ranked the Pacific Railroad above the Suez Canal as a triumph for its engineer over all the obstacles arrayed against him by Nature in her most formidable aspects across 1,775 miles of mountain and plain. The new American Consul-General to Egypt at his reception by Ismail in 1870 spoke of the U.S.A. and Egypt as two nations which had 'simultaneously accomplished the greatest triumphs of nineteenth century civilization'.[1] The prospective termination of the transcontinental railroad had revived the idea of a Darien Ship Canal:[2] its completion on 10 May 1869 encouraged proposals for a Panama Ship Railway[3] and for a Nicaragua Canal[4] in competition with the Colombian route. It also encouraged the publication of a handbook for intending voyagers round the world via the Pacific Railroad and the Suez Canal.[5] It inspired Whitman to sing in his *Passage to India*, composed between 1868 and 1871, of the modern wonders which outvied the antique seven, the 'Year of the marriage, of continents, climates and oceans', the rediscovery by the West of its Asiatic past and the destiny of America to fulfil all the hopes of mankind, 'not for trade and transportation only, But in God's name, and for thy sake O soul'. The Pacific Railroad also provoked the incorporation by special act of the New York State Legislature in May 1869 of the Mediterranean and Oriental Steam Navigation Company, to carry mail to Port Said and to import Indian and Chinese labour via the Suez Canal to the Southern States. The new company hoped thereby to solve the postwar 'labour shortage' and to make the Suez Canal for the defeated South what the Pacific Railroad promised to be for the North, East and West.[6] Thus the Canal seemed to offer new economic opportunities to the South as Ismail opened staff employment to ex-Confederate officers in 1870.

The completion of the Suez Canal revived the Saint-Simonian dream of Suez and Panama and inspired two youths, Theodor Herzl in Budapest and Philippe Bunau-Varilla in Paris,[7] to determine to imitate at Panama what Lesseps had achieved at Suez. The Americans who disliked being surpassed in anything hoped that 'Suez may finally yield to Darien',[8] through which peninsula a ship canal was recommended by the Secretary of State for the Navy on 1 December 1869. Five naval expeditions were despatched to Central America[9] but found the Darien route impracticable. Two new Canal Treaties between the U.S.A. and Colombia in 1869 and 1870 ignored British rights

---

[1] *Le Canal de Suez*, 23 Juin 1870, 268, 'Le Nouveau Consul des États-Unis en Égypte'.
[2] *Engineering*, 23 April 1869, 270.   [3] *The Engineer*, 11 June 1869, 409.
[4] *Engineering*, 13 August 1869, 112; *The Times*, 18 December 1869, 5i.
[5] C. C. Coffin, *Our New Way Round the World* (Boston, Fields, 1869).
[6] *The Times*, 8 April 1870, 10i; *Le Canal de Suez*, 30 Juin 1870, 283–4.
[7] P. Bunau-Varilla, *Panama. The Creation, Destruction and Resurrection* (London, Constable, 1913), 35. T. Herzl, *Tagebücher* (Berlin, Jüdischer Verlag, 1923), iii. 335, 21 Januar 1903.
[8] J. E. Nourse, *The Maritime Canal of Suez: Brief Memoir of the Enterprise from its Earliest Date, and Comparison of its Probable Results with those of a Ship Canal across Darien* (Washington, Philp, 1869), 50.
[9] *The Times*, 14 December 1869, 4i; 10 February 1870, 4vi.

under the Clayton-Bulwer Treaty of 1850 and encouraged the counter-proposal for a Tehuantepec Ship Canal[1] across the southern isthmus of Mexico. In Canada, which had been shocked by the speedy completion of the Pacific Railroad, proposals were made for Canadian ship canals either between Lake Huron and Lake Ontario[2] or between Quebec and Montreal, in order to divert the commerce of the American West into the St. Lawrence and the ships of Hugh Allan. One positive result was that the U.S. Government took over the Sault Sainte Marie Canal linking Lake Superior to Lakes Huron and Michigan from the State of Michigan in 1870 and converted it into a ship canal. American tours around the world became possible by the use of the new rail and steamship services in tours lasting from a year to ninety[3] days but using the overland route rather than the Suez Canal.

The successful completion of the first trans-isthmian canal produced a mania for cutting through isthmuses so as to provide vessels with a direct course, banish peninsulas and continents from the face of the earth and reduce the physical subdivisions of lands to islands. The success of Lesseps thus encouraged proposals for a Corinth canal,[4] a Holstein Intermaritime canal,[5] a Bridgwater–Exeter ship canal[6] and a Manchester–Liverpool ship canal.[7] Even a Calcutta–Calais canal was proposed by Sir Arthur Cotton,[8] the champion of irrigation canals for navigation and the bitter opponent of railways in India, in order to link India to Manchester by cheap water communication. In France proposals were made for a Darien Canal, a Susa or Gabes Canal in Tunisia and a sea-port of Paris. Those numerous proposals paid homage to the pioneer achievement of Lesseps who became 'the most celebrated civilian hero of our time',[9] at the expense of Linant, Enfantin, Negrelli and Voisin, and erased the stain on his honour left by the mission to Rome in 1849. He was not created Duke of Suez as had been expected[10] and he delivered an outspoken attack on the Imperial Government on 17 November for its delay in consenting to judicial reform in Egypt. He gave his name to nothing connected with his creation, though the inhabitants of Port Said spoke of the Place de Lesseps in defiance of his prohibition. His company survived the orgy of speculation which followed the issue of the delegations and drove down the price of Suez shares by 42 per cent from 615 francs on 1 August to 359 on 31 December. His dictatorship survived the protest made on 23 November

---

[1] *The Times*, 21 March 1870, 5i; *Manchester Guardian*, 26 March 1870, 6i. H. Stückle, *Interoceanic Canals. An Essay on the Question of Location for a Ship Canal across the American Continent* (New York, Nostrand, 1870), 137.

[2] *Engineering*, 17 December 1869, 408; *The Times*, 5 April 1871, 4ii; 10 April 1871, 4iii.

[3] Ibid., 17 January 1870, 9iii; 3 February 1870, 11ii.

[4] Ibid., 8 December 1869, 4i. *The Engineer*, 21 January 1870, 37–8; 18 February 1870, 98. *The Times*, 25 June 1870, 10i.

[5] *The Engineer*, 28 January 1870, 55, 'The Great Canal from the North Sea to Kiel'.

[6] *Engineering*, 18 December 1869, 399

[7] *The Times*, 29 April 1870, 5ii; 3 November 1871, 7v.

[8] *Engineering*, 10 September 1869, 178.

[9] H. K. Brugsch, *Mein Leben und Mein Wandern* (Berlin, 1894), 286.

[10] *London and China Express*, 19 November 1869, 917, 936.

by the twelve directors on board the *Péluse* and the resignation of five directors on 14 January 1870. The company remained a highly centralized autocracy, balanced uneasily between France and Egypt as a creation of the Empire and a personal fief of the Khedive, a quasi-state which aspired to the distinctive status of Belgium, Switzerland or the Vatican more than to that of the East India Company.[1]

The Company commemorated the inauguration by the issue of a medallion in 1869 and stamps in 1870. Then it discharged its contractors and workmen so that many Greeks were freed to make their way down both coasts of the Red Sea as the trading pioneers of Levantine civilization. It kept only one dredger in partial employment[2] and hired pilots in place of foremen. Its immediate task was to prove the prophets of doom wrong. It ended the free transit which had been granted to vessels arriving for the inauguration. It petitioned the Emperor on 17 December in favour of judicial reform in Egypt, in order to accelerate the flow of revenue from the sale of land, and so opposed itself even more to the merchant community of Alexandria. To draw Lesseps closer to the Liberal Empire Ollivier proposed his name on 12 February 1870 with that of Pasteur as a senator. The Company had accomplished the last great achievement of Imperial France. It had pierced the isthmus as it had promised and accordingly renamed its official journal from 1 January 1870 *Le Canal de Suez* instead of *L'Isthme de Suez*. It ceased to pay thereafter the statutory dividend of 5 per cent and so freed itself from a heavy burden. Its shareholders thereupon petitioned Lesseps to ask Ismail for a temporary guarantee of interest, which even the malleable Said had never granted. Thenceforward the Company entered on a new phase of its history as it shifted from enterprise to administration and waited for shipowners to use the Canal which it had built.

[1] C. Daleng, *L'Europe et l'Isthme de Suez* (Paris, Lachaud, 1869), 87–8.
[2] *Daily News*, 29 December 1869, 5 iv, 'The Suez Canal at Work'.

PART II

THE CANAL AS A TRADE-ROUTE, 1870–1876

6

THE COTTON TRADE OF BOMBAY IN 1870, AND THE CANAL'S FIRST TRANSITS

THE Canal of the Two Seas failed to attract much traffic during the first four months after its opening. Only nine of the forty-six vessels which passed through the Canal during its inauguration continued en route to the Indies. Those nine included warships as well as merchant vessels. The Prussian frigate *Herta* even made its way as far as Portland, becoming the first Continental ironclad to use the Canal and to breach the Anglo-French monopoly of the Red Sea. Commercial traffic was more cost-conscious than naval and proved slow to use the waterway, which was completely new and incompletely finished, more suitable for steamships than for sailing vessels, and highly taxed. Thus in November 1869 only one ship, the *Sin-Nanzing*, paid toll to pass through the Canal and in December only ten ships.

Cotton supplied the first cargo shipped through the Canal, although it had not been a main export of India when the Canal was first projected or first begun. It had become a staple export only during the Bombay boom of the 1860s induced by the American Civil War and the Cotton Famine in Europe. Then it had filled the gap left by American cotton with such success that the machinery of the cotton mills built in France and Germany after 1861 was specially adapted to handle its short staple. It remained so high in price after the end of the Civil War that it could be shipped by steamship via the overland route from 1867 and via the Cape to Liverpool from 1868–9. Most exports were however carried by sail via the Cape and reached Liverpool between May and September following the arrival of the American harvest between January and March. The small American crop of 1869 raised the imports of Indian above those of American cotton for the first time since 1862–6, enabling Surat to maintain a strong position in the Liverpool market and encouraging India to hope that it might use the Canal to export direct to the Continent and so become 'the cotton field of Europe'[1] in compensation for the increasing reversion of Lancashire to American cotton. Liverpool recognized that the use of the Canal would save three of the four months required by the Cape route and feared the loss of its entrepôt trade in Indian cotton. It also anticipated another short American crop, encouraged by American shippers who wished to maintain the price of their cotton. Accordingly its merchants made forward contracts in November and December 1869 for the shipment of Indian cotton via Egypt as it reached Bombay in order to maintain their existing trade with the Continent. The cotton brokers of London,

[1] *Manchester Guardian*, 3 January 1870, 4i, 'An Indian Cotton Trade with the Continent'.

whose cotton came from Calcutta and Madras rather than from Bombay, discounted the possibility of the large-scale use of the Canal for the shipment of cotton to England, because steam freights were so much higher than sail freights.[1] The cotton brokers of Liverpool, however, expected the first arrivals by the new Suez route in February–March 1870, a great increase in the shipments of cotton by the Canal and a large increase in the supply of Surat cotton, which would otherwise be very scarce in March and April.[2]

Liverpool's demand for cotton gave a new impetus to steam shipping in a port whose only steamship lines were those of Cunard, Inman, Holt and Bibby. Steam tonnage entering and leaving Liverpool, however, exceeded sail tonnage in the year ending 24 June 1869, uninfluenced by the Suez Canal. The port's first departures via the new route were advertised by Holt on 4 December for Calcutta[3] and by T. & J. Harrison on 27 December for Bombay.[4] The Merchants' Trading Company was formed in Liverpool for the specific purpose of trading to Bombay by the new Canal route so as to employ vessels displaced from the South American trade by the expansion of the Pacific Steam Navigation Company. That company provided the first two ships to use the Canal in December 1869, the *Brazilian* and the *Queen of the South*, and shipped out coal rather than piece-goods as cargo. The *Brazilian* had to discharge 40 per cent of its 4,000 tons of coal in Port Said in order to reduce its draught to 16 ft. 3 in. for the Canal and became the first English steamer to reach Bombay by the new route, in forty-nine days (6 November–25 December 1869) from Liverpool. English enterprise followed the example of France and incited Russia to emulation. The *Asie* of Fraissinet was the pioneer vessel of the first shipping line to adopt the new route, the first steamship built specially for the Canal and the first commercial vessel to pass through the Canal, on 29 November, although it did not pay toll. It became the first steamer to reach Bombay by the new route, in thirty-three days (11 November–16 December) from Marseilles.[5] A Russian steamship line was projected between Odessa and Bombay via the Canal with contracts from a Moscow firm for 4,000 bales of cotton per week, threatening Liverpool's entrepôt trade in cotton with the Continent.[6] India provided Europe with an effective weapon against America as well as Liverpool. The larger estimates of the Indian crop and the expectations of its early marketing through the Canal annihilated American hopes of a rise in cotton price, rendered the American cotton market dull and heavy throughout the first week of January 1870 and compelled London opinion to recognize that the decisive gain in the rapidity of transactions would in itself suffice to make the Canal a 'rude competitor' of the Cape route.[7]

[1] *Manchester Guardian*, 10 November 1869, 4 iv.
[2] Ibid., 2 December 1869, 4 iv; 1 January 1870, 5 ii.
[3] *The Times*, 4 December 1869, 2 i, 'Calcutta, via Suez Canal' (*Cleator*).
[4] Ibid., 27 December 1869, 2 i, 'Bombay via Suez Canal' (*Fire Queen*).
[5] *Le Canal de Suez*, 15–17 Janvier 1870, 24; 1 Février 1870, 38–40.
[6] *The Times*, 15 December 1869, 7 i.
[7] *The Economist*, 15 January 1870, 67, 'The Profit of Using the Suez Canal'.

From 17 January 1870 advertisements offering ships for the new route increased,[1] and orders began to flow to shipbuilders on the Clyde for screw-steamers for the new route. In Liverpool activity increased as the cotton-moving season approached, spurred by the fear of losing the entrepôt trade with Western India to accelerate the transfer of its trade from sail to steam and fill the void left by the demise of the Merchants' Trading Company. That company had lost the unseaworthy *Golden Fleece* off Cardiff on 10 September 1869 and was dragged through the courts by the underwriters, the Universal Marine Insurance Company Ltd. It had renamed four of its steamers *Port Said, Ismailia, Suez* and *Aden*. Its *Mauritius* drew 18 feet and passed through the Canal in 18 hours to reach Bombay in 50 days (23 December–11 February 1870) but the *Port Said* never reached Port Said although it left Liverpool on 16 January 1870 for Bombay. The enterprise of Liverpool encouraged imitation by Hull which hoped to benefit by its low port charges. The *Calypso* of Charles Henry Wilson (1833–1907), joint manager of his father's firm since 1867, became the first Hull vessel to pass through the Canal, in January 1870. Hull's first departure for Calcutta was advertised by Hornstedt & Garthorne from 21 January, four days after T. & J. Harrison had advertised their first departure for Calcutta. The first departure from Hull for Bombay was advertised from 31 January by C. M. Norwood.

The *Asie* of Fraissinet reached Marseilles from Bombay on 22 January after a round voyage of 70 days and became the first steamer to complete the round trip: the 813 bales of cotton it carried were less important than the 3,448 sacks of sesame because Marseilles was a market for oil-seeds as it was not for cotton. Fraissinet had nevertheless shattered the monopoly of overland freight transport held by the P. & O. and the Messageries. His freight-rates from Bombay to Marseilles at £2. 17s. to £3 per ton, were sharply competitive with overland freights, which had been £7 in 1869, and with sail freights via the Cape which were £3. 10s. in January 1870. The outward freights from London to Bombay also fell sharply from £2 in November 1869 to £1. 5s. by February 1870. Thus outward freights were reduced more than homeward freights, the reduction in which seems to have competed more with the overland route than with the Cape route. The growing concentration of steam shipping at Bombay eliminated the demand for sailing vessels. The mail of 12 February reported 70,000 tons of unfixed vessels in harbour at Bombay while that of 19 February confirmed that the demand for sail in Bombay was nil. The P. & O. was so alarmed by the growth of French and English competition that it considered the establishment of a line of cargo steamers via the Canal to India, the opening of a branch office in Liverpool[2] and even the replacement of Southampton by Liverpool as the port for the heavy mails. Thus the opening of the Canal brought a flood of English shipping into the Bombay freight market,[3] began

[1] F. E. Hyde, *Shipping Enterprise and Management 1830–1939. Harrisons of Liverpool* (Liverpool University Press, 1967), 36–7.
[2] *The Times*, 1 February 1870, 8 vi.   [3] Ibid., 11 May 1870, 12 iv.

the transfer of the trade of Bombay from sail to steam and encouraged the entry of the steamship into the country trade between Bombay and Calcutta. The Governor of Bombay expressed the appreciation of the merchant community in his invitation of 12 February to Lesseps to visit Bombay so that he might be presented to the city. British and French ships were followed in February 1870 by Spanish, Austrian and Italian vessels. The *Ebro* which passed through the Canal on 2 February was the pioneer of a Barcelona–Bombay line for J. Cassanova of Seville and entered the coasting trade of the Red Sea on its southward voyage. The *Apis* which passed through on 5 February pioneered the first service outside the Mediterranean of the Austrian Lloyd, which had followed the Messageries to Port Said and made it a port of call since 13 April 1869. The *Africa* which passed through on 1 March was the pioneer of a monthly service between Genoa and Bombay by R. Rubattino.

The failure to improve the quality of Indian cotton inspired Sir Thomas Bazley, a founder of the Cotton Supply Association, to hope that English agriculturists would use the Canal to visit India and help to improve its cotton cultivation.[1] Speedier shipment of the crop offered some compensation for its low quality. The 1869 crop supplied the cargo of the *Brazilian*, which reached Suez in 19 days and took 2 days to lighten cargo and pass through the Canal[2] but still grounded with its record length and cargo of 13,000 bales of cotton (including 1,000 for Le Havre) and 2,500 bales of wool: it required 58 days (31 January–27 March) to return to Liverpool. The transport of the 1870 crop was pioneered by MacGregor's *Danube* which carried 4,000 bales of cotton for Stoddard Brothers of Liverpool and was followed by a stream of other steamers, mainly English. The *Danube* reached Liverpool in 39 days (12 February–22 March) and discharged its cargo in the record time of 9 hours. On 25 March Learoyd Brothers of Huddersfield received some of the bales of cotton and promptly wove it into yarn: on 29 March the *Danube* left Liverpool, one week after its arrival and 45 days after leaving Bombay, with samples of the cotton yarn for the chambers of commerce in Bombay, Singapore, Hong Kong, Shanghai and Yokohama.[3] Thus the Canal Company received dues first on the raw cotton and then on the spun yarn.

The shipment of cotton dominated the traffic of the Canal during March 1870. In that traffic the southbound flow was supplemented for the first time by a comparable northbound movement, as those vessels which had passed southwards in January returned home with their cargo. Southbound vessels continued to outnumber northbound vessels despite the end of the one-way movement of the first four months. The Canal had established its basic pattern, a double flow through a waterway whose width restricted it to one-way traffic. The Company had acquired its first clients who were prepared to pay toll on both the outward and the homeward voyage. If the Company had been under less severe pressure to complete the Canal it might have delayed the opening

---

[1] *Journal of the Society of Arts*, 11 March 1870, 367.
[2] Ibid., 368, 370, 371.   [3] *Manchester Guardian*, 5 April, 7 iv.

for a full two months and further improved the channel in the interval. The cotton carried on the twenty-one northbound vessels during March proved the salvation of the Company in its hour of need after Lesseps had denied on 8 March the rumour of a new loan.[1] Receipts rose by 90 per cent and first exceeded £24,000, enabling the Company to begin from March the regular publication of its monthly receipts. Cotton also provided a bulk commodity precisely adapted to the needs of the new route because it required a large amount of ballast for stability and was best shipped in shallow vessels most suited to the shallow depth of the Canal. The trade linked Bombay closely to Liverpool, which built up its fleet of steamships, supplied the return freight of Manchester piece-goods and attracted shipments of cotton-seed from Egypt via Ismailia. The Canal was thereby established as a route for ships, commerce and passengers, who began to make large-scale use of it from March. Port Said established its first newspaper, the *Journal de Port Said*, on 10 March, and completed its new lighthouse on 20 March, while others began to operate from 1 May at Rosetta, Burlos and Damietta. On the Continent preparations were made in Amsterdam and Hamburg in March for steamship services via the Canal.

Cotton supplied the first commodity-season of the Canal's year. In April 1870 the cotton-moving season ended and the Canal experienced its first depression of traffic: no ships arrived at Port Said between 10 and 25 April. The number of transits was reduced by 34 per cent and their tonnage by 41·5 per cent. British tonnage fell by 60·5 per cent, reducing the British share of the total tonnage from 75 per cent in March to 50 per cent in April. Thus the seasonal pattern of Canal shipments was established, a busy season in spring followed by a slack season in summer. Bombay was the destination of the overwhelming bulk of the Company's first clients. Of the southbound transits, in the six months from November 1869 to April 1870, 45 out of 98 vessels went only to Bombay while 10 went to Calcutta, 2 to Singapore, 2 to Hong Kong, 2 to Yokohama and 6 to Shanghai. Those 45 vessels made 67 transits through the Canal, or 46 per cent of the total number of 145 transits, and so made short-haul traffic the source of most of the Company's revenue from tolls. The concentration on Bombay was a clear demonstration of the saving in distance by the Canal route, a saving which was 77 per cent of the distance from London to Bombay but only 44 per cent of that to Bengal.

The Canal undoubtedly enhanced the competitive capacity of Indian cotton in the markets of Europe in relation to American cotton. Even so the early expectations in Bombay that every bale of cotton would be exported as it arrived leaving no stocks were disappointed: when the monsoon began stocks remained at one-tenth of the crop. The Canal opened the markets of the Mediterranean markedly to Indian cotton, which was carried to Marseilles by Fraissinet and to Trieste by the Austrian Lloyd in competition with the overland route even more than with the Cape route. Liverpool did not lose its entrepôt

[1] *The Times*, 9 March 1870, 12i.

trade but began to import Indian cotton in the spring and early summer rather than in the autumn as thitherto, so placing it in competition with the cream of the American crop. Under the spur of Indian competition the American crop for 1870 exceeded the most sanguine expectations while the Bombay cotton crop proved short, fell short by the exact amount of the increase in supply from the U.S.A.[1] and so encouraged speculation by importers of Indian cotton in the Liverpool market. Thus India did not become the cotton field of Europe nor the destination of improving English agriculturists. The new s.s. *Suez* was employed not on the Suez route but in bringing cotton from Galveston to Liverpool, while Ismay also diverted his new White Star Line into the Atlantic trade.

The population of the isthmus showed as much enterprise as that of Europe in its use of the new route and was not discouraged by the Canal Company in the hour of its greatest need. During the first six months of the Canal's operation, from 21 November 1869 to 1 May 1870, 940 transits were made by Arab boats as well as 145 transits by ships.[2] The boats were far less profitable to the Company than the ships, each of which paid on the average 200 times as much in toll as a boat. The average tonnage of a boat was two-fifths of a ton while that of a sailing ship was 400 tons and that of a steamship 790 tons net (1,180 tons gross). The hope that sailing ships as well as steamships would use the route was disappointed. Only 6 of the 145 transits by ships were made by sailing vessels. Such maritime nations as Greece, Portugal, Scandinavia, Germany and the Netherlands remained committed to sail but supplied none of the 110 ships which made the 145 transits. The Company's Regulations would permit a sailing vessel to pass through only if it were towed, so adding a towage fee to the Canal toll. Steamships passed through under their own power and were taxed by the Company from 1 February 1870 on their net official tonnage (i.e. excluding their engines). The first sailing ship to use the Canal route, the barque *Noël* from Bordeaux, was wrecked on 28 November 1869 eighty-five miles south of Suez. Since sailing ships did not use the Canal they were not diverted from the Cape route as were the tea steamers of Holt and Robertson: Cape lines were still maintained by firms while they experimented with the Suez route. Nor did the Messageries or the P. & O. divert their vessels from the service of the Alexandria–Suez overland route. Thirty-two ships made sixty-seven of the transits: thus one-quarter of the ships furnished nearly half of the transits. Two-thirds of the 145 transits were southbound, a dominance of southbound traffic which remained characteristic of the Canal until 1886 and reflected the enterprise of Europe and the passivity of Asia.

The Canal Company fixed its attention and its hopes upon vessels from

---

[1] *The Economist*, 21 May 1870, 629, 'Cotton Prospects'.

[2] *Le Canal de Suez*, 12 Mai 1870, 164–5, E. Desplaces, 'Résumé de la Navigation sur le Canal au 1er Mai'. Ibid., 19 Mai 1870, 183–5, M. Fontane, 'Le Mouvement Maritime dans le Canal depuis l'Inauguration jusqu'au 30 Avril 1870'. Ibid., 19 Mai 1870, 187. M. Fontane, 'Recettes Mensuelles: Exploitation'.

France and Austria, encouraged by the anti-Prussian Franco-Austrian entente of 1869. France supplied at least four of the ships which passed through free from toll during the inauguration ceremony, including the *Asie* of Fraissinet and the *Thabor* of the Messageries. France also supplied the first warship to pay toll, the sloop *Adonis* en route in December 1869 from Réunion to Toulon. The first toll-paying French merchant vessel, the *Malta*, chartered by Rabaud of Marseilles for a voyage to Zanzibar, did not pass through until the end of December 1869. The sole port which despatched steamships by the new route was in France Marseilles, in Austria Trieste and in Italy Genoa. In Marseilles the firms which responded to the opening of the Canal were new firms established in the trade with Egypt such as Rabaud & Pastré and Fraissinet. Fraissinet was even compelled to seek freight in Glasgow for his line to Bombay but found fewer offers of freight there than in Marseilles. French enterprise proved better adapted to coaling British steamers at Port Said than to sending French vessels through the Canal. In Genoa Rubattino, whose ships had carried Garibaldi and the Thousand to Sicily, remained a new and isolated entrepreneur in a community still resentful of its incorporation in Piedmont. In Trieste the Austrian Lloyd was heavily dependent on the aid of the monarchy and on the cooperation of the Austrian railways. The Russian and Dutch schemes to establish a steam service via the Canal had provided orders to the shipyards of Britain but no clients to the Canal.

The lines established by the Austrian Lloyd and by Rubattino continued to exist when most of those of their English competitors had disappeared. They were the pioneers of a political civilization which regarded the Red Sea as an extension of the Mediterranean and thought in the limited terms of State-aid, mail-contracts, coaling-stations, colonial expansion, the naval protection of commerce and the traditional political economy epitomized in the belief that 'trade follows the flag'.[1] Italy was the first state which sought to acquire a port in the Red Sea, so compensating for the absence of her official representatives from the inauguration of the Canal. Giuseppe Sapeto, who had visited Abyssinia as a Lazarist missionary in 1838, was empowered by Victor Emmanuel in September 1869 to buy a suitable port in the Red Sea. In November he determined on Assab,[2] 40 miles north of the Straits of Bab el Mandeb on the inhospitable Danakil coast, as the best of five sites and a possible rival to Massawa and Obock. He concluded the Convention of 15 November 1869 with two Danakil sultans, who ceded seven square miles in return for the promise of payment within a hundred days from 3 December. On his return to Florence Sapeto was told to consider himself in the service of Rubattino, who signed the secret contract of 2 February 1870 with the head of an anti-colonial cabinet and paid cash for the purchase of Assab. Sapeto

[1] J. A. Froude, 'England and Her Colonies', *Fraser's Magazine* (January 1870), 4. A. Hamilton, 'On the Colonies', *Journal of the Statistical Society*, 19 March 1872, 112. *The Times*, 6 November 1875, 10 iii, W. E. Forster at Edinburgh.
[2] R. G. Woolbert, 'The Purchase of Assab by Italy' in D. C. McKay, *Essays in the History of Modern Europe* (New York, Harper, 1936), 114–29.

left Genoa on Rubattino's *Africa,* which became the first Italian steamer to use the Canal, and reached Assab on 9 March within the 100-day limit. There he signed a new convention on 11 March on board the *Africa,* raised the Italian tricolour on 13 March and planted boundary signs on 14 March. The Italian flag seems to have been accepted by the Danakil as reluctantly as the Egyptian.[1] The *Vedetta,* which passed through the Canal on 1 March, was sent by the Italian Government to explore the coast of Abyssinia and to help in the establishment of Italy's first coaling-station and colony. The first vessel of the Royal Italian Navy to use the Canal suffered a severe mishap on the shoals of Jedda and only reached Assab on 5 April.

The Italian activity on the west coast of the Red Sea provoked the forceful reassertion of Egyptian suzerainty over Assab[2] and the extension of French aspirations from Obock to the east coast. The voyage of the *Rethimo,* which became the first Turkish vessel to pay dues for its passage of the Canal on 7 February 1870, seems to have alarmed Ismail, because it was preceded and followed by the first Egyptian ships to pay toll for the use of the Canal. Its mission was to establish a quarantine and naval station on the coast of Arabia south of Bab el Mandeb. That intention was only fulfilled after Fraissinet's *Afrique* made its third transit through the Canal in May and landed two Europeans, an interpreter and a large supply of stores at Sheikh Said on behalf of the three merchant firms of Marseilles of Rabaud, Bazin and van der Bork.[3] Thus France masked her expansion behind merchant firms as Italy did behind a shipowner and encouraged even the Netherlands to consider the establishment of a similar station. Turkey replied by establishing a quarantine station with a garrison of 150 troops, and Ismail by appointing a Governor of the whole African coast from Suez to Cape Guardafui.

French expansion also alarmed Britain, whose vessels had predominated in both numbers and tonnage from the opening of the Canal to commercial shipping. British vessels led the way with the *Sin-Nanzing,* and supplied 100 per cent of the toll-paying tonnage in November 1869, 96 per cent in December and 80 per cent in January. Only in the depression of April 1870 did their contribution fall below their average share of 70 per cent over the whole of the first six months. Those British ships came from no single port but from Liverpool, Leith and London, Hull, Newcastle, Sunderland and Glasgow. They represented the enterprise of young shipowners in the service of a world commerce which extended to Shanghai and Yokohama. Twenty-nine of the sixty-eight British vessels were new, including some built specially for the Canal route. The average tonnage of the new vessels was 686 net (1,025 gross), or 13 per cent below the general average of 790 tons net. Most of the British ships were diverted from other trades, especially from the trades to the Baltic, the Black Sea, the North Atlantic, the Gulf of Mexico and South

[1] A. Codignola, *Rubattino* (Bologna, Cappelli, 1938), 338–43.
[2] *The Times,* 11 July 1870, 9v; 12 July, 12iii.
[3] H. Stephan, *Das Heutige Aegypten* (Leipzig, Brockhaus, 1872), 522–3.

America. Some used the Canal on a one-way voyage to service in Eastern waters while others were intended as the first of a regular line. As pioneers they proved that the compound engine was essential to gain the greatest profit from the new route pivoting around the 'great, long, straight, deep ditch'.[1]

The limited depth and width of that ditch necessitated care in navigation, while an occasional sandstorm provided an unusual hazard for ocean shipping. The difficulties of navigation were exaggerated by the merchants of Alexandria but were minimized by the Company. The Serapeum ridge restricted the use of the Canal to ships of 16 feet draught until a uniform depth of 19 feet was announced on 8 February[2] and ships up to 20 ft. 8 in. draught were admitted from March. The one-way channel would also have increased stoppages if traffic had been greater because the passing-stations were too few as well as too small and the Company insisted that vessels should load with coal at Port Said rather than at Suez. Steering was hampered by the limited width of the fairway, by two sharp curves at Guisr and Timsah and by a cross-section of half the necessary size. That restricted cross-section reduced the depth of water under the keel unequally, because a ship tended to 'sit down' in the trough between the bow-wave and the stern-wave, and compelled the use of more power to maintain a given speed than in the open sea. Steering was made more difficult by differential pressures created in the water by variations in the cross-section and by the eleven passing-stations. In the southern half of the Canal the velocity of the diurnal Suez tides was enhanced by the limited cross-section, making a passage with a following tide especially hazardous.

To limit the erosion of the banks the Company imposed a maximum speed of five knots, which was a half to one-third of the speed usual in the open sea and made a rudder's slow response to the helm more dangerous. The Company also applied to the Canal the railway block system of signalling invented in 1853 so that it might maintain central control of transit through the telegraph, the stations and the sidings. For that central regulation of transit a model of the Canal with miniature vessels was devised by Chartrey, who was Chief Superintendent of Transit at Port Said in 1870-1 and at Suez from 1871 to 1897. The Company insisted that its pilots should accompany each vessel to advise the captain and charged pilotage dues as well as transit dues. For pilotage it divided the Canal into northern and southern halves, a division of labour which enabled pilots to be changed half-way and gave Ismailia double the number of pilots possessed by either Port Said or Suez. The Company seemed to think that 'the commerce of the East is entirely under their

---

[1] *The Times*, 13 January 1870, 4 iv, J. B. Blow, builder of the *Sin-Nanzing*. Other accounts of pioneer transits through the Canal are those of J. B. Kennedy of the *Blue Cross* in *The Times*, 1 February 1870, 4 iii; Captain Nyberg of the *William Miller* in *The China Mail*, 26 March 1870, 4 v; 30 March 3 iii; J. Wolf of the *Cleator* ('An Engineer') in *The China Mail*, 5 April 1870, 3 iii–v; J. Steele of the *Erl King* in *The China Mail*, 11 April 1870, 3 iii–vi; 12 April, 3 iv–vi; S. P. Welch of the *Hibernia* in *Le Canal de Suez*, 1 Mai 1870, 153–4; R. Brenner of the *Marietta* in *Petermanns Geographische Mittheilungen*, 1870, 162, 353–7.

[2] *Le Canal de Suez*, 15–18 Février 1870, 49.

direction'[1] but failed to anticipate such an overwhelming British predominance as developed in the traffic because its pilots were not English, could not speak English and sometimes could not understand English.[2] They had been trained on ships with tillers rather than wheels and gave directions which were contrary to English custom, ordering 'port' for 'starboard' and vice versa. They also sought to travel faster than captains thought wise and were sometimes regarded as a curse rather than as a blessing. The combined difficulties of navigation under such conditions made groundings easy by the unwary, with a consequent blockage of the whole channel. The prudent sailor, however, found no unavoidable difficulties in his path. 'The river Avon to Bristol, or the Wye to Chepstow-bridge, or the Thames to Richmond, I think, would give a clearer idea of the Canal than any description I could give, unless you look at the Clyde from Dumbarton to Glasgow'.[3] An auxiliary rudder proved the best way of increasing control in the shallow channel rather than steam-steering, which had been first used in 1867 but would have proved too insensitive for the new waterway.

England found a common link at Suez between the new route and the overland route and began to transfer its familiarity with the overland route to the alien waters of the isthmus. Delane's prophecy of 1858 was justified by the predominantly British use of the Canal, facilitated by British resources for the building of steamships and by the accord between the British Government and a commercial people.[4] The bulk of the tolls imposed from 21 November 1869 was paid by British shipowners, for whose alleged convenience the Company on 13 January 1870 permitted tolls to be paid in Paris rather than in Port Said. The Company would not open a branch office in London and would not express its toll other than in French francs or its maximum permissible draught other than in metres. The dues which a French economist deemed exorbitant[5] were paid by the British as a tribute to the achievement of the French in creating 'this greatest naval work of modern times'.[6] Ninety per cent of the Company's receipts came from tolls, the other 10 per cent coming from passenger-dues and the rent of buildings and lands. The sale of lands[7] remained blocked by French resistance to judicial reform in Egypt. Transit revenues proved inadequate in the dead season of the second quarter of 1870 to meet the Company's expenses which remained high for the completion of the works and the settlement of accounts with the contractors, for which the Company resorted to arbitration.

[1] *The China Mail*, 12 April 1870, 3 vi, J. Steele.
[2] *The Times*, 11 October 1870, 4 iv–v, 'The Suez Canal'.
[3] Ibid., 1 February 1870, 4 iii, J. B. Kennedy, Captain of the *Blue Cross*, 'The Navigation of the Suez Canal'.
[4] Ibid., 3 February 1870, 5 vi, B. Frere, 'The Suez Canal and Trade with India'.
[5] C. Boissay, 'Le Canal de Suez. Historique et Description', *Journal des Economistes*, 16 (1869), 267.
[6] J. d'A. Samuda, 'On the Influence of the Suez Canal on Ocean Navigation', *Transactions of the Institution of Naval Architects*, 6 April 1870, 6.
[7] *The Times*, 30 May 1870, 9 i.

The Admiralty's surveyors, G. H. Richards and Andrew Clarke, thought that the limited width of 'a continuous dock ninety miles in length'[1] would necessitate the building of smaller troop transports than those constructed in 1864–5. One of H.M. Indian troopships then succeeded in passing through the Canal on 3–5 May.[2] That passage followed on the unfortunate transit by the *Nubia* which suffered one of the 'self-inflicted disasters of the P. & O.'[3] and was forced to return for repairs to Suez on 2 April. The 3,000-ton *Jumna* was given priority over all outward-bound steamers, became the largest ship to pass through the waterway during 1870 and proved that existing troopships could use it so that smaller ones did not need to be built. England communicated its intention to the Khedive but signed no convention and was not restrained by Ismail from sending through the Canal what were very close to ships of war. After the passage of the *Jumna*, which reached Portsmouth from Bombay in 40 days (15 April–25 May), a uniform centre depth of 24 feet was reported.[4] The Chairman of the P. & O. however declared to his sharcholders on 9 May that the waterway was not yet in a fit state for use by the Company, so causing a fall in Suez shares by 4 per cent (5–19 May). The Cabinet considered the wartime use of the Canal and inclined to think that England would be able to win any race for Egypt on the outbreak of war, although Childers urged neutralization of the Canal on condition that passage should be free at all times for troopships and warships.[5]

France and England began the military use of the Canal and set the example which was followed by the other imperial powers of Turkey, the Netherlands, Spain and Portugal. France sent the naval sloop *Surcouf* from Brest on 21 May through the Canal on 8 July to New Caledonia and the troopship *Sarthe*, with a draught of 20¾ feet, through the Canal on 5 July. The Canal was also used to link Lisbon to Macao by the Portuguese *Africana* (20–25 June), with 200 passengers, and by the transport *Saida* (1–13 July) of the Royal Portuguese Navy. The Messageries had lacked faith in the Canal like the P. & O. but had gained experience of it during the inauguration. It experimented with the use of the waterway for its monthly mailboat to China beginning with the departure of 17 April so that seven French steamers supplied 26 per cent of the total tonnage during April. In consultation with the Imperial Government it began a new fortnightly mail service to Indo-China on 23 July, so providing a weekly mail service in conjunction with the P. & O. The Messageries anticipated a saving of £120,000 per annum from the use of the Canal route over and above the Canal dues. It therefore made Marseilles

---

[1] G. H. Richards and A. Clarke, 'The Suez Canal', *Proceedings of the Royal Geographical Society*, xiv (15 August 1870), 270.

[2] *Le Canal de Suez*, 19 Mai 1870, 178, 195, 'Le Passage de la *Jumna*'.

[3] *The China Mail*, 18 March 1870, 3 iv–v; *The Times*, 8 April 1870, 5 iii.

[4] *The Times*, 6 May 1870, 10 i.

[5] *Camden Miscellany*, xxi (London, Royal Historical Society, 1958), part ii, 14, E. Drus, 'A Journal of Events during the Gladstone Ministry 1868–1874 by John, First Earl of Kimberley', 29 May 1870.

rather than Suez the home-port of its line to Indo-China, saving the cost of sending out its vessels for the first time to Asiatic waters and the higher wages required by sailors formerly in exile in Asia. That reorganization was associated with a revival of the oriental aspirations of France, apparent in its expansion in Syria, Arabia, Abyssinia, Zanzibar, in the erection of a memorial to Dupleix in Pondicherry in 1870, in its aspiration to make Saigon a counterpoise to Singapore and Shanghai and in the proposal to establish an Australian service of the Messageries via the Canal. Thus the energies suppressed in France under the Empire continued to be diverted outwards.

The Canal Company announced on 26 June 1870 the postponement of the payment of dividend and interest on its shares[1] and therefore also on the delegations. Its directors renounced from 1 July half of their annual fees until the resumption of dividend payments, cut the salaries of all Company employees by 10–15 per cent and disbanded the Advisory Works Commission from 1 September. In July a seasonal fall in transits, tonnage and receipts took place while passenger traffic declined from July to October during the heat of the Red Sea summer. In desperate need of financial help, Lesseps unveiled the bust of Waghorn on the Waghorn Quay at Suez[2] and visited England for the first time since 1857, disembarking at Liverpool on 25 June. In London he arrived at the height of the season and received ovations usually reserved for crowned heads of state. He was toasted by the Prime Minister at the Duke of Sutherland's banquet on 4 July[3] and presented with a gold medal by Lloyd's of London on 5 July. At the Lord Mayor's annual banquet to the archbishops and bishops on 6 July 230 guests heard the Lord Mayor toast Lesseps as one worthy of canonization.[4] The propagation of the Gospel which was the primary purpose of the banquet was subordinated to the celebration of Lesseps' achievement in placing Madras within twenty-one days' journey of London. Thomas Hughes, the chairman of the directors of the Crystal Palace, toasted Lesseps on 7 July at a great firework-display in his honour attended by 26,000. The achievement of Lesseps was given full recognition, despite its lack of financial success and Gladstone's reticence about a loan. 'It is a much grander exploit to make the Suez Canal than to make a railway between Pedlington and Muddletown.'[5] Lesseps was also presented on 8 July with the Albert Gold Medal by the Prince of Wales on behalf of the Society of Arts[6] and nominated on 11 July for the award of the G.C.S.I. and the honorary freedom of the City of London for the achievement of 'the wonder of the age. (Cheers).'[7] Thus England paid tardy homage to the creator of the work which it had so strongly opposed.

[1] *Le Canal de Suez*, 30 Juin 1870, 273.
[2] Ibid., 8 Septembre 1870, 410, 'Le Monument Waghorn'.
[3] *The Times*, 5 July 1870, 12 iv.   [4] Ibid., 7 July 1870, 5 iii.
[5] *Saturday Review*, 9 July 1870, 47, 'The Visit of M. de Lesseps'.
[6] *Journal of the Society of Arts*, 10 June 1870, 649; 15 July, 733.
[7] *The Times*, 12 July 1870, 10 vi.

THE FRANCO-PRUSSIAN WAR,
1870-1871

WAR broke out six months after the flurry of talk in Egypt about peace and universal brotherhood, so evoking pessimistic reflections by Ibsen and Flaubert. Ibsen discerned the similarity between the civilization of the Pharaohs and that of the Hohenzollerns. Flaubert recognised in the great collective work of the Suez Canal the harbinger of the unimaginable conflicts of the coming century between the whole East and all of Europe, a war of races between the old world and the new world.[1] The outbreak of war created a panic on 18–19 July in Liverpool which broke up speculation in the cotton market and reduced prices sharply. The heavy losses suffered by the importers of Indian cotton caused many failures and transmitted stagnation to Bombay, benefiting the Cape route at the expense of the Canal. The war also paralysed the markets for coffee and tea and thus for two other major components of the Canal's traffic. The paralysis of the silk trade in Shanghai from 10 August however reduced the traffic of the overland route more than that of the Canal.

Three days after France declared war on Prussia, Childers, who had been advised by Clarke to buy the Canal, urged on 22 July 1870 the purchase and neutralization of the Canal on Granville, so bringing Lesseps to London on 24 July. The Cabinet under Gladstone, Granville, Cardwell and Lowe peremptorily set aside the idea of purchase and found no reason to pursue the question of neutralization.[2] Lesseps received the Freedom of the City at Guildhall on 30 July, becoming the first Frenchman and the second foreigner after Garibaldi to be so honoured, while Lange was knighted on 9 August. Lesseps could secure no financial help, however, in England or in France, where the war prevented the Imperial Government from guaranteeing another loan to the Canal Company. The war did not bring Austria in on the side of France and so failed to consummate the entente of 1869. Eight months after his trip to Egypt the Crown Prince of Prussia as Commander of the German Army won the twin victories of 4 August and 6 August on the frontier of France which paralysed the French High Command and enabled the Empress Eugénie to end on 9 August the seven-month old ministry of Ollivier and the Liberal Empire. Ollivier went into exile as the scapegoat for the dynasty and the nation, resuming his post as the Commissioner of the Egyptian

---

[1] G. Flaubert, *Correspondance* (Paris, Conard, 1930), vi. 137–8, Flaubert à G. Sand, 3 Août 1870.

[2] R. H. Vetch, *The Life of General Sir Andrew Clarke* (London, Murray, 1905), 102, Childers to Clarke, 25 August 1870.

Government with the Canal Company which provided him with £1,200 per annum, his chief means of support during three years of exile.

The existence of the Canal enabled the French Navy to send a warship, the *Belligéreuse*, at full speed to Saigon, which first heard the news of the war on 5 August. No provision had been made to regulate the use of the Canal by the warships of belligerents. On 15 August a French and a German vessel of war met in Lake Timsah. Because Germany was not the first party to the war to send a warship through the Canal she might have complained of France. The warships, however, took no action against each other nor against the free use of the Canal: they saluted and passed on. The Canal Company took no stand on the issue, because France herself was a belligerent, and so condoned a precedent for the future use of the Canal by other belligerents. Neither the Porte nor Ismail took action to prevent the breach of the neutrality of the Ottoman Empire, implying by their inaction that the Canal was part of Egypt's maritime domain rather than of her landed domain. An important precedent was thereby set in a legal vacuum[1] in favour of the unrestricted use of the Canal by warships, troopships and military personnel, to the ultimate benefit of all imperial powers and the revenues of the Canal Company.

The war slowed down the immediate use of the new route by merchant shipping. In August fifty ships had been loading in the ports of Europe for Asia via the Canal. The French retreat from the Rhine to Metz and Sedan led to the suspension of all departures planned for the new route, diverting the ships of Italy, Austria, Spain and Russia and reducing the number of English ships. In September transits through the Canal fell to thirty-two, the lowest number since February, while receipts fell by 12 per cent from the level of August. Cotton shipments by the Canal went out of favour in Bombay, despite the low steamer freights, because Indian consigners hoped that shipment by the Cape would enable them to benefit by a further rise of price in the home market, where recovery from mid-August was inspired by the continued German successes.[2] The war diverted German interest from East Africa to home development, reduced German trade with China and postponed the formation of a direct German steamship line to the Far East. It also compelled the evacuation of the French garrison installed in 1849 from Rome to which Italian interest was diverted from the Red Sea. The Assab venture was buried by a parliamentary committee (8 May–5 June 1871) under Negri,[3] who had attended the inauguration of the Canal in his capacity as President of the Italian Geographical Society. Thus the war fixed the memories of Italy more than ever on the Risorgimento, restricting support of Rubattino's service to Bombay to a subsidy equivalent to the Canal dues under the contract of 1871. It also dampened French mercantile enthusiasm for the new route and ended the eastern ventures of Fraissinet and Rabaud. Fraissinet

[1] R. de Marees van Swinderen, *Het Suez-Kanaal* (Groningen, Huber, 1886), 229.

[2] *The Economist*, 24 September 1870, 1182, Bombay, 23 August.

[3] R. G. Woolbert, 'The Purchase of Assab by Italy' (1936), 125.

sold his pioneer steamers *Europe* and *Afrique* to British shipowners. The Messageries suspended from 16 October its new fortnightly service to Indo-China, reverting to a monthly service, and raised a fear that its monthly service to Mauritius might be suspended. French interests were diverted from Arabia, the Red Sea, Ethiopia and the Great Lakes, Madagascar, Annam and China. France could not follow up its 'occupation' of Sheikh Said and send the expedition planned to conquer Ethiopia in 1870. It could not even send a punitive expedition to China after the massacre of eighteen mission-aries at Tientsin. It abandoned Sheikh Said after the north-east monsoon drove several French ships on to the rocks in February 1871,[1] so relieving Gladstone's fears of a French rival to Aden. Thus the war reinforced all those influences which discouraged France from the fullest use of the Canal and diverted her energies from external expansion first to self-defence and then to reconstruc-tion at home. It ended the period when France had led the way in the use of the Canal by mailboats, removed the material content from the threat to British power represented by the Canal and so enabled English Liberals to denounce Palmerston for his well-founded opposition to the project. It re-duced the French share in the Canal tonnage from 19·4 per cent in 1870 to 11·7 per cent in 1871, reinforced the English domination of the new route and moderated Anglo-French friction in the Mediterranean and its new southward extension.

The French Navy established a partial blockade of the North Sea and Baltic coasts, to the benefit of neutral Holland and Belgium. It captured eighty German ships and removed German shipping from the sea. A single German army corps achieved the victory of Sedan, where Napoleon III capitulated on 2 September, making possible the immediate siege of Paris. Imperial Paris ended with the attack of 4 September on the Tuileries, where Lesseps was dining with Eugénie and was able to facilitate her escape.[2] A Spanish question ended the reign of the Spanish Empress, leaving her with only the hope of a restoration and the memory of her last great international appearance in 1869. The collapse of the Empire marked the end of an era for the Canal Company with the loss of its titular Protector in Prince Jerome Napoleon and of its Vice-President, Albuféra, who resigned on 4 September to retire into private life with the Empire he had served. The war also tightened the money-market at a time when the Company was in desperate financial straits and postponed the Company's revaluation of tonnage, which would have helped to rescue it from its plight. The war which was a catastrophe for Imperial France neverthe-less provided the Company with a welcome diversion since it remained within besieged Paris, unlike the Bank of France, and was cut off from communication with the departments as well as with Egypt. The Company was compelled

---

[1] Marston, *The Red Sea Area 1800–1878* (1961), 393.
[2] E. Malet, *Shifting Scenes, or Memories of Many Men in Many Lands* (London, Murray, 1901), 282. T. W. Reid, *Lord Houghton*, 234, 235, Lord Houghton to his daughter, 10 September 1870.

to suspend the publication of its journal after the issue of 15 September 1870 until that of 5 January 1871 and was hindered in its financial operations in so far as they depended on the collection of monies due. It could account to its shareholders for the slow growth of traffic and postpone its annual general meeting. It was, however, forced on 15 September to defer the payment of interest on its bonds and thenceforward came under the greatest pressure to redeem its reputation on the Bourse from the stigma of near-bankruptcy.

Two days after Bazaine surrendered at Metz on 27 October with 173,000 troops Russia denounced the Black Sea clause of the Treaty of Paris of 1856. The denunciation was not unexpected.[1] The clause had lasted for five years longer than the ten years allotted to it by Palmerston in 1856, but succumbed to the rise of Russian nationalism fifteen years after the humiliating treaty of peace. The opening of the Canal had increased rather than decreased the strategic importance of the Straits and had reinforced Russia's drive to Constantinople in quest of Saint Sophia as much as of the keys to her house and navigable ice-free water. The Russian ambassador at Constantinople secured Ismail's promise of neutrality at the beginning of a Russo-Turkish war.[2] The alarming prospect of a Russo-Egyptian alliance provoked Constantinople in November 1870 to send 10,000 Turkish troops to the Yemen, to threaten Ismail's rear.[3] In London fears were aroused for free access to the Canal and for the security of the Mediterranean against the threat of Russo-American Alabamas, which would make British vessels their first prey.[4] Thus the British fear of the use of the Canal by France against English interests gave way to the fear of a Russian threat to its free use by Britain. Derby, the reluctant Abyssinian Warrior of 1867, was prepared to go to war for the neutrality of Egypt but not for the neutrality of the Black Sea. Gladstone considered but dismissed the possibility of seizing the Canal. 'As long as the Canal is not fortified I do not see much to fear. It would be a less strong measure to seize it in war than to go to war about it: and this we ought always to be able to do. But never was there less danger or likelihood of our being overpowered in the Mediterranean.'[5] Sedan and Metz had transferred the military primacy of Europe from France which hated England by tradition to Germany which had never hated England.

The war destroyed French influence in Cairo, so increasing Turkish pressure on Egypt. It paved the way ultimately for the English purchase of Ismail's Canal shares, the French acceptance of judicial reform in Egypt, the German instigation of the deposition of the Khedive and the English occupation of the Nile valley. Immediately it brought about the return to France of a large

[1] *The Spectator*, 24 September 1870, 1133.

[2] F. J. Cox, 'Khedive Ismail and Panslavism', *Slavonic Review* (December 1953), 156.

[3] Ibid., 158.

[4] *The Economist*, 26 November 1870, 1425.

[5] A. Ramm (ed.), *The Political Correspondence of Mr. Gladstone and Lord Granville 1868–1876* (London, Royal Historical Society, 1952), i. 156, Gladstone to Granville, 13 November 1870.

number of Frenchmen from Port Said and accentuated the decline in its population. It moderated the French bias of the Company and so reduced friction with its British clients. It deprived the Company of Egyptian acquiescence in the 'French Canal' and encouraged a series of English proposals for its future management. In November 1870 Egyptian bonds declined in price and complaints began to be made in England about the Canal's capacity to handle traffic, followed by rumours in December about a sale of the Canal Company, its conversion into an English joint-stock company under the Duke of Sutherland[1] and the establishment at Bismarck's request of an English protectorate over the Canal.[2] The Company's receipts in December however rose by 36 per cent and first exceeded the record receipts of the cotton-moving month of March. The war also overcame the reluctance of the G.P.O. to use any route other than that through France and Marseilles. Thus it diverted the India mails, first from the Dover–Calais to the Newhaven–Dieppe route and then from Marseilles to the Ostend–Brindisi route from 21 October, after the Marseilles–Malta service by French steamers had been reduced from three to two per month. That shift to the Brenner route inspired Georges Nagelmackers, the Belgian engineer who sought from 1869 to become the Pullman of Europe, to introduce sleeping-cars on the through-route from Ostend to Brindisi. The Postal Convention of Florence was concluded between England and Italy on 7 December 1870 and came into operation from 1 January 1871, seven years after England's surrender of Corfu to Greece. The last mail-steamer for Marseilles left Alexandria on 11 December, the first steamer from Brindisi left on 18 December. Thenceforward the mail was diverted from Marseilles while the Great East India Hotel was opened for passengers on the quay at Brindisi in December 1870. Brindisi received its first ship direct from Bombay through the Canal on 26 December, and so became a port on the Canal route as well as on the express overland route.

Ismail's aspirations to take over the Canal Company were fostered by new rumours of its projected sale which were published on 29 December 1870 but were immediately denied by Lesseps.[3] Ismail suggested on 30 December to the English Consul-General, Stanton, the transfer of the Canal to an English company as the only way to make it really serviceable to general navigation.[4] T. H. Farrer, the Permanent Under-Secretary of the Board of Trade, recommended on 26 January 1871 neutralization and management by an international commission on the model of the Danube[5] and was prepared to encroach so far on the independence of Egypt in the interests of universal freedom of trade, if not to accept the expropriation by an English company favoured by Argyll at the India Office. The antiquary F. B. Zincke who chartered his own

---

[1] *The Times*, 5 December 1870, 5 iv.
[2] *Manchester Guardian*, 13 December 1870, 6 vi.
[3] *Le Canal de Suez*, 5 Janvier 1871, 3–8.
[4] *Egypt No. 2 (1876), Correspondence Respecting the Suez Canal* (C-1392), 133, Stanton to Granville, 30 December 1870.
[5] Ibid., 135–8.

small steamer at Suez in February 1871 to steam to Port Said encountered the little steamers of the Canal Company more frequently than any other vessel. He met only three large steamers on each of the two days on his transit and concluded 'The rarest object on the Canal is that for which it was constructed.'[1] Zincke learned that the Company's daily receipts were about £1,000 which represented the toll of 10s. per ton paid by only one 2,000-ton ship in 24 hours. He found that the Company could not meet a daily expenditure of £3,000 to complete and maintain the Canal nor offer any prospect of paying a dividend in the lifetime of the existing shareholders.[2] Finally, he noted the extreme unpopularity of the French in Egypt and in the three towns of the isthmus.[3] Since the Canal provided a defensible route through land-locked seas from Gibraltar to Hong Kong[4] and would have to be occupied in wartime by England he recommended on 13 May 1871 the establishment of a protectorate by England over Egypt as a fellow-Aryan race.[5]

In February 1871 the Canal Company sought an advance in vain from the Crédit Lyonnais and from the Crédit Foncier in order to maintain the payment of its bond interest and began to think again of charging toll on the real tonnage of ships. The Duke of Sutherland in his yacht *Cornelia* passed through the Canal (15–17 February 1871) en route from Brindisi to Suez and returned through the Canal on 20–21 February. Sutherland and John Pender then visited Port Said with Lesseps in March and offered a loan of £2,000,000 in return for reductions of toll, securing no support from Granville but renewing rumours of the Company's sale.[6] Farrer again suggested to Granville on 29 March management of the Canal by an international commission while Lange made on 3 April an unofficial and unauthorised proposal for British assistance and British management of the Canal, a suggestion which Granville discouraged on 4 May. Those suggestions were occasioned by the establishment of the Paris Commune which created a new crisis in the Company's affairs.[7] Lesseps returned from Ismailia to France with the subscription raised by the Canal Company personnel for the French wounded, widows and orphans. He suspended the publication of the Company's journal after its issue of 30 March and postponed the meeting of shareholders from 29 April until 20 July. He visited London on 18 April but failed to raise a loan of £600,000[8] because of his determination to avoid any British management of his enterprise. Lange then reported to Granville on 21 June Lesseps' reluctant consideration of a sale to the maritime powers for £12,000,000 plus £20,000,000 to the bondholders over the next fifty years,[9] a proposal which Granville dismissed as premature on 28 June. After the suppression of the Commune the Company resumed publication of its journal on 8 June and announced on

[1] F. B. Zincke, *Egypt of the Pharaohs and of the Kedivé* (London, Smith, 1871), 426.
[2] Ibid., 431.
[3] Ibid., 423.   [4] Ibid., 434.
[5] Ibid., 20, 30.   [6] *The Times*, 14 March 1871, 9v.
[7] J. S. Price, *The Early History of the Suez Canal* (London, Hazell, 1883), 26.
[8] Ibid., 29.   [9] Ibid., 34.

12 June a depth of 26 feet through the Canal, i.e. the depth scheduled in 1859. On 15 June Lesseps announced that the Company had no funds to pay the interest on its bonds and that an English loan would be proposed to the next meeting of shareholders, so evoking English complaints about the shallowness of 'the great Canal'.[1] The Company ended the transit service it had begun in 1866 and ceased to be a carrier from 15 July, relying thenceforward solely on its transit revenues, supplemented since August 1870 by the revenue from its telegraph and water-supply services. Its contemplated recourse to an increase in dues[2] encouraged Bagehot to find the best solution in the management of the Canal by Egypt as a Government enterprise rather than by the Company.[3]

The Company's shareholders were undoubtedly disappointed in their expectations when the first year's tonnage proved to be only 22 per cent of the expected 1,550,000, the first year's receipts[4] proved to be only 23 per cent of the £1,600,000 they had been led to expect by Lesseps' estimate of 1854, the losses of the Company totalled £383,570 and the price of the 500-franc share averaged 272·9 francs for the year 1870. They were disturbed by the end of the war which removed the last excuse for the Company's financial failure and by the rumour of an English loan contracted at 14 per cent. They were encouraged to revolt against the great Caesar of the Canal Company by the overthrow of Caesarism in France and by the failure of Lesseps to secure election as a deputy for Paris in 1871. The most outspoken dissenters far surpassed the malcontent directors of 1869 in the violence of their revolt against the Turkish despotism of Lesseps and were stigmatized as 'the Communist element' by friends of the administration.[5] Share prices opened at 190 francs on 18 July and fell steadily to close at 167·50: they reached their all-time low-point of 165 francs, or 33 per cent of par, on 20 July, the day of the annual general meeting. The shareholders at that meeting were too few in number to sanction the loan desired by the administration to pay the interest on the Company's bonds. They refused to accept Lesseps' financial report for the year 1870 and resolved to elect new directors.[6] Lesseps thereupon postponed the meeting for a month because modification of the statutes required a representation of one-tenth of the total number of shares. The directors then appointed on 22 August a commission of inquiry into the Canal tolls. In the heated session of the postponed shareholders' meeting on 24 August Lesseps repeatedly invoked the sovereignty of the General Assembly to impose the closure and to deny the floor to shareholders who wished to speak in favour of a ballot.[7] He successfully diverted the attack of the

---

[1] *The Times*, 20 June 1871, 10i; 22 June, 7ii.
[2] Ibid., 26 June 1871, 7ii; 17 July, 9i; 24 August, 7ii.
[3] *The Economist*, 29 July 1871, 903, 'The Financial Condition of the Suez Canal'.
[4] *Le Canal de Suez*, 9 Février 1871, 14, 19, 20.
[5] J. S. Price, *The Early History of the Suez Canal*, 26.
[6] *Le Canal de Suez*, 3 Août 1871, 190–3.
[7] Ibid., 31 Août 1871, 255–63.

dissenters against Egypt but was compelled to accept a ballot. The meeting adopted by 767 to 235 votes, amid sustained applause,[1] the base of 223,398 instead of 400,000 shares for questions requiring the representation of one-tenth or one-twentieth of the shares, depriving the Egyptian shares of their right to representation in view of the mortgage of their coupons in 1869. It then deprived the Egyptian shares of their voting-rights by a show of hands, although some shareholders vainly demanded a ballot. Thus it increased the voting-power of the shares held in France by some 44 per cent. The meeting also reduced the number of directors from thirty-two to twenty-four and their collective share in the profits from 3 to 2 per cent. That constitutional amendment made the board of directors almost wholly French in membership, reduced the vacant seats from sixteen to five and prevented the election of ten new members, who might have reduced the influence of Lesseps. It also increased the share of the profits available for the shareholders from 70 to 71 per cent. Those two meetings revealed Lesseps' capacity for surviving an initial assault on his position and for securing an ultimate victory over the forces of discontent.

A loan of £480,000 was necessary to pay the £600,000 due on three coupons of bond interest and to stave off legal action begun by the Company's creditors before the Commercial Court of Paris. The levy of a surtax of one franc per ton to pay the interest on the loan was sanctioned by both the Khedive and the Sultan, so enabling the Company to meet its current commitments out of its future revenue. The loan was sanctioned by the meeting of shareholders on 24 August and issued in the form of thirty-year bonds at the high nominal interest-rate of 8 per cent and a real interest-rate of 10 per cent. The Company was prepared to accept coupons in payment but received (9–18 September) subscriptions to only one-quarter of the total number of bonds. The Company kept the loan open and made an interim payment of the first coupon of bond interest from 25 October.[2] It did not levy the authorized surtax and remained for several months faced by the threat of liquidation and harassed by new rumours of a sale of the Company. Financial help by some of its directors made possible the payment of the second coupon from 15 December. Transit receipts began to grow rapidly from October 1871 when they first exceeded £40,000, with the aid of British vessels, and the Canal was definitely accepted as a preferable imperial route to a Euphrates Valley Railway.

A Select Committee of the House of Commons on Railway Communication between the Mediterranean, the Black Sea and the Persian Gulf was requested not by the Government but by a private member, Jenkinson, on 23 June and appointed under Northcote on 4 July. That defensive reaction to the new Russian advance into Central Asia after Sedan encouraged proposals for transcontinental railways in association with a Channel Tunnel. It stimulated the projection of railways via the Euphrates Valley, via Vienna and Salonika as

---

[1] *Le Canal de Suez*, 31 Août 1871, 262.
[2] Ibid., 19 Octobre 1871, 365.

the western complement to a Euphrates Valley line,[1] via Trieste and Constantinople to Karachi[2] and via the Black Sea coast of Asia Minor.[3] A wholly new proposal suggested a railway from the southern terminus of Port Said to Basra along the crescent demarcated by Jerusalem, Damascus and Palmyra.[4] In October 1871 the negotiations of the Admiralty for the purchase of an establishment at Port Said were finally concluded[5] and the Canal was first used by a British cruiser as well as by British troopships, to the full satisfaction of the Government of India. The *Iron Duke* en route from Plymouth to the China Station became the first capital ship and the first British ironclad to pass through the Canal. It drew 22 ft. 11 in., even with its fuel unloaded, and was towed through by three tugs in 51 hours (20–22 October 1871), coaling at Suez rather than at Port Said. The Admiralty's great white troopships also began to make regular use of the Canal from October 1871 for the transport of troops to India, confirming the military rather than the naval advantage enjoyed by Britain over Russia in India. The time for the journey from Portsmouth to Bombay was shortened by more than one day while its comfort was increased by the elimination of transhipment at Alexandria and Suez. The troopships available in reserve at Portsmouth during the summer were increased in number from two to five. The India Office reduced the overhead costs of the transport service substantially, closed the Victoria Military Hospital at Suez and coaled its ships at Port Said rather than at Suez or Aden. Indian revenues benefited by the decrease in married establishments and by the increased use of young recruits, who enlisted for six years under the Short Service Act of 1870 and proved best suited to stand the heat of the plains of India. The Indian Army nevertheless remained one of the most expensive in the world. The revenues of the Canal Company benefited by the payment of £1,400 per troopship per passage or by £28,000 per annum. The *Serapis* became the largest vessel to use the Canal from 1871 onwards. The number of military personnel using the Canal rose by 127 per cent from 15,535 in 1870 to 35,291 in 1871. The conversion of the Canal into a trooping route confirmed military opposition to the Euphrates Valley Railway because sleeping-cars could hardly be provided for soldiers crossing the Syrian Desert any more than Indian kit could be supplied to soldiers for the winter passage of the Red Sea. Ismail failed to prevent the use of the Canal either by warships or by troopships and did not even secure a limitation upon the number of troops passing through the Canal at any one time. Ismail and the Company interpreted the silence of the firman of 1866 as consent to such transits. The Sultan may have deemed it more politic to make England dependent on Turkey for the use of the Canal as a military route to India than to protest against the use of the

---

[1] *The Times*, 22 June 1871, 7 i–ii; 19 July, 10 v; 5 October, 4 v, W. P. Andrew.
[2] Ibid., 14 July 1871, 4 v, W. Low and G. Thomas, 'To India in Five Days'; *The Times*, 19 September, 4 iii–iv; 11 October, 12 ii.
[3] Ibid., 13 July 1871, 4 vi, R. M. Stephenson, 'The Euphrates Valley Line to the East'.
[4] Ibid., 28 October 1871, 6 vi, Colonel H. Drummond, R.E.
[5] Ibid., 12 October 1871, 7 v.

Canal by the warships of his potential protector against Russia. He thereby opened to the fleets of infidel Europe a naval highway flanking the birthplace of the Prophet and the holy cities of Islam. The British ambassador at Constantinople sought to maintain the tradition of Anglo-Turkish cooperation by opposing on 28 October Farrer's idea of the management of the Canal by an international commission. The example of England was followed by Portugal, whose *Estafania* first carried Portuguese troops through the Canal on 17–19 October 1871, to suppress a military mutiny in Goa and to avoid calling on Bombay for help. The subsequent disbandment of the Portuguese Indian Army increased the influence of the local Christians at the expense of the mestizos of Goa who had supplied the army's officers.

The Messageries Impériales renamed itself in 1871 the Messageries Maritimes in a dedication to the sea which was more fundamental and prudent than its earlier dedications to the Nation and the Empire. It resumed its fortnightly service to Indo-China from 9 July 1871 and extended its mail service to Shanghai with the *Meikong* which reached Shanghai in forty-two days (6 August–17 September 1871) from Marseilles. The postwar crisis of France was liquidated by the shipment of three condemned Communards with 260 convicts on the transport *Jura* through the Canal (26–28 November) en route to New Caledonia, which received more convicted Communards from Toulon in 1872. The Canal Company's shares were never at a lower annual average price than that of 208 francs during 1871. Lesseps admitted his readiness on 7 November to examine proposals for purchase made by interested Powers, especially by the Italian Government. A new rumour of the sale of the Company[1] aroused French opposition to the idea of a sale to the English and compelled Lesseps to disclaim the idea in a circular on 22 December. Lange then proposed on 29 December that Turkey should purchase the company's shares on behalf of the British Government. The Porte's rejection on 10 January 1872 of the idea of a sale or purchase forced the Company back upon its own resources, the greatest of which seemed to be its control of the Canal.

The Franco-Prussian War marked the end of a generation of change in Europe, precipitated by the Crimean War and dominated by the unification of the central powers of Germany and Italy. The remaking of Europe without British participation reduced English prestige and diverted the support of the national classes from Gladstone's Government to the Queen, the Prince of Wales and Disraeli, who in 1872 at the age of sixty-eight gained a popular reception for the first time in his career at Manchester, the home of the political economy which he had named in 1846 and had always rejected. The new military spirit diffused in Europe by the war was the antithesis of the spirit of free-trade and infected even the Canal Company, which elected in 1871 its first general in Clérembault, the hero of Solferino, to its board of directors as brutal Germany replaced perfidious Albion as the great object of French hatred.

[1] *The Times*, 20 December 1871, 5 ii.

United Germany gained with Alsace and Lorraine 4,781 shares in the Canal Company, or 2·6 per cent of the shares held in France. It also revived the idea of its own canal from the German Ocean to the Baltic.[1] Hamburg's pioneers of trade with the South Seas and East Africa supplied the first German transits through the Suez Canal. The *Sedan* of J. C. Godeffroy & Son became the first German toll-paying ship to pass through the Canal on 15–17 January 1871. The Canal Company pocketed the insult and the dues. The second German vessel was the *Africa* of Albrecht P. O'Swald & Co which passed through on 25–26 October 1871 en route to Zanzibar. The *Sedan*, which reached Shanghai in eighty-two days (8 June–28 August 1871), was the pioneer vessel of the German Steamship Line, Germany's first steamship line to the Far East and its first direct line to use the Canal. The Deutsche Dampfschiffs-Rhederei was founded in Hamburg in June 1871 under the stimulus of the competition of Trieste with no specific field of operations in its title and with a small capital raised with some difficulty by O'Swald. As a German line it offered goods for China and Singapore at freights which proved remunerative. It began regular departures every two months in 1872 with five small steamers but was compelled to load up in London. It paid a dividend of 4 per cent in 1874 and ranked Germany seventh in 1876 among the user-states of the Canal. In general German shipping to Asia remained sail rather than steam shipping so that Dutch and Austrian steamers filled the void left by Germany during the Canal's first fifteen years. Germany also extended its use of the transalpine route to Venice and Trieste and began the construction of the St. Gotthard Railway in 1872.

[1] *The Times*, 4 April 1871, 10 ii.

8

THE PORTS OF THE ISTHMUS AND THE
RED SEA, 1870–1873

THE successful completion of the Suez Canal realized the nightmare of the merchants of Alexandria by creating a Mediterranean rival to the historic export-port of Egypt. Alexandria nevertheless remained protected against any competition by its proximity to the rich cotton-growing region of the Delta, its communications via the Mahmoudieh Canal and the railway to Cairo, its virtual monopoly of warehouse accommodation and steampresses for cotton, its money-market and its financial support of the cotton markets of Mansura and Tanta. Its harbour, however, could not be entered either at night or in bad weather, unlike Port Said. The Canal Company hoped that Port Said would benefit by its cheap water-transport at the expense of the high-cost railway to Alexandria to become at the very least an Alexandria of the eastern delta and at the best the inheritor of all the trade of the Delta, breaking the monopoly of its rival and reducing it to a port of the second class. Thus Port Said would fulfil its destiny to become one of the chief seats of the future commerce of the world and the Queen of the Mediterranean. Even greater hopes were fixed on Ismailia than on Port Said in a revival of the aspirations of 1855 to make it an interior port appropriate to the capital of a future Egypto-Syrian kingdom.[1] Ismailia did attract many ships' chandlers and forwarding agents by 1870[2] but no cotton for export because Alexandria's monopoly left only the seed available for export via Ismailia and Port Said. The best brown seed was exported through Alexandria, leaving only the white seed for export via the Canal. That commodity was loaded on Arab vessels by Arab porters and carried along the Sweet Water Canal from Zagazig to Ismailia, whence it was shipped in Arab boats, sailing vessels and steamships to the seed-crushing mills of Europe. Ismailia exported cotton seed direct to Marseilles in 1870 and direct to Hull in 1871, hoping to become the business capital of Egypt as the most convenient landing-place when the Suez Canal became the highway of the world.[3]

The threat to Alexandria met with solid opposition from its pashas, its merchants and the Khedive. The pashas of Alexandria feared a decline in their ground-rents[4] as much as the merchants feared the competition of a free port. The merchants provided as fertile a seed-bed for anti-Canal propaganda

[1] C. Daleng, *L'Europe et l'Isthme de Suez* (1869), 15, 17.

[2] G. Ebers, *Durch Gosen zum Sinai. Aus dem Wanderbuche und der Bibliothek* (Leipzig, Engelmann, 1872), 27.

[3] *Daily News*, 9 November 1869, 5 ii.

[4] H. Couvidou, *Étude sur l'Égypte Contemporaine* (Le Caire, Barbier, 1873), 345.

as they had in the 1850s[1] and diffused with delight all reports of delays and disasters in the Canal. The offensive which they waged against the new water-way from November 1869 to March 1870 secured the support of Egypt's leading merchant, businessman and carrier. The Khedive gained revenue indirectly from the light-dues on the Canal and Red Sea[2] but lacked any great financial interest in the profits of the Canal Company, since he had surrendered the dividend on his shares for twenty-five years in 1869 and retained only the right to 15 per cent of the profits. He imposed no transit dues on goods shipped through the Canal or even on the coal imported to Port Said. He had, on the other hand, a direct interest in the revenues of the State railways and of the port of Alexandria. In anticipation of competition in the passenger traffic the State railways had reduced the first-class passenger fares between Alexandria and Suez from £10 to £4 10s. in 1869 and further to £3 in 1870. To restrict competition in the carriage of merchandise the railway from Cairo and Alexandria was pushed forward in 1869 to Damietta via Mansura. The Suez–Alexandria Railway could not expect to retain the transit trade in competition with the new sea-route. Ismail sought however to preserve the flow of Egyptian trade through Alexandria and ordered on 12 March 1870 an immediate start on the harbour works of the port by Greenfield and Elliot. Ismail laid the foundation-stone and the first block of the new breakwater on 15 May 1871. The blocks were the same type of 20-ton block used at Port Said and were deposited pell-mell on the same pattern: thus the techniques used in the creation of Port Said were imitated to enable Alexandria to repair the deficiencies of its harbour and to maintain its monopoly against its rival.

Neither Port Said nor Ismailia were free cities in the medieval tradition. Both were unwalled, exposed to attack from the sea and to encroachment on their liberties from the land. In a variety of ways the Government sought to curb the aspirations of both cities, to deprive them of any hinterland, to discourage the settlement of merchants and to restrict them to the supply of their own limited needs. Thus it questioned the right of the Canal Company to dispose of the ground at Port Said to foreign companies in perpetuity. To limit the trade of Port Said it levied high duties on vessels using Lake Menzaleh,[3] refused to permit the construction of a channel from Lake Menzaleh to Mansura and forbade the extension of the Sweet Water Canal to Port Said, leaving the port and its shipping dependent on the very expensive water carried by pipes from Ismailia. After the meeting of shareholders on 24 August 1871 deprived the Khedive of representation at the annual general meeting Ismail launched a many-sided attack on the Company. He was encouraged therein by the military defeat of France, by French opposition to judicial

[1] W. Simpson, *Meeting the Sun: a Journey all Round the World* (London, Longmans, 1874), 36–7.
[2] J. C. McCoan, *Egypt As It Is* (London, Cassell, 1877), 258.
[3] P. Fitzgerald, *The Great Canal at Suez* (London, Tinsley, 1876), i. 263, 269.

reform in Egypt, and by his own financial needs: he was not appeased by Lesseps' naming the second son born in 1871 from his second marriage Ismael. That attack was supported by German scholars[1] as well as by an English sailor[2] and an Alexandria banker,[3] who estimated the cost of the Canal to Egypt at £16,000,000, or the equivalent of 57 per cent of the Egyptian Debt, by including the cost of the outport and dry-dock of Port Ibrahim, the lighthouses and interest charges. The Government used its control of transportation to divert traffic from the Canal. Thus it raised freights on the Suez Railway by 20 per cent in the winter of 1871–2 in order to force the shipment of Egyptian produce through Alexandria. It carried Oriental produce over the Suez–Alexandria Railway for shipment to Europe throughout 1871 and 1872. It also pushed the railway forward in 1872 to Rosetta and Damietta while debarring Port Said from any rail link with the Delta. To restrict navigation and commerce on the Sweet Water Canal it allowed its level to fall in January and February 1872.[4] Ismail refused to develop the city named after himself, closed down the only newspaper in Port Said in January 1872 and contributed by his hostility to the decline of its population by one-third in 1871–2. His attempt in 1872 to levy duty on all the coal imported to Port Said was frustrated only by the combined resistance of all the European consuls. His approval of the organization of a Cotton Exchange in Alexandria in 1872 confirmed the failure of Port Said's attempt to capture the cotton market. Ismail also began from September 1872 to consider the construction of a fresh-water Suez Canal from Alexandria to Suez as a purely Egyptian undertaking. The response of the Company to the increasing pressure from Egypt was to improve the efficiency of its operation, to decide in 1872 to dismiss any employee responsible for an accident to a ship in the Canal, to reduce from 12 November 1872 the tariff for navigation to Ismailia by one-half and to resort to the levy of tolls on gross tonnage rather than on official tonnage in its quest for financial salvation.

Alexandria falsified the predictions made of its decadence, reduced Port Said's exports of cotton seed from their peak in 1872–3 and increased its predominance as the leading port and the national harbour of Egypt. Its continued expansion remained a function of the economic development of Egypt as well as of the suppression of the growth of the Canal ports. Although Alexandria never became a world harbour it remained the terminus for eight British shipping lines, none of which needed to extend their operations through the Canal. It supplied cargoes to the colliers which carried coal to

---

[1] H. Stephan, *Das Heutige Aegypten* (1872), 502–20, 'Die Finanzen der Suezkanal'. G. Ebers, *Durch Gosen zum Sinai* (1872).

[2] J. Steele, *The Suez Canal: its Present and Future. A Round-About Paper* (London, Simpkin, 1872).

[3] E. Dervieu, *Ce Que Coûte à l'Égypte le Canal de Suez* (Paris, Alcan-Lévy, 1871).

[4] *Reports of H.M. Consuls on the Manufactures, Commerce &c. of their Consular Districts* (London, H.M.S.O., 1872), 386, Report by Vice-Consul Barker upon the Commercial Position of Port Said, 21 March 1872.

Port Said and soon captured whatever trades Port Said developed. It remained the terminus of the overland route and developed its entrepôt trade with the Levant in Eastern produce carried by rail from Suez. Alexandria could not prevent Port Said from becoming a stage on the new tourist route from Cairo via Ismailia and Port Said to Jaffa and Jerusalem but it became the starting-point of a new route by rail to Ismailia and then by the Canal to Suez, so incorporating the Canal within the established pattern of its overland route at the expense of Port Said.

Port Said failed to become an Egyptian port and even less the maritime and commercial capital of the world.[1] It developed neither hinterland nor industry but remained essentially a port of transit, lacking land for warehouses on the scale of Alexandria. It gained neither a canal to Damietta nor a railway to the Delta and thus remained outside the system of the railway and the Sweet Water Canal, cut off from Egypt by the lagoons and marshes of Lake Menzaleh. It hoped to become the terminus of a railway to Syria and India, to deprive Kantara of its predestined function[2] and to acquire the strategic importance of Suez. Its inner harbour lacked deep foundations and deep-water berths, so that ships had to anchor in mid-channel by mooring posts and could not moor alongside a quay. Thus it provided a safe and accessible anchorage for small but not for large vessels.[3] Its harbour was seriously threatened by the rapidity of the silting on the Nilotic side of the western mole completed in 1869, accompanied by the erosion of the shore to the east of the eastern mole. That accumulation of sand was a danger which did not affect Alexandria to the west of the Delta. It created a new foreshore beyond the original sea-front, increasingly isolated the Eugénie Quay from commercial activity and gave the Government a fiscal interest in the reclaimed land. The Company considered building a small breakwater near Damietta but undertook instead a submarine extension of the western mole by one quarter of its length between 1872 and 1875 in order to counter the movement of sand into the entrance channel. It also acquired in 1873 the first marine dredger in the world to undertake the constant dredging necessary to maintain the depth of the harbour. To counteract the rapid deterioration of the blocks forming the harbour moles it began from 1875 to use masonry blocks in place of concrete blocks.

The function of Port Said was completely transformed after the opening of the Canal. It ceased to be a construction camp and became a port of transit whose essential function was to receive tolls and relieve passengers of their money. There ships paid their dues on arrival and took on a pilot for the first half of the Canal, together with the auxiliary rudder invented in 1872. They also took on the coal which formed the main import of the port and far

[1] C. Daleng, *L'Europe et l'Isthme de Suez* (1869), 31–4.
[2] H. Stephan, *Das Heutige Aegypten* (1872), 469.
[3] A. D. Taylor, *The India Directory, for the Guidance of Commanders of Steamers and Sailing Vessels* (London, Allen, 1874), Part i, 'The East Indies', 22.

outweighed its exports. Coal imports to the port paid no duty until 1874 because they were considered to be in transit: they increased most during 1870 and 1871, compelling the Company to build its first collier basin in 1873 on the Asiatic bank of the Canal. Coaling became the main function of Port Said, turning it into 'a coal depot between desert and marsh',[1] 'a big coaling station on the highway of nations, but outside all civilization'.[2] During the 1870s the port became the largest and most efficient coaling station in the world through the enterprise of its four coaling firms, which also dominated the coaling trade of Suez. Port Said benefited at the expense of Suez by the protective influence of the Canal dues on coal and by the proximity of Alexandria, which supplied return freight to the colliers from the Tyne. It also expanded at the expense of Algiers, where the local authorities hindered private efforts between 1869 and 1873 to supply bunker coal. It imported its coal from England because Egypt lacked coal and did not find it in the coalfields of Dranista, fifty miles south-west of Salonika, which were surveyed in vain by Ismail's English engineers in 1873. British ships nevertheless preferred to coal at Gibraltar and Malta rather than at a virtually French city, where the Canal Company sought to sell the waste sand for £2. 12s. per square yard.[3] The greater part of the coaling traffic was handled by the two French firms of C. & A. Bazin and Hippolyte Worms, the smaller part by the British firms of J. T. Wills and the Port Said & Suez Coal Company. Those four firms kept with the Canal Company in Paris a deposit account on which they could draw for the dues payable by vessels entering the Canal. Thus they facilitated passage through the Canal, limited their number to four and added financial commission to their high profits from the supply of coal. Worms developed into a powerful private banker, extending loans to Ismail and claiming on 21 July 1879 the right to import duty-free a small steamboat for the use of his firm in 'the neutral waters' of the Canal.[4]

Port Said captured many of the trades of Suez and became to shipping what the Company hoped Ismailia would become. The absence of fresh water raised the cost of living in 'this inhabited Sahara'.[5] The port nevertheless grew with a rude and vigorous life of its own while cosseted Ismailia wilted and declined. Its Europeans made the eligibility and price of city-sites into their universal topic of conversation. 'Port Said seems quite American.'[6] It remained the product of mushroom growth and a caravanserai rather than a city. The port became the town as nowhere else and the home of a cosmopolitan waterfront population free from the control of either Government or Company. Thus the town joined the character of a construction camp to that of a seaport and blended the vices of a Levantine population with those of migrant

[1] *The Times*, 9 April 1877, 6i.   [2] Ibid., 2 April 1880, 7v.
[3] H. Stephan, *Das Heutige Aegypten*, 512.
[4] O. Borelli, *Choses Politiques d'Égypte, 1883–1895* (Paris, Flammarion, 1895), 568.
[5] Couvidou, *Étude*, 345.
[6] O. R. Seward (ed.), *William H. Seward's Travels Around the World* (New York, Appleton, 1873), 575, 9 June 1871.

labour, sailors and passengers. From Suez Port Said inherited the blend of an Eastern population seeking its maintenance in the vices of the West[1] as well as the traditional appeal of the poor to the charity of the rich. Its commerce became essentially exploitative because its customers lacked any power of discrimination: they had been penned up on board ship for at least a week, stayed overnight before the introduction of night-time transit through the Canal and never returned. Its wares combined the maximum of uselessness and fragility while its native shops were even more squalid than the European ones. Its cafés were filled with the roulette-tables banned elsewhere in Egypt, made gambling and drink into their main sources of income and so flourished on what Islam anathematized. The lure of easy money attracted thieves and murderers, made killing as frequent in the European town as it was rare in the Arab village and compelled many men to carry revolvers after nightfall. The endemic vice fascinated visitors from Europe as much as the harems of Constantinople had an earlier generation and made the whole town into one of ill-fame as an African or Egyptian Wapping,[2] 'the Wapping of the Canal'.[3] Its first moral renaissance followed the establishment of a gas-works in 1875 and the introduction of gas-light in 1876: it reduced the incidence of murder and outrage but only for a short space of time. The port remained what Baden-Powell found it in November 1876 'wretched, stinking, filthy'[4] and was afflicted also by epidemic disease in small-pox from 1877.

Port Said became a new centre of contact between Christendom and Islam. Its Arab coal-heavers bunkered the ships of the infidel during the great fast of Ramadan. The Arabs in the Canal Company's workshops worked on the Christian Sunday rather than on the Moslem Friday but very rarely used a knife or showed their teeth, unlike the Levantines. Its Europeans combined arrogance towards the Egyptians with republican or socialist views.[5] The port nevertheless seemed destined to become 'the centre of human solidarity, the point of departure of new social laws'.[6] It wholly lacked public buildings. Its private buildings combined the inclined roof of Europe, to ward off the rains of winter, with the veranda of Asia, to moderate the heat of summer, and seemed to represent 'the architecture of the future'.[7] Its location on a low sand-bar prohibited drainage as well as burial. Its masonry cemetery was divided into three sections for Moslems, Greeks and Catholics (including Protestants and Jews)[8] and was replaced in 1881 by one in six feet of sand.

Ismailia remained the administrative and technical headquarters of the Company in Egypt, the Washington of the isthmus, with a superb baroque

[1] J. MacGregor, *The Rob Roy on the Jordan* (1869), 28. F. A. Swettenham, *Footprints in Malaya* (London, Hutchinson, 1942), 14.
[2] E. Dicey, *The Morning Land* (1870), ii. 199. *Daily News*, 29 December 1869, 5 iii. I. Burton, *Arabia, Egypt, India. A Narrative of Travel* (London, Mullan, 1879), 63.
[3] F. B. Zincke, *Egypt of the Pharaohs* (1871), 423.
[4] R. Baden-Powell, *Indian Memories* (London, Jenkins, 1915), 8.
[5] I. Burton, *Arabia Egypt India*, 63.
[6] H. Couvidou, *Itinéraire du Canal de Suez* (Port Said, Mourès, 1875), 57.
[7] Ibid., 46.   [8] Ibid., 65–6.

plan. 'Ismailia looks like a bit of Paris suddenly transported to the Desert.'[1] That town was the focus of the communications of the isthmus by railway, telegraph, Sweet Water Canal and maritime canal. It became the winter seat of Lesseps, whose chalet on the Mehemet Ali Quay became a place of pilgrimage for visitors. Its municipal services were provided by the Company which spent hundreds of thousands of pounds thereon and neglected Port Said.[2] The Company built houses of stone not of wood, as at Port Said, and macadamized its streets. It sought to protect the trade of Ismailia by equalizing the dues on vessels leading at any point in the Canal so that cargo loaded within two or three miles of Port Said paid the full Ismailia tariff. It also insisted that passengers for Cairo should disembark at Ismailia rather than at Port Said.

Ismailia failed however to fulfil the large expectations cherished by the Company. It gained no trade from the Canal and lost its small export trade to Port Said during the 1870s, together with its repair workshops and much of its retail trade. It attracted no merchant houses and inspired no local enterprise: the shops in its main street, the Rue Negrelli, were opened by Cairo retailers. It did not acquire a naval college or a staff college for the Army or an Institute of Egyptology. Its palace remained a monument without either master or guest since Ismail refused to honour it with his presence for an annual season. Ismailia did not even develop as a spa, an Egyptian Deauville, because it lacked an adequate supply of pure water to reinforce its attractive blend of desert air with sea air and of European accommodation with French cooking. The Company's Water Service nevertheless turned the Place Champollion into one vast garden in the 1870s and made the Garden of Fountains around the Waterworks the home of a gorgeous variety of subtropical trees, shrubs, plants and flowers. Ismailia could not become a centre of viticulture[3] in a land where the advent of Islam had banished the vine. It remained a garden-city and a paradise of colour amidst the sand, quite unlike Suez or Port Said. 'If the lake is the sapphire, Ismailia is the emerald, of the desert.'[4]

The Arab village of Ismailia remained distinct from the European town and was sited to the west between the Cairo Railway and the Sweet Water Canal. Its blocks were smaller than those of the French town and teemed with activity, focusing around the bazaar and the mosque, which was relatively more important than either the Catholic Church or the Greek Church were in the European town. Arab Ismailia became the real metropolis of the isthmus and was linked to the Delta as French Ismailia was not, providing a permanent market for food supplies, especially durra, from Zagazig as well as for fish from Lake Timsah. It became a centre for the contact of European and Oriental civilization as the Arabs recognized the superior power of Europe and adapted themselves to the needs of an alien civilization and the rewards

[1] *The Times*, 11 October 1870, 4v, 'The Suez Canal'.
[2] Couvidou, *Étude* (1873), 344. H. de Vaujany, *Description de l'Égypte* (Paris, Plon, 1885), ii. 244–50, Ismailia.
[3] F. de Carcy, *De Paris en Égypte, Souvenirs de Voyage* (Paris, Berger-Levrault, 1875), 414.
[4] Couvidou, *Itinéraire*, 119.

of a money economy.[1] It exerted no influence, however, upon the life of the fellahin of the Nile before 1928.

European Ismailia preserved its colonial tradition and society but lacked both walls and hinterland. Its roads were not used because they led nowhere except to Lake Timsah or the desert. Its trees halted sharply at the frontier of the waiting desert sand. The resulting contrast between civilization and the desert was sharp and sudden without any of the intermediate shades of the Midi beloved by the French. 'The *siroccos* blow the sands of the desert on the paved streets of Ismailia, and there is neither men nor money to sweep them out.'[2] The population declined markedly from 15,000 in 1869 to less than 2,000 in 1871. Reduced to a dormitory town for Company employees, it hoped that the enlargement of the Sweet Water Canal would tap the life of the Nile and develop its entrepôt function. 'Ismailia lies deserted like a city of the dead on the shores of Lake Timsah...At Ismailia one only sees houses without inhabitants and streets without traffic.'[3]

'Suez the Stony' faced the Red Sea with fewer prospects of growth than Port Said which faced Europe. It had doubled its area, trebled its houses and quadrupled its population between 1859 and 1869. It was however separated from the Canal to which it gave its name by the wide curve of the exit channel into the Gulf of Suez. The Canal Company hoped thereby to create a new French commercial settlement separate from the British merchant houses in Suez and built large financial hopes on the three miles of ground on either side of the new waterway. The new outport lay on the same western bank of the exit channel as Suez and thus could not be wholly conquered for French civilization: it was linked to Suez by an artificial mole two miles in length with a spur-railway, a wagon road, a foot-path and a water-main. That outport comprised the naval basin and dry dock of Port Ibrahim, which was named by Ismail after the father whom he revered. The Waghorn Quay separated that Egyptian port from the Canal proper and the Company's concession. The whole complex was named Terreplein because it was built on reclaimed land. Ismail expected a considerable increase in the local trade of Suez after the opening of the Canal. He therefore signed a contract in 1870 with Elzear Dussaud for the addition of a second basin for commercial vessels at Port Ibrahim and for the increase of its water surface by 62 per cent.[4] He also sought to develop the facilities of the Wells of Moses for visitors from passing steamers and took over the Aziziya Misriya Steamship Company, which concentrated from 1870 on its services in the Red Sea.

Those large expectations remained unfulfilled. The new harbour of Port Ibrahim did not attract local traffic because the Customs House did not move from Suez: it remained unused except by the P. & O. and earned no return

---

[1] G. Ebers, *Durch Gosen zum Sinai* (1872), 30–1.

[2] O. R. Seward (ed.), *William H. Seward's Travels Around the World* (1873), 487, 6 May 1871.

[3] *The Times*, 2 November 1875, 5 iii. Couvidou, *Étude* (1873), 341–2.

[4] *The Engineer*, 27 June 1873, 400, 'Construction of a New Port at Suez'.

on its capital cost of £1,250,000. Both Suez and Port Ibrahim remained without organic relation to the Canal. Terreplein did not become a port of call except for steamers to drop their Canal pilot and their auxiliary rudder so that passengers gained no time to visit the Wells of Moses. Suez became far more a port of transit than Port Said and suffered from the protective influence of the Canal tolls. Thus it lost to Port Said not only its trade in straw hats but also its coaling trade as it ceased to be the only coaling station on the Red Sea route to Aden. Coal prices at Suez fell by 1870 to half of their level in 1868 but were prevented from falling lower by the Canal tolls so that Port Said captured the bulk of the coaling trade. The imports of coal in 1871 were 25,000 tons to Suez but nearly 200,000 tons to Port Said. Suez also lost the provisioning as well as the bunkering of ships together with the workshops of the shipping companies. It gained the offices of Alfred Holt and the British Indian Submarine Telegraph Company while G. Beyts & Co. became the agents of the British India Steam Navigation Company. The P. & O. however began negotiations from 18 February 1870 for the purchase of lands at Port Said. The Messageries which had rented a plot of land at Port Said in 1868 transferred its agency there in March 1870 and reduced its establishment at Suez to a single sub-intendant. It left the houses built in the 1860s tenantless and let out its imposing premises built in 1863 in apartments, which were only partly occupied. Thus the Messageries abandoned Suez as its eastern home-port on the completion of the Canal, preferring to use La Ciotat near Marseilles for major repairs and Port Said for minor repairs.

Suez was burdened by the immediacy of the local authority, seated in the new Government House which Dussaud Brothers built as the most imposing structure in the town. The waters of the port remained Egyptian so that vessels in transit did not require a harbour-pilot as at Port Said. The 12 per cent ad valorem duty on fish effectively prevented the local inhabitants from becoming fishermen and restricted fishing to Greeks and Maltese. The high cost of living was an additional burden. The Canal reduced the price of some imported foodstuffs, such as potatoes, to the Cairo level as the Sweet Water Canal had reduced the price of water in 1863. Food prices in general remained high and were raised by the supply of large quantities of meat to passing steamers as in 1872. The French waterworks company proved a financial failure because the inhabitants were reluctant to pay its prices.

Suez failed to become an entrepôt or to retain its large European population.[1] European shopkeepers and artisans complained that they could no longer make a living and gradually went away. The Greeks alone survived to earn an independent livelihood in trade. Planned streets remained unbuilt[2] and houses became untenanted. Land values fell from the boom levels of the 1860s and landed property became unsaleable, although rents did not fall in

---

[1] G. West, 'The Trade and Commerce of the Port of Suez for 1872', *The Practical Magazine*, 1873, 447–63.

[2] Carcy, *De Paris en Égypte* (1873), 457.

the same proportion. The French Hospital had to appeal to the residents of Suez for funds to carry out essential minor repairs so that it might avert the fate of the English Military Hospital. The disappearance of roulette was a very bad sign, *rien ne va plus*.[1] English and American visitors in 1871 concurred in their verdict, 'Suez is in a state of rapid decay.'[2] 'Suez, like Omaha, is a great place in the future.'[3] The population, however, did not decline as much as that of Ismailia, falling from 17,000 in 1869 to 15,000 in 1871[4] and to 13,000 in 1872.

Suez remained in more direct communication with the East than with Europe from which it was cut off by the Canal. It was still the terminus of the overland route,[5] which inspired Consul West in 1872 to suggest the despatch of an Egyptian Trade Commission to India. As a port of export more than of import it remained the natural outlet of Lower Egypt to the Red Sea. Its trade remained stable and confined to the Red Sea, especially to the Hejaz. Its port continued in use not only by Moslem pilgrims en route to Mecca but also by English pilgrims such as Edward Palmer in 1869 en route to Sinai. Vessels in the coasting trade to and from Suez indeed paid the heavy Government lighthouse dues once only while vessels using the Suez Canal paid them twice. Port Ibrahim also became a base for Ismail's imperial ventures in the Sudan in emulation of his father and grandfather. The character of Suez was impressed upon the isthmus and the Company. 'Everyone struggles for profit and material comfort...Its mind is concerned with figures and quantities... Everyone has half given up his homeland but is not at home here and would let the world come to an end if he could only make a fortune as quickly as possible.'[6] The bazaar of Suez remained a great centre for the contact of East and West. 'The Europeans are buying goods from the East; the Orientals, those of Manchester and Birmingham.'[7]

The ports of the isthmus were Company towns rather than Egyptian cities. Economically the Company had become a parasite upon its Egyptian host as it failed to derive its expected sustenance from the shipping of Europe. Egypt's efforts to preserve its accustomed patterns of trade from diversion to the isthmus prevented the Canal from influencing the Nile valley for good as well as evil. 'Egypt is no more benefited by English ships passing through the Canal, than it would be by a flock of wild geese flying over the Isthmus.'[8] The Canal towns, especially Ismailia, increasingly concentrated their hopes on the summer influx of European visitors from Alexandria and on the completion of the Ismailia Canal which had been begun from the Nile in 1870. That

[1] Couvidou, *Étude* (1873), 339.
[2] F. B. Zincke, *Egypt of the Pharaohs* (1871), 425, February 1871.
[3] O. R. Seward (ed.), *William H. Seward's Travels Around the World* (1873), 483, 6 May 1871.
[4] H. Stephan, *Das Heutige Aegypten* (1872), 475.
[5] *Illustrated London News*, 19 October 1872, 383, 384, 'The Waghorn Monument at Suez'.
[6] G. Ebers, *Durch Gosen zum Sinai* (1872), 43.
[7] J. S. Cowan, 'From Port Said to Suez', *Canadian Monthly*, November 1875, 411.
[8] F. B. Zincke, *Egypt of the Pharaohs* (1871), 432.

canal was extended to Kassassin in 1874 and completed in 1877 by the entrepreneur Paponot over the eighty-three miles to Ismailia, where it was inaugurated unofficially on 15 April 1877 with a regatta.[1] Water was admitted on 6 June 1877 to the new canal so that the old Sweet Water Canal between Kassassin and Nefischa could be superseded and used for local irrigation. The Canal Company bought the Suez Waterworks in February 1877 for £8,600, placed them on a paying basis and fully amortized the purchase price by 1886: thus it centralized the control of the distribution of the water-supply of the whole isthmus in its hands. The new canal was fully navigable by vessels of 400 tons because it was quadruple the width and treble the depth of the old Sweet Water Canal. The Convention of 17 April 1878 fixed the level of tolls on the canal which was fully opened to navigation on 1 May 1878. The Mehemet Ali Quay at Ismailia did not however become an entrepôt as expected. The heavy charges for lock dues also shattered the hopes of Port Said, which turned instead to the idea of a railway or a salt-water canal to the Nile. Suez derived no benefit because the southern extension was not fully navigable. 'Poor Suez wears the appearance of a Red Sea settlement lately bombarded and not yet repaired.'[2]

The new canal failed to bring the expected 100,000 acres of desert under cultivation but sent 20,000 acres out of cultivation in the Wadi Tumilat by raising the water-table and encouraging saline percolations, which destroyed the fertility of the land of Goshen around Tel el Kebir.[3] Suez allowed the sea to receive enough water to irrigate 2,000 acres of desert because reclaimed land was not exempted from the land-tax. The canal also brought malaria to Ismailia, where 90 per cent of the summer visitors in 1877 caught fever and the Mixed Court was compelled to adjourn to Cairo. Thenceforward malaria remained endemic in the city until 1903 and flourished most in the last three months of the year at high Nile. Ismailia did not recover from the shock. Lesseps ceased to make it his winter seat. Its well-built houses fell empty while its streets became grass-grown. The canal also brought to Suez malaria by 1879 and bilharzia by 1882 while it added malaria to the other plagues of Port Said. That deterioration in the public health of the isthmus followed the assumption by the Company in 1876 of responsibility for maintaining public health services within the isthmus.

The opening of the Suez Canal converted the Red Sea into a through-way. That sea ceased to be an interior sea of the Ottoman Empire and became a highway for foreign shipping as never before in all its long history. Its ports were not the destination of the vessels which first used the Canal but ports of call at the best. Its indigenous maritime life had been far less vigorous than that of the Mediterranean because of its barren coasts and mountainous

[1] *The Times*, 9 April 1877, 6i.

[2] R. F. Burton, *Sind Revisited* (London, Bentley, 1877), 2. Idem., *The Gold Mines of Midian and the Ruined Midianite Cities* (London, Paul, 1878), 74.

[3] D. M. Wallace, *Egypt and the Egyptian Question* (1883), 250.

hinterlands. The seaboard populations prevented the penetration by European merchants into the interior, the construction of littoral telegraph lines and the development of its ports but could not resist the imperial expansion of either Turkey on the east coast or of Egypt on the west coast. European possessions, however, were bitterly contested and were restricted to the precarious footholds of Aden, Perim and Obock at the southern exit by Bab el Mandeb.[1]

Aden was found to have no seaward defences when Mayo inspected it in 1868. After Prussian, Dutch, Spanish, French and Austrian warships arrived in the wake of the inauguration of the Canal its perturbed Resident asked on 12 January 1870 for an ironclad and for large-calibre guns.[2] In the spring of 1870 Aden became a cable-station on the Suez–Bombay line and in the summer it manned its masonry forts with Armstrong guns to discourage any 'Isthmian Games' by France.[3] 'Aden is a fortification and harbor, and nothing more.'[4] 'This hell upon earth'[5] lacked tree, shrub, flower, leaf, grass or earth to redeem its sterility. This 'congeries of gigantic cinders or heaps of colossal coke'[6] made coaling its primary function and coal its main import. Coal imports were diverted from the sailing ship to the steamship and from the Cape route to the Canal route. Although the coal was imported direct from England its price was maintained at a high level by the Canal tolls. Thus Aden became the complement to Port Said as a coaling station but developed its general trade to a greater extent and began to export salt from 1870 to Bengal.

Ismail contemplated a 1200-mile Suez–Aden Railway to save 4–5 days on the Red Sea mail service. His real dream however was of a Greater Egypt which would control the lake-sources of the Nile discovered in 1862, assume suzerainty over Uganda, Zanzibar and Ethiopia and embrace a tributary area worthy of a line of rulers sprung from Mehemet Ali. Such an Egypt would inevitably restore the Arabian empire established by Mehemet Ali. Ismail appointed Sir Samuel Baker, who had discovered Lake Albert Nyanza in 1864, to command an expedition to the Great Lakes under a four-year contract from 1 April 1869.[7] Baker was ordered to suppress the slave-trade, to introduce legitimate commerce and cotton cultivation so as to provide the necessary exchange for Manchester goods, to open the Great Lakes to navigation and to establish a chain of trading-stations on the model of the Hudson's Bay Company, an administration on the model of Egypt and a labour-tax for the construction of roads on the model of Ceylon. Baker was raised to the rank of Bey in May and to that of Pasha in June 1869[8] and was armed with

[1] T. E. Marston, *The Red Sea Area 1800–1878* (1961), 392–3.
[2] Ibid., 388.
[3] *Punch*, 27 November 1869, 216.
[4] O. R. Seward (ed.), *William H. Seward's Travels Around the World* (1873), 472, 28 April 1871.
[5] G. F. I. Graham, *The Life and Work of Syed Ahmed Khan* (Edinburgh, Blackwood, 1885), 131, 17 April 1869.
[6] M. Monier-Williams, *Modern India and the Indians* (London, Trübner, 1878), 24.
[7] G. Douin, *Histoire du Règne du Khédive Ismail*, iii. 475, 'L'Empire Africain'.
[8] Ibid., 483.

despotic power never before entrusted by a Moslem to a Christian. His expedition was held up first by the absence of Ismail in Europe and then by the festivities of the opening ceremony of the Canal, when every available vessel, especially steamers, was pressed into the service of the Khedive's visitors. That delay in departure lost Baker twelve months of his four-year contract. On 5 December 1869 he left Suez on an Egyptian sloop for Suakin and the Sudan.[1] His expedition was supported by Ismail's instructions to Hawkshaw at Ismailia on 17 November to make immediate preparations for the canalization of all the cataracts of the Nile[2] so as to open up a great commercial highway into the heart of Africa. Ismail also ordered the construction of the telegraph which was completed in 1870 from Cairo to Khartoum, the centre of Egypt's military administration and military trade in the Sudan. Baker's expedition encouraged Menelik, Prince of Shoa, in self-defence to ask the Resident at Aden in September 1870 for instruction in the mechanical arts.

Egyptian expansion in Africa was accompanied by Turkish expansion in Arabia, especially in the Yemen where the monsoon rain created the true Arabia Felix as distinct from the Arabia Petraea of the north and the Arabia Deserta of the centre of the peninsula. The Turks had lost control of the Yemen since 1620 but had regained the port of Hodeida in 1840. The Asiri to the north of the Yemen, encouraged by Ismail, revolted from Turkish authority in November 1870 and attacked Hodeida on 2–3 December 1870. To suppress that revolt, to eliminate the need for any help from Aden or from Egypt and to reconquer the Yemen 10,000 Turkish troops were despatched in November and passed through the Canal in December 1870.[3] The transport of Ottoman troops through the isthmus of Suez disturbed Ismail deeply because it followed immediately upon his conclusion of an entente with the Russian ambassador at Constantinople and implied that it was unnecessary to call on his services in a traditional sphere of Egyptian interest. The Ottoman expedition also revealed the inadequacy of the shore-batteries established at Suez in 1863–4 and threatened Egypt's strategic control of the isthmus. Ismail therefore sought to enlist English support against Turkey for the protection of the Canal and sought the advice of his American officers on the military protection of the isthmus. General C. P. Stone recommended on 4 January 1871 the creation of a submarine fleet and a mine service and the construction of a military railway linking Alexandria to Port Said via Rosetta and Damietta.[4] Ismail ordered in January 1871 the construction of three forts of Attaqa stone to command the Suez roads in his first attempt to protect the Canal. He considered the fortification of Port Said on land for which the Admiralty was negotiating. He also ordered a reconnaissance of the desert

---

[1] S. W. Baker, *Ismailia. A Narrative of the Expedition to Central Africa for the Suppression of the Slave Trade organised by Ismail, Khedive of Egypt* (London, Macmillan, 1874), i. 24.

[2] A. Russel, *Egypt: The Opening of the Great Canal* (1869), 97, 124.

[3] G. Douin, ii. 585.

[4] F. J. Cox, 'The American Naval Mission in Egypt', *Journal of Modern History* (June 1954), 174.

route between Ismailia and Cairo. That survey was undertaken by Chaillé-Long, who recommended the construction of earth works at Tel el Kebir as the best point at which an enemy attack from the Canal could be met. Those works were promptly built while work on the Suez forts was suspended at the request of the Sultan.[1]

The Turks captured the Emir of the Asiri in his capital in May 1871 while from Bagdad they reduced Kuwait to submission and reoccupied Nejd, including the province of Hasa and Qatar. Facing eastward, upland Arabia could be penetrated from the Red Sea coast only with the greatest difficulty and was supplied either from the Persian Gulf or from Syria. Thus an overland advance combined with the seaborne assault to extend Turkish power over the uplands and coasts of Arabia and to frustrate Ismail's hopes of Arabian dominion. Aden's position became more precarious, the Resident beginning from 1871 to make in self-defence direct subsidy agreements with the tribes, by-passing the Sultan of Lahej, while the Government of Bombay began from 29 June 1871 to think in terms of a virtual protectorate over Lahej.

England lost her initiative as the chief protector of the integrity of the Ottoman Empire when she acquiesced in Russia's denunciation of the Black Sea clause of the Treaty of Paris and separated her interests from those of Austria. The Treaty of London of 13 March 1871 enshrined Russia's victory in the Black Sea and empowered her to maintain a fleet therein. Abandoned by England the Porte was compelled to come to terms with Russia and greatly improved Russo-Turkish relations. That Russo-Turkish détente precluded any possibility of a Russo-Egyptian combination and even portended a Russo-Turkish alliance against Egypt. The conflict between Cairo and Constantinople encouraged the new Permanent Under-Secretary to the Colonial Office to deduce from his experience in Australia that Cape Town was 'the true centre of the Empire...clear of the Suez complications, almost equally distant from Australia, China, India, Gibraltar, the West Indies and the Falklands'.[2] Ismail made warlike preparations against the Russo-Turkish combination. John L. Lay, an American manufacturer of mines, surveyed the Canal, the Red Sea and the Mediterranean coast in one of Ismail's steamers and contracted to mine all those waters to prevent the approach of any vessel. An agent was sent to buy a number of large-calibre Krupp guns for fortresses on the Canal, which progressed in defiance of the imperial veto.[3] 'What the Dardanelles are to the Russian Empire for military, political and commercial purposes the Suez Canal is to the British Empire... The Treaty of 1871 forms a new era for the policy of England which must be based on the free navigation of the Suez Canal.'[4] England was thus urged to abandon its preoccupation

---

[1] G. Douin, ii. 588.

[2] *Cambridge History of the British Empire* (Cambridge University Press, 1940), ii. 591, E. A. Walker, 'The Routes to the East, 1815–1870', quoting R. S. W. Herbert's minute of 31 May 1871.

[3] F. J. Cox, 174–5. G. Douin, ii. 565–6.

[4] *The Times*, 19 October 1871, 4 i–ii, 'The Suez Canal'.

with the Cape route, to secure international guarantees for the free navigation of the Canal in war as well as in peace and for its exemption from territorial belligerency, to impose on Turkey and Egypt its view of the Canal as an ever open international highway, and to declare that no war for control of the Canal would be fought without British participation. From Suez Consul West noted the ease with which the Canal could be entered, especially at night, and blocked by scuttling. He recommended the issue of a consular pass to all vessels through a branch consular office at Port Said as well as the introduction of floating booms at both entrances. In India C. U. Aitchison, the Secretary of the Foreign Department since 1868, regretted British acquiescence in the Russian victory as much as his equivalent in the English Foreign Office. 'I think the opening of the Suez Canal has made it ten times more our interest to be on good and intimate terms with Turkey than it ever was before.'[1]

Ismail renewed friendly relations with the Porte from the autumn of 1871 and secured the three firmans of 1872,[2] the abrogation of the highly restrictive firman of 1869 and the restoration of his right to raise foreign loans. That Turco-Egyptian rapprochement of 1872 was based on a tacit agreement which left Africa to the Khedive and Arabia to the Sultan. Before that agreement was reached the Porte complained in 1872 that an expedition to the Yemen had been held up at Port Said for twenty-five days. The Turks nevertheless reconquered the Yemen, capturing Sanaa in 1872[3] and deposing the last independent Imam in 1873 but maintaining the dominion of the Shiite Zaidi highlanders over the Sunni plainsmen. Thenceforward the Yemen passed under Turkish rule for the first time since 1620, preventing its annexation by Egypt and supplying a convenient place of exile for officials offensive to Constantinople. The Aziziya Misriya Steamship Company re-established from 8 July 1872 the service from Suez to Jedda, Suakin and Massawa and took over from the Austrian Lloyd in 1873 the contract for a monthly mail service between Constantinople and Jedda. The sea-route to the Yemen fostered the growth of Hodeida as the port for Sanaa and proved far superior to the difficult overland route. The opening of the Canal contributed to the establishment of Turkish hegemony over Arabia rather than to the prosperity and independence of the peninsula. Turkish control was established over the whole Arabian flank of the Suez–Aden route to the East. Turkey used the Canal for the transport of mail, troops and grain from Odessa to its garrisons in Arabia. It also imported through the Canal slaves, eunuchs, and Galla women from Abyssinia.

Ismail aspired to dominion in the south as a substitute for the sovereignty which he could not attain in Egypt.[4] *Aida* took as its theme the conflict

---

[1] Ravinder Kumar, *India and the Persian Gulf Region 1858–1907. A Study in British Imperial Policy* (London, Asia Publishing House, 1965), 114, 15 April 1872.
[2] G. Douin, ii. 638–65.   [3] T. E. Marston, 400.
[4] R. Gray, *A History of the Southern Sudan 1839–1889* (London, Oxford University Press, 1961), 70–119. R. Hill, *Egypt in the Sudan 1820–1881* (London, Oxford University Press, 1959), 106–52.

between Egypt and Abyssinia and directed attention southwards from Memphis to Thebes. That opera was first performed in Cairo in 1871 and in Milan in 1872, having been delayed and transformed in spirit by the Franco-Prussian War. It enlisted the music of Verdi and the civilization of the Pharaohs as interpreted by Mariette in the service of Khedivial Egypt. The military spirit of its Grand March was the very antithesis of the spirit of peace and commerce invoked at the opening of the Canal, to which the opera made no specific reference. Ismail used the most modern techniques in his southward expansion and projected from 1872 a 1,100-mile railway in the Sudan, which Werner Munzinger in 1871 called 'the little America of Africa'. The Khedivial Mail Line, as the Aziziya Company was renamed on its reorganization in 1873, established at the request of J. M. Cook a regular steamboat service as far as the granite-barrier of the First Cataract of the Nile at Aswan. The Khedive's engineering adviser, John Fowler, recommended the construction of a ship-incline, to by-pass the First Cataract, and a railway to the Red Sea. Ismail accordingly ordered in 1873 surveys for a Berber–Berenice Railway and for a Shendi–Massawa Railway, to link the Nile to the Red Sea and avoid the cataracts. By then Baker had carried the Egyptian flag as far south as Lake Albert and the powerful lacustrine kingdoms of Unyoro and Uganda. Thus Turkey and Egypt found a common frontier of expansion in the Red Sea and reconciled their thitherto divergent interests.

After Ismail's eighth visit to Constantinople and his payment of £900,000 he secured the firman of 8 June 1873[1] which restored the administrative autonomy of Egypt. Ismail failed, however, to secure a single attribute of that sovereignty in which contemporary Europe recognized no gradations[2] because Egypt remained a Turkish province wholly dependent on the Empire in external relations. The full restoration of the internal autonomy of Egypt nevertheless encouraged Vogüé, the French ambassador at Constantinople, to conclude: 'If I am not wrong, the centre of gravity of the Orient is tending to shift from the shores of the Bosphorus, the narrow route of a local trade, to the banks of the Suez Canal, the future route of general commerce. The political evolution of Egypt follows that economic evolution.'[3] That firman of 1873 was followed by the admission of Egypt to the Universal Postal Union at Berne in 1873, the beginning of the elimination of foreign post offices from Egyptian territory, the resumption of the campaign for judicial reform to restrict the extensive judicial privileges of Europeans in Egypt and the flotation of the monster loan of 1873.

The contract for the loan of 1873 was signed with Oppenheim & Co. That firm had floated the five successive Egyptian loans of 1862, 1864, 1866, 1867 and 1868 and exacted conditions onerous beyond all precedent[4] so that

[1] G. Douin, ii. 711–42.
[2] *Law Reports 42 Admiralty and Ecclesiastical Cases*, 1873, 17–41, Sir Robert Phillimore in the *Charkieh* case.
[3] A. Sammarco, *Le Règne du Khédive Ismail de 1863 à 1875* (1937), 225, Vogüé, 18 Juin 1873.
[4] J. C. McCoan, *Egypt under Ismail* (London, Chapman, 1889), 154, 156.

the loan became the most ruinous ever contracted by Ismail. The flotation even of the first part proved a failure in the crisis of 1873 and reduced the price of all Egyptian stocks.[1] The flotation of the second part left Oppenheim's syndicate with £3,750,000 of stock still on its hands. The loan raised £19,974,000 (including £9,000,000 in Treasury bonds) or 62·4 per cent of its nominal amount of £32,000,000 leaving a mass of floating debt still unredeemed. It closed the money-markets of England and France to further Egyptian loans until 15 July 1875 by a self-denying clause and compelled Ismail to turn from Oppenheim to the Crédit Foncier so as to permit a new expansion of his floating debt. The loan increased the annual charge on the Egyptian Treasury by £2,565,670 and the proportion of revenue devoted to the payment of interest from 35·8 per cent in 1873 to 58·6 in 1874. Its increase in unlegitimized interest-payments to the Franks aroused opposition in Nile-centred Egypt unlike the tribute to the Sultan. Its comparative failure encouraged Ismail's bid in 1874 to take over the operation of the Suez Canal and reinforced his drive for quick returns from his empire in the south, which was extended by the conquest of Darfur in 1874 and placed under Gordon as the successor to Baker.

The Turkish expansion in Arabia approached closer and closer to Aden which Frere found in danger of its existence when he arrived on 31 December 1872. The Sultan of Lahej refused to submit to Turkish rule and claimed British protection on 3 January 1873.[2] The establishment of such a protectorate was favoured by the Viceroy of India but was rejected on 11 October 1873 by Gladstone. After a Turkish raid into Lahej on 16 October[3] which reached within eighteen miles of Aden, its Resident complained both to Bombay and to London.[4] The Turkish Note of 28 January 1874 claimed sovereignty over Arabia including the Yemen and Lahej and implicitly Aden itself.[5] Derby's very strong reply of 30 April to Constantinople apparently implied a threat to the Ottoman Empire in the Balkans.[6] Aden survived the extension of Turkish power but was then threatened by the extension of Egyptian authority over the Somali coast between 1872 and 1874 and thereby over the supply of provisions from Berbera across the Gulf of Aden. The Egyptian efforts in November 1874 to close Bulhar and to make Berbera the staple port of the Somali coast doubled the price of provisions in Aden. Aden nevertheless expanded its entrepôt trade with Ethiopia as well as the Yemen. It developed its re-exports of gum and coffee from 1874, of ivory and spices from 1875 and of rubber and hides from 1876. Between 1870 and 1880 it increased the value of its coffee trade fivefold, re-exporting coffee to London, Marseilles, Trieste and New York. Aden also became a centre for the large-scale import of cotton textiles, especially from 1874. Its population increased

[1] A. M. Hamza, *The Public Debt of Egypt 1854–1876* (1944), 218–19.
[2] Marston, 403.   [3] Ibid., 417.
[4] R. J. Gavin, 'The Bartle Frere Mission to Zanzibar, 1873', *Historical Journal* (1962), 128.
[5] Marston, 429–30.   [6] Ibid., 440–1.

by 67 per cent from 21,000 in 1870 to 35,000 in 1880. Thus it grew faster than either Port Said or Bombay in the decade after the opening of the Canal.

In 1875 Ismail began the construction of the Sudan Railway from Wadi Halfa to Shendi on 15 January, founded the Khedivial Society of Geography on 19 May and was ceded by the Porte on 1 July Zeila, the last town with a Turkish garrison on the coast of Africa as well as Abyssinia's second outlet to the sea after Massawa. He extended his empire in the south through expeditions which reached as far as the Juba River on 16 October and were planned to link up the Indian Ocean with the Great Lakes and the headwaters of the Nile. Thus Egypt expanded from the Mediterranean to the Equator over 30° of latitude and an area as great as that of Russia in Europe.[1] That expansion took place at the expense of the Moslem sultanates of the Red Sea coast, of the pagan Negro tribes of the Upper Nile and of the Christian kingdom of Ethiopia. It established Egyptian suzerainty over the African coast of the Red Sea and especially over the ports through which the coffee from Harar passed. Berbera was equipped with a lighthouse, a wharf, a mole, coal bunkers and a piped supply of water from 1876 and grew as the Aden of Egypt at the expense of Massawa, which declined in trade and population, and of the Somali ports which reduced their exports. The commerce of Equatoria nevertheless remained a dream of the future while the Sudan did not become the cotton field of Lancashire. Ismail's claim to the Mareb as his frontier, moreover, brought him into conflict with Abyssinia while his aspiration to control Zanzibar created friction with England. His acquisition of an African empire benefited Suez as a base port and expanded its entrepôt trade. It ranked Egypt as the eighth largest user of the Canal in 1871–4 while Turkey ranked as the ninth largest user: Turkey and Egypt each supplied less than 1 per cent of the total tonnage of the Canal between 1869 and 1876. The extension of the Turkish peace opened up Arabia to European travellers[2] and encouraged the revival of the scheme for a Euphrates Valley Railway in 1873. Thus the Canal was used for imperial expansion first by the powers of Asia rather than by the powers of Europe and helped to divide Africa and Asia between Egypt and Turkey.

[1] M. Sabry, *L'Empire Égyptien sous Ismail...(1863–1879)* (1933), 375–552.
[2] D. G. Hogarth, *The Penetration of Arabia* (1904), 193–7.

9

THE ENTREPÔT TRADE OF THE MEDITERRANEAN, 1870-1874

THE Canal represented a great challenge by the Mediterranean world and especially by France to the domination of economic life by England. The saving of distance which its use would accomplish was the greatest of all from the Mediterranean and amounted to 61 per cent from Trieste and 59 per cent from Marseilles of the voyage to Bombay. Such a vast saving of time and capital would, it was hoped, create an economic revolution to the benefit of the economically weaker countries against the economically stronger England. The cities of the Mediterranean would become once more the centre of the world and regain the most profitable branch of economic activity in the entrepôt trade with all its enriching ancillary traffic in unloading, pilfering, warehousing, processing, distributing and financing and its associated freight, insurance, depot, consignment and transhipment charges. England would lose in succession its commerce, its merchant marine, its maritime supremacy and finally its Indian possessions. Thus Lesseps appeared as the avenger of a hundred seaboard cities ruined by the avarice of England,[1] and was accordingly decorated on the successful completion of the Canal by the rulers of the Mediterranean states of Russia, Greece, Austria, Italy, France and Belgium, which remained a northern outpost of Latin civilization. The main client-states of the Canal after England all lay in the Mediterranean: in 1870 France, Egypt, Austria, Turkey, Italy and in 1871 France, Austria, Italy, Turkey, Egypt.

In England informed opinion was compelled to recognize the achievement of the Canal but still doubted its profitability[2] and flatly disbelieved in the prospective transfer of economic supremacy to the Mediterranean because of the massive inertia of the capital invested in one of the great trades of the world and the necessary dependence of the capacity to export on the capacity to import. Each decade since the 1830s had increased the trade of the Mediterranean but also that of the Cape route in favour of North-West Europe and of the sailing ship. A trade of over £140,000,000 engaging 4,800,000 tons of shipping could not be transferred to states which had at the most a similar trade of less than one-twelfth of the amount, occupying about one-ninth of the shipping.[3] 'During the continuance of peace, and under an equal system

---

[1] *The Spectator*, 17 February 1872, 198 ii.
[2] *Manchester Guardian*, 20 November 1869, 4 vi; 8 December 1869, 5 vi.
[3] *The Economist*, 4 September 1869, 1043–6, 'The Probable Traffic of the Suez Canal'. Ibid., 4 December 1869, 1427–30, 'The Suez Canal and the Eastern Trade'. Ibid., 1 January 1870, 7–8, 'The Suez Canal'.

of charges for all nations, the greater part of the trade of the Canal will be conducted by English vessels. The Southern cities, which date their decline from the discovery of the passage round the Cape of Good Hope, will find that, although the course of trade may once more pass along their coasts, its destination depends on the fertility of producers and on the capacity of consumers.'[1] The superior power of the market over geography had been proved during the Cotton Famine when British steamships established their dominance in the Egyptian trade.

The Franco-Prussian War removed from the field of overseas expansion the greatest of the Mediterranean powers and stimulated the construction of steamships in Britain for the Suez route. It also diverted the express overland route to India from France to Italy. That shift from Marseilles to Brindisi was consolidated by the opening on 17 September 1871 of the Mont Cenis Tunnel which marked the completion of fourteen years of labour, made possible the full use of the land route through the Italian peninsula pointing south-east towards Egypt and aroused local hopes that Italy might thereby secure the monopoly of shipping to the Levant and Asia against the competition of Marseilles and Trieste on its flanks. The Mont Cenis Tunnel was first used by the Bombay mail from London of 5 January 1872 and by the China mail of 12 January. Its use avoided the break of gauge on the Summit Railway and linked Calais to Brindisi without change of vehicle over 1,390 miles and at speeds of 34–41 m.p.h. unequalled on any other railway in Italy. Its use saved 35 hours over the Marseilles route and 7 days 5 hours over the Southampton–Gibraltar route. The transfer of the express mail from the Brenner to the Mont Cenis route frustrated Nagelmackers' plan to run sleeping-cars from Ostend to Brindisi over the Brenner. The St. Gotthard Railway was begun on 1 October 1872 as Germany's reply to the Mont Cenis in order to benefit by Italy's central position in the Mediterranean, to give Germany access to that sea at Genoa and even to open an alternative route to the India mail.[2]

The Mont Cenis Railway followed on the completion of the Bombay–Calcutta Railway in 1870 and encouraged the revival of schemes for a Euphrates Valley Railway, a Salonika Railway and a Channel Ferry. The greatest beneficiary became Brindisi, where the number of British steamships arriving rose from five in 1870 to fifty-six in 1871. The P. & O. carried little or no export cargo from Brindisi, sought to prolong its voyage to Venice and replaced the Italian Adriatic and Oriental Steam Navigation Company on that route in 1872. Brindisi diverted some import trade from Venice and Trieste and increased the value of its imports by 178 per cent from £203,000 in 1870 to £564,000 in 1871.[3] Those imports mainly comprised silk and silkworms' eggs, which it had first imported in 1869 for shipment by rail to Lombardy.

---

[1] *The Times*, 31 December 1869, 6v.

[2] Ibid., 11 October 1871, 9iv–v.

[3] *Reports from Her Majesty's Consuls on the Manufactures, Commerce of their Consular Districts* (London, H.M.S.O., 1872), 442, Report by Consul Grant on the Trade and Commerce of Brindisi during the Year 1871, 28 February 1872.

Brindisi also imported hides direct from India for Naples in 1872. It imported coal in Italian sailing vessels from 1869 and in steamships from 1872. It first exported coral and straw hats made in Tuscany to Egypt in 1872, so supplying the shops of Port Said with topis and curios. Its population grew from 10,000 in 1869 to 13,755 in 1871 and to 18,000 in 1881. The crisis of 1873, however, halved the value of its exports in 1874. Its harbour could not be improved out of the high harbour dues, and its general trade could not be expanded because of its lack of a hinterland, the control of its trade, especially in olive oil, by the merchants of Naples, the proximity of Bari and the jealousy of Ancona as well as of Venice. Passengers remained the staple traffic of the port after mail: passengers for Alexandria numbered 6,625 out of 11,164 in 1872 and thenceforward formed a majority of the total using the port. For them Southern Italy became the highway it had been to the ancient Romans, and Brindisi became again 'the Gate to the East'.[1] Brindisi remained the mail port although Naples was used by passengers for Egypt and the East and the Southern Railway's main line from Bologna was completed in 1872 to Otranto, which was the nearest terminal port to Egypt but in need of extensive port works. Nor was Brindisi dethroned by Salonika to the east, despite the completion of the railway along the Vardar valley to Mitrovitza in 1874. The Calais–Brindisi–Alexandria route complemented the Suez–Bombay–Calcutta route as an achievement of the railway in combination with the steamship. Both routes confirmed the superiority of the overland route over the Suez Canal for all the passenger and mail traffic which could bear the cost of long-distance transport by land and of repeated transhipment.

The German defeat of France confirmed the triumph of Prussia over Austria and of Hamburg over Trieste. That victory stimulated the great economic boom of 1869–73 in Central Europe and the industrialization of Germany. The associated expansion of the railway and steamship network increased the activity of the ports of the Adriatic at the expense of the ports of France. The Adriatic opened a low-cost waterway deep into Central Europe and became the main focus of schemes intended to profit by the new outlet given to the Mediterranean and capture the great prize of the entrepôt trade through the improvement of harbours, the construction of railways and the provision of through-route facilities linking up with the Canal. Thus the Adriatic benefited most by the shortening of the voyage to the East and responded more fully than either the western or eastern basins of the Mediterranean proper to the opening of the Canal because Spain was prostrated by the civil war of 1868–74 while Genoa concentrated on its American trade. The great railway boom in Austria even encouraged a proposal in 1869 for a railway from the Danube to the Adriatic. The two seaports at the head of the Adriatic had become rivals more than ever since the transfer of Venice to Italy. Venice the rich had seemed decadent to Gautier in 1842 as well as to Twain in 1867 and less predestined than either Marseilles, Genoa or Trieste to profit from the opening

[1] *The Times*, 19 November 1875, 8i.

of the Canal.[1] Venice benefited, however, by the Italo-Prussian alliance of 1866 at the expense of Austrian Trieste, by its liberation from subordination to Trieste, by its historic commercial connexions with Germany and by the economic expansion of Germany and Austria during the cyclical boom of 1869–73. Its merchant community displayed unexpected energy in their efforts to make Venice the great entrepôt for Indian traffic via the Canal, Europe's key port of access to the Suez route and thereby once more the unrivalled emporium of Eastern trade and traffic as it had been before the full development of the Cape route. Venice began to construct a new harbour basin in 1869 to eliminate the use of lighters and regained its 1847 level of population in 1870–2. Its renaissance inspired the rediscovery in 1871 of an early Venetian proposal of 1504 for an isthmian canal in reply to the voyage of da Gama.[2]

Venice benefited especially by the establishment of a regular steamship service to Egypt from 20 July 1872 under the Convention of 14 April 1872 with the P. & O. and the renewal of the old relation between the two cities of St. Mark. That subsidized service to Egypt eliminated the competition of Ancona, which had ceased to be a free port in 1869 and suffered from the abrupt halt to the improvement of its harbour. It enabled Venice to profit more from the overland route than from the Canal route, to gain some passenger traffic for Egypt and to import gums, coffee and hides from the Red Sea as well as silk and spices from the East. Venice increased its imports by the P. & O. from India, China, Japan and Egypt in 1872 and 1873 beyond the most sanguine expectations. The P. & O. considered the establishment of a new harbour at Venice[3] and launched in 1873 the *Venetia*, the *Lombardy* and the *Adria*. From January 1873 it had to place auxiliary steamers in service to carry the accumulation of goods at Alexandria awaiting shipment to Venice for Germany and Switzerland. Venice also imported rice via the Canal from Rangoon and Akyab in 1872. It was reached on 3 January 1873 by the s.s. *Jeddah* with pepper, coffee, cinnamon, coconut oil and bar-lead direct from Singapore, so linking the modern and medieval entrepôts of the Eastern trade. It imported coal direct from England in fifteen steamers in 1873 and survived the abolition on 31 December 1873 of its free port. In 1874 it established a Chair of Japanese at the suggestion of the Italian ambassador to Japan. It responded more effectively to the opening of the Canal than its old rival, Genoa, or its new rival, Trieste. In 1876 it secured the reduction of freights by the P. & O. and established free warehouses. It lacked, however, bulk exports or control over its own trade to the East. Its shipbuilding industry had declined since 1869. It established no shipping line of its own to the East

[1] V. von Kalchberg, *Der Suez-Canal und die Zukunft des Directen Oesterreichisch-Ostindischen Handels* (Wien, Gerold, 1870), 7. C. Taglioni, *Deux Mois en Égypte. Journal d'un Invité du Khédive* (Paris, Amyot, 1870), 253.

[2] R. Fulin, ' Il Canale di Suez e la Republica di Venezia (1504)', *Archivio Veneto*, tomo ii, Anno I, 14 Giugno 1871, 175–99.

[3] *The Times*, 15 April 1872, 7 i.

before 1903, unlike Barcelona, Genoa, Marseilles or Odessa, and remained dependent for its Eastern trade on the alien line of the P. & O., which was bound to the port only by subsidy. The Italian flag was raised from the sixth client-flag of the Canal in 1870 to the fourth in 1871 by the enterprise of Rubattino of Genoa rather than by that of Venice. Italian trade with the East was, moreover, carried on mainly through the Canal of Constantinople and the ports of the Black Sea. Italian enterprise via the Canal was represented less by merchants than by the astronomer Respighi en route to view the solar eclipse of 12 December 1871 from Ceylon, the naturalist Beccari en route to New Guinea in 1871 and Nino Bixio, the Genoese hero of the Risorgimento, who sailed to the East to open new channels for Italian trade and died at Achin in 1873.

Trieste was stimulated by the competition of Venice for the German trade as well as of Odessa for the Russian trade[1] and by the prospect of saving a greater proportion of the journey via the Cape to Bombay by the use of the Canal than Marseilles. Trieste had its own shipping company, unlike Venice, in the Austrian Lloyd which was the oldest steamship company in the Mediterranean and began a line to Bombay in 1870. The *Apis* was the first toll-paying Austrian steamer to use the Canal on 5–6 February 1870. It carried only 130 tons of cargo, of which half came from Venice. It reached Bombay in 25 days (31 January–24 February) and returned to Trieste in another 25 days (10 March–3 April) with 4,200 bales of cotton and 25 bales of hides which were sold in the local market on 7 April. It was followed by the *Sphinx* which passed southwards through the Canal on 14 March to return with more cotton from Bombay. Trieste was also the base for the departure on 1 January 1870 of a Swiss-Austrian mercantile venture to Zanzibar in the tiny schooner *Marietta*. The Austrian Lloyd was harassed by the lack of export cargo and even briefly extended its service to London in 1870. It also began a second line from Port Said to Trieste to carry cargo transhipped from other vessels using the Canal. It did not build warehouses in Port Said, although it carried musicians from Bohemia to its cafés. Triestine capital preferred the profits of Egyptian finance to those of Egyptian commerce and benefited by the wartime eclipse of France to expand the financial interests of Austria in Egypt. The mail contract of 1871 enabled the Austrian Lloyd to double its Canal tonnage in 1871 and raised Austria from the fourth client of the Canal to the third after Britain and France. Under the new contract it gained a subsidy of £19,000 plus the refund of Canal dues in return for the despatch of twelve steamers per annum to Bombay. Thus Austria began the refund of Canal dues as a concealed subsidy and set the example followed by Italy, Russia and other protectionist states. Hungary refused to share in the payment of that subsidy, despite the change of the company's name in 1872 to that of the Austro-Hungarian Lloyd. It aspired to develop its own national harbour in Fiume and secured the extension of the railway to that port in 1873.

[1] *The Times*, 10 July 1867, 5 iii.

Trieste benefited by its earlier import of cotton via the overland route and imported 40 per cent more cotton than Venice from Bombay in 1872. It also imported coffee from Ceylon from 1870 as well as mother of pearl from the Red Sea. It preserved its free port for seven years longer than Venice but remained cut off from its hinterland by a great mountain barrier and wholly dependent on the Südbahn to Vienna. It could only develop its trade by a great reduction in German railway freights, the building of warehouses and the establishment of an East Asiatic Company.[1] Its rulers remained dominated by the territorial tradition of Vienna while its Italian population became a seed-bed of irredentist sentiment after the Italian entry into Rome. Its seafaring population was almost exclusively Dalmatian, recruited especially from the island of Lussin off the approaches to the Gulf of Fiume. Thus the city remained an epitome of the Habsburg Monarchy wherein the German élite used the subject Italians and Dalmatians to maintain its own dominion as well as the status of the monarchy as a great power.[2] 'Never was a maritime city less maritime.'[3] The hinterland of Trieste beyond two hours' walk was supplied from Hamburg with coffee and sugar even in 1875. After Austria was surpassed by the Netherlands in 1874 as the third client of the Canal the Südbahn reduced its railway rates and so encouraged two coffee importers from Mannheim to establish themselves in Trieste and import coffee to markets as far north as Bohemia by 1876. The Austrian Lloyd benefited by the completion in 1876 of the four breakwaters of the free harbour begun in 1867 to the north of the old city. That harbour remained wholly under the control of the Südbahn as well as open to the fury of the prevailing bora. The Austrian Lloyd supplied the overwhelming bulk of the Austrian vessels using the Canal and furnished the fourth largest tonnage of client lines in 1876 after the P. & O., the Messageries and the Wilson Line. It proved slow to adopt innovations and did not venture to expand beyond Bombay before 1878, despite its large reserves.

Marseilles was the main port of departure for ships for the inauguration of the Canal and for the *Asie* of Fraissinet which accomplished the first return voyage from Bombay. It did not undergo the anticipated maritime revolution and become a world port because of the opening of the Canal. It was much more dependent on the Algerian than on the Eastern trade, in relation to which it was complementary to Alexandria and committed to the overland route rather than to the Canal. It had begun to lose its privileged position as the port of entry to the Continent as railways began to span the Alps in the 1860s. Its enthusiasm for the Canal had declined in its growing fear of Italian, Austrian and Greek competition.[4] It had applauded its Government's systematic obstruction of the English efforts to develop the speedier

---

[1] Kalchberg, 33–4.   [2] Ibid., 42.
[3] I. Burton, *Arabia Egypt India* (1879), 31.
[4] L. Simonin, 'Marseille et l'Avenir de son Commerce', *Journal des Économistes* (Décembre 1871), 422.

route via the Mont Cenis to Brindisi. It had returned Gambetta rather than Lesseps as its deputy in 1869. The steam tonnage entering and leaving Marseilles exceeded the sail tonnage first in 1865–7 and permanently from 1869 under the influence of the Mediterranean trade of the port rather than of its Eastern trade. The English coal imported in increasing quantities was not primarily intended for use by steamships on the Canal route. The merchants of the port aspired to develop an entrepôt trade which would add the profits of processing to those of handling and would thus be more than a mere transit trade. Unlike those of Liverpool and Amsterdam they founded no company intended specifically to profit by the opening of the Canal. Fraissinet remained an isolated pioneer harassed by the lack of outward freight.

Marseilles imported by the new route cotton from Bombay on 22 January 1870, tea from China in March and coffee from Ceylon in May. Its merchants may have been spurred into emulation by the enterprise of A. Chalès of Bordeaux and Quesnel Frères of Le Havre who began services to Calcutta via the Canal in 1873. Schloesing first imported wheat from India in 1874, making available more raw material for the manufacture of macaroni and semolina. C. A. Verminck, who had been engaged in the Senegal trade since 1844, first imported sesame through the Canal from India in 1875.[1] The import of oil-seeds direct from India, especially linseed, sesame and ground-nuts, increased from 19·3 per cent in 1869 to 30·2 per cent of the total weight of the seed imports of the port in 1876. The use of Indian oil-seeds had been restricted to the manufacture of soap by their deterioration on the journey of 5–6 months by sail but was thenceforward extended to the manufacture of pure olive oil because they arrived fresh after a journey of thirty days. Marseilles developed the import of copra while England began to draw the cheaper palm oil from West Africa. It also imported rice from Indo-China and sugar from Java, so becoming a centre of the Eastern trade in succession to Lorient. It developed an entrepôt trade in tea which it re-exported not only to England but also to its neighbours and to other Mediterranean states. Marseilles could not, however, secure a strong hold on the Eastern trade because France preferred coffee to tea and produced her own silk. It lacked the proximity to the industrial North enjoyed by Le Havre and failed to become an entrepôt for the cotton of India or for the wool of India or of Australia.[2] Its associated lack of manufactured exports hindered its efforts to develop an entrepôt trade so that it remained a port of import rather than of export, limited in its hinterland to the Rhone valley and almost wholly dependent on the subsidized Messageries and P.L.M. Marseilles lacked a rail link to Strasbourg and the Rhine and complained of the very high rail freights charged by the P.L.M., but failed to reduce its own high harbour dues at the request of the Docks Company.[3] Thus the port failed to encourage either shipping, the carrying trade or the entrepôt trade. It may well have benefited

[1] J. Pierrein, 'Marseille et le Canal de Suez', *Annales de la Faculté des Lettres d'Aix*, xxx (1956), 84–5.   [2] Ibid., 77–8.   [3] Ibid., 81.

more than any other French port from the Canal but it benefited less than other ports in the Mediterranean and much less than it had originally expected.

Marseilles was representative of all France in its failure to take full advantage of the opening of the Canal. France as a rich and prosperous nation with continental, military and agricultural traditions remained averse to maritime pursuits. Its intermediate position in Europe encouraged the carrying trade of other powers, made its commerce passive rather than active, retarded the growth of its merchant marine and inhibited a rapid conversion from sail to steam as much as did its high-cost steam shipbuilding industry. Thus its maritime commerce and shipping were given no fresh impulse by the Canal which neither opened up new markets nor benefited French ports. France continued to use the Cape route to the East and its island outposts in the Indian and Pacific Oceans. In 1875 only 34·6 per cent of the 604,616 tons of shipping between France and Asia used the Canal and over 40 per cent of that third represented foreign tonnage. Thus France paid abroad £200,000 per annum in freights, mainly to England, for the transport of cotton and oilseeds from Bombay. The Canal did not lead to any place visited by French ships and trading with France, to the U.S.A., to New Orleans or to any French colonies other than Saigon and the penal colonies of Obock and New Caledonia. French tonnage using the Canal increased in every year after its opening but not as fast as the tonnage of other powers. Thus the share of France in the traffic of the Canal fell from 10·6 per cent in 1873 below 10 per cent for the first time in 1874 and to 7·7 per cent in 1875, although France remained the second largest client of the waterway until 1890.

The eastern basin of the Mediterranean was less affected than the west by the opening of the Canal, which gave no stimulus to the shipping of Greece, Turkey or Egypt or to the trade of their ports. The Greeks, who had engrossed the commerce of the Ottoman Empire, disappointed the expectations cherished by Western observers that they would benefit more than any other community from the opening of the Canal. Their shipping remained bound to sail and to the local trades: their great idea remained the liberation of their brethren from Turkish rule and the recreation of an Orthodox Greek Empire with its capital at Constantinople. Tobruk was made a free port in 1869[1] but failed to attract shipping to its natural harbour any more than Rhodes or Suda in Crete. Suda, which was made into a Turkish naval base after the suppression of the Cretan rebellion of 1866–9, aspired to rival Malta, to eclipse Syra and to become a port of call as well as an entrepôt for the Canal trade:[2] its hopes were doomed by the lack of rainfall, by the poor olive crops of 1871–3 and by the failure of the defeated Greeks to turn their economic enterprise to the support of Turkish dominion.

The ports of Syria lost much of their transit trade, especially to Bagdad, through the development of the route to the Persian Gulf via the Canal. The

---

[1] T. Bilbaut, *L'Isthme de Suez et les Intérêts Internationaux* (Douai, Crépin, 1869), 8, 24.
[2] Ibid., 24; *The Times*, 7 August 1871, 7i.

establishment of a direct Turkish line to the Gulf in British ships confirmed the Anglo-Turkish entente against Russia and created a new route encircling the great peninsula of Arabia because Turkey had thitherto used its own overland route to Bagdad and had never used the Egyptian overland route. The Suez route to the Gulf was pioneered by the *Babel* which inaugurated a service between Constantinople and Basra. The *Babel* had been built in 1866 as the *Mataura*, the fourth and largest steamship of the short-lived Panama New Zealand and Australian Royal Mail Company (1866–9). It passed through the Canal in December 1869 and reached Basra by 15 January 1870, returning to Smyrna with pilgrims. That new service did not make Mesopotamia, as expected,[1] a granary for the Mediterranean as well as for Western Asia. It enabled Turkey, however, to make more effective use of its Bagdad base in order to suppress Arab risings, to extend its imperial power and to consolidate the supremacy of the Sunni élite over the Shiite masses of Mesopotamia. It ranked the Turkish flag as the fifth client flag of the Canal in 1870 and 1871. It also encouraged the formation of two companies for the London–Basra service via the Canal in 1870 and 1871, especially by Gray, Paul & Company of London. The first steamer direct from England arrived in the Gulf in June 1870. The new steam route developed to the Ottoman rather than to the Persian shore of the Gulf. Persia was severed from the Gulf and the Levant by the Zagros Mountains as it was from India by desert and mountain. It carried on the bulk of its trade by overland caravan with Russia rather than by sea with England. The main centres of trade and piracy in the Gulf remained Oman and Muscat. Oman was in closer touch with East Africa and India than with Arabia from which it was cut off by the Oman Mountains and the Empty Quarter, 'the great middle East of the Arabian Peninsula'.[2] Muscat also remained a base of pirates whose dhows attacked the ninth toll-paying transit through the Canal, the diminutive steam-tug *Rocket* of 17 tons en route to Shanghai, when it was 400 miles east of Aden.[3]

Basra was nevertheless stimulated to improve its port, to dredge away its harbour-bar and to import sugar from Europe as well as from Java. It thereafter enjoyed a boom in trade without the anticipated slump, especially in its staple exports of wool, grain and dates. The Euphrates and Tigris Steam Navigation Company of Lynch Brothers replaced its two steamers on the Tigris by new ones brought out via the Canal in 1870: it survived the competition of a Turkish steam navigation company established in 1867 and even introduced deep-draught steamships on the shallow Euphrates in 1870–2. Bagdad remained the great centre of trade for Mesopotamia and Western Persia. There small merchants, especially Jews, began in 1870 to buy through commission-agents in the markets of Europe, so shattering with the help of the Canal the monopoly of the import trade from Europe thitherto held by a

---

[1] *Le Canal de Suez*, 15–17 Janvier 1870, 28.
[2] C. M. Doughty, *Travels in Arabia Deserta* (London, Cape, 1921), ii. 524.
[3] *North China Herald*, 2 June 1870, 413, 414; 25 August 1870, 152 ii.

few leading merchants. Those small merchants created alarming competition for the great merchant houses in 1871 and glutted the Bagdad market with all sorts of European goods, forcing prices down to the very lowest remunerative level. They used the new all-water route to Bagdad in competition with the expensive overland route from the Mediterranean and so competed with the merchants of Damascus, Aleppo and Mosul as to reduce the caravan trade from Beirut to one-fifth of its size between 1869 and 1871.[1] Thus Aleppo lost its transit trade to Bagdad and Southern Persia, decreased the volume of its imports of Manchester goods by 26 per cent in 1871 and suspended the construction of the Alexandretta–Aleppo road begun in 1860. It nevertheless rapidly regained its entrepôt trade in English merchandise through the enterprise of Indian Jewish merchants under British consular protection who opened branch houses in Manchester and cut the profit-margins of the Syrian merchants there drastically from their accustomed 20 per cent. Those merchants stimulated exports from Liverpool, even including coffee, to Aleppo. Mosul ceased to import direct from Europe and became dependent on Aleppo and Bagdad for Manchester goods but developed a direct export trade to Europe via Bagdad in wool, gall-nuts, linen and mohair.

Damascus had suffered increasing competition in the 1860s from Aleppo for the trans-desert traffic to Bagdad and from the transfer of the pilgrim traffic to the sea route to Jedda so that it lost some of its trade as the last halt for provisions before the desert. Pilgrims began to travel by the new all-sea route first by the Austrian Lloyd and the Aziziya Company and then by the British India Line from 1869, Rubattino from 1870, Holt from 1871 and Ruys from 1873. By 1873 the bulk of the pilgrim traffic had shifted to the Canal from the desert route. That desert crossing also served as the best of protective barriers against the spread of disease, which travelled by the Canal route with all the speed of steam. To restrict its spread disinfection stations were established at Suez in 1870 and at the Wells of Moses in 1871, the Canal was closed to all pilgrim ships in the Hejaz epidemic of 1872 and quarantine restrictions were imposed on pilgrim ships passing through the Canal in 1875. Some vessels carried pilgrims from Bombay to Jedda and there embarked a cargo of pilgrims returning to Algiers and Tunis via the Canal. The trade of Jedda thus increased at the expense of that of Damascus. The assertion that the trade of Damascus was annihilated by the opening of the Canal and did not revive thenceforth until after 1918 would, however, be as misleading as the assertion that the trade of the Mediterranean declined after da Gama's voyage around the Cape because it would emphasize the decline of European and long-distance trade at the expense of indigenous and local trade. The 'Holy' city increased its vast local trade and retained the overland trade in necessaries to Bagdad, the provisioning of hundreds rather than of thousands of pilgrims and the eight-day dromedary post to Bagdad.

[1] *Report from the Select Committee on the Euphrates Valley Railway* (322 of 22 July 1872), 72, Q 1162–3, R. Paul.

French enterprise had expanded in Beirut during the 1860s, but was checked by the Franco-Prussian War and by the decline in the overland trade so that projects by French capitalists for the construction of a port in 1869 and 1872 did not mature. Beirut attracted Arab merchants, however, and was linked from 1873 to the Constantinople–Red Sea service of the Aziziya Company, importing coffee from Mokka in competition with that shipped from Brazil via Liverpool. It became the chief financial centre of Syria as well as 'the Schoolmistress of the Levant'.[1] To the south Jaffa was linked by telegraph to Jerusalem in 1871[2] and to Bethlehem in 1873. The cattle trade from Syria to Egypt had been largely transferred from the caravan route via Kantara to steamships from Jaffa to Alexandria in the late 1860s before the opening of the Canal completed that shift. The caravans leaving El Arish for Egypt declined after 1870, reducing the number of livestock crossing the Kantara ferry between 1870 and 1875 by 56 per cent. By 1878 the route was used only by a few camel-drivers and by fewer cattle-traders.[3] The two main routes across the isthmus of Suez and the peninsula of Sinai still continued in use for eastward travel as though the Canal did not exist, the caravan route to Damascus using the Kantara ferry and that to Mecca using the Kubri ferry on the pilgrim's road ten miles to the north of Suez. Caravans leaving Egypt for Syria and for Arabia did not decline in number.

The 6,000 Beduin of Sinai were nevertheless adversely affected by the construction of the Canal, which cut them off from their raiding lands in Africa and restricted their mobility for warfare, if not for commerce. They were affiliated to the Beduin of Palestine and Arabia rather than to the Beduin of Egypt just as their peninsula of gravel plains and sand formed a geological 'compendium of Arabia'.[4] Egypt gained such an admirable moat for defence against the Beduin that Suez allowed its walls to fall into ruins. The Beduin of North Sinai lost a source of income from acting as guides and hiring out camels through the decline of the cattle trade. The few and poor Beduin of Tor-Sinai south of Nakhl, who had thitherto lived by the sale of dates and turquoises at Cairo and by the pilgrim trade to the Sinai monastery, were virtually ruined. They could cross the Canal by a ferry or bridge of boats but were forced to pay toll and were subjected to quarantine regulations for themselves and their animals. They were further harassed by the grant to a European company of the concession for the turquoise mines and by the assimilation of the whole peninsula to an infected district by the establishment of a quarantine station at Tor in 1877.[5] It is however doubtful whether those Beduin supplied any of the Canal beggars, who besought bakshish from passing ships and were especially numerous in the narrows just south of Kantara. The Canal also separated the Beduin of Charkia from those of Katia in North

---

[1] C. M. Doughty, ii. 362.   [2] *The Times,* 22 March 1871, 12v.
[3] (Archduke Ludwig Salvator of Austria), *The Caravan Route between Egypt and Syria* (London, Chatto, 1881), viii–ix.
[4] C. M. Doughty, ii. 422.
[5] W. S. Blunt, *My Diaries* (London, Secker, 1919), ii. 145–6.

Sinai, checked the State-fostered colonization of Palestine by the Beduin of Lower Egypt and encouraged them to settle down. Thus the Canal produced harmful rather than beneficial results on the use of land by the Beduin, whose interests were sacrificed to those of the developed economies of Europe.

Russia was the most distant state of all Europe from Asia by the sea route around the Cape but the nearest by the overland caravan route across its Siberian empire to China, finding in its roads, rivers and portages in combination an excellent substitute for the transcontinental railway built by the U.S.A. The rise of Slavophile sentiment from the 1830s in reaction against the westernizing policy of Petersburg had reaffirmed the dualist tradition of Russia. Westernizers and Slavophiles were both imbued with an aristocratic feeling of superiority to such merchant nations as England and France. They thought that such nations allotted to commerce a guiding role in their foreign policy and they preferred a policy of princes to a policy of merchants. Both were dominated in their foreign policy by a single aim, the aggrandizement of Russia, and in their world outlook by a Chinese belief that the power and the glory were inseparable. The Russian response to the completion of the Canal was thus more political than economic and extended from the Baltic to the Black and Caspian Seas. From Odessa the Russian Steam Navigation Company sent special agents in July 1869 to the ports of Asia to prepare for a line to Bombay, China and Japan by the new all-sea route. In Petersburg the Russian Government granted on 11–23 October 1869 a concession for the overland telegraph to Vladivostock to the Great Northern Telegraph Company. On the Caspian Sea the fort of Krasnovodsk was established in November 1869 as a new base for expansion into Central Asia.[1] There Henry Stanley in May 1870 found General Stoletoff determined to prove himself 'the de Lesseps of Turkestan'[2] by diverting the Amu Darya, the ancient Oxus, from the Aral into the Caspian Sea. Such a feat would not only restore life to the desert steppe of Turkestan but would also extend an impregnable water-route from the Baltic to the heart of Khiva.[3] The same imperial ambition inspired a proposal in 1871 for the construction of a canal from the Caspian to the Black Sea.

Odessa had enjoyed considerable expansion during the reform decade of the 1860s, being linked by railway to Kiev from 1870. It was stimulated by the opening of the Canal to seek to displace Trieste as the southern port of import for Russia because it could thereby save 70 per cent of the voyage to Bombay or a greater proportion thereof than any other port in Europe. The first Russian toll-paying transit was made by the small sailing ship *Hermes*, which passed south to Ismailia in March 1870 and returned north in April to Port Said en route to Liverpool with cotton-seed. Odessa supplied the first

---

[1] A. P. Thornton, 'British Policy in Persia, 1858–1890', *English Historical Review* (October 1954), 559.

[2] H. M. Stanley, *My Early Travels and Adventures in Africa and Asia* (London, Low, 1895), ii. 263,

[3] *The Spectator*, 1 January 1870, 2.

Russian steamships to make use of the Canal in a two-pronged attack on the trade of Bombay and Shanghai. Those steamships were routed to India and China rather than to regions of Russian interest such as Siberia, the Persian Gulf or even the Red Sea: thus they could not make Russian produce competitive with that from Hamburg or the U.S.A. in the markets of Siberia. The *Nakhimoff*, the pioneer steamship of the Russian Steam Navigation Company, left Odessa on 26 February 1871 and found Port Said thronged with pilgrims from the Moslem tenth of Russia's population en route to Mecca. It passed through the Canal on 7–9 March and reached Bombay on 24 March, eleven days after the Treaty of London had recognized Russia's denunciation of the Black Sea clause. It carried the name of a Russian admiral and the flag of a great power into the Indian Ocean, ending the British monopoly of the eastern seas and causing more concern to the Government of India than any other single vessel using the Canal. On 1 May it returned to Odessa with 7,000 bales of cotton and 530 sacks of coffee, pepper, gum and rice. The attack on the entrepôt trade was extended from cotton to tea by the voyage of the *Tchihatchoff*, which sailed outwards through the Canal on 19–21 March 1871 to inaugurate the Shanghai line of the Russian Steam Navigation Company. Those pioneer voyages of 1871 coincided with the completion of the cable to Vladivostock, Nagasaki, Shanghai and Hong Kong and ranked Russia as the eighth client of the Canal after the Netherlands. Their results were not very encouraging because the absence of an export cargo made the outward voyage unprofitable and high-cost Russian coal had to be shipped outwards to the coaling stations en route. The company nevertheless repeated the voyages in 1872 with cargo from the Mediterranean for India and with cargo from England for China. Its increase of Russia's tea imports via the Canal from 2,000,000 pounds in 1871 to 4,000,000 pounds in 1872 caused a sharp fall in re-exports from London in 1872–3. It also transhipped such Oriental produce as tea, coffee, incense, pepper and cinnamon at Port Said for Odessa. In 1872 the Grand Duke Alexis, the third son of Alexander II, became the first European prince to pass through the Canal since its inauguration.

Russian expansion into Central Asia, especially into the khanate of Khiva, encouraged Charles Cotard, a former engineer on the Suez Canal, to plan a Central Asiatic Railway. Such a railway of 2,400 miles in length from the terminus of Orenburg to Peshawar would link the railway systems of Russia and India through Turkestan, Tashkent and Samarkand. That railway was the first great project which Lesseps is known to have taken up after the Suez Canal, to the alarm of some of his more timid shareholders. On 1 May 1873 Lesseps broached the idea to Ignatiev, the Russian ambassador at Constantinople, claiming that it would extinguish the antagonism between Russia and England as the Suez Canal had reconciled France and England. He secured Ignatiev's recognition on 5 May of the railway as 'the natural corollary of the maritime route opened by the Suez Canal'. That railway was even more chimerical than the Euphrates Valley Railway because of the Himalayas,

Anglo-Russian hostility and Russia's policy of high protection.[1] Gladstone accordingly sanctioned the visit made to India and Peshawar in March–April 1874 by Victor de Lesseps who accomplished the journey east of Suez which his father never did.

The Franco-Russian railway scheme encouraged the revival of the Euphrates Valley Railway by Jenkinson and Andrew and an outburst of English enterprise in 1873 on the Persian Gulf route to India in efforts to enter the pearl-fishing trade, the resumption of archaeological excavations at Nineveh and the State visit by the Shah of Persia to London. The Select Committee of the House of Commons, reappointed in 1872, reported on 22 July in favour of a railway between the Mediterranean and the Persian Gulf as an alternative military route at a maximum cost of £10,000,000,[2] encouraging the first suggestion for an Acre–Kuwait Railway.[3] The British India Line was also encouraged to launch the *Bagdad*, the *Assyria* and the *Chaldea* in 1872 and to make its service to the Persian Gulf weekly. In 1873 it began a London–Basra service via Aden and Karachi, so threatening Bombay's monopoly of the entrepôt trade to the Persian Gulf at the very time that Bombay lost control to Calcutta of diplomatic relations with the Gulf. Karachi completed its Manora breakwater in 1873, doubling the depth of its harbour from 10 feet in 1868 to 20 feet in 1873. Jenkinson's motion in favour of a Euphrates Valley Railway was however defeated in the Commons on 4 April 1873 by 103 votes to 29.

After the apparent revival of the Holy Alliance of 1815 in the Dreikaiserbund of 1873 an Anglo-Russian détente was brought about by the marriage in Moscow of Alfred, Duke of Edinburgh, to the only daughter of the Tsar and by the visit of the Tsar to London in 1874. That Anglo-Russian rapprochement encouraged the pioneer British voyage from Dundee to the mouth of the Yenisei,[4] the formation of Pender's Black Sea Telegraph Company in 1874 to link Constantinople to Odessa and the experimental shipment of Crimean wines to India in 1874. Lesseps was left defenceless in his conflict with the maritime powers in 1874 by that détente which culminated in the support given by Russia and England to France against Bismarck in the war-scare of May 1875 and in the proposal to play out Lord Wellesley's Great Game on a larger scale and partition Asia between England and Russia.[5]

---

[1] *Saturday Review*, 31 May 1873, 704, 'M. De Lesseps's New Project'. *Le Canal des Deux Mers*, 16 Décembre 1873, 379, 'Le Chemin de Fer Indo-Européen'.

[2] W. P. Andrew, 'The Euphrates Valley Route to India in connection with the Central Asian Question', *Journal of the Royal United Service Institution*, 23 May 1873, 472–500. *The Practical Magazine* (1873), 177–80, 'India via the Euphrates Valley'. W. B. Kerr, 'From India by the Euphrates Route', *Fraser's Magazine* (October 1874), 424–36.

[3] G. E. Dalrymple, *The Syrian Great Eastern Railway to India* (London, Skeffington, 1878), 26.

[4] J. Wiggins, '"The Northern Waterway" or New Ocean Route to Siberia', *Journal of the Society of Arts*, 3 May 1889, 535–6.

[5] W. M. Thorburn, *The Great Game; a Plea for a British Imperial Policy. By a British Subject* (London, Simpkin, 1875), 173, 209.

In 1875 Russia began to import tea via the Canal to the Baltic as well as the Black Sea and 'Canton tea' imported via the Canal competed at the Fair of Nijni-Novgorod with the brick tea transported overland.

Russia did not increase her use of the Canal route faster than other states so that in 1876 the Russian flag still ranked eighth and the Russian Steam Navigation Company ranked fourteenth among the client-lines with its eight steamships, supplying 0·8 per cent of the net tonnage. Russia remained chary of a route to the East which was subject to hostile control from the Dardanelles to the Korea Strait, unlike the North-East Passage around the inaccessible northern coast of Asia. Russia lacked export staples suitable for the East, which did not want Russian wheat, wool, hides, hemp or linseed. Odessa did not want the cotton of Bombay and failed to displace Trieste as an entrepôt for the Russian market, perhaps because the Baltic barons at Petersburg preferred German Trieste to Russian Odessa. Odessa thus remained handicapped by the high freights of the Russian Steam Navigation Company and of the South Russian Railway. It was itself no less monopolistic than its railway and steamship companies since it strove to prevent the emergence in its vicinity of any rival port such as the grain port of Nicolaieff. It was stimulated far more by the rise of the grain trade than by the opening of the Canal, for which it could supply no staples nor even develop the export of coal. After the upheavals of the decade of reforms Russia remained at rest as the populists discovered in their crusade of 1872–4 and as Turgenev described in 1876 in *Virgin Soil*. Holy Russia could not be aroused from its interminable sleep by any superficial economic change. Even the rise of the oil trade of Baku after the gusher of 1873 was directed to the home market rather than to the export market.

Sailing ships from the Mediterranean early made experimental use of the Canal and provided 238 or 4·6 per cent of the 5,236 transits made during its first 6½ years from December 1869 to 1 April 1875. Italian sailing vessels supplied the largest single contingent. They carried English coal to Suez and returned through the Canal to the Black Sea. They even sailed through the Canal to Calcutta and Rangoon with either ballast or salt from Cagliari or Trapani to return via the Cape. Usually the Italian ships were restricted to short voyages. The sailing ships averaged only one-quarter of the tonnage of the steamships which swamped them: they paid a special pilotage surcharge and reached their maximum number in 1874. They served the needs of their rivals by supplying the coaling stations developed on the overland route at Malta and Gibraltar. Those prizes won in the Anglo-French duel for the Mediterranean became more valuable from 1869 because of the British preference for coaling in a British harbour. Malta became more important to merchant shipping than ever before in its history. Valetta aspired to capture the entrepôt trade of the East and reported regularly from January 1870 on ships calling or passing en route to the Canal.[1] The Anglo-Maltese Hydraulic

---

[1] *Ocean Highways* (April 1870), 40. *The Times*, 2 March 1870, 5 iii.

Dock Company Limited was registered in London on 20 July 1869 with half of its capital subscribed in Malta. It secured an Admiralty loan, opened Edwin Clark's hydraulic dock in 1871 and paid its first dividend in 1874.[1] In 1874 Malta finally completed the extension of its harbour begun in 1863 and so benefited merchant shipping more than the Admiralty. French Creek was then handed over to the Admiralty while merchant shipping moved into the newly extended waters of the Marsa end of the Grand Harbour. Malta survived the competition of Palermo, which completed its dock between 1863 and 1876. As a bunkering port Malta increased its coal imports from Britain and made coal its most valuable single import in 1874. As a port of call it centred its life increasingly around the harbour rather than around agriculture, itself as exotic as the soil imported from Sicily. It lost its direct mail service to England via Marseilles after the express India mail was diverted to Brindisi.

Gibraltar increased rather than decreased in value to England after the opening of the Canal. Its shipping increased markedly in 1871 and it dredged its harbour in 1873. Its coal imports rose in quantity until 1889 and in value until 1890, although its harbour lacked any coaling wharfs and used uneconomical coal hulks. Gibraltar retained its cosmopolitan population, which made it an epitome of Europe, Africa and Asia, while Malta treasured its old aristocracy. Malta preserved the strategic significance which Gibraltar was losing through the decline of sail and the improvement of artillery. Gibraltar nevertheless retained its proximity to Capes Trafalgar and St. Vincent as well as the heroic tradition of its fourteen sieges, especially that of 1781. Thus it remained a symbol of British power much more than Malta, was celebrated in verse by Trench, Browning and Blunt and survived the seditious talk in Manchester of surrendering the Rock. Even at the height of their importance as ports on the Suez route Malta and Gibraltar served, however, primarily as ports of call for Mediterranean shipping which was mostly sail.

The opening of the Canal was invoked to explain the depression of 1873–5 in England although as a contributory rather than as a primary cause. 'Fourth —The opening of the Suez Canal at the end of 1869 created during 1870–3 an urgent demand for a large fleet of steam vessels adapted to the new Indian route; and what is more, so altered and twisted many of the existing modes and channels of business as to create mischief and confusion among the parties engaged in them; and these derangements have been greatly intensified by the completion since 1868 of a very complete telegraphic system between all ports of the world, not excluding China, Australia and both sides of South America.'[2] In that process of readjustment Britain lost some of its entrepôt trade through the development of direct trade to the Continent, especially in silk and tea from China, in cotton from India, and in coffee from Ceylon.

---

[1] *Stock Exchange Year Book for 1876*, 217.

[2] *Supplement to The Economist*, 11 March 1876, 2i, 'Commercial History and Review of 1875'. R. Giffen, 'The Liquidations of 1873–76' in *The Fortnightly Review* (October 1877), 510–25, does not refer at all to the Canal.

That diversion of trade may even have begun on account of London firms to foreign ports, reflecting the capacity of the merchants of London to adapt to the new channels of commerce no less than those of Hamburg and Mannheim. The development of direct trade to the Continent had, however, begun before 1869 and was not caused only by the Canal. Thus the transfer of the raw silk market from London to Lyons had begun in the 1860s with the shipment of silk by the Messageries via the overland route to Marseilles. The export of rice from Burma direct to Europe had also begun in the 1860s especially in the sailing fleet of R. C. Rickmers of Bremerhaven. The decline of the entrepôt trade also affected commodities which could not have been influenced by the Canal such as cotton from the U.S.A. and coffee from Brazil.

London retained its entrepôt trade in Indian and colonial produce except in isolated commodities. In particular it retained its entrepôt trade in wool and jute as well as in tea and coffee. It even increased its re-exports of tea to the Continent with the growth of the tea trade. Liverpool also continued until 1876 to re-export more Indian cotton to Europe than the Continent itself imported direct from India. The exceptional growth of the entrepôt trade in the 1850s and 1860s had been caused by the adoption of a policy of free trade, and could hardly have been maintained into the 1870s, even if the Canal had never been opened. The entrepôt trade continued to grow thereafter but not as fast as population or as exports in general: thus it declined only by comparison with the expansion of the home market and of home industry. The real loss of the re-export trade was suffered not by England but by Egypt with the transfer of goods from the overland route to the Canal. The witnesses who gave evidence before the Royal Commission on the Depression of Trade and Industry in 1886 rightly denied that the Suez Canal was responsible for the economic depression in reply to leading questions from Stafford Northcote and Charles Palmer.[1] London seems to have retained its entrepôt trade through the inertia of a highly developed commerce,[2] the continued use of the Cape route by bulk commodities such as wool and jute and the capacity of its merchants and brokers to adapt their functions to the new channels, the new ports and the new commodities which began to enter into world trade under the stimulus of the increased facilities for traffic, including the Canal.[3] Those merchants were powerfully supported by the use of the bill on London as an international credit instrument and by the carrying trade undertaken by English ships for foreign lands, which remained the essential basis of the entrepôt trade. Thus England retained the hinterland lacked by Brindisi and

---

[1] *Royal Commission on the Depression of Trade and Industry*, 10 February 1886, Q4284, Iddesleigh to G. Gribble; 3 March, Q7329, C. M. Palmer to W. C. Brocklehurst; 31 March, Q10,716, J. Allport to C. E. Collyer; Q10,847, Iddesleigh to A. Scholefield; 8 April, Q11,907, Q12,039, C. M. Palmer and J. P. Corry to J. Scott.

[2] A. Marshall, *Money, Credit and Commerce* (London, Macmillan, 1923), 126.

[3] M. E. Fletcher, 'Suez and Britain: an Historical Study' (Ph.D. Thesis, University of Wisconsin, 1957), 219–55. Idem, 'The Suez Canal and World Shipping, 1869–1914', *Journal of Economic History* (December 1958), 566–7.

Odessa. The pioneer conversion of its mercantile marine from sail to steam provided the steamships lacked by Marseilles and Trieste and benefited London at the expense of Liverpool. London attracted to its port the merchant firms and steamship lines of the outports, including the Glen Line from Glasgow in 1873 and the P. & O. from Southampton in 1874. The lure of the great markets and the great cargoes, which London possessed as no other port did, also attracted the new steamship lines from the Continent, the Austrian Lloyd in 1870, the Messageries in 1871, and the Russian Steam Navigation Company as well as the German Steamship Line in 1872. English merchants thus gained access to foreign lines as well as to English lines and supplied foreign lands with goods cheaper than they could otherwise have obtained them.

The relative failure of the Mediterranean ports to capture the entrepôt trade proved the unimportance of a simple geographical advantage. 'The trade of the East has thus far not been wrested from England because commercial custom and the possession of the best markets of production and consumption influence the course of navigation more effectively than a saving of a few hundred miles in a long voyage.'[1] The Mediterranean's hinterland was severely limited by the mountain barriers of the Alps and by the lack of navigable rivers comparable to the Rhine. The Mediterranean's own markets were restricted by the influence of a rural and aristocratic culture which was not governed by the market as much as that of North-West Europe, could not be transformed by a simple change in geography and restricted the supply of capital and enterprise to profit by the opening of the new route. A large-scale expansion of Mediterranean shipping might have helped to capture the entrepôt trade but was hindered by the lack of the steam shipping and of the coal which were essential to the most effective use of the new route. The four Mediterranean states of France, Austria, Italy and Spain together supplied 18·2 per cent of the Canal's tonnage in the seven years from 1869 to 1876 while Great Britain supplied 72·8 per cent. France, Austria and Italy ranked behind Britain until 1874 when the Netherlands assumed third place, leaving Austria and Italy in the fourth and fifth places and confirming the triumph of North-West Europe over the Mediterranean first achieved by Britain. When the Canal Company began to distribute its first dividends for the year 1875 they were largely supplied by the client-states of the North in homage to the achievement of France. Britain increased its share of the total Canal tonnage from 74 per cent in 1875 to 80 in 1878: France, Austria, Italy, Spain and Russia together supplied 26·4 per cent thereof in 1870, 18·3 in 1874 and 13·3 in 1878.

The prosperity of the Mediterranean had been its own creation: its decline was fostered by external influence. Although the alien steamships were a minority of the total steamships of the Mediterranean and even more so of its total shipping their advent was disastrous to the local primary producers

[1] *Saturday Review*, 31 May 1873, 704; 25 April 1874, 521; 4 December 1875, 696.

because they facilitated competition by the primary producers of rice, cotton and silk in Asia. Thus Italy's massive increase of rice imports through the Canal between 1870 and 1873[1] contributed to the decline of rice cultivation in Lombardy from its peak acreage of 1870 and reduced Italian rice exports from 1871 onward, especially to Egypt, Turkey, Greece and England. The imports of rice from Cochin-China to France decreased Italian exports thereof to France. The seven-fold increase in the value of the imports of cotton from Bombay to Naples in 1873 over 1872 helped to decrease the cultivation of cotton in Southern Italy. The increased imports of Indian sesame to Marseilles helped to decrease the cultivation of sesame in Syria for export while those of Chinese silk helped to decrease the cultivation of the silk-worm in Southern France, Northern Italy and Syria. Even the Mediterranean triad was affected. The increased import of oil-seeds from India displaced the olive in the manufacture of cooking-oil and kept the Italian production of olive-oil stationary from 1871. The increased import of wheat from India displaced Italian wheat in the manufacture of macaroni as well as ending the export of grain from Kosseir to Jedda. Only the produce of the vine remained free from the competition of ascetic Asia. The tides of commerce flowing more strongly westward than eastward thus made the Canal more of an inlet than an outlet to the Mediterranean. In self-defence Italy, which abolished the free ports of Ancona in 1869 and of Venice in 1873, pioneered from 1878 the protectionist reaction in Europe against free trade and so prevented the Mediterranean from becoming an extension of Asia in its produce and its standards of living.

[1] G. Cantoni, *Il Canale di Suez e l'Agricoltura Italiana* (Milano, Il Sole, 1876), 8.

10

THE TRADE OF THE INDIAN OCEAN, 1870-1874

THE opening of the Canal strengthened more than it weakened the Indian Empire, 'the very boldest and most successful enterprise ever tried by mortal men',[1] and enhanced the influence of England on Hindu and even on Moslem civilization.[2] It seems nevertheless to have been less important than the Mutiny in the history of India, whose developing élite continued to regard England as the centre of its culture, the focus of its interest and effort, the great model for its emulation and the sole destination of foreign travel. 'All good things, spiritual and worldly, which should be found in man, have been bestowed by the Almighty on Europe, and especially on England.'[3] The English-influenced Brahma Samaj achieved its greatest success when Keshub Chandra Sen visited England and preached in the Unitarian chapel of Russell Martineau in Westminster on 10 April 1870,[4] so becoming the first Hindu to speak from a Christian pulpit. Sen was more impressed by the shortcomings of the English than by their greatness, unlike R. M. Roy, but nevertheless returned to found the Indian Reform Association in 1870. Indians of rank were discouraged from visiting Europe by the deaths in 1870 of those loyal servants of the British, the Rajah of Kapurthala near Aden and the Rajah of Kolhapur in Florence. They were however provided with colleges for the education of their sons in the Etons of India, the first of which was opened at Rajkot in 1870 under C. E. Macnaghten.

The completion of the Canal was the greatest of three simultaneous improvements in communications. For Bombay its opening was followed by the completion of the railway to Calcutta and the cable to Suez, which were both complementary to the overland route rather than to the Canal. The inauguration of the rail link to Calcutta at Jubbulpore on 7 March 1870 by the first member of the royal family to visit India placed Bombay within seventy hours of Calcutta. It made possible the combination of rail and steam services as never before and encouraged calculations of the possibility of a voyage around the world in eighty days. Bombay aspired to become the New York of the East but did not replace Calcutta as the Indian terminus of the P. & O.,

---

[1] J. Roach, 'James Fitzjames Stephen (1829–1894)', *Journal of the Royal Asiatic Society* (1956), 12, J. F. Stephen to his wife, 13 February 1870.

[2] W. F. V. Fitzgerald, *Egypt, India and the Colonies* (London, Allen, 1870), 1.

[3] G. F. I. Graham, *The Life and Work of Syed Ahmed Khan* (1885), 185, Letter from London, 15 October 1869.

[4] S. D. Collet (ed.), *Keshub Chunder Sen's English Visit* (London, Strahan, 1871), 64. K. C. Sen, *Diary in England February 15–May 21, 1870* (Calcutta, Brahmo Tract Society, 1886).

although it was 1,500 miles nearer England than Calcutta, or one-quarter of the average passage to England of thirty-two days. The P. & O. retained separate fleets for its services to Bombay and Calcutta as it did for its home and eastern services. The completion of the railway was the complement to the Bombay mail service of 1868 and to the Brindisi–Alexandria mail service of 1870: the improvement of the overland route formed the British reply to the French achievement of the Canal.

The Red Sea cable laid in 1870 succeeded where the cable laid in 1858 had failed, in a striking demonstration of the superiority of private enterprise to State enterprise by John Pender (1816–96). Pender was a textile merchant of Glasgow and Manchester who had been a supporter of Lesseps on his visit to England in 1857 as well as a founder-director of the Atlantic Cable Company in 1856. He became chairman of the Telegraph Construction and Maintenance Company Limited formed in 1864 but retired after the successful completion of the Atlantic cable in order to devote all his energies to the Indian cable. He founded the British Indian Submarine Telegraph Company Ltd., which raised the capital denied to the Anglo-Indian Telegraph Company of 1867 and was registered on 28 January 1869 to lay a cable to Bombay. The success of the French Atlantic cable, financed from London and completed on 14 July, quickened English interest in cable companies and encouraged the formation of two more companies to complement the intended Suez–Bombay cable, the Falmouth, Gibraltar and Malta Telegraph Company Ltd. on 19 July and the British Indian Extension Telegraph Company Ltd. on 20 October, to lay a cable between Galle and Singapore.

The twenty-fifth of the forty-six vessels which sailed through the Canal in the inauguration ceremony was the cable ship *Hawk* of the British Indian Submarine Telegraph Company. The companions of 'the great Manchesterian'[1] on board included many financiers, merchants, engineers and the journalist Edward Dicey, who gained from his trip and from Hawkshaw the strongest impression of the vital importance of the Canal to England. The captain of the *Hawk* was satisfied by the Canal enough to say that he would rather take a vessel through it a hundred times than up the London river once.[2] Pender then ordered on 20 November the Red Sea section of the cable to be sent via the Canal to Suez. He also registered two more cable companies in London, the China Submarine Telegraph Company Ltd. on 11 December 1869, to lay a cable from Singapore to Hong Kong and Shanghai, and the British Australian Telegraph Company Ltd. on 3 January 1870, to lay a cable from Singapore to Batavia and Port Darwin. The eastern cable companies reached working agreement with the Anglo-Mediterranean Telegraph Company, which had laid the Malta–Alexandria deep-water cable in 1868, and with the Falmouth, Gibraltar and Malta Telegraph Company. Out of twelve cable companies with a capital of £9,000,000 established in the cable company

---

[1] T. W. Reid, *Lord Houghton*, ii. 208, Milnes to his wife, 9 November 1869.
[2] A. Russel, *Egypt: The Opening of the Great Canal* (1869), 99.

boom of 1869 six were registered for cable communication with the East with a total capital of £4,065,000. Such was the English reply to the French achievement of the Canal and the refutation of the allegations of lack of enterprise in England. 'We are expending on oceanic telegraphs in a year about as much as the canal cost all the independent shareholders in ten.'[1] Thereby English capitalists found new avenues of investment for the capital liberated by the nationalization of the telegraph companies within England in 1869. They also revealed their enterprise, energy and judgment because cables changed the conditions of trade at small expense while offering large-scale profits. For the Canal by contrast Pender anticipated a maximum tonnage of 1,000,000 for some years to come and a maximum return of only $1\frac{3}{4}$ per cent on its capital to the proprietors.[2] Those British cable companies offered the prospect of competition to the Indo-European Telegraph Company Ltd. which had been registered in London in 1868 by Siemens Brothers. That company undertook to link London with Tehran and Karachi by a land line through Germany and Russia but suffered a sharp decline in its shares by 10 February[3] after three more cable companies had been formed to link Calcutta to Singapore, Marseilles to Malta and Manila to Hong Kong.[4]

The *Great Eastern*, the *Hibernia* and the *Chiltern* carried the 3,600 miles of cable around the Cape to Bombay. The *Great Eastern* landed the cable at Bombay on 7 February and at Aden on 2 March 1870, further depressing the shares of the Indo-European Telegraph Company. The *Hawk* and the *William Cory* passed through the Canal with their portion of the Suez–Aden cable for the Gulf of Suez. The *William Cory* had been built in 1857 as an iron screw collier for the Cardiff–London service and carried 253 miles of cable: it grounded three times and stuck fast the third time[5] so that its passage required five days (8–13 March). The transit of those ships symbolized the interrelation of cable and Canal in the communications revolution of the 1870s. No cable was, however, laid through the Canal and most of the 1,460 miles of the Aden–Suez cable was laid from the south by the *Hibernia* and the *Chiltern*, which spliced its cable with that of the *William Cory* at the Daedalus Light, 350 miles south of Suez, on 22 March.[6] Bombay was successively linked to Aden from 5 March, to Suez from 22 March and to London via Marseilles from 26 March. The *Hibernia* after the completion of its task passed northwards through the Canal with the *William Cory* and the *Hawk* at the end of March in a transit which was more significant than the first passage of the *Hawk*. With a net register tonnage of 2,164 the *Hibernia* became the second

[1] *The Economist*, 22 January 1870, 97, 'The Oceanic Telegraph Monopoly'.

[2] *The Times*, 13 January 1870, 7 iv.

[3] R. Ehrenberg, *Die Unternehmungen der Brüder Siemens* (Jena, Fischer, 1906), i. 257.

[4] The Calcutta and Singapore Telegraph Company Ltd. (31 January 1870), The Marseilles, Algiers and Malta Telegraph Company Ltd. (7 February 1870), The Manila and Hong Kong Submarine Telegraph Company Ltd. (9 February 1870).

[5] J. C. Parkinson, *The Ocean Telegraph to India. A Narrative and a Diary* (Edinburgh, Blackwood, 1870), 276.

[6] Ibid. 257.

largest vessel to navigate the Canal during its first year of operation and supplied the Anchor Line, which had sold it to Pender, with useful information on the Canal's navigability. Its captain, Septimus P. Welch, returned home via the Canal after steaming out via the Cape: he thereby became the first sailor to make use of the Cape and Canal routes in combination and the first circumnavigator of Africa on his homeward journey.[1] The voyage of Captain Welch followed in the tradition of da Gama because it was in the service of communication between East and West but was obliterated from history because the eastern cable appeared a prosaic achievement in contrast to the romance of the pioneer Atlantic cable. The *Hibernia* then laid a quarter of the Malta, Gibraltar and Falmouth cable, the remainder of which was laid by the *Scanderia*, the *Edinburgh* and the *Investigator*.

The Malta–Gibraltar–Falmouth cable was completed on 14 June 1870 and therewith the construction of an all-British cable between Falmouth and Bombay. That achievement was celebrated by Pender at a soirée offered to Lesseps in London on 23 June when messages were sent from the Viceroy of India in Simla across 8,442 miles in forty minutes to the President of the United States in Washington.[2] Further messages of congratulation were sent by the Prince of Wales and by Lesseps to Ismail, through whose territory the cable passed overland from Alexandria to Suez as a complement to the overland route rather than to the Canal. After the interruption of the Indo-European line by an earth tremor on 1 July the eastern cable system was dominated by England as much as the Canal was by France. That system employed six intermediate stations and gave a new function to such coaling stations as Gibraltar, Malta, Suez and Aden. A joint committee of the directors of the seven submarine telegraph companies to India was formed in February 1871 and secured an increase in the tariff by 58 per cent from 1 April 1871. Thus the Bombay cable became the basis for the profitable extension eastwards of Pender's system in 1871. The cable was more important than the railway or the steamship because it extended overseas the internal telegraph system of India completed in 1855 and carried information rather than goods. Thereby it facilitated the centralization of information as well as action and the emergence of large-scale structures of economic and political power. The Atlantic cable made possible the withdrawal of troops from Canada: the Indian cable produced no reduction of troops in India but permitted the Government of India to end from 1871 its monthly subsidy to the dromedary mail service across the Syrian desert.[3] The cable transmitted commercial and financial information, especially market-prices, commodity-orders and news of changes in the political structures of economic life. It thereby laid the mechanical basis for the emergence of a world market. It increased the

---

[1] *Le Canal de Suez*, 1 Mai 1870, 153–4.

[2] *The Times*, 24 June 1870, 12 iii.

[3] J. G. Lorimer, *Gazetteer of the Persian Gulf* (Calcutta, Superintendent Government Printing, 1915), i. 1461.

certainty of business, permitted the reduction of commission, facilitated the
entry of small merchants into the India trade, increased the use of the telegraphic transfer in place of the bill of exchange and encouraged the rise of
tramp shipping carrying goods 'to orders' received from Europe. Although
it gave a major hostage to the Mediterranean states it facilitated substantially
the expansion of British economic power in Asia.

Bombay benefited more than any other single port by the opening of the
Canal. The influx of steamers ended the era of profitable sailing-ship freights
and even forced the Bombay and Bengal Steamship Company into liquidation
in 1871. The shift of freights down to a lower level, accompanied by great
fluctuations, encouraged the transfer of the trade of the port from sail to
steam. The local merchant houses wound up their interests in sail shipping
and relied thenceforward on the specialized services of British steamship
owners. They benefited by the arrival of vessels in ballast and foreign lines
as well as by the emergence of the tramp. In 1873 the presence of a pool of
such 'irregulars' was first noted at Bombay, carrying sesame from Bombay,
Karachi and Calcutta and coffee from Batavia and Ceylon. Bombay became
a port for the recruitment of seamen as well as of ships. Its exports rose much
faster than its imports while its trade with the Continent developed much
faster than that of Calcutta. Its merchants pressed for the abolition of export
duties, for freight reductions on the Great Indian Peninsular Railway and for
the extension of railways in an effort to enlarge the port's hinterland. They
diverted the export of skins from the Central Provinces from Calcutta by 1872
after capturing much of the import trade of Karachi and Goa by 1871. The
imports of Bombay began to include ice from Trieste as well as the staple
piece-goods from Liverpool.

The heavy fall in cotton prices in the second half of 1870 caused by the
increase in the American harvest began a long-term decline in cotton prices
and reduced the supply of Indian cotton by an estimated 300,000 bales. The
fear of a glut of American cotton retarded the departure of steamships from
England via the Canal to bring cotton from Bombay.[1] Early in 1871 Manchester decided to wind up the Cotton Supply Association founded in 1857,
a decision justified by the imports from America which first reached in 1871
the volume of 1860.[2] The liquidation of the Cotton Famine thus threatened
to deprive Bombay and the Canal of a staple trade. The Great Indian Peninsular Railway therefore granted freight reductions on cotton from 1871 in
order to encourage its export. Bombay found new markets in Northern
Europe to replace in part the shrinking demand from Liverpool. The Wilson
Line's *Orlando* reached Bombay in $30\frac{1}{2}$ days (21 December 1870–21 January
1871) from London and became the first steamer to return to Hull direct from
India. The first Norwegian vessel to use the Canal, the *St. Olaf*, passed through

[1] *Manchester Guardian*, 2 January 1871, 2 iv.
[2] W. O. Henderson, *The Lancashire Cotton Famine 1861–1865* (Manchester University
Press, 1934), 35.

(1–9 February 1871) en route from Bombay to Liverpool and was followed by the first Swedish vessel in 1872. Another new customer appeared in the Bombay market when the direct shipment of cotton began to Russia in the *Nakhimoff*, which completed the round trip from Odessa and back in 65 days (26 February–1 May 1871). Thereby the transhipment of cotton via the ports of Liverpool, Hull and Cronstadt or Petersburg, which were accessible in summer only, began to decline in favour of year-round contact between Bombay and the cotton mills of Moscow via the Canal route and the port of Odessa. That Russian line also stimulated the subsidization of the Austrian Lloyd's service to Bombay for the transport of cotton to Trieste. The decline of the Russian trade was compensated in part for England by the growth of the Spanish trade as the line from Barcelona to Bombay was extended to Liverpool. In 1872 Bombay first shipped more cotton via the Canal than via the Cape, under the stimulus of high prices at Liverpool, although steamship freights by the Canal remained higher than sail freights until 1875–6. Those high freights combined with low prices to encourage the use of the steam press for baling so as to reduce the size of bales and thereby their cost f.o.b. Indian cotton was screwed so hard that it quickly became heavy goods instead of measurement goods while American cotton continued to require ballast if it was a full cargo. To compensate for the decline in cotton exports the Bombay Chamber of Commerce pressed in 1872 for the abolition of the export duty on wheat. English steamers also began to carry cotton in untaxed space intended to increase their seaworthiness and so precipitated the Canal Company's revision of the gauge in 1872, the Constantinople Conference of 1873, the Canal crisis of 1874 and the victory of the Liverpool shipowners in the defeat of the Tonnage Measurement Bill of 1874.

The surplus of India's cotton was absorbed by the new cotton mills of Bombay, which were founded by the Parsis in imitation of the cotton-spinning companies formed by the working-classes of Lancashire in 1872–3. In the boom of 1873–4 eighteen mill companies were formed in Bombay, encouraging English-sponsored mills from 1874 and a boom in jute mills in Calcutta in 1873–5. Those spinning mills were favoured by the beginning from March 1873 of the large-scale export of yarn to the Chinese market.[1] They increased in number from eighteen in 1873 to fifty-six in 1879 and created a forest of cotton mills below Amballa Hill, making Bombay appear like Wigan and apparently contributing to the industrial supremacy of Britain in the world.[2] They created a great demand for English machinery, English steam-engines, English coal and English supervisors. They also became a school for the education of Marathi labour by Lancashire technicians. They began to compete effectively with the mills of Lancashire after rather than before the opening of the Canal. Their production precipitated Manchester's appeal in 1874 for protection against Indian competition by the reduction of India's

---

[1] S. D. Mehta, *The Cotton Mills of India 1854 to 1954* (1954), 47, 54.
[2] I. Burton, *Arabia Egypt India* (1879), 124.

import duties on cotton piece-goods and yarn[1] and the defensive formation in 1875 of the Bombay Millowners' Association. The reduction of stocks in transit was caused not only by the use of the shorter Canal route but also by the reversion of Lancashire mills from Indian to American cotton. Between 1869 and 1875 the quantity of Indian cotton at sea for Europe fell by 250,000 bales at a time when India's cotton exports averaged about one million bales, the cotton harvest of the U.S.A. averaged about four million bales and the cotton consumption of Europe had risen to 108,000 bales per week. The simultaneous reduction in the quantity of cotton goods and yarn at sea for Eastern markets from 4–5 months' to 6–8 weeks' consumption was equivalent to another 250,000 bales of cotton.[2] The tonnage of ships carrying Bombay cotton contributed a rising share to the traffic of the Canal, 9 per cent in 1873, 10 in 1874 and 13 in 1875, at the expense of that of the Cape route.[3]

The increase in shipping necessitated the extension of the capacity of the best harbour on the west coast and the improvement of its defences on the arrival of two ironclad monitors in 1871. The expansion of the Bombay Corporation from the three members of 1856 to the sixty-four, (thirty-two members being elected), of 1872 helped to make the city 'evidently quite English in feeling and I should say as loyal as Liverpool'[4] as Northbrook reassured the Queen in 1872 after the assassination of Mayo. Albert Abdullah Sassoon was inspired by the Canal to build the first wet dock on the west coast of India at Colaba between 1872 and 1875. In 1873 Bombay established the first Port Trust in Asia. Bombay maintained in economic dependence Karachi, which was 200 miles nearer to Suez and aspired to independence through the Indus Valley Railway sanctioned in 1869, a steamship service to Basra and a Euphrates Valley Railway. Bombay also retained the entrepôt trade with the Persian Gulf developed by its Parsis. The British India Line suspended its direct line from London to Basra in 1874 and began a regular monthly but peripatetic service in 1875 between Bombay and Basra in association with Lynch's river navigation service. Thenceforward the Persian Gulf remained eccentric to the main steamship route via the Canal. Bombay survived the challenge of the Canal to its Gulf trade and retained the entrepôt trade in the pearls of Bahrein for the markets of London, Paris and New York as well as in the cotton of Karachi. After the Great Indian Peninsular Railway reduced the freight charges on oil-seeds and wheat in 1875 Bombay added those commodities to the cotton it exported to the Continent. The population of the port grew by 20 per cent from 644,400 in 1872 to 773,200 in 1881 and its character remained cosmopolitan. 'It is, and will be, more and more to all

[1] A. Redford, *Manchester Merchants and Foreign Trade* (Manchester University Press, 1956), ii. 27–9.
[2] *Manchester Guardian*, 30 November 1875, 4 iii.
[3] *Le Canal de Suez*, 12 Mars 1877, 2, 'Les Cotons de Bombay et le Canal de Suez de 1872 à 1876'.
[4] B. Mallet, *Thomas George Earl of Northbrook* (London, Longmans, 1908), 62.

this part of the world what Ephesus or Alexandria were to the eastern basin of the Mediterranean in the days of the Roman Empire.'[1]

Calcutta enjoyed a much smaller saving in distance by the new route than Bombay and became eccentric in its position in relation to Europe, like Cochin-China and New South Wales. It nevertheless enjoyed access to the whole hinterland of Bengal, the most populous and productive area in all India, the home of the only well-developed network of internal navigation and the great source of indigo, jute and tea. Its trade was dominated by the keenest entrepreneurs in India who were European merchants as they were not in Bombay. It lay 150 miles from the sea and so enjoyed the security from attack via the Canal lacked by Bombay. Above all, 'Hustlefussabad'[2] was the political capital of India and the seat of a newly reorganized administration which successfully reduced Bombay to greater dependence on itself through the railway and the cable of 1870. The Government of India remained a great landlord and tax-collector rather than a merchant and thought in terms of revenue rather than of population or commerce. It survived Manchester's agitation to add merchants to the Council of India[3] and maintained closer links with London than with Liverpool or Manchester. It maintained such effective control of economic life as to evoke in protest Nairoji's drain theory of economic exploitation. Nairoji therein made England responsible for a great and continuous drain of £12,000,000 per annum from a land where the average per capita income was £2:[4] he so revived the theme of Burke and of J. S. Mill and extended Proudhon's theory of property to international relations in the conclusion, *Le commerce c'est le vol*. The Government itself began to undertake the construction of railways in India after the completion of the Bombay–Calcutta line by private enterprise. It appointed a civil engineer in September 1870 to report on harbour improvement but took no action to convert any of the nine ports surveyed on the west coast into first-class harbours. It considered favourably a proposal made on 3 May 1871 for an Indian Ship Canal between India and Ceylon as part of the new steam route to Calcutta.[5] It established in 1871 a new Department of Revenue Agriculture and Commerce but gave revenue priority over the development of agriculture and commerce.[6] The same fiscal motive inspired the establishment of the Statistical Survey of India in 1871 and the Census of India in 1872. That Government reigned without a rival after the final dissolution of the East India Company in 1872.

[1] M. E. G. Duff, 'Notes of an Indian Journey', *Contemporary Review* (May 1875), 916.
[2] A. Davidson, *Edward Lear, Landscape Painter and Nonsense Poet (1812–1888)* (London, Murray, 1938), 227.
[3] A. W. Silver, *Manchester Men and Indian Cotton 1847–1872* (Manchester University Press, 1966), 249–54.
[4] D. Nairoji, 'The Wants and Means of India' (East India Association, 27 July 1870). D. Nairoji, 'The Commerce of India', *Journal of the Society of Arts*, 17 February 1871, 239–48, 301–7.
[5] *Engineering*, 5 May 1871, 325. *The Times*, 6 May 1871, 5 iii.
[6] A. W. Silver, 279–83.

Calcutta greeted the opening of the Canal with satisfaction and hoped that the Indian Navy promised to Mayo would be sent out by that route[1] before it abandoned the idea of such a resurrection. The Hooghly must have been first reached by the *Godavéry* of the Messageries which scraped over the Serapeum ridge after the inauguration. The *Godavéry* left Calcutta again for Marseilles with indigo, raw silk, shawls and silks on 11 January 1870, the day when the Viceroy wrote a letter of congratulations to Lesseps. The *India* of the British India Line which sailed on 24 January became the second vessel to leave Calcutta for the Canal: built in 1862 it returned home for new boilers and compound engines. It carried 400 chests of Jorehaut tea in accordance with instructions from London of 5 January[2] and became the first ship to reach London with Indian produce via the Canal, arriving in 48 days (24 January–13 March) from Calcutta. Calcutta was also the destination of the first English ship advertised for the new route, on 20 October 1869, and of ten of the ninety-eight vessels which navigated the Canal during its first six months. The *Blue Cross* of Thomas & William Smith of London became the pioneer of the first British line to use the Canal on 1–4 January 1870 and was followed by the *Waverley* of D. R. MacGregor of Leith. From Liverpool Holt sent the *Cleator* through the Canal on 9–10 January. T. & J. Harrison also began a steamship service to Calcutta in competition with Hull with the chartered *Cordova* which left Suez on 3 March and reached Calcutta in 51 days (6 February–29 March) from Liverpool. The *Volante* of Hornstedt and Garthorne represented Hull's first venture into the Eastern trade. It sailed from Hull on 14 February with 4,000 bales of Manchester goods, or less than the cargo of the *Cordova*, and passed through the Canal on 10 March, followed by the *Odessa* (15–20 March) of C. M. Norwood of Hull. The pioneer steamer of Rathbone Brothers' Star Line, the *Sirius*, reached Calcutta via the Cape by 9 May but returned to Liverpool via the Canal. Thus more ships sailed to Bombay while more lines were established to Calcutta. Calcutta exported through the Canal from 1870 expensive commodities which could bear the high steamer freights such as tea, indigo, raw silk, sesame and safflower. It even shipped jute via the Canal to Dundee, where two steamships arrived during November 1870, and indigo via the Canal and England to the U.S.A. Its imports did not fall in price except for ale, the price of which was sharply reduced by the appearance of new English exporters. Bengal also began to import salt from Massawa and Aden as well as from England and France.

From July 1870 British shipowners began to test the capacity of the Suez route from end to end. Their experiments established the full value of the route in August 1870 as the value of the Canal itself had been proved in March 1870. Calcutta was reached by the *Russia* in 48 days (8 June–25 July) and then by the *Arcturus* in 35 days (21 July–24 August),[3] so revealing the

---

[1] *The Times*, 17 January 1870, 9 iii.

[2] H. A. Antrobus, *A History of the Jorehaut Tea Company Limited 1859–1946* (London, Tea and Rubber Mail, 1948), 74.   [3] *The Times*, 6 September 1870, 4 ii.

full value of the Canal and beginning its use by the Star Line of Rathbone Brothers. The success of that voyage encouraged competitive emulation by other shipowners on the route to Colombo, Calcutta and Rangoon. The *Olga* of Norwood's Red Cross Line returned from Calcutta to London in 42 days (28 July–10 September).[1] The *Historian* of T. &. J. Harrison completed a fast outward voyage to Colombo in 27 days (31 August–27 September) although it reached Calcutta only in 42 days on 11 October. Those voyages firmly established Calcutta's interest in the Canal for a fast voyage to England.[2] They proved the value of the compound engine, encouraged the projection of more lines to Calcutta and stimulated the ordering of steamships on the Clyde. Experimental voyages were made via the Canal from September by ships of 1,500 register tons after the depth had reached 22 feet throughout so as to enable bigger ships to compete better with sailing vessels and with the Egyptian Railways. Thus the average tonnage of vessels using the Canal rose from 660 in February to 1,100 in September 1870.

The *Glengyle* of McGregor Gow & Co., which left Liverpool on 1 November 1870, made its maiden voyage to Calcutta, like the *Cleator*, before entering the China trade. During 1871 steamship lines via the Canal to Calcutta were begun by George Smith & Sons of Glasgow, Charles Palmer of Newcastle, Robert Alexander of Liverpool and Frederick Green of London. The *City of Brussels* which passed through the Canal on 16–17 December 1870 began the City Line from Liverpool to Calcutta for the tea and jute trade of George Smith. The *Holland* of the National Steamship Company established by Charles Palmer in 1867, reached Calcutta in 33 days (31 July–2 September)[3] including 2 days 5 hours in the Canal: it thereby broke the record of the *Arcturus* and established the National Line. The *Rydal Hall* was Robert Alexander's first steamer: it passed through the Canal on 20–21 September, reached Calcutta in 39 days (6 September–14 October) and so began the Hall Line. The *Viceroy* was the first of a new steamship line for F. Green & Co. of Blackwall:[4] it took no risks and arrived at Calcutta in 51 days (27 September–16 November) instead of the expected 34 days. The Blackwall Line began to earn preferential insurance premiums, like the City Line, the P. & O. and Holt.[5] All those sailing shipowners began to change over to steam and established steamship services through the Canal to Calcutta in competition with the sailing ships of Liverpool, cutting outward freights to the minimum and finding their profit in the homeward freights. Two other lines were begun to Calcutta in 1871 by the Queen Line from Liverpool and by Quesnel Frères of Le Havre. Further regular lines were begun in 1872 by the Red Cross Line, the Lloyd Italiano and Apcar & Co. In 1873 Carlyle's Ducal Line was begun

[1] *The Times*, 14 September 1870, 7 i.
[2] Ibid., 11 October 1870, 4 iv–v, 'The Suez Canal'.
[3] Ibid., 12 August 1871, 10 ii; 5 September 4 vi.
[4] Ibid., 28 September 1871, 3 i.
[5] F. Martin, *The History of Lloyd's and of Marine Insurance in Great Britain* (London, Macmillan, 1876), 382.

under the management of MacDiarmid, Greenshields & Co. and came into association with Green's Blackwall Line. Thus Calcutta was linked to the main ocean steam routes and added first-class British lines to the service of the P. & O. It compelled Bombay to fight for its trade and left it with the tramps and the foreign lines.

The P. & O. faced the greatest crisis in its history, like the Cunard Company in the 1870s. It was taken wholly by surprise by the success of the Canal and was quite unready to face a sudden, serious and sustained challenge to its monopoly from England as well as from France. Its weekly mailboat was faced by the competition of 280,000 tons of English shipping, which was placed on the new route in 1870 and 1871 and provided 2–3 commercial departures daily from England for the East. The compound engine reduced costs and freights, so extending competition to the cargo-trade. Silk freight rates fell by 65 per cent in 1870 and 1871. Specie was carried to the East by its Canal-using rivals at ¼ per cent from London and ⅓ per cent from Liverpool against the 1½ per cent charged by the P. & O. The passenger trade, especially the more democratic traffic, was diverted to other vessels and lines charging as little as £15.[1] The P. & O. was compelled in 1871 to end the privilege of 'free drinks', which had kept fares some 15 per cent above their economic level, and to slash its fares again by 20 per cent in March 1871, forcing the Messageries to follow suit in April 1871. It was seriously hampered in any attempt to make use of the Canal by its commitment to the overland route and by its extensive investment in separate fleets as well as in shore establishments in Egypt. Its mail contract which gave it so much prestige stipulated for the use of the Egyptian Railway and precluded the use of the Canal. The G.P.O. was determined to reduce the P. & O.'s subsidy in the general downward revision made possible by the development of the compound engine and refused to revise the mail contract without a reduction in its subsidy by £50,000. The use of the Canal would also add 120 miles, or 12 hours' steaming, to the sea-voyage and might expose the mail-boat to the possibility of a hold-up. The P. & O. paid a high price during the boom of 1868–72 for its lack of faith and foresight. Its receipts declined by £150,000 per annum from £2,549,000 in 1868 to £2,092,000 in 1871 as its monopoly profits were eliminated. Its reserves were low, unlike those of the Messageries. It was also forced to depreciate its existing fleet faster than it had intended. In order to adapt to the new competition the P. & O. sold off its older and smaller vessels. It built larger, cheaper and faster steamers.[2] It adopted the compound engine from 1870 to cut coal consumption by a half and to increase cargo space in proportion. It compounded the engines of the older vessels it retained and increased its boiler-pressures from 1871. It contemplated the adoption of the new route to India from 1871 when it built its first steamer designed for passage through the Canal in the *Khedive* and first used the Canal from October 1871 for its

---

[1] *The Times*, 14 December 1871, 4 iii, 'Cheap Travelling'.
[2] Ibid., 7 December 1870, 7 iv; 8 December 1871, 6 v.

steamer to China. Thomas Sutherland, who had been Assistant Manager since 1868, became Managing Director in 1872 and presided over its rebirth.[1] He had served in the ports of China between 1860 and 1866 and so was able to compete with Holt. The P. & O. brought the first of the new season's teas to London in July 1872 and began to use the Canal from September for its weekly mailboat to Bombay. In 1872 it also began its Italian Mail Service to Venice and experienced a rise in its revenues from their low-point of 1871. During the Coal Famine it began the large-scale use of Australian coal from 1872 and of Japanese coal from 1873. It also lengthened its vessels from 1873 to increase their cargo space and reduce their draught for the Canal. In 1873 it launched eleven new screw steamers in addition to the seven launched in the two preceding years. It was thus able to maintain the payment of high dividends until 1875.

The most valuable produce of Bengal was diverted from the Cape route by the growth of British steam shipping to Calcutta. During 1871 Calcutta increased the volume of its produce shipments through the Canal by 150 per cent over the level of 1870 and exported more cowhides, calfskins, indigo and tea via the Canal than via the Cape to Britain.[2] Thenceforward Calcutta increased its shipments via the Canal in every year until 1875 while decreasing its shipments via the Cape in 1872, 1873 and 1874. From 1872 it exported more poppyseed via the Canal than via the Cape, followed from 1873 by the majority of its shipments of ginger and shellac.[2] It even used the overland route through Egypt to carry hides, oil-seeds and cotton in 1872 as well as jute in 1873. From 1874 Calcutta shipped more cotton, linseed and rapeseed via the Canal than via the Cape, followed by the majority of its shipments of lac dye and turmeric from 1875 and of rice and wheat from 1876.[2] The abolition of export duties on wheat from 1873 and on oil-seeds and hides and skins from 1875 benefited Calcutta more than Bombay. Calcutta enjoyed a greater freedom of choice between the Canal and Cape routes than Bombay. Its greatly increased exports of jute from 1872 were shipped at low freights via the Cape. The jute clippers carried coal out to Bengal and reduced the time for their outward voyage to 80 days in 1873 and to 79 days in 1876. During 1875 69 per cent of the produce shipments to London were carried via the Cape while 30·92 per cent used the Canal:[2] the latter third was the more valuable part of the trade.

Indian wheat, which was unknown in Europe before 1870, became the object of a new trade after the opening of the Canal. The use of the Canal avoided the long voyage around the Cape and the double passage of the wheat through the tropics with its associated liability to ferment, to be consumed by weevil and to suffer a loss of up to 50 per cent during the five months at sea. After the Bombay Chamber of Commerce petitioned in 1872 for the

---

[1] *The Times*, 7 December 1872, 6 iii; 5 December 1873, 6 iii.

[2] *British Trade Journal*, 1 August 1883, Supplement, 'Produce Shipments from Calcutta to Great Britain for Thirteen Years, 1870 to 1882—Since Opening of Suez Canal'.

removal of the small export duty imposed in 1871 Northbrook removed the duty from 4 January 1873, producing a sharp rise in exports. Northbrook pleaded the need for railways as a protection against famine but refused to prohibit the export of grain during the Bengal famine of 1874. Wheat exports rose from 78,208 cwt. in 1869–70 to 394,010 cwt. in 1872–3 and to 2,498,185 cwt. in 1875–6, of which Britain imported 83 per cent. India's share in the total wheat imports of Britain rose from 2·1 per cent in 1874 and 1875 to 6·3 per cent in 1876. Indian wheat was also shipped to Marseilles from 1874 in 25 days via the Canal and supplied 7·6 per cent of French wheat imports in 1876. Bombay benefited by railway freight reductions from 1875 on the new export. Calcutta first exported wheat in 1876 and ranked first among Indian wheat-exporting ports from 1875–6 until 1880–1. It benefited by its links through the East India Railway with Delhi, Lahore and the United Provinces of Agra and Oudh in the Ganges valley. It nevertheless shipped one-third of its wheat via the Cape in 1876. Cereals replaced textile fibres by 1877 as the major northbound commodity in the traffic of the Canal, re-inforcing India's dominant position therein. The share of cotton in the volume of northbound cargo fell from 64 per cent in January–March 1872 to 18 per cent in January–March 1877: the share of wheat rose to 14·5 per cent and that of rice to 11·5 per cent.[1] India's export of wheat remained small and highly elastic, unlike that of the staple exporters of America.

Calcutta remained the pivot of the trade of Burma while its shipping also carried the produce of Madras and Ceylon. Rangoon was reached through the Canal by sailing ships which returned laden via the Cape. It was drawn into the orbit of long-distance steam shipping when the *Carolina* left Rangoon on 2 August 1870 for London via the Canal and the *Pei-ho* reached Rangoon in 40 days (19 August–27 September) from Glasgow.[2] Thus Patrick Henderson & Co. of Glasgow maintained the British-Burmese Line which they had founded with sailing ships in 1856. In 1871 they began a regular steamship service to Rangoon with the *Tenasserim* which passed through the Canal on 3–4 September 1871. William Thomson & Co. of Leith in cooperation with Henderson sent their first steamer, the *Benledi*, out with coal to Rangoon via the Cape and brought it back via the Canal (1–7 November 1871) with tea and rice to Liverpool. Burma thus first shipped rice by steamer to Europe in 1871. Its rice shipments via the Canal rose ten-fold in volume during 1872 when Henderson placed six steamers in regular service and made the trade thence-forward an 'established fact'. The bulk of the rice of Burma, however, con-tinued to use the Cape route, like the jute of Bengal. Ceylon gained an importance on the Suez route which it had never enjoyed on the Cape route. It benefited by the passage of shipping to Calcutta and Singapore and became a junction and coaling-point, like Aden. It also experienced a great expansion in its production and exports of coffee. Its first shipment of coffee via the

---

[1] *Le Canal de Suez*, 12 Mai 1872, 2; 2 Décembre 1877, 4.
[2] *The Times*, 20 August 1870, 11 ii ('*Petrio*'); 4 October 1870, 5 i.

Canal reached London on 8 July 1870 and was followed by the direct shipment of coffee to Trieste in 1870 as well as to Hamburg and Genoa in 1871. The pressure of a buoyant postwar demand in Central Europe on an inelastic supply maintained the rise in coffee prices between 1871 and 1875, despite massive shipments by the Canal. In Ceylon Galle lost ground because of its distance from the plantation hinterland. It lost the projected Singapore cable to Madras, through Mayo's decision, and ceased to be the cable terminus of Asia which it had been since 1858. It also lost the planned new harbour to Colombo, on Sir William Gregory's recommendation,[1] despite the support of the P. & O.

In defiance of the expectations of sailing shipowners in the Indian trade, the Canal brought many screw steamers into the Indian Ocean and ended the monopoly of the trade held by the East Indiamen. The Canal also ended the British monopoly of the Indian trade by enabling Mediterranean states to import direct from India. Austria and Italy developed a new steam-borne trade from India which had never been carried by sail around the Cape. The British share in the total value of India's foreign trade consequently fell from 66·3 per cent in 1868 to 59·6 per cent in 1876 while the entrepôt trade of London in cotton from India declined. Britain's trade nevertheless increased in absolute terms and its competitors reinforced rather than shattered its economic supremacy. They imported far more than they exported through the Canal and were therefore compelled either to export bullion to India or goods acceptable to England, which alone provided the manufactured textiles and iron acceptable to India. Thus India's increased exports to the Continent attracted foreign shipping to London and made India more rather than less dependent on Britain. The entrepôts of London and Calcutta established their supremacy over those of Trieste and Bombay. Britain benefited more than any other power by the opening of the Canal because she was the greatest maritime power in the world and the effective sovereign of the seas with the biggest navy and merchant marine. She was the pioneer of the steamship and of the tramp, the great builder of steamships for shipowners at home as well as abroad and the carrier of the world. She became the base for the reconstruction and repair of ships and steamers in the local trade of India as well as the home thenceforward of India's reserve shipping tonnage. She remained also the greatest trading power in the world, the main exporter of coal and of manufactures, the largest exporter to Asia and to India, the sole source of the piece-goods favoured by India, China and Japan, the greatest creditor of India and the centre of the cable system of the East. British shipping lines to Calcutta consolidated their supremacy by forming the Calcutta Conference in 1875 and introducing in 1877 the deferred rebate on the shipment of Manchester goods to Calcutta.

Britain was also the greatest colonial power in the world, the unchallenged

---

[1] L. A. Mills, *Ceylon under British Rule 1795–1932* (Oxford University Press, 1933), 245 note. *Papers Relating to Her Majesty's Colonial Possessions Part II—1873* (C.709-I of 1873), 6–7, W. Gregory, Ceylon, 3 August 1872.

ruler of India and the only state with established coaling stations on the new route to the Indies. The use of the Canal reduced the cost of troop transport per head by almost 25 per cent between the 1870–1 and the 1875–6 trooping seasons, saving £238,000 per annum to the Government and peasant of India.[1] The improved communications between England and India also facilitated the education at 'home' of the children of Anglo-Indian families.[2] Proposals were even made for the colonization of the hills by retired English soldiers to maintain law and order in the plains, so reversing the traditional relationship of hill and valley societies in India. Britain thus dominated India which dominated the traffic of the Canal by virtue of its geographical position, the fertility of its soil as well as of its population and the neo-mercantilist policies of its rulers. Indian trade and British steam shipping became the key to the economic history of the Canal for the next fifty years. By 1875–6 the share of steamships in the total tonnage of India's maritime trade had risen to 41 per cent while the steam tonnage via the Canal entering and leaving the ports of India had risen to 26·5 per cent of the total tonnage both steam and sail of those ports. By 1875–6 the Canal carried 50·2 per cent of the total value of India's trade (36·9 per cent of her merchandise exports but 69 per cent of her merchandise imports, including treasure) and 72·2 per cent of the total value of India's trade with Europe and Egypt (59·7 per cent of her exports thereto but 84·8 per cent of her imports therefrom).[3] Thus far more of India's imports than of her exports used the Canal. The southbound traffic of the Canal was governed by India's demand for imports, which in turn depended on the harvest. Thus the prosperity of the Canal Company became closely linked to the fortunes of the Indian harvest.

England's cultural domination of India was unrivalled by that of any other power but discouraged the English understanding of India. Improved communications reduced the supply of Eurasians,[4] the bridge between the English and Indian worlds, and separated those worlds more sharply from each other. Thus Maine seems to have identified India with Nature and Europe with Reason after his seven years of service in India. 'Except the blind forces of Nature, nothing moves in this world which is not Greek in its origin...It is this principle of progress that we Englishmen are communicating to India.'[5] Such cultural supremacy encouraged educated Indians to accept the English view of the Canal, a view which changed with the increasing British use of the new highway. What had been regarded at first as a nefarious device of French policy and recognized only reluctantly as 'a decided engineering

---

[1] Hansard, *Commons Debates*, 27 July 1883, 797, J. K. Cross.
[2] W. S. Lindsay, *History of Merchant Shipping* (London, Low, 1876), iv. 445 note.
[3] *Le Canal de Suez*, 12 Juillet 1883, 897–8, 'Le Commerce de l'Inde et le Canal de Suez'.
[4] *The Times*, 28 May 1872, 12i.
[5] H. S. Maine, *The Effects of Observation of India on Modern European Thought* (The Rede Lecture, 22 May 1875), (London, Murray, 1875), 38. A. V. Dicey, 'The Influence of India on English Opinion', *The Nation*, 3 February 1876, 82–3.

triumph in an age abounding in kindred triumphs'[1] became a growing channel for trade between England and India. The Canal became far more important for trade than for passengers because emigrants were not attracted to the populous East. The overland route also continued in use until 1888 especially by the wealthy and the famous while the young and the unknown travelled via the Canal. The overland route was also extended by combining the Alexandria–Cairo–Ismailia rail journey with the Ismailia–Suez voyage. The Viceroy-elect Northbrook visited the residence of Lesseps at Ismailia by that route and then proceeded via the Canal to Suez.[2] Northbrook's invitation to visit India enabled Edward Lear to 'purSuez eastern journey farther'[3] and to produce one of the earliest water-colours of the Canal after those painted at the inauguration.[4] The Canal was also used by travellers returning westabout from a voyage around the world, one of the first of whom saw nothing in 1874 but desolate sands.[5] For India the Canal became especially important from 1871 as part of the military highway from England. The British troops appreciated the elimination of the discomfort and inconvenience of the overland route and gave Lesseps three cheers from the deck of the *Malabar* as they passed him on 8 April 1875 on horseback at Lake Timsah.[6] The Canal made Egypt more than ever 'the half-way station between Southampton and Bombay'[7] and became to the Anglo-Indian the visible dividing-line between England and India:

> Just purge from your mind every English-formed notion
> Of Ind, ere you get to the Indian Ocean....
> Et caet'ra, et caet'ra—all rank fal-the-lal, sir:
> Just drop such ideas in the Suez Canal, sir![8]

The toll dispute of 1873–4 emphasized the new importance to England of 'the key of the passage between the East and West'.[9] 'The greatest enterprise of the present age'[10] remained, however, a symbol of human achievement rather than a specific British interest, 'the great new river which M. Lesseps has taught to flow through that dreary wilderness—a luxurious highway for all nations... vulgarly termed the Great Ditch'.[11] The spectacle of the P. & O.'s

---

[1] E. M. Martin, *Round the World* (London, Remington, 1883), 20, 1871.

[2] *The Times*, 10 April 1872, 12 iii.

[3] A. Davidson, *Edward Lear* (1938), 222.

[4] R. Murphy (ed.), *Edward Lear's Indian Journal* (London, Jarrolds, 1953), 37, 3 November 1873.

[5] T. W. Hinchliff, *Over the Sea and Far Away being a Narrative of Wanderings Round the World* (London, Longmans, 1876), 414–15.

[6] L. Bridier, *Une Famille Française. Les De Lesseps* (Paris, Fontemoing, 1900), 401.

[7] Hansard, *Commons Debates*, April 1873, 455, E. B. Eastwick.

[8] Aliph Cheem (W. Yeldham), *Lays of Ind: Second Series* (Bombay, 'Times of India' Office, 1873), 99–100, 'To a Griffin'.

[9] *Saturday Review*, 25 April 1874, 520–1. 'The Suez Canal'.

[10] Hansard, *Commons Debates*, 5 June 1874, 1036, Lord Houghton.

[11] Constance F. Gordon-Cumming, 'A Sail Down Old Egypt's New River', *Good Words* (1874), 851.

Surat passing through 'the grandest undertaking of modern times' was used by a Scottish Liberal M.P., amid the frequent applause of the working men of Dundee, as an illustration of human progress rather than of British power. 'The sight of a gigantic steamer like this wending her way through a channel cut in the sand impressed me more than the Pyramids...One vast ocean steamer after another came in or went out [to Port Said], or went up the canal, a noble sight, indicative of increasing comfort, civilization and international concord, in a higher sense grander than the pillars of Karnak.'[1]

[1] *The Dundee Advertiser*, 16 November 1875, 8 i–ii, W. E. Baxter, 'The Suez Canal'.

II

THE TRADE OF THE CHINA SEAS, 1870-1874

THE development of the Suez steam route altered the relative importance of the straits which dominated the great peninsula between India and China and gave access to the China seas. Thenceforward the Straits of Malacca rather than the Straits of Sunda became the shortest route between Europe and the East, benefiting Penang and Singapore at the expense of Anjer and Batavia and arousing Italian, Austrian, and Prussian interest in a coaling station.[1] Penang became a port of call for steamers and increased its shipping even faster than Singapore. It expanded its imports from Europe at the expense of its imports from India, developed its entrepôt trade in tobacco with Deli in North Sumatra and replaced its jetty by a wharf designed in 1872.[2] Singapore, however, benefited more than Penang and developed the full potentialities of its central location as an entrepôt. Singapore was reached through the Canal first by the *Thabor* from Marseilles in 61 days (6 November 1869-6 January 1870), the *Sin-Nanzing* from Glasgow in 57 days (11 November-6 January), the *Sakana* from London in 58 days (24 December-19 February) and the *William Miller* from London in 62 days (30 December-29 February). Then the *Shantung* arrived from Glasgow in 42 days (20 January-2 March),[3] one day ahead of the P. & O. mailboat, while the *Pei-ho* arrived from Marseilles in 29 days (15 May-12 June) and proved the full value of the new route. Sail tonnage entering Singapore declined from its peak of 1869 and was surpassed by steam tonnage in 1870. The port's imports of copper sheeting and nails for sailing vessels decreased sharply from their 1870 peak while its imports of coal from England increased from 1870. The New Harbour to the south-west of the original settlement on the Singapore River, used by the P. & O. since 1850, developed at the expense of the old harbour. The increase in shipping tonnage by one third between 1869 and 1871 compelled the expansion of dock facilities and probably saved the Tanjong Pagar Dock Company from bankruptcy.[4] That company found its warehouses congested for the first time in February 1870[5] and shifted increasingly from ship-repair into cargo-handling. After five years without a dividend it paid its first dividend in 1870

[1] *Le Canal de Suez*, 19 Mai 1870, 180.

[2] *Papers Relating to Her Majesty's Colonial Possessions*, Part i—1874 (C.882 of 1874), 176, G. W. R. Campbell, Straits Settlements, 5 June 1873.

[3] *The China Mail*, 17 March 1870, 3 v, 'The Suez Canal and the China Trade'. *Le Canal de Suez*, 1 Mai 1870, 153.

[4] G. Bogaars, 'The Effect of the Opening of the Suez Canal on the Trade and Development of Singapore', *Journal of the Malayan Branch, Royal Asiatic Society* (March 1955), 127-8.

[5] W. Makepeace, *One Hundred Years of Singapore* (1921), ii. 3.

and its first directors' fees in 1871. Singapore attracted Chinese immigration increasingly, appointed its first Chinese Municipal Commissioner in 1870 and acquired an agency of the Hong Kong Bank in 1870. The vast expansion of its general entrepôt trade far outweighed the loss of its small re-export trade in tea. Its position was consolidated by the failure of projects to tap the trade of China through Burma and to pierce the isthmus of Kra. It became a base for British expansion in Malaya and the Dutch East Indies under Sir Andrew Clarke, who hoped that Malaya would become a second India. Clarke appointed Residents on the Indian pattern on 14 December 1874 in three sultanates of Western Malaya, where tin production had begun in Perak in 1872.

The second colonial power of Asia divided the aristocratic Moslem Malay society of the archipelago with Britain. The Dutch East Indies enjoyed a more centralized government than India, based on the centre of population, production and export in Java and on 'animated coats of arms' in the outer islands.[1] They remained the model of an export-economy, an alien capitalism, a plural society and a dual administration: they suffered no revolution of their corporate tradition of economy, society and empire under the influence of the Suez Canal. The screw steamer *Curaçao*, with the historic name of the first ship to cross the Atlantic under steam power in 1827, passed northwards through the Canal after the opening ceremony but without paying dues: it reduced its draught to 18 feet by transferring its coal to the fore of the ship[2] and reached Port Said safely on 3 December. Prince Henry of the Netherlands was the only prince present at the inauguration who took positive steps to enable his country to profit by the new route, which saved 24 per cent of the voyage around the Cape to Batavia. He did as much for the maritime expansion of the Netherlands as Prince Henry the Navigator had done for that of Portugal. He promoted the foundation on 13 May 1870 of the Netherland Steamship Company under the patronage of King Willem III to establish a direct steam service to Java via the Canal. The only company founded in Europe as a direct result of the Canal was financed by the leading bankers and merchants of Amsterdam,[3] whose Chamber of Commerce had opposed the Canal in 1858. Prince Henry gave his name to the new *Prins Hendrik der Nederlanden* which sailed from Falmouth on 13 July 1870 via the Canal (10–16 August) with a full cargo of coal for Billiton. The Netherland Steamship Company lost its first ship, the *Willem III* off Portsmouth on 15 May 1871[4] but sent the *Prins van Oranje* from Amsterdam to Batavia in 41 days (30 July–9 September 1871).

For the Dutch East Indies the opening of the Canal was one of several

---

[1] J. S. Furnivall, *Netherlands India. A Study of Plural Economy* (Cambridge University Press, 1939), 178.

[2] N. J. den Tex, *Egypte en het Suez-Kanaal* (Amsterdam, Van Kampen, 1870), 41.

[3] M. G. de Boer, *Geschiedenis der Amsterdamsche Stoomvaart* (Amsterdam, Scheltema, 1921), i. 189.

[4] Ibid., i. 200.

changes in economic environment. The landing of the cable at Batavia in 1870 linked Java to the Eastern Telegraph system and made possible the extension of that system to Australia but did not produce the expected transfer of the 'pearl of the Indies' to Australian administration.[1] The expansion of private enterprise at the expense of State production was encouraged by the Agrarian Law and the Sugar Law of 1870. European private enterprise developed the production for export of tobacco, tin and cinchona from 1872. By the Treaty of 2 November 1871 England renounced all interference in Sumatra in return for the abolition of preferential duties. The tariff of 1872 threw open the trade of the 500 natural harbours of the Indies to the whole world and especially to Britain. British steamers increased their activity in the archipelago and benefited Singapore at the expense of Batavia, which lacked accommodation for steamers. Java began the large-scale import of rice from 1873 and even introduced Assam tea in 1873 in its quest for profitable exports. The Java Line was founded in the Netherlands in 1873 for the Suez route to Batavia and was followed by two new British lines, the Commercial Steamship Company in 1874 and the Star Ball Line in 1875. Dutch shipping increased its use of the Canal until in 1874 it supplied 4·6 per cent of the total tonnage and replaced Austrian tonnage in the third place after British and French. The Netherlands became the first power to build a warehouse at Port Said for the entrepôt trade, making the Dutch Commercial Establishment,[2] begun in 1874 and completed on 1 September 1876, Prince Henry's demonstration of confidence in the commercial future of the port. In 1875 only 21 per cent of the shipping tonnage between the Netherlands and Asia used the Canal while 79 per cent used the Cape route.[3] Willem Ruys & Sons of Rotterdam, who had maintained a service to the East since 1839 and had resolved in 1870 to introduce steamships, began their steamship service in 1875. The *Groningen* reached Batavia in 42 days (7 March–18 April 1875) but paid in Canal dues 9·85 per cent of the total expenses of its voyage. Thus Rotterdam began to compete with Amsterdam, whose Netherland Steamship Company paid its first dividend in 1875. Although the Cape route continued to carry the bulk of Dutch trade, especially in sugar, the Government allotted £3,000,000 in 1876 for the construction of a new harbour for Batavia. The growing use of the Straits of Malacca by steamships together with the development of tobacco cultivation by the Deli Company, established in 1869, inspired the Dutch to strengthen their hold over Sumatra as the British were strengthening theirs over Malaya across the Straits. From 1873 the Dutch waged war against the Achinese in their hope to convert the island into another Java. That war encouraged the Dutch to make increasing use of the steam route via the Canal and the Straits of Malacca but ended the financial surplus of the Dutch East Indies in 1877 and compelled the retention of the profitable crop of coffee under the culture-system.

---

[1] *The Spectator*, 14 August 1869, 947 ii. [2] M. G. de Boer, i. 215.
[3] *Le Canal de Suez*, 12 Avril 1877, 2.

British economic penetration into the Spanish Philippines was even greater than into the Dutch East Indies after the abolition in 1871 of differential duties against foreigners.[1] Williamson's *Waverley* which passed through the Canal in January 1871 with tobacco for Liverpool was the first ship with its entire cargo from the Philippines. Olano, Larrinaga & Co. of Bilbao imitated J. Cassanova of Seville who had established a steamship line to Bombay in 1870. They built their first steamship, the *Buena Ventura*, and sent it from Liverpool through the Canal on 8–10 June 1871 to Manila. From 1873 they made their Liverpool–Manila service monthly in basis, increasing markedly Spanish tonnage and tobacco shipments through the Canal. The expansion of British firms and British banks in Manila took place at American expense. Manila remained unconnected to the Eastern cable-system until 1880. The tradition of State-control remained as strong as the local influence of the great land-owners, debt-peonage and share-cropping.

The victory of the steamship was not foreseen in the China trade as it was in the Bombay trade[2] because the Canal reduced the distance between Europe and China proportionately far less than that between Europe and India. The great land empire of China also remained more self-sufficient than India with the best food, drink and clothing in the world in rice, tea, silk, cotton and fur. The carriage of China silk had already been accelerated by its shipment via the overland route from 1855. China tea had been carried faster first by the tea clippers from the 1850s and then by Holt's steamships from 1866 in competition with the clippers. The China clippers had reduced the record voyage from Foochow from 110 days in 1860 to 89 in 1869. They performed the voyage with the speed and regularity of the steamship, enabling the stocks of Congou in the bonded warehouses of London to be halved between 1866 and 1869 and encouraging their owners to launch twelve new tea clippers in 1869, with the support of the merchants who preferred tea carried in wooden hulls. China's staple exports of tea and silk were, however, so high in price that they were better adapted than the cheap bulk exports of India to the high steamer freights and Canal tolls of the Suez route. Tea formed a light cargo like cotton which required much ballast and was best carried by a shallow vessel adapted to a shallow waterway. Thus the Canal's influence on the trade of China became even greater than on the trade of India. The first toll-paying transit of the Canal was made en route to China rather than to India.

The Canal contributed to the triumph of steam over sail in the foreign and local trade of China. Its use saved one-quarter of the Cape voyage to Hong Kong and Shanghai. Its opening raised immediate expectations in Shanghai of reduced freights. Those expectations were fulfilled through a reduction in freight-rates and in passenger-fares by the four existing steamship lines intended to prevent the entry of competitive lines. The Canal helped drastically to reduce the tonnage of shipping and cargo in transit between England and

---

[1] *North China Herald*, 22 August 1871, 709.
[2] *London and China Express*, 25 November 1869, 961.

China: the number of vessels on the water from London and Liverpool to Shanghai was halved from twenty-eight in January 1870 to fourteen in January 1871.[1] The practice of storing merchandise at both termini in England and China declined, as in the Indian trade, further reducing the capital necessary for China merchants. Small men entered the trade, financed by the banks established in the 1860s. Even Chinese traders from Shanghai tried to establish branch houses in London for the exchange of tea and silk for piece-goods.[2] The Canal also encouraged an immense lateral extension of trade with China in so far as it stimulated trade between China and the Continent. Odessa, Hamburg and even Antwerp followed the example of Marseilles in establishing a direct steamship service to China. Thereby the Continent reduced its dependence upon Britain for the tea and silk of China. The share of British shipping in the external trade of China and the British share in the total value of China's exports declined. The English carrying trade and the English entrepôt trade were not, however, destroyed. The princely houses of the China coast were not submerged but strengthened by the concentration of trade in the larger ports. The alien control of China's foreign trade increased rather than decreased.

The opening of the Canal caused 'the greatest revolution that ever upheaved the affairs of Hongkong',[3] a revolution from a commercial rather than a political source. The first steamers to reach the island-colony direct from Europe were the *Sin-Nanzing* in 67 days (11 November–16 January) from Glasgow, the *Thabor* in 63 days (6 November–18 January) from Marseilles, the *William Miller* in 86 days (30 December–26 March) from London[4] and the *Chu-Kiang* in 66 days (22 January–29 March) from London. The *Cleator* arrived in 103 days (20 December–2 April) from Liverpool via Calcutta. Then the *Erl King* arrived in 55 days (15 February–11 April) from London, carrying the first shipment of bullion by the new route,[5] and became 'the gallant pioneer of a commercial fleet which will know nothing of seas south of the Equator between Europe and China'.[6] It was followed by the *Craigforth* in 54 days (12 April–4 June) from London and by the *Pei-ho* in 37 days (15 May–20 June) from Marseilles, the fastest passage on record.[7] The port became a growing coaling station as well as the great entrepôt of Southern China. Its shipping tonnage soared by 92 per cent from 1,974,299 tons in 1868 to 3,795,566 tons in 1872. The warehouses of Victoria were filled to overflowing to the embarrassment of the European merchants and the benefit of the Hong Kong and Whampoa Dock Company Ltd., which amalgamated on 8 March 1870 with its rival the Union Dock Company[8] so as to prevent the dissipation of the profits of the new trade through the curse of competition. The port

---

[1] *North China Herald*, 11 January 1871, 31 iii. [2] Ibid., 7 July 1870, 8 ii.
[3] E. J. Eitel, *Europe in China. The History of Hongkong* (London, Luzac, 1895), 571.
[4] *The China Mail*, 26 March 1870, 1 i, 4 v; 30 March, 3 iii. [5] Ibid., 6 April 1870, 3 i.
[6] Ibid., 12 April 1870, 3 i. [7] *North China Herald*, 7 July 1870, 8 ii.
[8] *The China Mail*, 18 January 1870, 2 v, 'The Suez Canal and the Dock Companies'; 17 February, 3 ii; 1 March, 3 iv; 3 March, 7 iii.

remained the terminus of the P. & O.'s trunk line from Suez and gained from Shanghai a branch of Butterfield & Swire on 1 May 1870 to support Holt against the crushing competition of the 'huge monopoly' of the P. & O.[1] Shanghai lay at the furthest limit of Europe's extended line of communications with the East. 'The first experiment of juxtaposing the progressive civilization of Western Europe and the stagnating finality of China'[2] took place in Shanghai rather than in Hong Kong and revealed the ability of the 'white Chinese' to turn the tradition of cultural superiority against its oldest exponents. The jelly-like alluvial subsoil of the city necessitated for both Chinese and European buildings of wooden lath and plaster which were copied from Hong Kong's imitation of the style of India. Those buildings contrasted with the sacred 'stones of Venice', its European prototype as a city of refuge, and seemed to presage an early decay. Shanghai nevertheless handled 71 per cent of the purely external trade of China in 1871 against the 13 per cent of Canton. It survived the competition of all rivals to the north and to the south, despite its shallow and restricted harbour, and remained 'the queen, the metropolitan and the regulator of all European commerce with the Celestial Empire'.[3]

Shanghai was reached via the Canal first by a vessel of the Messageries, which had summoned the *Alphée* from Réunion and the *Erymanthe* from Saigon to ascend the Canal northwards with the *Curaçao* and meet the *Aigle* in Lake Timsah on 18 November 1869. The *Thabor* passed southwards during the opening ceremonies and reached Shanghai in 90 days (6 November 1869–3 February 1870) from Marseilles. From Shanghai the *Hoogly* of the Messageries carried silk and tea through the Canal on 3 March 1870 in fourteen hours and so became the first mailboat direct from China to use the Canal without calling at Alexandria. At least seven other steamers arrived at Shanghai after the *Thabor* and before the first tea steamers left on 8–9 June. The most important of those was the *Sin-Nanzing*, the first commercial vessel to pass through the Canal and pay dues on its 722 register tons. That paddle-steamer was built by John Elder on the Clyde for J. F. H. Trautmann & Co., the managing agents of the North China Steamship Company established for the Tientsin trade in 1868, and gave on its trials the strongest demonstration to date of the immense superiority of the compound-engine.[4] The *Sin-Nanzing* left Greenock on 11 November 1869 under Captain L. B. Drage with its builder, J. B. Blow, the marine superintendent of the North China Steamship Company, but without cargo other than coals for its own use. It took on coal at Gibraltar and water at Malta, where Drage heard on 25 November that the Canal was open and a success.[5] It reached Port Said in 19 days from Greenock,

---

[1] F. E. Hyde and J. R. Harris, *Blue Funnel: a History of Alfred Holt and Company of Liverpool* (Liverpool University Press, 1956), 65.

[2] *North China Herald*, 16 June 1870, 438 i.

[3] Baron J. A. de Hubner, *A Ramble Round the World, 1871* (London, Macmillan, 1878), 466.

[4] *London and China Express*, 16 November 1869, 944 ii.

[5] *Le Canal de Suez*, 1 Janvier 1870, 10–11, J. Blow, 'Remarques sur l'Ouverture du Canal de Suez'.

two weeks after the inauguration and one week after Eugénie's departure. With a draught of 12 ft. 11 in. it grounded only once at Ballah for nine hours but required 3¾ days (30 November–3 December) to complete its passage, steaming at the fast speed of 8–10 knots and washing portions of the bank away in the narrows by its paddles. The *Sin-Nanzing* reached Bombay on 16 December in 13 days from Suez and in 35 days from Greenock, enabling Blow to give the world the first report of a complete voyage by the new route.[1] At Singapore on 6–9 January 1870 the steamer took on board 57 Chinese passengers for Hong Kong, where it was greeted with enthusiasm on its arrival on 16 January[2] because of the Chinese shareholders supporting Trautmann. It remained at Hong Kong for 31 days, left for the last lap of its voyage on 16 February and arrived at Shanghai on 24 February,[3] 106 days out from Glasgow including 53 days of actual steaming.

The *Sin-Nanzing* was not the first ship to reach Shanghai via the Canal because it arrived three weeks after the *Thabor*. The steamers which followed those pioneers completed their voyages in much shorter times, the *Shantung* in 58 days (20 January–19 March), the *Chu-Kiang* in 76 days (22 January–7 April) and the *Diomed* in 66 days (22 February–28 April). Nevertheless the *Sin-Nanzing* was the first commercial vessel to pass through the Canal and pay dues on a voyage which crossed the world from the Clyde to the China seas and in so doing pierced the land-barrier between East and West at the heart of the Old World. It was not a typical representative of the ships which were to use the Canal because it was a paddle-boat and not a screw-steamer. It was also intended for the coastal trade and not for the long-distance trade between Europe and China. For the Canal it was in reality less a carrier than a cargo, a self-transporting capital good, although it was classed and taxed by the Canal Company as a carrier. Its passage was thus a one-way passage like those of the *Savannah* in 1819 and of the *Royal William* in 1833 across the Atlantic and those of the *Thabor*, the *Shantung*, the *Chu-Kiang* and the *Hupeh* to Shanghai in 1870. The steamer was part-owned by Chinese and wholly Chinese by name, a symbol of the first Chinese and comprador response to the challenge of the West.

The *Sin-Nanzing* was nevertheless an instrument of East-West trade and of the three-cornered struggle between English, Americans and Chinese for the China trade, using steam as a technique of commercial warfare.[4] It demonstrated the capacity of the British to surpass the Americans in building steamships of light draught and high speed. Even the American-managed Shanghai Steam Navigation Company had the *Shantung* and the *Hupeh* built on the Clyde with their engines and hull on the American plan. John Elder made the

---

[1] *The Times*, 13 January 1870, 4 iv–v. *Le Canal de Suez*, 1 Mai 1870, 157–8, 'Le Sin-Nanzing à Bombay'.

[2] *The China Mail*, 17 January 1870, 2 vi, 'The Suez Canal and the East'.

[3] *North China Herald*, 1 March 1870, 156 i.

[4] Kwang-Ching Liu, *Anglo-American Steamship Rivalry in China 1862–1874* (Harvard University Press, 1962), 78–83, 'The Tientsin Route—Trautmann's & Jardine's'.

Sin-Nanzing sturdy enough to make the long ocean voyage to China under its own steam and a British crew so as to avoid sending the ship out in pieces for assembly by local labour at Shanghai. The new steamer was used for the coast and not for the river trade because of a self-denying agreement of 1867 among the local steamship companies. It had reached Shanghai four days after the first steamer had left with the spring supply of piece-goods for Tientsin, the outport of the capital and the focus of the commerce of 200,000 square miles. The *Sin-Nanzing* left for Chefoo and Tientsin the day before the Peiho was opened on 5 March on the end of the 'Great Cold' of the three winter months. It made four trips with opium and general cargo to Tientsin between 4 March and 25 May, averaging 18 days for the round trip of 1,500 miles, and then ten trips to Hong Kong between 3 June 1870 and 2 January 1871, again averaging 18 days for the round trip of 1,800 miles. Thus it served to link Shanghai to Hong Kong as well as to Peking and to unify the coast trade, which thitherto had been carried on by different types of vessels to the north and the south of Shanghai. Its activity also consolidated on the new basis of steam the pattern of Indo-Chinese trade created during the commercial revolution of the mid-eighteenth century. The opium which it carried to the Chinese supplied a gentle stimulant, relief from the monotony and insignificance of his existence and 'that solace which false economy and mis-government forbids him in his daily life'.[1] That trade supplied the revenue of British India as much as of China, placed the trade of the East in British hands and maintained steam communication throughout the East by the lucrative freights which it afforded.[2]

The opening of the Canal stimulated the improvement of the steamship and especially the adoption of the compound-engine so that it gave full value to the Yangtze route opened in 1861. The Canal made possible a direct voyage by steamship from Hankow to London, increased the competitive advantage of the steamship over the clipper and encouraged Holt to use the *Cleator* to test the full capacity of the Suez route. The *Cleator's* voyage of 1865 to China made possible the odyssey of the *Agamemnon* in 1866: its voyage of 1870 to Calcutta and Hong Kong inspired Holt to build six new steamers each of 1623 tons burden, for the Canal route.[3] Holt owned two of the four steamers which were waiting at Hankow when the tea season opened on 19 May 1870. The *Diomed* had steamed through the Canal on 10 March, three days after its rival the *Erl King*, while the *Agamemnon* had steamed via the Cape on 1 March, like the *Oberon*. The P. & O. advertised the *Sunda* as due to sail direct from Hankow to London via the Canal, perhaps to redeem its reputation from the charge of a fear of change,[4] but then withdrew its offer. The beginning of competition between ocean and river steamers caused a temporary depreciation

---

[1] *North China Herald*, 30 June 1870, 474 iii.
[2] *The Economist*, 12 March 1870, 320, 'The Opium Clauses in the Chinese Convention'.
[3] *The China Mail*, 2 April 1870, 5 iv, 'The Suez Canal'.
[4] *North China Herald*, 19 May 1870, 352 iii; 2 June, 415 i.

in the shares of the river steamer companies but no decrease in their activity. The Chinese maintained their freedom of choice between two competing markets and prevented Shanghai from recapturing the whole of the tea trade. The *Erl King* became the first steamer to leave Hankow on 4 June and Woosung on 8 June, being followed by two more on 9 June and 14 June. Advanced opinion in Shanghai thereupon began to acknowledge that the days of the China clipper were numbered and that the days of clipper racing were over,[1] despite the reintroduction in 1870 of the extra premiums for the first ship to arrive which had been discontinued after the dead heat of 1866. The first tea clipper did not leave until 24 June: the *Cutty Sark* earned for John Willis only half the freight rates of the first steamer, although it had been specially built for the trade in 1869.

Holt's new *Priam* arrived at Shanghai in 63 days (18 April–20 June) having passed through the Canal in seven days (2–9 May) because of the *Jumna* but without touching, despite its draught of 20 ft. 3 in. The arrival of his *Hipparchus* in 53 days (4 June–27 July) ended all doubts in Shanghai about the utility of the new route. By the end of July the arrival of steamers via the Canal had become as routine an event as arrivals via the Cape. The competition of ocean steamers inward-bound for Shanghai reduced the freights for coastal steamers. Four steamers had loaded and left Woosung while five others were loading or preparing to load for Europe via the Canal. Three regular steamship lines had been announced and Shanghai had been placed within sixty days of London. A fleet of some eighteen tea clippers had thereby been superseded. Freights had been reduced from £7 per ton to £2. 10s. per ton for steamships and from £3. 10s. to the lowest possible level of 30s. per ton for sailing ships, spreading panic among sailing shipowners.[2] 'Not even the invention of steam created such a revolution in trade as has done the cutting of a few tens of miles from Suez to Port Said. In the one case, the change was gradual; in the other a few months have been sufficient to effect a radical alteration.'[3] The first of the clippers from Foochow did not leave until the end of July, or nearly two months later than in 1869. The last of the clippers did not leave Foochow until 3 November. The tea clippers visiting that port were reduced from sixteen to eight in number, were threatened by the arrival of Holt's steamer *Achilles* and did not attract the visits of the resident merchants in 1870 as they had in 1869.[4] Shipowners were compelled by the reduction in freights to readjust themselves to the fact of the Canal and launched their last three tea clippers in 1870, two being for John Willis and one for Killick, Martin & Co. The Sailor's Home of Shanghai also suffered from the fall in homeward freights and from the decline in the demand for sail and for sailors. It lost the custom of many sailors because steamships stayed only a short while in port,

---

[1] *North China Herald*, 30 April 1870, 297–8; 16 June, 439 i.
[2] Ibid., 4 August 1870, 85 iii, 'The Suez Canal'.
[3] Ibid., 25 August 1870, 148 i, 'The Suez Canal'.
[4] Ibid., 16 June 1870, 443 i.

unlike sailing ships with their minimal overhead costs. The Home was therefore reorganized with a new superintendent, reduced accommodation and a lower rental in order to prevent it from becoming a burden upon the port instead of self-supporting as thitherto.[1] The shortage of sailors at Shanghai gave the port's name from 1871 to their recruitment by drugs or by force.[2]

The tea steamers inherited the tradition of racing established by the China clippers and revived under higher pressure the excitement of the clipper races from Foochow in steamer races from Hankow via Suez. The *Erl King* reached London in 54 days (8 June–3 August) from Shanghai and against the monsoon. It arrived four weeks earlier than in 1869, cut 31 days or 37 per cent off its voyage-time of 85 days via the Cape in 1869 and earned the bonus of an extra 10*s.* per ton freight for Robertson & Co.'s King Line. Holt's *Diomed* arrived second on 4 August and his *Agamemnon* third on 18 August, to find the London tea market increasingly paralysed since the outbreak of the Franco-Prussian War with the new season's teas selling slowly and lower. Thus the war by reducing demand accentuated the influence of the Canal in bringing supplies foward earlier. The Canal had achieved the result foreseen by one Shanghai merchant in 1869,[3] had shifted the carriage of tea from sail to steam and had transferred stocks of tea from China to London, frustrating the hope of Shanghai that the steady fall in prices might be remedied by the holding of stocks in China rather than in Europe. The London tea season was advanced a full month from September to August, which was a dull time because of the harvest and the holidays. Thus London reduced its prices to a permanently lower level, captured from Liverpool its tea imports and so finally ended the efforts made by the outports since the 1830s to capture the tea trade. Importers could confirm within eight weeks if the purchases on their account were such as they were described to be and needed no longer to accept the former excuse of 'deterioration on voyage' to shield exceeded limits.[4] Exporters in China anticipated that the rules and precedents of home business would apply increasingly in Shanghai, leaving little room for speculation and replacing the ideal of the nabob by the English ideal. They had ignored 'that great fact, the "Suez Canal"', had bought tea at the old scale of price without regard to home demand and had so competed to enrich the Chinese growers.[5] The year 1870 was made profitable for Shanghai only by the partial failure of the Assam crop. The saving of time by the use of the Canal also prevented the dissipation of the flavour of the lightly fired teas of China and made their depreciation in the London market less than it would have been in competition with the highly fired teas of India.

[1] *North China Herald*, 25 August 1870, 147–8; 4 October, 260 ii.
[2] M. Schele de Vere, *Americanisms; the English of the New World* (London, Trübner, 1872), 347, quoting 'shanghaied' from the *New York Tribune*, 1 March 1871.
[3] *North China Herald*, 11 January 1870, 26 i; 12 April, 268 i; 30 April, 304 iii; 9 June, 426 ii, 'The Suez Canal and the Tea Trade'.
[4] *The Times*, 21 March 1870, 6 iv, 'Spurious Tea'.
[5] *North China Herald*, 9 June 1870, 426 ii-iii, Hankow.

The clipper ships did not race home in 1870 but took double the time of the *Erl King*. The *Cutty Sark* arrived in a leisurely 110 days on 13 October. English tea clippers also began sailing to New York in 1870, together with steamships via the Canal. The *Magdala*, which was advertised as the first of a direct steam line to New York, arrived there via the Canal in 97 days (16 August–22 November 1870) against the 89 days of the sailing vessel *Harlaw* via the Cape in 1869. The s.s. *Riga* required 120 days (9 September–14 January 1871) to reach New York via Port Said (8 November) and was beaten by the clipper *Ariel* from Yokohama in 117 days, by the clipper *Lantra* from Macao in 110 days (30 September–24 January 1871)[1] and, above all, by the clipper *Surprise* from Shanghai in 83 days. Thus the American trade offered clippers a refuge from the competition of steam. The cheapest of all sea routes avoided the transhipment inevitable with the Pacific Railroad as well as the high steamer freights and the tolls of the Suez Canal.

Nearly one-third of the 1870 crop was carried by twenty-one steamers between 8 June 1870 and 18 January 1871, while more than two-thirds was carried by clipper. The shipments by steamship were shared between the Cape and the Canal routes so that the Canal carried only some 15 per cent of the crop. It was in 1871 rather than in 1870 that the Canal route triumphed in the trade of Shanghai. Alfred Holt began a regular weekly service between Liverpool and Shanghai from 1 October 1871. As an engineer he eliminated square sails from the main mast of his steamers after finding them of little use on the Suez route.[2] His large-scale shipment of cotton goods from Liverpool largely transferred to the Canal route the trade in piece-goods to Shanghai. The tea trade was stimulated by the revival of export demand to the Continent on the establishment of peace early in March and by the entry of the P. & O., the Glen Line, the Russian Steam Navigation Company and the German Steamship Line. The racing clippers were reduced from twenty-seven in 1870 to nine in 1871 while those loading at Foochow sank to three with the influx of steamers. Tea shipments via the Canal rose from 22,000,000 pounds in 1870 to 48,000,000 pounds in 1871, or to 34 per cent of the crop. The dead season in the traffic of the Canal became the months of June and July because of the seasonal gap between the passage of cotton in February–March and the passage of tea in August–September. Those changes were consolidated by the completion during 1871 of the submarine cables to Shanghai and Hong Kong.

The first tea steamers left Woosung on 6 June 1871, two weeks before the first clipper on 22 June. On 18 June the *Tchihatchoff*, which had steamed outwards through the Canal on 19–21 March, left Woosung for Odessa, so inaugurating the direct shipment of tea to Russia by the short all-sea route via the Canal. Most of the 2,664 tons carried on board for Moscow merchants were Ningchows, the best and dearest teas, because the Russian buyers valued

---

[1] *The Times*, 8 February 1871, 5 vi, 'Rapid Passages'.
[2] W. S. Lindsay, *History of Merchant Shipping* (1876), iv. 435.

quality above all else and paid the highest price for the highest quality, thereby quite excluding other merchants from the market for early teas. That pioneer shipment secured for Odessa 25 per cent of the total value of Russia's trade with China in 1871. It diverted trade from the Cape route more than from the route from Kiakhta overland across Siberia, whose colder latitudes preserved the delicate flavour of the tea so well that it remained superior in quality and price to that carried via the Canal. The *Tchihatchoff* began its homeward voyage from Hankow, like eight other ocean steamers, and thereby stimulated the Russian brick-tea importers from Tientsin to hire mosquito steamers on the Yangtze. Those steamers, largely owned by the Chinese but operated by a British firm, carried brick-tea down-river to Shanghai, whence it was carried up the coast to Tientsin and thence overland to Russia. The direct shipment of tea via the Canal enabled Odessa to compete with London for the entrepôt trade in tea to Russia, for the steamer freights on tea from London to Petersburg and for the very large insurance policies effected thereon at Lloyd's. The transfer of tea imports into Russia from Petersburg to Odessa made Hamburg fear that it might lose to Odessa the supply of tea to the Russian market and encouraged the passage of the *Sedan* from Hamburg through the Canal on 15–17 July 1871, the pioneer steamer of the German Steamship Line to Shanghai, ten years before the first German steamship line to India. One leading tea importer of Hamburg opened a branch in Odessa in 1872 in order to retain his Russian connexions. The first tea steamers to reach London on 30 July 1871 were the *Enterprise* of E. M. de Bussche, a Belgian merchant resident in England, the *Erl King* of Robertson & Co. and the *Australia* of the P. & O. The voyage time of fifty-four days achieved no advance on the 1870 record. The new teas were sold very slowly: tea prices and tea freights slumped. Four veteran British clippers deserted the London tea trade and loaded instead for New York, two at Yokohama and two at Shanghai, while two more loaded at Manila and Batavia.

The eastwards extension of the cable from India to China was the achievement of private enterprise rather than of governments, like the construction of the overland telegraph through Siberia. The Great Northern Telegraph Company Ltd., registered in London on 29 April 1869, sprang from the Anglo-Danish and Russian Telegraph Company Ltd., established in 1867 for cable communication to Denmark and Russia. It was granted a concession on 11–23 October 1869 by the Russian Government to lay a cable through Siberia to Vladivostock, which was completed in November 1870. It shipped ninety-six miles of cable on the Danish frigate *Tordenskjold*, which became the first Danish vessel to pay Canal dues (19–25 July 1870) en route to Hong Kong, where it arrived on 16 August. Pender's three companies formed on the opening of the Canal laid a chain of submarine cables to link up with the Russian system. The Madras–Penang cable of the British Indian Extension Telegraph Company was carried from London by the *Edinburgh* on 25 August 1870 via the Cape and by the *Scanderia* on 15 September via the Canal. That cable was completed on 31 December and opened on 5 January 1871. The cable to Batavia was carried by the *Hibernia* via the Cape (26 July–1 November 1870) and the cable to Singapore by the *William Cory*. The cable was landed at Batavia on 14 November 1870 and at Singapore on 4 January 1871. After that extension of the Indian cable via Penang to the Straits the *Hibernia* returned via the Cape, while the *William Cory* returned via the Canal. The cable from Hong Kong to Shanghai was completed on 29 March 1871 by the Great Northern Company and opened to the public on 18 April.[1] The 1,600-miles extension northwards from Singapore to Hong Kong was carried for the China Submarine Telegraph Company from London by the *Agnes* on 5 January 1871 and by the *Kangaroo* on 27 February. That cable to Hong Kong was carried from Singapore on 19 May and opened on 8 June,[2] so enabling Chinese merchants to send loyal greetings to the Queen[3] and linking Hong Kong to New York as well as to London. The China Submarine Telegraph Company reached agreement with the Great Northern Company for the use of the cable to Shanghai, which was thereby linked to London via Singapore and received at its Chamber of Commerce on 22 June 1871 a cable from London in twenty-four hours. That company also laid an extension to Saigon on 31 July 1871 at the request of the French Government. The Great Northern Company shipped cables from London on 2 May and 6 May on board the *Great Northern* and the *Africa* which reached Nagasaki on 22 July and 26 July: those cables were laid from Shanghai to Nagasaki on 4 August[4] and from Nagasaki to Vladivostock on 19 August.[5] That Japan cable made the first extensive use of William Hooper's vulcanized indiarubber core and linked Shanghai to London via Japan and Russia.

The eastern cable-system was completed by Danish, Russian and British enterprise without seeking the permission of either China or Japan.[6] The system excluded Africa south of Aden but was extended southwards to Port Darwin and thence overland to Adelaide in 1872. It made Singapore as a cable-junction for the lines to Hong Kong and Batavia more important than Aden. It alarmed Hong Kong as likely to benefit the Chinese more than the foreign merchant.[7] That network, however, remained peripheral to the life of China because it followed the sea coast and was not linked with an internal network as in India until 1898. Nevertheless it served as the carrier of the world-market to the East and helped to centralize trade in those great ports of Eastern Asia which became cable stations. It increased the severe competition in Shanghai and encouraged exporters in self-protection to transfer the silk

[1] *The Times*, 7 April 1871, 4i. *North China Herald*, 21 April 1871, 276, 'The Hong Kong & Shanghai Telegraph'.
[2] *The China Mail*, 10 June 1871, 5i.   [3] Ibid., 14 June 1871, 3i.
[4] Ibid., 8 August 1871, 3i. *The Times*, 9 August 1871, 8i.
[5] *The Times*, 12 September 1871, 5i; 23 November, 7v.
[6] C. Bright, *Submarine Telegraphs. Their History, Construction and Working* (London, Lockwood, 1898), 114 note.
[7] *The China Mail*, 20 April 1871, 3i, 'The Probable Effects of Telegraphy on the China Trade'.

trade to the Canal in 1871 and importers to generalize the new custom of selling the early season's silk 'to arrive'. It also encouraged the entry of new steamship lines into the Shanghai trade, the rise of shipment to order, the introduction in 1873 of the auction of imported cotton goods in Shanghai and the expansion of the London-backed Chartered Bank at the expense of the Hong Kong Bank. London became the focus of the world cable-system as well as the centre of the world-market, gained control of market prices from Hong Kong and Shanghai and reduced its tea stocks as well as its tea prices. The China cable became much more profitable than the Indian cable because it served a more profitable trade and avoided the competition of the lines via the Persian Gulf and Persia. The four companies which owned the cables to the west of Bombay, the Falmouth Gibraltar and Malta Telegraph Company, the Marseilles Algiers and Malta Telegraph Company, the Anglo-Mediterranean Telegraph Company and the British Indian Submarine Telegraph Company were amalgamated by Pender on 6 June 1872 in the Eastern Telegraph Company Ltd. with an inflated nominal capital of £3,800,000. The three companies operating to the east of India, the British Indian Extension Telegraph Company, the China Submarine Telegraph Company and the British Australian Telegraph Company were amalgamated on 24 April 1873 in the Eastern Extension, Australasia and China Telegraph Company Ltd. with a nominal capital of £3,000,000. Pender's companies, created to break the Indo-European monopoly, thus became the largest cable system in the world, with control of sufficient capital and shore facilities from Falmouth to Hong Kong to deter any competitor. In 1873 Pender even sought to establish a world cable monopoly through the Globe Telegraph and Trust Company.

Silk was even higher in price than tea but fell in price from March 1870 as tea rose. It was carried through the Canal for the first time in 1870 in Holt's steamers, which benefited at the expense of the P. & O.[1] After the silk famine of 1870[2] caused by the Franco-Prussian War the bulk of China's silk harvest used the Canal for the first time in 1871, eliminating the very high railway freight of £8. 5s. per ton between Suez and Alexandria, reducing the risk of pilfering and cutting total freights by 57 per cent, after their fall by 18 per cent in 1870. The establishment of daily telegraphic communication with London increased the severe competition in the silk trade of Shanghai and hurried forward most of the season's supplies by 2–3 months. Chinese silk began to compete in the Mediterranean market, benefiting by the ravages of disease among the indigenous silkworms and by the decline of silk production in South France and North Italy. Its import via the Canal reinforced the dominance established by Lyons in the silk market since 1863 and accentuated the decline of the London entrepôt in silk. Chinese silk helped to oust Italian silk from the French market but enabled Italy to increase its imports direct from

[1] *North China Herald*, 19 May 1870, 362, 'Silk via Suez Canal'.
[2] C. M. Dyce, *Personal Reminiscences of Thirty Years' Residence in the Model Settlement Shanghai* (London, Chapman, 1906), 69.

China, especially from 1872, and to decrease thenceforward its imports of raw silk from England.

In 1872 the last real racing took place among the fourteen tea clippers, which made a determined effort to retain their trade.[1] During the five weeks of the tea season thirty-nine steamers, excluding those of the Messageries, visited the ports of China. Steamers loading at Hankow fell from nine in 1871 to six in 1872 while those loading at Foochow increased markedly and nearly doubled the volume of tea shipment via the Canal. The Glen Line of Allan C. Gow & Co. of Glasgow began a regular service from London to Hong Kong and Shanghai with the *Glenroy* which passed through the Canal in mid-January 1872. The P. & O.'s *Deccan* reached London in 48 days (29 May–16 July) to break the record of 54 days established in 1870 and 1871. The London season was thereby advanced a further month to July, in which an accelerated supply still met a reduced demand. Amid general apathy the new season's teas proved difficult to sell, except for the finest. Importers suffered heavily from panic in August and failure in September. The triumph of the steamer in the tea trade was consolidated by its expansion in the river and coast trade of China through the succession of Jardine's in 1871 to Trautmann & Co. as the managing agents of the North China Steamship Company, the organization in 1872 of the China Navigation Company Ltd. by J. Swire & Sons in London for the Yangtze trade[2] and the establishment by Jardine's in 1873 of the China Coast Steam Navigation Company for the trade to Tientsin.[3] Those 'ships with fire wheels' decreased the opportunities of local boatmen for employment and increased the unpopularity of foreigners in the northern ports. The first Chinese steam shipping company was the China Merchants' Steam Navigation Company established in 1872 by the capital of Chinese merchants under the patronage of Li Hung-chang, Viceroy of Chihli, for the transport of the tribute-rice from Shanghai to Tientsin. Thus Shanghai became more than ever the great centre for the diffusion of Western technology to China.

The success of the Glen Line stimulated the establishment of other competitive steamship lines between London and Shanghai. The *Flintshire*, the first steamer of D. J. Jenkins' Shire Line, passed through the Canal in mid-January 1873. Other steamship services were begun in 1873 by T. Skinner's Castle Line and by Watts, Milburn & Co., compelling the Glen Line to move from Glasgow to London. The P. & O. abandoned differential freights graduated according to speed after it lost the *Drummond Castle* on 31 May en route from Hankow. For the last time it brought the first cargo of new teas to London, where they were received with great caution and lack of animation. Eleven tea clippers sailed from China to London while seven more sailed to

[1] B. Lubbock, *The China Clippers* (Glasgow, Brown, 1914), 332–46.
[2] S. Marriner and F. E. Hyde, *The Senior. John Samuel Swire 1825–98* (Liverpool University Press, 1967), 59–60.
[3] K. C. Liu, *Anglo-American Steamship Rivalry in China 1862–1874* (1962), 113–50.

New York. The fastest clipper arrived in the 1869 record time of eighty-nine days. Some clippers adjusted their schedules to steamer competition, loaded in November–December, when the monsoon was fair and insurance rates were low, rather than in June–July[1] and so made paying voyages in the tea trade until 1877. The remainder were compelled to find other employment. The tea trade to New York afforded cargo to some for a few more seasons. Others loaded in the Philippines for New York. Many entered the Australian trade. Some became colliers. Most passed into foreign hands and ended their days in the country trade of the Indian and Pacific Oceans. The direct export of tea to Hamburg began in 1873 after the establishment of a regular service by the German Steamship Line in 1872, the opening of the Deutsche Asiatische Bank in Shanghai in 1872 and the increase in Russian imports via the Canal in 1872. The volume of tea shipped through the Canal rose from 60,000,000 pounds, or 40 per cent of the harvest in 1872, to 70,000,000 pounds or 50 per cent in 1873 and to 102,000,000 pounds or 74 per cent in 1874. The stocks of Congou in the bonded warehouses of London declined from 49,000,000 pounds on 30 June 1869 to 33,000,000 pounds on 30 June 1874 or from $5\frac{1}{4}$ months' supply to $3\frac{1}{4}$ months' supply. That reduction in stocks testified to the even greater regularity of shipment achieved in the three years following the opening of the Canal. In 1874 the Glen Line carried the new season's tea to London in the record time of 46 days, which it reduced in 1875 to 44 days and in 1876 to 43 days, enabling Jardine's to re-emerge more powerful than ever in the China trade but placing Holt's at a growing disadvantage.[2]

China and Japan faced eastward across the Pacific, although their trade mainly flowed westward. The opposing seaboard of the U.S.A. remained a frontier-region while its most developed seaboard faced eastward across the Atlantic. The U.S.A. was uninfluenced by the opening of the Canal, except in its China trade. It had become a continent-state with less interest in foreign trade than the small maritime states of Europe. Its steam fleet was based on its great rivers and lakes rather than upon the oceans and therefore served home trade but not foreign trade. The Canal reduced the distance to the ports of Asia much less from New York than from London: the Canal route saved 21 per cent of the voyage to Calcutta but entered the sphere of American Pacific shipping beyond Hong Kong. The saving in distance was less in proportion than for Europe because America, like Australia, lay on the fringe of the Canal's sphere of influence. America's large fleet of merchant sail enjoyed the advantage of an uphill location in relation to India and China through the use of the great-circle routes and the trade winds.[3] Direct trade with the primary producers of Asia via the Canal would thus have been uneconomic and would have entailed competition with Britain in the entrepôt trade as well

---

[1] B. Lubbock, 347.
[2] S. Marriner and F. E. Hyde, *John Samuel Swire*, 115.
[3] J. E. Nourse, *The Maritime Canal of Suez* (Washington, Philp, 1869), 51–2. *New York Times*, 18 November 1869, 4v, 'The Suez Canal'.

as in the carrying trade. From 1870 New York imported tea by British clippers sailing round the Cape in record time as well as by slower British steamers through the Canal. The U.S.A. also used British shipping and the London entrepôt to import silk from China and indigo from Calcutta. It thereby benefited by the general reduction in price of oriental commodities in the emerging world-market of the 1870s. Above all, the U.S.A. used the new Pacific Railroad for its trans-Pacific trade with China.

The completion of the Pacific Railroad led the Pacific Mail Steam Ship Company to double the frequency of its monthly service to Japan and China in 1869. It also ended the trans-Pacific service of the Panama, New Zealand and Australian Royal Mail Company, encouraged a proposal for a steam and railway service between England and Australia in forty days,[1] and stimulated the beginning of a paddle-steamer service in 1870 from San Francisco to Sydney. That railway attracted many Shanghai merchants to travel home to England by the temperate route via Japan and the U.S.A. in preference to the Red Sea and captured many passengers for China and Japan from the P. & O., whose steamers took sixty against thirty-five days and were neither cheap nor well-managed.[2] Its competition forced down passenger-fares by the Messageries as well as by the P. & O. It also encouraged George Francis Train, who had helped to build the Union Pacific Railroad in reply to the Suez Canal, to seek to become the first man to travel round the world in the shortest possible time. He hoped to return to New York from a westabout journey in ninety days and he claimed in his autobiography to have travelled around the world in eighty days,[3] although his own dates showed him to have taken 81 days (1 August–20 October 1870) from San Francisco to Marseilles. His journey inspired Cook's first exploratory world-tour in 222 days in 1872 via New York, San Francisco and Suez. Train was transformed from an American merchant into an English aristocrat in the story which Jules Verne published as a serial in 1872 and as a book in 1873.[4] That story brought its creator fame, prosperity and the formula of the 'Extra-ordinary Journey' for literary success: it became influential enough to stimulate travel around the world.

The Pacific Railroad also helped to carry the mail in 1870 from Hong Kong to San Francisco in thirty-four days and to London in forty-eight days, or in three days more than the forty-five days necessary by the Suez route.[5] It did not divert much mail from the overland route, although it carried the mail faster from Japan and New Zealand to Europe. In 1871 the railway helped to carry 500 bales of silk from Yokohama via San Francisco and New York to

[1] *The Economist*, 29 January 1870, 133. *The Times*, 10 May 1870, 10i.

[2] C. H. Pearson, 'The Land Question in the United States', *Contemporary Review* (November 1868), 351.

[3] G. F. Train, *My Life in Many States and in Foreign Lands dictated in my Seventy-Fourth Year* (London, Heinemann, 1902), 301, 331.

[4] J. Verne, *Le Tour du Monde en Quatre-Vingts Jours* (Paris, Hetzel, 1873).

[5] R. Andree, 'Der Sieg der Pacificbahn ueber den Suezcanal', *Die Grenzboten*, 26 Januar 1872, 189. *The China Mail*, 16 February 1870, 3i.

Liverpool in forty-seven days or in thirteen days less than the Suez route required. It also became the favoured route for the shipment of green tea from China and Japan. The increasing import of tea and silk to Europe via San Francisco undoubtedly decreased the importance of the Suez Canal in the tea and silk trade. Americans hoped that the railway would divert from the Canal the bulk of the trade of Asia. Germans hoped that it would thus achieve another victory for German over Latin as the economic complement to Sedan.[1] The Canal remained, however, far cheaper than the railway for bulk-freight because it was an all-water route which avoided transhipment: it carried cargo to New York at one-fifth of the combined freight by sea and rail across the U.S.A.

Between 1870 and 1876 only eleven ships under the American flag used the Canal. The first American to propose its use was no representative ship-owner but the eccentric Captain Norton. He left Hong Kong on 20 March 1870 in a Chinese junk, hoping to emulate the feat of the *Keying* in 1847 and to reach London via the Canal.[2] Apparently he was compelled to abandon his plan after leaving Penang. The American flag was first carried through the Canal not by the junk *Fung Shuey* but by the corvette *Palos* of the U.S. Navy, which left Boston on 21 June and passed through the Canal (10–16 August 1870) en route to China and San Francisco. Its captain made on 22 August the first report on the Canal to the Secretary of the Navy.[3] Its southbound transit established the pattern followed by later American vessels, commercial as well as naval, and was followed by the appointment of an American Consul at Port Said.[4] The first American merchant vessels to pay toll for the use of the Canal were two large paddle-steamers of the Pacific Mail Steam Ship Company, the *Arizona* (27–29 January 1871) and the *Alaska* (5–8 March 1871) en route to Yokohama. Those ships were reported to be the pioneers of a new monthly line between New York and Hong Kong via the Canal[5] but they were the broadest ships to use the Canal and were followed by no further vessels of the company.

The Pacific Mail Company reverted to the use of the Straits of Magellan to reach San Francisco. In 1873 it diverted its main ships to Panama from the San Francisco terminus of the Central Pacific and Union Pacific Railroads. Those railroads thereupon incorporated in 1874 the Occidental and Oriental Steam Ship Company for the operation of a service between San Francisco and Hong Kong, in order to preserve themselves from discrimination in freights by the Pacific Mail Company. The new line chartered three ships from the White Star Line, which had a surplus of tonnage after the failure of its Liverpool–Valparaiso service. The first of those steamers, the *Oceanic*,

---

[1] R. Andree, 184.

[2] *North China Herald*, 9 June 1870, 430ii.

[3] J. E. Nourse, *The Maritime Canal of Suez, from its Inauguration, November 17 1869 to the Year 1884* (Washington, 1884), 82–4.

[4] *Le Canal de Suez* 16 Mars 1871, 40, 'Les États-Unis d'Amérique et le Canal de Suez'.

[5] *Le Canal de Suez*, 2–4 Mars 1871, 27.

was sent from Liverpool through the Canal (2 May) for which it had originally been designed as the first modern mail-steamer. The *Oceanic* made a record passage to San Francisco in 16 days 10 hours from Yokohama, in 25 days from Hong Kong and in 74 days (17 April–29 June 1875) from Liverpool. It was followed by the smaller and slower *Belgic* and *Gaelic*, which left Liverpool on 8 May and 29 May 1875. Thus employment was found in the Pacific for steamers surplus to the needs of the Atlantic trade during the depression of 1874–5. The Pacific Mail Company's speed-record and its monopoly of steam shipping were shattered by a company which continued in operation until 1906, sharing the service to San Francisco on a fortnightly basis with its rival. Their joint competition for the tea trade from Japan did not prevent a sharp rise in New York's imports of tea via the Canal by 124 per cent between 1874 and 1876. Those imports were increasingly of Japanese rather than of Chinese tea.

The Pacific Mail Company carried the first detachment of thirty Chinese boys from Yokohama to San Francisco in 1872 for fifteen years of study in Connecticut of the technical professions associated with the art of war. The Yung Wing educational mission increased American influence upon China as American trade with China declined: it reduced China from its traditional role of teacher to that of pupil but did not diminish its claims to supreme status in the world. Thus the Son of Heaven granted the foreign ambassadors their first formal audience in Peking in 1873 in the building used for the reception of tributary princes. The signature of the Chefoo Convention in 1875 after the disastrous Margary expedition to the frontier of China and Burma was followed by the creation of a Chair of Chinese at Oxford in 1875 and the establishment of the first Chinese legations in London and Berlin in 1877 and in Washington in 1878: the first ambassador to Britain was, however, a commoner instead of a nobleman. The same reverence for the traditions of the past inhibited the Chinese acceptance of foreign innovations. The first railway in China was sponsored by Jardine's as a tea-railway between Shanghai and Woosung. For that railway the *Glenroy* carried a locomotive-engine through the Canal in November 1875 and railway wagons in May 1876. The construction of the railway was begun without Chinese sanction and completed in ten months between 20 January and 1 December 1876. The Chinese then tore up the rails and shipped them to Formosa, to ward off a Japanese threat, and built on the site of Shanghai Station a temple to the Queen of Heaven. Steam navigation by river was, however, accepted as steam navigation by land was not. The purchase of the Shanghai Steam Navigation Company in 1877 by the China Merchants' Steam Navigation Company was a triumph for Chinese over American enterprise which also eliminated Jardine's great competitor. China's response to the challenge from the West could not be as speedy or as successful as that of Japan because its land was so large, its administration so decentralized and its economy so self-sufficient. Its traditions were continental rather than maritime. Its eighteen provinces were as independent as self-governing British colonies[1] but were administered without police, army, laws or lawyers. Its military tradition was weak and its ethic was persuasion, making it 'a State resting on moral force, a concept almost as alien to the Western mind as material progress is to the Eastern'.[2] Its ruling mandarins maintained respect throughout 'the country of courtesy and accommodation' for the ancestors, the family and the clan. They subordinated all economic activity to social ends while the alien Manchu dynasty lost control over the ports, the customs and the economic policy of 'All that is under Heaven'.

The impact of the West produced in China the Tai-Ping Rebellion and in Japan the revolution of 1868 which overthrew the Tokugawa shogunate with the support of the anti-foreign sentiment emerging fifteen years after the appearance of Perry's black ships in 1853. The Emperor Mutsuhito who took over the government in 1868 and died in 1912 profited by the centralization of administration, society and nation as much as by the tradition of uncondi-tional obedience to authority in order to claim a total competence for the new Meiji state as a moral entity. Japan preserved its independence because of its poverty, began to import the techniques of the industrial civilization of the West as formerly it had the techniques of the agrarian civilization of China and remodelled itself 'as it were on the field of battle and in front of the enemy'.[3] In that process Japan bought the first vessel to reach Shanghai through the Suez Canal for use in the construction of lighthouses, the *Thabor* leaving for Nagasaki with cotton on 7 February 1870.[4] Local purchase also awaited two steamers sent out by Gellatly, Hankey, Sewell & Co., the *Sakana* which passed through the Canal on 12 January, and the *Tszru* which passed through on 7 March. Japan imported those steamers via Shanghai, to which it exported coal from Nagasaki from 1870 and from Formosa from 1875. Japan imported capital goods rather than manufactures, so as to build up its own resources, and imported more than it exported through the Canal. It was nevertheless forced by foreign competition to produce those commodities for which its relative advantages were greatest, i.e., tea for export to the U.S.A. and raw silk for export to France. It resented French support of the Tokugawa shogunate, insisted on exporting all its silk to Lyons via London and Liver-pool and would accept in exchange only Birmingham and Manchester goods. Japan was as friendly towards England as it was hostile towards France. It floated its first foreign loan in London in 1870 for the construction of a railway between its new and old capitals[5] and completed in 1872 the first railway in Eastern Asia, between Tokyo and Yokohama. The maritime tradition en-gendered by its 600 islands and sixty ports inspired Japan in 1871 to send twelve naval cadets, including Togo, for training to England where it estab-lished a Consulate in London in 1872. Its orders to all farmers to keep and

---

[1] A. Michie, *The Englishman in China during the Victorian Era as Illustrated in the Career of Sir Rutherford Alcock* (Edinburgh, Blackwood, 1900), i. 408; ii. 372.
[2] Ibid., ii. 370.   [3] Ibid., ii. 84.
[4] *North China Herald*, 12 April 1870, 259ii.
[5] *The Times*, 15 April 1870, 12i.

breed the economical and productive pigs, to be sent out from England via the Canal, created a brief pig-boom in Yokohama.[1] In 1873 the first vessels under the Japanese flag passed through the Canal, two ships aggregating 1,004 tons, a response wholly unanticipated in Europe because Japan had made no use of the Cape route. Japan limited its use of the Canal until the Sino-Japanese War, although it built its first warship in 1875. Its reorganization seemed to the West to be a revolution based on liberal principles. That revolution was in fact planned as a reorientation of the nation in a military spirit antithetical to that of free trade. It took place under samurai leadership[2] and preserved the continuity of the aristocratic tradition by combining 'Eastern ethics and Western science' in order to create 'Rich Country and Strong Army'. It used foreigners for Japanese ends and never allowed them to use the Japanese for their ends. Thus it integrated all the imports from the alien West into a culture which continued to be specifically Japanese and increasingly divinized its Emperor in Hegelian terms.

[1] *North China Herald*, 18 January 1871, 39; 15 February, 103, Yokohama.
[2] E. H. Norman, *Japan's Emergence as a Modern State. Political and Economic Problems of the Meiji Period* (Institute of Pacific Relations, New York, 1940), 101.

12

THE CANAL, THE CAPE,
AND STEAM SHIPPING, 1870-1875

THE Canal was not only a product of the trade which had developed apace between Europe and Asia since the 1830s but also in itself a cause of economic change. As a commercial innovation its main effects were felt during its first decade when interlocking networks of steam shipping, railways and cables bound the continents of the world together under the technical supremacy of Europe. In that revolution in communications the Canal was a work without precedent designed to replace the old routes to the East by a whole new complex of facilities centring around itself. The new route did not offer better weather or a safer passage as its greatest advantages. Its hazards were strategic rather than nautical because the Red Sea was in effect one great canal free from the difficulties and dangers of a narrow canal. Many fine steamers were, however, lost on the new route through gross blunders in navigation. Insurance premiums were at first higher than had been expected and were higher for the homeward than for the outward voyage, because it was more risky and difficult to enter than to leave the Red Sea from the Indian Ocean. Homeward risks proved ruinous to the underwriters of insurance except in the Bombay trade.[1] The Suez route nevertheless afforded a more direct route to the largest continent in the world by eliminating the circumnavigation of the second largest continent.

The enormous saving in distance was all the more important because distance was covered only slowly at sea, so locking up large capitals in goods in transit. That economy was the greatest of all on a voyage from the ports of the Mediterranean to Bombay but was still substantial on one from the ports of North-West Europe to Calcutta, Singapore or Hong Kong. Such a reduction in distance shortened the time of voyage, increased the frequency of voyages per ship and enlarged the utilizable capacity of a given tonnage of shipping. Such short-term economies attracted shipowners and merchants who balanced the large saving in distance and time against the higher freights and insurance rates. The decrease in the time and distance of voyages reduced substantially the quantity of goods in transit. Thereby it saved in insurance and interest on the capital thitherto locked up at sea but thenceforward liberated for investment elsewhere. It also opened the Eastern trade to smaller merchants as quick returns on small stocks replaced slow returns on large stocks. It insured importers against the deterioration of goods in transit and exporters

[1] F. Martin, *The History of Lloyd's* (1876), 380–3, 'A Classification of Risks. V, Suez Canal and Indian Steamers'.

against adverse fluctuations of the market. Merchant speculators in the ports of India and China benefited by the arrival of goods six to seven weeks before the six-months bankers' drafts matured. Those bills were not replaced by bills at four months until 1879, thereby achieving the reform first attempted in 1866 and again in 1872.

The fall in freights in Eastern ports after the opening of the Canal was unexpected. The increase in shipping seeking cargo helped to extend the market in freights and to bring them down to a lower level. The average outward steamer freights by the Messageries from Marseilles to India and China were halved immediately, reduced to one-third within two years and to one-quarter within three years by 1873.[1] Shipowners were compelled to devise new answers to their basic questions. How far was a cargo to be carried? How much freight would a cargo bear and for how long without the fear of competitors spoiling the market? Shipowners responded to two successive falls in freights by creating in self-protection the shipping conference in 1875. The shortening of the time of voyage and the fall in freights also reduced the price of Eastern commodities, contributing to the long fall in prices between 1873 and 1896. That fall furnished a striking example of the interaction of supply and demand, enhancing the magical appeal of those concepts to the economists of the 1870s. The fall in price affected cotton, jute, indigo, rice and tea from India, gutta-percha, sago and tin from the Straits Settlements, coconut oil and cinnamon from Ceylon, silk and tea from China and wool from Australia. The fall in the price of primary produce thus affected commodities shipped by the Cape route as well as those shipped by the Canal. The emerging world-market used complementary rather than single routes to its European location. In that market prices tended to be equalized but were determined in the West rather than in the East. The increase of consumption in Europe was thus achieved at the expense of the reduction in the monetary returns to the primary producers of Asia, a loss which was only partly offset by the fall in freight rates and in import prices.

The Canal route offered better possibilities of freight than the Cape route by avoiding the vast extent of the unproductive coast of Africa with its regular coastline and consequent lack of harbours, its great rivers other than the Nile incapable of use either for navigation or for irrigation, its limited contact between seaboard and interior and its lack of new staple products to replace the old export of slaves. The new route avoided the sparsely peopled southern hemisphere and linked the two most populous of continents together through the inland seas of the northern hemisphere with their coaling stations, entrepôt ports and feeder trades. It thus extended the economies of water-borne trade to the oldest route between East and West and to merchandise, which suffered from transhipment as much as passengers appreciated it. It opened a

---

[1] L. Bian, *Rapport sur l'Inauguration du Canal de Suez* (Mulhouse, Bader, 1870), 17–18. E. Sax, *Die Verkehrsmittel in Volks- und Staatswirtschaft* (Berlin, Springer, 2te Auflage, 1920), 232.

new route from Gibraltar to Aden to the high-cost steamship rather than to the sailing ship, which preferred the free domain of the open ocean to a land-bound route of narrow and treacherous seas. The new route was peculiarly well-suited to steam navigation which was far more dependent on the land but enjoyed independent power to navigate enclosed waters, to sail through calms, to overcome contrary winds and to avoid the danger of lee shores such as that of Port Said. Thus in 1870 the Canal was used by twenty-seven sailing vessels, which supplied 5·5 per cent of the 486 transits but only 1·7 per cent of their total tonnage.

The opening of such a route created a revolution of expectations in both the shipbuilding and shipowning industries. It economized vastly in shipping tonnage by reducing the ratio of tonnage to cargo. By lowering the value of sailing vessels it discouraged in succession their sale, their completion, their building and their ordering. During the boom of 1858–69 in shipbuilding sail tonnage built in Britain had reached its peak in 1864 and sail tonnage registered in Britain its peak in 1865. The opening of the Canal ended that boom, especially in the building of composite wood and iron clippers for the China tea trade,[1] a more effective compromise with the new marine technology than the construction of 'mixed' vessels, or sailing ships with auxiliary engines. The number of ocean-going square-rigged vessels built in Britain sank from 132 in 1869 to 51 in 1870 and to 10 in 1871.[2] After the last tea clippers were launched in 1870 almost no large sailing vessels were built until the revival of 1873–4. The sailing fleet of both London and Liverpool reached its maximum size in 1870. In America the decline of the shipbuilding industry of Quebec was precipitated by the end of the English timber preference in 1867 and completed by the expectation-effects of the Canal. The Surveyor for Lloyd's Register appointed at Quebec in 1852 was therefore transferred in 1870 to Shanghai.[3]

The opening of the Suez route encouraged the building of steamships as much as it discouraged the building of sailing ships, first for the Bombay trade in 1870 and then for the China and Calcutta trades in 1871. The new route impressed contemporaries less as a shorter route than as a steam route and a new avenue for the dominant machine of the new technology. 'Coal, the stored-up sunlight of a million years, is the grand agent. Liberty lights the fire, and Christian civilization is the engine which is taking the whole world in its train.'[4] The Canal route even seemed to make feasible the replacement of coal by heavy shale-oil or by petroleum gas in steam vessels trading to the East. The losses suffered by the sail shipbuilding industry were more than counterbalanced by the benefits derived by the steam shipbuilding industry, in which the comparative advantages of Britain were especially great. The

[1] Lloyd's Register of Shipping, *Annals of Lloyd's Register, 1834–1884* (London, 1884), 86.
[2] Lloyd's Register of Shipping, *Report made to the Committee of Lloyd's Register...concerning the Dismasting of Large Iron Sailing Ships* (London, Lloyd's, 1886), 168.
[3] *Annals of Lloyd's Register, 1834–1884*, 107.
[4] C. C. Coffin, *Our New Way Round the World* (1869), 507.

shock of the opening of the Canal was nevertheless necessary to force English shipowners to adopt steam-power.[1]

The typical steamer built for the new route was made of iron and equipped with a compound engine and a screw propeller. The screw-steamer benefited at the expense of the paddle-steamer whose wheels were better suited than the screw to shallow water but added one-third to the beam of a vessel in a very narrow canal and created a more injurious wash to the banks than a screw. The coal-saving cost-cutting compound tandem marine engine had been first fitted by John Elder to a sea-going vessel in 1854, the year of the Canal concession. It was perfected only in the late 1860s so as to reduce coal consumption to one-third or even to one-quarter of that of an unimproved engine. Thus coincident with the opening of the Suez route it valorized that route by making possible the construction of steamers economically engined and economically fuelled from frequent coaling stations on a long voyage through Eastern seas where coal was dear. The typical steamer was larger than had been usual thitherto, although it was limited in size by the dimensions of the Canal, which became thenceforward an additional determinant of the size of ships. The Canal Company had thought in terms of sailing ships and had not considered the size of steamer which would prove most profitable on the Suez route when it adopted the revised profile of 1859. The limited size of the channel restricted the size of steamers and therefore the profits of trade, because small vessels could not pay on a long voyage in competition with sail. The Canal steamer was restricted in both draught and beam by the channel available and secured its increased capacity by a proportionate extension in length on the pattern of the long ships built by Bibby from 1861. That long, light and narrow vessel followed the new ratio of length to beam of 10:1 instead of 7:1 established by Bibby in 1867 and by Holt in 1868. Thereby its capacity and its speed were both increased without a corresponding increase in engine-power, although at the risk of running aground in the sharp curves of the Canal and at the expense of the visual appeal of the serpentine 'ditchers',[2] 'the ugly, black, snakey steamers which have come so much into vogue since the Suez Canal was opened'.[3] Shipbrokers foretold in 1870, when a 1,400-ton ship was considered large, that the 1,400-ton, 7-knot steamer would be replaced by the 2,000-ton, 9¾-knot steamer. Such a ship would burn 15–16 tons of coal per day to drive its 250 h.p. engine, accommodate forty passengers and cost £40,000, at £20 per ton.[4] J. Scott Russell, the builder of the largest ship in the world in the *Great Eastern*, even proposed 3,000-ton, 300 h.p., 10-knot steamers burning 24 tons of coal per day and carrying 4,600

[1] J. Steele, *The Suez Canal: its Present and Future. A Round-About Paper* (1872), 8.

[2] M. E. G. Duff, 'Notes of an Indian Journey, I', *Contemporary Review* (May 1875), 904, 27 November 1874.   [3] *The Times*, 25 April 1876, 13 i.

[4] *Le Canal de Suez*, 1 Mars 1870, 70, Buckley Offor & Co., The Freight Market in 1869. *The Economist*, 12 March 1870, 27, 'Commercial History and Review of 1869'. J. d'A. Samuda, 'The Influence of the Suez Canal on Ocean Navigation', *Transactions of the Institution of Naval Architects*, 6 April 1870, 2–3.

tons of cargo at half the maximum speed of the *Great Eastern* as the smallest capable of serving the future needs of trade with the East.[1] The immediate influence of the Canal was to accelerate the triumph of steam over sail, of the screw over the paddle and of iron over wood as well as to encourage the general acceptance of the larger steamship and the compound engine. Existing ships were also rebuilt, lengthened and re-engined to the profit of both the marine engineering and shipbuilding industries.

Some anticipatory orders for steamships for the new route were placed in 1869, providing 3·6 per cent of the tonnage launched on the Clyde during the year and making no extraordinary demands on shipbuilders.[2] From January 1870, however, such orders began to increase on Clyde yards. During 1870 53,887 tons were built on the Clyde for the Suez route, or 30 per cent of the total tonnage launched on the Clyde and eight-fold the 6,887 tons launched in 1869. In 1870 steam tonnage launched in Britain first exceeded sail tonnage while steam tonnage registered in Britain first exceeded one million tons. Sail tonnage entering the port of London reached its all-time maximum in 1870 as the new steamers shifted the bias from sail to steam and effected 'a complete revolution in the Eastern trade'.[3] During 1870 English shipowners learned that the best ship for the new route was one of 1,500 tons carrying 2,250 tons of cargo. The average gross tonnage of the ships launched for the Canal route in 1871 was 1,775 while that of transits through the Canal rose from 1,180 during the first six months (November 1869–May 1870) to exceed 1,775 tons only in 1873 and 2,000 tons only in 1876. During 1871 the Clyde launched for the Suez route 79,887 tons or 40·7 per cent of its total tonnage for the year. The example of the Clyde was followed at Newcastle, West Hartlepool, Hull and London. The boom of 1868–74 in steam shipbuilding encouraged Lloyd's Register of Shipping to recognize engines and boilers for the first time in 1869 as part of a ship's equipment but was not detonated by the opening of the Canal because expectations of the value of the route did not crystallize before January 1870. Nevertheless the growing use of the Canal powerfully reinforced that boom which doubled the steamship tonnage of England between 1868 and 1873. England's lead was followed by Holland, Germany and Russia but not by such sailing-ship nations as France, Norway and Greece. The British steam shipbuilding industry benefited by foreign as well as by home orders and received its greatest stimulus from the opening of the new route during 1870 and 1871 before the dispute over tolls began in 1872. By October 1871 50,000 tons of foreign steamships and 147,986 gross tons of British steamships had been brought into service in the Eastern trade and embarked in unsubsidized lines on the Suez route to the East: the British tonnage represented at £25 per ton a capital investment of £3,699,650 and

[1] J. S. Russell, 'The Fleet of the Future: For Commerce—For War', *Transactions of the Institution of Naval Architects*, 7 April 1870, 69.

[2] *The Engineer*, 3 December 1869, 341 iii; *Engineering*, 21 January 1870, 38 i–ii; *The Times*, 28 March 1870, 10 iii.

[3] *Mitchell's Maritime Register*, 6 December 1871, 17 iii.

was the equivalent not so much of 148 sailing ships of 1,000 tons each as of 370 such ships because the steamship was 150 per cent faster than the sailing vessel.[1] Thus the growth of steam shipping accompanied the increase in the traffic of the Canal and greatly depreciated the value of sail shipping.

Sailing shipowners bore almost the whole burden of the decrease in the demand for shipping. Some owners were bankrupted by the 20 per cent depreciation in the value of their ships. Others were reduced to carrying coal around the Cape to the coaling stations of the East. Most, however, survived the opening of the Canal as J. Samuda, C. H. Wigram and S. R. Graves[2] had anticipated in 1870 that they would. They did not attempt to send sailing ships through the Canal like Italian shipowners but responded to its challenge in their own way. They scrapped some tonnage and used the rest to carry on their old trade at lower freights. They continued to carry throughout the 1870s a greater aggregate value of trade around the Cape than that which passed through the Canal. They benefited by lower insurance rates and carried the cheap bulk commodities of rice and jute, wool and wheat in low-cost carriers using the long routes and the unbought wind of the open ocean. Other shipowners changed their front to face the foe and began, especially under the influence of younger partners, to build steamships. Such a use of the new technology to retain their established connexions with the markets of the East was made from 1870 by James MacGregor, Shaw & Maxton, William Ross, Thomas Wilson, T. & J. Harrison, from 1871 by Robert Alexander, Donald Currie, George Smith, William Thomson, Patrick Henderson, Frederick Green and from 1872 by D. J. Jenkins. Such a readjustment was less a triumph for steam over sail than a triumph for established firms in the maintenance of their accustomed status through the use of a new technology.

The rise of the steamship represented the transformation of a civilization as much as the emergence of a new technology. The sailing ship represented far less capital than the steamship, was linked to the land at infrequent intervals and served as a hard school of seamanship. The steamship was much less dependent on wind and current but represented a greater investment of capital, saddled the shipowner with heavy overhead costs and exposed the industry to depression which sailing ships could survive with their minimal overheads. Its spread assimilated the sea increasingly to the land on which it was so dependent. Shipping routes became 'ocean highways'[3] subject to a 'rule of the road' (1862) and to international regulation from 1879. Channels of commerce became 'trade routes' (1873).[4] The cable ended the freedom of the

---

[1] *Mitchell's Maritime Register*, 3 November 1871, 1391.

[2] *The Times*, 5 February 1870, 7 vi.

[3] T. Carlyle, *History of Frederick II of Prussia* (London, Chapman, 1864), 471. J. M. Dempsey, *Our Ocean Highways: a Condensed Universal Route Book* (London, Stanford, 1870), 367–70. *The Times*, 30 November 1869, 4 i. *Our Ocean Highways, the Monthly Geographical Record and Travellers' Register*, i, April 1870.

[4] T. T. Cooper, *The Mishmee Hills. An Account of a Journey made in an Attempt to Penetrate Thibet from Assam to open New Routes for Commerce* (London, King, 1873), 2, 15, 33.

ship's husband and subordinated the captain to the instructions of the home office as ambassadors and governors were similarly reduced to office-boys at the end of a wire. The subjugation of the sea by the land and its machine technology was also reflected in a rash of projects for ship-railways and in the conversion of the warship into what Nathaniel Barnaby called in 1879 a 'fighting machine'. Within the ship the compass replaced the stars for navigation while the engine-room telegraph, developed in 1875, mechanized the transmission of orders for power. The steamship inevitably revolutionized the skills of sea-faring personnel, replaced the sailor by the labourer, reduced able seamen to deck-swabbers and destroyed an ancient school of character training. The new passenger-liners became floating hotels which sought to make their clients forget that they were at sea and so closed off a whole realm of experience to landsmen. Land-time triumphed over ship's time, the clock over the ship's bell and the language of the mainland over the lore of the sea.

The spread of the steamship increased the demand for coal and for coaling stations on the new route. The frequency of coaling stations along that route saved bunker-space, increased cargo-space and enhanced the freights earned by steamships. The growth of coaling stations was more rapid after 1869 in the Eastern than in the Western seas and benefited Britain most of all because of her secure hold on the best locations on the capes and peninsulas of the Eastern sea-routes. In Asia new sources of fuel were sought, especially of coal, from Calcutta to Japan and from Natal to New South Wales. Labuan in particular was expected to supply from its estimated 400,000,000 tons half the needs of the steam navigation of the East and thereby to increase its value to the Empire.[1] The Oriental Coal Company, established in 1868 as the island's third coal company, produced 28 per cent less coal in 1870 than in 1869. The volume of Labuan's coal exports had declined in 1867–9 from their peak of £10,000 per annum in 1864–6. Those exports rose in 1870 but fell sharply in 1871 when Labuan lost its garrison and retained its mines only as a synonym for unsuccessful pretensions.[2] Thus coal exports were stimulated from England to the coaling stations along the new route both in the Mediterranean and in the Eastern seas. Colliers to Aden and even to Bombay were diverted from the Cape to the Canal route while colliers to ports beyond Aden used the Cape route and increased with the increase in steamships using the Canal. A steamer of 1,200 tons on a Calcutta voyage of 76 days burned 15 tons per day or a total of 1,130 tons, whereof 700 tons had to be sent by sail around the Cape. Such a steamer made two voyages in the time taken for one of the sailing ship and so created more employment for sail and more traffic around the Cape. The Canal Company did not exempt colliers from toll as had been recommended by the Cairo Commercial Congress of 1869. Colliers could thus avoid the payment of the high tolls on their bulk freight by using the Cape route and

[1] *The China Mail*, 18 February 1870, 3 vi.
[2] *Papers Relating to Her Majesty's Colonial Possessions, Part II—1874* (C-1102 of 1874), 144, 146, H. Bulwer, Labuan, 8 November 1873.

returning with rice or linseed. The opening of the Canal did not stimulate British coal-mining so immediately, so directly and so greatly as shipbuilding. The great demand for coal came from the iron industry rather than from the steam shipping industry. The increase in the building of iron steamships however increased the derived demand for iron and therefore the demand for coal. The limited initial use of the new route also restricted the demand for coal. Because the Abyssinian War had produced vast shipments of coal to the East, markets eastward of Suez imported less coal in 1872 than in 1867[1] while India's imports of coal decreased steadily from 1867–8 to 1870–1.[2] Thenceforward Calcutta's imports of coal rose tremendously, imports from Britain first exeeding imports from Australia in 1870–1 while coal production in India declined between 1869 and 1873.[2] When local coal production revived from 1873 English coal remained the fuel of English ships and found more extensive markets in Asia during the 1870s and 1880s than at any later time, in competition with the coal of Asia and of New South Wales.

The Canal thus created its own fleet which was built for, and adapted to, the new route as to no other. British shipowners were untormented by Flaubert's visions of the future and were indeed stimulated by the prostration of the greatest Mediterranean power in the Franco-Prussian War. They enjoyed the protection of British supremacy at sea, which secured British control of the new route to India, and they could therefore make massive investments not merely in shipping but also in the ideals of peace, free trade and universal brotherhood. Their construction of such a fleet of specialized cargo-vessels adapted to a single route and incapable of conversion into warships was a great act of faith which was economic in the short run but most uneconomic in the long run. Such a fleet was liable to be treated as a client- or captive-fleet either by the Canal Company or by the powers which flanked the whole length of the land-locked Suez route from Gibraltar to Aden. It was wholly dependent upon a canal which was wide enough for only one vessel and could easily be blocked. It would be useless for the Cape route if the Canal were blocked in the event of war with a Mediterranean power because its vessels did not have sufficient power to round the Cape with safety. In the event of a Mediterranean war it would require such massive cruiser protection that it would employ a large proportion of the Navy and leave few ships to protect the great bulk of British trade: it would then become the most expensive of cargo-carriers. Even in the Russian Black Sea Note of 1870 the threat emerged to the security of the Mediterranean which was to be made by the Franco-Russian alliance of 1892. Sir Alexander Milne, who had commanded the British squadron at the inauguration of the Canal, wrote the first Admiralty memorandum on commerce-protection as the First Sea Lord in 1874.

[1] D. A. Thomas, 'The Growth and Direction of our Foreign Trade in Coal during the Last Half Century', *Journal of the Royal Statistical Society* (1903), 485.
[2] D. R. Gadgil, *The Industrial Evolution of India in Recent Times* (Madras, Oxford University Press, 1924), 65.

By contrast to the Suez route the Cape route remained a secure ocean route in a world dominated by British seapower and by the British colonies at the Cape and Natal. The Cape route was a familiar route to the British Navy and was indeed its private thoroughfare. It did not pass by hostile states nor compel the British to flaunt their dominance in the very face of their rivals. The opening of the Suez route did not throw that old route into disuse, although it captured its steam traffic and deprived it of potential steam traffic for a decade. The Cape route was still used by steamships and auxiliary steamships en route to Australia but ceased to be used by the new steamers of the P. & O., outward bound since 1842, and of the Messageries, outward bound since 1861 to their Eastern stations for the service to Suez. It also lost the lines of fast steamers maintained by Holt and Robertson in the China tea trade. The steam route via the Cape could be used only by steamers of high steaming radius: it suffered from the great distances between its coaling ports and therefore from the sacrifice of cargo-space to unprofitable bunker-space. The steamship line to Calcutta via the Cape which was projected by Rathbone Brothers of Liverpool in December 1869 was transferred in 1870 to the Suez route. Cape Town's facilities were also limited for docking, coaling, shelter and repair. The new basin and dock opened to traffic on 17 May 1870 were first used by a sailing vessel and not by a steamship and were named the Alfred Basin and Dock by the Duke of Edinburgh when he opened them on 11 July.

The disadvantages of the Cape route for steam navigation were positive advantages for navigation by sail. The Cape route was the perfect all-water route, using the great expanses of the oceans, the great-circle technique of navigation and the favourable westerly winds of the high latitudes. The continued supremacy of sail over steam in world shipping ensured the continuing use of the Cape route[1] far more than did the technical deficiencies of the Canal or the heavy dues charged by the Canal Company. Such established merchant-shipowners as Brocklebanks carried only Brocklebank cargoes to and from Calcutta, never entered the freight market, and imbued the younger shipowners of Liverpool such as Donald Currie with their preference for the Cape route to India. The Cape route continued in use by the sailing vessels of the U.S.A., France, Germany, the Netherlands, Scandinavia, by clippers in the trade to Bengal, Java and China, by clippers in the trade from America to India and China and by ships in the Australian trade. Thus the Glasgow Shipping Company began the new Loch Line from Glasgow to Australia in 1867 under the management of Aitken, Lilburn & Co. The Cape route became a low-cost route in contrast to the high-cost Canal route and was used for the carriage of cheap bulk commodities which did not represent large investments of capital and a heavy burden of interest capable of reduction by the shorter route. Thus it was used for the shipment of jute, rice, wool, hides,

[1] G. S. Graham, 'The Ascendancy of the Sailing Ship 1850–85', *Economic History Review* (August 1956), 81, 84.

oil-seeds, sugar, salt-petre, cutch, timber and metal ores: it also competed in the carriage of tea, cotton and wheat.

The Cape route was even used in conjunction with the Suez route in experimental combinations by ships carrying tea, salt, coal and cables. Usually the Suez route was used for the outward voyage and the Cape route for the homeward voyage except by the cable-ships. Italian sailing ships used the Canal en route to Calcutta or Rangoon with salt and returned via the Cape to Europe. Even colliers travelled out via the Canal and returned via the Cape with bulk cargoes. Pender's cable-laying ships, however, steamed out via Cape Town (22–31 December 1869) to lay the Bombay–Suez–Aden cable, establishing the pattern which was repeated with the Singapore, the China and the Australian cables. The *Hibernia* returned via the Canal and so set the example for its use by discharged cable-ships on their homeward voyage in ballast. The other experiments in combining the Suez and Cape routes established no successful precedent for imitation. Australia, which was best adapted to combine the use of the two routes, continued to depend on sailing ships using the Cape route until 1877.

The Cape Colony, founded as a half-way house between the Netherlands and Java, had become an English colony by conquest, unsupported by any moral bond between English and Dutch. The mutual repulsion between the English who loved commerce and the Boers who loved the land had made the Cape the parent of the three other colonies of South Africa. Communications with England were restricted by the monopoly of the Union Line, which seemed to serve the interests of Cape Town almost to the exclusion of those of the Eastern Province and Natal. The opening of the Canal encouraged a suggestion in January 1870 to improve the mail service and to give Port Elizabeth and Durban similar benefits to Cape Town by the establishment of a new steam-route to England via the Canal. D. C. Stevens enlarged on his scheme in September after the success of the Canal was no longer in doubt, the cable had been laid from Suez to Bombay via Aden and gloomy predictions had been made about the future of the new Table Bay docks.[1] He proposed the despatch of every alternate mail steamer of the Union Company from Europe and the Cape through the Canal, each steamer making a complete circuit of Africa in alternate directions and so using the Canal both ways. Such a service would link the Cape with the telegraph at Aden in 22 days, against the 36 days taken by the Union Line on the Atlantic route, and with London via Brindisi in 36½ days, avoiding the English Channel and the Bay of Biscay. It would also link Natal with London in 30 days and with Aden in 15 days. It would be used, however, only by passengers without family encumbrances, with money to spare and with a desire to see the world. It would need subsidies from Portugal, Zanzibar and Cape Colony to enable the Union Company

---

[1] *East Coast of Africa. Correspondence respecting the Slave Trade and Other Matters* (C-657 of 1872), 65–8 quoting letter by Stevens in the *Cape Argus* of 3 September 1870. R. Coupland, *The Exploitation of East Africa 1856–1890* (London, Faber, 1939), 84.

to cover the cost of the Canal tolls and the extra 9 days' coal on a 45-day voyage. The proposal won the support of the *Cape Argus,* which hoped that it might develop the rich potentialities of the back country of East Africa, but failed to secure the substantial subsidies which alone would have tempted the Union Company.

During 1870 the full effect of the opening of the Canal on the Cape route became apparent. The overseas tonnage entering Table Bay had risen by 6 per cent in 1867 and by 5 per cent in 1868 but fell in 1869 by 1·7 per cent and in 1870 by 34,737 tons or by 22·4 per cent. The Governor of the Cape Colony reduced the decline in shipping tonnage to just over 10 per cent by combining coastwise with overseas tonnage.[1] He doubted whether the colony would suffer much loss from the end of the calling-trade, thought that the real shock had taken place when the overland route was first opened and Indian officers stopped spending their furloughs in Cape Town, and attributed the real prosperity of the Cape to its agriculture. The decline in total tonnage during 1870 was halved from 22·4 to 11·4 per cent by the expansion of the coasting trade under the stimulus of the discovery of the alluvial diamond deposits on the Vaal in January 1870 and of the first of the volcanic pipes south of the Vaal in August 1870. That new source of wealth compensated the colony for the loss of its unique position on the sea-road to the Indies and converted an expected government deficit of £60,000 for 1870 into a surplus of £35,000. It stimulated coastal more than overseas trade and encouraged new enterprise in shipping. The Cape and Natal Steam Navigation Company Ltd. was established in October 1870 by G. H. Payne to breach the monopoly of the Union Company in the interests of Port Elizabeth and Durban and to reach the Cape in 35 days en route to Algoa Bay and Port Natal. Stevens revived his scheme in the *Cape Argus* of 20 December after the Franco-Prussian War had made it likely that French steamers would stop running from Mauritius and the *Times of Natal* had argued on 12 November that a Durban–Aden steamer service would bring letters from England in 25 instead of 60 days. He calculated that the round-trip from Plymouth would take 96 days against the existing 88 days and suggested that larger and more powerful steamers might be built specially for the east-coast route to link up with others at Algoa Bay and to return via the Canal.[2] That purely mercantile scheme won the support of the Natal Chamber of Commerce for a subsidy in January 1871. Natal's aspirations to supremacy in South Africa were aroused by the marked revival of internal trade which moderated the sectional antagonisms within the Cape Colony, enabled Cape Town to reduce Port Elizabeth to subordination, and attracted diggers from Natal to the Free State. 'Look to your diminution

[1] *Reports on the Present State of Her Majesty's Colonial Possessions 1870, Part III. Cape of Good Hope* (C-617 of 1872), 80, H. Barkly, 23 June 1871. *Papers Relating to Her Majesty's Colonial Possessions 1871, Part II. Cape of Good Hope* (C-709-I of 1873), 228, H. Barkly, 27 May 1872.

[2] *East Coast of Africa. Correspondence respecting the Slave Trade* (C-657 of 1872), 68, quoting Stevens' letter from the *Cape Argus* of 20 December 1870.

of trade and people, ye Durbanites, within the last six months! Suppose, now, if Natal should federate with the Free State, open the different passes of the Berg, throw open her port to all the world by abolishing the Customs tariff, establish steam communication through the Suez Canal, do away with the excise.'[1] Those aspirations were frustrated by the Cape Colony which became the great beneficiary by the boom in imports and in shipping created by the trade to the diamond fields. Payne's Cape and Natal Line encouraged the development of the harbours of Port Elizabeth from 1870 and of East London from 1871 as well as a revival of interest in Natal coal in 1871, especially in compressed patent fuel which could bear the freight to Aden. Payne's vessels regularly outsteamed the ships of the Union Company. His *Sweden* reached Cape Town from Dartmouth in $27\frac{1}{2}$ days (10 March–6 April 1871),[2] or seven days before the mailboat. The Union Company was compelled in reply to buy the fast *Syria* from the P. & O., to lower the Cape record further to 26 days 18 hours (10 October 1871)[3] and so to reduce its unsubsidized competitor to bankruptcy. The acceleration of the voyage to the Cape remained a permanent gain.

Kimberley's annexation of the diamond fields to the Cape in 1871 prevented the shift of power from the historic centre of Cape Town to the Free State beyond the Orange River. That act provoked a Boer revival which made Bloemfontein more than ever the centre of Dutch politics, religion and nationality and deepened the contrast between the Boers rooted in the soil and the temporary English sojourners in Natal.[4] 'The English and Scotch in South Africa have gone there mostly to make fortunes and to return when they are made... The grain of the old oak is in New England. The English in South Africa are pulpy endogens.'[5] Kimberley's act ruined any possibility of confederation by agreement on the Canadian model of 1867 Annexation also estranged the Boers of the Cape as well as those of the republics while self-government provided the institutions for the formal expression of their resentment. Self-government had been refused by the Cape Legislature in 1870 but was pressed from 1871 by the imperial government on a reluctant colony. It was not associated with the extension of cable communication as in Canada because the Cape lacked the bulk exports to bear the cost of a cable which even Australia could afford. The inauguration of responsible government in the most isolated of British possessions in 1872 made any coercion of the republics of the interior impossible as intolerable to the Boers of the Cape. Thus Froude recommended in 1874[6] the fortification of the Cape Peninsula

---

[1] *Natal Mercury*, 6 June 1871, 3 i, 'A Voice from the Vaal'.

[2] *The Times*, 24 May 1871, 10 ii; 22 September 1871, 4 iii.

[3] M. Murray, *Ships and South Africa. A Maritime Chronicle of the Cape* (London, Oxford University Press, 1933), 48–9.

[4] J. A. Froude, *Short Studies on Great Subjects* (London, Longmans, 1877), iii, third series. *Leaves from a South African Journal*, 382, 6 December 1874.

[5] Ibid., 357, 8 October 1874; 366, 27 October 1874.

[6] Ibid., 345, 347, 373–4, 25 September 1874.

from Table Bay to False Bay on the model of Gibraltar, the restriction of imperial control to the harbours of South Africa, especially to Cape Town as the most important naval station in the world, and the abandonment of the rest of the country to its own destiny. Froude's pessimism was justified by the Boer revival of 1875–7 which produced the stereotype of the 'Great Trek' made by the 'Voortrekkers' of the 1830s as the one supreme nation-forming event in South African history.

The opening of the Canal created a new sea-route to East Africa and made possible a service linking the European colonies of South Africa with the Arab and Indian colonies of East Africa. The great island-entrepôt of East Africa which thitherto had been reached by sailing ship around the Cape became the destination of some of the first steamers using the Canal, although they were French and Austrian rather than British. Rabaud and Pastré of Marseilles chartered the British steamer *Malta* to pioneer a line to Zanzibar. That ship was the sixth toll-paying transit to pass through the Canal (27–30 December 1869) and the first toll-paying French transit. It carried £26,000 of cargo to Zanzibar and perhaps the cholera which killed 25,000–30,000 inhabitants. It returned through the Canal on 14 March, a week after the *Explorateur* had left Marseilles to follow up its voyage. The path of German trade in the Red Sea and East Africa was pioneered by the *Marietta*, a diminutive Austrian schooner-brig of seventy-seven tons which left Trieste on 1 January 1870, loaded to the scuppers with £8,000 of Austrian manufactures and Swiss cheese on an expedition financed by seven manufacturers of St. Gall led by Künzle, by the St. Gall Chamber of Commerce established in 1466 and by one Swiss merchant of Trieste. The *Marietta* passed through the Canal on 8–10 February and made its way slowly southwards to Zanzibar on 1 December: it circumnavigated Africa and returned to Germany after eighteen months.[1] The next German vessel to use the Canal (25–26 October 1871) en route to Zanzibar, the *Africa* of O'Swald & Co., came from Hamburg rather than Trieste.

The Canal enabled the Indian merchants in Zanzibar to deal direct with visiting steamers and to by-pass foreign, especially American, merchants. Thereby it 'raised the old scratch with our markets'[2] and presented a challenge to which American merchants responded with vigour and English statesmen with caution. British influence in Zanzibar had been destroyed by an unauthorized attack on the local slave-trade in 1868[3] and by the growth of Arab-Moslem opposition to the penetration of Indian merchants. An interdepartmental committee appointed to consider the slave-trade and British prestige in Zanzibar expressed the hope on 24 January 1870 that the island

---

[1] *Petermanns Geographische Mittheilungen* (1870), 161–2, 353–7; (1871), 69–70, 390–1, 'Richard Brenner's Expedition nach Ost-Afrika'. *Le Canal de Suez*, 14 Septembre 1871, 293–5, 'L'Expédition par le Canal de Suez dans l'Afrique Occidentale'.

[2] N. R. Bennett, *Studies in East African History* (Boston University Press, 1963), 38–9, 'Americans in Zanzibar: 1865–1905', Consul F. R. Webb to Roper, 6 October 1870.

[3] R. J. Gavin, 'The Bartle Frere Mission to Zanzibar, 1873', *Historical Journal* (1962), 126–7, 132–3.

would become the great central depot for liberated slaves and would gain more certain and regular postal communication, so encouraging an offer by William Mackinnon to establish a British-India service to Zanzibar for £15,000 per annum. The renewed agitation against the slave-trade from June 1871[1] encouraged the revival from October of Stevens' scheme which won more support for a steamship service via the Canal as part of a campaign against the slave-trade than the earlier efforts in the cause of commerce alone. 'I only hope that the opportunity will be seized to make Lesseps' grand work conducive to the civilizing of Eastern Africa by commerce, and from being, as hitherto, inimical to the Cape, to make it a means of reviving our hitherto waning trade and enriching colonies which have hitherto had a hard struggle against adverse circumstances.'[2] The reluctance of Zanzibar and the Cape to pay subsidies for such a service compelled Granville to send a circular despatch on 16 February 1872 to the Governments of Germany, France, the U.S.A. and Portugal, appealing to them to help to establish a line of mail steamers to Zanzibar.[3] On 19 August the Governor of the Cape Colony rejected the scheme on behalf of his colony[4] which would not pay £4,000 per annum for the almost exclusive benefit of Natal nor sacrifice Cape Town's monopoly of the mail terminus.

The entry of Donald Currie into the South African trade introduced competition which accelerated the creation of the Zanzibar service. Overseas tonnage entering Table Bay had declined during 1871 for the third successive year, especially that of vessels in ballast. In 1872 overseas tonnage, which had fallen in 1871 by 10·4 per cent, made its first gain since 1868 and rose by 52·5 per cent to the record level of 164,579 tons. The dispute with the Canal Company over tonnage measurement and the payment of tolls encouraged some English shipping to return in 1872 to the Cape route. The comparative stability in the total value of the Cape's exports between 1866 and 1869 was followed by expansion in 1870–1 and by a boom in 1872–4, especially in the exports of ostrich-feathers, mohair and wool while diamonds supplied a dynamic lure to Cape Town as the gateway to the interior. That boom attracted to the African periphery Currie's Castles which were suffering from the new steam competition in the Calcutta trade. Currie began his London Line of Cape Steamers with the chartered steamship *Iceland* from Dartmouth on 25 January 1872, so reviving the competition with the Union Company begun by the Cape and Natal Line. His fourth chartered steamer, the *Penguin*, reached Cape Town in 24 days 16 hours (7 April–2 May 1872)[5] and won him the support of the Cape merchants in London. Currie also cultivated the

---

[1] Gavin, 136–7.

[2] *East Coast of Africa. Correspondence respecting the Slave Trade* (C-657 of 1872), 70, quoting Stevens' letter from the *Cape Argus* of 19 December 1871.

[3] Gavin, 138.

[4] B. A. Le Cordeur, 'Natal, the Cape and the Indian Ocean, 1846–1880', *Journal of African History* (1966), 257–8.

[5] *The Times*, 11 June 1872, 12 v. M. Murray, *Ships and South Africa* (1933), 61.

support of the Boer Republics and used his East Indiamen to carry out coal for his steamships from Cardiff to Cape Town. His competition compelled the Union Company to submit in June 1872 a joint tender with the British India Line for a service to Zanzibar.

The mail contract with the British India Line was approved by Gladstone on 29 September 1872 and signed on 24 December 1872.[1] It provided for a subsidized monthly mail service between Aden and Zanzibar and brought the first British India steamer to Zanzibar on 15 December 1872, followed by the first Union steamer in February 1873. The supplementary mail contract of 8 May 1873 with the Union Company reduced the contract time from thirty-seven to thirty days, provided for a service from the Cape via Natal to Zanzibar and so created a chain of communication girdling Africa through the cooperation of the Union, the British India and the P. & O. Lines. The P. & O. however used the overland route rather than the Canal. Zanzibar rather than Port Elizabeth became the half-way port between the Cape and Suez routes and the meeting-place of the steamers of the British India and Union Lines. The Union Line thus linked the Cape indirectly to the new imperial cable route at Aden and enabled Cape Malays to go on pilgrimage to Mecca by steamship. Durban was linked by the new service of the Union Line to Zanzibar but did not develop as rapidly as Port Elizabeth, which served as the nearest port of import to the diamond fields. Currie's reply to the extension of the Union Company's mail contract was further to reduce the Cape record by the outward voyage of the *Windsor Castle* in 23 days 15 hours (24 April–17 May 1873).[2] He thereby earned a resolution of congratulations from the House of Assembly of the Cape and encouraged the Cape Government to grant speed-premiums from 1873. In 1874 he decided to concentrate on his colonial line and to lay down no more steamships for the Eastern trade.

The Zanzibar mail service was followed by Frere's mission to Zanzibar via Suez on 25 December 1872 to secure the prohibition of the slave-trade from the island. His mission failed to overcome French opposition during a stay of three months[3] and was accomplished by Kirk, a Consul-General from 1873, after the Cabinet decided on 14 May to go to war if necessary against the Sultan.[4] The Sultan accepted the Treaty of 5 June 1873 under the threat of a naval blockade, forbade the trans-oceanic commerce in slaves and closed on the same day the slave-market of Zanzibar, on the site of which the foundation stone of Christ Church Cathedral was laid on 25 December 1873. An increase in the slave-trade of the Red Sea followed its prohibition from Zanzibar. The growth of British interests in the island culminated in the Sultan's visit to England via the Canal in 1875. The entrepôt trade of Zanzibar remained much more important than its local trade. Its cloves were less valuable than those of Penang and suffered from uncertain harvests. Its ivory exports however increased to England but decreased to Bombay. Zanzibar became the base for

[1] Gavin, 173.   [2] *The Times*, 4 July 1873, 12 vi; 8 July, 5 ii.
[3] Gavin, 145.   [4] Ibid., 146.

V. L. Cameron's pioneer crossing of Africa from Bagamoyo to Benguela in 1873–5, when he took possession of the Congo basin in the name of Queen Victoria to the distress of the Foreign Office. Stanley had travelled via Zanzibar on his circuitous route from Port Said in 1869 to Livingstone at Ujiji, bringing him on 19 November 1871 the 'grand news' that 'the Suez Canal is a fact'.[1] From Zanzibar the embalmed body of Livingstone was carried by the British India Line to Aden and thence by the P. & O. *Malwa* free of charge to Southampton, en route to its interment on 18 April 1874 in Westminster Abbey. Livingstone's career was commemorated in the P. & O. *Zambesi* of 1873. His death inspired a new wave of English missionary expansion to Lakes Tanganyika and Nyasa and brought a steamship through the Canal in 1875 for the Lake Nyasa Mission, which blended commerce with civilization in the true spirit of Livingstone.

The Cape route increased its traffic as the overseas tonnage entering Table Bay rose by 15 per cent in 1873 and by 20 per cent in 1874. The rates of increase for the tonnage of Table Bay and the Suez Canal were very close in both 1872 and 1873,[2] indicating that the two routes had become complementary rather than competitive in the new equilibrium of world trade. Calcutta's shipments of produce to London via the Cape declined by 12·4 per cent in 1872 and continued to fall in 1873 and 1874. Shipments of China tea via the Cape sank markedly in 1873 because the tea-clippers had been driven by steamer competition out of the trade to London. The coal famine of 1872–4, however, raised the price of coal high enough to decrease the competitive capacity of steamships in the India and China trades to the immediate benefit of sail but to the ultimate advantage of the steamship because it encouraged the general acceptance of the coal-saving compound engine. From 1873 commodity prices began their long fall which encouraged exporters in Asia to use the sea and the long route via the Cape as a warehouse for their bulk commodities in the expectation of a rise. From 1874 a new fall in freights began to the benefit of sail rather than of steam. Effective competition between sail and steam began with the revival of sail shipbuilding in 1873–6. The tonnage of sailing vessels built in Britain in 1875 and 1876 exceeded that of steamships. Iron clippers were built in place of composite vessels: their size was raised from 1,500 tons to 1,700 tons and their length was increased at the expense of their sailing power and speed. In that boom sailing vessels were built by some shipowners who used the Canal such as Robert Alexander in 1873–4 and T. & J. Harrison in 1874. The pioneer vessels to use the Canal in 1869–70, the *Queen of the South* and the *Mauritius*, were even converted to sail in 1875. Thus the Cape route gained a new stream of low-cost shipping as its strategic importance was recognized anew in Carnarvon's campaign for South African confederation. In the Cape trade Currie achieved his greatest success by securing a half share

[1] H. M. Stanley, *How I Found Livingstone; Travels, Adventures and Discoveries in Central Africa* (London, Low, 1872), 415.

[2] In 1872, 52·49 and 52·44 per cent; in 1873, 14·89 and 17·84 per cent.

in the mail contract of 5 October 1876 which reduced the contract time further to twenty-six days.

The Cape route continued to be used by emigrants and passengers en route to Australia, by Indian coolies en route to the West Indies, by retiring Anglo-Indians and by invalided soldiers. It also remained an emergency trooping route which by 1875 could carry troops to Calcutta in only 14–15 days longer than the time taken via the Canal. It was used by the first 'globe-trotter' en route to Melbourne on the s.s. *Great Britain* in 1872 in combination with a return journey by the overland route in 1874.[1] It was also used by Pierre Loti in 1872 en route to Tahiti as a midshipman in the *Vaudreuil*, by Togo in 1875 on a voyage around the world in C. H. Wigram's *Hampshire*, by Rimbaud in 1876 en route to Le Havre with sugar from Batavia in W. Kinloch's *Wandering Chief*, by Rufus Isaacs in 1877 en route to Calcutta in Thomson and Grey's *Blair Athole* and by Joseph Conrad in 1878 en route to Sydney in the wool clipper *Duke of Sutherland*.

The Cape route of island-outposts pivoted around Table Bay, with additional ports of call to both east and west. Of those subsidiary ports St. Helena suffered more than any other from the decline of the Cape route but mainly from the general acceleration of communications rather than from the opening of the Canal.[2] Madeira became a coaling port for steamers and increased its British steam tonnage sharply between 1867 and 1871. The Seychelles became a naval sanatorium and depot from 1871, with a mail service to Zanzibar, and increased the export of their staple of coconut oil. Mauritius anticipated an increase in its isolation but raised its customs revenue to record heights in 1870 and first exported sugar through the Canal in the English steamer *Earl of Lonsdale* in September 1872, although India remained its main export market. Even Réunion enjoyed a sharp increase in the number of English vessels entering its harbour in 1870. St. Helena failed, however, to become a port of call for steamers or to develop a staple export from its barren perpendicular rock. As sailing vessels sailed faster around the Cape they either ceased to call at James Town or did not take on supplies if they did call or took on much fewer supplies than formerly. The shipping tonnage of St. Helena had increased by 4·3 per cent in 1869. In 1870 however a great depression was caused by the decrease in the shipping trade, by the reduction in military establishments and by the loss of the troop-ships to India: the number of vessels fell by 9·3 per cent and their tonnage by 6·7 per cent while the colony's revenue declined by 23·9 per cent and the value of its imports by 31 per cent. The Government received two public loans in 1869 and 1870 to reduce its deficit and hoped that the island would gain a staple export from the establishment of a cinchona plantation in 1869 and the collection of guano from 1870.

[1] E. K. Laird, *Rambles of a Globe-Trotter in Australasia, Japan, China, Java, India and Cashmere* (London, Chapman, 1875), ii. 355.
[2] J. C. Melliss, *St. Helena: a Physical, Historical and Topographical Description of the Island* (London, Reeve, 1875), 44.

Shipping tonnage fell by a further 8·5 per cent in 1871 and 14 per cent in 1872 when that of Table Bay revived.[1] Landed property depreciated in value and rents fell by an average of 33 per cent by 1872. Emigration from the island, which had begun to reduce its population during the 1860s, rose from an annual average of 62 in 1861–70 to one of 450 in 1871–3, mainly to the Cape to supply domestic servants and employees of the Cape Copper Company of Namaqualand. A third public loan was granted in 1872. When the cinchona tree was killed off in 1871–3 by the damp subsoil experiments were made with fibre plants, especially aloe and New Zealand flax, and even with coffee trees in 1872. The Governor ranked the importance of the island as no less than that of Malta or Gibraltar because in wartime the sinking of one ship might close the Canal while two or three steamers stationed on St. Helena might intercept the whole of the returning trade from the East.[2] In 1873 the island revived with the recovery in its shipping tonnage and revenues, aided by Kimberley's drastic reduction from July 1873 of the combined salaries of Governor and Colonial Secretary from £2,700 to £900, in an effort to transform a base into a self-supporting colony. The withdrawal of troops by the Colonial Office in 1875 left only a battery of artillery and a squadron of engineers amid ruined fortifications and encouraged the rumour of the impending cession of the island to Italy for use as a penal settlement.[3] James Town failed to benefit by the growing importance of South Africa and Australia because of the rise of steam shipping at the expense of sail. American vessels, however, developed the whale fishery from 1875, permitting the export of whale oil, as well as flax fibre, to London from 1876. The former Surveyor and Engineer of the colony painted perhaps too gloomy a picture because he was himself so near to the death which relieved the colony's revenues of his pension. 'The ships calling at the port, the chief trade of the place, lessen day by day.'[4]

[1] *Reports on the Present State of Her Majesty's Colonial Possessions, 1870, Part III*, 103, St. Helena, C. G. Patey, 20 April 1871. *Papers Relating to Her Majesty's Colonial Possessions, 1871, Part II*, 246, St. Helena, C. G. Patey, 14 March 1872.

[2] *Papers Relating to Her Majesty's Colonial Possessions, Part I—1874* (C-882 of 1874), 149, St. Helena, C. G. Patey, 17 March 1873.

[3] *Morning Advertiser*, 27 November 1875, 4 ii.

[4] J. C. Melliss, *St. Helena* (1875), 43.

13

THE REVOLT OF THE STEAM
SHIP OWNERS, 1872–1874

THE Canal Company remained on the verge of bankruptcy after two years of operating the Canal in competition with the Cape route and the Egyptian Railway, while its client shipping lines paid satisfactory dividends and merchants doubled both their turnover and their profits by using the new route.[1] The Company's receipts rose in 1871 to £475,000 but did not cover its expenses although its losses sank to £105,700, or to 28 per cent of those made in 1870. After the war and the Commune the Company came under growing pressure to produce dividends from its shareholders, from its bondholders and especially from the delegation-holders, who were entitled to receive dividends only for twenty-five years from 1869 and therefore wished their distribution to begin as soon as possible. The Company was also faced by a revolt of the middling shareholders against the large shareholders who habitually supported the administration. Shareholders had no voice in the affairs of the Company save through the general meeting which was, however, restricted to shareholders with twenty-five shares. The average French shareholding had been ten in 1858 and might have fallen to as low as five by 1864 with the increase in shareholders. In 1872 only 1,425 shareholders were eligible to attend the general meeting while 38,500 were incligible. The powers of that minority were further limited by the restriction of attendance at the general meeting to those who had registered their shares with the Company five days beforehand, by the constitution of a quorum by forty shareholders representing 5 per cent of the Company's capital, by the restriction of votes to a maximum per member of ten representing 250 shares on the basis of one vote for every twenty-five shares, and by the acceptance of proxy votes. A company so constituted could justify itself only by financial success. The continuing absence of dividends, aggravated by Lesseps' efforts to raise funds in England, aroused the discontent of the middling shareholders of the provinces. Those vehemently French shareholders detested the idea of a sale of the Canal and the Anglophile bias of the Company administration in Paris. They disliked the large shareholders and the delegation-holders, especially Jules Lebaudy, who held 5 per cent of the Company's shares and had become its financial saviour in January–February 1872 by subscribing to 60 per cent of the 1871 loan. They established their own opposition journal[2] under Charles

---

[1] J. Steele, *The Suez Canal: its Present and Future. A Round-About Paper* (London, Simpkin, 1872), 9.
[2] *Le Canal des Deux Mers*, 4 Janvier 1872–25 Février 1875.

de Lesseps, who was a distant relative of Ferdinand and had been the manager from 1858 to 1871 of *L'Isthme de Suez*.

The directors accepted the use of the Canal by a smaller tonnage than they had expected and sought to secure from that tonnage some return to their unruly shareholders. They therefore determined to capitalize on the huge capital investment made in steam shipping for the specific use of the Canal and to revise the basis on which tolls were levied, so that the same tonnage would yield a greater revenue. Such a revision was justifiable because real tonnage was invariably higher than the official tonnage on which harbour- and Canal-dues were paid. Shipowners had also constructed spaces adding materially to their carrying capacity but not to their tonnage-dues, had arranged their engine-spaces so as to increase deductible capacity unduly and had so exploited for monetary advantage concessions intended to make steamers more seaworthy.[1] The commission of inquiry into tolls reported after five months to the board on 20 January 1872. The board then defined on 4 March the ton of capacity referred to in the concession of 1856 as the real capacity of a vessel and decided to levy tolls from 1 July on that real capacity, using as a basis of measurement gross tonnage, which was not so easily tampered with as register tonnage. Thereby high-powered steamers, which were the best clients of the Company, would be taxed more in proportion than low-powered steamers.[2] Tolls would be increased by about 30 per cent on English ships, which supplied 71 per cent of the total tonnage during the first thirty months of the Canal's operation down to June 1872. The Company's income would also be increased by the postponement of improvement works and even by the suspension of dredging so that it would be able to declare the desired dividend.

Lesseps could not however avert a serious clash with his dissatisfied shareholders. 'The father of the Isthmus',[3] who regarded his employees as 'the family of Suez', always treated his shareholders as a grand seigneur treated his tenants. Usually he dominated the general meeting as he did the elected board of directors and the delegated executive committee, which remained an extension of his family, comprising Theodore Motet, a former Engineers officer in the service of the Pasha of Egypt, Lesseps' brother Jules, his brother-in-law Victor Delamalle and his eldest son Charles, who had been a director since 1869 and a vice-president since 1872. That small executive committee undertook the real management of the Company, met much more frequently than the monthly board, and was wholly under Lesseps' influence. Lesseps claimed to be President of the Company not by virtue of election by the shareholders but by virtue of the concession, and he claimed to hold that position for life rather than for the ten years from the opening of the Canal

---

[1] J. Steele, *The Suez Canal* (1872), 12. *Report from the Select Committee on Merchant Ships* (*Measurement of Tonnage*) *Bill* (C. 309 of 17 July 1874), Q.21 and Q.151, 2 July 1874, Colonel J. Stokes.

[2] J. Steele, 13.

[3] E. de Léon, *The Khedive's Egypt* (1877), 25.

prescribed in 1856. He thus enjoyed a position unparalleled by that of any other president. He never lacked the support of a strong group of loyalist shareholders, although he did not recruit his directors from the general body of shareholders, not even if they were as rich as Lebaudy. He used his highest arts as a diplomat to the full in the conduct of a general meeting. He delayed the distribution of the annual report and withheld information useful to discontented shareholders. He restricted the budget and the list of shareholders to the Company administration but did not discourage friends of the administration from forming a caucus to counter any dissidents. He framed the agenda of each meeting carefully and sought to avoid the raising of controversial issues. If he was forced to permit speech by a shareholder hostile to the administration he then invited speakers for the opposing view in order to prevent other shareholders from rallying to the rebel flag. If he was forced to accept controversial resolutions he sought to frame the questions put to the vote in the interests of the administration. He postponed voting or imposed the guillotine when either course seemed desirable in order to wring a favourable vote from a hostile assembly. He even adjourned a meeting rather than risk an unfavourable vote and so gained time to encourage the rally of his supporters. He could not however always succeed in diverting currents of opposition to reinforce his own dominance.

One week before the meeting of shareholders the Company with the aid of Lebaudy resumed the payment of interest on its bonds from 6 March 1872 together with interest on the deferred coupon (i.e. with interest on the interest), and so regained credit on the Bourse. The day before the meeting preparatory caucuses were held on 11 March by 150 opponents and by 33 friends of the administration. The meeting on 12 March was attended by 661 shareholders representing 51,749 shares. An attempt by ten shareholders to convert the Company into a French joint-stock company under the Law of 24 July 1867 was opposed by the board, because of the Company's obligations to the Khedive, and rejected by the meeting. The dissident shareholders then threatened to haul the directors before the courts. Lesseps refused to put to the vote a motion that sovereignty lay with the general meeting of shareholders and not with the board of directors. He emphasized that the shareholders had subscribed their money but were not petty sovereigns free to interfere in the administration of the Company. He flatly denied their freedom to vote on the taxation of shipping tonnage and so to encroach on the central mystery of the board. He secured approval of the board's action regarding tonnage only by asserting that defeat would mean legal action against the board and by a narrow majority of 810 to 722 votes, amidst confusion after 17 directors had cast 170 votes for themselves to convert a hostile majority of 82 into a safe one of 88. He then read out the names of four nominees to the board without specifying which were nominated by the board and which by the shareholders. The meeting nevertheless elected two directors hostile to the board by 796 and 786 votes and defeated by the large majorities of 413 and 408 votes the two directors recommended by the board, including Guichard. Lesseps was audibly moved by his defeat and closed the meeting amidst tumult.

The new regulations for the taxation of tonnage, published on 17 March to give the necessary three months' notice, were attacked in England as protectionist and as liable to drive shipping away from the Canal.[1] They were commended by the Board of Trade on 8 April because they provided for the calculation of gross tonnage by the British method of measurement. English shipping interests were, however, compelled to revise all their calculations of costs and expectations of profit: they began a sustained agitation against the new tariff, encouraged proposals for the purchase of all the Company's shares as well as for the creation of an English company and compelled Lesseps to deny on 20 April that the Company had offered to sell the Canal. The steamship owners led by Palmer, Donkin, Norwood and Sutherland protested to the Foreign Office on 8 June and raised the question in the Commons through Norwood on 13 June and Cochrane on 24 June. In France the Messageries Maritimes began a law-suit against the Company on 26 June, when loyalist shareholders formed the Union of Suez Shareholders in support of the new tariff. The Company rejected pleas from England and Egypt to postpone the introduction of the new tariff and brought it into force from 1 July 1872, so raising its receipts by 30 per cent. It discreetly returned on 2 July the voting rights of the Government of Egypt, which had repeatedly refused to accept disfranchisement at the annual general meeting. The general meeting of 31 July was not asked to approve the President's Report but approved the accounts by 1,459 to 704 votes in a complete triumph for the friends of the administration. It also refused by 1,410 to 669 votes to consider any alteration in the tariff and so preserved the statutory prohibition on the control of the tariff by the shareholders. That success for Lesseps was followed by a 20 per cent rise in the quotation of the Company's shares between 30 July and 8 August while the frustrated dissidents vented their wrath in a rash of pamphlets. The Messageries sent a circular to English shipowners on 4 September appealing for their support. The P. & O. thereupon drew up on 10 September a memorandum of protest, which alleged that the new tariff would increase the dues on its vessels by 67 per cent. The Messageries won its case in the Commercial Court of the Seine on 26 October and secured a verdict for the repayment of the excess dues plus interest, so reducing the Company's shares by 11·4 per cent in value in a single day. The Porte decided on 28 October to summon a conference on the tonnage question and protested on 15 December against the assumption of jurisdiction by the French courts between the Canal Company and the Messageries. Thenceforward Constantinople became the scene of diplomatic conflict, first between the representatives of the Canal Company and the Messageries and then between the French and English ambassadors.

The Cour de Paris heard the appeal of the Canal Company against the

[1] *The Engineer*, 22 March 1872, 207, 'The Suez Canal'.

verdict in favour of the Messageries and on 11 March 1873 recognized the Canal Company as foreign and therefore as non-justiciable before a French court, reversing the judgment of the lower court to a salvo of applause in the court-room and to the approval of the Bourse.[1] That judgment satisfied French opinion, which regarded the State-subsidized Messageries as the symbol of the high finance of the Pereiras and resented its invocation of the moral support of English shipowners in international financial comity. The P. & O., which had asked the permission of the G.P.O. on 5 March to use the Canal for its mailboats, continued the battle against the Canal Company. The law suit left a lasting bitterness between Lesseps and the Messageries. The favourable reception of the court's verdict gave the first hint that the Canal Company had been accepted in France as a symbol of the small investor and inspired the Alsatian novelist Erckmann to recapture for literature the story of the Canal's construction during his visit to Egypt in 1873 to recover from the shock of Sedan. Suez shares rose by 11·5 per cent (8–11 March). The Company received a letter of congratulations on 14 March from the President of the Republic and the support of Thiers for Lesseps' mission to Constantinople in his constant enthusiasm for the cause of France in the Levant. 'In all our dealings with the French Government we invariably encounter M. de Lesseps and in all our dealings with M. de Lesseps, we are immediately encountered by the French Government.'[2] In Paris the Company paid on 14 April the coupons for the first half of 1870 after a delay of nearly three years, as the first fruits of the new tariff. In Constantinople Lesseps suggested on 4 April the determination of 'real capacity' by a commission of maritime powers and on 27 April the submission of the question to a council of former Turkish Ministers but failed to secure a favourable compromise despite a sojourn of five months. He lost official support after the fall of Thiers and the advent of Macmahon, with Decazes as Foreign Minister under the anti-Imperialist Broglie. He therefore offered on 28 June to accept a surtax of 5 francs per ton additional to the toll of 10 francs per ton but rejected on 2 July the levy of dues on net tonnage (i.e. on gross tonnage less 20 per cent). The Porte urged in a Vizirial letter of 12 July to the Khedive the use of net tonnage on the English Moorsom system of 1854. The general meeting of 15 July was attended by only 380 shareholders, who accepted the reports unanimously for the first time since the opening of the Canal because the Company had made net profits for the first time of £82,851 in 1872 and had carried forward a surplus. That financial triumph for Lesseps was followed by decisive action by the Porte which warned the Company through the Khedive on 30 July not to oppose the just and legal decision of the Porte in the tonnage question. The Porte summoned on 21 August a conference on the measurement of ships' capacity in general and on the Canal tolls in particular.

---

[1] Voisin Bey, *Le Canal de Suez* (1902), ii. 103–4.
[2] J. Marlowe, *The Making of the Suez Canal* (London, Cresset, 1964), 284, Lyons to Granville, 18 April 1873.

The ensuing Conference of Constantinople was attended by twenty-three diplomatic and technical representatives of twelve powers,[1] including Colonel John Stokes, who had been from 1856 to 1871 the English Commissioner on the European Commission for the Danube. From its beginning on 6 October the conference became a debate between the English and the French, in which the French lost ground steadily and the Company's shares began to drift downwards from 13 October. The English representatives offered in private negotiations on 30 October–1 November a surtax of 3 francs while the French representatives held out for a surtax of 4.50 francs. On 4 November the first formal motion was carried against the French by 9 to 3 votes and decided in favour of the Moorsom system for the determination of gross tonnage. The French representatives thereafter abstained from attending the Conference. The delegates then voted on 2 December that there was no difference between utilizable capacity and net tonnage, so frustrating the French desire to investigate utilizable capacity. They offered in private nego- tiations on 3 December a maximum surtax of 4 francs to compensate the Company for any loss of revenue on the new basis of measurement of net tonnage. A condemnation of the Company's tariff was debated on 4 December but was not put to the vote because of Russian intervention. The threat implicit in that discussion coupled with the lack of support from Decazes compelled the return of the French representatives to the Conference, after their absence from eight sessions. After twenty-one public sessions and a month of private negotiations a compromise emerged with the withdrawal of the English suggestion that gross tonnage should become the basis of tax and of the French suggestion that the surtax should correspond to the difference between net tonnage and cargo capacity.

The Final Report of the Conference on 18 December 1873[2] adopted space not merchandise as its basic criterion of tonnage and the Moorsom ton of 100 feet cubic capacity as its unit of measurement of gross tonnage. It drew up general principles for the computation of tonnage and agreed on the deductions from gross tonnage which were necessary to determine net tonnage. It recommended the issue to every merchant ship of a certificate showing both gross and net tonnage calculated either according to its own recommendations or according to those of the Danube Commission. As a penal sanction it recommended that any deductible permanent space used for cargo or passen- gers should be added to the net tonnage and never again be allowed as deduct- ible. The report also provided for a surtax of 4 francs per net register ton, for its progressive reduction after the year in which the net tonnage reached 2,100,000 tons, for its extinction after the year in which net tonnage reached 2,600,000 tons and for the exemption from the surtax of all warships, troop transports and vessels in ballast. That report represented a triumph for the

---

[1] *Correspondence regarding Suez Canal Dues* (C-1075 of 1874). Voisin Bey, *Le Canal de Suez* (1902), ii. 127–232.

[2] Voisin Bey, *Le Canal de Suez* (1902), ii. 205–17

British Government and for the British shipping interests which it had championed. It was accepted by Decazes on 19 December but not by the Canal Company or by Lesseps because its recommendations seemed to frustrate the long-cherished expectations of his shareholders, to afford no relief to the delegation-holders, to limit the Company's receipts beyond reason and thereby to degrade its whole status.

Lesseps made his first protest to the Khedive on 22 December but received from Ismail on 29 January 1874 a copy of the recommendations of the Conference with three months' notice until 29 April in which to conform to them. The Company's shares began to fall in price while Ismail made plans to take over the operation of the Canal and European interests revived plans for its purchase.[1] Lesseps made counter-proposals on 31 January to Tewfik, Ismail's son and heir and Minister of the Interior, especially for the retention of the surtax until the shares had received an 8 per cent dividend. He was influenced by the imminence of the slack season in traffic after the end of the cotton-moving season in March and by the need to encourage future shareholders in the Central Asiatic Railway. The crisis of April 1874 became inevitable after the Grand Vizier rejected Lesseps' proposals on 7 March and Lesseps asserted on 20 March that he would hold the Porte responsible for all financial losses under the new tariff. The ambassadors of England, Austria, Germany and Italy demanded on 30 March the immediate enforcement of the decisions of the Conference. The Porte instructed the Khedive accordingly on 7 April, so as not to jeopardize Turkey's prospects of a foreign loan. After the Company's shares resumed their decline on 8 April Lesseps declared to Ismail on 11 April that he would oppose the passage of any vessel which did not pay dues based on the gross tonnage, refuse pilots to such ships, cut the telegraph wires, remove the buoys, extinguish the lights and so render passage through the Canal impossible. Ismail confidently replied, 'In that case I will take possession of the Canal and operate the passage for the Company.'[2] From Constantinople it was even reported on 17 April that Lesseps had told the Grand Vizier that he would put chains across the two entrances of the Canal and sink every ship that dared to navigate '*his* waters'.[3] Lesseps affected to believe *La Compagnie c'est moi*, having forgotten the implacable Turk. 'The suicide of the Company would never produce the death of the Canal.'[3]

From Petersburg Gorchakov refused any further support for Lesseps on 15 April because of the growing Anglo-Russian rapprochement. From Paris Decazes cabled his Consul-General in Egypt on 16 April to ask Lesseps to enforce the new tariff from the end of April and to reserve any objections to the future. Thereupon Lesseps exhorted the Company's workmen at Port Said to resistance, threatened to blow up the Canal approaches rather than

---

[1] *Manchester Guardian*, 19 January 1874, 4 iv.
[2] F. J. Cox, 'General Stone and the Suez Canal Incident of 1874', *Cahiers d'Histoire Égyptienne* (Octobre 1952), 200.
[3] *The Times*, 24 April 1874, 12 iv.

submit and left on 16 April for Jerusalem, promising to be back at his post on 26 April. In London letters from D. A. Lange were republished which had been written on behalf of Lesseps to the Board of Trade on 21 April and to the Admiralty on 22 April. Those letters affirmed that no ship would be allowed to enter the Canal without first paying the extra charges demanded by the Company and that any objectors might revert to the use of the Cape route or of the Alexandria–Suez Railway. Those letters alarmed the new Prime Minister Disraeli and stimulated him to consider the acquisition of the Company's shares by Britain, while his Foreign Secretary, Derby, favoured their acquisition by the maritime powers.[1] Delane publicly advised Lesseps to yield. 'M. DE LESSEPS is not afraid to face SULTAN and KHEDIVE, Ambassadors and Consuls, the Peninsular & Oriental and the Messageries Maritimes, the merchants of India and China and the Antipodes. It is M. DE LESSEPS contra mundum, but the ruler of the Suez Company will not flinch.'[2]

Ismail ordered 1,250 troops in three battalions under General Stone and two frigates under Captain H. F. M'Killop to Port Said. Those troops arrived on 23 April and were immediately deployed along the Canal on the basis of one battalion to each town, with the support of Beduin. General Stone conducted his sole active operation during thirteen years' service in Egypt with skill and tact.[3] He made no threats against Lesseps and permitted no interference with the officials of the Canal Company before the appointed date. He deployed his troops outside rather than inside the zone of the Company's concession.[3] He established an independent telegraph line and placed European and American officers in readiness to take over and manage the Company's offices and stations. Lesseps returned to Port Said on 24 April to find Egyptian troops at all the key-points of the Canal and deduced that they were prepared to treat the Company's workmen as Egyptians in defiance of all conventions and treaties. He therefore went from Ismailia directly to Cairo, saw Ismail on 25 April and agreed to apply the new tariff with effect from 29 April. He had no alternative save to surrender in the face of the resolute and united opposition of Britain, the Powers, the Porte and the Khedive. He had been abandoned by Decazes, Gorchakov, Vogüé, Ignatiev and even by Ruyssenaers, the oldest of his colleagues. His last weapon, which was publicity, crumpled in his hand when his threatened closure of the Canal provoked no response from French opinion but was only derided as a theatrical gesture by 'the Roland of the Isthmus'.[4]

The defeat suffered by Lesseps in 1874 was, however, far less severe than the catastrophe he had experienced in 1849, Lesseps submitted to Ismail in the spirit of Henry IV at Canossa, so preventing the administration of the

[1] G. E. Buckle, *Life of Disraeli* (London, Murray, 1920), v. 412, Disraeli to Derby, 23 April 1874.
[2] *The Times*, 23 April 1874, 5 iii; 24 April, 9 ii–iii.
[3] G. E. Hubbard, 'Suez Canal', *The New Englander* (May 1885), 316.
[4] *Le Canal des Deux Mers*, 5 Mai 1874, 59–60, 'Le Roseau Peint en Fer'.

Canal by Egypt and any contribution by it to the financial needs of the Khedive. Ismail was forced to withdraw his troops from the Canal by 1 May under the pressure of Decazes, Vogüé and the Sultan. His consequent anger against Lesseps and the French Government hardened Lesseps' opinion against judicial reform in Egypt and ushered in two years of Franco-Egyptian tension. The failure of Ismail's venture led him to try, to the alarm of South Wales, to impose an 8 per cent duty on the coal imported for Canal steamers,[1] to commission Fowler's preliminary study of a sweet-water ship canal from Alexandria to Suez via Cairo and to renew from 1874 his drive for empire in the equatorial south. The near-success of Ismail's coup encouraged Lesseps to take an interest in Roudaire's scheme of 1873 for a 150-mile Gabes Canal to create an inland sea in the Sahara. The new tariff sealed the fate of Lesseps' dream of a Central Asiatic Railway. The crisis also encouraged the publication of the first biography of Lesseps[2] and the composition by Lesseps of a self-justifying documentary history of the Canal.

Immediately after Lesseps submitted he protested to Tewfik on 26 April against the breach of contract with the Company inspired by 'a foreign coalition against public and private law'.[3] The new tariff fixed the toll from 29 April at its all-time maximum of 13 francs. The Canal Company did not accept that tariff without continuous protests. It stopped the publication of its monthly reports of traffic from Ismailia, refused to accept the official papers of vessels and remeasured them from 29 April in order to 'verify' their tonnage. It thus assumed the power to measure ships in defiance of the recommendations of the Conference. It also served each vessel paying dues with a protest and a claim for the amount due under the old tariff while it sent in from 2 May monthly claims on the Porte through the Government of Egypt for a financial indemnity for its losses under the new tariff. It also raised difficulties as to the dues on tugs accompanying troopships and warships and pursued a policy of reprisals towards British shipping. Thus the Company maintained what it held to be its legal rights, evaded or defied the recommendations of the Conference and reaffirmed its proprietary view of its clients and of what Lesseps called in 1875 'the fleet of the Canal'.

The resistance of the Company led Disraeli to introduce a bill in the House of Commons on 19 May to generalize the Suez Canal measurement of tonnage as agreed at Constantinople. He also made soundings in Paris through Sir Nathaniel de Rothschild for the purchase of the Company's shares, encouraging a recovery in share-prices from 20 May. Lesseps, who had become a vicomte on the death of his elder brother on 24 May 1874 and had so acquired aristocratic status in 'the republic of dukes', refused to consider a sale of the Company except at the prohibitive price of £40,000,000,[4] or

---

[1] *Manchester Guardian*, 21 August 1874, 7 ii. Hansard, *Commons Debates*, 5 August 1874, D. J. Jenkins.

[2] S. Berteaut, *Ferdinand de Lesseps et son Œuvre* (Marseille, Cayer, 1874).

[3] Voisin Bey, *Le Canal de Suez* (1902), ii. 254.

[4] Lord Newton, *Lord Lyons. A Record of British Diplomacy* (London, Arnold, 1913), ii. 93.

25 per cent more than in 1871, and so flatly rejected the English bid. At the general meeting of 2 June 1874 he protested against 'a political conspiracy formed against a free and private Company' to dispossess it of its property, 'the first example of the spoliation of foreign capital trustingly invested in the East'.[1] He used the crisis to eliminate dissension among his shareholders, to confirm his own personal ascendancy, to consolidate his power by a unanimous vote and so to ward off renewed demands for the redemption of the Canal tolls.[2] His new board of twenty directors included six members of his own family, three former members of the Foreign Service, four retired soldiers, two engineers, two former officials of the Company including Guichard, one journalist, one member of the Jockey Club and a former lawyer.[3]

After a long debate the meeting approved the creation of new 40-year 5 per cent consolidated-interest bonds to represent the seven coupons of interest which were still in arrears on the shares after the payment of the first coupon on 14 April 1873 and of the second coupon on 2 February 1874. Those bonds were a financial device of brilliant simplicity and marked a turning-point in the fiscal history of the Company. They enabled the Company to capitalize or fund the seven coupons due, increasing the ultimate total of payments by the addition of 5 per cent interest between 1874 and 1882 (or £68,000 per annum) but spreading its payment over the forty years from 1882 to 1921. Thus the Company again wrung immediate financial help from its future expectations of profit in order to regain full credit on the Bourse and to begin the regular distribution of dividends six years earlier than would otherwise have been possible, to the particular benefit of the holders of the delegations. Those delegations were admitted to joint quotation on the Bourse from 18 August 1874, when the coupons were exchanged for the new bonds.

After the general meeting of shareholders Lesseps, deprived of Russian support by the Anglo-Russian rapprochement, proposed on 11 July 1874 through the British ambassador in Paris the raising of a loan of £1,000,000–£1,500,000 from the Powers using the Canal, i.e. 75 per cent from Britain.[4] He also suggested the creation of a Twelve-Power Commission to decide on the works necessary for the Canal, to fix the amount of the loan necessary and to sign a convention for the guarantee of interest and sinking-fund in the event of the Company's resources proving insufficient. That proposal was supported in the Cabinet by Derby and Northcote but was opposed by W. H. Smith who thought that outright purchase would be safer.[5] The Cabinet dropped the idea of purchase and of a loan, hoping that the Commons

[1] Voisin Bey, ii. 259–60, 265.
[2] *The Times*, 12 June 1874, 4v.
[3] *Le Canal des Deux Mers*, 13 Juin 1874, 96–7, 'Composition du Nouveau Conseil d'Administration sur la Proposition de son Président'.
[4] Lord Newton, *Lord Lyons* (1913), ii. 93.
[5] H. E. Maxwell, *Life and Times of the Right Honourable William Henry Smith, M.P.* (Edinburgh, Blackwood, 1893), i. 279–80.

Tonnage Committee would settle the vexed question of Canal tolls permanently. Lange was so alarmed at the prospect that he appealed for protection against political pressure on 'a private and defenceless company'.[1]

The clash between the Company and its clients was not over a vital issue[2] but only over money. The Company was defending its future interests as well as its past achievements in resisting the pressure from its clients but so precipitated the first of the disputes over tolls which continued throughout its history. The question of tolls was not one of general concern to Britain but only to sectional interests and especially to British shipowners. Their response was ungenerous and narrowly economic, especially after England had recognized Lesseps' achievement in 1870 as one of the greatest of the age. Those shipowners had given Lesseps even less support during the construction of the Canal than had the P. & O. They recognized, however, their importance to the completed Canal in supplying, in 1873, 69 per cent of its transits, 71 per cent of its revenues and 72 per cent of its tonnage. They exaggerated the significance of the waterway to Britain although they could not prevent the increased use of the Cape route nor the revival of interest in the Euphrates Valley Railway. The Canal, which was 'one of the highways of the world' to Granville in 1873 and a 'great highway of nations' to Farrer in 1874, undoubtedly assumed the superficial appearance of an English highway because of the predominance of British shipping. Baillie Cochrane ranked the Canal on behalf of Southampton and the P. & O. as of 'deep interest' and 'vital consequence' to England.[3] The shipowners, however, sought their ends through the Chamber of Shipping of the United Kingdom and the Association of Chambers of Commerce and through questions in the Commons and petitions to the Foreign Office rather than through public meetings, public agitation or public correspondence. Nelson Donkin & Co. had the 2,145-ton steamer *Suez* built at Newcastle in 1874 but the public mind had little clear idea of the significance of the Canal and seemed more concerned with the significance of drunkenness in the streets. 'It is time for Englishmen to awake to a vivid perception that the early closing of the Suez Canal is a matter more urgently concerning them—even such of them as are cockneys—than the early closing of the Bull and Mouth, or the Goat and Compasses.'[4] The shipowners secured the use of political power for economic ends against a weaker state, prostrated by the Franco-Prussian War, in an act of virtual international brigandage. They ensured that the British Government fought to the utmost on their behalf and proved by their success that the Canal Company was no state within a state. They consolidated their victory by demanding a refund of the excess dues paid to the Canal Company since 1 July 1872 and by securing the rejection of the Tonnage Measurement Bill. That bill would have generalized

[1] *The Morning Post*, 14 July 1874, 5 iv.

[2] *The Economist*, 22 June 1873, 771, 'The Suez Canal Company's Rates'.

[3] Hansard, *Commons Debates*, 1 April 1873, 454, B. Cochrane.

[4] (W. M. Thorburn), *The Great Game; a Plea for a British Imperial Policy. By a British Subject* (1875), 210, 133, 164–5.

the Suez Canal measurement, although at the expense of an increase in net register tonnage, and was abandoned in deference to the opposition of the shipowners of Liverpool led by William Rathbone. The new measurement remained unique to the Suez Canal, an expedient elaborated for one waterway as Lesseps insisted rather than a stage towards the general unification of tonnage measurement.

The new tariff reduced navigation dues per net ton by 12·5 per cent to the benefit of the most regular and stable element in the Canal's traffic, the mail lines. The P. & O., which had sent eighty-six mailboats through the Canal during 1873, transferred its heavy mails from the overland route to the Canal from August 1874, after the Chambers of Commerce of Manchester and Bombay had cooperated in pressing for the acceleration of the mails to India and China.[1] The revision of the mail contract[2] reduced the subsidy paid by the G.P.O. to the P. & O. not by the £50,000 proposed in 1870 but by £20,000 to £430,000 and was regarded by Lesseps as a sharing of the plunder between two thieves. The renewal of the P. & O.'s contract was opposed by the shipping lines of Liverpool, especially by Holt, who offered to carry the mails to China in a special ocean yacht.[3] The P. & O., however, enjoyed the powerful support of the Government of India, which further adapted itself to the Canal route by reviving in 1873 the marine surveys it had stopped in 1862.[4] Thus Captain A. D. Taylor's 1874 edition of *The India Directory* included for the first time a limited chapter on the Mediterranean.[5] The P. & O. adopted the Canal route only after completing the reconstruction of its fleets between 1868 and 1873. After 1873 it ordered all its new ships of suitable dimensions for the Canal, ended its separate Home Station and generalized the employment of Indian crews, except on the express Brindisi service. It introduced automatic ventilators for the Red Sea and began to compete with the vessels of the Bibby Line in the Mediterranean. It reduced its establishments at Alexandria and Suez to the minimum and concentrated its workshops at London. From 1874 it made London its terminal port and so tapped a rapidly growing traffic. It continued to embark the mails at Southampton but reduced its establishment there to the minimum necessary for the performance of the mail contract and discharged 150 local employees in 1874. The consequent fall in the tonnage of Southampton by 12 per cent between 1873 and 1875 provoked Southampton to begin to discriminate against London cargo in favour of Southampton-direct cargo. The P. & O. had expected to raise its annual revenue by £100,000 through the use of the Canal but lost £150,000 through a new fall in freights and halved its annual

[1] A. Redford, *Manchester Merchants and Foreign Trade, 1850–1939* (1956), ii. 150.
[2] *The Times*, 5 December 1874, 7 vi.
[3] F. E. Hyde and J. R. Harris, *Blue Funnel* (1956), 42.
[4] *The Geographical Magazine* (April 1874), 27, 'The India Directory'; (July 1874), 135, 'Indian Marine Surveys'.
[5] J. Horsburgh, *The India Directory, for the Guidance of Steamers and Sailing Vessels* (London, Allen, 1874), 15–32, Gibraltar to Aden.

dividends for 1875. It calculated ruefully that if the Canal had not been opened it would have earned £2,500,000 per annum instead of £2,000,000 on its capital of £3,500,000 and would be able to pay a dividend of 20 per cent instead of one of 3 per cent.[1] It was forced to issue debenture stock and began to foster the creation of shipping conferences so as to maintain the level of freights and end the era of competition ushered in by the opening of the Canal.

The diversion of the Southampton steam packets to the Canal reduced the British steam tonnage entering Alexandria by 14·2 per cent in 1875 and left the shipping of Alexandria predominantly sail while that of Port Said remained mainly steam tonnage. After the completion of the new breakwater at Alexandria in May 1874 the management of the harbour dues was placed from 1 June under English naval officers to increase their yield. Suez ceased to be 'the western gate of India'.[2] The diversion of the heavy mail coincided with the end of the harbour works at Port Ibrahim in 1874. The consequent decrease in the demand for labour spread distress and dissatisfaction among the indigenous population of Suez and reinforced the anti-infidel and anti-Coptic sentiment reported by Consul West in 1874. The commerce of Suez was reduced to that of an English coaching town untouched by the railway, deserted by traffic and devoid of productive industry.

The Canal gained what the overland route lost and increased the share of subsidized mail tonnage to 31 per cent of its total tonnage. The transfer of the P. & O. mail to the Canal increased English interests in the Canal route and encouraged speculation in September–November 1874 in the Canal Company's shares, which first passed their pre-crisis level of 440 francs on 1 October and rose markedly from November onwards. The Canal Company gained revenue from both tonnage and passengers, including cargo which would never have used the overland route. The decline in trade by the overland route from its 1872 peak reduced English exports to 'Egypt', as recorded by the Customs, from £6,000,000 in 1868 to £2,000,000 in 1878, and English imports from 'Egypt' from £18,000,000 in 1868 to £6,000,000 in 1878. The exports of raw silk from 'Egypt' thus declined from £5,147,770 in 1871 to £48,572 in 1875 and ceased thereafter. The exports from 'Egypt' to England of goat's hair, wool and indigo similarly declined from their peak in 1871, exports of tea, jute, drugs, oil-seeds and manufactured silk from their peak in 1872 and exports of coffee from their peak in 1873. The Egyptian railways lost an estimated annual revenue of £300,000 on goods and passengers.[3] Egypt's imposition of a compensatory import duty on coal was accepted by the British firms at Port Said on 21 July 1874.[4] That duty made Holt decide to coal his ships in future only at Liverpool and Singapore, reduced the imports of coal to Suez by 13 per cent in 1874 and encouraged the bunkering trade of Malta.

[1] *The Times*, 6 December 1876, 7 v.
[2] M. E. G. Duff, 'Egypt', *Contemporary Review* (February 1874), 436.
[3] *The Times*, 28 April 1874, 12 ii.   [4] *Manchester Guardian*, 21 August 1874, 7 ii.

Passengers travelling to India continued to complain about the speed and facilities of the P. & O.[1] but those returning from India no longer needed to struggle for a seat in the Suez–Cairo train, which became thenceforward one of the slowest trains in the world. Civilian passengers using the Canal had increased from 5,657 in 1870 to 12,143 in 1873; their number rose by 36 per cent in 1874 and by a further 18 per cent in 1875 to 19,624. The outward flow of travellers through the Canal became especially marked from 1875. Meadows Taylor, who had reached Bombay in 1824 via the Cape and had returned to England through Egypt in 1837 and in 1860, revisited Hyderabad via the Canal in 1875 before his death in 1876.[2] The Duke of Connaught became the first English prince to pass from Suez to Port Said on the warship *Helicon* on 15 March 1875. Sultan Barghash of Zanzibar was escorted by Consul Kirk through the Canal and reached Gravesend in 37 days (9 May–15 June 1875) from Zanzibar for his state visit to England.[3] Mary Carpenter, whose father had attracted R. M. Roy to Bristol, made at the age of sixty-eight her fourth visit to India in the cause of social reform, travelling via the Canal on 3 October 1875 rather than via the overland route: 'I consider that transit through the desert the one event of the voyage; and I think it worth the voyage to anyone who has time and money, simply to go through it...I was full of admiration of the genius of Lesseps and this wonderful work, which is the work of the century, unless indeed Sahara should be made an inland sea.'[4] A Canadian traveller was more impressed by the mighty ditch than by its ports.[5] Monier Monier-Williams was also more moved by his first impressions of the Canal on 26 October 1875 than by those of Port Said: he had been brought to England at the age of three in 1822 via the Cape and he returned to the land of his birth as the Boden Professor of Sanskrit to enlist the support of the leading princes of India for his projected Indian Institute at Oxford.[6] Isabel Burton, who found the passage on 9 January 1876 through 'the last link riveted in the great belt of trade' like a river-picnic, heard the appeal for bakshish at Suez for the first time since her days in Syria in 1871 and heard it change to curses when it was left unanswered.[7] Thomas Brassey, the son of the great railway-contractor and millionaire, brought his steam-yacht *Sunbeam* through the Canal on 26–7 April 1876 on the last lap of a pioneer 35,393-mile circumnavigation of the world, the first to be completed by way of the Canal.[8] The overland route continued in use after 1874 by the express mail via Brindisi and Alexandria. After the Government of Italy purchased the railway line to Brindisi in 1874 Pullman sleeping-cars were introduced

[1] *The Times*, 8 December 1874, 12i.
[2] P. M. Taylor, *The Story of My Life* (Edinburgh, Blackwood, 1878), 466.
[3] R. Coupland, *The Exploitation of East Africa 1856–1890* (1939), 239.
[4] J. E. Carpenter, *The Life and Work of Mary Carpenter* (London, Macmillan, 1879), 443.
[5] J. S. Cowan, 'From Port Said to Suez', *Canadian Monthly* (November 1875), 407, 410.
[6] M. Monier-Williams in *The Times*, 26 December 1876, 9i–ii. M. Monier-Williams, *Modern India and the Indians* (London, Trübner, 1878), 12–20, 'The Five Gates of India'.
[7] I. Burton, *Arabia Egypt India* (1879), 68–9.
[8] Mrs. A. Brassey, *A Voyage in the 'Sunbeam'* (London, Longmans, 1878), 463–6.

on the Indian Mail Train while the Channel Tunnel scheme was revived to complete the rail link between London and Brindisi. The Canal Company introduced in 1874 an express boat service from Port Said to Suez, making the return trip in eighteen hours, in imitation of the express mail from Alexandria to Suez which the Company coveted for the Canal.

British shipping using the Canal had increased faster than other shipping until 1873, when the British rate of increase first fell below the general rate of increase. After the settlement of the dispute over tolls shipowners resumed building up their Canal fleet in 1875, encouraged by the fall in coal and iron prices and by the appointment in 1874 of the first engineer-surveyor by Lloyd's Register of Shipping.[1] Regular services were begun to Bombay by R. & F. Henderson's Anchor Line from Glasgow on 4 March 1875 and to Calcutta by T. & J. Harrison from Liverpool on 21 October 1875. The City Line doubled the frequency of its Calcutta service in 1875 and competed with the Queen Line, whose *Queen Margaret* reached Calcutta from London in under 29 days (24 August–22 September 1875).[2] The growth of steamer competition reduced return freights to Liverpool sharply and drove out of the Indian trade Currie in 1874 and Wilson in 1875. The Canal remained more important to Britain than to the world and more useful to British shipping than to British trade. Thus an estimated 3·6 per cent of the total value of British commerce and a larger share of its volume passed through the Canal in 1875 when the Canal carried 1,382,000 tons of cargo or 1·6 per cent of the total volume of world trade of 88,000,000 tons. Britain's Canal tonnage was not subsidized like that of other states but represented double the proportion of its steam fleet that the total Canal tonnage represented of the world steam fleet. Britain's gross Canal tonnage in 1874 represented 74 per cent of the total Canal tonnage but only 32 per cent of the total British steam tonnage, assuming three transits per annum to each vessel. British ships carried the trade of other nations with Asia as well as British trade and could thus be larger in size than the general average so that Britain supplied 71 per cent of the transits in 1874 but 74·2 per cent of the tonnage. In 1875 Britain employed 10 per cent of its gross Canal tonnage on routes to or from non-English ports.[3] The shipping tonnage between England and Asia and Africa beyond the Canal in 1875 totalled 4,863,420 tons net, of which only 1,384,900 or 28·47 per cent used the Canal while the remainder used the Cape routes.

From Suez Consul West calculated on 23 January 1875 that the new tariff had reduced the Company's income in the eight months from May to December 1874 by £74,602 or 11·65 per cent. Receipts which had risen by 35·3 per cent during 1873 rose by only 7·6 per cent during 1874 while gross tonnage rose by 16·2 per cent and British gross tonnage by 19·8 per cent. The British share of the total tonnage rose from 72 to 74 per cent and continued

[1] Lloyd's Register of Shipping, *Annals of Lloyd's Register, 1834–1884* (1884), 113.
[2] *The Times*, 24 September 1875, 12 ii; 25 September, 4 ii.
[3] *Le Canal de Suez*, 22 Mai 1877, 3, 'L'Angleterre et le Canal de Suez, 1860–1875'.

to rise from 1874 to 1878. Receipts for the year 1874 nevertheless first exceeded £1,000,000. The regular distribution of dividends was resumed from 1 January 1875, refuting the British charge that the Company was a commercial failure. Shares exceeded their par value of 500 francs for the first time since 1869 on 25 January 1875. After an extra-ordinary increase in traffic during January 1875 shares rose in February by 11·6 per cent to a premium of 15·5 per cent by 24 February. The first quotation of the shares on the London Stock Exchange from 23 February earned the Company a welcome as a prospective second New River Company and as an illustration of the great value of an absolute monopoly of an article of increasing use.[1] The Company's prospects for growth were recognized as favourable and were estimated not at the 15 per cent of 1874, which would have been unprecedented as a regular increase after the initial stage of development, but at a minimum of 5 per cent per annum, which was the rate of increase of traffic on railways in Britain and in the foreign shipping of Britain and was below the rate of increase in the steam shipping of Britain.

Lesseps' position was also strengthened by the end of the rival publication of *Le Canal des Deux Mers* after its last issue on 25 February. He resumed discussions with the Porte to increase the surtax. Charles Lesseps arrived at Constantinople on 1 April to undertake those negotiations with the aid of Vogüé and Decazes. His father wrote a personal letter to Disraeli on 9 May, to facilitate his son's task, and sent Marius Fontane, the new Assistant Manager of the Company, as his personal representative to London. Derby remained under mercantile pressure to secure a reduction in tolls and countered the proposals of the Company by asking it to give some assurance that the money raised by an additional surtax would be spent on improvement works and to accept some outside influence in its administration. Lesseps became alarmed at the threat to encroach on the internal administration of his Company and to establish external control of its budget, which he regarded as tantamount to the creation of an international commission analogous to the Danube Commission.[2] He therefore recalled Fontane from London on 17 May and Charles from Constantinople on 29 June and offered the French-reading public the historical justification of his policy in the first volume of his early correspondence.[3] With that first important contribution to the written history of his own creation Lesseps began to incorporate into the history of France what the French Treasury, the French Foreign Office and the French courts had recognized as a foreign company.

[1] *The Economist*, 6 March 1875, 273–5. 'The Financial Position and Prospects of the Suez Canal'.

[2] Voisin Bey, *Le Canal de Suez* (1902), ii. 281.

[3] F. de Lesseps, *Lettres, Journal et Documents pour Servir à l'Histoire du Canal de Suez (1854–1855–1856)* (Paris, Didier, 1875).

THE SALE OF THE KHEDIVE'S SHARES, 1875

'The riches of Egypt are for the foreigners therein.'
J. L. Burckhardt, *Arabic Proverbs* (London, Quaritch,
Second edition, 1875), 83, no. 262

IN the late summer of 1875 the reputation of the Disraeli Ministry was declining steadily with the health of its seventy-year-old head in an accumulation of embarrassments. Plimsoll's violent attack on Disraeli for postponing the Merchant Shipping Bill struck the first great blow on 22 July at the popularity of the Ministry. That scene 'without precedent in the annals of this assembly'[1] reduced 'the Sphinx' to utter distraction and inflicted a striking defeat on one who believed the conciliation of opponents to be more important than the reward of supporters. Then the ironclad *Vanguard*, the pride of the British Navy, while on a recruiting cruise off Ireland was rammed in error and sunk by its sister-ship, the *Iron Duke*, on 1 September[2] and so became the first capital ship in the annals of the Navy to be sunk by a collision. The decline of the Ministry's standing in the country was accelerated by the Admiralty Circular on Fugitive Slaves of 31 July, which was deplored first by Delane[3] and then by the country for its savour of the Fugitive Slave Laws of the American South in its inhumane restriction of the right of captains to receive slaves on board their 'floating islands' of English law. The Government felt an increasing need to restore its damaged prestige and its control over Parliament and the country. 'Water, I trust, will not prove fatal to the Government. Between Plimsoll, the Vanguard, and the Admiralty Instructions and Minute, we seem in a leaky state: but it is only October, and there is time, I hope, to caulk.'[4]

The means of deliverance was opportunely provided by the re-emergence of the Eastern Question. The revolt of the Christian peasantry of Herzegovina and Bosnia against their Serb Moslem landlords began to arouse the Panslav demon in Russia against the Turk. It also introduced the word 'moratorium' into English[5] and precipitated the bankruptcy of Turkey on 7 October after twenty-one years of foreign borrowing. The heavy fall in Turkish stocks on the London Stock Exchange produced a sympathetic decline in Egyptian

[1] H. W. Lucy, *A Diary of Two Parliaments. The Disraeli Parliament 1874–1880* (London, Cassell, 1885), i. 106–11.
[2] *Manchester Guardian*, 3 September 1875, 5 iv.
[3] *The Times*, 20 September 1875, 9 iv.
[4] G. E. Buckle, *Life of Disraeli* (1920), v. 433, Disraeli to Salisbury, 15 October 1875.
[5] *The Times*, 28 September 1875, 5 iii, Vienna.

stocks,[1] in Henry Oppenheim's unissued holdings of the 1873 Egyptian loan and, above all, in the floating debt which was held largely by the French. The French interests involved in Egyptian finance feared a similar moratorium in Egypt but hoped to turn the financial straits of the Khedive to their advantage. The Prince of Wales, the first crown prince to visit India, decorated Tewfik on 24 October with the Star of India and was asked by the anglophile Nubar on 30 October for an English financial official who might in effect give Egypt a certificate of solvency. While Turkish bondholders suggested the cession of Palestine for conversion into an independent Jewish principality by a limited company modelled on the East India Company,[2] Egyptian bondholders hoped that Egypt might become an English dependency as was publicly suggested first on 27 October by the Liberal Brassey[3] and then on 3 November[4] by the Conservative Greenwood, who assured Turkish bondholders that the tribute to Constantinople would nevertheless remain a first charge on the Egyptian Treasury.[5] Simultaneous rumours on the Bourse of the sanding-up of the Canal and of the imminence of an £8,000,000 loan reduced the price of Suez shares by 6·3 per cent (3–15 November), a sharper fall than that of 7·4 per cent which had followed the Turkish bankruptcy. Suggestions for a 4,550-mile overland telegraph from 'Cairo to Cape Town',[6] for a submarine cable to the Cape via West Africa,[7] and even for a railway from the Mediterranean to Natal[8] were also encouraged by Stanley's exploration of Central Africa and by Carnarvon's campaign for South African confederation.

In Cairo rival French financial groups sought to profit by plans for the restoration of Egyptian credit. The Crédit Foncier had agreed in February 1875 to advance the Government first £5,000,000 and then £8,000,000 against bills falling due for payment from 1 February 1876 to 1 January 1877. It thereby increased its investment in the Egyptian floating debt to £10,000,000, or to 56 per cent of the total of £18,000,000, and locked up in Egypt nearly four times the amount of its own paid-up capital. To restore and maintain the price of Egyptian stocks the Crédit Foncier envisaged a general consolidation of the debt with the Khedive's Canal shares as a guarantee. Its confidential agent was Jules Pastré[9] who had established the Anglo-Egyptian Bank in 1862 and bought the 341-ton *Glencairn* in 1875 to rename it *Suez*. For his part

---

[1] *The Times*, 28 October, 6 iii, J. Fowler, 'Egyptian Finance'.

[2] C. Warren, *The Land of Promise; or Turkey's Guarantee* (London, Bell, 1875), 5. *Manchester Guardian*, 27 November, 7 iv.

[3] *The Times*, 28 October, 6 v.

[4] F. Greenwood, 'Egypt for the English', *Pall Mall Gazette*, 3 November 1875, 1.

[5] F. Greenwood, 'Russians, Turks and Egyptians', Ibid., 8 November 1875, 2.

[6] *The English Mechanic*, 26 November 1875, 278, 373 quoted by L. C. Raphael, *The Cape-to-Cairo Dream. A Study in British Imperialism* (New York, Columbia University Press, 1936), 49–50, 409.

[7] D. Currie, 'Maritime Warfare', *Journal of the Royal United Service Institution*, 2 March 1877, 233, Currie to Carnarvon, 30 October 1875.

[8] W. M. Thorburn, *The Great Game* (1875), 201.

[9] J. C., *Histoire Financière de l'Égypte depuis Said Pacha, 1854–1876* (Paris, Guillaumin, 1878), 202.

Ismail desired financial relief free from any onerous conditions. He sought access to a fund of credit which would never run dry and would never demand control over his expenditure. He could never contemplate the introduction of a Western budget into an Oriental state nor accept restriction to a fixed income while Egypt remained liable to famine, flood and competition in the world market any more than Lesseps could accept external control of his budget while he remained under binding obligations of honour to his shareholders. Ismail wished to mortgage his shares rather than to sell them but to do so to a French banker to balance the appointment of an English financial official. He wished, however, to use his princely prerogative and to seek help from new financial syndicates rather than from the powerful Crédit Foncier. He accordingly accepted the services of André Dervieu of Alexandria to undertake the mortgage of the shares. His offer proved unattractive because the interest had already been mortgaged for twenty-five years in order to create the delegations in 1869. He therefore granted on 12 November an option to sell the shares.

On Sunday 14 November Henry Oppenheim, who had adhered to the Crédit Foncier's scheme of a consolidation of the debt[1] and wished to disrupt Dervieu's operations, invited Frederick Greenwood to dine at his home at 17 Park Lane in Mayfair and told him that negotiations were on foot in Cairo to raise a loan on the security of the Khedive's shares. Greenwood thereupon conceived the idea of a purchase by the British Government and passed the information on to Derby at the Foreign Office the next morning. First the inner Cabinet approved and then the whole Cabinet decided on 17 November 'by a sort of whirlwind of agreement'[2] in favour of the principle of such a purchase. Dervieu failed to raise the necessary funds despite the support of the 'irrepressible' Lesseps in Paris[3] and then proposed on 19 November a mortgage of the shares together with Ismail's 15 per cent share in the profits of the Canal Company. The Crédit Foncier, having succeeded in closing the Paris market to Dervieu, also proposed on 19 November to Ismail a general consolidation of the Egyptian Debt with a prohibition on any further loans, a control over expenditure and a guarantee in the form of the shares. Decazes supported the Crédit Foncier like Leon Say, the Finance Minister, but seems to have been moved by his passion for speculation rather than by any political motives since he made no use of his Consul in Egypt.[4] Ismail was determined never to grant the proposed control over his finances, least of all over his expenditure. He therefore permitted himself to be persuaded on 23 November to sell his shares to the British Government, which approved the purchase-price of £4,000,000 on the same day and offered a counterpoise to the French Government such as might enable the Khedive profitably to pursue a middle

[1] M. Sabry, *L'Empire Égyptien sous Ismail* (1933), 161.
[2] A. Hardinge, *The Life of Henry Howard Molyneux Herbert Fourth Earl of Carnarvon 1831–1890* (London, Oxford University Press, 1925), ii. 91.
[3] Lord Newton, *Lord Lyons* (1913), ii. 86, Derby to Lyons, 17 November 1875.
[4] J. C., *Histoire Financière de l'Égypte* (1878), 204.

course between two rival suitors. Ismail also wished to discourage the resistance of Decazes and Rouvier to the judicial reform embodied in the decree of 17 September 1875 which created the Mixed Courts and crowned eight years of effort by Ismail and Nubar to re-establish the control of the State over the foreign communities. The shares were thus sold as well as bought in a stroke of statecraft in the oldest Oriental tradition and worthy of the new serpent of old Nile. The Khedive thereby asserted Egyptian independence and made the first move in a planned campaign to enlist foreign credit in his service rather than the last fling in a career of riotous expenditure.[1] The purchase-price was equal to 37 per cent of his 1874 revenue of £10,800,000 but was a once-for-all payment. Ismail's aim was not simply to raise money nor to rid himself of the burden of the Canal shares but to secure continuing credit appropriate to his status and granted on his own terms.

The monies for the purchase were advanced by Nathan de Rothschild & Sons as the British Government asserted its independence of the Bank of England as well as of Parliament. The Rothschilds promised their cooperation on 17 November and so earned a commission of £152,319, or 14·47 per cent on their advance of £4,000,000 for three months[2] against the security not of the Egyptian Government but of the British Government itself. Their gains seemed to reduce British credit to the level of that of Honduras or Paraguay, to the concern of the Treasury, the Bank of England and the City. The gains made on the Stock Exchange by the manipulation of Egyptian stocks were, however, far more substantial. Late on Monday 15 November, after Greenwood had passed his information to Derby and had so informed Oppenheim, the buying of Egyptian stocks, especially of the 1873 loan, began on the Exchange. Those purchases were made by a very large buyer and continued steadily for the next ten days side by side with the negotiations for the sale of the shares while the market in foreign stocks remained on the whole unsettled until 20 November. The market quotation of the 1873 loan rose daily by an average of one point from 54–54½ on 15 November to 62¼ on Wednesday 24 November[3] before the largest rises of the whole fortnight occurred on the following two days. The quotation rose on Thursday by 4⅞ points as rumours of the purchase filtered through, necessitating an evening Stock Exchange, and on Friday by 4¼ points to 72¼ when the official news arrived at 1.35 p.m.[4] On Saturday 27 November when the 1873 loan had regained the pre-crisis level of 7 October it was estimated that Egyptian stocks had risen by more than £8,000,000 after the official announcement.[5] Enormous losses were sustained by the speculators for the fall who had oversold, enormous profits were

[1] J. Marlowe, *The Making of the Suez Canal* (1964), 293–302.
[2] Hansard, *Commons Debates*, 21 February 1876, 591, Gladstone.
[3] *Pall Mall Gazette*, 15 November 1875, 7 ii. *Manchester Guardian*, 20 November 1875, 6 i; 22 November, 4 i; 23 November, 4 i; 25 November, 4 i.
[4] *The Times*, 26 November, 4 i. *Manchester Guardian*, 26 November, 4 i. *Daily Telegraph*, 26 November, 3 i. *Morning Post*, 26 November, 2 i.
[5] *The Observer*, 28 November, 2 vi, 'City Topics. Egyptian Finance'.

made by the speculators for the rise who then unloaded their stock on to the general public in London and the provinces.[1] Everyone rushed to buy Egyptian stock as though England had just announced that she would pay the Egyptian Debt.[2] The despatch of the Cave financial mission to Egypt, rumoured from 26 November and confirmed on 29 November, reinforced those expectations. On Settlement Day, 30 November, transactions of nearly £300,000,000 (or 76 per cent of the total value of Consols), made during the previous fortnight, were settled through the Stock Exchange Clearing House.[3] Within the preceding eighteen days over £300,000,000 of Egyptian 1873 was estimated to have changed hands.[4] Egyptian credit was re-established in the money-markets of London, Alexandria and Cairo, greatly benefiting Ismail but vastly increasing English interests in the solvency of the Khedive.

There is no evidence of the identity of the English speculators for the rise in Egyptian stocks which is more than circumstantial. Nor would the knowledge of their identity be of more than antiquarian interest unless it could throw light on the antecedents of the share-purchase and reveal a consummate ability to turn a public transaction to private profit. It should therefore be emphasized that speculation for the rise required substantial funds unlike speculation for the fall and was usually undertaken by men of means. Such was Henry Oppenheim, the only loan contractor in London whose firm depended wholly on Egyptian finance and had become 'Rothschild in ordinary to the Khedive'[5] by issuing the six loans of 1862, 1864, 1866, 1867, 1868 and 1873,[6] which gave it an unrivalled proprietary interest in the funded debt. His firm had withdrawn at the last moment from the private Daira Loan of 1865 which with the Daira Loan of 1867 were the only Egyptian stocks which did not appreciate in value during the last fortnight of November 1875. As the sole expert in Egyptian finance in London Oppenheim alone was aware of the secret financial negotiations in Cairo and Paris and so possessed the information denied to all other members of the Stock Exchange as well as the motive to prevent a sale or a mortgage of the Khedive's shares through Dervieu. Oppenheim's Liberal political sympathies denied him the access to the Conservative administration which was necessary to capitalize his information in London but did not prevent him from passing on the information to the Conservative editor of a Liberal evening paper. Oppenheim may even have inspired Greenwood's clarion-call of 'Egypt for the English' on 3 November. He was certainly given the credit for the purchase by such well-informed contemporaries as Labouchere and Gavard. Labouchere, who had speculated

[1] *The World*, 29 December, 6 ii.   [2] *The Times*, 27 November, 6 ii.

[3] Ibid., 3 December, 4 ii, L. L. Cohen.

[4] *The Hour*, 1 December, 8 iii.

[5] Sidi Lokman el Hakim (John Ninet), *Les Milles Pertuis des Finances du Khédive et les Banques en Égypte* (Vienne, Agence Internationale, 1873), 125.

[6] A. M. Hamza, *The Public Debt of Egypt 1854–1876* (1944), 73, 88, 96, 143, 209, 218–19, 222, 249.

for a fall in Egyptians and had lost a reputed £80,000–£200,000,[1] published Oppenheim's own claim to have originated the idea of the purchase[2] and so provoked Greenwood to credit Oppenheim with the information as distinct from the idea.[3] Gavard, the French chargé d'affaires, called Oppenheim on 14 December 'the organiser of the Suez affair'.[4] Oppenheim never directly claimed any such credit, being 'a very retiring man who never bothered about kudos'.[5] He may have been discouraged by the pressure of contemporary opinion which disapproved of the manipulation for personal gain of the Stock Exchange,[6] and vastly more of the manipulation of the State for private ends. Granville's view that the share-purchase was a 'stock-jobbing transaction'[7] was shared by such other Liberals as Bright, Forster, Harcourt, Holms and Lubbock. Disraeli himself did not seek to deny in the debate of 21 February 1876 the occurrence of stock-jobbing but rather rejoiced in the charge by referring to the Stock-Exchange speculation on the glorious battle of Waterloo. The house of Rothschild was nevertheless forced to remain content with its financial profits and did not gain until 1885 the peerage which had been anticipated for its head amidst the first enthusiasm. Greenwood neither sought nor received any public recognition for his unpaid service, perhaps because he was held to have been used by others for their personal gain. Whether the State itself had been so used is another question which may at least be asked if it may not be conclusively answered.

The official announcement of the purchase provoked, at first, general surprise and then, after some hesitation, widespread satisfaction. Thus Delane allotted England a 'heavy stake' in Egypt which he increased the next day to 'an abiding stake'.[8] Many editors experienced a week-end conversion from neutral acceptance of the purchase to enraptured praise of its sagacity. Frank Hill elevated the act from 'bold and timely' to 'bold and wise'.[9] Alexander Russel was perturbed at first by the possibility of complications but then discovered the act to be both wise and fair.[10] The purchase was undoubtedly welcomed as much for its manner as for its content and for the energy, boldness, speed and secrecy revealed by a regime characterized until then by a spirit of square-toed humdrum, marred by blazing indiscretions. The act was regarded as a political achievement by a government even weaker in foreign policy than in domestic policy and as an emphatic assertion of British power

[1] H. O. O'Hagan, *Leaves From My Life* (London, Lane, 1929), i. 366. *The Englishman* (Calcutta), 27 December 1875, 3 iii.

[2] *The World*, 8 December 1875, 6, 'Who Suggested the Purchase?'; ibid., 15 December, 9 ii.

[3] *Pall Mall Gazette*, 8 December, 1–2, 'City Gossip and the Suez Canal'.

[4] C. Gavard, *Un Diplomat à Londres. Lettres et Notes 1871–1877* (Paris, Plon, 1895), 280–1.

[5] J. W. R. Scott, *The Story of the Pall Mall Gazette* (London, Oxford University Press, 1950), 203.

[6] *The Hour*, 24 November, 8 iv. *The Globe*, 1 December, 4 iii.

[7] A. Ramm (ed.), *The Political Correspondence of Mr. Gladstone and Lord Granville 1868–1876* (1952), 474, Gladstone to Granville, 28 November 1875.

[8] *The Times*, 26 November, 7 i; 27 November, 8 i.

[9] *Daily News*, 27 November, 4 vii; 29 November, 4 viii.

[10] *The Scotsman*, 27 November, 6 ii–iii; 29 November, 4 i.

to the states of the Continent which had grown too accustomed to ignore Britain. The purchase was especially popular among the national classes of newspaper editors, publishers, civil servants, army officers, Anglican clergy and railway directors in an inevitable reaction against the Liberal attack of 1868–74 on Church and State. It was also supported by the Liberal press and by Liberal M.P.s before the first Government representative spoke on Tuesday, 30 November. It gratified Northbrook, the Liberal Viceroy of India, as much as the Queen and the Prince of Wales.[1] Radicals such as Chamberlain recognized the act as a 'clever thing' done by the Tories.[2] Liberal M.P.s broke away from the express wishes of their leaders to voice their approval in public. The Liberal press of London, especially the *Daily Telegraph*, joined the Conservative press in 'a shout of triumph as if the world were conquered'.[3] The Liberal leaders were cowed into oracular ambiguity in public and provoked into fuming vexation in private. Gladstone was stirred to the roots of his being by the purchase which followed so closely on the Turkish repudiation. 'The manner in which it was received really makes me blush for my Countrymen and for their press.'[4] The applause of the London press was reiterated in Calcutta, Singapore, Hong Kong, Shanghai and Durban[5] but not in the Liberal press of the provinces.[6] The purchase was attacked in the Gladstonian spirit by Bagehot as incomprehensible,[7] by Lord Sandhurst, C.-in-C. in India from 1865 to 1870, as an unprecedented application of State resources and 'a mischievous anomaly'[8] and by City opinion as a purchase at a high price, low interest and bad security. The general acclaim of the metropolitan press however drowned the voices of dissent and won over the dubious Northcote to the policy of the purchase.[9] Such extensive press-generated approval reflected the rise of a new public opinion distinct from the older club-moulded opinion and the triumph of journalists over the clerisy.

The elation of the press was in part a reaction against the dullness of trade and politics during the parliamentary recess and was carried further by society. 'Society was far more excited than the papers, and was far less reticent of speech. Professional men, of middle age and sober habit, were beside

---

[1] G. E. Buckle (ed.), *Letters of Queen Victoria. Second Series* (London, Murray, 1926), ii. 428, Queen Victoria to Theodore Martin, 26 November 1875. S. Lee, *King Edward VII. A Biography* (London, Macmillan, 1925), i. 295.

[2] J. L. Garvin, *The Life of Joseph Chamberlain* (London, Macmillan, 1935), i. 223.

[3] J. Morley, 'Home and Foreign Affairs', *Fortnightly Review*, 1 January 1876, 143.

[4] A. Ramm, *The Political Correspondence of Mr. Gladstone and Lord Granville 1868–1876* (1952), ii. 474, 476, Gladstone to Granville, 10 December 1875.

[5] *The Englishman*, 29 November, 2 v; *Singapore Daily Times*, 14 December, 2 v; *China Mail*, 13 December, 2 vi; *North China Herald*, 16 December, 603 ii; *Natal Mercury*, 31 December, 3 i.

[6] *Leeds Mercury, Sheffield Post, Manchester Examiner, Liverpool Mercury, Dundee Advertiser, Gloucester Journal, Cheltenham Examiner, Cheltenham Express.*

[7] *The Economist*, 27 November 1930, 'The Political Effect of the Suez Canal Purchase'. *The Economist*, 4 December, 1417–19, 'The Suez Canal Purchase as Far as We Yet Understand it'.

[8] *The Times*, 3 December, 7 vi, Baron Sandhurst.

[9] A. Lang, *Sir Stafford Northcote* (1891), 274–5, Northcote to Disraeli, 26 November 1875.

themselves with glee. For ten days men the most sedate and cynical raved about Egypt and India, as schoolboys rave about Troy and the Achaean League. Diplomatists toasted the Nile. Clowns joked about the Khedive in the Christmas pantomimes. Ladies and curates put their savings into Egyptian stock.'[1] 'For the despondent the purchase was a ray of light; for the speculator Egyptian would be up; for the trader and shipowner the tolls were to be lowered and freights raised; for the politician it floated the "Vanguard"; for the philanthropist it liberated the fugitive-slave; for the patriot it was a peaceful triumph. To everyone the act came home with a feeling of pleasure and hope.'[2] The reputation of the Ministry and of the Premier was enhanced, despite criticism by the landed gentry of the southern counties.[3] In many ways the purchase seemed eminently characteristic of Disraeli who loved the calculated surprise, the hurried decision and the immediate triumph as much as he preferred peacocks to pheasants at Hughenden. His appeal to the pride and imagination of 'the most enthusiastic race in the world' stemmed from a deep yearning for the admiration of the multitude[4] as well as from a recognition of its political advantages. His earlier purchases of the Blacas gems for the British Museum for £48,000 in 1867 and of the Barker pictures for the National Gallery for £10,000 in 1874[5] were similar achievements on his own responsibility which he delighted to recall. His hand was detected behind the audacity of the act by Delane, Townsend, Pollock and Tenniel.[6] He claimed the credit for himself and Rothschild,[7] especially in winning over Derby as well as Northcote,[8] and earned the lasting admiration of Rothschild, Greenwood[9] and Delane.[10] Most journalists of repute, however, gave the credit not to Disraeli but to Derby as did the Liberals Morley and Levy,[11] the Radicals Labouchere and Arthur Arnold[12] and the Conservatives Dicey, Dixon, Wolff and Greenwood.[13] Greenwood explicitly refuted Delane's ascription of the credit to Disraeli, affirming 'The truth is that the hand is not the hand of

[1] W. H. Dixon, 'The Way to Egypt', *Gentleman's Magazine* (February 1876), 169.

[2] H. D. Wolff, 'The Suez Canal an International Highway', *Quarterly Review* (October 1876), 430.

[3] W. S. Blunt, *Secret History of the English Occupation of Egypt* (London, Unwin, 1907), 20.

[4] F. Greenwood, 'Characteristics of Lord Beaconsfield', *Cornhill Magazine* (November 1896), 590.

[5] *The Times*, 8 February 1867, 12 iii; *The Times*, 8 June 1874, 7 v.

[6] *The Times*, 26 November 1875, 7 i. *The Spectator*, 4 December, 1508 ii, 'Mr. Disraeli from a New Side'. *Saturday Review*, 27 November, 665, 'England and Egypt'; 4 December, 695, 'The Suez Canal Purchase'. *Punch*, 11 December, 245, 'Mosé in Egitto'.

[7] *Saturday Bristol Times and Mirror*, 27 November, 5 v. *Morning Advertiser*, 2 December, 5 vi, 'The History of the Suez Canal Bargain'.

[8] G. E. Buckle, *Life of Disraeli* (1920), v. 443, Disraeli to Queen Victoria, 18 November 1875. G. E. Buckle, *Letters of Queen Victoria, Second Series* (1926), ii. 428. Marquess of Zetland (ed.), *The Letters of Disraeli* (London, Benn, 1929), i. 306.

[9] H. M. Hyndman, *The Record of an Adventurous Life* (London, Macmillan, 1911), 233.

[10] *The History of The Times* (1939), ii. 506.

[11] *Fortnightly Review*, 1 January 1876, 144; *Daily Telegraph*, 27 November 1875, 4 vii.

[12] *The World*, 1 and 5 December. *The Echo*, 4 December, 2 v.

[13] *The Observer*, 28 November, 4 iii. *Gentleman's Magazine* (January 1876), 39. *Quarterly Review* (October 1876), 429–30.

Mr. DISRAELI, but of necessity.'[1] He not only gave full credit to Derby[2] but also revealed that Disraeli appeared at first unfavourable or pretended to be unfavourable to the project.[3] Disraeli may have wished as much as Derby to be converted to an idea which he already supported. His reasons for accepting the purchase were political, those of Derby were commercial.

The purchase was greeted by the stockbroker-socialist Hyndman as 'a splendid idea'[4] and welcomed by the craftsmen of London as much as by the newly enfranchised artisans, on whose behalf George Potter commended the act as 'wise, honest and useful'.[5] The working-man enfranchized in 1867 seemed essentially a civis Romanus who liked national prestige because it cost him nothing and flattered his vanity. Thus the gulf between the classes was bridged by the enlistment of patriotic sentiment in a common cause, as A. B. Richards, the chief promoter of the Volunteers of 1859, explained: 'Mr. Disraeli never accomplished anything in his life so likely to acquire popularity for his name and administration as this spirited bargain...There are paupers not in heart, but in pocket, who delight in hearing of a national purchase like this. It is their only taste of and participation in wealth; for are they not citizens of so mighty a community, humble sharers in this magnificence?'[6] The purchase was thus admired not only in Birmingham but also in Lancashire, the centre of the Conservative reaction in England, the territorial seat of the Foreign Secretary and the home of 'the great majority of the working people of these Isles'.[7] The working population welcomed the prospect of imperial expansion as an intoxicating substitute for the alcohol for which they supplied the great market. 'It is they who raise the money that buys the Suez Canal.'[7] In Manchester the delighted C. P. Scott equated the transaction with 'the purchase of the Suez Canal by England'.[8] There the first public statue to Cromwell who had made England powerful by the sword was unveiled on 1 December 1875. There on 8 December Northcote defended the purchase as an act of unselfishness amid repeated outbursts of applause from the Conservatives assembled in the Radical-Liberal foundation of the Free Trade Hall.

The swelling chorus of approval inevitably exaggerated the significance of the purchase and encouraged estimates that the shares would have been cheap at £40,000,000 or even at £400,000,000[9] and that the Government's act was 'the greatest financial achievement of modern times'.[10] Thus it was thought that England had prevented the establishment of Russian control over the Canal Company and had acquired supreme command of the Mediterranean

---

[1] *Pall Mall Gazette*, 26 November, 1.
[2] Ibid., 3 December, 1–2; 4 December, 1–2, 10.
[3] H. M. Hyndman, *The Record of an Adventurous Life* (1911), 164.
[4] Ibid., 163–4.
[5] *The Bee-Hive, the People's Paper and Organ of Industry*, 4 December, 9 ii.
[6] *Morning Advertiser*, 29 November, 4 iv.   [7] *The Times*, 8 December, 9 i.
[8] *Manchester Guardian*, 27 November, 7 iii–iv; 7 December, 5 i.
[9] *Herapath's Railway (& Commercial) Journal*, 27 November, 1234.
[10] *The Observer* (Bristol), 4 December, 5 i.

as well as the power to prevent Russian steamers from carrying arms through the Canal to the East, so as to settle the vexed Eastern Question. It was even thought that a British protectorate had been established in Egypt in preparation for one in Syria and that the first Resident appointed at Cairo was Cave. It was hoped that Port Said would be made a free port by the Khedive at the request of the British Government, attract British capital and become a vast depot for Eastern produce for reshipment to Mediterranean ports, so supplying the half of the entrepôt trade not supplied by London.[1] That sudden wave of interest in Egypt created a new picture of the Canal in the English mind, which had regarded it at first as an anti-English device of French policy and then as a triumph of engineering, a bond between East and West and a standing proof of the shortsightedness of English opposition but never as a vital British highway. Expectations could still be cherished of the imminent destruction of the Canal by the Deity which would spare His Englishmen the cost of construction of a work of which He disapproved.[2] The material importance of the Canal in 1875 was still far below its potential importance. In economic terms it was relatively unimportant either to world shipping or to world trade. The growth of trade with America had reduced the relative importance of the Eastern trade and had made the Atlantic the main highway of world commerce. The Eastern trade itself was carried along various routes of which the Canal was less important than the Cape. For Britain the waterway was more important to shipping than to trade and more important in military than in economic terms because the British hold on India was military rather than naval. Even for military purposes its utility could not prevent the periodic revival of projects for a Euphrates Valley Railway.

The news of the share-purchase encouraged the press, especially the Conservative press, to revalue the Canal as a peculiarly national route and an indispensable highway of empire. Thus Christopher Marlowe became a farsighted precursor of the engineer Lesseps[3] while the Canal became 'the world's most important highway'[4] and 'the greatest commercial highway in the world',[5] although it carried less than 2 per cent of the volume of world trade. It was elevated to 'the finest military and naval route in the world',[6] although it had never been used by troops of the two great military powers, Russia and Germany, it could not be used by the heaviest ironclads[7] and it remained as fundamentally insecure as any route along a defile. It acquired

[1] *Cook's Tourists' Handbook for Egypt* (1876), 232–3, quoting the *Planters' Gazette*, 1 December 1875.

[2] *Leading the Nation to Glory by Our Identification with Lost Israel*, 1 December, 346–9; 8 December, 352–6, 'Egypt and the Suez Canal'.

[3] J. H. Pepper, 'The Suez Canal' in R. Routledge, *Discoveries and Inventions of the Nineteenth Century* (1876), 163.

[4] *The Spectator*, 27 November 1875, 1476.   [5] *The Hour*, 27 November, 4 iv.

[6] *Daily Bristol Times and Mirror*, 29 November, 2 vii.

[7] C. N. Parkinson, *British Intervention in Malaya 1867–1877* (Singapore, University of Malaya Press, 1960), 373, on the grounding of the *Iron Duke* four times on its passage of 23 March 1875.

overnight a magical strategic significance without reference to any other route as 'the south-eastern key of the Mediterranean',[1] 'the key to the Red Sea and to India',[2] 'the key of our Eastern Empire'[3] and 'the key to the East'.[4] The Canal was exalted anew by free-traders at the expense of the Delta as 'the most valuable of all the public works of Egypt'[5] and as 'a glorious enterprise by which the world will profit when the pyramids have crumbled into the sands of the desert'.[6] Cave's conclusion that the Canal was all that Egypt had to show for Ismail's loans was accepted by most Englishmen but by few Egyptians. The Canal was also assimilated by the imperial vision of Conservatives to the sea as 'a liquid highway' accidentally bounded by Egyptian soil.[7] 'The Canal is, in fact, the sea.'[8] 'An Englishman feels proud now that he can "paddle his own canoe" on his own canal...No doubt we shall come to possess the whole property and build arsenals on the canal, whence we can supply India in any time of need.'[9] As the connexion between the two great seats of the human race the waterway seemed to be 'the gate of the East'[10] or the 'water-gate of the East'.[11] 'History repeats itself, though centuries may intervene between its lessons; and, as the first canal was constructed more as a defence against invasion than as a channel for transportation, it would be only a repetition of history if the Suez Canal became again the boundary line between Africa and Asia.'[12] Thus Egypt became almost an appendage to the necessary stepping-stone to India and increased in value as a dependent link in a chain of empire. 'Egypt is as necessary to England as Alsace and Lorraine to Germany.'[13] 'The Isthmus of Suez has become what Sir Walter Raleigh said the Isthmus of Darien was to Spain—the key of her Empire.'[14] 'What Acre was to Napoleon, or what he thought it, the Suez Canal is to us today, and as long as we hold that we have the key to Constantinople and India. Holding that we hold Turkey and Egypt in the hollow of our hands, and the Mediterranean is an English lake, and the Suez Canal is only another name for the Thames and the Mersey.'[15]

Lawyers encouraged the identification of property in the shares with property in the Canal and the Lord Chancellor Cairns concluded that a British seizure of the Canal in a future war would be the seizure of British property. Sheldon Amos, the philosophical radical and Professor of Jurisprudence since

---

[1] *Daily Bristol Times and Mirror*, 29 November, 2 vii.
[2] *Hampshire Advertiser*, 1 December, 2 ii.
[3] *The Observer* (Bristol), 4 December, 5 i.   [4] *China Mail*, 13 December, 2 vi.
[5] *Liverpool Mercury*, 2 December, 6 iii.
[6] *Journal of the Statistical Society* (September 1876), 504, W. Farr.
[7] *Sheffield and Rotherham Independent*, 29 November, 2 vii. *Manchester Courier*, 27 November, 5 ii.
[8] *The Times*, 11 February 1876, 8 ii, H. D. Wolff.
[9] *Birmingham Weekly Post*, 4 December, 4 vi, J. T. Bunce.
[10] *The Times*, 26 November, 7 i. *The Globe*, 26 November, 4 iii.
[11] *The Standard*, 27 November, 4 iv, W. H. Mudford.
[12] *The Hour*, 29 November, 4 v, 'The Way to the East'.
[13] *Cheltenham Free Press*, 4 December, 2 i.   [14] *Dublin Evening Mail*, 29 November, 2 v.
[15] *Daily Bristol Times and Mirror*, 29 November, 3 i.

1869 at University College, London, recognized that the logic of the purchase would compel the Government in the interest of the State to become directly or indirectly 'the supreme controller of the fortunes of the Canal'.[1] He could suggest no easy solution to the dilemma created by the conflict between the military and the commercial use of the waterway or to that between the divergent claims of Europe and Asia to the protection of international law.[2] Suggestions for the 'pacification' or 'neutralization' of the Canal on the model of the Clayton-Bulwer Treaty of 1850[3] were firmly rejected by Conservative opinion as entailing intolerable restrictions on British freedom of action: 'We must hold the Canal in trust for Europe and the world, but our legal responsibility for the management of our trust should be to God and Parliament alone.'[4] The expansion of English interests also precluded any redemption of the Canal dues on the model of that of the Sound dues in 1857.[5]

The new importance of the Canal was given visual emphasis in the illustrated lecture,[6] the diorama and the opera, in the diorama of 'The New Overland Route to India via Paris, Mont Cenis, Brindisi and the Suez Canal' which opened in the Egyptian Hall, Piccadilly, on 7 February 1876 and in the opera *Aida* which was first performed in England on 23 June 1876 at Covent Garden. Publishers consolidated the press-generated interest in the sea-route to India.[7] A full account of the P. & O. steam-route to India was published by an unsuccessful rival of the P. & O. in 1856.[8] Lesseps' letters and lectures were translated,[9] so importing his version of the Canal's history into England. The first English history of the Canal,[10] which remained without a rival until 1933, was published by a Catholic journalist with substantial help from Lesseps. It comprised a biography of Lesseps with chapters on the engineering and finance of the Canal and concluded that Egypt had gained enormously from the construction of a toll-gate of the most permanent kind.[10] It represented the Canal as a benefit to Britain and thus helped to keep the nation spellbound by a master magician and enthralled in 'its dream about the Suez shares'.[11]

---

[1] S. Amos, *The Purchase of the Suez Canal Shares; and International Law* (London, Ridgway, 1876), 31.   [2] Ibid., 27–9.

[3] *The Hour*, 29 November, 5 v; 2 December, 5 v; 5 December, 5 v; 9 December, 6 i, T. Twiss.

[4] *The Spectator*, 4 December, 1509–10, 'Europe and the Suez Canal'. *Gentleman's Magazine* (February 1876), 173.   [5] *Manchester Guardian*, 30 December, 5 vi.

[6] R. Routledge, *Discoveries and Inventions of the Nineteenth Century* (London, Routledge, 1876), 162–78, J. H. Pepper, 'The Suez Canal'.

[7] E. Ashley, *The Life of Henry John Temple, Viscount Palmerston: 1846–1865* (London, Bentley, 1876), ii. 325–8, 'Views about the Suez Canal Scheme', Palmerston to Russell, 8 December 1861. *Cook's Tourist Handbook for Egypt, the Nile and the Desert* (London, Cook, 1876), 220–33.

[8] W. S. Lindsay, *History of Merchant Shipping* (London, Low, 1876), iv. 416–46, 643.

[9] F. de Lesseps, *The Suez Canal. Letters and Documents descriptive of its Rise and Progress in 1854–1856* (London, King, 1876). Idem, *The History of the Suez Canal—A Personal Narrative* (Edinburgh, Blackwood, 1876, translated by H. D. Wolff). W. Chambers, 'Lesseps and the Suez Canal', *Chambers's Journal*, 19 February 1876, 113–17.

[10] P. H. Fitzgerald, *The Great Canal at Suez* (London, Tinsley, 1876), ii. 56.

[11] M. E. G. Duff, 'The Pulse of Europe', *Contemporary Review* (July 1876), 359, 363–4.

The news of the purchase roused Arab hopes that Britain had ceased to support Turkey, strengthened the anti-Ottoman aspirations of the first Arab liberation society founded at Beirut in 1875 and rallied support in favour of the annexation of Syria to Egypt.[1] A new stimulus was given to the hopes centred on Palestine by Jews and British Israelites. From Dublin the British Government was advised to seize Palestine, to promise protection to all Jews desirous of returning there and to buy the properties of all who wished to sell. 'Thus would be re-established a people, friendly to Great Britain and under her protection, on the only line by which Russia could have invaded Egypt.'[2] In Bristol a British Israelite concluded that God had given the British Nation suzerainty of the land of Egypt by the purchase and would shortly destroy the Canal on the restoration of the lost tribes to Israel.[3] In Sheffield a fellow-believer agreed that the Canal would suffer annihilation within six years but thought that the same act of God would open up the Akaba Canal and would divert the Nile into the Sea of Jerusalem: thus British ships would sail direct from Britain into the interior of Africa, the slave-trade would be abolished and the redemption of Africa accomplished.[4] The Porte was disturbed by both the form and the substance of the transaction. It was annoyed by the Khedive's failure to consult Constantinople and to pay the customary blackmail. It was alarmed by the interpretations of the English popular press and especially by its readiness to believe that England had renounced its faith in the integrity of the Ottoman Empire, recognized the inevitability of partition and staked its claim to Egypt if Russia should take Constantinople. 'We have shifted the point of gravity of the Eastern question as far as British interests are concerned, from Constantinople to Suez.'[5] 'The Suez Canal is at least worth fighting for while the preservation of the autonomy of Turkey is at best a mere shadow.'[6] Turkey remained so dependent on British support against Russia that it was forced to canalize its wrath into a week of warlike gestures and machinations for the dismissal of Nubar,[7] necessitating England's plea that it had merely refused 'to merge the Suez Question in the Eastern Question'.[8]

Russia was surprised by the move which could be seen as a delayed reaction to the denunciation of the Black Sea clause in 1870. The organs of commerce and the landed gentry approved the purchase while Panslav and military

[1] D. E. Lee, *Great Britain and the Cyprus Convention Policy of 1878* (Harvard University Press, 1934), 15 note.
[2] *Dublin Evening Mail*, 30 November, 4 vi. *Cheltenham Express*, 4 December, 2 iii.
[3] *Daily Bristol Times and Mirror*, 30 November, 4 i; 1 December, 4 i; 3 December, 4 i; 6 December, 4 i, Philo-Israel of Clifton (E. W. Bird). *Leading the Nation to Glory*, 8 December, 352–6, Philo-Israel, 'Egypt and the Suez Canal'.
[4] *Sheffield Daily Telegraph*, 6 July 1876, 8 iii, F. Newbery, 'The Suez Canal and the Passage to India'. *The Nation's Glory Leader*, 26 July 1876, 296–9.
[5] *The Observer*, 28 November 1875, 2 vi, E. Dicey.
[6] *Manchester Evening News*, 29 November, 2 iii.
[7] *Manchester Guardian*, 2 December, 4 vii, 6 iii.
[8] *Pall Mall Gazette*, 10 December, 2, F. Greenwood.

opinion opposed it as a unilateral English intervention in the Eastern Question. 'England most unceremoniously has taken the lead in partitioning Turkey' and pocketed 'the key to the whole of Southern and Eastern Europe'.[1] Gorchakov concealed his opinion from the British ambassadors in Petersburg and Berlin[2] but was not averse either to a rupture of the Anglo-French entente or to the creation of a precedent for Russian expansion at Ottoman expense. Russia replied to the transaction by sending to Egypt at the end of 1875 General Rostislav Fadeyev, a Panslav leader and aspirant to the command of the Egyptian Army.[3] The Grand Duke Alexis also toured the Canal on 23 March 1876 in the company of Lesseps in reply to Cave's proprietary tour on 6–8 January. Germany made no reaction save such as Bismarck dictated. Bismarck was delighted because the act offended Russia as well as France and shattered the Anglo-Russo-Austrian 'coalition' of May 1875 in defence of France. Thereby it increased English dependence on German goodwill and restored Germany's freedom of action in a world of five Great Powers in unstable equilibrium. Thus Bismarck was not annoyed by the purchase as Queen Victoria had hoped. He rather extended his hearty congratulations to the British Government on having done 'the right thing at the right moment'[4] and so became the first foreign statesman to offer congratulations. He was however no more inclined than Russia to accept a unilateral coup in the Levant and therefore designated Egypt as Britain's share in the event of a peaceful partition of the Ottoman Empire so as to avert conflict between England and Russia through the allocation of mutual compensation in non-competing spheres. The offer of Egypt made by Bismarck on 2 January and again on 19 February 1876[5] was not accepted by Derby, who thereby encouraged a closer association of Germany with Russia and Austria.

Decazes, who had asked on 25 November for Russian support to block any plans for a British occupation of Egypt, was infuriated by the purchase. He enacted on the same evening a ritual outburst of bad temper on first hearing the news in the presence of Blowitz but hoped in vain to repeat his earlier coup when he had secured publication in *The Times* of 6 May 1875 of an anti-German article on 'The French Scare'. He made soundings to muster support against England in Vienna, Rome, Athens, Constantinople and, above all, in

---

[1] *The Times*, 9 December, 5iv, quoting the *Moscow Gazette*. *The Times*, 10 December, 7i, 5ii. *Manchester Guardian*, 19 February 1876, 8i. G. B. Smith, *Ferdinand de Lesseps* (London, Allen, 1893), 180–2.

[2] A. Loftus, *The Diplomatic Reminiscences of Lord Augustus Loftus, P.C., G.C.B. 1862–79. Second Series* (London, Cassell, 1894), ii. 145–6. W. Taffs, *Ambassador to Bismarck. Lord Odo Russell First Baron Ampthill* (London, Muller, 1938), 116.

[3] F. J. Cox, 'Khedive Ismail and Panslavism', *Slavonic Review* (December 1953), 161–3.

[4] W. Taffs, *Odo Russell*, 112–16, 29 November 1875. *Manchester Guardian*, 2 December 1875, 6iii.

[5] G. H. Rupp, *A Wavering Friendship: Russia and Austria 1876–1878* (Harvard University Press, 1941), 92. A. O. Sarkissian (ed.), *Studies in Diplomatic History and Historiography in Honour of G. P. Gooch* (London, Longmans, 1961), 228, 232, W. N. Medlicott, 'Bismarck and Beaconsfield'.

Petersburg on 27 November.[1] He also sought to secure the dismissal of Nubar by the Sultan,[2] asked the British ambassador in Paris on 30 November whether Ismail had the right to sell the shares without the Sultan's consent and blamed the Bank of France for insisting on usurious terms for a loan. On 3 December he published in a justificatory Yellow Book the diplomatic correspondence conducted about the Canal between the British and French Foreign Offices since 1872. In the new year he replaced the French Consul in Egypt and began to work actively against Cave's schemes of financial reorganization. Throughout his remaining eighteen months of office Decazes retained a distrust of England. He was defended only by the official and Orleanist press and suffered immediate attacks from the Legitimist, the Bonapartist and the Catholic press. 'The Suez Canal is about to become a second East India Company... The seizure of the Suez Canal by the English Government inaugurates a new type of conquest...conquest by mortgage.'[3] 'Henceforth the Suez Canal has become an English possession, a new Gibraltar.'[4] Gambetta's organ demanded the resignation of Decazes for his lack of radical nationalism and his failure to understand the world function of the French flag:[5] it blamed Rouvier for Ismail's reluctance to resort to the Paris money-market because of the delay of his committee in reporting on judicial reform in Egypt. At Versailles a caucus of the Left discussed the purchase at great length on 27 November but decided that the time was not opportune to raise it in the Assembly.

France as a nation remained still paralysed by the shock of Sedan[6] and more dependent than ever on Britain for support against Germany since the war-scare of May 1875. Thus she could not regard the transaction as an affront comparable to the Hohenzollern candidature of 1870 or as an Asiatic Sedan. All her attention was concentrated on home rather than on foreign affairs, on the definitive acceptance of the Republic and the final rejection of the Monarchy after 1,000 years. The Canal was not yet deeply embedded in French traditions. It represented the traditions of the Empire rather than those of the Nation. It could not be defended without also defending the Bonapartist cause and was thus made vulnerable by the cloud of infamy which surrounded the Imperial party in the 1870s. 'The Suez Canal was made a national question formerly, and is again today. Yet there never was a question less national for France than this.'[7] The transaction was seen as a threat to

[1] *Pall Mall Gazette*, 6 December 1875, 7 ii. C. Bloch, *Les Relations entre la France et la Grande-Bretagne (1871–1878)* (Paris, Éditions Internationales, 1955), 251–2.

[2] *Documents Diplomatiques Françaises, 1ère Série*, ii. 27, No. 20, Decazes à Bourgoing, 29 Novembre 1875.

[3] John Lemoinne in the *Journal des Débats*, 27 and 29 Novembre, quoted by C. Lesage, *L'Achat des Actions de Suez (Novembre 1875)* (Paris, Plon, 1906), 228.

[4] A. Neymarck, *Finances Contemporaines* (Paris, Guillaumin, 1905), 80, 82, 'Le Canal de Suez'.

[5] *La République Française*, 30 Novembre, 2 iii; 1 Décembre, 1–2; 2 Décembre, 2 ii; 3 Décembre, 2 v–vi; 7 Décembre, 1 vi.

[6] *Pall Mall Gazette*, 11 December, 10 ii, F. Greenwood, 'France and Egypt'.

[7] *The Times*, 14 April 1876, 3 iii, Blowitz quoting a French statesman of 'high authority', perhaps Say or even Decazes.

Egypt rather than to Suez, which was identified with England in the tradition of Lamartine. France could recognize no national interest in the road to India before the imperial expansion of 1883–5. The Canal was used almost exclusively by English shipping, English warships and English troopships. Even if it was used by French warships, the Navy remained a costly exotic import into France, unlike the Army. Trieste and Brindisi had derived double the advantage from the Canal of Marseilles, Cette or Toulon. The failure of Dervieu and Lesseps to acquire the Khedive's shares for French interests affected French capitalists rather than the French nation. The 40,000 shareholders holding 178,659 shares, or 44·7 per cent of the total, were small investors rather than wealthy bankers. They were wounded in their pride by the transaction but benefited in their pocket as their shares rose by 150 francs or by 22·2 per cent between 24 and 29 November on the Bourse, where sentiment was at a discount. France also retained five-sixths of the Company's total assets of £24,000,000.

Egypt's credit was restored by the establishment of relations with the first financial power of the world and the leading financial house of Europe. Ismail was able to order on 1 December a punitive expedition of 11,000 to Abyssinia but remained short of cash and was faced by the prospect of a mission of enquiry under Cave instead of the single official he had requested. He mooted on 25 November the possibility of a sale of his 15 per cent share in the profits for £1,200,000–£1,600,000, an offer which was rejected by Derby on 6 December and left the way open for renewed competition between English and French financial interests. He succeeded in securing the promulgation by France on 25 December of the Law of Judicial Reform sanctioning the new Mixed Courts. He had also established direct financial relations with the British Government by the sale of what Bagehot perceived to be 'a very peculiar property.'[1] The shares had been deprived of their coupons in 1869 when the delegations were created. Thus they would receive no dividends before 1894 but only 5 per cent interest per annum from Ismail in lieu of their coupons. Nor would they receive the dividend on the participating shares which gradually replaced the capital shares through amortization from 1876. Their market-value was only 36·8 per cent of the actual purchase-price while the other 63 per cent was represented by the delegations.[2] They formed 44 per cent of the ordinary shares but secured only the ten votes allotted to the British Government by the Company on 8 December while each of the 270 shareholders attending the general meeting had at least one vote and a similar maximum of ten votes under the Company's statutes. Future friction became almost inevitable with France over 'an undefinable bit of England located in Egypt, subject to the laws of France'.[3] From mid-December a reaction against

[1] *The Economist*, 4 December 1875, 1418i.
[2] G. Campbell, 'Our Dealings with Egypt, and the Possible Results', *Fortnightly Review*, 1 February 1876, 158.
[3] *The Times*, 14 December 1875, 4i, C. Magniac.

the over-valuation of the purchase began to be voiced by northern Liberal M.P.s[1] and by the Newcastle Chamber of Commerce in its memorial of 16 December to the Foreign Secretary. On the day after Cave's arrival in Egypt on 16 December Derby addressed the Conservative Working Men's Association at Edinburgh and delivered a completely different interpretation of the transaction from that which had been generally accepted. His speech provoked thunders of applause as he first touched on the purchase but continued in a stunned silence as he demolished the popular press-generated illusions and minimized its significance to the last degree. He explicitly disclaimed such unjustified imputations as 'a wish to establish a Protectorate over Egypt, an interested reversal of our policy on the whole Eastern question, or an intention to take part in a general scramble [for that] which does not belong to us'.[2] He denied any deep-laid scheme and implied that the Government had taken a leap in the dark in self-defence. He disclaimed all ulterior motives other than that of the security of the passage through Egypt to India. 'We seek no exclusion, no monopoly, only a secure passage for ourselves, and the same security we are willing that all the world should enjoy.'[2] Derby did not reveal the source from which the security of passage was threatened nor, out of deference to Lesseps, the manner in which the purchase of the shares had increased that security. He concluded dryly that there was no reason why the State should lose a penny by the transaction in the end. His exposition had required considerable moral courage but disheartened all the enthusiasts for a spirited foreign policy, earned him rebukes from Greenwood, Dicey[3] and Townsend[4] and impelled Disraeli towards the more sympathetic Salisbury. His speech was intended as a reassurance to the offended susceptibilities of foreign powers and a warning that England would not permit 'the roguery of the Khedive'[5] to draw her into the vortex of Egyptian finance. It enabled Lesseps, who had followed Cave and Stokes to Egypt, to offer Ismail on 20 December a loan of £2,000,000 at 9 per cent on the security of the 15 per cent share in the Company's profits and so to begin the battle of the loans.[6] The full significance of Derby's speech was expounded by the irrepressible Harcourt on 30 December in language which shocked Delane.

Since the speech of the Foreign Secretary, the whole aspect of the question has been completely changed, both at home and abroad. Up to that time a sort of glamour had invested a very plain business with the unnatural haze that distorts the true

---

[1] *Hull News*, 18 December 1875, 4 v, C. M. Norwood.

[2] *The Scotsman*, 18 December, 8 i. *The Times*, 18 December, 6 iv.

[3] *Pall Mall Gazette*, 18 December, 5 ii. *The Observer*, 19 December, 4 vi. *The Times*, 20 December, 9 i. *Manchester Guardian*, 20 December, 5 ii.

[4] *The Spectator*, 25 December, 1617–18, 'Lord Derby on Turkey and Egypt'.

[5] A. T. Wilson, *The Suez Canal. Its Past, Present, and Future* (London, Oxford University Press, 1933), 53, E. Hammond to A. H. Layard, 30 November 1875.

[6] J. Tagher, 'Les Dessous de la Mission Cave', *Cahiers d'Histoire Égyptienne* (Octobre 1952), 220. J. Bouvier, 'Les Intérêts Financiers et la Question d'Égypte (1875–1876)', *Revue Historique* (Juillet 1960), 81–3. J. Bouvier, *Le Crédit Lyonnais de 1863 à 1882* (Paris, Imprimerie Nationale, 1961), ii. 668–76.

proportion of things. There was something Asiatic in this mysterious melodrama. It was like the *Thousand and One Nights* when in the fumes of incense, a shadowy genie astonished the bewildered spectators. The public mind was dazzled, fascinated, mystified. We had done, we did not know exactly what, we were not told precisely why, *omne ignotum pro magnifico*... England had at length resumed her lead amongst the nations. The Eastern Question had been settled by a *coup d'état* on the Stock Exchange. Turkey was abandoned to her fate. Egypt was annexed. The Bulls of England had vanquished the Bears of Russia. Moab was to be our washpot, and over Edom we had cast our shoe. France and M. de Lesseps were confounded. We were a very great people and we had done a very great thing; and to consummate the achievement, a Satrap from Shoreham, attended by a troop of financial Janissaries, was despatched to administer the subject provinces of the English Protectorate on the Nile... We, all of us, felt some six inches taller than before. We spread our tails like peacocks to the sun, and were as pleased as children at our soap-bubble, iridescent with many hues. But, all of a sudden, this beautiful vision melted away; the Egyptian mirage evaporated; the great political phantasmagoria faded like a dissolving view... Lord Derby is a great master of prose, and he has translated the Eastern Romance into most pedestrian English...And so the nine days' wonder is over, the enchantment is at an end, and the chariot of Cinderella relapses into its original pumpkins and mice. (Great laughter)...Now that this great affair is reduced to the moderate dimensions of a sort of post-office subsidy, we may criticise it.[1]

The shares reached Portsmouth on 31 December on the Indian troopship H.M.S. *Malabar*, whose captain was granted £500 or much less than he had asked for carrying 'treasure', and were stowed in the vaults of the Bank of England on 1 January. Lesseps signed a protocol of agreement at Ismailia on 3 January with Colonel Stokes. Nubar's resignation on 5 January after the speeches by Derby and Harcourt and the payment of the last instalment of the purchase-price by Rothschilds produced a sharp fall in Egyptian stocks in London. Sir George Elliot, the contractor for the harbour-works of Alexandria, presented Ismail on 12 January with a scheme for the consolidation of the Egyptian Debt and for its management by a specially created branch of the financial administration which would include two Englishmen. That scheme proposed to reduce the capital of the Debt by 20 per cent to £65,000,000 and its interest-rate by 1 per cent to 6½ per cent, so saving £250,000 per annum at the expense of the French. Cave's support for the scheme provoked the intervention of the new French Consul in opposition on 14 January. When Cave cabled on 24 January that he might be obliged to give provisional approval to Elliot's scheme Derby immediately forbade him to do so and ordered him on 26 January to return to London. Thus the English withdrawal from Egypt began, disappointing Ismail's hopes that he might benefit by the competition between English and French to lend him money.

Hostile analyses of the purchase as a bad bargain, a poor investment, a

[1] *The Morning Post*, 31 December 1875, 6 ii. A. G. Gardiner, *The Life of Sir William Harcourt* (London, Constable, 1923), i. 294–5.

political folly and a legal anomaly were published by leading intellectuals[1] while Bradlaugh began to deliver weekly protest lectures. The Canal itself was belittled as a calamity to English commerce and marine-insurance[2] and as a mere ditch in the desert which needed doubling in width to be worthy of its geographical position and future capacity.[3] Sir George Campbell, who had been Lieutenant-Governor of Bengal from 1871 to 1874 and a Member of the Council of India in London in 1874–5, delivered the most trenchant attack on the purchase of a large share in 'a great Egyptian property' as a loan to a foreign ruler at great risk but without the compensatory high interest-rate which Ismail would have been compelled to pay in any of the money-markets of Europe.[4] Such a direct subsidy or financial protectorate was the worst and most dangerous form of protectorate, encouraged creditors to seek usurious terms as well as their complete fulfilment and could only end in a political protectorate over a land where the ordinary land revenue was tenfold the average rate in India. Campbell recognized the lure of Africa as a possible 'gigantic Java or Ceylon'[4] but warned Britain against the belief that it was a matter of life and death to maintain the Canal route under all possible circumstances and against further official interference in Egyptian finances. 'We cannot so interfere without making ourselves in some sort responsible, and creating financial hopes and expectations, compared to which our own £200,000 per annum is a small sum.'[5]

On 8 February 1876 Queen Victoria, robed in the imperial purple, opened Parliament for the first time since 1871 and asked it to approve the act of her Ministers ten weeks earlier. Disraeli explained for the benefit of Lesseps that the world was governed by conciliation and compromise and for the benefit of the public that the Canal had increased the security of the great chain of fortresses between London and India, emphasizing English maritime rather than territorial interests in the Canal in a revival of his catenary metaphor of 1863. In Egypt the Mixed Courts were inaugurated on 1 February with £40,000,000 of foreign claims outstanding against the Government. On 8 February Ismail accepted with regret a loan of £2,000,000 from Pastré's Anglo-Egyptian Bank with his 15 per cent share in profits as a guarantee and on 10 February a loan of £700,000 from André Dervieu. The success of the Crédit Foncier encouraged Elliot to present his scheme in more detail to

---

[1] H. Reeve, 'The Suez Canal', *Edinburgh Review* (January 1876), 250–80. J. R. Jefferies, *Suez-Cide!! Or, How Miss Britannia Bought a Dirty Puddle and Lost her Sugar-Plums* (London, Snow, 1876, 20 pp.). S. Amos, *The Purchase of the Suez Canal Shares; and International Law* (London, Ridgway, 1876, 35 pp.). *North China Herald*, 3 February 1876, 91 i–ii, 'The Suez Canal'.

[2] C. Magniac, 'On the Commercial Aspects of the Suez Canal', *Journal of the Society of Arts*, 18 February 1876, 253–62, 277–84, 302–3, 341–3. F. Martin, *The History of Lloyd's* (1876), 380–3, 'Suez Canal and Indian Steamers'.

[3] *The Times*, 18 April 1876, 5 vi, J. Corbett, salt manufacturer and merchant of Droitwich.

[4] G. Campbell, 'Our Dealings with Egypt, and the Possible Results', *Fortnightly Review*, 1 February 1876, 167.

[5] Ibid., 173.

Ismail on 11 February[1] and Decazes to propose on 14 February an Anglo-French control of Egypt's finances. Derby refused on 19 February to join France in such a control. The criticisms of the purchase compelled the Government to present three successive batches of supporting parliamentary papers on 9, 11 and 14 February and to spread the debate over two days, 14 and 21 February. In the debate on 21 February the private member Henry Drummond Wolff was chosen to answer Lowe's attack on the Government as an authority on the Suez Canal, the translator of Lesseps' lecture-history[2] and the pseudonymous defender of the Government in *The Times*.[3] Gladstone attacked the transaction as obscure, unconstitutional and illusory. He ridiculed the Government's argument of the security of the road to the East by referring to the speech of a parliamentary candidate at Manchester. 'He said, is not the Prince of Wales in India, and is not the Princess of Wales in England, and are we going to put the Prince to the hazard of not coming home by the nearest route?'[4] Gladstone concluded that the best way to avoid future apprehension and embarrassment would be to distribute the shares among the members of the Cabinet as a small acknowledgement of their services in the transaction from a grateful country. He was so infuriated as to publish a syllabus of twenty-one questions from his speech on the purchase[5] and retained thenceforward an unconquerable distrust of the route-to-India argument. Sir George Campbell could not believe that English commerce could be carried on in wartime by the aid of a chain of fortresses through the Mediterranean separated by 2,000 miles. The Liberal Roebuck however defended the Premier and so earned membership of the Privy Council. Norwood, the shipowner and opponent of Plimsoll, was the only private Liberal member openly to deplore the principle of the purchase on behalf of the commercial community of Hull. The Liberal leaders recognized the support of their own followers for the Government and refused to force a division. Disraeli concluded that the English people wanted the Empire to be maintained and would not be alarmed even if it were increased. The cheers which greeted that assertion provoked Herbert Spencer to use 'the Suez Canal business' in association with British expansion in Fiji and Perak to illustrate a wider social metamorphosis, the reversion from the industrial to the militant type of society as much as from voluntary to compulsory cooperation and the tendency to disregard the principles of free government in the name of military exigency. 'Military officialism everywhere tends to usurp the place of civil officialism.'[6] Even the Canal Company attained a military unity under Lesseps.

---

[1] *The Observer*, 5 March 1876, 5 iii; 2 April, 3 iii. *Manchester Guardian*, 3 April 1876, 6 ii. *Revue Historique* (Juillet 1960), 88, J. Bouvier, 'Les Intérêts Financiers'.

[2] F. de Lesseps, *The History of the Suez Canal—A Personal Narrative* (Edinburgh, Blackwood, 1876).

[3] Memnon, 'The Suez Canal', *The Times*, 20 January 1876, 8; 26 January, 4.

[4] Hansard, *Commons Debates*, 21 February 1876, 598, Gladstone.

[5] *The Times*, 24 February 1876, 8 iii.

[6] H. Spencer, *The Principles of Sociology* (London, Williams, July 1876), i. 603.

'It was drilled under M. de Lesseps as an army under its commanding officer—they moved forward, halted or receded, just as he chose to give the word of command.'[1]

Lesseps signed with Stokes after four weeks of negotiations the Cairo Convention of 21 February 1876.[2] Lesseps therein accepted on behalf of the Canal Company the decisions of the Conference of Constantinople regarding the measurement of tonnage in return for the prolongation of the surtax, which the increase in traffic threatened immediately to reduce and then to abolish under the procedure laid down in 1873. The British Government agreed to undertake negotiations whereby the surtax would be eliminated through a sliding-scale of six successive stages at fixed dates independent of the increase of traffic. The surtax would be reduced first from 1 January 1877 and again from 1 January 1879 and would then be reduced four times more on 1 January of each year between 1881 and 1884. The original counter-proposals made by Lesseps in 1874 were thus partly met by making the reduction of the surtax more gradual. In return Lesseps agreed to spend £40,000 per annum for the next thirty years on the development of the Canal in addition to its ordinary maintenance. He also withdrew his claims against the Porte which had averaged £9,200 per month and totalled £1,921,700 for the period from April 1874 to January 1876. He ended his protests against the Convention of Constantinople and his four-year war against the clients of the Canal. The Convention of Cairo encouraged engineers to contemplate a double canal for northbound and southbound traffic at a cost of £10,000,000. Lesseps however limited the expenditure of the Company on improvement to the stipulated annual £40,000. On 28 February he abruptly dismissed his London agent, D. A. Lange, who after nineteen years of service to the Company had been revealed as 'too English in his feelings'[3] by the unfortunate publication on 9 February of his unofficial correspondence with Granville in 1871.[4] Thereby Lesseps demonstrated the absolute nature of his power, unrestrained by any influence which the British Government could exert, and his unswerving opposition to any English bid to take over the Company. The Exchequer Bonds Bill was passed on 6 March to raise a 35-year loan of £4,080,000 at 3½ per cent, or 1½ per cent less than Egypt was paying Britain in interest, from the Post Office Savings Bank. The Khedive's shares were thus bought with the money placed by the small investor in the institution created by Gladstone in 1861. The transaction was kept separate from the ordinary finance of the year on the inauspicious precedent of the payment of the Alabama indemnity. Northcote established a new Sinking-Fund and raised

[1] Hansard, *Commons Debates*, 21 February 1876, 595, Gladstone.
[2] *Egypt No. 9 (1876). Further Correspondence regarding the Suez Canal* (C-1525 of 1876), 14–18.
[3] Hansard, *Commons Debates*, 6 March 1876, 1427, Gladstone.
[4] *Egypt No. 2 (1876). Correspondence Respecting the Suez Canal* (C-1392 of 1876), 145–6, Lange to Granville, 3 April 1871. *The Times*, 29 February 1876, 9 vi; 1 February 1877, 11 vi. *Saturday Review*, 11 March 1876, 318–19, 'Incidents of the Suez Canal Discussion'.

the income-tax by 1*d*. from 3*d*., the first rise in the tax in peace-time since 1842. The financial cost of the shares remained far below their political cost.

Disraeli was determined to defend Turkey against Russia and to frustrate the Russian solution of the Eastern question implicit in Bismarck's offer of Egypt. He also became alarmed by the size of Ismail's liabilities and by the Khedive's inclination to accept a French financial solution. He therefore followed Northcote's express disclaimer of 6 March of any overt interference with Egypt's finances by the equally public refusal on 23 March to guarantee an £18,000,000 loan to consolidate the Egyptian Debt, declaring that Ismail did not wish the Cave Report to be made public. Thereby he finally disentangled his administration from the Egyptian morass into which he had unwittingly trodden in November 1875 and annihilated the expectations built up among the investors in Egyptian stock. The resulting panic on the Stock Exchange, where the 1873 loan fell from 62–63 on 23 March to 51½–52½ on 30 March, made the establishment of British control of Egypt and 'the true approach to our Indian possessions'[1] a moral obligation in the eyes of English bondholders. The defeat of the Egyptian troops in the valley of the Gura in Abyssinia on 6–8 March destroyed the prestige of Ismail's Circassian officers and generals and shattered his expectations of speedy returns from his new empire in the south. The publication of the Cave Report on 3 April and the failure of Pastré on 5 April to float an unguaranteed loan of £10,000,000–£14,000,000 precipitated Ismail's bankruptcy. His last wholly independent act of authority was to postpone on 7 April the payment of the Treasury bonds due in March and April for three months, so preferring the British to the French creditors. In Paris the Great Syndicate of bankers was therefore formed on 8 April under Hentsch, Joubert and Oppenheim to defend French interests while in London a panic fall on the Stock Exchange drove the 1873 loan down to 42–46 on 12 April and to 40–42 on 13 April, a decline in value of 33 per cent in three weeks. That financial collapse doomed Fowler's proposal for an Alexandria–Cairo–Suez Canal.[2] On 9 May the decrees of 2 and 7 May were promulgated, establishing a Commission of the Public Debt and a General Unified Debt of £91,000,000 and favouring the French holders of the floating debt at the expense of the British holders of the consolidated debt. Derby demonstrated his dissatisfaction with Ismail's acceptance of a French scheme. He replaced Stanton as Consul-General, after his cumulative neglect of British interests, by Vivian on 10 May. He refused to make official British appointments to the new Commission of the Public Debt. The London Stock Exchange also refused to cooperate with the Paris Bourse in the proposed reorganization of the Debt and so forced the French to negotiate anew with the English.[3]

The general meeting of the Canal Company on 27 June 1876 was attended

---

[1] G. C. Chester, 'Some Truths About Egypt', *Fortnightly Review*, 1 April 1876, 590.
[2] *Manchester Guardian*, 12 April 1876, 5 iii.
[3] *Revue Historique* (Juillet 1960), 95–6, J. Bouvier, 'Les Intérêts Financiers'.

by only 273 shareholders, or 40 per cent of the number present at the tumultuous meeting on 12 March 1872, and heard the Report for 1875 which showed a profit for the first time in the history of the Company. During 1875 receipts rose by 15·4 per cent to exceed the 1855 estimate of thirty million francs for the first time and to prove wrong the *Economist*'s forecast of a 5 per cent rise per annum. The average price of the 500-franc share for the year rose by 60 per cent to 674 francs and to a premium of 35 per cent. Net profits rose by 60 per cent, making possible the first full distribution of surplus profits for the year 1875. Derby had nominated on 26 June three English directors to the Company in Stokes, Rivers Wilson and Standen. Wilson had been a Treasury official since 1856 and Comptroller-General of the National Debt since 1874 and had become a great friend of the Rothschilds. Standen had been Stokes' old secretary on the Danube Commission. H. D. Wolff was not named a director and repeated his plea for an international administration of the Canal.[1] The three new official directors-elect were prevented by the Company from taking their seats on the board because they lacked the statutory qualification of 100 shares apiece. On 5 August Parliament therefore voted a further £9,200 to buy 300 more shares in the open market at a cost of over £8,000. The directors held those shares under bond and paid the dividends received thereon to the Treasury. A Treasury minute of 17 July fixed salaries of £800 for the resident director, Standen, and of £300 plus expenses for the two non-resident directors.

The acquisition of the shares stimulated a new activity along the Suez route by Anglo-Indian interests which increased its share of British trade and justified the purchase in retrospect. The improvement of the port of Bombay from 1875 was geared to the Canal's depth of 26 feet, as was that of the ports of Aden, Madras and Singapore from 1876. On the eastern flank of the Suez route Arabia aroused aspirations to open Mecca to the march of civilization.[2] It attracted Doughty to join the pilgrimage of 1876 from Damascus as a confirmed Nazarene in quest of Biblical inscriptions and reckless of the wave of indigenous unrest which swept Asia in 1872–5 and made the Maghrebi pilgrims unusually insulting to the Europeans at Suez in 1876 in defiance of the local authorities. Anglo-Indian policy sought to extend its control of the Suez route and to protect Aden against any renewed threat from Egypt, which Derby had warned off Somaliland on 23 November and off Abyssinia on 17 December 1875. The Treaty of 23 January 1876 with the Mahri Sultan of Qishn and Socotra precluded him from alienating his island except to the British Government. Aden also became the scene of the first official rite on the new route to India. Lytton's gaudy and theatrical ambition had been intoxicated by his transfer from Lisbon to Calcutta, by the introduction of the bill to bestow the imperial title on the Queen of India and by the

---

[1] H. D. Wolff, 'The Suez Canal an International Highway', *Quarterly Review* (October 1876), 455–6.
[2] I. Burton, *Arabia Egypt India* (1879), 93.

commissioning of H.M.S. *Orontes* as 'an Imperial troopship'.[1] He toured the Canal on 24 March on his overland passage through Egypt and landed from the *Orontes* in state on 1 April at Aden as the first point of his new dominions,[1] so seeking to impress the local population and creating the precedent followed by every later viceroy at Aden and Bombay. Northbrook became the first returning Viceroy to use the Canal in the Indian troopship *Tenasserim* en route to Brindisi in 1876. Pender's duplication of the Suez–Bombay cable followed the introduction in 1875 of duplex operation and the interruption of the line for eighty days in 1875–6. The cable-laying ships *Hibernia, Kangaroo* and *Seine* passed through the Canal to link Suez to Aden (27 October–11 November 1876), Aden to Bombay (23 February–7 March 1877)[2] and Penang to Rangoon on 7 April 1877. Pender then made in 1877 a joint-purse agreement with the Indo-European Telegraph Company and sought a subsidy from Zanzibar for an Aden–Natal cable,[3] so encouraging Donald Currie to renew his plea for a west-coast cable from England to South Africa.[4] The monthly service begun by Mackinnon in 1876 between London and Calcutta brought the British India Line out of the coastal trade and into the long-distance trade in direct competition with the P. & O. for the first time. In reply the P. & O. extended its China terminal from Hong Kong to Shanghai and adopted the auxiliary rudder for the better navigation of the Canal. The British India Line helped to increase Calcutta's shipments of rice via the Canal above those shipped via the Cape for the first time in 1876. The increase in steamer competition in the Calcutta trade stimulated the voyage of the clipper *Coriolanus* to Calcutta in sixty-nine days via the Cape, a record equalled but never beaten. Mackinnon also began from 1876 to project an East African Company[5] as an inland extension of his Aden–Zanzibar service and an essential organ of legitimate commerce in place of the slave-trade from the interior which was prohibited by the Sultan of Zanzibar on 18 April 1876.

The deterioration of the situation in the Balkans drew England inexorably but unaccompanied towards Constantinople. To avoid isolation as in the war-scare of 1875 Bismarck was compelled to become the associate of the revolutionary powers of Russia and Austria in their bid to subvert the *status quo* and to partition Turkey like Poland in the eighteenth century. Britain had no prospect of active French support for its conservative Turkish policy as in 1853 and experienced growing pressure to accept compensation for the expected gains of Russia and Austria, especially after the insurrection spread from Herzegovina to Bulgaria on 2 May, the news of the Bulgarian atrocities of the Turkish irregulars was published on 23 June and Gladstone's pamphlet

[1] E. H. Seymour, *My Naval Career and Travels* (London, Smith, 1911), 177.
[2] J. U. Bateman-Champain, 'Telegraph Routes between England and India', *Journal of the Society of Arts*, 10 May 1878, 529.
[3] R. Coupland, *The Exploitation of East Africa 1856–1890* (1939), 301–2, 323.
[4] *Journal of the Royal United Service Institution*, 2 March 1877, 230, D. Currie, 'Maritime Warfare'.
[5] Coupland, 302–3.

on *The Bulgarian Horrors* rallied Christian, Nonconformist and Liberal opinion to the side of Russia from September. Thus Bismarck in his memorandum of 20 October again assigned Egypt as Britain's share in any partition of Turkey in exchange for the liberation of Turkey's subjects north of the Balkans. The Tory–Turkish–Moslem interest in England was, however, more tempted by the emerging prospect of a new empire based on Constantinople and under the rule of an English duke, his Russian wife and Anglo-Indian administrators.[1] Disraeli's acceptance of partition in his letter of 4 September to Derby ushered in six months of debate within the Government as to where the British share should be taken. Disraeli firmly rejected Bismarck's suggestion of Egypt. 'Our strength is on the sea. Constantinople is the key of India, and not Egypt and the Suez Canal.'[2] Thereby he refuted Tenniel, completed his withdrawal from the Egyptian snare of 1875 and dissociated himself from the supporters of a forward policy in Egypt. He sought a naval base for a policy based on naval power, a Malta or a Gibraltar in the Aegean or even in the Black Sea rather than in the South-East Mediterranean. He considered such bases as Crete, Rhodes, the Dardanelles and Gallipoli in his wish to divert Anglo-Indian enterprise and English capital to Turkey rather than to Egypt, provoking pleas for the annexation of the Egyptian road to India. 'So surely as Russia is setting her face towards Constantinople must England concentrate her attention on Egypt, Port Said and the Suez Canal.'[3] 'Our gate to India is Port Said, the entrance of the Suez Canal.'[4] Disraeli, however, hoped to protect the Canal by naval power and sent H.M.S. *Fawn* to survey the Port Said entrance, so leading the Association of the Chambers of Commerce of the United Kingdom to submit a memorial to Derby on 12 December in favour of the neutralization of the waterway. British hopes focused on Constantinople rather than on the Canal and were drawn towards Cyprus after the Conference of Constantinople by Colonel Robert Home's suggestion on 8 February 1877 of the island as an alternative to the Dardanelles[5] and by Disraeli's preference for 'some unexpected act to the constant writing of State papers'.[6] Unofficial English interest remained centred on the Holy Land rather than on Egypt.

French interest in Egypt grew after the creation of the Commission of the Public Debt and the establishment by the Crédit Lyonnais, the largest bank of deposit in France, of a branch in Port Said in September 1876. The formation

---

[1] G. E. Buckle, *The Letters of Queen Victoria, Second Series* (1926), ii. 475–6, 27 Août 1876, King of the Belgians to Queen Victoria. *The Times*, 11 September 1876, 6 ii, M. E. G. Duff.

[2] G. E. Buckle, *The Life of Disraeli* (1920), vi. 84, Memorandum by Lord Barrington, 23 October 1876.

[3] *The Times*, 26 December 1876, 9 i–ii, M. Monier-Williams, 'The Suez Canal'. M. Monier-Williams, *Modern India* (1878), 18.

[4] H. M. Havelock, 'Constantinople and Our Road to India', *Fortnightly Review*, 1 January 1877, 121, quoting the advocates of Egypt against Turkey.

[5] D. E. Lee, *Great Britain and the Cyprus Convention Policy of 1878* (1934), 174–7.

[6] A. Hardinge, *The Life of the Earl of Carnarvon* (1925), ii. 355, 21 April 1877, Disraeli in Cabinet.

of the unofficial Anglo-French Dual Control of Egypt's finances by the Goschen-Joubert agreement of 18 November 1876 was welcomed by the French as a permanent basis of French influence in the administration of Egypt. That Control was determined to secure the deposition of Ismail if necessary.[1] It reduced the United Egyptian Debt from £91,000,000 to £59,000,000 and secured the payment of 78 per cent of Egypt's revenue in 1877 to the bondholders, although the Nile flood was the lowest in 150 years. It also brought Evelyn Baring to Egypt as the first British Commissioner on 2 March 1877. Baring encouraged Ismail to resist suggestions by the French Commissioner in 1877 and 1878 to suspend the payment of the 5 per cent interest to the British Government on the Canal shares. French influence however spread through the new Mixed Courts which were French in language, law and administration and extended their protection to the Canal Company. The new Mixed Civil Court of Ismailia could hardly function otherwise than as a Company court in a Company town, as the Company administration could hardly avoid giving speedy passage to French mail steamers and delaying the mail steamers of the P. & O.[2] Thus it showed a consistent tenderness in its decisions for the rights of the Company against individual litigants. It declared itself on 20 April 1876 competent to hear a suit for the price of land lodged by the Company against a French widow because the Company was neither French, Ottoman nor Egyptian but international.[3] Thus it sought to restore the legal Alsatia destroyed by Egypt in 1866. On the other hand it declared itself on 15 January 1877 incompetent to hear an action for damages against the Company because the Company was not a commercial company carrying on trade. The mortgage on 20 October 1877 of the Khedive's 15 per cent share in the Company's profits to the Great Syndicate of Paris bankers satisfied some of Ismail's richest creditors, especially the Crédit Foncier, at the expense of Egypt's last financial interest in the Company. The increase in Frankish influence evoked a growing demand for 'Egypt for the Egyptians'.[4]

The purchase of the Khedive's shares caused some unease in France which encouraged proposals for the repurchase of the Canal by means of a toll on French shipping[5] and the capture of the heroic legend of Suez from the Empire for the Republic, especially after the Republican victory in the elections of 1876. The incorporation of some study of the Canal into the educational curriculum was facilitated by the spread of the study of geography in French schools from 1872 and by the postwar efflorescence of geographical societies. Waddington as Minister for Education decided in 1876 that a lecture on the Canal should be given annually in every lycée in France by the Professor of

---

[1] *Revue Historique* (Juillet 1960), 97, J. Bouvier, 'Les Intérêts Financiers'.
[2] *The Times*, 14 January 1878, 7 vi.
[3] Y. van der Mensbrugghe, *Les Garanties de la Liberté de Navigation dans le Canal de Suez* (Paris, Pichon, 1964), 196–8.
[4] J. C. McCoan, *Egypt As It Is* (1877), 85.
[5] *The Times*, 28 June 1876, 5 i.

History and Geography and ordered a hundred models of the Canal.[1] Those models were small reproductions, on the scale of four feet to the hundred miles of the Canal, of the large-scale model made by Vice-Admiral Edmond de Paris, Curator of the Naval Museum of the Louvre and President of the Academy of Sciences. His model was displayed in the Suez Canal Room, the Salle de Lesseps, at the Louvre and described in a notice published on its first exhibition in 1875. Lesseps himself extended the basis of the French tradition of the Canal by publishing the first two volumes of his letters in 1875 and the third in 1877. In 1876 the first novel ever written about the Canal appeared[2] based on reminiscences by the foreman Montezuma Goguel to Erckmann in 1873. That national and popular work with an anti-clerical bias and an anonymous workman as its hero went through five editions in the year of its publication. It effectively extended the French affection for Egypt to embrace the isthmus of Suez as a little France, identified the Canal with France and urged its renaming the Canal de Lesseps. Thus the Canal was divorced from the imperial regime which had sponsored its creation and became a means of reconciling the new France to the old France amid the growing tension between Left and Right. As an achievement of eternal France, the pioneer of civilization and the benefactor of humanity, the Canal became part of the layman's new religion of republicanism which blossomed on the loss of the monarchy. The acceptance of the Canal into the pantheon of the Republic preceded the observance of Bastille Day from 1880 but coincided with the fall of French Canal tonnage in 1877 below the level of the preceding year after six successive years of increase, making the Canal seem to have been made by the French 'for the English in spite of the English'.[3]

The second great boom in sea-canal projects after that of 1869 extended French interest from Suez to Panama. That canal boom of 1876 was encouraged by the completion of the Dutch North Sea Canal (1865–76) with basin-intervals on the Suez model, the remarkable growth of traffic through the Suez Canal, the share-purchase by the British Government, the payment of the first dividends by the Canal Company and the distribution on 1 July 1876 of the first dividends on the founders' shares. At least ten schemes were outlined, including projects for a White Sea–Baltic Canal, a Black Sea–Caspian Sea Canal, a Samoyed Canal from the River Ob to the Kara Sea, a Channel–Mediterranean Canal, a Biscay–Mediterranean Canal, a Seine Canal, a Manchester Ship Canal, a Gabes Canal, a Congo–Zambesi Canal and a Nicaragua Canal.[4] That rash of projects perhaps encouraged the astronomer Schiaparelli to announce in 1877 his discovery of 'canals' on Mars. It also inspired some Arabs of Aneyza in Arabia, where no rivers existed, to ask

[1] *The Times*, 20 September 1876, 9v.
[2] E. Erckmann and P. A. Chatrian, *Souvenirs d'un Ancien Chef de Chantier à l'Isthme de Suez* (Paris, Hetzel, 1876).
[3] A. Léon, 'Le Canal de Suez et la Politique', *Journal des Économistes* (Juillet 1877), 145.
[4] *Appleton's Annual Cyclopaedia, 1876*, 252–6, 'Engineering'.

Doughty in 1878, 'Might there not be made a canal through Nejd?'[1] Lesseps himself favoured the idea of a Congo–Zambesi Canal to link Dakar to Madagascar but accepted the presidency of a committee formed on 24 March 1876 by the Paris Geographical Society to study the question of an American Interoceanic Canal after American interest had revived in the Nicaragua route. On his advice Lucien Napoleon Bonaparte Wyse, a grand-nephew of Napoleon I, was sent to explore the isthmus between November 1876 and April 1877, so diverting Bonapartist support to a Panama Canal.

Lesseps had thitherto been neglected by public opinion as manifested in elections but grew in status as the Republic accepted his creation as the greatest achievement of the century. His nomination was sought in 1876 as an opposition senator to the candidate of Marshal Macmahon, the President of the Republic, and again in 1877 as a government deputy for Paris by Macmahon and Decazes[2] after the coup of 16 May 1877 and Macmahon's attempt to govern through a junta of generals rather than through the Assembly. He became the President of the French National African Committee established on 24 March 1877 under the inspiration of Leopold of Belgium, lectured on the colonization of Africa at the Paris Exhibition of 1878 and so sought to divert the rising ardour of the Republic into colonial expansion. The incorporation of the Canal into the French tradition aroused opposition only from Bordeaux which complained on 11 February 1878 that the Canal was a cause of the decay of its trade. The ageing Flaubert remembered his unfulfilled ambition of 1862 to study the interpenetration of East and West, especially the 'barbarization of the West and the civilization of the East'. 'If I were younger and richer I would revisit the Orient in order to study the modern Orient. A great book about the isthmus-of-Suez Orient is one of my old dreams.'[3]

[1] C. M. Doughty, *Travels in Arabia Deserta* (1921), ii. 421–2, 438.
[2] L. Bridier, *Une Famille Française. Les De Lesseps* (1900), 413–19.
[3] G. Flaubert, *Correspondance* (Paris, Conard, 1930), viii. 94, Flaubert à Mme. Roger des Genettes, 10 Novembre 1877.

PART III

THE CANAL AS A HIGHWAY
OF EMPIRE, 1877-1903

15

THE RUSSO-TURKISH WAR, 1877-1878, AND THE SCRAMBLE FOR THE OTTOMAN EMPIRE

THE rebellion of the Balkan Christians stirred Holy Russia to its depths as the opening of the Suez Canal had never done. It united Orthodox, Panslav and military opinion in detestation of the Turk and created a growing Russian threat to the European provinces of the Ottoman Empire. Nubar Pasha expected a Russo-Turkish conflict, a Turkish defeat and an Anglo-Russian clash. He concluded that England should secure a territorial pledge against any Russian advance and accordingly visited London to urge the annexation of Egypt as well as his own restoration to power.[1] Thus the Eastern crisis continued to open new prospects of empire as well as new horizons of danger. The declaration of war by Russia on 24 April 1877 transformed the Canal into a potential scene of warlike operations and aroused concern in Britain for the right of passage acquired during the previous seven years. As a ditch in the desert the waterway could be blocked easily and quickly and rendered useless in twenty-four hours as natural straits could not.[2] Both belligerents were users of the Canal. Russia was the eighth largest user in 1876 when fourteen ships of 23,916 tons had passed through under the Russian flag. Turkey was the fourteenth largest user, supplying more troops than trade, while Russia had sent no troops through the waterway. The Canal belonged to Turkey as the suzerain of Egypt as much as the Caledonian Canal did to England. Turkey was therefore entitled to control its navigation and even to use it for warlike operations. She might halt all navigation either by scuttling ships in the channel or by removing the beacon lights in the Little Bitter Lake. Russia in reply might also seek to block the Canal or more feasibly to blockade its approaches. Thus English merchants and shipowners as well as shareholders in the Canal Company became concerned for the security of navigation.[3] English opinion sought to treat the Canal as an arm of the sea uniting the northern and southern oceans and thereby to bring it out of the sphere of land-power into that of sea-power. Advanced private opinion began to hope for the cession of the Canal by Turkey to England and the establishment of English rights over the isthmus or even over Egypt itself. Such ambitions exaggerated the value of the Canal, which carried only one twenty-eighth of the total commerce of Britain against the one-seventh carried by the Cape

---

[1] *Die Grosse Politik*, Band 2, 148, Munster to Bismarck, 24 April 1877.
[2] *The Times*, 22 May 1877, 8i.
[3] Ibid., 4 May 1877, 4vii; 19 May, 6vi, C. Magniac.

route[1] and had had far less strategic security than the Canadian rail link from the Atlantic to British Columbia.[2] They also assumed, as Gladstone emphasized in the debate of 7 May on the Eastern question, that the English had rights in the Canal quite distinct from those of the rest of the world and were entitled to assert their mastery without regard to the interests of the other portions of mankind. English opinion in Alexandria was content to urge the neutralization of Egypt and 'the denationalization of the Canal'.[3]

Derby's Note of 6 May expressed a Cabinet decision of 1 May and gave the world the first official intimation of the degree of British interest in the Canal. It asked Russia to respect as primary British interests the Suez Canal, Egypt, Constantinople, the Straits and the Persian Gulf, affirming 'the necessity of keeping open the communication between Europe and the East by the Suez Canal: an attempt to blockade or otherwise interfere with the Canal or its approaches would be regarded as a menace to India and a grave injury to the commerce of the world'.[4] Thus Britain did not deny Russia's right to blockade the Canal but asked Russia to refrain from the exercise of that right lest Britain should abandon her passive neutrality. Derby's Note evoked a conciliatory reply on 18 May by Russia who renounced therein her belligerent rights against the Canal, considered 'as an international work', and excluded Egypt from the sphere of her military operations. That renunciation was an act of grace rather than the acknowledgement of any legal obligation. It cost Russia very little while it avoided friction with England and the other users of the Canal. Russia lacked the interest, the desire and the means to undertake operations against Egypt or the Canal. She concentrated all her efforts and hopes on the Balkan approaches to Constantinople. She had only a limited direct interest in the Canal from which her base in the Black Sea was cut off by the Turkish Straits while her base at Vladivostock lay at the furthest end of her line of maritime communications.

The Anglo-Russian exchange of notes established that no hostilities should take place in the Canal and no blockade at its mouths and that the ships of war of belligerents might use the waterway under such conditions, including those of the belligerent territorial power. That bilateral arrangement infringed on the sovereign rights of Turkey, which was thereby expected to permit such free passage of her foe through the Canal as would be denied through a natural strait. The Canal was far less vital for commerce to Turkey or to Egypt than it was to Britain or even to Russia. Although its destruction would not have damaged the material interests of Turkey or Egypt the exclusion of Russian warships was deemed a sufficient safeguard of Ottoman imperial interests. By agreement between the Porte and the Khedive the Canal

---

[1] C. F. Goodfellow, *Great Britain and South African Confederation (1870–1881)* (Cape Town, Oxford University Press, 1966), 71, 237, C. H. Nugent's memorandum of 1 April 1877.

[2] J. C. R. Colomb, 'Imperial and Colonial Responsibilities in War', *Journal of the Royal Colonial Institute*, 15 May 1877, 321–2.

[3] *The Times*, 16 May 1877, 4iv, Alexandria, 29 April.

[4] Ibid., 25 June 1877, 5ii, 8i.

was therefore closed from 10 May to Russian warships and its entrances were placed under the surveillance of H. F. M'Killop.[1] Lesseps' proposal of 10 May for the neutralization of the Canal was rejected by Derby on 16 May: thus England resisted neutralization in 1877 as much as in 1856. British determination to defend freedom of transit through the Canal was shown in the arrival at Port Said on 16 May of a British squadron of six ironclads, the first such despatch of a foreign naval force to the Canal in history. Although no sailors or marines were landed, rumours of the movement of German and Italian squadrons to Pelusium showed the reluctance of the powers to permit a single state to establish itself as the guardian of the waterway. The British squadron left Port Said on 19 May, the day after the Russian renunciation of her belligerent rights against the Canal. The British withdrawal undermined Bismarck's plan of 27 May for an Anglo-Russian agreement which would establish British control of Egypt and Russian control of the Black Sea. Disraeli continued to focus his interest on the southern maritime approaches to Constantinople.

Five days after a cartoon in *Punch* showed a Russian approaching the Suez Canal lock with casks of dynamite[2] a plot was reportedly discovered to make the waterway unnavigable by blowing up its banks with nitro-glycerine.[3] That report coincided with a sharp increase in the threat to the Ottoman Empire as Russian troops crossed the Danube. Ismail promptly appointed on English advice a Commission of Supervision to prevent such attempts.[4] He was as much concerned to prevent the use of Turkish troops as to preserve the security of transit. He had no ironclads and could not use mines at Suez or in the waterway but he organized an Egyptian canal police by land and water at the cost of several thousands of pounds. Eight infantry stations on the banks escorted land travellers across the isthmus, to prevent damage either to the banks or to the water-pipe to Port Said. Six patrols of mounted police ranged from Suez to Port Said. Passing ships were watched night and day by two gun-boats, steam-launches and rowing-boats. M'Killop Pasha was appointed to take charge of the Surveillance Force and was raised to the rank of Field-Marshal for his services. Those symbolic precautions could not deter a determined and active foe. Lemasson, the Chief Engineer of the Canal Company since 1873, considered how best to deal with the blocking of the waterway by a sunken ship and decided that the easiest way would be to dredge a new channel around it in five to six days, so laying down the Company's tactics for any emergency. The Turkish Note of 21 June to Derby accepted the principle of the free navigation of the Canal by neutrals but reserved to the Porte the right to fight the enemy's vessels:[5] that note remained unpublished by the Foreign

[1] Hansard, *Commons Debates*, 11 May 1877, 726, G. Errington.
[2] *Punch*, 16 June 1877, 271, 'The Man in Possession'.
[3] *The Times*, 22 June 1877, 5vi quoting *Le Temps* of 21 June.
[4] *Manchester Guardian*, 9 July 1877, 8i. *The Times*, 1 April 1878, 4i; 12 June 1878, 11vi, H. F. M'Killop.
[5] *The Times*, 25 June 1877, 5ii, 8i.

Office. The scare-report of 22 June inspired a pamphlet published on 25 June urging the fulfilment of 'the mission of England in the Land of Egypt'[1] and ranking Gibraltar as a costly toy in comparison with the Canal.[2] That pamphlet recommended the purchase of the rights of the shareholders of the Canal Company for £20,000,000, the purchase of the suzerainty of the Porte over the Canal for £5,000,000, the establishment of a permanent alliance with the Khedive, and the extinction of the Egyptian Debt by a Government guarantee for £3,250,000 per annum. The establishment of England's territorial right to the Canal, supported by fortifications, observation posts and gun-boats, might then make possible the extinction of the bulk of the Canal tolls and perhaps the duplication of the channel.

In June Nubar returned to England and the friendliest reception from the Foreign Office, the India Office, the Treasury, the War Office and the City[3] but was given no encouragement by Derby for an English occupation of Egypt. His friend Edward Dicey, who had been interested in Egypt since his first visit in 1869, came to his help with an article like a trumpet-blast.[4] Dicey urged England to occupy the isthmus of Suez and the Nile Delta so as to profit by the prostration of France since the war of 1870, by the Russian threat to Constantinople and by her own policy of free-trade which would mollify Italy, Spain, Portugal and Holland. He asserted that England's choice lay between strengthening her hold on Egypt and weakening her hold on India, because a Russian fleet on the Bosporus could reach Port Said long before reinforcements could arrive from Malta. He thought it would be advisable to buy out the Canal Company for under £15,000,000 but that it was essential to hoist the British flag at Port Said and Suez, to undertake the military occupation of the Canal and the isthmus and to establish a British Resident at Cairo. 'The same causes which compelled us the other day to annex the Transvaal Republic in the south of Africa compel us also to occupy the Isthmus.'[5] Dicey was supported by the growing interest in the opening-up of Africa and by the Free-Trader Émile de Lavaleye who urged the occupation of both Egypt and Cyprus as the logical sequel to the purchase of the shares.[6] Bismarck renewed on 6 July his offer of Egypt to England in return for the Russian annexation of Armenia and the Russian freedom of the Dardanelles.[7] The crisis, however, became less urgent as the defence of Plevna blocked the Russian advance on Constantinople for four long months. The Government remained fixed in its determination to require an island base near Constantinople. Conservative opinion disliked Dicey's suggestion as presenting

[1] An Englishman, *England in Egypt. The Highway to India. A Proposal Submitted to the People of England by an Englishman* (London, King, 1877, 18pp.), 13.

[2] Ibid., 6.

[3] *Die Grosse Politik*, Band 2, 155, Munster to Bismarck, 28 June 1877.

[4] E. Dicey, 'Our Route to India', *Nineteenth Century* (June 1877), 665–85.

[5] Ibid., 685.

[6] E. de Lavaleye, 'British Interests in the Present Crisis', *Fortnightly Review*, 1 July 1877, 25–34.

[7] G. von Bunsen, 'Germany and Egypt', *Nineteenth Century* (September 1877), 167–75.

England to the world 'in the character of a sort of Methodist Pirate'.[1] The greatest spokesman of the Liberal Opposition rejected the proposal with a vehemence that was the greater since he had himself considered Dicey's idea in 1870. Dicey renewed his appeal for the occupation of the Canal as an expedient which was possible without war, cost, resistance or injustice. 'Since the abolition of West Indian slavery, no single act of our Government could do so much to lessen the sum of human misery and suffering as the establishment of a British protectorate in the isthmus.'[2] Gladstone however rebutted the fundamental premises of his argument by denying that Russian supremacy at Constantinople would imply the closure of the Canal, that the Canal was the only route to India or that India was of value to England as a source of tribute. He stressed the value of the Cape route which many had forgotten 'as completely as if that route lay by the North-West Passage'[3] and reduced the stoppage of the Canal to a mere question of profit and loss. Above all, he stigmatized the suggested occupation as a political crime which would end cordial relations with France and asked 'whether to protect a few score miles of Canal, we are to take the charge of two thousand miles of territory?':[4]

What I seek to impress is, that territorial questions are not to be disposed of by arbitrary limits; that we cannot enjoy the luxury of taking Egyptian soil by pinches. We may seize an Aden and a Perim, where there is no already formed community of inhabitants, and circumscribe a tract at will. But our first site in Egypt, be it by larceny or be it by emption, will be the almost certain egg of a North African Empire, that will grow and grow until another Victoria and another Albert, titles of the Lake-sources of the White Nile, come within our borders and till we finally join hands across the Equator with Natal and Cape Town, to say nothing of the Transvaal and the Orange River on the south, or of Abyssinia or Zanzibar to be swallowed by way of viaticum on our journey. And then, with a great empire in each of the four quarters of the world, and with the whole new or fifth quarter to ourselves, we may be territorially content, but less than ever at our ease.[5]

Goldwin Smith also became alarmed by projects to make England mistress of all the water communications of the globe and to recreate the Roman Empire in the nineteenth century. He perceived that the overland route pivoting around 'the fatal Canal' required Syria as well as Egypt and East Africa for its protection but still remained open to attack from every port between Cherbourg and Port Said. He blamed the share-purchase for having served as the signal for the demolition of the Ottoman Empire by powers each seeking their own interests. 'Already our nervous anxiety about the canal has brought an avalanche of calamity on the world.'[6] In rebuttal Dicey could only invoke

[1] *Saturday Review*, 14 July 1877, 33, 'England and Egypt'.
[2] E. Dicey, 'The Future of Egypt', *Nineteenth Century* (August 1877), 12.
[3] W. E. Gladstone, 'Aggression on Egypt and Freedom in the East', *Nineteenth Century* (August 1877), 156, reprinted in *Gleanings of Past Years, 1851–77* (London, Murray, 1879), iv, *Foreign*, 341–65.
[4] Ibid., 161.   [5] Ibid., 158–9.
[6] G. Smith, 'The Policy of Aggrandizement', *Fortnightly Review*, 1 September 1877, 321.

the manifest destiny of England to bear the burden of an Empire and the absence of set purpose in the growth of that Empire,[1] four years before Seeley's first lecture of 1881 on 'Tendency in English History'.

The debate over the expediency and morality of an English occupation of the Canal undoubtedly strengthened Ismail's determination to maintain his rights to the full in order to remove any possible pretext for British intervention in Egypt. On 5 July the Government of Egypt issued at the behest of the Porte a circular to Foreign Agents[2] closing the Suez Canal to Russian vessels for the duration of the war but keeping it open to neutral vessels. Such a declaration of the neutrality of the Canal was in accordance with international law but remained an isolated precedent so that the very existence of the circular could later be doubted.[3] After the mysterious arrest of an Armenian or Maltese with a chest of dynamite cartridges for blowing up the Canal, the steamers on watch were increased from two to four while the Admiralty ordered warships to Port Said, ostensibly to undertake a careful resurvey of the sandbank at the entrance.[4] In reply Russia authorized on 15 August the issue by her Consul-General in London of certificates of protection against seizure by Russian cruisers to ships clearing the British ports with coals for Port Said for commercial use.[5] Thus Russia asserted its belligerent rights over coal destined for belligerent use and by implication over coal for the guard warships at Port Said. The Institute of International Law at Zürich was sufficiently concerned to begin on 13 September to consider the legal status of the Canal.

English interest increased in Egypt after the end of Ismail's Abyssinian ventures, the establishment of the Anglo-French Control in 1876, Ismail's appointment in 1877 of Gordon as Governor-General of the Sudan and the conclusion of two Anglo-Egyptian Conventions. On 9 August 1877 Ismail accepted a convention for the suppression of the slave-trade.[6] The Convention of 7 September 1877 recognized Egyptian jurisdiction over the coast of the Red Sea as far south as Ras Hafun and gave England a diplomatic document wherewith to exclude other powers from the Red Sea but limited official concern with Egypt to her role as the guardian of the route to India. The creation of the Anglo-French Control reinforced the growing mystical interest in the monuments of Egypt and the widening appeal of Egypt as a winter resort, which led James Cook to open a hotel at Luxor in 1877 and the Australian author James Bonwick to ask 'what a future for Africa to contemplate,

---

[1] E. Dicey, 'Mr. Gladstone and our Empire', *Nineteenth Century* (September 1877), 295.

[2] H. D. Wolff, 'The Suez Canal and the Egyptian Question', *Quarterly Review* (October 1887), 448.

[3] B. Avram, *The Evolution of the Suez Canal Status from 1869 up to 1956* (Geneva, Droz, 1958), 30.

[4] *The Times*, 24 July 1877, 6i. *Manchester Guardian*, 26 July, 7iii.

[5] *The Times*, 25 August 1877, 8v. E. Hertslet, *Commercial Treaties* (London, Butterworth, 1880), xiv. 1150.

[6] H. L. Hoskins, 'British Policy in Africa 1873–1877. A Study in Geographical Politics', *Geographical Review* (January 1942), 147–8.

should Egypt be our colony in the North, as the Cape in the south?'[1] The shipment of the obelisk from Alexandria, sanctioned by Ismail on 10 March 1877,[2] was undertaken by private interests to symbolize England's growing concern with Egypt rather than with Turkey but was only completed after five months (21 September 1877–20 January 1878). The growth of interest in Egypt was countered by the revival of the project for a Euphrates Valley Railway from November 1877 after the completion of the Indus Valley Railway on 8 June 1877, the recurrence of friction between Bombay and Karachi and the publication of Burton's second study of Sind.[3] Sir Henry Hoare, as a member of an anti-Russian deputation to the Foreign Office on 28 November 1877, expressed in vain to Derby his fear of a Russian Euphrates Valley Railway competitive with the Suez Canal.[4] Lesseps was praised by a British archeologist for the energy which had enabled him as a single untitled individual to succeed where great kings with nations at their disposal had failed,[5] but was expected to be succeeded as President of the Company by an Englishman after the first three English directors took their seats on the board in 1877.[6] After the fall of Plevna pro-Turkish zealots in England depicted the resumed Russian advance as a menace to the Canal. On 9 January 1878 Turkey appealed for an armistice while the Commissioners of the Egyptian Debt demanded from Ismail a general inquiry into the finances of Egypt and so began a new phase of encroachment on the independence of Egypt. The annexation of Egypt was advocated on 14 January by the Radical Dilke at Chelsea while the Liberal Campbell urged the purchase of the full pecuniary interest in the Canal Company by fair and honest means.[7] Standen as Resident Director in Paris paid a long winter visit to Egypt (10 January–28 March 1878) ostensibly to inspect the Canal works.

After Russian troops entered San Stefano on 23 February in their advance on Constantinople Bismarck again urged Egypt on the British ambassador in Berlin.[8] The Treaty of San Stefano of 3 March annulled the Treaty of Paris of 1856 and created a Big Bulgaria which was expected to be a Russian satellite overshadowing Constantinople. To secure British acquiescence in the peace-treaty the German ambassador in London urged Egypt on Derby on 9 March, with some unofficial support. Thus Brassey urged a joint Anglo-French protectorate of Egypt with the Delta allotted to France and the Canal to England[9] while Sir George Elliot thought that the harbour he had built at Alexandria could serve as a British naval base for the protection of the

---

[1] J. Bonwick, *Pyramid Facts and Fancies* (London, Paul, 1877), 6, 28 August 1877.
[2] T. Mackay, *The Life of Sir John Fowler Engineer* (London, Murray, 1900), 266–7.
[3] R. F. Burton, *Sind Revisited* (London, Bentley, 1877), ii. 319.
[4] *The Times*, 29 November 1877, 6i.
[5] J. W. Grover, 'Suez Canals from the Most Ancient Times to the Present', *Journal of the British Archaeological Association* (December 1877), 448.
[6] E. de Léon, *The Khedive's Egypt* (1877), 39.
[7] G. Campbell, 'An Inside View of Egypt', *Fortnightly Review*, 1 January 1878, 47, 42.
[8] W. Taffs, *Odo Russell*, 218, 25 February 1878.
[9] *The Times*, 9 March 1878, 8ii.

Canal.[1] Disraeli then decided to summon troops from India as a substitute for Austria, to take Cyprus from Turkey and to compel Russia to submit the Treaty of San Stefano to a Congress of Europe. He capitalized on the upsurge of jingoism fifteen years after the humiliating retreat by Palmerston and Russell over Denmark and Poland and forced his decisions through the Cabinet on 27 March, compelling Derby to resign. The succession of Salisbury to the Foreign Office began a new era in British foreign policy and ushered in a new forward policy in Egypt, Asia Minor and the Levant in general. Dicey was encouraged to argue that Russia could not be allowed to dominate Egypt, the isthmus and the Canal. 'Our flagstaff, in other words, should be planted at Port Said—as it was at Perim.'[2] The collective protest by Austria, Germany, England, France and Italy on 28 March secured the appointment on 30 March by Ismail of a commission of enquiry into Egypt's finances. That commission was intended by Ismail to discover how he should pay his debts but by Baring to enquire into expenditure as well as revenue, to produce an unfavourable report and so to facilitate the deposition of the Khedive. Lesseps accepted the presidency of the commission in order to prove that Egypt was solvent[3] but after visiting the Canal (18–22 April) with Rivers Wilson he remained in Ismailia, leaving the effective presidency to Wilson. His retirement confirmed that Egypt's bankruptcy was due to the double disaster of the low Nile of 1877 and the high Nile of 1878 rather than to the Canal, because Lesseps would otherwise have felt bound to ensure that the commission returned a report favourable to the Canal Company.

The instrument of the new imperial policy was the Indian military contingent, whose movement Parliament was allowed to learn of from the newspapers on 17 April, the day after it had adjourned for the holidays. The troop movement was decreed by Disraeli, organized by Sir Richard Temple in Bombay and executed with the help of the P. & O. The demand for transports created employment for some of the steam shipping rendered idle in the harbours of India by the depression of 1878 but was mainly met by the transfer of home shipping from commercial to strategic use, causing a delay of at least twenty-five days. The India troop movement provoked a Russian naval reaction and the Tsar's decision on 8 April to equip American-built privateers with Russian crews at Philadelphia for operations against British merchant vessels.[4] The announcement on 2 May that three ironclads would meet the troopships at Port Said was followed by the British offer to Egypt of as many more ships as its Navy might require to protect the Canal and Red Sea,[5]

---

[1] B. F. Cobb, 'Egypt: its Commercial Changes and Aspects', *Journal of the Society of Arts*, 22 March 1878, 361.

[2] E. Dicey, 'England's Policy at the Congress', *Nineteenth Century* (April 1878), 796.

[3] *The Times*, 6 June 1878, 5 iv.

[4] L. I. Strakhovsky, 'Russia's Privateering Projects of 1878. A Page in the History of Russian-American Relations', *Journal of Modern History* (March 1935), 26.

[5] H. L. Hoskins, 'The Suez Canal as an International Waterway', *American Journal of International Law* (July 1943), 375, Pauncefote to Vivian, 3 May 1878.

encouraging speculation by the British colony in Egypt on a possible British occupation of the Canal in defiance of French susceptibilities. 'Port Said and Suez, it is said, are both without defences, either of casemates or earthworks, and the Canal will fall as easily as a ripe pear into the hands of any great naval Power that has a fancy for it.'[1] The thirty transports, including one dhow and sixteen sailing vessels with their better accommodation for horses, reached Aden on 9–10 May and began to arrive at Suez on 16 May. As the ships began to pass through the Canal on 18 May signs appeared of a Russian move from San Stefano on Constantinople and the Russian ambassador Shuvalov left Petersburg for London. The ships passed through between 18 and 21 May, facilitated by Egypt as well as by the Canal Company. The twelve steamers, including the s.s. *Suez*, passed through in thirty hours on the average while the sixteen sailing vessels were towed through by eight tugs in forty-four hours on the average. The last substantial use of the Canal by sailing vessels was thus made at a speed seldom before exceeded. Some of the former animation of Suez revived as the 8,412 Indian troops and followers passed northwards, seven years after the Canal had first been used for the transport of British troops.

The troops began to leave Port Said on 19 May not for Cyprus but for Malta, where they were concentrated at the end of May and reviewed on 19 June by the Duke of Cambridge. The first inspection of the Indian Army by the English C.-in-C. symbolized the partial fulfilment of the Crown's aspirations of 1857 to possess its own army. Those 8,000 troops could fulfil no practical purpose against the four million troops which the five Great Powers could bring into the field. They served, however, as both vanguard and symbol, intimating to Russia that she faced two empires rather than one and that Britain could draw on her military reserves in India with great facility. The expedition revealed England's capacity for the first time in her history to fight a great Continental war without an ally.[2] It proved the utility of the Canal to a fleet seeking to pass through very quickly[3] and the military value of the Suez route. It revived the demand for speedy communication by rail with India.[4] It also strengthened the need to neutralize the Canal in time of war by a treaty with Turkey on the model of the Clayton-Bulwer Treaty of 1850 so as to preserve the essential freedom of passage for troopships and warships.[5] It paralysed trade by the threat of war and especially deterred commerce from the use of the Canal route but achieved its political aim. The Salisbury–Shuvalov Protocol was signed in secret on 30 May, the day after the last transport had left Port Said. That agreement gave Russia Batum in

[1] *The Times*, 15 May 1878, 5 vi.   [2] Ibid., 27 May 1878, 9 v.
[3] Ibid., 10 June 1878, 4 i; 18 June 1878, 10 iv.
[4] F. J. Goldsmid, 'On Communications with British India under Possible Contingencies', *Journal of the Royal United Service Institution*, 14 June 1878, 675–98. *The Times*, 25 June 1878, 11 vi.
[5] J. Macdonell, 'The Legal Position of the Dardanelles and Suez Canal', *Fraser's Magazine* (May 1878), 662.

compensation for her renunciation of the Big Bulgaria of San Stefano and for the English gain of Cyprus under the secret Convention of Constantinople of 4 June. Russia replied to England's use of her Indian reserves by despatching on 13 June a Russian mission from Tashkent under 'the De Lesseps of Turkestan' to Kabul. Lytton's violent reaction to that mission produced the disastrous Afghan War of 1878–9 and the endless quest thenceforward for a 'scientific frontier'.[1] Britain replied to the threat of Russian privateers by completing inland telegraph lines across Canada and South Africa in 1878 and by fortifying from 1878 Aden, Karachi, Bombay, Rangoon, Singapore and Table Bay.

The Malta Expeditionary Force was the first military expedition ever sent from India to Europe. The summons of such a force by a constitutional state from despotic Asia was without precedent in peace-time and aroused alarm in England[2] comparable to that of the Roman Senate on the crossing of the Rubicon by the legions. Goldwin Smith attacked the appearance on the European scene of such barbarian mercenaries as the harbingers of a third Indian war and of an orientalized England.[3] Meredith Townsend deplored the removal of the greatest single restraint on arbitrary government by the separation of the army from the nation. In his view Disraeli understood and loathed the British Constitution, which he had subordinated to the Indian Empire. Disraeli had opened up an inexhaustible recruiting-ground in Asia which cost nothing but money. He had so accomplished the greatest innovation in the military history of England since she had replaced feudal retainers and train bands by regular regiments. He had brought a seventh Great Power to the very doors of a jealous Europe, so enormously enhancing the powers of the Crown within the Empire outside the British Isles. Such a Carthaginian use of mercenary swords in the service of empire reflected the 'deep, inner vulgarity of soul'[4] of those whom Macaulay had thought the 'hereditary nobility of mankind'. The temptation to conquer the Turkish Empire in Asia from the European side without the sacrifice of a single Englishman seemed to reveal the new spirit of a degenerate society:

> We don't want to fight;
> But, by Jingo, if we do,
> We won't go to the front ourselves,
> But we'll send the mild Hindoo.[5]

In the debates in Parliament the Liberal leaders remained timid or apathetic, although the move was attacked by Lord Selborne on 20 May for its infringement of the Mutiny Act and by Sir George Campbell on 23 May for its use of the Indian Exchequer to bypass parliamentary control of supply. Those

---

[1] G. E. Buckle, *Life of Disraeli*, vi. 390, 9 November 1878.
[2] *The Spectator*, 20 April–25 May 1878, 493–4, 556–7, 588–9, 624–5, 656–8.
[3] G. Smith, 'The Eastern Crisis', *Fortnightly Review*, 1 May 1878, 652.
[4] M. Townsend, 'The Summons to the Sepoys', *The Spectator*, 4 May 1878, 556.
[5] *The Spectator*, 1 June 1878, 687.

protests ensured that the cost of £748,000 (or £100 per soldier) was not borne by the revenues of India and permitted the Commons reluctantly to accept the move on 23 May by 347 to 226 votes.[1]

The troop movement raised the question of the dividing-line between the British and Indian Governments and between the constitutional and despotic armies of the State, showing how the isthmus of Suez had superseded the old charter limits of the East India Company at Alexandria. A. J. Balfour thought that it could not be dangerous to bring Indian troops to Malta if it was not dangerous to bring them to Aden. 'What mystic virtue was there in the Isthmus of Suez, that it should be so wrong and unconstitutional to bring Indian troops through it?'[2] Gladstone disagreed and asked 'What lessons shall we send back to India with our regenerated native armies? Shall we have one level for Englishmen and Indians on this side of the Isthmus of Suez, and two levels on the other?'[3] The Indian soldiery and press, especially the Moslem press, received the order with the same cordial approval as Calcutta, as indicating the confidence of the Crown in the Indian Army and erasing the stigma of disloyalty left by the Mutiny of 1857. The approval of India largely counterbalanced the disapproval of England. The move converted a threat to British power in India into a bastion thereof, enlisted the martial ardour of India in the cause of imperial prestige and inspired even orthodox Hindus with the will to cross the sea in defiance of their religion.[4] India desired, however, more than to attain military equality with England: she wished to pit a trained Indian army against a trained European army in Europe itself.

The passenger tolls levied by the Canal Company on the troops provoked a protest by the P. & O. on 11 June but were levied again when the troops were repatriated in August and September 1878. The expedition raised the number of military personnel using the Canal in 1878 by 18,827 or by 47·7 per cent to 58,292 and the total number of passengers by 36·2 per cent to 99,209. The protection of the passage of the Canal from acts of war by an International Act was demanded in August 1878 by the Association of the Reform and the Codification of the Law of Nations meeting at Frankfort-on-Main and including merchants and shipowners as well as jurists[5] and again on 9 September 1878 by the Institute of International Law meeting at Paris.[6] Twiss' proposal on 4 September to exclude from the Canal all vessels of an enemy of Turkey and to sanction Turkey's use of the Canal itself to achieve such exclusion was opposed by Russia and was not accepted by the Institute. No perimeter was drawn to confine Indian troops to Asia and the isthmus

---

[1] *The Times*, 21 May 1878, 11i; 27 May, 9 iii–iv. *Punch*, 25 May 1878, 235, 'Our "Imperial" Guard'; 8 June 1878, 258–9, 'The Dark Horse' (Sepoy).
[2] Hansard, *Commons Debates*, 21 May 1878, 410, A. J. Balfour.
[3] W. E. Gladstone, 'Liberty in the East and West', *Nineteenth Century* (June 1878), 1166.
[4] *The Times*, 1 April 1878, 5i; 15 July, 5 i–ii; 16 July, 9i.
[5] T. Twiss, 'The Protectorate of the Suez Canal', *Nautical Magazine* (October 1878), 876.
[6] *Revue de Droit International* (1878), 380–1, 'Pacification et Protection Internationale de l'Isthme de Suez'.

remained a highway rather than a barrier. 'Henceforth England and India are one for purposes of offensive or defensive warfare, and are definitely leagued together against all possible antagonists, whether on this or on the other side of the Suez Canal.'[1]

The summons of Indian troops to the Mediterranean aroused expectations of British expansion throughout the Levant, in Egypt, Syria and Asia Minor. The English occupation of Cyprus raised land values in Beirut, attracted a rush of Greeks from Alexandria and encouraged Ismail to send for Nubar. Salisbury sanctioned the Anglo-French cooperation against Ismail which Derby had rejected and secured on 28 August the appointment of a consti-tutional ministry under Nubar with two European Ministers, including Rivers Wilson. The appointment under alien aegis of the Armenian Christian Nubar as Prime Minister of the Khedive for the first time raised the price of Egyp-tian bonds in Europe. The obelisk which symbolized the new interest in Egypt was raised into position on the Victoria Embankment on 12 September by hydraulic jacks decorated with the Union Jack: thus 'Cleopatra's Needle' followed the Thames-ward path of the Arundel and Elgin Marbles. The Nubar Ministry achieved its greatest success in securing through Rothschild on 31 October the 5 per cent £8,500,000 Domains Loan under the political guarantee of England and France, so extending substantially the interests of English bondholders in Egypt. The Ministry lacked, however, the confidence of Ismail even more than of the country, which was increasingly offended by its policy of retrenchment, the halving of the Army, the discharge of Egyptian officials and the employment of European officials. Thus the choicest pearl in the Sultan's crown passed under the joint protection of England and France, who refused any share in the Dual Control to Germany, Austria or Italy.

The Cyprus Convention also encouraged the revival of Indo-Mediterranean railway projects as instruments for the regeneration of Asia. The acquisition of Cyprus pointing towards the Gulf of Alexandretta favoured a northern route for such a railway from Ayas,[2] Alexandretta,[3] Suedia or even from Tripoli via Palmyra.[4] The rebirth of interest in Palestine encouraged the idea of a more southerly route from Acre[5] as well as a scheme for a colony in Gilead with railways to Haifa, Ismailia and Akaba.[6] Above all, the hope of a new empire in Asia Minor favoured R. M. Stephenson's plan for a Constantinople–Sivas–Mosul–Bagdad line along the Tigris Valley. That route was adopted

---

[1] H. M. Hyndman, 'The Bankruptcy of India', *Nineteenth Century* (October 1878), 585.

[2] *The Times*, 11 July 1878, 6 vi, J. L. Haddan, 'Cyprus and the Euphrates Valley Railway'. Ibid., 12 July, 10 iii, V. L. Cameron, 'The Syrian Coast'.

[3] Ibid., 25 July, 5 vi, G. Geary, 'Asiatic Turkey'.

[4] F. J. Goldsmid, 'On the Occupation of Cyprus as a *tête du pont* for the Euphrates Valley Railway', a lecture given on 14 June 1878 under that title according to *The Times*, 11 July 1878, 6 vi, but published as 'On Communications with British India' in the *Journal of the Royal United Service Institution*, 14 June 1878, 675–98.

[5] G. E. Dalrymple, *The Syrian Great Eastern Railway to India* (London, Skeffington, 1878, 26pp.).

[6] L. Oliphant, *The Land of Gilead* (Edinburgh, Blackwood, 1880), 302.

by the Association for the Asia Minor and Euphrates Railway[1] which was formed at the Duke of Sutherland's Stafford House on 8 July, the day when the news of the Cyprus Convention was made public and a British squadron anchored in Larnaca Bay. V. L. Cameron argued that an Indo-Mediterranean Railway was more valuable in imperial strategy than the Suez Canal[2] and would link London to Karachi in 200 hours.[3] He left Portsmouth in the *Orontes* in September 1878 in order to survey on behalf of Disraeli the route for a Tigris Valley Railway from Tripoli via Mosul. Those schemes provoked a rival Russian project for an Indo-European railway from Tiflis to Peshawar.[4] They also failed to gain the sanction of the Ottoman Government or the financial support of the British Government, which was refused on 1 October,[5] even in the form of an Asia Minor and Syria Railway loan modelled on the Suez Canal share-loan.[6] The imperial interest in railway routes to India, however, benefited Karachi and encouraged C. W. Cayzer, who had served the British India Company for fifteen years (1861–76) in Bombay, to establish the Clan Line's fortnightly cargo service to Bombay and Karachi with the *Clan Alpine*, which left London on 26 October 1878. The Canal maintained its position as Britain's great military highway and was navigated by the *Euphrates*, the last troopship of the season, in the fastest passage ever made, of fourteen hours when the average passage required over thirty hours.[7]

The Brindisi–Alexandria–Suez route maintained its supremacy over the Euphrates and Tigris Valley routes through the award of the India and China mail contract of 7 February 1879 to the P. & O. with the support of the India Office and the Colonial Office against a competitive bid from Holt. The new contract reduced the subsidy by £80,000, or by 17·8 per cent, to £370,000 and replaced the port of Calcutta by that of Bombay, that of Galle by Colombo, and that of Southampton by London. The P. & O. took full advantage of the Bombay–Calcutta Railway completed in 1870, made Bombay its terminal port for mail and passengers, discontinued its Calcutta line and combined its Suez–Calcutta fleet with its Suez–Bombay fleet. The P. & O. also faced the competition of the Austrian Lloyd's new service to Calcutta and began to cooperate from 1879 with the Wagons-Lits Company founded by Nagel-mackers in 1873, so that passengers could travel from Calais to Bologna by Wagons-Lits and change into a Pullman for the Bologna–Brindisi journey.

[1] *The Times*, 17 July 1878, 5 iii; 5 August, 5 iv; 30 August, 6 ii.
[2] Ibid., 1 August 1878, 4 ii, V. L. Cameron, 'The Suez Canal'.
[3] V. L. Cameron, 'The Indo-Mediterranean Railway', *Macmillan's Magazine* (September 1879), 417. Idem, *Our Future Highway* (London, Macmillan, 1880), ii. 292–302, surveys ten routes via Orenburg, Constantinople, Alexandretta, Tripoli, Palmyra, Tyre, Sidon, Seleucia, El Arish and Peshawar.
[4] *The Times*, 19 September 1878, 3 iii.
[5] D. E. Lee, *Great Britain and the Cyprus Convention Policy of 1878* (1934), 142. *The Times*, 17 September 1878, 4 vi.
[6] H. Clarke, 'On Railways to India and Turkey', *Journal of the Society of Arts*, 13 December 1878, 51.
[7] *The Times*, 12 May 1879, 12 i.

The P. & O. made Brindisi the exclusive port for mails from 1881. In 1880 it decided to convert its branch lines to Australia and to China into trunk services, so as to compete with the Austrian Lloyd's projected service to Hong Kong and provide through-services direct from London to Sydney and Shanghai. Its financial position was strengthened by the extinction of its debenture debt in 1881 and by the high rate of depreciation of the ledger-value of its fleet. It built steel vessels from 1881, two years after the first ocean-going steel ship had been launched. It also profited by the rise of Antwerp and the revival of the Scheldt–Thames axis to abandon its use of Southampton after a connexion of forty years. The *Rome* became the first passenger-steamer to leave from the Tilbury terminus of the London, Tilbury and Southend Railway on 5 October 1881: the last P. & O. steamer sailed from Southampton in January 1882. The importance of the Suez route in imperial communications was further enhanced by the extension of the operations of the Survey of India along the Bombay–Suez route in 1878–9, using electro-telegraphic signals through the submarine cables, and by the extension of Pender's cable network southwards from Aden to Durban after the annihilation of a British army by Zulu spears. The news of the disaster of Isandlwana required 20 days (22 January–11 February 1879) to reach London and led to the despatch of reinforcements to Natal in 24 days 8 hours (19 February–16 March).[1] The Government concluded on 9 March a convention with the Eastern Telegraph Company and the Telegraph Construction Company for the construction, laying and operation of a cable to South Africa. Pender formed the Eastern and South African Telegraph Company Ltd. on 19 August 1879.[2] The completion of the cable from Aden via Zanzibar to Durban established direct telegraphic communication with the Cape from 8 March 1880. It eliminated the possibility of independent local action by another Frere as well as the need for an overland telegraph from Egypt to the Cape as proposed in 1875. Thenceforward Aden became a main cable-junction like Singapore, with a southern as well as an eastern cable. In the path of that cable the British India Line extended its service southwards in 1881 from Zanzibar to Lourenço Marques, so replacing the Union Line, extending the watershed between the Cape and Suez routes to Delagoa Bay and encouraging the Natal shipping lines to shift from sail to steam.

The Cyprus Convention, which stimulated a reappraisal of imperial communications and won for Disraeli the title of 'Duke of Cyprus',[3] sought to realize Napoleon III's dreams of Asiatic empire of 1860. The Convention was not designed to secure a new market for cotton goods, a coaling station for Indian steamers or a base for the defence of the Suez Canal against attack from the north, although the Government's acquisition was often defended as a bastion intended to protect the Canal. It was in reality intended to

---

[1] *The Times*, 20 February 1879, 10iii; 7 April, 10i.
[2] Ibid., 26 November 1879, 7ii.
[3] Ibid., 17 July 1878, 5v.

establish an English protectorate over Asiatic Turkey[1] and to reinvigorate Asia Minor through the infusion of English money, English officers and English energy. Such a protectorate would open up one of the finest recruiting-grounds in the world for soldiers and make possible the resettlement of Syria by the Jews.[2] The assumption of the administration of such another India for the benefit of the Sultan would, however, extend England's frontier with her Russian foe and require the free navigation of the Dardanelles. It would also arouse the jealousy of Austria, Italy and France and so destroy the security of the Mediterranean route. The Convention indeed encouraged those other powers to encroach on the Mediterranean provinces of the Ottoman Empire. It suggested the transfer of Bosnia to Austria and the return of Macedonia from Bulgaria to Turkey. It enhanced the uneasiness of Spain and seriously offended Italy because of the historic Italian connexion with 'the divine island...sold by the eunuchs of Constantinople to the usurers of London'.[3] It deeply disturbed France which pressed for compensation in Syria and Egypt, compelling Salisbury to promise Tunis to Waddington on 21 July 1878 and to accept France as co-protector of the Khedive. It ushered in a new phase in the competition between France and Italy for Tunis and in Italian expansion in the Red Sea. Thus the Cyprus Convention precipitated the great partition of Africa among the European Powers which the occupation of Egypt only accelerated. For Europe it marked the beginning of a new phase of imperial expansion and for England, Wilfrid Blunt concluded, the start of 'a new policy of spoliation and treacherous dealing in the Levant foreign to her traditional ways. To the Cyprus intrigue are directly or indirectly referable half the crimes against Oriental and North African liberty our generation has witnessed.'[4]

The Cyprus Convention ended the Sultan's brief honeymoon with 'liberal Europe' dating from the Crimean War and more than anything else ruptured the Anglo-Turkish entente established against Russia in 1833 and renewed in 1853. England's first territorial encroachment on Turkey marked the end of her policy of maintaining the integrity of the Ottoman Empire without thought of recompense. The eyes of the Sultan were opened to the dangers of English cooperation and of the English alliance, which thenceforth outweighed

---

[1] M. Townsend, 'An English Protectorate over Asiatic Turkey', *Spectator*, 1 June 1878, 688. *The Times*, 10 August 1878, 10 ii, 'England and Asiatic Turkey'. E. Dicey, 'Nubar Pasha and our Asian Protectorate', *Nineteenth Century* (September 1878), 548. R. H. Patterson, 'The New Routes to India', *Blackwood's Edinburgh Magazine* (October 1878), 494. J. C. McCoan, *Our New Protectorate. Turkey in Asia. Its Geography, Races, Resources and Government* (London, Chapman, 1879), i. 1–2. L. M. Penson, 'The Foreign Policy of Lord Salisbury 1878–80. The Problem of the Ottoman Empire', in A. Coville and H. Temperley (eds.), *Studies in Anglo-French History* (Cambridge University Press, 1935), 128–9, 134–5. W. N. Medlicott, 'The Gladstone Government and the Cyprus Convention, 1880–85', *Journal of Modern History* (June 1940), 186–7.
[2] B. L. Tuchman, *Bible and Sword. England and Palestine from the Bronze Age to Balfour* (1956), 168–74.
[3] *The Times*, 20 July 1878, 7 iii, quoting the *Bersagliere*.
[4] W. S. Blunt, *My Diaries* (London, Secker, 1919), i. 36.

its utility to Turkey. England threatened Turkey not merely with territorial annexation like Russia but also with reform, which would subvert Ottoman dominion in the remaining territories of the Empire. Even Russia became preferable to England, whose whole influence for good in the Empire was destroyed at a critical moment. The Porte became permanently alienated from England and the Sultan hardened his heart to a policy contrary to English advice as well as to English interests. Thenceforth Turkey began to move out of the British and into the German orbit.

Bismarck was left by the Congress of Berlin with a deeper fear than ever of Russia, because he had helped to deprive her of the gains of San Stefano. His growing fear of a war on two fronts produced those insurance policies which bound Austria to Germany in the Dual Alliance of 1879 and France to anti-Russian England in the deposition of Ismail, so precluding both Austria and France from an anti-German entente with Russia. Ismail's political capacity received its greatest testimony in the demand of the Powers for his deposition after his failure to serve as a docile instrument of the Anglo-French Control, his skilful dismissal of the Nubar Ministry and his rally of Egyptian support against the foreigner. The Powers refused to permit him to repudiate any part of his debts, even in the name of the nation, denied him the great fiscal privilege of princes and insisted on his personal responsibility for his debts, in accordance with Baring's aim. Bismarck's demand on 18 May 1879 that he should settle with his German creditors was followed by the demand of England and France on 19 June that he should abdicate. His deposition by the Sultan on 26 June sacrificed him to the maintenance of the precarious balance of power in Europe.[1] On the steam-yacht, which had been built by Samuda for Said in 1862 and had become the symbol of Ismail's programme of progress and civilization, 'the last of the Pharaohs'[2] and the first of the Khedives sailed into exile with £3,000,000 and a sublime faith in the inevitability of his own restoration by the repentant Powers. Thomas Chenery, Professor of Arabic at Oxford (1867–77) and editor of *The Times* since 1877, exonerated him from the charge of misgovernment and oppression made by Baring and the Dual Control.[3] The major achievement of Ismail's viceroyalty was preserved, the establishment of primogeniture and of succession in the tail male, which the Sultan himself had failed to secure at Constantinople. Ismail's successor was unlike his father in so far as he was a faithful Moslem and had seen nothing of Europe beyond Vienna. Caring deeply for money, Tewfik determined to conciliate the bondholders who had dethroned his father and so became 'an ornamental Khedive under Anglo-French tutelage'.[4]

---

[1] W. Windelband, 'Bismarcks Ägyptenpolitik', *Bulletin of the International Committee of the Historical Sciences*, xii (1942–3), 123–4.

[2] M. Eyth, *Lebendige Kräfte* (Berlin, Springer, 1904), 227, 'Ein Pharao im Jahrhundert des Dampfes'.

[3] *The Times*, 27 June 1879, 9 iii.

[4] C. de Malortie, *Egypt: Native Rulers and Foreign Interference* (London, Ridgway, 1882), 200.

The deposition of Ismail however deprived the Khedive of that prestige which was the very basis of his rule: it undermined the principle of authority essential to government in Egypt as much as in the Sudan and so replaced a financial by a political crisis. The succession of a weak to a strong ruler encouraged Europe to dictate to Egypt, the Egyptian Army officers in consequence to revolt and the Mahdi to usurp the power of the Khedive in the Sudan.

The influence of England and France was immediately strengthened by the restoration on 4 September 1879 of the Dual Control. The Mixed Courts which had delivered judgments against Ismail in his own land were prolonged in existence for a further five years and developed the theory of 'mixed interest' by the judgment of 20 May 1880 in the Mixed Court of Alexandria. Thereby they widely extended their competence in the praetorian tradition and brought the Canal Company out of the sphere of the Egyptian courts into their own jurisdiction, preventing its complete assimilation to an Egyptian company. Lesseps secured the tacit prolongation of his term of office as President after the expiry of his ten-year term in 1879 but continued to hope for a restoration of Ismail. The Dual Control sold on 21 March 1880 the Egyptian Government's share of 15 per cent in the profits of the Canal Company in order to settle a debt of £4,250,000 of which 56 per cent was owed to the Crédit Foncier.[1] That sale was not made under fiscal pressure because the Government reduced taxation in 1880 and still enjoyed a surplus of over £1,266,000, repaid the loan of £320,000 made by the Canal Company to Paponot and took over the operation of the Ismailia Canal from the Company from 15 July 1880. Baring apparently intended to placate France, to atone for the occupation of Cyprus and to facilitate the negotiation of a commercial treaty between England and France, which was not in fact concluded, despite the efforts of Rivers Wilson as a commissioner. The Crédit Foncier formed on 21 April 1880 a French company, the Civil Society for the Receipt of the 15 per cent of the Profits of the Suez Canal Company Allotted to the Government of Egypt, with a capital of £881,600 so divided into 84,507 shares that each would receive as much as a participating share of the Canal Company. As a French company it was taxed on a different basis from the Canal Company and was able to issue bearer-shares, which benefited by a lighter tax and earned a higher dividend than the participating shares on which they were modelled. The Crédit Foncier thus secured compensation for Ismail's coup of 1875, consolidated its Egyptian interests, and formed the Crédit Foncier Égyptien in 1880. Egypt lost another link with the Company because the sale was not for a limited term of years but for the whole duration of the concession. Egypt retained its founders' shares but ceased to exercise its right to appoint the President of the Company. The £1,200 for its Commissioner with the Company was received by Ollivier, the dividend on its shares by the

---

[1] J. Rabino, 'The Statistical Story of the Suez Canal', *Journal of the Statistical Society* (September 1887), 543. P. Crabitès, *The Spoliation of Suez* (London, Routledge, 1940), 187–203, 'Cromer's Fatal Mistake'.

delegation-holders and its 15 per cent share in the profits by the members of the Civil Society, while from 1880 the Company began to pay magnificent dividends. Egyptian rulers and statesmen inevitably acquired a deep-rooted sense of the loss and injury inflicted on the concessionary power by 'the French Canal'.

The growth of the influence of England and France in Egypt weakened their influence at Constantinople as much as it strengthened German influence.[1] After the Cyprus Convention the Porte developed an ineradicable suspicion of every English enterprise, whether commercial, financial, postal, railway or humanitarian. It turned all its considerable powers of obstruction and procrastination against England throughout Asia and Africa. Turkey was increasingly drawn into the German orbit and became another counter for Bismarck to use against Russia and France. The Congress of Berlin shifted the basis of Turkish power from Europe to Asia, from its Navy to its Army and from its subject Christians to its subject Moslems. Thereby the heterogeneous elements of the Empire gained an incomparable bond of union in Islam which united spiritual and temporal dominion in the person of the Caliph as the successor of the Prophet, the keeper of the keys of the Kaaba, the shadow of God on earth and the keystone of the whole legal structure of the Moslem commonwealth. Thenceforward the Sultan asserted his authority as Caliph, developed pan-Islamic views and used the Mecca pilgrimage from 1880 to spread amongst the faithful the cry 'the Caliph in danger'. The pilgrims carried to Jedda for profit by the European steamship firms returned to diffuse the word which undermined the rule of the English, French and Russian infidel over the Moslem community and transformed the Achinese campaign in Sumatra into a holy war. Increasingly indigenous firms carried the pilgrims via the Canal, through which the average annual number of pilgrims rose sharply from 7,000 in 1870–7 to 25,000 in 1878–97. Even the Egyptian caravan adopted the sea-route in place of the land-route from 1880.

The reawakening of the Arab peoples was fostered by English sympathizers, by Blunt and Townsend as much as by Doughty. In reaction against the urbanization and industrialization of contemporary England they revived the idealization of the Arab by Alexander Dow in 1768, by Karsten Niebuhr in 1770 and by Alexander Kinglake in 1844. Thus the anti-Turkish bias fostered by Gladstone was transferred from the liberated Christian peoples to the still subject Arabs in the hope to shift the whole centre of gravity of Islam from Constantinople to Mecca. The Sussex squire Wilfrid Blunt became a breeder of Arab horses from 1877 and opposed in 1878–80 the construction of a Euphrates Valley Railway through the pastures of the Beduin Arabs.[2] He

---

[1] W. Taffs, *Odo Russell* (1938), 326–34.

[2] W. S. Blunt, *Secret History of the English Occupation of Egypt* (London, Unwin, 1907), 29. Lady Anne Blunt, *Bedouin Tribes of the Euphrates* (London, Murray, 1879), ii. 277–83, 'Euphrates Valley Railway'. Idem, *A Pilgrimage to Nejd, the Cradle of the Arab Race* (London, Murray, 1881), vol. i. p. xxii.

came to regard Arabia as 'a sacred land, the cradle of Eastern liberty and true religion'[1] and aspired to free it from Turkish rule.[2] He first described the Moslem revival to the East as well as the West in 1881[3] when he became an Egyptian landowner. Meredith Townsend paraphrased Blunt's sonnet 'To the Bedouin Arabs' in order to offer to the money-grubbing middle class of England an alternative ideal. 'The Arabs do not believe one word of all that Mr. Bright gives to the world as solidly sensible advice, and they are content, and among their rivals noble. They despise industry, put wealth by as meaningless, keep the tradition of the past as possession, and, without decay as without progress, live on for ever, as they were in ages of which history tells us nothing.'[4] The revival of Arab consciousness was fostered even more by the new eccentricity of Constantinople within the Empire and by the new importance of Mecca to the Caliph.

European interest began to grow in the coasting trade of the Red Sea under the stimulus of Gordon's administration in the Sudan between 1877 and 1879 when trade was diverted from the Nile to the Red Sea ports of Massawa, Suakin and Kosseir. Suez began to import immense quantities of gum arabic and ivory for re-export. Suakin shipped more gum arabic through the Canal to Liverpool for the British market than any other single source of supply. Italy's exclusion from the Berlin round of compensations ended the decade of quiescence which had followed Sapeto's acquisition of Assab. Rubattino began a new service to the Red Sea from Genoa on 28 September 1878 and facilitated the Italian settlement of Assab from January 1879. He concluded three successive conventions with the Danakil Sultan in 1879 and 1880 which vastly extended the limits of Italian settlement and encouraged its bid to capture the export trade of Massawa. As the station became an unofficial colony the Italian Government began to assume responsibility, appointed the first Governor of Assab in January 1881 and sent its first troops through the Canal in 1881. The creation of that colony took place at the expense of Turkey as well as Egypt and despite the opposition of the British, the French, the Ethiopians and the Danakils. The Italian initiative extended French interest from East Africa to the Red Sea. The shipowners of Marseilles had developed services via the Canal to East Africa and Madagascar, led by Joseph Valéry in 1878, Cyprien Fabre in 1879 and Marc Fraissinet in 1880. French enterprise thus replaced the service maintained by the British India Line from Zanzibar to Madagascar between 1874 and 1879. From 1880 France also sought to develop Obock as a coaling station as well as a base for trade with Abyssinia,

---

[1] W. S. Blunt, *My Diaries, 1888–1914* (London, Secker, 1919), i. 157, 1880.
[2] Ibid., i. 80, 26 June 1880.
[3] W. S. Blunt, 'The Sultan's Heirs in Asia', *Fortnightly Review*, 1 July 1880, 16–30. Idem, 'The Future of Islam', *Fortnightly Review*, 1 August 1881–1 January 1882. Idem, 'The Egyptian Revolution: a Personal Narrative', *Nineteenth Century* (September 1882), 328.
[4] *The Spectator*, 21 May 1881, 667, M. Townsend, 'The Arabs of the Desert' (a review of Blunt, *The Love Sonnets of Proteus*) reprinted in *Asia and Europe* (London, Constable, 1901), 305–6.

reinforcing Menelik's efforts to resist European expansion with the aid of European technology.

The Eastern crisis contributed to the first depression in the traffic of the Canal in 1878–9 after its continued expansion during 1874–7, despite the economic crisis of 1873 in Europe and the recession of 1874–7. The fall in freights made Canal tolls seem burdensome and called forth the first complaints since 1874, although the surtax was reduced from 5 April 1877 under the agreement of 1876. Thus D. J. Jenkins asked the Chancellor of the Exchequer on 13 March 1877 to secure a reduction in the Company's excessive pilotage charges. Holt was compelled to reduce his outward freight rates, estimated that Canal tolls were sometimes 50 per cent more than his coal bill on the voyages to China and 'only wished he could apply the compound principle to the Suez Canal'.[1] Rathbone pressed on 27 February 1878 for the introduction of navigation by night. Those complaints by the shipowners of the outports coincided with a sharp reduction in shipping losses by the Canal route in 1877, the decrease of insurance rates to the equivalent of the Canal toll and the building of 'water tramps'[2] at depression-prices from 1877–8. The 'ocean tramp' (1880) was a screw-steamer rather than a paddle-steamer and was first developed on the Tyne and Wear. It carried cargo rather than passengers or mail, captured the trade pioneered by the liner and carried it from port to market in accordance with orders sent by cable, without the heavy overhead costs of the liner. It began to create a world-market in freights, with its low running-costs, to the great discomfort of the P. & O., which began to encourage the general public to travel for pleasure in order to supplement its small passenger traffic with India and its limited cargo trade. No concession was made to the demands for a reduction in toll by the Company, which profited from the final ending in 1878 of the tonnage controversy detonated in 1872. Lesseps reaffirmed in a letter sent to the British directors on 8 January 1878 the right of the Company to 'verify' that deductible spaces for the use of officers and crew were not misused for revenue-earning and encouraged British ships to obtain a Board of Trade Suez Certificate which would avoid such verification. Thus the Suez gauge was not unified with other gauges but remained separate from those already in existence. The Company became in effect a measuring agency in its own right and effectively captured the principles of 1873 for use in its own interest. The Company's revised Navigation Regulation was adopted on 12 March 1878 in place of the controversial one of 1872 and came into force from 1 July.[3]

The war suspended Russia's use of the Canal, especially for the direct import of tea from China to Odessa between 1877 and 1879. Thus it revived the re-export of tea from London to Russia. It also cut off the export of wheat from

---

[1] A. Holt, 'Review of the Progress of Steam Shipping during the Last Quarter of a Century', *Proceedings of the Institution of Civil Engineers, 1877–8*, Part 1, 73, 13 November 1877.

[2] E. Arnold, *India Revisited* (London, Trübner, 1886), 40.

[3] *The Times*, 14 June 1878, 5 iv.

the Black Sea ports of Russia, raising its price in London by 25 per cent. Thereby it stimulated the export of wheat through the Canal and enabled India to supply 9·6 per cent of the total volume of British imports in 1877. The war also increased the exports of hides and skins from India in 1877–8 to supply material for the boot and shoe industry of the U.S.A. and thereby American footwear for the troops at war. It diverted British shipping from the ports of the Black Sea to India and the Persian Gulf. It also closed the northern trade-routes from Russia to Persia, stimulating trade between South and North Persia, traffic through the Canal to the Gulf, projects for an Indo-Mediterranean Railway and efforts to open the Karun to European trade. Sailings from London to the Persian Gulf were increased in 1878 from a monthly to a fortnightly basis. Direct consignments via the Canal were made from England to Tabriz in Azerbaijan and in 1880 to Tehran via Bushire as an alternative to Trebizond.

The Eastern crisis brought more loss than gain to the Canal by rendering insecure the new route to the East. The depression of 1878–9 was also caused by the famines in China and India, which reduced exports and freights, and by the fall in passenger traffic after the heavy military traffic of 1878. The decline in exports depressed sail freights in the Eastern trade and the building of sailing ships from Moulmein to Baltimore. Non-British tonnage using the Canal declined more than British tonnage so that the British share of the total rose to the record proportion of 79·91 per cent in 1878. The depression encouraged the formation of the first shipping conferences in 1879 in the China trade, the Straits trade and the East African trade. It also provoked Glover & Son to protest on 13 January 1880 to the Board of Trade against the high pilotage and light dues on the Canal and on 18 June against 'the extortions of which English ship-owners are the chief victims', both of which protests were rejected by the English directors on behalf of the Company. The depression ended the Canal's first phase of eight successive years of expanding traffic. Receipts declined more than tonnage and dividends much more than receipts. Gross tonnage sank by 3·7 per cent in 1878 and by 1·7 per cent in 1879 but dividends sank by 19·4 and 24·3 per cent. After ten years' trial the Company's shareholders had realized $1\frac{1}{4}$ per cent on their investment,[1] or less than the return foretold by Pender in 1870. Such was the inauspicious background for the International Scientific Congress which assembled in Paris on 15 May 1879 under the presidency of Lesseps, voted on 29 May in favour of the construction of a sea-level canal at Panama and offered Lesseps the presidency of the new enterprise as a work of peace in revulsion from the war of 1877–8.

Turkish command of the Black Sea had compelled Russia to fight a mainly military war. Russia's use of the land-route to Constantinople had compelled her to depend on the Rumanian bottleneck and therefore on the favour of

[1] *Report on the Trade of Port Said for the Year 1879 by Acting Consul Wolff*, 31 March 1880. Parliamentary Papers 1881, lxxiv, 1219.

Austria. Russia's wish to assert her freedom from such dependence encouraged her maritime and naval renaissance. The remilitarization of the Black Sea gave material content to the symbolic gain of 1870 while the cession of Batum by Turkey gave Russia a free port, essentially rather than exclusively commercial. The Russian Volunteer Fleet established in 1876 ordered the construction in England of a fleet of high-speed ships capable of 13–15 knots. Those ships were manned by Russian naval officers and crews and were military transports rather than cargo-carriers. They could each carry 2,000 troops. They passed the Straits in peacetime under the merchant flag and then changed it to the war-flag. Thus Russia circumvented the restrictions on the military use of the Straits, prevented her navy from being penned up in the Black Sea, exposed British commerce to the possibility of destruction in wartime by Russian Alabamas and faced the British Navy with the prospect of war in the Mediterranean basin. Russia resumed and extended her use of the Canal from 1879 when she began to reimburse the Canal dues paid by Russian vessels as an indirect subsidy. The first 700 Russian convicts were shipped through the Canal in 1879 to the penal colony of Sakhalin and Eastern Siberia, reducing their journey from eighteen months overland to sixty days by sea. The circum-navigation of Asia by the Finn A. E. Nordenskiold in the *Vega* achieved the first successful voyage through the North-East Passage and so fulfilled the great dream of the sixteenth century. The *Vega* did not sail around the triple continent of Asia, Africa and Europe but returned through the Canal in February 1880 while Nordenskiold travelled overland through Egypt. Thenceforward Russia enjoyed the possibility of access to her Siberian colony by the North-East as well as by the South-East Passage but found the Canal of more immediate value.

Russian statesmen had resented the wartime exclusion of Russian ships from the Canal and believed that the Canal was an international work which should not be allowed to fall into the hands of any strong power.[1] Russian lawyers therefore sought to secure international guarantees against a repetition of the events of 1877 and 1878. The Russian Professor T. T. Martens demanded at the Institute of International Law on 2 September 1879 that the Canal should be closed in wartime to the warships of both belligerents, including Turkey, on the model of the neutralization of the Black Sea in 1856. He was supported by the Austrian Professor Naumann, who suggested the creation of a 'marine Belgium', but by no one else so that agreement was precluded in 1879 as in 1878 and 1877. The reports of attempts to dynamite the Canal led a Study Commission of the Institute to propose on 4 September an international agreement to avert damage to the Canal in the event of war and to ensure the repair of the Canal works by the Power which damaged them, so diverging from inter-state relations to relations between states and the Canal Company.[2]

---

[1] D. M. Wallace, *Egypt and the Egyptian Question* (1883), 94.

[2] M. L. Camand, *Étude sur le Régime Juridique du Canal de Suez* (Grenoble, Allier, 1899), 109–18.

The rise of Russian naval power and of Russian interest in the Canal increased concern in Britain over the security of her colonies and her routes of communication. The secret Carnarvon Commission on Colonial Defence of 1879–81 foresaw the abandonment of the Mediterranean route by unarmed merchant vessels in wartime,[1] encouraged Gordon to denounce the Canal as a great danger to the Empire in the event of war,[2] increased interest in the alternative routes via the Cape and Canada and stimulated Currie to urge the construction of a graving-dock at Simon's Bay.[3] The Canadian Pacific Railway began from May 1881 to open a 'Euphrates' route in the West to supplement the British military route via the Canal.

[1] A. Hardinge, *The Life of the Earl of Carnarvon* (1925), iii. 39–40.
[2] H. W. Gordon, *Events in the Life of Charles George Gordon* (London, Paul, 1886), 171. D. M. Schurman, 'Chinese Gordon and the Suez Canal', *Journal of the Society for Army Historical Research* (1964), 80–3, quoting C. G. Gordon, Memorandum on Colonial Defences, 1881.
[3] D. Currie, 'Maritime Warfare: the Adaptation of Ocean Steamers to War Purposes', *Journal of the Royal United Service Institution*, 5 March 1880, 93.

THE REVOLT OF THE DELTA, AND THE OCCUPATION OF EGYPT, 1882

THE advance by the British Government under Disraeli to Kabul, Pretoria, Cyprus and Cairo divided Britain and enabled the Irish voters to inflict the greatest electoral defeat on the ministry in power since 1841. The Liberal assault upon imperialism encouraged Justin McCarthy to deride the enthusiasm aroused by the share-purchase in 1875 when 'England saw a few middle-aged or ancient gentlemen gravely trying to persuade themselves and their friends that they were Elizabethan conquerors of new worlds, Heaven-ordained makers of new Empires'.[1] Towards the end of his first Midlothian tour Gladstone denounced anew on 5 December 1879 the doctrine of safeguarding the route to India which had reappeared on the occupation of Cyprus: he dismissed the share-purchase as 'a financial operation' of a 'ridiculous description' rather than 'the offspring of consummate human wisdom'.[2] Thereby he incurred the disapproval of the shipping jingoes who saw the Canal as 'the neck which connects the head with the extremities of our Empire. (Cheers.)'[3] Gladstone refused to recant his condemnation of the share-purchase and showed that the rise in the price of the shares since 1875 was £4,750,000[4] and not the £10,242,916 claimed by one Conservative,[5] but conceded that his objection 'had no reference to the financial operation, considered as a financial operation, conceived and executed by a stock broker'.[6] His new Government was more concerned with Ireland than with the greater Empire and acted only slowly to liquidate Disraeli's imperial legacy. Salisbury had recognized the failure of the policy of reforming Asia Minor through British administration before the election of 1880: Gladstone was prevented from surrendering Cyprus by the defeat of the British by the Boers at Majuba Hill. The island became neither a naval base nor a commercial entrepôt and remained the meaningless vestige of an awe-inspiring but abortive imperial policy. There Britain remained the tax-gatherer, the tributary and the vassal of the Sultan whom its Cyprus policy had permanently alienated.

[1] J. McCarthy, *A History of Our Own Times from the Accession of Queen Victoria to the General Election of 1880* (London, Chatto, 1880), iv. 436, 438.
[2] *The Times*, 6 December 1879, 11 i. Grant Allen, 'Why Keep India?', *Contemporary Review* (October 1880), 544, 549.
[3] J. Cowen, *The Foreign Policy of England* (Newcastle, Reid, 1880), 8, 22, 31 January 1880.
[4] Hansard, *Commons Debates*, 31 March 1881, 348, Gladstone in reply to Lord George Hamilton.
[5] *The Times*, 26 March 1881, 10iv; 31 March 1881, 10vi. E. Dicey, *England and Egypt* (London, Chapman, 1881), 8.
[6] Hansard, *Commons Debates*, 8 April 1881, 1022, Gladstone in reply to Baron Henry de Worms.

In Egypt the reconstitution of the Anglo-French Control after the deposition of Ismail multiplied the number of European officials through the rivalry of the two Controllers for influence and encouraged English efforts at reform on the Anglo-Indian model. The Europeanization begun under Ismail was thus accelerated, separating the regime increasingly from the traditional beliefs of the population[1] and provoking an indigenous revolt which was both nationalist and Moslem. That revolt embraced the Beduin, the Copts and the notables as well as the fellahin but drew its leaders from the Army, the primary vehicle of the modernization of Egypt. It was no more a purely military revolt than the Indian rebellion of 1857 had been. The fellah-colonels who had suffered in the Turco-Circassian reaction under Ismail enlisted the support of the Nile-bound fellahin. They also rallied the Copts in opposition to their Syrian and Maltese competitors for public employment. They won the support of 'Young Egypt', which imported from Europe the concept of the 'Fatherland' in order to oppose the Turkish Khedive, the Turkish pashas, the Turco-Circassian officers and the Ottoman connexion. That movement of national regeneration found its fullest expression in religious terms, in the opposition of the faithful to the infidel, the European officials, the Dual Control and the whole process of Europeanization. The Moslem peasantry hoped that the thirteen hundredth year of the Hegira would witness the general triumph of Islam. Their debts had increased sharply, with the fall in the price of cotton and sugar, to the benefit of their Greek, Syrian and Coptic creditors who were invariably Christian. They deeply resented the extension of the usury prohibited by the Koran, the increase in loans on the mortgage of their land in defiance of the Shariah and the erosion through the Mixed Courts of their rights in the land of Islam.[2] Above all, they loathed the increased taxes demanded for the benefit of the infidel bondholders. They found their inspiration in religious reformers more than in political reformers, their ultimate security in the sacred right of rebellion[3] and their true leader in 'the only one' Arabi Bey, who was more an alim than a soldier.

The military revolt of 1 February 1881 ended Turco-Circassian domination of the Army and produced a flow of petitions from the peasantry of all the provinces to Arabi. Tewfik determined to imitate his father's tactic in 1879 and to use the Army under Arabi to overthrow his Minister, Riaz Pasha, so as to free himself from consular tutelage. The French expedition to Tunis in May 1881 gave France its compensation for Cyprus. It contrasted sharply with the British withdrawal from Asia Minor, encouraged India Office jingoes to seek recompense for England in Egypt and re-awakened interest in the isthmus of Suez, 'the key-stone of our position as an Imperial Power'.[4] Lesseps

---

[1] N. Safran, *Egypt in Search of Political Community, 1804–1952* (Harvard University Press, 1961), 50.

[2] J. Ninet, 'Origin of the National Party in Egypt', *Nineteenth Century* (January 1883), 124–5.

[3] G. Campbell, 'The Situation in Egypt', *Fortnightly Review*, 1 May 1879, 797.

[4] E. Dicey, *England and Egypt* (1881), 27.

accompanied Tewfik on the Khedive's first visit to the isthmus between 28 April and 4 May. He asked his permission on 3 May to form an Egyptian joint-stock company to extend the Sweet Water Canal from Ismailia to Port Said and secured the sanction of the British Cabinet on 28 May to such an enterprise. The expedition to Tunis detonated a wave of indigenous unrest throughout Moslem Africa, in eastern Tunis, in the Algerian Sahara, in the Senussi hinterland of Tripoli and in the Sudan, where Mohammed Ahmed proclaimed himself the Mahdi on 29 June 1881. In Egypt the second military revolt of 9 September 1881 enabled Tewfik to dismiss Riaz but made Arabi the real ruler of the land and ushered in a political revolution. Colvin, the successor of Baring as Controller of Finance, was outwitted by Tewfik and appealed for British intervention, bringing the first British warship to Alexandria on 19 October. Chérif Pasha, the successor of Riaz, believed that Britain desired only 'the undisturbed and peaceful enjoyment of the great Indian highway which passes through our country'[1] and arranged a meeting of the Chamber of Notables in order to rally the landowners against the Army. The Dilke–Gambetta Note of 8 January 1882, devized by Rivers Wilson, expressed the support of England and France for the Khedive against the notables who therefore rallied to the support of the Army. That joint Anglo-French intervention distinct from the Control weakened instead of strengthening Tewfik's position. Samuel Baker suggested a joint occupation of the Canal because the share-purchase had allied England and France 'in a partnership which necessitated a protectorate' best embodied in alternate French and English garrisons in a chain of military posts from Port Said to Suez.[2] Lesseps gave public support on 22 February to the new nationalist ministry in which Arabi was Minister of War. His campaign for a new Sweet Water Canal concession had achieved no success, although on 19 January he had renamed Terreplein Port Tewfik in the presence of the notables of Suez, which seemed like an English coaching town honouring a railway which had robbed it of its prosperity.[3]

The Anglo-French encroachment on the independence of Egypt disturbed the other European Powers, whose consular delegates in the reorganized Egyptian Maritime and Quarantine Council of Health blamed British ships for bringing cholera from India and imposed quarantine on ships from Aden on 11 September 1881, on those from Bombay on 27 September and on those from India on 29 September. Those restrictions increased the strain on the pilot service of the Canal Company and the number of accidents, strandings and stoppages in the waterway, especially from 14 November. They also raised the time of transit, the charges for pilotage and towage and the income of the agents and ships' chandlers of Port Said. The increase in congestion and delay provoked sustained complaints against the efficiency of the Canal Company which were first voiced on 17 December by the North of England Steamship

---

[1] *Pall Mall Gazette*, 13 January 1882, 2i, Chérif Pasha as transmitted by Malortie.
[2] *The Times*, 18 January 1882, 10vi, 'The Affairs of Egypt'.
[3] Ibid., 20 February 1882, 8i, 'M. de Lesseps in Egypt'.

Owners' Association. Shipowners even revived the idea of suing the Canal Company for the return of the excess dues paid in 1872–4. The representatives of the P. & O. met those of its chief competitors, the Glen, Castle, Ocean, Orient, Harrison, Hall and Anchor Lines, at the P. & O. offices on 25 February. That meeting sent a deputation led by Thomas Sutherland, the chairman of the P. & O. since 1880, to the Foreign Office on 27 February. Granville accepted their view of 'the great block on the Canal'[1] and asked the Government of Egypt to see that its sanitary regulations did not disturb British trade unnecessarily. Quarantine restrictions were lifted between 23 February and 27 March after the transit time reached its all-time peak of 80 hours 32 minutes during February 1882, despite an increase in the number of pilots from 39 in 1881 to 100 in 1882. Lesseps denounced the quarantine system on the Canal to the Academy of Sciences on 21 March and was refused on 26 March the concession for the extension of the Sweet Water Canal or any hope of the relaxation of the restrictions on the commercial use of the Ismailia Canal. Thenceforward he ranged himself against Tewfik in virtual alliance with Arabi who promised to grant him the concession for the Sweet Water Canal extension without payment.[2] The isthmian population continued to live complacently on the memory of its past prosperity and the hope of similar future wealth, arousing English ire and ambition. 'A serious collapse of the Suez Canal is urgently needed to stir up the towns it has created.'[3] English interests aspired to take over the Canal and drastically widen the deep-water channel from 25 to 60 yards[4] so as to make possible two-way traffic.

The promotion of 500 Egyptian officers, including Arabi who rose from Bey to Pasha on 5 April, caused a revolt by the old guard of Turkish officers and a breach between Tewfik and his nationalist ministry. That rupture of relations led many European families to leave Cairo and encouraged Freycinet timidly to contemplate intervention in Egypt in alliance with England and with the authority of a European mandate. England joined France after the 'Invincibles' murdered the son of the Duke of Devonshire in Phoenix Park, Dublin, on 6 May as a sacrifice to the cause of 'Ireland, Her Own'. Under pressure from Hartington, the elder brother of the victim, the Cabinet equated Egyptian nationalism with Irish nationalism and decided on 12 May to depose Arabi as an adventurer and to send two ironclads to Alexandria so as to achieve a success in Egypt which might atone for failure in Ireland. French and English warships arrived in the Canal ports as well as at Alexandria between 17 and 27 May. The Canal was thus placed under naval protection while Admiral Seymour arrived at Alexandria on 20 May to repeat his success at Dulcigno. Arabi was dismissed but was then reinstated under popular pressure the next day, so frustrating the intentions of England and

---

[1] *The Times*, 28 February 1882, 8 vi, 'Quarantine in the Suez Canal'.
[2] S. Gwynn and G. M. Tuckwell, *The Life of the Rt. Hon. Sir Charles W. Dilke* (London, Murray, 1918), i. 465.
[3] S. Lane-Poole, *Egypt* (London, Low, 1881), 119.
[4] *The Times*, 25 March 1882, 4 i–iii, 'The Suez Canal'.

France. The menace implicit in the arrival of the ironclads strengthened the position of Arabi and precipitated a rapid deterioration of relations between Egyptians and Europeans, who began to make a general exodus. The Egyptian Army began to construct earthworks at Alexandria opposite the ironclads from 29 May, to lay mines around the anchorage of the warships in the Canal from 30 May and to concentrate forces along its banks. The withdrawal of those troops on 7 June ended the only military demonstration made against the waterway during 1882.

The anti-Christian riots in Alexandria on Sunday, 11 June seem to have been arranged by Tewfik in a bid to discredit the Army and Arabi,[1] whom they left in the outcome stronger than ever. Those riots turned Christian opinion in England against Egypt and especially horrified Manchester.[2] They threatened the overland mail service but not the Canal route.[3] They neverthe-less provoked questions in Parliament demanding protection for vessels using the Canal[4] and equating English interests in Egypt with its shipping using the waterway.[5] Gladstone reluctantly conceded the importance of the Canal but refused to make its security an object of British policy.[6] He secured a decision by the Cabinet on 15 June against the beginning of preparations for the despatch of a force to the Mediterranean but so aroused the opposition of the service departments. At the War Office Childers received a report on 16 June that the Canal was vulnerable and should be occupied at Port Said and Suez: he therefore held a secret meeting with Cambridge, Wolseley and Adye to discuss the organization of an expedition to Egypt.[7] From the India Office Hartington also proposed military measures to Granville to protect the Canal and told Ripon to be prepared for an order to send a force from India to Suez. At the Admiralty Northbrook began on 17 June preparations for a naval force to hold the Canal as a preliminary to its occupation by troops,[8] so envisaging its use as a base for military operations.

The rise of anti-foreign sentiment in Egypt compelled the Canal Company to transfer its offices from Cairo to Ismailia on 16 June. The influx of refugees trebled the population of the three isthmian towns by 18 June and turned Port Said into a port of embarkation, especially for Malta. The waning of European influence in the Delta strengthened the agitation for intervention to end the anarchy in Egypt. No threat then emerged to the Canal to justify

[1] W. S. Blunt, *Secret History of the English Occupation of Egypt* (London, Unwin, 1907), 312–15, 498–512, marshalled the evidence which Cromer dismissed without any explicit reason. Lord Cromer, *Modern Egypt* (London, Macmillan, 1908), i. 287 note.

[2] Hansard, *Commons Debates*, 14 June 1882, 1168, 1170, J. Bright and W. F. Ecroyd.

[3] Ibid., 14 June 1882, 1128, R. Bourke.

[4] Ibid., 12 June 1882, 820, D. R. Onslow; 13 June, 982, C. M. Norwood; 14 June, 1155, Onslow.

[5] Ibid., 14 June 1882, 1141, E. A. Bartlett.

[6] Ibid., 14 June 1882, 1146, Gladstone.

[7] S. Childers, *The Life and Correspondence of the Right Hon. Hugh C. E. Childers 1827–1896* (London, Murray, 1901), ii. 89.

[8] P. H. Colomb, *Memoirs of Admiral the Right Honble. Sir Astley Cooper Key* (London, Methuen, 1898), 458.

either the request for its neutralization in time of war[1] or the public acknowledgement by Government spokesmen of England's enormous interest in the Canal,[2] the last such statement made during the crisis. Gladstone remained firmly opposed to any exaggeration of the value of the Canal and at first declined to allow the Conference of Constantinople to consider the Canal or its neutralization.[3] In the Cabinet on 21 June he refused to agree to the request for a British occupation of the Canal and thereby to ratify the unauthorized actions of the service departments. He accepted as a compromise the proposal that two battalions of troops should be sent to the Mediterranean and that the War Office and Admiralty should consider how best to protect the Canal if it should prove necessary. He did not intend thereby to authorize military preparations for the protection of the Canal but held it impermissible to propose or to frame a plan for occupying the Canal or landing in Egypt without any sanction from or reference to Europe. Thus he conceded that the Conference might embrace the peace and security of the Canal as a part of Egyptian territory.[4] At the opening session of the Conference on 23 June Italy proposed the protection of the Canal by a permanent international maritime police, to the alarm of Egypt, the Canal Company, France and England. Northbrook ordered Admiral Hewett from the East India station on 23 June to Suez.[5] Arabi reportedly considered sending cannon to the banks of the Canal as well as powder-laden barges into the fairway[6] but took neither course of action. Lesseps believed that the waterway was safe and only in danger from foreign intervention to protect it: nevertheless he cabled to the Prime Minister of Egypt on 24 June for a guarantee that the waterway would not be endangered. Armed Beduin then formed a cordon along the banks and inspired Northbrook on 27 June to entrust the Arabic scholar, Edward Palmer, with a secret mission of pacification intended to prevent the destruction of the Canal by the Beduin sheikhs of Sinai. The first troops left England on 29 June when insurance brokers doubled the war-risk premium on freight carried via the Canal, so recognizing a threat from England rather than from Egypt. On the same day Hartington told Ripon to make all the necessary preparations short of moving troops and taking up transport while Childers quietly decided to establish a Confidential Mobilization Committee.[7] That committee first met on 30 June, approved Wolseley's basic plan for an Egyptian expedition and submitted it to Childers on 3 July, meeting thenceforward almost daily.

[1] Hansard, *Commons Debates*, 16 June, 1421, E. A. Bartlett; *Lords Debates*, 19 June, 1551, Lord Lamington who, as Baillie Cochrane, had magnified the value of the Canal in 1873.
[2] Hansard, *Lords Debates*, 19 June, 1554, Granville; *Commons Debates*, 20 June, 1762, Dilke.
[3] Hansard, *Commons Debates*, 19 June, 1608, 1609; 22 June, 63, Gladstone.
[4] A. Ramm, *The Political Correspondence of Mr. Gladstone and Lord Granville, 1876–1886* (Oxford, Clarendon Press, 1962), i. 380, Gladstone to Granville, 21 June. Hansard, *Commons Debates*, 22 June, 55, Gladstone.
[5] Colomb, 460.
[6] Ramm, i. 381, Gladstone to Granville, 24 June.
[7] J. F. Maurice, *Military History of the Campaign of 1882 in Egypt* (London, H.M.S.O., 1887), 4. Childers, ii. 90, 137.

Lesseps visited England as 'a flaming Arabist'[1] and assured Gladstone on 4 July that no danger to the Canal had yet arisen. Hartington, Northbrook and Childers, who had sent out secret orders to prepare for mobilization,[2] then told Gladstone that they wished to send troops at once to ensure the safety of the Canal and secured a Cabinet meeting for the following day. The decisions taken by the Cabinet on 5 July together with those taken on 20 July determined the destiny of Egypt for the next seventy years and were forced through against the opposition of Gladstone. On 5 July Gladstone reluctantly agreed to the despatch of military reinforcements to the Mediterranean, so ratifying the secret movement orders sent out on the previous day.[3] He nevertheless refused to agree to the occupation of the Canal and drew up a forceful memorandum in justification.[4] Therein he concluded that Egypt had the strongest motives to avoid antagonizing the whole world and did not desire or even contemplate blocking the Canal. He emphasized that England had no separate rights in the Canal and could not claim such rights without creating a precedent for American claims at Panama and Russian claims at the Straits. He had nevertheless weakened his position by sanctioning the bombardment of the forts of Alexandria and faced growing pressure thenceforward from the supporters of a forward policy. He successfully opposed a proposal by Hartington and Childers that the bombardment would justify independent action to occupy the Canal.[5] He forced the withdrawal of orders to Seymour to send warships into the waterway. Then he sought to ensure the protection of the Canal first by the Porte and then by the Great Powers assembled in conference.[6]

The bombardment of the forts of Alexandria was decreed in order to restore European prestige in Egypt in the most economical way. In preparation Seymour warned British ships on 10 July not to enter the Canal in the event of hostilities since he could spare no force to guard them. His warning halted eleven ships and produced panic in both Port Said and Suez, the complete suspension of business by Europeans, the flight of 360 Europeans to vessels in the port, and a protest by Victor de Lesseps against the violation of the neutrality of the waterway. The bombardment of 11 July proved as influential as the riots of 11 June in strengthening the hand of the war-party in England. 3,200 shells and 33,000 bullets killed 2,000 Arabs[7] but failed to destroy the Egyptian artillery, to break the spirit of the Egyptian officers and gunners or to make Egypt habitable once more by its Levantines. In revenge the Arabs destroyed the commercial heart of Alexandria by fire. The United Egyptian Debt declined sharply by 12 per cent on 13–14 July. Egypt united under Arabi in Cairo against the infidel and utterly abandoned Tewfik at Alexandria. Port Said became the last frontier of European power and influence, a

---

[1] Gwynn and Tuckwell, *Dilke*, i. 464–5. *The Times*, 3 July 1882, 5vi.
[2] Maurice, 5–6.   [3] Ibid., 5.
[4] Ramm, i. 385–6, Gladstone to Granville, 5 July.
[5] Ibid., 387, Gladstone to Granville, 7 July.
[6] Ibid., 389 note, Gladstone to Granville, 10 July.
[7] *The Times*, 15 July 1882, 7ii.

no-man's-land and a half-way house between Khedive and Pasha. Its coal heavers refused to coal European vessels from 11 July until 16 July. The bombardment created an immediate danger of Egyptian retaliation against the Canal as Bright and Blunt had foretold.[1] The Canal, however, survived undamaged and unthreatened. Spain sent a frigate to Port Said on 12 July to protect its interest in the Canal while Lesseps departed post-haste for Egypt on 13 July in a frenzy of possessiveness over his creation. At Alexandria Arabists cut the telegraph line between England and the East, making the Red Sea cables useless and bringing into use again the Indo-European line through Persia in the absence of any reserve cable other than the Siberian. Gladstone angrily declined to allow Pender to lay a cable at the Government's expense from Alexandria to Port Said and Suez.[2] He also opposed Hartington's attempt to eliminate the sanction of the Powers as the essential preliminary to any measures to protect the Canal.[3] Nevertheless he defended the bombardment in the Commons on 12 July by the precedent of Navarino and by three references to the unavenged 'massacre' of 11 June. Thereby he sought to repeat the success of his agitation against the Bulgarian Horrors with that new phrase which was borrowed from the Conservatives[4] and repeated by Dilke four times on the same evening. Only when he was assured of French co-operation and a mandate from the Conference did he admit that an Anglo-French operation to protect the Canal was practicable and might be accepted in principle under the authority of the Conference given in answer to an Anglo-French initiative.[5] He sought even then to limit any protective measures purely to naval action.[6] Admiral Hoskins was sent to Port Said on 13 July to concert with the French admiral but not to act without his agreement except to defend British subjects. Hoskins used gunboats from 14 July to escort British vessels through the waterway and was imitated therein by Italy, Spain and Germany. Thus he calmed the fears expressed for the security of traffic[7] and facilitated the diversion of the P. & O. express mail leaving on 14 July from Alexandria to the Canal. Gladstone's intention was frustrated by Childers who ordered Woolwich Arsenal on 14 July to prepare for an expedition of 21,000 and by General Alison who believed in accordance with the plan of 3 July that the bombardment was to be the signal for the occupation of the Canal.[8] Alison arrived in Cyprus on 14 July and left with his two battalions for the Canal without any orders to do so. At Port Said he was very properly obliged by Hoskins to depart for Alexandria in order to avoid provoking attacks on Europeans or the blocking of the waterway by Lesseps.

[1] Blunt, *Secret History*, 556, 11 July 1882.
[2] Ramm, i. 390, Gladstone to Granville, 11 July.
[3] Ibid., 392, Gladstone to Granville, 12 July.
[4] Hansard, *Commons Debates*, 14 June, 1172, H. D. Wolff; 14 July, 455, Dilke.
[5] Ramm, i. 394, Gladstone to Granville, 13 July.
[6] Colomb, 462.
[7] Colomb, 460–1. Hansard, *Commons Debates*, 14 July, 451, 454, 504–5, Campbell-Bannerman, H. Peek, W. H. Smith.
[8] Maurice, 7, 11.

Gladstone discounted an alarmist report that Arabi might make a diversion against the Canal but agreed that Hoskins might act with the French admiral in the event of sudden and immediately impending danger.[1] He refused to agree to the use of either British or Indian troops.[2] On 20 July Arabi allotted an army corps to the defence of the Canal after the publication of Wolseley's plan of attack via the Canal.[3] He made no attempt to undertake any reprisal against the Canal itself. On the same day Gladstone was forced by his Cabinet to agree to the despatch of an army corps for operations in Egypt, so making the fundamental shift from the use of the Navy to the use of the Army. Gladstone refused however to allow the Government of India to take up transport because the use of Indian troops would be unnecessary if England acted with France or with any other powers.[4] He remained unmoved by a panic-born rumour that Arabi had turned the salt water of Lake Timsah into the more elevated Sweet Water Canal. He sanctioned negotiations with France for common action to impose a fresh brake on his Service ministers.

Lesseps recognized the hostility of the French Chamber to such common action and asked Freycinet on 20 July to protect the Canal by a French naval expedition, assuring him that 50,000–60,000 troops would be necessary to conquer Egypt and would require at least six months. Thus he sought to protect both Arabi and the Canal. He informed Seymour that the passage of British ships through the waterway constituted a breach of its neutrality but appealed on 22 July to Arabi to exclude the Canal from his military operations. An Anglo-French agreement of 23 July confined cooperation to the protection of the Canal and to the occupation of certain points on its banks but only in the event of its security being threatened. Thus France was unprepared to play the role for which Gladstone had hoped. The Cabinet then decided on 24 July to authorize the Government of India to take up transport to carry Indian troops to Suez and Seymour to prepare to occupy Port Said, Ismailia and Nefischa.[5] That decision made India the substitute for France but was coupled with Gladstone's proposal to invite Italy to cooperate. Gladstone recognized that the traffic of the Canal had not been disturbed or even threatened and declined to restrict the Egyptian question to the defence of the Canal, whose insecurity was only a symptom of the anarchy in the interior of Egypt and could only be ended by the restoration of law and order in the Delta.[6] The Admiralty expected that English action might endanger the Canal and therefore chartered a salvage vessel to clear the waterway of sunken vessels if necessary. From 25 July a committee of the Cabinet comprising Hartington, Childers, Northbrook and Granville met daily as a war-cabinet to deal with

[1] Ramm, i. 397, Gladstone to Granville, 16 July.
[2] Ibid., 398, Gladstone to Granville, 18 July.
[3] *The Times*, 19 July 1882, 7 iii. Hansard, *Commons Debates*, 19 July, 975, E. T. Gourley.
[4] Ramm, i. 398, 401, Gladstone to Granville, 18 and 22 July.
[5] Maurice, 15.
[6] Hansard, *Commons Debates*, 24 July 1882, 1585–6, Gladstone; 1611, Campbell-Bannerman; 25 July, 1719, Dilke.

Egyptian affairs. The invitation to Italy encouraged France reluctantly to agree on 26 July upon a joint occupation of the Canal with the French in Port Said and Kantara and the British in Ismailia and Suez.[1] Panic recurred at Port Said on the same day after the Arabist chief of police took over from the Governor and began to prepare the defences of the town. Lesseps succeeded in preventing the landing of troops and secured a guarantee of the safety of the Europeans from the new Governor. His efforts were rewarded by the thanks of Arabi and a promise to respect the Canal.

On 27 July the British warship *Orion* entered the waterway and the vote of credit for the expedition was passed in the Commons by 275 to 19 votes, which were cast mainly by Irish members. Italy refused however on 28 July to cooperate with England and Freycinet's proposal for the protection of the Canal was rejected on 29 July by a massive 417 to 45 votes, an unprecedented defeat in the parliamentary annals of France for the size of the majority and the minority in a vital vote.[2] France was determined not to leave its Rhine frontier defenceless for the sake of the Canal nor its foreign policy as an independent state at the mercy of Bismarck, who had been infuriated by the bombardment of Alexandria.[3] Clemenceau thus ended Freycinet's second ministry and earned the approval of Lesseps for his 'perfect speech'. Lesseps did not agree with those pessimists who anticipated the establishment of an English protectorate and suggested as compensation the renaming of the Canal as Lesseps Strait.[4] He assumed that he could protect the Canal and that Arabi would defeat the British. On 1 August the troop trains began to leave Cairo for 'the Egyptian Plevna' at Tel el Kebir while the French ironclads began to leave Port Said, as they had left Alexandria before the bombardment. Bismarck favoured Turkish rather than Anglo-French intervention and hoped to eliminate the need for British action. He therefore took advantage of Italy's 'extra-ordinary pretensions of predominant interests in the Suez Canal, next only to those of England'[5] and permitted her to present a plan to the Conference of Constantinople on 2 August[6] for the collective naval protection of the Canal. He recognized however that England's national pride had been committed to action in Egypt and therefore was not prepared to make a formal protest against unilateral British action.

For England the Canal had become its highway to India and was undoubtedly more important in 1882 than in 1875 as well as more familiar, being by then 'as well known as the Rhine'.[7] The need to protect it was an argument publicly used to justify military preparations[8] and military intervention but

---

[1] *The Times*, 27 July 1882, 10i.
[2] C. de Freycinet, *La Question d'Égypte* (Paris, Calmann-Lévy, 1905), 312.
[3] W. Taffs, *Odo Russell*, 319, Russell to Granville, 15 July 1882.
[4] *The Times*, 28 July 1882, 5iv.   [5] Ibid., 2 August 1882, 9i.
[6] L. E. Roberts, 'Italy and the Egyptian Question, 1878–1882', *Journal of Modern History* (December 1946), 327, 330.
[7] Hansard, *Commons Debates*, 22 June, 57, J. C. M'Coan.
[8] *The Times*, 26 June 1882, 7ii.

seems to have been intended to serve as an excuse for the occupation of Egypt. Thus E. P. Bouverie, a barrister and a director of the P. & O., claimed a right of necessity for England in the Canal comparable to the right of way to and from one's own land if it were entirely enclosed by the land of another.[1] John Morley, who had become editor of the *Pall Mall Gazette* when Greenwood had been dethroned after the Liberal victory in the general election, converted his paper from Cobdenism to jingoism[2] and justified English intervention as necessary to protect a channel of world commerce from the Beduin and from the organized rapacity of some hostile European power.[3] Chenery even equated the Canal with Constantinople. 'For us the Eastern question is the Suez Canal, and all that it implies.'[4] Such judgments undoubtedly exaggerated the importance of the Canal which carried only 13·2 per cent of the value of British exports in 1879[5] but was represented by Chamberlain as carrying one-seventh of the whole foreign trade of Britain.[6] Even for naval purposes the waterway could not be used by warships above 23 feet in draught. Nor had it thrown into disuse the older routes to the East. The great ocean highway via the Cape continued in use. The Euphrates Valley Railway as advocated by Lord Lamington[7] received little support beyond the knighthood bestowed upon W. P. Andrew. The overland route had however been maintained and improved under the mail contracts of 1874 and 1879: it was a peculiarly English route, unlike the Canal, and was liable to be affected by any political convulsion in the Delta.

The crisis of 1882 centred around Cairo and not Suez: it was described by contemporaries as an Egyptian crisis and not as a Canal crisis. Little concern for the Canal was expressed in Parliament, in the press, in periodicals or in books: the subject never dominated debate in public or private but remained on the periphery. The disintegration of law and order in the Delta was the central problem because it threatened the whole status of Europeans in Egypt[8] together with that of the Khedive, the Dual Control, European officials and foreign bondholders. Egypt provided the largest market in Africa for Lancashire cotton goods and the long-stapled cotton for the fine spinning industry of Bolton and presented no threat to English interests. The economic interests of the Levantines and the financial interest of the Rothschilds in the unsold half of their Domains Loan of 1878[9] were, however, directly and immediately threatened by the revolt in the Delta whereas any danger to the Canal was contingent and remote. 'If Arabi is allowed to prevail, the country must go

---

[1] *The Times*, 30 June 1882, 8i.
[2] F. Harrison, *The Crisis in Egypt* (London, Clarke, 1882), 21.
[3] J. Morley, 'Egyptian Policy: a Retrospect', *Fortnightly Review*, 1 July 1882, 120–1, 403.
[4] *The Times*, 26 July, 5ii; 18 September, 7ii.
[5] Ibid., 6 July, 4iv.
[6] Hansard, *Commons Debates*, 25 July, 1800, Chamberlain.
[7] Hansard, *Lords Debates*, 17 July 1882, Lamington. *The Times*, 21 July, 3iv, W. P. Andrew; 2 September, 9i, W. Campbell.
[8] *The Times*, 27 July, 9ii.
[9] Blunt, *Secret History*, 21, 267, 12 May 1882. Blunt, *My Diaries*, i. 343.

from bad to worse, and no European interest in it, not even the Canal itself, will be safe.'[1] The claims of sectional economic interests could only divide the nation whereas a threat to the Canal, even if imaginary, might serve to unite it and especially to rally Liberals, Free-Traders and commercial radicals behind the Conservatives in support of the war. The commercial value of the Canal was depreciated by such Liberal shipowners as C. M. Norwood[2] and William Rathbone[3] as well as by J. C. R. Colomb[4] and W. E. Baxter.[5] Most Liberals seem however to have been as ready to approve intervention in 1882 to protect the Canal as they had been to applaud the purchase of the shares in 1875. To such Liberals the Canal seemed 'the gate and the key to India'[6] and made Egypt in practice for England 'part of the sea':[7] thus it was deemed a necessity to England in time of war[8] which had to be under her 'supreme and paramount influence'.[9] Their concern was shared by H. D. Wolff, who first proposed measures for the pacification of the Canal which were intended to preserve its use to England in wartime[10] and were incorporated in the Convention of Constantinople in 1888. The conscience of such Liberals might be salved if intervention could be justified in the name of world communications and free trade. Their capitulation to such argument reveals the extent to which the militarization of English culture had proceeded since the war-fever of 1878 which transformed the Christian Mission into the Salvation Army. That new military spirit pervaded the whole of society and inspired the foundation of the Drake Memorial Committee on 19 July 1882 as well as of the Royal Colonial Institute on 26 September. It infected even the police, who began to wear helmets and to speak of the population as 'civilians'.[11] It sapped the very basis of the Liberal ethos and rallied cotton jingoes,[12] shipping jingoes, Nonconformists and Radicals to support the national classes and the police-action against military despotism in Egypt. Thus under a Liberal Government elected to oppose imperialism the British and Indian Armies each travelled 3,000 miles in order to attack in its own land the organized Army of Egypt. That attack inevitably appeared to the reborn nation of the Nile as an armed aggression against its newly won independence. Thus the crisis of 1882 became a clash between two renascent military powers. Technical superiority lay on the side of England. Wolseley knew that the occupation of the Canal

[1] *The Times*, 4 July, 9 vi.

[2] Hansard, *Commons Debates*, 22 June, 65–6. *The Times*, 10 July, 6 vi, C. M. Norwood.

[3] Hansard, *Commons Debates*, 26 July, 1861, 1865. W. Rathbone, 'Great Britain and the Suez Canal', *Fortnightly Review*, 1 August 1882, 239–40. F. Egerton, W. Rathbone and C. M. Norwood, *Great Britain, Egypt and the Suez Canal* (London, Chapman, 1884), 5–24.

[4] *The Times*, 6 July, 4 iv; 27 July, 9 iii.

[5] Ibid., 2 September, 8 ii–iii.

[6] Hansard, *Commons Debates*, 25 July, 1758, M'Coan.

[7] Ibid., 25 July, 1748–9, A. Arnold.   [8] Ibid., 26 July, 1850, T. C. Bruce.

[9] Ibid., 27 July, 2051, H. Labouchere.   [10] Ibid., 25 July, 1842, H. D. Wolff.

[11] H. Spencer, 'The Militant Type of Society', *Contemporary Review* (September 1881), 352–3. Idem, 'The Industrial Type of Society', *Contemporary Review* (October 1881), 527–8. Idem, *Principles of Sociology* (London, Williams, 1882), ii. 681, 722.

[12] Hansard, *Commons Debates*, 12 July 1882, 171, W. Lawson.

without that of the Delta was a military illogicality[1] and aimed to attack Arabi's position from the rear via Ismailia so as to avoid the cotton-growing districts of the Delta with their impassable maze of rivers and canals. Thus he sought to avoid any damage to the cotton harvest but subordinated the commercial function of the Canal to the military exigency of a flank attack. He took advantage of the lack of legal protection of the Canal[2] to use it as a tactical highway in order to resolve the crisis in the Delta and re-establish the happy state of 'safety to Europeans and to the canals'.[3]

The Egyptian revolution had not in fact endangered the Canal nor interfered with the passage of shipping when the decisions of 5 and 20 July were taken. The Canal remained unfortified and undefended, the most vulnerable section of the whole Suez route, but was separated from the Delta by fifty miles of impassable and uninhabited desert. It depended on the Nile only for fresh water, whose flow to the isthmus remained uninterrupted and unadulterated. No attempt was made to block the Canal. Nor was the threat to block it used or apparently contemplated, even in retaliation for the bombardment of Alexandria. Vessels, cargoes and passengers continued to pass without hindrance from Egypt, the threat of hindrance or even the threat of discrimination against a particular flag. Such discrimination might have been deemed a useful diplomatic weapon but was never used because Arabi did not wish to antagonize Europe and trusted Lesseps to preserve the essential interests of Egypt. Transit rights were thus not limited by any attempt to restrict access or to search for contraband of war. The Canal Company remained in full control of operations, was not disturbed by any massacre or riot in the towns of the isthmus and enjoyed a steady rise in its revenues through the increase in traffic. No shipping association petitioned the British Government to protect the Canal or even held an extraordinary meeting to consider the matter. Some shipowners blamed the rise of insurance rates on the military preparations of the Government. No official or unofficial plans were devised for the use of alternative routes or even for the protection of the Canal itself. No shipping line diverted its vessels from the Suez route except for the Orient Line, whose vessels had been designed for the Cape route to which they returned from 11 July while the P. & O. diverted its express mail-ships into the Canal. No prohibition or restriction was imposed by Egypt on the passage or stationing of warships despite the recommendation made by Blunt's agent to Arabi.[4] In short there was no imminent danger to the waterway in any form when the Cabinet sanctioned the invasion.

Gladstone never stated that intervention was necessary to protect the Canal and would not permit other ministers after 20 June so to justify British action lest a damaging precedent should be created for independent American and

---

[1] Maurice, 3.
[2] *The Law Times*, 22 July, 1882, 209–10.
[3] S. Childers, *Hugh Childers*, ii. 89, Halifax to Childers, 2 July 1882.
[4] Blunt, *Secret History*, 547.

Russian action. His views remained as much opposed to aggression as in 1877 and were given forceful expression by Frederic Harrison. 'All this wild and criminal bluster is supposed to be justified by the one word—the Canal. Well, the Canal is not a British river; it is an ocean highway open to the world.'[1] Gladstone assumed that it was impossible permanently to destroy or even to injure the Canal. He refused to be swayed by the flow of alarmist rumours and never believed or pretended to believe that the Canal was in any danger whatsoever. He had however been broken in spirit since the Phoenix Park murders and he failed to keep the service departments in due subordination. The effective decisions were therefore taken in 1882 as in 1878 by the great departments[2] rather than by the Cabinet, which acted under pressure from Hartington, Northbrook, Chamberlain and Dilke. Hartington was eager to avenge his brother in Egypt, Northbrook to conceal the disastrous outcome of the bombardment of Alexandria and Chamberlain to strengthen Gladstone in a resolute policy towards Ireland as well as to enhance the power of the State. Dilke was not in the Cabinet but, if Blunt is right, was intended by Gladstone as his successor and virtually controlled the Foreign Office, the Foreign Secretary and foreign policy. Colvin represented in Egypt Anglo-Indian opinion, which regarded the Canal as even more important than Ireland[3] and feared a general Moslem rising spreading from the west. He served as the Egyptian correspondent of the *Pall Mall Gazette*, the only paper read attentively by Gladstone. His reports were accepted without question by Morley, who hoped for a seat in Parliament through the patronage of Dilke and Chamberlain. With the support of Dilke Colvin took 'exactly six months to get the British Government to act'.[4] Under such combined aristocratic and radical pressure Gladstone was forced to yield ground, to invent successive stratagems for procrastination and then finally to recognize that he had been driven into a corner. Therein he twice used his ultimate weapon, the threat of resignation, but failed to restore his control over the Cabinet. In that extremity he preferred to accept intervention rather than to resign and thereby to lose any chance of success in pacifying Ireland. Thus he accepted the Cabinet decisions of 5 and 20 July for military action to relieve the gnawing sense of the failure of his policy in Ireland. He nevertheless excluded the Canal from his explicit statement of the ends of British policy on 16 August[5] as he had on 14 June. He publicly recognized Egypt and not the Canal as 'the great gate between the Eastern and Western hemispheres'.[6] He remained determined that intervention should not lay the egg of a North African empire. He openly repudiated Hartington, who asserted in the debate of 18 May 1883

[1] F. Harrison, *The Crisis in Egypt*, 19.
[2] A. A. H. Knightbridge, 'Gladstone and the Invasion of Egypt in 1882' (B.Litt. Thesis, University of Oxford, 1960), 103–23.
[3] *The Times*, 3 July, 5i.
[4] (C. F. M. Bell), *Khedives and Pashas* (1884), 235.
[5] Hansard, *Commons Debates*, 16 August, 1940–51.
[6] *The Times*, 10 August, 6ii.

that British action was intended to protect the Canal.[1] 'Our interest in the Suez Canal was not the immediate cause of the war of last year... The warlike operations of last year had assumed a character higher than that of any question of mere interest. It had become a question directly involving the honour and the fame of the British Government.'[2]

On 31 July the Khedive authorized the British occupation of as much of the Canal as was necessary for the expulsion of the rebels. He thereby supplied a legal basis for British action and enabled Northbrook to authorize Hewett to occupy Suez if necessary but forced Lesseps to assume 'the character of an independent potentate'.[3] Hewett did not wait for the arrival of Indian troops as he had been instructed but on 2 August occupied Suez, which had been abandoned first by its European population and then by its Egyptian population, who did not wait to welcome their liberators from military despotism. Britain thereby anticipated the deliberations of the Conference of Constantinople and increased the activity in Constantinople and Cairo for the protection of the Canal. Lesseps protested immediately against the 'flagrant violation of the neutrality of the Canal'.[4] The Egyptian Council of War sent 2,000 horsemen from the Nile Beduin to occupy the Canal in force and decided on 5 August to block the Canal in four places at Ras el Esh, Kantara, Guisr and Chalouf. Arabi secured information of British movements from Lesseps as well as from the telegraph to Syria. He withdrew his garrison and administration on 7 August from Ismailia to Cairo in anticipation of Tewfik's belated proclamation naming him a rebel on 8 August. He thereby entrusted Lesseps with the defence of his own creation and placed the responsibility for any damage to the Canal on the shoulders of the English. Palmer left Suez on 7 August for Nakhl with £3,000–8,000 in English sovereigns to buy the protection of the Canal from the sheikhs of Sinai: he was captured on 10 August and shot the next day by the Haweitat in the Wady Sudr.[5] After the transports began to arrive simultaneously at Alexandria and Suez on 10 August the Admiralty bought on 12 August the Dutch Commercial Establishment in Port Said, which had been closed in 1880 after the death of Prince Henry. That building became Navy House, the first official British foothold in Egypt outside its consulates, and was immediately linked by Pender by cable to Alexandria although not to Suez because of the opposition of Lesseps. Granville invoked the authority of the Convention of 1866 to the directors of the Canal Company on 14 August for the British military operations undertaken with the authority of the Khedive and in alliance with the Sultan. On the same day the Powers signed a protocol at Constantinople for the protection of the Canal by an international naval squadron as a diplomatic warning to Britain against any encroachment upon their rights.

The Khedive informed the authorities in the isthmus on 15 August that

[1] Hansard, *Commons Debates*, 8 May 1883, 308.
[2] Ibid., 27 July 1883, 794, 807.   [3] *The Times*, 2 August 1882, 9i.
[4] Ibid., 8 August, 5vi; 12 August, 4vi.   [5] W. S. Blunt, *Secret History*, 400–12.

the British Admiral and C.-in-C. were authorized to restore order in Egypt and to occupy all points necessary for their military operations against the rebels. Arabi complained that the Canal Company was permitting the passage of munitions through the Canal as well as the construction of fortifications and ordered the coal-heavers out on strike on 15 August, preventing vessels coaling at Port Said and diverting coaling to Malta and Naples. Admiral Hoskins professed to regard Port Said and Lake Timsah as Egyptian waters in which he might act as he liked without regard to the Canal Company, in preparation for the arrival of the transports from England. He repeatedly affirmed on 17 August 'M. de Lesseps is an enemy of England' and threatened to hang Victor de Lesseps from the yard-arm if he interfered with operations when the British fleet entered the Canal.[1] When the first transport arrived at Port Said on 18 August Admiral Hewett in the name of the local sovereign ordered the Canal to be considered closed and a gunboat to anchor in its mouth to prevent entrance, in disregard of the protest of the commander of a French gunboat. Thus the Navy effectively demonstrated that the Canal was not a narrow strait between two open seas as English publicists had been wont to argue. Arabi's troops cut the telegraph along the banks of the waterway on 18 August, so interrupting the passage of steamers. 'The old rogue' Lesseps[2] publicly announced that he would with his own hand kill the first Englishman who dared to land at Ismailia.[3] He so provoked exasperated Englishmen to prove that the Canal was not neutral,[4] that it had cost Egypt £52,000,000 or even £70,000,000[5] and that the Canal Company was an Egyptian company.[6]

Early in the morning of Sunday, 20 August British sailors and marines occupied Port Said and Ismailia.[7] The Arab coal-heavers and the Arab work-men on the Company dredgers and barges immediately went on strike. Lesseps was faced by a far more serious threat than Ismail's coup of 1874. He felt more outraged by the occupation of Ismailia than by that of Suez and con-demned the sailors who had acted 'like barbarians'. Strong Arabist forces were defeated at Nefischa and Chalouf in the first battle of the Canal which was fought for the control of the locks on the Sweet Water Canal.[8] Arabi's Council of War ordered on the evening of 20 August the damming of the Sweet Water Canal and the temporary destruction of the maritime Canal, twenty-four hours too late. Lesseps sent a final telegram to Arabi on 21 August forbidding any attempt 'to block my Canal' and so saved it from destruction. Commercial

---

[1] W. S. Blunt, *My Diaries*, i. 264, 23 January 1896.

[2] Lord Edmond Fitzmaurice, *Earl Granville* (London, Longmans, 1905), ii. 272, Granville to Spencer, 18 August 1882.

[3] Childers, ii. 106, Wolseley to Childers, 19 August 1882.

[4] *The Times*, 8 August 1882, 5 vi; 12 August, 4 vi; 19 August, 4 vi.

[5] Ibid., 11 August 1882, 4 vi, 'What the Suez Canal has cost Egypt'.

[6] Ibid., 9 October 1882, 8 ii.

[7] Ibid., 21 August, 3, 4, 'The War in Egypt. Occupation of Port Said and Ismailia'. J. F. Maurice, *Military History*, 29–32, 'The Seizure of the Maritime Canal by Admirals Hoskins and Hewett'.

[8] *The Times*, 1 September, 6 i–ii, 'The Capture of Chalouf'.

traffic was halted at 11 a.m. on 20 August at the termini and at the passing-stations. A fleet of thirty-two vessels entered the waterway on 21 August[1] and proceeded to land their troops at the single small pier of Ismailia, their base of operations and the one town in Egypt ravaged by malaria. The Company refused to provide pilots or to accept dues and resumed the operation of the Canal after thirty-two hours at 6.40 p.m. on 21 August. After the Indian transports entered the Canal from Suez on 22 August the armies from Bombay and from Portsmouth made their appointed rendezvous in the Canal. On 24 August the traffic of the waterway resumed its normal course while Wolseley was forced to fight his first action earlier than he had anticipated for the possession of the dams across the Sweet Water Canal. Lesseps left Port Said with his son Victor on 27 August, leaving Egyptians with the feeling that he had betrayed the Canal to the English, as in 1849 his pacific promises had permitted the French assault on Rome. Lesseps had been as over-confident in Arabi in 1882 as in Mazzini in 1849. He had misled French politicians as to Arabi's power but had embarrassed Hoskins as much as Oudinot in 1849 and had limited British action to the minimum necessary by his repeated protests and his refusal to take orders from the British or from Tewfik or from any source but the French Government. 'I have remained master of the Canal, where none receive orders not emanating from me.'[2] His defence of the Canal was deemed to have probably forfeited the Company's charter[3] and earned him the bitter hostility of the London press, the applause of the Paris press and the gratitude of the merchants of Amsterdam.

Arabi's hesitation in acting against the Canal completed the destruction of confidence in his military leadership by his own lieutenants. He was systematically betrayed by the sheikh in charge of scouting, Saud el Tihawi of Salhia, who was the grandson of a client sheikh of Bonaparte and had been corrupted by a long association with Lesseps and the French into playing the gentleman and hunting the gazelle. Wolseley had to wait three weeks for his troops to complete disembarkation through the bottleneck of Ismailia but replaced strategic surprise by tactical surprise. Arabi was defeated in twenty minutes at Tel el Kebir and was even accused by Suez shareholders of accepting English bribes to surrender at 'Tel el Bakshish'.[4] The defeat of Arabi marked the defeat of Egypt, the Army, the notables, the fellahin, the ulema, the Sultan, the Ottoman Empire and Islam. The British victory was the victory of the Khedive, the Khedivial party, the Turco-Circassian élite, the Copts, the Jews, the Rothschilds, the bondholders, the Levantines and Christendom. Port Said remained the sole centre of resistance after the fall of Fort Ghemil on 20 September and Damietta on 23 September. There the coal-heavers returned to work by the end of September but refused to work

[1] *The Times*, 23 August, 9 ii.
[2] Ibid., 5 September 1882, 5 iii.   [3] Childers, ii. 129, 15 September 1882.
[4] E. Hennebert, *Les Anglais en Égypte* (Paris, Jouvet, 1884), 72. W. N. Medlicott, 'The Gladstone Government and the Cyprus Convention', *Journal of Modern History* (June 1940), 202.

at night and demanded double pay for their unwilling work during the day. The coaling firms resorted to a lock-out on 27 October, compelling vessels to use their crews for coaling and the coal-heavers to migrate to Damietta. They then imported on 13 November 150 European labourers from Alexandria to replace the Arabs, engaged them to work on the terms refused by the Arabs and secured the protection of a gunboat which was sent to Port Said for the winter.[1] Their action secured a return to work on the employers' terms on 20 November and the resumption of coaling at the usual speed.

Egyptian stocks rose rapidly in London between 15 and 18 September. The Army which had been the hope of Young Egypt and the bearer of the country's destiny was dissolved on 17 September in the hope that order could be maintained by a reformed police. Tewfik returned to Cairo in the baggage of the English on 25 September amid a chill silence broken only by the curses of the Egyptians.[2] Turco-Circassian rule was re-established amid a reign of terror and the rejoicing of the European colonies.[3] 'The English are in Cairo, and the usurers are again in the villages. God is great!'[4] Three-quarters of the cattle of the peasantry, their sole capital, were killed by the rinderpest, which was introduced from Odessa with the sheep and cattle for the British forces and raged from March 1883 amid the administrative anarchy created by the disbandment of the army and police. Blunt helped to save Arabi from the judicial murder which was his intended fate.[5] From prison Arabi recommended to Dufferin a programme of reforms including a general and joint protectorate of the European Powers over the Canal.[6] Dufferin would have preferred to cure all the evils of Egypt through the masterful hand of a Resident and more European officials but was forced by Gladstone to recommend on 6 February 1883 the creation of a reformed native government as the essential preliminary to evacuation. The news of Baring's appointment as British Agent and Consul-General on 21 May 1883 raised the price of Egyptian stock. Baring arrived on 11 September 1883 by special train from Suez to take up his post which was raised in the salary-scale to that of Lisbon, Rio and Tokyo.[7] Egypt became a new sphere of Anglo-Indian administration[8] and a little India[9] under 'Evelyn the First',[10] whose aspirations to an Austinian sovereignty were curbed by the capitulations. D. M. Wallace recognized the total misconception of the Egyptian revolutionary movement by the English Cabinet[11]

[1] *The Times*, 28 October 1882, 11; 14 November, 5i; 21 November, 7iv; 22 November, 4vi; 1 May 1883, 7i.

[2] W. S. Blunt, *India under Ripon* (London, Unwin, 1909), 166.

[3] W. S. Blunt, *Secret History*, 376, 542.

[4] D. M. Wallace, *Egypt and the Egyptian Question* (London, Macmillan, 1883), 293.

[5] Ramm, i. 429, Gladstone to Granville, 22 September 1882.

[6] W. S. Blunt, *Gordon at Khartoum* (London, Swift, 1911), 35.

[7] *The Times*, 12 September 1883, 9ii.

[8] R. L. Tignor, 'The "Indianization" of the Egyptian Administration under British Rule', *American Historical Review* (April 1963), 636–61.

[9] *The Times*, 31 May 1883, 4vi, G. Schweinfurth.

[10] (C. F. M. Bell), *Khedives and Pashas* (1884), 245.

[11] D. M. Wallace, *Egypt and the Egyptian Question* (1883), 104–7, 395–6.

but nevertheless provided the first text in the literature of the justification of British rule in Egypt. The rule of a conqueror over the conquered opposed thenceforward an unavoidable and insurmountable barrier towards any approach to a relationship of equals. British rule was marred by the general ignorance and disdain of Arabic inherited by British officials from the Turkish élite and reinforced by Baring's reputed hatred of Arabic,[1] his preference for Turkish and his love of the classical languages. Baring recognized material interests as the sole bond between governors and governed in Egypt, believed in low taxation as the cure for social discontent,[2] sought to maintain the golden mean of a scientific administration and remained unsure which extremist was the greater nuisance 'the man-and-a-brother or the damned nigger'.[3]

Britain established its control over the key point in the Suez route to the East as the complement to the control which it had established over the Cape between 1795 and 1806. Cyprus became less important than ever while Aden extended its influence through the protectorate established over the Kamaran Islands opposite Massawa after the Italian Government bought Assab from Rubattino on 10 March 1882. The passage of the Canal under the control of the ruler of the seas enabled British power in Egypt to be maintained on a naval basis: British troops could be reduced from 31 October 1883 to a symbolic presence of 6,700 because of the 20,000–30,000 troops which passed through each year on their way to or from India and formed a mobile reserve available at call. Egypt remained in such subordination to India that the Canal soon seemed to have been the cause of the occupation of the Delta.[4] The British route to India nevertheless began to be transformed from a chain of isolated stations into a continuous territorial bloc. The integrity of the Ottoman Empire was shattered. Britain shouldered a far greater burden than that of Cyprus. She became, by conquering a Moslem community, both the supreme object of Turkish hatred and a standing rock of offence to the Mahdi. She had no fear of a Turkish military or naval assault upon the province of the Nile but could no longer rely on Turkey to defend Constantinople against Russia or on Egypt to defend the Sudan against the Mahdi. Moslem hostility provided the core of the tidal wave of indigenous unrest which swept Africa and Asia between 1883 and 1886. Wilfrid Blunt began to move towards the intellectual acceptance of Islam and vented his anger in prophetic pentameters:

> Thou sellest the sad nations to their ruin.
> What hast thou bought? The child within the womb,
> The son of him thou slayest to thy hurting,
> Shall answer thee 'an Empire for thy tomb'. . . .[5]

[1] H. H. Johnston, *The Story of My Life* (London, Chatto, 1923), 127–8.
[2] R. L. Tignor, 'Lord Cromer: Practitioner and Philosopher of Imperialism', *Journal of British Studies* (May 1963), 146.
[3] F. Petrie, *Seventy Years in Archaeology* (London, Low, 1931), 158.
[4] *The Times*, 8 January 1883, 7 vi, C. Beresford, 'Were Arabi's Demands Legitimate?' G. Campbell, 'Reconstruction in Egypt', *Fortnightly Review*, 1 January 1883, 49–50.
[5] W. S. Blunt, *The Wind and the Whirlwind* (London, Paul, 1883), 34, Stanza 81.

The occupation could have been justified with the greatest difficulty as a temporary measure but lost that slender justification in the eyes of the world as it became permanent. It disturbed Russia as well as the U.S.A. and offended Italy but paralysed France with anger at the loss of a second Algeria which contained the intellectual capital of Islam. The end of the Dual Control made France again the defender of Egyptian liberties and therefore the unwearying opponent of any 'reform' of the Egyptian administration under British aegis. The cultural domination of Egypt by France was reinforced by the reform of the Egyptian courts in 1883, which condemned British officials to administer French law in Arabic, to teach French law in English, to argue French law in French and to conduct all their official correspondence in French. The French-language press in Cairo gained a new daily paper from 1882 in Octave Borelli's *Le Bosphore Égyptien*, whose title served as a constant reminder of French interests in the isthmus and whose editorials proved thorns in the flesh of the administration. The loss of the legacy of Bonaparte, Champollion, Lesseps and Joubert inflicted what seemed an intolerable humiliation on the French nation,[1] for which compensation seemed no more conceivable or acceptable than for the loss of Alsace-Lorraine. The rising tide of French nationalism was diverted into anti-English channels, so uniting a society otherwise deeply divided and making perfidious Albion the focus of French hatred in place of brutal Germany. The Anglo-French entente of the 1870s was thus replaced from 1882 by Anglo-French hostility which extended throughout Africa and Asia. France launched the scramble for Africa at Tajura and on the Congo from November 1882,[2] on the Niger from March 1883,[3] in Madagascar from May and in Tunis from June. Thus France sought compensation for the loss of Egypt at the expense of England and of its satellites in Portugal, Belgium and Italy. It accelerated its construction of new empires in the hinterland of Senegal and Tonkin and extended England's frontiers of insecurity around the world. Thus Sir Andrew Clarke, appointed Inspector-General of Fortifications in 1882, found it necessary to recommend the fortification of Sierra Leone, St. Helena, the Cape and Mauritius as well as of Aden, Trincomalee, Singapore and Hong Kong. Within the Mediterranean the occupation of Egypt did not safeguard the route to India but destroyed its security by antagonizing France, Turkey and Russia and creating the threat of a combined French, Russian and Turkish onslaught on the British Fleet in the Mediterranean.[4] Thus it diverted the attention of the Navy from home waters to the impossible task of protecting a country which could

---

[1] M. E. Fournier de Flaix, *L'Indépendance de l'Égypte et le Régime International du Canal de Suez* (Paris, Guillaumin, 1883), 58.

[2] J. Stengers, 'L'Impérialisme Colonial de la Fin du XIXe Siècle: Mythe ou Réalité?', *Journal of African History* (1962), 474, quoting Lesseps to Leopold of Belgium, 12 October 1882.

[3] Ibid., 479–80.

[4] *Engineering*, 6 July–10 August 1883, 1–3, 27–8, 51–4, 80–4, 111–12, 133–4, 'The Story of the Battle of Port Said. A Chapter in the History of the Future'.

not be held with or without naval ascendancy in the Mediterranean. England was simultaneously driven into the diplomatic orbit of Germany,[1] which had no need of Anglo-French cooperation after the Dreikaiserbund was renewed in 1881 and became the great beneficiary by Anglo-French friction and by the Franco-German entente made possible in 1883–5 by the diversion of French interest under Ferry away from the Rhine. The increased dependence of England on the Triple Alliance from 1885 encouraged the Franco-Russian understanding which annihilated the security of both the eastern and western basins of the Mediterranean. In order to appease her foes England was forced to recognize in succession German claims to East Africa, French claims to Morocco and Russian claims to Constantinople. Such was the heavy political price paid between 1885 and 1915 for the victory of Tel el Kebir.

[1] *The Times,* 6 October 1882, 4i, E. A. Bartlett.

17

THE AGITATION FOR A
BRITISH CANAL, 1883

THE occupation of Egypt marked a turning-point in the history of the Canal Company and ushered in an immediate crisis in its fortunes. Its shares began to decline from their peak quotation six days after Tel el Kebir while the Civil Society discovered that its new one-fifth shares had been created to meet a demand which no longer existed. The Canal had twice been closed by warlike operations in defiance of the wishes and protests of the Company. Its staff had been temporarily superseded in the operation of the waterway as they had never been before. It suffered a loss of moral authority in the isthmus even more than in the Delta. It was forced to operate thenceforward under the aegis of British troops so long as they remained in Egypt. The traffic brought by the invasion to Lake Timsah was more than it had seen since the inauguration of the Canal but could afford only temporary and monetary consolation. Ismailia's shipping in 1882 amounted to over 270 steamers of nearly 600,000 tons gross, exclusive of 5,800,000 tons gross of transit traffic. The British Government voluntarily paid £95,000 in dues on the 155 warships and troop transports of 207,885 net register tons and 37,239 troops which had used the Canal without paying between 16 July and 31 August. It refused to pay for the long stay of its ships in Lake Timsah on the ground that the lake was original water. The Company's receipts for August 1882 were adversely affected by the insecurity of the waterway but nevertheless totalled £224,423, or more than in any previous month except April 1882.

Lesseps' future expectations were transformed as profoundly as they had been in 1849. He ceased to visit Egypt and diverted his interests to the Panama Canal, the Kra Canal[1] and the Corinth Canal which would all work to the disadvantage of England, like the Biscay–Mediterranean Canal. He could not pursue any of those schemes with success unless he maintained the profits of the Suez Company at their highest level. His alliance with Arabi had however opposed him to both Tewfik and the British Government. He had found the British admirals flatly hostile and even the British directors insubordinate. He had in effect suffered defeat at Tel el Kebir with Arabi. He lost his faith in the Egyptian Garibaldi but continued to hope for the replacement of Tewfik by Ismail. He was faced by an English desire to exploit their new position as the quasi-suzerain power. He refused even to consider negotiation and hoped only for their expulsion from Egypt. The reverence of the English

---

[1] V. G. Kiernan, 'The Kra Canal Projects of 1882–5: Anglo-French Rivalry in Siam and Malaya', *History* (February 1956), 148–51. Idem, 'Britain, Siam and Malaya: 1875–1885', *Journal of Modern History* (March 1956), 1–20.

for the sanctity of contract placed the Company in a strong legal position in England if not in Egypt. The English were compelled to contemplate the increase of their influence over the Company through indirect expedients such as the acquisition of Port Said, the purchase of more shares in the Company or even the construction of a competing canal. After Tel el Kebir the Lord Chancellor, Selborne, sat up all night composing a memorandum on the legal position of the Canal.[1] Therein he concluded that the British occupation of the Canal on 20 August had been illegal but recommended that the Canal Company should be moved from Paris to Cairo and that its concession should be modified by the Khedive to increase the number of British directors. The Cabinet thereupon appointed on 14 September a committee of Childers and Dilke with Granville as chairman to consider the future status of the Canal in wartime.[2]

Eight days after Tel el Kebir Chenery denounced Lesseps for his 'attitude of an independent sovereign'[3] and alarmed the Company by mentioning the possibility of a second canal. Lesseps retorted on 23 September that he had a monopoly through the grant of exclusive power in the concession.[4] Granville thereupon proposed to Gladstone the purchase of more Canal shares and the creation of faggot-votes.[5] Gladstone was unwilling to consider anything less than 'a clear and complete job'[6] and was deterred by Lesseps' 'front of brass'.[7] Bismarck was delighted to offer any advice embarrassing to France and suggested that the British Government might declare Canal shares trustee stock or even replace Lesseps by an English president such as Admiral Seymour.[8] Chenery immediately denied that England would ever seek the overthrow of Lesseps through such 'a gigantic Stock Exchange intrigue'[9] or that the Canal was an investment promising the security and stability required of trustee stock. Lesseps suggested on 14 October that the English purchase of more Canal shares would be illegal from an international viewpoint and that the British directors would be the last to accept his resignation. He dismissed Chenery's rebuke on 18 November with wounded majesty, 'If I have spoken as a sovereign it is as the sovereign of the Canal'.

The rash of new enterprises proposed for the regeneration of Egypt included new canals in competition with the Suez Canal.[10] Proposals were made for a Damietta–Cairo–Suez Canal by Cairo interests, for an Alexandria–Cairo–Suez Canal by Alexandria interests, for a second Sweet Water Canal for

[1] Roundell Palmer, Earl of Selborne, *Memorials, Part II, Personal and Political, 1865–1895* (London, Macmillan, 1898), ii. 67–8.
[2] A. Ramm (ed.), *The Political Correspondence of Mr. Gladstone and Lord Granville, 1876–1886*, i. 425, 440.
[3] *The Times*, 21 September 1882, 9i; 27 September, 7ii–iii.
[4] Ibid., 27 September, 6i.
[5] Ramm, i. 431, Granville to Gladstone, 25 September 1882.
[6] Ibid., 433, Gladstone to Granville, 27 September 1882.
[7] Ibid., 442–3, Gladstone to Granville, 5 October 1882.
[8] *The Times*, 11 October, 5i.   [9] Ibid., 11 October, 9i.
[10] *The Engineer*, 29 September 1882, 239, 'A Second Suez Canal'.

navigation,[1] for a Delta canal system on the Indian model[2] and for an Akaba Canal.[3] The British directors thought that a second canal would be preferable to a widening of the existing channel and were authorized by Granville on 17 November to discuss the idea with the Company. The Company was thereby encouraged to hope for a fifty-year extension of its concession and for protection from attack under the Stokes–Lesseps 'Treaty of Peace' of 1876. It decided to spend the £920,000 remaining of the £1,200,000 allotted in 1876 for improvement over thirty years. Its recreated Works Committee adopted on 9 January 1883 a more precise version of the scheme of 1876 which included stone-facing of the banks, implicitly precluded any future widening of the channel and postponed to an indefinite date in the future a survey for a second canal. Thus the Company closed its ranks against attack from outside and affirmed that no negotiations for a second canal could be undertaken without the assent and support of the British Government. Lesseps was not succeeded by an English president: even Victor de Lesseps was not succeeded as Principal Agent in Egypt by an Englishman as the British directors had suggested on 28 November. Roualle de Rouville had earned the cross of a chevalier of the Legion of Honour for keeping the services of the Canal intact during the Egyptian crisis. He was promoted on 1 January 1883 from his post as Chief of Transit and Navigation to succeed Victor. Petitions for an alternative canal through Egypt under English control were presented to Granville by the Chamber of Shipping of the United Kingdom on 19 December and by the General Shipowners' Society of London on 22 December, supported by similar memorials from Glasgow on 29 December, North Shields on 11 January and Cardiff on 15 January 1883. By 3 January Suez shares had lost 18·5 per cent of their market price on 18 September 1882. General Rundall's proposal on 24 January[4] for a parallel Sinai Canal from the Serbonian Lake to the Bitter Lake was followed by the resolution of the Chamber of Shipping of the United Kingdom on 14 February in favour of an alternative canal. Lesseps then asserted on 18 February that it would be impossible to construct a second canal outside the main channel of the isthmus and that if a second channel were necessary the Company would excavate it itself.[5]

The strong inter-departmental committee on the Canal had recommended on 4 November 1882 that the maritime powers should agree on free navigation as an alternative to a British protectorate over Egypt or over the Canal, that warships should be free to pass through at all times, that no hostilities should

---

[1] *The Times*, 13 October, 3–4, 'Ship Canals Through Egypt'; 26 December, 4 ii–iii, 'The Proposed Alexandria to Suez Canal'. J. Fowler and B. Baker, 'A Sweet Water Ship Canal Through Egypt', *Nineteenth Century* (January 1883), 166–72.

[2] F. H. Rundall, *The Highway of Egypt, is it the Suez Canal, or any other Route between the Mediterranean and Red Sea?* (London, King, 1882, 14 pp.).

[3] W. Beck, *Our New Waterway to the East by a Valley of Passengers* (London, West, 1882, 18 pp.).

[4] F. H. Rundall, 'The Suez Canal: its Engineering, Civil and Political Aspects', *Journal of the Society of Arts*, 26 January 1883, 206.

[5] *The Times*, 23 February 1883, 5 ii.

take place in Egypt's territorial waters and that no fortifications should be created on the Canal.[1] On those bases Granville's circular letter of 3 January 1883 invited France, Germany, Austria, Italy and Russia to conclude a Treaty on the free navigation of the Canal. Such a Treaty would have infringed on Egyptian independence but would have made no mention of international control or neutralization or any specific restrictions on British freedom of action in Egypt. Granville's proposal to give the occupying power such an advantage over other powers was defeated by the opposition of Germany[2] as well as of France, especially by Bismarck's dislike of a collective guarantee and his wish to exclude warships from the Canal.[3] The proposal encouraged European jurists to assimilate the Canal to the open sea rather than to the land, in the hope to protect it from appropriation, and French and Russian diplomats to contemplate the neutralization of Egypt rather than of the Canal alone.[4] It revealed England's isolation from the Continent and compelled British shipowners to wage their campaign against the Company without the moral approval of Europe.

The dispute between the Company and its clients in 1883 was thus only superficially similar to that of 1872–4 over the Canal tolls. It roused deeper passions in both England and France and effectively ended the compromise based on the share-purchase and the Stokes–Lesseps agreement of 1876. The enormous growth in traffic during the cyclical expansion of 1880–3 made the Canal as important a maritime highway as the Straits of Gibraltar.[5] British shipowners, serving as the carriers of the world as well as of Britain, dominated the traffic more than they were ever able to do again. They employed on the Suez route in 1881 shipping to the capital value of £23,000,000,[6] or one-quarter of the capital invested in the British steam fleet. British tonnage reached its all-time peak proportion of 82·9 per cent of the total tonnage in 1881 and supplied 81·3 per cent of the tonnage in 1882. The Canal had established its superiority over the Cape route and in 1881 carried £104,000,000, or 63·5 per cent, of the £164,000,000 of British trade with the lands eastwards of Suez.[7] British clients thus provided the French shareholders with unprecedented dividends, swelled by the surtax which had been divorced from the increase in traffic by the Stokes–Lesseps agreement and was to be maintained until 31 December 1883. One-ninth of the tolls covered the expenses

---

[1] *Truth*, 5 October 1882, 489ii, H. Labouchere. C. J. Lowe, *The Reluctant Imperialists. British Foreign Policy 1878–1902* (London, Routledge, 1967), 20, Report of Cabinet Committee, 4 November 1882. Ramm, i. 474, Gladstone to Granville, 22 December 1882. Gwynn and Tuckwell, *Dilke*, i. 543–4. R. H. Vetch, *The Life of General Sir Andrew Clarke*, 256.

[2] W. Taffs, *Odo Russell* (1938), 321, Russell to Granville, 12 January 1883. *Documents Diplomatiques Français* 1ère Série, iv. 582, no. 602, Courcel à Duclerc, 16 Janvier 1883.

[3] O. Borelli, *Choses Politiques d'Égypte, 1883–1895* (1895), 557–8.

[4] F. Martens, *La Question Égyptienne et le Droit International* (Bruxelles, Muquardt, 1882), 43–4.

[5] *Nautical Magazine* (July 1883), 499, 'A Second Suez Canal'.

[6] *Le Canal de Suez*, 22 Juillet 1882, 129.

[7] *The Times*, 6 December 1882, 8iv, Liverpool Chamber of Commerce.

of the Company, leaving 89 per cent available in 1882 for allotment to interest, sinking-fund, reserves and profits. The jealousy aroused among shipowners by the vast increase in dividends paid by the Company was heightened by the fall in freights since 1880 and transformed their view of the Canal and the Company. Lesseps in their jaundiced vision appeared as a successful speculator rather than as a benefactor of the world. The Canal seemed to be less a new channel for commerce than a fiscal barrier, 'the great toll-gate between the East and the West'.[1] The Suez Canal tonnage certificate was seen as an invention for the sole benefit of the Canal Company and a source of infinite annoyance and loss to shipowners.[2] Canal dues formed 20–25 per cent of the gross freight of a steamer on a round voyage to India[3] and appeared as blackmail of 4s. on every ton of coal and 1s. on every quarter of Indian wheat[4] rather than as a modest fee for the use of a great utility. Such dues were most burdensome to the small shipowners. The large shipowners recognized that high dues were paid by the consumer and protected their trade from their smaller rivals: they wanted a second channel which would tap the high profits of the Canal Company without any risk and extend enormously the facilities for existing lines without increasing competition. Both large and small shipowners were united in opposition to the inadequacy of the Canal as a one-way rather than a two-way channel under the plan of 1859. They were reluctant to make use of the Cape route which would have necessitated the rebuilding of their fleets and raised their costs of operation to unprofitable levels. They complained that the Canal was too narrow in width, that it could only be used during the hours of daylight and that it had not been improved in proportion to the increase in traffic. The increase in the clients of the waterway from a daily average of $1\frac{1}{2}$ ships in 1870 to one of 8 in 1882 created growing congestion in a single-file ditch. The delay in transit was further increased by the imposition of quarantine restrictions in 1881. Thus the Company could not properly fulfil its function of welcoming the arriving client and speeding the departing client, who paid tolls on tonnage rather than on the time of transit.

The agitation against the Company was as much non-economic as economic in its origin, originating in the national humiliation of the successful opening of the Canal fourteen years earlier and in the irritation aroused by Lesseps' Arabist alliance. Britain had made the Canal into an imperial highway, had supplied 60 per cent of the soldiers using it in 1882 and had acquired a new power over the Canal Company by its conquest of Egypt. The real burden of the English complaints against the Company was that it was a French company which was as centralized as a French Government Department and would not decentralize its administration from the sacred heart of Paris nor make any reasonable concessions to its foreign clients. The Company

---

[1] G. W. Vyse, *Egypt: Political, Financial and Strategical* (London, Allen, 1882), 210.
[2] *The Times*, 24 May 1883, 11 ii, Angier Brothers.
[3] Ibid., 21 July 1883, 13 ii, T. V. S. Angier.
[4] Ibid., 14 July 1883, 10 iii–iv, John Glover.

employed only 3 English pilots out of 117 and employed many other pilots who could speak no English. It gave preference to the steamers of the Messageries over those of the P. & O. and to French warships over British troopships. It was alleged to deliver arbitrary and biased judgments in disputes and to permit its officials to accept bribes from British captains.[1] Above all, it imposed taxation without representation and gave its British clients no voice in management. The shipping interest attacked the three British directors as a 'triumvirate of dummies' and mere tools of a dictator and despot.[2] It demanded that England should possess 'the key of the Water Avenue that leads to her Eastern Empire'[3] and create an independent Suez Canal as a national canal under an English company which would be able to tap the lucrative monopoly profits of the existing 'mismanaged and exorbitant French ditch'.[4] It enjoyed the support of the imperial sentiment which inspired the erection of statues to Drake at Tavistock in 1883 and at Plymouth in 1884. It even inspired Edwin Arnold to claim the Canal for England as much as the mail 'Bridge to Asia' built by Waghorn[5] and so exaggerated the importance of the waterway to England. T. H. Farrer revealed the vast gulf between the economic and the military significance of the Canal[6] and so revenged the Free Trader William Rathbone for the aspersions cast by Chenery in 1882.[7] Farrer estimated that the Canal was used in 1880 by 8·7 per cent of the total value of British imports and exports (or barely 10 per cent, including bullion) and in 1881 by 11–12 per cent thereof (or 12·9 per cent according to the Liverpool Chamber of Commerce). He concluded that 'the Canal does not appear to have given any great stimulus to trade', that the material gain had gone to the shareholders of the Canal Company while the material loss had been borne by English capitalists as well as by English shipowners and that the Canal was fivefold as important in the foreign trade of India as in that of Britain.[6] Chenery retorted that the Canal, if unimportant in 1883, was nevertheless 'the pivot of the larger relations of the future' as the direct route to the markets of the future in the teeming regions of the East.[8]

The Canal Company clung to its legal rights as enshrined in the concession.

---

[1] Hansard, *Commons Debates*, 31 July 1883, 1144–5, E. A. Bartlett.

[2] *The Times*, 30 May 1883, 13 ii; 14 June, 12 ii; 21 July, 13 ii; 18 August, 8 iii–iv.

[3] F. H. Rundall, 'The Suez Canal', *Journal of the Society of Arts*, 26 January 1883, 208.

[4] *The Graphic*, 4 August 1883, 110 i, 'The Suez Canal Debate'.

[5] *Daily Telegraph*, 19 May 1883, 5 iii–iv, viii. *The Times*, 31 May 1884, 6 ii.

[6] T. H. Farrer, *Return Showing What Proportion of the Trade of the United Kingdom with the East goes through the Suez Canal, and what Proportion round the Cape. Return to an Order of the Honourable the House of Commons dated 1 December 1882 (Mr. Rathbone)* (C-41 of 1883), 4, 6, 8.

[7] *The Times*, 27 July 1882, 9 iii, 'Of Mr Rathbone's singular and almost whimsical attempt to disparage the importance to England of the Suez Canal, both in a commercial and a military sense, it is sufficient, perhaps, to say that the relevancy of his arguments was as little apparent as their cogency.'

[8] Ibid., 21 February 1883, 9 iii–iv. The Return was also criticized by G. Anderson in the Commons on 2 March 1883 and by Joseph Rabino in the *Journal of the Statistical Society*, 14 June 1887, 536–40.

It defended the net profits of 16 per cent on the nominal value of its shares as a legitimate return to its shareholders on their investment and the transit dues as a tax of less than 1 per cent of the value of the goods in transit while commerce saved 2 per cent in insurance charges. It enjoyed more support from French sentiment in 1883 than in 1874. France's Canal tonnage had grown very slowly since 1876 so that its share of the total had declined from an average of 8·3 per cent in 1870–80 to 4·8 per cent in 1881. Thereafter French tonnage increased by the unprecedented rates of 44 per cent in 1882 and 95 per cent in 1883 as new French lines were begun to the English colonial ports of Sydney, Calcutta, Hong Kong and Basra and the French share of the total tonnage rose from 5·6 per cent in 1882 to 9·7 per cent in 1883. The Canal united the pecuniary and the sentimental interests of the French because it reminded France of its greatest achievement in defiance of England. Lesseps had given a new hostage to the Bourse in the Panama Canal Company, so widening the circle of small investors in his enterprises. He could not halt the glorious financial career of the Suez Company without sacrificing the dream of a dynasty of Lesseps astride the main trade-routes of the world. He had won the support of the press and acceptance by the reviving spirit of a great nation as the most illustrious living Frenchman while Paris praised Lesseps' history of his own enterprise[1] and considered no other work so essentially French or so fundamentally popular as the Canal.[2]

The campaign against the Company was resumed when two deputations met Granville at the Foreign Office on 26 April. The deputation from the Associated Chambers of Commerce under its president C. J. Monk, Liberal M.P. for Gloucester, requested increased Government representation in the Suez Canal Company and a second canal only as a last resort. The deputation from the Chamber of Shipping of the United Kingdom under its president James Laing, whose father had become a shipbuilder at Sunderland in 1793, requested a new and British Canal, which Chenery welcomed as 'our new Indian highway' under British control.[3] As the Paris Bourse recognized the onset of a new attack by the traditional foe Suez shares declined steadily by 12·2 per cent between 26 April and 1 May. Lesseps made overtures on 30 April for the opening of negotiations but held out no hope of a second canal, adding on 4 May that he cared as little as the English would if French merchants asked for a tariff reduction on the South-Eastern Railway. He secured the recognition of the Company's monopoly on 7 May by the legal advisers to the Government of Egypt led by Octave Borelli. Thereupon shipowners representing 3,000,000 tons of shipping using the Canal met in London with

---

[1] L. Alloury, *Comment s'est fait le Canal de Suez. Pages d'Histoire Contemporaine recueillies sur les documents de M. de Lesseps* (Paris, Challamel, 1882). B. Girard, 'L'Egypte en 1882. Le canal maritime de Suez', *Revue Maritime* (Août 1883), 423–83.

[2] *The Times*, 7 May 1883, 5iii; 12 May, 8i, 'France and the Suez Canal'.

[3] Ibid., 27 April 1883, 9–10. E. C. P. Hull, *England and the Suez Canal: the Situation Reviewed. A Brief Statement showing that a Parallel British Canal has now become an absolute necessity* (London, Spottiswoode, 1883, 72 pp.).

five M.P.s under the presidency of Laing and formed on 10 May the Association of Steamship Owners Trading with the East. Stephen Ralli, a French merchant and president of the Société Nationale Française de Londres, raised the only voice in favour of negotiation with the Company in order to demand half of the seats on the board of directors for the English, alternate meetings of the board in London and Paris and the substantial widening of the Canal. The meeting assumed that both political parties had committed themselves respectively in 1875 and in 1882 to the importance of the Canal to England and hoped that the British Government might take up the same shareholding in a British canal company as it held in the French company. Resolutions proposed by Thomas Sutherland and John Pender in favour of another canal were passed with only Ralli in opposition. John Glover, George Elliot, Sutherland and Pender were elected to the executive committee of the Association with Laing as chairman. After Chenery dismissed Lesseps' claim to a monopoly as a preposterous, mischievous, monstrous, intolerable perpetuity in restraint of trade,[1] T. E. Holland, the Chichele Professor of International Law at Oxford since 1874, made available his helpful interpretation on 11 May of 'exclusive power' as an exclusive right to form a Suez Canal Company but not as an exclusion of competition to the Company,[2] encouraging the Association to seek and find the backing of legal advice against Lesseps. The difficulty of passing through the Canal within a reasonable time led to the announcement of earlier departures by the P. & O. on 11 May and by the British India Line on 15 May so as to reinforce the Association's arguments.

An array of potential competitors to the Canal appeared in order to profit by the sense of injustice under which British shipowners laboured and to provide new outlets for British capital seeking investment. Those schemes added to the Damietta–Red Sea Canal and the Alexandria–Suez Sweet Water Canal proposed after Tel el Kebir a Keneh–Kosseir Railway,[3] a Euphrates Valley Railway[4] and a Palestine Canal.[5] The railway schemes would have necessitated the double transhipment of merchandise. The canal schemes would have required an enormous capital investment, two new entrance-ports and thrice as much excavation as the Suez Canal. They would have necessitated the consent, cooperation and financial assistance of the British Government and crystallized British political commitments in the Levant whilst exposing the leading sea-power in the world to overland attack by any great land-power. None of those schemes came within measurable distance of being properly promoted. None could serve the shipping interest as an effective

[1] *The Times*, 11 May 1883, 9iv.
[2] Ibid., 14 May, 12i. T. E. Holland, 'The International Position of the Suez Canal', *Fortnightly Review*, 1 July 1883, 39–49, reprinted in *Studies in International Law* (Oxford, Clarendon Press, 1898), 270–93.
[3] D. M. Wallace, *Egypt and the Egyptian Question* (1883), 49–50.
[4] W. Campbell, 'Postal Communication with the East', *Proceedings of the Royal Colonial Institute*, 8 May 1883. *The Times*, 9 May 1883, 6vi, W. P. Andrew. Hansard, *Lords Debates*, 12 and 20 July 1883, Lord Lamington.
[5] *The Times*, 17 May 1883, 10iv, 'A Proposed Palestine Channel'.

substitute for the Canal or even as a lever with which to bend the Canal Company to its will. The importance of the Canal was further increased when cholera appeared at Port Said on 23 June and the mails reaching Suez on 9 July abandoned the Suez–Alexandria Railway to pass direct through the Canal without communication with the shore.

Gladstone decided on 10–12 May to begin negotiations with Lesseps for lower dues rather than for an increased share in management[1] and authorized the British directors to begin negotiations with the Company for a substantial reduction in tolls in return for political help to secure the prolongation of the Company's concession. The beginning of conversations on 20 May aroused fears in England that the Government might make a bad bargain by not first consulting the shipping interest. Angier Brothers expressed the hope on 23 May[2] that the Government would make no hasty agreement with Lesseps and set out the demands of the shipowners for the reduction of dues preliminary to any second channel: the predominance of British control of the existing Canal, the establishment of the board offices of one Canal in London; the abolition of the pilotage charges, the Suez Canal tonnage certificate and the quarantine regulations; the reduction of dues to a maximum of 5s. per net register ton with a rebate thereon for a round voyage; the institution of a board of arbitration, half composed of competent Englishmen, for cases of accidents in and damage to the canals.[3] Chenery added his own warning to the Government and dismissed the 1854 concession as a bit of parchment conveying powers which the donor, as the tributary governor of a province with no independent existence, had never possessed and forming 'this gigantic claim, this unheard of embargo upon the activity of man, this tremendous mortgage upon the future'.[4] He urged Lesseps to recognize that 'the thing he has constructed is too great, too successful and of an influence too commanding over the affairs of the world to be treated as a mere joint-stock company'.[4] 'England's road to and from India—nay, the traffic between Europe and the Eastern Hemisphere—is too big a thing to be left to the will, pleasure, caprice or even to the justice, of any individual, however eminent or meritorious, or even to be settled so as to suit shipowners only. For England indeed it is the essence of the Eastern Question. If we ever had a British interest in that this is it, and its solution is now in our own hands.'[5]

At the meeting of shareholders on 4 June Lesseps ranked the convention of 1876 as second only to the concession itself, dismissed the English protests as 'sterile agitation' worked up by speculators and justified the right of the shareholders to their dividends by the sacrifice of the first investors who had ruined themselves and by the very magnitude of the service rendered to the world in the construction of the waterway. He hinted that a dividend level of

[1] Ramm, ii. 49, Gladstone to Granville, 13 May 1883.
[2] *The Times*, 24 May 1883, 11 ii.
[3] Ibid.   [4] Ibid., 2 June 1883, 11 iv.
[5] Ibid., 2 June, 12 vi, J. Glover, 'The Second Suez Canal—Who Shall Make It?'

20 per cent might justify concessions to the shipowners.[1] The Association of Steamship Owners Trading with the East, having increased its representation to 4,000,000 tons from the original 3,000,000 tons of shipping, felt most dissatisfied with Lesseps' remarks and with the open alliance between the British directors and the Canal Company which brought on England the odium attached to the Company by Egyptians as 'a gigantic job by which their country was robbed'.[2] That condemnation was mitigated by Ismail when he passed through Paris on 25 June en route to London in quest of the succession to Tewfik. 'I think that when I gave the concession, I did the worst thing for myself, and the most useful thing for Egypt, for England and for France who has had the glory of carrying it out.'[3] The ex-Khedive confessed himself bewildered by the dispute whether the Canal was French or English. 'It is neither French nor English, it is Egyptian. The reversion belongs to Egypt, not merely because at the expiration of the concession it reverts to Egypt, but because it is made on her soil, her inalienable soil.'[3]

The satisfactory progress of negotiations with the British directors encouraged Lesseps to announce on 21 June his intention to introduce electric light on the Canal. The bases of an understanding between the Government and the Company were announced by the Company on 5 July and by Childers in the Commons on 11 July. Under the agreement of 10 July a second canal was to be constructed parallel to the first and completed by 1888 if possible. Tolls were to be reduced on a sliding-scale in proportion to the increase in dividends beyond 100 francs, or 21 per cent on the nominal value of the share, and decreased to 5 francs per ton in the year after 51 per cent thereon was paid in dividend. The British Government was to lend its good offices to secure land for the construction of the second canal, authority to extend the Sweet Water Canal to Port Said, and the prolongation of the Company's concession by twenty years so as to make a new term of ninety-nine years from the completion of the second canal. The Government was also to lend the Company £8,000,000 at 3¼ per cent for fifty years. Childers was competent in the field of finance, shipping and communications as the great-great-grandson of the financier Sampson Gideon, as the chairman of the Royal Mail Steam Packet Company in 1874–80 and as the minister responsible for the installation of the telephone in Government offices in 1880. He had been concerned with the Suez Canal since 1869 but was ill-informed on the subject, undertook no preparatory presentation of papers and offered no explanation of the terms of the agreement. He announced the agreement on the first anniversary of the bombardment of the forts of Alexandria, coincident with the news of the French bombardment of Tamatave in Madagascar, to an ominously cold reception and to a flurry of questions, more from Liberals than from Conservatives. The

[1] *The Times*, 5 June, 6 i–iii.
[2] Ibid., 4 June, 5 vi–6 i, O. C. Waterfield, 'The Projected Suez Canal'. O. C. Waterfield, 'The Negotiations with M. de Lesseps', *Fortnightly Review* (August 1883), 171.
[3] *The Times*, 28 June, 5 ii.

demand for Suez shares, thitherto active in the City, fell off immediately on the news of the terms.

The agreement made what seemed excessive concessions to the Canal Company and to France in relation to the proprietary rights acquired by the English occupation of Egypt. It was the work of the Government and not of private commercial interests and made substantial economic sacrifices for political motives. It coincided with the appointment as the new French ambassador to London of Waddington, who had made the English alliance the pivot of his foreign policy in 1877–9. It was intended to renew the Anglo-French Entente whose rupture ended the tunneling under the Channel at Sangatte on 18 March and at Dover on 1 July. It might also enable Gladstone to repeat Disraeli's stroke of 1875 in the hope of a parliamentary vote of £8,000,000.[1] The agreement delighted the French and encouraged Suez shareholders to hope for a capitalization similar and perhaps superior to that of British Consols.[2] The Canal Company had made no real concessions and had refused to transfer its domicile to England, to admit English directors in preponderant numbers or to reduce tolls at any earlier time or to any greater extent. The Company had even asked that the loan should be amortized out of the dividends due to the British Government, a request which the British directors refused. The agreement gave the Company all that it wanted, together with effective insurance against accidents, bad management or reckless expenditure. It recognized implicitly the exclusive powers claimed by Lesseps and granted the Company the patronage and protection of the new paramount power in Egypt. It proposed to recognize the Company's absolute and permanent supremacy, to double its power and property and to sacrifice British freedom of action for the future. It provided English capital for the construction of a second canal which would be through foreign soil but would remain under French control for a further twenty years after 1968. It enabled the Company to avoid an appeal to the French capital market in accordance with the wish of the French Government[3] and provided English capital at an interest-rate which could not have been secured in any capital market, was absurdly low for a foreign investment and caused Gladstone grave concern. That interest-rate was most probably as much as $1\frac{1}{4}$ per cent below that which the Company would have had to pay in the market,[4] so extending a concealed subsidy of £100,000 per annum, or £2,500,000 over twenty-five years. The proposed reduction of rates was not as substantial as desired by Granville but was so small, gradual and remote, beginning in 1886, as to be inoperative and

[1] Ramm, ii. 65–8, Gladstone to Granville, 21 July 1883.

[2] *The Times*, 14 July 1883 quoting *Journal des Débats* of 13 July.

[3] *Documents Diplomatiques Français*, 1ère Série, v, 69, no. 59, D'Aunay à Challemel-Lacour, 8, Juillet 1883.

[4] The differential in interest between the $3\frac{1}{4}$ per cent on the proposed loan and the rate at which the Company could raise money was estimated at $1\frac{3}{4}$ per cent, or £140,000 per annum, by Childers and Ralli but at only $\frac{1}{2}$ per cent, or £40,000 per annum, by Gladstone. *The Times*, 14 July 1883, 10ii, Childers; 19 July, 10iv, Ralli. Ramm, ii. 66, Gladstone to Granville, 21 July 1883.

worthless. Dues were to be reduced immediately only on ships in ballast (i.e. on 10 per cent of the tonnage) from 1 January 1884. Worst of all, the whole concession was to be prolonged in return for the payment of a niggardly 1 per cent share in the profits to the Government of Egypt. The agreement provoked the protest of the Turkish ambassador on 18 July, treated the great shipping interest with studied contumely and offended the financial interests excluded from the profits of the £8,000,000 loan, which it was intended to raise from the Post Office Savings Bank as in 1876. It made no fundamental alteration in the balance of power between Britain and the Company. It secured only the quick and cheap construction of a second canal but paid no homage to the dream of an English canal cut through Egyptian soil, 2,000 miles from Beachy Head. It failed to satisfy the new expectations aroused in shipping and commercial circles after Tel el Kebir when sectional interests were emerging in strength in Parliament.

Public opinion opposed the Government as much as it had supported it in 1875. Between 12 and 30 July thirty-two protest meetings were held throughout the country by associations of shipowners and by Chambers of Commerce while questions in the Commons averaged eight every day, mainly from the Conservative benches because the issue immediately became a party question. The Conservative opposition, which had been placed at a disadvantage by the Ministry's success in securing its vote of war-credit in 1882 and in winning a military victory for the nation, found in the Canal issue a golden opportunity to harass the Government. It took up the cause of the shipowners, who were not content to follow the Duke of Manchester's suggestion that they should combine to send their outward-bound ships round the Cape, as a protest-strike against the Company in emulation of the working-classes, and so reduce British shipping through the Canal by a half and the Company's receipts by three-eighths.[1] It recognized the national appeal of a national canal built under British influence by British subjects with British capital as more than a question for shipowners. 'It is essentially a national one, and its proper solution will affect very largely the well-being of the working and labouring classes of the country.'[2] Thereby the Conservatives won the support of many chambers of commerce and compelled a leading supporter of the Government to urge that the balance of the revenues derived from the Suez shares from 1894 should in all justice be returned to the shipowners.[3] The agitation was regarded as justifiable in Germany[4] but delayed agreement with a suspicious France over the Madagascar incident. 'The object of the Gallophobes across the Straits seems to us to be Suez more than Madagascar.'[5]

Gladstone was dismayed by the national outburst of 'pride, greed, ignorance

---

[1] *The Times*, 23 July 1883, 12 ii.

[2] Ibid., 27 July, 2 i, W. T. Marriott, Liberal M.P. for Brighton.

[3] R. Tangye, *Reminiscences of Travel in Australia America & Egypt* (London, Low, 1883), 253.

[4] *The Times*, 18 July 1883, 7 ii–iii.

[5] Ibid., 18 July 1883, 7 ii, quoting *Le Temps* of 17 July.

and passion'[1] but remained determined not to sacrifice Lesseps to the shipowners or to the Conservatives. His Administration was placed at a disadvantage in negotiations with the Company by the Government's shareholding in the Company, by its public profession of faith in an early evacuation of Egypt and by its respect for the sanctity of contract which was so important to the British in other lands. Gladstone therefore asserted in the Commons on 12 July that Lesseps held 'an exclusive right to make a Canal, as far as the Isthmus of Suez is concerned'.[2] That recognition of Lesseps' claim to a monopoly, buttressed by the advice of the Lord Chancellor and the Law Officers of the Crown, led the shipowners, lawyers and Conservatives to concentrate their attack on the Company's monopoly as a right non-existent in law or in fact, never conceded in 1854 nor claimed before 1872 and incapable of assertion against the State. 'Exclusive power', as Mark Napier stressed, had a magical but not a legal importance and was printed by the directors of the Company in type of extraordinary size and clearness, like a brilliant beacon on a dangerous shore.[3] Salisbury in a professedly unpremeditated denunciation of 'this improvident Agreement' on 17 July appealed to 'the natural access to means of transit which as a prima facie right is possessed by the commerce of the world' and doubted the competence of any Sultan or Khedive 'to make an Agreement that would debar Nations from the natural right of passage across the Isthmus of Suez for the commerce of the world' and would forbid the British 'by the aid of British capital to secure a British Canal from sea to sea'.[4] Salisbury's exaltation of the rights of commerce over the rights of sovereignty astounded Selborne, Gladstone and T. J. Lawrence, Deputy Professor of International Law at Cambridge, as well as all upholders of the rights of property.[5] At a special meeting of the London Chamber of Commerce on 18 July a Royal Commission of Enquiry was urged into Lesseps' claim to a monopoly. The Conservative M.P. Alderman W. J. R. Cotton thought that Lesseps could not expect to retain proprietorship of the Canal for ever as his own if an inventor was grudgingly allowed a patent for only fourteen years. 'A second Suez Canal ought to be carried out in English interests and in English interests only. (Cheers.) Ostensibly—at least, it is so to my mind—Egypt is England's property. ("Oh").'[6] Such a revival of 'the antiquated principles of Tartar international law'[7] led Morley to support a German proposal for a Danube Commission for the Suez Canal,[8] provoked Lesseps to reassert on 20 July the Company's claims to an exclusive monopoly for ninety-nine years and aroused more concern in England than in the colonies.

[1] Ramm, ii. 64, Gladstone to Granville, 14 July 1883.
[2] Hansard, *Commons Debates*, 12 July 1883, 1231–2, Gladstone.
[3] *The Times*, 17 July 1883, 4iii–vi; 18 July 1883, 4–5.
[4] Hansard, *Lords Debates*, 17 July 1883, 1671–2.
[5] *The Spectator*, 21 July 1883, 922, 'The Ethics of Neo-Toryism'.
[6] *The Times*, 19 July 1883, 10iii.
[7] D. M. Wallace, *Egypt and the Egyptian Question* (1883), 512.
[8] *Pall Mall Gazette*, 18 July 1883, 1, 'The Abating Storm'; 19 July 1883, 1, 'The Canal in the City'.

The crisis became the first Canal crisis to arouse the feeling of the Empire against the Company. Sir Julius Vogel, the ex-Premier and Agent-General of New Zealand, suggested on 14 July the expropriation of the Company by the Government of Egypt in the name of the superiority of the State to private interests and on the precedent of the purchase of the lines of the telegraph companies.[1] Sir Thomas McIlwraith, the Premier of Queensland, cabled his intense dissatisfaction with the agreement to London on 18 July. In the Cape House of Assembly Rhodes reflected the contemporary English exaggeration of the importance of the Canal by describing Bechuanaland on 18 August as 'the Suez Canal of the trade of this country, the key of its road to the interior'.[2] From Port Said George Royle, the agent of the P. & O., returned on 20 July a formidable indictment of the administrative 'blackmail' of the Company.[3] After thirteen days of growing protest and no approval even from Manchester[4] or Birmingham[5] Gladstone announced on 23 July without debate or discussion the withdrawal of the Agreement of 10 July in order to preserve the supremacy of the Cabinet in the Commons. He again explicitly recognized the monopoly of 'this great Canal Company' and disowned Salisbury, Cotton & Co. who asserted English dominion over the waterway of the isthmus. Thus he defended the Canal Company's monopoly of the land against the interests of British commerce, shipping and industry. He then rebuked the shipowners and Conservatives who exaggerated the importance of the Canal to England by denying that the British interest in the Canal had been the immediate cause of the war of 1882. Gladstone, whose father had sent the first ship from Liverpool to India in 1814, amplified Farrer's judgment that the Canal was far more important to India than to England in both the moral and the material sense. 'For India the Suez Canal is a connecting link between herself and the centre of power—the centre of the moral, social and political power of the world.'[6] Northcote's motion denying Lesseps' claim to a monopoly received, however, 183 votes to 282 on 30 July, reducing the normal Government majority of 130 to 99. The Liberal shipowners Norwood, Palmer and Monk rescued the Government from defeat but only by rejecting Gladstone's strict interpretation of the monopoly. Norwood suggested an equal partnership of French and English in the administration of the Canal Company on the model of the Crimean alliance against Russia. 'England and France had stood shoulder to shoulder on the Alma heights, and it would be a grander sight to see them jointly protecting a maritime highway that would last as long as the fabric of the Globe.'[7]

[1] *The Times*, 16 July 1883, 8 iii.

[2] 'Vindex' (J. Verschoyle), *Cecil Rhodes. His Political Life and Speeches 1881–1900* (London, Chapman, 1900), 62.

[3] *The Times*, 23 July 1883, 5 ii–iii.   [4] *Manchester Guardian*, 17 July 1883, 7 i–iii.

[5] *The Times*, 18 July, 13 v.

[6] Hansard, *Commons Debates*, 27 July 1883, 808, Gladstone. *The Times*, 30 July 1883, 10 i, 'India and the Suez Canal'.

[7] Hansard, *Commons Debates*, 30 July 1883, 984, C. M. Norwood.

The assault on the Company's monopoly turned English opinion against Lesseps and his claims to equitable treatment.[1] In April 1883 Lesseps had been ranked for his vitality with others of seventy and eighty years of age such as the Emperor William, Moltke, Hugo, Ranke and Gladstone:[2] in July he had become a representative captain of industry of the sensate civilization of the age, a realist Iago, a Sancho Panza rather than a Don Quixote and 'the Adam of the terrestrial Eden' of Paris. 'Both as egotist and as patriot, M. de Lesseps bodies forth the age... His energy, his tact, his indomitable perseverance, his courage are all tainted with selfishness. And this selfishness is of the senses, is sensuous and luxurious.'[3] Lesseps acted to maintain his monopoly and summoned Lemasson on 20 July to come to Paris immediately and to bring with him plans for a second canal. Gladstone, however, ordered the British directors on 7 August to abstain from making any proposals to the board of the Canal Company.[4] He then expressed on 20 August the determination of the Government not to renew negotiations and recommended the trading interests to open up direct communications with the Company, as meeting the Company's expressed desire. Lesseps' monopoly could not be circumvented, not even by a canal from the Mediterranean linked to another canal from the Red Sea by a quarter-mile of ship-railway[5] rather than by a continuous cut. Captain Rice's Report to the Admiralty on 28 August alleged that only 20 of the 117 pilots were competent and denounced the inefficiency and partiality of the Company's administration. 'English commerce is controlled by a French Company.'[6] That report inspired the Company to decide on 4 September to reduce the toll on ships in ballast from 1 January 1884, as in the abortive agreement of 10 July, a concession which benefited French ships more than English because of the French lack of exports.

Gladstone's reaffirmation of the Company's monopoly encouraged the revival of the Akaba Canal first suggested in 1855, either with locks as proposed in May 1883 by the Duke of Marlborough, the Duke of Sutherland and Admiral Inglefield, or without locks, as proposed on 17 August by Captain G. M. F. Molesworth.[7] The shift of interest from Egypt to Palestine blended with the apocalyptic vision of 1876, the imperial aspirations of 1878 and the general reverence for the Holy Land of Anglicans, British Israelites, engineers, statisticians and soldier-ascetics such as Gordon[8] and Kitchener. A Jordan Valley Canal would enable England to abandon Egypt to self-government, so liberating her foreign policy and her conscience. It would also permit her to recognize the pluck and energy of Lesseps by leaving to him and his successors

[1] R. T. Reid, 'The Suez Canal Question', *Contemporary Review* (August 1883), 163.
[2] *The Times*, 17 April 1883, 9iv.
[3] *The Spectator*, 28 July 1883, 958ii, 'M. Ferdinand de Lesseps'.
[4] Ramm, ii. 73, Gladstone to Granville, 7 August 1883.
[5] *The Times*, 25 August 1883, 7v, C. M. Ramus.
[6] Ibid., 20 September 1883, 9ii.
[7] Ibid., 18 August 1883, 7vi, 'A Jordan Canal'; 20 August, 4v; 7 September, 8iv; 11 September, 3iv; 15 September, 11v.
[8] H. W. Gordon, *Charles George Gordon* (1886), 283–4.

in perpetuity the existing Suez Canal. Above all, it might be crowned by the transfer of the capital of the British Empire to the very centre of the world in the new seaport, naval base and Jewish colony of Jerusalem.[1] It would however have to cross a watershed 780 feet above sea-level at a cost of 32 times as much per mile as the Suez Canal[2] and totalling some £223,000,000[3] rather than the £8,000,000 estimated by Molesworth. Its creation would submerge the Lake of Galilee, the River Jordan and 300 square miles of the Holy Land in an inland sea. It would also bring the pilgrim road to Mecca within the range of infidel warships and might well deprive the Ottoman Empire of Syria, as the Suez Canal seemed to have cost it Egypt. The hopes which it embodied were nevertheless strong enough to revive the idea of the Euphrates Valley Railway.[4] The British Association discussed plans for a Palestine Canal on 21[5] and 25[6] September while the Palestine Exploration Fund subsidized a survey of the Canal's route via the Wadi Araba by Kitchener who left Suez on 20 November 1883.

The economist Mongrédien sought to remedy the disproportion between the 10 British votes and the 8,400 French and Continental votes at the annual meeting of shareholders through his suggestion for the transfer of the Government's shares to 700 private persons in lots of 250 shares each through the medium of a private limited company, a Suez Canal Syndicate Limited,[7] a proposal which attracted Granville as much as in 1882 but neither Gladstone nor Derby.[8] The complete purchase of the Company for £30,000,000 was also urged in British interests.[9] The Association of Steamship Owners Trading to the East wrote a stiff letter to Granville on 12 October, raising again the question of a second canal, but was recommended on 30 October to enter into direct negotiations with the Company as the agency for any operations in the isthmus. The Association was as reluctant as Chenery to recognize the very special position of the Company. 'They are tenants with fixity of tenure and unquestioned right to compensation for disturbance, but they are not tenants, ground landlords, lords of the manor and sovereigns all in one.'[10] Lesseps was advised by the British directors on the instructions of Gladstone to enter into

---

[1] *The Future Capital of the British Empire. A Possible Solution of the Suez Canal and Eastern Questions. A Political Study by a Conservative-Radical* (London, Ridgway, 1883), 7–12.

[2] *The Times*, 22 September 1883, 6 ii, Canon H. B. Tristram.

[3] C. R. Conder, 'The Canal Dilemma', *Blackwood's Edinburgh Magazine* (September 1883), 278.

[4] *Report of the Fifty-Third Meeting of the British Association in September 1883* (London, Murray, 1884), 632–3, J. B. Fell, 'On the Euphrates Valley Railway'. *The Times*, 21 September 1883, 5v. J. B. Fell, 'The Euphrates Valley Railway as an Alternative Route to India', *Journal of the Society of Arts*, 28 September 1883.

[5] *Report of the Fifty-Third Meeting of the British Association*, 617–18, C. Walford, 'On the Palestine Channel and Canal Scheme'. *The Times*, 22 September 1883, 6 i–ii.

[6] *The Times*, 26 September 1883, 6 iv.

[7] A. Mongrédien, *The Suez Canal Question* (London, Cassell, 1883, 48 pp).

[8] Ramm, ii. 108–9, Gladstone to Granville, 20 October 1883.

[9] E. Dicey, 'Why Not Purchase the Suez Canal?', *Nineteenth Century* (August 1883), 203–5. C. Waring, 'The Trusteeship of the Suez Canal', *Fortnightly Review* (November 1883), 747–8.

[10] *The Times*, 6 November 1883, 9 iii.

direct negotiations with the English shipowners and crossed the Channel to attend the Lord Mayor's banquet at Guildhall on 9 November when he appealed in French to the English tradition of 'le fair play'.[1] Waddington told him that all his efforts to modify English opinion would be fruitless, that the Egyptian Government was under great pressure to grant a concession for a second canal to the English and that such a grant was imminent. The Egyptian Government was not in fact under pressure from the British Government[2] but seems to have begun to force the Canal Company on to the defensive. It disregarded the plea of the exile Arabi from Colombo on 5 November that the Canal should be internationalized and that Egypt should abandon all her sovereign rights over the isthmus as soon as possible in return for a money indemnity.[3] Its Note of 17 November to the British Government affirmed its right to be heard in any fresh arrangements with the Company and its Circular of 27 November to the Consuls made a fresh concession the essential pre-liminary to any modification in the *status quo* of the Canal. Lesseps was thus hamstrung by Egyptian hostility. He undertook a tour of the chief ports of England between 15 November and 20 November in a bid to by-pass the Association but failed to recapture the admiration of 1870 or even the sympathy of 1857. He was compelled to face the necessity for the compromise urged on him by Ferry and Waddington. At Newcastle Charles de Lesseps made the first offer of concessions to the shipowners in the form of a sharing of profits above the level of a 20 per cent dividend.[4] Lesseps then left his son in England on 26 November to begin discussions on the next day with the hard-headed members of the Executive Committee of the Association.

The shipping interest was denied the support of the Government and was reduced to negotiation with the Company on the basis of the 'exclusive power' which it had denounced. Thus it failed in its attempt to be both accuser and judge in its own quarrel but it succeeded in bringing the Company to the conference table and in negotiating directly rather than through the official directors. The Association demanded voting rights in the share-holders' meeting proportionate to the number of shares held by the British Government (i.e. a block 44 per cent vote), at least half of the seats on the board of directors as well as of the personnel in Egypt, a seat of administration in England as well as in France, substantial reductions in the tariff and the acceptance of English jurisdiction for any disagreement between English ship-owners and the Company. The Company wished to limit the dividend accruing to the British Government's shares to 5 per cent from 1894, to secure a loan of £8,000,000 at 3 per cent from the British Government and to admit no more English directors.[5] A compromise between those opposing aims emerged after

[1] *The Times*, 10 November 1883, 7 ii.
[2] Ramm, ii. 114, Gladstone to Granville, 23 November 1883.
[3] *The Times*, 13 December 1883, 8 iii. W. S. Blunt, *Gordon at Khartoum* (1911), 620.
[4] Ibid., 21 November 1883, 10 iii–iv.
[5] Ibid., 16 November 1883, 5 ii, 'The Suez Canal Question'.

seven meetings of the committee and was embodied in a minute signed on 30 November in the board-room of the P. & O. beneath the portrait of Thomas Waghorn.

The seven signatories represented shipping lines which supplied 4,000,000 tons annually to the Canal, or 91 per cent of the total British tonnage through the Canal. They were Thomas Sutherland of the P. & O., William Mackinnon of the British India Line, J. G. S. Anderson of the Orient Line, J. B. Westray, the representative of the City, Hall, Clan, Glen, Shire, Harrison and Ducal Lines, John Glover, R. S. Donkin and James Laing. In the minute the Canal Company agreed to enlarge the Canal at its own expense or to build a second canal at a cost of £8,000,000, as decided by a special commission of engineers and shipowners, half English in its membership. It also agreed to increase the number of English directors from three out of twenty-four to ten out of thirty-two, the seven new directors being chosen from English shipowners and merchants, one of whom was to become a vice-president of the Company. It agreed to create an advisory committee of the English directors sitting in London, to establish a branch office of the Company in London, to employ in the future in its transit service a greater number of English-speaking officials, to abolish the last surtax from 1 January 1884, to eliminate the pilotage dues from 1 July 1884 and to assume expenses arising from accidents in the waterway. Above all, it agreed to decrease the Canal tolls by 50 centimes per ton to 9 francs 50 centimes from 1 January 1885, to apply to the reduction of tolls half of the surplus profits after an 18 per cent dividend (including the statutory 5 per cent interest) had been reached and all of the surplus profits after a 25 per cent dividend had been reached until the toll reached a minimum of 5 francs or 4s. It agreed to limit the amount carried to the statutory reserve to 3 per cent of the net profits after the reserves had reached £200,000. The voting power of the British Government's shares was explicitly left undecided.[1]

The provisions of the agreement were less numerous but more significant than those of the agreement of 10 July. Great changes were made by Article 8 in the reduction of dues, which was regarded as of central importance by most shipowners. The article provided for immediate reduction from 1 January 1885 whatever the state of traffic as against the date of 1 January 1888 anticipated under the first Agreement. It arranged for the reduction of toll in the year following the payment of dividends over 18 per cent, a starting-point 7 per cent lower than the 25 per cent fixed on 10 July. The Agreement recognized the relation between toll reductions and the afflux of new traffic whilst avoiding the rigidity of toll reductions on fixed dates. It imposed an upper limit of 25 per cent at which dividends were to be frozen until the dues became 5 francs per ton and a barrier on the transfer of profits to reserve and therefore on the evasion of toll reduction. It excluded a provision included on 10 July

[1] *The Times*, 1 December 1883, 5 vi; 3 December, 6 ii. *Le Canal de Suez*, 12 Décembre 1883, 506–7.

for raising the dues if the dividend declined and so precluded any sharing of losses. It abolished the pilotage-dues of £150,000–170,000 per annum 2½ years earlier than the date of 1 January 1887 anticipated under the first Agreement. It excluded the loan which the Company had sought, freeing the British tax-payer of the cost of a political subsidy and forcing the Company back on the ordinary capital market. It avoided any infringement on the concession or on the monopoly of the Company but made no mention of any extension of the concession and failed to secure for Egypt any share in the profits of the Company. Above all, it granted seats on the board to the shipowners and so passed beyond the sharing of profits to the sharing of power, against the flat opposition of the three official directors. The British directors elected in 1877 purported to fear the creation of separate parties on the board, constant voting and an English minority but really feared a diminution in their own status. Thus the Agreement established the London Programme for the future de-velopment of the Canal and installed watch-dogs to ensure its execution as well as to watch over Company policy in general. It ended the crisis of 1883 when the waterway had become the focus of the rival nationalisms of England and France in the press, pamphlets, periodicals, public meetings and parlia-mentary debate: eighty-two separate publications appeared on the subject of the Canal in 1883, against thirty-one in 1882 and forty-one in 1884.[1] The Association of Steamship Owners Trading to the East dissolved itself on the achievement of its substitute-aims.

The Agreement was criticized by Egypt in its note of protest of 3 December 1883 and by the London press because it did not give the British Government equal influence to the private shareholders[2] and surrendered the attack on the Company's monopoly for a reduction in toll.[3] It was also attacked by the shipowners' associations of the outports as the work of a self-elected conven-tion in London. The criticism of the North of England Steam Ship Owners' Association on 11 December was echoed during the next month by the Cham-bers of Commerce of Newcastle, Cardiff, Hull and Liverpool. The Agreement was also attacked by merchants[4] as a shipowners' convention and by both Liberal and Conservative M.P.s[5] as a sacrifice of the national interest. It was communicated to the British Government on the day of its signature, together with Lesseps' request for a letter from the Cabinet as a security against future demands. Gladstone became alarmed at the possibility of the Government being forced to become negotiators between the Company and the Government of Egypt.[6] Granville despatched official letters of approval on 4 February 1884,

---

[1] J. Charles-Roux, *L'Isthme et le Canal de Suez* (1901), ii. 517–24.

[2] *The Times*, 1 December 1883, 9 ii.

[3] *Pall Mall Gazette*, 1 December 1883, 1, 'The Shipowners' Surrender'.

[4] *The Times*, 22 January 1884, 10 ii, C. Magniac.

[5] Hansard, *Commons Debates*, 8 February 1884, C. Magniac and C. M. Norwood; 15 Feb-ruary, C. Magniac; 18 February, C. M. Norwood; 6 March, H. D. Wolff; 10 March, W. A. Smith and H. D. Wolff; 17 March, H. D. Wolff. H. B., *The Suez Canal and the Liberal Govern-ment; or, the 'Policy' of Deceit* (London, Wilson, March 1884, 23pp.).

[6] Ramm, ii. 126–7, Gladstone to Granville, 12 December 1883.

so supplying Lesseps with his desired letter but in six pages rather than in the six lines he wanted.

The news of the Agreement was received in France with general stupefaction because the English Government had reaffirmed the rights of the Company and was regarded by the French as as absolute as the French Government. The new Agreement represented a defeat for the Canal Company as well as for the French Government and a permanent alteration in the balance of power between English and French interests. As soon as the news reached Paris on 1 December Suez shares were offered for sale. As the shares sank to 1,858 francs on 17 December, or to 14·6 per cent below their level of 15 November, Lesseps condemned such culpable manoeuvres as damaging to the interests of all shareholders. At Abbéville on 23 December Lesseps repeatedly affirmed that the Canal would never cease to be French during his lifetime or that of his sons.[1] The delegation-holders were threatened more than any other interest by the proposed limitation on dividends because their rights expired in 1894. They established on 28 January 1884 at the Canal Company's offices the Mutual Association of the Suez Delegation Holders, which was legally constituted on 4 February with four of its eight directors drawn from the board of the Canal Company, to undertake the amortization of the delegations. A group of rebel shareholders formed the Suez Canal Defence Committee on 25 February to oppose any reduction in tolls. That committee devised a scheme for the lease of the Canal by England and the payment of an 8-francs toll to the shareholders.[2]

At the annual meeting on 12 March 433 shareholders, including 130 small shareholders without votes in the gallery, were present or more than the number at any meeting since the rebellion of 1872.[3] Lesseps explained that the document signed in London was a simple minute setting out a programme, not a contract, convention or treaty but that its articles could not be voted upon separately. He argued in favour of the proposed reductions in toll that such a policy would stimulate an increase in the traffic of the Canal and would especially attract cargo still held back in the export markets of Asia by the high cost of transport. He looked forward to a rapid reduction from 10 francs to 5 francs and to the enjoyment by the Company thenceforward of all the fruits of an increasing traffic. In the discussion women and shareholders of 1858 protested against the sacrifice of their expectations to English egoism and attacked the Agreement as a one-sided contract and an attempt to turn the French shareholders out of their own house. 'The English are like a mendicant who, not satisfied with alms, requires a written agreement to bestow alms every day.'[4] Lesseps conceded a demand for a ballot but did not ask the shareholders directly to approve the exchange of views with the shipowners. Instead he asked them to approve the President's Report for 1883 and the

---

[1] *The Times*, 24 December 1883, 5 iv.   [2] Ibid., 29 February 1884, 5 iii.
[3] Ibid., 13 March 1884, 5 ii–iv, 'The Suez Canal Question'.
[4] Ibid., 13 March 1884, 5 ii, Philippon.

Agreement only by implication, explaining that a negative vote was not a vote for rejection but a vote for the postponement of the decision. After $4\frac{1}{2}$ hours of discussion the Report was approved through the personal influence of Lesseps and by a reluctant 843 to 761 votes, a very narrow majority in the Company's history. The meeting then closed amidst confusion. The renewed resistance offered to the great Frenchman provoked a loyalist reaction in his favour. The Union of Suez Shareholders was formed on 27 March by secession from the Suez Canal Defence Committee in order to approve the Agreement and support Lesseps. Another meeting of shareholders was held ten weeks later on 29 May and was attended by 593 shareholders representing 279,805 shares or an all-time peak proportion of 70 per cent of the privately held shares. A stream of faithful Lessepsites poured into the hall to rout the dissidents and adopt the closure against the last opposition speaker.[1] The resolutions of the board were carried by overwhelming majorities and announced amid loud cheers. The increase in the board of directors from 24 to 32 was accepted by 2,608 votes to 506, i.e. by 82 per cent of the 3,167 votes present or by 500 votes more than the necessary two-thirds majority. The first industrialist was elected to the board in Émile Darier, the creator of the oil-cake industry of Marseilles which produced cattle-fodder from cotton seed. The crushing majority votes were assumed to be a personal triumph for Lesseps at the climax of his career and a remarkable example of the powers of the President of a Company which far surpassed the combined authority of the Speaker and the Leader of the House of Commons.[2] They were also a triumph for the organization of the large shareholders and a proof that the supporter of Lesseps was a special type of shareholder. 'He is the only one who is not exclusively governed by his interest, and who would prefer to lose with M. de Lesseps rather than to win without him.'[3]

The Advisory Commission of Engineers and Shipowners created under the London Programme first met in Paris on 16–19 June 1884, with the representatives of eight nations on the international pattern of the 1855 commission. It included eight English members out of the total of twenty-two instead of the eleven laid down in the London Programme. The eight French members included Voisin Bey and five of his colleagues from the 1860s. The London office of the Company was opened on 29 August 1884 under Henri Chevassus who remained in charge of it for the following thirty years. On the same day N. M. Rothschild & Sons of London was first authorized to receive payment of Canal tolls. The three official directors secured the regular publication of returns of Canal traffic by the Board of Trade from 1884. The seven new directors were virtually self-appointed and comprised the shipowners Sutherland, Mackinnon and Alexander, the shipbuilders Palmer of Jarrow and Laing

---

[1] *The Times*, 30 May 1884, 5 ii–iii, 'The Suez Canal'.
[2] Ibid., 30 May 1884, 9 i. G. Rouanet, *Les Complicités du Panama* (Paris, Savine, 1893), 14–15 note.
[3] *The Times*, 30 May 1884, 5 ii.

of Sunderland and the merchants John Slagg and C. J. Monk. They included only three of the seven signatories of the London Programme. They lacked the perfect French and the official status of the three directors appointed by the Government. In Paris on 2 September 1884 they took their seats for the first time on the board, which they transformed into a Franco-English body. They still cherished their unfulfilled hopes and wanted to go to Egypt to decide the question of doubling the Canal, causing Victor de Lesseps to call the new board 'impossible'.[1] They first met on 10 November 1884 in the London Committee whose chairman was at first Laing and then from 1887 Sutherland who had become M.P. for Greenock in 1884.

The Canal Company retained its monopoly and its concession, despite the agitation for their abrogation. It was freed from the threat of competition and absorbed its potential competitors. It remained under effective French control with a French administration, a French personnel and a French centralization of operation. Its sacrifice of the dues on ships in ballast reduced receipts by 4·6 per cent in 1884. Tolls were reduced below 10 francs per ton for the first time from 1 January 1885. The sacrifice of dues was offset by the continued increase in traffic down to 1886, which proved the only year of the decade failing to surpass the tonnage of the previous year. That slump reduced tonnage and receipts by 9 per cent and dividends by 17 per cent. Dividends were slightly reduced in 1886–7 and formed less than half of the receipts for the first time since 1882. The dividend for 1883 was exceeded only by that for the boom year of 1888. The introduction of night-time transit from 1887 reduced delays and the complaints of inadequate facilities, although tolls were not reduced again until 1893. Thus the Company surmounted the gravest crisis in its history and retained in the Canal the finest colony in the world acquired without the sacrifice of a single French soldier.[2]

[1] T. Barclay, *Thirty Years. Anglo-French Reminiscences (1876–1906)* (London, Constable, 1914), 60.
[2] *Le Canal de Suez*, 2 Septembre 1885, 918, quoting *Le Figaro*.

18

EUROPE'S EGYPTIAN CAMPAIGN, AND THE CONVENTION OF CONSTANTINOPLE, 1888

THE occupation of Egypt plunged Europe into a paroxysm of jealousy. It gave mortal offence to the Sultan as well as to France, which assumed the leadership of the Powers in a campaign to force England out of Egypt. It compelled England to offer Europe repeated assurances of an early evacuation and of the free navigation of the Canal. It eroded her capacity to resist a further Russian advance on Constantinople and increased her diplomatic dependence upon Germany. England was also lured into the Sudan by the apparent ease with which she had crushed the Arabist military revolution. Thereby she asserted her claim to the Egyptian dominion over the Sudan and made her policy gradually an Egyptian policy, so justifying Lesseps' belief that the Egyptians could never be subjugated because a fellah woman never bore a child by a European.[1] England imprisoned herself in the Egyptian house of bondage and sacrificed her freedom of action elsewhere in the world to maintain her new position in Africa whilst suffering successive defeats at the hands of an invincible religious revolution.

The despatch of Hicks Pasha to Khartoum provoked the Mahdi first to raise the Eastern Sudan in rebellion, so closing the escape-route from Khartoum to Suakin, and then to annihilate Hicks and his whole force of 10,000 Egyptian troops. The news of that disaster led the British Government to decide to withdraw the Sudan from Egyptian control and to establish a strong personal government in Khartoum like that of Rajah Brooke in Sarawak. The despatch of Gordon to Khartoum was thus intended to add another province to the British Empire and to 'Sarawak the Soudan'[2] rather than to evacuate it. The same feudal conception inspired a suggestion for the creation of a separate Canal principality as a Lilliputian Oriental Belgium,[3] whose population could have no history or literature, no common religion or language, no bond of blood and no community of sentiments or interests. The plan ignored the strength of support for the Mahdi in the Sudan and the absence of any basis for a feudal regime. It also extended the British commitment to the Suez route to India in defiance of Lord Randolph Churchill's emphatic warning against

[1] *The Times*, 12 February 1885, 3 iii.
[2] W. Stone, *Shall We Annex Egypt?* (London, Low, 1884), 12, quoting Rajah C. A. J. Brooke from the *Pall Mall Gazette*.
[3] T. J. Lawrence, 'The Suez Canal in International Law', *Law Magazine and Review* (February 1884), 117–43, reprinted in *Essays on Some Disputed Questions in Modern International Law* (Cambridge, Deighton, 1884), 37–71.

the over-valuation of that route by the heirs of Disraeli as 'a terrible and widespread delusion'. 'Egypt is not the high road to India.'[1] The plan also flouted Egypt's deep attachment to its Nilotic empire and precipitated the resignation of Chérif Pasha on 7 January 1884, the succession of Nubar Pasha, the deterioration of Egypt's finances into a critical condition and the abandonment of the idea of handing over a reformed Egypt to a strong native Government as a preliminary to evacuation. Thus Britain's commitment to Egypt could be exploited to the full by a jealous Europe.

Gordon intended to reach Khartoum via the Canal and Suakin in a symbolic assertion of the Sudan's independence of Egypt. The strength of Egyptian resentment compelled Baring to halt Gordon at Port Said on 24 January 1884 and divert him via the safer Nile route. The continued Mahdist successes necessitated the reinforcement of the garrisons at Port Said and Alexandria on 18 February. Britain's Egyptian dilemma strengthened the case for evacuation and encouraged proposals for the purchase of the Canal,[2] for a Euphrates Valley Railway,[3] a Jordan Valley Canal[4] and even for an Akaba Ship Railway,[5] so increasing English interest in Arabia[6] and Syria. The collapse of the Egyptian empire in the Sudan increased the interest of the Powers in the Red Sea and compelled Britain to undertake the defensive acquisition of territory opposite Aden. After a visit by Egyptian troops to Obock in June 1883 and the refusal of coal at Aden to French transports en route to Tonkin France developed from October 1883 a coaling station at Obock, which lay on the Gulf of Tajura at the same distance from Port Said as Aden. France also sought to establish a protectorate over Madagascar, with its base of Diego Suarez, and to add Massawa to Obock. Britain in reply fortified Aden and occupied Zeila, opposite Obock, in August 1884. France raised the tricolour in place of the Egyptian flag at Tajura on 17 November after its evacuation by Egyptian troops.[7] Italy then occupied Massawa on 5 February 1885 and so secured the best natural harbour in the Red Sea, an acquisition which Mancini was compelled to defend as the key of the Mediterranean. Massawa became the base for immediate expansion into the highlands of the interior by the 15,287 Italian troops which passed through the Canal in 1885–6. The Italian initiative roused the French desire for Jibuti, opposite Tajura, and the German desire for Zanzibar. Britain occupied Berbera and so secured control of Aden's food supply. France created at Obock in 1885 a penitentiary especially for Arab convicts and shipped 100 Arab nationalists there in 1886.

The financial crisis in Egypt was aggravated by the reinforcement of the

---

[1] *The Times*, 19 December 1883, 7 iii, Lord Randolph Churchill at Edinburgh, 18 December 1883.   [2] W. Stone, *Shall We Annex Egypt?* (1884), 11.

[3] J. B. Fell, 'On the Necessity of an Improved Means of Communication with India by the Euphrates Valley Route', *Journal of the Royal United Service Institution*, 28 March 1884.

[4] L. Oliphant, *Haifa or Life in Modern Palestine* (Edinburgh, Blackwood, 1887), 204–7, 10 November 1884.   [5] W. S. Blunt, *Gordon at Khartoum* (1911), 340, 3 November 1884.

[6] Gwynn and Tuckwell, *Dilke* (1918), i. 530, 24 May 1883.

[7] A. Ramm, 'Great Britain and the Planting of Italian Power in the Red Sea, 1868–1885', *English Historical Review* (May 1944), 231.

Army of Occupation, whose charge on Egypt Gladstone sought to reduce by proposing to raise a loan on the future value of the Suez Canal shares.[1] Such was the first Liberal bid to turn the shares to fiscal advantage and to secure revenge for the Conservative coup of 1875. The Cabinet rejected the idea on 2 April 1884 and decided to approach the Powers for financial concessions to Egypt and especially for a reduction of the interest on Egyptian bonds, which could be balanced by a remission of the interest due to England on her Canal shares. The London Conference of the Powers refused to allow any such reduction in the interest on the Egyptian Debt and so achieved a great success for Bismarck, who wished to reduce British opposition to German colonial expansion. The Cabinet then decided to send a relief expedition to Gordon in Khartoum and a financial mission to Egypt under Northbrook. Northbrook proposed that the interest paid on the Canal shares by Egypt should be reduced from 5 to 3 per cent or at least to $3\frac{1}{2}$ per cent so as to meet Egypt's wish to reduce it to $3\frac{1}{4}$ per cent.[2] Gladstone proposed to use the future profits of the Canal shares to make up the full interest to the bondholders.[3] The reduction in interest was pared down by Childers on 24 November from $1\frac{1}{2}$ to $\frac{1}{2}$ per cent so that Britain's financial sacrifice was reduced to the same level as that of Europe and Egypt paid $4\frac{1}{2}$ per cent interest for the two years from 1 December 1884 to 30 November 1886.[4] The British attempt to achieve a purely financial settlement of the Egyptian question compelled Ferry to insist on a simultaneous regulation of the passage through the Canal, so taking up the question which had remained in suspense since Granville's circular of 1883.

The series of British defeats in the Sudan was crowned by the fall of Khartoum to the Mahdi and the death of Gordon. The failure of Wolseley's Nile expedition was the price paid for his easy victory at Tel el Kebir. The destruction of Khartoum ended the Turkish era of 1820–84 in the Sudan and made Omdurman its new capital. It set the seal upon the creation of the Mahdi's empire but shattered English hopes of creating a feudal empire on the Nile. It reduced the trade of Suez much more than that of the Canal. It enhanced the martial reputation of the Arab in English eyes but inspired England with a determination to smash the Mahdi and avenge the death of Gordon. A meeting at the Mansion House decided on 14 March 1885 to commemorate Gordon by erecting a Memorial Hospital at Port Said which would be visible to all passengers through the Canal and be open to Oriental and European alike on the fringes of Asia and Africa, the two continents where Gordon had won his fame.[5] Thus Admiral Sir Edward Inglefield secured support for his

---

[1] Gwynn and Tuckwell, *Dilke*, ii. 46, 59.

[2] A. Ramm (ed.), *The Political Correspondence of Mr. Gladstone and Lord Granville, 1876–1886* (1962), ii. 283, Gladstone to Granville, 14 November 1884. J. O. Ronall, 'Julius Blum Pasha, An Austro-Hungarian Banker in Egypt 1843–1919', *Tradition* (April 1968), 72.

[3] Ramm, ii. 283, Gladstone to Granville, 14 November 1884.

[4] *The Statist*, 18 September 1886, 314, 'British Financial Interests in the Suez Canal'.

[5] *The Times*, 16 March 1885, 10 iv, 9 iv, 'The National Memorial to General Gordon'; 20 March, 10 iv; 25 March, 7 vi.

idea of an English sailors' hospital which he had first proposed in 1882.[1] The site offered by the Canal Company in 1882[2] proved, however, totally unsuitable because it was too far from the Canal, too near the Arab town and apparently 'selected with no small care as about the worst site possible for a hospital or for any other building'.[3] The proposal which had already been deemed inadequate as a memorial to a hero of Gordon's stature was thereupon abandoned on 30 May by the Mansion House Committee.[4]

The first news of the disaster of Khartoum had led the Cabinet to decide to reconquer the Sudan and to retain control of it by building a Suakin–Berber Railway. Military aid was offered to England by the Australasian colonies but was refused by Canada in such a 'wretched business'. 'The Suez Canal is nothing to us.'[5] That second expedition to Suakin was liquidated under the pressure of Russia and Germany more than under the attacks of Beja tribesmen. In 1884 Russia had occupied Merv on the frontier of Persia east of the Caspian. In 1885 her forces advanced south from Merv and expelled the Afghans from Penjdeh, so first expressing her interest in the three questions of the Sudan, Egypt and the Canal.[6] The Russian advance on the North-West Frontier of India produced an attack of what Argyll called 'Mervousness' in England, which wished to preserve its Afghan buffer-state but feared another disastrous Afghan war. Russia was fully protected by the buffer-states of Denmark, Turkey and Persia and could not be directly attacked by the British Navy.[7] The Cabinet decided on 14 April to occupy Port Hamilton in South-West Korea as a base for an assault on Vladivostock[8] and on 15 April to evacuate the Sudan, retaining only Suakin. Nineteen miles of railway built in seven weeks at a cost of £866,000 were abandoned to the Beja. The Canal Company benefited by the dues paid on those rails which were returned to England without ever being landed at Suakin. The rapid liquidation of the Sudan venture provoked Australian claims to an equal voice with the English in determining whether Egypt and the Canal should be left to anarchy.[9]

Britain's isolation from the Continent was revealed in the Conference of Berlin on Africa, in the Paris Conference on the Suez Canal and in the Rome Conference on Quarantine after cholera had been transmitted through the Canal on the British troopship *Crocodile* to France, Italy and Spain in 1884[10] and so aroused 'the fantastic fears and the unscientific theories' of the Continental

[1] *The Times.*, 13 March 1882, 8 iii.

[2] Ibid., 8 March 1882, 4 ii.

[3] Ibid., 1 June 1885, 9 ii, 8 i, quoting the reports of Colonel Maitland, Surgeon-Major Greene and Lieutenant-General F. Stephenson of 4 and 5 May 1885.

[4] Ibid., 11 July 1885, 10 iii.

[5] J. Pope, *Correspondence of Sir John Macdonald. Selections* (London, Oxford University Press, 1921), 338, J. A. Macdonald to Sir Charles Tupper, 12 March 1885.

[6] W. S. Blunt, *Gordon at Khartoum*, 436.

[7] Ibid., 420.

[8] Ramm, ii. 363, Gladstone to Granville, 26 April 1885.

[9] Lord Lorne, *Imperial Federation* (London, Swan Sonnenschein, 1885), 37.

[10] W. F. Miéville, *Under Queen and Khedive. The Autobiography of an Anglo-Egyptian Official* (London, Heinemann, 1899), 153, 160–3.

Powers.[1] Those powers accepted the reorganization of Egyptian finances only upon condition that the status of the Canal was given simultaneous consideration and that representatives of Russia and Germany were included on the reorganized Commission of the Public Debt, so imposing a great restraint on Baring's fiscal freedom in Egypt. The Conference on the Suez Canal Convention met in Paris rather than in Cairo, which England rejected, or in London, which France rejected. The representatives of the ten Powers intended to prevent the reduction of the Canal to an appanage of the British Empire, to reaffirm its essentially universal, European and international character and to secure its neutralization by a Convention, so provoking the reiterated expression of concern by shipowners and Conservatives in the Commons.[2] The Turkish ambassador also submitted on 30 March, the opening day of the Conference, a declaration reserving the full rights of the Sultan to take the necessary measures for the defence of Egypt against either external attack or internal disorder. France sought to defend its rights at Panama as well as at Suez by a guarantee of the freedom of navigation, by the substitution of Europe's guardianship of the Canal for that of England and by the establishment of a Canal Commission comparable to the Danube Commission, which had become a virtual heptarchy with its own financial, legislative and judicial powers.[3] France wished to make the power of any Canal Commission as extensive as possible, to authorize the maintenance of warships at the entrances and the inclusion of their commanders on the Commission, and to extend the definition of the Canal region as widely as possible. Britain objected to the extension of protection beyond the Canal itself, its ports and a three-mile radius beyond. She also opposed the inclusion within the Canal Convention of any lateral zone not covered by water, the Sweet Water Canal, the establishments of the Canal Company or the maritime approaches to the Canal, lest that should imply the Red Sea. Britain's representative also objected on 3 April to the word 'guarantee' and on 2 May to the word 'neutrality'. Thus Britain sought to limit the scope of the Convention as much as France sought to extend it, so as to preserve its complete freedom of action without the restraint of international control. Granville's circular of 1883 which embodied the unchanged British proposals paid so little respect to the wishes of Europe that it was virtually black-balled by the Conference.[4] A sub-commission of the Conference in consultation with Ferdinand and Charles de Lesseps[5] found that sixteen sessions extending over seven weeks from 30 March to 19 May were too few to reconcile the English and the French proposals. France sought

---

[1] *Saturday Review*, 6 June 1885, 738–9, 'Quarantine at Suez'.

[2] Hansard, *Commons Debates*, 23 March 1885, Norwood, Onslow, Wolff, Gibson, Cowen, Gourley; 24 March 1885, Gibson, Northcote, Wolff.

[3] M. L. Camand, *Étude sur le Régime Juridique du Canal de Suez* (Grenoble, Allier, 1899), 235.

[4] A. d'Avril, 'Négociations Relatives au Canal de Suez', *Revue d'Histoire Diplomatique* (Janvier 1888), 14.

[5] Ibid., 162–3.

also to restrict as far as possible the disembarkation of troops along the Canal in peacetime and the reinforcement of the defending forces from outside. The Russian delegate suggested on 4 May the restriction of the defence of the Canal by the phrase 'by their own forces' so as to exclude any allies of the Khedive such as Britain. The Netherlands delegate secured the insertion on 4 May of a most important clause whereby any measures in defence of the Canal were not to hinder its free use. Such anti-British proposals provoked a new series of questions from Conservative M.P.s, especially from R. A. Cross.[1] Although the British representative had objected on 6 May to the analogy between the Danube and the Canal on the grounds that the Canal Company was no different from an Egyptian Railway Company,[2] the sub-commission adopted at its last session on 19 May the French proposal for a permanent Canal Commission, in harmony with the resolution to establish an international financial commission if Egypt should not have met its regular debt payments by 1887. Britain therefore felt compelled to append a reservation to the draft convention reserving its freedom of action during the existing transitory and exceptional condition of Egypt. A Russian proposal on 9 June to extend the proposed convention to include the Red Sea which was narrow enough to form 'the natural continuation of the artificial passage'[3] and far easier to blockade than the Mediterranean was successfully opposed by the Italian delegate in order to preserve Italian freedom of expansion from Massawa. France was strongly supported at the Conference by Germany, which used the British commitment in Egypt to restrain Britain's Russophobia.

The Paris Conference produced after ten weeks (30 March–13 June 1885) a draft convention largely directed against Britain. Its activity inspired the application of international law to the Canal, the production of the first university thesis on the legal status of the Canal[4] and the legal justification of encroachment on Egypt's control of the Canal. Sir Travers Twiss upheld the empirical tradition of England against the juridical tradition of the Continent and maintained that the Canal was unique and could not be judged by the analogies favoured on the Continent. 'The Suez maritime canal is the sphinx of European diplomacy.'[5] The French lawyers Fournier de Flaix, Octave Borelli and Pradier-Fodéré nevertheless introduced into legal thought Salisbury's concept of the supremacy of commercial over territorial interests to justify the expropriation of local sovereignty in the interest of humanity. Fournier de Flaix applied Hautefeuille's principle of the free strait[6] to the

---

[1] Hansard, *Commons Debates*, 5 May 1885, Puleston; 8 May, Cross and Puleston; 11 May, Cross; 12 May, Dixon-Hartland; 19 May, Ashmead-Bartlett; 21 May, Cross; 8 June, Wolff and Cross.

[2] A. d'Avril, 174. [3] Ibid., 166.

[4] R. de Marees van Swinderen, *Het Suez-Kanaal* (Groningen, Huber, 1886).

[5] T. Twiss, 'Le Canal Maritime de Suez et la Commission Internationale de Paris', *Revue de Droit Internationale* (1885), 615.

[6] L. B. Hautefeuille, *Des Droits et des Devoirs des Nations Neutres en Temps de Guerre Maritime* (Paris, Comon, 1848), i. 248, Mers fermées, 'La mer libre, le détroit est libre; la mer commune à tous les peuples, le détroit est commun à tous les peuples'.

Canal considered as an artificial strait.[1] Pradier-Fodéré extended the super-session of local law to permit the pacific use of the Canal by warships.[2] Borelli argued that the ruler of Egypt had recognized the Canal as an arm of the sea,[3] making it international, universal, free and neutral and accepting an international servitude which would continue beyond 1968.[4] The Argentinian Calvo generalized the freedom of the Suez Canal into a freedom of maritime canals in general as integral parts of the sea.[5] Thus the lawyers of Europe sought to protect the interests of the international community against Britain but inevitably did so at the expense of Egypt and Turkey.

The war-scare of 1885 revealed England's isolation and forced her into closer dependence upon Germany to maintain her position in Egypt. Britain was forced to barter for German goodwill Dar-es-Salaam, the hinterland of Zanzibar and the interests of the 6,000 British Indian merchants who con-trolled 90 per cent of the local trade at Zanzibar. Germany had paid 3 per cent of the Canal's transit-receipts in 1885 against the 77 per cent paid by Britain but thenceforth extended its use of the waterway. Its enterprise ushered in the European phase in the history of Dar-es-Salaam and began to build up a German India in East Africa. It also began to import cotton direct from Bombay to Hamburg in 1886 and inaugurated the first German mail services to China and to Australia under the Subsidy Law of 1885. The *Oder*, which left Bremerhaven on 30 June 1886, began a monthly mail service to China and reduced the voyage-time by four days to thirty days. The North German Lloyd thus expanded from the Atlantic into the Far Eastern trade. Its steamers began to call at Brindisi from 1886 and so entered into the Mediterranean trade. They failed however to capture Austrian cargo from the Austrian Lloyd, were forbidden to carry agricultural produce on their return voyage and made heavy losses until 1896. Their deep draught encouraged coaling at Suez rather than at Port Said and increased the volume of coal imports to Suez by 60 per cent during 1887. Their inaccurate tonnage-certificates compelled the Canal Com-pany to enter into diplomatic negotiations with the German Government between 1887 and 1890.

The crisis of 1885 also ushered in a new era in the development of overland communications. The English threat to Siberia from Port Hamilton produced the first Russian plan in 1885 to place Vladivostock by railway within thirty days of Petersburg by 1893, the creation from 1886 of a Russian Navy and the establishment of a service via the Canal to China by the Russian Steam

[1] M. E. Fournier de Flaix, *L'Indépendance de l'Égypte et le Régime International du Canal de Suez* (Paris, Guillaumin, 1883), 111.

[2] P. Pradier-Fodéré, *Traité de Droit International Public Européen et Americain Suivant les Progrès de la Science et de la Pratique Contemporaines* (Paris, Pedone-Lauriel, 1885), ii. 203–6, 'Les canaux artificiels communiquant avec la mer'.

[3] O. Borelli, *Choses Politiques d'Égypte, 1883–1895* (1895), 554–7, 'Le Régime des Eaux du Canal de Suez au Point de Vue du Droit Public International Maritime (Février 1885)'.

[4] Ibid., 560–3.

[5] C. Calvo, *Le Droit International Théorique et Pratique* (Paris, Guillaumin, 1887, 4ème édition), i. 507.

Navigation and Commercial Company. The appearance of a Russian naval squadron in the Mediterranean compelled Britain to reconsider the value of the Suez route, which was also threatened by the postwar resurgence of French power and by British isolation from any Continental allies. In that debate a sharp difference appeared between military and naval opinion. Soldiers trans-lated the adage 'Time is money' into 'Time is victory' and were hypnotized by the tremendous advantage of the short sea-route using the Canal for naval and military movements. 'If you draw a line from the Land's End to Cape Comorin, on the south of India, the centre of that line is about the Suez Canal.'[1] 'It is recorded that when Cromwell assumed the Protectorate, the news was 13 or 16 days in reaching Devonshire. In 16 days in this year of Grace you may go to America and back; in 16 days the Home and Australian Fleets might concentrate in the neighbourhood of Suez. So much for dis-tance.'[2] For the Navy the saving in distance was less important than the con-ditions of warfare along a route which could be commanded from the land far more easily than from the sea. The narrow seas between Gibraltar and Aden virtually formed a long canal through land-locked straits where English control was highly localized and the gigantic military might of a hostile Europe created the greatest threat. That land-locked route through an inland sea could not be held open without an overwhelming concentration of force unless the Navy abandoned the defence of home waters or increased its strength to unprecedented levels. Even if Gladstonian finance permitted such a revolution no navy could really compensate for the inadequacy of British military forces within a land-locked sea. Flanked by the hostile naval powers of France, Italy and Russia the route was well-adapted to the operation of torpedo-boats from the ports of Spain, Algiers and Sicily.[3] Its central link could not be used by cruisers with a draught above 24 feet and could be blocked with fatal facility. Its southern half had become so insecure through French and Italian expansion that Kitchener urged the construction of a railway from Port Said to Suez, the fortification of Perim, the establishment of a lighthouse at Cape Guardafui and the maintenance of the British position at Berbera, Zeila and Socotra. To counter the Franco-German threat to the English position at Zanzibar from Diego Suarez and Dar-es-Salaam Kitchener recom-mended the immediate acquisition of Mombasa.[4]

Naval opinion concluded that the Canal had shortened the route to the East for all potential enemies while making England's route the longest. The Canal would, however, require a far smaller concentration of force to keep it closed

[1] *Journal of the Royal United Service Institution*, vol. 31, 6 May 1886, 526, General Collin-son, R.E.

[2] Colonel Sir Charles H. Nugent, 'Imperial Federation', *Journal of the Royal United Service Institution*, vol. 30, 30 June 1886, 881.

[3] *Royal Commission on the Depression of Trade and Industry* (1886), ii. Appendix E, 72, V. L. Cameron, 8 March 1886.

[4] R. Coupland, *The Exploitation of East Africa 1856–1890* (1939), 470–1, 'Notes by Lieu-tenant-Colonel Kitchener on British lines of communication with the Indian Ocean, 12 De-cember 1885'.

than to keep it open and would be most valuable to Britain if it were closed against her foes. The Navy thus reverted to the negative tradition of Palmerston because it could not command either the Mediterranean or the Red Sea against France without an Italian alliance as a substitute for a greatly enlarged fleet. In wartime high insurance rates would transfer British trade to neutrals and eliminate British shipping from the Canal. The Navy could not spare the thirty first-class cruisers which would be essential to protect commerce in wartime between England and Port Said. It would have to destroy the whole of the French Fleet before insurance rates fell and reopened the Canal route to British shipping. The Navy also denied the vital importance to British trade of the Canal, which in 1885 carried £120,000,000 or 16·4 per cent of the total value of British trade of £642,442,000. The first Director of Naval Intelligence concluded that Britain would have to close the Canal to traffic on the outbreak of war after sending through the first reinforcements to India and rely on the Cape and even on the Canadian Pacific routes.[1] Britain would have to take charge of the Canal, to the exclusion of all but friendly nations and in defiance of objections from France and Russia, by forts at Port Said and Suez, a couple of block ships at Ismailia and a few intermediate posts, a patrol of gun-boats and British control of the management of the Canal.[2] Thus Britain would deny her enemies access to the Eastern seas, harming them most and herself the least.

The British Government revived the association between the Navy and the mail-boat lines, sanctioned annual naval manoeuvres for the first time and established a Colonial Defence Committee. It also strengthened the defences of Aden, Karachi, Bombay, Singapore and Cape Town in 1886 and annexed the island of Socotra to Aden on 30 October 1886. It added 30,000 British troops to the permanent strength of the Indian Army and created a vast railway and road system for the strategic concentration of troops on the North-West Frontier. The threat to that frontier revived from 1885 the idea of a Euphrates Valley Railway[3] which was countered by a brilliant French proposal for a Euphrates Valley Navigation from Antioch to Basra.[4] The Russian war-scare brought the troopship *Euphrates* into the harbour of Karachi for the first time on 6 March 1886 and first led the Government to charter vessels of the P. & O. for trooping in 1886, so supplementing the Admiralty's troopships which had been used for twenty years. The plantation from 1886–9 onwards of canal colonies of ex-soldiers in the Punjab created military frontier colonies on the Roman and Byzantine model which would also serve to reduce English

[1] C. H. Nugent, 'The Advantages and Disadvantages of Different Lines of Communication with our Eastern Possessions in the Event of a Great Maritime War', *Journal of the Royal United Service Institution*, vol. 31, 6 May 1886, 525; 528–9, Captain Hall; 530, Admiral Boys; 530–1, Admiral Sir John Hay.
[2] C. H. Nugent, 516–17.
[3] A. F. Baillie, *Kurrachee: (Karachi) Past: Present: and Future* (Calcutta, Thacker, 1890), 208–9. C. H. Nugent, 512.
[4] J. S. Jeans, *Waterways and Water Transport in Different Countries* (London, Spon, 1890), 276.

dependence on Russian wheat. The completion of the railway to Quetta in 1887 increased British strength one hundred-fold on the Afghan frontier.

The discovery of gold at Barberton and the Witwatersrand produced a steep rise in gold exports from Cape Town from 1886, a marked expansion of trade and shipping to South Africa and a renewed interest in the broad ocean highway via the Cape. That route remained open to Britain, free from hostile control and incapable of obstruction or destruction like the Canal. It was valorized by the triple-expansion engine, which opened up the possibility of a steam voyage to India in thirty days and to Australia in thirty-five days. Its use was advocated by Dilke, who suggested that the Mediterranean might have to be sealed off at Gibraltar unless the Navy were increased.[1] Lord Charles Beresford reaffirmed the Navy's loyalty to the Cape route at the Imperial Federation League on 2 April 1887. 'The point of importance in the world is, in my opinion, no longer Constantinople but the Cape...It will never do for England to think she is going to be what she has been if she goes in for defending ditches. (Laughter and cheers).'[2] The Prime Minister of the Cape Colony agreed at the first Colonial Conference that the Cape Government had no interest whatever in keeping open the Suez Canal.[3] A bold and radical proposal to evacuate the Mediterranean, abandon Malta and surrender the Canal[4] provoked Samuel Baker to an impassioned plea for the continued control of 'this thin silver line'[5] and Rear-Admiral P. H. Colomb to a more sober plea for Port Said as a necessary British naval base between Malta and Aden.[6] 'Every colony would join the mother country in the struggle, from Australia to Ceylon, to preserve the passage that would be fatal to their interests and even to their existence, should the Suez Canal fall to the possession of a hostile power.'[5] Salisbury had, however, no intention of abandoning Constantinople and even less of retiring from the Mediterranean.

An alternative imperial route across Canada was opened when the first transcontinental passenger-train reached Port Moody on the Pacific in $5\frac{1}{2}$ days (28 June–4 July 1886) from Montreal. The Canadian Pacific Railway thus opened a North-West Passage to the Indies and one to Brisbane in a possible thirty-two days.[7] It would permit the speedy despatch of troops to the East if the British hold on the Canal were temporarily loosened[8] and would open an alternative route for mails if 'that narrow gut'[9] were blocked in wartime.

---

[1] C. W. Dilke, 'The Present Position of European Politics', *Fortnightly Review*, 1 February 1887, 173, 178–9; ibid., 1 June 1887, 810.

[2] *The Times*, 4 April 1887, 10iv.

[3] *Proceedings of the Colonial Conference 1887* (C. 5091 of 1887), i. 414, 225, 30 April 1887, J. H. Hofmeyr.

[4] *The Times*, 3 August 1887, 3vi, Sir H. W. Gordon.

[5] Ibid., 9 August 1887, 3ii, 17 August, 13ii, S. Baker, 'Maritime Routes to the Eastern Seas'.

[6] Ibid., 17 August 1887, 13iv, P. H. Colomb.

[7] C. H. Nugent, 521.

[8] R. Kipling, *From Sea to Sea* (London, Macmillan, 1900), ii. 57, 1889.

[9] *The Times*, 26 September 1887, 9iii.

'The Empire's answer to a "blocked" Suez Canal has been given by Canada.'[1] The C.P.R.'s offers in 1885 and 1887 to provide a mail service to Hong Kong were opposed by the P. & O. and were not accepted by the British Government.[2] The Admiralty nevertheless approved the specifications of the White Star Line's armed merchant cruiser *Teutonic* which was laid down in March 1887 with a capacity of 20 knots so that it could reach Halifax in 5 days, Bombay in 14 days and Calcutta in $17\frac{1}{2}$ days. The C.P.R. gained its first oceanic extension in Sir William Pearce's Canadian Pacific Steamship Line, which was begun in 1887 by three ex-Cunard steamers sent out via the Canal. A Pacific Cable was urged in vain as a logical extension of the C.P.R. in order to free imperial communications from Pender's monopoly which 'like a huge octopus has fastened its tentacles upon almost every part of the eastern and southern world'.[3] Des Voeux, the son-in-law of Pender and the new Governor of Hong Kong, reached his colony in 1887 by the new 'Empire route'[4] and so maintained the tradition established by Pottinger in 1841 of using the most modern route to the East. The British Government decided to reinforce the defences of the new Canadian route as well as of the old Cape route by the construction of defensive works at Simon's Bay and Mauritius, by the supply of armament at Table Bay, Ceylon, Singapore, Hong Kong and Esquimalt and by the fortification of the coaling stations at Sierra Leone and St. Helena.

France remained the gravest threat to the security of the Mediterranean route. It sent its first African troops through the Canal in 1886 to the 'Indo-China' which it created out of Cochin, Annam and Tonkin in 1887. It sought compensation for German expansion in Zanzibar and made the Canal into a steam-route to Madagascar from 1886, used especially by the Compagnie Havraise Péninsulaire from 1887 and by the Messageries from 1888. The possibility of a Franco-Russian combination in the Mediterranean was opened by the Bulgarian crisis of 1885–7 which threatened to create a new Big Bulgaria as a Russian province in defiance of the Berlin settlement of 1878. Salisbury thereupon concluded the Mediterranean Agreements of 1887 with Italy and Austria in order to hold Russia off from Constantinople and France from North Africa, increasing British dependence on the German pivot of the Triple Alliance. Salisbury also offered the Sultan in the Drummond Wolff Convention of 22 May 1887 the evacuation of the Sudan and Egypt in exchange for a right of re-entry if necessary, a legal title to the political surveillance of the Canal and access through the Straits to the Black Sea for British warships. The prospective evacuation of Egypt thereunder encouraged a revival of the project of 1878 for a Cyprus–Karachi Railway via Tripoli, Palmyra and

[1] J. C. R. Colomb, 'Imperial Federation—Naval and Military', *Journal of the Royal United Service Institution*, vol. 30, 31 May 1886, 857.
[2] H. A. Innis, *A History of the Canadian Pacific Railway* (London, King, 1923), 138.
[3] H. Heaton, 'The Postal and Telegraphic Communications of the Empire', *Proceedings of the Royal Colonial Institute*, 13 March 1888, 185.
[4] *The Times*, 4 October 1887, 4i–iii, 'The New Route to the East'; 17 October, 3 iii–iv; 19 October, 10iv–v, 'Comparison of the Various Routes to the East'.

Bagdad.[1] The threat to the independence of the Canal sent Lesseps to Berlin, where he was received by Bismarck on 11 March 1887 as well as by his imperial shareholders in the Suez and Panama enterprises, the Emperor, the Empress, the Prince Imperial and the Crown Princess.[2] That visit was ostensibly intended to secure either a German contribution to the Paris Exhibition of 1889 or Lesseps' sponsorship on his promotion in the Legion of Honour of Jules Herbette, the French ambassador in Berlin and a director of the Canal Company since 1882.[3] The mission may really have been intended to renew the Franco-German entente so as to force 'these English beggars' out of Egypt,[4] ensure the failure of the Wolff mission and facilitate the return of Ismail to Cairo. It certainly alarmed the Russian Foreign Minister, who had just renewed the Dreikaiserbund with Bismarck. Lesseps failed to elicit the desired response from Bismarck[5] but returned to proclaim that France was the natural friend of Germany.[6] He was thereupon attacked by the Republican press as a conservative Bonapartist nearly forty years after the Legitimists had condemned him in 1849 as a dangerous republican. He failed to reinforce Franco-German amity, which declined as Boulangist nationalism was encouraged by the Schnaebelé affair.

The influence of France and Russia combined to prevent the ratification of the Wolff Convention by the Porte. No Franco-Russian rapprochement followed but separate French and Russian efforts to improve relations with Britain.[7] France and England finally reached agreement on the Canal Convention after Freycinet had accepted on 24 March 1886 the English form of a Canal Commission[8] and Salisbury had accepted in October 1886 an annual meeting of the Commission.[9] France linked the Canal question with that of the New Hebrides on 8 August 1887 and concluded successive agreements with Britain on the Canal Convention on 24 October and on the Condominium of the New Hebrides on 16 November 1887. She chose to regard the agreement as a sequel to the rejection of the Wolff Convention and as a step towards eliminating the British from a neutral Egypt. Britain however turned from France to conclude the second Mediterranean Agreement of 12 December

---

[1] F. Goldsmid, 'Traffic Routes to the East', *Journal of the Society of Arts*, 11 March 1887, 402–14.

[2] *Bulletin du Canal Interocéanique*, 15 Mars 1887, 1733, 'Voyage de M. Ferdinand de Lesseps'.

[3] *Documents Diplomatiques Françaises*, 1ère Série, vi. 483, no. 472, Flourens à Laboulaye, 17 Mars 1887; vi. 484, no. 473, Herbette à Flourens, 18 Mars 1887.

[4] J. R. Rodd, *Social and Diplomatic Memories 1884–1893* (London, Arnold, 1922), i. 111, quoting Lesseps to the Crown Princess in 1887, 'Ces gueux d'anglais, nous allons bientôt les chasser de l'Égypte'.

[5] *Documents Diplomatiques Françaises*, 1ère Série, vi. 479, no. 467, Herbette à Flourens, 12 Mars 1887.

[6] *The Times*, 16 March 1887, 5iv.

[7] Colin L. Smith, *The Embassy of Sir William White at Constantinople, 1886–1891* (London, Oxford University Press, 1957), 84–5.

[8] M. L. Camand, *Étude sur le Régime Juridique du Canal de Suez* (1899), 161.

[9] Ibid., 164.

1887 with Austria and Italy at Constantinople, so preserving its Egyptian interests and the political security of the Mediterranean from Gibraltar as far as the Straits and the Canal. The Canal Convention of 1887 originated as an Anglo-French agreement, which was accepted by Italy, the Netherlands and Spain while the three Great Powers of Germany, Austria and Russia waited for the assent of the Porte.[1] The Porte delayed its signature for a year in an effort to enforce the conclusion of a preliminary convention for the evacuation of Egypt[2] but was forced to remain content with securing protection for the Ottoman rights of access to Arabia and of presidency over the Canal Commission.

The Convention of Constantinople was signed on 29 October 1888 to regulate the passage through the Canal of warships and not of merchant vessels. In its first and primary article it proclaimed absolute freedom of transit through the Canal. 'The Suez Maritime Canal shall always be free and open, in time of war as in time of peace, to every vessel of commerce or of war, without distinction of flag.'[3] That freedom of passage had been guaranteed in the concession of 1856 but had been infringed in 1877 and in 1882. It was extended in 1888 to warships which were exempt from all territorial jurisdiction, could decline the competence of Egyptian courts and were not even required to ask the permission of Egypt before passing through her territorial water. That freedom became primarily freedom of military transit, being extended to belligerent warships and even to belligerent fleets in accordance with international law which accepted as legitimate the passage of belligerent warships through the territorial waters of a neutral state and their entry into the ports and harbours of such a state. It was further extended to all nations and not only to the nine signatory powers in defiance of the doctrine that treaties might neither benefit nor injure third parties. It could be maintained that it was even extended by implication to belligerent enemies of the territorial power because it was a right which, in the ambiguous wording of Article XI, was not to be hindered by any action whatsoever, not even by measures in defence of Egypt or of the Canal itself. Thus Egypt seemed to be denied any discretionary power to deny passage.

The Convention made the Canal a corridor for all belligerents but incorporated the rules built up to govern the stay of belligerent ships in neutral ports. It restricted the revictualling and provisioning of warships and their time of transit to the minimum necessary and their stay in the ports of the Canal to twenty-four hours at the utmost. It used the modes of 'pacification' applied first in the Geneva Convention of 1864 to doctors, wounded and

---

[1] A. d'Avril, 'Négociations Relatives au Canal de Suez', *Revue d'Histoire Diplomatique* (Mars 1888), 185–6.

[2] *Documents Diplomatiques Français*, 1ère Série, vii. 114, no. 103, Montebello à Goblet, 21 Avril 1888; vii. 120–1, no. 108, Waddington à Goblet, 25 Avril 1888; vii. 129–30, no. 117, Montebello à Goblet 17 Mai 1888.

[3] *Commercial No. 2. (1889). Convention...respecting the Free Navigation of the Suez Maritime Canal* (C-5623 of 1889), 5.

hospitals and extended in 1868 to include ships and military transports carrying only the wounded. It forbade the exercise of the rights of war including the rights of blockade, of prize and of search within the waters of the Canal or within three miles of its ports of access. The Canal had been liable to blockade for eighteen years until the Convention freed it from that threat and did so in the most specific and absolute terms to the benefit of all neutral powers. Britain failed to secure the adoption of its proposal that warships should be forbidden to bring their prizes into and through the Canal, despite the widespread hostility of Continental lawyers to the right of commercial prize and the exclusion of prizes from their territorial waters by many states. The British proposal would have offered the greatest protection to British merchant vessels and would have made the Canal into a bulwark of British commerce because such prizes would presumably be British and their captors non-British. The Convention assimilated prizes to warships and permitted the transport of enemy vessels under enemy flag through the Canal as the Berlin Act of 1885 permitted their transport on the Congo and the Niger. No specific provision was however made in 1888, as the Netherlands had suggested in 1885, for the ports of the Canal to offer asylum from their pursuers to 'ex-prizes'[1] and to hunted merchant ships without any limit of time.[2] The Convention further forbade the embarkation or disembarkation in wartime of troops, munitions or materials of war, the maintenance of warships within the waters of the Canal and the erection of permanent fortifications. It left those rules dangerously general and made no provision for difficulties of interpretation. It forbade the search of vessels which might be potential block-ships and laid down no conditions under which belligerents should coal, although Russia had raised the question in 1877. It made no explicit use of the word 'pacification',[3] although it excluded part of Egypt from acts of war and precluded any European power from attacking Egypt via the Canal, even though Egypt might be actively engaged in warfare with that power. Such pacification would have created an irreconcilable clash between the belligerent capacity of the territorial power and the pacified portion of its territory. The Convention did not demilitarize the Canal because it did not forbid temporary as distinct from permanent fortifications.

The Convention revealed the enormous extension assumed by the concept of a right of way outside Europe. That temporary territorial right had been steadily restricted in Europe through the growth of opposition to military transit and the rise of an organic view of sovereignty in opposition to its classification as a bundle of separable rights. Thus the doctrine that a belligerent might force a passage for its troops over neutral territory if the neutral refused permission declined before the rise of the new doctrine that a neutral

---

[1] T. M. C. Asser, 'La Convention de Constantinople', *Revue de Droit International* (1888), 545–6.

[2] M. L. Camand, 202–3. A. d'Avril, 171.

[3] F. E. Liszt, *Das Völkerrecht Systematisch Dargestellt* (Berlin, Haering, 1898), 217.

state would commit a gross violation of its neutral duties if it granted such a passage. The right to regulate or refuse passage across territory was acknowledged as one of the complex of rights of territorial sovereignty in the city-states of ancient Greece, in the small states of medieval Europe, in the territorial states of modern Europe and Asia and in the tribal areas of desert, mountain and jungle where no Hegelian state existed. Egypt was master of the territory of the Canal and therefore of the passage, as Britain was of the Caledonian Canal. Her right to regulate the passage of the Canal was the same as her right to regulate the navigation of the Nile or the use of the overland route but suffered restriction in the name of freedom of transit and of 'mare liberum', whose rising tide repudiated even the idea of territorial waters as a useless fiction.[1] The Convention of Constantinople considered the isthmus of Suez as a whole as destined to serve international communications for ever and as available to an imprescriptible right of passage.[2] It was unlimited by the duration of the Canal Company's concession and was therefore intended to continue in effect after 1968. It infringed on Egyptian rights to control transit through its own territory and territorial waters.[3] It assimilated the Canal to a neutral maritime territory,[4] to an artificial strait or even to a 'second Bosporus'. It applied to Egyptian soil the customary regime of the high seas and especially their capacity for use but not for appropriation. It seemed to bear that soil out of the sphere of national law into that of international law and out of the realm of territorial law into that of maritime law in an age when the sea was in general being assimilated to the land. It limited Egypt's control over the Canal much more than the concessions of 1854 and 1856 had done. It forbade Egypt to fortify the Canal, to fight in its own waters, to exercise the right of blockade or to prohibit the passage of foreign warships through the Canal. Those restrictions were in reality directed against England, whom the powers understood to be the 'Egypt' referred to in the Convention. They nevertheless imposed on Egypt obligations tantamount to a 'servitude' such as Christian Wolff had first conceived in 1749 and Immanuel Clauss was first fully to study in 1894. The concept of 'servitude', with its overtones of subjection, was irreconcilable with sovereignty as understood by the states of contemporary Europe and was not used in the text of the Convention. 'Neutrality' was repeatedly invoked by the French negotiators as their aim but was expressly excluded from the text at the British request. Neutralization had been applied to the Black Sea in 1856 as a diplomatic solecism in order to mask the insult to Russia and was not applied to the Canal in 1888 unless neutralization meant freedom of passage. 'Free passage has been assured (not guaranteed) by a mutual servitude of partial internationalization through limited neutralization.'[5] The Canal Company glossed the text to affirm that

---

[1] M. L. Camand, 63. [2] Ibid., 222.

[3] H. Wheaton, *Elements of International Law* (London, Stevens, 1889, Third English Edition), 308.

[4] L. M. Rossignol, *Le Canal de Suez (Étude Historique et Juridique)* (Paris, Giard, 1898), 204.

[5] A. d'Avril, 26. M. L. Camand, 172.

the Convention provided the international recognition of the neutrality of the Canal[1] as well as of the absolute inviolability of the property of the shareholders.

The affirmation of transit-rights was unsupported by any sanctions. The powers assumed no positive obligations to prevent interference with the Canal by others. They affirmed their desire to 'assure' the freedom of navigation but they avoided using the word 'guarantee' and enumerated no penalties for contravention, because no power would assume the responsibility for enforcing penalties upon Great Britain. They were granted the symbolic right to station two warships each at the entrance to the Canal and to attend meetings of the Canal Commission. That Commission had been intended by France to supervise the execution of the Convention and thus to provide an effective international guarantee. Britain was however opposed to the establishment of an international control commission which might form an Areopagus of the Powers in permanent session of judgment on British policy in Egypt like the Debt Commission of 1885 and the Mixed Courts, with their Palace of Justice opened at Alexandria in 1886 and their General Assembly established in 1889. She was able to secure acceptance of her form of the Commission by France, deprived of German support after 1885. In Article VIII[2] the Commission was thus reduced to an extraordinary meeting of the representatives of the Powers in Cairo in circumstances which threatened the security of, or free passage through, the Canal. Its purely advisory function was to warn the Government of Egypt of the danger: it had none of the powers of the Danube Commission and not even the right to communicate with the Powers as a collective body. To prevent Article VIII from falling into disuse the Commission was to meet once a year under the presidency of an Ottoman commissioner and in the presence of an Egyptian commissioner, an arrangement which Salisbury accepted as unnecessary but harmless,[3] because English interests were protected by the rule that a collective resolution of diplomatic representatives was only valid if unanimous.

The Government of Egypt was left to devise the necessary measures for ensuring the execution of the Convention and the strict adherence of warships to the regulations prescribed for their passage through the Canal. Its powers were defended by Britain against excessive encroachment by Europe. Britain failed to secure the explicit acknowledgement of Egypt's right to call on allies for help and was the object of the deliberate restriction of Egypt's activity in defence of the Canal to the use of 'its own forces'.[4] She restricted the Sultan's power of intervention to the specific case in which it was requested by the

[1] A. Milner, *England in Egypt* (London, Arnold, 1892), 349, 'The Future Outlook'. G. B. Smith, *Ferdinand de Lesseps* (1893), 201. H. Resener, *L'Égypte sous l'Occupation Anglaise et la Question Égyptienne* (Le Caire, 1896), 190.

[2] A. d'Avril, 172–8.

[3] *Egypt. No. 1.* (*1888*) *Correspondence respecting the Proposed International Convention for Securing the Free Navigation of the Suez Canal* (C-5255 of 1888), 41, Salisbury to Egerton, 21 October 1887.

[4] A. d'Avril, 178–80.

territorial power in Egypt because of its inadequate forces. The Powers insisted that the Sultan should then consult them and so deprived Egypt of the right to call on an ally of its own choice. Britain however secured the explicit mention of the rights of the Khedive in opposition to the Turkish wish. The Convention assured Egypt against any attack via the Canal by a self-denying ordinance of the Powers[1] and, by Article XIII, explicitly preserved the sovereignty of Egypt where it was not subjected to specific restrictions. Throughout it sought to isolate the Canal from Egypt. It did not demilitarize, pacify, neutralize, denationalize,[2] internationalize,[3] universalize or extraterritorialize the Canal. Thus Britain defended the rights of Egypt which under Palmerston she had sought to restrict and maintained her position in Egypt, in India and on the high seas. She preserved her right of search by excluding it from the general prohibition of the first article, her access to India in war and peace and her right to send warships and troopships through the waterway. She even gained in a large innovation in international law the right to embark and disembark troops in peacetime without special authorization in the event of an accidental obstruction of the Canal.[4] She diverted her express India mails from the overland route through Egypt to the Canal route in the same year that she signed the Convention of Constantinople. As in 1885 Britain explicitly reserved her absolute liberty of action in Egypt because of the transitory and exceptional state of that country and refused to bring the provisions of the Convention into practical operation during the British occupation. She thus explicitly repudiated the limits imposed on British power in Egypt. She reserved the right to act as interpreter of the Convention's applicability, to admit or to refuse the ships of any other power entrance to the Canal and to 'run an iron-clad through the treaty, just as one drives a four-in-hand through an Act of Parliament'.[5] The British reservation was not however renewed at the time of signature or of ratification on 22 December 1888 and did not become part of the Convention because it was not accepted by the Powers.[6] It nevertheless satisfied British opinion because no questions were asked in the Commons about the Canal from 1887 until 1892 after an annual bout of such questions ever since 1870.

The compromise of 1887–8 was one achieved in harmony with international law as developed in Europe but at the expense of the powers of Asia.[7] The Convention was signed by Turkey but by no other state of Asia or Africa. Unlike the bilateral Clayton–Bulwer Treaty of 1850 for the Central American

[1] A. d'Avril, 187.

[2] W. Cunningham, *The Growth of English Industry and Commerce in Modern Times* (Cambridge University Press, 1907), 871.

[3] H. D. Wolff, 'The Suez Canal and the Egyptian Question', *Quarterly Review* (October 1887), 453.

[4] M. L. Camand, 221.

[5] A. F. Baillie, *Kurrachee: (Karachi)*, 252.

[6] K. Mostofi, 'The Suez Dispute: a Case Study of a Treaty', *Western Political Quarterly* (March 1957), 31–2.

[7] M. L. Camand, 242.

Canal the Convention bore from the first the character of a great international act and was thought worthy to rank beside the Geneva Convention of 1864.[1] It was not signed by Belgium, Greece and Sweden which had been represented at the Conference of Constantinople in 1873 but which had made virtually no use of the Canal. It recognized the equality of all the nine signatory powers in its benefits and invited the accession of non-signatory powers. Thus it recognized the utility of the Canal to the states of the West for war as much as for commerce and enshrined a worldwide extension of territorial rights to the benefit of all Europe. The exclusion of the Red Sea and the Gulf of Aden from its purview immediately placed Ethiopia, which lacked a navy, at a disadvantage in relation to the naval powers of Europe. The Convention confirmed the function of the Red Sea as a corridor to the East, facilitated the extension of European influence along its shores and imposed no restrictions on European expansion in the East. Thus it exposed the states of Asia to the unrestrained erosion of their security and their independence by the commercial and imperial powers of the West. The Convention was, however, riven by the ambiguity and omission inevitable in view of the delicacy of the problem, which was only less complex than that of the Dardanelles. It created the inconceivable, a right of way in time of war as well as in time of peace, open to all and abused by none. That right of way lay through a narrow shallow channel cut through the soil of the richest province of the Ottoman Empire between two seas and at the junction of two continents, which Kipling made into the cross-roads of three continents.

[1] M. L. Camand, 243.

19

THE FROZEN MEAT TRADE OF AUSTRALASIA 1877–1896

ENGLISH predominance in the traffic of the Canal was all the more remarkable because the only English colonies beyond Suez did not use the waterway before 1877. Australia was divided among five colonies with five capitals, lacked the unity imposed on India from Calcutta since 1833 and remained a continent of outposts or an Africa in miniature. Its fringe of settlement faced the Pacific rather than the Indian Ocean while Western Australia remained sparsely peopled. Its colonies lacked the high-priced commodities and passenger-traffic most suited to rapid transit. Their staple product of wool was a bulk commodity in no need of speedy carriage to market: it supplied the freight of a season rather than of a year and was best carried by sailing vessels such as those of George Thompson's Aberdeen White Star Line established in 1825. The Australian route with its great distances and its consequent lack of coaling stations and of profitable ports of call was dominated by the sailing ship. The great westerly gales which stormed almost unchecked around the world in the latitude of 40° south provided the best and cheapest form of power for the voyage outwards via the Cape of Good Hope and also for that homewards via Cape Horn because they discouraged westward voyages via Table Bay. Emigrants also preferred the repose of a sailing ship to the continual shiver, smell and heat of a steamship.[1] The gold rush to Victoria had led to the foundation of new clipper lines such as the Orient Line in 1853[2] while the trade of New Zealand attracted the Albion Shipping Company of Patrick Henderson of Glasgow from 1855 and Shaw Savill & Co. from 1858. From 1852 a branch line of the P. & O. carried the mail and gold of Australia by the Suez overland route first via Singapore, then from 1859 via Port Louis and finally from 1861 via Galle. During the 1860s sailing ships increased their speed on the route to Australia with the building of composite and auxiliary or mixed ships. Australia gained the services of the Loch Line in 1867[3] and the Colonial Line of Watts Milburn & Co. in 1869 so that it was well supplied with the shipping best suited to its needs when the Suez Canal was opened: it became the first call on the triangular England–Australia–China trade route and was even linked by barque direct to the inland tea market of Hankow from 1870.

The ironclad monitor *Cerberus* made the first transit through the Canal on 21–23 December 1870 en route from Newcastle to Melbourne on a one-way

---

[1] J. Berry, *New Zealand as a Field for Emigration* (London, Clarke, 1879), 35.

[2] B. Lubbock, *The Colonial Clippers* (Glasgow, Brown, 1921), 146.

[3] Ibid., 219–20.

voyage in the cause of colonial defence.[1] The use of the Canal saved 545 miles in distance on the Australian route. That saving in distance was much less than the comparable saving on the route to India, was less to the homeland of the colonists than to ports in the Mediterranean and formed only a small proportion of the total length of the voyage, being 4·3 per cent of the 12,700 miles from London to Sydney.[2] Australia's location on the very edge of the Canal's zone of influence explains its slowness to use the new route better than any dissatisfaction of a democratic community with either the aristocratic P. & O. or the heavy tolls charged by the Canal Company. The Pacific Railroad completed in the same year as the Canal also offered an improved overland route to Australia, increased the fascination of the re-established power of the U.S.A. for Australia[3] and made possible the beginning of a service from San Francisco to Sydney from April 1870. The British response to that American enterprise was to extend their eastern cable system to Australia. The British Australian Telegraph Company Ltd. was formed on 3 January 1870 to connect Singapore with Port Darwin via Batavia. The cable was carried around the Cape by the *Hibernia* and *Edinburgh* in eighty-five days (3 August–27 October 1871) while the technical staff travelled out on the *Investigator* through the Canal.[4] After the cable was laid over 1,082 miles to Banjoewanji in fourteen days (7–20 November), the *Edinburgh* and *Hibernia* returned via the Canal. The completion of the land line across 1,973 miles on 22 August 1872 and the repair of the submarine cable on 21 October united the Australian colonies with the world cable-system and the world-market. Those colonies had already developed their own colonial nationalism sufficiently to secure an end to the despatch of convict ships after 1868. The independent Australian Britons who emerged in the 1870s as the sons of the Australian soil and opponents of the Anglophile Australian gentry secured full control over their own tariff policy in 1873 and thereby the power to protect themselves if necessary against the world-market. The laying of the cable from Singapore encouraged the development of steam navigation from Singapore via the Torres Strait rather than via the west-coast route followed by the P. & O. Before the renewal of the P. & O. contract in 1874 at least three steamship companies were registered in London in 1873 for the Australian service. The Eastern and Australian Mail Steamship Company Ltd.,[5] which was formed on 3 May 1873, began its service from Singapore with the *Sun Foo*, which pioneered the steam navigation of the Torres Straits and reached Sydney in thirty days (18 November–17 December 1873). That service

---

[1] *Le Canal de Suez*, 30 Mars 1871, 50–1, 'Les Avantages du Passage par le Canal'.

[2] J. Rabino, 'The Statistical Story of the Suez Canal', *Journal of the Statistical Society* (September 1887), 526.

[3] *Le Canal de Suez*, 26 Mai 1870, 203, 'L'Australie et le Canal de Suez'.

[4] F. Clune, *Overland Telegraph* (Sydney, Angus, 1955), 211.

[5] W. Lawson, *Steam in the Southern Pacific* (Wellington, Gordon, 1909). W. Lawson, *Pacific Steamers* (Glasgow, Brown, 1927). D. Gregory, *Australian Steamships Past and Present* (London, Richards, 1928).

encouraged Singapore to import coal from New South Wales, whose hostility restricted the P. & O. to its mail contract with Victoria.

Australia supplied neither regular nor occasional traffic to the Canal before 1877 except for a tug, a coastal steamer and a dredger. Its harbours attracted sailing tonnage which was forced out of the trades of Asia by steamer competition after the opening of the Canal, as in the China trade from 1872 and in the Calcutta trade from 1878. The consequent reduction in freights made competition by steamships even less economic than before and encouraged shipowners in the England–Australia trade to form in 1876 the first association to maintain outward freights from London in imitation of the steamship lines in the Calcutta trade. The fall in freights affected the fast clippers of the Orient Line more than other vessels. That line began negotiations in February 1877 to charter four steamers from the Pacific Steam Navigation Company, which was thereby relieved of its surplus capacity caused by over-building. Those steamers were used to begin a monthly service by the cool-weather route of the Cape to Adelaide, with postal subsidies from the government of New South Wales and South Australia and with all-white crews in accordance with the 'White Australia' policy which was elaborated between 1876 and 1885. The fast clippers of the Orient Line had averaged 80 days on their outward voyage but 95 days on their homeward voyage. Its pioneer steamer, the *Lusitania*, reached Melbourne in 40 days 6 hours (28 June–8 August 1877) from Plymouth, and so began a sustained assault on the postal monopoly of the P. & O. The *Lusitania* returned to England via the Canal, reached Suez on October 17 in 26 days 12 hours 40 minutes and London in 40 days from Adelaide, so proving the capacity of the Suez route to equalize the time of the homeward with that of the outward voyage.

The success of the Orient Line encouraged the reduction of the Cape record to 19 days 8 hours in 1877 and compelled imitation by the auxiliary screw-steamers of Watts Milburn & Co., whose pioneer mixed vessel the *Whampoa* of 1873 followed the *Lusitania* through the Canal in October 1877, and by those of Money, Wigram & Sons whose mixed vessel the *Kent* returned from Melbourne in March 1878 via the Canal rather than via Cape Horn. Regular voyages through the Canal from Australia began with the seven steamers which passed through in the six months between October 1877 and March 1878. Those steamers established the characteristic Australian use of the Canal for the return voyage to England rather than for the outward voyage[1] via the Cape and enabled Australia to enjoy the advantages of both routes. They also established the pattern of large vessels appropriate to the long voyage from Australia, supplying an average tonnage of 3,311 or 61 per cent above the average gross tonnage of 2,056. They carried 1,252 passengers as well as 18,000 tons of cargo, making a relatively greater contribution to the passenger traffic of the Canal than to its cargo tonnage. They began the

---

[1] *Le Canal de Suez*, 12 Mai 1878, 1–2; 12 Mars 1880, 2–4; 12 Juin 1902, 4095, 'L'Australie et le Canal de Suez'.

shipment through the waterway of Australian wool and may have contributed to the depression of wool prices in Bagdad in 1877. Wool was followed by flour, copper and even wheat during the bad harvests of 1878–9. The steamers using the Canal from Australia rose from three in 1877 to twenty-seven in 1878. The £11,244,000 of British trade with Australia passing through the Canal in 1878 included the cargo carried by the P. & O. and represented 17 per cent of the total British trade through the Canal. Relations between England and Australia were drawn closer by the visit of the first English team of professional cricketers to Australia in 1877, the visit of the first Australian cricket eleven to England in 1878, the organization of exhibitions at Sydney in 1879 and at Melbourne in 1880 and the opening of an office by Thomas Cook in Melbourne in 1879. After the first test match in England in 1880 and the defeat of the English team on their home ground at the Oval on 29 August 1882 the nationalism of both peoples was reinvigorated on the field of sport, where representative teams came to personify 'England' and 'Australia'.

The Orient Steam Navigation Company Ltd. was formed on 12 February 1878 by Anderson, Anderson & Co. and Frederick Green & Co. of Blackwall. It sent the *Garonne* from England on 7 March 1878 via the Cape and bene-fited by the Russian war-scare of 1878, building its first liner as an armed merchant cruiser to the specifications of the Admiralty.[1] James Laing became the first shipowner to make use of the Canal for the outward voyage to Australia when the *Syria* left London on 24 May 1878. The example of the *Syria* was followed by the *Lyttelton* in September 1878, a paddle-tug outward bound to Lyttelton Harbour Board in New Zealand, and by the *Cairnsmuir* of Houlder Brothers in March 1879. The use of the Canal for the outward voyage combined with the development of the Orient Line to usher in a great expansion of Australasian traffic via the Canal from 1878. Steamships were first chartered by such established sailing lines as the Albion Line in 1878 and Shaw Savill in 1879, while the British India Line began negotiations for a mail service via the Canal outwards and homewards.

The competition of the Orient Line stimulated the P. & O. to announce on 16 May 1879 a new fortnightly service of 39 days between London and Melbourne in place of its monthly service. One week later the Orient Line's *John Elder* brought advices from Adelaide which reached London via Suez and Brindisi in 34 days (19 April–23 May) and so saved 10 days on the contract-time of the P. & O. The pioneer clipper *Orient* of 1853 was sold and its name was given to the first specially built steamer of the Orient Line launched in June 1879 by John Elder, inventor of the compound-engine and builder of the compound-engined vessels chartered from the Pacific Steam Navigation Company in 1877. The *Orient* could steam for 40 days without refuelling and reached Adelaide in 37 days 22 hours. The Orient Line then

---

[1] W. J. Loftie, *Illustrated Guide of the Orient Line of Steamers between England and Australia* (London, Orient Steam Navigation Company Ltd., 1880), 2.

arranged with the Pacific Steam Navigation Company a joint fortnightly service to New South Wales in reply to the P. & O.[1] That service saved the Pacific Steam Navigation Company from the excess capacity created by the Pacific War of 1879, opposed democratic Sydney to aristocratic Melbourne but still used the Canal only for the homeward voyage. The new fortnightly service was begun by the Orient-Pacific Line in January 1880 and by the P. & O. in February 1880. The Orient Line employed the best vessels of the Pacific Steam Navigation Company and maintained the same sailing dates as the P. & O. until 7 December 1883. The *Orient* made its first transit of the Canal in March 1880 in a triumph of pilotage because its gross Suez tonnage was 5,438 when the average gross tonnage was 2,192. The Orient Line could not however recognize the Canal as a triumph of engineering because of its limited size and desired to supplement it by a second and more commodious British Canal.[2] The *Orient* then broke the Cape record, reaching Table Bay on 22 April 1880 in 17 days 21 hours from Plymouth against the contract-time of 26 days, and arrived at Adelaide on 9 May in $34\frac{1}{2}$ days, the fastest passage on record.[3]

The fortnightly service increased the Orient steamers using the Canal from fourteen transits in 1879 to twenty-four in 1880. The enterprise of Anderson and Green stimulated competitive emulation by other shipowners in the colonial trade and encouraged the boom of 1880–3 in English shipbuilding. The P. & O. began to build a superior type of liner for its Australian mail service with the two 5,000-ton, 15-knot *Rome* and *Carthage* in 1881. George Thompson ordered his first steamship with the triple-expansion engine invented in 1878 as an even more economic engine than the compound-engine of the *Orient*. The Greenock Steam Ship Company was formed in 1879 and built in 1880 as its pioneer steamers the *Gulf of Finland*, the *Gulf of Panama* and the *Gulf of Suez*. The *Gulf of Finland* left London on 14 December 1880 to pioneer its outward service via the Cape to Australia and first passed through the Canal in August 1881. William Lund began his Blue Anchor Line of steamships via the Cape early in 1880. With the *Aconcagua* on 5 January 1881 the Orient Line began to send out one outward steamer in three via the Canal during the winter season and so began to transfer outward traffic from the Cape route. The hostility of the P. & O. made coaling at Aden very difficult for the Orient Line and compelled it to rent from Mauritius in 1882 the two palm-covered islands of Diego Garcia, largest of the Chagos atolls. Diego Garcia was thenceforward used as a coaling station by the Orient Line and also by Lund's Blue Anchor Line.

The *Merkara* of the British India Line began a new mail service from London via the Canal (28 February) to Queensland, arriving in sixty-two days (11 February–13 April 1881).[4] That service was created to replace the service

[1] *The Times*, 28 October 1879, 7 i; 30 October, 7 ii; 3 November, 7 i.
[2] W. J. Loftie, *Illustrated Guide of the Orient Line* (1880), 41.
[3] *The Times*, 11 May 1880, 9 vi.
[4] *The Times*, 20 January 1881, 11 vi. G. Blake, *B.I. Centenary 1856–1956* (London, Collins, 1956), 113.

of the Eastern and Australian Mail Steamship Company, which had refused to make Brisbane its terminal port in Australia. At the request of the Premier, Sir Thomas McIlwraith, Edwyn Dawes founded the British India Associated Steamers to undertake the 44-day service, the longest mail service in the world, in return for an annual subsidy of £55,000. Thus the British India Line encircled the Indian Ocean with its services extending from Delagoa Bay to Brisbane. The new service became the first independent mail service to Australia via the Canal. The British India Line also began to carry emigrants when the *Almora* left London in September 1881 with 161 emigrants for Queensland via the Canal. The use of the route via the Torres Strait was intended to prevent the loss of emigrants to Adelaide, Melbourne or Sydney and encouraged Queensland boldly to annex South-East New Guinea on 4 April 1883, to the dismay of the Colonial Office.

The pioneer steamer of George Thompson's line the *Aberdeen* reached Melbourne via the Cape in forty-two days in 1881, giving a great impetus to the use of the Cape route by large and economically engined steamers. Table Bay Docks were accordingly improved in 1882 by the completion of the Robinson Graving Dock and the building of a 500-foot coaling jetty to supply the needs of such large steamers. Thus Cape Town preserved its function as the half-way house to Australia. The Cape route became thenceforward the most formidable competitor of the Canal as a route for both steam and sail: during the dispute of 1883 it even attracted tea-steamers outward bound to China. The growing competition of steam forced passenger-carrying sailing ships to transfer from 1881 from the colonial into the jute trade. The rise in the proportion of the wool shipped through the Canal from 10 to 20 per cent during 1881 followed direct purchases in Sydney from 1879 by the manufacturers of France and Belgium and began the advance of the London sales to January. Steamers for the Australian trade were first ordered in 1882 by Money, Wigram & Sons, by William Lund and by Archibald Currie. The P. & O. began a through service to Australia via Colombo in place of Galle and began to shift from the Indian and China trades into the Australian trade. Colombo became a port of call first for the Austrian Lloyd from 1879 and then for the P. & O. and the Messageries from June 1882. Its south-western breakwater, built by an imperial loan between 1874 and 1886, gave it protection against the south-west monsoon and the basis of a great artificial harbour in place of its open roadstead. Its facilities for coaling ended the use of Diego Garcia as a coaling port by 1888. Colombo became the great bunkering port of the Indian Ocean, raising the value of Ceylon's imports of coal to equal the value of its cotton textile imports in 1890. Its harbour dues were used from the very first year to repay the imperial loan and thereafter provided the Government of Ceylon with a growing source of revenue. Colombo benefited by its proximity to the plantation hinterland of the island at the expense of Galle, which it replaced on the route to the East as well as on that to Australia. It attracted the merchant-houses of Galle but did not develop a large entrepôt trade or become the emporium of the East as Sir William Gregory had hoped in 1877.[1] As it grew in population and activity Ceylon gained a new commercial administrative focus in addition to its cultural centre at Anurudhapura.

The British monopoly of the Australian trade was broken by the Sloman Line and the Messageries. Robert M. Sloman, who had founded Hamburg's first steamship line in 1839, established a service to Australia in 1879, began to use the Canal from 1882 for the return voyage in the winter wool-moving season and thenceforward developed Australia's trade with the Continent, especially with Germany and Belgium. The interest of France in Oceania increased with its commitment to the Panama enterprise. The island of New Caledonia had been a penal colony since 1864 and recruited its population on the original Australian pattern despite strong protests to France from Australia. Its minerals entered into world trade with the successive discovery of copper in 1872, nickel in 1874, cobalt in 1876, chrome in 1878 and lead in 1883. The French company formed by the Rothschilds, Le Nickel, mined the nickel from 1876, smelted it on the island from 1879 and supplied the world market before the discovery of the Sudbury ores in Canada in 1883. The Messageries began a new monthly mail service via the Canal in 1882 to Noumea in New Caledonia. The service began from Marseilles, despite the protests of Le Havre, Bordeaux and Dunkirk, whose sailing ships carried the minerals of New Caledonia. It linked together the island-outposts of the French empire, calling at Mahé in the Seychelles, Réunion and Mauritius as well as at Melbourne and Sydney, and increased the French pressure on Madagascar. It gave Australia the advantage of another first-class passenger service and helped to increase its trade with France. The hope of the Chamber of Commerce of Marseilles that their port might become the wool entrepôt for Switzerland, Alsace and Northern France was, however, frustrated by the equal rates charged by the Messageries on the transport of wool to Marseilles and to London. The sailing ship continued to compete for the transport of the minerals of New Caledonia and carried the island's first shipment of silver to the Clyde in 1886.

Emigrants were not as conspicuous in the traffic of the Canal as in the contemporary Atlantic trade because Asia held forth little prospect for colonization while the Cape route carried the one great stream of emigrants to Australia. After the Orient Line had begun to use the Canal for outward passages during the winter season Government emigrants to New South Wales began to use the Canal route during 1882, when their numbers exceeded those of both pilgrims and convicts. In 1883 the Orient Line contracted with the Government of New South Wales to carry emigrants and thenceforward abandoned the use of the Cape route completely. It thereby benefited at the expense of the P. & O. which never carried emigrants and was deemed less Australian than the Orient Line. Perhaps 40 per cent of the second great wave

[1] Lady Gregory, *Sir William Gregory, K.C.M.G., Formerly Member of Parliament and Sometime Governor of Ceylon* (London, Murray, 1894), 268, 316, 386.

of emigrants, which brought 38,000 every year to Australia between 1876 and 1890, followed the Canal route to their new home. In summer they were exposed to the heat of the Red Sea but they benefited in health, comfort and morality by travel on the fast steamships[1] and were fortified by compulsory church services and the exclusion of all but religious works from the ship's library. Emigrants to Queensland perhaps fared worse than those to New South Wales: certainly George Lansbury found the conditions of an emigrant on board Westray's *Duke of Devonshire* in 1884 as appalling as those of a passenger on his return voyage on the *Merkara* of the British India Line in 1885.[2] The Canal Company followed the example of the Atlantic shipping lines which distinguished first-class 'passengers' sharply from steerage 'emigrants'. It ranked the emigrants to Australia together with Arab pilgrims and Russian and French convicts under the general designation of 'Pilgrims, Emigrants, Convicts' and separated them clearly from 'Civilian Passengers'. The emigrant traffic confirmed the predominance of non-military passengers using the Canal in 1880–4. It supplied some compensation for the lack of cargo on the outward voyage and enabled more Australian exports, especially wool, to be shipped via the Canal to London from 1882. The bulk of the emigrants came from Britain and not from the Continent, although the lands of the Mediterranean did supply some. The Breton Marquis de Rays was revolted by the rise of republican sentiment in France which brought 2,000 Communards in 1879 back through the Canal from New Caledonia. He launched a scheme to establish a Catholic, Royalist and Legitimist colony at Port-Breton in 'New France' in the south-eastern corner of New Ireland, to the east of New Britain and New Guinea and on the highway between Australia and China. He raised £200,000 and sent out four batches of emigrants, the first via the Cape and the other three via the Canal in the *Génil* in March 1880, the *India* in July 1880 and the *Nouvelle Bretagne* in April 1881 to a non-existent settlement. The disastrous failure of the scheme earned the little colonel, 'Charles I', four years' imprisonment on his conviction in 1884 for fraud and freed the surviving Italian emigrants to establish 'New Italy' in New South Wales.[3]

The British emigrants were more easily absorbed into the fixed mould of Australian life. The returning flow of colonists swelled the ranks of the 'civilian passengers' using the Canal and brought far more profit to the shopkeepers of Port Said than the outward-bound emigrants.[4] Those travellers paid homage to England as 'the focus of the highest form of earthly civilization'[5] and

[1] J. Rabino, 529.

[2] G. Lansbury, *My Life* (London, Constable, 1928), 59–60, names the *Mercaro* which is not recorded in *Lloyd's Register* for 1885.

[3] J. H. Niau, *The Phantom Paradise. The Story of the Expedition of the Marquis de Rays* (Sydney, Angus, 1936).

[4] W. J. Loftie, *Orient Line Guide. Chapters for Travellers by Sea and by Land* (London, Low, 1890), 157–65, 'The Suez Canal'.

[5] W. Thorburn, *The Great Game* (1875), 24.

included colonial aspirants to wider recognition for their abilities, like the outward flow of Anglo-Indians. They were quite distinct from the Anglo-Indian officials, who had no need to enquire the nationality of 'the vulgar riff-raff which lands at Colombo, and which goes to see the large tortoise, and then to see Arabi'.[1] The Australians and Anglo-Indians found however a common meeting-ground in the cricket game which became a custom at Colombo from 1887. They were also united by a common tradition of independent loyalism, a common aversion to General William Booth's plan of 1890 to settle in Australia paupers and reclaimed criminals from Darkest England and a common hostility to free trade, to economic liberalism and to the Suez Canal Company as a private French enterprise.

The pattern of Australia's use of the Canal was largely established between 1879 and 1883 when the number of its passengers rose by 360 per cent, the number of its transits by 410 per cent and the net Australian tonnage by 680 per cent while cable messages rose by only 105 per cent.

Fig. 1. *Australian Traffic through the Suez Canal, 1877–1883*

Year	Transits	Net Australian tonnage	Annual per cent increase	Per cent of total tonnage	Emigrants	Passengers including emigrants	Annual per cent increase	Per cent of total passengers
1877	2	4,904		0·21	—	417		0·57
1878	27	46,248	843	2·04	—	3,509	740	3·54
1879	42	71,600	54·8	3·16	—	6,865	95·5	8·12
1880	51	107,553	50	3·5	—	5,367	− 21·8	5·29
1881	98	208,570	94·3	5·04	337	9,770	82	10·79
1882	166	343,006	64·5	6·76	13,499	20,862	113	15·92
1883	226	488,735	42·5	8·46	22,686	31,420	50·5	26·36

SOURCE: *Le Canal de Suez*, 12 Juin 1902, 4095, 'L'Australie et le Canal de Suez'.

Thus Australia added another stream of traffic to the Canal as the ship-owners first supplemented their sailing ships by auxiliary engines then chartered steamships and finally ordered steamships, in competition amongst themselves without any disturbing influence from outside their ranks. Australian traffic proved a welcome addition which buttressed the prosperity of the Canal Company in 1884, a year of economic depression in Europe and the U.S.A. That traffic had its own distinctive features. It supplied more homeward than outward shipping and cargo to the Canal and never supplied outward tonnage to the Canal in ballast alone but used the Cape route for the outward voyage. Thus it reinforced the dominance of northbound tonnage established in the traffic of the Canal from 1886. It also brought to the Canal its largest steamers and to the Canal Company its largest individual payments including by 1886 £1,800 per single transit[2] and 8s. 4d. on each of 34,000

[1] Lady Gregory, *Sir William Gregory* (1894), 393, Sir William to Lady Gregory, 14 February 1884.
[2] *Saturday Review*, 5 February 1887, 188.

passengers. Australia supplied more passengers than any other country. Its postal traffic increased the pressure for speedier transit and especially for night-transit by electric light. Australia became the only part of the Empire of settlement to use the Canal and so developed interests distinct from those of the Cape and of Canada, which would benefit by the closure of the Canal. It was drawn within the sphere of the Canal after its colonial nationalism had crystallized: it developed no special interest in Egypt or the Canal as such, despite the development of Egyptology in Australia since the 1850s. Thus it paid no contribution to the cost of the 1882 expedition to Egypt,[1] despite hints in the Commons[2] and in the press. 'To nobody is the Canal more useful than to our countrymen in Australia.'[3]

The rise of steamship traffic was so sudden and unexpected that some sailing shipowners expected the ultimate loss of their trade[4] and cast the whole blame upon the Suez Canal. 'I am speaking with some prejudice, but I entertain a very strong opinion that, speaking especially for this country, I consider it is an unmitigated nuisance. I say it has altered our profits, it has altered our trade altogether, it has prevented our being the *entrepôt* that we used to be, and I think that the world would have been happier and better without it. That is my opinion. I am quite aware that I am considered very retrograde in my views, but the British shipping interest would have been very much better without it.'[5] Many shipowners followed the example of the Andersons and converted to steam, especially between 1884 and 1890. Others developed the capacity and even the speed of their vessels. Thus the *Maulesden* reached Tasmania from Greenock in sixty-one days and Brisbane in sixty-nine days (2 March–10 May 1883) to establish a record which was never approached.[6] The *Cutty Sark* reached Ushant in sixty-seven days from Sydney (17 October –23 December 1885)[7] and established its reputation in the wool trade of Australia rather than in the China tea trade for which it had been built: it carried eight tea cargoes (1870–7) but twelve wool cargoes (1883–94).[8] Throughout the 1880s wool was carried by sail as the ideal clipper cargo which required far less stiffening by shingle ballast than tea. The last wool-clippers were launched in 1891 during the boom of 1889–93 in the construction of large steel sailing ships of 2,000–3,000 tons, which T. Jenkins Hains christened 'wind-jammers' in 1899. Thus Australia preserved its sail fleet and the advantage of choice between two competing routes.

The Russian war-scare of 1885 and the despatch of two warships to defend

---

[1] *The Times*, 2 September 1882, 4i.

[2] Hansard, *Commons Debates*, 27 July 1883, 801, 804, Arthur Arnold and Gladstone.

[3] J. Morley, 'The Expansion of England', *Macmillan's Magazine* (February 1884), 250.

[4] *Royal Commission on the Depression of Trade and Industry, Third Report: Minutes of Evidence*, Q 10,307, 25 March 1886, T. L. Devitt.

[5] *Royal Commission on the Depression of Trade and Industry*, 25 March 1886, W. R. Price, Q 10,091a.

[6] B. Lubbock, *The Colonial Clippers* (1921), 325.

[7] B. Lubbock, *The Log of the 'Cutty Sark'* (Glasgow, Brown, 1954), 227–32.

[8] Ibid., 326–7.

King George's Sound, the best harbour on the Suez–Melbourne route, ended seven successive years of expansion in Australia's Canal tonnage. A new phase in the development of its trade began with the discovery of the silver-lead-zinc mine of Broken Hill in 1885 and the rise of the frozen meat trade. Germany also established a new subsidized mail service after it had occupied New Guinea and the Bismarck Archipelago in 1884 and the Marschall Islands in 1885. That service by the North German Lloyd was begun by the *Salier* from Bremen on 14 July 1886 and compelled the Sloman Line to end its unprofitable and irregular service and return to the New York trade. The P. & O. began a direct through service from Aden to Australia in 1886 in order to compete with the C.P.R. as well as with the Lloyd. It also decided to enter the democratic emigrant traffic to Australia after finding its passenger-receipts for 1886 inadequate: in 1887 it first began the large-scale transport of second-class passengers and even tried a sixty-day tourist cruise to India.[1] The Orient Line secured after ten years of competition a division of the mail contract of 1887 with the P. & O. when the mail was transferred from the overland route to the Canal, and the Orient Line abandoned Chagot for coaling in favour of Colombo. It suffered most of all by the new competition and paid no dividend for the financial year 1887: it advertised in 1889 the first ocean liners for cruising to the Norwegian fjords and paid no dividend for the four years from 1891 to 1894.[2]

The dynamic element in Anglo-Australian trade in the 1880s was supplied by the new commodity of frozen meat. The growth of population and industry in Britain had increased the pressure on the supply of food while the growth of wealth had increased the consumption of meat per head as prices rose.[3] The import of meat from overseas necessitated the extension of the techniques of refrigeration to the transport of large quantities over long distances and through the tropics. The successful development of refrigerating machinery gave the Canal a new traffic, which was a northbound rather than a southbound trade, although a shipment of fresh meat in ice was made from Glasgow to Rangoon via the Canal in the *Irrawaddy* by June 1876, six months before the pioneer shipment of meat from Rouen to Buenos Aires. The successful transport of frozen meat from Buenos Aires to Le Havre in 1877–8 inspired McIlwraith, McEacharn & Co. to charter the s.s. *Strathleven* and install on board the Bell-Coleman dry-air compression machine patented in 1877. The *Strathleven* carried the pioneer shipment of 40 tons of frozen meat, 70 beef and 500 sheep carcasses, at 12° F. through the Canal on 14 January 1880 and reached London in sixty-four days (29 November 1879–2 February 1880) from Sydney.[4] The sale of the meat in Smithfield Market at treble its price

---

[1] *The Times*, 7 December 1887, 10v.

[2] *Stock Exchange Official Year Book, 1898*, 1122.

[3] M. G. Mulhall, *England's New Sheep-Farm* (London, Stanford, 1882), 5.

[4] *The Times*, 9 February 1880, 11i; 12 February, 10vi; 9 March, 10v, 'Fresh Meat from Australia'. J. T. Critchell and J. Raymond, *A History of the Frozen Meat Trade* (London, Constable, 1912), 30–2.

in Australia made the venture a commercial success in contrast to earlier shipments made in 1873 and 1876. Another shipment followed so that two of the thirty-five steamers which passed through the Canal from Australia in 1880 carried frozen meat in bulk. Refrigerating equipment was installed on board the vessels of the Orient Line from 1881 and in the new mail-steamers ordered by the P. & O. in 1881 for its Australian service. Frozen meat companies were formed in Melbourne from 1880 and in London from 1881, when freezing machinery supplied the first outward cargo of the *Merkara* to Brisbane. The first cold store was opened at Victoria Dock, London, in 1882. The reduction of the sheep flocks of England by 15 per cent between 1879 and 1882 by liver fluke stimulated the development of the new trade, the development of Queensland and New Zealand, the shift from sail to steam and the extension of the freezing technique to other commodities. The first shipment of 100 tons of butter reached London in sixty-four days (18 November 1880–20 January 1881) from Melbourne in the *Protos*. A shipment of frozen fish was even carried in the Orient Line's *Lusitania* through the Canal in May 1881 to Melbourne, although the appropriate technique of quick-freezing was not developed before 1933. Australia's example was followed by New Zealand from 1881 and by Argentina from 1882.

New Zealand's first cargo of 5,000 frozen sheep carcasses was carried not by steamship but by the fast iron clipper *Dunedin* of the Albion Shipping Company. That shipment of 130 tons reached London in ninety-eight days (15 February–25 May 1882) and sold at double its price in Dunedin, Scotch meat having reached famine prices at Leadenhall.[1] 'The fact is prodigious.'[2] Sheep-farming, until then the last reserve of English agriculture, seemed to be threatened, opening up the possibility of an aristocratic emigration to New Zealand and offering emigrant farmers an alternative destination to Texas and Virginia.[3] The Albion Line suffered competition from the New Zealand Shipping Company, established in 1873, and from the Sloman Line. The New Zealand Shipping Company's iron barque *Mataura* carried the second shipment of meat in 103 days (12 June–26 September 1882) while the Sloman Line entered the trade from New Zealand via the Canal from September 1882.[4] The Albion Line was bought on 6 November 1882 by Shaw Savill from P. Henderson & Co., which thenceforward abandoned its interest in the New Zealand trade and concentrated on its trade to Burma. The Shaw Savill and Albion Company Ltd. was then registered on 10 November 1882[5] as a defensive amalgamation of the British interests in the trade against the competition of the New Zealand Shipping Company. The new firm continued to equip sailing ships to carry frozen meat but also began to shift from sail to steam and

---

[1] M. G. Mulhall, 3.   [2] *The Times*, 27 May 1882, 11 v.
[3] M. G. Mulhall, 13.
[4] F. C. Bowen, *The Flag of the Southern Cross. The History of Shaw Savill and Albion Co. Limited 1858–1939* (London, Shaw Savill, 1948), 46.
[5] S. D. Waters, *Shaw Savill Line. One Hundred Years of Trading* (Christchurch, Whitcombe, 1961), 69.

acquired its first steamship in 1883, when New Zealand first supplied England with more mutton than Australia. The New Zealand Shipping Company also ordered five steamships for the frozen meat trade from the Fairfield Shipbuilding Yard under the influence of Sir William Pearce, who held interests in both the shipping and shipbuilding firms. The competition between the two lines accelerated the voyage to New Zealand as much as that to the Cape had been in the 1870s. The *British King*, which reached Wellington via the Cape in fifty days (1 January–19 March 1883), was the first steamer of the New Zealand Shipping Company fitted with refrigerating machinery and the first steamer to carry frozen meat to London via Cape Horn in the path of the *Dunedin*. The Company's chartered steamer *Ionic* reduced the voyage to Wellington to 43 days 22 hours (26 April–11 June 1883) while its *Ruapehu* reached Plymouth on 14 May 1884 in 39 days.[1] By October 1884 it had acquired the largest refrigerated fleet in the world but found its fast 15-knot steamers uneconomic in competition with sailing vessels. It was compelled to sign with Shaw Savill the joint mail contract of 30 October 1884 for round the world sailings via Cape Town to New Zealand and back to England via Cape Horn: thus the pattern established by the sailing ship was maintained by the new high-powered steamships such as Shaw Savill's *Arawa* which was fitted for 25,000 carcasses and reached Hobart in thirty-eight days (5 November–19 December 1884) and Otago in forty-three days.[2] The new service reduced the time of the voyage by more than half and greatly stimulated trade.

From 1884 the large-scale shipment of frozen meat was begun from New Zealand by Nelson Brothers Ltd., who used the English railways from 1885 for distribution and made forward contracts from 1887 with the sheep farmers. Exhibits at the Lord Mayor's Show in 1885 and at the Colonial and Indian Exhibition in 1886 stimulated the consumption of 'New Zealand Frozen Mutton—the Meat of the Future'.[3] The trade raised the value of New Zealand's exports above that of its imports in 1886 and so gave the colony its first export surplus. The large sheep owners were saved from the low wool prices of 1875–81 and from the burden of excess capacity in flocks and herds. The creation of smaller farms in the plains was encouraged by the introduction from 1886 of the small grazing lease.[4] The industry was pioneered in Otago and then taken up in Canterbury, Southland and the North Island, which was colonized through the use of the Romney Marsh breed with its capacity to rear a large proportion of lambs under a heavy rainfall. The carcass was improved by crossing the merino with the English Leicester and Shropshire so as to develop the cross-bred dual-purpose sheep, whose meat appeared bright red on thawing while that of the merino remained dark. Cross-breeding increased the demand for the English Leicester as a stud sheep and stimulated

---

[1] *The Times*, 15 May 1884, 6ii.
[2] F. C. Bowen, 58.   [3] Critchell and Raymond, 279.
[4] J. D. Gould, 'The Occupation of Farm Land in New Zealand, 1874–1911: a Preliminary Survey', *Business Archives and History* (August 1965), 133.

the competitive improvement of the lean merino sheep of Argentina while leaving the production of fine merino wool to Australia. Frozen-meat factories began their extensive and continuous development as the industrial appendage of the pastoral community from 1889 onwards when Australia was harassed by droughts. Those farmers' companies developed under the paternal guidance of the Department of Agriculture established in 1892. New Zealand remained bound to England by navigation and commerce as well as by emigration and investment, despite the protective tariff of 1888. The 'Britain of the South' became a powerful counterbalance to the nationalist colonies of Australia.[1] The growth of the new trade enabled the Government of New Zealand to discontinue the mail subsidy after 1889 in favour of a poundage-payment. Thereafter the New Zealand Shipping Company found its fast steamers more uneconomic than ever and had to be reorganized after paying no dividends for the four years down to 1888–9. Edwyn Dawes, who had especially identified himself with the frozen-meat trade of the British India Line, acquired Pearce's interest in 1890 and became chairman of the Company. He removed its head office from Christchurch to London, disposed of all its sailing ships and replaced between 1891 and 1899 its fast steamers by more profitable cargo vessels.[2] On the death of William Mackinnon in 1893 Dawes succeeded him as Chairman of the British India Steam Navigation Company and as a director of the Suez Canal Company.

Australia began the regular commercial shipment of frozen meat in 1883. The new product never rivalled Australia's older staple of merino wool but increased the security of the woolgrower by providing an overseas market for mutton as well as for wool. The new trade created an outlet for surplus meat additional to canning and refining for tallow and reduced canning to the secondary function of treating meat below prime quality. In general Australia preserved its merino stock but produced through cross-breeding a large-bodied sheep with a fleece of cross-bred wool. Freezing machinery, especially the Haslam compressed dry-air machine developed in 1880, was imported from London via the Canal. The necessary investments were undertaken by local rather than by English capital down to 1912–14. The export of frozen mutton from New South Wales and of frozen beef from Queensland concentrated economic activity more than ever in the ports but increased the value of rural land and the strength of the landed interest. The trade helped to develop inland tropical Queensland, which established freezing enterprises from 1883, especially along the Brisbane River, made its first shipment from Brisbane in 1884 on the British-India *Dorunda*,[3] and became the home of the bulk of Australia's cattle, with a higher proportion available for export than the other colonies.

The meat was shipped solely to England exclusively under the English flag

---

[1] G. R. Parkin, *Imperial Federation. The Problem of National Unity* (London, Macmillan, 1892), 229.

[2] Critchell and Raymond, 361–3.   [3] Ibid., 36.

and largely in bulk shipments, so offsetting the growth of direct trade, especially in wool, between Australia and the Continent. It was carried by the P. & O. from 1887[1] at freights reduced from $2\frac{1}{2}d.$ to the round $1d.$ per pound. Refrigeration was also extended to fruit in 1888 and to butter in 1889. The trade provided the Canal with a new commodity-season because the frozen meat was shipped largely between December and May. It encouraged an increase in the number and size of steamships trading with Australia. The meat competed in the English market more with American meat than with English meat and proved less damaging to home producers of meat than the import of wheat was to the home producers of wheat. The advent of the low-cost primary producers of meat restrained the rise in price of home-produced meat under the pressure of growing demand. Meat prices reached their peak in 1882–3. Beef prices fell from 1883–4 side by side with declining imports because of an increase in home production and the expectation of competition.[2] Mutton prices fell more sharply from 1883–4 than beef prices because the mutton of New Zealand was more competitive than the beef of Australia. Existing channels of commerce were so reluctant to handle the new commodity on a large scale that shipowners were compelled to invest in cold stores on land, such as the Central Markets Cold Air Stores Limited formed in 1884,[3] as well as in cold chambers on shipboard. The multiple shops opened by John Bell & Sons from 1879 favoured the trade on a cost-including-freight basis rather than a consignment basis. The c.i.f. trade which developed from 1888 encouraged grading by the producers from 1890, forward-purchasing by the buyer and shipment by steam rather than by sail: thereby the retailer was assured of his supply for six months ahead.[4] The urban-industrial markets of the Manchester and Cardiff areas were conquered by frozen meat, especially by 'prime Canterbury' meat with its familiar though deceptive name. Those markets accepted cheap meat as they did the cheap tea of Assam and the reborn shoddy cloth of Batley. The imports from Australasia did not compete directly with home production but served a separate market. They reduced the import of live cattle from its peak of 1890 and the import of live sheep from its peak of 1895. Sheep land was abandoned to the deer over large tracts of the Scottish Highlands.[5] British farmers were discouraged from slaughtering their stock before maturity[6] and encouraged to concentrate on the highest quality of production as well as on the highly profitable breeding of pedigree stock for the world-market.[7] The landed interest of Britain thus survived the deluge of antipodean meat as it had that of transatlantic wheat.

After the experiments in the 1870s and the expansion in the 1880s the 1890s became a decade of organization for the trade under the impact of the

[1] Critchell and Raymond, 129.
[2] R. H. Hooker, 'The Meat Supply of the United Kingdom', *Journal of the Royal Statistical Society*, 18 May 1909, 337–8, 344–5.
[3] Critchell and Raymond, 167.
[4] Ibid., 102–5.
[5] Ibid., 324.
[6] M. G. Mulhall, 8.
[7] Critchell and Raymond, 323–4.

Australian crises of 1892–3 and 1896–8. The crisis of 1892–3 followed a fall in wool prices from 1891 and a financial crisis in 1892. It harassed shipowners by a lack of freight and farmers by a glut of stock, for which frozen-meat export was recommended as a remedy. It stimulated a shift from wool to beef and a rapid increase in the number of cattle to a peak in 1894. It encouraged producers to try and bypass the London entrepôt by developing direct exports to Liverpool from 1892 and to open up other markets in India, Germany and the British Army after France imposed import restrictions in 1892. The market of Port Said was supplied for the first time from 1892 by McIlwraith, McEacharn & Co., Wills & Co. and Nelson & Sons. Thus frozen meat began to compete with the live cattle imported from Syria for the supply of passing ships and was supplemented by the import of butter and fruit from 1894. Frozen meat was supplied to the garrisons of Gibraltar and Malta from 1895, when it was also first marketed in Colombo. Thus the ports of the Suez route provided additional markets for Australian produce. For the Mediterranean trade a special thawing process using a current of hot dry air was patented in 1894 by C. A. Lichtenberg of Wills & Co. of Port Said.[1]

Producers were encouraged to agitate for a reduction in freights in 1893–4, to experiment with the shipment of live cattle and sheep in 1894[2] and to ship chilled beef at high speed for the first time from Sydney in 1894 and from Wellington in 1895. The extension of refrigeration from meat to other commodities proved more successful, especially to fruit and butter. Fruit had first been exported in 1888 from South Australia by the Orient Line and in 1891 from Victoria and Tasmania by the P. & O.: thenceforth the English market was increasingly supplied during the English winter with apples from the antipodes. Butter shipments had been made in 1889 to London but only began on a large scale from 1892 after the establishment of the first butter factory: thenceforth butter was shipped from November to April when the milk-yield in Europe was declining. The first shipment of cheese from New Zealand to London took place in 1893. Rabbits were first shipped from Australia in 1895, so turning a nuisance into a benefit. The exceptionally heavy meat imports from Australia in 1895 compelled the London importers to establish the Frozen Meat Trade Association in order to control prices. The first direct shipment to Manchester was made in 1895 after the opening of the Manchester Ship Canal, which failed however to become a highway for argosies laden with the frozen produce of the antipodes because of price-cutting by the importers to Liverpool from the River Plate.[3]

While English farmers benefited by the rise in prices from 1896 the drought of 1896–1902 ended the great sheep boom which had begun in Australia in the 1860s and reduced the number of sheep in Australia by 45 per cent, the number of cattle by 42 per cent and the number of cattle in Queensland by

---

[1] Patent Number 1489 of 23 January 1894.
[2] Critchell and Raymond, 408.
[3] Ibid., 215–16, 223.

70 per cent.[1] The crisis of 1896–8, ushered in by the drought, provoked the first Australian protest in 1896 over the Suez Canal tolls, which prevented cargo-steamers from using the Canal on their outward journey to Australia, imposed a heavy tax on their homeward journey and served the same alien ends as the high freights exacted by English shipowners. Australian producers imitated the London importers and formed the Australian Meat Export Trade Association in September 1896. They also benefited by the weekly transmission of Smithfield prices by cable from 2 July 1897, the introduction of the first frozen meat insurance tariff in 1898 and the appointment of the first Refrigerating Engineer Surveyor by Lloyds.[2] The crisis reduced British imports from Australia between 1897 and 1900 but increased those from New Zealand, which passed the General Meat Inspection Act of 1900 and so ended the era of 'unsatisfactory cargoes' of 1885–99. It also encouraged the extension of refrigeration to the transport of eggs by 1900 but paved the way for the establishment of the supremacy of Argentine beef in the British market. Argentina benefited by its proximity to that market, by the greater centralization of its commerce and by its continuous operations around the year. Australia could not compete with such a low-cost producer nor rescue England from dependence on foreign beef as effectively as India had freed it from dependence on foreign tea. The frozen meat trade thus became a main factor in the economic growth of Australia between 1890 and 1910[3] but 'revolutionized agriculture in New Zealand'[4] and greatly diversified the traffic of the Canal.

[1] R. Duncan, 'The Australian Export Trade with the United Kingdom in Refrigerated Beef, 1880–1940', *Business Archives and History* (August 1962), 110.
[2] G. Blake, *Lloyd's Register of Shipping 1760–1960* (1960), 81.
[3] Critchell and Raymond, 300.
[4] Critchell and Raymond, 305, quoting Sir Joseph Ward, Prime Minister of New Zealand from 1906 to 1912.

20

THE EXPORT TRADE OF INDIA, 1882–1896

T HE greatest technical change in the history of ocean shipping since the voyage of da Gama had won acceptance by 1879, ending the role of the Canal as an innovation and ushering in the greatest expansion in traffic that it had ever known. Passengers became familiar enough with the waterway to dispense with the admiration of its first observers: by 1880 they pronounced the Canal a dull affair as their ship steamed through the vast solitude at the regulation 5 knots[1] and were no longer impressed by their first sight of the Southern Cross in the Red Sea. Clients began to plead for increased facilities and for lower tolls. The creator of the Canal turned from the routine administration of a successful enterprise to win new laurels through the canalization of the isthmus of Panama. After the depression of 1878–9 the traffic of the Canal experienced continuous expansion until 1886 with its greatest expansion in the years 1880–2 and 1885. Lesseps' estimate of 1854 of an annual traffic of 3,000,000 tons was first exceeded in 1880 while his revised estimate of 1862 of 4,000,000 tons was exceeded in 1881. The time of transit which had fallen gradually between 1873 and 1879 began to rise sharply under the afflux of traffic. Between 1879 and 1883 the number of transits increased by 124 per cent, the net register tonnage by 155 per cent and the annual revenues by 121 per cent but share-values rose by 228 per cent and dividends by 1200 per cent.

In that sustained expansion the steamship established its supremacy over the sailing ship, and North-West Europe its dominance over the Mediterranean. The expansion of the world-ports of the North Sea was sharply reflected in the traffic of the Canal. In 1881 the mercantile élite of Bremen founded the German Steamship Company 'Hansa' which began a direct cargo service via the Canal to Calcutta for jute and to Bombay for cotton, so pioneering the first German steamship line to India, ten years after the establishment of the first German steamship line to China. The enterprise of the Hansa Line began the rapid growth of German Canal tonnage, which rose tenfold between 1879 and 1883 so that it first surpassed that of Austria, Italy and Spain in 1882 to rank Germany as the fourth client of the Canal after Britain, France and the Netherlands. Germany also gained a new ally after France occupied in Tunis Italy's predestined inheritance and the key of the Mediterranean. The day after Italy became the Mediterranean member of the Triple Alliance the St. Gotthard Railway Tunnel was completed on 21 May 1882 as a new link between Germany and Italy and was used by the first train

[1] *The Times*, 2 April 1880, 7 v, 'The Suez Canal'. A. E. Nordenskiöld, *The Voyage of the 'Vega' Round Asia and Europe* (London, Macmillan, 1881), ii. 441.

from Lucerne to Milan on 1 July. That new transalpine route competed with the circuitous Rhone route via Marseilles and with the Mont Cenis route: it made Genoa virtually a German port, helped to reconcile the Genoese to Piedmontese rule and extended German influence into the heart of the Mediterranean. The economic expansion of Northern Europe thus frustrated the hopes cherished by Mediterranean states since the 1850s. The decrease in the British share of the Canal's traffic from 1882 was caused by the growth of German and Dutch tonnage and not by that of Mediterranean tonnage. The inland sea became a great highway for the shipping and trade of North-West Europe while its ports specialized more in passengers and mail than in general cargo. Marseilles was thus reduced to a port of call by the Netherland Steamship Company from 1882, by the P. & O. from 1883 and by the Anchor Line from 1885. The entrepôt trade was developed most by ports under alien control such as Malta and Suez. The shipping of the Mediterranean increasingly required mail subsidies to protect it from competition and its sea-captains found employment less on the Suez route than on the Canal itself, where the pilots were French, Italian, Greek, Austrian and Maltese. From 1883 emigrants from Malta, Sicily, Greece and Italy used the Canal en route to the Australian colonies founded by the English.[1]

The expansion of trade with Asia stimulated the transfer to the Canal route of such bulk commodities as the sugar of Java, the jute of Bengal, the hemp of the Philippines, the rice of Burma and the dates of Basra as well as the export of such new staples as tea from Ceylon, cinchona from Java, sugar from Fiji, tin from Malaya and frozen meat from Australasia. European technology extended its influence in Asia through the spread of the cable, the telephone, the railway and the coasting steamer. The widespread improvement of harbours geared the ports of Asia to the needs of the steamship and the dimensions of the Canal. Japan continued to adopt European technology with greater success than China. The steam war-corvette *Seiki*, built by the Japanese in 1875 and manned by Japanese, passed through the Canal under the Japanese flag and arrived in the Thames in June 1878 to denote 'an epoch in the history of the civilisation of the human race'.[2] The first Japanese merchant-house was established in London under Buhierosan Tannaker in 1879, twenty-four years after the first Indian merchant-house, but remained unsupported by any Japanese shipping line to Europe before 1896. The Russo-Chinese war scare of 1880 brought through the Canal the first Russian troops and the first Russian naval squadron from Cronstadt en route to Chinese waters as well as the first ships under the Chinese flag in 1881.[3] The *Mei Foo* reached London on 6 December 1881[4] with 3,000 tons of tea and the first Chinese merchants to arrive in London, as the managers of a Chinese line

[1] C. A. Price, *Southern Europeans in Australia* (Melbourne, Oxford University Press, 1963), 83, 98, 118, 126.
[2] T. Twiss, 'The Protectorate of the Suez Canal', *Nautical Magazine* (October 1878), 877.
[3] J. L. Rawlinson, *China's Struggle for Naval Development 1839–1895* (Harvard University Press, 1967), 92.   [4] *The Times*, 8 December 1881, 6 vi.

from Shanghai for the China Merchants' Steam Navigation Company. Liu Shao-tsung even attended the annual dinner of the Cobden Club on 1 July 1882 and praised Cobden in Chinese to the assembled merchants of London.[1] The new line failed to overcome the opposition of the British merchants in China but nevertheless ushered in a new phase of competition in the China trade.

The Canal also established its supremacy over the Cape route, first carried in 1882 more of the total volume of Calcutta's shipments to London[2] than the Cape route and was first used in 1883 by more shipping tonnage than the Cape route. The Cape route, however, came into increasing use by steamships en route to Australia, by new medium clippers built for capacity up to 1,800 tons rather than for speed and by the new steamship services to Natal of Bullard King from 1879, the Clan Line from 1881 and J. T. Rennie from 1882. In that economic expansion of the 1880s India became the great focus and the Indian voyage the representative voyage through the Canal. The acceleration of communications permitted Northbrook to become in 1880 the first ex-Viceroy to occupy a seat in the Cabinet as the First Lord of the Admiralty. Travel to India was facilitated by Thomas Cook, who opened offices in Bombay and Calcutta in 1880, and by the P. & O., which began from 1881 to issue cheap return tickets and circular tickets, making possible the first holiday-tours to India by the English and the first visits to India by M.P.s during the parliamentary recess from 1881. Even the Salvation Army appeared in India in 1882 under Major Frederick Tucker, the scion of an old Anglo-Indian family. The viceroyalty of Ripon, 'the only Whig who ever showed real sympathy with Eastern liberty',[3] gave English power in India a new moral basis and a renewed lease of life. It did as much to shift Indian consciousness to a new level[4] as the Vedantist revival from 1881 and the spread of the Arya Samaj at the expense of the Brahma Samaj. The Indian response to the opening of Monier-Williams' Indian Institute at Oxford in 1884 was the foundation in 1885 of the Indian National Congress, which began to divert popular loyalty away from England's allies in the princes.

The shipping of India had adapted itself to the Canal immediately; its trade followed suit only in the 1880s. The abolition in March 1882 of all general import duties in India was a triumph for Baring as the Financial Member of the Viceroy's Council and achieved Lytton's dream of making the country one great free port. It marked the highest point in the import of free-trade doctrine into protectionist India, following on the commercialization of the Indian railway system from 1880. It removed import duties from a society which approved of them and replaced indirect taxes by direct taxes, leaving the Government wholly dependent on the land revenue and with no remedy

[1] *The Times*, 3 July 1882, 10 iv.
[2] *Supplement to the British Trade Journal*, 1 August 1883.
[3] W. S. Blunt, *My Diaries, 1888–1914* (1919), ii. 264.
[4] H. A. L. Fisher, *James Bryce* (London, Macmillan, 1927), i. 268.

against revolt save in the reduction of taxation. That reform of the tariff followed the marked expansion of the cotton mills of Bombay during the 1870s and was partly intended to prevent a revival of indigenous industry on a modern factory-basis so as to avoid a clash between the commercial interests of India and those of Lancashire. It stimulated the establishment of the Bombay Native Piece-Goods Merchants' Association in 1882 after the introduction of the deferred rebate by the Bombay Conference in 1881. It also encouraged the competitive adoption of ring-spinning in the cotton mills of Bombay from 1883 and the first shipment of cotton yarn from Bombay to Italy in 1883. It reflected the belief that capacity to export was dependent on capacity to import and confirmed India's economic function as the largest single market for the piece-goods of Lancashire. Those piece-goods became the instrument which succeeded where the mere reduction of export duties had failed to create an export economy. They converted the trade of India to bulk exports and increased the share of the Canal more rapidly in the exports of India than in its imports.[1] They accelerated the erosion of its indigenous handicrafts and began the remoulding of its whole economic structure to the export of primary produce. The new media of communication, which had destroyed the protection thitherto afforded by distance, thus brought the full competitive power of the developed secondary producers of Europe to bear on the secondary producers of India. They became instruments of economic warfare, fulfilling the function thitherto performed by hostile tariffs or trading companies but with far greater efficacy. Thus they effected the de-industrialization of a world whose products had embodied the training of countless generations of the past and had attracted the bullion of the world for centuries. They created in place of a balanced economy unbalanced economies on a continental scale kept in precarious poise through international trade.

India entered on its second phase as an exporter of wheat in the 1880s after the short harvests of 1878 and 1879 and the war-scare of 1878, which made England wary of relying upon foreign wheat, especially from her traditional foes of Russia and America. The attempted corner in wheat in the U.S.A. in 1881 so increased exports from India that it supplied 10·2 per cent of the total imports of wheat into the United Kingdom in 1881, or double the contribution of Russia. Bombay in particular increased its exports in 1881 as in 1880,[2] benefiting by the extension of the railway from the west coast to Agra and Delhi in 1881. Bombay displaced Calcutta as the leading wheat-port of India between 1881–2 and 1888–9, supplying 53 per cent of India's total wheat exports for the five years ending on 31 March 1888. The wheat corner of 1881 encouraged the Government of India to try and raise the export surplus of India from 20,000,000 cwt. to 40,000,000 cwt. so that India might replace America in the British market to the extent of two-thirds. Thus British dependence

---

[1] *Le Canal de Suez*, 12 Juillet 1885, 897–8, ' Le commerce de l'Inde et le Canal de Suez '.
[2] C. P. Wright, ' India as a Producer and Exporter of Wheat ', *Wheat Studies of the Food Research Institute, Stanford University* (July 1927), 362.

on American price-manipulations as well as on an alien source of supply might be reduced. Wheat would replace cotton as the offspring and bond of empire. India as a primary producer would form a symbiosis with Lancashire as a secondary producer in the interests of British industry, British trade, British shipping and the British Empire. The Government of India accordingly in 1883 reduced the railway freight-rates on wheat substantially and abolished the duty on gunny-bags to encourage the export of wheat as well as of oil-seeds. It increased the fiscal pressure on small farmers to plant wheat and granted subsidies to the shipping lines which carried wheat.

The export of wheat at first restricted its indigenous consumption by men and cattle, encouraging the substitution of rice and millets for wheat. Then wheat began to replace other crops in cultivation, so fostering an expansion in its production. A drain of foodstuffs was thus created from India, as it had been in the eighteenth century from Ireland, leaving the peasantry to subsist on a substitute-diet. Wheat was, however, an alien and a minor crop in India, unlike rice or millets. India consumed the bulk of its own wheat even in good years: its consumption per head was low but immense in the aggregate be-cause of its vast population. Its export surplus fluctuated with the harvest in India, with the harvest of millets, rice and barley and with the wheat harvests elsewhere in the world. Its surplus was comparatively small, like that of Russia and the U.S.A., and unlike that of the new countries of settlement such as Canada, Argentina, Australia: exports averaged 13 per cent of its total crop in the five years ending on 31 March 1888. Its exports surplus was handled by the European merchants in the Presidency towns and was carried by rail, unlike all other bulk commodities, which moved by river and were financed by Indian merchants. The export trade made only small profits and would have made less without the subsidies levied on the Indian tax-payer and criticized by such economists as Nairoji and Dutt.

India's share in the total wheat imports of Britain rose to 10·9 per cent in 1882, 13·9 per cent in 1883 and 12·8 per cent in 1884, helping to reduce Russia's share in English imports from 17 per cent in 1875 to 8 per cent in 1884. India's share in those imports between 1881 and 1887 averaged 12·6 per cent and reached the peak proportion of 16·7 per cent in 1886.[1] America's share in English imports was not, however, reduced. 'India has in fact been used as a lever whereby the whole weight of American enterprise has been rolled with increasing velocity upon the English wheat-grower.'[2] India raised its acreage under wheat by 68 per cent from 16,000,000 in 1871 to 27,000,000 in 1888. It became the third largest producer in the world in 1885 after the U.S.A. and Russia. Its exports supplied 10 per cent of world wheat exports in 1884–8 and were stimulated in 1885–6 by the depreciation of silver.[3] India

---

[1] J. McDougall, 'Indian Wheats', *Journal of the Society of Arts*, 14 June 1889, 639.

[2] A. K. Connell, 'Indian Railways and Indian Wheat', *Journal of the Statistical Society*, 19 May 1885, 256.

[3] A. F. Baillie, *Kurrachee: (Karachi) Past: Present: and Future* (1890), 238.

also shipped wheat increasingly to Italy from 1886–7 after France raised its duties in 1885. It raised the proportion of its wheat exports shipped to the Continent from 5·9 per cent in 1879–80 to 48·6 per cent in 1887–8: the high gluten content of its durum wheat made it especially suitable for the manufacture of macaroni. Although only half of India's shipments to Europe in 1886–7 used the Canal attempts were made in 1883–5 to export wheat from India to 'the race of beans' via the port of Suez.

Wheat cultivation developed in the drier regions of India, especially in the north-west which enjoyed more regular spring rains than the monsoon area to the south and could therefore grow wheat as a winter crop. In the Punjab where winter rains were abundant wheat became the main crop and a general staple of consumption as in no other of the provinces of India. Wheat was elsewhere compelled to adjust to the monsoon regime as well as to the much shorter growing-season. It remained closely dependent on rainfall in an arid region and stimulated the development of perennial irrigation from 1890. In the Punjab 'canal colonies' were first established in 1886–9 by Sikh ex-soldiers, raising the area under irrigation from 2,300,000 acres in 1888 to 5,200,000 acres in 1898 but diffusing malaria and salinifying the soil as in Egypt. Thus the Punjab became the great centre of wheat-production for export. Karachi became the outlet for its harvests, raising its share in the wheat exports of India from 10 per cent in 1881–2 to 20 per cent in 1883–4 and to 25 per cent in 1884–5 through the agrarian colonization of its hinterland. From 1887 it agitated for a desert railway to Delhi via Rajputana to facilitate the competition of the Punjab with the U.S.A. in the world wheat-market.[1] It raised its population from 56,750 in 1872 and 73,560 in 1881 to 105,200 in 1891. It surpassed Bombay in its wheat exports for the first time in 1890 and ranked as the first wheat-port in 1889–90 and in 1890–1 but was displaced by Bombay in 1891–2 and 1892–3. Thereafter Karachi became India's leading wheat-port and shipped wheat especially to Hull as Bombay did to Liverpool and Calcutta did to London.[2] The port benefited by its very low rainfall, which facilitated the storage of grain awaiting shipment in the open air. It never built elevators on the American model, which were often proposed from 1890 onward, because Karachi Port Trust preferred to avoid such specialized capital investment. It shipped its wheat wholly in bags and never in bulk, so maintaining the demand for the jute bags manufactured in Bengal. It derived its supremacy as a wheat-port from its proximity to the centres of production but did not extend its hinterland beyond the Indus valley and the Punjab. It remained a highly specialized port, lacked any commerce of its own apart from the transit trade[3] and never developed the large-scale general trade of Bombay. Thus it used tramp shipping to a far greater extent than Bombay or Calcutta and fluctuated in its contribution to the traffic of the Canal much more than Bombay. It became more dependent on the Canal than any other

---

[1] A. F. Baillie, *Kurrachee* (1890), 227.
[2] C. P. Wright, 366. [3] A. F. Baillie, 237.

port in the whole world and so suffered the annihilation of its long-cherished expectations as the Indian terminus of a Euphrates Valley Railway. Its merchant-houses and banks remained dependent on their parent Bombay firms and lacked strong local associations.[1]

Wheat exports were increased in weight by the admixture of dirt by Indian merchants, as in the cotton trade, to the anger and despair of European merchants. Exceptionally heavy exports as in 1877, 1882 and 1891 stimulated the passage of ships southwards in ballast through the Canal. Shipments began in April and May after the harvest was gathered from March onwards and were made mainly in June, July and August, which were otherwise slack months in the traffic of the Canal. Indian wheats thus brought a welcome counter-seasonal addition to the traffic of the waterway and arrived in the markets of Europe when the winter wheats of the U.S.A. were their chief competitors. Indian wheats could not compete with American wheats but provided another source of supply for the urban consumers of industrial Europe and for the flour millers of Europe, especially of London and Liverpool, which so gained some compensation for the loss of its entrepôt trade in Indian cotton and oil-seeds and China tea. The qualities of Indian wheats were recognized by McDougall in his report of 1882[2] as deriving from the dry climate which made their skin thinner and their flour drier than the humid wheats indigenous to England. Those wheats afforded unprecedented yields of flour in comparison with other wheats because of their thin skin, a larger yield of bread than other flours and therefore larger margins of profit to both miller and baker. They were used not by the many small millers but by the few large millers who bought them the cheaper as 'dirty' and developed elaborate cleaning machinery to reduce their high content of dirt, techniques of blending to take full advantage of their cheapness, dryness and stability, the bleaching of flour to conceal their unattractive colour and the art of 'conditioning' to offset their poor baking qualities.[3] Those large millers prevented through their powerful London Corn Trade Association the reduction of the fixed allowance for impurities from 5 to 2 per cent proposed by Liverpool at the conference of 8 May 1889 at the India Office[4] and so preserved the advantage which they enjoyed in their machinery over their smaller competitors.

Wheat exports reached a peak of 30,307,000 cwt. in 1891–2 because of bad harvests in Europe and a famine in Southern Russia. In that year wheat became the most valuable export of India, supplying 14·2 per cent of the total value of its seaborne exports.[5] Those exports made 1891 a boom year for the Canal, helping to increase its net register tonnage by 26·25 per cent and raising India's share thereof to the peak proportion of 56·41 per cent. Thereafter

[1] Baillie, 198–9.
[2] J. McDougall, 'Indian Wheat', *Journal of the Society of Arts*, 29 June 1883, 807–8.
[3] C. P. Wright, 375.
[4] J. McDougall, 'Indian Wheats', *Journal of the Society of Arts*, 14 June 1889, 644.
[5] C. P. Wright, 363.

wheat shipments fell off by 43·5 per cent during 1892 and by 54·5 per cent during 1893, reducing the net register tonnage of the Canal by 11·3 per cent in 1892, its sharpest fall in twenty-two years. Exports sank in 1894 for the third successive year as the wheat harvest shrank to a new low level in 1894–5. India's export surplus declined to an average of 5·1 per cent of its crop in 1892–7. The depression of 1892–4 completed the diversion begun in 1889 of the wheat exports of the United Provinces to Bombay, ended the importance of Calcutta as a wheat-exporting port and established the supremacy of Karachi, which exported 298,535 tons in 1894 or 77 per cent of the total wheat exports of India against 30 per cent from Bombay and 3·3 per cent from Calcutta. India's second phase as a wheat exporter drew to a close with the drought, famine and plague of 1896. Its exports of wheat to Britain declined by 73 per cent between 1895 and 1897 and helped to reduce the net register tonnage of the Canal by 7·7 per cent in 1897, the second depression of the 1890s. Wheat exports to Britain revived in 1898 when good harvests in India coincided with short harvests in Europe: the recovery of freights again attracted shipping in ballast through the Canal to Bombay and Karachi. The short harvests in Western and Central India in 1899–1900 however reduced the trade of Bombay and reversed the flow of cereal shipments through the Canal. Thus southbound shipments of maize were made from Sulina in Rumania to Bombay in October 1899, January 1900 and April 1900, one shipment of maize was even made from the U.S.A. to Bombay in June 1900, while Australia increased its wheat shipments through the Canal to England markedly in 1899 as a substitute source of supply. Those short harvests eliminated India's shipments of wheat to Europe in 1900 and diverted the rice exports of Burma from Europe to India.

The cultivation of tea had developed during the 1860s in the Brahmaputra valley of Assam which pointed like a finger towards China and supplied the profitable markets of Central Asia through Amritsar and Kabul. Calcutta began the export of tea from Assam in 1869 after the reduction of the import duty in England in 1864 and 1867. It shipped tea through the Canal in 1870, and first shipped more via the Canal than via the Cape in 1871. Indian tea was not a bulk commodity like wheat or rice or jute: it was dear enough to bear the cost of steamer freights but cheap enough to blend with China tea so as gradually to educate the public in a new flavour. That flavour was more robust, rich, pungent, penetrating and lasting than that of the delicate product of China, whose imports into England reached their maximum quantity in 1877.[1] Indian tea increased its share in the total tea imports of England from 10·6 per cent in 1873–4 to 33·1 per cent in 1877–8. The new trade developed apace despite the long-term fall in tea-prices which it encouraged. It benefited by the depreciation of silver which reduced working expenses. It compensated Calcutta for the decline of its silk exports from their peak in 1875–80. Ceylon first exported tea in 1875 after the import duty was halved in 1874 but

[1] P. Griffiths, *The History of the Indian Tea Industry* (London, Weidenfeld, 1967), 125.

only began its large-scale export from 1880, finding therein compensation for the decline of its coffee exports from their peak in 1874–6.

The production of tea on a plantation basis expanded greatly during the 1880s, encouraged by the Government and by the Chartered Bank of India, which granted open credits on the crop from 1878 in defiance of its Charter. Exports were extended from Calcutta to Chittagong from 1879. The shortage of labour created abuses in the recruitment of coolies, which were only partly checked by Ripon's Inland Emigration Act of 1882. The development of the tea plantation was even more rapid in Ceylon from 1884 than in Assam. The produce of both areas, classified in grades with Chinese names,[1] shattered the Chinese monopoly of the tea market. The process of substitution was facilitated by the systematic adulteration of Chinese tea and by the systematic blending of Indian with Chinese tea in London. New markets were also tapped as stronger tea was found to supply an acceptable alternative stimulant to alcohol and as its consumption was popularized through the chain-stores of Thomas Lipton from 1871–4 and through the use of advertisements from 1874. Thus the share of China in the tea consumption of England sank from 97 per cent in 1865 to 59 per cent in 1886 while the share of British-grown tea rose from 3 per cent in 1865 to 19 per cent in 1877 and to 41 per cent in 1886.[2] Tea became the most valuable single export from Ceylon in 1887, exceeding the value of coffee exports for the first time. England's imports of tea from India and Ceylon first exceeded the weight of tea imports from China in 1888.[3] Thenceforth India became the major source of supply of tea for the British market as well as for the entrepôt trade. The revenue from import duties was reduced because Indian tea was strong and went half as far again as China tea, as the Chancellor of the Exchequer, Goschen, complained to the Commons on 21 April 1887. Tea became incomparably the most popular drink ever known in England and the national beverage as it had never been before. The increased consumption of tannin, however, aroused the concern of doctors from 1891 because of its effects on health.

A new field for enterprise was opened up in the cultivation, preparation and marketing of tea. Lipton was encouraged to enter the tea trade in 1888, to transfer the headquarters of his firm from Glasgow to London in 1889 and to acquire plantations in Ceylon from 1889. Joseph Lyons began to retail his dark and strong brew at exhibitions from 1887–90 and in tea-houses from 1894. British entrepreneurs gained that control over the actual production of tea which they had always lacked in China. The tea planters established their homes in India and became the backbone of opposition to Ripon's liberal

---

[1] A. Burrell, 'Indian Tea Cultivation: its Origin, Progress and Prospects', *Journal of the Society of Arts*, 9 February 1877, 199–215. S. Baildon, *The Tea Industry in India* (London, Allen, 1882). H. W. Cave, *Golden Tips. A Description of Ceylon and its great Tea Industry* (London, Low, 1900), 167.

[2] J. B. White, 'The Indian Tea Industry: its Rise, Progress during Fifty Years and Prospects', *Journal of the Society of Arts*, 10 June 1887, 740.

[3] D. M. Forrest, *A Hundred Years of Ceylon Tea 1867–1967* (London, Chatto, 1967), 169.

policy, because they lacked any official position and derived their status from their colour alone. They formed the Indian Tea Districts Association in London in 1879 for marketing[1] and the Indian Tea Association in Calcutta in 1881 for labour questions. They created the demand for the Assam–Bengal Railway, which was begun in 1892 and completed to Chittagong in 1895. They served the Government of Calcutta as willing instruments of its neo-mercantilist policy to win 'a victory of race over race, of progress over stagnation, of the spirit of enterprise and innovation over that of conservative contentment'.[2] A new trade was also opened to British shipping. The Calcutta Tea Conference fixed freights to London from 1886, applied the deferred rebate even to the homeward trade and so aroused the opposition of the Indian Tea Association.[3] That conference was entered by T. & J. Harrison when they acquired Rathbone Brothers' Star Line of four steamers in 1889.[4] The freight-rates fixed by the Conference aroused the opposition of the Tea Association anew in 1891[5] and were reduced in 1892. The Indian Tea Association established its supremacy over its London counterpart in 1894 and secured new freight concessions in 1895. Ceylon benefited by the experience of India and developed much more rapidly, raising its share of the British tea market from 2 per cent in 1885 to 33 per cent in 1895. The Colombo Tea Conference was established in 1902 as the complement to the Calcutta Tea Conference, whose freight-rates determined its own.

The rise of the Indian tea trade disrupted the triangular trade in opium, tea and piece-goods between India, China and England. The tea of China lost the British market to India at the same time that it lost the American market to Japan, which also replaced China as a cheaper source of supply of Oriental curios to the West. The China merchants remained undisturbed by the loss of that trade and spoke of China to Kipling in 1889 as 'a place where fortunes were made—a land only waiting to be opened up to pay a hundred fold'.[6] Hong Kong increased in importance relative to Shanghai, which nevertheless remained independent of any single staple export. Tea-ports such as Foochow declined with the fall in tea freights from China and the end of the shipment of Chinese teas by racing steam clippers. The decline in tea freights from China depressed the profits made by Holt's between 1883 and 1892, broke up the China Conference of 1879–88 and produced a rate-war until 1891. Killick Martin & Co. sold their ships in 1885 and 1886[7] and retired from the China tea trade into ship-broking and insurance-broking, on behalf of the Ben Line from 1883 and of Holt's from 1887. Skinner's Castle Line paid the price

---

[1] P. Griffiths, *The History of the Indian Tea Industry*, 513.
[2] A. Michie, *The Englishman in China during the Victorian Era* (1900), i. 185.
[3] Griffiths, 132.
[4] F. E. Hyde, *Shipping Enterprise and Management 1830–1939. Harrisons of Liverpool* (Liverpool University Press, 1967), 43.
[5] Hyde, 73. Griffiths, 132.
[6] R. Kipling, *From Sea to Sea* (London, Macmillan, 1900), i. 367.
[7] D. R. MacGregor, *The China Bird. The History of Captain Killick* (London, Chatto, 1961), 232.

for the expensive speed records it had established in 1882–3 and ceased to exist after 1890. Holt's, however, discarded sails after 1885, adopted the triple-expansion engine from 1888, three years after the P. & O., and entered the trade of the Dutch East Indies from 1891. They began rebuilding their fleet to carry heavy cargo from the Midlands rather than light-weight textiles from Lancashire: their three-island superstructure of 1892 permitted the carriage of relatively large deadweights in relation to the dimensions of a steamer as well as deck-passengers in the centre-castle space.[1] The neo-mercantilist policy of England enabled Russia to dominate the market for the finest black tea of China, to benefit by the growing Chinese resentment against foreign merchants and to profit by the opening-up of China from the land rather than from the sea. For the Canal the westward shift of the tea trade offered protection against the potential competition of the Panama Canal begun in 1881 as well as against the actual competition of the Canadian Pacific Railway completed in 1886.[2] Tea shipments through the Canal do not seem to have increased in volume, perhaps because of the greater strength of Indian tea. The tea season remained unaltered in July–August. The replacement of China by India insured the Canal Company, however, against over-dependence on any single source of supply.

Jute had been first shipped through the Canal from Calcutta in 1870 but was too cheap to bear high steamer freights. The growth of world trade in primary produce increased the demand for the cheapest of natural fibres for use as sacking. As a cheap bulk product jute was better suited to shipment via the Cape during the 1870s when freights remained high. Shipments via the Canal declined markedly in 1875 and 1876 under the influence of the depression of trade. The share of the Canal in Calcutta's jute shipments to England rose only from 10 per cent of the total volume in 1870 to 18·6 per cent in 1878. From 1880 more jute was shipped via the Canal, which increased its share of the total shipments from 27 per cent in 1880 to 33 per cent in 1882. That proportion was sufficient to control the market-price because jute prices rose in the carpet-making town of Kidderminster on 8 July 1882 when traffic through the Canal seemed threatened by Anglo-Egyptian friction. In 1882 the German Hansa Line began the direct shipment of jute from Calcutta to Bremen and so began to capture the Continental trade from the jute clippers, many of which entered the Australian trade in 1884. Steamer freights between Calcutta and London were reduced by the import of Cheshire salt from Liverpool at ballast freights and first fell below sail freights in 1886. Thenceforth jute shipments shifted increasingly to the Canal from the Cape route, which retained only shipments to Argentina, Brazil and Boston. The last jute carriers were launched in 1886–8 and in 1891–3[3] but were compelled to increase their

---

[1] F. E. Hyde, *Blue Funnel* (1956), 67–93, 174–5.

[2] H. A. Innis, *A History of the Canadian Pacific Railway* (1923), 193.

[3] B. Lubbock, *The Last of the Windjammers* (Glasgow, Brown, 1927), i. 467–79, 'Register of Chief Sailing Ship Fleets'.

speed so as to average 125 days in 1890 between Calcutta and Dundee. There-after sail was diverted into the grain trade from San Francisco and then into the case-oil trade from New York and Philadelphia. The jute exported to Dundee in 1894–5 was carried by forty-nine steamers and by four sailing ships. The season for Canal shipments became October–February following the harvest in July–September. Those shipments were made exclusively through Calcutta and Chittagong and remained highly susceptible to the influence of economic depression.

Jute was the pre-eminent export staple of Bengal, which enjoyed a world monopoly of its production and export. Its cultivation expanded greatly from the 1880s at the expense of cotton, safflower and indigo. Jute supplied the peasants of Bengal with a secondary crop to supplement rice, to fill a gap in their crop-rotation and to bring in ready money as a cash-crop. Its cultivation increased the hunger for land in Eastern Bengal and enhanced the value of inferior soil. From 1880 jute sacks, which had been manufactured in Calcutta since 1859 and exported increasingly since 1873, were shipped to England for the bagging of flour and salt. From 1884 they were also ex-ported to the Levant for bagging wheat and sugar as well as to Suez, where they replaced Dundee gunnies for the bagging of sugar in 1890–1. Those sacks formed the first manufactured commodity to be shipped northwards through the Canal and were more stable in volume than the shipments of jute fibre, because they supplied a more direct demand. The agricultural produce of India and Asia also passed through the Canal in jute sacks, which as containers were not classed by the Canal Company as a separate commodity.

The great expansion of rice cultivation which had begun in Burma in the 1860s continued in the 1870s when the Cape route carried the bulk of rice exports to Europe. From 1872 increasing amounts were shipped by English steamer through the Canal: such steamers often carried coal through the Canal between February and April to return with rice and linseed between March and May. The colonization of the Irrawaddy delta inspired France from 1870 to develop the Mekong delta and Siam to develop the Menam delta, though without the assistance of Burma's public works or its labour-migration. Siam increased its output of rice not for export to Europe but for export to the markets of Asia thitherto supplied by Burma, especially to Singapore and Hong Kong. Thus a division of export markets developed from the 1870s, enabling Siam to preserve its society of small independent farmers in which all adult males were warriors. Java replaced the export of rice by its import and concentrated on the more profitable cash-crops for the Dutch market. In 1880 shipments via the Canal from the rice ports of Rangoon, Bassein, Akyab and Moulmein rose to 34 per cent of Burma's total shipments of rice to Europe because of the spread of the potato blight in England, the export of potatoes from Germany and the Netherlands to England, the substitution of rice for potatoes in Germany and the Netherlands and the partial failure of the harvest in Italy. The increased demand in Europe raised the number of steamers loading in the rice ports in 1881 to equal the number of sailing ships and brought the first shipment of rice from Japan through the Canal in March 1882. From 1883 rice was shipped increasingly to Hamburg to supply the distilling industry with a new raw material. The Canal consolidated its hold on the rice trade in 1884 when rice prices rose while steamer freights for Burma rice to Europe fell to the same level as sail freights via the Cape.

The enormous increase in exports stimulated the colonization of the valleys of Burma by the hill people of Upper Burma, who lacked the protection of the caste system and became converted to economic civilization and to Buddhism.[1] The balance of population was thereby shifted from the interior dry zone to the monsoon delta. The simultaneous immigration of Indian merchants and labourers increased Indian at the expense of Chinese influence in that frontier-region between India and China. Indian influence only triumphed with the conquest of Upper Burma in reply to Ferry's seizure of Tonkin (1883–5), the re-unification of the kingdom under foreign rule and the introduction of the village-system for administrative convenience into a society based on the township or county. The conquest of the kingdom of Ava was accomplished in a campaign of three weeks which included the rapid advance by steamboat to Mandalay (14–28 November 1885). The war created a boom in Rangoon and Singapore and increased the shipments of Burma rice via the Canal from 40 per cent of the total shipments to Europe in 1884–5 to 53 per cent in 1885–6. The Burmah Oil Company was also registered in Edinburgh by Glasgow merchants on 22 July 1886 and began drilling operations in 1887. The annexation of Burma encouraged the transfer of its trade from the sailing ship and the beginning of steamship services by Rickmers from 1889, the Hamburg –Calcutta Line from 1890, Brocklebanks from 1890 and the Bibby Line from 1891. The share of the Canal in Burma's rice exports to Europe was thereby increased from 58 per cent in 1888 to 66 per cent in 1889 and from 70 per cent in 1893 to 84 per cent in 1895.

Burma exported more polished than unpolished rice from 1890, replacing its cargo rice by white rice. Steam rice-mills grew in number in the rice-ports, especially in Rangoon. The millers were mostly British and eliminated the fine millers of London: they reaped most of the profits of the trade and formed their own combination in 1892 when the Rangoon Shipping Conference was organized. Their mills cleaned the rice for export so effectively that they removed the vegetable oil and the vitamin B_1 in the bran and so devitalized the most nourishing cereal in the world.[2] As Burma replaced Java as the rice-granary of the Malayan archipelago steam-milled rice ousted hand-milled

[1] J. S. Furnivall, *An Introduction to the Political Economy of Burma* (Rangoon, Burma Book Club, 1931), 42, 47, 'The Reclamation of the Delta'. E. R. Leach, 'The Frontiers of "Burma"', *Comparative Studies in Society and History* (October 1960), 53.

[2] H. B. Proctor, *Rice: its History, Culture, Manufacture and Food Value* (London, Dunham, 1882), 38–9.

rice and the vitamin-deficiency disease of beri-beri spread throughout the region. The correlation between the consumption of polished rice and the incidence of beri-beri was established only by research begun by Christiaan Eijkman in Java in 1888–97 and completed by Casimir Funk in 1911.[1] The rice-eating communities of the Asian seaboard also became dependent on the power which controlled the seas and the seaborne trade in rice. The staple item in the diet of the poorest and most populous communities in the world was used to solve Europe's population-problem: it was shipped westward to the richest communities in the world and turned into beer, spirits, starch and feed-cake as much as into human food for the poor below the potato level.[2] Shipments through the Canal formed a higher proportion of the world trade in rice than of the world trade in wheat because rice was grown largely in the East whereas wheat was grown largely in the West. Rice shipments through the Canal remained more stable than those of wheat which always remained liable to competition from the great producers of the West. The rice-season in the traffic of the Canal from March to May intervened between the cotton and tea seasons. Malta developed an entrepôt trade in rice shipped 'to orders' via the Canal and increased the pressure of Burmese competition on the rice-growers of Italy, who were forced to reduce their exports. The growing embarrassment of the primary producers of the Mediterranean region was relieved when France and Italy raised their import duties on rice in 1895, so making Germany thenceforward the largest single market for the rice of Burma.

Bengal and Burma thus came fully within the range of the Canal's influence. The Canal's shipping tonnage with Calcutta and Eastern India surpassed that with Bombay and Western India first in 1892 and permanently from 1894. Calcutta became the representative destination of the cargo steamer using the Canal because it lay midway between Bombay and Shanghai. The expansion of India's exports increased the share of Asia in world trade and reduced after the 1880s the relative importance of passenger-traffic to cargo-traffic in the Canal. Trade between East and West was transformed less in value than in kind. The most valuable trade remained that in tea, silk and specie while that in bulk commodities provided the expanding volume. The exchange of foodstuffs, raw materials and minerals for the manufactures of Europe supplied the Canal with an increasing flow of traffic and insured it against the failure of any single source of supply. The balance of freight was weighted heavily in favour of northbound cargo even before 1886 when for the first time the number and tonnage of ships entering from the Red Sea exceeded the number and tonnage of those entering from the Mediterranean. The bulky nature of the raw materials and foodstuffs exported from Asia gave northbound vessels a higher load-index than southbound vessels with their light-weight and high-priced manufactures. Exports of manufactures from Europe proved more

[1] *Bulletin of the Imperial Institute* (1917), 259–60, 'The Production and Uses of Rice'.
[2] H. B. Proctor, 25.

susceptible to reduction during economic depression than the agricultural exports of the primary producers of Asia. The fluctuations of traffic through the Canal were nevertheless determined from 1895 more by the variations in northbound than by those in southbound cargo. Those fluctuations down to 1888 had followed by one or two years the fluctuations in English railway traffic and in the industrial economies in general. Between 1890 and 1895 they coincided with the fluctuations in English railway traffic while after 1895 they preceded them.[1]

Commerce united Asia during the nineteenth century but proved more disruptive than any previous military conquest. The 700,000 village-communities of India which had survived all previous invasions formed the basic units of society, together with the family and the caste. Those little republics were economically invulnerable because they were founded upon subsistence agriculture and supplied essential support against omnipotent Nature. Economic man was therein submerged beneath social man and individual enterprise was enclosed within the group although social mobility was not so closely confined to economic channels as in contemporary Europe. All-purpose crops proved as useful to the peasant as the all-purpose camel and horse to the nomad. Cattle were far more than sources of food or beasts of burden. River boats and junks were the homes of the owner and the crew as well as means of transport. Above all, religion created 'a fixed, crystallised sacro-economic system' which could assimilate a new steam-plough only as a new divinity and idol.[2] It also inhibited the taking of risk, the exaction of interest and the untrammelled use of wealth by the individual. It imposed social obligations on the wealthy, making charity a primary duty and alms a divine right. Thus social pressure restrained the pursuit of money just as mutual help avoided its use. Wealth was hoarded within the house rather than invested outside and apportioned therein on the basis of needs rather than of earnings so as to maintain the economic independence of the family. More money was thus spent on social than on economic functions. Large-scale commerce remained a branch of government confined to the periphery of community, city and state and to the sphere of the foreigner. Indigenous commerce was carried on by networks of merchant families, who lacked status in their aristocratic society and prospered only through economic activity in proportion to the density and extent of their personal relationships because commerce was based on the inviolable unwritten agreement.

The growth of bulk exports remoulded the life of village-India. Fiscal pressure encouraged such subsistence economies to yield place to a market economy and transformed self-contained into dependent communities. Their inhabitants were drawn into economic activities wholly independent of the rest

[1] Institut National de la Statistique et des Études Économiques, *Études et Conjonctures Économie Mondiale* (Janvier–Février 1949), 61–2, ' L'Évolution du Trafic du Canal de Suez et son Rôle dans la Conjoncture Mondiale'.

[2] G. Birdwood, 'Indian Pottery at the Paris Exhibition', *Journal of the Society of Arts*, 28 February 1879, 309.

of local life and found in the market-place their sole contact with the alien culture of a dual society. Cash-crops for export replaced subsistence-farming. Specialization even developed between the production of raw materials and that of foodstuffs while monoculture appeared in the production of rice and sugar. Economies based on an all-purpose staple such as the date, the coconut, and the oil-seed were undermined through the development of a one-sided export trade. Neither machinery nor artificial fertilizer were introduced while the natural fertilizer of oil-cake was exported, destroying the equilibrium between technology and resources in the central sector of the economy. The plantation provided no model which peasants could imitate but rather the ideal type of the dual economy, with its fundamental division of labour between an alien administration and local labour. The plantation eliminated the irrational dis-economies of peasant-farming and organized indigenous labour to mine the sacred soil for the profit of alien gods. The associated migration of labour replaced the slave-trade by the coolie-trade, which recruited labourers through indentures from non-literate societies and treated them primarily as instruments rather than as men. That trade extended the Indian diaspora in Burma and East Africa as it did the Chinese diaspora in Malaya and the Dutch East Indies.

The commercialization and secularization of agriculture revolutionized rural life far more than did the plantation, exposing the villagers to the fluctuations of an uncomprehended and alien market-mechanism. Their monetary returns sank with the fall in prices between 1873 and 1896 while their currency and ornaments were devalued by the depreciation of silver. Nor were they offered the compensation of a rise in social status, the protection of a trade-union or even the comfort of the myth of progress. They suffered from the unprecedentedly rigorous justice with which the land-tax was exacted and the legal claims of money-lenders enforced. Their traditional society was eroded through the land-tax, the judicial system, Manchester cottons, English education and missionary activity. Thus they were impoverished rather than enriched through the spread of a money-economy. They bore their growing burden of poverty patiently and bequeathed it to their children without blaming fate and without condemning gods or men. Their ordeal nevertheless so impressed William Cunningham on his visit to India in 1882 that he concluded that trade was the great solvent which broke up social organization. 'Every step of progress means the impoverishment of some class. We really are nihilists, overthrowing the institutions of society and helpless to develop anything in their stead.'[1] England's first great teacher of economic history was confirmed in his new-born suspicion of free trade as he observed its effects in a country whose economic defences had been undermined. In the succeeding generation of accelerated economic change the indigenous commercial élites of Asia began to adapt their operations to the new mechanical

---

[1] W. Cunningham, 'From Julumdun', *Cambridge Review*, 8 March 1882, 223. Idem, *Christian Civilisation with Special Reference to India* (London, Macmillan, 1880), 117–18.

media of communication[1] and to inherit the revolutionary function of the Western élites of the colonial ports. They became the ablest instruments of the expansion of Asiatic trade and the self-perpetuating agents of a continuing economic transformation. They became the great vehicle for the transmission of Western culture to the peasant hinterland of the ports and for the conversion of Asia to the economic civilization and the export technology of Europe.

[1] D. A. Wells, 'The Great Depression of Trade. A Study of its Economic Causes', *Contemporary Review* (August 1887), 278 note.

21

THE UNION OF EAST AND WEST, 1880–1885

WHEN Europe was united by the railway the Saint-Simonian Heine foretold in 1842 'the European or the world Revolution, the gigantic battle of the disinherited with the inheritors of fortune, and in that there will be no question of nationality or of religion for there will be but one fatherland, the Earth, and but one religion, that of happiness in *this* life'.[1] Heine's prophecy was fulfilled in the early 1880s when the world was united under the leadership, the flag and the faith of Europe as the Mediterranean world had been under Rome. Mechanical communications imposed a linear and maritime unity upon the continent of Asia. The new unity was not the product of international cooperation but the achievement of Britain, France, Russia and the U.S.A., which built up railway-empires in place of the road-empires of 1870 and imposed on the world the symbols of their technical supremacy in their railway gauge, cable network, shipping lines and monetary standard. The new media of communication served military as much as economic ends but also helped to militarize economic life and to extend it from a national to an international basis. International organization also expanded under European aegis through the foundation of the first foreign refinery by Standard Oil in 1882, the first transatlantic trade-union in 1883 and the first international industrial cartel in 1884, such private organizations filling the void left by the State in the international sphere. The drawing of the International Date Line through the uninhabited wastes of the Pacific Ocean in 1884 made possible the introduction in 1885 of an international standard time and completed the conquest of the world by metric time. The first artificial international language was devised between 1878 and 1887 by the Lithuanian Jew Ludwig Zamenhof who as 'Doktoro Esperanto' aspired to restore the linguistic unity of the ancient world. The technical foundations of a visual international language were laid in the telephotography of S. Bidwell (1881), the zoopraxiscope of E. Muybridge (1881) and the cine-camera of E. J. Marey (1888).

The world of Asia was united through the emergence of new power-structures, new capital cities and new social élites as well as through the growth of new staples of production. The British Empire, imitated from the 1860s by France and Russia, spread peace, law and order throughout the East. As Russia expanded into the Moslem sultanates of Central Asia Britain encroached on the Moslem sultanates of India, Malaya, East Africa, the littoral of the Arabian Sea and the Red Sea although not upon Arabia itself. The new

[1] H. Heine, *French Affairs. Letters from Paris* (London, Heinemann, 1893), ii. *Lutetia*, 304–5, 12 July 1842.

imperial peace freed the population from one Malthusian check on its growth, relieved the monarchs of Asia from their fear of insurrection, encouraged in consequence misgovernment and then sanctioned intervention in the name of 'reform'. The imperial powers refused to distinguish between commerce and ethics and suppressed as far as possible piracy, banditry and slave-trading. Thus they established an alien control over the main channels of indigenous trade, narrowed the economic outlets open to the rising generation and closed up traditional avenues of social mobility. They eroded the social hierarchies as well as the political structures of Asia, replacing the dominant military élites by new administrative and commercial élites and spreading the veneer of an alien commercial culture over a peasant civilization. Thus the foreign port became sharply separated from the village-community, the municipality from the village and the town from the country. That Manichaean world vividly exemplified the distinction drawn by Tönnies in 1887 between a Gesellschaft and a Gemeinschaft. 'In the Gemeinschaft they [human beings] remain essentially united in spite of all separating factors, whereas in the Gesellschaft they are essentially separated in spite of all uniting factors.'[1]

The colonial ports created along the whole periphery of the continent new centres of commerce and administration distinct from the traditional centres of culture[2] and similar to the Hanseatic cities along the coast of North-West Europe in the fifteenth century. Those ports were foreign to Asia in their origin, nature and function. They were usually won and maintained by military power until land-power began to retreat before sea-power during the nineteenth century. They were far more numerous than the few naval bases and stations which provided when necessary a protective gunboat. They represented a massive investment of political power as well as capital and remained centres of power more than of commerce until the 'consular city' (1847) emerged into full autonomy as the 'treaty port' (1881).[3] Those new foci of European activity in a townless civilization remained urban islands in a peasant-ocean. They developed on sites neglected beforehand when capital cities had been located more centrally. Sometimes they were established as compulsory entrepôts, like the Naukratis which Petrie excavated in 1884–5. Usually they were founded with a protective barrier of water in their early years and often on an island like Suakin, Massawa, Zanzibar, Bombay, Penang, Singapore and Hong Kong. The traditional cities of Asia had sought to reproduce the universe in their circular or rectangular shape: the European cities in Asia reproduced the universe of the West in their wharf where the

[1] F. Tönnies, *Community and Association* (*Gemeinschaft und Gesellschaft*) (London, Routledge, 1955), 74.

[2] Thus the cultural dichotomy emerged between Beirut and Damascus, Alexandria and Cairo, Massawa and Axum, Basra and Bagdad, Bombay and Poona, Colombo and Anurudhapura, Calcutta and Benares, Rangoon and Mandalay, Singapore and Kuala Lumpur, Saigon and Hué, Haiphong and Hanoi, Bangkok and Ayudhia, Hong Kong and Canton, Shanghai and Nanking, Tientsin and Peking, Tokyo and Kyoto.

[3] J. Hatton, ' *The New Ceylon*'. *Being a Sketch of British North Borneo, or Sabah* (London, Chapman, 1881), 114.

foreign ships arrived, loaded and departed. Those cities possessed only one of all the functions of a city and made trade far more important than it was in the ports of Europe. Usually they grew up near an important delta of monsoon Asia where they enjoyed maximum access to cheap water-routes for the bulk-transport of produce by both land and sea. They became centres of a network of communications and trade by water and grew at least as fast as the cities of the West during the nineteenth century but with a marked maritime orientation and at the expense of the indigenous towns. They were centrally located in maritime terms between Asia and Europe, although grossly eccentric in relation to their own hinterland, whose produce they channelled towards the sea through economic structures oriented towards the West. As centres of the world-market, they remained economic not sacred centres and cities of the technical not of the moral order.

Their European élites, recruited especially from Scots mercantile connexions, became the standard-bearers of an export technology and expanded at the expense of the trading companies of the West as well as of the indigenous military élites. The creed of commerce which inspired them gained a new clarity of formulation in proportion to its world-wide diffusion. That creed pivoted around a belief in the market, the price-mechanism, a money economy and free trade. It assimilated all products to commodities and assumed the separation of business and household as well as the pressure of unlimited wants on limited means. Although such assumptions formulated in Europe were invalid in Asia, its dogmatic conclusions were deemed valid for the whole world. Barriers to trade, which served to protect the production of small local societies and to prevent the survival of the cheapest, were condemned as an unnatural and uneconomic diversion of resources. Comparative accounting was exalted over national accounting on a universal scale and comparative costs over national costs. The principle of comparative costs created by Ricardo in 1817 and by Mill in 1848 was used to explain the virtue and even the necessity of trade between different lands. The creed of commerce assumed that free trade among the nations would divert energy from military into economic activity, so as to make the market the only battlefield of the world. It thus located the moral basis of a new world-order in the satisfaction of material necessity and of individual egoism. Its golden age was envisaged as one of universal trade in place of the traditional age of universal autarchy. The principle of comparative advantages became the foundation of the new discipline of commercial geography and the central assumption of G. C. Chisholm's *Handbook of Commercial Geography* in 1889. Commerce appeared less a source of profit than an instrument of civilization, a vehicle of progress, the surest bridge from barbarism to civilization and the great social leveller. Commerce was identified with civilization by mystic, preacher and agnostic in the anti-aristocratic and anti-militarist tradition of the eighteenth century under the influence of the drive to reunite the United States after the Civil War as the basis for world unity. No contemporary American was so influenced by Oriental thought as Emerson, who nevertheless concluded in 1870 that 'the greatest meliorator of the world is selfish, huckstering Trade'.[1] Flavius J. Cook proclaimed in 1878 'God is making commerce his missionary.'[2] Robert G. Ingersoll agreed in 1882 with his inveterate opponents. 'Honest commerce is the great civilizer. We exchange ideas when we exchange fabrics.'[3] That millenarian outlook made free trade the key to a new world such as it had seemed in England between 1846 and 1853. It could never believe that foreign trade might appear to be a source of exploitation as Nairoji and Hyndman maintained in their drain-theory.

The doctrine of free trade exalted market-demand as the great determinant of agricultural production and climate as the great determinant of comparative advantages in defiance of its bias towards north–south rather than east–west trade. The doctrine of comparative costs ignored, however, nine-tenths of the life of village-Asia as well as the categorical insistence on charity of all the religions of Asia. It also neglected the warning of Malthus in 1817 that the division of labour which made one state the manufacturer and carrier of others was generally accidental and temporary rather than natural and permanent. By assuming that comparative advantages would be permanent it reserved manufacturing industry, transportation services and the world-market to the developed economies of the West. The primary producers were thereby condemned to eternal poverty and denied in modern industry an insurance against harvest failure, a key to world-power and the material symbols of modern civilization. The movement of commodities was exalted above that of the factors of production. The fictitious commodities of capital and labour manufactured in Europe were however exported to Asia there to assume the disproportionate forms of the great merchant-house and the poor rickety coolie and to become ideal types of foreign capital and local labour such as could not be found in the homeland of capitalism.

The merchant firms lost their power to determine prices locally after the completion of the world cable-network in 1870–2 but found their holdings of real estate a growing source of income as their ground-rentals rose with the growth of population. They were able to restrain the entry of competitors from Europe through their monopoly of the best sites in each port. They developed a whole complex of economic activities through the medium of the joint-stock company and the managing-agency. They extended their interests from trade into the associated activities of the docks and warehouses, marine insurance, banking and local steam shipping but opposed the construction of competing railways for the sake of their shipping. They revived the historic tradition of the merchants of Europe and Asia in their use of political connexions and administrative influence for economic advantage. They sought

[1] R. W. Emerson, *Society and Solitude* (London, Routledge, 1883, Riverside Edition), 159, 'Works and Days'.

[2] F. J. Cook, *Boston Monday Lectures: Conscience* (Boston, Houghton, 1879), 91.

[3] R. G. Ingersoll, 'To the Indianapolis Clergy', *The Works of Robert G. Ingersoll* (New York, Dresden, 1909), vii. 138.

the prestige as well as the material benefits of association with the governments of the imperial powers. Regarding political boundaries as barriers to their progress and the State in Asia as their foe, they became instruments of imperial expansion and made commerce appear to Asia as the main influence in the policy of the West. Where political guarantees were strongest for the investment of capital they expanded into plantation-production and into mining, as in British India from the 1860s, and even into manufacturing industry as in the treaty-ports of China from 1878 to 1883. From their concessions they sought to maximize their entrepôt trade by developing the local feeder-trades. They tried to extend their hinterland to the maximum, to attract as many of the local streams of commerce as possible so as to avoid excessive dependence on any single source of supply, to eliminate local restrictions on alien trade and to reduce 'unfair' competition by indigenous ports and merchants. They sought to establish direct contact with the producers of the interior and to develop direct shipment from the producer to the market. Their activity helped to eliminate the smaller harbours from oceanic commerce and reinforced rather than shattered the old entrepôt-monopolies of Zanzibar, Bombay, Calcutta and Canton. They thus compelled the indigenous merchant-family networks to adopt Western techniques in self-defence and endowed the colonial ports with Asian élites in succession to their European élites.

The merchants became the first élite to dominate Asia which never became acclimatized to the continent. They focused their activity around the wharf, the warehouse, the office and the bank. Their contacts with the old city were restricted because they had no knowledge of the local language, knew the local population only as servants or criminals, relied on indigenous intermediaries and were excluded from any contact with the most cultured orders of Asian society. They lacked any common social centre other than the club, the racecourse and the chamber of commerce, membership of which was however sedulously shunned by the great firms, which formed in themselves a small treaty-port community. Their strongest bond of union became their compound-mentality of aversion to the local population on whom they may even have projected their own shortcomings. Their 'restricted, protected, quasi-aristocratic, half-socialistic society'[1] was sheltered by the privilege of extra-territoriality. They cultivated an aggressive parochialism within the cocoon of the club, with the support of the local press and frequent communication with Europe. They centred their life around 'home' and maintained contact with Europe through the cable, the mail-boat and regular leave. The influx of women from Europe prevented their absorption into the teeming mass of waiting Asia more effectively than the traditional seclusion of the local women folk. In the same way the French developed from 1887 the concept of 'association' in place of that of 'assimilation' as an acceptable ideology for a republican empire in full expansion. Europeans in Asia were thereby burdened by the high cost of educating their children at home and debarred from any

---

[1] A. Michie, *The Englishman in China* (1900), i. 261.

contact with the cradle of civil progress in the domestic hearth.[1] They were precluded from exerting any direct beneficial influence in Asia and condemned to believe in the indirect benefits ensuing from their activity.

The merchants readily accepted stereotyped opinions which exaggerated the difference between themselves and the Asian. In their consistent depreciation of local custom they explained any indigenous revolt as a military rebellion, an outburst of fanaticism or a food-riot: thus they deprived them of any political significance and implicitly denied the continuity of Asian history except in terms of ignorance, despotism and superstition. They recognized the material needs of the Asians for food and clothing but they could neither feed nor clothe their souls and were inevitably inclined to doubt their existence. Their concentration on trade in the least durable of material goods reduced their image of the Asian to the lowest biological level and prevented their recognition of him either as a brother in mankind or as an equal in Christ. They resented adverse judgments made by the press at home, by visiting princes or by noble governors on the communities which had grown up around the nucleus of their commercial activity. They made little contribution to the corporate life of those towns because they could not afford to cherish a strong sense of local responsibility. Thus they developed no communal facilities except for self-preservation. Extending the technique of police-control, they introduced Sikh police into Hong Kong in 1867, into Singapore in 1881 and into Tientsin in 1896 while China itself survived without any police or army. The port trust also spread from Bombay (1873, 1879) to some of the main ports of India such as Karachi in 1886, Aden in 1889 and Calcutta in 1890. In general the merchants founded no other institutions except in Tientsin under the stimulus of the three months' hibernation enforced by the 'Great Cold'. Nor did they engage in any charitable activity. 'I am not aware that the monied men of Kurrachee ever combined to found one single institution in that town.'[2] Their model foundation was the capital of Bengal, India and the East, the ill-planned, ill-serviced and ill-regulated Petersburg of Asia. 'Calcutta is thus not a city: it is only a capital.'[3]

Those merchants were creatures and captives of their own culture as much as ruthless exploiters of the helpless Asian. They functioned as happy cogs in the great machine of commerce. Regarding the Asian as impoverished they had no measure of the depth of their own impoverishment and no memory of the Asiatic past of their own culture. They retained, however, an abiding sense of the reality of monetary values and made money their criterion of social status to a greater extent than the members of any other social hierarchy. Tending to reduce all relationships to the cash-nexus and the whole of life to pecuniary terms they measured their success by the yard-stick of profit and

[1] G. F. I. Graham, *The Life and Work of Syed Ahmed Khan* (Edinburgh, Blackwood, 1885), 399.

[2] A. F. Baillie, *Kurrachee: (Karachi) Past: Present: and Future* (1890), 124.

[3] J. Darmesteter, *Nouvelles Études Anglaises* (Paris, Lévy, 1896), 281, Calcutta.

never expected gratitude, like the colonial administrator. 'Commerce was the beginning, the middle and the end of our life in China.'[1] Traders appeared as 'little folk of little soul'[2] to such exponents of the heroic tradition as Kipling who rarely praised the British merchant[3] as he did the British official or soldier. Their commerce exploited opportunities for monetary gain to the utmost without regard to the local controls of tradition, status and morality. Its high monetary returns were bought at substantial economic and social cost in a high turn-over of personnel. The partnership became the representative structure of economic power rather than the family firm because the hereditary transmission of economic power was impossible. The greatest firms, however, strove to attain to the ideal of the corporation as the pattern of the past, the guarantee of immortality upon earth and the best protection against Asia's ensnaring web of personal relationships.

Europeans in Asia were inspired above all else by faith in the superiority of their civilization. Europe however impressed Asia more as a source of power than of culture, as the home of the new machine-technology, the centre of the world-market, the cradle of the master-races and the seat of the world-empires. Its world-wide commerce inhibited any understanding of the non-commercial patterns of life of Asia's peasantry. Its military and naval power restrained the westward spread of Asiatic ideas. Its dualistic world-outlook prevented the acceptance of any monistic view of reality and facilitated the acceptance of an East–West antithesis. Its classical education made Greece the fountain of the civilization of the whole world but inhibited the understanding of the extra-classical civilizations, identified peoples without a history with peoples without a civilization and used philology to prove the disunity and discontinuity of Asian history. Its growing faith in evolution hindered the understanding of a thought-world lacking the principle of progress and decadence. Thus Maine divided the world between the realms of the rational and irrational and held the principle of progress, 'the continued production of new ideas', to be absent from most societies then existing in Asia and to be peculiar to Greece.[4]

The great expansion of travel in the 1880s reflected European supremacy and was facilitated by the pacification of the world and by the abolition of the extra insurance premium thitherto levied for foreign travel. The spread of travel agencies and travellers' clubs established the travel season and the travel habit, which was also fostered by the proliferation of travel tales and travel literature. Travel around the world was stimulated by Verne's best-selling novel of 1873, by the Prince of Wales' visit to India in 1875 and by Brassey's

[1] C. M. Dyce, *Thirty Years' Residence in the Model Settlement Shanghai, 1870–1900* (1906), 95.
[2] Kipling, 'The Miracles' (1894); 'A Tale of Two Cities' (1887).
[3] Idem, 'Our Overseas Men', *The Times*, 30 July 1892, 8i–iii, reprinted in *Letters of Travel, (1892–1913)* (London, Macmillan, 1920), 47–58.
[4] H. S. Maine, *Lectures on the Early History of Institutions* (London, Murray, 1875), 225–7, 'The Growth and Diffusion of Primitive Ideas'.

world-cruise in 1876–7. Kalakaua I, King of the Hawaiian Islands since 1875, became in 1881 the first sovereign to travel around the world:[1] he did not use the Canal but the railway from Suez to Alexandria, where he toasted Cook's frigate *Resolution* anchored as a coal-hulk in the harbour.[2] The first organized cruise round the world took place via the Canal in the *Ceylon*, which had been built in 1858 as a pure passenger-vessel for the Southampton–Alexandria service of the P. & O. and was bought by the Inter-Oceanic Steam Yachting Company after Brassey's world-cruise.[3] The *Ceylon* sailed outwards through the Canal with sixty passengers in December 1881 and returned to Southampton after covering 36,000–37,000 miles in ten months (27 October 1881–22 August 1882). From 1884 world tours by individual English travellers became fashionable, using the westward route across the Atlantic and the homeward route via the Canal rather than the eastabout route. Thus the aristocratic institution of the grand tour was extended and democratized, providing a new occupation for the parliamentary recess and a new refuge from the English winter.

Travel replaced face-to-face contacts by face-to-place contacts, became an act of devotion to the modern pilgrims of the travelling nations of the world and achieved the functional autonomy best expressed by Stevenson. 'For my part, I travel not to go anywhere, but to go. I travel for travel's sake. The great affair is to move.'[4] 'There is always a new horizon for onward-looking men... To travel hopefully is a better thing than to arrive, and the true success is to labour.'[5] Travel extended the nature-conquering outlook of the West to Asia where man was dwarfed by the immensity of space, by hills that could not be subdued and by rivers that could not be spanned unlike the 'small river' of the Nile.[6] The Western mind ceased to divide space between the sacred and the profane but appropriated the whole to utilitarian ends, represented it in geometrical terms and sought to delimit it by scientific frontiers in flat opposition to the Asian aversion to fixed boundaries. The growth of travel did not enhance international understanding because the best interpreters of the East to the West did not visit India or China, while missionaries in the East discouraged travel to Europe by their converts and pupils. Thus the world became divided between the travelling nations and the toured nations, between the culture-bearers and the culture-sufferers. The travellers from the West reached into the spatial depths of Asia more than into its cultural heart They made the holy places of Asia less sacred but their own persons increasingly more sacred in the pursuit of their curiosity. They praised security for travellers as the greatest achievement of local rulers and identified social

---

[1] W. N. Armstrong, *Around the World with a King* (London, Heinemann, 1904), 282.
[2] Ibid., 194.
[3] *The Times*, 19 September 1881, 8iv, 'A Cruise Round the World'.
[4] R. L. Stevenson, *Travels with a Donkey in the Cevennes* (London, Chatto, 1920), 63, Cheylard and Luc, 1879.
[5] Idem, *Virginibus Puerisque* (London, Chatto, 1891), 172, 178, El Dorado, 1881.
[6] *Cornhill Magazine* (May 1870), 583, 'A Chinese Commissioner's Foreign Tour'.

and geographical immobility with oppression. The sessile civilizations of Asia used barriers of physical as well as of social distance in self-protection and sought self-realization through immobility, seeing the world as a bridge and change as an illusion. They derived no stimulus from travel and discouraged unnecessary movement in order to conserve social energy. They could not understand the restless activity of the English and Americans and suspected them of hostile designs against their independence. They understood travel only in terms of a pilgrimage to their holy places or to the tombs of their forefathers. Thus the new media of communication divided the world between the parents and the foundlings of the human family: 'The Ruler of the world has brought the inborn sentiment of curiosity and benevolence in the more highly-favoured parts of the earth to bear on the darkness and isolation of the more remote and obscure.'[1]

The influence of Europe upon Asia was reinforced through the spread of Christianity which achieved its greatest territorial extent in the 1880s, when China and Africa were brought within the Christian fold. Two waves of Christian missionaries had followed the road to the East since the Nestorians of the sixth century and before the fourth wave of the nineteenth century. Those missionaries carried a universal gospel to regions where religion was inseparable from land and people. From the 1860s they penetrated far beyond the fringe of European settlement on the coast into the continental interior. Their preaching of the virtue of self-imposed poverty produced no effect in a society which did not separate acts from beliefs. They sought to convert the heathen from Confucian ethics to Greek theology and Hebrew morality. They tried to arouse them to a sense of sin of which they were ignorant and to the need for atonement which they could not recognize. They preached individual salvation to a society which esteemed the family above all else. Inevitably they failed to separate the Chinese from a religion which was the core and emanation of their society. Their recruits comprised only the out-castes of society, 'only the worst, the feeblest, the poorest and the most vicious of Chinese'[2] who 'ate Christianity' in return for rice and judicial protection from 'pagan customs'. In order to achieve more success the missionaries began to combine social reform with Christianity: they founded schools, hospitals and even universities from the establishment of the Shantung Christian University in 1882. Thus they diffused Western education in China much more than in India and tended to adopt the short-term viewpoint of the merchant and the soldier in their increasing concern with first things rather than with last things. Their reports emphasized the worst rather than the best features in the life of Asia so as to facilitate the raising of funds in Europe. Their activity recreated the revolutionary power of primitive Christianity, subverted the whole structure of Chinese society and made their religion

---

[1] A. P. Stanley, 'The Mission of the Traveller', *Good Words*, 19 April 1874, 357.
[2] A. Chih, *L'Occident 'Chrétien' vu par les Chinois (1870–1900)* (Paris, Presses Universitaires de France, 1962), 157, quoting Ku Hung-ming in 1891.

appear as a political instrument to the literati. Their converts became second-hand foreigners and the object of the silent hatred of all true Chinese. They themselves became the object of ceaseless guerrilla warfare by the officials and of active outrage and massacre by the people from time to time. In general they lived only on the tolerance of a tolerant civilization and under the protection of the same alien power which sheltered the merchants in the treaty-ports. Their function was to identify the diffusion of European civilization with that of Christianity: their achievement was to make the cathedral the supreme symbol of the European metropolis in Asia.

The newly united world was sharply divided by Kipling, who commemorated the annexation of the kingdom of Ava in *Mandalay* in 1890 and so brought Suez into the world of literature as well as into the sub-literary world of the popular imagination. 'East of Suez' had been used as a phrase as early as 1867[1] but was transformed by Kipling into an idea-force. Kipling first distinguished 'East and West' at the age of twenty in 1885 under the influence of the Afghan crisis.[2] He first coined the phrase 'East of Suez' in 1887 as a synonym for Asia in contrast to Europe. 'East of Suez men do not build towers on the tops of hills for the sake of the view, nor do they stripe the mountain sides with bastioned stone walls to keep in cattle.'[3] He used the expression in the same way in a study of the Calcutta police in 1888 after his first visit to Calcutta. 'They are, despite the wearing climate they work in and the wearing work they do, as fine a five-score of Englishmen as you shall find east of Suez.'[4] In 1890 Kipling first gave that journalistic formula a religious content in order to explain the horrors of life in a hot and heathen world. 'East of Suez, some hold, the direct control of Providence ceases; Man being there handed over to the power of the Gods and Devils of Asia, and the Church of England Providence only exercising an occasional and modified supervision in the case of Englishmen.'[5] Thus the grandson of two Methodist ministers displayed his irreverence for the comfortable certainties of Anglican England as well as for the narrow piety of the Evangelical tradition. In the ballad which catapulted Kipling into the first rank of contemporary writers in 1889 he also affirmed the primal unity of mankind as personified in those rare heroes who formed the brotherhood of the brave:

There is neither East nor West, Border, nor Breed, nor Birth,
When two strong men stand face to face, though they come from the end of the earth![6]

To the ranks of such universal men Kipling added children, in whose hearts there was neither East nor West.[7] Most people were however above the age

---

[1] Hansard, *Commons Debates*, 1 August 1867, 674, 677.

[2] L. L. Cornell, *Kipling in India* (London, Macmillan, 1966), 108-9.

[3] Kipling, 'Letters of Marque, No. ii' (1887), reprinted in *From Sea to Sea* (London, Macmillan, 1900), i. 8, 208, 432.

[4] 'The City of Dreadful Night, No. v, With the Calcutta Police' (1888), reprinted in *From Sea to Sea* (1900), ii. 238.

[5] 'The Mark of the Beast' (1890), in *Life's Handicap* (London, Macmillan, 1891).

[6] 'The Ballad of East and West' (1889).   [7] 'To James Whitcomb Riley' (1890).

of caste and had to recognize the essential diversity of creatures. Their perceptions were given lasting form by Kipling.

Kipling's love of place-names enabled him to give a local habitation and a name to the lure of the East in his portrayal of the homesickness of all who had once fallen beneath the spell of Asia. He had earlier expressed the traditional lament of the exile, whether a private soldier[1] or a younger son,[2] for his lost heritage of London life. In 1889 he left India forever at the age of twenty-three and travelled eastwards until he reached the heart of the world once more in London. That journey via Rangoon, Moulmein and Penang bore fruit in *Mandalay* in 1890.[3] Therein Kipling portrayed the appeal of the heathen world to an ex-soldier who had served in the Burma War of 1886 and was overcome in the English drizzle by a sickening aversion to London and an overpowering attraction to a cleaner, greener land of palm-trees, sunshine and silence. The road to Mandalay became the ex-soldier's golden path to romance, the way of escape from the urban house of bondage and the road back to an heroic past, transfigured by the imagination of the exile.[4]

> But that's all shove be'ind me—long ago an' fur away,
> An' there ain't no 'buses runnin' from the Bank to Mandalay;
> An' I'm learnin' 'ere in London what the ten-year soldier tells:
> 'If you've 'eard the East a-callin', you won't never 'eed naught else.'

To bridge the gulf between the austerity of Christian Europe and the hedonism of heathen Asia Kipling invoked the god of motion:

> Ship me somewheres east of Suez, where the best is like the worst,
> Where there aren't no Ten Commandments an' a man can raise a thirst;
> For the temple-bells are callin', an' it's there that I would be—
> By the old Moulmein Pagoda, looking lazy at the sea;
> > On the road to Mandalay,
> > Where the old Flotilla lay,
> > With our sick beneath the awnings when we went to Mandalay!
> > O the road to Mandalay,
> > Where the flyin'-fishes play,
> > An' the dawn comes up like thunder outer China 'crost the Bay!

Thus Kipling powerfully revived the Romantic homesickness for Asia, for the eldest of all the Gods and for the temples of the East. Those verses appeared in the year of his sudden success in London and achieved the maximum penetration of a culture deriving, as Arnold had maintained, from the Hebrew

[1] 'The Madness of Private Ortheris', in *Plain Tales from the Hills* (1888).
[2] 'The City of Dreadful Night, No. 1' (1888), in *From Sea to Sea*, ii. 202.
[3] *The Pioneer Mail*, 8 May 1889, 584–5, 'From Sea to Sea, No. ii, The River of the Lost Footsteps and the Golden Mystery upon its Banks'.
[4] J. K. Stanford, 'Some Lesser-Known Aspects of Kipling in the East', *Kipling Journal* (July 1947), 10–11, *Mandalay*. B. Gutteridge, 'The Road to Mandalay', *Kipling Journal* (April 1951), 9–10; (July 1951), 6–7.

mind rather than from Greek thought. *Mandalay* was written to an old waltz tune, was first set to music in 1892 in England as well as in the U.S.A.[1] and also inspired Beverley Bewicke's 'Mandalay Waltz' of 1892. Set to better music than the other *Barrack-Room Ballads*, it assumed a martial air and reached through the urban music-hall large audiences unaffected by verse, penetrating in depth even more than in extent. It won the approval of such bitter critics of Kipling as Francis Adams,[2] Robert Buchanan[3] and Richard Le Gallienne.[4] It infected even the stern unbending Cromer with fascination for the call of the East.[5]

'East of Suez' had been used only in prose before Kipling: used in verse and song it passed quickly into literature. It ceased to be a euphuism for Asia and assumed the power of an incantation by its association with heroic deeds of conquest and with such other evocative idioms as 'the road to Mandalay' and 'the call of the East'. Within that single sibilant saying Kipling compressed all the mystery of the Orient, the splendour of the gorgeous East and the magic of the Arabian Nights. He expressed the fascination exerted upon him by Asia during his own formative years and conjured up a vision of a world of warmth and light and colour. His affection for Asia was rooted in his dislike of the cold damp climate of England as well as of the provincialism of London, in his sensitivity to new environments and in his lack of patriotism[6] beneath the superficial content of his verse. As a child he had absorbed the lore of India: as a man he opened for the West a magic casement on the faery lands of the East and revealed it as larger, older and stranger than the mind of Europe cared to conceive. 'And the wildest dreams of Kew are the facts of Khatmandu.'[7] Kipling shifted the frontier of Europe eastwards from the Danube and the Balkans to the isthmian junction of Asia and Africa, which he made the focus of three continents instead of two. Thereby he subsumed the division of the Mediterranean world between East and West within the larger unity of Europe west of Suez. He brought the Levant within the pale of Europe but consigned its civilization to that limbo he reserved for the mixed breeds. Above all, he replaced the traditional religious barrier between East and West by a geographical barrier located at Suez, which Flaubert had identified with the modern Orient. It is not clear whether Kipling meant by 'Suez' the isthmus, the Canal or the town because he used the phrase like a

[1] G. F. Cobb, 'Mandalay' (London, Sheard, 1892). A. Thayer, 'Mandalay' (Philadelphia, Presser, 1892). F. W. Mackenzie-Skues, 'Kipling Poems Set to Music', *Kipling Journal* (December 1932), 118.

[2] F. Adams, 'Mr. Rudyard Kipling's Verse', *Fortnightly Review*, 1 November 1893, 602–3, 593.

[3] R. Buchanan, 'The Voice of "The Hooligan"', *Contemporary Review* (December 1899), 799–800.

[4] R. Le Gallienne, *Rudyard Kipling. A Criticism* (London, Lane, 1900), 29–32, 40–1, 47, 162.

[5] Earl Cromer, *Modern Egypt* (London, Macmillan, 1908), i. 8.

[6] G. K. Chesterton, *Heretics* (London, Lane, 1905), 47, 'On Mr. Rudyard Kipling and Making the World Small'. L. L. Cornell, *Kipling in India* (1966), 11, 44.

[7] 'In the Neolithic Age' (1893).

magician[1] and avoided that definition which would have shattered its power. He never honoured Suez with a description as he did Port Said but most probably referred to the town through which he had travelled via the overland route as often as via the Canal. Thus in the phrase 'east of Suez' he resurrected the old division of the services of the P. & O. shortly after the extinction of the overland route.

Kipling endowed Suez and the Canal with an importance which they could never have assumed without him. In particular he rendered the Canal holy in the imagination of a culture which was losing touch with the sacred things of its own past. For the Canal Kipling did as much as the Greek Orthodox priest who on the solemn festival of the Epiphany on 6 January 1884 blessed the Canal and cast a golden cross into the sea at Port Said.[2] That service Kipling performed for an isthmus which had become almost as unhealthy as that of Panama and for a Canal whose waters had lost their clarity of the 1870s and had become uninviting either to fish or to passengers. The opaque waters of the Canal remained unscoured by any current, unpalatable to man or beast and polluted by sewage from the Company stations as well as from passing ships in defiance of the Company's Regulations. The banks had only scanty vegetation, never having been planted with trees, and had even been used by ships' captains as natural cemeteries for the burial of corpses.[3] The cholera epidemics of 1883 and 1884[4] reinforced the impact of the endemic mosquitoes from the Sweet Water Canal. The great maritime Canal thus deteriorated into 'a stinking ditch', 'a home for disease and mischief...a mere sewer',[5] 'a dirty ditch with nothing remarkable'.[6] 'This was the foulest cesspool that ever existed.'[7] Such a waterway threatened to become 'a centre of infection for Europe and the East'.[8]

Balfour had asked rhetorically in 1878 what mystic virtue resided in the isthmus of Suez: Kipling used his memories of 1882 and 1892 to confer magical significance upon the isthmus and the Canal and to purify its waters in the mind of Europe as the works programme of 1886–96 purified them in fact. He stressed its function as the common frontier of two civilizations, as the meeting-place of East and West and as a stage on the road to Mandalay. In the Canal globe-trotters en route to a five-weeks' Cook's tour of India were shown leaving their English manners.[9] Port Said formed in his view a universal

[1] R. G. Collingwood, *The Principles of Art* (Oxford, Clarendon Press, 1938), 70.

[2] H. W. Lucy, *East by West. A Journey in the Recess* (London, Bentley, 1885), ii. 356–7.

[3] *Le Canal de Suez*, 2 Juillet 1879, 1.

[4] E. C. Wendt (ed.), *A Treatise on Asiatic Cholera* (New York, Wood, 1885), 61, John C. Peters, A History of Asiatic Cholera.

[5] *The Times*, 9 May 1883, 6 vi; 29 June 1883, 4 iii, W. P. Andrew.

[6] W. S. Churchill, *Lord Randolph Churchill* (London, Macmillan, 1906), i. 555, Lord Randolph to his wife, 18 December 1884.

[7] Hansard, *Lords Debates*, 29 July 1884, 839, Lord Lamington.

[8] E. M. Clerke, 'Maritime Canals', *Journal of the Manchester Geographical Society* (1886), 54.

[9] *The Pioneer Mail*, 17 April 1889, 494, 'From Sea to Sea, No. 1, Of Freedom and the Necessity of Using Her'.

rendezvous, like Charing Cross Station and Nyanza Docks. 'There are three great doors in the world where, if you stand long enough, you shall meet anyone you wish... At each of these places are men and women looking eternally for those who will surely come.'[1] There those who waited long enough might see 'most of the men and women you have known in this life' and there all the races of East and West were available for study by the journalist.[2] There the lingua franca of the Levant gave place to the lingua franca of the East which 'runs from Port Said eastwards till east is west' beyond Japan. Port Said also marked the beginning of 'the well-remembered smell of the East, that runs without a change from the Canal head to Hong-Kong',[3] 'the smell of the East, One and Indivisible, Immemorial, Eternal, and, above all, Instructive'.[4] Thus Port Said concentrated in itself the function of the Canal as 'the gate of East and West'.[5]

Through the Canal the Exiles' Line took out and brought back the exiles' line.[6]

> Bound in the wheel of Empire, one by one,
> The chain-gangs of the East from sire to son,
> The Exiles' Line takes out the exiles' line
> And ships them homeward when their work is done.

In the Canal the father retiring from Indian service passed his son going out to take up the family duties.[7] The Canal Company's garden at Port Said, which marked the exact division between East and West, was haunted by djinns and afrits to dispirit the young griffin but by the good spirits of the East to inspire the sons of families who had served India for five or six generations.[8] Kipling thus transformed a mundane waterway into a romantic highway and a sacred stream which remained to Asia an illusion of illusions. He focused attention upon the Canal rather than upon the desert, the Sinai Peninsula, the Red Sea or the Gulf of Suez, which was rarely visited and was garnished in 1895 by 'a continuous jetsam of empty brandy and rum bottles cast up by the waves and marking the unholy track of Western civilization'.[9] Thus Kipling introduced into literature the idea of the waterway as the great divide between East and West and so recognized the large difference in temperature between Port Said and Suez. That dividing-line was recognized by Dulip Singh in 1886, by Bryce in 1888[10] and by Blunt in 1892.[11] Kipling

---

[1] 'The Limitations of Pambé Serang' (1889), in *Life's Handicap* (1891).
[2] *The Light that Failed* (1891), ch. iii.
[3] Ibid., ch. xv.
[4] *The Times*, 2 July 1892, 12 ii, 'The Edge of the East', reprinted in *Letters of Travel* (*1892–1913*), 39.
[5] G. W. Steevens, *Egypt in 1898* (Edinburgh, Blackwood, 1898), 22.
[6] 'The Exiles' Line' (1892).
[7] 'The Tomb of his Ancestors' (1897).
[8] *Nash's Magazine* (July 1914), 481–2, 'Egypt of the Magicians'.
[9] W. S. Blunt, *My Diaries, 1888–1914* (1919), i. 207.
[10] H. A. L. Fisher, *James Bryce* (1927), i. 254–5.
[11] W. S. Blunt, *My Diaries* (1919), i. 94, 27 September 1892.

endowed the Canal with the sanctity which only a Palestine Canal could otherwise have acquired and so achieved for the Canal route what W. P. Andrew failed to do for the Euphrates route. He made Suez into a new Jerusalem, increasingly sacred to the West as Mecca, Meshed and Benares were to the East. Thus he restored to Suez the mystic aura bestowed upon it by Enfantin and destroyed by Lesseps.

22

THE RISE OF PORT SAID, 1887-1914

PORT Said began its real expansion as a half-way house, a bunkering port and a toll-gate after the abandonment of the overland route in 1888 rather than immediately after the opening of the Canal. Its population had risen to 12,300 in 1879 and to 15,000 in 1882, when it first exceeded that of Suez. Its aspirations revived on the destruction of the commercial centre of Alexandria in 1882 and the influx of European refugees but were restrained by the British invasion and occupation, the strike of its Arab coal-heavers and the cholera epidemic of 1883 which reached Port Said a month before it struck Suez, so reversing the pattern of the 1865 epidemic. Wolseley's invasion of Egypt via the Canal first revealed the strategic importance of Port Said and stimulated its anglicization as well as the construction of an Alexandria–Port Said–Suez cable by the Eastern Telegraph Company. That cable was sanctioned by the Canal Company in October 1882 and opened on 28 June 1883, so making the cable to India wholly submarine. Port Said became increasingly a port of disembarkation by English passengers for Cairo because the Company refused from 1883 to permit disembarkation at Ismailia and so reversed its previous policy. The agitation by English shipowners against the Company in 1883 encouraged C. A. Lichtenberg and C. E. Stephens of Port Said to propose a second competitive ship canal. The Company thereupon decided to introduce gas light into the harbour from 1884[1] and to experiment with the navigation of the Canal by night in order to reduce congestion and the complaints of its clients. Port Said experienced a second moral renaissance after the fire of 4 April 1884 led to the establishment of an international fire-brigade, a Treaty of Commerce with Greece in 1884 ended the smuggling of Greek tobacco and Baker Pasha's police made the town no longer 'a den of thieves and assassins'.[2]

Port Said became an important destination for English colliers, which were intended to benefit by the Convention of 18 December 1884 whereby the Government of Egypt agreed to halve the tolls on the Ismailia Canal from Cairo to Ismailia. The Company halved its tolls on the Port Said–Ismailia half of the Canal from 15 May 1885 in order to encourage colliers to pick up return freight at Ismailia. The four existing coaling firms lost their monopoly with the establishment of the new firms of John Carrara & Co., the Anglo-Egyptian Coaling Company and the Port Said International Coaling Company Ltd., which was registered in London on 13 October 1884 but was wound up on 14 May 1887. Land prices rose by 27 per cent from £2. 12s. to £3. 6s. per

---

[1] *The Times*, 28 April 1883, 13 vi.

[2] E. Arnold, *India Revisited* (1886), 27–8, November 1885.

square yard while coal prices fell from 24*s.* to 21*s.* per ton between 1884 and 1886 and were thenceforward kept low by competition between the French and English firms. Coal imports, which had risen from under 200,000 tons in 1871 to 310,000 tons in 1879, soared to exceed 500,000 tons in 1883 and 750,000 tons in 1887. The proportion of ships in transit bunkering at Port Said increased steadily. The other coaling stations of the Mediterranean sought in vain to preserve their trade at its peak level of the early 1880s. In 1885 Gibraltar sanctioned night coaling, while Algiers admitted bunker coal free of duty. Coal imports reached their peak quantity to Malta in 1885 and to Gibraltar in 1889 but continued rising to Port Said. Malta suffered most from the competition of Port Said and provided emigrants for Australia by the Canal route. The annual value of the coal supplied at Port Said to ships in transit rose from £480,000 in 1885 to £1,200,000 in 1890. The English coaling firms adopted the company form of organization. Wills Manché & Co. Ltd. was registered on 4 April 1887 by John Trenwith Wills, C. A. Lichtenberg and Henry Weissenburg of Liverpool to take over the business of J. T. Wills and became Wills & Co. Ltd. on 24 October 1887. The Eagle Coal Company Ltd. was formed on 25 August 1891 by Cory Brothers Company of Cardiff to take over the business of Carrara.

The coal came largely from England, first from the Tyne and then from South Wales, whose exports first exceeded those from the North-East coast in 1881. Coal formed the overwhelming bulk of the total volume of imports into Port Said, 94 per cent thereof in 1882 and 96 per cent in 1884, and made it one of the most highly specialized of all ports. 'Port Said is coal—the Clapham Junction of nations, the gate of East and West, the coaling-station of the world.'[1] Apart from sand as ballast Port Said could supply no return freight which had to be sought at Alexandria, in Syria, in the Black Sea or even at Jedda. Thus Cardiff–Port Said freights were regulated mainly by Black Sea grain freights. The coal firms paid a substantial rent to the Company and a transit duty of 1 per cent to the Government from 1874. The import duty of 8 per cent ad valorem on coal, with a rebate of seven-eighths on its re-export, restricted import for domestic consumption. The loading and unloading of the coal gave employment to a fleet of barges and to a small army of labourers. In 1880 7,000 Arabs worked in teams of fifty, each of whom carried 55 pounds at a time. Coaling took place to the rhythm of a chant and was very rapid, supplying mail-boats with up to 100 tons an hour,[2] which was faster than a warship could be coaled at sea. The activity covered ship, passengers and crew with a fine dust, although every door, port and scuttle was sealed. It prevented passengers from sleeping and drove them ashore to escape the noise and the dust, to the benefit of local shopkeepers. The Arab coal-heavers were driven by land-hunger to work for low and stable wages and do not seem to have benefited immediately from the competition between the coaling firms.

[1] G. W. Steevens, *Egypt in 1898* (Edinburgh, Blackwood, 1898), 22.
[2] J. Steele, *The Suez Canal: its Present and Future* (1872), 20.

After the agreement on the London Programme of 1883 a sub-commission of the Advisory Commission of Engineers created in 1884 visited Egypt between 21 November and 3 December 1884. Lesseps then paid his forty-ninth and last visit to Egypt, secured the all-important permission on 13 December to extend the Sweet Water Canal to Port Said and concluded two Conventions on 18 December relating to tolls on the Ismailia Canal and to the administration of the Common Domain. The full Advisory Commission decided on 11 February 1885 against the construction of a second canal and in favour of the enlargement of the existing canal as suggested by Lemasson. A second canal would completely eliminate sidings as well as the danger of collisions and greatly reduce the risk of a total blockage of the waterway.[1] It would not however create a more favourable cross-section whilst it would require new negotiations with the Government of Egypt, more labour and more expense for supervision, administration and repairs: it would also give Lesseps two Suez Canals in addition to his projected Panama Canal and Kra Canal. The Commission therefore drew up an ambitious three-phase programme which would enable ships to pass one another without stopping in the enlarged channel,[2] reduce the transit-time to the minimum and increase the day-time capacity to 100 ships when the average number was nine per day in 1883. The Company would gain absolute security against any future demands for enlargement by the excavation at a cost of £8,118,000 of 124,000,000 cubic yards, including 85,000,000 cubic yards deposited on the banks during the original excavation. The Commission proposed a general increase in bottom width by 49 feet from 72 feet to 121 feet, an increase in surface width to 213 feet for vessels with a maximum beam of 48 feet and a general deepening, first from 26 feet to 28 feet and then to 29½ feet, for vessels with a maximum draught of 24½ feet. Thus it overrode the British wish for a minimum depth of 31 feet,[3] which would have admitted vessels with a draught of 27 feet or even of 28–30 feet. Its programme was accepted on 20 May 1885 by the board of directors which sanctioned the first phase of the works to add 49 feet to the width and 20 inches to the depth in five years. The board believed that the mere enlargement of the Canal would not require the sanction of the Government of Egypt and decided at the same time to seek approval from the shareholders on 4 June for a bond issue of £4,000,000 to spread the cost of the works programme over seventy rather than over seven years.

The Government of Egypt considered itself the real loser by the London Programme, which had been concluded without consultation by the Company. It therefore limited the Company strictly to the terms of its Concession, refused to sanction either the works or the loan and maintained that the Company could not improve the Canal beyond a surface width of 144 feet

---

[1] C. Hartley, 'A Short History of the Engineering Works of the Suez Canal', *Proceedings of the Institution of Civil Engineers*, 13 March 1900, 164–84.

[2] J. Rabino, 'The Statistical Story of the Suez Canal', *Journal of the Statistical Society* (September 1887), 542.

[3] Hartley, 174, 196.

without special authority. The Company argued that the Canal was not Egyptian territory and appealed to the Customs Regulation of 2 April 1884 placing the customs frontier on the boundaries of the Canal.[1] It also refused to pay the duty claimed by the Customs in June 1884 on the dredgers, tugs and barges which it had imported from Europe for the improvement works. The Civil Court of Alexandria rejected the Company's plea on 18 May 1885. The Government then brought a legal action against the Company on 27 May for the customs dues on its plant and again won its case in the Mixed Courts.[2] It also refused from 1885 to pay for land in the Common Domain occupied for public services. Only in 1886 did Nubar's Ministry reach agreement with the Company. The Convention of 10 May 1886 approved the modification of the Company's Statutes necessary to float the £4,000,000 loan. The Convention of 20 December 1886 sanctioned the works programme and sold the Company 4,000 hectares of land for £80,000. The Government imposed in 1886 a tax of 12 per cent on buildings but applied it only to those which paid rent to the Company. From 1887 it encouraged litigation against the Company. It also nullified the effect of the Convention of 1884 which had been intended to develop the trade of Ismailia, and then denounced the Convention on 23 March 1887, together with a similar Convention of 31 December 1886. Thus it counteracted the effect of the Company's successive reductions in the Ismailia tariff in 1885 and 1887, discouraged the growth of trade via Port Said, protected the revenues of the State railways and forced the Company back upon its own resources.

The Company pushed ahead experiments which had been conducted with the use of electric light since 26 January 1884.[3] Therein Lesseps was opposed by his own technical personnel but supported by the P. & O. whose first vessel above 5,000 tons gross, the *Carthage*, made the first transit with the aid of a searchlight from Port Said to Suez in eighteen hours on the night of 22–23 March 1886. Four months later the *Océanien* of the Messageries passed through and was portrayed in the first engraving ever published in the Company's Bulletin.[4] By December 1886 ninety-five guide-lights had been installed on buoys along the Canal. Transit by night remained limited to mailboats and warships and was undertaken mainly by the vessels of the P. & O. but during 1886 averaged 20 hours 42 minutes or 43 per cent less than the general average time of 36 hours 11 minutes. The North German Lloyd made its first night transit on 16–17 January 1887. Regulations published in the London Gazette on 18 February permitted night-time transit by all ships provided with a searchlight from 1 March 1887. The proportion of such continuous transits rose from 12·6 per cent in 1887 to 71·7 per cent in 1889,

[1] O. Borelli, *Choses Politiques d'Égypte, 1883–1895* (1895), 567.

[2] *The Times*, 7 January 1886, 5v. Hansard, *Commons Debates*, 25 January 1886, 304, C. W. Dilke and T. Sutherland.

[3] T. Holmes, *Heart and Thought. Memories of Eastern Travel* (Bolton, Gledsdale, 1887), 110.

[4] *Le Canal de Suez*, 22 Septembre 1886, 1327. G. Weisbrodt, 'Die Erste Nachtfahrt durch den Suez-Kanal', *Das Ausland*, 27 Dezember 1886, 1034–5.

when they formed a majority for the first time, and then to 83·5 per cent in 1890 and 95 per cent in 1895. The searchlight which had been developed to enable warships to detect torpedo-boats proved superior to lighting the banks by gas-lamps or the channel by buoys: its use differentiated the Suez Canal from the North Sea Canal, which was not lighted, and from the Kiel Canal, whose banks were lighted by electric light. The searchlight was modified for the Canal by Sautter and Lemonnier of Paris, who enjoyed a virtual monopoly of its manufacture, so as to produce through a prismatic lens a long triangular beam with an emission-angle of 15° and a range of three-quarters of a mile. Competition was fostered in the manufacture not of searchlights but of port-able power-plants driven by boilers under low pressure and steam-engines at the low r.p.m. imposed by the low speed mandatory in the Canal, such as the slow-speed dynamo developed in 1888 by S. Charlesworth & Co. of Oldham.[1] Port Said gained a new industry in the hire by shipping agents of searchlights and small dynamos to ships without their own generators. The electric light was introduced into the town itself in 1891 although not into the harbour before 1912. The demand increased for the subsidiary fuels of oil and gas, for the oil used in the lights on shore and in the buoy lamps in the lakes as well as for the gas in the Pintsch light used in the outer harbour at Port Said. Pilots earned an additional fee from the double pilotage rates charged for night-time transit.

The introduction of night-time transit first reduced the average duration of overnight stops in the Canal by 88 per cent from 16 hours 36 minutes in 1885 to 2 hours 21 minutes in 1890 and then wholly eliminated them.[2] The general absence by night of wind, heat-haze and mirage facilitated steering. Navigation became continuous, saving much more time than the hours of night and largely eliminating complaints by clients of the Company. It thus made possible the most effective use of the waterway by mail-boats and the decision to send express mails direct through the Canal. It harmed the trade of the shopkeepers of Port Said because passengers no longer needed to spend the night drinking in port while waiting to pass through the Canal. It also damaged the trade of the Canal-beggars, increased the number of accidents to Arab boats as well as to Company tugs between 1885 and 1889 and compelled the Company to forbid night-time navigation by sailing boats in the Canal. The searchlight added an element of unparalleled visual beauty to the prosaic operation of the waterway. The dazzle produced between two ships approaching in opposite directions as they emerged from the horizon at 12½ miles distance, however, drove pilots to seek refuge behind the fore-mast and increased the possibility of errors in navigation. The searchlight with a divided beam was therefore invented in 1892, trisected the beam into three 5° segments, leaving the central one dark, and was made compulsory from 1 October 1893.

The Company demonstrated that the average delay had been reduced from

[1] Patent No. 13,954, of 28 September 1888 by S. Charlesworth and J. P. Hall.
[2] J. Charles-Roux, *L'Isthme et le Canal de Suez* (1901), ii. 148–58.

23 hours 37 minutes in 1876–86 to 5 hours 30 minutes in 1887–1900 and so concealed the effective reduction in transit times by 33 per cent between 1882 and 1886 before the general introduction of night-time transit. The average transit-time was reduced by a further 33 per cent between 1886 and 1890 so that it fell for the first time below thirty hours in 1889 and below twenty hours in 1894.[1] The record transit-time fell by 38 per cent from 13 hours 53 minutes in 1886 to 8 hours 45 minutes in 1894. Night-time transit more than doubled the effective carrying-capacity of the Canal at a cost of one-tenth of the radical widening programme of 1884. Thus it proved an effective substitute for that programme and the most economic solution to traffic-congestion. It permitted the extension of the enlargement works over twelve years from 1887 to 1898 instead of the six years recommended in 1885.[2]

After the complete replacement of the Company's dredging equipment between 1881 and 1886 the improvement of the channel began in 1887 when a new Advisory Works Commission first met on 4–5 November 1887. The thirteen members of that Commission included no shipowners but were all engineers who met annually under the presidency of Voisin Bey to submit their recommendations to the Company. The 3 per cent £4,000,000 loan of 1887 was floated over thirteen years at a real interest-rate of £3. 18s. 10d. per cent against the 1880 interest-rate of 4½ per cent. In 1888 the Company first used the Lobnitz rock-breaker, which had been patented in 1886 after Bunau-Varilla used concussion rock-dredging at Panama in 1885: chisel-pointed rams were therein used to break up the hard limestone of Chalouf without drilling or blasting which might have endangered passing ships.[3] The improvement of the channel in 1887–8 destroyed the original Canal save in the narrowest cuttings and permitted passing at any point, but was achieved in depth rather than in width in accordance with the requests of shipowners who wished to build deeper and more economical vessels. The depth of 26 feet attained in 1871 was first surpassed in 1890. The channel remained adapted to one-way rather than to two-way navigation. The Orient Line imitated the Inman Line, which had introduced the twin-screw on the Atlantic route in 1888, and built the twin-screw *Ophir* to the maximum dimensions permitted by the waterway.[4] The first twin-screw vessels passed through the Canal in 1891, the *Cheshire* of the Bibby Line, the *Ophir* and the Empress liners of the C.P.R. The P. & O. remained doubtful about the suitability of a twin-screw for the limited fairway and introduced a twin-screw only on the *Candia* in 1896 and the *Plassey* in 1900 while the Holt Line introduced a twin-screw only on the *Bellerophon* in 1906. The improvement of the channel encouraged the growth of traffic and benefited the larger shipowners. Its deepening reinforced the natural deepening of the Bitter Lakes through the dissolution of

[1] *Le Canal de Suez*, 12 Juillet 1908, 5119–20, 'La Durée du Transit des Navires (1870–1907)'. *Le Canal de Suez*, 22 Septembre 1909, 5316–17, 'La Navigation de Nuit, dans le Canal de Suez'. J. Charles-Roux, ii. 156.   [2] C. Hartley, 176–7.
[3] *The Engineer*, 9 March 1888, 197, 'Subaqueous Rock Dredger for the Suez Canal'.
[4] W. J. Loftie, *Orient Line Guide* (1900), 177.

their salt bed and reduced the salt content of the Canal waters as well as of the lakes.[1] The increase in the tidal scour purified the waters of the Canal at the same time as Kipling sanctified them in the imagination of the West. The decrease in the salinity of the Canal facilitated the migration into the Mediterranean of marine fauna from the Red Sea, especially the littoral erythraean fauna rather than the deep-sea fauna. Thus the pearl oyster reached Tunis by 1895 and decapod crustaceans were found at Fiume by 1896.[2] The swimming crab was caught in the Bitter Lakes first in 1889 and at Port Said first in 1898. The resulting increase in the marine population along the coasts of Syria and Palestine enriched and diversified the catches of Mediterranean fishermen. A local fishing industry developed in the Canal, especially in Lake Timsah and the Great Bitter Lake, supplying fish and shell-fish to the markets of Port Said, Ismailia and Suez, to mail-boats in transit and even to the markets of Cairo and Alexandria.[3] The simultaneous conclusion of the Sanitary Conventions of 1891–7 made Egypt and the Canal a key point in the defence of the West against epidemics from the East. Quarantine restrictions saved Egypt and Europe from the cholera epidemic of 1890 and 1891 in the Hejaz but severely damaged the trade of the Syrian cities. After preparatory work by the Institute of International Law at Hamburg in 1891 the Anglo-Austrian Protocol of London of 29 July 1891 and the Convention of Venice of 30 January 1892 established regulations to stop epidemics on the threshold of the Canal. In the cholera epidemic of 1893 a sanitary cordon of military and camel posts was established all along the Canal.[4] A lazaretto was established at the Wells of Moses in 1896 while that at Tor was linked to Suez by telegraph between 1895 and 1897.

After the failure of the Wolff negotiations at Constantinople in 1887 the British administration established itself more firmly in Egypt through Baring's Gladstonian policy of retrenchment. The Egyptian budget was first balanced in 1886 and the first surplus was manufactured in 1887, partly by the remission of interest on the Canal shares sold in 1875.[5] That achievement banished the spectre of a new international financial commission and made

---

[1] G. Wüst, 'Über die Abnahme des Salzgehalts im Suez-Kanal von 1869 bis 1937', *Erdkunde* (Juli 1951), 243.

[2] C. Keller, *Die Fauna im Suez-Kanal und die Diffusion der Mediterranen und Erythräischen Thierwelt. Ein Thiergeograpische Untersuchung* (Zürich, 1882). H. M. Fox, 'Zoological Results of the Cambridge Expedition to the Suez Canal, 1924', *Transactions of the Zoological Society of London*, xxii (1926–9), 1–64, 843–63. H. M. Fox, 'Marine Migrations Across the Isthmus of Suez', *Nineteenth Century* (May 1926). H. M. Fox, 'Where East Meets West. Migrations through the Suez Canal', *Century Magazine* (August 1928). *The Times*, 22 July 1929, 15 iv, 'Perilous Passages'. R. Gurney, 'Animal Migration through the Suez Canal', *Illustrated London News*, 12 February 1949, 210.

[3] *Le Canal de Suez*, 22 Décembre 1909, 5352–3, 'La Pêche dans le Canal de Suez'. A. Gruvel, *Contribution à l'Étude de la Bionomie Générale et de l'Exploitation de la Faune du Canal de Suez* (Le Caire, Imprimerie de l'Institut Français d'Archéologie Orientale, 1936).

[4] W. F. Miéville, *Under Queen and Khedive* (1899), 271.

[5] R. L. Tignor, *Modernization and British Colonial Rule in Egypt, 1882–1914* (Princeton University Press, 1966), 81.

possible the creation of a reserve-fund in 1888. The Canal Company was granted no special protection under the Convention of Constantinople but consolidated its position under the aegis of the theory of mixed interest, which the Mixed Courts elaborated between 1880 and 1887 and the Court of Aix accepted in 1896. It extended its central administration by creating new departments for Litigation (Egypt) in 1887 and for Health on the inauguration on 19 July 1888 of the new St. Vincent de Paul Hospital near Ismailia, which became the centre of its medical services. It created Chief Agents at Port Tewfik in 1885 and at Port Said in 1888. Its Canal pilots were freed from responsibility for navigation by the judgment of the Mixed Court of Cairo on 19 April 1890 in the case of the *Hindustan* of the Compagnie Nationale de Navigation, which left absolute authority and responsibility to the captain unless the Canal lacked depth or the pilot gave a false indication of the route. The Canal pilots thus added legal security to their light work. They enjoyed only limited pension-rights but supplemented their salaries by premiums from the Company and the shipowners. Those advantages combined with the proximity of the Canal to Europe encouraged Conrad after eight years as a British master-mariner to apply in vain to the Company for a post as a pilot just before he left the merchant navy for ever in 1894.[1]

The diversion of the express mail to the Canal route reduced the quarantine difficulties inseparable from the overland route and so avoided friction with the representatives of the Powers in Egypt. The P. & O. mail contract of 18 March 1887 stipulated for the use of the Canal by the Brindisi mails and for a speed of $12\frac{1}{2}$ knots between Brindisi and Bombay. It reduced the subsidy to the P. & O. by 26 per cent from £360,000 to £265,000.[2] The transfer of the mails to the Canal followed the introduction of night-time navigation in 1886–7 and the co-ordination by the G.P.O. in 1887 of the Australian mail services by the P. & O. and Orient Lines. The alternative overland route was last used by the dromedaries of the British consular mail service between Basra and Damascus in 1885 after 102 years of intermittent use since 1784. Curzon, who first travelled in Persia in 1889, rejected the reopening of the Syrian route as unnecessary and even dangerous to British hegemony in the Persian Gulf.[3] On the end of the overland route through Egypt its most famous pioneer was commemorated at Chatham in a statue unveiled by Northbrook on 10 August 1888 and in Waghorn Terrace inaugurated on 1 October 1888. The transfer of the mails to the Canal increased the British interests in the Canal route symbolized by the association in the new London Shipping Exchange opened in 1891 of the trade of the Levant with that of India, China and Australia. The India mails had so increased in bulk that it was announced on 23 December 1887 that for the first time they would be conveyed from

---

[1] G. J. Aubry, *The Sea Dreamer: a Definitive Biography of Joseph Conrad* (London, Allen, 1957), 195, 200. J. Baines, *Joseph Conrad. A Critical Biography* (London, Weidenfeld, 1960), 132.   [2] *The Times*, 7 December 1887, 10 vi.

[3] G. N. Curzon, *Persia and the Persian Question* (London, Longmans, 1892), i. 635.

London to Dover by special train and thence to the Continent by special steamer.[1] The overland route across the Continent to Brindisi was maintained and improved. The Wagons-Lits sleeping cars attached to the Indian Mail Train replaced the Pullmans on the Bologna–Brindisi line in 1888 on the expiry of the contract of 1874 and thenceforward ran right through to Brindisi. In 1890 the Wagons-Lits and the P. & O. created the Brindisi Peninsular and Oriental Limited Express for the carriage of mail to the exclusion of passengers. The Wagons-Lits also organized the Bombay Express in 1890 between Calais and Marseilles, which so regained its passenger traffic to the East.

From 1888 the Egyptian overland route established in the 1830s ended its official existence, stimulating Alexandria to improve its harbour facilities in 1889–91 and ending an era in the history of Suez. Suez benefited by the stabilization of Egypt's frontier with the Sudan, enjoyed a boom down to 1894 and increased the value of its trade by 32 per cent between 1890 and 1893. The Company port of Terreplein, named Port Tewfik by Lesseps in 1882, was provided with municipal services by the Company like Port Said and Ismailia. After it was linked to Suez in 1884 by the first suburban railway-service in Egypt it attracted one or two merchant-houses from Suez by 1886, acquired coaling firms in 1887 and even aspired to become 'a new Venice'.[2] After the death of Consul West, who made his last annual report on 5 February 1887, Suez was reduced to a vice-consulate and placed under the British Consul at Port Said: the merchant-house of Beyts increased in local influence thenceforth at the expense of the Vice-Consul. The French community acquired the Church of Sainte Hélène which was inaugurated at Port Tewfik on 1 July 1888 to complement that of Sainte Eugénie built at Port Said between 1886 and 1890. The Company created a harbour basin in 1888–90 by a new embankment across the Suez Channel. A lighthouse was completed on 15 January 1889 on Shadwan Island, at the entrance to the Gulf of Suez, to supplement that lighted on the Brothers Rocks opposite Kosseir on 4 June 1883 and to serve the traffic of the Canal rather than that of the overland route for which the first lighthouses had been built in the Red Sea in 1862–3. The Company built offices in 1891 at Port Tewfik which was thenceforward linked by telephone to Suez. The Bonded Warehouse Company, organized by Beyts & Co., built a very large store near the ex-Suez Hotel in 1892 and enjoyed a large increase in trade during 1893, especially in jute sacks from Calcutta but also in gum from Suakin. The town of Suez ceased to depend wholly on lanterns and was partly lighted by oil lamps by 1892: it even acquired Egyptian houses in the European style from 1894. Thus Suez survived the loss of its transit traffic by developing its entrepôt trade, not only with the Sudan but also with India in gunnies, rice and wheat.

The replacement of Alexandria by Port Said as the entrepôt for the express

[1] A. F. Baillie, *Kurrachee* (1890), 243.
[2] *Saturday Review*, 5 February 1887, 188, 'How the Suez Canal is Worked'. *The Times*, 28 January 1890, 8i.

mails gave additional employment to the Arab labourers of Port Said in the unloading and loading of the mails. It increased English influence in Port Said where a small British prison was arranged in 1887, the Lady Strangford Hospital was opened on 18 June 1887, and a Protestant Church was founded in 1888, supplemented in succession by a Sporting Club in 1889, the Minerva Baths in 1890, the Port Said Club in 1891 and the Khedivial Theatre in 1892. It so increased English interest in 'the greatest of Egyptian public works since the Pyramids'[1] and 'the most successful industrial enterprise of modern times'[2] that one English firm proposed to erect and lease advertisement hoardings along the banks of the Canal.[3] Port Said never failed to impress even experienced travellers as 'the first stage of the real Orient'[4] and was rivalled only by Colon[5] in moral degradation as an 'odious little town'[6] and 'a dreadful place for Englishmen to live in'.[7] After four days at Port Said (2–6 October 1882) Kipling crystallized the impressions of all his predecessors of a 'sand-bordered hell' where all things were for sale. 'There is iniquity in many parts of the world, and vice in all, but the concentrated essence of all the iniquities and all the vices in all the côntinents finds itself at Port Said.'[8] Kipling thereby gave the town a reputation as bad as that enjoyed by Acre in the thirteenth century. He diffused through an unsuccessful novel, which became in 1903 a less successful play, an image so close to the reality in 1890 of 'an unspeakably filthy, noisy, disease- and vice-infected town',[9] that it proved almost indestructible by later iconoclasts. Frenchmen such as André Chevrillon in 1889 agreed with English travellers. 'The place is a cosmopolitan hotel, where all ships set ashore their passengers... There is nothing so sad and so unsightly as these commonplace cross-roads which have no existence of their own, and live only by the continuous passage of strangers in search of amusement. There is nothing here but a little European scum jettisoned upon the edge of the desert, in which all the streets come so strangely to an end.'[10] The port, used by 150,000 sailors and 150,000 passengers every year in the 1880s, added to its range of illicit trades the export of contraband to Odessa to bypass the high tariff walls of Russia, the import of gunpowder from Cyprus for reshipment via Aden to the dervishes of the Sudan[11] and

[1] J. C. McCoan, *Egypt under Ismail* (1889), 107.

[2] J. S. Jeans, *Waterways and Water Transport in Different Countries* (1890), 189, 265.

[3] *The Times*, 24 June 1892, 5 iii, 'Advertising in Egypt'.

[4] P. Neubaur, 'Port Said und der Suezkanal', *Westermanns Illustrierte Deutsche Monatshefte* (Oktober 1891), 28.

[5] *The Spectator*, 25 March 1893, 392, 'Recollections of Panama'.

[6] M. E. G. Duff, *Notes from a Diary Kept Chiefly in Southern India 1881–1886* (London, Murray, 1899), i. 5, 18–19 October 1881.

[7] R. Tangye, *Reminiscences of Travel in Australia, America and Egypt* (1883), 230, 1882. E. A. W. Budge, *By Nile and Tigris. A Narrative of Journeys in Egypt and Mesopotamia* (London, Murray, 1920), i. 77 note.   [8] R. Kipling, *The Light That Failed* (1891), 31.

[9] P. F. Martin, *Egypt—Old and New* (London, Allen, 1923), 90–1.

[10] A. Chevrillon, *Dans l'Inde* (Paris, Hachette, 1891), 326, 7 Janvier 1889.

[11] E. Starkie, *Arthur Rimbaud in Abyssinia* (Oxford, Clarendon Press, 1937), 112, quoting Dufferin to Foreign Office, 7 May 1890.

the import of white slaves from Europe for re-export to the ports of the East.[1]

The shopkeepers were mainly Greek, Italian and Jewish rather than Egyptian and included Simon Artz from the 1890s. They adapted the hours of their shops to the times of arrival of the passenger-ships and made the whole town into one vast market. They used English and French coins rather than the new coinage introduced by the Government of Egypt in 1886. The town was more cosmopolitan than other ports because it was created in Egypt by Europe, controlled by its foreign colonies and devoid of any life other than that of its harbour. Its Levantines included the Maltese who formed the bulk of the British colony. Their interests were wholly economic and their aspirations were to make the port into an Egyptian Shanghai. Thus they resisted taxation by Egypt as they had in 1868 and 1874. They refused to pay the 1886 tax on buildings and hired a lawyer to defend their interests against the demand in 1889 for their arrears of taxes. The Government's reply was to complete in 1890 the construction of new Government offices, barracks and prison in the centre of town, enabling the Governor to move out of the house built originally for a Company official. Egypt's claims were also recognized in the Anglo-Egyptian Commercial Convention of 29 October 1889 which empowered the Government to place guards on board any British ship in an Egyptian port or the Suez Canal without notification to the British Consular authorities. After the Government failed to raise funds either by the attempt in 1889 to auction 60,000 square yards of beach or by the transformation in 1890 of the Abbas Bazaar into a modern central market, it closed down all public gaming-tables in 1890, so threatening the income of the Levantine café proprietors, improving the morality of Egypt and honouring the precepts of Islam but driving gambling in the port into secrecy. The foreign colonies centred their activity around their church, their school and their national day.[2] They owned the port's fifteen carriages in 1891 and read its five newspapers (two being in French, two in Italian and one in Greek), in 1895. The Greeks kept Epiphany and Easter as their great festivals. The Italians celebrated 20 September, the anniversary of the Italian entry into Rome, and inaugurated thereon in 1888 a luminous fountain in the Place de Lesseps. The Austrians celebrated the birthday of their Emperor Francis Joseph on 18 August. Bastille Day served as the festival day for the whole port as well as the French national day. Friction between the communities was restrained by the common interests which usually united them against Egypt. The Greek–Jewish riot of 13 March 1892[3] revealed however the inability or the reluctance of the Egyptian authorities to protect the Jews, caused a large Jewish emigration from Port Said and may have been provoked by Paul Friedmann's attempt in 1891–2 to create a Jewish colony in Sinai.

---

[1] P. G. Elgood, *Egypt and the Army* (London, Oxford University Press, 1924), 256.
[2] L. Dori, 'Esquisse Historique de Port-Said', *Cahiers d'Histoire Égyptienne* (Janvier 1956),
11   [3] *The Times*, 13 May 1892, 5 vi.

The Company experienced in 1894 its first serious labour trouble since the opening of the Canal. Its harbour workmen at Port Said had asked in 1891 for bonuses after the Company revised their wage-rates, had suffered retrenchment in 1892 and had again requested bonuses in 1893. On 21 August 1894, 190 workmen on the marine dredgers and barges, led by the Greeks, went on strike to secure a minimum of ten months' employment for 1895 and the elimination of the lay-off for 2–3 months during the winter season. The Company decided after an inquiry to take back into employment all who pleaded intimidation but to dismiss the ringleaders who had preached revolt in the workshops of Port Said and had failed to respect their comrades' freedom to labour. After the Company sacked 139 out of 2,000 its Chief Engineer was assassinated on 29 September at Ismailia. All the dredgers as far as Ismailia were abandoned by their crews and the police of Port Said had to be reinforced on 3 October by eighty men.[1] The dismissed workmen were then repatriated at a cost of £5,200 to the Company. Lemasson was commemorated by a monument erected at Ismailia in 1898 with the subscriptions of the remaining workmen as well as by the Avenue Lemasson leading to the Hospital. He was succeeded by Édouard Quellennec (1894–1901) under whom the work of the Company continued unimpaired by any trade-union among 'the Suez family'.

The expansion of the decade trebled the number of houses between 1890 and 1899[2] and gave the port its first modern buildings. The Eastern Exchange Hotel and Clubhouse was the first really fine building, with seven massive stories of brick and iron imported from England in 1888 by Wills & Co. and erected in 1890. It was the only hotel in Egypt under English management as well as the first with electric light and a lift. Its domination of the town was ended by the new offices of the Canal Company which were begun in 1890 and completed in 1895 to the design of Charles Marette in the Arab style with cupolas, arcades, lawns and flower-beds plus a giant flag-staff for signalling instructions to ships in harbour. Those offices provided the port with its most impressive and characteristic building while a bust of Lesseps unveiled in the Place de Lesseps on 16 June 1895 became his first posthumous memorial. The expansion of the 1890s was facilitated by the completion of the Sweet Water Canal and the tramway. The Abbassieh Canal sanctioned in 1884 was begun on 27 March 1887, close to the maritime canal so that the trough-dredgers could still discharge their spoil in Africa. Its construction led the Company to consider the possibility of a tramway to Ismailia and encouraged the formation in London of the Port Said Carrying Company Ltd., which was registered on 4 June 1892 but was wound up on 1 August 1894. That canal first brought the water of the Nile north from Ismailia to Port Said on 13 April 1893, thirty years after its arrival at Suez. Its completion coincided with the transfer of the

---

[1] *Le Canal de Suez*, 22 Octobre 1893, 2585–7; 22 Septembre 1894, 2751–2, 2764.
[2] B. Girard, 'Le Canal Maritime de Suez', *Bulletin de la Société de Géographie Commerciale de Bordeaux* (1901), 80.

noisome unloading of coal to the new Abbas Hilmi basin on the Asiatic bank of the Canal from 1893. It made the central stem of the Ismailia Canal from Cairo more important than ever and encouraged A. Prompt's imaginative proposal on 2 March 1894 for a maritime canal from Ismailia to Alexandria so as to make Cairo a virtual sea-port with three out-ports. The waterworks ancillary to the new canal began the distribution of water in Port Said on 3 May 1895.[1] Port Said was freed from dependence on the Ismailia Water-works and on the Arab water-carrier. The water was at first of worse quality but was reduced from quintuple to treble the Alexandria price. It made pos-sible the cultivation of fruit and vegetables which had been imported from Damietta but were thenceforward supplied to ships, especially strawberries and grapes. The Abbassieh Canal was used only for the supply of water and not for navigation, ships taking over one-quarter of the deliveries of water in 1898.

The tramway to Ismailia was authorized on 3 December 1891 by the Govern-ment of Egypt, which also regulated the occupation of Common Domains land on 5 December 1891. That 30 in. Decauville line was inaugurated on 2 Dec-ember 1893, giving Port Said its own railway-station and introducing the tramway into the isthmus for local purposes rather than for the overland route. Its construction encouraged proposals to link Port Said to Syria[2] and to Arabia, although its use was confined to the carriage of passengers, mail and Company officials. The tramway linked the French community of Port Said to Ismailia which added to its Company headquarters a hospital in 1888, a cooperative society in 1892, an improved small harbour on Lake Timsah in 1894 and a club in 1895 on the Place Champollion. It also linked Port Said to Cairo, Suez and Alexandria by a joint service with the State railways from 1 May 1895 but it remained unused for commercial purposes before the Convention of 17 May 1896 so that it did not infringe Alexandria's monopoly. It completely eliminated the passengers on Arab boats between Port Said and Ismailia, who had provided the Company with some of its first revenues and had averaged 5,500 per annum between 1887 and 1893. From 1894 passenger-transport through the Canal became confined to long-distance passengers. Neither the tramway nor the Abbassieh Canal diverted the trade of the Delta from Alexandria. The population of the port nevertheless grew from 20,000 in 1886 (63 per cent Egyptian) to 42,300 in 1897 (57 per cent Egyptian) and to 49,000 in 1899 (49 per cent Egyptian). The security of the European colonies was enhanced by the suppression of the Mahdiya. In 1891 the Euro-pean town was reserved to Europeans while its Arabs were limited to work-men, boatmen, coal-heavers and police, in European-style uniform at every junction. By 1900 Arab and European mingled in the streets while the coal-heavers had doubled their productivity and trebled their pay.

Port Said failed to expand its Egyptian trade but developed an entrepôt trade by 1892–3 in coffee, tea, pepper, spices, ginger and even in dates from

[1] J. Charles-Roux, *L'Isthme et le Canal de Suez* (1901), ii. 210.
[2] L. Oliphant, *Episodes in a Life of Adventure* (Edinburgh, Blackwood, 1887), 5.

the Persian Gulf. Wills & Co. began to import frozen meat from Australia from 1892, in competition with meat from Syria, and butter and fruit from 1894. France competed with England to supply her outlanders and trebled her exports of flour from Le Havre to Port Said between 1894 and 1896. Cigarettes began to be exported on a large-scale from 1893-4 after the cultivation of native tobacco was forbidden in 1890 and half the duty on imported tobacco was refunded on its re-export in manufactured form from the end of 1891. The basic trade however remained one in coal. The port first imported over 1,000,000 tons in 1890 and first bunkered over 1,000,000 tons in 1896. Its general character remained many degrees worse than that of Alexandria.[1] 'There are no sights, no amusements, no society; everybody is saving his money for a summer somewhere else... Port Said today is just coal and boredom.'[2] Its moral renaissance of 1890 proved as short-lived as those of 1876 and 1884 so that it appeared in 1899 to Uzanne 'the Subura of Egypt', to Meinertzhagen 'a sink of immoral filth',[3] and to Ballin 'a typical brigands' den, the best adapted to the modern mailboat'.[4]

The epidemic of plague in 1900 was part of the third pandemic which began in Yunnan in 1892 and spread to Hong Kong in 1894, Bombay in 1896, Jedda in 1897, Calcutta in 1898 and Alexandria in 1899. The disease was perhaps introduced by an Arab stoker from India, because such stokers could be engaged at Port Said for the Red Sea voyage and returned later. Between 20 April and 15 July 1900 ninety-two persons were affected and thirty-seven died.[5] The plague compelled ships and pilots to cut off relations with Port Said and the Company to place some pilots in isolation. It increased the average time of transit by 36 minutes in 1899 and 1900 to 18 hours 38 minutes and deprived the shopkeepers of the trade of steamers passing in quarantine. The epidemic led to the gradual tightening of quarantine regulations for the Canal through rigorous inspection of homeward-bound ships in the Suez roads and again at Port Said, strict regulation of the discharge and disinfection of firemen and seamen, disinfection of suspected vessels, transit in quarantine and supervision of mooring and coaling. Those regulations achieved as much as was possible without the taxation of the local European community but they increased the fees paid by ships passing in voluntary quarantine and the complaints of shipowners as well as of travellers from Cairo.[6] Port Said gained a lazaretto whose cost of £8,320 was shared between the Company and Egypt. It exiled the establishments of the rue Babel to special quarters at the far west of the Arab town on the edge of Lake Menzaleh and so facilitated a fourth moral renaissance which made the town no longer the wickedest place on

---

[1] W. C. Ford (ed.), *Letters of Henry Adams (1892-1918)* (Boston, Houghton, 1938), 155, 12 March 1898.
[2] G. W. Steevens, *Egypt in 1898* (1898), 27-8.
[3] R. M. Meinertzhagen, *Army Diary 1899-1926* (London, Oliver, 1960), 12-13, 4 April 1899.
[4] B. Huldermann, *Albert Ballin* (Berlin, Stalling, 1922), 123, 16 Januar 1901.
[5] J. Charles-Roux, *L'Isthme et le Canal de Suez* (1901), ii. 272-82.
[6] Hansard, *Commons Debates*, 5 June 1902, 1529; 8 July 1902, 1076-7, J.G.Weir.

earth, 'the international dumping-ground of refuse villany',[1] but 'slightly quieter than Westgate'.[2]

Malaria had ravaged Ismailia since 1877, defeating all efforts made by the Company and even provoking a proposal to abandon the town.[3] The Company finally sought the advice of the Scot who had discovered the oocysts of the malaria parasite in the anopheles mosquito in 1897. At the invitation of Prince Arenberg, Ronald Ross visited the isthmus (17–29 September 1902) during the malaria season. Ross found no malaria in either Port Said or Port Tewfik because there were no anopheles, but found Ismailia swarming with anopheles and malaria.[4] His recommendations were accepted by the Company on 27 December 1902, although Arenberg preferred to give the credit to the Company doctors who carried out Ross's instructions.[5] The destruction of the mosquito larvae by draining marshes and spraying oil on their breeding-grounds in the drainage-cisterns and cesspools eliminated the mosquitoes as if by magic and made mosquito-nets unnecessary from 1903, even for children. The cases of malaria sank from 1,990 in 1901, and 1,551 in 1902, to 214 in 1903 and to 90 in 1904. The four deaths from malaria in 1903 were all of Egyptians. No new case of malaria occurred in 1905. The death-rate fell substantially, especially among infants. Thenceforward Ismailia developed as a health resort as well as the capital of Arenberg's principality. William Gorgas visited the isthmus in 1903 to learn how to reduce the ravages of malaria and so made it a training-ground for the great medical battle of Panama.

The continued growth of trade strained the capacity of Alexandria to the limit, necessitated the scheme of 1893–6 to improve its harbour and curbed the hostility of its merchants to Port Said. Cromer's quest for an entente with France overrode the hostility of the Government of Egypt to the development of the local trade of Port Said. After the appointment of E. P. C. Girouard as Traffic Manager of the State railways in 1899 and the repeated recommendations made during the 1890s for a Port Said railway the Convention of 1 February 1902 sanctioned the construction of a rail link to Cairo from Port Said parallel to the Canal rather than across Lake Menzaleh. That Convention also sanctioned the creation of a free port area excluding the town proper and the construction of a coal and oil basin on the Asiatic shore whilst it restored the privilege withdrawn in 1869 of the duty-free import of the machinery necessary for the improvement and maintenance of the Canal. The expectations so aroused encouraged the development in 1902 of a new suburb on the north foreshore, where roads were laid out and new-made land was sold for

---

[1] M. L. Todd, 'The Amherst Eclipse Expedition', *The Nation*, 30 May 1901, 432, 3 April 1901.

[2] R. Storrs, *Orientations* (London, Nicholson, 1937), 19, 5 October 1904.

[3] R. Ross, *Memoirs* (London, Murray, 1923), 471.

[4] R. Ross, *Report on Malaria at Ismailia and Suez* (Liverpool School of Tropical Medicine, Memoir IX, Longmans, 1903, 24 pp.). Idem, *Studies on Malaria* (London, Murray, 1928), 113–20, 'Ismailia'.

[5] *Le Canal de Suez*, 22 Mars 1904, 4389–90, 4427. Arenberg, 'Expérience faite à Ismailia pour la Suppression du Paludisme par la Destruction des Moustiques'.

building at prices of up to £2 per square yard. Thus the hopes of the 1870s came near to realization and the centre of the town began to shift northwards. Port Said also began to export cotton in the winter of 1902 from the eastern provinces of the Delta, especially from Charkia, to Japan as well as to Liverpool and increased its shipments markedly in 1902–3. Salt became the chief manufacture of the port and its ideal export, a cheap bulk commodity which provided payable ballast for southbound vessels. The Port Said Salt Association Ltd., registered in London on 14 December 1899, laid out 200 salt pans in the eastern part of Lake Menzaleh modelled on those of Provence. It employed Arab workmen under skilled Sicilian foremen and began to export salt through the Canal to Calcutta from 1901.[1]

Egypt increased its influence in Port Said through the Convention of 1902. The Government laid the foundation-stone of an Egyptian Post Office on 2 January 1902 and inaugurated it in 1903. It took over the tramway built in 1893 from the Company, whom it agreed to pay in return £E 19,930 every year until 1968. It built the railway to Ismailia from 1902 on the normal gauge as part of the Egyptian rail-network. The opening of that railway on 1 June 1904 created a line parallel to the whole length of the Canal, along which Lloyd's established wireless telegraphy in 1904. The railway reduced the journey to Cairo to five hours and encouraged the establishment in Port Said of branches of the new National Bank of Egypt in 1904 and of the Comptoir National d'Escompte in 1905. Although the railway made the isthmus into the hinterland of Port Said it produced no large diversion of trade from Alexandria. In fact exports of cotton from Port Said sank in 1905 while the value of the port's trade, which had risen by 14 per cent in 1903 and by 23 per cent in 1904 declined by 11 per cent in 1905. The free port area was demarcated by an iron railing erected in 1905 along the Francis Joseph Quay, which then gained the first pavement laid in the town. The free port stimulated smuggling more than the entrepôt trade and was disliked by the Customs. Alexandria undertook the further improvement of its harbour in 1905–7. The reduction of the import duty on coal and oil from 8 to 4 per cent from 25 November 1905 was intended to encourage the bunkering trade of Port Said rather than its general trade. Efforts to extend the import trade achieved only a limited success. A concession was granted in 1904 for the establishment of a frozen meat depot at Port Said to supply the towns of Egypt with New Zealand mutton at 30 per cent below the price of native mutton but was used only to supply the needs of the Army in Cairo and Alexandria from 1905. In 1904 a concession was also granted for a navigation service through Lake Menzaleh to the New Egyptian and Menzaleh Canal and Navigation Company, which hoped to divert some of the trade of the Delta to Port Said. A channel from 'Rasswa' (Port Said) to Matarieh was opened through Lake Menzaleh in February 1906 and was extended to Damietta in February 1907. The Port Said and Cairo Navigation Company Ltd. was registered in London on

---

[1] L. Dori, 'Esquisse Historique de Port-Said', 45–6.

29 September 1907 to exploit the new traffic but was wound up on 19 September 1912. The doubling of the harbour's capacity benefited the traffic of the Canal rather than the local traffic of the port. The arrival of a floating dock on 4 October 1904, five years after Alexandria had acquired a graving dock for the Khedivial Mail Line, relieved the Company from dependence on the graving dock completed in 1866 at Suez. The trade of Port Said revived during 1906, despite the decline of its cigarette exports to Germany after a heavy import duty was imposed. Suez, however, suffered a sharp fall in the value of its trade in 1906 and 1907: it began to lose its gunny imports to Port Said from 1906, its coal imports to Port Said from 1907 and its oil imports to Alexandria from 1907.

As Port Said became a leading world-port by the tonnage in transit its bunkering trade reached new heights, despite a one-day strike by the Arab coal-heavers on 2 April 1907 and a three-weeks' strike from 19 December 1907 to 5 January 1908. The subsequent rise in coaling rates from 1 January 1908 diverted some of the bunkering trade to Malta and reduced the quantity of coal imports to Port Said by 25 per cent during 1908. That coaling crisis encouraged the foundation of the port's last two coaling firms after the establishment of the Deutsches Kohlen Depot in 1902. British Coaling Depots was established as a partnership by Frank C. Strick & Co. Ltd., J. & C. Harrison Ltd. and Harrison, Tidswell & Co. It began operations towards the end of 1908 and prevented the other coaling companies from fixing the selling-price for 1909 before it was registered as a private company in London on 26 May 1909. The English Coaling Company Ltd. was also registered as a private company on 23 October 1911 by seven shipowner-directors, including three directors of the Canal Company, Inchcape, F. D. Green, O. Sanderson, J. Caird, A. W. Bibby and A. S. Williams. In the peak year of 1911 Port Said first imported over 2,000,000 tons of coal. It also became an oiling port and thenceforward increased its imports of oil at the expense of those of coal. The Standard Vacuum Oil Company, founded in 1904 as an export refinery by Standard Oil, established on the Asiatic shore in 1910 three new oil tanks, which were fed by pipeline under the Canal. Marcus Samuel established oil tanks in 1911 at Port Said to which he imported fuel from Rumania as he imported fuel from the East Indies to Port Ibrahim and so transferred the burden of Canal tolls to his clients.

The expansion of Port Said did not alter its character. The new railway-station opened on Navy House Quay on 29 December 1908 enabled passengers to arrive or depart without passing through the town and saved much trouble with their baggage. The port remained 'a very poor and dishevelled place'[1] where 'the sin of the East links itself in your arm immediately you have paid your landing fee to the Arab at the jetty'.[2] After twenty-eight cases of plague

[1] Lord Hardinge of Penshurst, *My Indian Years 1910–1916* (London, Murray, 1948), 8, November 1910.
[2] J. R. Macdonald, *The Awakening of India* (London, Hodder, 1910), 12.

with thirteen deaths in 1910 and the destruction of 17,000 rats by the Public Health Department the Port Said Municipality was created by the Khedivial Decree of 2 January 1911 with five official members (including two representatives of the Canal Company), and ten elected members (five being Egyptian and five European), under the Governor. Its primary function was to undertake drainage and to accept voluntary taxation unlike the Alexandria Municipality created in 1889 which required the sanction of the Powers to tax Europeans.[1] After forty-two more cases of plague in 1911 the new municipality concluded agreements on 25 June and 2 July 1912 with the Canal Company and borrowed thereunder £E180,000 at 4 per cent. The municipal drainage works were begun by Hughes of Lancaster and the Egyptian Engineering Company at an imposing inauguration ceremony on 29 March 1913 in the presence of Lord Kitchener. The municipality also established a municipal fire-brigade, created a municipal park and paved sixteen streets. The Company cooperated by reducing the price of water in 1910 and introducing in 1911 into its Port Said Waterworks the Puech-Chabal process of slow filtration through five beds of sand which had been used first at Paris in 1899, at Ismailia in 1907 and at Suez in 1909. The Company also began from 1911 to construct a new community for its workshops on the Asiatic bank, which was linked by a cross-harbour ferry to the main port from 1912. Thus it accelerated the development of the eastern bank begun by the Port Said Salt Association and carried further by the Standard Vacuum Oil Company. It was able to proceed with the enlargement of the harbour, to make Port Said commercial and to devote its new town to engineering. The floating dock was moved from the west bank to the east bank. The creation of a new French community also countered the English influence which had increased through the foundation of a Rowing Club in 1908, a new English Hospital in 1912 and a branch of the British and Foreign Bible Society in 1912 as well as through the increase in the imports of flour from British India in 1911–12 at the expense of imports from France. Both English and French élites met in the huge Casino Palace Hotel for which the concession was granted in 1907.

Port Said exported gold in ingots to England from 1909 and imported from 1910 common soap from Turkey, which replaced in that year England as the main source of its imports. Its main import nevertheless remained coal and its main export salt. The Port Said Salt Association increased salt exports from the port through the Canal by 89 per cent in 1909. In 1910 it supplied 91·5 per cent of the total quantity of Port Said's exports and 21 per cent of the salt shipments through the Canal. It decided in 1911 to increase the number of its salt-pans by 27 per cent and paid a dividend of 12½ per cent in 1912. It benefited by the Government's reduction of export dues and increased its shipments through the Canal by 27 per cent in 1913. Its salt pans increased their share of the salt exported through the Canal from 25 per cent in 1912 to 32 per cent in 1913, enabling Port Said to replace Britain as the

[1] L. Dori, 'Port Said (1900–1914)', *Cahiers d'Histoire Égyptienne* (Juillet 1956), 330.

leading source of southbound salt, which supplied 4 per cent of the Canal's southbound cargo in 1913. The construction of a small canal through Lake Menzaleh in 1910–13 to Matarieh and Damietta was intended to divert the trade of Mansura from Alexandria to Port Said. The continued expansion of the port's trade from 1910 to 1913 reflected a vast expansion in Europe's trade with Asia but no diversion of the trade of the Delta. The increase of its trade during 1912 and 1913 contrasted with the shrinkage of the trade of Suez, whose harbour Gaston Jondet planned in 1913 to modernize.[1] In 1913 Port Said nevertheless imported 10·1 per cent of the total value of Egypt's imports but exported only 1·3 per cent of the value of her exports. Port Said began to rival Alexandria by 1912 but only as a seaside resort. It preserved its great market for coal and vice but had begun between 1890 and 1912 to reflect developments in the Delta and to lose many of its former liberties. The improvement in its public health reduced the death-rate but not the birth-rate, so ushering in a marked expansion of its Arab population. By 1912 its inhabitants had risen to 56,534, or to 65·5 per cent of the population of the isthmus, and its European and Arab towns, still separate in 1900, had joined together. The Arab coal-heavers derived less benefit than the Europeans from the boom of 1900–13: they appeared 'almost indistinguishable from apes'[2] and earned 8*d.* per ton for coaling, under the pressure of relentless competition.[3] As the living tools which operated the port's greatest industry they maintained the decisive superiority of European Port Said over Egyptian Suez. Thus Port Said became as much as Suez the clearest dividing-line between East and West.[4]

[1] G. Jondet, *Le Port de Suez* (Le Caire, Imprimerie de l'Institut Français d'Archéologie Orientale, 1919).
[2] A. B. Spens, *A Winter in India* (London, Paul, 1913), 5, 9 December 1912.
[3] Earl Brassey, *The 'Sunbeam' R.Y.S.* (London, Murray, 1917), 364, 25 March 1914.
[4] R. Kipling, 'Egypt of the Magicians', *Nash's Magazine* (July 1914), 481–2.

23

THE PANAMA CRISIS OF 1889-1893, AND THE REORGANIZATION OF THE CANAL COMPANY

THE financial returns of the Canal Company from 1880 were unparalleled by those of any other engineering enterprise because of the absolute monopoly of the shortest route between East and West granted to it by the Khedive, protected by the Mixed Courts and recognized by its greatest client since 1883. The Canal increased its traffic with every increment of population, every expansion of trade between East and West and every increase in shipping. After the depression of 1878-9 the Canal increased its tonnage in every single year of the 1880s except in 1886 and began to earn monopoly profits for the Company. The tolls on shipping supplied almost all the Company's income and were paid in cash. The Company gave no credit but was itself given credit as shipowners began to keep a Suez Canal account with the Company's bank. The prior charges on its profits which had to be met before dividends were distributed comprised the costs of maintenance and administration, the payment of interest on its bonds, the payment of 5 per cent interest on its ordinary shares, the allotment of 4 per cent of the original capital to a sinking-fund for the amortization of shares and the allocation of 5 per cent to reserve.

The costs of maintenance and administration remained stable between 1875 and 1887 while receipts expanded tremendously. The Company enjoyed the low coefficient of operation common to canals and great estates rather than the high coefficient of railway companies, whose working expenses rose in proportion to their income and absorbed over 50 per cent rather than 20 per cent of their receipts. The burden of interest was undoubtedly heavy on the 5 per cent fifty-year lottery loan of 1868, the 8 per cent thirty-year loan of 1871 and the 5 per cent consolidated-interest loan of 1874 which reached par only in 1878. The Company preferred its own shareholders to subscribe to its bonds so as to limit the extent of a separate bondholder-interest. It also incorporated a sinking-fund in its loans so as to lighten the interest-charges year by year until the loan was wholly repaid, whereupon it diverted the annuity to repay another loan. Thus it reduced its fixed charges to the minimum and could distribute a higher proportion of its receipts than any other corporation.

The remaining net profits were distributed in the proportion of 71 per cent to the shareholders, 15 per cent to 'the Egyptian Government', 10 per cent to the founders, 2 per cent to the directors and 2 per cent to the staff. The transfer of the 15 per cent royalty of the Egyptian Government in 1880 extended substantially the interest of French investors in the Company's profits, like the creation of the delegations in 1869. The 2 per cent of the profits distributed to the thirty-two directors on the pattern of the Crédit Mobilier provided from 1881 a substantial per capita income unlike the 2 per cent of the profits allotted to the staff which the Company used to increase its non-contributory pensions so as to enhance the benefits accruing to long service. The capital of the shareholders which received 71 per cent of the profits was not excessive but below the cost of the Canal because of the indemnities paid by Egypt under the Award of 1864. The combination of maximum income with maximum security in the great wish-dream of every investor was marred only by the limited duration of the concession and by the London Programme of 1883. The Company therefore sought to arrange for the repayment of its nominal capital within its allotted ninety-nine years from 1869 and began the regular amortization of its ordinary shares in 1876. Every year it drew by lot 161 of its 400,000 shares, repaid the nominal capital of £20 and replaced them by participating shares which lost only the right to the fixed interest of 5 per cent but retained the right to the much larger dividend. Those participating shares preserved the same rights as the other shares, including the right to vote at meetings, unlike other such shares or founders' shares, as well as the right to a proportionate share of the payments made by the Government of Egypt on the liquidation of the concession. That device of amortization served in effect as a concealed distribution of profits which diminished the apparent size of the dividends while avoiding taxation on the repayment of capital out of revenue. Thus the French State was led to claim from the Company in 1887 the 3 per cent tax on the revenue of the premiums of amortization with retrospective payment from 1 July 1873. The Company concealed one great reserve through the consistent under-valuation of its Paris offices, which remained at the same value in its balance-sheets from 1877 to 1889 despite the massive appreciation of its central metropolitan site.

Financial success transformed the Company and almost deprived it of a history. The steady rise in the price of its shares affected both ordinary and participating shares to the special benefit of the small shareholders who held their shares in inelastic supply. Small investors benefited by the extension in 1879 of the 3 per cent share-tax over all shares, whether the coupons were cashed in France or abroad: thus large shareholders were prevented from shifting the burden of payment on to the French and foreign shareholders by going abroad. The rise in prices however carried shares beyond the reach of new small investors and made the general meeting more plutocratic than ever, attended in the 1880s by a declining number of those rich enough to hold twenty-five shares.

The success of the Company encouraged the projection of twenty-five or more maritime canals in the enthusiasm of the years 1880–3 when ten were proposed in 1880, six in 1881, four in 1882 and five in 1883.[1] All those projects sought to improve and extend maritime communication and to convert isthmuses into banks for canals. They relied on 'the new-born sense among nations that the earth is their common possession, and that they who open up its resources may trust to it to recompense them for their pains... The Suez Canal proprietary has fastened a mortgage on the world's industry, ingenuity and hurry; and its success is inflaming the emulation of a host of competitors.'[2] The example of Suez inspired all those enterprises and provided the specific model for the greatest of all so that the history of Suez promised to repeat itself in Panama. The concession secured by L. N. B. Wyse from Colombia in 1878 was largely modelled on the Suez Canal concession of 1854. Lesseps took over that concession in 1879 and broke off relations with Wyse as in 1855 he had with Enfantin. He chose the right route for a canal across Central America because the direct Panama route was as superior to the Nicaragua route as the Pelusium route had proved in Egypt to the Alexandria route. There he aspired to recreate Suez on a larger scale by the methods which had succeeded in Egypt. He regarded the Panama Canal as the complement of the Suez Canal which he used as a touchstone and a yardstick. His 'interoceanic Bosphorus' would be a similar sea-level canal without locks or tunnels. Its dimensions would be identical to those of the Suez Canal with a depth of $27\frac{1}{2}$ feet, a width at bottom of 72 feet, sloping banks and a half-way basin. The cube of excavation of 99,000,000 cubic yards would be the same for both canals. The cost would be £40,000,000 against £8,000,000 but the time would be eight years as in the revised estimate of 1864 for the Suez Canal. A similar toll of ten francs per ton was envisaged while preliminary funds were again raised from a small group of founders, whose shares were allotted 15 per cent of the net profits instead of the 10 per cent allotted to the founders of the Suez Canal Company.

Lesseps again revealed his distrust of the great bankers by choosing the same £20 denomination of share and by making his first appeal for funds direct to the public. He relied solely upon the power of his name and did not win the confidence of high finance or of the press.[3] The failure of his first Panama flotation was far greater than that of his Suez flotation because he received subscriptions to 7·5 per cent of the shares offered in 1879 but to 71 per cent thereof in 1858. Lesseps thereupon resorted to the techniques of publicity which he had used in his Suez campaign, began the issue of a bimonthly journal[4] and held a series of meetings in France. In 1880 'the Duke of Suez'[5] paid his first ceremonial visit to Panama, held meetings in the U.S.A.

[1] F. N. Newcome, 'Canal Projects of the Day', *Nautical Magazine* (February and March 1883), 96–105, 168–76. *Appleton's Annual Cyclopaedia* (1880), 247–9; (1881), 244–5; (1882), 279; (1883), 306–9, 'Engineering'.

[2] *The Times*, 10 June 1881, 9v–vi.   [3] *The Times*, 14 May 1879, 11vi.

[4] *Bulletin du Canal Interocéanique*, 1 Septembre 1879.

[5] E. H. Yates, *Celebrities at Home* (London, 'The World', 1879), Third Series, 211–19, 'M. De Lesseps in the Rue de Richepanse'.

as well as in England, Belgium and the Netherlands and reduced substantially the estimated cost of the enterprise. The Universal Interoceanic Canal Company was then successfully launched on 20 October 1880. £86,000 or 7·2 per cent of the total number of its shares were issued through the offices of the Suez Canal Company and brought £28,000 in commission to the parent company or over one-third of the year's receipts of its financial service. Marius Fontane who reorganized the finances of the Suez Company in 1879–82 brought his financial talent to the aid of the new company to eke out its capital which was insufficient from its very foundation. Fontane had been a collaborator of Lesseps since 1858 and had publicized the inauguration ceremonies of 1869.[1] He had become head of the secretariat from 1873 and Assistant Manager from 1875 under Lesseps as Manager. He became the collaborator of Charles de Lesseps in the Panama Company first as Public Relations Officer (1883–6) and then as Assistant Manager from 1886, so that he served as Assistant Manager of both the Suez and Panama Companies under Lesseps as President-Manager. Lesseps tried to create out of his 102,230 shareholders the family of Panama, 'younger brothers' of the Suez family as he termed them in 1883, and maintained their confidence by constant appeals to the experience of Suez. 'The Panama Canal will be easier to begin, to finish and to maintain than the canal of Suez.'[2] 'The Panama Canal will cost double but will bring in treble that of the Suez Canal.' The hopes focussed on Panama were magnified out of proportion to those fixed on Suez by the very success of the parent enterprise and especially by the Suez dividends for the year 1880. Dividends had remained at a modest level from their first distribution for the year 1875 until 1880 when they rose out of all proportion to the increase in traffic and in receipts. They rose in 1880 by 350 per cent, a rate of increase which was without precedent or sequel in the history of the Company and came immediately after the reduction in dividends for 1878 and 1879. That large increase did not benefit either the Egyptian or British Governments but the French shareholders, the French founders, the French delegation-holders and the French shareholders in the new Civil Society. The shareholders in the new Panama Company were given a striking example of the success of Lesseps' first company and were inevitably encouraged to expect a similar golden harvest from his second enterprise. From 1881–3 the Suez Company began to pay out the bulk of its receipts in the form of dividends, which rose from 8·9 per cent of the total receipts for 1879 to 52·3 per cent for 1883. The statutory dividend of 5 per cent was reduced to the proportion of one-third of the gross dividend. Thus the Company became a dividend-earning machine without equal in the world of commerce while its shares became one of the best investments of the age. Its shares were first quoted at

[1] M. Fontane, *De la Marine Marchande à propos du Percement de l'Isthme de Suez* (Paris, Guillaumin, 1868). Idem, *Le Canal Maritime de Suez Illustré. Histoire du Canal et des Travaux* (Paris, Marc, 1869). Idem, *Voyage Pittoresque à travers l'Isthme de Suez* (Paris, Dupont, 1869).

[2] F. de Lesseps, 'The Interoceanic Canal', *North American Review* (January 1880), 14.

1,000 francs, or double their par value, on 7 May 1880, at 2,000 francs on 22 September 1881 and at 3,000 francs on 11 December 1881.

The hopes of Lesseps became as great as those of his shareholders as his status was increasingly enhanced by his new enterprise. The projection of the Panama Canal at the Paris Congress of 1879 earned for him the praise of the ageing Hugo and Littré, the appellation of 'the great Frenchman' from Gambetta, the presidency of the Geographical Society of Paris through the influence of Gambetta and honorary membership of the Institution of Civil Engineers.[1] The *Stad Haarlem*, built in 1875 for the Netherland Steamship Company, was acquired in 1880 by the Compagnie Générale Transatlantique, renamed the *Ferdinand de Lesseps* and placed in service between Marseilles and Colon. Lesseps City was founded in the summer of 1881 outside the village of Gatun. His name was also given to the Rio de Lesseps, as it sexplorer Dr. J. N. Crevaux (1847–83) named the 650-mile Guayabero tributary of the Orinoco in 1881. The Swiss zoologist Conrad Keller named a new species of sponge discovered in Lake Timsah in 1882 *Lessepsia violacea*.[2] The achievement of Lesseps at Suez was celebrated in Verdi's *Aida*, which was first performed at the Paris Opera in 1880. It was glorified in two tableaus of Luigi Manzotti's ballet *Excelsior*, which was first presented in Milan on 11 January 1881 and personified in Lesseps the forces of Light and Civilization:[3] it enjoyed 103 performances during 1881 and was even performed in London in 1885. Lesseps completed in 1881 the publication of his *Lettres Journal et Documents*, which was awarded the Marcel Guérin prize of the French Academy and gave ample proof of his tenacity of purpose. He thereby provided a solid personal frame for the history of the Suez Canal, which was related increasingly in terms of the efforts made since the Pharaohs to remedy so obvious an error in Creation. He attended the unveiling on 18 April 1882 of a memorial plaque erected on his birthplace by the municipality of Versailles. He was ranked among the greatest of Latin pioneers, such as Cortez and Pizarro[4] or da Gama and Columbus,[5] as well as with Washington and Rowland Hill as an 'energetic performer of impossibilities'.[6] Lesseps became at that time an international figure as never before and helped by his activity to bring the word 'trans-isthmian' into English in 1885. He remained however one great man in an age of great men: his biography was published in 1883 as the twenty-third in a series of lives of contemporary celebrities.[7]

---

[1] *Proceedings of the Institution of Civil Engineers*, 13 April 1880, 132–3; 4 May 1880, 66.

[2] C. Keller, *Die Fauna im Suez-Kanal und die Diffusion der Mediterranen und Erythräischen Thierwelt. Ein Thiergeographische Untersuchung* (Zürich, 1882), 19–20.

[3] L. Manzotti, *Excelsior* (London, Ricordi, 1885), 13, Eighth Tableau, 'The Isthmus of Suez'; 16, Tenth Tableau, 'The Great Frenchman'.

[4] B. d'Harcourt, *Diplomatie et Diplomats. Les Quatre Ministères de M. Drouyn de Lhuys* (Paris, Plon, 1882), 56.

[5] M. Hélène, *Les Nouvelles Routes du Globe* (Paris, Masson, 1883), dedication. W. W. Kiddle, 'The Panama Canal', *Nautical Magazine* (January 1884), 25.

[6] A. Mongrédien, *Wealth-Creation* (London, Cassell, 1882), 281.

[7] A. Pinard, *Célébrités Contemporaines. Ferdinand de Lesseps* (Paris, Quantin, 1883).

Lesseps failed to reconcile American opinion to a project which would compete with the trans-continental railways, bridle the U.S. Navy and create a French principality in America. President Hayes reaffirmed the Monroe Doctrine in 1880 and began negotiations in 1881 to amend the Clayton–Bulwer Treaty so that the U.S.A. would control the projected canal alone rather than in cooperation with Britain. American strategists deduced the need for a large navy to maintain control of the isthmus. American investors failed to subscribe to the 50 per cent of the shares offered to them by Lesseps. American engineers proposed in 1880 a Nicaragua Canal and a Tehuantepec Ship Railway across Mexico as preferable alternatives to the Panama project. American publicists also attacked the existing Suez Canal. Thus P. H. Morgan, who had been in exile from his beloved Louisiana as judge of the Mixed Court in Egypt from 1877 to 1879, propagated in America the hostility of the Alexandria élite to Suez and so strengthened his own position as envoy extraordinary and minister plenipotentiary to Mexico (1880–5). Morgan first blamed Egypt's bankruptcy on the Canal, 'the greatest scheme of plunder that was ever conceived' or executed,[1] and asked where Lesseps was to find the money to cut through the isthmus of Panama. Lesseps in his indignant refutation blamed Ismail's bankruptcy on his expenditure on territorial expansion and economic improvement rather than on the Canal,[2] 'the only profitable concern he ever encouraged'.[3] The U.S. Government was even advised to buy a controlling interest in the Panama Canal Company in imitation of the British Government's action in 1875.[4]

The founder-president of the Suez and Panama Companies achieved the greatest distinction of his life on his election on 21 February 1884 to the Académie Française in succession to the historian Henri Martin by twenty-two votes to eleven blank votes. Lesseps presented Bartholdi's statue of 'Liberty illuminating the world' to the U.S. ambassador in Paris on 4 July 1884 as a gift from the French nation to America in memory of the Franco-American alliance of 1778. He also gave his name to the Quai Lesseps which was unveiled on 5 March 1885 by the Rouen Municipality. On his reception at the Académie Française on 23 April 1885 he was ranked by Renan next to Lamartine as 'the most beloved man of our century—the man upon whom the greatest number of legends and dreams have been built'. 'You were born to pierce isthmuses… You have thus marked out a great battlefield for the future.'[5] Lesseps' companies began to secure acceptance as an unofficial *corps d'état* from 1885 when the Suez Company began to recruit the chief officers

[1] P. H. Morgan, 'The Suez Canal. A History', *Appleton's Journal* (April 1880), 309; (May 1880), 465.

[2] *Le Canal de Suez*, 22 Avril 1880, 3–8, 'Une prétendue Histoire du Canal de Suez'.

[3] C. H. Rockwell, 'The Suez Canal and Egyptian Finances', *Appleton's Journal* (July 1880), 84.

[4] J. E. Nourse, *The Maritime Canal of Suez, 1869–1884* (Washington, 1884), 153 note.

[5] E. Renan, *Discours de Réception de M. F. de Lesseps. Séance de l'Académie Française du 23 Avril 1885* (Paris, Lévy, 1885), 40–1, 25, 34. F. de Lesseps, *Recollections of Forty Years* (1887), ii. 319, 305, 315, 'The French Academy'.

of its traffic department from the French Navy, and the Panama Company began to recruit its engineers direct from the École des Ponts et Chaussées. Lesseps enlisted in the support of Panama deputies, senators and ministers, members of the Institute and the Academy and representatives of literature and the Church. He also gained increasing popular support for his new company. When Lesseps left Paris with Jules Charles-Roux of the Compagnie Générale Transatlantique for his second visit to Panama he declared on 27 January 1886, 'I cannot die before opening my second canal' while 200 spectators responded 'Vive Lesseps.'[1] In Southampton which hoped to benefit even more than the Atlantic ports of France by the Panama Canal he was banqueted on 28 January by the mayor and corporation as well as by Baron Montagu while the bells of the parish churches rang out in his honour from early in the morning.[2] 'The greatest figure of our century'[3] made a triumphant return to Paris[4] and then presided over the French delegation to New York for the official inauguration of the Statue of Liberty on 28 October.[5] When Lesseps returned to Paris on 15 November he again became the object of the collective adulation[6] which he increasingly enjoyed: thus he was transformed from an entrepreneur into a prophet honoured in his own country and during his own lifetime. The year 1886 proved, however, to be the last year of real hope and enthusiastic hard work for his new enterprise. The Panama Company was unfavourably affected by the London Programme imposed on the Suez Company in 1884 and by the depression of the traffic of the Suez Canal in 1886. The London Programme prevented the accumulation of reserves in good years to cushion dividends in such lean years as 1886. It provided for the future halving of tolls, retarded the rise in share-prices and diminished the prospective earnings of Panama.

Lesseps failed to unlearn his Suez experience although Panama was similar to Suez in very few respects apart from its situation and location. At Suez he had linked together the greatest primary and secondary producers in the world by the shortest possible route, so improving the oldest and most frequented trade-route. At Panama however he proposed to create a new trade-route by piercing a canal into a vast and empty ocean and by opening up to commerce the barren western coast of South America. The enterprise of Panama does not seem to have been ruined by mal-expenditure, by excessive profits made by the contractors, by the abandonment of unused machinery[7] or even by the

---

[1] *The Times*, 28 January 1886, 5 vi.

[2] Ibid., 29 January 1886, 10 iv. *Bulletin du Canal Interocéanique*, 1 Février 1886, 1390–6.

[3] R. de Marees van Swinderen, *Het Suez-Kanaal* (1886), 4.

[4] *Bulletin du Canal Interocéanique*, 1 Avril 1886, 1438–47.

[5] *Bulletin du Canal Interocéanique*, 1 Novembre 1886, 1634–5; 15 Novembre 1886, 1642–7, 'L'Inauguration de la Statue de la Liberté à New York'.

[6] *Le Canal de Suez*, 22 Novembre 1886, 1352. *Bulletin du Canal Interocéanique*, 1 Décembre 1886, 1661–3.

[7] P. Bunau-Varilla, *Panama. The Creation, Destruction and Resurrection* (London, Constable, 1913), 535–50, Appendix A, 'Exposure of Certain Falsehoods Deeply Rooted in Various Minds'.

ravages of yellow fever. What seems to have doomed it as an engineering venture was the sheer lack of capital to construct a sea-level canal without locks through the long and high Culebra Cut and along the bottom of the great natural line of drainage of the Chagres River, which had been formed by tropical rains during the course of ages. Lesseps who had launched the enterprise in 1879 at the age of seventy-four lacked the energy which had made him ubiquitous at Suez. He disregarded the advice of his relatives and friends, believed that good faith could move mountains of granite and visited the isthmus only twice, in 1880 and 1886. His son and heir Charles became Vice-President of the Panama Company and its effective head[1] but lacked his father's power to charm as well as his fierce drive to action, perhaps since the death of his son in the cholera epidemic of 1865. Lesseps also lacked local support either from Panama or from Colombia and found no malleable potentate comparable to Said in Egypt. Thus he could not secure the conscription at Panama of an army of born navigators and was forced to employ from the start expensive machinery together with workers who cost fifty times as much as a fellah and did half as much work.[2] The opposition of the U.S.A. made him completely dependent on the French capital market and retarded the grant of a lottery-loan. The estimate of cost had been reduced four times from 1,000,000,000 francs to 500,000,000 francs.[3] The flotation of 1880 asked only for 300,000,000 francs instead of for 1,000,000,000 francs for fear of another failure like that of 1879. Such a substantial initial shortage of capital made inevitable the raising of regular loans, the private subsidization from 1885 of the press and of politicians, the repeated incantation of the magical name of Lesseps,[4] the reluctant modification of the original scheme in 1887 to one of a lock canal and the final reliance on political help to save an uneconomic enterprise. The seven successive Panama loans were issued with diminishing success and at real rates of interest rising from 5·75 per cent in 1882 to 7·7 per cent in 1888. Lesseps nevertheless raised 1,336,000,000 francs, or seven times as much as he had for the Suez Canal, from French investors of the bourgeoisie whose sober heads had been turned by the dazzling financial success of Suez.[5]

The three-year political struggle for a lottery-loan on the pattern of 1868 ended with success for the Company in 1888. That loan was publicized by the naming of a Marseilles quay after Lesseps at the instigation of Charles-Roux:[6] it was offered at a discount of 10 per cent and was expected to be subscribed 4–5 times over but failed because of the opposition of high finance.

[1] Bunau-Varilla, 71, 434.
[2] *The Times*, 11 September 1891, 3i, 'The Panama Company'.
[3] *Bulletin du Canal Interocéanique*, 15 Novembre 1880, 274.
[4] A. Bertrand and E. Ferrier, *Ferdinand de Lesseps, Sa Vie Son Œuvre* (Paris, Charpentier, 1887). F. de Lesseps, *Recollections of Forty Years* (London, Chapman, 1887; New York, Appleton, 1888).
[5] G. Sorel, *Les Illusions du Progrès* (Paris, Rivière, 1920, 1947), 342 note.
[6] L. M. Floridian, *Les Coulisses du Panama* (Paris, Savine, 1891), 224.

On 23 June hundreds of telegrams falsely announced to all Europe the death of Lesseps and the collapse of the enterprise while financial syndicates offered hundreds of thousands of Panama shares in the market:[1] on 26 June the issue closed as a failure with only 42·5 per cent of the bonds taken up. A lecture-tour by the 84-year old Lesseps and his eldest son appealed in vain to the public of twenty-six cities. Boulanger had eclipsed Lesseps who remained a disciple of Liberty, could not become a generalissimo and fell a victim to the more warlike spirit of the age. The death-bed flotation of the unsold lottery bonds was frustrated by the combination of Boulangism with high finance and by the anticipated reduction of the Suez toll from ten francs to five francs under the London Programme.[2] The subscription-lists remained open for two weeks from 29 November to 12 December but attracted subscribers to only 18·4 per cent of the total number of bonds. No saviour like Lebaudy in 1872 appeared to avert disaster. The subscriptions were therefore cancelled and the Company suspended payment on 14 December.[3] The Governor of the Crédit Foncier refused to extend financial help, securing revenge for the reverse suffered in 1875 and compelling Lesseps to agree on 15 December to the cessation of works in the isthmus as well as to the dissolution of the Company 'provided that honour is intact'. The great Frenchman aged by ten years during the next two months[4] before the dissolution of the company on 9 February 1889. Lesseps had taken success for granted and had suffered the complete collapse of the hopes which he had shared with a whole generation. The minor ship-canals of Corinth, Manchester and Kiel were completed in 1893, 1894 and 1895 but the dream of an American interoceanic sea-level canal proved too great for the timid bankers of the 1880s. The 'Great Bubble on the Isthmus'[5] lost its clients £70,000,000, a sum far in excess of the capital of the Suez Company plus the whole of its earnings since 1869. 'M. de Lesseps' impossible canal'[6] was not, however, an engineering failure. It bore the overhead costs of a great pioneer work, excavated 72,000,000 cubic yards out of the 120,000,000 estimated as necessary in 1884 and succeeded in substantially lowering the Culebra Cut. The very success of the French created a deep-rooted American aversion to Panama and a preference for an all-American canal through Nicaragua.

The financial failure of the Panama Company proved disastrous to the fortunes of the whole Lesseps family and shattered the dream of a Lesseps dynasty in control of the trade-routes of the world. It also contrasted strikingly with the success of the Suez Company: it encouraged litigation in Cairo from 1889 to secure founders' shares as well as a proposal to reassert the power of the Viceroy of Egypt to nominate the President of the Suez Company. The

[1] *The Times*, 28 June 1888, 5 ii–iii. *Bulletin du Canal Interocéanique*, 2 Juillet 1888, 2073–4.
[2] F. Paponot, *Suez et Panama. Une Solution* (Paris, Baudry, 1889), 62–5.
[3] *Bulletin du Canal Interocéanique*, 17 Décembre 1888, 2181.
[4] F. Bridier, *Une Famille Française. Les De Lesseps* (1900), 448.
[5] E. Whymper, 'The Panama Canal', *Contemporary Review* (March 1889), 323, 340.
[6] W. Nelson, *Five Years at Panama. The Trans-Isthmian Canal* (London, Low, 1891), 286.

Suez Company had become such a successful distributor of dividends that it was compelled in 1888 to offer each shareholder present at the start of the annual general meeting a silver medal exchangeable for ten francs, so trebling the number attending the meeting on 15 May 1888 to 483. It nevertheless felt compelled to elect Charles-Roux to its board in 1889 and to publish a massive statistical estimate of its own stability: the Canal had been used between 1869 and 1888 by 40,297 ships of 64,917,092 tons as well as by 2,031,379 passengers, had produced £28,921,050 in transit- and passenger-receipts and had necessitated expenses of only £100,000.[1] The failure of Panama inevitably diminished the status of Lesseps. The tide of French nationalism which thitherto had carried him to success turned against his German-Jewish associates,[2] enabling Édouard Drumont to condemn him as a scoundrel and a criminal, tenfold guiltier than the Marquis de Rays and more anti-French than anyone except Gambetta and Ferry, the most monstrous egoist ever known and 'the great corrupter' rather than the great Frenchman.[3] The opposition within the Company to the London Programme revived. One group of small shareholders requested the board of directors on 17 May 1890 to suppress toll remissions, not because receipts were falling but because share quotations were stationary in contrast to the steady rise in those of the Canal's client shipping companies. That group mustered the representatives of 150 shareholders at a preliminary meeting on 28 May[4] but secured only 200 votes at the annual general meeting on 4 June against the 1,244 votes cast in favour of the annual report by the large shareholders. The English directors agreed in 1890 that the word revenue in Article 8 of the London Programme meant net revenue (i.e. the dividend after the deduction of tax) and that each toll-reduction should be at least 1.50 francs. Thus the Company reduced the impact of the increase in the share-tax from 3 to 4 per cent in 1891 while the English directors made their first surrender of the principles of 1883 to their French colleagues and remained models of discretion throughout the succeeding crisis.

Legal proceedings on the charge of fraud were ordered on 11 June 1891, revived Lesseps' memories of 1849 and 1874 and produced a marked deterioration in his health. After his interrogation on 22 June by the magistrate Prinet, of which no transcript was ever published, Lesseps took to his bed, never spoke for three weeks and even thought of suicide which thitherto he had held in abhorrence.[5] On an investment of £14,480,672 his Suez Canal Company had repaid France by 1891 £75,765,286 (31·2 per cent thereof in gross dividends to 1 July 1891, 40 per cent in the appreciation of the Company's shares to 18 June 1891 and 19 per cent in wages, salaries and purchases

[1] *Le Canal de Suez*, 6 Juin 1889, 1820.

[2] E. Demachy, *Le Scandale de Panama. Les Juifs Allemands et le Parlement Français. Le Rôle de Charles de Lesseps* (Paris, Demachy, 1892), 7, 11.

[3] E. Drumont, *La Dernière Bataille. Nouvelle Étude Psychologique et Sociale* (Paris, Dentu, 1890), 339, 394, 420, 425, 'Une Entreprise au XIXe Siècle. Panama'.

[4] *The Times*, 4 June 1890, 5i.   [5] E. Drumont, 18–19. L. Bridier, 444.

of materials).[1] It was nevertheless condemned by the Court of the Seine on 29 January 1892 to pay the tax on the premiums of amortization claimed by the State since 1887. The London Programme eliminated any transfer to its reserve in 1892–3 and doomed Paponot's attempt to revive Panama by a financial transfusion from Suez. In 1891 Paponot had urged the suspension of the London Programme for eight years, the loan of the tariff reductions on the Suez Canal to the Panama Company and the guarantee of a Panama loan by the Suez Company.[2] In 1892 he again urged the loan to the Panama Company of part of the revenues due to be remitted to shipowners using the Canal after the large increase in traffic in 1891–2.[3] The shareholders' meeting on 31 May 1892 approved by 1,542 to 47 votes the report for the boom year of 1891, when receipts rose by 23 per cent and dividends by 29 per cent to the critical level of 18 per cent on the nominal value of the share prescribed under the London Programme: it made no offer of help to the Panama Company. Such single-minded concentration on pecuniary gain seemed to assure a magnificent future to Suez shares, even in the distant year 1950 when the French railways would have been nationalized but the Suez Company would be peacefully pursuing its career.[4]

Panama was transformed from a private enterprise into a public scandal by the campaign of the Boulangist Right and the Socialist Left against the Republican Centre. That campaign was directed against the élites of society, the State and the Assembly, which had become the sole repository of public faith since the 1870s because of the decline of belief in a God, King, Emperor, General, Leader or Party and the lack of any real equilibrium between the executive, judicial and legislative powers. The impact of the scandal thus became far greater than that of the Ouvrard, Teste or Jecker scandals under the three previous regimes. The Government appointed a commission of enquiry into Panama and issued summonses on 21 November 1892. Thus it diverted the attack on the parliamentary republic into an attack on the Panama Company and on Lesseps with his Orleanist sympathies, his Bonapartist affiliations and his capitalist associations. Prince Victor Bonaparte, the son of the first Protector of the Canal Company, rallied his Bonapartist followers to the assault on the State, proclaiming 'The Empire built Suez, the Republic Panama.' The State was saved only by the sacrifice of one of its greatest sons. Lesseps became the scapegoat of an investigation which gave the public the impression that corruption was exceptional rather than the general rule.[5]

---

[1] *Le Temps*, 22 Juin 1891, 4 vi. *The Times*, 12 September 1891, 9 ii.

[2] F. Paponot, *Le Canal de Panama. A M. Ferdinand de Lesseps. Solution de la Question Financière* (Paris, Baudry, 1891), 11–15. J. B. Dumont, *Les Grands Travaux du Siècle* (Paris, Hachette, 1891), 169–208, 'Le Canal de Suez'; 209–45, 'Le Canal de Panama'.

[3] F. Paponot, *Canal de Panama. Son Relèvement par le Suez. Appel aux Armateurs de toutes les Nations* (Paris, Baudry, 1892), 6–7.

[4] R. Lahaye, *Les Dividendes Prochains de l'Action Suez et l'Avenir du Canal* (Paris, Chaix, 1892), 5.

[5] V. Pareto, *The Mind and Society. A Treatise on General Sociology* (New York, Dover, 1935, 1963), iv. 1637.

Panama thus became a great symbol of corruption, which was the most damaging offence against a parliamentary democracy. Lesseps was also accused of fraud of which he was innocent in order to save the Republic and became the representative 'speculator' who used the 'rentiers' of modern society without any scruple.[1] Thus his second career was suddenly blighted as his first had been in 1849.

The arrest on 16 December 1892 of Charles de Lesseps at his home and of Fontane at the Suez Canal Company office on the charge of corrupting public officials galvanized the Suez Company into a convulsive response. Suez and Panama were like Siamese twins which were born of the same parent but had to be separated by surgery so that Suez might not be infected by the taint of Panama. Vice-President Guichard wrote immediately to the Syndic of the Paris Bourse that the Company's satisfactory progress was absolutely assured and that shareholders had no cause for anxiety. He became acting President of the Company from 17 December. As Principal of the Company's Agricultural Service between 1861 and 1866[2] he had supervised the resettlement of the Wadi Tumilat and acquired a firm belief in France's colonial genius and its mission in Africa. He had served as the first Principal of the Company's Transit Service between 1866 and 1871. He was elected a director in 1874, a vice-president in 1887 and President in 1892. He replaced Lesseps who remained nominal President but was virtually dethroned and abandoned by the Company of his own creation. Thus the Company lost at one blow its king, its heir-apparent and its chancellor. Five of its directors most closely connected with the Panama Company resigned after the extraordinary meeting of the board on 21 December. Charles de Lesseps could no longer be envisaged as the predestined successor to his father, ceased to be a vice-president but remained a director: his role was assumed by Charles-Roux[3] who had sought to revive the Panama Canal works in 1892 and carry them to completion. Thus ended the reign of Lesseps and the Lesseps connexion, after the death of Jules de Lesseps in 1887 and of Victor Delamalle in 1889. The Panama scandal ended the era of the Company as a family-firm and deferred the apotheosis of Lesseps to posterity.

On 7 February 1893 Fontane was found guilty of fraud and was sentenced to two years' imprisonment. On 9 February Ferdinand and Charles de Lesseps were found guilty of fraud and condemned to the maximum penalty prescribed by the law of five years in prison and a £200 fine, an unexpectedly severe sentence which inspired Rouen hastily to rename the Quai de Lesseps the Quai de Bois-Guilbert. On 21 March Fontane was acquitted of the charge of bribery on which Charles de Lesseps was sentenced to one year in prison. The Supreme Court quashed on 15 June the conviction of Charles de Lesseps

---

[1] V. Pareto, *The Mind and Society, A Treatise on General Sociology* (New York, Dover, 1935, 1963), iv. 1637.
[2] J. Guichard, 'Colonisation de l'Isthme de Suez 1861–1866', *La Nouvelle Revue*, 1 Février 1882, 241–52.   [3] L. M. Floridian, 223.

for fraud on a legal technicality but maintained that for bribery. Ferdinand de Lesseps was freed from his sentence by the special procedure for criminal proceedings against grand officers of the Legion of Honour: he did not appeal and his sentence stood, though 'morally quashed'.[1] Lesseps was hurt by the ingratitude of the Suez Canal Company[2] but retained the affection of the Republican peasantry of Berri.[3] 'The old man who does not grow old'[4] and had been ranked for his vitality with Newman, Gladstone, Radetsky, Moltke, Bismarck, Littré and Chevreuil[5] became the victim of senile amentia as age which he had thitherto defied caught up with him. He degenerated into 'a witless, speechless thing'.[6] The greatest of optimists became overpowered by an unalterable sadness: he read his *Souvenirs* all day long together with year-old newspapers, waited for Queen Victoria to arrive and make all things right and expected her arrival with every visitor.[7]

At the shareholders' meeting on 6 June 1893 Ferdinand and Charles de Lesseps were absent for the first time but attendance was larger than usual and some uproar occurred,[8] because the annual receipts had fallen in 1892 for the first time since 1887 while the first toll-reduction since 1885 had taken place with effect from 1 January 1893. Six candidates including Waddington were proposed by Guichard for the six vacant directorships. Waddington was the product of French industry and of an English education: he had studied at Cambridge, become fully bilingual and had married an American. He had been Minister for Education in 1873 and in 1876, when he had ordered the distribution of models of the Suez Canal and an annual lecture on the Canal in every lycée. As Foreign Minister in 1877–9 he had been responsible for the bargain at Berlin which gave France Tunis in compensation for the English occupation of Cyprus. He was Prime Minister in 1879 and then ambassador to Britain from 1883 to 1893. In that most unenviable of embassies he was condemned to exile from France and committed to the impossible task of getting England out of Egypt. He was the first ex-Premier and ex-ambassador to London to be proposed for election to the board of the Company. His nomination was however opposed by that of Delort de Gléon, the President of the Suez Canal Defence Committee established in 1884, who urged the abandonment of the London Programme of Charles de Lesseps and an end to personal rule. Waddington was elected by only 1,122 votes to 700 cast for Gléon, while Voisin Bey was elected by 1,791 votes and Arenberg by 1,771 votes. Loud cries of 'sold to the English' made Waddington's election a humiliation rather than an honour.[9] French prejudice against England reached a peak in

[1] *The Times*, 16 June 1893, 5 ii. *Saturday Review*, 17 June 1893, 652, 'Panama the Irrepressible'.
[2] R. H. Sherard, 'The Count de Lesseps of Today', *McClure's Magazine* (June 1893), 89–90.   [3] Ibid., 85.
[4] E. de Léon, *The Khedive's Egypt* (1877), 25.
[5] C. H. Pearson, *National Life and Character* (London, Macmillan, 1893), 324.
[6] R. H. Sherard, 93.   [7] Ibid., 92.
[8] *The Times*, 7 June 1893, 5 i–ii.
[9] C. R. Wilson, Chapters From My Official Life (London, Arnold, 1916), 80.

the naval crisis of 1893 and esteemed Tunis no compensation for the loss of Cyprus. That Anglophobia caused Waddington's defeat for re-election to the Senate on 7 January 1894 and contributed to his death on 13 January. The election of Voisin was also a triumph for French national sentiment. The buil-der of the Canal had fallen victim to Lesseps' distrust of engineers and was elected to the board only after the fall of Lesseps from power. Voisin Bey had been the Chairman of the Advisory Works Commission from 1887 to 1893 and an abstainer from the Panama venture. Arenberg had been asked by Guichard and Charles-Roux to join the board in order to serve the national interest.

The Company began to reorganize its administration to prevent any re-currence of the Panama disaster. Its executive committee was purged and enlarged by the addition of three new members in 1893, Voisin, Boucard and Charles-Roux so that it ceased to be the emanation of a single autocrat. Fon-tane resigned on 30 June after eighteen years as Assistant Manager. The new office of Manager was created on 1 August so as to separate the presidency from the management and assimilate the Company's organization to the pat-tern of most of the great French companies. Roualle de Rouville (1839–1901), who had arrived in Egypt in 1860, had succeeded Guichard as head of the Transit Service in 1872 and had been Principal Agent of the Company in Egypt since 1883, became the first Manager. He was succeeded in Egypt by the Comte de Sérionne, who was the first aristocratic representative of the Company in Egypt since 1867 and remained its Agent there for thirty-one years. Rouville became General Manager of the Company from 6 March 1894 after the nomination on 13 February of Guichard as President, Arenberg as Vice-President and Ferdinand de Lesseps as Honorary President. The posi-tion of the Company in Egypt had rested on the personal relations of Lesseps with the ruler and was seriously weakened by his virtual deposition. A legal action was even begun in Paris on 12 May 1894 by the heirs of two leading members of Said's army and household against Lesseps for fraud and em-bezzlement.[1] The leading French lawyer-journalist in Egypt recognized the right of the Government of Egypt to expropriate the Company for public utility,[2] as he had in 1883, and denounced the Canal as a work of 'blood and gold' which had ruined Egypt and enriched Europe.[3]

The verdict of the French courts on Lesseps was accepted readily in Eng-land and the U.S.A. The Rear-Admiral who had helped to occupy Port Said in 1882 condemned 'this Napoleon of canalisation' for his wish to be alone in dividing the continents of both worlds. 'He alone could have produced such a mighty financial disaster.'[4] Lesseps was attacked by a Liberal financial

[1] J. Charles-Roux, *L'Isthme et le Canal de Suez* (1901), ii. 462–3, 'Principaux Procès Soutenus par la Compagnie de Suez—VIII Parts de Fondateur'.
[2] O. Borelli, *Choses Politiques d'Égypte, 1883–1895* (1895), 112, 'Le Canal de Suez', 10 Oc tobre 1894.   [3] Ibid., 122, 'Sir Charles Dilke et l'Égypte', 19 Novembre 1894.
[4] E. H. Seymour, 'The Present State of the Panama Canal', *Nineteenth Century* (February 1892), 309.

expert as a 'grandiose charlatan' and 'a slave-driver, a briber of princes and politicians, a man sunk all his life long in the ugliest forms of financial intrigues and who fittingly brings that life to a close as a convicted felon'.[1] Those sweeping judgments were countered in the first English biography of Lesseps by a journalist who thought that Lesseps had enjoyed more prestige than any other Frenchman of his generation save only Hugo and resembled in the extremity of his days Marius among the ruins of Carthage.[2] American writers attacked the British as well as the French and especially criticized the share-purchase.[3] The finance of the construction of the Canal became 'one of the most gigantic robberies of history' as Panama cast its shadow backwards over Suez. The directors of the Company became 'successful bandits' and the Canal itself 'the death-blow to Egyptian foreign commerce'[4] as well as the cause of Ismail's bankruptcy and deposition. Suez gave its name, in the story planned by a Southern novelist in 1889–90 and written in 1890–3, to an imaginary town in the old plantation-state of Dixie which had become a meeting-place of North and South and a focus of postwar reconstruction on Northern and economic lines through a similar finance company.[5] America's new historical tradition of the Canal separated itself from the English tradition which was itself largely derived from French sources. It became anti-French, anti-British and pro-Egyptian: its humanitarian bias condemned the Canal Company as a representative of financial capitalism.

The shareholders' meeting on 5 June 1894 voted pensions to the Lesseps family by 1,299 to 486 votes. Those pensions were of £2,400 per annum to Madame Hélène de Lesseps and of £2,400 to the thirteen children of Ferdinand, who had lost all his own savings in the bankruptcy of Panama.[6] Lesseps celebrated the twenty-fifth anniversary of the opening of the Suez Canal on 17 November 1894 with his family and not with his Company, whose shares rose above 3,000 francs for the first time since 1881 on 30 November. He died on 7 December at the age of ninety at the country-house in Berri where forty years before he had heard of the death of Abbas and had then begun to emerge from the obscurity of retirement on to the stage of world history. His last years had been one long-drawn-out agony, like those of his father, and his end was not unlike that of Columbus. His will made in 1889 expressed the wish that his descendants should retain the title of Count bestowed by Napoleon on his father in 1815. The Republican Government refused him burial in the Pantheon and kept many friends and relatives away from the funeral service by means of 'police protection'. 'His coffin, unattended, traversed an

[1] A. J. Wilson, 'Mr. Milner on Egypt', *Investor's Review* (May 1893), 211.

[2] G. B. Smith, *The Life and Enterprises of Ferdinand de Lesseps* (London, Allen, 1893), 438, 261. I. Bowes, *Rails and Waterways. George Stephenson and M. Ferdinand de Lesseps* (Manchester, Heywood, 1893).

[3] C. Whitehouse, 'England's Right to the Suez Shares', *Fortnightly Review*, 1 September 1893, 409.

[4] G. T. Ferris, 'The Romance of the Great Canal', *Cosmopolitan* (April 1894), 672.

[5] G. W. Cable, *John March, Southerner* (New York, Scribner, 1894; London, Low, 1895).

[6] G. E. Bonnet, *Ferdinand de Lesseps* (Paris, Plon, 1959), ii. 317, 349.

indifferent crowd.'[1] Lesseps was buried on 15 December at the Company's expense in the Père Lachaise Cemetery, the national cemetery for the self-made great men of the land. In his funeral oration Guichard foretold that the Canal he had created would become the Lesseps Canal.[2] Contemporary English verdicts were unsympathetic. 'His name will be linked for centuries to come with the greatest engineering success and the most disastrous engineering failure recorded in the history of nations.'[3] In Egypt, however, Gaillardot Bey recognized him as 'the Creator' of the Suez Canal,[4] using the capital letter reserved for the Deity, while Borelli Bey called him 'the immortal Frenchman'[5] and Gabriel Charmes 'the incarnation of the spirit of enterprise in the highest sense, the initiator of the greatest material revolution which has taken place in the world'.[6] Gustave Le Bon ranked Lesseps in 1895 with St. Paul, Mohammed and Columbus amongst the greatest leaders of humanity, 'the true founders of religions and great undertakings', because of his strong and continuous will and his personal magnetism. 'His life teaches how prestige can grow and how it can vanish. After rivalling in greatness the most famous heroes of history, he was lowered by the magistrates of his country to the ranks of the most abused criminals.'[7] Movements were set on foot in England and Calcutta to raise a statue in his honour. At the Académie Française on 25 December 1896 Lesseps' successor, Anatole France, praised both the dream and the resulting creation of 'the greatest entrepreneur of the century' and refused to accept the verdict of the French State. 'Such a man has only one judge: the Universe.'[8]

The Canal Company reorganized itself under the pressure of hostile public opinion in France and Egypt. It began to replace the charisma of one man by the impersonal logic of finance. It introduced in 1893 the telephone between the Company offices and its signal stations along the Canal, refused to consider Conrad's application in 1893 for a post as a pilot and first experimented in 1894 with the suction-dredger which had been developed since 1861. It drew up in 1895 the first cadastral plans of the three towns of the isthmus in order to determine the occupation of buildings and sites and to end any irregular occupations. It elected to the board on 6 June 1895 Jules Cambefort of the Messageries Maritimes and so broke the ban imposed by Lesseps after the lawsuit of 1872. In 1896 the Lesseps dynasty ended its reign when Charles fled to London to avoid the payment of a £36,000 fine and Victor died at the age of forty-eight. After the sudden and unexpected death of Guichard on

[1] G. Le Bon, *The Crowd. A Study of the Popular Mind* (London, Unwin, 1900), 156.

[2] *The Times*, 17 December 1894, 5 v; 8 December 1894, 61–v, 9 iv.

[3] *The Engineer*, 14 December 1894, 532. *The Times*, 20 November 1894, 10 iii, 'The Twenty Fifth Anniversary of the Suez Canal'. I. Bowes, 'The Suez Canal', *Journal of the Manchester Geographical Society*, 7 January 1895. J. Fowler, 'Owen and Lesseps. A Reminiscence', *The Minster* (February 1895), 117–33. W. S. Blunt, *My Diaries* (1919), i. 264, 23 January 1896, 'Lesseps was a vain old fool'.

[4] *Revue d'Égypte*, 1 Avril 1895, 685.   [5] Ibid., 725.

[6] Ibid., 695.   [7] G. Le Bon, *The Crowd*, 139, 155–6.

[8] G. E. Bonnet, *Ferdinand de Lesseps* (1959), ii. 352–3.

17 July 1896 the board elected Arenberg on 3 August as President of the Company. Augustus Louis Albéric, Prince of Arenberg (1837–1924) stemmed from an old family of Eifel in the Rhineland, some of whose members had become French with the French Revolution and more French than the French themselves under Napoleon. The personification of Franco-German comity, Arenberg was a determined opponent of the radical nationalism of Gambetta and of the republican policy of continental hegemony. As a great landowner in Le Cher he became the monarchist representative of that department in the Assembly from 1877 to 1881 and a constant voter with the conservatives against all Republican Cabinets and all Republican legislation. A grand seigneur and a natural leader of men, he failed to secure re-election in 1881 or in 1885. On his re-election in 1889 he became the founder-president of the Committee of French Africa, which included Charles-Roux. Thenceforward he became the apostle of empire in the Assembly, the vice-president of the colonial party and the leader of the movement for the diversion of French interest from Alsace-Lorraine to colonial expansion. He secured the rejection of the Franco-Congolese partition of the Upper Nile on 3 January 1893, was re-elected to the Assembly as a liberal republican in 1893 and became a supporter of the movement to reconcile the Republic and the Catholic Church.

Arenberg was elected a director of the Canal Company in 1893, a vice-president in 1894 and President in 1896 at the age of fifty-nine in fulfilment of the intention and hope of Guichard. His reign restored prestige to the Company in its administration of 'the greatest and most fruitful work of modern times'.[1] He secured the appointment to the administration of its first Inspector of Finances in Edgar Bonnet who had served as such for seventeen years and undertook in 1896–1900 a financial reorganization comparable to that accomplished by Fontane in 1879–82. In that reorganization Bonnet was restricted by the judgment of the Cour de Paris which ruled on 25 November 1895 against the Eastern Railway Company that a debt amortized by lot could not be repaid by anticipation, unless the borrower had specifically reserved such a right to his own benefit. Thus the Company could not imitate the action of a prudent government in consolidating its bonds and unify its past debts in order to benefit by falling interest-rates and spread its overhead costs uniformly over the whole span of its existence. The Company created a Special Reserve Fund in 1896 and reformed its accounting procedures, first in Egypt in 1896 and then in Paris in 1898. It made a complete inventory of its equipment in Egypt in 1899 and established in 1900 an amortization fund for its buildings and equipment. Bonnet preserved the book-value of the Paris offices of the Company at the level of 1890 for twenty-two years until the Company changed its site in 1913. Arenberg refused to consider doubling the number of shares when requested to do so at the shareholders' meeting on 6 June 1899: he thereby maintained Suez shares as luxury-shares and discouraged speculation. From 1900 he ceased to reserve to the shareholders a first option on the

---

[1] *Le Canal de Suez*, 12 Juin 1897, 3218, Arenberg on 9 June 1897.

bond issues of the Company. He secured the consent of the London directors in 1900 to the end of the limitation of dividends under the London Programme: he thereby regained fiscal freedom for the Company, restored unanimity to the annual general meeting and made possible a slow building-up of the Company's investments from 1901. Bonnet was promoted on 21 May 1900 from his position as head of the Company's financial section to that of Assistant Manager. He was designated on 5 August 1901 by the board as the future General Manager, occupied that post from 1909 and functioned as the real administrator of the Company from 1900 until 1926.

Arenberg coopted all his directors in the presidential tradition and recruited to the board in 1897 Robert Guichard, the son of Jules, François Charmes, a former permanent head of the French Foreign Office, and Charles Jonnart, the chief agent of Ferry's imperial policy in Algeria between 1881 and 1889. Arenberg was elected a member of the Academy of Fine Arts in 1897 and a director of the Paris–Orleans Railway Company, the Anzin Mines and the Parisian and Neapolitan Gas Company. He also became Vice-President of the Jockey Club and President of the Philanthropic Society of Paris. He was even ranked as a supernumerary Minister after the French Cabinet,[1] an honour never allotted to his predecessor or successor. In France a prince without a principality, Arenberg found in the isthmus of Suez a French principality without a prince[2] and therefore withdrew from the republic of comrades to his isthmian kingdom, especially after he failed to secure re-election to the Assembly in 1902 and 1906. For the subjects of his realm he willingly approved the new pensions regulations of 3 November 1896, which increased pensions from 50 to 60 per cent of the salary at retirement, and the regulations of 1900 which eliminated the differentials between French, Greek and Egyptian pensions. At Ismailia he built the Residency on the Mehemet Ali Quay next to Lesseps' chalet and inspired the creation of its gardens and tree-shaded boulevards. He revived the tradition of Lesseps and made a practice of spending the two winter months of each year at Ismailia. He suggested the opening of free dispensaries for the poor at Ismailia and Port Tewfik in 1896, encouraged the campaign against ophthalmia and malaria in the isthmus and favoured the elementary education of the children of the station employees. Thus he made possible the consolidation of the family dynasties of the isthmus. He restored relations with Egypt but remained averse from close relations with England and preferred an entente cordiale with Germany. The eleven wide passing-stations which were created on his initiative at every six miles of the Canal in 1897–9 permitted the crossing of very large ships, which were mainly German vessels. Arenberg secured the election of the first German director of the Company in 1899. He also favoured as the Company's banker the Banque de Paris et des Pays-Bas which enjoyed affiliations with German financiers.

[1] J. Whitaker, *An Almanac for the Year of Our Lord 1897* (London, Whitaker, 1896), 545.
[2] F. Charles-Roux, *Souvenirs Diplomatiques d'un Âge Révolu* (Paris, Fayard, 1956), 200.

Arenberg benefited by the reaction of opinion against the condemnation of Lesseps for political reasons. He suggested the erection of a memorial to Lesseps at Port Said which the Company decided on in 1897 in relief at the decline of the demand for its expropriation.[1] On 17 November 1899, the thirtieth anniversary of the opening of the Canal, a 24-foot bronze statue of Lesseps was unveiled on a 31-foot pedestal on the jetty at Port Said.[2] The figure wore the grand cordon of the Legion of Honour, bore a map of the Canal in its left hand and half-extended its right arm towards the Canal entrance, the town of Port Said and the East. Its assertion of the French achievement in Egypt was a necessary response to the British conquest of the Sudan and of the science of Egyptology. Port Said thus gained its greatest monument through the Company's desire to erase the stain of Panama. Lesseps was thenceforward translated into the realm of myth as the hero-martyr of the Canal. 'Beyond all others Lesseps was the representative man and the necessary servant of our nineteenth century.'[3] The occasion was enshrined in literature as well as in statuary so as to turn to account the brilliant financial performance of the Canal Company,[4] to exorcize the shade of the 'colossal swindle' of Panama[5] and to depict Lesseps as a type of the hero rather than of the great capitalist bourgeoisie.[5] Friends and associates helped to rehabilitate Lesseps by portraying him in the French tradition as a paterfamilias[6] and the greatest representative of a family of servants of the nation.[7] Thus he was placed in the perspective of a history ranging back to a l'Essep of the fourteenth century and seemed like Columbus and Galileo to have come before his appointed time.[8] His achievement was given due recognition in Germany[9] and the Netherlands.[10] He was defined as the personification of moral power with the capacity of an apostle more than of a prophet by Charles-Roux,[11] who

---

[1] L. M. Rossignol, *Le Canal de Suez (Étude Historique et Juridique)* (Paris, Giard, 1898), 210–11.

[2] Compagnie Universelle du Canal Maritime de Suez, *Inauguration du Monument de Ferdinand de Lesseps le 17 Novembre 1899* (Paris, Berthaud, 1899). *The Times*, 29 November 1899, 12i. J. Charles-Roux, *L'Isthme et le Canal de Suez* (1901), ii. 335–78. Voisin Bey, *Le Canal de Suez* (1902), iii. 272–97.

[3] *Le Canal de Suez*, 2 Décembre 1899, 3658, E. M. de Vogüé.

[4] A. Neymarck, 'Le Canal de Suez (1869–1899)', *Journal de la Société de Statistique de Paris* (Octobre 1899), 363–6.

[5] P. Lafargue, 'Socialism and the Intellectuals', *International Socialist Review* (August 1900), 87, 91, 95.

[6] T. Batbedat, *De Lesseps Intime* (Paris, Juven, 1899, 1901), 179, 204, 230.

[7] L. Bridier, *Une Famille Française. Les De Lesseps* (Paris, Fontemoing, 1900).

[8] Ibid., 453.

[9] G. Steindorff, 'Dreissig Jahre Suezkanal', *Die Woche*, 24 März 1900, 512–15.

[10] J. R. W. Conrad, 'Het Suez-Kanaal', *Tijdschrift van het Koninklijk Instituut van Ingenieurs* (1902–3), *Verhandelingen*, 1–169.

[11] J. Charles-Roux, 'Le Canal de Suez, I, 1854–1898', *Revue de Paris*, 1 Octobre 1899, 505–46. Idem, 'Le Canal de Suez, II, L'État Actuel-L'Avenir', *Revue de Paris*, 15 Octobre 1899, 759–97. Idem, 'Le Canal de Suez, III, L'Œuvre Sociale—L'Œuvre Financière', *Revue de Paris*, 1 Novembre 1899, 92–130. Idem, *L'Isthme et le Canal de Suez. Historique-État Actuel* (Paris, Hachette, 1901), vol. i, p. ii. *The Nation*, 4 January 1900, 7–8, 'The Suez Canal'. A. Rambaud, 'L'Isthme et le Canal de Suez', *Revue des Deux Mondes*, 1 Février 1904, 624–54.

shifted the emphasis of his history from Lesseps to the isthmus and traced the earlier projects for a canal in terms of evolution as well as of French inspiration. Charles-Roux first emphasized the creative social and financial function of the Company. His bibliography of 1550 items in 13 languages (including 908 in French, 378 in English, 108 in German), published between 1766 and 1901 included 147 items by Lesseps himself.[1] That bibliography was compiled by the cataloguer G. T. Petrovitch in the Company's own Library[2] but was not apparently used in the preparation of the text of Charles-Roux's own work. Its length, its range and its scholarship created a permanent framework for the history of the Canal and extended the influence of its sources far into the future. The Company acquired another sacred text in the history of Voisin Bey,[3] who began not with the Pharaohs but with the concession of 1854. His seven volumes formed a magnificent contribution to the literature of engineering and the justification of his own life as well as of the Company's existence. The works of those practical men Charles-Roux and Voisin marked the highest peak of scholarship on the subject of the Canal although they could not wholly restore the tarnished prestige of the Company. Thus the Panama Scandal proved the greatest forcing-house for the historical study of the Canal since the debate over its construction.

[1] J. Charles-Roux, *L'Isthme et le Canal de Suez*, ii. 465–540.
[2] Ibid., ii. 464.
[3] F. P. Voisin, *Le Canal de Suez, I, Historique Administratif et Actes Constitutifs de la Compagnie* (Paris, Dunod, 1902, 3 vols.). Idem, *Le Canal de Suez, II, Description des Travaux de Premier Établissement* (Paris, Dunod, 1904, 1906, 3 vols.).

24

THE FRANCO-RUSSIAN
ENTENTE, 1888–1894, AND THE
RUSSIAN OIL TRADE

THE security of the Mediterranean route was increasingly undermined by the postwar resurgence of France and Russia. The successive naval crises of 1888, 1891 and 1893 established a new Franco-Russian unity of the Mediterranean at the expense of Britain, which regarded the inland sea as the cradle and citadel of its sea-power, the theatre of its greatest naval victories, the keystone of its position in Europe and the basis of its status as a world-power. Salisbury's Mediterranean Agreements of 1887 provoked France to concentrate its whole fleet at Toulon in 1888,[1] revealing the utter inadequacy of England's Mediterranean squadron, even with the support of Italy, to hold the inland sea against France. In reply England sent its Channel Fleet into the Mediterranean and passed the Imperial Defence Act of 13 August 1888, whereby Goschen appropriated the future dividends of the Government's Canal shares to the redemption of a loan to improve the defences of the ports and coaling stations of the Empire. That Act diverted to anti-French purposes the shares which Bradlaugh dismissed as 'utterly unsaleable at any price at all'.[2] It also prevented any future Liberal administration from appropriating dividends to Egyptian ends such as Gladstone had proposed in 1884. It aroused much Liberal criticism and compelled Goschen to borrow from the Sinking Fund in 1889 to accelerate the repayment of the £4,000,000 loan of 1876 within eighteen instead of thirty-six years so as to free the shares from all other commitments by 1894. It failed to deter France but forced her immediately into closer relations with Russia. Hamilton's Naval Defence Act of 1889 sought to establish by 1894 a Two-Power Standard against France and Russia and began a new race in naval power.[3] The naval scare of 1888 also enabled the C.P.R. to secure its long-desired contract in 1889 for a monthly mail service from Halifax or Quebec to Hong Kong[4] and to order three 14-knot liners capable of rapid conversion into armed merchant cruisers on the pattern of the *Teutonic*. The C.P.R. also agreed to employ R.N.R. men as far as possible and to carry all troops to the East at cost price, so maintaining British interests against the U.S.A. as well as against Russia. The P. & O. also paid homage to the new importance of the Navy when the London Committee

[1] C. J. Lowe, *Salisbury and the Mediterranean 1886–1896* (London, Routledge, 1965), 35–6.
[2] Hansard, *Commons Debates*, 4 June 1888, 1133, Bradlaugh.
[3] A. J. Marder, *British Naval Policy 1880–1905* (London, Putnam, 1940), 119–43, 'The Naval Defence Act of 1889'.
[4] H. A. Innis, *A History of the Canadian Pacific Railway* (1923), 138–9.

of the Canal Company, under its new chairman Sutherland, appointed in 1889 as the successor to John Slagg, who had been the godson of Cobden, Lord Brassey, who had been the editor of *Brassey's Naval Annual* since 1886.

France opened new harbours at Saigon in January 1888 and at Jibuti in March 1888, compelling Britain to strengthen the defences of its 'Arabian cinder-hole, so ugly and so useful'[1] and to conclude treaties of protection with eight neighbouring sheikhs and sultans in 1888, so laying the basis of the Eastern Aden Protectorate. Italy brought 55,759 Italian troops through the Canal during its war of 1887–9 against Ethiopia. It cut Ethiopia off from the Somali coast in 1889 and created Eritrea in 1890 as the last link in the littoral barrier around its prey. Menelik established his capital at Addis Ababa between 1887 and 1890 in the isolation of the central plateau and called on Orthodox Russia for support against Catholic Italy and its aspirations to establish a protectorate. France declined, however, to permit the establishment of a 'New Moscow' in the bay of Tajura and ended the history of the first Russian settlement in Africa after thirty days.[2]

England encouraged German as well as Italian expansion in Africa in order to restrain French expansion. Germany developed its trade to the Levant from 1888 and to the East from 1890, after Hamburg and Bremen entered the German Customs-Union in 1888. As German shipping became converted from sail to steam Hamburg founded in 1888 the Hamburg–Calcutta Line as a complement to the Hansa Line and the German Australian Line as a rival to the North German Lloyd. The Hamburg–Calcutta Line began operations in 1890 after the Rickmers Line had established a steamship service via the Canal for the transport of rice from Rangoon to Bremerhaven. The German Australian Line began its service, which avoided English harbours, in 1889. The resignation of Bismarck removed a great restraint on German colonial enthusiasm and encouraged German aspirations to empire in Equatoria as well as the foundation in Hamburg on 19 April 1890 of the German East Africa Line.[3] That company was the only German steamship company founded at the invitation of the Government and in the almost certain prospect of a subsidy under the Mail Steamer Subsidy Act of 1890.[4] It was financed by the great German banks and was managed in close association with the Woermann Line to West Africa. Its first steamer reached Zanzibar in thirty-six days (23 July–27 August 1890). German expansion was regulated by the Anglo-German Agreement of 1 July 1890, which partitioned East Africa as the Conference of Berlin in 1885 had partitioned West Africa. Although that agreement shattered the dream of 'a continuous band of British dominion' from the south to the north of Africa[5] its exchange of Heligoland for Zanzibar, Uganda and the Nile Valley seemed the best bargain made by any British

[1] E. Arnold, *Seas and Lands* (London, Longmans, 1891), 524, 13 February 1891.
[2] C. Jesman, *The Russians in Ethiopia. An Essay in Futility* (London, Chatto, 1958), 10, 13.
[3] K. Brackmann, *Fünfzig Jahre Deutscher Afrikaschiffahrt* (Berlin, Reimer, 1935), 22.
[4] O. Mathies, *Hamburgs Reederei 1814–1914* (Hamburg, Friedrichsen, 1924), 121.
[5] *The Times*, 22 August 1888, 8ii, H. H. Johnston, 'Great Britain's Policy in Africa'.

Government 'since Lord Beaconsfield made the Suez Canal a mainly English property'.[1]

In the 1890s rather than in the 1870s East Africa ceased to be a backwater and was drawn into the sphere of European influence at the expense of that of Bombay. In March 1891 the German East Africa Line began a four-weekly service from Hamburg via the Canal to Zanzibar together with a local feeder-service. In 1892 it extended its services southwards to Lourenço Marques and Durban as well as eastwards from Zanzibar to Bombay. It made the Beira–Durban zone the competitive region between the Suez and the Cape routes because Bullard King and Rennie had extended their lines northwards from Durban to Beira in 1891 and 1892, to compete for the traffic of the new Rhodesia. The British India Line suffered most by its expansion south of Zanzibar, ended its service to Lourenço Marques during the bitter Anglo-Portuguese dispute of 1889–90, inaugurated a new service in 1890 from London to Mombasa as the port of entry to Mackinnon's long-desired inland empire and began to press for the construction of a Uganda Railway. The German East Africa Line became the pacemaker for shipping services to East Africa in the two decades before a comparable British line was organized. German expansion increased the flow of German shipping through the Canal. Germany, the fourth largest client of the Canal since 1882 rose to the third place in 1888, when it surpassed the Netherlands, and to the second place in 1890 when it surpassed France. The German share of the Canal's tonnage rose from 3·7 per cent in 1886 and 4·2 per cent in 1889 to 7·1 per cent in 1890. Only in 1892 did German Canal tonnage end the twelve successive years of expansion which had begun in 1879. Thus Germany replaced Austria and the Netherlands as the bearer of Germanic culture to Asia and Africa. A traveller to Zanzibar in 1890 published the first account of the Canal by a German tourist.[2] Germany introduced into Tanganyika the cultivation of coffee in 1892 and of sisal in 1893: it also became the largest single market for the raw hides of India from 1891–2 and for the raw cotton of India from 1891 to 1896. It expanded with England into East Africa rather than into the more populous and economically valuable West Africa. England thus overcame the obstacles to the penetration of Africa by the Navy in its crusade against the slave-trade. It gained a new empire which could be approached only by salt water and could not be threatened directly by the great military powers of Europe. It acquired a buffer-continent for Egypt and the Canal, whose opening could thenceforth be ranked by the geographer as a notable event in the partition of Africa.[3]

England's close association with Germany in Africa and with Italy in the Mediterranean brought about the Franco-Russian entente of 27 August 1891

[1] *Saturday Review*, 21 June 1890, 755, 'The New African Empire'.
[2] P. Neubaur, 'Port Said und der Suezkanal', *Westermanns Illustrierte Deutsche Monatshefte* (Oktober 1891), 28–47.
[3] J. S. Keltie, *Applied Geography* (London, Philip, 1890), 14. Idem., *The Partition of Africa* (London, Stanford, 1893), 110.

after the fall of Bismarck and the end of his secret Reinsurance Treaty of 1887 with Russia. That entente ended the long diplomatic isolation of France and encouraged her to aspire to dominate the Mediterranean, to adopt a ten-year naval programme, to begin the fortification of Bizerta as an African Toulon athwart the Sicilian narrows and to finance the construction of the Great Siberian Railway. That railway was decreed by the Tsar on 17 March 1891, fourteen years after Russia's humiliation in 1878, and was begun on 19 May by the Tsarevitch at Vladivostock, which imported its railway material through the Canal in the Russian Volunteer Fleet. The line would form the longest railway in the world and would, in Witte's view, supersede the Suez Canal as the leading route to China. The overland trade between China and Russia through Kiakhta had declined substantially in 1889, especially in tea, while tea shipments from Hankow to Odessa had increased in weight by 130 per cent between 1886 and 1890. The Russian merchants in Kiakhta therefore complained that the Canal had left them with only the fur trade while enabling the English to establish a monopoly of the China trade. The economists of Nijni even professed to fear the peaceful conquest of Siberia by the British. Thus the railway was seen as both a counter-balance and a rival to the Canal.

The Dardanelles scare of September 1891[1] followed the growing use of the Straits by the fast well-armed merchant-cruisers of the Russian Volunteer Fleet[2] and Salisbury's refusal on 3 August to consider a Turkish request for the evacuation of Egypt. German hints of a possible Russian seizure of the Suez Canal and of large-scale Russian purchases of Suez shares[3] sought to heighten British fears. A British naval demonstration in the Aegean on 13 September was intended to warn Turkey against permitting the Dardanelles to become a Russian naval highway. The Porte's circular of 19 September however allowed vessels of the Russian Volunteer Fleet to use the Dardanelles provided that they did not carry troops. That circular complemented the Turkish fortification in 1889 of the Dardanelles which was directed even more obviously against Britain. The new Russian threat produced the last British proposals for a protective Euphrates Valley Railway.[4] It increased unofficial support for reliance on the Cape as 'our true route to India',[5] for the conciliation of Russia by the surrender of Constantinople and for the appeasement of France by the evacuation of Egypt. 'It is not India, but the insisting on one particular road to India, that binds us with hampering chains to the volcanic Eastern Question, big with all its tremendous potentialities for disaster.'[6]

[1] W. L. Langer, *The Franco-Russian Alliance 1890–1894* (Harvard University Press, 1929), 201–6.

[2] *The Times*, 12 September 1891, 10vi, W. L. Clowes.

[3] Ibid., 3 September 1891, 3iv. C. L. Smith, *The Embassy of Sir William White at Constantinople, 1886–1891* (1957), 145.

[4] *The Times*, 14 September 1891, 3v–vi, T. Frame Thompson. *Proceedings of the Institution of Civil Engineers*, cxi (1892–3), Part 1, 24–30, H. Hayter, Presidential Address, 8 November 1892.

[5] *The Times*, 15 September 1891, 7ii.

[6] Ibid., 17 September, 12iii; 25 September, 2vi, Major-General W. J. Stuart, R.E.

Curzon however dismissed the Euphrates Valley Railway as supererogatory to the Suez Canal and urged the improvement of steam communication with the East so as to place British soldiers in Karachi three weeks after leaving Portsmouth.[1] Salisbury would not tolerate Russia as the mistress of Constantinople because it would preclude the use of the Suez route to India except in conditions of the profoundest peace. The crisis thus confirmed Dilke's judgment of 1889. 'The canal, considered as a means of communication in time of war, is as delicate as a thread of a spider's web.'[2] The Admiralty concluded that it could not support the traditional Straits policy of the Government against the overwhelming power of the French Fleet nor ensure the safety of the Mediterranean even in alliance with Italy.[3] It abandoned its policy of seeking superiority to the French Fleet in the Mediterranean and so encouraged more advanced opinion to contemplate withdrawal from the Mediterranean and even the surrender of Gibraltar itself.[4]

The accession of the new Khedive Abbas Hilmi was greeted by the visit of French and Russian naval squadrons to Alexandria and encouraged Turkey to make what Baring regarded as an attempt to advance to the very edge of the Canal by placing the frontier of Egypt on the traditional line from Suez to El Arish. Abbas was infuriated by Milner's *England in Egypt*[5] which was published in December 1892 and widely read in an Arabic translation in Cairo. Milner's plea for the maintenance of a veiled protectorate in the cause of civilization carried further the tradition of the justification of British policy pioneered by D. M. Wallace in 1883. Abbas manifested his indignation so forcefully that the British garrison in Cairo had to be doubled, by a telegram of 22 January from Gladstone which stopped a regiment on its way home from India at Suez.[6] The Egyptian crisis of January 1893 thus reinforced rather than ended the occupation, although it encouraged proposals to withdraw the garrison to the Canal or to Suez,[7] which was depicted as a potential Aden in Egypt, with Kosseir as a substitute port on the Red Sea. The same depreciation of the value of the Suez route inspired the request by Lord Stern, a Gladstonian Liberal, for a Return of Trade from the East via the Suez Canal in continuation of that secured by Rathbone in 1883.[8]

The Franco-Russian military convention of 18 August 1892 was followed

[1] *The Times*, 19 September, 7 iv; 24 September, 6 i; 26 September, 12 iii. G. N. Curzon, *Persia and the Persian Question* (London, Longmans, 1892), i. 631–6.
[2] C. W. Dilke, *Problems of Greater Britain* (London, Macmillan, 1890), 657.
[3] *The Times*, 28 September 1891, 9 iv.
[4] W. L. Clowes, 'The Uselessness of Gibraltar', *Fortnightly Review*, 1 February 1893. J. W. Gambier, 'An Exchange for Gibraltar', *Fortnightly Review*, 1 May 1893, 731.
[5] W. S. Blunt, *My Diaries, 1888–1914* (1919), i. 107.
[6] T. B. Miller, 'The Egyptian Question and British Foreign Policy, 1892–1894', *Journal of Modern History* (March 1910), 5.
[7] E. Martin, *La Question d'Égypte. L'Angleterre et le Canal de Suez* (Paris, Michaud, 1892), 34–5. W. S. Blunt, *My Diaries*, i. 80, 19 May 1892, Harcourt; 110, 15 February 1893, Blunt; 116, 7 March 1893, Riaz Pasha. Idem, 'Lord Cromer and the Khedive', *Nineteenth Century*, 1 April 1893, 584.
[8] Hansard, *Commons Debates*, 24 April 1893, S. J. Stern.

by an Anglo-French clash at Bangkok on 28 July 1893 and Russia's announce-ment on 6 August of her intention to send a naval squadron to Toulon. The Admiralty reinforced its China squadron by the despatch of a first-class battleship from the Mediterranean on 8 August and sanctioned the construc-tion of the *Renown* with a draught of 26¾ feet so that it might use the Canal as well as the rivers of Asia. British supremacy in the Mediterranean finally ended when the Russian Baltic Fleet anchored at Toulon on 13 October 1893 and was joined by one warship which had passed the Straits.[1] The system of the Mediterranean agreements was thereby shattered and the security of the inland sea was annihilated in both east and west. The Mediterranean had become the meeting-place for the two Powers which flanked Germany and thenceforward encircled the Triple Alliance by sea as well as by land. Ger-many's pre-eminence in Europe was ended and the Bismarckian security of Britain's sole friend on the Continent was destroyed. Britain was threatened even more than Germany by the Franco-Russian demonstration because the British Army could not assume the offensive and its Navy was already sup-posed to be ubiquitous. France and Russia had clearly proved that the dominion of the sea was divisible and had increased the strain on the British Navy beyond all measure. The keys of the Mediterranean still controlled access to the sea but not movement within it. Thus control of the Canal even in defiance of the Convention of Constantinople became pointless without control of the whole associated sea-route. The British Navy could not defeat the French Navy and reopen the Mediterranean route in wartime without some 60–70 additional warships.[2] The price paid for the large-scale capital investment in merchant shipping in 1870–4 became the large-scale capital investment of the 1890s first in cruisers for commerce-protection under the Hamilton programme and then in battleships under the Spencer programme. Gladstone's policy of financial retrenchment faced its greatest crisis just after the United Egyptian Debt first rose above par on 16 March 1893 and pro-mised to end the burden of Egypt on the Exchequer.

The naval scare of 1893 reinforced the bonds between the Navy and the mail lines. It renewed interest in the C.P.R.'s capacity to girdle the globe in seventy-three days or even in sixty-four days[3] and to carry troops free from attack to Singapore or even to India in forty days.[4] It stimulated record-breaking voyages by the P. & O. as well as by the Union Line and Shaw Savill. The *Oriental* had carried the mail from London to Hong Kong in 23 days 16½ hours (7 April–1 May 1893),[5] in response to the competition of the C.P.R. from 1891. The *Australia* had reached Adelaide on 4 May 1893 in 26 days 16½ hours. The *Himalaya* carried the mail to Bombay on 12 November 1893 in 10 days 20 hours from Brindisi and in 13 days 1 hour from London. The

---

[1] *The Times*, 31 October 1893, 12i. A. J. Marder, 174–205, 'The Navy Scare of 1893'.
[2] W. S. Blunt, *My Diaries*, i. 145–6, 28 November 1893, Colonel J. Stokes.
[3] *Nautical Magazine* (October 1892), 918, 'Round the World in Seventy Days'.
[4] Ibid. (November 1893), 1011–15, 'War Routes to India'.
[5] *The Times*, 16 June 1893, 8iv, 'Round the World in Sixty-Two days'.

Admiralty despatched the Channel squadron to Gibraltar in November 1893 and appointed a full admiral to command the Mediterranean squadron in place of the usual vice-admiral. The secret Franco-Russian alliance of 4 January 1894 ratified the military convention of 1892 between the two great enemies of Britain and exposed Malta to the threat of a combined attack by the French Fleet from the west and by the Russian Fleet from the East. Gladstone became the first Prime Minister to be driven into private life by a Conservative attack on the Naval Estimates. His resignation made possible the adoption of the secret five-year Spencer programme and the fortification of Gibraltar and Malta. After H.M.S. *Centurion* with a draught of 27½ feet successfully passed through the Canal on 16–17 March en route to China the Admiralty decided on 10 May 1894 to guard the entrances to the Canal in wartime, in order to deny access to the Red Sea to the enemy whilst preserving its use to the British. After the Mediterranean Fleet was routed by the 'Toulon fleet' in naval manoeuvres on 3–5 August 1894 in the Irish Sea before reinforcements from the Channel had arrived the Admiralty announced on 4 October that the Channel squadron would winter at Gibraltar and so sought to avert a similar disaster in a real war.

The revelation of the existence of the Franco-Russian alliance brought the Mediterranean debate to its peak in the spring of 1895, when Laird Clowes urged the immediate evacuation of the Mediterranean, bag and baggage, because the Canal could not be kept open against an enemy, even if both banks were held by the entire military force of the Empire. 'Our road is across the ocean or our own territory, and not through other people's ditches.'[1] That advice was rejected by all authoritative naval opinion, by Spencer and by Admiral Sir G. H. Richards, who as a captain had inspected the Canal for the Admiralty in 1870. Sir George Clarke, who had been secretary to the Colonial Defence Committee from 1885 to 1892, asserted that the abandonment of all attempt to defend the Suez route 'would shake the very foundations of the Empire and imperil the allegiance of great colonies'.[2] Clarke's suggestion that the Canal could be protected by placing a guard on all merchant ships in transit was however dismissed by Clowes as ineffective unless ships passed through with no persons on board and in a dry dock or on a pontoon to prevent contact between the ship and the Canal.[3]

The naval scares of 1893 and 1895 reflected the new enthusiasm for the Navy apparent in the unveiling of the Armada Memorial on Plymouth Hoe in 1890, the organization of the Royal Naval Exhibition at Chelsea in 1891 and the foundation of the Navy Records Society in 1893. Spencer introduced continuity in naval policy from 1893, so raising the Navy above parties, as

---

[1] Nauticus (W. L. Clowes), 'The Millstone Round the Neck of England', *Nineteenth Century* (March 1895), 373.

[2] G. S. Clarke, 'England and the Mediterranean', *Nineteenth Century* (April 1895), 545. *The Times*, 29 March 1895, 9iii.

[3] W. L. Clowes, 'Braggadocio about the Mediterranean', *Nineteenth Century* (May 1895), 881–2.

Rosebery had raised foreign policy. The Navy League was established in 1894 and promoted the general celebration of the ninetieth anniversary of Trafalgar. The sailor was celebrated in ballad, ode and song, poem, play and opera, painting, history and advertisement as never before and first assumed a dominant position in the national consciousness. Naval Estimates which had remained stationary between 1858 and 1893 first exceeded the Army Estimates in 1895 and doubled between 1888–9 and 1899–1900. The presiding spirit behind that great transformation was Mahan,[1] who drew lessons from British naval history for the intended benefit of the U.S.A. but became the harbinger of the Anglo-American cooperation of the 1890s and America's gift to England in exchange for Herbert Spencer. In the lectures which he wrote in 1886 and published in 1890 he developed a specifically western interpretation of the sea based on control rather than on comprehension. Mahan based his theory of naval strategy on the militarization of warfare at sea, on the precision movements of a steam fleet and on the global continuity of the oceans.[2] He associated English security with its fleet rather that with the military moat of the Channel. 'Those far-distant, storm-beaten ships, upon which the Grand Army never looked, stood between it and the dominion of the world.'[3] Mahan thus gave the Royal Navy a philosophy of history and England the magical assurance that its sea-power would not suffer the fate of that of Tyre, Carthage, Venice and Genoa, at the very time that the decline of the sailing ship and of the sailor was undermining that maritime supremacy. His influence encouraged the attribution of the Indian empires of England[4] and Portugal[5] to their sea-power rather than to their military power. It did not, however, directly magnify the importance of the Canal, 'for British commerce the most important piece of water in the world outside of our own home waters'.[6] It could neither restore the vanished security of the Suez route nor prevent the Admiralty adopting a negative approach towards the Canal as an instrument of strategy. Thus England's policy in Africa became based on land-power rather than on sea-power. After Kitchener's victory in the second crisis with Abbas Hilmi in January 1894, Rhodes decided that England would never withdraw from Egypt and aspired to create 'a British boulevard from Table Bay to the Suez Canal'.[7] The declaration of a protectorate over Uganda on 12 April 1894 encouraged the ambition in the tradition of Ismail to link Uganda to the Nile. Campbell-Bannerman made the last public profession of the Government's

[1] W. L. Clowes, 'Sea Power, its Past and its Future', *Fortnightly Review*, December 1893, 853.
[2] W. D. Puleston, *Mahan* (Yale University Press, 1939), 46, was apparently misled by the use of the overland route through Suez to affirm that Mahan passed through the Canal within a month of its formal opening.
[3] A. T. Mahan, *The Influence of Sea Power upon the French Revolution and Empire 1793–1812* (London, Low, 1892), ii. 118.
[4] A. C. Lyall, *The Rise and Expansion of the British Dominion in India* (London, Murray, 1894), 1–4, 341.
[5] W. W. Hunter, *A History of British India* (London, Longmans, 1899), i. 134, 165–6.
[6] G. R. Parkin, *Round the Empire* (London, Cassell, 1892), 194.
[7] H. W. Lucy, 'From Cape Town to Cairo', *Fortnightly Review*, 1 March 1894, 410.

intention to evacuate Egypt on 9 October 1894. The lure of Africa thus helped to convert Liberal England from Cobdenism to the imperialism of 'the empire-builders' (1894) and 'the flag-wavers' (1894).

As the Canal lost its strategic function it acquired a new fiscal function as a source of revenue to the Treasury. The imperialist Ashmead Bartlett extorted from the new Liberal administration the admission that the Government's Canal shares had an estimated value of £17,750,000[1] and so encouraged the revaluation of the share-purchase as 'one of the most brilliant strokes of finance ever accomplished either by financier or statesman'.[2] Milner cast a cold Germanic eye upon the Canal Company as a gigantic French profit-making enterprise on Egyptian soil and argued that England should provide the £4,000,000 necessary for the construction of a Nile Dam at Aswan as one-quarter of the clear profit made on the purchase of 1875.[3] No new financial bond was however created between England and Egypt. The end of Egypt's payments of 5 per cent interest on the Canal shares removed one existing link after Egypt had paid a total of £3,635,188, or nearly the purchase-price of the shares, to the British Government by 1 July 1894. The realization of the full value of the investment made in 1875 encouraged an American attack on the transaction as a mortgage of property which belonged to Egypt and not to its Khedive.[4] The transfer of that financial interest to England increased anglophobia in Paris because the growing dividends were paid thenceforward to the British Government rather than to the delegation-holders, who received their last payment of interest on 1 July 1894 and wound up their Mutual Association established in 1884. Thenceforward the British Government received both dividend and interest on the shares, together with the expectation of their continuation from 1894 until 1968. The £4,000,000 loan of 1876 in Exchequer bonds which had been repaid at an accelerated rate since 1889 was fully amortized by 20 March 1894, so liquidating the last debt in connexion with the share-purchase. The shares rose from a nominal value of £3,532,040 on 31 March 1894 to their full market value of £23,892,955 on 1 January 1895. The Government became entitled to receive 44 per cent of the total dividends distributed by the Company on its shares, or 31 per cent of the total distributed profits, because the Company's shares received 71 per cent of the total profits. In the year ending 31 March 1896 the Government received the substantial income of £673,418. That income, independent of taxes and of the taxpayers' consent, was very largely a transfer-payment by the British shipowners who supplied 74·6 per cent of the Company's receipts in 1894.

The valorization of a Conservative achievement under a Liberal administration occasioned a conflict over the use of the dividends which Goschen had

[1] Hansard, *Commons Debates*, 19 June and 11 December 1893, E. A. Bartlett.

[2] *The Times*, 30 September 1893, 11v, John Scott.

[3] A. Milner, *England in Egypt* (1892), 261–2, 340, 179, 287, reviewed in *The Investor's Review* (May 1893), 210–12.

[4] C. Whitehouse, 'England's Right to the Suez Shares', *Fortnightly Review*, 1 September 1893, 409. *The Spectator*, 9 September 1893, 343–4, 319.

appropriated to the cause of imperial defence in 1888. Goschen suggested in 1892 that the appreciation of 'that splendid asset of the nation'[1] to their full market value would enable the purchase-price of £4,000,000 to be repaid and the National Debt to be reduced by £15,000,000. 'I should like to do it now. I should like to anticipate some right hon. Gentleman perhaps on the other side of the House, but I am too modest to make this entry at the present moment.'[2] Goschen's anticipation of the increased revenue to borrow £1,870,000 in the financial year 1892–3 aroused the concern of Liberal financial experts[3] while an Irish Liberal on the trail of jobbery attacked the new custom whereby the three official directors received directors' fees in addition to their salaries:[4] thereafter Rivers Wilson resigned from his post as Comptroller-General of the National Debt in 1894 and from his official directorship in 1896. The naval scare launched by the Conservatives inspired Labouchere to suggest in 1893 that Harcourt should reduce the Government's holding in the Canal Company in order to meet the increased naval expenditure.[5] The Liberal Government decided to appropriate the Suez Canal dividends to the general revenue instead of to the extinction of Goschen's imperial defence loan. Sir Richard Temple, the former Governor of Bombay, forced a division on the issue in the debate on the Army Estimates on 6 July 1894 but secured only twenty-six Conservative votes against ninety-three Liberal votes. The Finance Act of 31 July 1894 consequently authorized the payment into the Exchequer of all dividends received in respect of the Suez shares by the Treasury. That victory for Liberal finance created a powerful Treasury interest in the dividends which were thenceforward consistently preserved from departmental appropriation, even after the return of a Conservative ministry. Thus Chamberlain's attempt in 1895 to appropriate the dividends to the guarantee of loans for colonial public works[6] failed to secure the approval of the Treasury or of the Chancellor of the Exchequer. The Treasury also began to receive an additional income as the shares were amortized, payments which had thitherto been retained by the Company but which were applied to debt-redemption, like the New Sinking-Fund, under the Finance Act of 9 May 1898. Thus the fiscal ingenuity of the Canal Company made England a substantial sharer in its great enterprise while neither its directors nor its management were subjected to the English domination which French pessimists had feared. Even the strictest Liberals were forced to recognize the great financial success of the share-purchase so that the political nation became united in its enjoyment of the income from 'this enormous national property'.[7]

As the Canal became a source of revenue for England it also became an oil

[1] Hansard, *Commons Debates,* 11 April 1892, 1149, Goschen.
[2] Ibid., 11 April 1892, 1149, Goschen.
[3] Ibid., 16 May 1892, S. Buxton and W. Harcourt.
[4] Ibid., 9 June 1892, C. K. Tanner.
[5] Ibid., 14 December 1893, Labouchere.
[6] J. L. Garvin, *The Life of Joseph Chamberlain,* iii. 176, 25 November 1895.
[7] Hansard, *Commons Debates,* 9 June 1892, 639, J. E. Gorst.

route for Russia. The bulk oil trade which gave material content to the Franco-Russian alliance began as a southbound rather than as a northbound traffic and carried refined paraffin rather than crude oil. The demand for paraffin arose first in the West and not in the East, where vegetable oil in the traditional lamp supplied cheap and adequate light in a climate where wax candles melted easily and gas-light was restricted to the colonial cities.[1] The first great flow of paraffin from the West came from the U.S.A. which first shipped it to China in 1867 and increased its exports to Asia as Baku increased its competition in the home market of Russia. Baku produced oil without the need for a pump and reduced the U.S. exports of oil to Russia from their peak of 1873. It increased its competition on the abolition of the Government excise in 1877 and so encouraged the U.S.A. to seek new markets and to ship oil for the first time direct from New York to Batavia via the Canal in 1877.[2] The success of that shipment encouraged Rockefeller to organize the Standard Alliance in 1878 and the Standard Oil Trust in 1881. He thereby made the export market of Asia a safety-valve to preserve the balance between home production and consumption and prevent any weakening in Standard Oil's monopoly of the home market. The oil imports of India and China rose sharply from 1878, especially after India abolished its $7\frac{1}{2}$ per cent import duty in March 1878. Oil was shipped via the Canal to Bombay from 1879 but was carried increasingly by sail via the Cape because speed was not essential and engines might ignite gases. The oil was assimilated to ordinary cargo, being packed in rectangular tin cans and shipped in wooden cases. The rise of the case-oil trade stimulated the expansion of tin-mining in Malaya to supply the tin-plate industry of South Wales, which manufactured the containers. The other British interests which became bound up with the export trade of Standard Oil included the sailing-ship owners, the London shipping brokers and the London financiers.

The trade in lamp-oil encouraged the search for oil in Asia where it was first found in Sumatra in 1885 and at Gemsa on the Red Sea coast of Egypt in 1886. The American monopoly of production and export was destroyed by the full development of the fields of Baku, especially after the Baku–Batum Railway[3] was completed in 1883 with the aid of the Rothschilds of Paris in order to open up the markets of the Black Sea and the Mediterranean. In 1886 Batum was released from the free-port restrictions of 1878 and the Rothschilds founded the marketing company of B.N.I.T.O. (The Caspian and Black Sea Naphtha Commercial and Industrial Company).[4] Oil gave the Black Sea a staple export which drew it more completely into world trade than the export

---

[1] Gas-lighting was introduced into Bombay in 1835, Sydney in 1836, Calcutta in 1854, Hong Kong in 1864 and Alexandria in 1865.

[2] *Le Canal de Suez*, 12 Juin 1877, 3.

[3] C. Marvin, *The Petroleum of the Future. Baku: the Petrolia of Europe* (London, Anderson, 1883).

[4] B. Gille, 'Capitaux Français et Pétroles Russes (1884–1894)', *Histoire des Entreprises* (Novembre 1963), 19.

of grain had done. The expansion of Baku sharply reduced the American share in world production between 1880 and 1885, made Batum the greatest oil-port in the world and opened new opportunities to English enterprise.[1] Baku oil reached the ports of the Baltic in 1882 when American oil was first shipped through the Canal to Jedda, Karachi and Calcutta. It reached Beirut and India for the first time in 1885. The sea route from Batum through the Straits and the Canal provided convenient access to the markets of Asia, which were inaccessible by the mountain-barred route from the Caspian to the Persian Gulf. Those markets were captured increasingly from Standard Oil by Russia, which also began to export oil to Port Said from 1886, forcing down the price of American oil and importing Egyptian cotton in exchange. From 1888 the export of Russian oil was stimulated by the high excise duty imposed on the domestic sales of paraffin in Russia and was made in bulk from Batum to Bombay, which it reached in thirty days. Russian paraffin proved a low-cost competitor of American paraffin and forced an immediate reduction in its price in the markets of Bombay, Madras and Calcutta. Standard Oil supplied the Europeans and the Westernized élites while Russia supplied the indigenous population and extended its exports to Singapore and Japan from 1888 and to Java from 1889. The oil imports of India from Russia first exceeded the value of those from the U.S.A. in 1891–2, ranked Russia second to Britain in the supply of India's imports and created a substantial seaborne trade between Russia and India at the very time that the North-West Frontier was being heavily fortified against the threat of a Russian overland advance. Thus Russia developed a staple export through the Canal to compensate for its imports from the East both by sea and by land.

Russian competition forced Standard Oil further to reduce its prices from 1889 and to consider the economies of bulk transport by the steam-tankers built since 1884 as an alternative to the cases, which were costly to make and handle, easy to damage and prone to leak. Bulk transport would necessitate capital investment in tankers, pumps and storage-tanks but would reduce freight-costs and permit retail distribution by the cheap labour of Asia, so combining the capital of the West with the labour of the East. In 1890 first Standard Oil and then B.N.I.T.O. applied in vain to the Canal Company for permission to send tankers through the Canal.[2] In response to the Russian challenge Standard Oil extended its control of marketing outside the U.S.A. through its own distributing companies established in England in 1888, in Germany in 1890 and in the Netherlands in 1891. Thereby it began to concentrate increasingly on Western Europe, reduced its case-oil shipments to Asia from 1890 and diverted the oil ousted from the Indian market in 1890–2 to the China market. Thus Russia increased its share of the total number of

---

[1] C. Marvin, *The Coming Deluge of Russian Petroleum and its Bearing on British Trade* (London, Anderson, 1886).

[2] F. C. Gerretson, *History of the Royal Dutch* (Leiden, Brill, 1953, 1955), i. 214–17; ii. 144–52.

cases of oil shipped through the Canal from 22·6 per cent in 1889 to 41·6 per cent in 1891. The increase in shipments to Asia encouraged the quest for local sources of supply which were located in 1889 in Burma and in Java. The Royal Dutch Petroleum Company was chartered in 1890 to supply the export markets of Asia from the oil of Sumatra.

The carriage of case-oil from Batum to the East by British steamers brought Marcus Samuel into the trade.[1] Samuel had established with his brother in 1878 the merchant house of Samuel, Samuel & Co. which became the leading British firm in Japan and marketed in 1888 the first cargo of Russian case-oil in Japan. Samuel's first application in 1890 for permission to send a tanker through the Canal was unsuccessful. After tank-lighters were admitted to the Rhine in 1890 he renewed his application through Henri Goudchaux, the Chairman of Worms & Co., the leading coal firm of Port Said. On 20 April 1891 Samuel informed the Company that he proposed to establish a direct oil-tanker service between Europe and Asia and submitted Fortescue Flannery's plans for a tanker. The Canal Company granted permission on 18 August 1891, two months after Samuel had been elected an Alderman of the City of London. Probably on the same day B.N.I.T.O. contracted to supply Samuel with 'Anchor' paraffin for a period of nine years. Thus B.N.I.T.O., the second largest refiners in Baku since 1889, sought to improve its position in the markets of Asia and its prospects of agreement with its chief rival by turning against Standard Oil its own habitual technique of price-cutting and by using Samuel as its instrument.[2] In return Samuel agreed not to market Russian paraffin west of Suez, which so became a dividing-line between the world-markets of Asia and Europe. He ordered his first tanker from William Gray & Co. of West Hartlepool, and may have encouraged William Doxford of Sunderland to develop the turret-steamer from 1892 for the oil as well as the grain trade.[3] He sent two nephews through the Canal to arrange for the establishment of storage tanks in eight ports of Asia, including Singapore, Bangkok, Hong Kong and Kobe.

The Canal Company's concession to Samuel was a concession to greater freedom of trade made against the most powerful combine in the world by a company which had been portrayed since 1883 as a monopoly hostile to trade. The price of case-oil fell immediately, bringing together all the interests associated with the case-oil trade of Standard Oil, whose interest in its export market increased when legal action by the State of Ohio caused the Standard Oil Trust to decide in 1892 voluntarily to dissolve and the independent producers began to export by pipeline in 1892. Standard Oil wished to maintain its monopoly of the Cape route, like Britain in the 1850s, and to preserve the Canal as a barrier against the competition of Russian oil in bulk. Of its

---

[1] R. Henriques, *Marcus Samuel First Viscount Bearstead and Founder of The 'Shell' Transport and Trading Company 1853–1927* (London, Barrie, 1960), 67.
[2] B. Gille, 43–4, 48.
[3] *Nautical Magazine* (January 1892), 103.

ancillary interests in Britain the tin-plate manufacturers of South Wales had also lost 80 per cent of the American market through the McKinley Tariff which came into operation from 1 July 1891. All the threatened interests united to protest on 30 October 1891 to Salisbury and then on 20 November to 'the Signatory Powers of the Suez Canal Company's Charter' (i.e. the signatories to the Convention of Constantinople of 1888).[1] Their protest on behalf of the 'regular and safe', the 'convenient and safe' case-trade against a 'perilous and precarious' bulk-trade was inspired by their prospective loss of profits but was ostensibly made against the danger to all users of the Canal from oil-tankers. They enlisted the support of shipowners who were not primarily interested in the case-oil trade. They did not advocate the prohibition of the oil trade but only that of the bulk oil trade through the Canal. Thus they sought protection for the case-oil trade, a less efficient and more expensive mode of transport, in the homeland of political economy and free trade. Shipowners in the bulk oil trade had never shown that they regarded it as especially dangerous and had secured the admission of tankers to the Thames itself.[2]

The regulations for the new tanker traffic were considered at the Foreign Office on 17 December 1891 by an interdepartmental committee of five including Rivers Wilson, Stokes and representatives of the Foreign Office, the Home Office, the Board of Trade and the Admiralty. They were then discussed and adopted on 22 December by the Executive Committee of the Company and were finally approved by the full Board on 5 January 1892. The Company opened its first small oil basin at Port Said in January 1892 on the Asiatic bank south of the coaling basin and therefore in similar isolation from the shipping in transit. The opponents of tanker traffic took legal action, organized petitions of protest,[3] inspired alarmist articles in half of the newspapers of England, arranged for questions to be asked in Parliament and enlisted the support of expert opinion. A lawsuit was begun in Alexandria against the Company on 1 January 1892 by Chambers & Co., carriers of case-oil for Standard Oil, to secure a ruling that the Company's new regulations were illegal, null and void. Stereotyped petitions of protest were sent to the Foreign Office from Newcastle on 21 January, from Hull and Cardiff on 22 January and from Glasgow on 13 February.[4] At Newcastle the North of England Steam Ship Owners' Association protested on 16 February against the Company's excessive dues as well as against the threatened admission of bulk petroleum and suggested the construction of a second canal in order to avert danger to other users. Further protests followed from West Hartlepool on 29 February, from Sunderland on 1 March, from Leith and Hull on 10 March, from the

[1] *Correspondence respecting the Passage of Petroleum in Bulk through the Suez Canal* (C-6556 of 1892), 6, 10.
[2] *The Times*, 8 March 1892, 4 iii, M. Samuel, 'Petroleum in Bulk in the Suez Canal'.
[3] Ibid., 28 December 1891, 5 vi.
[4] *Correspondence respecting the Passage of Petroleum in Bulk through the Suez Canal* (C-6556 of 1892), 47–56.

United Kingdom Chamber of Shipping on 16 March, from Liverpool on 18 March, from Belfast on 22 March, from Glasgow and Cardiff on 28 March and from Bristol on 7 April.[1] Those protests represented 250 owners of over 5,000,000 tons of shipping but did not include the P. & O. On 24 March Captain Grice-Hutchinson, the Conservative M.P. for Aston Manor, raised the question in the Commons and so began the attack on the Company and on Samuel from a third flank. Samuel was defended only by *The Economist*[2] and *The Nautical Magazine*[3] which were however the highest authorities on the commercial and technical aspects of the question. 'It looks, indeed, very much as if the tank steamer were destined to do for the case-trade what Stephenson's locomotive did for the coaching industry.'[2]

The technical attack on behalf of the shipowners was mounted by the eminent chemists Sir Frederick Abel and Professor Boverton Redwood in their report of 7 May which carried great weight with those outside their profession, emphasized the risk to other shipping and deemed the Company's regulations insufficient. Salisbury refused on 16 May to interfere in the regulation of traffic by the Company because he was a firm believer in freedom of transit. A substantial command paper was presented to the House on 10 June to justify the Government's policy of non-intervention.[4] Between 12 May and 21 June nineteen different M.P.s had asked thirty questions on the subject, fourteen being from Conservatives, nine from Liberals and seven from Irish M.P.s. The campaign against the use of the Canal by tankers was the first such agitation in history. In so far as it was a defence of the case-oil trade of Standard Oil its failure did not envenom Anglo-American relations because Standard Oil had fallen from favour in the U.S.A. Nevertheless it ensured the highest possible standards of safety for the new traffic in the Provisional Regulations introduced by the Company on 1 July in the first supplement to its Navigation Regulations. Its combination with an agitation against tolls may have encouraged the general meeting of shareholders on 31 May to accept the first reduction of toll since 1885. The Royal Dutch Company secured the exclusion of Samuel's tanks from the Dutch East Indies, opened its first refinery on the harbourless east coast of Sumatra and began the export of 'Crown oil' on 2 April to nearby Penang. The prospect of competition drove its shares below par from mid-April and made its new capital issue of 15 June a total failure.

The tanker *Murex* was launched on 27 May 1892 and left West Hartlepool on 26 July under Captain John R. Coundon. It embarked paraffin at Batum

---

[1] *Correspondence respecting the Passage of Petroleum in Bulk through the Suez Canal*, 57–70.
[2] *The Economist*, 9 January 1892, 37, 883, 'Petroleum in Bulk and the Suez Canal'.
[3] G. H. Little, 'Petroleum in Bulk to the East, Via the Suez Canal', *Nautical Magazine* (March 1892), 208–17. Idem, 'Transport of Petroleum through the Suez Canal', *Nautical Magazine* (June 1892), 497–504. Idem, 'Improvements in Petroleum in Bulk Steamers', *Nautical Magazine* (March 1893), 193–201. Idem, 'Petroleum Traffic through the Suez Canal', *Nautical Magazine* (April 1893), 297.
[4] *Correspondence respecting the Passage of Petroleum in Bulk through the Suez Canal.*

and passed through the Canal on 24 August en route to Singapore and Bang-kok, the first such transit by a tanker. The *Murex* was classified as a first-class risk in Category A.1.100 at Lloyd's and became the first of a fleet designed by Flannery to the Canal Company's Regulations. It established the pattern followed by all later tankers until the 1930s. Its crew accommodation was forward and its tanks amidships. Its engine-room was aft rather than in the usual central location and was separated from the tanks by a coffer-dam of two transverse bulwarks. Its five cargo tanks each had a maximum capacity of 200 tons and were in non-communicating compartments separated by water-ballast tanks which were filled before entering the Canal so that the tanker might be lightened if necessary by pumping out water rather than oil so as to avoid any pollution of the Canal or jettisoning of cargo. The Company's Regulations also insisted that tankers should be convoyed by a tug-tanker during their transit and that their cargo should exclude products with a flash-point below 73 °F (23 °C), the standard English flash-point for petro-leum by the Abel close-test of 1879. Those regulations recognized that paraffin had a high flash-point of 100–120 °F. and was less dangerous to transport than crude oil: in effect they limited the cargo of tankers to refined products and so excluded crude oil from the Canal.

The *Murex* carried oil for the lamps of Asia around half the world on a voyage which proved that the bulk oil trade was no more dangerous than the coal or grain trade. Its voyage produced an enormous fall in prices in the autumn of 1892. In Singapore Samuel's agents, Syme & Co., opened the first petroleum tank station in Asia on 16 September 1892[1] and offered to buy ten cargoes yearly of unmarked paraffin in cases from the Refinery of the Royal Dutch Company, a minority of whose directors favoured negotiations for a sale of the Company to Samuel or to the Rothschilds.[2] Standard Oil itself did not seek to follow Samuel's example of bulk shipment and was deterred from direct investment in Sumatra by an Achinese raid in 1893 on the Royal Dutch Refinery. It established however from 1893 its own Asiatic Stations as whole-sale outlets, with the largest of the former importers as its agents. Above all, it concentrated increasingly on the market of Europe which Russia had sur-rendered in exchange for the market of Asia, perhaps by mutual agreement in 1891. Thus it increased its exports from 43 per cent of its production in 1892 to 57 per cent in 1894 and maintained its power to fix prices both in the U.S.A. and in Europe. The shipments of oil from Batum to Asia, especially to India, rose markedly in 1893. The exports of case-oil did not fall but rose: bulk shipments of case-oil through the Canal rose by 55·5 per cent in 1893 while the imports of case-oil to Port Said more than doubled and were captured by Russia from America. The ten tanker transits through the Canal between 24 August 1892 and 20 May 1893 paid the Company an average of £1,168 on each passage but carried only a very small share of the total oil exports

[1] W. Makepeace, *One Hundred Years of Singapore* (1921), ii. 97, 601.
[2] F. C. Gerretson, *History of the Royal Dutch* (1953), i. 149–56.

from Batum. Nevertheless the cost-cutting innovation of bulk transport had been made through rational organization by Samuel in the very prime of his life. He placed eight new tankers on the Suez route from Batum to Asia with the supporting capital of ten Eastern merchant houses organized in the Tank Syndicate of 1893 and the short-term financial support of the Chartered Bank of India. Those tankers carried oil but were themselves steamships, the largest steam-tankers in the world. They were built by William Gray & Co. of West Hartlepool, by Armstrong Mitchell & Co. of Newcastle and by Sir James Laing & Co. Ltd. of Sunderland, whose head had been a director of the Canal Company since 1884 and the first chairman of its London Committee. They helped to make the building of oil tankers a speciality of the North-East coast. They were operated with the day-to-day advice of only their designer, Flannery, but brought no danger to other shipping using the Canal because their Chinese crews served under a discipline almost as strict as that on board a warship. The Regulations of the Canal Company were exacting enough in the interests of safety to be upheld by the Mixed Court of Alexandria in its judgments of 17 January 1893 and 17 May 1894. After unloading their paraffin at the oil tanks established from Yokohama to Bombay the tankers were ventilated, steam-cleaned and whitewashed. They then returned with bulk cargoes of tea, coffee, sugar, rice and tapioca, which remained unaffected by the outward cargo. Thus Samuel earned homeward as well as outward freights while the Canal Company received full dues rather than ballast dues. Samuel became a large-scale shipowner as well as a general merchant and earned profits from freights as well as from cargo. He became a great oil-carrier and the operator of the largest and most modern fleet of tankers in the world. Increasingly a merchant-banker rather than a merchant he became Sheriff of London in 1894 and bought a landed estate near Maidstone in 1895.[1]

The attempt to distribute paraffin in drums failed because the consumer insisted on the traditional tin and refused to supply his own container.[2] Samuel could carry oil in bulk but could not sell it in bulk. He was compelled to re-introduce tins and to begin their manufacture in Asia, although Singapore did not develop a tin-plate industry but exported its tin and imported its tin cans. He was able to sell at a price including that of the tin, which seems to have been even more desired than its contents. The tin can was assimilated into the domestic economy of monsoon Asia more readily and quickly than its contents because it was an all-purpose receptacle similar in its manifold uses in transport, marketing, manufacture and building to the all-purpose crops of Asia. In the arid zone of Western Asia it also began to displace the traditional water pot from the 1890s. The paraffin can thus became the great symbol of the acceptance of the technical veneer of Western civilization by the indigenous civilizations of Asia. Because it was sold with the precious container the oil of the West competed effectively with the cheaper vegetable oils of Asia from the 1880s, releasing oil-seeds for shipment from India to Europe. Oil became

---

[1] Henriques, 121. [2] Ibid., 138.

a chief agent in the spread of a money economy in the peasant world. It satisfied a demand unaffected by the vagaries of fashion and spread to backward as well as to advanced communities. It thus became the most widely diffused of products, the first commodity with a true world market and the basis of the first world marketing organizations.

Samuel's venture encouraged the Burmah Oil Company and the Royal Dutch Company to begin large-scale production in Asia from 1893. The Government of India preferred Burmese to Russian oil as it preferred Assam to Chinese tea and Punjab to American wheat: it therefore excluded Samuel from both Rangoon and Aden. Burmese oil was free from import duty, competed more with Russian than with American oil and began to oust its rival from Calcutta and the Ganges valley. The Royal Dutch Company began to export oil to China from 1894, paid its first dividend for 1894 and raised its dividend from 8 to 44 per cent for 1895. It ordered its first tanker in 1896 in order to profit by Samuel's experience and to eliminate the long haul from Batum as well as the double payment of Canal dues. After the failure of negotiations with Samuel in 1896 the Company began to build its first tanks at Hong Kong and Shanghai in 1897: thus it undertook the expansion of its operations from the well to the wick and supplied the outer provinces of the Dutch East Indies with their first great staple export. Witte's aspiration to bring the transport of Russian oil under the Russian flag led him in 1896 to confine the coastal trade from Batum to Vladivostock to Russian vessels, so devalorizing the two large tanks erected at Vladivostock by the Tank Syndicate. To retain the loyalty of its members Samuel transformed the syndicate into a private company, The Shell Transport and Trading Company Ltd., on 18 October 1897.

Samuel also began to seek in Borneo from 1896 for oil which would be independent of both Russia and B.N.I.T.O. After the investment of £1,000,000 a gusher was brought in in 1898, so extending Samuel's interests from transport to production and placing him in a similar position to the Royal Dutch Company which had expanded from production into transport. The oil of Borneo proved to be too heavy for paraffin and best suited for fuel oil whose markets were limited, unlike the large market for lamp-oil, and lay west rather than east of the Canal. Samuel therefore launched in 1898 his first oil-burning tanker and a campaign to convert the Navy from coal to liquid fuel. The assistance of a Shell tug in refloating on 15 February 1898 the stranded warship *Victorious* at Port Said earned Samuel a knighthood in lieu of a salvage fee of £5,000[1] and shamed the Canal Company into ordering a tug of 3,000 H.P. or more power than any other in the world. In April 1899 Samuel sent his first shipment of fuel oil from Borneo through the Canal without the permission of the Canal Company for trial by the Navy. He bought land at Port Ibrahim in 1898 and had three oil tanks built there in 1899 by Worms & Co. He began to import fuel oil from Borneo in 1899 and loaded his first

---

[1] Henriques, 228–9.

oil-burning steam-tanker with 200 tons of fuel oil at Suez on 23 December 1899 for the Suez–Colombo voyage.[1] He failed to develop either the internal market of Egypt or the oil-bunkering trade on a large scale, despite the marked price-differential for oil between Alexandria and Suez. Increasingly he became interested in the development of oil-fields in British possessions because the Navy would abandon British coal only for British oil. His enterprise had brought a new trade to the Canal and a new industry to Suez and had begun to tilt the balance weighed down by coal away from Port Said.

[1] J. Charles-Roux, *L'Isthme et le Canal de Suez* (1901), ii. 198.

25

THE PARTITION OF ASIA AND AFRICA, 1895–1903

I N the 1890s the religious revival which had begun in the 1830s ended and all the creeds collapsed. In the resulting void flowered militarism, navalism, racialism, imperialism,[1] the progress-ethic, the religion of sport, the Social Darwinism of Pareto, the machine-theology of Kipling[2] and the political Zionism of Herzl. The new culture identified space with the Deity[3] and produced the geopolitics of Ratzel, Kjellen and Mackinder, the frontier-theory of Turner and the continental aspirations of Rhodes. It measured the comparative status of empires by the area they occupied, extended the definition of the coastwise trade as well as of territorial waters and renewed the quest for the ends of the earth. It reinterpreted Asia in terms of distance and divided it not merely into 'the Further East' and the 'Nearer East' in 1891[4] but also more precisely in 1894[5] into 'the Near East', 'the Far East' and 'the Central East', which became in 1902 'the Middle East'. Thus the complex societies of Asia were reduced to geometrical order in the mind of the West and became the object of dominion rather than of conversion. The sympathy cherished in the West since the time of the Romantics for the East died away in a European revolt against the Oriental mirage.[6] Inspired by its new faiths Europe began to penetrate from the coastlands into the heart of Asia four centuries after the voyage of da Gama and assumed the whole continent to be its predestined province. In that expansion the Canal became a route of world empire as never before while Britain made growing use of the Cape and Canadian routes to the East.

The Canadian Pacific Railway linked the Pacific port nearest to China with the Atlantic port nearest to Europe. It became the basis for James Huddart's 'all-red route' around the Empire, projected in 1894–5 but denied a transatlantic mail contract.[7] As an imperial highway the C.P.R. became essentially an extension of sea communications rather than an independent link in itself: it would have entailed for its full use an uneconomic diversion of force away

---

[1] C. G. Robertson, 'A Note on the New Imperialism', *Time* (March 1891), 227–33.

[2] Kipling, 'The Bridge-Builders' (1893); 'The Liner She's a Lady' (1894); 'M'Andrews' Hymn (1894); 'Romance' (1894) ('The King', 1896); 'The Ship that Found Herself' (1895); '·007' (1897); *The Day's Work* (London, Macmillan, 1899).

[3] H. Spencer, *Facts and Comments* (London, Williams, 1902), 204–5, 'Ultimate Questions'.

[4] J. L. Kipling, *Beast and Man in India* (London, Macmillan, 1891), 84.

[5] G. N. Curzon, *Problems of the Far East* (London, Longmans, 1894), 7.

[6] S. Reinach, 'Le Mirage Oriental', *L'Anthropologie* (1893), 551.

[7] J. H. Hamilton, 'The "All-Red Route", 1893–1953: a History of the Trans-Pacific Mail Service between British Columbia, Australia and New Zealand', *British Columbia Historical Quarterly* (January–April 1956), 41–8.

from the Cape route. As a trade-route it could not compete with the all-sea routes via the Cape or the Canal except in the carriage of such high-priced commodities as tea and silk which could bear the cost of transhipment. For passengers it could serve only as a seasonal route, being as intolerable in winter as the Red Sea was in summer. At best the C.P.R. could offer an alternative but high-cost route: at the worst it could give another hostage in war to the military power of the U.S.A. The P. & O. thus survived the colonial challenge to its monopoly and retained the passenger traffic of Australia as well as of India. It benefited by Sutherland's close links with the China merchant-houses, which formed the China Association at its London offices in April 1889. It enjoyed an incalculable advantage over the C.P.R. in the location of its head office in the capital of the empire. Sir James Fergusson, who had been Governor of Bombay (1880–5) and had become a director of the P. & O. as well as of the Royal Mail Steam Packet Company, resigned from the board to become Postmaster-General in 1891 and defended Pender as well as the P. & O. against attack.[1] Thus the P. & O. remained the 'Unofficial Fleet' of the Empire[2] and paid a regular annual dividend of 10 per cent from 1890 to 1900.[3]

After the main Shanghai and Japan mails had been diverted to the C.P.R. the P. & O. ended in 1894 the direct service from London to the Far East which it had begun in 1880. It was stimulated by the competition of the C.P.R. and the construction of the Trans-Siberian Railway[4] to accelerate its carriage of mail to Shanghai. Between 1889 and 1893 it accelerated the London–Melbourne mail by 9 per cent to 32 days 9 hours, the London–Bombay mail by 15 per cent to 14 days but the London–Shanghai mail by 22·6 per cent from $37\frac{1}{2}$ days to 29 days. The P. & O. *Caledonia*, which coaled at Port Said on 11 November 1894 with 602 tons in 70 minutes to break all previous records, reached Bombay in $12\frac{1}{2}$ days from Marseilles. The P. & O. also cooperated in the military reforms which in 1894 abolished the separate military commands of the three Presidencies of India. It began to transport troops to India in mail-boats which it chartered to the Government for the first time in the 1894–5 season. Thus it secured the entry to the trooping service which it had sought in vain in the 1860s. In the 1895–6 season the British India Line was admitted to share in the service, which from the 1896–7 season was carried on wholly by the private enterprise of the two rival lines. Thenceforward the fleet of five thirty-year old Government transports was scrapped, so ending the conflict between the Army which had travelled in the ships and the Navy which had operated them. The P. & O. suffered a reduction in its subsidy but retained the supreme privilege of the India mail contract

[1] H. Heaton, 'Imperial Telegraph System. Cabling to India and Australia', *Contemporary Review* (April 1893), 539, 545.
[2] E. Arnold, *Seas and Lands* (1891), 524, 13 February 1891.
[3] T. Skinner, *Stock Exchange Year Book for 1901*, 820.
[4] *The Times*, 25 February 1897, 12v. 'The Siberian Railway as the Shortest Road to the Far East'.

and even secured in 1896 special railway trains from Calais to link up with its mail-boat berth at Marseilles. From 1 January 1898 its vessels called at Marseilles on the homeward as well as on the outward voyage so that it could dispense from 1900 with the mail service maintained between Venice and Egypt since 1872. Its passenger-fares had moved closer to those on other mail-routes apart from the North Atlantic but still remained high. It proudly maintained its leisurely pace,[1] its 'chain-gang regulations', 'the comforts of a coolie-ship and the prices of a palace'.[2] It paid its Canal dues all the more willingly because they replaced the barrier against competition formerly provided by the isthmus.

A new era in the competition for empire in Asia was ushered in by the Sino-Japanese War. The successes of Japan and especially its capture of Port Arthur by storm at prodigious cost alarmed the new Tsar, whose voyage to the East in 1891 had confirmed his belief in Russia's mission in Asia. Two torpedo-boats were sent by Russia at full speed to the East and were enabled by the Canal Company to complete the transit to Suez on 24 December 1894 in $8\frac{3}{4}$ hours, the fastest passage on record. The war falsified Curzon's prediction in 1894 that the British might emulate the Mongols and Manchus in the conquest of China but justified Charles Pearson's prophecy in 1893 of the doom of the white man's empire. 'The black and yellow belt, which always encircles the globe between the Tropics, will extend its area, and deepen its colour with time... We shall wake to find ourselves elbowed and hustled, and perhaps even thrust aside by peoples whom we looked down upon as servile, and thought of as bound always to minister to our needs.'[3] The war demonstrated Japan's success in adopting the techniques of Europe and in militarizing her peasantry in self-defence against the naval power of the West. The shock of defeat by the 'dwarfs' of Japan shattered the confidence of the mandarin bureaucracy in the past 4,000 years of Chinese history. It deprived the middle kingdom of its only effective element of national cohesion, purpose and direction and transformed its status from a receiver of tribute into a seeker of alliances. The Powers of Europe aspired to reduce China to full equality with other states and sanctioned missions by chambers of commerce from 1895 to examine the market-potential of the land of '400 million customers'. Japan's victory led the Admiralty to sanction the construction of first-class cruisers of the *Diadem* class in its 1895–6 programme and of first-class battle-ships of the *Canopus* class in its 1896–7 programme, all with a reduced draught so that they might use the Canal. Thus the Admiralty pursued the adaptation of the Navy to the use of the Canal which had begun with the approval of the *Centurion* class in 1891 and of the *Renown* class in 1893: it simultaneously increased the value of the Cape route by the construction of harbour works from 1896 at the Cape and Mauritius.

---

[1] Kipling, 'The Exiles' Line' (1892).   [2] Idem, *From Sea to Sea* (1900), i. 261.

[3] C. H. Pearson, *National Life and Character. A Forecast* (London, Macmillan, 1893), 64, 85. A. C. Lyall, 'Permanent Dominion in Asia', *Nineteenth Century* (September 1895), 381–96.

The Sino-Japanese War stimulated the economic expansion of Japan which exacted an indemnity of 50 per cent more than the cost of the war and so financed its industrialization for the next generation. Japan raised its domestic production of cotton yarn above its imports in 1891 and its exports thereof above its imports in 1897. It raised its output of machine-made silk above that of hand-made silk in 1894 and its exports thereof above its imports in 1899. From 1896 its shipbuilding industry was fostered by the grant of loans at low interest-rates and its ocean shipping by the grant of operating subsidies. The Nippon Yusen Kaisha, which had been established by the Mitsubishi interests in 1885, secured admission to the Bombay-Japan Shipping Conference in 1896 after a three-year rate-war waged by the P. & O. and made Japan thenceforward the largest single foreign market for Indian cotton in place of Germany. It also began in 1896 three long-distance services to Seattle, Australia and Europe. Its regular service from Yokohama to London and Antwerp via the Canal compelled the P. & O. to inaugurate from 1896 an intermediate service from London to Japan. It increased the Canal tonnage under the Japanese flag from 0·5 per cent of the total tonnage in 1896 to 1·3 per cent in 1897 and to 2·8 per cent in 1898. It raised Japan from the eleventh client of the Canal in 1896 to the seventh in 1898, when its tonnage surpassed that of Russia, Norway, Denmark, Italy and Spain. The Nippon Yusen Kaisha ranked in 1899 as the thirteenth client-line of the Canal, immediately after the Shell Company in twelfth place. Its subsidized mail tonnage formed a higher proportion of Japan's Canal tonnage than such tonnage did of that of any other power except Spain. Thus the Canal first came into continuous use by an Asiatic shipping line as well as by Japanese soldiers from 1891 and by Japanese cruisers from 1897. Unlike the Chinese line of 1881, the Nippon Yusen Kaisha worked in cooperation with European merchants, especially with Samuel, Samuel & Co., which had supplied much of the wartime needs of the Japanese Government. Marcus Samuel became the London banker of that Government and floated its first sterling loan in 1899. Thus an Anglo-Japanese entente became a political possibility in reply to the Russo-Chinese entente established in 1896.

The reawakening of Asia was marked by peasant-risings in 1896 in Shantung, the Philippines, and Madagascar as well as in Rhodesia. The consequent increase in troops using the Canal ended the dominance of non-military passengers in 1888–94 and raised the total number of passengers above 200,000 in 1895 and above 300,000 in 1896. The 198,520 military passengers helped to mask the decline in commercial traffic through the waterway in 1896 but deepened the depression of 1897 when the number of passengers was reduced by 38 per cent. The revolt of the Philippines compelled Spain to send 27,501 troops through the Canal in 1896, or tenfold her average annual number. After the Ethiopians under Menelik defeated the Italians in 1895 with the aid of French rifles and Russian doctors Italy sent 74,094 troops through the Canal, supplied 4·6 per cent of the total tonnage for 1896 and displaced the Netherlands as the fourth client of the Canal for that year. Italy also decreed the effective blockade of the Red Sea without even notifying the Powers, contrary to international custom. Despite that blockade and an English diversion in the Sudan Italy suffered an overwhelming defeat at Adowa on 1 March 1896 and was forced to abandon the 'protectorate' established in 1889. Italy's defeat precipitated the decision of the British Government on 12 March to advance to Dongola, with the diplomatic support of Germany for such an ambitious anti-French move. Kitchener's entry into Dongola on 23 September laid the basis of a new Anglo-Egyptian empire in the Sudan and ended fourteen years of vacillation over the question of evacuation. From 1896 England accepted its mission in Egypt as a permanent obligation and began another renaissance of life in a land which had already witnessed ten renaissances. The beginning of the construction of the Aswan Dam made British engineers and officials into servants of the Nile rather than of the Public Debt. France became more hostile than ever to Britain and sought by the conquest of Madagascar to acquire a base athwart both the Cape and Suez routes as well as a tropical Normandy.

The rapid expansion of gold-mining on the Rand powered the economic boom of 1892–6 in South Africa and encouraged Jameson's raid into the Transvaal in a bid to bring the gold mines under the British flag as the diamond fields had been annexed in 1871. The failure of the raid was regretted by the passengers in the British ship who cheered Jameson and his fellow-officers as he passed through the Canal on his way from Durban to Plymouth (21 January–23 February 1896). The Kaiser sent a telegram of congratulations to President Kruger and then sought to repair the resulting damage to Anglo-German relations by warning the British ambassador in Berlin on 4 March that Russia and France would attack in concert Persia and the Suez Canal and could only be discouraged by a gesture of solidarity from England with the Triple Alliance. Paul Cambon, the French ambassador at Constantinople, was asked by the French Foreign Minister to suggest a demonstration in the Levant as a reply to the British decision to advance in the Sudan. He proposed on 31 March a plan for the occupation of Port Said as the sole point on the Egyptian coast where a French demonstration could be effective with the aid of the French outlanders of the isthmus.[1] That bold and imaginative plan was inspired by Jameson's raid and justified the Kaiser's suspicions of France but paid no respect to the rights of either the Khedive or of the Powers under the Convention of Constantinople. The ambiguous status of that Convention was used by Prince Lobanov, the Russian Foreign Minister, to bring pressure on England and to aggravate Anglo-French relations. Lobanov offered the French ambassador in Petersburg on 29 March his most energetic support to secure the neutralization of the Canal under the Convention[2] and told the British

---

[1] *Documents Diplomatiques Francaises*, 1 ère série, xii, 550, No. 362, Cambon à Bourgeois, 31 Mars 1896.

[2] Ibid., xii, 545, No. 361, Montebello à Bourgeois, 31 Mars 1896.

ambassador on 4 April that the neutrality of the Canal would remain illusory until the British had evacuated Egypt. The French ambassador in Berlin was less impressed than the French Foreign Minister by Lobanov's sudden interest in the Canal but nevertheless recommended on 8 April that France should ask England to abandon her reservation of 1885 and 1887.[1] Salisbury expressed his willingness to abandon that reservation on 15 July, three months after France had approved a raid upon Fashoda by Marchand. Thus France committed herself to a race with England for trans-African dominion as well as for Mediterranean supremacy and to an ultimate collision on the Upper Nile.

Britain's determination to remain in Egypt was reinforced by the crises in Anglo-Turkish relations caused by the successive Armenian massacres which began in August 1894, fifteen years after the failure of the Cyprus project of 1878-9, and were resumed in October 1895 and August 1896. Those crises brought the 'Near East' as a term into general use in 1896. They forced Britain to recognize that Turkey had passed under Russian influence and that Constantinople could no longer be defended against the opposition of Russia, Turkey and France. Salisbury failed to rouse the country as Gladstone had in 1878-80 in protest against the massacre of a Christian community by the Turks. He was compelled finally to liquidate Palmerston's policy of 1833 as well as his own policy of 1878 and to fall back upon Egypt as the guardian of the road to India. The permanent occupation of Egypt was recommended by General Ardagh, the new Director of Military Intelligence, on 13 October 1896[2] as well as by the Director of Naval Intelligence, who argued that Russia could be checked by a fleet based on Alexandria, as the French fleets were by the fleets based on Gibraltar and Malta, and that the Canal could be blocked, guarded and commanded if Egypt were strongly held and Alexandria turned into a naval base comparable to Gibraltar and Malta. 'If there was no Suez Canal, it would not be long before there was no India.'[3] Thus the decision to remain in Egypt, to advance into the Sudan and to maintain control of the Canal reduced the Indian Empire almost to a dependency of the Canal and completely inverted Palmerston's assumption that India's security depended on the absence of such a Canal. The Navy adapted its strategy to the waterway twenty-seven years after its opening. The guardian of the Canal was to be Britain rather than the Sultan, who had fallen under Russian influence, had ceased to rely on British protection and could no longer fulfil his duties under the Convention of Constantinople. The function of Egypt as 'the natural resting-place, the natural stepping-stone, between England and India'[4] re-emerged in proposals for the construction of an Indo-Egyptian Railway as an alternative to a Euphrates Valley Railway and as an eastern counterpart to

---

[1] *Documents Diplomatiques Francaises* 1ère série, xii, 563-4, No. 370, Herbette à Bourgeois, 8 Avril 1896.   [2] A. J. Marder, *British Naval Policy 1880-1905* (1940), 572-3.

[3] A. J. Marder, 247, 12 November 1895; 579-80, 13 October 1896, Captain Lewis A. Beaumont, Director of Naval Intelligence.

[4] Hansard, *Commons Debates*, 6 July 1896, 811, Lord George Hamilton.

the all-red route through Canada. The construction of a 2,400-mile railway on the Indian broad gauge from Port Said to Basra and Karachi with a possible extension to Singapore, might so develop Port Said as to compensate the Canal Company for any loss of traffic by the Canal.[1] An alternative railway from Alexandria via Basra and Kuwait to Karachi might cross the Canal at Ismailia either by subway or by a swing-bridge[2] and could transfer the commercial frontier of the Indian Empire from Sind to Alexandria at one sweep. Such proposals would have benefited the Moslem community of India, especially of Sind, and might have established a new Indian troop depot at the northern end of the Canal between Port Said and the Syrian frontier.[3] They represented a new form of overland route, with its terminal port shifted eastwards from Brindisi to Port Said. Freights would have been prohibitive by comparison with sea-transport and would have made the route even less economic than the Euphrates Valley Railway.[4] Theodore Herzl, who founded the World Zionist Organization in 1897, even concluded that the Zionist cause would benefit if the British were forced to leave Egypt and lose control of the Canal so that a modern Jewish Palestine with a Jewish railway from Jaffa to the Persian Gulf might replace the Canal as the British road to India.[5] During his visit to Palestine in 1898 Herzl remembered his ambition at the age of ten to achieve a Lessepsian work and construct the Panama Canal: he was more impressed by the Suez Canal 'this shimmering strip of water extending into infinity' and by the colossal will it symbolized than by the Acropolis.[6] Thenceforward he sought to replace it by a new route under Jewish control.

The defeat of China by Japan produced the first peasant rising in China since the Tai-Ping Rebellion, a new wave of encroachment by the Powers on China and a marked expansion in the trade and shipping of the Far East. The anti-Christian revolt of the peasants of Shantung enabled Germany to secure Kiaochow and Russia to secure Port Arthur. The infuriated Japanese began to build up a large navy and made the Pacific Ocean the focus of a gathering storm. The battle of the concessions for the development of the resources of China encouraged Sutherland of the P. & O. to hope that China would break the monopoly of India by developing the cultivation of oil-seeds, indigo and jute, and Charles-Roux to hope that China would provide an incalculable reserve for the future of the Canal.[7] Between 1894 and 1898 traffic with China and Japan rose by 42 per cent and its share of the total Canal tonnage rose from 16·8 to 20 per cent. The traffic of the Canal benefited especially by the

[1] C. E. D. Black, 'The Railway to India', *Contemporary Review* (April 1895).

[2] A. T. Fraser, 'An Egypto-Assyrian Railway, or the New Overland Route to India', *Journal of the Society of Arts*, 4 September 1896.

[3] C. E. D. Black, 'The Railway to India', *Journal of the Society of Arts*, 7 May 1897.

[4] G. N. Curzon, *Persia and the Persian Question* (1892), i. 637–8.

[5] T. Herzl, *Tagebücher* (Berlin, Jüdischer Verlag, 1922), i. 603–4, 24 März 1897; ii. 275, 18 März 1898.

[6] Ibid., ii. 204, 27 Oktober 1898.

[7] J. Charles-Roux, 'Le Canal de Suez. L'État Actuel-L'Avenir', *Revue de Paris*, 15 Octobre 1899, 792.

entry of Germany on its era of world-policy and the extension of the Teutonic peace to Asia. The Atlantic liners of the North German Lloyd, diverted for a round voyage to the Australian service, became the largest vessels to use the Canal. The *Friedrich der Grosse* made its historic transit in December 1896 with a tonnage of 10,785, or quadruple that of the average transit, and a displacement almost twice as great as the largest ship previously to use the Canal. Its successful passage proved the fears of the transit-service unfounded and encouraged the Lloyd to ask the Company to take immediate steps to deepen the waterway, so beginning a generation of technical pressure on the Company to adapt the Canal to the growing size of ships.[1] The Company welcomed its new giant clients because the *Friedrich der Grosse* had made the historic payment of £2,880 in transit-dues plus passenger-dues.[2] The monopoly of the Bremen line was challenged by the Hamburg American Line which absorbed in 1897 the unprofitable Hamburg–Calcutta Line and discontinued its service. In 1898 the Hamburg American Line exceeded the tonnage of the P. & O. to become the largest shipping line in the world and entered the trade with Asia. The *Andalusia*, which left Hamburg on 25 January 1898, established a monthly cargo service from Hamburg to Shanghai and Yokohama via the Canal. The Hamburg American Line also established the United States and China–Japan Steamship Line in cooperation with R. M. Sloman and T. B. Royden. It absorbed the German Steamship Line which had first carried the German flag through the Canal in 1871 but had failed to secure the mail contract either for China under the 1885 law or for East Africa under the 1890 law. Finally it reached a working agreement with the Lloyd, which doubled the frequency of its mail service to China by arranging with the Hamburg American Line for alternate departures from Hamburg and Bremen. The new fortnightly service began with the *König Albert* which left Bremen on 4 October 1899, paid £3,400 in Canal dues on its 7,195 tons[3] and extended the direct mail service from Shanghai to Yokohama. The Lloyd entered the coasting trade of the Dutch East Indies in 1898 and that of the Bay of Bengal as well as of the South China Sea in 1899. The Hamburg American Line resumed in 1899 the cargo service to Calcutta and Bombay which it had suspended in 1897, and entered in 1900 the coasting and river trade from Shanghai, 'the New York of the East'.[4] Its first specially built mail-steamer, the *Hamburg*, sailed for China on 21 March 1900. It cooperated with the Lloyd until 1903 and so stimulated the Hansa Line to expand its service from 1898 to Rangoon for the carriage of rice to Germany, the largest customer of Burma since 1895.

The German share of the total Canal tonnage rose from 10·9 per cent in 1897 to 15·1 per cent in 1900 while the continued expansion of Dutch and Austrian tonnage further increased the share of Germanic shipping. German

[1] P. Neubaur, *Der Norddeutsche Lloyd, 1857–1907* (Leipzig, Grunow, 1907), i. 206.
[2] P. Neubaur, 'Der Suezkanal, seine Entstehung und seine Entwicklung', *Meereskunde* (1910), 14–16.
[3] G. Steindorff, 'Dreissig Jahre Suezkanal', *Die Woche* (1900), 515.
[4] B. Huldermann, *Albert Ballin* (1922), 129, 6 März 1901.

vessels captured the highest class of passenger traffic to the Far East and began to compete in the cargo trades. Germany began to import phosphates from Christmas Island to Stettin from 1900 and so introduced a new traffic to the Canal. She imported far more than she exported through the Canal and enjoyed a favourable balance of trade only with Japan in Asia. The increase in German tonnage encouraged the election to the board of the Canal Company of the first German director in 1899. George Plate had been a raw cotton merchant since 1870 and the President of the Bremen Cotton Exchange as well as the Chairman of the North German Lloyd since 1892.[1] His election was a further recognition by the Company of the principle that user-interests should be represented on the board. The North German Lloyd rose from the fifth client of the Canal in 1899 to the second in 1901, the Hansa Line from the sixth to the fourth and the Hamburg American Line from the eighteenth to the sixth. The associated trebling of the value of the coal imports from Germany to Port Said between 1900 and 1902 was crowned by the establishment at Port Said in 1902 of the German Coaling Depot, which used British coal in 1902 but imported more coal from Westphalia than from Wales from 1903. The expansion of Germany in Asia was welcomed by England as that of a possible ally against Russia.

The U.S.A. entered the contest for Pacific dominion in its war against Spain which was provoked by the revolt against Spanish rule of Cuba in 1895 and of the Philippines in 1896. The U.S.A. had developed direct steamship links to the Cape from 1893, to Calcutta from 1897 and to the Far East from 1898 via the Canal. Spain was the oldest colonial power in Europe but was virtually denied the wartime use of the Canal by Britain, which permitted Admiral Dewey before the outbreak of the war to use Hong Kong as an American base and to buy British colliers, steamers and coal. British sympathy with the U.S.A. was also reflected in Salisbury's 'living and dying nations' speech on 4 May 1898, three days after Dewey had forced an entry into Manila Bay without the aid of a single ironclad. America's main effort was concentrated against Cuba, where Cervera's fleet was blockaded in Santiago from 29 May and an American attempt to block the harbour entrance on 3 June failed to free any ships to reinforce Dewey. After the U.S. expedition sailed for Cuba from Florida on 12 June the Spanish Government ordered its reserve squadron to Manila via the Canal on 15 June. The U.S.A. thereupon ordered all patrol vessels from its northern coasts to help in the blockade of Cuba and decided that it could not weaken or divide its fleet off Santiago before Cervera's fleet had been defeated and Cuba conquered. Its War Board first advised Dewey to be prepared temporarily to abandon Manila Bay on the arrival of the Spanish squadron but then decided to despatch three ironclads if necessary to reinforce Dewey and announced on 24 June that a fast squadron would cross the Atlantic and bombard Spain's Mediterranean ports if its squadron entered the Canal. Hay, the ambassador of the U.S.A. in

[1] P. Neubaur, *Der Norddeutsche Lloyd* (1907), ii. 603–4, George Plate.

London, was instructed on 25 June to ask Salisbury whether the Canal might be used by warships of the U.S.A., a non-signatory power to the Convention of Constantinople.

The Spanish reserve squadron under Admiral Camara left Cadiz on 16 June, passed both Gibraltar and Malta and arrived at Port Said on 26 June, four days after American troops had landed near Santiago. The Navy Board thereupon announced on 27 June that a U.S. squadron was to leave without delay to harass the coasts of Spain, hoping that the Spanish Government would recall Camara and that the Canal Company would obstruct Camara's passage on the grounds of interference with navigation. The Canal Company demanded the payment of the dues of £52,000 in cash and in advance so delaying Camara at Port Said. Above all, the Government of Egypt on the application of the U.S. Consul at Port Said on 27 June forbade the supply of coal to the squadron and prevented the engagement of stokers in Port Said until a decision had been reached on the question of principle involved in its passage. The State Department heard from Salisbury that there was no distinction between signatory and non-signatory powers in their right to use the Canal, but found from an examination of the Convention that it could not protest against the passage of the Spanish fleet through the waterway lest it should establish a precedent debarring its own warships from the use of the Canal en route to the Far East.[1] The Government of Egypt decided that the squadron must state its destination before entering the Canal. It then refused on 29 June to permit the supply of coal except for a return voyage to the nearest home port in a most restrictive interpretation of international law. By 30 June the Canal dues had been paid but all the 20,000 tons of coal in Port Said had been quietly bought by the U.S. Consul,[2] so limiting the Spaniards to the 7,000 tons on board their own Trasatlantic liner-colliers. On the arrival of two more Spanish colliers at Port Said on 30 June the Spaniards began coaling from their own colliers. The Government forbade them to do so and ordered them to leave port because they had greatly exceeded the 24-hours' limit laid down in the Convention. The Spaniards thereupon stated that their ships needed repairs and began discharging coal to effect repairs.[3] On 1 July Camara sent two transports to Suez but was refused permission to send local colliers from Port Said with them so that they might coal in the Red Sea. The Government refused to permit repairs and compelled Camara on 1 July to move outside the harbour of Port Said with his eleven ships. In the Commons that evening Michael Davitt asked whether Egypt or Britain was responsible for the long stay of the belligerent warships in Port Said contrary to the Canal Convention. Curzon used a Foreign Office memorandum of 28 June, which concluded that it had never been distinctly stated whether the Convention was or was not in operation, and replied that the provisions of the

[1] *New York Times*, 28 June 1898, 2 ii–iii, 'Camara and the Suez Canal'.
[2] Ibid., 1 July, 1 vii.
[3] *The Times*, 1 July, 5 ii.

Convention had never been brought into operation and that the question was one primarily for the Egyptian Government.

After Camara's squadron coaled from their own colliers in heavy seas beyond the three-miles' limit off Port Said Cervera's squadron made a sortie on 3 July from Santiago without fear or hope and was destroyed, freeing the American fleet from its close confinement. Camara returned to Port Said on 4 July and was again requested to leave within twenty-four hours. He then decided to send back to Spain three destroyers, which could not weather the monsoon of the Indian Ocean, and to take the remainder through the Canal in the hope of refuelling in a Red Sea port. The Government allowed on 5 July two destroyers to take on twenty tons of coal each and a third to be repaired in Port Said after exacting a written guarantee that they would return direct to Port Mahon, the nearest Spanish port. The Spanish squadron then passed through the Canal on 5–6 July after being delayed for ten days. The Government had almost exhausted its range of pretexts but could not deny entrance point-blank. It nevertheless gave the squadron notice on 6 July to quit Suez within twenty-four hours and refused to permit the supply of coal at Suez, compelling Camara to proceed seven miles out to sea outside territorial waters. After Camara's entry into the Canal Commodore Watson was detached from service off Santiago on 7 July and ordered to cross the Atlantic in the hope that he might earn enough on his way through the Mediterranean, perhaps by the capture of Cadiz, to pay his Canal tolls.[1] The Spanish Government then decided to recall Camara's squadron to protect the Canary Islands and the homeland against Watson's depredations. On 8 July Camara received his recall orders before Watson was even ready to sail and re-entered the Canal.[2] His implicit confession of the failure of his mission freed Dewey from the threat of attack from the rear and permitted Watson to postpone his departure. His squadron returned through the Canal on 9–10 July and was allowed on 10 July to transfer 600 tons of coal from a collier in the harbour of Port Said on the written assurance of Camara that they were returning home. On 11 July the squadron left Port Said after two weeks of sustained obstruction.

England had virtually denied coal and the effective use of the Canal to the Spanish warships.[3] Her actions implied a new legal thesis of the refusal of coal to a belligerent and furthered the assimilation in law of coal to armaments of war as well as of Port Said to an Egyptian harbour in regard to the coaling of belligerents. She had been forced to act through Egypt and to use her control of the Canal rather than of Gibraltar or Malta in order to harass Spain and favour the U.S.A. She had acted as the guardian of the Canal rather than of the Canal Convention. She had made herself the sole interpreter of the

[1] *New York Times*, 8 July 1898, 1 vii.
[2] Ibid., 9 July, 6 iii, 'The Return of Camara'.
[3] L. Le Fur, 'Espagne et États-Unis. Rapports entre les Belligérants et les Neutres', *Revue Générale de Droit International Public* (1899), 216–19.

Convention, using it or disregarding it in the sole interests of herself and the U.S.A.[1] which was not a signatory power like Spain and had shown no intention of being bound by it. The Convention was used to force the Spanish squadron out of the Canal ports because it was in operation and to justify British obstruction of that squadron because it was not in operation. Thus Curzon replied on 12 July to T. G. Bowles, an English disciple of Mahan and a crusader for maritime rights, that the Convention was certainly in existence but had not been brought into practical operation owing to the reservations made in 1885 and 1887, so justifying the conclusion that it was 'a dead letter'.[2] Britain's support of the U.S.A. contrasted with the hostility of all Europe to the U.S.A. as the first non-European Power to defeat an imperial power. It was not acknowledged, however, by Mahan who professed to see in Camara's expedition a vagabondage beyond his understanding.[3] It infuriated Madrid which regarded the neutral British as greater enemies of Spain than the belligerent Americans[4] and decided to mount permanent batteries opposite Gibraltar, so creating a new threat to the security of the Mediterranean route at its entrance-strait. The surrender of Santiago on 17 July determined the War Board to re-establish the U.S. Fleet in the Pacific by sending a squadron to Manila via the Canal, escorted by the entire battle-fleet as far as Gibraltar. After the armistice of 12 August over 8,000 Spanish troops were withdrawn from Manila through the Canal while nearly 8,000 American troops were sent there by the same route. The war encouraged the formation of the concept of economic imperialism in terms of the investment of capital in decaying lands[5] and cast the spell of Kipling's realm to the east of Suez over America.[6]

The Anglo-Egyptian reconquest of the Sudan was followed by the fourth and greatest crisis in Anglo-French relations since 1882, centred on the Shilluk village of Fashoda, where Marchand hoisted the tricolour on 12 July and Kitchener the Egyptian flag on 19 September. An English hint on 29 September that a French retreat from Fashoda might be followed by the neutralization of the Nile from its mouth to the lakes on the model of the Canal provoked protests by lawyers such as T. E. Holland against the misuse of the term 'neutralization' in reference to the Canal.[7] French nationalism reached a peak in 1897–8, fifteen years after the loss of Egypt to England, and refused to accept the extension of the Canal's regime to the Nile as an

[1] M. L. Camand, *Étude sur le Régime Juridique du Canal de Suez* (1899), 217–19.

[2] A. S. White, *The Expansion of Egypt* (London, Methuen, 1899), 315.

[3] A. T. Mahan, *Lessons of the War with Spain* (London, Low, 1899), 197. H. W. Wilson, *The Downfall of Spain. Naval History of the Spanish-American War* (London, Low, 1900), 164.

[4] *The Times*, 1 July 1898, 5 ii.

[5] C. A. Conant, 'The Economic Basis of "Imperialism"', *North American Review* (September 1898).

[6] Kipling, *Mandalay* (New York, Buckles, 1899), the first separate edition of the poem which was set once more to music by R. W. Damrosch, 'Mandalay' (Cincinnati, Church, 1898) and by W. Hedgecock, 'On the Road to Mandalay' (London, Sheard, 1899).

[7] *The Times*, 4 October 1898, 4 v; 5 October, 9 iv; 6 October, 5 iii; 8 October, 14 iv–v; 11 October, 5 v; 15 October, 10 iv. A. Loria, *The Economic Foundations of Society* (London, Sonnenschein, 1899), 267.

effective guarantee against England. France was however compelled by the inferiority of its Mediterranean Fleet[1] and by the lack of support from Russia to order Marchand on 3 November to evacuate Fashoda, where the French flag was lowered on 11 December and the Union Jack was hoisted beside the Egyptian flag. Thus the Anglo-Egyptian Condominium of the Sudan was established on 19 January 1899 by Britain in a virtual San Stefano with no succeeding Congress of Berlin. That crisis ended the century-long struggle between England and France for Egypt which had begun in 1798. It aroused French fears of English encroachment on the Canal and brought Suez shares down by 6·6 per cent between 2 September 1898 and 5 January 1899. It encouraged French scholars to resurrect the oral tradition of an offer of the Khedive's shares made in 1875 to the French Government, which was thereby condemned for letting slip an opportunity to win a great French creation wholly to France.[2] One French lawyer assembled together all the sixty pledges given by the British Government since 1881 of its disinterestedness in Egypt,[3] while another recommended in 1899 the neutralization of the Red Sea as well as of Egypt and the creation of an effective and permanent international Canal Commission with police, judicial and diplomatic powers:[4] he even considered the replacement of the Canal Company by an international syndicate[5] under the growing pressure of British aspirations to reclaim the Company for Egypt.[6]

The destruction of the Mahdist dominion by Kitchener's Maxim guns facilitated the recognition that the Canal had shattered the community of Islam.[7] It left the cause of Islam to be taken up in Arabia by the Wahhabi, in Tripoli by the Senussi and in Somaliland by the Salihiya. The reconquest of the Sudan was a military rather than an economic achievement, permitted the British Empire to enlist the Southern Sudanese in its military service and encouraged the revival of projects for a Suakin–Berber Railway,[8] for a Cape-to-Cairo Railway[9] and even for an Alexandria–Shanghai Railway.[10] The trade of the Sudan was drawn towards the ports of the Red Sea and away from the Nile although the new tropical empire was subsidized and serviced by Egypt. The Egyptianization of England proceeded apace in Egypt under 'the great

---

[1] A. J. Marder, *British Naval Policy 1880–1905* (1940), 320–40, 'Fashoda: a Lesson in Sea Power'.

[2] E. Driault, *La Question d'Orient depuis ses Origines jusqu'à nos jours* (Paris, Alcan, 1898), 341. J. Cocheris, *Situation Internationale de l'Égypte et du Soudan* (Paris, Plon, 1903), 74. C. Lesage, *L'Invasion Anglaise en Égypte. L'Achat des Actions de Suez* (Paris, Plon, 1906), 238–9.

[3] J. Cocheris, 531.

[4] M. L. Camand, *Étude sur le Régime Juridique du Canal de Suez* (1899), 249, 259, 289.

[5] Ibid., 259–65.

[6] A. S. White, *The Expansion of Egypt* (1899), 59.

[7] E. Driault, 332.

[8] R. W. Felkin, 'The Soudan Question', *Contemporary Review* (October 1898), 490.

[9] J. T. Wills, 'The Cape to Cairo', *Contemporary Review* (February 1899).

[10] C. A. Moreing, 'An All-British Railway to China', *Nineteenth Century* (September 1899), 486–7.

firm of Messrs. Cromer and Cook that now rule it, in succession of Saladin and Haroun al Rashid'.[1] The P. & O. introduced a new express service from Brindisi to Port Said with the *Osiris* of 1898 which covered the 1,000 miles at a phenomenal average speed of 18–20 knots. The increased security of the Red Sea route to India which Curzon contemplated as Viceroy-elect on his way to govern 'the noblest fabric yet reared by the genius of a conquering nation'[2] left the Persian Gulf as the sole avenue for any maritime threat to India. The geographer Arthur Silva White concluded that Egypt was committed to the protection of the leading maritime Power by an inexorable law of history[3] and urged the necessity of the proclamation in or before 1905 of a British Protectorate throughout the Nile Valley.[4] 'The Suez Canal is the Bosporus of the modern Mediterranean world... The Suez Canal being the nexus between East and West, Egypt necessarily becomes the chief nodal point of International commerce, as well as the principal strategic base of sea-power and world-dominion.'[5] 'Egypt is the fulcrum of our foreign policy. She stands about midway, in Diplomacy and Naval Strategy, between our Eastern and Western Empires... The Colossus that bestrides the isthmus of Suez necessarily holds a commanding position. Egypt is the Gate of the East.'[6]

Britain was equally determined to maintain the security of its dominion in Southern Africa as well as of the Cape route, which still carried 37 per cent of the total value of British trade with the East in 1898. The Boer War revealed the isolation of Britain from the Continent where opinion was largely pro-Boer. The outbreak of the war on 12 October led France to move a large fleet to the Mediterranean and to send it through the Canal on 2 November en route to Madagascar, alarming Curzon for the security of the Persian Gulf. Britain was compelled to settle her differences with Portugal, Germany and the U.S.A. and to divert her Indian troopships from the Canal to the Cape route. The number of outward-bound British troops using the Canal declined from 19,000 in 1898 and 15,000 in 1899 to 5,600 in 1900. The reduction of the minimum safe garrison in India by over 15,000 encouraged Russian expansion towards the Persian Gulf. The P. & O. suffered a reduction in its passenger-revenue but built its first troopships in 1899–1900 with wide decks for parades and a speed of 15 knots. During 1900 British Canal tonnage declined by 14·9 per cent while non-British tonnage rose by 25 per cent. The predominance of British tonnage was such that the total tonnage declined by 1·6 per cent. The British share in the total tonnage nevertheless declined from 66·6 per cent in 1899 to 57·6 per cent in 1900. After the defeat of the organized forces of the Boers the European volunteers returned home, greeted on their

[1] W. C. Ford, *Letters of Henry Adams (1892–1918)* (Boston, Houghton, 1938), 152–3, 6 March 1898.
[2] G. N. Curzon, *Persia* (1892), v, Dedication.
[3] A. S. White, *The Expansion of Egypt* (1899), vii.
[4] Ibid., 59.   [5] Ibid., 76.
[6] Ibid., vii, 440.

passage by the foreign population of Port Said, while President Kruger was saluted by every passing ship, unless it was English, from Jibuti to Suez and was cheered by the passengers on board those which came close enough to the Dutch warship *Gelderland*.[1] In splendid isolation from the Continent Britain established her new empire on a Calcutta–Cairo–Cape Town axis. The establishment of such a land-empire by a sea-power was only possible because the two arms of the ocean pierced into the heart of the island-continent of the Old World while the Suez Canal united the sea-power of the eastern and western oceans[2] and shifted 'the Cape of Good Hope to the head of the Mediterranean'.[3] The Canal provided a maritime interior line of communication as well as the sole bridge between two great oceans, whose possession by Britain could force an enemy to make the great circuit around the Cape but demanded an enormous exertion of force for its retention. Mahan's preference for an offensive rather than a defensive strategy enabled him to recognize the superior importance of Western Asia to Eastern Asia as a strategic centre of overmastering and permanent influence and Suez as the heir to the supreme importance of Alexandria and Constantinople in the past. 'To our own age the like meaning is conveyed more impressively by the word Suez; for in that little isthmus and its canal is concentrated for western Europe the question of access to the greater East.'[4] Thus Mahan began to formulate the new definition of the Levant in relation to Eastern Asia which he achieved in 1902.

In China the Boxer Rebellion made a supreme effort to sweep the foreigners into the sea. The Boxers attacked Christians, foreigners, European goods, European machinery and the European legations at Peking in the last and greatest movement of democratic resistance to the aristocratic West.[5] The Peking Expeditionary Force was fêted by the foreign colonies of Port Said on its way to China and on its return voyage. It comprised 37,377 Russian troops, 34,522 French troops and 24,478 German troops. The increase in German troops passing the Canal was especially marked because only 4,000 had passed through in 1898 and 2,000 in 1899. The increase in German Canal tonnage encouraged German efforts to secure a coaling station in the Red Sea. The China expedition compensated for the decline in military traffic caused by the Boer War, raised the number of military passengers by 42 per cent to over

---

[1] P. Kruger, *The Memoirs of Paul Kruger Four Times President of the South African Republic Told by Himself* (London, Unwin, 1902), ii. 362–3.

[2] H. Mackinder, 'The Great Trade Routes', *Journal of the Institute of Bankers* (March 1900), 153. G. S. Robertson, 'Political Geography and the Empire', *Geographical Journal* (October 1900), 455.

[3] A. T. Mahan, 'The Problem of Asia III', *Harper's New Monthly Magazine* (May 1900), 939. Idem, *The Problem of Asia and its Effect upon International Policies* (London, Low, 1900), 138.

[4] Idem, 'The Problem of Asia II', *Harper's New Monthly Magazine* (April 1900), 756. Idem, *The Problem of Asia* (1900), 82–3.

[5] M. Townsend, 'The Dislike of Asia for Europe', *The Spectator*, 23 June 1900, 868–9. Idem, 'Asiatic Courage', *The Spectator*, 30 June 1900, 916–17. Idem, 'The Contempt of Asia for Europe', *The Spectator*, 4 August 1900, 136–7. Idem, 'The Effects of the Shrinkage of the World', *The Spectator*, 15 September 1900, 329.

150,000 for the first time and brought £180,000 in revenue to the Canal Company, or 4·8 per cent of its receipts for 1900. The increase in the number of warships on the China Station maintained the shipment of coal through the Canal, depleted the strength of the Mediterranean Fleet and produced a Mediterranean scare in June–July 1901 after France announced in May that it intended to move fourteen battleships into the Mediterranean for special manoeuvres.[1] The successful relief of the legations revived Europe's ambitions to conquer the most fertile and tempting of all the continents, although it lay at the very end of its maritime line of communications and would have imposed an intolerable strain on its military and civil power. Such enormous ambitions provoked warnings against the dangers of an extension of empire as well as against its existing administration. 'You have humiliated the proudest nation in the world... You are arming a nation of four hundred millions!'[2]

The partition of the world between the U.S.A., Britain and Russia gave a new stimulus to trade, transport and communication. The Spanish–American War had greatly reduced the trade of the Philippines in 1898, the exports of Spain to the Philippines in 1898–9 and the tonnage of Spanish shipping using the Canal by 24 per cent in 1899. It also created an American empire in the Pacific, made the U.S.A. an Asiatic Power and increased U.S. tonnage using the Canal tremendously from 1,531 in 1898 to 67,690 in 1899. The revolt of the Filipinos which began in February 1899 brought 10,269 U.S. troops through the Canal while 12,812 Spanish troops returned home. The U.S.A. imported more that it exported through the Canal like France and Germany but unlike Britain. It imported jute from India, sugar from Java, hemp from Manila and nickel from New Caledonia. Its first export through the Canal in 1899 was coal, which was shipped to Colombo and Manila for the U.S. Fleet: in 1900 it first exported coal to Port Said. It first shipped phosphates from Florida through the Canal to Japan in May 1901. Its trade with Asia was carried largely by European, and especially by German, shipping. In the general stimulus given by the war to Pacific trade new trans-Pacific services were established via the Canal in 1900, and the first shipments of wheat from Tacoma were carried through the waterway in 1901 as steamers began to encroach on the Pacific wheat trade. The first trans-Pacific cables were laid in 1902 by Britain and in 1903 by the U.S.A., reinforcing the Anglo-Saxon monopoly of cable communication and stimulating the German development of 'wireless telegraphy'.

The Spanish–American War also encouraged the revival of the project for an isthmian canal under American auspices, although American pride preferred the Nicaragua to the Panama route and denigrated the Suez Canal.[3]

[1] E. Robertson, 'The Mediterranean Scare', *Nineteenth Century* (August 1901), 311.
[2] G. L. Dickinson, *Letters from John Chinaman* (London, Johnson, 1901), 55, 63. Idem, 'From the Chinese Point of View', *Saturday Review*, 12 January 1901, 47–8; 19 January, 78–9; 26 January, 109–10; 2 February, 140–1. M. Townsend, *Asia and Europe* (Constable, 1901), 4–5.
[3] F. C. Penfield, *Present Day Egypt* (New York, Century, 1899), 184–217, 'The Story of the Suez Canal'.

Such a ship canal would supplement America's possession of the Sault Ste. Marie Canals, which had exceeded the tonnage of the Suez Canal in 1889 and compensated the wheat producers of the American West for the injury inflicted by the Suez ditch in facilitating the competition of Indian wheat. It was however designed for strategic purposes like the Kiel Canal and unlike the Suez Canal or the Manchester Ship Canal. The Boer War ended British opposition to an American Canal. The second Hay–Pauncefote Treaty of 1901 gave the U.S.A. a position combining that of the territorial power with that of the Suez Canal Company, recognized that the U.S.A. was not prepared to accept the Convention of 1888 as a precedent for the neutralization of its isthmian canal[1] and alarmed Germany at the prospect of a purely American canal.[2] The Hay–Herran Convention of 1903 first referred to a Canal Zone under American control and was rejected by Colombia, which wished any Canal to be either Colombian or non-existent. The Republic of Panama was then established in independence of Colombia and adopted as its national anthem the 'Isthmian Hymn', having been created under foreign patronage to permit the building of an isthmian canal by foreigners and for foreigners. Bunau-Varilla, who had helped to establish the new republic, recommended the application of his salary as its ambassador to the U.S.A. to form the nucleus of a monument to Lesseps, the source of his inspiration since 1869. The prospect of future competition encouraged the Suez Canal Company to begin the publication from 1902 of statistics of its traffic by regions.

The sacrifice of the New World to the U.S.A. united Anglo-Saxondom against the world and enabled the British Empire to establish itself firmly in Asia, Australasia and Africa. Military, naval and imperial sentiment was aroused by the Boer War and further stimulated by the establishment of the Australian federation. Australia became a large-scale exporter of wheat through the Canal from 1899 after the famines in India and attracted from 1901 the enterprise of new shipping lines, which used the Cape route on the outward and the Canal on the homeward voyage. The Parliament of the new federation was opened by the Duke of York, who passed through the Canal on 31 March 1901 on the *Ophir* of the Orient Line.[3] That line had used the Cape and Suez routes for its steamships since 1877 and secured its first direct representative on the board of the Canal Company in 1901 when Frederick Green was elected as the successor to Sir James Laing. British aspirations extended southwards from Australia with the revival of Antarctic exploration from 1901. After Scott's *Discovery* was trapped in the Ross Sea the sealer *Terra Nova* was equipped with stores by Shackleton and rushed out on a relief-

---

[1] W. B. Munro, 'The Neutralization of the Suez Canal', *Annals of the American Academy of Political and Social Science* (May 1901), 31–4. J. Westlake, *International Law* (Cambridge University Press, 1904), i. 321–31, 'Interoceanic Ship Canals'.

[2] H. Schumacher, 'Deutsche Schiffahrtsinteressen im Stillen Ozean (Oktober 1901)', *Weltwirtschaftliche Studien* (Leipzig, Veit, 1911), 463–97.

[3] D. M. Wallace, *The Web of Empire. A Diary of the Imperial Tour of their Royal Highnesses the Duke and Duchess of Cornwall and York in 1901* (London, Macmillan, 1902), 46–9.

mission, being towed by a cruiser through the Canal on 8 September and down the Red Sea to reach Hobart in sixty-five days (27 August–30 October 1903). The *Loongana*, which was built ten years after the *Turbinia* of 1894 for the Tasmanian service of the Tasmanian Steam Navigation Company on the model of Channel steamers, became the first turbine-steamer to undertake a long ocean voyage from Glasgow to Melbourne, the first to navigate the Canal, on 10 September 1904, and the first to reach Australia. Australian produce made increasing use of the short Suez route to the home market, although the Boer War had enabled Argentina to exceed Australia for the first time in 1900 in the supply of the beef imports of Britain and to retain that market by chilling its beef from 1901. The Cape route remained the great route for sail and came into use by new steamship lines to South and East Africa as well as to Australia and India. To safeguard that route new docks were begun in 1900 at Simon's Town after its cession to the Admiralty for exclusive use as a naval base and the end of its commercial activity. The harbour works of 1895–1905 also made 'the Rock' a first-class naval base as never before, the symbol of world rather than of Mediterranean empire and the guardian of the Cape as well as of the Suez route. Durban benefited more than Cape Town by the postwar boom and by the growing interest in East Africa as the link between the Sudan and the Transvaal: it bunkered steamships homeward bound from Australia as Cape Town bunkered them on the outward voyage and began the export of Natal coal from 1905, contributing to South Africa's first export surplus in that year.

The surest link between Europe and its colonies was provided by the mail steamers which served as auxiliary fleets and formed the aristocracy of the merchant marine using the Canal.[1] Those mail lines confirmed the military as much as the commercial value of the Canal and carried mail under long-term contracts with regularity, precision and speed. The subsidies they thereby earned insulated them to some extent from the freight market and made them the most stable element in the traffic of the Canal so that they provided 31 per cent of its tonnage in 1874 and 23 per cent thereof in 1889 as in 1899. The Canal had a far larger proportion of liners than any other trade-route because their transits were more frequent as well as more regular than those of cargo-vessels. Mail steamers enjoyed priority of passage over all non-mail steamers and became the first beneficiaries by the introduction of night-time transit in 1886. The mail lines supplied the largest vessels to use the waterway and benefited most by the deepening of its channel. They were invariably the leading carriers of their national flags and predominated in the Canal tonnage of protectionist states. In 1899, 75 per cent of the Canal's tonnage was contributed by forty-four shipping lines, of which twenty-seven were English and seventeen non-English. At least eleven of the seventeen non-English lines were mail lines while twenty-five unsubsidized British lines provided 86 per cent of British tonnage, the P. & O. 10·8 per cent thereof and the Orient Line

[1] J. Charles-Roux, *L'Isthme et le Canal de Suez* (1901), ii. 315.

2·8 per cent. British shipping carried cargo for other states as well as for home ports and enjoyed its biggest invisible subsidy through the British dominion of India while other states paid monetary subsidies in the form of a rebate of Canal dues. The Netherland Steamship Company did not dominate Dutch shipping using the Canal nor the North German Lloyd German shipping but in 1899 the Messageries supplied 73 per cent of French tonnage, the Austrian Lloyd 84 per cent of Austrian tonnage, the Danish East Asiatic Company 90 per cent of Danish tonnage, the Navigazione Generale Italiana 92 per cent of Italian tonnage and the Trasatlantic 99 per cent of Spanish tonnage. The Nippon Yusen Kaisha was the only Asiatic mail line and supplied 96 per cent of Japanese tonnage.

The European mail lines undoubtedly inhibited the development of indigenous shipping in Asian waters. The liner companies also enjoyed the protection of the Canal tolls against competition by smaller shipowners and made the London Committee their own peculiar organ under Sutherland. No Holt, Cayzer or Smith was elected to the board of the Company despite the substantial contribution to the tonnage of the Canal made by the Ocean Steam Ship Company, the Clan Line and the City Line. The repeated attempts by Holt to secure a share in the China mail-contract seem to have debarred his firm from direct representation on the board, despite the very large Canal tonnage supplied by his firm. The mail lines enhanced the status of the colonial ports which served as their terminals at the expense of the lesser ports. They carried out not only servants of empire but also crown princes on tours of their future dominions although never reigning monarchs before 1911. The third improvement programme of the Canal Company was drawn up in 1901 for a general widening and deepening in order to permit the passage of mammoth mail-boats as well as of armoured warships. That programme inspired the Company to acquire in 1902 an improved rock-breaker with chisel-pointed rams treble the weight of its first rock-breaker of 1888. It enabled the P. & O. to construct its new 'M' line to the maximum limits permitted by the Canal, beginning with the *Moldavia* which was its first mail-steamer with overlapping screws and made its first transit in October 1903. The increase in the depth of the waterway followed the dredging of the harbours of Liverpool, Antwerp and New York to a depth of 30 feet at low water and stimulated the dredging of all harbours east of Suez, especially of Aden, Karachi, Colombo, Calcutta, Hong Kong, Fremantle and Melbourne. The resulting concentration of trade in the giant entrepôts of Asia stimulated the development of transhipment and contributed to the decline of the lesser ports. It made the Red Sea more than ever a thoroughfare, with only Aden, Massawa and Jibuti as suitable harbours: it encouraged the Arab merchants of Jedda to blame the Canal for the decline of their trade and the British to choose in 1903 a new outlet for the trade of the Sudan thirty-five miles north of Suakin so as to divert the trade of the Sudan from the Nile to the Canal and the profit of the reunification of the Nile valley from Egyptian into

British hands. The associated increase in the draught of ships was stimulated by the expansion in the volume of trade and by the competition of sailing ships, which were unlimited by the dimensions of the Canal. Deeper ships offered substantial economies of scale and spread working expenses over more freight without decreasing speed or increasing tolls in proportion. They made the ship-railway no longer an economic engineering enterprise and exerted constant pressure on the Canal Company as sustained expansion during the 1900s replaced the repeated depressions of traffic in the 1890s.

The establishment of British power in Egypt exposed Britain to the threat of an overland descent on Port Said by Turkey and even by Russia.[1] It extended British interests to the vulnerable frontier of Sinai, beyond which the Hejaz Railway was begun in 1900 to link the Holy Places to Damascus by a route beyond the range of the British Navy. Sinai was coveted by Herzl as the ante-chamber to a future Jewish state of Palestine which in his vision of *Altneuland* in 1902 was to become the centre of the railway network of the world, replacing the Canal as the natural junction between Europe, Asia and Africa, diverting from it mail liners and passenger traffic and leaving it with only tramps and freighters. Herzl's request to Chamberlain on 22 October 1902[2] for part of untenanted Sinai for a self-governing Jewish colony was encouraged by the postwar reconstruction in South Africa which was based on the establishment of Jewish control over the Rand.[3] Herzl felt so certain of success that he no longer wished to buy a family vault in a Viennese cemetery. He asked the British Government on 12 November to support the establishment of a Jewish Colony in the South-East Mediterranean and to guarantee to it 'Colonial Rights'.[4] Lansdowne's reply on 8 December reflected his fear of a Jameson raid from El Arish upon Palestine and asked for clarification of 'colonial rights' but encouraged Herzl to envisage an 'Egyptian province of Judaea'. Such plans were, however, opposed by Abbas, by Cromer and by the Foreign Minister, Boutros Ghali Pasha, so that Chamberlain was compelled from 21 December to consider East Africa as a possible alternative to Sinai. Herzl requested in his reply to Lansdowne on 6 January 1903 civic liberty for 'free and respected citizens on the soil of a definite homestead'. He lacked any mysticism of the soil, had never dared to mention any place to the north of El Arish, least of all Jerusalem, and had acquired faith during his five years in the Budapest Technical School in the power of engineering to reclaim the desert for civilization. He envisaged the settlement of the Pelusian Plain by a colony of 100,000 Jews under a chartered company of colonization, its irrigation in winter as well as in summer by an extension of the Sweet Water Canal across the maritime Canal and the dredging of a new harbour in the Serbonian Lake to the east of Port Said.[5] Thus he aspired to

[1] L. M. Rossignol, *Le Canal de Suez (Étude Historique et Juridique)* (1898), 212.
[2] T. Herzl, *Tagebücher* (Berlin, 1923), iii. 295–9.
[3] J. Amery, *The Life of Joseph Chamberlain* (London, Macmillan, 1951), iv. 256–70, Zionism.
[4] O. K. Rabinowicz, 'Herzl and England', *Jewish Social Studies* (January 1951), 27–32.
[5] T. Herzl, *Tagebücher* (1923), iii. 335, 339.

create a Jewish rival to Port Said and a base under the Egyptian flag for a Zionist assault upon the Ottoman Empire. Abbas refused on 17 February to grant a charter of colonization and conceded only municipal rights. Herzl failed to gain any concession from Cromer on 25 March and thought him 'the most disagreeable Englishman' he had ever met.[1] Sir William Garstin, the head of the Public Works Department, reported on 6 May that the laying of pipes beneath the Canal would interfere with traffic for several weeks and that five times as much water would be necessary as had been estimated by Herzl's engineers.[2] Such a diversion of the water of the Nile to non-Egyptian ends could not be permitted by the Government of Egypt. Cromer rejected the plan on 11 May and Herzl acquired on 16 May a vault in the Viennese cemetery.[3] The offer of 'Uganda' as an alternative to Sinai was embodied in a charter prepared by Lloyd George, Roberts & Co.[4] but was virtually rejected at the Sixth Zionist Congress by the massive opposition of the Jewry of Eastern Europe, educated in Jewish tradition and organized by Chaim Weizmann. Thus ended the first contact of the British Government with Zionism, whose founder died in 1904. The Canal remained unflanked by an Ottoman Jewish colony to the east and Port Said remained without a competitor in its immediate vicinity. Thus the world was partitioned to the advantage of the established powers rather than to that of the disinherited.

[1] M. Lowenthal, *The Diaries of Theodor Herzl* (London, Gollancz, 1958), 382.
[2] T. Herzl, *Tagebücher*, iii. 420, 426.   [3] Ibid., *Tagebücher*, iii. 429.
[4] A. Bein, *Theodore Herzl. A Biography* (London, East and West Library, 1941), 443.

PART IV

THE BRITISH EMPIRE OF THE MIDDLE EAST, 1904-1947

26

THE ANGLO-FRENCH ENTENTE
AND THE BRITISH AGITATION FOR
LOWER TOLLS, 1904-1905

THE foundations of the Anglo-French Entente were laid before the Russo-Japanese War precipitated its conclusion. That agreement was intended to end the friction which had been constant since the occupation of Egypt and had become acute with the reconquest of the Sudan. After the retreat from Fashoda France concentrated upon expansion in the Western Sudan and Morocco and so sought to find in the richest province of North-West Africa another great colonial opportunity as well as a complement to Algeria and a counterpoise to Gibraltar. The decline of the French Navy from 1902 enabled the Anglo-French naval antagonism to yield place to the Anglo-German. In that growing rapprochement the Suez Canal became to England 'a monument to the genius and courage of an inspired son of the great friendly nation across the Channel'.[1] The French directors of the Canal Company transformed their shotgun wedding with the British directors in 1884 into an entente cordiale[2] while the British administration in Egypt reconciled itself to the economic development of Port Said through the Convention of 1902. Cromer seems to have desired a quasi-dynastic security in Egypt and a permanent mayoralty of the palace, hereditary in his own family.[3] To achieve that end he renamed Fashoda in 1903 Kodok so as to obliterate the memory of France's humiliation together with the name and suggested to Lansdowne on 17 July 1903 the barter of Morocco for Egypt, especially through the abolition of the Debt Commission.[4] After Cambon, the French ambassador to London, asked Lansdowne on 26 October to guarantee the free use of the Canal according to the principles of 1888 Cromer insisted on 30 October that Article VIII of the Convention of Constantinople providing for the consular commission of supervision and for its annual meeting should remain suspended because he still opposed the idea of another international commission in Egypt. When Cambon expressed on 9 December his inability to understand how Article VIII could be incompatible with the British occupation of Egypt Cromer agreed to yield to the French but expressed his dislike of the

[1] *Le Canal de Suez*, 12 Décembre 1901, 4005, The Prince of Wales at Guildhall on 5 December 1901.

[2] *Le Canal de Suez*, 12 Janvier 1904, 4361-2, Henri Boucard, director since 1891 and vice-president since 1893, as President of the Board of Directors on 4 January 1904.

[3] W. S. Blunt, *My Diaries, 1888-1914* (1919), ii. 75, 90.

[4] G. P. Gooch and H. Temperley, *British Documents on the Origins of the War 1898-1914* (London, H.M.S.O., 1927), ii. 285-401, 'The Anglo-French Treaties of April 8, 1904'.

permanent presence of the Ottoman Commissioner specified in clause 2 of the article. Cambon told Lansdowne on the same day, 11 December, that it would be a mistake to denounce Article VIII and that it would cause England no practical inconvenience to retain it, so securing the triumph of French legalism over English empiricism.

The Russo-Japanese War does not seem greatly to have reduced French bargaining-power, although Balfour had no confidence in Japan and Delcassé feared lest England should give active support to its new ally against Russia and so turn Germany against France in Europe. The British draft agreement of 14 March 1904 proposed that the commission and its annual meeting should remain in abeyance during the British occupation. Delcassé's insistence secured the acceptance of the French draft text of 21 March, i.e. the commission but without its annual meeting under an Ottoman commissioner. On 31 March Cromer yielded but affirmed that executive action rested entirely with the Egyptian Government. In the Declaration of 8 April 1904 the British Government affirmed its adherence to the provisions of the Convention of 1888 and to their operation. Thus it renounced the reservation explicitly made in 1887 to the effect that the whole Convention remained inoperative so long as the British occupation continued. It proposed to bring the Convention into operation for the protection of the Canal and might no longer permit its Navy to close the Canal to a foe. It nevertheless refused to agree to the annual meeting of the commission and accepted only its meeting in the exceptional event of a threat to the Canal. By a secret article Britain's renunciation of the reservation was to remain intact even if the British Government was compelled to modify its policy in respect to Egypt, i.e. if Britain was compelled to annex Egypt. Lansdowne explained to the British ambassador in Paris[1] that the purpose of the article was to eliminate the doubt left by Salisbury in 1888 and by Curzon in 1898 as to the extent to which Britain held herself bound by the Convention and to dissipate any possible misunderstanding by specifically declaring the adhesion of the Government to the Convention. Earl Percy revealed in answer to a question by the navalist T. G. Bowles in the Commons on 14 April that none of the other seven Signatory Powers had been consulted. Thus the legal basis of the annual meetings remained unchanged because England and France could not bind the other seven powers. England proposed in effect to hold itself relieved from the obligations of the Convention in relation to the supervisory commission but to require the fulfilment of its remaining stipulations. Thus England deprived the Convention of its sole effective guarantee and remained the virtual guarantor of the freedom of passage. Although France helped to secure for Russia more liberal treatment than Spain had enjoyed in 1898, Russia reminded France as well as England of her right to be consulted about the Canal.[2] Germany was affected more than Russia because the entente deprived her of the Egyptian truncheon for use

---

[1] Gooch and Temperley, ii. 369, Lansdowne to Monson, 8 April 1904.
[2] *The Times*, 30 April 1904, 7v.

against Britain and liquidated the Egyptian mortgage which had burdened British policy since 1882. Since 1890 the German flag had also ranked second in the traffic of the Canal which was used in 1904 by two-thirds of the German sea-going fleet.[1] In 1903 the North German Lloyd, which had taken over the mail service to China wholly from the Hamburg American Line, supplied 33 per cent of Germany's total Canal tonnage while the Hansa Line supplied 31 per cent and the Hamburg American Line 16 per cent. The increase in German cargo tonnage replaced the Lloyd in 1904 by the Hansa Line which assumed first place in Germany's Canal tonnage and second place after the P. & O. in the total Canal tonnage. Germany was expected by Cromer to demand a coaling station either in the Red Sea or in Morocco.[2]

The Debt Commission was not abolished as Cromer had originally intended but was neutralized by pledging nearly all the land tax to the service of the Debt under the Khedivial Decree of 28 November 1904 and by confining the operations of the Commission to the payment of that interest. Its anti-British intervention in general administration ended so that the Government of Egypt gained the free disposal of its 'own' resources. Thenceforward England was released from her sixty pledges to withdraw from Egypt[3] and was assured of French support against Germany in Egypt. Cromer was immensely pleased with the entente,[4] contemplated the withdrawal of the British garrison from Cairo and proposed in 1905 to remain for six more years in Egypt. A company-flotation boom was encouraged by the new security for foreign investment, by an influx of French capital intended to prevent the total sacrifice of French Egypt and by the creation of numerous English joint-stock companies in 1904–6. The British Government appointed in succession to Stokes in 1902 its last soldier-director to the board of the Canal Company in General Sir John Ardagh, who had mapped the Wadi Tumilat for Wolseley in 1882 and had urged the annexation of Egypt as Director of Military Intelligence at the War Office in 1896.[5]

For England the agreement, reinforced by the Anglo-Spanish entente of 1906, restored the security of the Mediterranean route in the west but not in the east where Turkey and Russia remained hostile. For France it restored the position in the Atlantic which she had lost at Trafalgar and the position in Africa which she had lost at Tel el Kebir. German resentment provoked the Moroccan crisis of 1905, which was followed by the extension of French power in Morocco from 1907. Thus France gained compensation for the expansion of the Anglo-Saxon world in America. The French Atlantic ports expanded their hinterland at the expense of Marseilles and gained their first

---

[1] *The Times*, 17 January 1905, 4ii.
[2] Lord Newton, *Lord Lansdowne* (1929), 286, Cromer to Lansdowne, 27 November 1903.
[3] J. Cocheris, *Situation Internationale de l'Égypte et du Soudan (Juridique et Politique)* (1903), 531.
[4] E. Dicey, 'The Anglo-French Compact and Egypt', *Fortnightly Review*, 2 May 1904, 788.
[5] A. J. Marder, *British Naval Policy* (1940), 572–3, Memorandum on Naval Policy, 13 October 1896.

representative on the board of the Canal Company in Paul Mirabaud, President of the Chargeurs Réunis of Le Havre, in 1905. The Messageries co-ordinated its services with those of the Chargeurs Réunis, launched the *El Kantara* in 1904 and sent it through the Canal in May 1905 en route to China. In January 1905 it began a new service from Antwerp to China and extended its terminus to Japan by a joint service with the Chargeurs Réunis. Thus it extended its operations from Marseilles in order to compete with the rival ports which had been encouraged by the Suez Canal.[1] In 1906 it supplied André Lebon to replace Cambefort on the board of the Canal Company.

The entente achieved by England under a Conservative administration was followed by an immediate attack by the Liberals on the Canal Company in the interest of the small shipowners and the Indian wheat trade. The wheat export trade from India had stimulated shipbuilders to develop a special type of ship designed during the fall in freights of 1890–4 to minimize Canal tolls on a marginal cargo. The turret-deck was patented in 1891 by C. D. Doxford of Sunderland and was first used in the *Turret* of Petersen, Tate & Co. of Newcastle, which made its maiden voyage in February 1893. The turret-ship was specially adapted to the Canal trades[2] and especially to the carriage of grain from India to Europe. Its turret-deck reduced the measurable deck-space to mere cat-walks above bulbous sides, reducing measurement-tonnage and making possible the carriage of deck-cargo in the shelter-deck free from toll. The trunk-steamer developed by R. Ropner & Co. in the *Trunkby* (1895) and also built by Sir James Laing from 1895 similarly reduced register tonnage through the use of a central or trunk deck. Both trunk- and turret-steamers facilitated competition by the tramp-steamer with the aid of the Canal Company which in 1899 renounced the effort to define an 'easily closed' space and proposed to add any space formed by a construction on the upper deck to the taxable tonnage each time cargo was carried therein. Some shipowners thereupon increased the size of their deck spaces up to a capacity of 800 tons covering almost all the deck and so benefited at the expense of shipowners in general. Holt's built their ships with a three-island superstructure of poop, bridge and forecastle from 1892.[3] The Clan Line which had first chartered a turret-steamer in 1896 scrapped almost all its fleet and had new turret-steamers built by Doxford under techniques of large-scale production. Even the P. & O. launched a turret-ship in 1900.

The ingenuity of shipbuilders and shipowners compelled the Canal Company to reach a new agreement with the London Committee as a necessary prelude to a revision of its regulations. The London Programme of 1883 had provided for an end to the sharing of profits between the Company and its clients after the dividend reached 25 per cent and for the total application

---

[1] L. Pierrein, 'Marseille et le Canal de Suez', *Annales de la Faculté des Lettres d'Aix* (1956), 77.

[2] S. O. Kendall, 'Turret-Deck Cargo Steamers', *Transactions of the North-East Coast Institution of Engineers and Shipbuilders*, 12 March 1895, 242, 273, 325.

[3] F E. Hyde, *Blue Funnel: a History of Alfred Holt and Company* (1956), 175, 180.

of profits thereafter to the benefit of the shipowners until the dues were reduced to 5 francs per ton. After the dividend for the year 1898 had been fixed at 100 francs, or at 20 per cent on the nominal value of the 500-franc share, a shareholder expressed his concern at the general meeting on 6 June 1899 at the prospect of a sequence of years of toll reductions which would reduce the dividend below 125 francs. Arenberg thereupon met the London Committee on 18 May 1900 and revised the agreement of 1883 in the interests of the shareholders. The large shipowners on the London Committee accepted such a revision in order to maintain an effective toll-gate at Suez and so reduce competition by tramp steamers: thus at the lunch at the P. & O. offices after the meeting Sutherland insisted on the great identity of interest between the Canal Company and British commerce and called the Canal a bond of union between France and England which would last for ever. The English directors took into account the decline in the number of original shareholders and the rise in the market-price of the 500-franc share to an average price of 3,620 francs for the year 1899. They therefore permitted dividends to be related to that market-price rather than to the nominal value of the share as provided for by the London Programme. They agreed not to insist either on the reduction of the toll to 5 francs or on the limitation of dividend under that programme. They thus surrendered their control over dividends for the future and abandoned a principle of general interest to all shipowners. They accepted the Company's new principle that any future reduction in dues should be preceded by a dividend increase, that it should take place in the second year following the increased dividend and that it should equal the total increase in dividends in place of the reduction equal to half the increase in dividends stipulated in 1883. That agreement of 1900 was intended to benefit the shareholders rather than to permit the further improvement of the channel and was followed by Arenberg's denial that there was any need for such improvement after the programme completed in 1898.[1] At the shareholders' meeting on 4 June 1901, however, Arenberg recognized that the improvement works could not be considered finished and would have to be continued under the pressure of the growth of shipping: he was authorized to raise a loan of £1,000,000 and to use to pay its interest the £40,000 per annum which would become available from 2 September 1901 on the repayment of the thirty-year bonds of 1871 and would service a loan twice as great as that of 1871. The third improvement programme of 1901 recognized that the Canal had not attained finality of construction and undertook its deepening for the benefit of the large shipowners. The primary purpose of the agreement of 1900 was fiscal: it liberated dividends from restraint and from their close relation to receipts. It permitted the payment of a net dividend of 125 francs for the year 1901 or 25 per cent on the nominal value of the share: it enabled the dividends distributed for the year 1903 to exceed 60 per cent of the Company's receipts for the first time.

[1] *Le Canal de Suez*, 2 Avril 1901, 3887–8.

In May 1902 Arenberg reached an agreement over the measurement of taxable tonnage with the President of the Board of Trade and General Ardagh. Thereunder ships without a special tonnage-certificate would have the spaces formed by their poops, bridges and forecastles measured and added to their tonnage unless their owners formally declared to the Board of Trade that such spaces were not intended to receive cargo. Ships with a special tonnage-certificate which had such spaces not included in their special certificate but which carried cargo therein on any transit of the Canal would have such spaces added thenceforward to their tonnage under a new Board of Trade certificate which would replace the old one.[1] Thus the Company sought to withdraw its concession of 1899, to end the occasional taxation of shelter-deck spaces, to restrict to defined proportions the capacity of poop, bridge and forecastle exempt from measurement in those ships with a three-island type of superstructure and to include in the tonnage of ships with a shelter-deck all the space beneath the shelter-deck. The Company approached other certificate-issuing authorities and accompanied its new regulations by a reduction of dues by 5*d.* per ton from 1 January 1903. The Company's decision was explained to the United Kingdom Chamber of Shipping on 23 June 1903 by Sutherland, who had succeeded Stokes as a vice-president of the Company. The Chamber, however, asked the Board of Trade on 15 March and again on 21 July 1904 for a conference to be held in London on the question of tolls and on all other questions of the administration of the Company. Thus began the crisis of 1904–5 which ended twenty years of peace between the Company and its clients. The conflict followed on the triumph of two Liberal M.P.s who had capitalized on the postwar sensitivity to any confusion of public and private interest and had secured the resignation of a Government director of the Company. C. W. Fremantle had been Deputy-Master to the Mint from 1870 to 1894 and had succeeded his friend Rivers Wilson as an official director of the Canal Company in 1896, so securing appointment to a much more responsible position than the one from which he had retired. He was then elected to the board of four other companies in 1897–8 and became Vice-President of the Corporation of Foreign Bondholders in 1898. He drew a pension of £950 as well as a salary of £800 as a director of the Canal Company: as a Secretary to the British Embassy in Paris and a commercial attaché in France, Belgium and Switzerland he held five different offices in three different countries. He resigned after questions in the House[2] and so followed the example of Rivers Wilson, the first official director to resign. The conflict of 1904–5 was fought largely outside the House of Commons and allied the economic élites of England and France together against their smaller competitors so that it did not become an Anglo-French dispute like that of 1883.

The sharp rise in wheat exports from India in 1902 continued in 1903 when a good wheat harvest in Europe coincided with a decrease in exports from the

---

[1] *Le Canal de Suez*, 12 Mai 1902, 4073–5.

[2] Hansard, *Commons Debates*, 21 April 1903, 98, 100–2, J. H. Dalziel and J. H. Whitley.

U.S.A. and Australia. During 1903 wheat shipments through the Canal re-attained their peak level of 1891–2 while tramp shipping increased to over 35 per cent of the total Canal tonnage. Those tramp ships included trunk-steamers, nineteen of which had been built between 1894 and 1898, and turret-steamers, of which seventy-nine had been built by 1902, including nineteen for the Clan Line. The small shipowners were separated more visibly from the large shipowners by the rapid growth in the size of ships. The large shipowners were harassed by the depression of freights produced by the liberation of a mass of tonnage from war-service. The shipping interest was thus seriously divided although British shipping recovered from its wartime diversion from the Canal to form 60·2 per cent in 1902 and 62·2 per cent in 1903 of the total tonnage. Nor could it be reunited by appeals to national sentiment against France, such as Bowles made when he enquired the percentage of British pilots employed by the Canal Company in comparison to the percentage of British shipping passing through the Canal.[1]

After the Company duly promulgated the amendment to the Suez rules on 2 August[2] and so seemed to threaten the wheat trade from India[3] the Chamber of Shipping repeated on 7 November its request to the Board of Trade for a conference. That request was rejected on 19 November by Arenberg with the support of the London Committee, which he affirmed was representative primarily of the shareholders of the Canal Company.[4] At the annual general meeting of the P. & O. on 13 December Sutherland expressed amidst general approval his gratitude to the Canal Company that the tolls of £322,000 paid in 1903 were not more and his belief that no other company English or foreign was so generous to its clients. His satisfaction was not shared by the smaller shipowners who revived the idea of a British Canal and proposed an El Arish–Akaba Canal,[5] an idea which found some support in Germany but none in France. The Nautical Society of Hamburg condemned the new rules most severely on 9 January 1905 and called for an international conference on the Company's regulations.[6] Holt's secured the unanimous support of the Liverpool Steam Ship Owners' Association on 6 February 1905 for Government efforts to secure a reduction in the Company's charges.[7] A deputation of shipowners to Lansdowne on 9 February achieved, however, no results. Howard Vincent, who was Conservative M.P. for Sheffield, a supporter of tariff reform and a director of Bucknall Steamship Lines Ltd. which paid £40,000 per annum to the Canal Company on their traffic to India and the Persian Gulf, addressed a general meeting of the London Chamber of

[1] Hansard, *Commons Debates*, 28 July 1904, 1446, T. G. Bowles.
[2] *Le Canal de Suez*, 2 Août 1904, 4455.
[3] *The Times*, 13 December 1904, 14i.
[4] Ibid., 24 November 1904, 7i–ii.
[5] C. E. H. Vincent, *The Suez Canal, its Origins, Constitution and Administration* (London, Soulden, 1905), 34.
[6] *The Times*, 17 January 1905, 4ii, 'German Shipowners and the Suez Canal'.
[7] F. E. Hyde, *Blue Funnel* (1956), 130.

Commerce on 13 February. He rebuked those English who thought 'that the Canal was dropped from Heaven for the benefit of England'[1] and excused Lesseps for appearing as 'a St. Peter of the Oceans with the keys of the East and of the West in his hands'.[2] He noted that the British Government had received in interest and dividends on its Canal shares a total of £12,956,149 between 1876 and 1904[3] and recommended the Government to reimburse 2 francs per ton to an industry employing £120,000,000 of capital.[4] He so placed emphasis on the income from the Government's shares rather than their capital appreciation and diverted the attack of the Liberal shipowners from the Company to the Government. In the Commons Vincent appealed on 10 April for relief to the British shipowners out of the £1,040,000 dividend received per annum by the Government. When Vincent asked the Government on 30 May to consider the refund to British shipping using the Canal of 5–10 per cent of the dividend of 28 per cent which the Company had announced on 22 May, Austen Chamberlain replied that a substantial reduction of dues would be proposed at the next meeting of the Company's shareholders.

At that meeting on 6 June Arenberg explained to his shareholders that the Company had only become one of the most prosperous enterprises in the whole world through the close association of shareholders and clients.[5] He supported the London Committee against the attacks made by other English shipowners and alleged that one promoter of the scheme for a second canal through the isthmus was a disappointed aspirant for a seat on the board of the existing Canal Company. He promised that no reduction in toll would ever be made without a corresponding increase in the dividend of the shareholders and so concluded that tariff reductions were the best proof of the Company's prosperity. After he had won the unanimous support of his shareholders the board of directors decided on 1 September to reduce the toll by $7\frac{1}{2}d.$ from 1906. At a banquet given on 6 November by the London Committee to the French directors Sutherland suggested that 'the entente cordiale of Suez has been like the prologue and precursor of the entente cordiale between France and England'. Arenberg, however, expressed his dislike of the application of the term 'entente cordiale' to the Company, having secured the election to the board in 1902 of Casimir-Périer, who as Premier had concluded the anti-British Franco-Russian Alliance and became the first ex-President of the Republic to serve as a director. Gorst on behalf of the Foreign Office confirmed on 30 November to the Chamber of Shipping that the British directors had surrendered control over the Company's dividends in 1900. The shipowners were thus deprived of any legal ground for their agitation and could secure no political support from the London Committee, the official directors, the Foreign Office or the Treasury, which formed a united front with the

[1] Vincent, 31.   [2] Ibid., 17.
[3] Ibid., 37.   [4] Ibid., 19.
[5] *Le Canal de Suez*, 12–13 Juin 1905, 4595–8.

Company. The Treasury gave its first clear proof of interest in the Government's dividends and repelled an Australian assault in 1906 even more decisively than the British protests in 1905.

The Company bought off the opposition by a further reduction of dues and maintained its monopoly unchallenged. Its new regulations made the turret- and trunk-steamers much less useful than they had been thitherto, benefited the larger lines at the expense of the smaller and stimulated a further increase in the size of ships using the Canal. In 1904–5 India's wheat exports reached the maximum proportion of 22·3 per cent of the crop and Karachi exported its maximum of 2,150,025 tons of wheat, so achieving through a single port the export tonnage of wheat desired for all India by the neo-mercantilist policy of 1882. British tonnage regained in 1904 its 1899 proportion of 66 per cent of the total Canal tonnage while India's share of the net register tonnage rose above 50 per cent for the last time in the history of the Canal. Thenceforward tramp shipping declined from 31·3 per cent of the total tonnage of the Canal in 1904 to 26·7 per cent in 1905 and to 21·8 per cent in 1906. Three turret-ships were built for the British India Line in 1905 but for use in the coal and rice trade in Asian waters. The last trunk-ship was built in 1907 and the final turret-ship in 1911, the last of 158 such vessels. The Company increased the depth of the Canal from 1906 and so increased the facilities for the great liner companies. From 1906 it began to calculate the depth of the waterway in feet and inches rather than in metres in a large concession to the illogical English. Vincent did not convert the Government to the cause of tariff reform nor secure election to the board of the Company but was presented in September 1905 with the Cross of the Legion of Honour by the President of France. In 1905 the board elected John W. Hughes of T. & J. Harrison, which had used the Canal first in 1870 and regularly since 1875. Thus Liverpool was granted an additional representative to Robert Alexander while Holt's and the tramp interests remained excluded. The Company entered upon a new phase as a distributor of dividends as the depressions of the 1890s were succeeded by the most buoyant decade in the history of the Canal's traffic. Dividends which had fallen off under the influence of depression in 1892–4 and in 1897 rose in every year above the level of the previous year from 1898 to 1913 inclusive, although receipts declined in 1900, in 1905–6, in 1908 and in 1913. Thus the Company emerged from the shadow cast by Panama to become a model of international financial cooperation and an apparent basis for international concord.

The conflict of 1904–5 was followed by a lasting reconciliation under the influence of the Entente which recognized the overwhelming supremacy of British over French traffic in the Canal,[1] established British rule in Egypt and the Sudan on a firm political basis[2] and fashioned the English image of the

---

[1] E. Lavisse and A. N. Rambaud, *Histoire Générale du IVe Siècle à Nos Jours* (Paris, Colin, 1901), xii. 763, A. Viallate, 'La France Économique de 1870 à nos Jours'.

[2] E. A. W. Budge, *Cook's Handbook for Egypt and the Sudan* (London, Cook, 1905), 370–83.

Canal in a French mould. That image was built up largely in the years 1905–10 through an unprecedented efflorescence of histories and biographies after the religious crisis of the 1890s, the introduction of general education from 1902, the emergence of the profession of history-teachers and their union in the Historical Association in 1906. The new histories used secondary sources, especially the superior journalism of Fitzgerald, Cameron and Dicey,[1] rather than the primary sources made available by Charles-Roux and Voisin Bey.[2] They did not diffuse any detailed knowledge of the Canal's history which they reduced to the three episodes of the construction of the waterway by Lesseps (who was often made into an engineer), the inauguration by Eugénie and the share-purchase by Disraeli.[3] The last great revival of the free-trade gospel ensured the triumph of liberalism in the writing of history as well as in the general election of 1906 and in fiscal policy. Thus contemporary histories accepted the axioms of classical economics and underestimated the contribution made by Egypt in capital to the construction of the Canal while over-emphasizing its contribution in labour.[4] Palmerston's opposition was revealed as strong enough to have overridden the views of his Cabinet colleagues[5] and of the editor of *The Times*[6] but was usually denounced for its short-sighted failure to foresee Sedan. The opening of the Canal was assumed to have marked a new era in the economic development of the world.[7] 'Two continents were divided in order to unite the whole world.'[8] Traffic was thought to have been suddenly diverted from the Cape route, with disastrous consequences for the colonies of St. Helena and Mauritius,[9] and to have returned to the Mediterranean route as in the days before da Gama. Contemporaries were apparently overpowered by the stimulus given to British exports by the Canal whose economic function they stressed at the expense of its military function.

The share-purchase had remained controversial down to the 1890s when it was first revealed how much dislike it had excited in the Cobdenite Northcote,[10] the Duc de Decazes[11] and the Panslavs of Moscow.[12] The first full

---

[1] P. Fitzgerald, *The Great Canal at Suez* (London, 1876, 2 vols.). D. A. Cameron, *Egypt in the Nineteenth Century* (London, Smith, 1898). E. Dicey, *The Story of the Khedivate* (London, Rivington, 1902).

[2] J. Charles-Roux, *L'Isthme et le Canal de Suez* (1901, 2 vols.). F. P. Voisin, *Le Canal de Suez* (1902–6, 7 vols.).   [3] P. G. Elgood, *Egypt and the Army* (1924), 70.

[4] A. Colvin, *The Making of Modern Egypt* (London, Seeley, 1906), 7–8.

[5] Duchess of Argyll, *George Douglas Eighth Duke of Argyll* (1906), i. 568–9.

[6] A. I. Dasent, *John Thadeus Delane, Editor of " The Times "* (London, Murray, 1908), i. 324–328.

[7] Earl of Meath, M. H. C. Legh and E. Jackson, *Our Empire Past and Present* (London, Harrison, 1905), ii. 678.

[8] M. Voss, *Der Suezkanal und seine Stellung im Weltverkehr* (Wien, Lechner, 1904), 75.

[9] C. Bruce, *The Broadstone of Empire. Problems of Crown Colony Administration* (London, Macmillan, 1910), ii. 404.   [10] A. Lang, *Sir Stafford Northcote* (1891), 274–5.

[11] H. S. de Blowitz, 'Reminiscences of a Journalist', *Contemporary Review* (February 1893), 229–30.

[12] A. Loftus, *The Diplomatic Reminiscences of Lord Augustus Loftus* (London, Cassell, 1894), ii. 145–6.

histories of the transaction in 1905 stressed its political rather than its financial significance. An angry French account sought to defend the French Government for its failure in 1875.[1] A jubilant English account written with the help of Henry Oppenheim gave credit in the assimilationist fervour of the decade to the Jewish contribution of Disraeli, Rothschild and Oppenheim to the British Empire and elevated the Cairo contract of 1875 into 'one of the decisive documents of latter-day European history'.[2] Although the reactions of the Liberal leaders[3] and of the French[4] were more fully revealed the controversy which had surrounded the transaction for twenty years was wholly eliminated, together with its very kernel in Egypt's active bid for British financial support. The act became a simple purchase rather than a sale, made by due parliamentary process[5] rather than by extra-parliamentary procedure and intended to secure the route to India by an act of high statesmanship. Greenwood gave repeated credit to Derby rather than to Disraeli at the public dinner of 1905 in his honour.[6] Most writers, however, attributed the purchase to Disraeli,[7] ranked it as his greatest act of policy where earlier biographers[8] had ignored it and so encouraged other claimants[9] to share in the credit. Oppenheim left £500,000 when he died in 1912[10] whereas Greenwood died so poor and so forgotten in 1909 that two whole days elapsed before *The Times*, under Northcliffe since 1908, published the obituary[11] of 'the greatest journalist of our time'[12] and 'the creator of New Journalism in this country'.[13] The chapter on Disraeli in the *Cambridge Modern History* which Acton had persistently asked Greenwood to write since 1896[14] was transformed into the article on

[1] C. Lesage, 'L'Achat des Actions de Suez 1875', *Revue de Paris*, 15 Novembre 1905. Idem, *L'Invasion Anglaise en Égypte. L'Achat des Actions de Suez (Novembre 1875)* (Paris, Plon, 1906).

[2] L. Wolf, 'The Story of the Khedive's Shares', *The Times*, 26 December 1905, 11, reprinted in L. Wolf, *Essays in Jewish History* (Jewish Historical Society of England, 1934), 287–308, and followed by seven weeks of intermittent correspondence in *The Times*, 27 December 1905, 8i (Greenwood); 28 December, 4i (Wolf and Oppenheim); 29 December, 5iv (Wolf); 13 January 1906, 6iii–v (Greenwood); 18 January, 4ii–iii (Wolf); 26 January, 4ii–iii (Greenwood); 29 January, 8ii (Wolf); 30 January, 14vi (A. P. B. Loftus); 10 February, 13i–ii (Greenwood).

[3] Lord Edmond Fitzmaurice, *Earl Granville* (London, Longmans, 1905), ii. 158–9.

[4] Lord Newton, *Lord Lyons* (1913), ii. 85–93.

[5] J. Redlich, *The Procedure of the House of Commons* (London, Constable, 1908), iii. 132.

[6] *The Times*, 10 April 1905, 8ii, 'Dinner to Mr. Frederick Greenwood'. Ibid., 10 February 1906, 13ii, 'The Story of the Khedive's Shares'.

[7] H. Paul, *A History of Modern England* (London, Macmillan, 1905), iv. 190–1. H. Maxwell, *A Century of Empire 1801–1900* (London, Arnold, 1911), 48–9. J. A. Todd, *The Banks of the Nile* (London, Black, 1913), 104–5.

[8] *Dictionary of National Biography* (London, Smith, 1888), v. 1006–22, T. E. Kebbel, 'Benjamin Disraeli'.

[9] R. H. Vetch, *Life of Lieutenant-General The Hon. Sir Andrew Clarke* (1905), 102. H. S. de Blowitz, *My Memoirs* (London, Arnold, 1904), 343–50.

[10] D. S. Landes, *Bankers and Pashas* (London, Heinemann, 1958), 309.

[11] *The Times*, 17 December 1909, 11iii.

[12] H. Lucy, *Sixty Years in the Wilderness. More Passages by the Way* (London, Smith, 1912), ii. 14. W. R. Nicoll, *A Bookman's Letters* (London, Hodder, 1913), 272.

[13] H. Lucy, *Lords and Commoners* (London, Unwin, 1921), 190.

[14] J. W. R. Scott, *The Story of the Pall Mall Gazette* (1950), 291, 299, 311.

Beaconsfield in the *Encyclopaedia Britannica*, where Greenwood again affirmed of the purchase: 'It was not a Disraeli conception, nor did it originate in any government department.'[1] The Disraeli-myth was nevertheless accepted by the editor of the *Cambridge Modern History*[2] and was widely popularized by Louis Napoleon Parker, the creator in 1905 of the historical pageant on an episodic basis. Parker's play *Disraeli* centred around the episode of the purchase, depicted it as a triumph by England over Russia and was first performed in Montreal on 20 December 1910 and in New York on 11 September 1911. Edwardian England, freed from the disapproving presence of Gladstone, became overpowered by the magnitude of the profits accruing since 1894 from 'the great turnstile between West and East'[3] and readily assumed that the financial profits of the Treasury abundantly justified the purchase, especially after the Government's dividends first exceeded £1,000,000 in the financial year ending on 31 March 1906. Such revenues exhilarated Conservatives, converted Liberals to acceptance of the British dominion in Egypt and persuaded anti-imperialists to rank the shares as a main imperial asset.[4] Lloyd George became the first Liberal Chancellor of the Exchequer to accept the financial justification of the purchase when he singled out the dividends as 'not a bad test of the prosperity of the country'.[5]

The occupation of Egypt remained unexplained[6] or was interpreted in deterministic terms as the inevitable culmination of its history since the construction of the Canal, being deemed necessary 'to save an ancient civilisation and a modern canal'[7] and to keep free 'the waterway of the nations'.[8] The occupation was justified in the terms favoured by Cromer and Milner of the material benefits resulting to the population. That interpretation necessitated the unmitigated vilification of Ismail as a spendthrift tyrant who had dragged his country down to ruin and rebellion. It blamed him for the accumulation of the Egyptian Debt by minimizing the Debt at his accession and ignoring his extensive programme of economic development. That fixed bias against 'the Egyptian Verres'[9] diffused by Milner was entrenched by Cromer. Milner's work went through eleven impressions and four editions between 1892 and 1904 and converted not only all British historians but even the radical economist Hobson to the belief that the British entered Egypt as deliverers rather than as conquerors. Cromer supplied the national epic of the national idyll,[9]

---

[1] F. Greenwood, 'Beaconsfield', *Encyclopaedia Britannica* (Cambridge University Press, 1910, 11th edition), iii. 568.
[2] S. Leathes, 'Great Britain', *Cambridge Modern History* (Cambridge University Press, 1910), xii. 32.
[3] F. C. Penfield, *East of Suez* (New York, Century, 1907), ch. i, 'The World's Turnstile at Suez'.
[4] J. G. Godard, *Racial Supremacy* (Edinburgh, Morton, 1905), 290.
[5] Hansard, *Commons Debates*, 19 April 1910, 1914, Lloyd George.
[6] J. Morley, *The Life of William Ewart Gladstone* (London, Macmillan, 1903), iii. 72–86.
[7] H. Paul, *A History of Modern England* (1905), iv. 252.
[8] H. Maxwell, *A Century of Empire 1801–1900* (1911), iii. 106.
[9] Earl of Cromer, *Modern Egypt* (London, Macmillan, 1908), i. 46; ii. 443.

supported by the histories of the other chief actors in the crises of 1882 and 1893,[1] and established his reputation as the greatest colonial administrator of all time and his work as the final authority on modern Egypt, in the U.S.A.[2] as well as in England. The new history provoked protests against its injustice to Ismail,[3] to Derby and to Egypt,[4] against the overvaluation of the Canal[5] and of the share-purchase,[6] against Cromer's composition of his official reports in the style of the first chapter of Genesis,[7] against the systematic neglect of Egypt's past history and current aspirations and against the extension of its economic exploitation.[8] The most powerful of these protests was penned by Blunt in the first volume of his five Secret Histories[4] which he wrote for the specific benefit of future historians. That whole eddy of dissent was however eclipsed by the tidal spread of the interlocking myths of Disraeli, the Canal and the route-to-India. The Mediterranean route was inevitably overvalued[9] while the Canal was dissociated from Egypt in the English mind[10] and transformed into 'the one pivot of the world of the sea'[11] and a 'vital necessity' to England,[12] although the British trade of £200,000,000 via the Canal in 1911 was only 16·4 per cent of the total value of British trade, or the same proportion as in 1885. The Convention of Constantinople was thought by the English[13] as well as by the French to have neutralized the Canal but not to have deprived England of her primary role as its guardian.[14]

The importance of the Canal was enhanced by the general diffusion of the magical phrase 'East of Suez', devised by Kipling between 1887 and 1890, as a title for short stories[15] and tales of travel[16] as well as a refrain in new musical

[1] A. Colvin, *The Making of Modern Egypt* (1906). A. Milner, *England in Egypt* (1892).

[2] A. L. Cross, *A History of England and Greater Britain* (New York, Macmillan, 1914), 1002-3.

[3] E. Ollivier, *L'Empire Libéral* (Paris, Garnier, 1902, 1904), vi. 508; ix. 2-3.

[4] W. S. Blunt, *Secret History of the English Occupation of Egypt* (1907). E. E. Farman, *Egypt and its Betrayal* (New York, Grafton, 1908).

[5] D. A. Thomas, 'The Growth and Direction of our Foreign Trade in Coal during the Last Half Century', *Journal of the Royal Statistical Society* (1903), 485.

[6] S. Walpole, *The History of Twenty-Five Years 1856-1880* (London, Longmans, 1908), iv. 1876-1880, 92-3.

[7] W. S. Blunt, *Gordon at Khartoum* (1911), 60.

[8] T. Rothstein, *Egypt's Ruin* (London, Fifield, 1910). R. Luxemburg, *Die Akkumulation des Kapitals* (Leipzig, Franke, 1913), 406. H. N. Brailsford, *The War of Steel and Gold* (London, Bell, 1915), 120.

[9] A. J. Sargent, *The Sea Road to the East. Gibraltar to Wei-hai-Wei. Six Lectures Prepared for the Visual Instruction Committee of the Colonial Office* (London, Philip, 1912), 20, 32. A. E. McKilliam, *The Highways of the World* (London, Bell, 1912), 128-37, 'Overland Routes to India and the Suez Canal'.

[10] D. Sladen, *Egypt and the English* (London, Hurst, 1908), i. 502.

[11] T. Fraser, 'A Century of Empire'. *Fortnightly Review*, June 1905, 1112.

[12] Hansard, *Commons Debates*, 4 July 1912, 1368, Colonel Hickman.

[13] H. Paul, *A History of Modern England* (1906), v. 117.

[14] A. S. White, *The Expansion of Egypt under Anglo-Egyptian Condominium* (1899), 59.

[15] Alice Perrin, *East of Suez* (London, Treherne, 1901).

[16] F. C. Penfield, *East of Suez, Ceylon, India, China and Japan* (New York, Century, 1907). Idem, *Wanderings East of Suez in Ceylon, India, China and Japan* (London, Bell, 1907).

versions of Kipling's verse.[1] The influence of Kipling reached its zenith and extended the frontiers of the European mind across the Mediterranean. 'Egypt, in spite of the maps, lies in Europe.'[2] Kipling himself recognized the claims of Venice or even of the St. Gotthard to be the frontier of Asia but preferred to locate its exact beginning in Port Said.[3] Suez however remained far more evocative in the world of the imagination than Port Said, provided the core of the counter-phrase 'west of Suez' coined in 1907[4] and was recognized as the barrier between East and West by Indians[5] as well as by Europeans. Thus the Edwardian era crystallized imperial emotions around Suez and moulded the outlook of later generations, in defiance of successive changes in the actual function of the Canal. The waterway was accepted as the fount of Britain's Egyptian policy as well as the key to its Eastern Empire so that a passage through it acquired new interest for Americans as well as English[6] and the role of Canal pilot secured recognition as a highly specialized profession.[7] Biographers associated their subjects with the Canal as never before[8] while E. J. Howarth, a fine cotton spinner of Farnworth, built the new Suez Mill in 1906 and incorporated his firm as the Suez Mills Company Ltd. on 5 December 1910. The Canal Company benefited most of all by England's acceptance of the French tradition[9] because Lesseps remained beneath the cloud of Panama while old Anglo-Egyptians still remembered Egypt's lack of financial benefits of any kind from the Canal.[10] 'Never yet, in as far as I am acquainted with financial history, has there been a concession granted, so profitable to the grantee, so costly to the grantor, as that given by Said Pasha to the Suez Canal Company.'[11]

[1] Oley Speaks, 'On the Road to Mandalay' (Cincinnati, Church, 1907). Charles Willeby, 'Mandalay' (Cincinnati, Church, 1911).

[2] Morley, *Gladstone* (1903), iii. 76.

[3] Kipling, 'Egypt of the Magicians', *Nash's Magazine* (July 1914), 481–2. Idem, *Letters of Travel (1892–1913)* (1920), 220, 222, 'A Return to the East'.

[4] I. Z. Malcolm, *Indian Pictures and Problems* (London, Richards, 1907), 210. C. M. Pepper, 'The West in the Orient', *Scribner's Magazine* (April 1908), 449, 'westward to Suez'.

[5] G. L. Dickinson, *An Essay on the Civilisations of India, China and Japan* (London, Dent, 1914), 27.

[6] E. B. Wright, 'The Canal', *Scribner's Magazine* (December 1905), 692–4. J. D. Crace, 'Through the Suez Canal with M. de Lesseps', *Cornhill Magazine* (August 1909). S. E. White, 'On the Way to Africa', *Harper's Magazine* (January 1913), 218–22.

[7] L. Tillier, 'La Navigation dans le Canal de Suez', *La Revue du Mois*, 10 Novembre 1907, 587–605; 10 Décembre 1907, 700–12. *Le Canal de Suez*, 22 Mars–22 Avril 1911, 5538–9, 5541–2, 5550–1, 'Le Pilotage dans le Canal de Suez'.

[8] G. M. Fenn, *George Alfred Henty. The Story of an Active Life* (London, Blackie, 1907), 172.

[9] A. B. Spens, *A Winter in India* (1913), 1–22, 277–99, Count Charles de Lesseps, 'The Suez Canal'.

[10] F. M. Sandwith, 'Egypt and the Egyptian Sudan (1841–1907)', *Cambridge Modern History*, xii (1910), 430–3.

[11] E. Dicey, *The Story of the Khedivate* (1902), 40.

27

THE RUSSO-JAPANESE WAR, 1904–1905, AND THE RE-AWAKENING OF ASIA

RUSSIAN expansion in Asia was fostered by the building of the Trans-Siberian Railway and by the expansion of its oil shipments through the Canal. As Russia became the largest oil producer in the world between 1898 and 1901, the price of its oil sank from 1900 and reduced the value of the stocks which the Shell Company had built up in the ports of Asia. Shell had also suffered from the competition of the tankers of the Royal Dutch Company and of Standard Oil which had used the Canal since 1899.[1] Marcus Samuel secured a renewal of his contract of 1891 with B.N.I.T.O. in 1900 but lost the exclusive right to market B.N.I.T.O. oil east of Suez.[2] In 1902 he offered the control of Shell to the British Government,[3] citing Disraeli's action in 1875 as a precedent and asking only that the Royal Navy should undertake conversion from coal to oil, a condition which proved unacceptable. He had sought to bring a cargo of petrol from Sumatra through the Canal in 1901 but had been turned back by the Company under the safety regulations of 1892.[4] In 1902 he therefore brought the *Murex* around the Cape with 8,000 tons of petrol, to supply the storage tanks of Thameshaven with their first consignment and to prove that its bulk transport was not dangerous.[5] The rise of petrol production in the outer provinces of the Dutch East Indies, together with the competition of Russian and American oil, brought Shell and Royal Dutch together in the Asiatic Petroleum Company in 1903. That sales-association united the oil of Royal Dutch with the tankers of Shell, recognized the central location of the Dutch East Indies in relation to the Eastern market, established the primacy of Royal Dutch in production as well as in sales and limited B.N.I.T.O. to the supply of one-seventh of the estimated annual consumption of the East.[6] Thereafter Shell's Canal tonnage sank in 1904 to a level 23 per cent below that of 1903 and 60 per cent below that of 1901 as Samuel diverted his tankers to the carriage of heavy oil from Texas.

Britain's distraction by the Boer War encouraged Russian expansion in the Persian Gulf. The despatch of a Russian cruiser to establish a coaling station at Bandar Abbas in 1900 prompted the competitive despatch of British battle-ships to the Gulf.[7] Russia developed its trade to the Gulf by refunding from 1900 all Canal dues to Russian ships for ten years and so extended the

---

[1] R. Henriques, *Marcus Samuel* (1960), 321–4.
[2] Ibid., 320.
[3] Ibid., 400–1, 13 March 1902.
[4] Ibid., 366–7.
[5] Ibid., 386.
[6] F. C. Gerretson, *History of the Royal Dutch* (1955), ii. 248.
[7] J. G. Lorimer, *Gazetteer of the Persian Gulf, Oman and Central Arabia* (Calcutta, Superintendent Government Printing, 1915), i. 327–8, 375–7.

50 per cent rebate made since 1876 to the Russian Volunteer Fleet. The Russian Steam Navigation and Commercial Company began a service from Odessa to Basra which linked up at Aden with the Russian Volunteer Fleet. The *Korniloff*, the first steamer of the new line, reached Bushire on 21 March 1901 and Basra on 4 April.[1] Russian exports to the Gulf of oil, sugar and manufactures benefited by the 'Persian tariff' of 1901 on manufactures shipped for export to Odessa and by the establishment of Russian consulates on the Gulf in 1901. The unofficial British response to the Russian advance was to secure the D'Arcy oil concession in 1901 and to begin a service from Manchester to the Gulf by the *Haddon Hall* of the West Hartlepool Steam Navigation Company, which passed through the Canal in March 1902. The Russian advance on the approaches to India inspired Mahan to distinguish in September 1902 the 'Middle East' centred around Persia from the 'Near East' and the 'Far East' as 'that portion of the Suez route to the Further East which lies between Aden and Singapore'.[2] He thereby transmuted Curzon's 'Central East', itself an offshoot of the Central Asian Question, closed a major gap in the geographical imagination of space and created the concept popularized by Valentine Chirol.[3] British interests were equally opposed to the Bagdad Railway because it would open the Gulf to Germany as the Suez Canal had opened the Indian Ocean to France. The P. & O. helped to frustrate an official scheme for British participation in the Bagdad Railway Company[4] by joining with the Euphrates Steam Navigation Company, the Turkish bondholders and the Smyrna–Aidin Railway Company, whose chairman, Baron Rathmore, had also been a director of the Canal Company since 1896. The diversion of passenger traffic by such a line would have affected only 2 per cent of the Canal Company's receipts but the diversion of the mail lines would have deprived the Canal of nearly one-quarter of its tonnage.[5] British interests in the Gulf were protected against both its rivals by the Monroe-type doctrine laid down by Lansdowne in the Lords on 5 May 1903,[6] by the contract of 10 November 1903 for the addition of a slow service to the fast weekly service of the British India Line[7] and by the unprecedented vice-regal tour of the Curzon lake in November 1903.[8] Curzon benefited by the diversion of

---

[1] Lorimer, 333–4.

[2] A. T. Mahan, 'The Persian Gulf and International Relations', *National Review* (September, 1902), 38, 39. 'The Middle East, if I may adopt a term which I have not seen, will some day need its Malta as well as its Gibraltar.' R. H. Davison, 'Where is the Middle East?', *Foreign Affairs*, July 1960, 667–8.

[3] V. Chirol, 'The Middle Eastern Question. The Persian Aspect of the Asiatic Problem', *The Times*, 14 October 1902, 6i: The pressure applied by Russian statesmen 'in Persia is perhaps not infrequently meant to be felt as much in the Far East or in the Near East as in what Captain Mahan has aptly christened the Middle East'. V. Chirol, *The Middle Eastern Question or Some Political Problems of Indian Defence* (London, Murray, 1903), 5.

[4] *The Times*, 24 April 1903, 5v, 9v. R. Kumar, *India and the Persian Gulf Region 1858–1907* (1965), 173–6.

[5] *Le Canal de Suez*, 22 Juin 1903, 4269–70.

[6] Lorimer, i. 367–77.   [7] Ibid., 2441.

[8] Ibid., 2626–62.

Russia's interest from the 'Middle East' to the Far East and became in 1904 the first Viceroy of India to take leave in England.

Expansion across Siberia into Manchuria brought Russia into collision with Japan, which could not accept Russian condominium in Korea and hungered to regain the Port Arthur which it had won in 1894 and lost in 1895. The Trans-Siberian Railway carried mails from London to Peking in 23–26 days from November 1903 and extended Anglo-Russian rivalry from the political to the economic field. England placed an Asiatic bridle on the Russian bear in the Anglo-Japanese alliance of 1902 and continued to aid the growth of Japanese power. The shipment of coal and provisions to the Far East in October–December 1903 was undertaken in anticipation of the coming conflict and raised English coal exports east of Suez by 16·3 per cent to 1,149,000 tons in 1903. The boost to the traffic of the Canal more than compensated for the depression in traffic of the first half of 1903 so that the estimate for the traffic in 1903 made in 1900[1] by projecting the 15 per cent rate of increase of 1884–98 was exceeded by 8 per cent. Lansdowne arranged with Samuel for the coaling of the Japanese fleet outside its territorial waters.[2] As an island-power Japan enjoyed the advantage of short sea-communications over the long lines of communication of Russia, which had to send its forces across 120 degrees of longitude to defend Port Arthur, to sever Japan's communications with the mainland and to destroy the Japanese Fleet. Such conditions placed the land-power at a great disadvantage in relation to the sea-power. Mackinder's exaltation of land-power over sea-power was an inevitable reaction against Mahan but also an act of faith rationalized by the suggestion that the mobility of sea-power in relation to land-power during the preceding generation had been more apparent than real because of the advent of steam and the Suez Canal.[3]

A Russian squadron of fourteen vessels under Rear-Admiral Virenius passed through the Canal in January 1904, followed by two Japanese cruisers built in Genoa and bought by British brokers on behalf of Japan. On the news of the departure of Virenius from Suez on 4 February for the Far East Japan broke off diplomatic relations with Russia on 6 February and thereby recognized Suez as the Rubicon between Europe and Asia. After the arrival on 9 February of the news of Togo's surprise attack on a Russian squadron at Port Arthur the Foreign Office issued Neutrality Rules on 10 February and Egypt a Neutrality Order on 12 February with new restrictive regulations on coaling. Thereunder no coal might be supplied without a written authorization from the port authorities and without a written declaration from the captain of his destination and of the coal already on board his vessel. Those regulations, intended to give effect to the Convention of 1888, applied ostensibly

[1] J. Charles-Roux, *L'Isthme et le Canal de Suez* (1901), ii. 327.
[2] R. Henriques, *Marcus Samuel*, 480, Lansdowne to Samuel, 31 December 1903.
[3] H. Mackinder, 'The Geographical Pivot of History', *Geographical Journal* (April 1904), 431, 434.

to both belligerent powers but practically only to Russia with its long line of maritime communications. They were more liberal than the 1898 ruling because they permitted a vessel to reach the nearest accessible port at which supplies necessary for the continuation of her voyage might be obtained. Earl Percy, the Under-Secretary of State for Foreign Affairs, stated in the Commons on 18 February that the Government adhered to the opinions of Lord Derby's Note of 6 May 1877 in relation to the navigation of the Canal in wartime. Thereby the Foreign Office retreated beyond the Convention of 1888 to the unilateral anti-Russian declaration of 1877.

Virenius was ordered by his Government to return to the Baltic and began his return voyage from Jibuti up the Red Sea on 18 February. On the way he stopped and searched merchant-vessels, detaining on 19 February three east-bound neutral ships as prizes. Thus Russia replied to the new Anglo-Egyptian coaling regulations because the three vessels were all colliers and two were British. Virenius did not escort his prizes through the Canal but brought them on 25 February to Ras Sudr, twenty miles south-east of Suez. He used that anchorage as a base from which to overhaul other neutral ships in the Gulf of Suez where the navigable channel was no wider than eight miles. Thereby he controlled the passage of the Canal almost as effectively as if he had occupied the town and harbour of Suez and showed that the three-mile limit of protection for the Canal under the Convention of 1888 was too restricted for the essential interests of seaborne commerce.[1] His blockade of the route which carried 60 per cent of the trade with the Far East began to divert many ships, especially English colliers, to the Cape route. Egypt protested against what it thought a gross and open violation of its neutrality and of its territorial waters. Earl Percy explained in reply to a question from Bowles in the Commons on 25 February that the Government had signed and ratified the Convention of 1888 subject to reservations and that the other signatory powers had therefore taken no steps to bring the Convention into active operation. The Foreign Office thus advanced within a week from the English position of 1877 to the European position of 1888. The Tsar then ordered the release of the colliers on the ground that coal had not been declared contraband of war at the time of their capture. Virenius released his cumbersome prizes after four days on 28 February, entered the Suez roads and took his whole squadron through the Canal by 6 March. His activity led the Government of Egypt to authorize on 2 March new Rules regarding Belligerent Vessels in Egyptian Ports and Territorial Waters, which introduced a three-months' interval between supplies of coal to the same vessel within Egyptian waters, forbade the carriage of any prize into Egyptian territorial water or port and prohibited the recruitment of soldiers and sailors within Egypt.

The *Dimitri Donskoi*, one of Virenius' warships which had been allowed to remain at Suez for repairs until 10 March, secured 500 tons of coal at Port Said

---

[1] T. J. Lawrence, *War and Neutrality in the Far East* (London, Macmillan, 1904), 112–19, 'The Russians in the Red Sea'.

for the stated purpose of steaming to Cadiz. It left Port Said on 12 March but used the coal to cruise off the approaches to the Canal for four days (13–16 March), overhauling six neutral merchant-vessels and examining their papers. It continued the same practice off Alexandria a few days later and so extended the Russian offensive against contraband from the Red Sea to the Mediterranean. Its activity compelled British shippers to Japan to place their cargo-manifests on board ship before leaving England instead of at Suez as thitherto.[1] It clearly revealed the difficulties in the use of the Canal route by merchant-vessels in wartime as well as the advantages of a consular commission of supervision of the Canal which England had denied herself. It provoked indignant protests to Balfour and Percy in the Commons against the Russian use of Suez and Port Said for belligerent operations.[2] The maritime activity of Russia thus aroused hostility in the West while the Japanese victory on the Yalu River on 1 May enhanced sympathy for a brave little people whose concentrated power was concealed from the West by Puccini's screen of geishas, gardens and cherry-blossom.

Russia was debarred from using her Black Sea Fleet against Japan by the closure of the Straits. Lansdowne and Balfour decided on 29 April that even if that fleet passed the Straits it could not be permitted to pass through the Canal. The determination of the Foreign Office to bottle up the Russian Fleet even at the price of contravening the newly operative Convention of Constantinople was circumvented by the use of the Russian Volunteer Fleet. Two vessels of that fleet passed the Straits as merchantmen and then transformed themselves into the cruisers *Petersburg* and *Smolensk*. They coaled at Port Said on 7 July and passed through the Canal on 8 and 10 July. In the Red Sea they overhauled neutral vessels in accordance with their commission from the Tsar to search and seize foreign vessels. They first captured on 13 July near the exit to the Red Sea the P. & O. *Malacca* which was bound for China and Japan with 3,000 tons of general cargo and 40 tons of explosives for the British China Squadron at Hong Kong.[3] The *Malacca* was brought back 1,250 miles to Suez on 19 July with a Russian prize crew under the Russian naval flag and taken through the Canal in defiance of the decision of the Cabinet in Cairo but was refused coal at Port Said on 20 July.[4] Four other British and German vessels were stopped between 15 and 19 July by the Russian cruisers in the Red Sea. Thus Russia renewed the indirect blockade of the Red Sea and of the Canal, captured mail-boats as well as colliers and escorted prizes through the Canal for the first time in its history. She extended her belligerent rights at the expense of neutrals and restored her maritime prestige at the expense of England and Germany but refrained from halting French vessels. Britain could take no action against Russia lest she limit her own future

[1] D. R. MacGregor, *The China Bird. The History of Captain Killick* (1961), 241.
[2] Hansard, *Commons Debates*, 7 March 1904, J. L. Walton; 9 March, G. Renwick; 17 March, B. Jones for Walton; 18 March, E. R. P. Moon.
[3] *The Times*, 18 July 1904, 5iii; 19 July, 5iii; 20 July, 5iii–iv; 21 July, 5i; 22 July, 3i.
[4] Ibid., 23 July 1904, 7i.

freedom of action as a belligerent power. Lansdowne nevertheless made a strong remonstrance to Russia on 20 July while the Admiralty ordered the Mediterranean Fleet to Alexandria. The Tsar then ordered on 21 July the release of the *Malacca*, which was en route to Libau. The Mediterranean Fleet reached Alexandria on 22 July and detached a cruiser to Suez on 23 July and a gunboat to Port Said on 24 July, when the Tsar revoked the commissions granted to the two warships. Balfour admitted to Bowles in the Commons on 25 July that legitimate prizes might be taken through the Canal, even if they included a British vessel and its crew. On 27 July the Russian prizes were released including the *Malacca* at Algiers, where the British Consul certified that the military stores on board were the property of the British Government and that the rest of the cargo was not contraband. Thus ended one of the most humiliating incidents in the history of the P. & O. The Mediterranean Fleet then left Alexandria and called at Port Said on 29 July while the *Petersburg* and *Smolensk* returned through the Canal. Ten of the forty-eight merchant-vessels seized or sunk during the war were captured between 19 February and 27 July 1904[1] in the Red Sea, where nine others were stopped. Russia extended its surveillance of the routes to the East to the Cape, off which the *Smolensk* cruised for a month and stopped Harrison's *Comedian* eighty miles off East London on 22 August before it returned via Zanzibar and Suez towards the end of September.

The war diverted both the Nippon Yushen Kaisha and the Russian Volunteer Fleet from their regular services via the Canal and reduced the total mail tonnage of the Canal by 6·5 per cent during 1904. The number of Russian troops using the Canal remained the same in 1904 as in 1903 because the Trans-Siberian Railway was the main route used by the Russian Army. The massive concentration of Japanese power against Port Arthur reduced Japan's Canal tonnage much more than that of Russia. Russian tonnage declined by 56 per cent in 1904 while Japanese tonnage sank by 90 per cent and disappeared completely during 1905. The traffic of the Canal was also reduced by bad harvests in Western India and the slackening of normal trade with North China and Japan. The war however provided the Canal with compensatory traffic and so averted depression during 1904. In particular it stimulated southbound coal shipments which rose by 62·5 per cent to 1,484,000 tons in 1904 while another 100,000 tons of coal for the war were shipped via the Cape. In the depression of 1905 coal shipments sank back by 48·5 per cent to 764,000 tons. Samuel's help in coaling the Japanese fleet earned him the decoration of Commander of the Order of the Rising Sun in 1904[2] and his firm another fortune comparable to that made by the Hamburg American Line in coaling the Russian Baltic Fleet.

The Second Pacific Squadron under Admiral Rozhestvensky sailed from the Baltic via French ports of call. The resulting Dogger Bank crisis in Anglo-Russian relations led Fisher to plan the withdrawal of the British Far Eastern

---

[1] *The Times*, 29 August 1904, 10 ii.   [2] R. Henriques, *Marcus Samuel*, 483.

Fleet so as to concentrate the fleet in home waters and to provide in the war orders of 1905 for the Channel Fleet to safeguard the military reinforcements for India as far as the Cape. Felkerzam left the main fleet at Tangier on 5 November with a squadron of thirteen smaller vessels which could navigate the Canal. The supply of coal to Felkerzam at Port Said provoked the complaint by H. W. Wilson, the naval historian of the Spanish-American War and the assistant editor of the *Daily Mail*, that England had abandoned its precedent of 1898 in favour of Russia.[1] Felkerzam passed through the Canal on 25–26 November with his men standing by their guns and their torpedo-tubes in his fear of Japanese torpedo-boats in the confined waters of the Great Bitter Lake and the Gulf of Suez. He was escorted by two Egyptian coast-guard cruisers from Suez to Shadwan at the exit from the Gulf. He reached Madagascar on 28 December, thirteen days before Rozhestvensky arrived and learned of the fall of Port Arthur after a siege of seven months. The consequent increase in Japanese power necessitated the despatch of reinforcements which reached Rozhestvensky in two instalments through the Canal under Botrovsky on 10–13 January 1905 and under Nebogatov on 24–26 March. The passage of Nebogatov's Third Pacific Squadron of thirteen old Baltic hulks was aided by the Canal Company and by the Government, which detained homeward-bound merchant-vessels at Suez, gave priority to the warships over the merchantmen and so provoked a new complaint of favouritism towards the Russians as compared with the Spanish in 1898.[2] England recognized however that Russia was not Spain while Cromer concluded that the Convention of 1888 worked well during the war, needing revision only in points of detail.[3] Rozhestvensky left Madagascar on 16 March as Nebogatov entered the Mediterranean. He was joined by Nebogatov off Indo-China on 9 May and then set off on the last lap of his 11,000-mile voyage around the world. Togo met the combined Russian fleets of thirty-two vessels off the Island of the Donkey's Ears in the Yellow Sea between Korea and Japan. There he annihilated them with the aid of British gunners[4] and of thirty years' training in the naval technology of the West. The news of Tsushima reached London on the same day as Jawaharlal Nehru,[5] who had arrived at the age of $15\frac{1}{2}$ to pursue his education at Harrow. Nehru's rejoicing was shared by the whole of Asia. The Admiralty recognized that Russia had been reduced from a first-class to a third-class naval power, concluded that Tsushima was the equivalent of Trafalgar and replaced Russia by Germany in their calculations of the two-power standard.

Peace was concluded on 5 September while munitions were still flowing towards the theatre of war. On the night when the Treaty of Portsmouth was signed a collision took place in darkness in the Canal twelve miles south of

[1] *The Times*, 28 November 1904, 4iv.
[2] Hansard, *Commons Debates*, 17 April 1905, Weir.
[3] Lord Cromer, *Modern Egypt* (1908), ii. 387.
[4] O. D. Rasmussen, *The Reconquest of Asia* (London, Hamilton, 1934), 147–8.
[5] J. Nehru, *An Autobiography* (London, Lane, 1936), 17.

Port Said. The *Clan Cumming* was coming up too fast from the south[1] to avoid collision with the *Chatham* of Watts & Co.'s Britain Steam Ship Company Ltd. The collision caused the lamps in the forecastle of the *Chatham* to fall and set fire to the ship, whose cargo for Yokohama included seventy-nine tons of dynamite, nitroglycerine and detonators as well as pig-iron, coke and superphosphates. The Canal Company sought to avert the realization of the worst nightmare of amateur strategists and took charge of the vessel in order to extinguish the fire. The vessel sank on 6 September as the result of the actions of the Company's officials. Whether the Company intended to sink the vessel is doubtful since it had no power to do so. Probably its agents flooded the fore-hold as a precautionary measure[2] and so unwittingly sank the seven-year-old vessel, whose bows had been damaged and whose bulwarks were not watertight. The sinking of the *Chatham* made the dynamite even more dangerous and partly closed the Canal from 7 September to traffic, which the Company sought to facilitate by widening (13–17 September) the channel between the ship and the western bank. A special representative of Nobel's Explosives Company, summoned from Glasgow to Port Said, reported that spontaneous decomposition of the dynamite was possible at any moment. The Canal was then entirely closed to traffic from 20 September. Nobel's representative assessed any attempt at salvage as dangerous and recommended blowing up the wreck, although he could not predict the exact effect because such a vast quantity had never been exploded before. His recommendation alarmed the Company but was carried out with military precision under the controlled conditions of an experiment, without damage to either the Sweet Water Canal or to the railway, without any destruction of property and without any loss of life. From a distance of four miles the *Chatham* was blown up on 28 September[3] and was so removed from *Lloyd's Register*. The bay created by the explosion was twice as large as expected, the Canal was blocked for about 900 yards and its depth at the centre of the explosion was reduced from 33 to 11 feet. After the dredging by night and day of 23,500 cubic yards the Canal was reopened to daytime transit on the morning of 8 October. Vessels had been compelled to wait in Port Said, enabling passengers to visit Cairo but raising food prices in the port. By 11 October 109 ships, 53 southbound and 56 northbound, had passed through the waterway. Night-time transit was not resumed until 25–26 October when all fragments of the wreck and 400 tons of scrap-iron had been removed. The Company's shares did not decline during the blockage because tolls were still paid as the ships queued up at the terminal ports. They declined after the reopening by 5·6 per cent between 11 October and 8 December, because the

---

[1] *Aspinall's Reports of Maritime Cases* (London, Cox, 1908), x. 189–94, Admiralty Court, 7 December 1905; 436–8, Court of Appeal, 11 March 1907, *The Clan Cumming*.

[2] Idem, 190.

[3] *Le Canal de Suez*, 2–3 Octobre 1905, 4653. Lord Edward Cecil, 'A Day on the Suez Canal (1905)', *National Review* (September 1921), 133–40, reprinted in *The Leisure of an Egyptian Official* (London, Hodder, 1921), 199–211.

incident had interrupted transit for a month and revealed the terrifying vulnerability of the Canal and therefore of the whole Canal route. Although Arenberg claimed that the Canal could be cleared quickly even in the most unfavourable conditions, the incident suggested the need for a second channel and the possibility of the destruction of the projected Panama Canal. Belated questions in the Commons[1] revealed that the Canal Company had no regulations for ships carrying explosives and that Grey refused to take any action on behalf of the Government. The Company was left to take the necessary action and elaborated appropriate safety-regulations on the model of those for petroleum tanker steamers.

The war stimulated the production of the first German treatise on the Canal since 1870[2] and the first study of its military significance,[3] especially of its role in the newly-ended war.[4] The ratification of the peace-treaty permitted the return through the Canal of nine Russian warships, of Japanese prisoners from Russia via Hamburg and of Russian prisoners from Manchuria. During 1906 2,516 Japanese passed through in English ships while 127,533 Russians passed through in German ships. Thus passengers increased by 39·6 per cent from 252,693 in 1905 to 353,881 in 1906 and first exceeded the 1896 record. Military passengers first exceeded 200,000 and rose from 43·6 per cent of all passengers in 1905 to 62·5 per cent in 1906. That large military contingent stimulated the Company to prove that the Canal had been a very important military route as well as an incomparable commercial highway and had been used between 1870 and 1907 by 3,133,000 troops, by 4,200 warships and by 1,600 troop-transports.[5] Military personnel had provided 49·6 per cent of the 6,305,535 passengers using the Canal between 1870 and 1907. England had contributed 34 per cent of those troops; England, France and Turkey had together contributed 70 per cent and, with Russia, 81 per cent of the total. Troops had formed the largest single group of passengers in every year down to 1879 and in eighteen of the thirty-eight years between 1870 and 1907. Troops had, however, been exceeded by non-military passengers in 1879–84, in 1886, in 1888–94, in 1897, and in 1899. Their transport created useful employment for the vessels of the mail lines while their tolls provided a welcome supplement to the revenues of the Canal Company, especially in years of economic depression.

The war increased manganese shipments from India to fill the gap left by Russia and stimulated the rise of soya shipments from Manchuria through the Canal from 1909. Above all, it transformed the oil trade of the Canal by enabling the U.S.A. to recapture the oil markets of Asia from Russia and to increase its share of the world oil market. From December 1904 strikes broke

[1] Hansard, *Commons Debates*, 15 and 22 November 1906, 7 March 1907, Dr. V. H. Rutherford.
[2] A. U. E. von Öthalom, *Der Suezkanal, seine Geschichte, seine Bau- und Verkehrs-Verhältnisse und seine Militärische Bedeutung* (Wien, Hartleben, 1905).
[3] Ibid., 74–82.   [4] Ibid., 82–104.
[5] *Le Canal de Suez*, 12 Septembre 1908, 5143–5, 'Transit des Passagers'.

out in Baku and U.S. case-oil began to flow to Asia, accelerating the collapse of Russian oil shipments through the Canal in 1905–6. Tanker transits reached their peak tonnage of 650,000 in 1904, a record which was not surpassed until 1920, and then sank by 54 per cent to 300,000 tons in 1905. Shell which had carried over 90 per cent of the oil shipped through the Canal since 1892 supplied very little tonnage to the Canal in 1905–6. Samuel was compelled to choose between the source of oil for his tankers and his markets in Asia. He chose to sacrifice his source of supply to his markets and his Russian to his Japanese connexions so that he lost the opportunity of benefiting by the Anglo-Russian Entente of 1907. The U.S.A. increased its share in the value of India's oil imports from 19·2 per cent in 1905 to 54 per cent in 1906. Standard Oil concluded long-term sales contracts in order to debar Russian oil from any speedy return to Eastern markets and increased its exports at the expense of Royal Dutch as well as of Shell. Its shipments used the Cape route rather than the Canal. Russia's export trade was resumed when the *Spondilus* loaded 10,000 tons of lamp-oil at Batum for the Far East on 19 October 1905. Samuel was, however, so harassed by a reduction in the flow of oil in Texas and by a price-war waged by Standard Oil in the German market that he was compelled to accept the amalgamation of Shell with Royal Dutch in 1907 on the 60–40 terms of Royal Dutch and so suffered a major defeat.[1] That amalgamation brought together two rivals into a smaller version of Standard Oil but based on the export trade as Standard Oil was on the home market. The first great Anglo-Dutch combine became the first true international firm, created in a juridical vacuum and benefiting in its operations in British territory as well as in Egypt by the belief that Shell controlled and managed Royal Dutch rather than vice versa.[2]

The admission of petrol tankers to the Canal in 1907 followed the rise of the automobile industry, the growth in demand for petrol and the expansion of its production.[3] Shell had been compelled to transport petrol to Europe from the Dutch East Indies via the Cape since 1902 and had discovered a rich field in Borneo in 1905. In March 1907 the *Cardium* passed northwards through the Canal with 6,700 tons of petrol with special permission.[4] It was the first petrol-tanker to use the waterway and like the *Murex* in 1892 was operated by Samuel. On 8 April the Board of the Canal Company lifted the prohibition on petrol with a flash-point below 23°C and sanctioned the publication of Regulations for Navigation by Ships laden with Petroleum Oil in Bulk, under which petrol tankers had to be towed and might not navigate by night. That achievement crowned two years of effort by L. H. Ruyssenaers, who was the son of Lesseps' closest friend in Egypt, the Dutch Consul-General. Ruyssenaers had been a director of the Canal Company since 1905 and was elected a director of the Royal Dutch in 1907 as a token of

[1] R. Henriques, *Marcus Samuel* (1960), 491–3.
[2] F. C. Gerretson, *History of the Royal Dutch* (1957), iii. 239.
[3] Ibid., 259–60.   [4] *Le Canal de Suez*, 2 Juin 1907, 4928.

appreciation,[1] although less pressure had been necessary on the Company than in 1891. The use of the Canal saved freight, fuel oil and so much time as to double the capacity of the tanker-fleet.[1] It opened up the market of Europe to the petrol of Sumatra, for which no market existed in Asia, and increased the competition of petrol from the Dutch East Indies with that of Standard Oil. It greatly stimulated the export trade of the Dutch East Indies, which supplied all the petrol shipped through the Canal until 1911. Thus it made possible the rise of the Royal Dutch to world-power and the reduction of the Dutch East Indies to one province of an oil empire of world-wide range. It also stimulated the development of the entrepôt trade of Port Said in petrol. In 1908 Britain became the largest consumer of petrol in Europe and replaced Germany as the chief consumer of petrol from the Dutch East Indies. Shell Spirit became a household name and the fuel of the omnibuses and trams of London. The Canal dues however prevented the manufacture of lamp-oil in the refineries of Sumatra for the markets of the Mediterranean and encouraged the transfer of shipments of petrol to the Cape route from June 1909 to delay their arrival in Europe, after the economic crisis of 1908.

The Anglo-Russian Entente of 1907 was a product of Russia's defeat and of the growth of common anti-German interests during the postwar surge of German power against France in Morocco and against England in the Persian Gulf, to which the Hamburg American Line began a service with the *Canadia* on 14 July 1906 in association with the plan for a Berlin–Bagdad–Basra Railway. The entente sacrificed Persia in order to save India from Russia and provided for its pacific division. It removed the threat of an attack on India from the north and increased the security of the British Empire, eliminating the need on the outbreak of war to block the Canal or to despatch heavy military reinforcements to India. It made possible a future withdrawal of most of the Indian Army to a front in France against Germany. Thus it conferred a positive strategic value on the Canal, restored the full security of the Mediterranean and made the *Duncan* class of 1903–4 the last warships to be built with a reduced draught for the Canal. The entente recognized the eastward shift of British interest from the Near East of Turkey to the Middle East of Persia, where Germany remained the sole formidable rival. It entailed the final estrangement of Britain from the Ottoman Empire, transformed her from the defender into the foe of Turkey and permitted her to consider a Russian acquisition of Constantinople or even of the Canal,[2] so completing the reversal of alliances begun in 1878. It enabled Britain to move towards the support of the subject Arabs against their Turkish overlords as Russia had supported the subject Christians during the previous century. The entente between the two allies of France enhanced French security and ushered in the greatest age of the Republic and of the Canal Company.

[1] F. C. Gerretson, iii. 259–60.
[2] J. E. Barker, 'The Future of Turkey', *Fortnightly Review*, 1 October 1908, 561.

The victory of a second-class Asiatic power over a first-class European power united the world of Asia in rejoicing. It created a new sense of the unity of Asia in opposition to Europe and detonated a widespread resurgence of the old cultures of the East[1] coincident with a sharp differential increase in the population of Asia and Africa in contrast to that of Europe. The defeat of Russia thus proved more important than the defeat of China and made the year 1905 rather than 1895 the true beginning of a new era in world history. If the Seven Years' War began the permanent revolution of modern Europe, the Russo-Japanese War began the permanent revolution of modern Asia, where six previous waves of indigenous unrest had established no permanent organization save in India. The revolts of the nineteenth century culminating in those of 1896 had been conservative revolts seeking to restore an ancient pattern: the revival of 1904–6 sought for the first time to create a future on the Japanese model, Asia's new and effective pattern for imitation. The adoption of the boycott in 1905 against American goods in China and against British goods in Bengal extended the national revival to the economic field. The expansion of the economic ambitions of India in 1907 encouraged the floating of the Tata Iron and Steel Company with a wholly Indian capital, the foundation of the Indian Merchants' Chamber of Commerce in Bombay and the first shipment of 50,000 bales of cotton yarn from Bombay to Europe.[2]

Japan enjoyed a great postwar boom until the crisis of 1907. From 1905 new shipping services were begun to Japan by Brocklebanks of Liverpool, by the Messageries jointly with the Chargeurs Réunis, by the Prince Line from the U.S.A. and by the North German Lloyd from Australia. The shipping tonnage to and from Japan via the Canal doubled from 1,168,000 tons in 1904 to 2,290,000 tons in 1905. The Nippon Yushen Kaisha resumed its use of the Canal from March 1906 and its mail service via the Canal from June 1906, four months before the reappearance of the Russian Volunteer Fleet. The Canal tonnage under the Japanese flag remained mainly mail tonnage and rose from 1·7 per cent of the total in 1907 to 2·3 per cent in 1909. Japanese ships using the Canal came to exceed German ships in size by 1913 and so became the largest ships using the Canal, both naval and commercial. Japan rose from the seventh client of the Canal to the sixth in 1913. It continued to develop its agriculture and industry for export and increased its import of fertilisers. From 1905 Japan developed its export of raw silk to Europe and first exceeded the total volume of Chinese shipments in 1909, competing powerfully in the French market with the staple export of Syria. Thus it expanded towards the Suez

[1] W. S. Blunt, *My Diaries* (1919), ii. 121, 12 March 1905. I. Spector, *The First Russian Revolution. Its Impact on Asia* (Englewood Cliffs, Hall, 1962), 29–30. J. D. Thijs, 'The influence on Asia of the Rise of Japan and her Victory over Russia', *Acta Historiae Neerlandica* ii (1967), 156. M. Townsend, 'The Dislike of the East for the West', *The Spectator*, 20 April 1907, 606. Viator, 'Asia Contra Mundum', *Fortnightly Review*, 1 February 1908, 185–200.
[2] *The Times*, 11 December 1907, 16 ii.

entrance to the West[1] and proved 'the Suez East'[2] to be more than a market for Western products.

The Japanese victory ended the conflict with Russia which had made the Pacific the storm-centre of the world since 1895. It diverted Russian interest back from Asia to Europe but alarmed Australia, New Zealand, Western Canada and the U.S.A. and stimulated Britain to improve its imperial communications. Kitchener undertook the reorganization and redistribution of the Indian Army from 1905 while Fisher's withdrawal of the Far Eastern Fleet in 1905 entrusted the defence of British interests in Asia to Japan and left the Indian Ocean without battleships or even first-class cruisers. Fisher derived another lesson from the war by making the summer manoeuvres of the Home Fleet in 1906 the first trade exercise which sought to protect merchant shipping against commerce-destroyers. The G.P.O. accelerated the mail service to Cape Town, Calcutta, Hong Kong and Sydney by concluding new contracts with the Union-Castle Line, the P. & O., the C.P.R. and the Orient Line. The U.S.A. was so alarmed by the growth of the 'yellow peril' that it sought to build up its naval defences in the Pacific and even to organize a round-the-world railway service under American control.[3] It asked the Canal Company's permission in September 1905 to send a large floating dock through the Canal. The Company granted permission so as not to lose the 135-feet wide dock to the Cape route. The 12,000-ton *Dewey* dock made the first transit by such a dock in the history of the waterway, squeezed through in 107 hours (27 April–1 May 1906)[4] and reached Manila in 6$\frac{1}{2}$ months from Chesapeake Bay. The U.S.A. divided its fleet in 1907 into separate Pacific and Atlantic Fleets so as to protect its exposed Pacific seaboard and accelerated the construction of the Panama Canal from 1907 in order to reunite its seapower. The U.S. White Fleet toured the world from 1907 to 1909, showed the flag in the Pacific and brought Sperry's fleet of sixteen warships northwards through the Canal on 4–6 January 1909, the most powerful naval squadron ever to have used the waterway.

In Western Asia the indigenous revival of 1904–5 centred around Arabia and Persia. That revival facilitated the reconstitution of the Saudi domain but radiated a spirit of unrest outwards into the Yemen, Aden, Syria and Sinai and compelled Cromer in self-defence to extend the frontier-dykes of Egypt far beyond the Canal. The arrival of the Hejaz Railway at Ma'an in September 1904 encouraged a German idea for a Beirut–Ma'an–Akaba Railway in competition with the Canal, and a Turkish plan for a Ma'an–Akaba branch line, with extensions eventually to Port Said and Suez. Such a branch railway to Suez would have followed the Sinai section of the Cairo–Medina pilgrim

---

[1] C. M. Pepper, 'The West in the Orient. iv—The Westward Tide of Commerce through Suez', *Scribner's Magazine* (April 1908), 435.　　　　[2] Ibid., 443.

[3] G. Kennan, *E. H. Harriman. A Biography* (Boston, Houghton, 1922), ii. 13, 12 October 1905.

[4] Pepper, facing page 444, W. J. Aylward, The Dry-Dock Dewey Aground in the Suez Canal.

route and would have strengthened the pan-Islamic appeal of Turkey while a branch railway to Port Said would have joined up the railways of Egypt and Syria across Egyptian territory. The increased English interest in Sinai aroused by Turkish enterprise was archaeological as well as strategic. A first excursion by Petrie made possible the Exhibition of Sinai held in London in July 1905 but taught him the importance of the shipping agents of Suez. 'To anyone in Sinai it may be said that Beyts is Suez and Suez is Beyts.'[1] Cromer appointed an Inspector of Sinai with his H.Q. at Nakhl and sent him in January 1906 to define the frontier at Akaba, so moving wholly outside the administrative frontier of Egypt which extended from Suez to El Arish, excluding East and South Sinai as part of the Hejaz province of the Ottoman Empire.[2] Cromer may have hoped to annex the mouth of the Wadi Araba and certainly proposed to bestow on the Beduin of Sinai such benefits as irrigation and a mosque, barracks and police-station at Nakhl.[3] The Sultan complained on 12 January and ordered the occupation of Taba, nine miles from Akaba, and the fortification of Akaba. Egyptian troops were prevented from landing at Taba and disembarked on Faroun Island. When the Turkish Commandant at Akaba demanded their withdrawal Cromer sent a gunboat in reply on 14 February.

The first question in the Commons about the dispute with Turkey was put to Grey on 8 March.[4] After the Turkish ambassador laid claim to Taba as a dependency of Akaba on 21 March, Grey in the Commons on 27 March first claimed the Sinai Peninsula, including Taba, as under the administration of Egypt. Grey refused on 4 April to publish any papers on the territorial limits of the Khedive's authority east of the Canal. Turkey's claim of 11 April to Sinai south of the Suez–Akaba line was supported by Egyptian opinion as well as by tradition and would have preserved most of the peninsula under Turkish administration. It would, however, have left the Gulf of Akaba as a Turkish sea and a possible base for torpedo-boats on the flank of the Suez route. It would have pointed a huge Turkish salient at Suez and was regarded by Cromer as a serious menace to the liberties of Egypt and the Khedivial dynasty as well as to freedom of transit through the Canal.[5] Grey favoured strong action like Cromer, whose Private Secretary he had been in 1884. He was opposed in the Cabinet of 25 April by the Lord Chancellor, Lord Loreburn, who as R. T. Reid had pleaded in 1883 for the equitable treatment of Lesseps. Campbell-Bannerman recognized that the British case was 'pretty

[1] W. M. F. Petrie, *Researches in Sinai* (London, Murray, 1906), 4.

[2] H. F. Frischwasser-Ra'anan, *The Frontiers of a Nation. A Re-examination of the Forces which Created the Palestine Mandate and determined its Shape* (London, Batchworth, 1955), 35–40, 'Economic Partition 1906–14'.

[3] *Egypt No 1. (1906). Reports by H. M. Agent and Consul-General on the Finances, Administration and Condition of Egypt and the Soudan in 1905, March 8 1906* (Cd. 2817 of 1906), 13–15.

[4] Hansard, *Commons Debates,* 8 March 1906, 631, W. W. Ashley.

[5] *Correspondence on the Turco-Egyptian Frontier in the Sinai Peninsula* (Cd. 3006 of 1906), 26, Cromer to Grey, 21 May 1906. W. S. Blunt, *My Diaries, 1888–1914* (1919), ii. 138–75, 'The Beginning of Grey's Blunders—Akabah'; ii. 457–60, 'The Akabah Quarrel'.

fluid', 'thin and technical'[1] and refused Cromer's request for the landing of British troops in Sinai but nevertheless decided to defend 'the independence of Egypt and the international interests of the Canal'.[1] The Turkish reaction extended from the south to the north of Sinai where a Turkish detachment pulled down the boundary pillars at Rafa on 25 April and prevented the commander of a gunboat from Port Said from landing.[2] Grey then announced in the Commons on 26 April an increase in the Egyptian garrison. A special Cabinet on 27 April sanctioned an ultimatum to Turkey demanding the evacuation of Sinai and Taba within ten days. That ultimatum was delivered to the Porte on 3 May and was supported by the arrival of the Mediterranean Fleet under Beresford at the Piraeus on 4 May.

The Navy undertook to defend the Canal against any possible Turkish raid in a considerable extension of the blue-water school of thought which saved the Liberal Government from any military expenditure. Military Intelligence estimated that 5,000 men and 2,000 camels would have difficulty in crossing Sinai under normal conditions because of the shortage of water and that the Canal itself was the obvious line of actual defence for the eastern frontier of Egypt. Thus Sinai was regarded as a barrier rather than as a highway because of its mountains and its waterless uninhabited desert. A powerful squadron arrived at the Canal in readiness for an appeal for help from the Government of Egypt and carefully respected for the first time the provisions of the Convention of 1888.[3] On 7 May Fitzmaurice in the Lords and Grey in the Commons affirmed that the British stand was one in defence of the freedom of the Canal, Egypt and the Khedivial dynasty. Fitzmaurice explained that intervention in 1882 had been necessary to protect the Canal from danger from the west and that the British stand in 1906 was necessary to protect the Canal from a similar danger from the east. Grey affirmed on 10 May, in reply to a penetrating eight-pronged question, 'We cannot refer the safety of the Canal and of Egypt to arbitration.'[4] The Admiralty completed the necessary arrangements to occupy six Aegean islands and Rhodes and to stop all Turkish ships in the Mediterranean outside the limits of the Canal.[5] On Sunday 13 May the ten days of the ultimatum expired and a naval demonstration was made in the Bosporus. Confined to the Foreign Office in London, Grey was deprived of his customary visit to the beech trees of Hampshire, which were in full leaf on the second Sunday in May, a loss which he never forgot and for which he never seems to have forgiven Turkey. After six days of prevarication the Porte ordered on 14 May the evacuation of Sinai and Taba because it lacked the support of Germany against England, backed by France, Russia and the

---

[1] J. A. Spender, *The life of the Right Hon. Sir Henry Campbell-Bannerman* (London, Hodder, 1923), ii. 266–7, Campbell-Bannerman to Grey, 25 and 28 April 1906.
[2] Hansard, *Lords Debates*, 1 May 1906, 375, Lord Fitzmaurice in reply to Lord Monkswell.
[3] *Correspondence on the Turco-Egyptian Frontier in the Sinai Peninsula*, 28–9.
[4] Hansard, *Commons Debates*, 10 May 1906, 1472, Grey in reply to Lupton.
[5] G. P. Gooch and H. Temperley, *British Documents on the Origins of the War 1898–1914* (H.M.S.O., 1928), v. 191, G. H. Fitzmaurice, The Sinai Boundary Dispute, 11 May 1906.

Khedive. France did not intervene to protect its interests in the name of the Canal Company.[1] The humiliation of Turkey contributed to the Denshawai incident in Egypt and to the Young Turk Revolution at Salonika in 1908.

The Akaba crisis proved the baptism of fire for the new Liberal Cabinet. The frontier of Sinai was demarcated by a joint commission and by concrete pillars from Akaba to El Arish, with the approval of Turkey on 11 September and of England on 1 October. Thereby the administrative frontier of Egypt was extended eastwards from El Arish to Rafa and, in a large advance, from Suez to Taba and to within three miles of Akaba. Kossaima was left to the west of the new frontier but El Auja, with the intersection of all the main routes into Sinai, remained on the Turkish side. Turkey abandoned its plan to build a branch line to Akaba and completed one in 1906 from Der'a to Haifa. The extension of Egyptian administration to the Beduin was facilitated by the terrible drought of 1906. From 1906 the Survey of Egypt was extended to the peninsula, which Cromer protected from economic exploitation[2] and brought under the administration of the War Department.[3] The Akaba crisis fostered the rise of pan-Islamic sentiment in the Egyptian press and necessitated a permanent increase in the Egyptian garrison two years after Cromer had aspired to govern without any army of occupation. The attack on the British officers who had gone pigeon-shooting at Denshawai near Tantah on 13 June 1906 marked a stage in the elevation of the Egyptian peasantry to full humanity. The attack was regarded in England as entirely unprovoked and as a small-scale Moslem revolt stimulated by the mischievous action of the Turks on the Egyptian frontier and by the incitements of their emissaries in Egypt.[4] For the death of one British officer the lives of four Egyptians were claimed in sentences which Cromer described in 1906 as 'just and necessary'[5] but in 1915 as 'unduly severe'.[6] The erection of the scaffolding for the executions before the conviction of the accused villagers[7] revealed the extent to which British rule in Egypt had become militarized. Blunt strove to publicize the Egyptian case through questions asked in the Commons by Dillon,[8] through a pamphlet written by himself[9] and through a preface published by Bernard Shaw.[10] 'The Denshawai Horror' stimulated the rise of Egyptian

---

[1] R. de Saint-Exupéry, 'Au Sujet de l'Incident d'Akaba', *Bulletin du Comité de l'Afrique Française* (Juin 1906), 156.

[2] W. S. Blunt, *My Diaries* (1919), ii. 80, 12 November 1903.

[3] *Annual Report on Egypt for 1906* (Cd. 3394 of 1907), 3.

[4] *The Times*, 28 June 1906, 9iv.

[5] *Correspondence Respecting the Attack on British Officers at Denshawai* (Cd. 3086 of 1906), 20, Cromer's Memorandum of 12 July 1906.

[6] Earl of Cromer, *Abbas II* (London, Macmillan, 1915), x.

[7] W. S. Blunt, *Atrocities of Justice under British Rule in Egypt* (Unwin, 1906, 42 pp.), 23.

[8] Hansard, *Commons Debates*, 18 June 1906, 1366–7; 21 June 1906, 361, J. Dillon.

[9] W. S. Blunt, *Atrocities of Justice under British Rule in Egypt*, reviewed in the *Manchester Guardian*, 12 September 1906, 4ii and *The Times*, 13 September 1906, 6iv.

[10] G. B. Shaw, *John Bull's Other Island* (London, Constable, 1907), xliv–lix, 'The Denshawai Horror', the proofs of which Blunt read on 24 January 1907.

nationalism as no other event had done for twenty-five years against a background of rising real income.

The new nationalism compelled Cromer to appoint as Minister of Public Instruction Saad Zaglul, who had been imprisoned in 1883 as an Arabist but had become the son-in-law of the Prime Minister. Fourteen years after Cromer's humiliation of Abbas in 1893 a new generation had emerged to whom the Turks were a memory and the British a reality. Its greatest representative was the Francophile Mustapha Kamil, who was thoroughly impregnated with French culture and held the basic political unit to be the nation rather than the Islamic community. He coined the phrase 'Cromerism' to divert attention from what he regarded as the delusive pursuit of Pan-Islamic and Pan-Arab ideals. He benefited by the deep hold of French culture on the élites of Egyptian society and won the loyalty of the professional classes, the journalists and the Khedive. The retirement of Cromer gave a further stimulus to the new national movement. Cromer held Abbas responsible for the nationalist agitation, sought in vain to secure his deposition by his fellow-ruler, Edward VII,[1] and then told Grey on 28 March 1907 of his intention to retire. Grey's announcement of the news in the Commons on 11 April quite demoralized the financial and commercial markets of Cairo on 12 April, deprived the Levantine communities of their great protector and ended the cotton boom of 1907 by a sharp crisis. The Principal Agent of the Canal Company in Egypt helped to launch on 15 April a project for a Cromer Memorial. At his farewell speech on 4 May at the Cairo Opera House, which was attended by the foreign communities and by three Egyptians,[2] the great Pharaoh of modern Egypt declared that the British occupation would continue for an indefinite period. The continued presence of British troops was in fact essential to preserve Cromer's great achievement for the foreign bondholders, his balancing of the budget and his maintenance of the United Egyptian Debt at par since 1893. Cromer had however failed to reconcile Egypt to British rule and drove through deserted streets when he departed on 6 May.[3] He was condemned by the oldest advocate of a British protectorate over Egypt for his attempted 'Anglification' of the land through British officials.[4] He had failed to establish an administrative dynasty in Egypt like the British in India or the French in the isthmus of Suez. Nor was he immortalized in a Cromer Memorial or ever again consulted by the Foreign Office on Egyptian affairs.

Cromer's successor Gorst was chosen to introduce a policy of conciliation. He could speak Arabic and gave the Khedive more freedom of action. He could not, however, check the national movement which enlisted the workers, inspired strikes by the Arab coal-heavers at Port Said in 1907–8 and survived the death of Kamil in 1908, when leadership passed to Mohammed Farid.

[1] W. S. Blunt, *My Diaries* (1919), ii. 185, 13 August 1907. S. Lee, *King Edward VII. A Biography* (London, Macmillan, 1927), ii. 534–5.
[2] W. S. Blunt, *My Diaries* (1919), ii. 177, 198, 6 May and 24 December 1907.
[3] P. G. Elgood, *Egypt and the Army* (1924), 24.
[4] E. Dicey, *The Egypt of the Future* (London, Heinemann, 1907), 5.

Gorst then imitated Minto's policy in India and appointed the Copt Boutros Ghali Pasha, Foreign Minister since 1894, as Prime Minister on 13 November 1908, so ending the entente between Moslem and Copt which Kamil had sought to promote. The nationalist movement gave a great stimulus to education in Arabic, especially through the foundation of the 'Popular University' of Cairo in 1908. It achieved its greatest immediate success with the rejection of the Government's plan to prolong the concession of the Canal Company beyond 1968.[1] Sixty years before 1968 the Company sought once more to achieve what it had failed to accomplish in 1883. It was encouraged to hope for such a renewal of its concession without substantial alteration by the rising tide of foreign investment in Egypt which followed the Anglo-French Entente. Early in May 1909 it was rumoured that the Company also hoped to purchase the Khedive's right to a 15 per cent share in the profits,[2] which had been allotted until 1968 to the Civil Society created in 1880. Thereupon John M. Robertson, the historian of free-thought and Liberal M.P. for Tyneside since 1906, asked in the Commons on 20 May what the Government's intentions were, enabling Grey to deny that negotiations were then in progress between the Company and the Government of Egypt.

Gorst unlike Cromer favoured negotiations, in order to supply the Government with ready cash to finance the Sudan and public works. The Government's Financial Adviser carried on long and laborious discussions with the Company, involving the British official directors, the Foreign Office, the Treasury and the Board of Trade but not apparently the seven unofficial British directors. The Company's shares rose in price by 4 per cent (1–8 October), a fortnight before the Financial Adviser's Memorandum of 21 October outlined possible heads of agreement for a 45-year extension of the concession. Farid published details of the proposed new Convention with the Company and the Legislative Council asked for its submission to a specially convoked General Assembly. Boutros Ghali was forced to agree, although he approved the idea of such a Convention. Grey was obliged to admit in the Commons on 4 November that negotiations were proceeding but refused on 25 November to say that the Commons would be consulted. In Egypt Gorst hoped that the Assembly would respect the wishes of the Khedive and his Ministers while the Company relied on the support of Prince Hussein, who was the second son of Ismail, the uncle of Abbas and the founder in 1898 of the Khedivial Agricultural Society. Hussein was appointed President of the Assembly and gave his name to the Hussein Basin which the Company opened in 1909 to the south-east of the Abbas Hilmi Basin at Port Said.

Egypt had no direct interest in the navigation of the Canal, through which only three Egyptian vessels passed in 1907 and two in 1909. She nevertheless had an overriding interest in the terms of the Canal Company's concession

---

[1] J. Alexander, *The Truth About Egypt* (London, Cassell, 1911), 251, 283–329. A. T. Wilson, *The Suez Canal* (1933), 95–107.

[2] *L'Économiste Européen*, 14 Mai 1909, 635.

and bitter experience of the price of public works undertaken by Europeans in Egypt: the new Aswan Dam so disturbed the immemorial regime of the Nile that the cotton crop of 1909 was completely ruined by the high and early flood. The Egyptian Cabinet therefore sought to improve the terms of the proposed Convention against the opposition of the Canal Company.[1] On 27 January 1910 it decided on essential amendments, especially the reduction of the extension of the concession by five years and the elimination of the Company's right to a minimum income of £E2,000,000 from 1969. The Assembly referred the proposed Convention to a Committee on 9 February. The Convention proposed to extend the Company's concession for forty years from 31 December 1968 to 31 December 2008.[2] In return the Company would pay £E4,000,000 in cash between 1910 and 1914 as the discounted benefits due to the Government after 1968. The Company also proposed to pay a share of its net revenue to the Government beginning at 4 per cent in 1921–30 and rising by four decennial increases of 2 per cent to 12 per cent in 1961–8 and to 50 per cent in 1969–2008. The Government would thus divide the net profits with the Company for the period of the extension and also gain the right to nominate three directors to the board from 1968 onward but would surrender its statutory right to a 15 per cent share in the Company's profits.

The scheme was not ungenerous towards the Company and was approved by the British official directors, especially by H.T. Anstruther who had succeeded Fremantle in 1903. It was also approved by Hartley Withers, the City editor of *The Times*,[3] and by Cromer, who recommended it to the Foreign Office on the one occasion after retirement when he volunteered his advice. It was a considerable achievement for Arenberg and a proof of the enterprise of French investors,[4] although it was not submitted to the shareholders whose interests it so greatly extended. Little opposition was raised in Germany.[5] The scheme alarmed English shipowners lest it should prevent a reduction in Canal tolls which were considered to be too high by small shipowners[6] and were criticized by Edward Hain in his presidential address to the Chamber of Shipping of the United Kingdom on 25 February 1910. Egypt feared that the £4,000,000 compensation would be used for the Sudan and for new barracks in the Delta in the absence of any control over the Government's expenditure while the nationalist press estimated the resulting loss to the land at £650,000,000.[7]

---

[1] *Manchester Guardian*, 5 November 1909, 6vi; 9 November, 7iv. J. Alexander, *The Truth About Egypt* (1911), 302.

[2] J. Alexander, *The Truth About Egypt* (1911), 300–2.

[3] *The Times Financial and Commercial Supplement*, 18 February 1910, 13iii.

[4] A. Neymarck, 'Le Canal de Suez, 1869–1909', *Journal de la Société Statistique de Paris* (1910), 70. R. Puaux, 'Le Canal de Suez', *Revue Économique Internationale* (1910), 365–85.

[5] P. Neubaur, 'Der Suez-Kanal', *Meereskunde* (1910), 1–35. W. Hess, 'Der Suezkanal', *Archiv für Post und Telegraphie* (1910), 321–35. F. Magnus, *Aegypten* (Tübingen, Laupp, 1913), 117.

[6] *The Times*, 21 June 1909, 8vi.

[7] J. Alexander, *The Truth About Egypt* (1911), 287.

The scheme was therefore strongly opposed by the press, by public opinion and by the Assembly on its sole appearance on the forefront of the political stage. On 20 February the Anglophile Boutros Ghali, who had signed the Condominium Agreement of 1899 with Cromer, presided over the Denshawai Tribunal as Minister of Justice in 1906 and attended the inauguration of Port Sudan in 1909 in his official capacity as Prime Minister of Egypt, was assassinated by a member of the Society of Mutual Brotherhood, which had been formed by Moslems to rid Egypt of the British occupation. The first bloodshed by an Egyptian nationalist occurred eight months after the assassination by a Punjabi student of Curzon Wyllie, a leading Anglo-Indian Political Agent. It was justified by the assassin as necessary to save his country from the danger represented by a prolongation of the Company's concession.

Prince Hussein, the principal advocate of the Convention, abandoned hope of instilling order and moderation into the deliberations of the Assembly and resigned as its president shortly before its Committee submitted its report on 12 March. In that report the scheme was described as premature and one-sided in relation to the enormous profits in prospect for the Company while its 'supporting' data were thought to lack any rational foundation or even any high degree of probability. The stability of the Company's coefficient of operation was contrasted with the elasticity of its receipts. 'Statistics prove that all crises and conflagrations have contributed to the enhancement of its regular receipts.'[1] The Committee concluded that the scheme would entail a loss to Egypt of £130,598,000 in capital and interest combined and would dispossess all future generations of their patrimony in return for an immediate and insignificant compensation. In short its report revealed an 'entire lack of confidence in the intentions and good faith of the Government'.[2] Zaglul Pasha was the only Minister to defend the scheme in the Assembly. He had been one of the three Egyptians present at Cromer's farewell speech and was the spokesman for the landowning pashas of the Anglophile People's Party, which he had founded in opposition to Kamil's National Party. In vain he argued in favour of the Convention on 16 March that Egypt would probably have to make the passage of the Canal free when the concession expired. The new Ministry announced on 5 April amid loud cheers that it would abide by the decision of the Assembly.[3] On 7 April the Assembly, after restricting discussion as far as possible, rejected the project by sixty-six votes to one vote, which was cast with explicit reservations. Thereby it manifested the hostility of public opinion towards Britain, evoked great popular enthusiasm for the first victory of Egyptian nationalism since 1882 and strengthened the demand for a Constitution.[4] Egypt anticipated that the occupation would end before the expiry of the Company's concession in 1968 and therefore avoided establishing

[1] T. Rothstein, *Egypt's Ruin: a Financial and Administrative Record* (London, Fifield, 1910), 396.

[2] *Egypt. No. 1. (1910). Reports by H. M. Agent and Consul-General on the Finance, Administration and Condition of Egypt and the Soudan in 1909* (Cd. 5121 of 1910), 3–4.

[3] *The Times*, 6 April 1910, 5 iii.   [4] Ibid., 8 April 1910, 5 iv; 11 April, 5 v.

a precedent for further renewals which would have made the Company permanent in Egypt. The Company's shares weakened on the Paris market until the publication of the receipts for the first ten days of April on 12 April sent share-prices higher than ever on a Bourse preoccupied with the short-term rather than with the long-term. The Company had nevertheless been denied the supreme privilege of the corporation and, recognizing its mortality, sharply reduced the quantity of sand dredged from the Canal. Shipowners were warned not to expect the redemption or extinction of the Canal tolls while large shipowners were reassured that their freights would not thereby be reduced through consequent competition. The British Government was also given notice that the expiry of the concession would end its annual dividends of £1,000,000.

The snub to British prestige in Egypt provoked Gorst to recommend in his Annual Report in April 1910 evacuation as the sole alternative to rule by force. Bitter attacks began to be made in the English press and Parliament on the Egyptian Assembly and on the incapacity for self-government of Egypt and all Oriental countries.[1] The five successive requests made by Radical and Irish M.P.s to secure the submission to Parliament of the Government's correspondence on the renewal of the concession were all rejected by Grey.[2] Even a shareholder of the Canal Company who exercised his statutory rights and raised the question at the annual meeting on 6 June 1910 was ruled out of order by Arenberg.[3] Unknown reasons seem to have prevented the publication in Cairo of the second part of an extensive statistical analysis of the Company's financial performance.[4] Farid declared in Paris on 13 June that 'Egypt would sacrifice all her benefits from the Canal in exchange for her liberty and independence' but would maintain a minimum right of administration and control of transit after the expiry of the concession. In the Commons on 13 June Grey solemnly recanted amidst rapturous Conservative applause his whole policy of conciliation in Egypt inaugurated in 1907.[5] Dillon's attack on 21 July on the 'organized conspiracy of abuse' by 'the ignorant Jingo Press' against the Egyptian Assembly and his attribution of all the troubles of Egypt to 'the horrid incident' 'the atrocity of Denshawai'[6] provoked Grey to great anger and was as ill-received by the Radicals as by the Conservatives.[7] Grey's policy of evasion and repression was, however, lamented by Captain G. J. Sandys, the Conservative M.P. for Wells, because of 'the supreme importance of the Suez Canal, both to this country and the British Empire generally'.[8]

---

[1] *The Spectator*, 30 April 1910, 717–18, 'The Discharge of our Egyptian Trust'.

[2] Hansard, *Commons Debates*, 23 February 1910, Wedgwood; 17 March, Mooney; 7 April, Hazleton; 14 April, Hall; 5 July, Dillon.

[3] *The Times*, 7 June 1910, 7i–ii.

[4] I. G. Lévi, 'Tableaux Statistiques sur les Résultats de l'Exploitation du Canal Maritime de Suez depuis son Ouverture au Trafic', *Égypte Contemporaine* (Janvier 1910), 170.

[5] W. S. Blunt, *My Diaries* (1919), ii. 324, 14 June 1910.

[6] Hansard, *Commons Debates*, 21 July 1910, 1554–5, Dillon.

[7] W. S. Blunt, ii. 328.

[8] Hansard, *Commons Debates*, 21 July 1910, 1569, G. J. Sandys.

In his reply Grey thought it essential to leave no uncertainty in people's minds that the British Government intended to remain in occupation of Egypt.[1] Blunt's address of 13 September 1910 to the Egyptian National Congress encouraged it to hope for support from the Mediterranean powers of Austria, Italy and even France to wrest from England 'the Eastern key of their dwelling, their door of direct communication with the Indian seas'. Blunt also financed the publication on 24 October of Rothstein's *Egypt's Ruin* which included a thitherto unpublished English translation of the Committee's report on the proposed Convention and denied that the Egyptians were xenophobes who would 'seize and close against all the world the Suez Canal'.[2] Abbas consolidated the Assembly's victory by creating in 1911 the Port Said Municipality with its elected majority and boasted to Blunt that he had caused the rejection of the Convention by the Assembly.[3] Thus Abbas was recaptured for the nationalist movement. When George V arrived at Port Said in the P. & O. *Medina* on 20 November 1911 he received State visits from Abbas as well as from Kitchener on board the vessel moored in the place of honour by the Canal Company offices but did not land on the soil of Egypt which the nationalist agitation had dishonoured in his eyes. The *Medina* was then escorted through the Canal on 22 November by four cruisers as it carried the King-Emperor en route to the Coronation Durbar in his new capital of Delhi. Such was the first transit of the Canal by a reigning British monarch, who had passed through as a midshipman in 1882, as the Duke of Cornwall in 1901 and as the Prince of Wales in 1906.

[1] W. S. Blunt, *My Diaries* (1919), ii. 328.

[2] T. Rothstein, *Egypt's Ruin: a Financial and Administrative Record* (1910), 365, 371–408, reviewed in *The Spectator*, 12 November 1910, 799, and mentioned by W. S. Blunt, *My Diaries* (1919), ii. 334.

[3] W. S. Blunt, ii. 369, 18 July 1911.

28

THE NEW TRADES OF ASIA, 1909–1913

THE Canal was insulated against any depression of its traffic by its favourable location close to the greatest centres of population, agriculture and industry. Thus it could tap the commerce of the world rather than of a single country and might enjoy a whole succession of harvest seasons. The entry of new areas and new products into international trade prevented excessive dependence on a single crop or land and provided new stimuli to traffic in almost every year and season. Substitutes even appeared for some commodities when vegetable oil began to compete with oil-seeds and sisal with hemp. The traffic of the Canal was also stabilized by the shipment of oil-seeds and oil, which did not undergo any seasonal fluctuations, and by the trade in rice, which did not suffer from cyclical depression. The Canal was further insured against depression by its hard core of postal traffic as well as by its use by warships and troopships during wars when commercial traffic might suffer a depression. Thus in only nine of the forty-four years between 1869 and 1912 did the Canal's tonnage fail to exceed the level of the year immediately preceding. The decade of the 1900s was one of tremendous expansion which doubled the Canal's tonnage between 1900 and 1912, despite very slight recessions in 1900 and 1905 and a serious recession in 1908 which revealed the continuing dependence of traffic on the trade of India.

Northbound traffic began to decline from June 1907 under the influence of famine in Bengal. Southbound tonnage was reduced from April 1908 by the impact of the financial crisis of 1907 in the U.S.A. and Europe. The demand for cloth in India was reduced by the Swadeshi movement and by the coincidence of 1908 with that one year in twelve when no orthodox Hindu might marry. The depression affected merchant tonnage exclusively, reduced the share of tramp shipping sharply and raised the share of liners to 80·5 per cent of the total tonnage. Total shipping tonnage declined during 1908 by 7·5 per cent while that of Western India sank by 34 per cent. Southbound cargo declined by 4·3 per cent whereas northbound cargo fell by 11·2 per cent. The depression sharply reduced the role of sail shipping in the trade with Australia and enhanced the competitive capacity of the steamship therein. It also provoked P. A. Molteno, the son of the first Prime Minister of the Cape Colony, the son-in-law of Donald Currie and a manager of the Union-Castle Line formed in 1900, to ask a series of seven questions in the Commons about the Canal Company.[1] Molteno argued that British East Africa lacked shipping services because of the enormous tolls on the Canal. 'The Suez Canal earned

---

[1] Hansard, *Commons Debates*, 28 May 1908, 1339; 3 June, 18; 23 June, 1492; 29 June, 330; 23 July, 326–7, 329–30, P. A. Molteno.

enormous dividends, but like the old robbers on the Rhine, they descended upon all trade which passed them and levied enormous tolls.'[1] Arenberg sought to maintain the entente cordiale between the Company and its shipowner-clients and visited England for the Franco-British Exhibition of 1908 at the White City, where the Company arranged a Suez Canal section at the junction of the French and British galleries with a replica of the statue of Lesseps, one-twelfth of its size, at the threshold. The exhibition brochure was the Company's first statistical compendium and covered the years from 1870 to 1907:[2] it maintained the standards established by Charles-Roux and Voisin Bey while demonstrating the progressive reduction in toll paid by a ship of 8,000 tons burden in relation to its cargo tonnage between 1874 and 1908.[3] In the Commons Molteno however asked in succession for details of the dividends paid to the British Government, for a more acceptable division of the Company's surplus revenue and for a return to the limitation of the Company's dividends to 25 per cent.[4] Such requests were not unreasonable because the Company's receipts declined during 1908 by 7·2 per cent while its dividends rose to form 64 per cent of its receipts, a higher proportion than ever before in its history. They were however made in vain against a solid Anglo-French union, 'a real entente cordiale',[5] and could not be as effective as the prospect of competition from the Panama Canal. The Company thenceforward undertook the statistical study of its traffic in prosperity as well as in depression, began the regular publication of cargo statistics from 1910[6] to supplement the information it had published since 1870 on shipping, since 1895 on passengers and since 1902 on the regions of traffic, and supplied the technical information necessary for the celebration of the jubilee of the Canal.[7]

The depression of 1908 was not general or prolonged, because Austrian and German traffic continued to increase. The Austrian annexation of Bosnia on 8 October 1908 took place three months after the revolution of the Young Turks and produced a Turkish boycott of the Austrian Lloyd, which was thereby compelled to increase its voyages to Karachi, Colombo and Calcutta. German shipping benefited by the inauguration in 1908 of the Lloyd Express from Hamburg to Genoa via the Gotthard and reduced the British share of the total Canal tonnage from 64·5 per cent in 1907 to 60·9 per cent in 1908. The depression in the trade of Asia was heavily concentrated on India which echoed

[1] Hansard, *Commons Debates*, 28 May 1908, 1339, Molteno.
[2] Compagnie Universelle du Canal Maritime de Suez, *Exposition Franco-Britannique Londres 1908. Le Canal Maritime de Suez. Note, Tableau et Planches* (Paris, Publications Périodiques, 1908).
[3] Ibid., table XI.
[4] Hansard, *Commons Debates*, 23 June, 29 June and 23 July 1908.
[5] *Le Canal de Suez*, 12 Juillet 1909, 5287, Arenberg, 3 July 1909.
[6] Ibid., 22 Juillet, 2 Août, 22 Août, 2 Septembre 1909, 'Le Trafic du Canal en 1908'. Ibid., 22 Juin 1910, 5249–31; 2 and 12 Juin 1911, 5566, 5580; 2/4 Juin 1912, 5742; 12 Juin 1913, 5897; 12 Juin 1914, 6052.
[7] *The Engineer*, 30 April 1909, 440–1, 'The Present Condition of the Suez Canal'.

the complaints made in England against the heavy Canal tolls.[1] The famine of 1907 however made India the world's largest exporter of hides and skins in 1908. Traffic with the Dutch East Indies, Malaya, China and Japan continued to expand during 1908. Northbound traffic began to revive in the second half of 1908 and rose by 16 per cent during 1909. The subsequent boom of 1909–13 followed the last great territorial expansion of European power in Asia: it united political and economic penetration more closely than ever before through the widespread building of railways inland from the ports of Asia, the large-scale export of capital from Europe and the growth of private loans to the governments of Asia. The traffic of the Canal enjoyed a record expansion. Between 1908 and 1912 northbound cargo rose in tonnage by 52 per cent, southbound cargo by 20 per cent, total cargo by 38 per cent, shipping by 49 per cent and British shipping by 55 per cent. The expansion of British, German and Dutch shipping relegated France in 1910 from the position of the third to that of the fourth largest client of the Canal.

The Canal extended its range to the maximum, drew in the trade of the Red Sea, East Africa and the Persian Gulf and benefited by the growth of the trade of Australia, Malaya, the Dutch East Indies and Manchuria. That extension of trade reduced the dependence of its traffic on the Indian harvests.[2] In 1909–13 India supplied 45·5 per cent of the Canal's tonnage, China and Japan 22·2, Australia 9·9, Malaya and the Dutch East Indies 9·1, East Africa 5·2 and the Persian Gulf 1·5 per cent. Round-the-world services pioneered by the Chargeurs Réunis from 1907 passed through the Canal as well as the Straits of Magellan. The first cruise vessel to navigate the Canal was the *Cleveland* of the Hamburg American Line on 3 November 1909 en route from New York to San Francisco, while the first cruise round the world via the Canal was made by the *Empress of Russia* of the C.P.R., which made its transit on 14 April 1913. The greatest expansion was, however, in cargo rather than in passenger traffic, in the revival of tramp shipping and its extension into the Australian trade, and in the expansion of Scandinavian shipping from the interconnected ports of Oslo, Gothenburg and Copenhagen. The 25,775,000 tons of cargo carried through the waterway in 1913 represented 6·4 per cent of the total volume of world seaborne trade. Cereals formed 27·6 per cent of the volume of northbound cargo in 1913, oil-seeds 18·3, textile fibres 11·5, minerals and metals 10·8 and tea 2·4 per cent. The old staple of spices still supplied 36,000 tons of northbound cargo in 1909 but was far outweighed by the shipments of wheat, rice, jute and oil-seeds as well as by the new commodities of soya beans, manganese, rubber and oil. The growth of rubber and oil shipments was stimulated by the advent of the motor-car and of the Diesel oil-engine. Southbound shipments also expanded but to a smaller extent than northbound cargo. Metals and machinery formed 20·3 per cent of southbound cargo in 1913, coal 10·6, railway material 5·3, petroleum 4·5, salt 3·9 and cement 3·9 per cent.

[1] *The Times Empire Supplement*, 24 May 1909, 53 iv.
[2] *Le Canal de Suez*, 12/13 Juin 1911, 5569, 5575.

In the staple traffic of oil-seeds the soya bean supplied a new and dynamic element. The soya bean had supplied China with food and light for centuries, being low in fat but rich in protein. It replaced meat in the diet of Asia and fulfilled an even greater variety of functions than oil-seeds in general. The Russo-Japanese War had greatly stimulated its production in Manchuria to supply food for men and horses, but had left the producers of a cash-crop at the end of the war without a market appropriate to their increased capacity because the Japanese market was closed by tariffs and postwar depression. In Europe the shortage of cotton-seed had first led English oil-seed millers to use soya in 1906. The short harvests of linseed and cotton in the U.S.A. and of linseed in Argentina in 1908 encouraged them to develop new sources of supply of oil-seeds. In November 1908 Mitsui & Co. made the first experimental shipment of soya beans from Dalny and in February 1909 the first large cargo of 5,200 tons passed through the Canal en route from Vladivostock to the oil-seed mills of Hull. That cargo was followed by the soya boom of 1909 which made Europe a new market and the Canal a new route for soya beans and even for soya-cake. High freights attracted southbound tonnage in ballast in October–December 1909 and diverted a huge tonnage of shipping from the Black Sea. The shipments of soya through the Canal during 1909 totalled 442,000 tons of which 84 per cent was carried in bulk by 67 ships which paid £66,160 in dues to the Canal Company or nearly £1,000 each. Those 442,000 tons provided 18 per cent of the total oil-seed cargo shipped through the waterway and the chief event of the economic year for the Canal Company.[1]

The cultivation of the soya bean was extended in Northern and Central China where it ousted the poppy frowned upon by the Government. The soya of the Yangtze valley, however, absorbed humidity during its transport by river and fermented in the Indian Ocean: it could not stand the long voyage to Europe and was generally exported to Japan. Manchuria with its dry climate and alkaline soil produced beans which arrived dry at the ports of export and survived the long voyage in perfect condition. The opening of the European market thus benefited Manchuria, encouraged the agricultural colonization of the Amur valley by the Chinese and attracted the enterprise of European merchants into the north. Vladivostock became the port of export for Northern Manchuria and first shipped zinc through the Canal in 1909, followed by wheat in 1910 and yellow pine in 1911. Dalny had been built from 1899 by Russia as the southern terminus of the East China Railway and became the port of export for Southern Manchuria. It was declared an open port in 1907 and first shipped the bulk of its soya exports to Europe in 1909. The development of those two ports stimulated Japan to annex Korea in 1910, to promote the Japanese colonization of Korea as well as the Korean colonization of Manchuria and to undertake the competitive development of the port of Fusan from 1911. China gained a new export, supplemented by frozen produce

[1] *Le Canal de Suez*, 12 Juin 1910, 5364, 5422.

(such as shelled eggs, game and pork), from 1909 and by raw cotton from 1910. The exports of soya bean so increased that they surpassed in value China's exports of tea in 1910 and ranked second to silk. The beans were shipped in jute sacks from Bengal which afforded India some compensation for the decline of its opium trade. The export of the great source of soya oil and soya cake encouraged the import of lamp-oil and of ammonium sulphate to supply respectively light and fertilizer. The introduction of Manchuria into world trade increased the tonnage of shipping between Europe and the Far East, especially that of tramp shipping for the loading-season between December and July, and encouraged speculation that China might become a maritime power on the model of Japan to the benefit of the Canal.[1]

The new traffic disorganized the copra trade of Russia in 1909–10 but benefited the trade of Germany and fostered the expansion of Scandinavian shipping. The Danish East Asiatic Company, established in 1897, pioneered the import of soya beans to the Continent in cooperation with the Swedish East Asiatic Company founded in 1907. It built a factory at Copenhagen in 1910 to process beans into cake for cattle-feed and subsidized the establishment of a similar factory at Stettin. Those factories made feed-cake their main product for the markets of Denmark, Sweden and Germany with oil as a by-product for re-export. Germany's abolition in 1910 of its import duty on soya beans encouraged Rickmers to extend their service to Eastern Siberia for the new traffic. Soya shipments from Dalny fell off in 1911 with the outbreak of plague in Southern Manchuria, reducing Canal shipments by 14·4 per cent and leaving the 1910 shipments unsurpassed in volume until 1924. That depression encouraged efforts to extend the market for soya.[2] It also increased the shipments from 1912 of soya oil, which expanded more rapidly than bean shipments, became a substitute for the dearer ground-nut oil and competed with other oil-seeds after the development in 1909 of the process of hydrogenation for the conversion of oils into fats. Europe thus gained a supplementary food, a vegetable oil, a flour and a feed-cake. China gained a new export to Europe to fill the gap left by the declining tea and silk trades, and in 1909–13 shipped 57 per cent of its soya exports through the Canal[3] to supply 14 per cent of its total cargo of oil-seeds and 49·2 per cent of the world trade in soya beans. The Canal gained a new staple trade and did not suffer much competition therein from the Trans-Siberian Railway.

In the boom of the 1900s manganese also began to be shipped through the Canal. That mineral which gave steel its malleability and tenacity had been mined since 1893 in the north of the Madras Presidency but was only exported after production began in 1899 in the Central Provinces, whose rich deposits enabled India to surpass Brazil and to rank as the second greatest producer

[1] R. Puaux, 'Le Canal de Suez', *Revue Économique Internationale* (1910), 369.

[2] *Le Canal de Suez*, 22 Janvier 1913, 5836. Li Yu-ying, *Le Soja, sa culture, ses usages alimentaires, thérapeutiques, agricoles et industriels* (Paris, Challamel, 1912).

[3] R. C. Julien, *Le Trafic du Canal de Suez* (Paris, Sirey, 1933), 252.

FEA

in the world after Russia from 1903. Exports from India remained restricted by the cost of transport over 500 miles of railway as well as by high shipping-freights. The Russo-Japanese War, however, caused labour disturbances in the Russian mines in the Donetz basin and Caucasus and enabled India to increase its shipments through the Canal by 167 per cent from 31,600 tons in 1903 to 84,500 tons in 1905. F. C. Strick & Co. began a new service between Mormugao, the port of export in Goa, and England. In 1907 India attained its peak production of 916,000 tons, which was exceeded only in 1926, and manganese shipments became of major importance in the traffic of the Canal. From 1908 to 1911 India displaced Russia as the world's leading producer. The mineral was produced pre-eminently for export and 84 per cent of India's production in 1909–13 was exported through the Canal. Those exports were made through the ports of Bombay and Mormugao, which was improved by the Government of Portugal from 1909. The manganese was shipped to England, the U.S.A., Belgium and France but only in small quantities to Germany. The rise of Indian production took place under European control and attracted the Carnegie Steel Company to acquire mines in the Central Provinces in 1908. The U.S.A. increased its imports via Suez markedly in 1912 and 1913. From 1912 until 1954 manganese dominated the northbound mineral traffic of the Canal which thereby gained a stabilizing element. Manganese shipments did not decline in the recession of 1913 but were raised by the Balkan Wars, which hindered the exports of Caucasian manganese. The Canal shipments of 869,000 tons in 1913 represented 37·4 per cent of the world production of manganese.

Rubber came into increasing use after the development of the pneumatic tyre for cycles in 1888 and for cars in 1895. The demand was at first supplied wholly by wild rubber from the Amazon and Congo basins for which Liverpool became the world market and entrepôt. The rubber plant was transferred from America to Asia through British enterprise. The first plantations were established in Malaya in 1898 and in Ceylon in 1899 but required a six-year period of growth before their trees matured in the seventh year. The automobile boom of the 1900s created the rubber famine of 1905 when the rubber trees of Malaya reached maturity, the first shipments of plantation rubber passed through the Canal and the first sale of plantation rubber took place in the U.S.A. In the rubber boom of 1910 the trees planted in 1898 began to reach their maximum production at thirteen years of age and the Dunlop Rubber Company first established plantations in Malaya. Rubber shipments through the Canal rose from 7,000 tons in 1910 to 37,000 tons in 1912 and to 65,000 tons in 1913, of which 46 per cent was destined for the U.S.A. Thus rubber was added to jute and manganese as a third staple import through the Canal by the U.S.A. Britain gained a new re-export which replaced wool as its most valuable single re-export from 1910. The new trade extended the plantation from the tea to the rubber industry and made the rubber firms into pioneers of an international economy. In Ceylon the rubber industry gave the planters security after years of depression and opened up employment to Sinhalese labour unlike the tea plantations in the hills which employed immigrant Tamil labour. Malaya was influenced more powerfully than any other single region because it acquired for the first time an agricultural staple after the failure of efforts to cultivate sugar, coffee and pineapples. Plantations replaced the jungle in West Malaya where roads and railways had developed in the tin-mining areas of Perak. The spread of rubber plantations, especially in the truly British and democratic boom of 1910,[1] followed the passage of tin-mining in Malaya from Chinese to European control between 1894 and 1906. It crystallized British interests in the 'Middle East' as delimited by Mahan[2] after the creation of the Federated Malay States in 1909 achieved the last territorial extension of the British Empire. Singapore became a world centre of the rubber trade as well as an entrepôt with its own local auctions from 1911. In its new plantation hinterland rubber replaced food crops so that rice had to be imported. The new industry brought a flood of Chinese immigrants to Malaya but developed in the west rather than in the east, where the predominant Malayan peasantry remained independent of the world-market. The British monopoly of plantation rubber ended in 1912 when the first plantation rubber from the Dutch East Indies appeared on the world market. British capital, however, financed production by the rubber companies of the Dutch East Indies and so maintained the dependence of the U.S.A. on British production. The British share of the production of plantation rubber declined only to 87 per cent in 1914 when the tonnage of plantation rubber first surpassed that of wild rubber and the East Indies first dethroned Brazil as the major source of the world's rubber. Thus the English and the Dutch added a monopoly of rubber to that of diamonds and gold and to their world trade in oil.

The trade of the Canal ceased to be concentrated on India and China with the economic development of the littoral of the Persian Gulf and the Red Sea, where phosphates were discovered at Safaga in 1907, oil at Gemsa in 1909 and manganese at Abu Zenima in 1910. The first oil-field in Africa was discovered near deep water and inspired Marcus Samuel to decide in 1911 to build a refinery for fuel oil at nearby Suez[3] and to form on 6 July 1911 the subsidiary company of Anglo-Egyptian Oilfields Ltd. Oil production began at Gemsa in 1911 and was extended to Hurghada in 1914. Phosphates were exported from Safaga to Japan from 1912 in ships which passed through the Canal in ballast. They were also mined from 1913 at Kosseir which so acquired a new industry. Across the Red Sea the Hejaz Railway was laid throughout its 1,042 miles from Damascus to Medina with rails from the U.S.A., Russia and Belgium but not from England. It was built by Turkish soldiers and was

[1] *The Spectator*, 23 April 1910, 522, 'The Rubber Boom'.
[2] A. Wright and T. H. Reid, *The Malay Peninsula. A Record of British Progress in the Middle East* (London, Unwin, 1912), 283–301.
[3] R. Henriques, *Sir Robert Waley Cohen 1877–1952* (London, Secker, 1966), 176.

intended to decrease Turkish military dependence on the British-controlled Canal. 'The Hedjaz line will be of the same importance for the Mohammedan world as was the Suez Canal for the economic world.'[1] The railway was completed on 1 September 1908 and reduced the number of Turkish troops using the Canal during 1908. It also replaced the hardships of the pilgrimage by comfort and helped to reduce the number of pilgrims using the Canal by 56 per cent during 1909. In general it could not compete with the Canal. It caused financial loss to the Arabs who lived on the hire of their camels. It also increased the power of the central government in Arabia and enabled the Sultan to appoint Sherif Hussain as Grand Sherif of Mecca in December 1908. It encouraged both the Ottoman aspiration to link the Hejaz Railway to the Bagdad Railway and the contrary British aspiration to link Port Said to Basra and Quetta by a trans-Arabian railway.[2] Anglo-Sudanese interest was attracted towards Arabia along the Suakin–Jedda route as the trade of the Sudan was increasingly diverted to the Red Sea route. The Nile–Red Sea Railway was built in 1904–5 from Atbara to Suakin[3] and was officially opened by Cromer on 27 January 1906. That railway made the Sudan increasingly dependent on the Canal, whose tolls proved as burdensome as the commission of the Cairo merchants on the Nile route. The new Port Sudan opened its Custom-house in May 1906, began to levy its port dues on the basis of Suez tonnage and became a port of call for four British lines from 1906–7. The *Prince Abbas* of the Khedivial Mail Line moored at the unfinished port on 9 November 1907 with the London mail of 31 October and so placed Khartoum via Brindisi within ten days of London. The completion of two 30-foot berths enabled the Khedive formally to open the port on 1 April 1909. By 1911 the new port handled two-thirds of the value of the imports and exports of the Sudan. 'The new gate of Africa'[4] ranked third after Jibuti and Massawa among the ports of the Red Sea in its contribution to the traffic of the Canal. It did not however precipitate the decline of Suakin nor divert the indigenous trade in cattle and durra from the Nile route but created a dualism in the economic life of the Sudan between the indigenous commerce of Suakin and the Government trade of Port Sudan. The introduction of irrigated cotton cultivation in the Gezira through the agency of the Sudan Plantations Syndicate Ltd., established in 1904, took place on a large scale from 1913 when the Sudan's budget was first balanced without aid from Egypt. Thus England sought to separate the Sudan from Egypt and to enlist the Nile more fully in the service of Lancashire.

The Turco-Italian War followed upon growing friction between the two powers in the Red Sea. Five Turkish gunboats which failed to leave the ports of the Canal within twenty-four hours of the outbreak of war on 29 September

[1] A. Stead, 'Great Britain and Turkey', *Fortnightly Review*, 2 March 1908, 426, quoting *Ar Raid el Misri*.

[2] C. E. D. Black, 'A Railway to India', *Nineteenth Century* (January 1909), 163–9.

[3] *The Times*, 2 November 1905, 5 vi.

[4] S. Low, *Egypt in Transition* (London, Smith, 1914), 86–94.

1911 were disarmed without publicity, so preventing Turkey from closing the Canal to Italy. The protest by the Italian Consul on 5 October against the continued presence at Port Said of the Turkish transport *Kaiseri* since 30 September nevertheless proved ineffective. The *Kaiseri* was carrying soldiers to replace time-expired troops in the Yemen and was considered to be unaffected by the twenty-four hours' rule: it was therefore allowed to remain at Port Said and to pass south after quarantine. The African shore of the Canal was, however, occupied to prevent Turkish infiltration overland from Syria into Libya. The Italian occupation of Tobruk on 4 October produced in reaction the Egyptian occupation of Sollum, the definition of the western frontier of Egypt and the complaint by *El Ahram* that Tobruk was the door to the Suez Canal and Syria. The Italian occupation of the Dodecanese in May 1912 established Italian power on the northern flank of the route from Malta to Port Said and beyond the control of the Mediterranean Fleet at Malta. Kitchener kept the Canal open to Italian warships and so permitted its belligerent use for operations against its suzerain. Turkey did not exercise the rights explicitly guaranteed to her under the Convention of Constantinople and reduced her vessels using the waterway from eighty-five in 1911 to one in 1912 while her troops sank in number from 46,320 in 1911 to 33 in 1912. Italian vessels increased by 64 per cent from 87 in 1911 to 143 in 1912 and their tonnage by 82·5 per cent while Italian troops increased thirteenfold from 984 to 12,406. Italy even brought a battalion of askaris from Eritrea to Tripoli in February 1912. Italy also declared a blockade of the coast of Turkish Arabia, where the lights were extinguished to the inconvenience of passing shipping. That blockade provoked a new plea for the pacification of the Red Sea as well as of the Canal.[1] The final partition of the Ottoman provinces in North Africa among the infidel caused a Moslem renaissance which extended from Morocco to Java and aroused hostility in Egypt against her largest colony of infidels after the Copts. The Italian acquisition of Libya aroused the French desire for Syria and precipitated a general encroachment on Turkey in Asia. It also devalued the British base of Malta and encouraged Churchill to announce on 18 March 1912 the decision to withdraw most of the Mediterranean Fleet and to concentrate the Navy opposite the ports of Germany. The first revolutionary shift in the location of the Navy since the battles of the Nile and Trafalgar left the Mediterranean to France and Italy, the ally and the client of Britain, in flat contradiction of Blunt's hopes in 1910. In the debate in the House of Lords on 2 July Ellenborough lamented that the substitution of the Cape route for the Canal was 'the first step in the abandonment of our position as a Great Power'.[2]

In Egypt Kitchener aspired to bring Southern Syria as far as Haifa and Acre under British influence in fulfilment of his survey of 1883 and of the scheme for an Ismailia–Kuwait Railway, to link up with a Trans-Persian

[1] T. Barclay, *The Turco-Italian War and its Problems* (London, Constable, 1912), 97.
[2] Hansard, *Lords Debates*, 2 July 1912, 318, Ellenborough.

Railway from Basra to Baluchistan.[1] The Balkan Wars of 1912–13 confirmed the neutrality of Egypt in relation to the Sultan although they aroused the enthusiasm of the whole foreign colony of Port Said and inspired many young Greeks to volunteer for service against the Turk. The renewed defeat of the last great Moslem power strengthened the British hold on Egypt, the Canal and Sinai. The isthmus of Suez was first mapped by the Survey of Egypt in 1912–13 while the Canal Company published its first geological and archaeological map in 1913. Kitchener then launched S. F. Newcombe with C. L. Woolley and T. E. Lawrence on a survey of the Gaza–Akaba region, especially of the Wadi Araba,[2] while the British ambassador in Constantinople sought a concession for a Suez–Kuwait Railway.[3] The emergence of British aspirations to establish an Arab empire from an Egyptian base doomed any hope such as that expressed in May 1914 that the surrender of Port Said might secure the evacuation of the rest of Egypt by Britain.[4] The reactive nationalism of Lutfi al-Sayyid crystallized in 1913–14 around the 'pharaonic core' of 3,000 years of ancient Egyptian history. The Khedive recognized that new spirit by appointing an Egyptian as Commissioner of the Egyptian Government with the Canal Company on the death of Ollivier in 1913 after fifty years as Commissioner. Mohammed Izzat Pasha was appointed on 20 November 1913 to the post thitherto held by two Europeans in succession and became the first pasha to serve as Commissioner. Thus Abbas exercised one of his remaining prerogatives while the Company paid homage in lieu of taxes to the Government of Egypt.

The Anglo-German crisis precipitated by the leap of the *Panther* to Agadir in 1911 accelerated the German drive to Bagdad, increased the German use of the Canal and ushered in a new era in the historiography of the Canal. German shipping using the Canal increased its cargo tonnage as Germany increased its imports from Asia. The Canal tonnage of the mail line of the North German Lloyd was surpassed by that of the Hansa Line in 1904 and by that of the Hamburg American Line in 1912. Philipp Heineken nevertheless succeeded Plate in 1912 as a German director of the Canal Company and also as General Manager of the Lloyd, which supplied only 19 per cent of Germany's Canal tonnage in 1913 against the 31 per cent of the Hansa Line and the 24 per cent of the Hamburg American Line.[5] The growth of German trade and shipping via Suez aroused German concern for the security of

[1] C. E. D. Black, 'A Proposed Railway from the Mediterranean to India', *Journal of the Royal United Service Institution* (November 1911), 1409–28. H. H. Johnston, 'Railway Projects in Africa and the Near East', *Nineteenth Century* (September 1912), 568–9.

[2] *The Home Letters of T. E. Lawrence and his Brothers* (Oxford, Blackwell, 1954), 280, 4 January 1914, 'We are obviously only meant as red herrings, to give an archaeological colour to a political job.'

[3] H. F. Frischwasser-Ra'anan, *The Frontiers of a Nation* (1955), 38, 54.

[4] H. N. Brailsford, *The War of Steel and Gold. A Study of the Armed Peace* (London, Bell, 1915), 120.

[5] *Le Canal de Suez*, 2 Juillet 1914, 6060–1, 'L'Allemagne et l'Au-Delà de Suez'.

transit which seemed completely dependent on the will of England[1] so that the Canal question remained inseparable from the Egyptian question.[2] The Convention of 1888 was therefore regarded as having pacified the Canal[3] and was specifically excepted as a norm of international law from the freedom claimed for a newly independent state from the treaties which had bound the old state.[4] Britain had however succeeded in capturing a Mediterranean creation, in achieving a triumph for the Teutonic over the Latin races[5] and in making Suez into the porter's lodge of its planetary empire[6] by its bilateral division of the spoils of empire with France at the expense of Europe. Lesseps' predecessors were therefore resurrected after the long campaign for founders' shares waged by Maria Grois-Negrelli from 1894 to 1910.[7] Alfred Birk, the Austrian engineer, revived the memory of Negrelli as the hero-martyr of the Canal and fired from the borderland of nationalities in East-Central Europe the first shot in a campaign for the revision of the history of the Canal.[8] His attack on Lesseps and the French tradition was pressed home by two Saxon patriots, the son and the grandson of two supporters of the Canal in the 1840s. Their collection of letters written between 1845 and 1862[9] made public the first documents since those of Lesseps in order to prove that his real inspirers were Enfantin, Arlès-Dufour, Georgi, Dufour-Feronce and Negrelli. That documentary approach reflected the historical spirit of the decade and secured the rapid acceptance in Germany of the new anti-French thesis. '*Sic vos non vobis*, such has been the fate of the German effort and labour for the Suez Canal.'[10] German scholars who had given due credit to the genius of Lesseps down to 1911[11] ceased thenceforward to accept him as the true progenitor of the Canal and paid homage instead to the Austrian Negrelli.[12] Sombart was inspired by the memory of Panama to rank Lesseps as one of the great entrepreneurs richly endowed for the 'French speciality' of speculation in a long tradition from Jacques Coeur to Saccard.[13] Rosa Luxemburg carried further

[1] C. H. Jacobs, *Die Schiffahrtsfreiheit im Suezkanal* (Göttingen, Huth, 1912), 104–6. F. Magnus, *Aegypten. Seine volkswirtschaftlichen Grundlagen und sein Wirtschaftsleben* (Tübingen, Laupp, 1913), 100.

[2] R. Dedreux, *Der Suezkanal im Internationalen Rechte* (Tübingen, Mohr, 1913).

[3] Ibid., 81–93.

[4] W. Schoenborn, 'Staatenzukzessionen', *Handbuch des Völkerrechts* (Stuttgart, Kohlhammer, 1913), 45.

[5] A. W. Kirkaldy, *British Shipping* (London, Paul, 1914), 317, 'The Suez Canal'.

[6] R. Kjellen, *Die Grossmächte der Gegenwart* (Leipzig, Teubner, 1914), 118.

[7] *The Times*, 11 January 1909, 5iv.

[8] (A. Birk), *Die Geschichte des Suezkanals. Nach bisher unveröffentlichten Dokumenten. Herausgegeben von der Schriftleitung der 'Rundschau für Technik und Wirtschaft'*. (Prag, Calve, 1912, 26 pp.)

[9] R. Georgi and A. Dufour-Feronce, *Urkunden zur Geschichte des Suezkanals* (Leipzig, Weicher, 1913).   [10] Ibid., 8.

[11] H. Thurn, 'Die strategische Bedeutung der Kanäle, insbesondere des Suezkanals', *Deutsche Kolonialzeitung* (1911), 487–8, 506–7. K. Wiedenfeld, 'Suezkanal', *Wörterbuch der Volkswirtschaft* (Jena, Fischer, 1911), ii. 1021–4.

[12] R. Hennig, *Die Hauptwege des Weltverkehrs* (Jena, Fischer, 1913), 23.

[13] W. Sombart, *Der Bourgeois. Zur Geistesgeschichte des modernen Wirtschaftsmenschen* (München, Duncker, 1913), 59, 178.

Hilferding's study of finance-capital and used the Canal to illustrate the absorptive power of European capitalism. 'With the building of the Suez Canal Egypt became caught up in the web of European capitalism, never again to get free of it.'[1] Thus the attack on the French tradition of the Canal was made by both nationalists and socialists. The emergence of an independent German historical tradition of the Canal in 1912 was one aspect of a general onslaught on the conventional myths of civilization by Sorel, Boeke, Petrie, Malinowski and Beard. Thus the unity of Europe disintegrated in the world of the mind before it did so on the battlefield.

In the southbound oil traffic of the Canal American shipments to Asia maintained the supremacy over Russian shipments established during the Russo-Japanese War. The first southbound shipments from Rumania appeared in the Canal in March 1907 in anticipation of the Rumanian Refineries Law of 1908 which prevented Standard Oil from dominating the home market. Oil exports through the Canal from the U.S.A. increased in 1911 after the Supreme Court upheld the conviction of Standard Oil in Texas in 1909 under the Sherman Anti-Trust Act. The first northbound shipment of oil from Persia became possible after the discovery of oil on 26 May 1908 near the site of an old temple of fire in the oil-bearing limestone of the Zagros mountains, which shut off the nearest market for oil in trans-montane Persia. The beginning of oil production in the 'Middle East' of Mahan thus created a third centre of oil production for export in Asia additional to those in the Dutch East Indies and Burma, which first shipped fuel oil through the Canal to England in December 1908. The demand for oil was extended by the appearance of the first oil-fuelled ship in the Canal in 1908 and by the laying-down of the first oil-burning destroyer by the Admiralty in 1909. The Anglo-Persian Oil Company was registered on 14 April 1909 with capital provided by Lord Strathcona of the C.P.R. and by the Burmah Oil Company. It began the construction of a refinery on the island of Abadan on a site mapped and delimited by Arnold Talbot Wilson, whose Bengal lancers had protected the Canadian oil-drillers working for the Burmah Oil Company in Persia. Wilson discovered that Asia began on the Indus[2] and contemplated British intervention in Persia by a Liberal Government on the model of Egypt in 1882. Such action might resurrect the Arabistan of the Shatt el Arab under the Sheikh of Muhammerah as another British protectorate to the east of the Ottoman Empire.[3] The Government granted British protection to the Sheikh on 16 July 1909 and thus undertook diplomatic activity outside its own sphere of influence in South-West Persia in order to protect British interests in the oil located in the neutral zone as delimited in 1907.

Marcus Samuel in vain offered a vast loan to the Persian Government in

[1] R. Luxemburg, *Die Akkumulation des Kapitals* (Leipzig, Franke, 1913, 1921), 406.
[2] A. T. Wilson, *S.W. Persia. A Political Officer's Diary 1907–1914* (London, Oxford University Press, 1941), 49.
[3] Ibid., 86–7.

return for a share in the management of the Anglo-Persian Oil Company.[1] He brought in his first well in Sarawak in 1910 and offered his Borneo fuel to the Royal Navy in 1911 but without success. 'It would be the case of the Suez Canal Shares over again if the Government bought this huge British oil supply!'[2] The *Selandia*, of the Danish East Asiatic Company, became the first motor-vessel to use the Canal in March 1912 en route to Siam with 8,000 barrels of cement and proved the suitability of the improved Diesel engine of 1910 to a long ocean voyage. In April 1912 the Admiralty decided to include five oil-fired super-dreadnoughts in the 1912–13 estimates and to rely upon oil as the Navy's main source of fuel for the future. Oil fuel had a higher thermal efficiency in relation to weight than coal, extended the range of warships by 40 per cent and gave a large excess of the speed which was vital to the new battle-fleet. The increase of British interest in the Shatt el Arab relieved the Navy from dependence on Shell and confirmed British opposition to the Berlin–Bagdad Railway, which threatened to breach the maritime frontier of India in the Persian Gulf and carry the Turkish oil of Mesopotamia to Europe free from the control of the Navy. The refinery of Anglo-Egyptian Oilfields which began operations on 10 September 1913 gave Suez the basis of a new industrial complex and imported oil from Persia as well as from Gemsa. The refinery of the Anglo-Persian Oil Company also began to function in 1913, drawing its oil through the pipeline completed in 1911 over the 130 miles from the oil-field. After the *Queen Elizabeth*, the first oil-burning cruiser of the Navy, was launched in October 1913 the first shipment of 6,000 tons of oil from Abadan was carried through the Canal in November 1913 in the Japanese tanker *Soyo Maru* under charter to F. C. Strick & Co. and was landed at Sheerness for the Navy on 24 November. Thus the flow of fuel oil from Abadan gave the Gulf a staple export through the Canal and attracted tankers southwards in ballast.

The British Government bought a controlling interest in Anglo-Persian for £2,200,000 by the contract of 20 May 1914[3] after the miners' strike of 1912 and the triple alliance formed in April 1914 by the miners, the railwaymen and the transport-workers. Churchill defended the purchase in a seven-hour debate in the Commons on 17 June by reference not to the purchase of the Khedive's shares but to the need to secure the Navy's supply of fuel oil, to preserve the independence of Anglo-Persian and to prevent its absorption by the alien combine of Royal Dutch, which had launched a flanking attack in Mesopotamia through the Turkish Petroleum Company established in 1912. Lord Charles Beresford in the most trenchant attack declared that the defences of the Mediterranean, the Suez Canal and the Persian Gulf would thereby become a thousand times more necessary to England than thitherto.

[1] F. C. Gerretson, *History of the Royal Dutch* (1957), iv. 185.

[2] A. J. Marder, *Fear God and Dread Nought. The Correspondence of Admiral of the Fleet Lord Fisher of Kilverstone* (London, Cape, 1956), 353, Fisher to McKenna, 21 January 1911.

[3] M. Jack, 'The Purchase of the British Government's Shares in the British Petroleum Company 1912–1914', *Past and Present* (April 1968), 163.

Churchill recognized that the Cape route might be used from the start of the delivery of oil but suggested that diversion to the Cape would only increase the cargoes afloat at any one time by two or three and would counterbalance the cost of transport over the extra fourteen days by the saving of Canal dues. Thus the Government acquired virtually a national oilfield within 'the danger zone of the whole world'[1] and gave to Russia an invaluable hostage. It became the first government to assume a controlling interest in an oil company and appointed Inchcape as one of its first two official directors on the board of Anglo-Persian. The oil of Persia was diverted from what Samuel considered its natural outlet in Asian markets to England which had made its export of steam coal from the world's best and largest supplies into 'the key to the Suez Canal'.[2] Coal reached its all-time maximum of production and export in 1913. It was thenceforward dethroned as the fuel of the Navy, which became as dependent on foreign fuel as sailing ships had been on the Baltic for naval stores. Oil was added to cotton, wheat and meat as a new import from abroad and began to supplement coal in the bunkering stations along the ocean routes whose security became more vital than ever to Britain. Anglo-Persian also benefited by the Anglo-German agreement of June which ended British opposition to the Bagdad Railway and made the projected new port of Basra into a joint Anglo-German enterprise but preserved the British monopoly of the Gulf. It secured a half share in the reconstituted Turkish Petroleum Company which was then granted a lease of oil in the vilayats of Mosul and Bagdad. Its competitive position was further strengthened by the reservation to the British Government of the oil of Kuwait in 1913 and of the oil of Bahrein in 1914. It built its first oil bunkers at Aden in 1914 but paid no dividends from 1909 until 1916.

The fusion of the P. & O. with the British India Line was the sequel to the centralization of the Indian administration under Curzon, the reorganization of the Indian Army under Kitchener and the transfer of the Indian capital from Calcutta to Delhi under Hardinge in 1912. The P. & O. had moved increasingly into the cargo trade of Asia and into the China and Australian trades as competition grew in its traditional Indian preserve. In the carriage of passengers the P. & O. suffered from the competition of the Hamburg American Line to China from 1904, the Netherland Steamship Company with its new tourist class from 1906 and the North German Lloyd. In the protected field of the trooping service the British India Line built two fine troopships in 1906 and compelled the P. & O. to place some of its troopships built in 1899-1900 in normal commercial service after 1908. Even in the carriage of mail the P. & O. was threatened by a possible all-red route via Canada to Australia and New Zealand using the turbine-driven express liners *Lusitania* and *Mauretania* of 1907 as well as by the new mail service of the Orient Line from 1909. In the Bombay cotton trade it had lost ground rapidly

---

[1] Hansard, *Commons Debates*, 17 June 1914, 1174, A. A. Ponsonby.
[2] E. Crammond, *The British Shipping Industry* (London, Constable, 1917), 23.

to the Nippon Yusen Kaisha.[1] In the Calcutta trade it suffered with the British India Line from a freight war waged from 1905 by the Hansa Line with the aid of the Well Line, which had been inaugurated in 1907 by the Tyzack and Branfoot Steam Ship Company of Sunderland.[2] In reply the P. & O. began to carry jute from Calcutta to London and Dundee from December 1907. The Calcutta trade was also entered by the Nippon Yusen Kaisha from 1911 and by T. & J. Brocklebank, who bought the Calcutta Conference rights of the Anchor Line in 1912. The P. & O. under the ageing Sutherland faced the competition of the younger entrepreneurs J. R. Ellerman and Inchcape. Ellerman had benefited by the Boer War boom in shipping and had acquired control in 1901 of the City and Hall Lines, which had both used the Canal since 1871. He re-embarked those lines in the Indian passenger trade from 1905, began to speed up the passage to Calcutta in competition with the P. & O.[3] and entered the manganese trade from 1906 in cooperation with Strick. The P. & O. thereupon signed mail contracts in 1907 and 1908 for a contract speed of 16 knots instead of $14\frac{1}{2}$ and for the acceleration of the mail from London to Bombay by twenty-four hours to thirteen days. It launched in 1908 the 20-knot *Salsette* with a tonnage treble that of its *Osiris*-prototype for a shuttle-service to Bombay from Aden, where it linked up with the Australian mail steamers. Thus it accepted the challenge made by the City Line.[4] Ellerman then added to his group in 1908 Bucknall Steamship Lines which ranked third in Canal tonnage in 1909. His group displaced Holt from the second place in Canal tonnage in 1911 and the P. & O. from the first place in 1912 and 1913.[5] Thus it dethroned the P. & O. from the premier position which it had held since 1874.

The P. & O. increased its tonnage, its receipts and its dividends as well as its reserves. It expanded its tonnage by 79 per cent between 1899 and 1912 while the British India Line expanded its tonnage by 68 per cent. It paid 14 per cent of its receipts in Canal dues in 1908-9 against 22 per cent in 1897-8, a payment which was virtually offset by its mail subsidy and served as an insurance premium against competition by smaller shipowners east of Suez. It made profits from marine insurance as well as from shipping and so became a financial corporation. It paid a dividend of 10 per cent per annum for the twenty-five years down to 1914-15 with a bonus of 3 per cent for each of the eleven years down to 1910-11, rising to 5 per cent from 1911-12.[6] Perhaps the P. & O. expanded too fast and paid out too much in a decade of growing competition, especially from the British India Line under the dynamic management of J. L. Mackay, a partner in Mackinnon Mackenzie & Co.

---

[1] *The Times*, 11 December 1907, 16ii; 27 December, 15v; 8 January 1908, 14iv, S. R. Bomanji, 'The P. & O. Company and its Japanese Competitors'.

[2] *Report of the Royal Commission on Shipping Rings* (Cd. 4685 of 1909), IV, 258, Q. 19,686, J. L. Mackay.

[3] *The Times*, 2 November 1905, 8vi, 'Fast Passage to India'.

[4] Ibid., 11 November 1908, 5iv.   [5] Ibid., 11 October 1913, 17v.

[6] *Stock Exchange Year Book for 1922*, 1170.

of Calcutta since 1878 and senior partner since 1905. Mackay had become a director of the Canal Company on 11 April 1904 after his first presidency of the United Kingdom Chamber of Shipping, and Baron Inchcape of Strathnaver in 1911 after his retirement from the Council of India. Inchcape limited the dividends of the British India Line to a regular $7\frac{1}{2}$ per cent for each of the eleven years down to 1912[1] and so built up its capital reserves. He extended its interests by the purchase of the Shah Line in 1910 with its Hejaz trade, the Apcar Line in 1912 with its China trade and the Currie Line in 1913 with its Australian trade. The P. & O. acquired only the Blue Anchor Line in 1910, with its emigrant traffic to Australia via the Cape, after the loss of the *Waratah* in 1909. The lack of enterprise of the P. & O. was perhaps inseparable from its vast size and centralized organization but was chided by Kipling in 1913 as in 1889 and 1892. The P. & O. seemed to Kipling to conceal its inadequacies beneath a semipontifical ritual, to exist strictly for itself, and to regard its ships as though they were annexes of Westminster Abbey. His American fellow-passengers in 1913 found the voyage from Marseilles to Port Said 'like sailing with Columbus'. 'Time and progress had stood still with the P. & O. ... Today it neither feeds nor tends its passengers, nor keeps its ships well enough to put on any airs at all... What it really needs is to be dropped into a March North Atlantic, without any lascars, and made to swim for its life between a C.P.R. boat and a North German Lloyd—till it learns to smile.'[2] His criticisms endorsed that made by the Royal Commission on the Dominions in 1914.

By the contract of 27 May 1913 the P. & O. and the British India Line were to be amalgamated with effect from 1 October 1914. The fusion united the home and the country shipping interests of the Indian Ocean and brought under the control of one man 1,250,000 tons of shipping and a capital of £12,600,000. Inchcape became a director of Pender's Eastern Associated Telegraph Company as well as the Chairman of the British India Steam Navigation Company in 1913 and Managing Director of the P. & O. from May 1914 in succession to Sutherland.[3] Sutherland, who had visited Paris 268 times between 1885 and 1909 for board meetings of the Canal Company, remained Chairman of the London Committee and emerged every month from his retirement in Hampshire to visit his second home in Paris for the meeting of the board. The P. & O. supplied 1,292,000 tons to the traffic of the Canal in 1913, of which 52 per cent was non-postal and 48 per cent postal tonnage. Of its Canal tonnage 30 per cent was in the trade with Australia, 28 in the trade with Bombay, 25 in the trade with the Far East and only 19 per cent in the trade with Calcutta. Even in its postal tonnage 53·6 per cent was with Australia and only 45·6 with Bombay. In the passenger traffic of the Canal the P. & O. ranked second to the Orient Line which carried 21 per cent of the

[1] *Stock Exchange Year Book for 1914*, 906–7.
[2] Kipling, 'Egypt of the Egyptians', *Nash's Magazine* (June 1914), 277–8, 281.
[3] *The Times*, 10 July 1914, 20v; 14 October 1914, 14i.

total passengers in 1913 against the 17 per cent carried by the P. & O. The British India Line carried more cargo than mail or passengers, retained its solid basis in the coasting trade of the Indian Ocean and made indigenous competition more difficult than ever. Of the 581,000 tons which it contributed to the Canal traffic in 1913, 43·4 per cent was in the Calcutta trade, 37·5 in the Bombay trade, 15 in the Australian trade and 4·1 per cent in the East African trade. The new group increased its share of the Canal's tonnage from 8·5 per cent in 1913 to 11·3 in 1914, regained the lead from the Ellerman group and retained it until 1932. The Ellerman group was denied both a share in the mail contract and a seat on the board of the Canal Company.

The competitive capacity of the P. & O. group in the Australian trade increased as the rise of the steamship extended Australian use of the Canal, especially after the North German Lloyd introduced the large cargo boat in 1905 and so began a steady decline in homeward freights. The appeal of the new federation on 15 May 1906 for a reduction in Canal dues in the interests of inter-Empire trade and migration was rejected by the three official directors on 31 August and by the Colonial Office on 31 October in order to preserve the revenues of the Exchequer. The antipodean democracy was then supported by the shipping democracy of England when Oswald Sanderson, the Managing Director of the Wilson Line of Hull and retiring President of the Chamber of Shipping of the United Kingdom, attacked the exclusive representation of the liner interest in the London committee in a resolution adopted by the Chamber on 15 February 1907.[1] At the Colonial Conference of 1907 Sir Joseph Ward, the Prime Minister of New Zealand, professed his mortal hatred of the toll-bar and appealed for the exemption of British and French but not German ships from the 'high and almost prohibitive' Canal dues which debarred tramps from the use of the waterway. 'We ought not, from the sordid point of view, or from the point of view of the interest upon the shares, to allow this Canal to stand in the way of the Empire's progress.'[2] The idea of a competitive Akaba Canal was revived but was dismissed by Arenberg as a melancholy prospect for any capital invested therein.[3] Howard Vincent then asked Asquith in the Commons on 18 June to consider offering a proportion of the Government's Canal shares at the current market rates to the colonial governments. His hope that the Treasury's interest in high tolls would thereby be diluted was frustrated by the opposition of the liner companies and by the reluctance of Conservative M.P.s to subsidize free-trade shipowners through a reduction in tolls. The colonies gained only a faster mail service by the Orient Line, whose *Orsova* accelerated the Brindisi–Adelaide service from 1909 by 58 hours to 26 days 14 hours. The main shipping lines in the Australian trade refused on 9 August 1911 to reduce freights in proportion to a

---

[1] *The Times*, 16 February 1907, 6v.
[2] *Minutes of the Proceedings of the Colonial Conference, 1907* (Cd. 3523, 1907), 275, J. Ward, 1 May 1907.
[3] *Le Canal de Suez*, 12 Juin 1907, 4935, Arenberg, 4 June.

reduction in Canal tolls because of the extra expenses incurred by their employment of Australian labour. The Royal Commission on the Dominions
whose chairman was Edgar Vincent, the brother of Howard, reflected Australian hostility to the Canal in its Second Interim Report of 16 January 1914.
That report emphasized the waterway's lack of the depth necessary for fast
ocean vessels and the high cost of carrying the mails overland across Europe.
'This route is essentially hybrid and cosmopolitan and cannot be regarded
as a final and satisfactory solution of a great Imperial problem.'[1] The Commission therefore recommended that the Cape route, which was used in 1912
by 75 per cent of outward-bound steam tonnage to Australia, should be used
for a combined mail service to South Africa and Australia. Such a service
would save Canal dues, create an auxiliary fleet of fast mail steamers and end
the quasi-monopoly of the P. &. O. and Orient Lines.

Four years of uninterrupted expansion in the traffic of the Canal from 1909
to 1912 ended after the Chinese Revolution of 1911–12. That revolution
followed China's loss of the tea trade to India and of the silk trade to Japan.
Sixteen years after the catastrophic defeat by Japan the alien Manchu dynasty
was replaced by the Chinese Republic in an apparent triumph for Western
civilization. The divorce between East and West became apparent as southbound cargo tonnage rose by 15·7 per cent during 1913 while northbound
cargo tonnage declined by 7·7 per cent as Asia began to divert its energies
from economic into revolutionary channels. Northbound cargo shipments
stagnated between March 1912 and January 1914. Sugar shipments from Java
sank by 50 per cent during 1912 under the influence of the Moslem and
Chinese renaissances as well as of the competition of Continental beet-sugar
in the English market. During 1913 wheat exports from India declined by
25 per cent, soya shipments by 25, British tonnage by 6·2, total tonnage by
1·2 and receipts by 7 per cent. Dividends however continued to rise and
formed 67·6 per cent of total receipts at the close of an unprecedented sequence
of sixteen years from 1898 to 1913 of continuously rising dividends. The threat
of competition nevertheless compelled the anticipatory reduction of toll during
the last years of the Canal's unchallenged monopoly. Thus shipping tonnage
rose by 49 per cent between 1908 and 1912 but receipts only by 25·5 per cent
and dividends only by 22 per cent.

In the decade of the most rapid growth in size of the steamship the U.S.
Congress adopted a lock-type of canal for Panama in 1906. The third isthmian
canal commission, established in 1907, decided in January 1908 to build its
locks 1,000 feet in length with a width of 110 feet and a depth of 40 feet over
the sills, so ushering in a new epoch in the history of shipping. The Suez Canal
Company expected that the influence of the Panama Canal would extend as
far west as Singapore[2] and immediately decided to undertake a five-year

---

[1] *Second Interim Report of the Dominions Royal Commission on the Natural Resources, Trade
and Legislation of Australasia* (Cd. 7210 of 1914), 31, paragraph 69.
[2] F. C. Penfield, *East of Suez* (1907), 21.

improvement plan from 1909 to deepen its waterway to 36 feet so as to increase the maximum permissible draught from the 28 feet authorized in 1906 to 30 feet. It was thereby compelled to issue from 1909 its third 3 per cent loan and to defer the reduction of transit dues desired by shipowners. It was also encouraged to seek an extension of its concession, rumours of which began to circulate from the end of 1908. The construction of the Panama Canal encouraged a new wave of American denigration of the French achievement at both Suez and Panama as well as of Lesseps and the Canal Company.[1] 'No Lorelei ever lured more souls to destruction than the sand waste between Port Said and Suez.'[2] 'Egypt derives no more advantage from the great Suez Canal than an imaginary kingdom existing in an Anthony Hope novel.'[3] The American Consular Agent in Egypt from 1875 to 1883 described the Canal as the primary cause of the ruin of Egypt and contrasted the treatment of the small Powers of America by the U.S.A. with the treatment of Oriental countries by Europe.[4] Roosevelt's action at Panama in 1903 seemed, however, to England to offer a possible example to follow in making the Canal an *imperium in imperio* under British control if Egypt should ever be allowed 'to masquerade with a Parliament and without an English Occupation'.[5]

The Canal Company created an extraordinary reserve fund after it failed to secure an extension to its concession in 1910. It also made from 1 January 1911 the first of three successive annual reductions of toll by 5*d.* per ton. The shareholders' meeting on 12 June 1911 agreed with Arenberg that their shares had become an 'appreciating rente'[6] and authorized a new loan of £4,000,000 for further improvement works. The programme of 1908 was still incomplete when the 1912 scheme was drawn up to deepen the channel to 39 ft 3 in. and to increase the maximum permissible draught to 33 feet. L. S. Amery, who had become an M.P. in 1911 and had raised the question of the burden of Canal tolls on British shipping on 17 May 1911, pleaded on 3 April 1912 for a reduction of the heavy tolls handicapping imperial trade in the light of the coming Panama Canal. The third toll reduction was authorized on 5 August 1912 and came into effect on 1 January 1913 after the announcement on 14 November 1912 of the schedule of tolls on the Panama Canal. Suez tolls had been reduced in three stages by 19·3 per cent, sacrificing a large element of quasi-rent and bringing them just below the level of the Panama tolls. That reduction of toll was the more significant because the Panama Canal was not designed primarily as a commercial route and could not charge a heavier toll than that of the Suez Canal. The U.S.A. thought it necessary to introduce protective import duties into the Philippines in 1913 so as to give U.S. goods

---

[1] W. E. Curtis, *Egypt, Burma and British Malaysia* (New York, Revell, 1905), 16–17, 212–14.

[2] F. C. Penfield, 'Suez and Panama', *North American Review* (June 1905), 817.

[3] Idem, *East of Suez* (1907), 10.

[4] E. E. Farman, *Egypt and its Betrayal* (1908), 286, 211–12.

[5] D. Sladen, *Egypt and the English* (London, Hurst, 1908), 1, 502.

[6] *Le Canal de Suez*, 12/13 Juin 1911, 5569, 5575.

a preference. In 1913 Edgar Bonnet, the General Manager since 1909, and Paul Solente, the Chief Engineer since 1907, paid the first visit ever made by Company officials to the ports of Asia so as to relate the improvement of the Canal to their capacities. From 1 January 1914 the maximum permissible draught was increased to 29 feet. By 27 June Suez shares had fallen to 5,000 francs, a reduction of 29 per cent from their peak of 6,505–6,600 francs on 10 February 1912.

On 1 August 1914 the first American ship passed through the Panama Canal, which was opened to commerce on 15 August. The new canal had been completed in ten years, like the Suez Canal, rather than in the sixteen years anticipated in 1908 by Arenberg. It had been built in a newly created State and not like the Suez Canal in one of the oldest States of history. It was 47 miles in length against the 100 miles of the Suez Canal and was also wider and deeper. 270,000,000 cubic yards had been excavated at a cost of £75,000,000, whereas 99,000,000 cubic yards had been excavated at Suez at a cost of £18,000,000. The Panama Canal incorporated 29,700,000 cubic yards extracted by the two French companies, or 38 per cent of their total cube of excavation and 10 per cent of the American cube. The Suez Canal had been built by the enterprise of a private company under a 99-year concession. The Panama Canal was built under a concession in perpetuity by the U.S. Government for its strategic ends and for the protection of the U.S.A. That Government combined the functions of Company and Government, bore the capital cost and met the operating deficits for the first fourteen years of its operation. It also built fortifications from 1911,[1] naming one fort after Lesseps, and administered its Canal Zone through a Governor. Navigation through the Panama Canal was more difficult than through the Suez Canal because it was a locked canal, rising by three sets of locks to a height of 85 feet above sea-level. Those locks postponed the fulfilment of Lesseps' vision of a sea-level canal from sea to sea, limited the number as well as the size of ships and increased the coefficient of operation. Ships could nevertheless pass one another while under way and could pass through in half the time required at Suez.

The Panama Canal was a continental and naval canal rather than a global and commercial canal.[2] As a strategic enterprise it achieved its ends immediately instead of over a period of time. It doubled the power of the U.S. Navy, eliminated the need for two separate fleets and facilitated the defence of American interests in the Pacific against Japan. The opening of the Panama Canal was denied the publicity given to the opening of the Suez Canal, because it was not a pioneer transisthmian canal but a prosaic imitation, the achievement of a republic rather than of a monarchy, and because war had broken out in Europe eleven days earlier. That war halved the tonnage

[1] *The Saturday Review*, 17 September 1910, 351–2, 'Panama'.
[2] L. Hutchinson, 'The Panama Canal and Competition for Trade in Latin America, the Orient and Australasia', *Journal of the Royal Statistical Society* (March 1913), 359–60.

expected by the new canal, but created a great demand for shipping and so absorbed the surplus tonnage which would otherwise have been created by the use of the new route. The war also postponed the beginning of competition between the Suez and Panama routes. The Suez Canal Company nevertheless increased the maximum permissible draught from 1 January to 30 feet, an increase of 3 ft. 8 in. since 1902 in the most refractory of dimensions. The war also stimulated the creation of a U.S. merchant marine and so valorized the construction of the new canal. It led the U.S. Government to issue the Regulations of 13 November 1914 which expressly permitted transit by belligerent warships. No Convention of Constantinople restricted American control over the Panama Canal and no provision existed for freedom of passage in time of war as in time of peace. The Regulations of 1914 however reflected the spirit of 1888 and assimilated the Panama Canal to the Suez Canal.

In the new climate of impending competition and of worsening Franco-German relations Arenberg yielded his place as President of the Company to Charles Jonnart (1857–1927), a true Frenchman of rural origins and interests. Jonnart had served as one of Ferry's three agents in colonial expansion together with Galliéni and Lyautey: he had been Principal Private Secretary to the Governor-General of Algeria from 1881 to 1885 and then Director of Algerian Services at the Ministry of the Interior from 1885 to 1889. He was elected as a Social Progressive deputy for the Pas de Calais (1889–1914) and became Minister of Public Works in the Ministry of Casimir-Périer from December 1893 to June 1894. As Governor-General of Algeria from 1900 to 1910 he was reputed to have amassed a fortune.[1] Jonnart succeeded Arenberg as President of the Committee of French Africa in 1912 and became Minister of Foreign Affairs in the third Briand Ministry in 1913. A member of the board of the Canal Company since 1897 and a vice-president since 1907 he became President at the age of fifty-six on 19 May 1913 when Arenberg was named Honorary President after eighteen years as President. Jonnart secured the appointment of Charles de Lesseps as Honorary Vice-President on 2 June. He became a senator in 1914 and fulfilled special wartime missions for the Government at Algiers, Athens and Rome. Thus he restored the good relations between the Company and the Republic which the Panama Scandal had impaired.

[1] W. S. Blunt, *My Diaries* (1919), ii. 402.

29

THE WAR IN THE SINAI DESERT, 1914-1918

AFTER the assassination of the heir to the Habsburg Monarchy the shares of the Canal Company shrank in market-value by 14 per cent from 5,000 francs on 27 June to 4,300 on 29 July. On 30 July the *Helgoland* of the North German Lloyd en route from Singapore to Bremen became the first German vessel to remain in harbour at Port Said, in the hope of asylum, and was soon joined by other large German vessels. On 3 August the Canal Company became most reluctant to accept the payment of Canal dues in London rather than in Paris because of the disruption of the exchange market[1] but confirmed that the Canal was open at all times to ships of all nationalities without distinction. The Egyptian Foreign Minister at the same time reaffirmed the Convention of 1888 while bringing into force the coaling regulations of 10 and 12 February 1904. The Company and Egypt thereby revealed their wish to insulate the Canal from the influence of the war. The English declaration of war on Germany on 4 August did not destroy the German hope that Egypt would remain neutral because Egypt did not declare war. Port Said remained in law until 5 November a neutral Ottoman port in which only warships were forbidden by the Convention of 1888 to stay for more than twenty-four hours. The Government of Egypt then decreed on 5 August that commercial vessels were free to pass through the Canal without risk of capture or detention whatever their nationality. The same decree empowered British forces to exercise the rights of war in Egyptian ports and to bring ships and cargo captured there before a British prize-court, but granted days of grace until sunset on 14 August to ships of not more than 5,000 tons gross.[2] On the same day the British deprived the German vessels of their wireless sets to prevent the communication of British naval movements in the Canal to the two German warships in the Mediterranean. The British did not occupy the German and Austrian buildings in Port Said and sited their military posts behind the stations of the Canal Company, which declined to be publicly associated with any military preparations.[3] On 17 August the Government of Egypt forbade the *Barenfels* of the Hansa Line bound for Calcutta to pass through the Canal lest it should block it.[4] The *Südmark* of the Hamburg American Line, which had been seized as prize in the Red Sea

---

[1] Hansard, *Commons Debates*, 6 August 1916, 2067, C. Cory.
[2] G. Douin, *Un Épisode de la Guerre Mondiale. L'Attaque du Canal de Suez* (3 Février 1915). (Paris, Delagrave, 1922), 15.
[3] G. Arthur, *General Sir John Maxwell* (London, Murray, 1932), 132.
[4] G. Douin, 16.

and kept in the Suez roadstead from 17 August for eight hours longer than the maximum of twenty-four hours prescribed in the Convention of 1888, was taken through the Canal on 19 August with a prize crew to Alexandria.

The German advance into France compelled the Cabinet to order on 18 August the diversion of the two Indian divisions intended for the defence of Egypt to Marseilles. Britain also withdrew the last imperial troops from Cape Town on 27 August, evacuated Sinai and concentrated the Egyptian Camel Corps on the western bank of the Canal on 31 August. Thus Cromer's great territorial gain of 1906 was surrendered to its 25,000 Beduin while the Canal was converted into a defence-barrier for the Delta. The uncertainty over whether Egypt or the Canal was being defended revealed the degree to which British policy had become Egyptianized.[1] In effect the main line of British communication with the East ceased to be an object of defence and was hastily degraded into a moat in front of a fire-trench. Such was the panic reaction to the threat from Turkey, where Enver Pasha had ordered the preparation of a plan for an attack on the Canal two days after the secret Turco-German Alliance of 1 August. The sinking by a German submarine on 4 September of the *Natal Transport* off Crete, two days out from Port Said, marked the advent of an even graver threat to the security of the whole Mediterranean route.

The first Indian troops reached Suez on 8 September in eighteen days from Bombay and passed through the Canal en route to Marseilles and Flanders. The movement of the bulk of the Indian Army to France fulfilled the promise of the symbolic troop-movement of 1878 and also restrained Egypt from any pro-Turkish demonstration. Territorial divisions replaced the regular troops in both Egypt and India. The Canal Company seems to have been reluctant to believe in the possibility of an attack on the Canal but was forced to interrupt night-time transit for the first time on 4–5 October after a report of eight Beduin and eighteen camels approaching the Canal from Sinai.[2] On 13 October the Government of Egypt first sent Egyptian troops on board the German ships in the Canal ports and then placed crews on board. The German vessels were ordered on 15 October to put to sea, where they were seized as prize by a cruiser waiting outside the three-mile limit and taken to Alexandria by 20 October.[3] Altogether fifteen vessels were captured in the region of the Canal, five of the Hansa Line, three of the North German Lloyd, three of the German Australian Line, three of the Austrian Lloyd and one of the German Levant Line. The Canal Company refused to associate itself with those captures. A British Note of 23 October informed the representatives of the maritime powers in London that the Government of Egypt had detained the enemy ships either for their hostile acts or for their hostile intentions or for their refusal to leave the ports of the Canal and denied the right to make use of the Canal to escape capture. Thus Britain assimilated the ports of the

---

[1] P. G. Elgood, *Egypt and the Army* (1924), 120–1.
[2] G. Douin, 31–2. [3] Ibid., 33–4.

Canal to Alexandria, eroded their privileged position under the Convention of Constantinople and placed that Convention under its first great trial, ten years after it had come effectively into operation.

Turkey maintained its neutrality for three months after its secret alliance with Germany with masterly diplomacy. On 2 November Abbas Hilmi from Constantinople asked Egyptians to oppose the British armies and martial law was proclaimed as a precaution in Egypt. The British declaration of war on Turkey on 5 November enabled Britain on the same day to annex Cyprus, to bombard Akaba and to occupy Abadan Island so as to protect the oil refineries, the tanks and the pipelines of the Anglo-Persian Oil Company. On 11 November Britain also destroyed the fortifications of Sheikh Said opposite Perim as the Aden Protectorate passed under Turkish influence. The establishment of a blockade of the Turkish coast completed the triumph of the Canal over the Syrian desert route. The Turco-Egyptian frontier became, however, a frontier of hostilities, arousing fears for the safety of the Canal and producing a temporary restriction in chartering. The Canal Company cabled its Principal Agent in Egypt on 9 November to cooperate without restriction with the Defence Forces. Four months of non-cooperation thereupon ended as the Company began to help England and France to defend the Canal against the suzerain power. The Company made available its telegraph, telephone and wireless services for communication and agreed to make no profit on its war services provided that it suffered no loss: it did not dismiss the Austrian pilots in its employment. Asquith's doom of the Ottoman Empire in Asia pronounced at Guildhall on 9 November raised Allied expectations of political gains so high as seriously to complicate the task of waging war to an end.[1] Zionist hopes were transformed into practical politics for the first time since the Boer War.[2] Russia demanded Constantinople on 18 November in return for her approval of a British protectorate in Egypt while France despatched a naval squadron to Port Said in support of her claims to Syria[3] and Indian troops occupied Basra on 21 November to stake the British claim to Mesopotamia.

An Indian patrol met a force of 200 Turks and Beduin twenty miles east of Kantara on 20 November and withdrew after a sharp fight. Kitchener immediately ordered the Australian and New Zealand troops which had left Albany on 1 November to disembark and train in Egypt because of the Turkish threat. The first contingent of the Australian Expeditionary Force reached Egypt on 1 December after a voyage of 6,700 miles and beheld the first signs of actual warfare as they passed through the Canal en route to Alexandria. Lloyd George, who had been introduced to Weizmann by C. P. Scott, in vain urged the defence of Egypt and the Canal by the landing of 100,000 troops on the coast of Syria so as to cut off the Turks in Sinai. Resources remained so

[1] P. G. Elgood, 222.
[2] A. Hyamson, 'The Future of Palestine', *New Statesman*, 21 November 1914, 163–4. C. Sykes, *Two Studies in Virtue* (London, Collins, 1953), 171, 'The prosperity of his servant: a study of the origins of the Balfour Declaration of 1917'.
[3] P. G. Elgood, 178.

limited as to deprive the defenders of the Canal of any strategic or even tactical freedom. They had to undertake a passive rather than an active defence and to hold the line of the Canal in strength throughout. They were thus deprived of the power of counter-attack against an enemy which could conceal its points of attack to the last moment. The length of the front to be watched was reduced by twenty miles by flooding four areas east of the Canal as far south as Ballah with sea-water. The great dredgers of the Canal Company began to flood the Plain of Tineh on 25 November in order to protect Port Said itself. Along the remaining front of 60–70 miles defence posts were established on the east bank covering the ferries while trenches were dug on the west bank in the intervals between those posts. A flotilla of armed launches was manned by the Navy to patrol the Canal. A military aerodrome was established at Ismailia in November for an R.F.C. detachment from India while Port Said became a base for the seaplanes despatched on 1 December from France. The isthmus was isolated from the rest of Egypt in December 1914 as a further precaution against the impending attack by Turkey.[1] The proclamation of a protectorate over Egypt on 18 December was a unilateral act by Britain and not the result of a joint agreement between Britain and Egypt. The deposition of Abbas Hilmi on 19 December gave Egypt in the person of Hussein a Sultan for the first time since 1517 to rival the Sultan of Turkey.

The war was the first time since the Russo-Turkish War which injured the Canal's traffic rather than benefited it. Commercial tonnage sank by nearly 40 per cent between 1 August and 31 December 1914. The flags of Germany, Austria and Turkey, which had ranked as the second, fifth and ninth largest users of the Canal and had together supplied 26·2 per cent of its tonnage in 1913, were eliminated. Germany suffered the greatest losses by the end of its trade with Asia and with Egypt, by the cutting-off of its supplies of rice, oil-seeds, jute, copra, soya bean, cotton, manganese and hides, by the enforced liquidation of its merchant-houses in the ports of Asia, by the closing-down of the Deutsches Kohlen Depot Gesellschaft in Port Said on the first day of the war and by the capture of twelve of its large merchant vessels. The vessels were condemned as prize by due process of H.M. Supreme Court for Egypt in Prize,[2] where Mr. Justice Cator ruled on 5 February 1915 that it was not the Court's duty to enforce the Convention of 1888 or to release the

---

[1] P. G. Elgood, 246. V. Chirol, *Fifty Years in a Changing World* (London, Cape, 1927), 64.

[2] *The Times Law Reports*, 32 (1915–16), 433–5, 7 April 1916, *Gutenfels, Barenfels, Derfflinger. Law Reports, Appeal Cases* (1916), 2, 112–21, 7 April 1916, *Gutenfels;* 186–93, 13 April 1916, *Marquis Bacquehem;* 193–7, 13 April 1916, *Pindos, Helgoland, Rostock. The Law Times Reports*, 114, 953–6, 7 April 1916, *Gutenfels, Barenfels, Derfflinger;* 958, 13 April 1916, *Marquis Bacquehem;* 960–2, 13 April 1916, *Pindos, Helgoland, Rostock. The Law Times Reports*, 116, 804–5, 3 August 1917, *Südmark;* 120, 102–6, 13 December 1918, Deutsches Kohlen Depot Gesellschaft. *Lloyd's Reports of Prize Cases*, IV, 336–59, 17 April 1916, *Gutenfels, Barenfels, Derfflinger;* V, 69–78, 13 April 1916, *Pindos, Helgoland, Rostock;* 79–91, 13 April 1916, *Marquis Bacquehem;* VI, 343–70, 3 August 1917, *Südmark;* VII, 394–400, 15 March 1918, *Derfflinger;* VIII, 138–57, 13 December 1918, Deutsches Kohlen Depot Gesellschaft; 458–67, *Derfflinger.*

Südmark because of its breach. The flag of Russia, which had ranked seventh in 1913, also disappeared from the traffic of the Canal because the Baltic was closed by Germany and the Straits by Turkey. The southbound shipment of oil from Russia and Rumania ended to the benefit of American exporters of oil to India. The end of wheat exports from the Black Sea increased the importance of cereal shipments from India, including barley as well as wheat. The end of beet-sugar exports from Germany and Austria stimulated the export of cane-sugar from Java and Mauritius. The Canal began to shift over from a peacetime to a wartime function. The neutral flags of the Netherlands and Norway increased their tonnage, Norwegian tonnage first exceeding Swedish between 1914 and 1919. The Canal became an Allied highway although the Brindisi overland route ended when British shipping was diverted from Brindisi first to Taranto, the base of the main Italian Fleet, and then to Marseilles, which so regained the Indian mail it had lost in 1871. Military traffic increased at the expense of commercial traffic. Although Canal tonnage declined by 3·1 per cent during 1914 British tonnage rose by 7·1 per cent and raised the British share of the total from 60 to 66·5 per cent. The flag of France, which had occupied the fourth place since 1910, replaced that of Germany in the second place with the Netherlands in the third place and Japan in the fourth place. Passengers increased in number by 39 per cent and troops by 158 per cent, ending the civilian ascendancy of 1902–13. Shipments of rice, oil-seeds, mineral ores and jute declined because of the loss of one of their great markets in Germany. Northbound cargo however declined less than southbound cargo, in which manufactures fell off much more than either coal or salt. Coal prices rose as freight-rates soared to Port Said, which even imported coal from Bengal from August 1914. The Company's expenditure rose while transits and receipts fell. Improvement expenditure under the 1912 programme was curtailed and was concentrated for wartime purposes upon the harbour of Port Said, despite an increase in 1914–15 in the average size of vessels. For the year 1914 receipts declined by 3·7 per cent but dividends were reduced by 30 per cent by the transfer of £148,000 to reserves. Dividends thereby fell below the level of the preceding year for the first time since 1897 and below 50 per cent of the year's receipts for the first time since 1887.

The Eighth Ottoman Army Corps of three Arab divisions under Turkish officers left Beersheba on the night of 14–15 January 1915[1] and crossed Sinai in night-marches by the difficult central route via Kossaima and Hassana in preference to the northerly caravan route from Gaza or the southerly pilgrim route from Akaba. The 25,000 troops were led by Achmet Jemal Pasha, who had been hailed as the 'Saviour of Egypt' on his departure from Constantinople. Their transportation, supplies and services were superbly organized by the Bavarian lieutenant-colonel of artillery, Freiherr Kress von Kressenstein. They achieved their greatest success in enlisting the support of every Beduin

---

[1] T. Wiegand, *Sinai* (Berlin, Gruyter, 1920), 12, Kress von Kressenstein, 'Die Kriegführung in der Wüste'.

sheikh in Sinai except one and in crossing the 187 miles in numbers fivefold those estimated possible by the War Office in 1906 and 1910, so proving that the desert was no barrier or ally of England. On the morning of 23 January the troops were able to see the British on the Canal from a distance of twenty-five miles. Kressenstein made a reconnaissance to the waterway on 27 January, ending night traffic, halving transit facilities at a single blow and arousing uneasiness in Charkia. Everyone in the Moslem world believed that the attack would succeed and would usher in a new epoch for Islam. The Turkish forces were however inadequate to realize their aims. Their highest hope was to restore the province of the Nile to the rule of Constantinople, their least to close the Canal by a dam of sand-bags which dredgers would be unable to extract, so as to compel England to use the 21-day route via the Cape to India. On 3 February 12,000–15,000 Turkish soldiers launched their main attack on the section between Toussoum and Serapeum, with feint attacks on Kantara and Kubri. Three pontoons made a surprise crossing before the British opened fire. Twelve Allied warships berthed as floating batteries in the Canal inflicted no damage, unlike the Turkish artillery. The 30,000 troops in defence, especially the 24 Indian battalions, nevertheless repelled the attack and inflicted the heavy casualties of 1,000 killed, 1,500 wounded and 700 taken prisoner. The Egyptians failed to rise in a holy war. Even fanatical Port Said remained apathetic,[1] although its garrison had been reduced to one weak battalion. Jemal's failure left him so uncertain of the temper of his Arab troops that he retired but with his guns and in good order. Maxwell was similarly restrained from risking a counter-attack by the pro-Turkish sentiment of Egypt.[2] The simultaneous Arab attack on the pipelines of the Anglo-Persian Oil Company on 5 February was far more successful, interrupted production at Abadan for five months[3] and necessitated the reinforcement of Basra from the Canal. The battle of Ismailia has been assessed as 'an event of first-class importance in the history of the war, since it averted once and for all the danger of a permanent interruption of the sea-route to the East'.[4] Traffic through the waterway was resumed on 5 February. The battle proved to be a successful defence of Egypt but nevertheless made the Canal itself into a war 'zone'.[5] The Turks remained in complete command of Sinai, prevented the re-establishment of the security of the Canal and compelled Britain to maintain large forces in Egypt to counter the threat of another attack. Kressenstein organized flying columns to make harassing pin-prick

---

[1] P. G. Elgood, 140.

[2] G. Arthur, *Maxwell*, 167.

[3] A. T. Wilson, *Loyalties. Mesopotamia 1914–1917. A Personal and Historical Record* (London, Oxford University Press, 1930), 24.

[4] C. E. Fayle, *History of the Great War. Seaborne Trade* (London, Murray, 1923), ii. 33.

[5] The phrase 'Canal Zone' was apparently borrowed from Panama and was used in the *Manchester Guardian*, 18 February 1915, 9v ('Canal Zone Quiet'), and in General Maxwell's despatches of 1 August 1915 and 1 March 1916: *Naval and Military Despatches Relating to Operations in the War, Part VI* (London, H.M.S.O., 1917), 103, 109. P. G. Elgood, 246.

demonstrations against the waterway and made such a reconnaissance to Kubri on 22 March. Shipping in transit was exposed to snipers from the water's edge to the alarm of neutral maritime nations. The military authorities therefore established control over the passage of commercial shipping against the opposition of the Company: they forbade navigation after dark as well as entry without a military permit and insisted on the protection of the bridge of steamers by sandbags. The Turks carried their first mine, manufactured in France, through the inundated area along a footpath revealed by the Beduin and anchored it on 8 April in the fairway between El Cap and El Kantara, with the technical advice of a former Canal pilot.[1] The mine was discovered on 10 April, presenting a new threat to the Canal which caused infinite annoyance to the defence and to the Company. Turkey had not attempted publicly to justify its attack of 3 February because it was debateable whether it was in violation of the Convention of Constantinople. It issued on 28 May an explanatory circular to neutral governments, proclaiming the Canal a war zone.[2] The laying of mines raised insurance premiums and compelled the British greatly to increase their patrols, especially their night patrols on the east bank, which was thoroughly searched at daylight each morning.

The Turkish attack proved the futility of trying to defend the Canal from the African bank and encouraged proposals for the partition of the Empire among Russia, France and Britain. The Russian claim to Constantinople was accompanied by a Russian suggestion that the Canal might become British property instead of an international enterprise.[3] The French claim to Syria alarmed T. E. Lawrence, because it would expose the Canal to attack by 100,000 within twelve days from the declaration of war.[4] It also disturbed the Zionists, because it would give Palestine to France rather than to Britain. The entry of Italy into the war on the Allied side was secured by the offer of territorial compensation in Asia Minor and Africa as well as in Europe. The Dardanelles expedition which thereby became possible was based on Egypt and was partly intended to lighten the defence of the Canal. From 7 April troops were drawn increasingly out of Egypt for the landings on 25 April. Those forces included Rupert Brooke, who caught at Port Said on 2 April the infection from which he died three weeks later at Scyros. In reply to the landings on Gallipoli the Turks increased their pressure on the Senussi to invade Egypt. They also tried to capture Perim from Sheikh Said on 14–15 June and occupied Sheikh Othman on 5 July. They thereby established control over the water-supply of Aden and compelled the despatch from the Canal of an infantry brigade for the offensive of 21 July which recaptured that village.

[1] P. G. Elgood, 155.

[2] U.S. Naval War College, *International Law Documents* (Washington, Government Printing Office, 1918), 1917, 221–2, 'Circular relating to Hostilities in Egypt and the Suez Canal, May 1915'.

[3] *Manchester Guardian*, 3 March 1915, 9iii.

[4] D. Garnett, *Selected Letters of T. E. Lawrence* (London, Cape, 1938), 85, Lawrence to D. G. Hogarth, 18 March 1915.

They also organized a Beduin Irregular Force in Sinai and increased their efforts to disrupt the use of the Canal. On 30 June the Holt liner *Teiresias* struck a mine near the south end of the Little Bitter Lake, revealing the ineffectiveness of the naval patrol and blocking the channel for fourteen hours until the ship could be towed away to Alexandria for repair. Air attacks were also made on Suez on 21 July and on Port Said on 1 September for the first time in their history. Those attacks sank no ships but presented a new threat to the security of the Canal, which lacked locks and was therefore less vulnerable than the new Panama Canal. Dynamite cartridges were planted on 13 August on the railway north of Kantara West, so compelling the defence to watch both banks of the Canal. Jemal Pasha was inspired to contemplate a strong diversionary assault on the Canal, which was approved in September by Enver and gave the sons of Sherif Hussain an excuse to raise troops in the Hejaz. German submarines were attracted by the Gallipoli expedition to the East Mediterranean by midsummer. They intensified their campaign from September and destroyed the security of the inland sea all the more easily because Britain lacked cruisers and destroyers for commerce-protection after Fisher's reforms. Their campaign necessitated security precautions in Port Said and the prohibition on 21 September of passengers from landing at Port Said unless they were of British or allied nationality.[1]

The junction of the German, Austrian and Bulgarian troops took place on 5 November 1915 after the destruction of the Serbian barrier to through communication between Germany and Turkey, reviving the Berlin-Bagdad dream as much as did the failure of the Dardanelles and Salonika ventures. German interest was also aroused in the Canal by the death of Prussian officers in Sinai and by the removal of Heineken, the sole German director of the Company, from the board by the decision of the shareholders' meeting on 14 June 1915. German literature on the Canal originated in military history[2] and carried further the revision of the Canal's history in the German interest which had begun in 1912. It resolutely attacked the Anglo-French tradition and used its revised version of history to stake out new claims for the future. It encouraged the production of the first biography of Negrelli by Alfred Birk in 1915 and condemned Lesseps as the betrayer of the international Study Society of 1846.[3] Above all it condemned England for opposing the construction of the Canal and then for adapting her policy to its existence by buying the Khedive's shares and infringing the neutrality of the waterway in order to occupy Egypt. German scholars identified the Canal Company with the British Government and assumed that control of the Canal was the precondition for the control of Egypt.[4] They inherited the imperial bias of Edwardian England and overemphasized England's dependence on 'the door

[1] P. G. Elgood, 208.

[2] E. Serman, *Mit den Türken an der Front* (Berlin, Scherl, 1915).

[3] A. Demiani, 'Deutschlands Anrecht an den Suezkanal', *Süddeutsche Monatshefte* (September 1916), 736.

[4] A. Gottlob, 'Das Eindringen Englands in Ägypten', *Die Grenzboten* (April 1915), 24.

and hinge' of her Cape–Cairo–Calcutta empire,[1] assuming that its closure would cut off England's imports, immobilize her shipping and shatter her prestige in the East. They deplored the confiscation of German vessels in the harbours of the Canal but did not propose to close the waterway to warships. They blamed the limited trade of Trieste and Fiume with Asia on the high level of Canal tolls,[2] hoped for the transfer to the Central Powers of some of the French and Italian possessions in the Red Sea[3] and so built up an Adriatic–Suez dream to complement the Berlin–Bagdad dream. They used the documents published by Birk and Georgi and the claims of Maria Grois-Negrelli[4] to support the German demand for Suez shares in reparation for the injustice done in the 1850s. They hoped for the transfer of some of the founders' shares, for the cession of the shares held in France as part of any war-indemnity and for the allotment of five seats on the board of directors to Germany as well as of seven seats to Austria.[5] They also suggested the abolition of the Egyptian administration in Sinai so as to establish the Turkish frontier on the Canal itself and prepare for the brilliant economic future in store for the peninsula.[6] The German agitation of 1915–16 was not so violent as the British agitation of 1883. It was directed not at the Canal Company but at the German and Austrian public, whom it sought to re-educate in a more national approach to the Canal. Neither England nor France found it necessary to defend their interest other than by force of arms. Effectively defended by England rather than by France the Canal remained a symbol of the French genius for civilization[7] and 'a great work which is one of the factors in the progress of the world and in the economic emancipation of the nations'.[8] The needs of wartime propaganda were served by the diffusion of the Disraeli-myth of the share-purchase from the stage in England[9] and from the screen in America.[10] The sympathetic understanding in the U.S.A. of England's defence of 'the weakest link in the Empire'[11] was restrained by the hostility of its large German-American population, by its affection for Turkey[12] and by its colonial distrust of the old country's imperial tradition.[13]

[1] A. Dix, 'Die Verkehrspolitische Bedeutung des Suezkanals', *Geographische Zeitschrift*, 18 Februar 1916, 90.

[2] D. von Wannisch, 'Der Suezkanal und dessen Beziehungen zur Europaischen Mächtegruppierung', *Deutsche Revue* (März 1916), 273–5.

[3] Ibid., 275.   [4] Demiani, 738.

[5] Ibid., 732.

[6] G. Steindorff, 'Die Ostgrenze Ägyptens und der Suezkanal', *Zeitschrift für Politik* (1917), 194.

[7] G. E. Bonnet, 'Le Canal de Suez', *La Science et la Vie* (Février 1916), 204.

[8] *Le Canal de Suez*, 9 Juin 1916, 6095, C. Jonnart, 5 June 1916.

[9] L. N. Parker, *Disraeli* (Royalty Theatre, London, 4 April 1916). E. A. Parry, *Disraeli* (Gaiety Theatre, Manchester, 9 October 1916). *Manchester Guardian*, 10 October 1916, 6 ii.

[10] Percy Nash, *Disraeli* (23 February 1917).

[11] W. A. Anderson, 'Soldiers, Sand and Sentiment', *Harper's Magazine* (August 1916), 352. C. Johnston, 'The Problem at Suez', *North American Review* (February 1916), 227–34.

[12] A. H. Lybyer, 'The Ottoman Turks and the Routes of Oriental Trade', *English Historical Review* (October 1915), 577–88.

[13] H. M. Allen, 'How England Got the Suez', *Sewanee Review* (April 1917), 139–43.

The failure of the Dardanelles expedition encouraged Kitchener to propose to Asquith on 11 November 1915 the defence of the Canal at Alexandretta with troops withdrawn from Gallipoli, as an alternative to the uneconomic defence of Egypt in Egypt. Kitchener deplored the administrative surrender to the west bank's monopoly of transport facilities and the use of the Canal as a means to its own defence. On 16 November he ordered the defence of the Canal seriously and in depth on an active rather than a passive basis.[1] The shift towards the idea of defence in depth encouraged Herbert Sidebotham, military critic of the *Manchester Guardian* since 1895, to suggest the creation of a Jewish Palestine as a bridle on French aspirations to a Greater Syria, a buffer-state against the Ottoman Empire and a bastion for the protection of the most vital and vulnerable spot in the whole imperial system. 'A Suez Canal which is a battlefront between two armies is of no use for any other purpose. . . In the long run there can be no satisfactory defence of Egypt or the Suez Canal so long as Palestine is in the occupation of a hostile or possibly hostile Power.'[2]

The retreat from the Dardanelles precluded the possibility of similar landings in Syria, lowered British prestige and exposed the Levant and the Canal to a new surge of Turkish power. During December 1915 six of the giant troopships of the Cunard, White Star and Shaw Savill Lines used the Canal in order to avoid German submarines after returning from the Dardanelles. Egypt became an armed camp as well as a gigantic hospital for the sick and wounded, for whom a new English Hospital was inaugurated at Port Said on 8 November 1915. General Maxwell professed to fear a Gallipoli in reverse in the Canal Zone and asked for thirteen divisions to defend Egypt against a possible onslaught by 250,000 Turks. That threat was no mirage because the Canal remained the British lifeline to the East throughout the war and necessitated some dispersion of military force in order to facilitate its continuing concentration.[3] The defences of the Canal therefore began to be organized as Kitchener had decreed. Orders were issued on 25 November for the doubling of the Zagazig–Ismailia Railway so as to facilitate the movement of vast numbers of troops from Alexandria to the Canal Zone. A meeting of the chief officials of the Ministry of Public Works on 1 December marked the transition to an engineer's war[4] waged by a works organization established on 4 December with its H.Q. in Ismailia. Major-General H. S. Horne chose a front line of defence 6¼ miles to the east of the Canal, in order to free it from long-range artillery fire and cabled his decision to Kitchener on 10 December,

---

[1] G. C. A. Arthur, *Life of Lord Kitchener* (London, Macmillan, 1920), iii. 206 note, 22 November 1915.

[2] *Manchester Guardian*, 22 November 1915, 6 ii, 'The Defence of Egypt'. H. Sidebotham, *Great Britain and Palestine* (London, Macmillan, 1937), 22, 38.

[3] F. Maurice, *British Strategy. A Study of the Application of the Principles of War* (London, Constable, 1929), 108.

[4] E. H. Lloyd, 'Work in Connection with the Suez Canal Defences in 1916', *Proceedings of the Institution of Civil Engineers*, ccvii (1918–19), Part 1, 349–50.

so requiring the extension of supporting communications seven miles into the desert from the west bank.

The Rotterdam Lloyd diverted its service from the Canal to the Cape route in December 1915 because the British denied coal supplies to vessels refusing to submit to restrictions on their trade with Germany and because the price of coal at Port Said had quadrupled, coal freights to Port Said having risen to tenfold their peacetime level.[1] The Dutch line preferred to reap the high wartime profits accruing from the neutral status of the Netherlands and so set the example followed by the Netherland Steamship Company in March 1916. Allied shipping was adversely affected by the intensified German submarine warfare. The submarine U-38 first sank the *Yasaka Maru* in the Mediterranean on 21 December, compelling the Nippon Yusen Kaisha to divert its service to the Cape route,[2] and then sank five British steamers within eight days. Lloyd's declined to insure ships between Port Said and Aden from 25 December, the day when the harbour of Port Said was closed[3] and the landing of women without authority was forbidden.[4] Thus the competitive advantages of the Cape route were greatly enhanced.[5] The tonnage of the Canal and the receipts of the Canal Company declined by the unprecedented proportion of 21 per cent during 1915, when military traffic supplied 20 per cent of the total tonnage. Dividends for the year suffered hardly any reduction after the massive decrease for 1914. The intensive bombing of the Canal region from the air in January–March 1916 increased the insecurity of the waterway. The greatest threat to the Canal route came neither from the land nor from the air but from the submarine, which after nineteen months of war compelled the diversion to the Cape route from 7 March 1916 of the British cargo-boats and the mail-boats of the P. & O. and Orient Lines en route to Australia.[6] That diversion coincided with the introduction of defensive armament on merchant-ships carrying war-stores and troops to the Mediterranean. Guns were mounted by the workshops of the Canal Company and transferred at Port Said from eastbound to westbound liners. Passengers from England for India wore life-belts throughout the day, slept in their clothes at night and attended frequent religious services as far as Port Said. The German submarines operated in a sea where only Austria, Turkey and Bulgaria were friendly while France and Italy were the allies of Britain. They served at an immense distance from their home bases and operated from Cattaro and Pola high up in the Adriatic, despite the barrier of trawl-nets across the 45–70 miles of the Straits of Otranto from 1915. Those submarines employed Germany's

[1] *The Times*, 16 December 1915, 9iii. Hansard, *Commons Debates*, 20 December 1915, P. Alden.

[2] *The Times*, 30 December 1915, 7v.

[3] R. Hennig, 'Die Bedeutung des Suezkanals für das englische Wirtschaftsleben', *Deutsche Kolonialzeitung* (1916), 5 note.

[4] P. G. Elgood, 227.

[5] *The Field*, 15 January 1916, 118–19, 'The Cape Route v. the Suez Canal'.

[6] A. J. Marder, *From the Dreadnought to Scapa Flow. The Royal Navy in the Fisher Era, 1904–1919* (London, Oxford University Press, 1965), ii. 336.

best commanders and inflicted heavy losses out of all proportion to their small numbers. Their activity inspired Japan to send eight destroyers to the Mediterranean in order to win Allied support for its claim to all the German possessions in the Far East.

The diversion of ships to Australia from the Canal route decreased the average size of vessels using the Canal from 1916. That rerouting of traffic increased costs, coal-consumption and cargo-space required, eliminating all the economies made available by the opening of the short Suez route in 1869 and raising shipping freights because of the longer route, the fewer ships and the reduced cargo-space. The Canal Company was compelled from 1915 to borrow money at 5 per cent instead of at 3 per cent, and to impose its first wartime surtax from 1 April 1916 in order to raise more revenue from the diminished traffic, in which the British share rose to 79·4 per cent, a proportion unequalled since 1882. The Company thereby made its tolls less competitive with those of the Panama Canal and destroyed the balance carefully established in 1913. During 1916 its receipts sank by 9 per cent while its dividends sank by 29 per cent. The Cape route gained what the Suez route lost. Overseas steam tonnage entering the harbours of South Africa rose by 81 per cent during 1916.[1] That tremendous afflux of tonnage created serious bunkering difficulties because the Union lacked adequate coaling facilities and rolling-stock to carry coal to the ports. The resulting long delays to shipping further increased the strain on the limited amount of tonnage available and attracted Dutch shipping to the Panama route. The restriction of trade between Europe and Asia reduced the competition of European manufactures in the East and facilitated the wartime industrialization of India, South Africa, Australia, Japan and the treaty-ports of China. Japan expanded its trade in Asia and in South America through the new westbound lines begun via the Cape by the Osaka Shoshen Kaisha in 1916 and the Nippon Yusen Kaisha in 1917. It reaped an especially rich harvest in the Egyptian market, dumping inferior flour, matches and tobacco in the Canal Zone in the absence of competition from Europe.[2] The end of the shipment of phosphates from Oceania in 1916 encouraged the beginning of phosphate exports from Kosseir through the Canal in 1917. The submarine menace reduced shipments of rubber through the Canal from their peak in 1915 and compelled the U.S.A. to accumulate stocks. As a neutral power the U.S.A. was able to increase its use of the Canal during 1916 and 1917 after the U.S. Hydrographic Office published in 1916 the first edition of *The Red Sea and Gulf of Aden Pilot* and the U.S. Steel Products Company sent its first vessel through the Canal in April 1916.

On 29 December 1915 Lieutenant-General Sir Archibald Murray, the C.I.G.S., was appointed G.O.C.-in-C. of the Mediterranean Expeditionary Force which was to defend the Canal and serve as a general strategic reserve

---

[1] *Official Year Book of the Union of South Africa* (Pretoria, 1918), No. 1, 1917, 558.
[2] P. G. Elgood, 288.

for the Empire. He assumed command on 10 January 1916 and carried forward the preparations which had been begun in December in fulfilment of Kitchener's decree. The railway to Ismailia was doubled over forty-nine miles in five weeks (1 December–6 January) and carried the first contingent of the Egyptian Labour Corps to the Canal Zone on 7 January, a Camel Transport Corps on 13 January and the Egyptian Army Reserve on 20 January, so placing all the resources of the Government of Egypt at British disposal. On 13 January Murray ordered three Army Corps to the Canal to take up their positions according to a revised scheme of defence in three lines of depth along a front divided into three sections. On 22 January Murray established his G.H.Q. at Ismailia, where the French Club was swamped by British officers and the shopkeepers began to enjoy unprecedented prosperity. Thenceforward the Canal Zone became a war area as never before in its history. In the desert seven miles east of the Canal a deep line of trenches and redoubts was built over the eighty miles from Kantara to the Wells of Moses and protected by matting hurdles manufactured in Port Said as well as by thirty million sandbags. Those defences introduced the trench warfare of the Western Front into Sinai and were manned by massed troops but were never put to the test of battle. Nevertheless they prevented Turkish patrols from approaching the Canal itself after February 1916 and especially from bombarding it as Kressenstein had planned since 1915. Ancillary services were developed to supply the needs of the defence forces. Water was carried from the Sweet Water Canal across the maritime Canal in syphon-pipes to six points. Eight short light railways were begun to defence-points east of the Canal in order to free the roads for the movement of troops and guns. The Canal itself was spanned by three floating heavy-load bridges and by six light pontoon boat-bridges. Two armoured trains with mountain-guns and Maxims patrolled the railway along the west bank. To relieve the strain on the railways the first main roads were built in the Canal Zone from Tel el Kebir to Ismailia and Port Said as well as from Suez to Kubri and Chalouf. Thenceforward it became possible for the first time to travel by car from Port Said to Cairo.

Murray decided that the defence of Egypt by a strong position built close to the Canal was a waste of men and material over a front of 80–90 miles and therefore proposed on 15 February the forty-five miles between El Arish and Kossaima on the eastern fringe of Sinai as the true strategic base for the defence of Egypt.[1] He recommended an initial advance to a suitable position east of the water-bearing basin of Katia, twenty-three miles from the Canal, the construction of a railway to Katia and the maintenance there of a force of 50,000. He began to advance on 20 February and secured permission on 27 February to advance to Katia. He benefited by the Russian entry into Erzerum on 16 February, which interrupted Turkish plans for attacking the Canal and led to the gradual reduction of the garrisons in Syria from 250,000

---

[1] G. Macmunn and C. Falls, *Military Operations. Egypt and Palestine. Official History of the War* (London, H.M.S.O., 1928), i. 170–4.

to 60,000. During March the strategic reserve of the Empire in the Delta and the Canal Zone was reduced from thirteen to seven divisions after the German onslaught on Verdun. From 10 March the Sinai Military Railway was pushed forward from Kantara over sixteen miles into the desert in four weeks. That railway was accompanied by a pipe-line carrying water from the Nile and was supplemented by the extension to Kantara West of the Salhia Railway built in 1869. It advanced north-eastwards from Kantara East to follow the caravan route along the coast under the protection of the Navy. It was built on the expensive standard gauge of 4 ft. 8½ in. rather than on the economic metre gauge. Thus Murray sought to emulate Kitchener's successful use of the railway in warfare in the Sudan and South Africa while Britain sought to lay the material foundation of a new empire. Jemal Pasha's reply was to accelerate the building of his own light 'Egyptian Railway' which he intended to extend westwards from Beersheba to the Canal at Ismailia so as to conquer Sinai by rail.

Murray took over command of all troops in Egypt on 19 March and ordered on 7 April a mounted yeomanry brigade of gentry and farmers to Romani, twenty-five miles east of the Canal, and so opened the Sinai campaign of one master-race against another. The advance of the railway encouraged the German aircraft, newly arrived at El Arish, to bomb Katia on 20 April and Romani on 21 April. Then a reconnaissance in strength of 1,600 troops under Kressenstein launched surprise attacks on 23 April on the hazardous forward positions held by the British at Oghratina and Katia. Those attacks were unmatched throughout the campaign for their combined speed, skill, daring and success.[1] The whole force of yeomanry was killed or captured, compelling the War Office to conceal the details for many months. The progress of the railway was delayed while the earthworks of the Turkish railway reached El Auja in May. Murray immediately sent the Anzacs across the Canal on 24 April to Romani and asked the War Office on 3 May for at least three divisions, or 50,000 men, for operations east of the waterway. German aircraft first bombed Port Said on 8 May and intimidated the civilian labourers. The British in reply bombarded the German air-base at El Arish from the sea and air on 18 May and rigorously restricted entry into the Canal Zone by the military proclamation of 18 May, which closed Port Said once and for all to the general public of Egypt.[2] Thenceforward Port Said was governed by English officials, save for the Governor and his deputy, and by the British Army and Navy in close cooperation. The trade in drink was controlled by the military proclamation of 3 January 1916 and the trade in hashish forbidden by that of 7 July 1916.

The most effective British reply was to encourage the Arab revolt through the Arab Bureau established in Cairo in January 1916 and through emissaries who left from Suez for Arabia as they had under Mehemet Ali and Ismail. The Hejaz had suffered more than any other land in Arabia from the effects of the war, from the blockade of its seaports, and from the end of the pilgrim

[1] G. Macmunn, i. 162. [2] P. G. Elgood, 249–50.

traffic to Jedda in 1915. Sherif Hussain had served the Imperial Government since 1908 but declared that he could not participate in Jemal's projected onslaught on the Canal. He fired the first shot in the revolt from his palace in Mecca on 2 June and proclaimed Arab independence outside Medina on 5 June. His aspirations to dominion over fertile Syria and Palestine were doomed by the Sykes–Picot agreement of 16 May which recognized a French zone of influence from Cilicia to Mosul and an English zone of influence from Sinai to Persia, so as to link Egypt to India. To support Hussain's revolt Murray was, however, instructed on 29 June seriously to prepare for the occupation of El Arish which might be held with fewer troops than the Canal, since he had sent away 200,000 troops for the summer offensive on the Western Front and retained only four weak Territorial divisions. The Arab revolt denied Germany the use of the Red Sea coast as a submarine base[1] and protected the British in Sinai from an attack on their right flank. It severed Turkish communications with the Yemen, diverted the interest of Jemal from the Canal to the Hejaz and locked up 65,000 Turkish troops. Above all, it undermined the loyalty to Turkey of the Arabs of Southern Syria through their sympathy with the cause of Hussain. To retain their loyalty Jemal was forced to launch another offensive in Sinai under unfavourable conditions. That advance by a Turkish Expeditionary Force of 16,000 under Kressenstein was also intended to celebrate Kressenstein's appointment to the command of a field army[2] and to drive the British back across the Canal.[3]

The advance began from El Arish on 16 July in the full heat of summer and remained unobserved by the R.F.C. until 19 July. The Turks transported six-inch howitzers along an artillery-road built of brushwood trenches and reached Katia on 3 August, when German aircraft attacked G.H.Q. at Ismailia. On 4 August they launched a surprise attack on Romani, the railhead since 15 May, against two very raw divisions.[4] The Anzac Mounted Division paid the price for the excessive caution of a British general under Murray's command[5] and suffered the bulk of the British losses of 1,130, including 202 killed and 882 wounded. Their magnificent battle-discipline nevertheless enabled them to repel the attack and to inflict 5,500 casualties, including 4,000 taken prisoner. The battle of Romani proved more important than that of Ismailia but was eclipsed from history because no French fought there to defend the Canal. That decisive defeat enforced Turkish recognition of British superiority, ended the two-year siege of the Canal and even encouraged a proposal to prohibit the use of the waterway to German and Austrian vessels for ten years after the end of the war.[6] It changed the desert campaign from a defensive into an offensive operation. 'The Battle of Romani was the decisive

[1] H. S. Gullett, *The Australian Imperial Forces in Sinai and Palestine 1914–1918* (Sydney, Angus, 1923), 80.

[2] P. G. Elgood, 278.

[3] Kress von Kressenstein, 'Die Kriegführung in der Wüste' (1920), 32.

[4] H. S. Gullett, 142–93.   [5] Ibid., 117–18, 134–5, 152.

[6] *Manchester Guardian*, 11 September 1916, 4v.

engagement of the whole Sinai and Palestine campaign.'[1] The Turks evacuated their forward positions in good order and returned to El Arish. Work on the railway was resumed on 10 August and accelerated, while the Arabs sabotaged the Hejaz Railway which Turkey had used for communication with Arabia since the outbreak of the war denied her the use of the Canal. Murray decided to establish closer relations with the civil authority and reported on 17 August his intention to transfer G.H.Q. to Cairo. He was informed on 4 October that policy in Egypt was to be mainly defensive, though preparations might be made for an advance on El Arish. G.H.Q. was transferred on 23 October to Cairo from Ismailia, where Moascar the nearby 'camp' remained a brigade-concentration point for France and Sinai.

The advance across Sinai by railway, water pipe-line and cavalry patrol took longer than any other in history. The completion of a locomotive cable-ferry at Kantara between 16 July and 27 October encouraged the revival of the idea of a Cape-to-Cairo Railway, which might be extended to link up with an Asiatic Railway.[2] The advance on El Arish was ordered on 11 November and completed on 21 December, after its evacuation by the Turks. Two days after Lloyd George became Prime Minister a War Office telegram of 9 December asked Murray what additional troops he would need to act beyond El Arish. Thus Lloyd George aspired to liberate the Holy Land from Egypt and realize the Zionist ideal. The Sinai Railway reached El Arish on 4 January 1917. The battle of Rafa on 9 January captured the last village of Sinai from the enemy and effectively freed Egypt from the Turk. The end of the Sinai campaign permitted a reduction in the number of troops allotted to the direct defence of the Canal but reduced Egyptian interest in the prosecution of the war beyond her frontiers. The War Office ordered Murray on 11 January to release one or two divisions for France and to postpone operations in Palestine until the autumn. After the loss of Bagdad the Turks reinforced Gaza, which Murray failed to take by surprise assault on 26 March. The War Cabinet then decided on 30 March on the occupation of Jerusalem but without reinforcements.[3] Murray's second defeat before Gaza on 17–19 April became inevitable after the British failed to send reinforcements and the Turks strengthened their defences. The 10,000 casualties in the unsuccessful battles of Gaza were the price paid for the advance across Sinai, which had progressively extended the British lines of communication and shortened the Turkish lines so that in the summer of 1917 the two armies re-enacted with roles reversed the confrontation of 1915 on the Canal.

The German submarine campaign in the Mediterranean increasingly diverted traffic to the Cape route, which itself became insecure after the start of unrestricted submarine warfare. The Corfu Conference which began on 27 April decided to divert shipping to the Far East from the Mediterranean

---

[1] H. S. Gullett, 189.
[2] A. M. Hyamson, 'Egypt and Palestine', *Quarterly Review* (October 1916), 428–9.
[3] G. Macmunn, i. 322.

to the Cape route and to introduce a fast convoy-system in the Mediterranean. The first westbound convoy started from the Mediterranean on 10 May and reached England without loss on 20 May. The first eastbound convoy of four ships left Malta for Alexandria on 22 May.[1] Port Said became a centre for the transhipment of cargo to fast vessels especially after ships bound for Bombay were diverted to the Cape route by June. Its harbour became so crowded with shipping that vessels had to be moored for 15–20 miles up the Canal.[2] Its quays became so filled with cargo that acres of fresh and distant ground had to be covered with goods. Its merchants established the Port Said Chamber of Commerce in 1918 as coal reached nearly tenfold its pre-war price. The needs of the war restricted international trade via the Canal to the minimum during 1917 when net register tonnage sank to 42 per cent, cargo to 26 per cent and civilian passengers to 10 per cent of the 1913 level. Four successive increases in toll raised dues 36 per cent above the level of 1913 or to the pre-Panama level of 1903–5. Dividends declined to 33 per cent of their 1913 level in the fourth successive reduction, a sequence thitherto unknown to the Company. The market value of the British Government's shares only declined by 31 March 1917 to 70·4 per cent of their value on 31 March 1913.

Murray was recalled on 11 June 1917[3] and returned to London infuriated at his supersession because he had obeyed every demand by the War Office to yield up troops for France. On 11–12 June Jonnart, the President of the Canal Company and the envoy of the Allies, presented an ultimatum in Athens and so secured the abdication of the King of Greece, the accession of Venizelos to power and the entry of Greece into the war on the side of the Allies, raising Greek shipping using the Canal from 55,000 tons in 1916 to 358,000 tons in 1917. Allenby's assumption of command of the Egyptian Expeditionary Force impressed Turkey with the imminence of a large-scale offensive against Palestine. For that offensive Allenby was given the troops denied to Murray and built up a vast base at Kantara, which gained ocean wharves and became an alternative seaport to Alexandria as well as an immense unhealthy garrison town extending for four miles along the Canal and for four miles into the desert. Oswald Sanderson, who had been a director of the Canal Company since 1910 and the organizer of Mediterranean shipping so as to increase its capacity, arranged for the construction of a railway swing bridge at Kantara. The first Through Mediterranean Convoy sailed from Liverpool on 3 October for Port Said, losing only two of its eleven large ships between Crete and Alexandria. After the first United Kingdom Convoy left Port Said on 16 November priority cargo from India and the Far East could be carried by a fleet of 90 instead of 130 steamers, so freeing 40 for the North Atlantic route. The submarine campaign proved a far graver menace than the hussar-raids on the Canal itself. 5,000,000 tons or 38·5 per cent of the

[1] R. H. Gibson and M. Prendergast, *The German Submarine War 1914–1918* (London, Constable, 1931), 256.
[2] P. G. Elgood, 66–7.   [3] G. Macmunn, i. 368.

13,000,000 tons of Allied and neutral shipping sunk by submarine during the war was lost between Gibraltar and Port Said.

Allenby's advance with the largest army ever to enter Palestine began on 27 October 1917 and frustrated Enver's plan to launch a great offensive in Sinai. Gaza fell on 7 November but did not become the Cannae which Allenby had intended. The Balfour Declaration of 2 November committed the British Government to the support of a Jewish National Home, by which the Zionists understood the Jewish State of Herzl. Jerusalem was captured on 8 December by Christian soldiers for the first time since 1187 and provisioned from Egypt. Allenby's campaign encouraged a revival of Brugsch's theory of 1874, which had chosen the northern route for the Exodus of Israel from Egypt, the location of the 'crossing' of the Pelusiac branch of the Nile in the Salhia–Kantara region, the location of the destruction of Pharaoh's Army in the Serbonian triangle of land flooded in 1914 and the identification of Israel's route across North Sinai with that followed by the Desert Column in 1916.[1] Russia's surrender of the heartland of Eastern Europe at Brest-Litovsk made possible the German occupation of the Ukraine and the Crimea. Thereby Mitteleuropa threatened to outflank both the Canal and the Euphrates Valley Railway,[2] which had been revived in 1917[3] together with the idea of a Hindu Kush Railway between London and Delhi. Germany might either open a new route to India via Batum, Baku, Bokhara or follow the westward advance of Persian, Macedonian, Roman and Turk along that fertile crescent between the Mediterranean and the desert which formed an intercontinental bridge 'strategically like a four-hundred-mile prolongation of the Isthmus of Suez northward'.[4] To preclude such a danger Britain was urged to establish a protectorate over Palestine, Syria and Armenia as well as to fortify the Taurus and Amanus tunnels above Alexandretta as an Asiatic Gibraltar protecting Suez, the key of the Pacific[5] and 'the crossways of the world'.[6]

The collapse of the Ottoman Empire made possible the last and greatest expansion by the Christian West at the expense of Islamic power. It enabled Britain partially to fulfil the dreams of Disraeli and Salisbury of 1878, although in the southern rather than in the northern provinces of the Empire.[7] Arabia gave England its war-hero while Sinai, Palestine and Mesopotamia supplied territorial compensation for the catastrophic loss of life on the Western Front.

---

[1] W. Willcocks, *From the Garden of Eden to the Crossing of the Jordan* (London, Spon, 1919), 67–76.

[2] J. A. R. Marriott, *The Eastern Question. An Historical Study in European Diplomacy* (Oxford, Clarendon Press, 1918, 2nd edition), 491, 510.

[3] H. C. Woods, 'The Bagdad Railway and its Tributaries', *Geographical Journal* (July 1917), 32–57. *Quarterly Review* (October 1917), 487, 'The Bagdad Railway Negotiations'.

[4] J. H. Breasted, 'The Bridgehead of Asia Minor', *The Nation*, 8 June 1918, 676.

[5] Ibid., 677–8.

[6] H. J. Mackinder, *Democratic Ideals and Reality. A Study in the Politics of Reconstruction* (London, Constable, 1919), 143.

[7] L. Bashford, 'Allenby's Victories and Britain's Opportunity', *Nineteenth Century* (December 1919), 1017–25.

The extension of British power eastward from Egypt was symbolized by the completion of the railway swing-bridge across the Canal three miles north of Kantara between 22 November 1917 and 29 April 1918. That bridge restricted the width of the fairway to 138 feet, sacrificed the interests of long-distance traffic to the exigencies of local empire-building and was built in defiance of the opposition of the Canal Company. It replaced the time-consuming locomotive-ferry and encouraged the Ministry of Shipping in May 1918 to consider building a port at Kantara. It was used for the first through-train from Jerusalem to Cairo on 15 June 1918 and functioned so well as to encourage the idea of replacing it by a permanent bridge.[1] The Sinai Military Railway became the first railway link between Africa and Asia and was extended to the port of Haifa in December 1918, when the British occupation of Palestine as a strategic buffer was justified by Curzon to the War Cabinet as necessary for the most effective and economic defence of Egypt and the Canal. The Sinai and Palestine campaign converted Australian hostility toward the Canal into fealty and gave Australians an intimacy which they had never known before with the Canal region as distinct from the Canal towns:[2] it also brought them into touch with their non-Australian past and earned them the embarrassing appellation of the new Crusaders.[3] Thus British interests in the Canal were reinforced by the interest of the two white dominions east of Suez, to which 56,000 troops were repatriated via the Canal in 1919.

The protection afforded to the Canal by the Convention of Constantinople had suffered erosion during the war. Britain began by respecting the Convention as far as possible but found it necessary to fortify the waterway and to mount coastal-defence artillery at its ports of access. She stationed warships in its interior waters and forbade the nocturnal transit of merchant-shipping. She also established search-stations and searched ships with their consent within the three-mile limit from March 1915.[4] In effect Britain blockaded the Canal against hostile shipping and restricted the freedom of navigation to freedom of passage alone at the expense of freedom of approach and of sojourn. The purpose was to prevent enemy ships from blocking the Canal by sabotage, the result was to exclude enemy ships from the Canal and to preserve its exclusive use to the Allies and to Britain in particular. Britain increased her share of the tonnage to a peak of 79·5 per cent in 1918. She made the Canal Zone a theatre of war but did not detach it from Egypt as Panama had been from Colombia. She disembarked and assembled troops along the length of the waterway, developed communications in the zone and built 200 miles of metalled roads. She created at Kantara a vast base for the invasion of Palestine. In effect Britain treated the Canal at least from 1916 as a British

---

[1] *The Engineer*, 22 August 1919, 176, 'Temporary Swing Bridge over the Suez Canal'.

[2] J. Pichon, *Sur la Route des Indes. Un Siècle après Bonaparte* (Paris, Société d'Éditions Géographiques, 1932), 18.

[3] R. E. C. Adams, *The Modern Crusaders* (London, Routledge, 1920).

[4] E. A. Whittuck, *International Canals* (London, H.M.S.O., 1920; Peace Handbook no. 150), 82–4.

territorial possession with the compliance and cooperation of the Canal Company. Thereby she proved that the Convention of Constantinople could not be maintained in any respect which was contrary to the policy of the territorial power and might even become 'a scrap of paper'. Britain infringed almost every article of the Convention, systematically restricting the rights thereunder of neutrals and even of signatory powers. British lawyers provided the legal formulae which justified such an extension of belligerent rights. They ruled that Port Said was a port enemy to Germany within the meaning of the Hague Convention whose protection they denied to German vessels.[1] Their judgments interpreted the Convention restrictively and refused to impose penalties for its violation because the Convention itself made no such provision. They nevertheless paid homage to the Convention by classifying the prizes taken in 1914 as seizures on the high seas rather than as seizures in port[2] and by holding the seizure in 1916 of the unseaworthy fleet of lighters and tugs of the Deutsches Kohlen Depot Gesellschaft to have taken place on Egyptian soil outside the waters of the Canal.[3] In the peace treaties of 1919–20 Britain assumed the rights of the Porte over the Canal, ending the juridical links between Turkey and the Canal as well as the special position of Turkey under the Convention. Thereby the formal structure of British preponderance over the Canal was completed and her wartime policies in defence of the Canal were given retroactive justification. The Convention remained in force, although Britain strengthened its privileged territorial position in relation to the Canal and favoured a revision of its restrictive eighth and ninth articles.[4] She even sought to extend the absolute freedom of navigation through the Canal to the Kiel Canal and, in the abortive Treaty of Sèvres in 1920, to the Dardanelles.

---

[1] *Law Reports*, 7 April 1916, 2 *Appeal Cases*, 118, *Gutenfels*, Lord Wrenbury.

[2] *Lloyd's Reports of Prize Cases*, VIII, 465–7, 5 June 1919, *Derfflinger*, Lord Phillimore.

[3] *The Law Times Reports*, 120, 103–6, 13 December 1918, Deutsches Kohlen Depot Gesellschaft, Lord Sumner.

[4] E. A. Whittuck, *International Canals*, 97.

30

THE BRITISH EMPIRE OF THE
MIDDLE EAST AND THE PERSIAN
OIL TRADE, 1920-1930

THE collapse of the Ottoman Empire enabled Britain to extend its
influence over the land-bridge between the Mediterranean and the
Persian Gulf and to establish its power in the Euphrates Valley. Thereby it fulfilled the aspirations of generations of Anglo-Indians and realized the
imperial dream of a Southern Asia British from Suez to Singapore, with
vassal-states extending from Palestine to the Pamirs. In Persia a British protectorate seemed essential to control the gateway to India against the new
revolutionary threat from the Bolshevik north. 'The Persian revolution may
become the key to the revolution of the whole Orient, just as Egypt and the
Suez Canal are the key to English domination in the Orient. Persia is the
"Suez Canal" of the revolution. By shifting the political centre of gravity of
the revolution to Persia, the entire strategic value of the Suez Canal is lost.'[1]
The renaissance of indigenous Asia in 1919-20 frustrated the full realization
of Britain's imperial ambitions. The war which impressed the East as a civil
war within Christendom began the deglorification of Europe in Asia. The
postwar renaissance of Asia depressed northbound cargo shipments between
November 1919 and August 1921 and attracted Indian enterprise into the
field of shipping through the Scindia Steam Navigation Company, Ltd., which
was founded on 27 March 1919. The *Empress of India*, laid up by the C.P.R.
in 1914, was renamed the *Loyalty* and left Bombay on 5 April 1919 with seven
rulers of Indian states on board, so beginning the first steamship service
between Bombay and London beneath the Hindu swastika flag.[2] Japan benefited from the wartime suspension of the services of the German lines and
from the wartime needs of the Allies for shipping to expand its tonnage using
the Canal markedly in 1918-20. In 1919 the Osaka Shoshen Kaisha launched
the *Suez Maru* and the Kokusai Kisen Kaisha the *Portsaid Maru*. Japan
which had ranked sixth in 1913 and fourth in 1915 rose to assume the second
place in 1919 and 1920 with 9·1 per cent of the Canal's tonnage. Thus its
Canal tonnage expanded outside the sphere of trade with Japan and far beyond
the limited basis of subsidized mail tonnage. Its tonnage failed however to
maintain Japan in the second place to Britain after the peak year of 1920. The

---

[1] I. Spector, *The Soviet Union and the Muslim World 1917–1958* (University of Washington
Press, Seattle, 1959), 84–5, quoting K. Troyanovsky, *Vostok i Revolutsiya* (1918).

[2] T. S. S. Rao, *A Short History of Modern Indian Shipping* (Bombay, Popular Prakashan,
1965), 81–2.

renewed expansion of European enterprise in Asia and Africa was reflected in a sharp increase in the export to Britain of sugar from Mauritius in 1919 and in the beginning of the shipments of soda from Lake Magadi in Kenya in April 1920, chrome from India and Africa in 1920, bauxite from India in 1921 and wattle-bark residue from Durban in June 1921. The wartime growth of industry in Asia made possible the increasing shipment of jute sacks from Calcutta, which exceeded from the year 1919–1920 the weight of raw jute exported. Coconut oil was also carried in tankers from Batavia and Manila from 1919 in competition with soya oil. Cast iron was first exported through the Canal from Bengal to the U.S.A. in April 1923. Eggs were first shipped from China in 1922: the first bulk shipment of preserved eggs from Hankow to Liverpool passed through on 20 September 1923.

Egypt like other primary producers had benefited from the wartime inflation of prices and especially from the boom in cotton. Its delegation or Wafd of twelve was led by Saad Zaglul, the secret adviser of Sultan Fuad since 1917, to ask the British High Commissioner for independence for Egypt and the Sudan and the end of the protectorate proclaimed in 1914. The request was refused and Zaglul was deported with three other leaders to Malta. The resulting rebellion surprised the remaining nationalist leaders by its scale, its speed and its force, showing that Egypt had gained a new national symbol in the Wafd and a new leader in Zaglul. Determined efforts in the Canal Zone to enlist the support of the Egyptian Labour Corps[1] compelled the Government to order the Anzacs on 17 March 1919 from Rafa to the Canal. Sir William Garstin, who had been greeted with enthusiasm by the fellahin on a farewell tour of the Delta when he retired as Director of Public Works in 1908, felt compelled to resign the position he had held for twelve years in succession to Ardagh as an official director of the Canal Company, provoking a question in the Commons which remained unanswered. Jonnart explained that his resignation at the age of seventy was due to the rigid age-limit fixed by the Government,[2] which then appointed as Garstin's successor Lord Downham, who was seventy-six. The revolt encouraged Colonel Meinertzhagen, a sympathizer with Zionism since 1917 and a member of the British Delegation at the Peace Conference, to recommend to Lloyd George on 24 March the annexation of Sinai beyond the Canal as an insurance against the rise of Jewish and Arab nationalism and as a prelude to the construction of an Akaba Canal.[3] That proposal was in accordance with Zionist aspirations to include Sinai within the boundaries of historic Palestine in the belief that the area east of the Canal was indefensible by Egypt. After Zaglul and his companions were released a strike of the Canal Company's employees broke out on 13 May. The stoppage of work in Port Said spread to Suez and Ismailia

[1] P. G. Elgood, *Egypt and the Army* (1924), 241.

[2] Hansard, *Commons Debates*, 20 March 1919, Earl Winterton. *Le Canal de Suez*, 20 Juin 1919, 6135, C. Jonnart, 16 June.

[3] R. Meinertzhagen, *Middle East Diary, 1917–1956* (London, Cresset, 1959), 17–19, 24 and 25 March 1919.

to become the first general strike in the history of the Company since 1882. It reduced share prices by 9 per cent between 2 and 23 May. It compelled the Company and the Government to maintain transit through the Canal in its fiftieth year of operation with naval and military help, including that of the Egyptian Labour Corps in coaling.[1]

The unrest in Egypt led the Government to appoint Allenby as High Commissioner and Balfour to affirm in the Commons Britain's refusal to surrender any of its responsibilities in Egypt and the Sudan. 'In our view the question of Egypt, the question of the Sudan and the question of the Canal, form an organic and indissoluble whole... British supremacy exists, British supremacy is going to be maintained, and let nobody either in Egypt or out of Egypt make any mistake upon that cardinal principle of His Majesty's Government.'[2] Balfour's statement bound together in an indivisible trinity the three regions which Cromer had maintained in discreet separation and was as unequivocal as the succeeding boycott of the Milner mission by the whole of unofficial Egypt. Meinertzhagen as Chief Political Officer in Palestine, again urged the annexation of Sinai on Allenby so as to give Britain 'a stranglehold on the Canal'.[3] The use of Sinai as a base and the evacuation of British troops to Kantara was also urged by Zaglul when he was persuaded to visit London on 7 June. Milner rejected that demand because the permanent occupation of the Canal Zone by British troops might be challenged as a breach of its neutrality and because Egypt had become a nodal point for imperial communications by land and air as well as by sea.[4] Australia even ranked as a vital imperial interest the whole hinterland of the Canal as well as Egypt.[5] After further strikes in 1920 had convulsed the great family of the Suez Canal the Company raised the wages of its 2,500 workmen substantially, increased their sick-pay, introduced an eight-hour day and a six-day working week, granted holiday-pay to workmen with two years' service and admitted workmen to an indirect share in the 2 per cent of the profits reserved for the staff.[6] Those concessions recognized the effective establishment of trade unions in the isthmus and compelled the Company to build up its pension funds from 1920.

The new empire of Western Asia was built upon the Cairo–Bagdad axis because Mesopotamia became more important than Arabia after Hussain's regular army was destroyed in 1919 by the Wahhabis of Saudi Nejd. Churchill transferred the administration of Palestine, Transjordan and Mesopotamia from an interdepartmental conference of the Foreign Office, the India Office

---

[1] Hansard, *Commons Debates*, 22 May 1919, G. Hirst; 4 June, T. Griffiths and F. Roberts.
[2] Ibid., 17 November 1919, 771, Balfour.
[3] R. Meinertzhagen, 68, 115, 5 January 1920.
[4] A. Milner, *Report of the Special Mission to Egypt, December 9 1920*, 28–29, 'The Defence of Imperial Communications'.
[5] W. M. Hughes, *The Splendid Adventure. A Review of Empire Relations* (London, Benn, 1929), 181–2.
[6] I. Malcolm, 'The Suez Canal', *National Review* (May 1921), 366.

and the Colonial Office to a Middle East Department created on 1 March 1921 within the Colonial Office. The 'Middle East' which had emerged in 1902 as a designation for the region of India and the Persian Gulf was thereby extended to Western Asia while 'Near East' was restricted from 1920 to the Balkans.[1] The unity of the whole region became strategic rather than ethnic or religious and enhanced the pivotal role of the Canal Zone. Churchill was converted to a land-based loyalty to the Canal which he could not give to the Canal as a maritime artery: he provided for the construction of aerodromes in the Canal Zone in anticipation of the beginning of a desert air route over the 860 miles from Cairo to Bagdad.[2] That service was first opened by the R.A.F. on 23 June 1921 and first carried the public air mail to the East from London on 13 October 1921. It became the core of the projected imperial air route to India as 'a Suez Canal of the air' and made Palestine as well as the Canal Zone into links in the imperial system of communications. Above all, it enabled Mesopotamia to be reinforced in twenty-four hours from Egypt or Palestine, permitted the reduction of local forces to a minimum and facilitated the use of the R.A.F. as an air-police. The rail route between Egypt and Palestine encouraged the projection of a Calais–Constantinople–Kantara Railway, which would link up with a Cape-to-Cairo Railway across the barrier of the Canal. 'Africa is not an island to be cut off from Eastern Europe or Asia by a ribbon of water one hundred odd feet wide!'[3] The Canal Company however sought to restore the pre-war function of the waterway as a highway between East and West and as an unbridgeable barrier between Africa and Asia. The railway bridge completed in 1918 across the waterway was therefore condemned on 9 November 1920 by the International Advisory Works Commission of the Company and was removed in March 1921 after a prolonged visit paid by Jonnart to Egypt. The premises of the Canal Company in the Canal Zone were also evacuated by British troops in 1921 after a definite date had been fixed for the beginning of the payment of rent. The disintegration of Kantara as a military metropolis in 1922 destroyed the hope that it might become a port on the trade-route between Egypt and Palestine. The Canal remained the customs- and quarantine-frontier of Egypt while the Sinai Military Railway was taken over by the Palestine Administration.

Renewed disturbances in Alexandria on 23 May 1921 accelerated the end of the protectorate. Britain's intention to replace the protectorate by a treaty of alliance encouraged the Canal Company to propose a prolongation of its concession for a further forty years on the model of the Convention of 1909 as an appropriate clause for inclusion in such a treaty.[4] Thus the Company

[1] R. H. Davison, 'Where is the Middle East?', *Foreign Affairs* (July 1960), 668.

[2] *The Times*, 8 March 1921, 13 iv.

[3] L. Weinthal, *The Story of the Cape to Cairo Railway and River Route from 1877 to 1922* (London, Pioneer Publishing Company, 1923), ii. 510.

[4] I. Malcolm, 'The Suez Canal', *The National Review* (May 1921), 366–7. G. Douin, 'Le Canal de Suez', *La Revue Maritime* (Décembre 1920), 491. P. G. Elgood, *The Transit of Egypt* (London, Arnold, 1928), 282 note.

sought to obtain security for its sixth improvement programme for a general deepening of the channel to 42 ft. 7 in. The negotiations of 1921 failed because Curzon could not accept the restriction of British troops to the Canal Zone but insisted on freedom of movement for them throughout Egypt. 'Egypt lies upon the main line of communications between Great Britain and the King's dominions to the east. The whole territory of Egypt is indeed essential to those communications, since the fortunes of Egypt are inseparable from the security of the Suez Canal zone.'[1] Zaglul's deportation via Suez on 29 December to the Seychelles inspired Egypt to imitate the passive resistance of India in Port Said and Suez as well as in Cairo and Alexandria. Allenby then visited London on 9 February 1922 to compel Lloyd George to make concessions to Egyptian opinion, reducing the value of the Canal Company's shares by 7 per cent between 6 and 20 February. The Declaration presented to Sultan Fuad on 28 February was a unilateral act by Britain and a poor substitute for an Anglo-Egyptian Treaty. It recognized Egypt as a sovereign and independent State, ended the employment of British officials in the internal administration of Egypt and terminated England's mission to bring civilization to the land of the Pharaohs. It insisted however that the Government should preserve internal order and security, i.e. repress the nationalist agitation, whilst it reserved to the absolute discretion of the British Government four great rocks of offence to the nationalists in imperial communications, defence, foreign minorities and the Sudan. The reservation of imperial communications first implicitly assumed that the Canal was a major imperial highway and that its free use was a permanent and vital interest of the British Empire.The Declaration did not explicitly mention the Canal and seemed to neglect the securities already provided by the Convention of 1888. In effect imperial communications had expanded from the Canal, the mail-lines and the cable to include the air-service from Cairo to Bagdad and those air-services projected from Cairo to Karachi, Khartoum and Cape Town as well as the Sinai Railway with its projected extensions from Cape Town to Cairo and from Haifa to Bagdad. The Canal undoubtedly appealed far more to the imagination of Britain than the other means of communication. 'We talk about the Suez Canal with as much emotion as we do about the Strand.'[2] The whole of Egypt however as the central junction of the Empire seemed best fitted to become 'a barracks for the Empire'.[3] Thus imperial communications were elevated above the interests of Egypt, above the interests of the Powers and above all other considerations of the international function of the Canal.

The end of Cromerism in Egypt compelled Jonnart to explain to his shareholders on 4 June 1923 that the rights and organization of the Company rested on concessions and statutes independent of the Egyptian regime.[4] The

---

[1] *The Times*, 5 December 1921, 14 iv, Curzon's letter of 3 December to Sultan Fuad.

[2] Ibid., 24 April 1922, 13–14, Lord Northcliffe, 'The Main Artery. Suez Canal Today. Some Facts and Reflections'.

[3] D. H. Cole, *Imperial Military Geography* (London, Praed, 1924), 39, 192.

[4] *Le Canal de Suez*, 5 Juin 1923, 6542.

emergence of Egypt as a new nation-state inspired Meinertzhagen to recommend on 6 July that the Canal should be made an International Waterway under the control of an international commission.[1] His renewed suggestion for a British base in Sinai was however rejected on 12 July by the Committee of Imperial Defence. Transit through the Canal was in effect protected against the new nation-state by the International Court of the Hague in its decision in the *Wimbledon* case. The majority of judges ruled on 17 August 1923 that transit through the Canal was free without distinction of time, flag, destination or cargo and that the free use of the Canal by belligerents was not incompatible with the neutrality of Egypt. Judges Anzilotti and Huber in their dissenting judgment argued that freedom of transit was absolute only in peacetime. The Egyptian delegation led by Zaglul to Lausanne had demanded on 21 November 1922 the confirmation of the neutrality of the Canal in accordance with the principles of 1888 and the independence of Egypt as the surest protection for that neutrality. The Treaty of Lausanne of 1923 restored Turkey and Russia to their historic position in the Eastern Mediterranean by establishing freedom of passage through the Dardanelles and eroding the quarantine-belt established around Soviet Russia by Clemenceau and Churchill. The flag of Imperial Russia which had continued to use the Canal between 1920 and 1922 gave way to the flag of Soviet Russia which was first carried through the waterway by the *Dekabrist* on 19 June 1923 en route with salt from Eupatoria to Vladivostock and by the *Lenin* in November 1923 en route from Vladivostock to Petrograd.[2] Thenceforward Russian oil began to oust American oil from the markets of Asia, where it had reigned unchallenged from 1915 to 1923.

The defeat of British policy in Turkey and Persia made Mesopotamia increasingly important. Bagdad was linked to Damascus by a motor-car service pioneered across the 513 miles of Syrian desert by two ex-New Zealand officers, N. and G. Nairn.[3] That service linked up with the P. & O. and the Kantara–Haifa Railway and carried the weekly mails in the contract time of sixty hours from Port Said to Bagdad, which they reached from London in nine days against the twenty-four days taken by the sea-route. The first mails left London on 22 November 1923 and furnished Bagdad with the benefits of rapid communication which Khartoum had known since 1907. The new route did not however carry mails to India, because it was extended to Tehran not by the Nairns but by Lebanese enterprise. The new British empire of the Middle East failed to create a continuous territorial bloc between Egypt and India. As a land-empire it could only be defended from the land and not from the sea. Its basis remained strategic more than economic because the mandated territories failed to develop any staple export. Its structure magnified the

---

[1] R. Meinertzhagen, 132.

[2] *Le Canal de Suez*, 15 Janvier 1924, 6634, 'Le Rôle de la Russie dans le Trafic du Canal de Suez'.

[3] C. P. Grant, *The Syrian Desert. Caravans, Travel and Exploration* (London, Black, 1937), 270–89, 'The Establishment of Motor Transport'.

function of the region as a transit-route at the expense of local interests. Its creation entailed the frustration of Arab aspirations to an Arab empire, the suppression of Arab revolts in Syria and Mesopotamia, the division of the Moslem world into artificial territorial states with no moral basis in the eyes of their inhabitants and the exclusion of the Moslem Arabs from the political community of their own historic domain. The empire was imposed by force in defiance of wartime promises of independence and maintained by indirect rule through the mandate and the treaty of alliance. Local rulers and local élites were supported by British power, the R.A.F. and a network of strategic communications. Wahhabi Nejd and Zaidi Yemen alone remained in possession of their full independence. The frontiers imposed on the other states failed to recognize that the Arab was, above all, a believer. The reappearance of the first pilgrims in the Canal in July 1922 under the Syrian flag marked the return of the Arab world to its fundamental allegiance at the same time that a romantic vision of an Arabia of the sheikhs was built up in the mind of the West through history, novel, play, song, film and opera. The 'Middle East' was detached from Asia in the Western mind as effectively as 'Mesopotamia' from Iraq. The Shiite masses of Iraq were offended by the support extended to the Sunni notables while the Sunni Arabs of Palestine were mortified by the amputation of 'Transjordan' and by the creation of a Jewish National Home as a buffer for the eastern flank of the British base in Egypt and a staging-post between Cairo and Bagdad. That Home never enjoyed the active support of any British Government after the fall of Lloyd George in 1922 or of any British officials reared in the imperial tradition of Mogul India. The Arabs feared that such a Home would become the basis of Jewish territorial expansion. France was already embittered by the failure of her previous struggles against England for empire in India and the Levant. She regarded the whole of historic Syria as her heritage but was compelled to accept inferior status in the Levant and thenceforward made Tripoli a bitter rival of Haifa. She no longer required British support against Germany in Europe while England no longer required France as a counterpoise against Russia in Western Asia. She became increasingly envious of the British Empire and the British 'masters of the sea, the coal and the oil'.[1] Her resentment restored to the Egyptian nation the support of a Great Power and undermined the security of the Mediterranean route through the Franco-Italian rapprochement, whose creator Camille Barrère, French ambassador at Rome from 1897 to 1924, was elected to the board of the Canal Company in 1923. Within the new structure of power the Canal and the Canal towns ceased to be eccentric and became a potential central base of operations by virtue of their pivotal location. The vulnerability of the Canal to attack from the land was increased[2] while the position of the Canal Company was threatened more

---

[1] J. Audemar, *Les Maîtres de la Mer, de la Houille et du Pétrole. L'Impérialisme Anglo-Saxon* (Paris, Nouvelle Librairie Nationale, 1923).
[2] D. H. Cole, *Imperial Military Geography* (1924), 205–7.

by the overwhelming victory of the Wafd in Egypt's first parliamentary elections in 1923 than by the threat of the new Egyptian Communist Party to nationalize it. Inchcape was elected Chairman of the London Committee on 9 January 1922 and a vice-president of the Company on 6 February after the death of Sutherland at the age of eighty-eight. He advised against a proposal by the Foreign Office in September 1922 that the Company should be asked to increase the number of British directors on the board. Thus he maintained Sutherland's Francophile policy.

Negotiations were renewed between England and Egypt after Ramsay Macdonald and Zaglul gained supreme office. Zaglul's claim that the British Government should abandon their claim to share in any way in protecting the Canal helped to reduce the value of Suez shares by 34 per cent from 14,900 francs on 7 March to 9,900 on 27 March 1924. England's first Labour Premier explicitly based imperial defence on the Canal as no Liberal or Conservative Premier had ever done and affirmed that the free use of the Canal in peace and war was 'the foundation on which the entire defensive strategy of the British Empire rests'.[1] Zaglul suggested that the defence of the Canal might be undertaken from Palestine or entrusted to the League of Nations as an international route under the Convention of Constantinople. Britain proved unwilling to accept 'a scrap of paper' as a sufficient material and positive guarantee of her imperial communications[2] because security of passage through the isthmus appeared 'a matter of life and death to the Empire'[3] and because a possible loss of the Canal seemed only less grave than the destruction of the Fleet or of the Army. After Zaglul broke off negotiations over the Sudan and returned from London empty-handed, Egyptian nationalists assassinated on 19 November Sir Lee Stack, Sirdar of the Egyptian Army and Governor of the Sudan. The resulting crisis in Anglo-Egyptian relations enabled Fuad to dismiss Zaglul and dissolve the Chamber. Britain annexed the Sudan, Sudanized its administration, army and trade and so discarded Cromer's dogma that the Nile was Egypt's river. At the same time French hostility undermined the security of the Mediterranean through the development of the submarine and the aircraft. Percipient military observers concluded that the Canal could not be the 'vital artery of the British Empire'[4] and that the Mediterranean had become the Achilles' heel of England.[5]

The Canal nevertheless remained in the public imagination a corner-stone of the Empire and an 'English stream'.[6] The Canal Zone became increasingly

---

[1] J. R. Macdonald, *Despatch to H. M. Commissioner for Egypt and the Sudan, October 7 1924* (Cmd. 2269 of 1924), 3.

[2] *The Times*, 21 October 1924, 13 v.

[3] P. G. Elgood, *Egypt and the Army* (1924), 79, 223.

[4] F. Maurice, 'British Policy in the Mediterranean', *Foreign Affairs* (October 1926), 111–12.

[5] B. H. Liddell Hart, *Paris or the Future of War* (London, Paul, 1925), 66–8. D. H. Cole, *Imperial Military Geography* (1924), 44–7.

[6] P. Crabitès, 'The Suez Canal as an International Waterway', *Current History* (May 1926), 221.

integrated from 1926 into imperial communications by road, rail and air[1] while the Canal Company became a reluctant and unofficial servant of the Empire. Port Fuad was inaugurated on 21 December 1926,[2] to provide houses on the Asiatic bank for the 1,300 employees in the workshops of the Canal Company to avoid a daily ferry journey for them across the harbour and to create a model township like Ismailia but insulated from postwar Port Said.[3] It was also intended to replace Kantara as the railhead of the Palestine Railway and to attract traffic from Syria and Mesopotamia. The Company hoped that Port Fuad would be linked by rail to Kantara as well as to Akaba and was prepared to lay a short link line over the thirty miles to Romani. Experimental shipments of oranges from Palestine were made via Port Said at higher prices than those made via Jaffa and were followed by a growing re-export of Jaffa oranges as well as by the import of goods for Palestine. From 1927 Port Said was also linked to Cairo by a Pullman service which connected at Kantara with the Palestine Railway to Haifa and at Cairo with the Star of Egypt Express inaugurated in 1926 to Luxor. The resumption of negotiations between England and Egypt in 1927 encouraged Egypt to hope for the withdrawal of British troops from Cairo to the Canal Zone and for the transfer of the Canal to the League of Nations, while Palestine hoped to incorporate Sinai as part of the same bargain. A Zionist Radical even recommended the occupation or lease of Sinai with a six-mile strip to the west of the Canal in exchange for Egypt[4] and, after negotiations broke down over the Sudan, the withdrawal of the Army to the Canal and the protection of the Canal by the Fleet.[5] Hoare's flight from Croydon to Delhi which carried him over Kantara on 1 January 1927 inaugurated a civilian service by Imperial Airways from Cairo to Basra in place of the military service. The establishment of a direct-beam radio service to Australia, South Africa and India in 1927–8 ended the great age of cable communication and encouraged the Canal Company to introduce radio-telegraphy and radio-telephony in 1927.

The Company replaced eight of its directors in 1925–8 as well as its President. Jonnart who died in 1927 after fifteen years as President was succeeded by Vogüé. The Marquis Louis de Vogüé (1868–1948) was a grand seigneur, like his father-in-law, Arenberg, and a scion of one of the oldest families of France. He was a landowner at Oizon in Arenberg's department of Le Cher and became the third landowner from Berri to preside over the Company.

[1] M. B. Stratton, 'British Communications in the Middle East 1885–1939. The Development of Imperial Railways, Motor Roads and Air Lines' (Ph.D. Thesis, University of Pennsylvania, Philadelphia, 1942).

[2] *The Times*, 21 December 1926, 13–14, 'Port Fuad'.

[3] H. Lorin, *L'Égypte d'Aujourd'hui. Le Pays et les Hommes* (Le Caire, 1926), 114–15, 175. J. Cattaui, *L'Égypte. Aperçu Historique et Géographique* (Le Caire, 1926), 320–50, G. Douin, 'Les Ports et la Navigation Maritime'.

[4] J. C. Wedgwood, 'The Occupation of Egypt', *Contemporary Review* (February 1927), 155. *Manchester Guardian*, 23 February 1927, 8v.

[5] *Manchester Guardian*, 4 June 1927, 7ii. J. C. Wedgwood, *The Seventh Dominion* (London, Labour Publishing Company, 1928), 3.

His grandfather had been a Legitimist who had retired to his estates after the revolution of 1830. His father had been an archaeologist and a diplomat, the ambassador of France at Constantinople (1871–5) and at Vienna (1875–9) and the French representative at the Conference of Constantinople of 1873. Vogüé became President of the Société des Agriculteurs de France, which had been founded by his grandfather and presided over by his father. He also became President of the Union Centrale des Syndicats Agricoles and a member of the Academy of Agriculture. Elected to the board of the Canal Company in 1919 he was chosen as President on 4 April 1927 at the age of fifty-nine, the same age as Arenberg had been on his election to the presidency in 1896. Vogüé was a traditionalist who aspired to a conscious emulation of the presidency of Arenberg and of the Company's golden age. Immediately his election was welcomed by the Bourse, where the value of the Company's shares rose by 6 per cent between 4 and 28 April. Vogüé developed a special affection for the 'great family of the Suez Canal'. He sought to maintain the entente cordiale and became President of the Association France-Grande Bretagne established in 1916. He was also honoured by a visit paid by King Fuad to the Company offices in Paris on 21 October 1927, the first visit by a ruler of Egypt since that by Ismail in 1867. Like Arenberg, Vogüé became a director of the P.L.M. and the Anzin Mining Company. He also joined the board of the Péchiney Company, a leading aluminium and chemical firm. He represented the agricultural interest as regent of the Bank of France from 1928 and became one of the three directors of the Bank for International Settlements established in 1929. The excellent administration of the Company under his regime strengthened its resistance to any suggestion for the transfer of the Canal to an international commission.[1] His reign nevertheless saw a serious weakening in the moral foundations of the Company in Europe.

The division of the postwar world between the satisfied and the unsatisfied Powers was reflected in a new interpretation of the history of the Canal sharply opposed to the accepted tradition of the victor-powers reiterated by Vogüé, who recognized the waterway as an 'instrument of progress and peace put in your hands by the genius of a Lesseps'.[2] The established Francophile tradition was given new vitality by the exaltation of the Allied victory and was crystallized in the form of literary history,[3] diplomatic history[4] and economic history. The pre-war biographical framework of its history gave way to a more impersonal approach which stressed the economic function of the Canal and the financial success of the Canal Company.[5] Thus economists and economic historians helped to embed the Canal in the impersonal framework of the

[1] J. Benno, *La Situation Internationale du Canal de Suez* (Lyon, Bosc, 1929), 170.

[2] *Le Canal de Suez*, 15 Juin 1927, 7169.

[3] R. Sencourt, *India in English Literature* (London, Simpkin, 1925), 434, 449, 450, 452, 456.

[4] J. A. R. Marriott, 'The Egyptian Factor in European Diplomacy (1798–1898)', *Edinburgh Review* (July 1924), 41–2.

[5] P. Dupont-Ferrier, *Le Marché Financier de Paris sous le Second Empire* (Paris, Alcan, 1925), 13–14.

shipping-routes of the Empire[1] and the commercial development of England, India and China.[2] The older biographical approach shifted in focus when Voisin Bey was first given by his grandson the credit he had been denied under Lesseps for the construction of the Canal.[3] Lesseps was also attacked from the U.S.A.[4] but was reincarnated as a type of the Latin genius in contrast to Rhodes, a type of the Anglo-Saxon genius.[5] 'Ferdinand de Lesseps had built one canal; another destroyed him. Here is a theme for Shakespeare.'[5] The postwar friction between England and France encouraged emphasis on the French achievement in the wartime defence of 'the main artery through which circulates the life-blood of the world and particularly that of the British Empire'.[6] French scholars also investigated the origins of the deep-seated English hostility to the opening of the Suez route.[7] Such shifts of emphasis however all took place within the pre-war framework.

A fundamentally alien tradition of historical interpretation was born from the Asian renaissance and was fostered rather than stifled by the intellectuals of the West, who, in their postwar insecurity accepted as inevitable Asia's recapture of the Eurasian and its menace to the expatriate European,[8] pleaded for a human rather than a political basis to relations between England and India[9] or shifted the precise dividing-line between East and West southwards from the Canal to the Gulf of Suez. 'Here, here and nowhere else, is the vestibule between the Levant and the Tropics.'[10] The new tradition of history denied the creative role of the Canal, emphasized the politics behind its

[1] A. J. Sargent, *Seaways of the Empire. Notes on the Geography of Transport* (London, Macmillan, 1918), 45–86. A. W. Kirkaldy, *The Trade, Commerce and Shipping of the Empire*, in Hugh Gunn (ed.), *The British Empire A Survey* (London, Collins, 1924), vii. 77–84. A. C. Hardy, *Seaways and Sea Trade* (London, Routledge, 1927), 59–79, 'Ship Canals'.

[2] A. Marshall, *Money, Credit and Commerce* (London, Macmillan, 1923), 126. L. C. A. Knowles, *The Industrial and Commercial Revolutions in Great Britain during the Nineteenth Century* (London, Routledge, 1921), 142, 194. L. C. A. Knowles, *The Economic Development of the British Overseas Empire* (London, Routledge, 1924), i. 316–19. V. Anstey, *The Trade of the Indian Ocean* (London, Longmans, 1929), 39–53. C. F. Remer, *The Foreign Trade of China* (Shanghai, Commercial Press, 1926), 38–41.

[3] E. Micard, *Le Canal de Suez et le Génie Francais* (Paris, Société Mutuelle d'Édition, 1922: Roger, 1930).

[4] P. Crabitès, 'Ferdinand de Lesseps and the Suez Canal', *Nineteenth Century* (October 1926), 586–93.

[5] J. Cournos, *A Modern Plutarch. Being an Account of Some Great Lives in the Nineteenth Century, together with Some Comparisons between the Latin and the Anglo-Saxon Genius* (London, Thornton, 1928), 336.

[6] G. Douin, *Un Épisode de la Guerre Mondiale. L'Attaque du Canal de Suez (3 Février 1915)* (Paris, Delagrave, 1922). P. Chack, 'L'Attaque et la Défense du Canal de Suez (Février 1915)'. *Revue des Deux Mondes*, 15 Janvier 1926, 418.

[7] F. Charles-Roux, *Autour d'une Route. L'Angleterre, l'Isthme de Suez et l'Égypte au XVIIIe Siècle* (Paris, Plon, 1922). Idem, *L'Angleterre et l'Expédition Française en Égypte* (Paris, Plon, 1925). L. Auriant, 'L'Angleterre et le Canal de Suez (1854–1855)', *Mercure de France*, 1 Novembre 1924, 646–67.

[8] Somerset Maugham, *East of Suez* (London, Heinemann, 1922).

[9] E. M. Forster, *A Passage to India* (1924).

[10] Idem, *Pharos and Pharillon* (Richmond, Hogarth Press, 1923), 55–6. H. M. Tomlinson, 'Through the Eastern Gate', *Harper's Magazine* (March 1924), 450.

economics, interpreted its opening as harmful rather than beneficial to the economic interests of Egypt, Syria,[1] India[2] and China and regarded the share-purchase as the first event in a chain which had led directly to the Great War.[3] Egypt was inspired to make its own contribution by Fuad's zeal for history after the birth of his son Farouk in 1920 and the discovery of the tomb of Tutankhamen in 1922. The history of the Canal was thereby associated with the unexplosive sciences of Egyptology[4] and zoology[5] rather than with the aspirations of Wafdist Egypt. The first university theses by Egyptians provided the first distinctively Egyptian histories of the Canal.[6] Muhammad Kassim emphasized the influence of Lesseps upon the historiography of the subject, recorded the contemporary hostility of the élites of Egypt to the concession of 1854 and used unpublished documents to defend the Egyptian case against the Company as well as against Britain.

The hostility of Egypt and France to Britain was reinforced by that of Germany and the U.S.A. Thus the German biographer of Negrelli and a publicist of the Bagdad Railway joined forces to attack England and France in their resentment at England's addition of the Bagdad Railway to the Suez Canal and in their desire to reveal 'the grossest international financial misconduct of the nineteenth century'.[7] The German scholars Heymann and Schoenwaldt however made a great contribution to history rather than to polemics when they raised the historical analysis of the Canal's economic function to a new level,[8] with the support of more traditionalist accounts.[9] Max Schoenwaldt became the first scholar to study the cyclical fluctuation of traffic. He related the variations in northbound traffic to the harvests of Asia and those in southbound traffic to the industrial production of Europe. He also detected in the variation in Europe's imports through the Canal and in the related tonnage of southbound shipping in ballast an important diagnostic, and even prognostic, tool for the measurement of the European conjuncture,

[1] P. K. Hitti, *The Syrians in America* (New York, Doran, 1924), 49.

[2] D. R. Gadgil, *The Industrial Evolution of India in Recent Times* (1924), 65.

[3] W. S. Blunt, *My Diaries, 1888–1914* (1919), ii. 479, Appendix VIII.

[4] C. Bourdon, *Anciens Canaux, Anciens Sites et Ports de Suez* (Le Caire, Imprimerie de l'Institut d'Archéologie Orientale Français, 1925).

[5] H. M. Fox, 'Zoological Results of the Cambridge Expedition to the Suez Canal, 1924', *Transactions of the Zoological Society of London*, xxii (1926–9).

[6] H. Husny, *Le Canal de Suez et la Politique Égyptienne* (Montpellier, L'Économiste Méridional, 1923). M. Kassim, 'The History of the Suez Canal Concession, 1854–1866' (M.A. Thesis, University of London, 1924). F. Yeghen, *Le Canal de Suez et la Réglementation Internationale des Canaux Interocéaniques* (Dijon, Bernigaud, 1927).

[7] A. Birk and K. H. Müller-Hamburg, *Der Suezkanal, seine Geschichte und seine wirtschafts-politische Bedeutung für Europa, Indien und Ägypten* (Hamburg, Boysen, 1925), v.

[8] E. Heymann, 'Der Verkehr im Suezkanal 1912–1914 und 1919–1926', *Weltwirtschaftliches Archiv* (Januar 1927), 86–104. M. Schoenwaldt, 'Die Konjunkturschwankungen im Verkehr der grossen Seeschiffahrtskanäle: ein Beitrag zur Erkenntnis internationaler Konjunkturen: Der Suezkanal', *Weltwirtschaftliches Archiv* (April 1927), 185–229.

[9] W. Glücks, *Die Handels- und Verkehrsbedeutung des Suezkanals für die deutsche Volkswirtschaft nach dem Weltkriege* (München Gladbach, Rixen, 1929). H. Spangenberg, *Die Veränderungen des Seeverkehrs im Indischen Ozean seit dem Weltkriege* (Stuttgart, Fink, 1930).

except in years of bad harvests. His work fanned no national passions and was largely ignored.

American scholars made their homeland the centre of historical revisionism in their urge to preach against the sins of economic imperialism. They powerfully supported the anti-British interpretation of the Canal's history, under the influence of the isolationist reaction of the 1920s and the ready postwar interpretation of history in terms of economics and geopolitics. Thus Earle ranked the Canal as a source of conflict as well as of civilization with the Bagdad Railway and the Trans-Siberian Railway.[1] The Irish-American scholar Moon shattered the Edwardian bond between the Canal and the occupation of Egypt, which he attributed to the influence of Ireland and the bond-holders as well as to that of the Canal.[2] Jenks closed his superb study of the migration of British capital with the share-purchase,[3] which he regarded with Delane as the first step to empire in Egypt. He carried the revisionist spirit of the decade to its height and first drew attention to the Stock Exchange manipulations associated with the purchase in order to refute the gratuitous assertion[4] that 'no one in the secret used his knowledge for personal gain'. The influence of geopolitical thought stimulated by successive wars encouraged historians to stress the value of communications in terms of distance and bases and to view systems of communications as a whole in the tradition of the Saint-Simonians.[5] Hoskins first related the history of the Canal to the whole context of its function as one of many alternative routes to India and based British policy in Egypt since the 1870s on the need to keep open the Canal.[6] The Swiss Reinhard focused attention not on the Canal itself but on the British Empire in Asia of which Suez had become the 'central fortress' and the 'hinge of world policy'.[7] Thus the revisionist historiography of the 1920s carried further the trend initiated in Germany in 1912 and shattered the comforting certainties of Edwardian history. It revealed a widespread dissatisfaction with the accepted assumptions of the Anglo-French tradition, with the continuing predominance of Britain within 'independent' Egypt and with the unilateral interpretation of the Convention of Constantinople. Its materialist assumptions reduced peoples from moral communities to statistical aggregates and eroded the idealist tradition. Its greatest contributions comprised Elgood's history of the Canal during the Great War,[8] Schoenwaldt's

---

[1] E. M. Earle, *Turkey, The Great Powers and the Bagdad Railway. A Study in Imperialism* (London, Macmillan, 1923), 4.

[2] P. T. Moon, *Imperialism and World Politics* (New York, Macmillan, 1926), 228.

[3] J. W. Jenks, *The Migration of British Capital to 1875* (New York, Knopf, 1927), 325, 409–10.

[4] *Cambridge History of British Foreign Policy 1783–1919* (Cambridge University Press, 1923), iii. 158, W. H. Dawson, 'Forward Policy and Reaction 1874–1885'.

[5] Lajard de Puyjalon, *L'Influence des Saint-Simoniens sur la Réalisation de l'Isthme de Suez et des Chemins de Fer* (Paris, Chauny, 1926).

[6] H. L. Hoskins, *British Routes to India* (New York, Longmans, 1928).

[7] E. Reinhard, *Kampf um Suez* (Dresden, Kaden, 1930), 72, 325.

[8] P. G. Elgood, *Egypt and the Army* (1924).

study of its traffic as an economic barometer and Hoskins' study of the Suez route as a geopolitical base of the British Empire.[1] Its high achievement was to reinforce the interest of East and West in 'the greatest cross-road in the world'[2] but also to associate the Canal more with power than with civilization.

After the return of the Labour Government to office under MacDonald conversations were renewed between the Prime Minister of Egypt and the Foreign Secretary. Those talks were announced on 10 July and encouraged a Liberal supporter of the League of Nations to ask in the Commons whether the Canal was to be placed under the control of the League.[3] They compelled Lord Lloyd, the British High Commissioner in Egypt, to resign rather than accept the transfer of British troops in Egypt to the Canal Zone.[4] The official notes which were exchanged on 3 August and published on 6 August outlined a draft agreement terminating the military occupation of Egypt by British forces in name and in outward appearance.[5] In order to protect the Canal Britain was authorized to maintain forces in Egypt to the east of longitude 32° East, but those forces would not constitute in any way an occupation and would in no way prejudice the sovereign rights of Egypt. The draft agreement thus sought to make the virtually impossible shift from an occupation to an alliance. It made a great advance on the draft agreements of 1921, 1924 and 1927 in so far as it isolated British troops completely from the Delta[6] and first recognized the Canal as an integral part of Egypt. The prospect revived the memory of the bad reputation acquired by Kantara during the war and alarmed Australia for the safety of 'the Achilles heel of the Empire'.[7] I. Z. Malcolm, who had been Private Secretary to Salisbury and Balfour and official director of the Canal Company since 1919, thought that Britain could never surrender her strategic highway to India.[8] Churchill, who had first expressed his doubts in public at Toronto on 16 August, returned home to renew his attack on a policy by which the British garrison was 'to dig itself in along the Suez Canal' and leave Egypt to confusion, retrogression and foreign intrigue.[9] He was supported in the Lords on 11 December by Lord Salisbury and Lord Lloyd, who thought that the Canal could only be defended economically and adequately against Egyptian disorder from Cairo. Churchill renewed his attack at a Conservative meeting at the Hotel Cecil on 16 December under the presidency of J. F. Flannery, the designer of the *Murex* in 1891. 'Our

[1] H. L. Hoskins, *British Routes to India* (New York, Longmans, 1928).

[2] P. Morand, *Rien que la Terre. Voyage* (Paris, Grasset, 1926), 246, translated as *Earth Girdled* (London, Knopf, 1928), 167.

[3] Hansard, *Commons Debates*, 17 July 1929, Mander.

[4] *The Times*, 27 July 1929, 12ii.

[5] Ibid., 7 August 1929, 9i–ii, 11ii. E. W. P. Newman, 'The Defence of the Suez Canal', *Journal of the Royal United Service Institution* (February 1930), 159–62.

[6] D. H. Cole, *Changing Conditions of Imperial Defence. Essays on Military Geography* (London, Praed, 1930), 120.

[7] *The Times*, 31 July 1929, 13iii, quoting the *Melbourne Argus* of 30 July.

[8] I. Z. Malcolm, 'The Suez Canal. When East Met West. Sixty Years of a Sea Link', *The Times*, 15 November 1929, 15vi.

[9] W. Churchill, 'The Peril in India', *Daily Mail*, 16 November 1929, 10iii.

soldiers are to leave the scene of their patient, peaceful duties and drink distilled water in desert fortifications "east of Line 32".[1] In the Commons debate on the Adjournment on Egypt on 23 December Churchill added that the separation of the British from the Egyptian Army consequent upon an evacuation to the Canal Zone would be 'simply manufacturing explosive in a retort'[2] and would make a clash inevitable between the two armies. Captain Eden argued that the Canal Zone was only twenty miles deep and could not therefore be defended in the depth necessary to its significance. 'If the Suez Canal is our back door to the East, it is the front door to Europe of Australia, New Zealand and India. If you like to mix your metaphors, it is, in fact, the swing-door of the British Empire, which has got to keep continually revolving if our communications are to be what they should.'[2]

The draft agreement of 1929 was doomed by the electoral victory of the Wafd which had opposed it. New talks between Nahas Pasha and the Foreign Secretary began on 31 March 1930 but almost broke down on 14 April when the Egyptian negotiators insisted on the concentration of the British garrison of 11,000 in the Canal Zone not in Ismailia but on the Asiatic bank of the Canal, either in Port Fuad or in Kantara.[3] The Egyptians then conceded Moascar but broke off discussions over the Sudan. Australia was alarmed by the attempt to restrict British rights to garrison even the Canal. 'The Egyptians must be clearly given to understand that the Canal is vital to Australia's existence. That fact transcends all other considerations.'[4] Military opinion was prepared to accept control of the Canal from its entrances[5] while naval opinion thought that it could be defended by the Navy even if the Canal Zone were evacuated.[6] Both were firmly opposed to Fuad's idea of international control through either the League of Nations[7] or a new international police.[8] Resumed negotiations by Nahas produced an agreement on 7 May 1930 on the defence of the Canal and the transfer of the R.A.F. base from Aboukir to Port Fuad but also broke down over the Sudan. Thus England failed to secure a Treaty of Alliance with Egypt comparable to the Anglo-Iraqi Treaty of 1930. Ismail Sidky Pasha succeeded Nahas Pasha as a royalist Prime Minister and provoked the worst riots since 1921, directed especially against the police, at Suez on 21 July and Port Said on 22 July 1930. Under his administration 75,000 feddans of the public domain were allotted in 1932 for a British base in the Canal

[1] *The Times*, 17 December 1929, 11 iv.

[2] Hansard, *Commons Debates*, 23 December 1929, 1998, Churchill; 2047, Eden.

[3] *The Times*, 17 April 1930, 14 vi.

[4] Ibid., quoting the *Melbourne Argus* of 16 April. J. M. Holmes, 'Egypt, the Sudan and the Suez', *Australian Geographer* (May 1931), 62.

[5] D. H. Cole, *Changing Conditions of Imperial Defence* (1930), 78–131.

[6] J. M. Kenworthy, 'The British Empire and the Suez Canal', *Saturday Review*, 3 May 1930, 546–7.

[7] A. Schiarabati, *De la Condition Juridique du Canal de Suez avant et après la Grande Guerre* (Lyon, Bascou, 1930), 137–45. Earl Winterton, 'England and Egypt', *Nineteenth Century* (June 1930), 769.

[8] D. Davies, *The Problem of the Twentieth Century. A Study in International Relationships* (London, Benn, 1930), 466, 471.

Zone, so committing the British to the defence of the Canal in the Canal Zone instead of in the Mediterranean and the Red Sea.[1]

British rights in the Canal were defended by the Liberal Norman Angell as in the economic interests of Manchester and Liverpool against the unreal claims of 'a small Arabian tribe'. 'What the Chinese Eastern Railway is to Russia, the Suez Canal may well be to Britain.'[2] The Allied defence of the Canal was commemorated in the War Memorials unveiled by the Canal Company on 3 February 1930 near Lake Timsah and by the Anzacs on 23 November 1932 at Port Said.[3] The construction of a British base in the Canal Zone enhanced British interest in the Canal. 'The half-way halt where the future meets the past'[4] attracted Evelyn Waugh on a Mediterranean cruise in the winter of 1929–30, enabled him to visit his first Oriental town and inspired him to compile the first travel-book on the port.[5] Egyptian Ismailia rather than cosmopolitan Port Said made the strongest response to the expansion of European civilization and destroyed whatever support existed amid the local population for such a British base. European Ismailia had acquired during its great expansion in the 1920s a holiday-resort by the sandy beach of Lake Timsah, becoming 'a paradise in the midst of the desert'.[6] Egyptian Ismailia, however, established its moral independence of the European city under Hasan al-Banna, a teacher in the Government Preparatory School from 1927 to 1933. He felt deeply disturbed by the subjection of entrance and exit to 'a truly Egyptian city' to the approval of the Canal Company, by the street-nomenclature 'in the language of the economic occupation' even in the Arab quarter with its Rue de la Mosquée, by the contrast between the magnificent houses of the European officials of the Company and the small cheap houses of the Arab employees and by the hierarchy of status ranking Arabs and Moslems below even the servants employed by the foreign community.[7] He could oppose to the economic and military power of the West only the community of the faithful, which he sought to recreate as a living reality on a secret, popular, proletarian and revolutionary basis. The Association of Moslem Brethren which he founded in Ismailia in March 1928 was inspired by the Wahhabi renaissance 'South of Suez'.[8] It succeeded in capturing the lower orders of society, which were unimpressed either by the ideology of liberal

[1] A. Baird Smith, 'The Defence of the Suez Canal', *Journal of the Royal United Service Institution* (May 1932), 308–13.

[2] N. Angell, *The Unseen Assassins* (London, Hamilton, 1932), 200, 201, 202, quoted by A. P. Thornton, *The Imperial Idea and its Enemies* (London, Macmillan, 1959), 300.

[3] *The Times*, 3 February 1930, 11 i; 4 February, 13 iii, 24 November 1932, 11 iii.

[4] H. Brown, *Both Sides of Suez. Some Collected Verse 1923–1928* (London, Douglas, 1930), 44, 'Half-Way House'.

[5] E. Waugh, *Labels. A Mediterranean Journal* (London, Duckworth, 1930), 67–97.

[6] G. Douin, 'Le Canal de Suez', *Revue Économique Internationale* (1929), 603.

[7] I. M. Husaini, *The Moslem Brethren. The Greatest of Modern Islamic Movements* (Beirut, Khayat, 1956), 11–12. C. P. Harris, *Nationalism and Revolution in Egypt. The Role of the Muslim Brotherhood* (Hague, Mouton, 1964), 148–9.

[8] A. Rihani, *Around the Coasts of Arabia* (London, Constable, 1930), chap. i, 'South of Suez'. W. J. Makin, *South of Suez* (London, Jarrolds, 1930).

nationalism or by the pharaonic renaissance of the 1920s. It was created
officially on 11 April 1929 and established branches in 1930 at Abu Sueir,
Port Said and El Ballah and in 1931 at Suez. Those branches among the
workers were linked by the bond of fraternity to the house of the Brethren
in Ismailia, like the branches in the Delta. Thus a secret counter-organization
was created within the isthmian kingdom of the Canal Company at the very
time that the construction of a permanent British base in the Canal Zone began.

The empire of the Middle East with a military base in Egypt, a mandate
in Palestine and a treaty of alliance with Iraq was extended by an economic
empire in South-West Persia as the oil resources of the geosyncline of the
Persian Gulf discovered in 1908 were exploited to give the region a staple
export. The war had stimulated northbound shipments of oil to supply the
needs of the Allied fleets, especially for fuel oil which had begun to use the
Canal in 1912–13. During 1914 northbound shipments of oil surpassed southbound shipments for the first time in the history of the Canal and so reversed
the balance established by the shipment of lamp-oil to the markets of Asia.
The wartime shortage of tonnage necessitated the convoying of petrol tankers
through the Canal from 1915 instead of the towing prescribed in 1907 and
compelled the Anglo-Persian Oil Company to form the British Tanker Company in 1915. The economy of transporting refined rather than crude oil
encouraged the refinery at Suez to double its capacity and that at Abadan to
quintuple its capacity between 1915 and 1919.[1] While southbound oil shipments dwindled away in 1917–18 fuel oil exceeded the volume of petrol from
the Dutch East Indies in northbound shipments of oil in 1916–18. Oil shipments from Persia rose from 2 per cent of northbound oil shipments in 1913
to 50 per cent thereof in 1919 while oil shipments from the Dutch East Indies
sank from 74 to 24 per cent of the total. Oil exports reduced to comparative
insignificance the Gulf's exports of dates, barley, rice and liquorice-root[2] and
stimulated its import of capital equipment and building materials. Persia
replaced Iraq as the leading exporter from the Gulf through the Canal.
British shipping became dominant in the Gulf through the wartime elimination of German, Austrian and Russian vessels and raised the British share in
the Canal's tonnage with the Gulf from 54 per cent in 1913 to 90 per cent
in 1922. The growth of oil exports from Abadan encouraged the inclusion of
oil-rich Mosul within Mesopotamia and the attempted establishment of a
protectorate over Persia in 1919. The refusal of Persia under Reza Khan to
ratify the treaty of 1919 compelled Anglo-Persian to form the National Oil
Refineries Ltd. in 1921, in order to construct refineries in Britain instead of
at Abadan and so to carry on the most profitable process of production in the
security of a British port.

[1] A. T. Wilson, *Mesopotamia 1917–1920. A Clash of Loyalties* (London, Oxford University
Press, 1931), 49.
[2] *Le Canal de Suez*, 25 Mai 1921, 6219, 'Les relations avec le Golfe Persique par le Canal
de Suez'. Ibid., 25 Mai 1924, 6686–7, 'La Mésopotamie et le Canal de Suez'.

The growth of the oil trade produced a rapid rise in the northbound traffic of the Canal to the pre-war level by 1923. After the war the demand for fuel oil was maintained by the demand of the Navy at Malta and by the rise of the motor-vessel using the improved Diesel engine of 1921. The passage of the first Danish motor-vessel through the Canal in 1912 had been followed by that of the first motor-vessels from the Netherlands in 1913, from England in 1914, from Italy in 1916 and from Sweden in 1919. The Danish East Asiatic Company converted its whole Canal fleet of fourteen ships into motor-vessels. The motor-vessel had more space for cargo than the steamship, spread Canal tolls over more cargo and became more important in Canal traffic than in world shipping. The oil-fired engine used oil in place of coal as the fuel of a steamship and came into greater use on the Suez route than the Diesel engine, although it did not become as important as on the Panama route. Conversion from coal to oil fuel was encouraged in Europe by the desire for freedom from dependence on British coaling-stations and in England by the militancy of the Miners' Federation, which demanded in 1919 the nationalization of the coal industry. British exports of coal through the Canal had been reduced to one-third of their pre-war level in 1915–17 by the wartime rise in freights and by the increased import of coal from India to Port Said as well as from Durban to Aden. The miners' strike of 1921 reduced coal shipments through the Canal to a trickle in May–July 1921 and increased the southbound shipments of non-English coal as well as the northbound shipments of oil. It also encouraged the Admiralty to decide on 25 May 1921 to make oil the exclusive fuel of all new warships and more British shipping lines to acquire their first motor-vessel. The first motor-vessels under the flags of Japan, Norway and the U.S.A. passed through the Canal in 1921, followed by the first German motor-vessel in 1922.[1] Southbound coal shipments nevertheless rose to tenfold their 1920 volume in 1921 and reached the all-time record in 1922 of 1,663,000 tons, which however represented only 2·6 per cent of the total coal exports of Britain. British coal never regained its pre-war monopoly of the markets of Asia and thenceforward faced the competition of the low-cost coal producers east of Suez which enjoyed the increasing protection afforded by the Canal tolls as the collier sailing-ship declined.

The demand for oil west of Suez was met by the producers east of the Canal, although Trinidad shipped fuel oil through the waterway in 1919. Suez itself began new port works in July 1918 and gained its first oil basin in 1919, twenty-seven years after Port Said. It became a base for oil companies founded in 1920–3 and benefited by the exploration of the Gulf of Suez, whose trade was extended through the Canal by the export of phosphates from Kosseir from 1917, of manganese from Abu Zenima from October 1918 and of phosphates from Safaga from February 1922. A State refinery was established at Suez in 1922 to refine the oil received as a royalty from Hurghada and gave

---

[1] *Le Canal de Suez*, 25 Juillet 1926, 7030, 'Progrès de la Navigation à Moteurs sur la route de Suez'.

Egypt its first State industrial enterprise since the time of Mehemet Ali and Ismail. Thus Suez began to develop at the expense of Port Said as oil replaced coal. It even aspired to replace its northern rival as the great bunkering-station on the Canal route as the protective influence of the Canal dues which had fostered the coal trade of the northern terminal was transferred to the oil trade of the southern terminal.

Tanker tonnage using the Canal surpassed the record volume of 1904 by 1920. Persia became the major source of oil in northbound cargo from 1919 because of the high productivity of its wells, their long life and the high quality of their crude oil. The Gulf's share of the tanker tonnage of the Canal rose from 6 per cent in 1913 to 70 per cent in 1920 and 88 per cent in 1922. Persian oil increased its share to 66·6 per cent of the northbound oil shipments in 1921 and to 74·4 per cent in 1922, reducing the share of the Dutch East Indies in proportion. Oil shipments from the Dutch East Indies reached their peak in 1923 and declined thenceforward. They even included less petrol than that supplied by Persia from 1923. The Gulf's cargo tonnage became predominantly export cargo, reducing the export-bias of the other export-economies of Asia to comparative insignificance. Its contribution to the traffic of the Canal mainly comprised tankers, which from 1921 were no longer obliged to pass through in convoy. From 1922 the tankers established new records for the volume of cargo per ship carried through the Canal, although they remained below the average size of vessels using the waterway. In 1923 the 120 tankers of 700,000 gross tons employed in the bulk transport of oil through the Canal represented 14 per cent of world tanker tonnage but 34 per cent of that of Shell and 89 per cent of that of the British Tanker Company.

On 13 and 26 March 1921 28,216 tons of crude oil passed through the Canal to the refinery at Llandarcy which was officially opened on 29 June 1922 by British Petroleum, Anglo-Persian's marketing company in England.[1] Thus Swansea gained a return cargo for the coal which it had shipped through the Canal since the 1880s and which never exceeded its peak volume of 1922 in southbound shipments. Britain acquired its first important refinery and a new industry additional to the shale-oil industry of Scotland. Crude oil outweighed petrol in northbound oil cargo for the first time in 1922 and maintained that superiority until 1929. The British Tanker Company became the intermediary which ferried crude oil six thousand miles from Abadan to Swansea for refining. The transfer of refining from Abadan to Britain was carried further by the opening of a second refinery at Grangemouth in 1924. The British Tanker Company rose rapidly from the eleventh client-line of the Canal in 1919 to the seventh in 1921, the fourth in 1922 and the third in 1923, with 11 per cent of British Canal tonnage: thus it replaced Holt's in the third place after the P. & O. and the Ellerman Groups. It increased its share of British tanker tonnage using the Canal to 50 per cent in 1922 and its share of the total tanker tonnage from 42 per cent in 1922 to 65 per cent in

---

[1] *The Times*, 30 June 1922, 19 vii.

1923. Its tankers so increased the speed of their turn-round that some made 9–10 transits each through the Canal during 1923 or double the average number of transits per tanker and treble the average number of transits of an ordinary vessel. Anglo-Persian's domination of the oil traffic of the Canal was reinforced from 1922 by the tankers of the Association Pétrolière, the tanker subsidiary of its French affiliate created in 1921, the Société Générale des Huiles de Pétrole. Shell declined from the sixth client-line of the Canal in 1918 and the eleventh in 1922 to the thirty-seventh in 1926 as it developed its interests in Venezuela and the U.S.A. The British Tanker Company dominated the tanker traffic of the Canal from 1923 and carried the British name as well as the British flag on every transit. Its first motor tankship the *British Aviator* passed through the waterway in August 1924. During 1924 its Canal tonnage reached 1,844,000 or 12·3 per cent of British tonnage and surpassed that of the Ellerman Group to give it second place after the P. & O.

In 1924–6 Asia was convulsed by a wave of indigenous unrest which diverted the energies of the continent from economic into political activity and reduced the northbound cargo of the Canal by 12 per cent and its shipping tonnage by 3 per cent during 1926. Reza Khan enforced the submission of the Sheikh of Muhammerah in 1924 and terminated the British protectorate of Arabistan established by Arnold Wilson in 1909. Iraq became more important than ever to Britain and permitted the dredging of a canal, which between December 1924 and May 1926 made Abadan accessible to gunboats as well as to ocean-going tankers and eliminated the use of lighters for loading. Anglo-Persian became a leading shareholder in the reorganized Nairn Eastern Transport Company (20 September 1926) and benefited by the regular air-mail service which was introduced from Cairo to Basra on 27 December 1926.

The miners' strike of 1926 lasted seven months, reduced British coal shipments through the Canal from April and eliminated them in August–September 1926. It reduced the volume of coal shipments through the Canal by 57 per cent during 1926 and cut British exports of coal through the Canal in greater proportion than total British exports of coal. It stimulated the southbound shipment of German coal and the northbound shipment of coal from Bengal and Natal. Above all, it gave a great impetus to the oil market and to oil shipments during 1926. It produced a sharp increase in transits by southbound tankers in ballast, in the proportion of the oil production of Persia shipped through the Canal and in the share of Persian oil in the total exports of the Gulf as well as in the total oil cargo of the Canal. It encouraged Norway to develop its tanker traffic via the Canal, Aden to open a third oiling berth and Port Said to increase its import of oil to orders from 1926. The northbound oil cargo of the Canal in 1926 reached a volume tenfold that of 1913 and surpassed the volume of cereals to become the largest single item in northbound cargo with 19·35 per cent of the total tonnage, while the tonnage of crude oil surpassed that of wheat. Burma then made its last shipments of oil through the Canal. The shipping tonnage contributed by the Gulf to the

Canal successively surpassed that of East Africa in 1921, Australia in 1924, the Dutch East Indies in 1925 and Western India in 1926. Thereby the Gulf rose from the sixth client-region of the Canal in 1921 to the third in 1926, with 13 per cent of the Canal's total tonnage and 18 per cent of its total northbound cargo, a share exceeded only by those of the Far East and Eastern India. Of the 2,796,000 tons of exports from the Gulf through the Canal in 1926 oil formed the peak proportion of 96·57 per cent.[1]

The conversion of the Canal into 'one of the principal gateways to Europe for oil'[2] was recognized in the election to the board of the Canal Company of the first representative of the industry in Sir John Cadman, who had been Professor of Mining at Birmingham University from 1908 to 1920 and the signatory of the San Remo Oil Agreement of 1920 which secured Mosul for Mesopotamia. He became a technical adviser to Anglo-Persian in 1921, a director in 1923, a vice-chairman in 1925 and chairman in 1927. He was then elected a commercial director of the Canal Company by the London Committee under Inchcape, who had resigned as an official director of Anglo-Persian in 1925. Cadman in effect enlarged the unofficial representation of the British Government on the board of the Canal Company. During 1927 shipments of crude oil reached a peak tonnage of 1,665,000, which remained unsurpassed for twenty years. Western Europe, a net exporter of energy until 1927, became a net importer from 1928 as oil replaced coal. Its imports also fuelled increasingly the vessels which carried the oil as motor vessels grew at the expense of steam tankers. The British Tanker Company became the leading supplier of motor tonnage to the Canal, although its motor vessels remained a minority of its fleet. Thus the rise of the oil trade confirmed the British domination of the traffic of the Canal and extended that supremacy to the motor-vessel developed in Germany.

The discovery of oil at Baba Gurgur on 14 October 1927 first revealed the immense Kirkuk field of Northern Iraq. That field lay so far inland that its economic exploitation was only possible by the construction of a pipeline to the Mediterranean coast so as to avoid the construction of a pipeline to the Gulf, the circuitous route around Arabia and the heavy Canal dues on oil tankers. The discovery of the oil of Iraq also encouraged exploration by American oil interests and the formation in 1928 of the Near East Development Corporation by Standard Oil (New Jersey) and Socony-Vacuum Oil Company. That corporation secured one of the four major shares in the reorganized Turkish Petroleum Company, the others being held by Anglo-Persian, Royal Dutch-Shell and the Compagnie Française des Pétroles established in 1923. Four of the seven great oil companies of the world thus joined together in what was renamed from 1929 the Iraq Petroleum Company Ltd. The Red Line Agreement of 1928 established the complete monopoly of those four partners throughout the area of the Ottoman Empire as it had been in

---

[1] *Le Canal de Suez*, 25 Juin 1927, 7181–3, 'Les Pétroles de la Perse'.
[2] A. C. Hardy, *Seaways and Sea Trade* (1927), 110.

1914 (i.e. excluding Persia, Kuwait and Egypt), tended to promote a buyer's monopoly in the purchase of concessions as well as of oil and made the British and the French automatic partners in any American oil venture in Iraq or Saudi Arabia. Royal Dutch-Shell, Anglo-Persian and Jersey Standard adopted by the price-agreement of Achnacarry in 1928 Gulf of Mexico prices for high-cost Texas crude oil as the base-point for world oil prices. Thereby they established an oil-shed, or line of equal prices, to the east of Italy and so restrained the rise of the low-cost oil production of the Middle East. That agreement crowned twelve years of diplomacy by Standard Oil which thereby turned the British capture of Bagdad to its own ultimate advantage. It contributed to the reduction in Persian oil output in 1928 but did not affect shipments through the Canal, which amounted to less than 1 per cent of world production in 1928. The tanker cargo carried through the Canal in 1929 nevertheless represented 6·25 per cent of the total tanker cargo carried by the world fleet in external trade.

The oil trade through the Canal had begun as a southbound traffic from New York and Batum. Southbound shipments revived after the war. Oil became Russia's most important export through the Canal in 1927, supplied 61 per cent of Russia's southbound exports through the waterway in 1928 and exceeded the volume of American oil for the first time since 1905.[1] The crude oil of Persia supplied however a growing volume of northbound cargo to the Canal and reinforced the dominance of northbound over southbound cargo. The creation of an Anglo-Persian oil empire compensated for the nationalization of the oil industry of Russia in 1920 and for the decline of coal exports from Britain. Oil thus created an economic empire in the sphere of influence long coveted by Anglo-Indians. It became the basis of a great corporation, a source of imperial prestige and a buffer against excessive dependence on the U.S.A. It also became the source of the foreign trade and government revenues of Persia, where Abadan became an alien capital of economic empire on the pattern of the colonial ports of Asia. Thus the oil-producing regions inherited the social problems of the coal-mining areas as oil advanced at the expense of coal.

The new trade increased the role of the tanker, the motor-vessel and the Persian Gulf in the traffic of the Canal. It increased the proportion of tanker tonnage from 6 per cent of the total in 1920 to 16·5 per cent in 1930. It increased the tonnage in ballast, the number of short hauls and the frequency of transit, raising the receipts of the Canal Company in proportion to the increased efficiency of the tanker companies in turning their vessels around. It converted the Mediterranean into an oil highway and made the Cape route more uneconomic than ever in terms of time and money. Egypt gained no direct profit from the emergence of the first great export staple of the Middle East. Suez however benefited more than Port Said, survived the end of oil

---

[1] *Le Canal de Suez*, 15 Juillet 1934, 8316, 'Le Trafic Nord-Sud des Pétroles via Suez (1913–1933)'.

production at Gemsa in 1927 and grew faster than the new Port Fuad. It shipped the first asphalt from its refinery through the Canal in December 1927 and gained a new oil basin and harbour, which was opened on 29 September 1930 by King Fuad.

The growth of the Persian oil trade gave the traffic of the Canal a new and firmer basis. The dominance of crude oil in northbound shipments from 1922 to 1928 ended as refining techniques improved at Abadan and the spread of the internal-combustion engine increased the demand for petrol. Petrol shipments increased, mainly from Persia, until they exceeded shipments of crude oil in October–November 1928. Oil had no harvest season so that its shipment became a pure response to demand unaffected by the fluctuations in supply peculiar to the agricultural produce of Asia. The oil trade displayed a remarkable capacity for expansion and became a main factor in the postwar growth of traffic, increasing between 1922 and 1929 at an annual average rate of about 250,000 tons, which represented one-third of the general increase in northbound cargo and one-quarter of the general increase in total cargo. Its dynamic growth helped to insulate the Canal against depression. In the twenty-eight years between 1907 and 1934 northbound shipments of oil fell below the level of the preceding year only three times, under the influence of war in 1916 and of economic depression in 1909 and 1931. Thus the economic security of the Canal Company was immensely reinforced as the Canal became an Anglo-Persian as well as an Anglo-Indian highway.

31

THE WORLD DEPRESSION, 1929-1932, AND THE BRITISH CAMPAIGN AGAINST THE CANAL COMPANY

THE boom of the 1920s marked the culmination of the economic expansion of Europe in Asia which had begun in the 1830s and assumed a new intensity from the 1890s. That expansion had transferred to the Canal the bulk of the world trade in jute, tea, tin, rubber, copra, soya and silk but only a small proportion of the world trade in manufactures. Traffic had increased in proportion to the development of trade between Europe and Asia: in only fifteen of the sixty-one years between 1869 and 1929 did its shipping tonnage fail to rise above the level of the preceding year. It enjoyed a large freedom from the pressures of economic depression, whether secular or cyclical, until the world depression of 1929–32. It had thitherto suffered depression of its traffic either after bad harvests in Asia or during the seasonal lull in summer between the spring shipments of cotton, rice, wheat, oil-seeds and sugar and the autumn shipments of jute and wool. The cyclical depression of 1929–32 was the first great crisis with which the new President of the Canal Company had to cope.

During the 1920s the traffic of the Canal recovered from its severe wartime depression and expanded without interruption except in 1926, although northbound cargo increased more slowly than southbound cargo throughout the years 1918–22 and in 1924. The Canal drew Australia, East Africa and the Red Sea more fully within its orbit and successfully adapted itself to the competition of the Panama Canal. In 1922 shipping tonnage first surpassed the record of 1912, while British tonnage first exceeded its volume of 1914. In 1924 northbound cargo first surpassed its record volume of 1912. The record cargo figure of 1913 was first exceeded in 1925 when Europe regained its pre-war level of industrial production, justifying Jonnart's view of the Canal as 'the barometer of world trade'.[1] Southbound cargo first surpassed the record volume of 1913 in 1928. The memory of the dividend-reductions of 1914–17 was obliterated by the successive increases in dividend from 1918 to 1929. Dividends for 1925 reached the level of those distributed for 1913 while dividends for 1926 first formed more than 80 per cent of the Company's annual receipts. The war had eliminated German and Austrian shipping from the Canal. The Allied victory secured the transfer of much German and Austrian shipping to Allied flags so that the Austrian Lloyd became converted into the Lloyd Triestino. New flags first appeared in the traffic of the Canal

[1] *Le Canal de Suez*, 15 Juin 1922, 6386; 5 Juin 1923, 6541.

from India in 1919, Czechoslovakia in 1920, Monaco and Yugoslavia in 1921, Finland, Soviet Russia and Panama in 1923 and Danzig in 1924. The great maritime powers, nevertheless, continued to dominate the traffic of the water-way. Germany's postwar recovery proved remarkably rapid. After the *Albany* of the German Australian Line steamed northwards on 3 August 1914 no German vessel appeared in the Canal for eighty-six months until 23 October 1920 when the *Hamburg* of the same line passed through en route to Java. In December 1920 the *Frauenfels* of the Hansa Line passed through en route to India. Thus the use of the Canal was resumed first by the cargo lines before the mail lines. In January 1922 the Hamburg American Line re-established its service to the Far East and began the first overseas motor-vessel service under the German flag. On 5 February 1922 the North German Lloyd re-sumed its service to China and Japan. In May 1922 Rickmers re-established their line to China and Vladivostock. In January 1923 the *Pfalz* resumed the mail service of the North German Lloyd to the Far East. The transit of the *Usambara* of the German East African Line on 26 June 1923 re-established the round-Africa service. The transit of the *Hohenfels* of the Hansa Line on 19 March 1924 began a service to the Persian Gulf which had been maintained from 1906 until 1914 by the Hamburg American Line. Thus Germany steadily regained its pre-war position[1] and rose from the sixth client of the Canal in 1922 to the fourth in 1923, thereby overhauling Italy, while Japan fell back to sixth place from 1923. In 1924 Germany displaced France from the third place after Britain and the Netherlands. The value of German trade to the lands east of Suez first surpassed its level of 1913 in 1925[2] when Germany employed only 8·4 per cent of its shipping tonnage on the Suez route against the 11·5 per cent of 1913. The expansion of the Hansa Line at the expense of the Hamburg American Line increased the Canal tonnage of Bremen. Germany's recovery took place despite the surrender of its colonies beyond the Canal but may have been assisted by the loss of its imperial status in the eyes of Asia. That revival was regarded by Jonnart as a threat to world peace[3] and did not secure the re-election of a German director to the Canal Company.

The end of the war ushered in a new golden era for the Company as the French franc depreciated in value between 1919 and 1926 and became divorced from the gold franc. The Company which had thitherto derived the bulk of its income from tolls on shipping found that profits on the exchange of Egyptian into French currency formed a growing share of its income, 0·5 per cent thereof in 1918 but 20 per cent in 1919. It decided on 1 April 1920 that its dues would be paid from 15 April in gold and in Egypt in order to preserve the essential equality of all user-nations. The Compagnie Havraise

---

[1] *Le Canal de Suez*, 25 Septembre 1923, 6590, 'L'Effort Maritime Allemand sur la Route de Suez'. Ibid., 15 Juillet 1928, 7344, 'La Navigation Allemande par Voie de Suez'. W. Glücks, *Die Handels- und Verkehrsbedeutung des Suezkanals* (1929), 109–13.

[2] W. Glücks, 35, 114.

[3] *Le Canal de Suez*, 15 Juin 1925, 6854.

Péninsulaire, which lacked the representation on the board of the Canal Company possessed by the Messageries since 1895 and by the Chargeurs Réunis since 1905, tried in vain to pay its dues in Egypt in French paper francs. Its legal action for reimbursement was then rejected by the Civil Court of the Seine on 7 February and 7 July 1922 and by the Paris Court of Appeal on 15 February 1924.[1] Thus the Company secured the payment of its tolls in gold and raised the share of exchange-profits in its receipts from 38 per cent in 1920 to 54 per cent in 1923 and to 62 per cent in 1924. Those profits offered security against the depreciation of paper currency and attracted savings into the Company's shares. They enabled the Company to build up a special reserve against the fluctuation of the franc but diverted its attention from the slower recovery of the traffic of the Canal.

The increased investment in the Company's shares raised their price steadily from 6,000 francs on 12 June 1922 to 10,000 francs on 3 January 1924, 14,000 francs on 4 March 1924 and 16,000 francs on 14 October 1924. That marked rise in price decreased the negotiability of the shares and necessitated the division of each 500-franc share into two 250-franc shares. Prices declined slightly after the division was made on 15 October 1924 and then resumed their upward trend to reach 16,000 francs again on 15 July 1926. The Government of Egypt revised the statutes of the Company so that each of the new 800,000 shares had the same rights and obligations as the old shares. The French Government doubled its share-tax in 1925, provoking a suggestion for the creation of bearer-shares which would pay no share-tax and compelling the Company to explain that as a foreign company it could not benefit from the creation of such shares under existing French law.[2] The demand by foreign investors in the Company's shares for exemption from French taxes was stubbornly opposed by the Company administration but was supported by the opposition of Egyptian bondholders to the increase in French taxes on the bond-interest paid in Egypt. The Mixed Court of Cairo ruled on 26 January 1925 in favour of the Company's bondholders that the Company should pay interest on its bonds in gold francs and rejected the Company's plea that it had issued its bonds in Paris in French francs and could only remunerate them in French francs. The Civil Court of the Seine thereupon refused on 1 April 1925 to enforce payment of interest on the Company's bonds in gold francs and authorized the Company to pay its creditors in French francs in accordance with the Civil Code, raising the price of Suez shares by 10·6 per cent between 30 March and 2 April. On 13 May 1925 the Court of Alexandria held Egyptian courts free from any obligation to resort to French law to determine the nature of an Egyptian company such as the Suez Canal Company. The Mixed Court of Appeal of Alexandria upheld on 4 June 1925 the judgment of 26 January. During 1926 the Company's receipts rose by 22·7 per cent, 71 per cent being supplied by exchange-profits, while the Canal's tonnage

---

[1] G. de Saint Victor, *Le Canal de Suez* (Paris, Sirey, 1934), 235–6.
[2] *Le Canal de Suez*, 15 Juin 1924, 6703.

declined by 2·6 per cent after the revolutionary upheaval of 1925 in Asia. Thus the rise in the value of the livre by 50 per cent over 1925 offset the depression of traffic. From 1926 the French franc remained stable in value. From 4 June 1928 the Company began to publish its receipts in French francs, three weeks before the legal stabilization of the French franc, so that 1927 became the last year of exchange profits. The Company had become more than ever a financial trust, so enhancing its reputation in France that its service became equated with security for life.

The inauguration of the Panama Canal did not divert much traffic from the Suez Canal. The new interoceanic canal was essentially different from the first trans-isthmian canal: it was an American strategic highway more than a highway of world commerce and its trade was more intercoastal than interoceanic. The maritime expansion of the U.S.A., stimulated by the opening of Panama, by the profits of trade as a neutral from 1914 and by the U.S. Shipping Board established in 1916, benefited the Suez Canal as well as the Panama Canal. The American share in the carrying trade between the U.S.A. and Asia via Suez so increased as to raise the U.S.A. from the sixteenth client of the Canal in 1913 to the fifth in 1920, when the U.S.A. first incorporated the concept of an 'essential trade route' into its law. The end of the war made possible the establishment of the first true competitive equilibrium between the two routes: the increase in the traffic of the Suez Canal between 1913 and 1922 had been exactly the same from India as from the eastward zone formed by China, Japan, Java and the Philippines and competitive with the Panama Canal. The Suez Canal Company was precluded by its concession from imposing differential tolls to favour particular areas or cargoes or to draw traffic from such a competitive zone. It reduced its dues from 1920, though not fast enough for such shipowners as Holt's. It decided to deepen its channel as an effective alternative to a drastic reduction of dues and adopted in 1921 another programme of improvement to achieve a depth of $42\frac{1}{2}$ feet, equal to that of the Panama Canal. The two canals proved non-competitive except on the very margin of their zones of influence. The Panama Canal competed more with the trans-continental railways across America than with the Suez Canal. It certainly competed with the Suez Canal in the trades from Europe to the Pacific coast of North America and to Australasia, especially to New Zealand. It competed most of all with the Suez Canal in the trade of New York to the Far East. Those three streams of traffic contributed only 15 per cent of the Suez Canal's tonnage in 1913 and 19 per cent in 1922.[1] Panama captured the developing trade of British Columbia which had first shipped wheat from Saskatchewan through the Canal in 1909. For the trade of Western Europe to Asia the threshold of competition between the two routes lay east of

---

[1] *Le Canal de Suez*, 15 Novembre 1923, 6611, 'Le Canal de Panama. Son influence sur le trafic du Canal de Suez'. Ibid., 25 Juin 1924, 6707–9, 'Le Trafic Sud–Nord au Canal et les Éléments de sa Stabilité'. Ibid., 25 Décembre 1924, 6780–1, 'L'Élasticité des Ressources Économiques de l'au-delà de Suez'.

Yokohama. For the trade of the Eastern U.S.A. to Asia the watershed lay east of Hong Kong, Manila and Fremantle. In the severe competition for the export trade of the U.S.A. Panama captured from Suez the exports of manufactures, railway material and oil to the Far East as well as those of phosphates from Tampa in Florida to Kobe. American shipments of metals, machinery and cottons via the Suez Canal, however, maintained their level throughout the expansion of the 1920s. The U.S.A. also began to pioneer new trades via the Suez Canal through its shipment of sulphur to Madras and Calcutta from September 1921, of wheat to Bombay from November 1921 and of beet sugar from April 1922: it even began to export raw cotton to India from 1926 when the local harvest proved short.

The imports of the U.S.A. via the Canal became much more important than its exports after the opening of Panama. From 1922 the tonnage of U.S. imports via Suez became double the tonnage of its exports via Suez instead of roughly equal thereto as in 1913. Such primary produce as jute, silk, rubber, sugar, tea, dates and manganese formed the bulk of its imports from Asia while gunnies for bagging its cotton exports supplied its only manufactured import. The opening of Panama diverted the copra exports of the Philippines more than their hemp and sugar exports from 1922 onwards.[1] Rubber, which had been a very small import via Suez to the U.S.A. before the war, was imported in rapidly increasing amounts to supply the expanding automobile industry. In 1921 for the first time over half the tonnage of rubber carried through the Canal was shipped to the U.S.A., thenceforward the world's chief rubber market. From 1922 rubber became the main Suez cargo for the U.S.A., which raised its share of the Canal's rubber cargo from 31 per cent in 1919 to 55·6 per cent in 1921 and to 73 per cent in 1924. American capital was invested in the plantations of the Dutch East Indies rather than in those of British Malaya. The focus of U.S. trade via Suez shifted westward from China to India, the Philippines and the Dutch East Indies. Rubber, gunnies and sugar formed 47 per cent of the volume of U.S. imports via Suez in 1925.[2] The Panama Canal also made possible round-the-world services using both Canals such as those of the Silver Line of Stanley and John Thompson of London from 1925, the Prince Line from 1926 and the American and Oriental Line of Andrew Weir & Co. Although such British lines continued to carry the bulk of American trade via Suez, U.S. lines increased their role, especially in the carriage of linseed, manganese, gunnies and rubber.[3] Thus the Dollar Steamship Line, established in 1901, began a round-the-world mail service from San Francisco, sent the first of its 'President' line of ships through the Suez Canal in June 1924 and carried a substantial

---

[1] *Le Canal de Suez*, 25 Août 1925, 6887, 'Les Échanges des Philippines via Suez'.

[2] Ibid., 15 Mai 1926, 6989–91, 'Le Commerce des États-Unis par la Route de Suez'. Ibid., 25 Juin 1928, 7335–7, 'Trafic avec les États-Unis via Suez'. Ibid., 15/17 Juillet 1933, 8152–3, 'Le Commerce Américain via Suez'.

[3] Ibid., 25 Juillet 1927, 7194; 25 Septembre 1935, 8507–8, 'La Navigation Américaine au Canal de Suez'.

proportion of the growing rubber imports of the U.S.A. The Panama Canal never exceeded the shipping tonnage of the Suez Canal, although it surpassed its cargo tonnage in April–August 1923. It cost four times as much as the Suez Canal but carried less traffic and only paid its way from 1928. The Suez Canal enjoyed the unrivalled advantages of proximity to the centres of population, commerce and industry. It was used for luxury cruises from 1923 by Cunard liners excluded from the Atlantic trade by depression and for round-the-world cruises from 1924 by C.P.R. liners from New York.[1] It was also favoured for the round-Africa cruises pioneered by the *Orca* of the Royal Mail Line which reached the Mediterranean in March 1926 from New York via Cape Town and the Canal. It was preferred by Japan to the American-controlled Panama Canal while Australia preferred the Cape route as an alternative to the Suez route. Thus the Panama Canal became the complement rather than the competitor of the Suez Canal and became linked to it by round-the-world services pivoting on the U.S.A.[2]

The cargo tonnage of the Suez Canal first exceeded 3,000,000 in the month of December 1928, while its shipping tonnage first exceeded 3,000,000 in January 1929, whereas Lesseps had estimated its *annual* capacity at 3,000,000 tons. The depression which prevented the establishment of new records was foreshadowed almost two years before its onset when southbound shipments of railway material reached their all-time peak in December 1927. Northbound shipments of jute reached their peak during 1927, after the record harvest of 1926, and those of maize and copra during 1928. Vessels making their first transit through the Canal reached their peak during 1928 and declined thenceforward in number and tonnage. Transits in ballast excluding tankers reached a peak in September 1928. Southbound cargo began to decline from February 1929 in sympathy with English industrial shares as well as with Suez shares, which reached their peak quotation of 26,500 francs on 7 February 1929, having trebled in price since 1924. Southbound shipments of metals and machinery began to decline from March 1929 when English coal prices began to fall. Southbound shipping tonnage in ballast excluding tankers, which served as the most reliable indicator of subsequent northbound tonnage, began to fall from May 1929. After U.S. production indices reached their peak between April and June the normal depression of traffic in June became very marked. From June, four months before the financial crash in October in the U.S.A., a decline began in the total number of transits, in the total tonnage of shipping, in the tonnage of northbound shipping and in the volume of northbound cargo excluding oil and cereals: the number of transits in ballast also began to rise from June.[3] July proved to be the first month whose shipping tonnage was

[1] *Le Canal de Suez*, 25 Février 1921, 6181; 25 Mars 1923, 6508; 15 Avril 1932, 7933, 'Les Croisières de Tourisme par la Voie de Suez'.
[2] A. C. Hardy, *Seaways and Sea Trade* (1927), 155, 68–70, 79.
[3] R. C. Julien, *Le Trafic du Canal de Suez* (1933), 136.

lower than that for the corresponding month in 1928. The autumnal recovery in traffic proved to be slight. Northbound shipments of manganese from Abu Zenima began to decline from September while those from India with their higher manganese content did not begin to decline until the start of 1930.

The financial crash of 24 October 1929 raised the value of Suez shares, as a gilt-edged security, between 24 and 28 October. The general depression of prices then reduced their price by 6 per cent on 29–30 October and pushed them below 20,000 francs on 25 November, a decline of 10·7 per cent from the level of 30 September and of 25 per cent from the peak quotation of 7 February. The Canal's tonnage fell below the corresponding level for 1928 for each succeeding month from September to December 1929 so that the Company sought to prove the fundamental stability of the northbound traffic.[1] The world depression which marked the end of Europe's greatest wave of economic expansion began as a decline first of economic activity and then of prices. The fall in prices was far more severe than the reduction in the volume of trade but proved catastrophic to societies geared to the making of money and the pursuit of profit. That depression justified the economic interpretation of history by its profound reactions on society and politics. It destroyed the market-economy and the liberal civilization of the nineteenth century, together with neo-classical economics and its reverence for economic man. It began the great transformation from an international economy to the new mercantilism of autarchic empires, from market-prices to administered prices, from a money-economy to barter trade, from the gold standard to paper currency, from the Commonwealth to the sterling area and from the export market to the home market. It provoked a fierce attack on international capitalism, the money-power, high finance and usury as well as on the bourgeoisie and parliamentary democracy. It enlisted the enthusiasm of the rising generation into extremist political causes and polarized society between Left and Right. It replaced the economic man of the nineteenth century by political man and encouraged the emergence of a new totalitarian front of the Fascist dictators and all their imitators from Syria to China.

The depression wiped out all the gains in traffic made by the Canal since 1923, encouraged widespread demands for a reduction in tolls and provoked a growing onslaught on the Canal Company as a representative of financial capitalism. In the traffic of the waterway it was characterized by a decline in shipping tonnage, by a decrease in the number of new vessels, deep vessels and coal-fuelled steamers, by an increase in ballast tonnage, by a decline in southbound cargo, especially in capital goods, and by an increase in competition from the Cape route. During 1930 the shipping tonnage for every month fell below the corresponding level for 1929 except in February and July while southbound cargo declined by a massive 27 per cent. During 1931 the shipping tonnage fell below the corresponding level for 1930 in every single month

---

[1] *Le Canal de Suez*, 15 Décembre 1929, 7563–5, 'Grandes Bases du Trafic Sud–Nord via Suez'.

apart from April while southbound cargo declined by a further 22 per cent to its lowest level since 1921. During 1932 transits and tonnage fell to their lowest level since 1926, tonnage falling in every month below the level of 1931 except in April and October–December: southbound cargo declined by 14·4 per cent to its lowest level since 1919. The decline of tonnage in three successive years was without precedent in the peacetime history of the water-way. Between 1929 and 1932 shipping tonnage declined by 15·6 per cent, cargo tonnage by 31·4, passengers by 19·5, receipts by 30, dividends by 31·4 and share-values by 38·5 per cent. The Company's investments also shrank in value between 1928 and 1931 by 38 per cent.

In Asia the depression affected least of all the autarchic states such as China and most of all the export-economies, which provided the bulk of Canal traffic. Thus in 1929 Ceylon supplied 34 per cent of the shipments of tea through the Canal, Java 52 per cent of the sugar, the Straits Settlements 60 per cent of the rubber, Burma 65 per cent of the rice and Australia 98 per cent of the wheat. Such trading-states paid the price in 1929–32 for their over-dependence on European markets. The reduction of traffic was greatest from the Dutch East Indies, enabling German tonnage to exceed Dutch in 1931 and Germany to replace the Netherlands in the second place in Canal traffic. The world-wide fall in the price of primary produce exacted a very high price from Asia for its development of monoculture in place of balanced agriculture. It reduced the monetary incomes of the primary producers and turned the terms of trade against Asia in so far as northbound cargo declined by only 19·9 per cent between 1929 and 1932 while southbound cargo sank by 51 per cent. Its effects were more incomprehensible in the East than they were in the West and rallied the support of the peasantry in a widespread reaction against European influence. It fostered a military renaissance in Japan and a rebellion by the southern peasantry against the landlords of newly reunited China. It encouraged the foundation of Communist Parties in Indo-China, Malaya and the Philippines in 1930. Immediately the fall in prices benefited the great imperial combines and the industrial importers of raw materials and foodstuffs in Europe. International rivalry prevented the con-clusion of international commodity-agreements on the production of sugar and tin until 1931, on that of tea until 1933 and on that of rubber until 1934. The depression encouraged each colonial producer to develop its export of those products in which its comparative advantages were the greatest. Thus Java extended the cultivation of the high-yielding variety of sugar-cane P.O.J. 2878 discovered in 1924. Malaya developed the export of pineapples from 1929 and that of latex in bulk from 1934, after the invention in 1928–29 of latex foam for use in upholstery. Australia made its first successful shipment of chilled beef to Britain in 1933 in competition with that from the Argentine. France sought to turn Indo-China into another Java or Malaya and reduced its Canal tonnage far less than the Netherlands, Germany, the U.S.A. or Britain.

Mail lines experienced the least decline in their Canal tonnage and cargo lines the greatest. The P. & O. displayed remarkable resilience during the depression. It had diverted its five vessels on the Cape route to the Canal route from April 1929 because of severe competition from the Australian Commonwealth Line. It had also declined to invest in airships or aeroplanes and suffered competition from the air-mail service established by Imperial Airways from April 1929 between London and Karachi. That service extended the Cairo–Bagdad air services created in 1921 and 1926, using the coastal route through the Persian Gulf by permission of Persia.[1] The first great imperial air route carried the highest class of mail, commodities and passenger-traffic from London to India within a week but did not divert from the P. & O. the viceroys, officials and merchants of India, who regarded the homeward voyage as an essential preliminary to their leave. The P. & O. ended its passenger-service to Calcutta in 1929 and its expensive and unpopular Aden–Bombay ferry service in 1930. In 1929 it adopted oil fuel and sent the first turbo-electric ship through the Canal in the *Viceroy of India*. It rationalized its ancillary establishments at Port Said, registering the Suez Canal Lighterage Company in London on 1 March 1929 in association with the directors of the three British coaling firms of Port Said. It decided to install a tourist-class in ships on the Australian and Indian service[2] and arranged in 1932 for its Australian and China mailboats to sail in alternate weeks and to call at Bombay, so eliminating its independent Bombay line. It suffered a far smaller reduction in its Canal tonnage than the most recent entrants into the Eastern trades: between 1929 and 1932 its Canal tonnage sank by 10·4 per cent but that of Ellerman sank by 37·7 per cent. It was able to pay successive annual dividends of 12, 10 and 6 per cent before it was forced to pass the dividend for 1931–2.[3]

The depression forced shipowners to retrench and make more economical use of shipping space. It rewarded the cost-cutting enterprise of Cayzer, Bibby and Weir who expanded their Canal tonnage. It encouraged Norwegian shipowners to make more use of the Suez route especially on the northbound voyage. Shipowners bunkered coal in the ports of Europe in order to avoid paying freight on coal to Port Said. They also made increasing use of oil-fuel in place of coal so that oil imports to Port Said almost equalled coal imports in volume by 1933. The increase in oil-bunkering at Port Said extended the operations of the existing coal firms, displaced labour engaged in coaling and made the port more pleasant for passengers. The depression also hastened the decline of British coal exports through the Canal to India, China and Ceylon: it replaced Cardiff coal by Natal coal at Aden and Suakin.

The traffic of the Canal was much less affected by the world depression

[1] H. Burchall, 'The Political Aspect of Commercial Air Routes', *Journal of the Royal Central Asian Society* (January 1933), 77–8.

[2] *The Times*, 3 December 1930, 16iii.

[3] Ibid., 12 December 1929, 23; 11 December 1930, 25; 10 December 1931, 21; 8 December 1932, 21.

than it had been by the Great War.[1] The collapse of southbound cargo was counterbalanced by the buoyancy of northbound cargo. The loss of the old staples of sugar from Java and silk from Japan together with such new staples as the cotton of the Sudan was partly offset by the appearance of such new exports as bananas from Italian Somaliland in 1929, copper from Northern Rhodesia in 1930, manganese from Postmasburg in 1930, steel from Calcutta for South Wales in 1932 and cast iron from Japan, also for South Wales, in 1932. Northbound oil shipments continued to expand throughout 1930 and displaced oil-seeds as the main item in northbound traffic: their volume fell off only in 1931 when Persia reduced its output for the first time since 1928. In southbound oil shipments Russian ousted American oil from the Indian market and from southbound cargo after 1931. Frozen meat exports from Australia continued to rise throughout 1929, 1930 and 1931, declining only in 1932. The reduction of laden tonnage between 1929 and 1932 by 32 per cent was partly offset by the increase in ballast-tonnage by 26 per cent as well as by the increase in mail-tonnage, cruise-tonnage and State-tonnage. The volume of cargo sank during 1930 more than that of the Panama Canal and more than that in world trade so that the share of the Suez Canal in world trade was slightly reduced from 7·4 per cent in 1929 to 6·5 per cent in 1930. During 1931, 1932 and 1933 however the reduction in its cargo was less than the general reduction in world trade so that the Canal's share therein recovered steadily to 7·5 per cent in 1933.

Annual Percentage Decline in Volume of Cargo, 1930–1932

	Suez Canal	Panama Canal	World Trade
1930	17	11·5	6·4
1931	11·4	20	13·6
1932	6·7	13·9	7·9

Between 1929 and 1932 shipping tonnage through the Panama Canal declined by 23·6 per cent but that through the Suez Canal by only 15·6 per cent.

The income of the Canal Company was insulated against a depression of prices because its tolls were levied on tonnage and not on the value or even on the quantity of cargo and were paid in gold francs. Its reserves enabled it to maintain its dividends and the payment of its bond-interest in paper-francs. The retrenchment of its improvement programme and the decline in salt exports from Port Said through the Canal by 26 per cent between 1929 and 1932 did not check the house-building boom in Port Said.[2] The Company's first response to the decline in traffic was to decide on 19 May 1930 to reduce the toll on ships in ballast from 1 September 1930 to one-half of the toll on laden ships, a proportion maintained thenceforth until 1951. That concession

---

[1] Graph I, p. 749, Shipping Tonnage of the Suez Canal, 1870–1955.
[2] A. Solletty, 'Port-Said', *Annales de Géographie*, 15 September 1934, 519.

encouraged an increase in the tonnage in ballast so that it equalled in December 1930 the figure for May 1929.[1] It coincided with a reduction in gross dividend in contradiction of the principle of 1900 but did not prevent an enquiry in the Commons about the main sources of supply of the Company's requirements.[2] In the spring of 1931 the shipowners began a campaign to secure a general reduction in tolls. They were harassed by the fall in commodity-prices, in load-indexes and in employment-opportunities. They had laid up 15 per cent of British ocean-going tonnage by 31 December 1930.[3] They were reluctant to yield to the heavy pressure to reduce freights before they had exhausted all opportunities of sharing the burden of the depression. They had benefited by the successive increases in the maximum permissible draught in the Canal from 30 feet in 1915 to 31 feet in 1922 and 32 feet in 1925 but could no longer find enough cargo to profit by the last increase to 34 feet in 1930. Harbour and canal dues had also increased their share in total costs so that they became a burden in a depression such as they were not during a period of expansion. Canal tolls had undergone seven successive reductions between 1920 and 1929 but had not yet reached their pre-war level. They bore most heavily on bulky goods which were low in price, could not pay the same high toll as luxury products and suffered the greatest reduction in price during the world depression. Thus tolls as a proportion of market-price were heavier on wheat than on rice or sugar, on soya than on copra or ground-nuts, on jute than on wool, on coal than on manganese or cement and on fuel oil than on petrol.[4] Those tolls also bore more heavily on short-haul traffic than on long-distance traffic, on the manganese of Abu Zenima, the phosphates of Kosseir, the cotton of the Sudan and the coffee of Tanganyika. Thus they taxed the produce of those regions for which the Canal enjoyed a monopolistic position and for which its use was compulsory. The zones on the margin of the Canal's orbit preserved a freedom of choice denied to the zones at the very gates of the waterway. Shipowners thus regarded the tolls as a burden on trade, a tax on the consumer and an obstacle to economic recovery. They recognized that France was neither a shipowner nor an exporter like Britain, that British shipowners supplied 56 per cent of the tonnage and Britain with the Dominions 75 per cent of the cargo of the Canal, and that the British Government owned 44 per cent of the Company's shares. They may also have feared a new bid to extend the Company's concession in the interests of the shareholders[5] rather than of the clients to whom Lesseps had dedicated his creation.

Under the inspiration of Alfred Holt & Company the Liverpool Steam Ship Owners' Association protested on 10 February 1931 against the high level of Canal dues as the equivalent of 13 per cent of the gross freights, outward and homeward, in the Eastern trade and as superior by 15–25 per cent to the

[1] R. C. Julien, 83 note, 125.
[2] Hansard, *Commons Debates*, 27 May 1930, Hannon.
[3] *The Times*, 11 February 1931, 9 ii.
[4] G. de Saint-Victor, *Le Canal de Suez* (1934), 239.
[5] I. Z. Malcolm, 'The Suez Canal, 1859–1929', *Quarterly Review* (January 1930), 111–12.

Panama Canal dues.[1] The Association's resolution urging a reduction in dues was supported by the Swansea Chamber of Commerce on 20 February as well as by both Conservative and Liberal M.P.s.[2] The proposal revived the spirit of 1883 and enlisted support from chambers of commerce and shipping deprived of direct representation in the London Committee, which had become under the 79-year-old Inchcape almost wholly a shipowners' committee. The Shipping Merchants' Committee of the Manchester Chamber of Commerce requested Government action on 10 March to secure a reduction in dues by 25 per cent to five gold francs per ton in accordance with the London Programme of 1883. Support for that demand came from European planters' associations, beginning with the Conference of Coffee Growers of the Northern Province, Tanganyika, which approached the Joint East African Board on 5 March. The Imperial Merchant Service Guild and the Council of the Mercantile Marine Service Association also urged on 11 March the reduction of dues to 5 francs.[3] The Liverpool Steam Ship Owners' Association, led by F. J. Marquis and Major L. Cripps of Holt's, protested to the Board of Trade on 23 March against the dues and urged their immediate reduction to 5 francs.[4] That British protest caused the sale of some 2,000 Suez shares in Paris and a fall of 4 per cent in Suez share-quotations between 23 and 26 March.

After the Canal Company deplored the aggressive approach of the British traders A. M. Samuel, who had been Minister of Overseas Trade in 1924–7 and Financial Secretary to the Treasury in 1927–9 began to ask repeated questions in the Commons about the Canal Company from 30 March, when he requested an inquiry into the effect of Canal dues on British exports to the East. Fifty-two parliamentary questions were asked about the Company during 1931 after a single question thereon during 1930. Those questions were asked by Liberal and Conservative M.P.s not by Labour M.P.s, and mainly before the end of MacDonald's ministry on 9 June. Twelve were asked by Samuel. Twenty-two sought to secure a reduction in Canal dues while eight, beginning with Samuel's question on 31 March, sought to increase the Company's purchases of British materials, a response which reflected the rise of unemployment in the traditional export industries and the desperate quest for new markets at any price. Those enquiries also urged from 20 April an overhaul of the administration of the Company and a reform of the composition of the London Committee to include directors more acquainted with the needs of the export trade. On 20 April Arthur Henderson revealed that inquiries, mostly unofficial, had been made to the Government by the six Governments of Germany, Italy, Belgium, the Netherlands, Sweden and Norway to discover whether Britain proposed to take any action to secure a reduction of Canal dues. On 21 April seven M.P.s asked questions about the Company, including the

[1] *The Times*, 11 February 1931, 19ii.
[2] Hansard, *Commons Debates*, 19 February 1931, Sir B. Peto; 26 February, Hore-Belisha.
[3] *The Times*, 13 March 1931, 11iii.   [4] Ibid., 24 March 1931, 11i.

shipowner Sir Charles Cayzer who alleged that the Company's funds were being used to finance an industrial trust company in Luxemburg. The next day Inchcape met a deputation from the Liverpool Steam Ship Owners' Association at the offices of the P. & O. and reluctantly agreed to raise the question in Paris. On 11 May the board of directors in Paris decided against any immediate reduction of dues and was supported by Inchcape, who explained that the interests of the British directors in shipping were subordinate to their general interest as directors of the Company.[1] The Liverpool Association thereupon expressed their bitter disappointment and questioned the right of the successor-shareholders to expect the maintenance of a high level of profits.[2] The Joint East African Board resolved on 20 May that the Canal dues were one of the causes preventing a reduction in shipping freights.[3] Samuel raised the question in the debate on the Adjournment on 22 May on behalf of the Association of British Chambers of Commerce. The Quaker manufacturer H. L. Tangye urged the use of the Treasury income from the Suez shares to relieve the charges paid by British goods so as to stimulate the power of employment rather than to help pay the dole.[4] In Paris Vogüé refused on 1 June to yield to the pressure of ill-informed and self-interested opinion and denied the existence of any necessary connexion between the level of tolls and the world economic depression.[5] Thus he maintained the legal rights of the Company against its clients and enabled the Company to pay a dividend for 1930 reduced by only one-half of the fall in tonnage. The Baltic and International Maritime Conference at Brussels representing twenty-one maritime nations decided on 1 June to seek an amendment of the Suez rules which bore unduly heavily on steamers in ballast.

The agitation had achieved no success when the Company was rudely shaken on 21 September 1931 by the devaluation of the pound sterling, in which the Company received 95 per cent of its receipts and paid out 35 per cent of its dividends. The Company had liquidated its sterling assets during the summer but nevertheless suffered a decrease in the value of its liquid assets by 6 per cent between the balance-sheet of 31 December 1930 and that of 31 December 1931. Its shares were reduced in price by 24 per cent between 24 August and 21 September. It was compelled to decide that from 22 September pounds sterling would only be received for their gold value in payment of Canal dues. Thereby it restored the value of its shares but increased Canal dues in sterling by over 25 per cent. That increase in the financial burden on British shipowners compelled the Company to revise its dues downwards. That decision was less influenced by the rising tide of anti-capitalist sentiment which revived the memory of 'the greatest fraud of the nineteenth century'[6] than by the beginning of the diversion of traffic, especially tankers, from the

[1] *The Times*, 13 May 1931, 17v.   [2] Ibid., 18 May 1931, 13v.
[3] Ibid., 21 May 1931, 26iii.
[4] Ibid., 25 May 1931, 6i; 24 April, 10v.
[5] *Le Canal de Suez*, 5 Juin 1931, 7796–7.
[6] Guy de la Batut, *Panama* (Paris, Carrefour, 1931), 1.

Canal to the Cape route and by the continued decline in Canal tonnage without any prospect of a return in prosperity. On 9 November 1931 the Company announced a temporary reduction in dues by 10 per cent from 15 November without the usual notice, as an exceptional measure of relief. It thereby made its biggest single reduction in dues since 1905 and first brought them below the pre-war level. It reduced them however to 6 francs, not to the desired 5 francs, and claimed to limit the period of reduction to $7\frac{1}{2}$ months until 1 July 1932. It had failed to help shipowners to keep their ships running by a timely reduction in dues but had forced them to lay up their ships. Its tardy reduction in dues was nullified by the devaluation of sterling through the losses incurred on exchange in the purchase of gold francs. In effect dues were increased for British shipowners by 17·7 per cent in 1932 over 1931. Thereby the revenue of the British Government from its Canal shares was increased by 30 per cent from £1,882,945 in 1931 to £2,440,251 in 1932, opposing its fiscal interests more sharply to those of British shipowners. The Company could well afford to begin buying British cement from 1931.

The Company's announcement of the reduction in dues provoked the Sinai Mining Company to suspend its production of manganese rather than pay $33\frac{1}{3}$ per cent on the market value of the ore f.o.b. at Abu Zenima[1] and the Egyptian Phosphate Company to complain of the Canal Company's lack of provision for the equitable treatment of local industries.[2] During 1931 600,000–700,000 tons, or 2·1–2·5 per cent of the total tonnage of the Canal, was diverted to the Cape route and 450,000 tons, or 1·4 per cent, to the Panama Canal. That diverted tonnage carried oil from Russia to Dalny, sugar and molasses from Java and the Philippines, oil from the Persian Gulf and wheat from Australia to the Mediterranean, so that the Canal's share in Australia's wheat exports to Europe sank from 52 to 25 per cent. During 1931 the Canal's tonnage fell by 5 per cent, the Company's receipts by 11 per cent and its dividends by 15 per cent. During 1932 1,000,000 tons of shipping was diverted to the Cape route while the Canal's tonnage declined by 6 per cent, receipts by 15 per cent and dividends by 17·5 per cent. The continued depression of traffic compelled the Company to renew its temporary reduction of dues on 6 June 1932 for a further six months and on 7 November for a further $13\frac{1}{2}$ months. From April 1932 almost all the prodigal tankers of the British Tanker Company returned from the Cape to the Suez route. Petrol shipments continued to surpass the volume of northbound crude from 1929 until 1936. During 1932 the Persian Gulf became the sole client region of the Canal to increase its tonnage while the British Tanker Company first surpassed the P. & O., which had been the leading line of the Canal since 1874 except in 1912–13. India's Canal tonnage also declined by 25 per cent between 1929

---

[1] *The Times*, 17 November 1931, 21 i.

[2] Ibid., 19 November 1931, 21 iv. Hansard, *Commons Debates*, 2 December 1931, J. T. C. Moore-Brabazon; 19 December, J. R. Robinson.

and 1932 and was first surpassed by that of China and Japan in 1932–5. Morand's judgment of 1936 thus applied to the economic history of the era 1870–1931 more than to the 1930s. 'If the Suez Canal is the essential artery of world commerce, if the *Bulletin de la Compagnie* and the *Panama Record* register the temperature of our planet it is because the road to India is the aorta of the universe.'[1] The P. & O. passed its dividend at the same time as it lost its supremacy in the traffic of the Canal. It further rationalized its services after it lost its great helmsman in Inchcape, who had presided at his last annual meeting in December 1930. It was inspired by a reprint of Kipling's *East of Suez*[2] to quote the poet in its advertisements ('And the temple bells they say...') and to adapt his formula to its own use in the proud claim 'East of Suez is the realm of the P. & O.'

The British devaluation precipitated the competitive devaluation of the Japanese yen in December 1931. Thereby the export industries of Japan were encouraged in the markets of Asia at the expense of the industries of Europe. The simultaneous increase in the burden of Canal dues on Japanese exports to Europe discouraged Japanese purchases in Europe and ended the expansion of Japanese Canal tonnage which had continued between 1929 and 1932. Devaluation also compelled the Egyptian pound to follow sterling and provoked the foreign creditors of Egypt to demand payment in gold of the debt coupons. The Canal Company yielded to local criticism that it collected dues in gold and paid wages in paper and decided on 9 November 1931 to pay salaries and wages in Egypt in gold, a gain of 30 per cent for its employees which was only partly offset by a 5 per cent reduction from 1 December 1931. The French Law of Finances of 27 December 1927 had extended the exemption from the share-tax to foreign-deposited shares, equating them with French bearer-shares from 1 January 1929 and leading Egyptian shareholders to claim a similar exemption for shares which were not deposited but circulated in Egypt. The Mixed Court of Cairo ruled on 17 February 1930 in favour of the Egyptian shareholders and against the deduction by the Company of any French tax from its dividends. It decided that the capital of the Company was in Egyptian gold francs and that the statutory dividend was payable in Egyptian gold francs and not in French francs. That decision inspired Vogüé to claim on 2 June judicial immunity for the Company from the Mixed Courts. The Court of Alexandria upheld on 25 May 1931 the judgment of 17 February 1930, allotted the Mixed Courts exclusive competence and annulled all clauses authorizing foreign courts. Thus the Company's arbitration clause under articles 73 and 74 of its statutes for disputes with shareholders, with an appeal to the Cour de Paris, was annulled and the jurisdiction of the Mixed Courts was correspondingly extended. The Mixed Court of Appeal at Alexandria ruled on 18 June 1931 that the Company should

---

[1] P. Morand, *La Route des Indes* (Paris, Plon, 1936; London, Hodder, 1937), 15.

[2] R. Kipling, *East of Suez* (London, Macmillan, 1931), a low-priced presentation volume of six poems which did not include 'Mandalay'.

pay its statutory interest in gold francs and should not deduct French taxes from shares held outside France, so ending the system introduced in 1879, raising the repayment-value of a capital share held outside France fivefold and concentrating the burden of the share-tax on the French shareholder.[1] Thus the Mixed Courts sought to protect the dividends of Levantine shareholders and the future earnings of Egypt.

The world economic depression proved the best forcing-house for the study of the Canal since the Panama crisis and enhanced the understanding of its economic functions. Its influence favoured a mechanistic interpretation of the Canal's function, revived Jonnart's metaphor of 1922 and first made the waterway appear as an economic barometer, which registered the pulse of an artery of the world's circulation, 'a recording barometer whose indications we have to interpret and whose mechanism we have to keep in good repair'.[2] Thus the Canal Company assumed the role of a physician to a sick world but preserved its function as a servant of civilization. The head of the Company's statistical department was inspired by Schoenwaldt's work and by an interest in the trade in agricultural produce appropriate to an agricultural engineer to publish in October 1933 a study of the Canal in the great tradition of Charles-Roux and Voisin Bey.[3] Julien used the analysis of time-series of statistics to determine the limits of the depression and sought to use traffic indices as the basis for a prophecy of economic recovery. He discovered that the highest correlation existed between the monthly movement of wholesale prices in Europe in 1924–9 and the southbound movement of ballast tonnage excluding tankers through the Canal four months beforehand.[4] Traffic indices were however more useful for the diagnosis of prosperity than for the prognosis of recovery because the Canal was more 'a focus of world commerce'[5] than a barometer.

The Canal continued to appear in the Anglo-French tradition as a triumph of French civilization,[6] in the English tradition as the cornerstone of the British Empire[7] and in the legal tradition as a triumph for Western civilization as well as for free trade.[8] In Britain the Disraeli-legend obliterated Jenks' revelations and was entrenched by the third film of Parker's play[9] as well as by the publication of a selection of Disraeli's own letters.[10] The depression

[1] G. de Saint-Victor, *Le Canal de Suez* (1934), 212.

[2] *Le Canal de Suez*, 15 Juin 1932, 7962, Vogüé, 5 June 1932.

[3] R. C. Julien, *Le Trafic du Canal de Suez. Conjoncture Économique et Prévisions* (1933).

[4] Ibid., 119.

[5] G. Mehrlin, *Der Suezkanal als Konjunkturanzeiger der Weltwirtschaft* (Zürich, Girsberger, 1945), 107, 192, 202.

[6] J. M. Carré, *Voyageurs et Écrivains Français en Égypte* (Le Caire, 1932), vol. i, p. xix; vol. ii, p. 343.

[7] F. V. de Fellner, *Communications in the Far East* (London, King, 1934), 310.

[8] F. A. Vali, *Servitudes of International Law* (London, King, 1933), 18, 19.

[9] *Disraeli* (Vitaphone, 1929), which provoked a correspondence in *The Times*, 12 March 1930, 15v; 13 March, 10iv; 15 March, 8v (E. L. Woodward); 17 March, 8iii; 20 March, 12v.

[10] Marquis of Zetland, *The Letters of Disraeli to Lady Bradford and Lady Chesterfield* (London, Benn, 1929), i. 305–9.

favoured the acceptance of the economic interpretation of history which made the creation of 'the greatest enterprise of general utility ever accomplished on the earth' the sole dividing-line in world-history[1] as well as a turning-point in the economic history of Burma,[2] the Dutch East Indies[3] and India.[4] The extension of the economic interpretation of history together with the rise of anti-capitalist and anti-British sentiment exposed the Company to sustained attack and undermined its moral basis in the mind of Europe, the U.S.A. and Asia. The first diplomatic history of the Canal by a German-American pupil of Parker T. Moon documented the sustained British opposition to its construction.[5] American opinion still saw the Canal as a calamity for every local interest of Egypt because it had established 'a piece of England on Egyptian soil'[6] and necessitated a British garrison for the *Wacht am Suez*.[7] The anti-British studies by Americans were reinforced by those of Egyptian scholars, provoked by the reduction of Egypt to a link in world communications. Fuad sponsored from piety and political interest the historical rehabilitation of his father Ismail, whom Crabitès defended against Lesseps as well as against the Milner school.[8] Georges Douin, an official of the Canal Company, produced the greatest contribution of the decade to the history of the Canal and first told the full story of the repeated conflicts between Lesseps and the Pasha.[9] The same Abdin archives revealed to Mohammed Sabry the outlines of 'an unknown Panama' and the economic penetration of Egypt from 1854 as a prelude to the occupation of 1882.[10] 'The history of the Canal from the start until after its completion has been nothing but a succession of financial crises from which the viceroys rescued the Company with the piastres of Egypt.'[11] Sabry's conclusions were widely diffused by the German-American scholar

---

[1] G. Hanotaux, *Histoire de la Nation Égyptienne* (Paris, Plon, 1931), tome I, p. iii, lxxxvii.

[2] J. S. Furnivall, *An Introduction to the Political Economy of Burma* (1931), 42–9.

[3] Idem, *Studies in the Economic and Social Development of the Netherlands East Indies. I. An Introductory Survey, 1815–1930* (Rangoon, Burma Book Club, 1933), 12, 15. Idem, *Netherlands India. A Study of Plural Economy* (1939), 174, 196, 428, 433.

[4] I. D. Parshad, *Some Aspects of Indian Foreign Trade 1757–1893* (London, King, 1932), 159–75. C. R. Fay, *Imperial Economy and its Place in the Formation of Economic Doctrine, 1600–1932* (Oxford, Clarendon Press, 1934), 115. P. Ray, *India's Foreign Trade since 1870* (London, Routledge, 1934), 19, 37–42.

[5] C. W. Hallberg, *The Suez Canal, its History and Diplomatic Importance* (New York, Columbia University Press, 1931), reviewed by H. L. Hoskins in *The American Historical Review* (1932), 155–6.

[6] W. E. Hocking, *The Spirit of World Politics with Special Studies of the Near East* (New York, Macmillan, 1932), 118. H. Feis, *Europe, the World's Banker 1870–1914* (Yale University Press, 1930), 382–97, 'The Financing of Egypt'. P. Crabitès, 'American Thoughts on the Suez Canal', *Asia* (January 1931), 40–5, 61.

[7] W. E. Hocking, 133. C. W. Hallberg, 269.

[8] P. Crabitès, *Ismail the Maligned* (London, Routledge, 1933), 47–69.

[9] G. Douin, *Histoire du Règne du Khédive Ismail* (Roma, Istituto Poligrafico dello Stato, 1933–6, 3 vols.).

[10] M. Sabry, *Épisode de la Question d'Afrique. L'Empire Égyptien sous Ismail et l'Ingérence Anglo-Française (1863–1879)* (Paris, Geuthner, 1933), 51–83, 'La Conquête Économique et la Compagnie de l'Isthme (1854–1863)'; 258–314, 'Ce qu'a coûté à l'Égypte le Canal de Suez'.

[11] Ibid., 82.

W. L. Langer and were reinforced by Abdel Maksud Hamza's definitive history of the Egyptian Debt. 'So far as Egypt is concerned, the Canal proved politically and financially a loss... The Suez Canal lies right at the root of Egypt's financial troubles.'[1] Thus Egypt carried on the tradition of the khedivate, whose last representative blamed the Canal as 'the principal cause of Egypt's misery'.[2] The Asian renaissance inspired its spokesman Nehru to credit the achievement of the Canal to the Pharaohs of 1400 B.C. instead of to nineteenth-century Europe.[3] The Canal remained a dividing-line to Nehru so that such English words as 'democratic' 'seem to change their meanings when they cross the Suez Canal'.[4] It was made by Antun Sa'ada, the founder of the Syrian Popular Party in 1932, the southern boundary of his Greater Syria which extended north as far as the Taurus. Thus it remained a frontier to which Europe might even anticipate in face of the resurgence of the East the withdrawal of its legions from Africa[5] and from Asia.[6]

The great representative in England of the anti-capitalist tradition of the Continent became the radical imperialist, Sir Arnold Talbot Wilson, who attacked the Canal Company as 'a parasitic growth on the shipping industry'[7] in a speech at an Individualist luncheon on 8 March 1933. He was encouraged to extend his attack by the 40–50 letters he received in the next few weeks and by questions asked in Parliament from 23 March, when Robert Rankin, a Liverpool shipowner, requested an international review of the Canal charges. Sir Arnold had first learned about Canal dues from commercial juniors on a P. & O. vessel bound for India in 1907[8] and cherished as little respect for the Canal Company as for the Burmah Oil Company, 'these faint-hearted merchants, masquerading in top hats as pioneers of Empire'.[9] He had helped to protect Anglo-Persian in its most difficult early years and had even worked his passage as a stoker up the Red Sea in 1913.[10] As Assistant Civil Commissioner in Mesopotamia he had helped to extend its frontiers to include Mosul. Thereafter he had served Anglo-Persian from 1921 until 1932. A disciple of Curzon and a Tariff Reformer since 1908 he had an invincible faith in expert administration and an unrivalled capacity for administration. Exalting trade above transportation and politics above economics, he regarded the Canal as a great international public utility and its operation by a private

[1] A. M. Hamza, *The Public Debt of Egypt 1854–1876* (Cairo, Government Press, 1944; completed in 1935), 27, 253.

[2] Abbas II Hilmi, *A Few Words on the Anglo-Egyptian Settlement* (London, Allen, 1930), 33.

[3] J. Nehru, *Glimpses of World History* (London, Luzac, 1936), 607, 11 March 1933.

[4] Idem, *An Autobiography* (London, Lane, 1936), 501, 'Democracy in East and West', commenting upon a speech by Lytton in the House of Lords on 17 December 1934. A. S. P. Ayyar, *An Indian in Western Europe* (Bangalore, Maniam, 1929), i. 75, 'Europe begins with the west of Suez'.

[5] E. Waugh, *Remote People* (London, Duckworth, 1931), 191.

[6] O. D. Rasmussen, *The Reconquest of Asia* (1934), 9.

[7] *The Times*, 9 March 1933, 22iv.

[8] A. T. Wilson, *S.W. Persia. A Political Officer's Diary, 1907–1914* (1941), 12.

[9] Ibid., 40.   [10] Ibid., 232–3.

profit-making company as an anachronism. His criticism of the Company was encouraged by Britain's departure from free trade in 1932, by the rise in the tonnage of unemployed shipping to a peak in the middle of 1932 and by the rise in unemployment to a peak in January 1933. To the Central Asian Society on 5 April Sir Arnold emphasized that the high tolls of the Canal Company encouraged self-sufficiency in Asia, discouraged trade between Europe and Asia and in effect subsidized the trade of Japan and the U.S.A.[1] The abandonment of the gold standard by the U.S.A. on 19 April lowered dues on the Panama Canal to a level 32 per cent lower per ton of shipping and 28 per cent lower per ton of cargo than those on the Suez Canal, enabling U.S. ships to compete with British ships as far east as Calcutta. In the Commons Captain Peter Macdonald revived Sir Herbert Cayzer's suggestion of 21 June 1932 and requested on 25 April 1933 a refund of tolls to British shipping from the Government's revenue from its Suez shares. To the Royal Empire Society Sir Arnold urged on 16 May the sale of the Government's shares to the Governments of the Empire from East Africa to Shanghai so as to establish a collective imperial control of the voting power of the Company,[2] a suggestion which J. B. Whyte urged on the Prime Minister in the Commons on 24 May. From 31 May questions in the Commons began to attack the inadequacy of the Government's directors of the Canal Company. In a trenchant article Sir Arnold dismissed the Annual Report on the Suez Canal laid by the official directors before Parliament as an insult to its intelligence and as apparently designed to hide the essential financial aspects of the Canal.[3] He affirmed that the Company had charged as much as the traffic would bear since 1900 so that it could easily halve the existing dues and still pay shareholders an annual dividend twice as great as that earned by any gilt-edged investment in the world.[4] 'The canal today is not a highway, but a barrier.'[5] He also condemned the extravagant management, salaries and pensions of the Company and its employment of one officer to every five men of its great army of employees.[6] He urged a reconstitution of the British directorate in the interests of the British Empire and pressure by the British Government on the Egyptian Government to persuade its mandatory to reduce its tolls as Ismail had done in 1874. Thus he began to propose more fundamental remedies than those of the shipowners.

Sir Arnold Wilson extended his criticism in the first complete history of the Canal which had been published in England since 1876.[7] That polemic

---

[1] *The Times*, 6 April 1933, 19i, A. T. Wilson, 'The Suez Canal Dues', a lecture not reprinted in the Journal of the Royal Central Asian Society.

[2] *The Times*, 17 May 1933, 11iv; 24 May, 26ii.

[3] A. T. Wilson, 'The Suez Canal: Barrier or Highway?', *Nineteenth Century*, 1 June 1933, 663–78. Idem, 'The Suez and Panama Canals—A Comparison', *Journal of Royal Society of Arts*, 9 June 1933, 679–94.

[4] A. T. Wilson, 'The Suez Canal', *Nineteenth Century*, 1 June 1933, 671.

[5] Ibid., 669.   [6] Ibid., 676.

[7] A. T. Wilson, *The Suez Canal, its Past, Present and Future* (London, Oxford University Press, 1933, 1939), reviewed in *The Times*, 1 December 1933, 20i.

did not end its story in 1869 because the Company had only begun to function as a toll-collecting concern after the inauguration of the waterway. Sir Arnold's account of British policy towards the Company served in effect as a warning of the need for a new compromise and laid special stress on the 1875 purchase, the British agitation of 1883 and the Egyptian agitation of 1910 against the concession. H. W. Macrosty (1865–1941), the author of *The Trust Movement in British Industry* (1907), the Chief Statistical Officer to the Board of Trade until 1930 and the Honorary Secretary to the Royal Statistical Society since 1928, supplied Sir Arnold with statistical and comparative tables of the Canal dues and the Company's finances. Sir Arnold argued that the £43,206,683 received by the Government in interest and dividends between 1876 and 1932[1] had encouraged the Government to sacrifice its political interests to its financial interests in the Company. By relating the dividends paid by the Company to the nominal value of the share rather than to its market-value he was able to show that the dividend had reached a level of 44·32 per cent in 1930[2] in contrast to the 7 per cent of the genuine public utility corporation. He condemned Vogüé's tenderness for his shareholders as an extreme capitalist viewpoint. 'One might say with truth that the old Canal has long ago, and several times, disappeared, and that the Canal of today has been built with the money of shipowners and their clients.'[3] He renewed his appeal for the distribution of the Government's shares in blocks of 250.[4] His criticism provoked Vogüé's memorandum of rebuttal to the British public of 9 June and his condemnation on 12 June of the accusations as 'a monument to error and ill-will'.[5] Vogüé denied that the Canal was a monopoly and defended the right of his shareholders to a superior reward because of the courage and tenacity of their predecessors. 'The cutting of the isthmus of Suez was the greatest enterprise ever attempted with private capital.'[6] Vogüé insisted that the waterway had to be maintained at the highest level of efficiency for its ultimate return to Egypt and that the Canal tolls represented only 1–2 per cent of the value of the merchandise carried through the Canal, and very exceptionally 3 per cent.

Sir Arnold's crusade encouraged M.P.s to urge a reduction by drastic means in the management expenses of the Company and in its tolls.[7] Sir Arnold addressed the Economics Section of the British Association on 8 September on the advantages enjoyed by U.S. shipping against British in the Eastern trade through the lower tolls on the Panama Canal.[8] Twenty-eight questions were asked in the Commons during 1933 about the Canal after only two questions thereon during 1932. The revival of trade from the autumn of

[1] A. T. Wilson, *The Suez Canal* (1933), 58.   [2] Ibid., 123.
[3] Ibid, 164 note.   [4] Ibid., 170.
[5] *Le Canal de Suez*, 15 Juin 1933, 8125.   [6] Ibid., 8126.
[7] Hansard, *Commons Debates*, 29 June 1933, Burnett; 4 July, G. Hall. *The Times*, 28 July 1933, 22 iv.
[8] *The Times*, 11 September 1933, 15 ii, A. T. Wilson, 'The Effect of Suez Canal Dues on Intercontinental Trade'.

1932 had however removed the economic basis of any agitation. The Canal's tonnage began to expand from October–December 1932 after the recovery began in the U.S.A. in July. During 1933 its tonnage rose in every month save in January above the level for 1932 and recaptured 57 per cent of the 1,000,000 tons of shipping lost to the Cape route during 1932. At the close of 1933 the volume of world trade remained 35 per cent below the level of mid-1929 while that of the Canal was scarcely 20 per cent below that level, because the new closed economies built up in the retreat from free trade often included a colonial empire beyond the Canal such as the French empire in Indo-China. The Company had forced British shipowners to adapt their freights to the level of the world market and announced in January 1934 a reduction of its dues from 1 April. Those dues were defended against attack by a French nobleman[1] while Vogüé compared his Company to 'a kind of League of Nations'.[2] Sir Arnold Wilson as a new M.P. asked his first parliamentary question about the Canal Company on 14 June but was refused a Colonial Office committee of investigation into the effect of the Canal dues on the trade of the African and Asiatic colonies of Britain. By then he had found another focus of interest and an example of efficiency in the new Germany.[3] Thus the Canal Company preserved full control over its administration, its directorate, its dividends and its tariffs and remained 'the most resilient company of the slump the world over'.[4]

[1] G. de Saint-Victor, *Le Canal de Suez* (Paris, Sirey, 1934), 238. F. Tuohy, 'The Golden Profits of Suez', *Current History* (September 1934), 676–81.
[2] *Le Canal de Suez*, 5/7 Juin 1934, 8287.
[3] *Manchester Guardian*, 24 May 1934, 10vi.
[4] F. Tuohy, 679.

32

THE ETHIOPIAN WAR, 1935-1936, AND ITALY'S NEW ROUTE TO EMPIRE

The Suez Maritime Canal shall always be free and open, in time of war as in time of peace, to every vessel of commerce or of war, without distinction of flag.

Consequently, the High Contracting Parties agree not in any way to interfere with the free use of the Canal, in time of war as in time of peace.

The Canal shall never be subjected to the exercise of the right of blockade.

The Convention of Constantinople, 29 October 1888, Article I.

THE abandonment of the market-economy and of the gold-standard of the nineteenth century was followed by the destruction of the peace-settlement by Italy, Germany and Japan. The Carthaginian Peace of Versailles had despoiled and disarmed the defeated Powers and had sought to maintain the temporary gains of the victors by eradicating the old balance-of-power system and creating a League of Nations as a league of victors in order to maintain a new collective security. France gained most by the peace-settlement and became the most insecure power during the ensuing truce, in her fear of another contest between forty million Frenchmen and seventy million Germans. She therefore sought to enlist the support against resurgent Germany of the eastern Slavonic powers through Barthou, the Foreign Minister in the Doumergue Ministry. That right-wing ministry of national unity identified the Canal Company as closely with the French State as it had been under the Empire, because Barthou had been a director since 1924 and Doumergue a director since 1932. On 9 October 1934 Barthou was assassinated at Marseilles with King Alexander I of Yugoslavia by a Croat terrorist trained in Italy and furnished with a passport by Italy's Hungarian ally. Barthou was succeeded as a director of the Canal Company by General Weygand and as Foreign Minister by Laval, who abandoned Barthou's policy of a grand alliance against Germany and sought to win the support of Italy in place of Yugoslavia as a step toward the establishment of a Latin bloc against Germany. Thus France was compelled to recognize Italy's aspirations to an Ethiopian Empire in order to safeguard her Alpine frontier.

Victorious Italy had been greatly disappointed by the allotment in the peace-settlement of all the German colonies in Africa to Britain, France and Belgium. Its proletarian imperialism was inspired by a wish to rival France, by a thirst for status rather than a hunger for bread and by a burning desire to erase 'the shame of Adowa'. No economic motive impelled Italy to expand from its bases in Eritrea and Somaliland because neither colony had developed an export staple. Somaliland had no harbours and Eritrea only Massawa.

Italy became, with Japan and Norway, one of the three states which increased their Canal tonnage during the world depression. In that expansion the colonial trade was less important than the oil trade, which made Italy from 1930 the third largest importer after Britain and France of oil from the Persian Gulf. Somaliland nevertheless began to export bananas through the Canal from 1929 in order to save Italy foreign exchange. From 1930 Eritrea attracted vessels in ballast to load with salt from the newly-created salines of Assab. Somaliland began to export bananas from Merka from 1931 and salt from Ras Hafun from January 1932. The King of Italy passed through the Canal in the yacht *Savoia* on 28 September 1932 en route to Massawa and returned on 12 October, preceded through the waterway on both occasions by an Egyptian cruiser in homage paid by Fuad to the land of his education. Emilio de Bono, the Minister of Colonies, accompanied the King and undertook a confidential mission of exploration in Eritrea, reporting to Mussolini on his return that no surprise attack on Ethiopia was possible because of the Canal, where arms and troops would be exposed to the espionage of all the nations of Europe.[1] An Ethiopian expedition would make great demands on Italian shipping, which was reorganized in 1932 into four large combines, the Lloyd Triestino based on Trieste, the Italia based on Genoa, the Adriatica based on Venice and the Tirrenia based on Naples. The Italia first appeared in the Canal on a large scale in 1933. The Tirrenia handled Italy's African and colonial trade and carried the mail to Massawa in nine days,[2] while the Lloyd Triestino maintained the long-distance services to Asia and Africa. Italy's Canal tonnage rose by 9·4 per cent during 1933 and by 18·7 per cent during 1934 when Italy exceeded the rate of growth of all other nations except Greece, and replaced France as the fourth client of the Canal after thirteen consecutive years in the fifth place. The growing export of bananas from Somaliland attracted specialized banana-boats from 1932 and small high-speed motor-vessels beginning with the *Merka*, which first passed through the Canal on 28 September 1933. Somaliland was also visited by the King of Italy, who passed through the Canal with de Bono on 25 October 1934 and returned on 26 November. The Canal however carried only 17 per cent of Italy's foreign trade in 1934 while 70 per cent passed via Gibraltar.

On 7 January 1935, when Laval in Rome gave Mussolini a free hand in Ethiopia in return for Italian support against Germany, de Bono sailed quietly for Massawa.[3] He was followed by the shipment via the Canal, which had been devalorized by air-power,[4] of the first bombing and scout planes in January and the first troops in February. The Italian flag rose from the fourth place in January to the second place in February, leaving the German, Dutch and French flags far behind and helping to conceal the decline in commercial traffic which began in January–February 1935. The growth of Italian military

[1] E. de Bono, *Anno XIIII. The Conquest of an Empire* (London, Cresset, 1937), 10.
[2] Ibid., 139–40.   [3] Ibid., 56.
[4] H. Bolitho, 'Beside the Canal', *Fortnightly Review* (January 1935), 101.

traffic through the Canal provoked questions in the Commons[1] and the Admiralty's announcement on 7 March of the reinforcement of the Mediterranean squadron. Hitler's repudiation of the disarmament clauses of the Treaty of Versailles, however, united England, France and Italy on 11 April in the anti-German Stresa Front, which encouraged Mussolini to hope for Ethiopia as the price of his support of France and England. The British Government could not aid Italy to conquer Ethiopia but would not aid Ethiopia to resist conquest and sought to deter Italy by diplomacy. On 15 May Sir John Simon told Geoffrey Mander, the Liberal M.P. for Wolverhampton and an enthusiastic supporter of the League, that no representations had been made to the Italian Government regarding the use of the Canal by Italian vessels in the event of war with Ethiopia but that the Italian Government was well aware of Britain's obligations. After that indirect menace de Bono was instructed on 18 May to anticipate difficulties of transit through the Canal and to build up a three-years' supply of victuals and munitions in preparation for the worst eventuality.[2] After the pro-Italian *Morning Post* in an inspired report[3] claimed that the British Government was obliged by the Convention of Constantinople to keep the Canal open, Mander asked Simon on 5 June whether Italy was aware that the first clause of the Convention of 1888 had been abrogated by Article 20 of the Covenant of the League of Nations. On 7 June Attlee asked the new Prime Minister, Baldwin, for the closure of the Canal to the military forces of Italy and was supported by Mander, who invoked Baldwin's principle of 1934. 'Wherever the peace of the world is likely to be disturbed there lies our frontier... Our frontier lies at the present time in the Suez Canal and the Red Sea.'[4] Such a closing of the Canal was opposed by Sir Arnold Wilson as 'of all possible sanctions the most complicated, the most dangerous, and, quite possibly, the most ineffective' because it would place an intolerable strain on the French administrators and on the Government of Egypt.[5] The speeches by Attlee and Mander aroused resentment in France where Vogüé proclaimed on 8 June 'absolute neutrality' to be the law of the Company. Italy and France were further offended by the Anglo-German naval agreement of 18 June which was necessary to permit English naval concentration in the Mediterranean.

The policy of Hoare, the new Foreign Secretary, was to negotiate with Italy, cooperate with France and so preserve the peace of Europe at the expense of Ethiopia. The democratic, humanitarian and pacifist conscience of the postwar Anglo-Saxon world, especially of the younger generation, opposed secret diplomacy as much as overt aggression. Both Christian and humanist therefore supported proposals to avoid war and to defend aristocratic Ethiopia through collective peaceful pressure on Italy by the closure of the Canal to

[1] Hansard, *Commons Debates*, 25 February 1935, Wilmot.
[2] E. de Bono, 161.
[3] *Morning Post*, 23 May 1935, 13 vi, 'Closing the Suez Canal. A Mischievous Report from Geneva'.　　　[4] Hansard, *Commons Debates*, 7 June 1935, 2198, G. Mander.
[5] Ibid., 2202, A. T. Wilson.

Italian troopships, either by a commission of the League of Nations, or by an international Canal association, or by Britain under mandate from the League.[1] Thus a debate began over freedom of transit through the waterway and focused around the question whether free transit was all-important without respect to other considerations. The lawyers of Italy, France and Germany affirmed that free transit was all-important, that free transit had been assured by international agreement and that international agreements were made to be kept. The Convention of Constantinople had been signed by both Britain and Italy and had been concluded for an unlimited period of time. It had made no distinction between licit and illicit wars. It had specifically excluded in perpetuity blockade of the Canal and provided no ground at all for closing the Canal but every ground for keeping it open. It had been brought into effect by England from 1904 and had been imposed on the defeated powers in the Peace Treaties of Versailles, Saint-Germain and Lausanne. It could not be overridden by the Covenant of the League of Nations because it was an earlier and specific agreement and because respect for freedom of transit seemed to represent the very basis of international order.[2] Nor did the League possess any specific authority to close the Canal. Lord Robert Cecil, President of the League of Nations Union since 1923, had himself moved the resolution of 16 September 1931 which explicitly reserved the right of free navigation through the Canal in the Geneva Convention for the Better Prevention of War of 27 September 1931 and so averted its infringement by any order to invading forces to retire within their own territory. Austen Chamberlain, the author of the Locarno Treaty guaranteeing the frontiers of France, Belgium and Germany, had affirmed in the Commons on 28 March 1928 that the Convention of Constantinople was still in force and had explicitly reserved British rights in the Canal by the Note of 19 July 1928 after the Briand–Kellogg anti-war pact. England could not, however, assert in peacetime the control of the Canal which she had established during the war. She had no legal right to close the waterway to Italy,[3] which endangered neither the security of the Canal nor of navigation through it, paid its dues punctually and could as a signatory power rightfully claim the rigorous observance of the Convention of 1888. Nor could England close the Canal without giving mortal offence to Italy and so destroying the security of her Mediterranean communications with India, Australia and New Zealand.[4] She could not violate

---

[1] *The Times*, 5 July 1935, 10 iii, V. Adams. *Manchester Guardian*, 18 July 1935, 20 iii, R. C. Hawkin.

[2] G. Scelle, *Précis de Droit des Gens. Principes et Systématique* (Paris, Sirey, 1934), ii. 64, ' Le Libre Commerce Internationale Norme Fondamentale du Droit des Gens'. C. Rousseau, 'Peut-on fermer le Canal de Suez?', *Le Temps*, 26 Septembre 1935, 4 i. G. de Saint-Victor, 'Peut-on fermer le Canal de Suez?', *Le Temps*, 22 Septembre 1935, 2 i–ii.

[3] 'The Suez Canal', *Law Times*, 27 July 1935, 54–5; 3 August 1935, 88. S. A. Heald, ' The International Status of the Suez Canal', *Bulletin of International News*, 17 August 1935. W. Landecker, 'Suezkanal und Italienisch-Abessinischer Konflikt', *Revue de Droit International* (Juli 1935), 204–20. *The Times*, 21 August 1935, 6 iv; 22 August, 13 v; 24 August, 6 iv.

[4] G. W. Baer, *The Coming of the Italo-Ethiopian War* (Harvard University Press, 1967), 177.

the sovereignty of Egypt and assume the mantle of a Protecting Power thirteen years after the abolition of the protectorate. 'We have lost control of the artery which unites the British Commonwealth and gives it life in every real sense of the word. It has passed to the country which is at the moment the most militant despotism in Europe.'[1] In the last resort England had no wish to create a binding precedent whereby the Canal might be closed to an aggressor and valued the free use of the Canal more than the continued existence of Ethiopia as an independent state. England had recognized Italian interests in Ethiopia on five separate occasions in 1906, 1910, 1919, 1924 and 1925.[2] She had no economic interest in Ethiopia, where Japan had replaced her by 1930 as the chief source of supply of cotton goods and cotton yarn. She was, moreover, disarmed and could take no action without the aid of the French Navy. France would not sacrifice her new entente with Italy to placate the English conscience[3] and separated herself from Britain more than at any time since 1924.

Britain still hoped to deter Italy by non-military measures. On 24 August the Cabinet resolved and declared that Britain would uphold its obligations under its Treaties and under the Covenant. Its decision to move the Mediterranean Fleet from Malta to the Levant alarmed Churchill lest it should presage the abandonment of the Mediterranean, so making it possible for Mussolini to land in Egypt in force and seize the Canal.[4] In the resulting crisis in the Mediterranean Mussolini made it clear on 26 August that the closing of the Canal would be a *casus belli*. Reinforcements were thereupon despatched to Malta, Aden and Egypt, where they were welcomed by the Egyptians for the first time in history, especially after the first of three Italian divisions began to land at Tripoli on 10 September. No reinforcements however could enable Malta with its twelve old anti-aircraft guns to protect the Fleet from attack from the air. The departure of the Fleet on 29 August shifted the axis of British power sharply from the west to the east of the Mediterranean. The C.-in-C. arrived at Port Said on 2 September with his second-in-command, Cunningham, to draw up plans for a possible war with Italy[5] and for the closure of the Canal to Italy. The Government chartered three vessels from Holt's to carry boom defence gear to the Canal[6] and may have hoped to become the executive of the League in superseding the Convention of Constantinople[7] but was compelled to act in cooperation with France. At Geneva on 10 September Laval refused to associate France with Britain in closing the Canal

[1] *The Times*, 29 August 1935, 11v, Abe Bailey.
[2] C. Cito de Bitetto, *Méditerranée Mer Rouge Routes Impériales* (Paris, Grasset, 1937), 169–71.
[3] P. Gentizon, 'Autour de Suez', *Le Temps*, 16 Août 1935, 6i–ii.
[4] W. S. Churchill, *The Second World War* (London, Cassell, 1948), i. 133–4, Churchill to Hoare, 25 August 1935.
[5] A. B. Cunningham, *A Sailor's Odyssey* (London, Hutchinson, 1951), 174.
[6] D. R. MacGregor, *The China Bird* (1961), 254.
[7] *Sunday Times*, 1 September 1935, 12, 'The Suez Canal: Can It Be Closed?' H. L. Hoskins, 'The Suez Canal in Time of War', *Foreign Affairs* (October 1935), 101.

and ruled out both military sanctions and a naval blockade because they could not be achieved collectively.[1] He reluctantly accepted limited economic sanctions, enabling Hoare publicly to affirm on 11 September the intention of the British Government to fulfil its obligations under the Covenant. On 16 September Laval told Mussolini's representative in Geneva that the French Government would on no account agree to the closing of the Canal.[2] On 23 September Hoare secretly promised Mussolini through the British ambassador in Rome that Britain would neither apply military sanctions nor close the Canal but would apply if necessary 'merely economic sanctions'.[3] A British request to France on 24 September for help in naval precautions was left unanswered until 5 October, two days after the invasion of Ethiopia. Thus no Anglo-French naval blockade of the approaches to the Canal ever matured. In France only the Communists campaigned for the closure of the Canal.[4] The threat nevertheless raised insurance rates from 2s. to 5s. per cwt. on 30 September, diverting traffic to the Cape route and reducing the value of Suez shares. Mussolini reaffirmed on 2 October that the closure of the Canal would mean war and mobilized his hundred submarines against the Mediterranean Fleet. Britain was not prepared to lose six or seven warships or the possibility of an Italian alliance against Germany and relied thenceforward on collective in place of bilateral action.

Between 1 February and 2 October 1935 193,200 passengers passed southwards through the Canal in Italian vessels and Italy paid an estimated £750,000 in Canal dues, wholly through French banks.[5] Suez shares rose as Italian troops crossed the Mareb on 3 October and de Bono planted the tricolour over Adowa on 6 October. The Canal Company declined to close the Canal or to increase the tolls[6] or to indemnify Italian shipping lines for the hypothetical cost of diverting their vessels around the Cape.[7] Sanctions were unanimously recommended by the fourteen members of the Council of the League of Nations and were accepted by fifty-one of the fifty-four members of the General Assembly on 10 October. Those sanctions were minor not major sanctions such as the closing of the Canal or an oil embargo. They were restricted to economic sanctions at the initiative of Eden and could therefore have no immediate effect. They did not compel Italy to choose between peace and war but became a symbolic device which saved the face

---

[1] A. Werth, *The Destiny of France* (London, Hamilton, 1937), 179.

[2] S. Hoare, *Nine Troubled Years* (London, Collins, 1954), 171.

[3] *Documents on German Foreign Policy 1918–1945* (London, H.M.S.O., 1962), Series C, IV, 674–5, Neurath to Embassies in Italy and Great Britain, 1 October 1935; 681–3, Bismarck, Chargé d'Affaires in Great Britain to Foreign Minister, 2 October 1935.

[4] A. Werth, 191.

[5] *The Times*, 15 October 1935, 13i; 9 October, 13iv; 10 October, 15v; 16 October, 10iv.

[6] L. Villari, *Storia Diplomatica del Conflitto Italo-Etiopico* (Bologna, Zanichelli, 1943), 112, quoting *L'Intransigéant* of 8 October. *The Times*, 16 October 1935, 10iv, Bosworth Goldman.

[7] C. H. Zeit, 'Les sanctions et le canal de Suez', in *Berliner Börsen-Zeitung*, 12 October 1935, translated in *Revue de Droit International* (1936), 367.

of Europe and of Britain in particular.[1] Europe's resort to siege-warfare against an outlaw-power reinforced the unity of Italy around its leader in opposition to such 'unjust, inhuman and illegal' measures.[2] After the British Government announced officially on 18 October that it would not close the Canal to Italian ships the Company's shares rose by 4·7 per cent between 18 and 25 October. The League itself lacked any authority to disregard the Convention of Constantinople as Sir John Fischer Williams, the international lawyer and authority on the League, explained. 'It cannot block, still less can it direct the Suez Canal Company to block, the canal against Italian ships.'[3] In the Commons on 22 October Hoare refused on behalf of the Government to block the Canal to Italy. The next day the Government announced a general election within three weeks and made the League of Nations the keystone of British foreign policy in its election programme. The Government's decision was influenced by the transfer of the leadership of the Labour Party from the pacifist Lansbury, the greatest vote-collector of his party, to Major Attlee, the advocate of military sanctions. Its spokesmen gauged well the war-weariness of the electorate and emphasized that closing the Canal meant war because Mussolini had said so. Attlee's policy produced no favourable response from public opinion in the first general election fought on foreign policy since 1880.

During the first month of the war the tonnage of the Canal first surpassed the record tonnage achieved in January 1929. Between February and November 1935 250,000 Italians passed southwards while only 20,000 passed northwards. Each Italian convoy was greeted with tremendous enthusiasm by the large Italian colony of Port Said, which gained that hour upon the stage of history denied to the Italian colony of 1869. The younger Italians donned black shirts, gathered on the breakwater and sang the Fascist anthem 'Giovinezza' to the passing troopships, whose troops replied with the salute 'Duce! Duce!'[4] They professed to protect the Canal against any attempt at sabotage by Ethiopian agents. Their elders subscribed their gold and jewels to pay the Canal dues as well as to buy oil and provisions in Egypt for Italy.[5] One Italian who had lived in Port Said since 1918 was inspired to begin in 1936 the compilation of a history of the Italian colony and so became the first annalist of the port.[6] English troops in the Canal Zone became depressed by the contrast between Italian power and English impotence and intolerant of the restraints of the Convention of Constantinople. During 1935 Italian military

[1] *Documents on German Foreign Policy, 1918–1945* (1962), Series C, IV, 637, L. von Geyr, Military Attaché in Great Britain to Reich War Ministry, 16 September 1935.

[2] G. Molfino, *Il Canale di Suez e il suo Regime Internazionale* (Genova, Orfini, 1936), 109.

[3] *Manchester Guardian*, 23 October 1935, 20 iii, 'Closing the Suez Canal. Legal Aspects of the Plan'.

[4] W. J. Makin, *War over Ethiopia* (London, Jarrolds, 1935), 19–30. M. Junod, *Warrior Without Weapons* (London, Cape, 1951), 22–3. A. B. Cunningham, *A Sailor's Odyssey*, 174.

[5] *The Times*, 16 December 1935, 13 iii.

[6] L. Dori, 'Esquisse Historique de Port-Said', *Cahiers d'Histoire Égyptienne* (Octobre 1954, Janvier 1956, Juillet 1956).

traffic more than compensated for the decline in the commercial traffic of the Canal which took place during the months of January, February, May and August–December. The volume of world trade expanded by 7 per cent while the volume of Canal cargo declined by 7·4 per cent, the tonnage of non-postal commercial vessels sank by 7·1 per cent to the level of 1932 and British tonnage sank by 8·7 per cent. The volume of northbound cargo declined by 15 per cent, especially in oil-seeds, cereals and oil. The completion of the pipelines from Kirkuk across Syria to Tripoli and Haifa exposed the Canal to its first competition from a pipeline. Their construction in 1932–4 had encouraged the Canal Company to introduce in 1934 night-time transit by tankers with the aid of special searchlights. Their use saved 1,522 miles of the voyage from Europe to Iraq, first opened up the great oil-field of Kirkuk and made possible the emergence of the Iraq Petroleum Company as an international producer of crude oil. Iraq began the export of oil over 532 miles to Tripoli on 14 July 1934 and over 620 miles to Haifa on 14 October 1934. The formal opening of the pipeline on 14 January 1935 reduced the volume of crude oil shipped through the Canal by 68 per cent during 1935. France was relieved from dependence on high-cost American crude oil and imported its first cargo of Mosul or French crude to Le Havre on 16 August 1934.[1] It reduced during 1935 the tonnage of French tankers using the Canal by 82·5 per cent and the Canal tonnage of the Association Pétrolière by 94 per cent. The French flag declined from the fourth to the fifth place in Canal traffic as Marseilles drew its oil thenceforward from Tripoli.

The depression in the traffic of every important region served by the Canal was counterbalanced by the sharp rise in Italian traffic and by the increase in southbound cargo by 12 per cent, especially between June and November. Italy's Canal tonnage trebled from 2,089,003 in 1934 to 6,077,376 in 1935. Its share in the total tonnage rose from 6·6 to 18·5 per cent and reduced the British share below half for the first time in the history of the Canal. Its flag ranked second above those of Germany, the Netherlands and France. The Lloyd Triestino became the fifth largest user of the waterway and the Italia the sixth. The 319,504 Italian troops who passed through during 1935 formed 51 per cent of the total number of passengers, who increased by 138 per cent to 625,465 and so exceeded the record figure for 1919. Passenger-receipts first exceeded the record figure for 1929 and rose from 1·3 per cent of the Company's gross receipts in 1933 to 3·2 per cent in 1935. Those unprecedented receipts for passengers were paid to the Company in gold francs. The total dues paid by Italian shipping rose from £700,000 to £2,000,000, insulating the Company against depression and raising its receipts above the prolonged low levels of 1932–4. The ports of the southern Red Sea, Aden, Berbera, Jibuti, Assab and Massawa, experienced such prosperity as they had never known. The Canal tonnage of East Africa expanded by 26 per cent and that of the Red Sea by 122 per cent while that of every other region declined. The

[1] R. F. Kuisel, *Ernest Mercier, French Technocrat* (University of California Press, 1967), 43.

number of transits grew by 5·8 per cent because Italian traffic was short-haul traffic. Total tonnage increased by 3·3 per cent to reach the highest level since 1929 while southbound tonnage first surpassed the record level of 1929. The Company's receipts rose by 3·6 per cent, enabling it to increase its dividends by 6 per cent as well as to add to its extraordinary reserve.

The sanctions which came into force from 18 November prevented air-flights across the Sudan from Libya and compelled Italy to carry out all its air transport by sea through the Canal.[1] The Italian demand for oil at Massawa helped to reduce the oil cargo of the Canal, gave an abnormal stimulus to the production of the Anglo-Egyptian Oil Refinery at Suez[2] and attracted the first shipment of oil through the Canal from Curaçao in June 1935. The proposal to extend sanctions to oil provoked Italian talk on 25 November of a surprise attack from the air on the British Mediterranean Fleet. The Hoare–Laval Pact of 9 December, concluded by Laval in consultation with Mussolini, secured the indefinite shelving of the oil sanction. It also handed over the substance of Ethiopia to Italy and left Hailie Selassie with only a shadowy remnant linked to the coast by a corridor for camels but not for a railway. That plan was regarded as a betrayal of the Government's election-pledge of support for the League of Nations and was overwhelmingly rejected by British opinion, which hounded Hoare from office and compelled his replacement by Eden. The champion of the League was prepared to consider the closure of the Canal in defiance of international law[3] in defence of Ethiopia, which had become what 'little Belgium' had been in 1914. Such a move could no longer affect the outcome of the war. 'By putting his great army the other side of the Suez Canal, Mussolini has tied a noose round his own neck and left the end hanging out for anyone with a Navy to pull.'[4] Mander was however rebuffed by Cranborne on 20 December when he suggested an appeal to the International Court of Justice at The Hague for its opinion on Italy's legal position with regard to the Canal. The Convention proved its value for the first time in its history and kept open 'the sluice-gate of the war'[5] to the troops of Italy. The end of war insurance rates early in January 1936 produced no revival in commercial traffic.

Within three days of the collapse of the Hoare–Laval peace plan Italy first used mustard gas in Ethiopia on 22 December. Before the end of February the Italians openly declared the passage of 260 tons of mustard gas through the Canal and Britain seemed 'almost ready to close the Suez Canal—almost, but not quite'.[6] The large-scale use of gas began in March with greater psychic than physical effect, shattering the morale of the Ethiopians and making possible an end to the war before the rains began. The moral impact was

[1] E. W. P. Newman, *Italy's Conquest of Abyssinia* (London, Butterworth, 1937), 278.

[2] *The Times*, 30 November 1935, 11 iv.

[3] W. Rees-Mogg, *Sir Anthony Eden* (London, Rockliff, 1956), 59.

[4] K. Feiling, *The Life of Neville Chamberlain* (London, Macmillan, 1946), 273, 8 December 1935.   [5] M. Junod, *Warrior Without Weapons* (1951), 22.

[6] John T. Whitaker, *Fear Came on Europe* (London, Hamilton, 1937), 295.

great in Europe as well as in Ethiopia and revived the demand for the closure of the Canal for a fifth time.[1] On 2 May Hailie Selassie ceased to stand guard in what he called 'the last citadel of collective security' and left by train for Jibuti. On 4 May he sailed from Jibuti on board a British cruiser which proceeded at full speed and in the greatest secrecy with an escort of six other warships to the British base at Haifa, where he disembarked on 8 May to visit Jerusalem before making his way to Geneva and Bath. The destruction of the oldest of Christian kingdoms and of the last black empire in Africa made Ethiopia a symbol of African independence and Negro freedom such as it had not been during its lifetime. British policy had preserved neither the existence of Ethiopia nor the friendship of Italy. The Canal Company's policy of benevolent neutrality towards Italy had made it an impartial accomplice in the Italian conquest: it thereby suffered grave moral damage[2] although its shares rose by 7 per cent between 29 April and 8 May. The war had revealed the inadequacy of international law in relation to the Canal.[3] It also destroyed the surviving framework of security in Europe. The outbreak of civil war in Spain created a new region of insecurity in the West Mediterranean as well as the Rome–Berlin Axis, which brought Italy out of the Stresa Front into the German camp and deprived Austria of its sole protector against Germany. On 6 May Eden explained that the only effective sanction would have led inevitably to war. 'You cannot close the Canal with paper boats. (Ministerial cheers).'[4] Sanctions were discontinued by Britain on 18 June, the anniversary of Waterloo, and by the League on 15 July, after 241 days. In the interests of collective security Baron David Davies, the coal-lord and founder in 1932 of the New Commonwealth movement for an international police force, suggested once more in September 1936 that the Canal should not be used as 'an international shuttle-cock' but internationalized and garrisoned by an international police modelled either on the Saar Police Force or on the French Foreign Legion.[5]

The war made possible a new relationship between Egypt and the Canal Company and the British Government. Egyptian influence had grown in the isthmus with the development of the fishing industry, the increase of Coptic and Egyptian shopkeepers in Port Said, the renaming of the Place de Lesseps the Place Saad Zagloul and of the Eugénie Quay the Rue Safia Zagloul, and the construction in 1934 of a Suez–Cairo Railway along the direct desert route of 1858. That new railway benefited Suez at the expense of Port Said as a port of import, especially for produce from the Sudan and Australia, and

---

[1] *The Times*, 21 April 1936, 15 v; 22 April, 15 v; 23 April, 10 iii; 25 April, 8 i; 29 April, 15 v.

[2] Hansard, *Commons Debates*, 7 May 1936, Sandeman Allen; 11 May, Leach; 25 May, O. Locker-Lampson; 26 May, Leach; 29 May, E. Rathbone.

[3] H. Rheinstrom, *Die völkerrechtliche Stellung der internationalen Kanäle* (Budapest, Revai, 1937).

[4] Hansard, *Commons Debates*, 6 May 1936, 1735–6, Eden. *The Times*, 7 May 1936, 8 ii.

[5] Lord Davies, *Nearing the Abyss. The Lesson of Ethiopia* (London, Constable, 1936), 110, reprinted as *It Need Not Have Happened* (London, Staples, 1942), 88.

carried tourists to Cairo as well as the middle class of Cairo to the Suez littoral. The motor-car also liberated the Europeans of the isthmus from dependence on the railway and therefore from contact with Egypt, as the railway had liberated overland travellers in 1858. The extension of the Port Said–Ismailia road to Suez between 1932 and 1934 enabled pilots to travel to duty by car to or from Ismailia. The growing rift between the Company and Egypt was widened by a series of lawsuits in the interests of the bondholders. The Egyptian decree of 2 May 1935, a long-term consequence of the devaluation of 1931, annulled the gold-clause in all international contracts by and with Egyptian companies, including the Canal Company, and affirmed that the francs referred to in its concession were Egyptian and not gold francs. The same national spirit inspired the recommendation of an Egyptian lawyer on 18 May 1935 that the Canal Company should be expropriated and the Canal administered as an international public utility.[1] The subsequent recession in the Company's shares compelled Vogüé to assert on 3 June that the Company's dividends and interest were not subject to any gold-clause but were payable in an 'international' franc, one-twentieth of the gold louis and 'the last refuge of timid capital in quest of security'.[2] On 7 July the Company announced however that it would pay its coupons in Egyptian francs and hold the balance for later payment if possible and that the Canal dues would be payable from 8 July in sterling, while passenger dues would remain fixed at 10 gold francs. From 8 July the Company expressed its dues in both Egyptian piastres and English shillings rather than in gold francs. The decree of 2 May ushered in a year of negotiations between the Egyptian Finance Minister and the Company's Principal Agent in Egypt, Baron Louis de Benoist who had succeeded Sérionne in 1929. Sir Arnold Wilson was encouraged to renew his attack upon the Company[3] in his concern lest its concession should be prolonged on the lines advocated in 1910.[4] Egyptian opinion proved more hostile to the Company in 1935 than in 1910. The Appeal Court of Alexandria recognized on 18 February 1936 the validity of the decree of 1935 to the dismay of the Company and rejected any reference to gold in the francs stipulated in Egypt. A decree of 30 April made the Egyptian piastre the legal money of the Company and compelled the Company to charge passenger dues in the piastre-equivalent of ten gold francs from 4 May. An agreement between the Company and the Government was reached on 1 July 1936 providing for the Company to pay the Government a royalty of £E200,000 per annum and to increase its Egyptian personnel to 25 per cent of the total by 1958. That convention was not approved before Egypt had finally reached agreement with Britain.

[1] Ahmed Moussa, *Essai sur le Canal de Suez. Droit et Politique* (Paris, Jouvé, 1935), 134, 137–8.
[2] *Le Canal de Suez*, 5 Juin 1935, 8450.
[3] A. T. Wilson, 'Some International and Legal Aspects of the Suez Canal', *Transactions of the Grotius Society*, 22 October 1935, 143–4.
[4] Hansard, *Commons Debates*, 19 December 1935, A. T. Wilson.

The Anglo-Egyptian Treaty of 26 August 1936[1] was negotiated by the Wafd after the death of Fuad and sought to defend Egypt against the threat of Italian aggression implicit in the use of the Canal to create a new empire at the expense of Moslem power on Egypt's southern flank, in Italy's claim to the free use of the air above the Canal Zone and in her identification of Egyptian with Italian interests.[2] The accession of the first English-educated ruler of Egypt in succession to the Italianized Fuad brought to a peak such royalist sentiment as Egypt could tolerate for its Turkish monarchs. The Treaty was modelled on the Anglo-Iraqi Treaty of 1930 and changed the whole basis of Anglo-Egyptian relations while seeming in appearance to change nothing. It elevated Egypt to full equality with Britain and removed all restrictions on Egyptian sovereignty save for British rights in the Canal Zone. It embodied Egypt's acceptance for the first time since 1882 of the presence of British troops, which ceased to be an army of occupation and became the forces of an allied power admitted under treaty. The Treaty explicitly recognized the essential nature of the Canal to Britain but also recognized it as an integral part of Egypt. The Canal was to be thenceforward defended by British troops until such time as the Egyptian Army could defend it by its own resources. The British military occupation of the Canal Zone thus replaced that of the Delta. Egypt insisted on her own responsibility for the defence of the Canal and refused England the right of Turkey to defend the Canal as suzerain under the Convention of Constantinople.[3] Thus the crucial eighth article accepted the presence of British troops only as the servants of Egypt and only on the periphery of the land. It restricted their location to specific areas and their number to 10,000 troops, 3,000 airmen and 400 pilots. Above all, it insisted that British forces were not to infringe the sovereignty of Egypt by their presence. Thus the Treaty transformed the occupation into an alliance and became as fundamental to the British base in the Canal Zone as the Convention of 1866 was to the Canal Company. The Treaty was signed on behalf of England by Eden, MacDonald, Simon, Halifax and Lampson and on behalf of Egypt by twelve pashas led by Nahas, the true creator of the agreement. Eden defended the Treaty as one entitling Britain 'to be assured that the canal will be adequately protected by the Alliance for all time'.[4] The 'permanent military defensive alliance' of 1936 was concluded, however, in the first instance for twenty years, was regarded as only temporary in Egyptian eyes and was bound to suffer erosion because Egypt remained the injured partner in the alliance, haunted by the ineradicable memory of the occupation. The Treaty marked an era in the liberation of Egypt from alien influence through the constitution of an independent national army, the opening of the

[1] *The Times*, 19 March 1936, 15–16, 'Egypt and the Canal'. J. J. Chevallier, 'Le Traité d'Alliance Anglo-Égyptien du 26 août 1936', *Revue Générale de Droit International* (Mai 1937).
[2] R. Tritonj, 'A Chi Appartiene il Canale di Suez?', *Nuova Antologia*, 1 Maggio 1936, 81–91.
[3] Mahmud Y. Zayid, *Egypt's Struggle for Independence* (Beirut, Khayats, 1965), 166, 172–3.
[4] Hansard, *Commons Debates*, 24 November 1936, 259, Eden.

Military Academy by the Wafd Government to youth irrespective of social origin or wealth, the suppression of the capitulatory regime from 1937, the abolition of the Egyptian Maritime Council of Sanitation and Quarantine in 1938 and the admission of Egypt to the League of Nations and thereby to the community of independent states in 1937. The Treaty was criticized by extreme nationalist opinion because it burdened Egypt with the cost of construction of barracks in the Canal Zone, created a massive reinforcement of British military power in the isthmus, maintained the occupation under cover of the defence of the Canal and so prevented Egypt from becoming the neutral and international Switzerland of the Middle East.[1] Italy resented the Treaty because it removed the protection of the capitulations from her 55,000 nationals, implied a perpetual alienation of the Canal Zone and prohibited the passage of aircraft thereover except through the Kantara air-corridor on the east–west route. Above all the Treaty regulated the Canal on an Anglo-Egyptian basis without reference to the comity of nations and allotted England a special position in the Canal Zone in defiance of the Convention of Constantinople. It only reconciled the opposed interests of the British Empire and Egypt in the Canal at the expense of the interests of Europe as embodied in 1888 in that Convention. The Treaty carefully avoided any mention of the Convention, with which it could be reconciled only with the greatest difficulty.[2]

The increase of Italian power in the Mediterranean and Red Sea presented the greatest threat to the British lines of communication to India since Bonaparte's Egyptian expedition.[3] Those narrow seas formed ideal hunting-grounds for the submarine and were made even narrower by aircraft with a range of 400–500 miles and by the impending threat of bombers with a radius of 800–1,000 miles. The security of Port Said, 350 miles from the Italian Dodecanese, was destroyed as effectively as that of the whole Mediterranean route. 'Thereby the 100-mile canal from Suez to Port Said has been extended into a 2,000-mile "canal" from Port Said to Gibraltar'.[4] From 1936 increasing use of the Cape route was made and the Cape record of 1893 was first broken when the *Stirling Castle* reached Cape Town in 13 days 9 hours (21 August– 4 September 1936), to inaugurate an accelerated mail service in $13\frac{1}{2}$ days in place of the $16\frac{1}{4}$ days' service, unchanged since 1912.[5] On the Suez route Britain sought to strengthen its position by developing closer relations with Turkey as well as with Egypt, by building up Malta as a sea-plane base and Alexandria as a naval base, by transferring Aden from the control of the India Office to that of the Foreign Office and by formally defining in 1937 the

[1] B. Aglietti, *Il Canale di Suez ed i Rapporti Anglo-Egiziani* (Firenze, Carlo, 1939), 85, quoting Hafez Ramadan Bey, 26 September 1937.

[2] A. T. Wilson, *The Suez Canal* (second edition, 1939), preface, b.

[3] F. J. C. Hearnshaw, *Prelude to 1937* (London, Murray, 1937), 130.

[4] B. Liddell Hart, *Europe in Arms* (London, Faber, 1937), 109, 'The Future of the Mediterranean'. S. Colman, 'The Suez Canal', *National Review* (February 1937), 206–8.

[5] M. Murray, *Union-Castle Chronicle 1853–1953* (London, Longmans, 1953), 202.

Western and Eastern Aden Protectorates. Above all, Britain sought to develop Haifa as the potential Singapore of the Middle East because its harbour, built between 1929 and 1933, was one of the best in the Levant as well as the furthest from the Italian air bases in Libya and the Dodecanese. To its mail service to Bagdad and its oil pipeline of 1934 were added an oil dock in 1935, an air terminal in 1935–7 and a light naval base in 1937. Haifa might thus become the terminus not only for a Bagdad Railway but also for an Akaba Railway proposed in 1935 and an Akaba Canal suggested in 1936. The increasing strategic integration of Alexandria, Suez, Haifa, Basra and Aden compelled Britain to conciliate Arab and Moslem opinion at Zionist expense in order to preserve its communications through the Middle East after the Arab Revolt broke out in Palestine in 1936, fifteen years after the 'betrayal' of 1921.

The end of the era of the capitulations subjected foreigners to Egyptian law and taxation, closed the French Post Office in Port Said on 1 April 1937 after seventy years and reminded the Canal Company of the third interest in the Canal apart from those of the client and concessionaire. Vogüé expressed the hope on 7 June that Egypt would use its new-found liberty with moderation and with respect to the duties imposed by the moral solidarity of civilized peoples.[1] Egypt placed its relations with the Canal Company on a new basis by the Convention of 9 June 1937. The Company thereby agreed to exempt vessels of the Egyptian Government passing through the Canal wholly from toll if they were under 300 tons net burden and to exempt such ships above 300 tons up to a total of 3,500 tons per annum. Two Egyptian directors were to be included on the board. From 1 May 1938 a voluntary annual rental of £E 300,000, or 50 per cent more than the £E 200,000 of the original agreement, was to be paid as a token compensation for the loss of revenue resulting from Egypt's disposal of her shares. Egyptians were to be taken increasingly into the employment of the Company so that by 1958 33 per cent instead of 25 per cent of its clerical staff in Egypt would be Egyptian. New strategic roads were to be built in the Canal Zone, especially a Suez–Port Said road, at a cost to the Company not exceeding £E 300,000. That Convention was concluded when Egypt's balance of payments was in difficulties and may have been intended to win Egyptian support against possible Italian claims on the Company. It recognized Egyptian rights and interests in the Company and first fixed the Canal tariff in Egyptian money of account. It ended the custom whereby Egyptian Government vessels flying the Egyptian flag had to pay tolls to pass through Egyptian territory, but it precluded the use of the Egyptian flag as one of convenience by limiting the concession to Government vessels under 300 tons. The Egyptian Treasury gained a share in the Company's profits for the first time since 1880 in theory and for the first time since 1858 in practice. The Company built the Port Said Medical Centre in 1937 and began the increased employment of Egyptians on the new terms from 1 January 1938. Egypt became a junior partner in the enterprise which it was

[1] *Le Canal de Suez*, 15 Juin 1937, 8781.

to inherit in 1968, no question having been raised about any renewal of the concession. After the fall in the gold price of the French franc during 1937 increased the interest on bonds and shares the Mixed Court of Cairo decided on 3 January 1938 that the Company should pay its dividends and amortize its bonds on a gold basis, raising the value of Suez shares on the local Stock Exchange. From 1 September 1938 the Company was subjected to Egyptian taxation at the rate of 7 per cent in addition to French taxation. Egypt had been offered and had refused in 1910 three seats on the board from 1968: in 1937 she secured two seats forthwith but not the third of the thirty-two seats foretold by Sir Arnold Wilson.[1] The first Egyptian directors became in 1937 Chérif Sabry Pasha, the brother of the Egyptian Queen Mother, and in 1938 Ismail Sidky Pasha, the Minister of Finance in 1937–8. Egypt still retained the memory of the material loss suffered from the opening of a waterway[2] which had encouraged the economic renaissance of Western Asia.[3]

Italian traffic continued to expand during the first half of 1936 while commercial tonnage continued to decline below the 1935 level in every month from January to June. When commercial tonnage revived in July and September military traffic began to decline. The result was that shipping tonnage rose above the level for 1935 in January–March but fell below that level in April–November: for the year as a whole tonnage declined by 1·3 per cent, transits by 1·9, cargo by 2·9, northbound cargo by 3·9 and British tonnage by 4·3 per cent. Although the volume of world trade rose by 5 per cent and that of industrial production by 14 per cent the share of the Canal in world trade declined from 6·4 to 5·9 per cent. The cargo tonnage of the Panama Canal even exceeded that of the Suez Canal, although no diversion of tonnage from Suez to Panama seems to have occurred as in 1931–2 and 1935. The Cape route however gained 1,800,000 tons of shipping from the Canal or 7·5 per cent of the Canal's traffic and nearly double the tonnage diverted during the depression of 1932. That route enjoyed freedom from war-risks as well as from toll, so that overseas steam tonnage entering the harbours of South Africa rose by 27 per cent during 1936.[4] Three hundred thousand tons of shipping from the Dutch East Indies, Indo-China and the Far East were diverted to the Cape route, together with 1,500,000 tons from Australia. Australia made the sharpest cuts ever in its use of the Canal, reducing its Canal tonnage by 38 per cent, its wheat shipments via Suez by 40 per cent, its homeward tonnage by 42 per cent and its cargo tonnage by 67·2 per cent. Its share in the tonnage of the Canal sank from 9·6 to 6 per cent, or to its lowest peace time proportion since

[1] A. T. Wilson, 'An Artery of Commerce. De Lesseps and the Suez Canal', *The Times Egypt Number*, 26 January 1937, xx, reprinted as *The Times Book of Egypt*, 67.

[2] A. E. Crouchley, *The Economic Development of Modern Egypt* (London, Longmans, 1938), 114–15, 118–19, 140.

[3] C. P. Grant, *The Syrian Desert* (1937), 261–95. J. Gottmann, 'L'Homme, la Route et l'Eau en Asie du Sud-Ouest', *Annales de Géographie*, 15 Novembre 1938, 594.

[4] *Union of South Africa, Official Year Book of the Union*, No. 19 (Pretoria, Government Printer, 1938), 488.

1881. Such mail lines as the Orient Line became much more sensitive to the burden of Canal dues based on gold, despite their reduction from 1 July 1936.[1] The burden of those tolls was especially increased by the loss of passengers during the Red Sea summer and by the growing demand of passengers for more and more taxable deck-space for their pastimes.

Italy brought through the Canal 1,333,000 tons in ballast during 1936 as its transports returned from the war and raised its share in the total traffic to 20·2 per cent. The 399,885 Italian troops and 200,000 workmen who passed through the waterway formed 76·5 per cent of the total passengers, of whom 59 per cent were military. The Italia rose from the sixth to the third client-line of the Canal. The Italian steamships reduced the share of motor-vessels in the total tonnage from the peak of 30·1 per cent in 1934 to 25·3 per cent in 1936. The Company's receipts would have fallen by 5 per cent if the devaluation of the franc had not raised them by 6·3 per cent for the year. Receipts in sterling rose on conversion into francs after the Poincaré franc ceased to exist from 1 October 1936. Devaluation raised Suez shares by 19·8 per cent in price between 25 September and 21 October, enabled the Company to increase its dividends for 1936 by 13·2 per cent and led to the appointment of the economist Charles Rist to the Company's executive committee on 5 April 1937. During 1937 300,079 Italian troops passed through the Canal, raising the total for the three years 1935–7 to 1,019,468. The Lloyd Triestino became the leading Italian line and passed both the British Tanker Company and the P. & O. to become the first client of the Company instead of the fifth. Never before in the history of the waterway had a non-British line assumed the first place. Italy's tonnage declined by 11·5 per cent to 16·1 per cent of the total but maintained its flag second to that of Britain.

The conquest of Ethiopia created an Italian colonial empire in North-East Africa but did not create an Anglo-Italian front, as Sir Arnold Wilson had hoped,[2] with a common interest in keeping open the Canal in all circumstances. Italy's new empire controlled the source of the Blue Nile, flanked the Straits of Bab el Mandeb from Massawa to Assab and threatened the security of Aden, especially through the establishment of friendly relations with the Yemen. Thus the Canal became an imperial highway for Italy as well as for Britain, whose former client was transformed into its rival. As a Mediterranean power Italy straddled the British lines of communication in the inland sea but remained wholly dependent on its extended line of communication to the Red Sea as Britain was not. Relative distances made the Canal far more necessary to Italy than to England: Naples was 2,178 miles distant from Massawa via the Canal but 10,850 miles distant via the Cape. Italy's demand for the use of what was a natural monopoly was thus inelastic. Tolls formed 1 per cent of the total cost of the Ethiopian campaign[3] but bore more heavily on

---

[1] *The Times*, 2 December 1936, 16iv, I. C. Geddes, Chairman of Anderson, Green & Co.
[2] E. W. P. Newman, *Italy's Conquest of Abyssinia* (1937), 5–6.
[3] H. J. Schonfield, *Italy and Suez* (London, Hutchinson, 1940), 52.

the short-haul traffic to the Red Sea than on long-haul traffic. Nor were Italian ships in ballast which would have entitled them to pay half rather than full dues. After the conquest it was essential to develop Ethiopia, to supply the occupation forces and the civilian settlers with their needs and to expand trade with the new metropolis. Thus Italy became more dependent than ever on the Canal and more insecure than ever before. She had placed a vice around her neck and did not even become a satisfied Power within the sea which carried the bulk of her trade. Her 2,500 miles of vulnerable coastline made her to Mussolini 'most blockadeable Italy' and a prisoner of the inland sea whose keys were Gibraltar, Malta and Suez. After Mussolini declared on 1 November 1936 'the Mediterranean is simply a highway for others but for us Italians it is life itself' the Anglo-Italian Declaration of Rome of 2 January 1937 sought to create a new Mediterranean equilibrium.

The growth of Italy's power and insecurity revived the debate over the road to India[1] and encouraged its publicists to supply their new society with its own national viewpoint and claims on the Canal. The literature produced during the crisis was essentially popular,[2] nationalist and Latin, discarding the scholarship of the literature of the 1920s whilst retaining and increasing its nationalist bias, especially against Britain.[3] Angelo Sammarco, who had served Fuad since 1922 as an historian, wrote the first authoritative history of the Canal from the Egyptian viewpoint.[4] After the reiterated English demands for the closure of the Canal Italy sought some guarantee for the freedom of its communications to Ethiopia and some influence over the Canal Company through representation on its board. As the second client of the Canal since 1935 Italy provided in 1937 more than double the tonnage of Germany in 1898 and 16 per cent of the total tonnage against the German proportion of 10·5 per cent in 1898, when the first German director had been elected. Italy's efforts to justify the election of Italian directors were made despite its anti-capitalist ethos and its aversion to the plutocratic nations of France and Britain as well as to such an organ of high finance as the Canal Company. Those efforts were supported by more historical research than either the English agitation of 1883 or the German agitation of 1915.

The new Italian historiography appealed in the Roman tradition to

[1] R. la Bruyère, 'Les Routes des Indes', *Revue des Deux Mondes*, 1 Décembre 1935. P. Morand, *La Route des Indes* (Paris, Plon, 1936). L. C. A. Knowles, *The Economic Development of the British Overseas Empire* (London, Routledge, 1936), iii. 274–6.

[2] M. O. Williams, 'The Suez Canal: Short Cut to Empires', *National Geographic Magazine* (November 1935). R. L. Baker, 'Britain's Hold on the Suez Canal', *Current History* (December 1935), 287–9.

[3] Jacques-Vincent, *Le Canal de Suez. Ferdinand de Lesseps Intime* (Paris, Nouvelles Éditions Latines, 1935). E. Morand, *Le Canal de Suez et l'Histoire Extérieure du Second Empire* (Paris, Figuière, 1936). J. von Kunowski, *Der Suezkanal Geschichte, Land und Leute* (Berlin, Schönfeld, 1936).

[4] A. Sammarco, *Les Règnes de 'Abbas, de Said et d'Ismail (1848–1879) avec un aperçu de l'histoire du Canal de Suez* (Roma, 1935). Idem, 'Canale di Suez', *Enciclopedia Italiana*, vol. 32 (1936), 958–62.

geological law as the real basis of canal-construction. It assimilated the Canal to the Mediterranean as a veritable artery rather than a mere means of communication. From the French tradition Italy inherited a juridical outlook with an emphasis on the creative role of the Corsican Bonaparte and on the Franco-Italian entente of 1859–66. From the Germanic tradition it inherited its emphasis on the Study Society of 1846 as well as on Negrelli and Revoltella whom it transformed from Austrians into Italians. From those sources it built up its own tradition which represented Italy as the great creator and England as the great opponent of the Canal. Those Italians who were elevated into precursors, prophets and apostles of the Canal did not include the Lazarist Sapeto, the founder of Assab.[1] Negrelli was converted from a Trentino Austrian, commemorated by a monument unveiled at Trento in October 1930 and honoured in Sammarco's revisionist studies as the true technical creator of the Suez Canal, the mind and soul of the Study Society and the author of the project adopted by the International Commission in 1856.[2] Gioia was praised as the engineer responsible for the most difficult of the Canal works at El Guisr and the miners of Piedmont as the conquerors of the rock of Chalouf. Monti used unpublished documents, like Georgi in 1913, and transformed the Canal into a national achievement through Italy's initiative, schemes, labour and propaganda, even attributing Lesseps' failure at Panama to his lack of Italian collaborators. Negrelli had been given due credit for his contribution in 1858[3] but as an engineer and not as an entrepreneur, since he lacked the driving-force which built up in Lesseps after his mission to Rome and distinguished him from Enfantin. Lesseps had not only grasped the essence of the Canal as an engineering project but had transformed it into reality. The Italian magnification of Negrelli implied a belief in the heroic theory of invention, which made a single progenitor responsible for each innovation and recognized neither the instrumental role of technology nor the organizing power of the master-builder using materials provided by others. The envy of the mass-man for the aristocrat and the alien also inspired the Italian denigration of Lesseps.

The divergence of Italy's national history of the Canal from the common French tradition reflected the shipwreck of collective security in Ethiopia. That history regarded the opening of the Canal only as the beginning of a new era in British hegemony in the Mediterranean[4] and preferred to see in

---

[1] A. Monti, *Gli Italiani e il Canale di Suez. Lettere inediti di P. Paleocapa, L. Torelli, E. Gioja, F. di Lesseps, B. Voisin, J. Conrad, B. Saint-Hilaire etc. etc.* (Roma, Vittoriano, 1937), reviewed by A. Sammarco, ' Gli Italiani e il Canale di Suez' in *Rivista Storica Italiana* (1937), 30–44. A. Monti, *Storia del Canale di Suez con un Diario di Luigi Torelli ed altri documenti inediti* (Milano, Istituto per Gli Studi di Politica Internazionale, 1937), 173.

[2] A. Sammarco, *Histoire de l'Égypte Moderne depuis Mohammed Ali jusqu à l'occupation britannique (1801–1882). III. Le Règne du Khédive Ismail de 1863 à 1875* (Le Caire, 1937). Idem, *Suez Storia e Problemi* (1943), 83–177.

[3] F. W. Conrad, *Reizen naar de Landengte van Suez* (1859), 320, 'His memory will live in the great work to which he was one of the most potent contributors'.

[4] L. Federzoni, 'Hegemony in the Mediterranean', *Foreign Affairs* (April 1936), 392.

1935 a turning-point in the history of a natural monopoly.[1] It emphasized the cost of the Canal to Egypt and dismissed French interests as financial rather than commercial or maritime. It argued that the interests of world trade and Mediterranean peace should take precedence over the interests of the shareholders in the cause of equity as well as in that of 'civilization and commerce', so invoking Lesseps' watchword against his heirs. Thus Italy demanded a radical revision of the Company's concession or of its statutes[2] and revived the German claim for founders' shares as well as for seats on the board. England produced no counter-propaganda apart from a biography in the French tradition by a Jewish scholar who had early found a spiritual home in Egypt.[3] Italy could hardly expect to achieve very much when the British agitations of 1931 and 1933 had achieved so little. France was even more disturbed by the establishment of the Italian Empire than England. The French directors of the Canal Company had no wish to repeat the exclusion of a member of the board which had taken place in 1914. Italian traffic had moreover grown far more rapidly than German traffic and may well have seemed less stable in its basis. Italy desired a Mediterranean naval agreement with England as well as a greater share in the control of the Canal and was even prepared to consider a surprise landing at Port Said and Suez.[4] Egypt was so disturbed by her exclusion from the Anglo-Italian talks and by the use of the Canal as a bargaining-counter in the politics of Europe[5] that her Government began to study measures for the defence of the Canal Zone in the event of war so as to proclaim herself the real mistress and the sole defender of the waterway.

The disintegration of the Versailles settlement occurred amid recurrent crises which undermined the security of the victors of 1918 and of the Canal Company. The incorporation of Austria in Germany alarmed Italy as well as France and reduced Suez share-prices by 12·2 per cent between 9 March and 16 March 1938. The Anglo-Italian Agreement of 16 April then reaffirmed the intention of Britain and Italy to abide by the provisions of the Convention of Constantinople. That Easter Pact was the first triumph of the new policy of appeasement and equated the Italian Empire with the British Empire as a user of the Canal, although in March 1938 Italy supplied only 12·2 per cent of the total tonnage and Britain 51·6 per cent. Britain was thus forced to accept a reaffirmation of the Convention which it had studiously excluded from the Anglo-Egyptian Treaty. Egypt adhered to the agreement and so recognized the Convention which she had not signed in 1888. Britain then made on 30 May its strongest appointment to the board of the Canal Company

---

[1] U. Toschi, 'Il Canale di Suez', *Bollettino della Società Geografica Italiana* (Agosto 1939), 587, 598.
[2] E. Anchieri, *Il Canale di Suez* (Milano, Lombarda, 1937), 169–70.
[3] H. J. Schonfield, *Ferdinand de Lesseps* (London, Joseph, 1937).
[4] M. Muggeridge, *Ciano's Diary 1937–1938* (London, Methuen, 1952), 75, 14 February 1938.
[5] *The Times*, 26 February 1938, 11 ii.

in Sir Maurice Hankey, who until his retirement had been Secretary to the Committee of Imperial Defence since 1912, Secretary to the Cabinet since 1916 and Clerk to the Privy Council since 1923. The Munich crisis brought the Mediterranean Fleet to Alexandria on 22 September in order to defend the Canal. Duff Cooper, the First Lord of the Admiralty, authorized on 23 September the despatch of 1,900 men to bring the Fleet up to establishment and to man the defences of the Canal. He urged the Cabinet on 24 September to ask the Government of Egypt to put into force the precautionary period for the protection of the Canal but was strongly opposed by the Prime Minister.[1] Marine insurance rates rose steadily to become prohibitive by 27 September for cargo shipped via the Canal, while the Company's shares slipped by 14·5 per cent between 23 August and 28 September. The crisis ended with a great diplomatic triumph for Germany, the revival of the Anglo-French entente and the general approval of the Munich agreement by the board of the Canal Company,[2] whose shares rose by 23·5 per cent between 28 September and 3 October.

The growing insecurity in both the West and the East contributed to the severe depression of the traffic of the Canal in 1938–9 and cost the Company far more than it had gained in war-profits in 1935. During the expansion of 1937 tonnage first surpassed the record level of 1929. Commercial tonnage however reached its peak in April 1937 after the prices of primary produce began to fall in March and April. During 1938 the Canal's tonnage fell below the level of 1937 in every month save in March and September. The depression reduced total tonnage by 6 per cent and affected most severely the traffic of the Red Sea, the Far East, the Persian Gulf and India. Italian tonnage sank by 21 per cent and so accounted for 59 per cent of the total reduction in traffic for the year. Receipts however rose by 23 per cent because of the depreciation of the French franc. The expansion of Japan in Asia developed Dalny at the expense of Shanghai and revived the scheme of a Kra Canal to by-pass the new naval base at Singapore.[3] Japan, a disappointed victor-power like Italy, attacked China fifteen years after her humiliation at the Conference of Washington in 1922. She undertook the systematic industrialization of Manchukuo and the de-industrialization of the China coast. She curtailed the commercial value of the treaty-ports to all other Powers and restricted the international trade of Free China. The Far East thus declined from the second place in the traffic of the Canal to the third place during 1937 and to the fourth place during 1938 when India regained the first place for the last time. The great westward migration of the Chinese into the valleys of Sikang, where railways were non-existent and modern roads were few,

---

[1] D. Cooper, *Old Men Forget. The Autobiography of Duff Cooper* (London, Hart-Davis, 1953), 235.

[2] *Documents on British Foreign Policy 1919–1939, Third Series*, iii (London, H.M.S.O., 1950), 87–90, M. Hankey to E. Phipps, 3 October 1938.

[3] W. J. Ronan, 'The Kra Canal: a Suez for Japan?', *Pacific Affairs* (September 1936), 406–15.

ended the Western dream of China as a substitute for India and began the de-Westernization of China, its economic retrogression and its cultural revival. The growing insecurity nevertheless increased traffic in the munitions of war and brought through the Canal its first shipments of bauxite from Bintang in January 1936 as well as the first shipments of manganese to the U.S.A. from Abu Zenima in 1936 and from Durban in 1937. During 1937 the volume of northbound oil first surpassed the level of 1934 after two years of depression caused by the Iraqi pipelines. Iran increased its Canal cargo tonnage by 36 per cent and assumed second place from the Far East. The Anglo-Iranian Oil Company, as Anglo-Persian had become in 1935, exported through the Canal 47 per cent of its production from Abadan which was becoming the largest oil-refinery in the world. Fuel oil replaced petrol in the first place in northbound shipments from December 1936. Basra regained as a port the importance it had lost to Bahrein as a base in 1935 and became, with Abadan, as important as the Canal to the British Empire. The oil imported by Britain through the Canal in 1937 was, however, worth less than one-third of the value of the tea imported via Suez. American interest in the oil trade increased when oil was first discovered in Saudi Arabia in March 1938 and in Kuwait in May 1938. The commercial production of oil began on 15 September 1938 for shipment from Saudi Arabia to Bahrein. The first overseas shipment left Ras Tanura on 1 May 1939 on the tanker *D. G. Schofield* of Standard Oil of California. Thus the Canal gained its first new source of oil since the shipment of oil had begun in 1912–13 from Persia and in July 1935 from Bahrein.

From 1938 German scholars and publicists renewed their contribution to the historiography of the Canal as their interest revived in the Berlin–Bagdad axis. They sought to reduce French conceit, to expose English machiavellianism and to support Italian claims, although Kressenstein's memoirs of the 1915–16 war, 'a chivalrous struggle against a chivalrous opponent',[1] passed implicit judgment upon Mussolini's techniques of warfare. German propaganda habitually stressed the military rather than the economic value of the Canal, portrayed England as the relentless opponent of the Canal[2] and criticized the Disraeli-myth of the share-purchase.[3] It attacked capitalism, Judaism and the Canal Company as a leech on the world-economy, if not the greatest robber-band of modern times. British scholars studied alternative routes to the Canal, especially the Cape and Syrian routes, and revealed the limited economic role of the waterway as the channel for only 9 per cent of the total value of British imports.[4] Soldiers reluctantly recognized the Mediterranean route as a luxury comparable to freedom from invasion, complete individual independence and cheap electric power which might have to be sacrificed in

[1] K. von Kressenstein, *Mit den Türken zum Suezkanal* (Berlin, Schlegel, 1938), 305.

[2] H. Hummel, *Vor dem Ziel steht England. Ferdinand de Lesseps* (Darmstadt, Vorwerk, 1939).

[3] S. Helander, 'Disraelis Erwerb der Suezkanal-Aktien. Kritik einer Legende', *Orient-Nachrichten* (April 1939), 99–103.

[4] E. Monroe, *The Mediterranean in Politics* (London, Oxford University Press, 1938), 12, 249.

the event of war.[1] The Italian case[2] was supported by an Italian translation of Sir Arnold Wilson's onslaught on the Canal Company as a toll-collecting parasite, but was refuted in the first paper-back published in England on the Canal.[3] The mass-medium of the film also carried the story of Suez around the world.[4]

Italy had been encouraged by the Munich agreement to hope for British support to secure a reduction in Canal tolls[5] and the appointment of an Italian director while France also sought English aid against Italian pressure. After England recognized the Italian Empire the spontaneous anti-French manifestation of the Italian Chamber on 30 November reduced share-prices by 12·5 per cent between 1 and 12 December and encouraged the Company in self-defence to suggest that Egypt had exclusive competence to negotiate on the Canal.[6] The Italian Note of 17 December to France declared void the Mussolini–Laval agreement of 1935 and demanded the settlement of Italian demands over Tunisia, Jibuti and Suez. Sir Arnold Wilson made a full-scale onslaught on the Company in the debate of 19 December on foreign policy, reinforced the protest of the Orient Line[7] and urged the reduction of its dues by one-half. A director of Holt's envied the annual dividend of 60 per cent paid by a public utility whose assets were indestructible sand and water.[8] Mussolini decided on 8 January 1939 to demand a strong Italian share in the administration of the Canal.[9] Edgar Bonnet, the vice-president of the Company since 1925, found little official support against Italy's claims and therefore emphasized on 13 January the Company's duty to obtain the approval of Egypt for any change in its constitution. 'Whatever some may think, the Suez Canal cannot be made the object of a diplomatic bargain.'[10] Sir Arnold Wilson even recommended the expropriation of the Company by the Egyptian Government with the support of the French and British Governments as the best solution to Italy's claims.[11]

[1] H. Rowan Robinson, *Imperial Defence. A Problem in Four Dimensions* (London, Muller, 1938), 287. H. W. Richmond and E. H. Carr, 'Strategy in the Mediterranean', *The Listener*, 15 December 1938, 1289–91.

[2] A. Sammarco, 'La verità sulle questione del Canale di Suez', *Oriente Moderno* (Gennaio 1939), 1–30. G. Ambrosini, 'Il Canale di Suez', *Annali dell'Africa Italiana* (Marzo 1939).

[3] H. J. Schonfield, *The Suez Canal* (Penguin Special, 1939), reviewed by H. L. Hoskins, 'Suez Canal Problems', *Geographical Review* (October 1940), 666.

[4] *Suez* (Twentieth-Century Fox, 1938).   [5] *The Times*, 23 November 1938, 14 ii.

[6] Ibid., 16 December 1938, 16 vi.   [7] Ibid., 14 December 1938, 25 iii.

[8] R. H. Thornton, *British Shipping* (Cambridge University Press, 1939), 111, in a footnote removed from the second edition of 1959.

[9] M. Muggeridge, *Ciano's Diary, 1939–1943* (London, Heinemann, 1947), 8. *Documents on British Foreign Policy, Third Series, iii.* 512. J. B. Firth, 'Italy and the Future of the Suez Canal. Is Her Claim to Share in Control Justified?', *Daily Telegraph*, 6 January 1939, 12 iv–vi. *The Times*, 11 January 1939, 9 ii.

[10] *The Times*, 14 January 1939, iiiv. *Le Canal de Suez*, 15 Janvier 1939, 9043.

[11] A. T. Wilson, 'The Suez Canal and its Future', *Spectator*, 13 January 1939, 44–5. Idem, 'The Suez Canal', *Contemporary Review* (March 1939), 280–7. Idem, 'The Suez Canal', *International Affairs* (May 1939), 380–95. Idem, *The Suez Canal* (1939), f–g, Preface dated 6 June 1939.

The annihilation of Czechoslovakia reduced share-prices by 12·8 per cent between 10 and 20 March and led Churchill to declare that command of the Mediterranean had to be the prime objective in wartime, in order to reinforce and supply all European land forces on the shores of North Africa. Mussolini's speech at Rome on the twentieth anniversary of the foundation of Fascism on 26 March repeated Italy's three demands as 'Tunis, Jibuti, the Suez Canal', reducing Suez shares by 5·2 per cent (24–30 March) and increasing uneasiness in both Egypt and England. The British Cabinet which had thitherto abstained from infringing the Convention of 1888 then invited the Government of Egypt at the end of March to mount guns at Suez and Port Said, where they were placed by 13 April without any protest by Italy.[1] Thus the Canal followed the example of the Straits in 1936. A new command-structure for the Middle East began to emerge from March when the post of Air Officer Commanding in Chief, Middle East, was created. Italy's invasion of Albania compelled the Mediterranean Fleet to leave Malta on 8 April for Alexandria and reduced the Company's shares by 10 per cent between 5 and 19 April. Italy's unofficial request on 25 April for two seats on the board of the Canal Company[2] produced no response from France. After Germany and Italy concluded their Pact of Steel, Vogüé hinted on 5 June at the Company's willingness to accept Italian directors when the time was ripe but emphasized that the Company had to defend Egypt's rights as well as its own.[3] As tension increased during the summer Admiral Cunningham arrived at Alexandria on 5 June to become C.-in-C. Mediterranean, but found the newly mounted defence batteries at Port Said most inadequate,[4] especially if the Italian Air Force contemplated bombing a vessel in the Canal to block it upon the outbreak of war.[5] The British Government ordered the despatch of troops from India to Egypt on 22 July[6] and appointed General Wavell G.O.C.-in-C., Middle East, on 24 July. The Indian troops reached Suez in twelve days (3–15 August) and began to train at Fayid, while the Company's shares sank by 7·2 per cent between 1 and 22 August. Sir Arnold Wilson appealed in desperation for Germany and Italy to recognize that 'the Mediterranean is our Lebensraum'.[7] In France Weygand at the age of seventy-two was recalled to service on 22 August and appointed C.-in-C., Middle East, resigning from the board of the Canal Company and even contemplating the conduct of operations in the Canal Zone.[8] Egypt issued its first decree on 25 August to render help to its ally under the Treaty of 1936.

[1] I. S. O. Playfair, *The Mediterranean and Middle East* (H.M.S.O., 1954), i. 37.

[2] *British Documents on Foreign Policy 1919–1939, Third Series*, v, 347, E. Phipps to Halifax, 27 April 1939.

[3] *Le Canal de Suez*, 5/7 Juin 1939, 9107–8. M. Pernot, 'Le Canal de Suez et les Relations Internationales', *L'Esprit International*, 1 Juillet 1939, 373–87.

[4] A. B. Cunningham, *A Sailor's Odyssey* (1951), 208.   [5] *The Times*, 4 July 1939, 14 iv.

[6] P. C. Bharucha, *The North African Campaign 1940–1943. Official History of the Indian Armed Forces in the Second World War 1939–1945* (1956), 35.

[7] Hansard, *Commons Debates*, 31 July 1939, 2043, A. T. Wilson.

[8] M. Weygand, *Recalled to Service* (London, Heinemann, 1952), 3.

The rise of Italian power had prevented the evacuation of British troops from the Delta in accordance with the Anglo-Egyptian Treaty and compelled Britain to defend its Middle Eastern empire against the Eurafrican empire of Italy and in defiance of the geopolitical advantages of the Axis powers. Thus Britain created a new military command in the Middle East, divided its forces between two fronts and accepted the burden of its entente with France, the reluctant support of Egypt as well as of India and the opposition of the Jews of Palestine. The Ethiopian War had undermined the Canal Company's moral basis[1] as seriously as the depression-inspired attacks on capitalism. The subsequent decline in the price of Suez shares had been far more severe than during the world depression. Those shares declined from 24,500 francs on 21 October 1937 to 13,000 francs on 22 August 1939. The British Government's shares had exceeded their market-value of 1929 in 1934 but then declined from £93,199,777 on 31 March 1935 to £27,683,263 on 31 March 1939. Italy's campaign had failed to achieve the election of a single Italian or German director, although nine new directors were elected in 1937–9. The Canal was also exposed to keener competition than ever before from the Cape route through the reduction in South African harbour dues from 1937. The Convention of Constantinople had been gravely weakened in its moral authority[2] and was infringed anew from 1939 as the Canal became an artery in the new military unity of Middle East Command.

[1] G. Schwarzenberger, *Power Politics* (London, Cape, 1941), 46.
[2] G. T. Garratt, *Gibraltar and the Mediterranean* (London, Cape, 1939), 140. H. von Richthofen, *Der Suez-Kanal im Weltkrieg und in der Nachkriegzeit: Eine völkerrechtliche Studie* (Berlin, Siegismund, 1939).

33

THE WAR FOR THE MIDDLE EAST, 1939-1945, AND THE CREATION OF THE CANAL ZONE BASE

THE war which broke out in 1939 affected the traffic of the Canal much more than the Great War had done. It followed a decade of depressions rather than one of expansion and dislocated the organization of the Canal Company as no earlier conflict had done. It did not break out suddenly as in 1914 nor did it encourage any Axis vessels to seek refuge in the Canal ports as in 1914. The Mediterranean route had become so insecure that British control of the Canal had become pointless except as a base from which to re-establish the security of the whole route. British ships bound for the Red Sea were therefore held at Aden on 26 August 1939 and those bound for the Mediterranean at Gibraltar on 27 August. The Government of Egypt introduced on 28 August inspection of all ships in its ports and proclaimed a state of siege on 1 September so that the land passed under the rule of a Military Governor. On 31 August all British ships were diverted around the Cape except for ships on Government charter and ships with a speed of 15 knots. That diversion of commercial traffic to the Cape route was cancelled on 3 September when Italy did not follow Germany into the war but was still maintained for ships whose first or last port of call lay east of Rangoon. The result was a sharp and sudden fall in Canal traffic by over 50 per cent during September, followed by a revival in October, November and December. To preserve the security of the Canal and of navigation the Military Governor issued a series of decrees. On 3 September double floating booms were placed in position at Port Said as well as Suez and the search of merchant vessels was introduced, but outside the three-mile limit in compliance with the Convention of Constantinople. Vessels carrying explosives or petroleum were evacuated to the wide spaces of the Great Bitter Lake. The Military Governor made compulsory on 10 September a detailed declaration of all cargo on board vessels in transit. He closed on 14 September the ports of Suez and Port Said between sunset and sunrise, established a special service on 19 September to control the wireless operations of commercial vessels passing through the Canal and enforced on 25 September a strict black-out in the Canal Zone, so bringing navigation under military control.[1]

The War Cabinet decided on 15 January 1940 to establish base organizations in Egypt and Palestine and to accumulate material reserves for a force

---

[1] B. Avram, *The Evolution of the Suez Canal Status from 1869 up to 1956. A Historico-Juridical Study* (Geneva, Droz, 1958), 92–3.

of nine divisions. The first Australian and New Zealand brigades began to arrive on 12 February after a 10,000-mile voyage in the track of their fathers and were welcomed at Suez by Eden as Dominions Secretary. The German invasion of Norway brought a million tons of Norwegian shipping to England and increased the use of the Canal by Norwegian vessels. It also increased the danger of war between England and Italy, compelling Britain to reinforce its fleet in the Mediterranean when all its ships were needed in the North Sea. The division of British forces between England and the Middle East increased the strain on shipping after vessels were diverted around the Cape on 27 April and the Admiralty decided on 29 April to form a fleet for the East Mediterranean in order to protect the British base in the Middle East and to facilitate the landing of British troops from Port Said in Crete 24–30 hours after an Italian attack on Greece.[1] The deterioration of relations with Italy led to the introduction on 4 June of dusk and dawn patrols in the Gulf of Suez and the examination of ships at a special anchorage before their entry into the Canal. The fall of France finally brought Italy into the war on 10 June when a boom-ship was established to close the Canal at night. On 11 June 400 Italians were arrested in Port Said and two Italian military transports, which had been successfully delayed from entering the Canal, were captured outside the three-mile limit.[2] In Egypt the Prime Minister, Aly Maher, sought to establish Egypt's independence of Britain but failed and resigned office on 23 June. In that crisis of confidence Cunningham was instructed by the Admiralty on 17 June to be prepared to block the Canal if the Mediterranean Fleet were withdrawn and the Army lost control of the Canal.[3]

Italy's entry into the war completely transformed the British position in the Mediterranean, created a new Axis unity in the western basin and threatened the British position in the eastern basin by virtue of the total superiority of air-power to sea-power. The whole 2,000 miles from Gibraltar to Port Said was converted into the narrowest of sea-lanes commanded by the aircraft and submarines of Italy. The inland sea became virtually closed to Allied shipping, trade and communications, necessitating reliance on the Cape route for cables as well as for commerce. Italian warships, aircraft and bases in East Africa also destroyed the security of the Red Sea route and even threatened the Cape route as well as Kenya and the Sudan. The fall of France carried with it the French Fleet and the French colonial empire, including Syria, which ceased from 30 June to serve as a barrier of defence in depth for the Canal and Egypt. It also ended the use of the Canal by the French flag and by French trade, produced the capitulation of two French liners in the waterway and immobilized a French squadron in Alexandria. Light buoys and searchlights ceased to be used on night transits as the black-out was extended to the Canal after nine months of war, halving its facilities for traffic. The passage of the Indian mail through France to Marseilles ended, together

---

[1] A. B. Cunningham, *A Sailor's Odyssey* (1951), 230, 29 May 1940.
[2] B. Avram, 93–4.   [3] A. B. Cunningham, 240–1.

with the westward flow of Iraqi oil from Tripoli. The head office of the Canal Company in Paris came under German influence if not under German jurisdiction because the Company, thitherto a 'great Allied corporation',[1] did not imitate Royal Dutch-Shell or the Norwegian fleet. The exclusion of the ships of the Canal's second largest client reduced the gross receipts of the Company from a monthly average of £750,000 to almost nil. Between January and May 1940 traffic had fallen by only 23 per cent compared with the average for 1933–7. The number of transits which had been 458 in August 1939 fell however in August 1940 to 43 or to less than four days' normal traffic. Tonnage which had fallen in 1939 by 14 per cent plummeted in 1940 by 54 per cent, the greatest single fall in the history of the Canal. The Company held its last shareholders' meeting on 3 June[2] but sought as far as possible to maintain communication with Egypt and to protect its assets against Germany. Thus it opened an office in 1940 at Châtel-Guyon in the unoccupied zone of France in order to maintain contact with Egypt and to remove part of its financial activity from the control of the Army of Occupation. That decentralization of administration from Paris, where the board continued to meet, enabled the Company to maintain contact with Benoist in Egypt for a further eighteen months, although it could not remit him the necessary funds to maintain the state of his 'virtual miniature Versailles'.[3] Benoist therefore reduced the salaries of the Company staff, closed down the Company's workshops, ceased to hire daily labourers, dismissed many employees and suspended the payment of the interest due on 1 August.[4] He also became the President of a very active French National Committee in Cairo. The interests of Egypt and Farouk were forcefully defended against a vulnerable Company by the Creole Pierre Crabitès, who had been a judge of the Mixed Courts since 1911 and argued that Egypt had been deprived of a potential aggregate revenue of £33,138,000 between 1880 and 1932.[5] In England the ambiguous status of the Company came under attack[6] as the members of the London Committee increased in importance. Sir Rupert de la Bère, the chairman of Hay's Wharf Ltd. and M.P. for the City of London since 1935, enquired in the Commons on 6 August about the assets of the Company. The Chancellor of the Exchequer replied that the greater part of the Company's assets and reserves were held in Britain and the U.S.A. That incorrect reply concealed from the House that most of the Company's assets were in France but effectively prevented any wartime action against the Company. Sir Rupert then asked repeatedly for future Government directors to represent British export

[1] *New York Times*, 19 May 1940, 34 vii.
[2] Ibid., 9 June 1940, E 2 vii; 27 June, 9 i.
[3] P. Benoit, *Lunegarde* (Paris, Michel, 1942), 41.
[4] *New York Times*, 21 July 1940, 26 viii; *The Times*, 25 July 1940, 3 iii; *New York Times*, 3 August 1940, 22 vii.
[5] P. Crabitès, *The Spoliation of Suez* (London, Routledge, 1940), 203.
[6] Hansard, *Commons Debates*, 6 August 1940, 13 August, 20 August, 19 September, Sir Rupert de la Bère.

industry rather than British politics and society. 'We do not want politicians as directors.'[1] From Paris the Company announced on 16 September the suspension of dividend and interest until further notice for the first time since 1874.[2]

The fall of France and the entry of Italy into the war left the new Middle East Command as a beleaguered garrison, connected with England only by a perilous roundabout sea route of 12,900 miles. The War Cabinet did not even discuss the question of abandoning the Middle East, whose defence was assumed to be as axiomatic as that of India in 1857. It revealed a magnificent confidence in the defensibility of England and the invincibility of the English people. It decided to fight for Gibraltar and Alexandria, to uproot the East African empire of Italy, to facilitate the return of Hailie Selassie, to contest the central Mediterranean with Italy, to operate aircraft from Malta and to inaugurate the Takoradi air-reinforcement route. That decision made Malta more than Gibraltar or Suez the key to Mediterranean dominion because of its function as an unsinkable aircraft-carrier astride the communications between Italy and North Africa. It also dispersed British forces between two widely separated fronts, left Germany and Italy free to dominate Europe and delayed the opening of a second front in the West. The use of the Cape route increased the strain on the Navy, doubled the length of the voyage to India and quadrupled the length of the voyage to Egypt. It entailed an enormous investment of shipping in the long voyage from the Clyde around the Cape to Suez, which took a convoy six weeks and a fast motor-vessel five weeks. The Cape route thus came fully into its own once more and acquired an extension in the Red Sea and even in the Canal, which became a back-door to the Mediterranean in place of a short-cut to the East. South Africa became a rear base for the supply of the Middle East and attracted to its waters German submarines and surface-raiders from their great hunting-ground off West Africa.

Hitler offered Mussolini aerial assistance to bomb the Canal.[3] Mussolini preferred to act alone and told him on 7 July of his plan for the reorganization of the Middle East whereby Italy was to inherit the British position, abolish the Canal Company and create a special regime for the Canal area. 'Suez spells escape to empire and the open sea, to life, and food, and freedom.'[4] Eritrea, cut off from Italy by the Suez barrier, conquered British Somaliland and Berbera between 3 August and 19 August, so completing the construction of Italy's East African empire and establishing Italian control over the southern flank of the route through the Gulf of Aden. On 22 August the first Winston Spencer, or W.S., convoy left England with England's only armoured

[1] Hansard, *Commons Debates*, 13 August 1940, 604, R. de la Bère.

[2] *New York Times*, 17 September 1940, 9ii.

[3] M. Muggeridge, *Ciano's Diary 1939–1943* (1947), 273, 2 July 1940.

[4] H. J. Schonfield, *Italy and Suez* (London, Hutchinson, 1940), 25. A. Sammarco, 'Storia Sincera del Canale di Suez', *Annali dell'Africa Italiana* (1940), 47–165. A. Monti, *Il Canale di Suez e le Rivendicazioni Italiane* (Roma, Libro Italiano, 1940), 82.

division of fifty tanks on the 34-day voyage to beleaguered Suez. Italy launched its first air-raids on Port Said on 28 August and on Suez on 5 September as naval reinforcements with an aircraft-carrier to protect the Fleet berthed at Alexandria from Gibraltar. It then invaded Western Egypt on 13 September in a limited offensive designed to coincide with the projected German invasion of England. Admiral Raeder told Hitler of his doubts whether Italy alone could accomplish the capture of the Canal and pressed for German partici-pation in a two-pronged drive to eliminate the Mediterranean pivot of the British world-empire.[1] Hitler met Mussolini at the Brenner Pass on 4 October, then withdrew his order for the invasion of England and decided instead to invade Crete in order to secure an air base against the British Fleet and the Canal. The Italian invasion of Greece compelled Hitler to decide on 4 Novem-ber to send German bombers to mine the Canal[2] as an alternative to reaching it from the East through Turkey and Syria.[3]

Base services in the Middle East, as an undeveloped theatre of war, had necessarily to be more extensive than elsewhere, to the increasing concern of Churchill from September 1940 over the small proportion of fighting men in the total forces in the region. Main depots were established in the Tel el Kebir–Kassassin area. A supply depot was established at El Firdan, an am-munition depot at Abu Sultan, airfields at Abu Sueir and a repair-station for the Fleet Air Arm at Fayid. As a port of entry to that developing isthmian base Suez proved incapable of handling traffic suitable only to a great port such as Alexandria. Its limited dock and railway facilities increased the delay in unloading shipping and thereby the amount of tonnage locked up on the Glasgow–Suez route. It also created in Suez Bay a congested mass of shipping, which remained highly vulnerable to air attack. To ease the strain on the port and reduce the chaos of its docks to order, deep-water berths were built between June 1940 and January 1941, doubling its capacity. Lighterage wharves were built along the Canal and a railway marshalling yard at Port Said.

The Board of the Canal Company announced on 1 October an increase in Canal dues of 2s. 3d. per ton, or of 39 per cent, to 8s. from 1 January 1941 so as to compensate for the decrease in traffic. The Government of Egypt there-upon reserved its rights on 19 October and made that increase the last for the whole war. The Company's revenue declined from £8,000,000 in 1939 to £800,000 in 1940. At the end of 1940 the board decided to send to Algiers a large part of the Company's liquid assets in France and so removed them thenceforward from German control. The Government of Egypt demanded and obtained from 1 January 1941 a share in the defence of the Canal. In January 1941 it imposed a moratorium on the payment of bond-interest by the Company. That proclamation was the more objectionable to bondholders

[1] *Brassey's Naval Annual* (1948), 140, 'Fuehrer Conferences on Naval Affairs', 26 Sep-tember 1940.   [2] Ibid., 146, 156.
[3] L. Hirszowicz, *The Third Reich and the Arab East* (London, Routledge, 1966), 95.

because the Mixed Court of Appeal in Alexandria had given final judgment on 26 February 1940 in favour of the bondholders and against the Company. Its decision that bonds should be paid interest on the basis of the gold franc had made the Canal Company almost alone in the world in having a gold debt and had produced an immediate rise in the price of its bonds.

The start of a British counter-offensive in Libya on 9 December 1940 inspired Hitler to order the German Air Force on 10 December to Sicily,[1] from which it closed the Mediterranean to through-traffic. The bombing of the Mediterranean Fleet's sole aircraft-carrier on 10 January deprived the Fleet of fighter-cover, left it helpless against air attack and compelled the Admiralty on 12 January to order the carrier *Formidable* from the South Atlantic around the Cape to Alexandria. The movement of the German Air Force to the Dodecanese enabled them to make their first raid on the Canal on 17 January, leaving unexploded bombs in the fairway and holding up traffic for twenty-four hours. After the British captured Tobruk on 22 January German aircraft from Sicily via Rhodes made the most successful raid of the war on the Canal on 30 January. Guided by a former German pilot of the Canal Company they dropped eleven parachute mines in the navigation channel and nine on the banks between Ismailia and Suez. Those mines defied detection because they were a new delayed-action type of acoustic-magnetic mine. They wreaked havoc which was wholly unanticipated and caused thirteen days of stoppages and accidents between 30 January and 11 February. They destroyed four vessels in four days (3–6 February) and damaged a fifth. The fairway was reduced in consequence from 197 feet to 85 feet in width and the draught of vessels in transit from 34 feet to 26 ft. 3 in. Above all, the passage of the *Formidable* to Alexandria was prevented, diverting Cunningham's attention from Malta and bringing him to inspect the Canal on 10 February.[2] Thereafter Egyptian sentries came into employment from 13 February. A second minelaying raid suspended navigation for a further nineteen days from 18 February to 9 March. A Canal Security Conference on 21 February considered proposals for the protection of the waterway, including the idea of a net. Reinforcements arrived after a further heavy attack on 22 February and made possible the establishment of observation-posts at fifty-yard intervals from 24 February.

The highly successful air attacks on the Canal seem to have precipitated the decision at a secret meeting of the board in Paris to transfer full control to the British directors comprising the London committee under a vice-president, Sir Harrison Hughes, who had been the first English shipowner to succeed his father on the board in 1920. That committee established effective control of the Company,[3] replaced the board during the period of the

---

[1] *Brassey's Naval Annual* (1948), 167.

[2] A. B. Cunningham, 312.

[3] Hansard, *Commons Debates*, 21 October 1942, 1941–2, Eden in reply to Hannah. *The Times*, 25 January 1946, 9vi. *New York Times*, 20 January 1945, 3v.

occupation of Paris and prevented Germany from influencing the operations of the Company in any way. It managed the Company's affairs for nearly three years in the same spirit as that of the Paris directors and protected the essential interests of the Company while pursuing the board's traditional policy in the general interest of the Allies. Egypt's aspirations to establish control of the Company were also encouraged, especially after the dissolution in 1940 of the Commission of the Public Debt. The complaints of the bond-holders were voiced in the Egyptian Parliament on 25 February and 4 March 1941, when the Government was urged to take over the Company if it continued to default on the payment of the interest on its bonds. The Prime Minister, Hussein Sirry Pasha, was the uncle of Farouk by marriage and as true a friend of the Company as of England. His father Sir Ismail Sirry Pasha had been Egypt's first fully-qualified Minister of Works and the third Egyptian Commissioner with the Company from 1919 to 1937. Hussein defended the Company in the Egyptian Parliament[1] as effectively as Sir Kingsley Wood did in the English Parliament.

After the *Formidable* squeezed through the Canal on 7 March to reach the Fleet at Alexandria renewed attacks closed the waterway for a further eleven days from 11 to 22 March and hastened the manufacture of a protective net in Moascar. The hazards of the British expedition to Greece were considerably increased because over fifty ships were needed to move 68,000 British troops to Greece between 4 March and 24 April when all the troopships lay south of the Canal. Over a hundred ships were held awaiting discharge in Suez Bay, delaying cargo of all kinds, especially coal for the Greek railways, fuel oil for the Fleet and war materials for Greece and Turkey. Thus it became necessary further to increase the capacity of the port of Suez and to provide unloading places for ships other than the Canal ports. In order to limit the strain on the Canal it was decided to develop the port of Suez to its utmost capacity, to double the railway between Suez and Ismailia, to develop Attaqa, eight miles south-west of Suez, as a lighterage port, to enlarge Akaba and link it with the Hejaz Railway and to lay a pipeline along the whole length of the waterway so that up to 1,000 tons of fuel oil could be pumped daily from near Suez to Port Said and tankers for the Fleet would not need to enter the Canal. Those extensive works were essential to convert an interoceanic highway into a local feeder route for the expanding military base.

Rommel counter-attacked on Cyrenaica on 31 March, seven days before the German invasion of Yugoslavia and Greece. He benefited by the diversion of forces to Greece and drove the British back to the frontier of Egypt by 11 April, regaining in eleven days what Wavell had won in fifty. The speedy elimination of Italian power in Ethiopia by South African and Indian troops removed the Italian threat to the eastern half of the Suez route and enabled Roosevelt to reopen the Red Sea to American shipping on 11 April. It even enabled American convoys to reach Greece direct through the Canal but

---

[1] *New York Times*, 26 February 1941, 6 iv; 6 March 1941, 4 ii.

aroused American distrust of Britain's imperial purposes in maintaining its long line of communications to the Middle East. It also engendered excessive optimism about the security of the British position in the Middle East and encouraged Churchill to impose four other simultaneous campaigns on Wavell, beginning with the expedition to Greece. The fall of Athens on 27 April forced the U.S.A. to contemplate the possible loss of Suez by Britain, the resulting closer attraction of Spain and France within the German orbit[1] and the passage of the whole Gibraltar–Suez route to the Axis. As long as Britain held Suez, however, Franco could resist German pressure to declare war because he might plead that it was useless to close one end of the Mediterranean while the other remained open.[2] The Chiefs of Staff recommended to Churchill on 7 May that the Canal should be blocked if it proved necessary to abandon it.[3] Ceaseless attacks on the waterway from 8 to 11 May suspended traffic for twenty days (8–27 May) while the German invasion of Crete on 20 May achieved a striking success for air-power. On 11 May Roosevelt assigned thirty American ships to carry Lend-Lease cargo along the 15,534-mile route from New York to Suez, which was reached on 17 May by the giant Cunard liners and the *Ile de France* for the first time in history, with the second convoy from Australia. The Axis gained a great triumph when the British evacuated Crete on 31 May: they moved their air-bases southward to the island and vastly increased their threat to the Canal, 400 miles to the south. The Greek fleet of over one million tons came over to the Allied side and supplied 12 per cent of the Canal's tonnage in 1941. The decline in British prestige throughout the Middle East encouraged the Iraqi nationalists to risk open conflict with British forces, necessitated the diversion of an Indian brigade from Malaya to Basra on 18 April so as to secure the western sea-approach to India and compelled Eden publicly to express on 29 May the Government's sympathy with Arab aspirations for independence.

Mussolini proposed to Hitler in May that German forces should capture the Canal through Turkey. He agreed with Hitler at the Brenner Pass on 3 June on a supreme effort to close the Mediterranean by the seizure of Gibraltar and Suez in order to counteract possible U.S. intervention. Britain raised its Middle East forces from nine to fourteen divisions to oppose the expected attack by the Axis. A special Cabinet Minister for Middle East Affairs, appointed on 28 June as a political commissioner, created a local Middle East Defence Committee and reorganized the Middle East Supply Centre by November 1941 so as to economize in shipping and divert Egypt's resources from production for export to war-production. Wavell was also replaced on 5 July as G.O.C.-in-C., Middle East, by Auchinleck, whose baptism of fire had been on the Canal in February 1915. During July more mines were

[1] *The Times*, 29 April 1941, 3 iv; 9 June 1941, 4 v.
[2] E. L. Woodward, *British Foreign Policy in the Second World War* (London, H.M.S.O., 1962), 127, The Spanish Ambassador to Eden, 8 May 1941.
[3] J. R. M. Butler, *History of the Second World War. Grand Strategy* (London, H.M.S.O., 1957), ii. 579.

laid by air in Suez Bay as well as along the Canal, adding greatly to the delays to shipping. Suez harbour became the object of a supreme attack on the night of 13–14 July when 135 ships lay there at anchor and the largest liner, the White Star Line's *Georgic*, was sunk.[1] Cunningham thereupon decided that only one of the four great Atlantic liners might be allowed in Suez roads at one time and even then only during the day.[2] Further steps were taken to ease the strain on Suez and the Canal. A large volume of non-essential goods lying at the port was carried by army lorry into the desert to form the 'Suez Dump'. The small lighterage port of Safaga beyond the air-range of the enemy was expanded and linked to the Nile valley by an improved road to Keneh. Deep-water berths were begun at Adabiya Bay as well as at Safaga while Port Sudan was also prepared for emergency use. Defended anchorages were provided at Abu Zenima and Gemsa in case Port Tewfik became unusable. The boom in Suez encouraged the establishment of the Suez Chamber of Commerce in 1941.

Syria passed under Allied control after the occupation of Iraq. Troops embarked at Port Said and landed in Syria on the night of 7–8 June[3] at the same time as a British column advanced from Iraq along the pipeline. Vichy France lost its dominion in the Levant together with its consulate in the Canal Zone which had thitherto co-existed with the Free French Forces in Port Said. The establishment of a form of Anglo-French condominium in Syria shifted the defence of the Canal 250 miles northwards and helped to counterbalance the gains made by the German invasion of Russia. It also made possible a survey for a strategic railway between Palestine and Syria, so as to facilitate the rapid movement of troops from the Delta against a possible German invasion through Turkey and to complete the missing link between Haifa and Tripoli during the eclipse of France.[4] Air-raids on the Canal Zone reached their peak between July and September 1941 when thirty-three raids were made, or three per week, against weak defences. Long-range Focke-Wulf even penetrated in September some distance down the Red Sea to threaten the security of the reserve anchorages south of Suez. By 3 August three miles of the waterway had been covered by a suspension-net, which was designed to catch parachute-mines and to protect the vulnerable Chalouf cutting, where dredging round a wreck was impossible because of the rock. That net was extended over six miles between the Bitter Lakes and Suez, being drawn across the Canal each evening by a special naval unit.[5] By the time of its completion parachute-mines had been abandoned so that the net became an indicator-net, encouraging the Italians to drop blocks of salt which created the impression of a mine but condemned the

[1] C. Dewhurst, *Limelight for Suez* (Cairo, Schindler, 1946), 133–4.

[2] A. B. Cunningham, 403.   [3] Ibid., 397, 422.

[4] O. Lyttelton, *The Memoirs of Lord Chandos* (London, Bodley Head, 1962), 243.

[5] D. V. Duff, *May the Winds Blow! An Autobiography* (London, Hollis, 1948), 354–70, 'Work on the Suez Canal'. R. G. Mills, 'The Net', *Blackwood's Magazine* (November 1958), 387.

defenders to search in vain for what the water had dissolved while traffic remained held up. During 1941 the Canal was closed to through-traffic by forty-eight air-raids for a total of eighty-two days, or for nearly one-quarter of the year.[1]

British and Russian troops invaded Iran on 25 August 1941 and secured the abdication of Reza Shah. Middle East Command was extended to include Persia as well as Iraq from 5 January 1942. After Rommel launched his second counter-offensive on 21 January 1942 British fortunes reached their lowest ebb[2] after reverses in Cyrenaica as well as in the Pacific and attacks on Alexandria and Malta. The increased probability of an Axis victory encouraged Farouk to dismiss Hussein Sirry Pasha because he had broken off relations with Vichy France without his approval. The 'Satrap of the Middle East' was as determined as the British ambassador to prevent a return to power of Aly Maher[3] and sent light tanks and infantry through the gates of the Abdin Palace at 9 p.m. on 4 February. A deed of abdication had been drafted by Monckton, the road to the Canal was cleared for the waiting cars and a cruiser lay ready to bear the 22-year old monarch into exile.[4] That *coup d'état* forced Farouk to accept a Wafd Ministry under Nahas Pasha. It followed the coups of 1941 in Afghanistan, Iraq, Syria and Iran as the tactical necessities of war compelled the Allies to sacrifice their long-term to their immediate interests. The humiliation of Egypt in the person of her king proved as far-reaching as the enforced abdication of Ismail had been in 1879. Although the Egyptian coup was kept secret until 1946, it destroyed the moral foundations of the Anglo-Egyptian alliance of 1936 and undermined the British position in the Delta. It turned the officers of the Egyptian Army against the Wafd and even inspired Farouk to seek support against the Wafd in the cause of Arab unity. Immediately it encouraged Raeder to recommend to Hitler on 13 February an attack on Egypt and the Canal because 'Suez and Basra are the western pillars of the British position in the East'.[5] Hitler agreed to launch an offensive against Egypt and Persia in order to link Germany and Italy with Japan and to complete the Axis unity of the Mediterranean. Auchinleck expressed his fear on 23 February lest a German advance across the Caucasus might make possible a drive through Persia and Turkey on the Persian Gulf and Suez Canal: he secured the increase of the Middle East Command to twenty-three divisions in March.

The Canal remained relatively free from attack in January and February[6] when German plans were dislocated by a Russian winter offensive. It

---

[1] C. B. A. Behrens, *Merchant Shipping and the Demands of War* (London, H.M.S.O., 1955), 241.

[2] A. B. Cunningham, 437, 515.

[3] O. Lyttelton, *The Memoirs of Lord Chandos*, 223, 275–6, 278.

[4] Duff Cooper, *Old Men Forget* (1953), 308.

[5] A. Martienssen, *Hitler and his Admirals* (London, Secker, 1948), 123. *Brassey's Naval Annual* (1948), 264, 266.

[6] A. B. Cunningham, 445, 447.

suffered renewed attack in March, April and May when the maximum permissible draught was reduced from 18 May from 34 feet to 32 feet, before Rommel's panzers lunged on Hitler's orders for Cairo and Suez on 27 May. The fall of Tobruk, 200 miles from the Canal, on 21 June was a great disaster for the British and encouraged Hitler to believe that Rommel might capture Egypt and the Canal without the conquest of Malta. It compelled Churchill to send 50,000 troops on a fast voyage in twenty-two transports from Glasgow to Suez and even to contemplate accepting the aid of a U.S. Armoured Division specially trained in desert warfare in California. Auchinleck ordered on 25 June a withdrawal to the superb defensive position prepared at El Alamein under Wavell in 1941 while Mussolini received from Libya on 27 June the password which was to be sent only when the Italian troops were certain of their advance up to the Canal.[1] Mussolini immediately ordered the seizure of Suez and the closing of the Canal. Auchinleck disagreed with the South African general who urged withdrawal into the wilderness behind the Canal.[2] He issued orders on 28 June for the defence of Alexandria and Cairo. He prepared for a last-ditch defence of the Delta and the Canal, for an ultimate withdrawal if necessary from the Delta southwards down the Nile towards the Sudan as well as eastwards into Palestine and for a transfer of G.H.Q. from Cairo to Gaza.[3] The Mediterranean Fleet retreated from Alexandria to Haifa, Port Said and Beirut but was forbidden by the Admiralty to pass southwards through the Canal. Churchill and Roosevelt decided, like Arabi in 1882, to destroy the Canal rather than allow it to pass under enemy control and to block it so effectively that it would require six months to reopen.[4] Air H.Q. Egypt moved from Cairo to Ismailia on 1 July and was joined there the next day by Admiral Harwood and his operations staff, although the French Admiral at Alexandria refused to sail his ships through the Canal to an American port without orders from Vichy. The fellahin expected land-reform on the arrival of the Germans and a run took place on the banks, the note issue of the National Bank of Egypt reaching a peak on 4 July. Suez shares dropped from 25,000 francs to 23,000 francs at the end of June and then to 21,000 francs in the first week of July, a decline of 16 per cent. 'The battle for Suez is now joined. The movement towards Suez constitutes the right arm of the pincers, while the left reaches deeply into the Ukraine.'[5] Germany's drive into Russia, however, divided its war-effort between two fronts and deprived Rommel of support. After Auchinleck repelled him at El Alamein on 2 July Suez shares recovered between 6 and 20 July by 5,200 francs or by 25 per cent to 26,200 francs as well-informed French investors concluded that the Canal would not change

    [1] M. Muggeridge, *Ciano's Diary, 1939–1943* (1947), 488, 21 July; 490, 23 July 1942.
    [2] J. A. I. Agar-Hamilton and L. C. F. Turner, *Crisis in the Desert, May–July 1942* (Cape Town, Oxford University Press, 1952), 276.
    [3] I. S. O. Playfair, *The Mediterranean and Middle East* (1960), iii. 334.
    [4] R. E. Sherwood, *Roosevelt and Hopkins. An Intimate History* (New York, Harper, 1948), 595, quoting Roosevelt to Marshall, 30 June 1942.
    [5] *The Times*, 30 June 1942, 5 ii, 'The Threat to Suez'.

hands.[1] The sixty-fourth air-raid on the Canal on 27 July reflected the failure of the Axis Powers which once more sought to destroy what they could not capture. The crisis had been the most acute of the whole war and compelled the American Chiefs of Staff to inform Churchill on 24 July that they thought the British Empire was making too many sacrifices to maintain an indefensible position in the Middle East, which they ranked in the lowest of all priorities.[2] English propaganda stressed the value of Malta rather than that of the Canal which both German and Italian publicists ranked as the key to empire in the Mediterranean, the Middle East and Africa. Axis propagandists emphasized the egoism of British policy[3] and the high finance behind the Canal Company.[4] They even discovered in 1941 a German project of 1792 for the Canal which when completed had become 'the Ulster of Anglo-Egyptian difficulty'.[5]

The crisis in the Middle East followed the rapid expansion of Japan in the Pacific and the opening of a third front for the British Empire. The destruction of the United States Fleet at Pearl Harbour enabled Japan to conquer without hindrance in twelve weeks Hong Kong, Manila, Singapore, Batavia and Rangoon, so destroying the British, American and Dutch island-empires. The destruction of European prestige begun in 1905 was carried a stage further, so liberating Asia from the cultural as well as the military dominion of the West, whose withdrawal was symbolized by the departure of the C.P.R.'s White Empresses of the Pacific after fifty years. Australia was forced to withdraw its troops from the Middle East, which England refused to sacrifice to the Far East. The frontier-march of South-East Asia Command was garrisoned from 1943 against Japan, creating a new strategic unity of 'South-East Asia' comparable to that of the 'Middle East'. Shanghai was replaced by Colombo and Cocos as the most easterly cable station of Cable and Wireless Ltd., the successor to Pender's Eastern Telegraph Company. The Japanese flag was excluded from the traffic of the Canal after 1941 until 1951. The oil, tin and rubber of Sumatra, Java and Malaya were diverted from Europe to Japan, encouraging the U.S.A. to produce synthetic rubber from oil, nylon in place of silk and paludrin in place of quinine as well as the soya bean. Fast long-distance U-boats also carried tin, rubber, wolfram and molybdenum to Germany and so created a submarine route around the Cape, whose surface waters were dominated by the Allies. Six German U-boats also operated against Allied commerce from Penang. Madagascar was occupied by Allied forces between 5 May and 23 September 1942 to deprive Japan of a possible base for action against the sea route to Suez and Basra.

[1] *The Times*, 15 July 1942, 3 iii; 22 July, 3 ii.

[2] W. L. Langer and S. E. Gleason, *The Undeclared War, 1940–41* (London, Oxford University Press, 1953), 591.

[3] A. Sammarco, 'Come l'Inghilterra ha impedito la Definizione e il Funzionamento di un securo regime giuridico internazionale del Canale di Suez', *Oriente Moderno* (Dicembre 1942), 485–98.

[4] G. Herrmann, *Der Suez-Kanal* (Leipzig, Goldmann, 1941), 77–84. R. Huber, *Der Suez-kanal einst und heute* (Berlin, Junker, 1941), 87–8.

[5] H. L. Stewart, 'The Suez Canal in World Politics', *Dalhousie Review* (April 1942), 46.

The German threat to the Canal and even more to the Delta inspired Churchill to fly to Cairo, where he decided on 6 August to replace Auchinleck and to transfer him to a new Middle East Command of Persia and Iraq separated from a new Near East Command by an impossible administrative boundary along the Canal.[1] The waterway was bridged at El Firdan by a steel railway swing-bridge which was built in June 1942 and opened on 7 August, so sacrificing the original function of the Canal to local imperial necessities as in 1918. That bridge replaced the Kantara Ferry for the railway and linked up with the 175-miles railway built between Palestine and Syria so that a through-journey became possible from Cairo to Beirut.[2] Kantara East became the terminus of the alternative route from India via Basra, Bagdad and the pipeline to Haifa. It was also linked by the first railway line along the Asian bank of the waterway to El Shatt, which became a lighterage port and relieved Suez and the Canal of traffic for Palestine. The strain on the Canal was also eased by the construction of a Cairo–Suez pipeline. The strategic unity of the original Middle East of 1902 was revived by the development of a supply-route to Russia via the Persian Gulf. After the U.S.A. created the Persian Gulf Service Command on 11 August 1942 the oil of the Gulf was freed from the rigid price-control established in 1928 through the formula 'U.S. Gulf plus'. The Persian Gulf became the centre of a separate marketing territory and its oil prices were cut by almost two-thirds. From 1942 the U.S. Navy was supplied by Caltex with bunker fuel at a price below U.S. Gulf quotations. From 1943 the British Navy was supplied with bunker fuel from Abadan at an f.o.b. price equal to the U.S. Gulf f.o.b. price.[3] The emancipation of the Persian Gulf from the price-control of the U.S. Gulf permitted a large-scale expansion of the Abadan Refinery, especially for the manufacture of aviation fuel, so as to replace the lost oil of Burma and the Dutch East Indies. That expansion combined with the closing of the Japanese market to petrol from Europe to reduce the Canal's southbound cargo of petrol and refined oil products.

The full tide of the war turned against the Axis in the autumn of 1942. At the second battle of El Alamein Montgomery, endowed with a Napoleonic sense of the importance of morale, decisively defeated the Axis bid for the dominion of the Middle East. The Axis then lost the initiative after the Anglo-American invasion of North Africa on 8 November and the Russian break-through at Stalingrad on 19 November. After the liberation of all North Africa from Dakar to Suez the French Admiral at Alexandria brought his squadron over to the Allies but sent his heaviest ships via the Canal and the Cape to Dakar. The Allied victory was won on the land but reopened the sea-route from Gibraltar to Port Said from the end of April. The Gibraltar–

[1] A. Bryant, *The Turn of the Tide 1939–1943. A Study Based on the Diaries and Auto-biographical Notes of Field Marshal The Viscount Alanbrooke* (London, Collins, 1957), 444, 448.

[2] *The Times*, 15 August 1942, 3 iv.

[3] W. A. Leeman, *The Price of Middle East Oil: an Essay in Political Economy* (Ithaca, Cornell University Press, 1962), 91–3.

Alexandria convoy of 17–26 May 1943 became the first since 1940 to be free from incident. The first unopposed convoy reached Malta on 24 May. From 4 June Mediterranean insurance-rates fell below those of the Cape route by 2·5–5 per cent for the first time since 1940 and the traffic of the Canal began to revive. Middle East Command became thenceforward a base and transit-centre and, above all, a training-centre for warfare in Europe. Thus the invasion of Sicily was rehearsed in assault craft which sailed from Suez on 10 June to land 23,000 troops on 13 June on the shore of the Gulf of Akaba. At Suez 46,500 troops were embarked in the three days from 29 June to 1 July for the invasion of Sicily on 10 July. A rehearsal by Indian troops in the Gulf of Suez for landing on Japanese-held islands in the Pacific made the Canal Zone also a training-centre for warfare in the East. The conquest of Sicily by 17 August enabled the Mediterranean to be fully reopened to shipping and Suez shares to bound upwards to 60,000 francs. The reopening of the whole Canal route coincided with a revisitation of plague to Suez in November 1943, Ismailia in March 1944 and Port Said in May 1944.

The war had depressed the traffic of the Canal much more severely than the Great War. Shipping tonnage had fallen by more than half in 1940, by 39 per cent in 1941 and by 15 per cent in 1942 to 7,027,763, or the lowest tonnage since 1890, representing a reduction of 80 per cent from the pre-war level against the reduction of 58 per cent in the trough of 1917. The waterway had lost its second, third, fourth, fifth and seventh largest clients in Italy, Germany, the Netherlands, France and Japan, which had together supplied 38 per cent of the total tonnage in 1938. British tonnage declined in 1942 to its lowest level since 1887 although its share rose from 51 per cent of the total in 1939 to 68 per cent in 1941. The Greek flag ranked second to that of Britain in 1941–2 but was replaced by the U.S. flag from 1943. The Company made only one increase in its tariff, unlike the four increases in 1916–17. It was forced to suspend the payment of dividend and interest as well as to use up its reserves, which had equalled one-quarter of its annual receipts by 1938. Its receipts for 1942 were 36 per cent of those for 1938. The Cape route had re-established its supremacy over the Suez route and had been used by 400 convoys of a million tons of shipping and 6,000,000 men, although German submarines sank 133 ships of the 155 lost in South African waters. The traffic of the Canal began to revive from 1943 when its tonnage rose by 40 per cent, a rate of increase known before only in 1871 and 1919. The resumed military use of the waterway increased the number of passengers from the all-time low point of 590 to 173,269 and markedly expanded the local tonnage of Port Said from 1943. The restriction upon draught to a maximum of 32 feet was lifted after 28 October 1943. The Canal's tonnage recovered to 34 per cent of its prewar level in 1943, to 55 per cent thereof in 1944 and to 76 per cent thereof in 1945 when receipts first exceeded the level of 1938.

The war had been fought partly for rights of transit through and dominion over the Middle East, which had been a major and not a minor theatre of war as in 1914–18. The region had been unified on a strategic basis as never before through the creation of Middle East Command in 1939, a Cabinet Middle East Committee in 1940, the Cabinet Minister for Middle East Affairs in 1942 and the Middle East Supply Centre in 1942. Homage had been paid increasingly to the Arabic culture of the region through the foundation of the Arab News Agency in 1941, the Near East Broadcasting Station in 1942 and the Middle East Centre for Arabic Studies in 1944. Within that strategic unity the Canal had lain at the very axis of empire between 1940 and 1942 so that Vogüé inferred that the Canal might even have been 'the whole stake of the struggle'.[1] From 1940 to 1942 the Canal was defended for its military, not for its economic, value: from 1943 to 1946 it served as a great military highway. The Canal Company in Egypt had collaborated much more fully and openly with the Allies than it had during the Great War. The Canal Zone itself had become a vast military base with 150 depots, of which the greatest at Tel el Kebir had a circumference of twenty-eight miles.[2] The construction of that base in defiance of the Convention of Constantinople turned to advantage the central location of the Canal within the Middle East as a whole for operations against Africa, Asia or Europe, its convenient double-approach by sea, its structure of internal communications and its access to the resources of the Delta. In building up such a state within the state Britain had made the Canal more vital than ever[3] but had inevitably exceeded the limitation on the numbers of troops and on the area occupied imposed by the Treaty of 1936. She had reinforced her occupation of the Delta and had thrice intervened to prevent the exercise of Egyptian power against her own interests. She had also destroyed the Italian menace to Egypt's security which had compelled Egypt to conclude the Treaty of 1936. She had prevented a land-reform under German auspices and had become as odious to the fellah as the Turk had been. Thus the war destroyed the basis of British rule as the 1914–18 war had destroyed the basis of Ottoman rule and seemed to entitle Egypt to ask for the evacuation of British troops as a reward for her war-time services.

Britain was wholly unprepared to entrust the defence of the Canal to any international authority or to abandon her newly regained empire, whose defence had become a purely British responsibility in place of the joint Anglo-French commitment envisaged in 1939. Britain had defended the region with the aid of India, Australia, the U.S.A. and South Africa, which was won over to the defence of the Canal as Australia had been during the Great War. She seemed nevertheless to have fought both great wars from start to finish by her own power. She had incurred large wartime debts to the U.S.A. while India had accumulated sterling credit-balances of £1,020,000,000 and Egypt balances of £325,000,000. The Middle East theatre had given Britain her sole independent victory of the war and her sole British hero-general. The Middle

---

[1] *The Times*, 25 January 1946, 9vi, Marquis de Vogüé's Report for 1945.
[2] Ibid., 8 May 1946, 3i, 'Defence of the Suez Canal. Alternative Stations Available'.
[3] F. Cox, 'The Suez Canal', *National Review* (May 1944), 417–18.

East had been a particular focus of interest for Eden, Macmillan and, above all, for Churchill. The last of the paladins saw the region as the basis of Britain's position as a Great Power and had preserved it at the expense of Singapore and of a very high turn-over of generals. He was disturbed by the conferences held after Yalta by Roosevelt in the U.S. cruiser *Quincy* in the Great Bitter Lake on 12–14 February 1945 with Farouk, Ibn Saud and Hailie Selassie and prevented the substitution of the American 'Near East' for 'Middle East' in official nomenclature in 1945.[1] The region had become the focus of memory for a whole generation of British soldiers[2] who joined in the annual democratic Alamein Anniversary Dinner from 1945[3] in the inspiring belief that the Mediterranean and Middle East had been the hinge of victory and that the Suez Canal had been almost as important as Britain itself.[4] Although their experience in the region had been even more limited than that of British officials they could not believe that the war-created unity of the region should dissolve. The military basis of Middle East Command even seemed the best possible foundation for a wider unity of the whole region.[5] Thus the Middle East Supply Centre sponsored the Middle East Agricultural Development Conference of Cairo in 1944, became the British Middle East Office in 1945 and appeared a potential basis for a Middle East Bank and a Middle East Customs Union.

The British Empire in the Middle East had however been undermined by the rise of the great land-powers, the withdrawal of American support, the resumption of Russian expansion and the rebirth of Asia between 1905 and 1943. The land-powers had devalorized sea-power, extending the range of their aircraft to close the Mediterranean to warships without air-protection and reducing the strategic importance of the Suez Canal below that of the fortified Panama Canal. Asia moreover regarded the war as a civil war fought for empire over the world outside Europe and aspired to establish its own independence from Europe and its imperial ambitions, its programme of collective security under Western policemen, its gospel of economic progress and its white liberalism which was strictly 'limited to West of the Suez Canal'.[6] The wider use from 1943 of the phrase 'west of Suez' after its earlier use in 1907, 1929, 1930 and 1938 commemorated the Allied battle for the Mediterranean[7] but also revealed the opposition of Asia to the white man's

[1] Lord Rennell of Rodd, 'Address at the Annual General Meeting', *Geographical Journal* (March 1946), 85–6.

[2] Lord Strabolgi, *From Gibraltar to Suez* (London, Hutchinson, 1941). C. B. Brown, *From Suez to Singapore* (New York, Halcyon House, 1943).

[3] A. P. Thornton, *The Imperial Idea and its Enemies* (1959), 330–1.

[4] A. Bryant, *The Turn of the Tide, 1939–1943* (1957), 244.

[5] W. B. Fisher, 'Unity and Diversity in the Middle East', *Geographical Review* (July 1947), 414–35.

[6] Lin Yutang, *Between Tears and Laughter* (New York, Day, 1943), 18, 'The Emergence of Asia'.

[7] The Admiralty, *East of Malta West of Suez. The Admiralty Account of the Naval War in the East Mediterranean. September 1939 to March 1941* (London, H.M.S.O., 1943), also in French and Spanish).

aspiration to resume his burden of empire in the East.[1] The victories of Japan over Europe in Asia had made the 'rimland' rather than the heartland the key to world dominion.[2] They had been facilitated more by indigenous discontent than by the closing of the Suez route and encouraged a new recognition of the Canal as an Egyptian achievement,[3] as well as the strongest link in the chain binding India to Britain.[4] Egypt's aspirations to independence revived as the war receded from her frontiers and were embodied in the explicit demands of her political leaders for the evacuation of British troops, the union of the Sudan with Egypt and the establishment of full control over the Canal.[5] The greatest American historian of the Canal denied however that the waterway was a great asset and recommended the establishment of an international canal commission to avoid leaving Egypt with 'one of the most ponderous of white elephants'.[6]

Egypt's hopes were frustrated by the re-establishment of the Canal Company on its prewar basis, despite rumours that a large number of shares had been acquired by Germany and Russia.[7] The administrative H.Q. of the Company were transferred from London back to Paris in December 1944, more than two years before Royal Dutch-Shell returned to The Hague. Thus ended the tripartite division of administration between London, Paris and Châtel-Guyon. The membership of the board was reorganized more thoroughly than it had been in the crisis-years of 1870 or 1893. Seven French directors resigned and were succeeded by men chosen for their patriotism as well as for their economic interests, such as Marcel Lebon and Ernest Mercier. To enable those new directors to acquire the necessary shares, the director's qualification was reduced from 18 December 1945 from 100 to 25 shares. Apart from that sweeping change in the directorate the Company resumed the prewar pattern of its existence. Vogüé continued to preside over it as he had during its greatest ordeal and restored its highly centralized administration. No change in administrative personnel took place. Michel Homolle, Assistant General Manager from 1926 to 1945, became General Manager when George Edgar-Bonnet, General Manager from 1935 to 1945, succeeded his father as a director in 1945. The interests of France necessitated the restoration of the Company as they necessitated the nationalization of the great economic fiefs of the State in France itself in 1945. The Company was recognized as an Egyptian company[8] which had enjoyed a return of 67·2 per cent between 1928

---

[1] J. S. Badeau, *East and West of Suez: the Story of the Modern Middle East* (New York, Foreign Policy Association, 1943).

[2] N. J. Spykman, *The Geography of the Peace* (New York, Harcourt, 1944), 40–3.

[3] K. K. Ardaschir, 'The Marriage of the Seas. The Tale of the Suez Canal' in G. Orwell (ed.), *Talking to India* (London, Allen, 1943), 58–64.

[4] K. M. Panikkar, *India and the Indian Ocean. An Essay on the Influence of Sea Power on Indian History* (London, Allen, 1945), 72.

[5] *New York Times*, 9 September 1944, 9i.

[6] H. L. Hoskins, 'The Suez Canal and the Outlook for Egypt', *American Political Science Review* (February 1944), 117. [7] *New York Times*, 20 January 1945, 3v.

[8] R. Vaux, 'A Legal Curiosity', *Law Quarterly Review* (July 1944), 227–9.

and 1939 on its capital of £7,600,000.[1] It was not however conjoined with nor supplanted by an international canal commission. Nor was it bought up by the World Bank on behalf of the United Nations, as Henry Morgenthau, the U.S. Secretary of the Treasury, had recommended. Nor was the Canal placed under the control of the United Nations as Truman proposed at Potsdam in order to persuade Russia to accept international control of the Straits.[2] From the beginning of 1946 the resumption of communications between France and Egypt enabled the Company to return to its peacetime organization. Its wartime ordeal in German-occupied Paris was obliterated from memory with the same facility with which the Company represented the Canal as having suffered interruption of navigation for only seventy-six days,[3] although the Canal route had been closed for at least thirty-two months. The Company's successful re-emergence was almost as miraculous as the transformation of France itself into a victor-Power. Its moral basis had nevertheless been weakened by the ambiguity of its wartime status and its shares remained much below the average level of French shares from 1944.

The growth of Zionist ambitions in Palestine encouraged the creation in 1944 of the Arab League, which seemed to offer Britain a new Egyptian vehicle of influence in the Arab world but aroused deep-seated French fears and hostility. French fears seemed justified when French troops were forced under British pressure to evacuate Syria and the Lebanon in 1946. Egypt and the isthmus of Suez became thenceforth the last remnant of the French Empire in the Levant. The French colony of the isthmus under the leadership of two officials of the Canal Company, Alfred Fontaine and Jean-Édouard Goby, formed the Society of Historical and Geographical Studies of the Isthmus of Suez, which was the first learned society of the region and held its first meeting at Ismailia on 6 January 1946. The isthmus was then in process of administrative integration into Egypt. Both the Public and the State Domain for the provinces of the Canal and of Suez were merged with those for Charkia from the beginning of 1946 while the Municipality of Port Said became wholly Egyptian. The Company had appointed its first Egyptian pilot in 1944 and Mahmoud Fakhry, the son-in-law of King Fuad and the ambassador to France from 1922 to 1945, to its board of directors in 1945. It also admitted its readiness to increase its Egyptian staff, Egypt's share in its profits and the privileges of Egyptian coastal navigation.

After the wartime moratorium on the Company's debts lapsed on 1 February 1946 the Egyptian Government drew up a bill which confirmed its decree of 2 May 1935 nullifying gold clauses in international contracts and allowed the Company to discharge its payments due between 1935 and 1946 on the basis of the official price of gold in London on each due date. The

---

[1] M. M. Hamdi, 'A Statistical Survey of the Development of Capital Investment in Egypt since 1880' (Ph.D. Thesis, London University, 1943), 8, 344.

[2] H. S. Truman, *Year of Decisions 1945* (London, Hodder, 1955), 304, 22 July; 313, 26 July 1945.

[3] *The Times*, 25 January 1946, 9 viii.

bondholders however claimed payment by the Company on the basis of the commercial price of gold on the Egyptian market on each due date, which would increase coupon payments substantially, especially in the case of the coupons due in 1944, 1945 and 1946. The Mixed Court of Cairo considered that the Company's enormous resources could well bear a considerable increase in payments of bond-interest and authorized on 20 May 1946 payment on the basis of the price of gold in Cairo for the period after 22 June 1940. The Company condemned that judgment as contrary to equity and to reason because it sanctioned the gold price of a local and restricted market lacking the international status of London or New York. Because its reserves would be inadequate to meet the payments ordered the Company postponed the payment of dividend as distinct from the statutory interest and threatened to consider raising the Canal dues above the existing rate of 8s. per ton. From 1 July 1946 it paid its arrears of statutory interest for the period from 1940 to 1945 on the basis of the Egyptian franc excluding the gold basis until the outcome of an appeal to the Mixed Court of Alexandria.[1]

That legal judgment reflected the rising tide of Egyptian opposition to the British occupation, encouraged by the growth of American interest in the Middle East and exacerbated by Britain's rejection on 26 January 1946 of the formal request made on 20 December for the evacuation of British troops and for the end of the restrictions on Egyptian sovereignty imposed by the Treaty of 1936. After Sidky Pasha became Prime Minister for the first time since 1933 a general strike took place in Cairo on 21 February accompanied by anti-British riots in which the demand for immediate evacuation first emerged as a popular slogan. In the riots in Port Said the bust of Lesseps erected in 1895 in the Place de Lesseps was destroyed. The Labour Government hoped to replace the Treaty of 1936 by a military alliance which would permit the use of Palestine and Sinai as a regional H.Q. for the Middle East. Attlee's unexpected announcement in the Commons on 6 May that the Government had decided to withdraw its forces from Egyptian territory by negotiation with the Government of Egypt alarmed opinion in Australia, New Zealand and South Africa.[2] It also provoked a storm of Conservative protests, especially from Churchill. 'Things are built up with great labour and cast away with great shame and folly.'[3] Churchill argued that only the presence of troops in the Canal Zone could safeguard the Canal as a treaty right of re-entry could not. Eden affirmed that the British troops were in Egypt for an imperial, an Anglo-Egyptian, a world purpose rather than for a purely British one. 'The issue of the security of the Canal is still a matter which concerns us and cannot be ignored or prejudged, however strong Nationalist feeling may be.'[4] Sir Ian Fraser, a director of Frasers Ltd. of South Africa, suggested that the advent of the atomic age might necessitate a strategic reappraisal in favour of the Cape

---

[1] *The Times*, 22 June 1946, 8vi; 30 July, 10i–ii.   [2] Ibid., 10 May 1946, 3i.
[3] Hansard, *Commons Debates*, 6 May 1946, 782, Churchill.
[4] Ibid., 852, Eden.

route for imperial purposes. 'It may be that what we should defend now and henceforth is not so much the Canal as Durban.'[1] That debate emphasized the defence of the Canal rather than of Egypt or the Middle East, the role of the Canal in world rather than in imperial strategy and the function of Egypt as 'the hub of the strategic centre of the globe'.[2]

Field-Marshal Montgomery arrived in Egypt on 10 June as C.I.G.S.-elect and decided that the Delta might be evacuated in 2-3 months as Bevin wished but the Canal Zone only within five years and that Britain might still dominate the Mediterranean without holding Egypt from Libya, the Sudan, Transjordan, Cyprus and, above all, Palestine.[3] From the summer of 1946 British troops and stores began to move into Southern Palestine while camps were built at Rafa as a forward base. The Zionists had begun large-scale military operations against the British from 9 October 1945 and resorted to terrorism from 22 July 1946.[4] Although Egypt refused to lease territory in Sinai between the Canal and the frontier of Palestine the Bevin–Sidky Agreement of 25 October 1946 provided for a phased withdrawal from the Delta by 1 March 1947 and from the Canal Zone by September 1949 and for a joint advisory council for common defence. The negotiations had been opposed from the start by the Wafd and the Moslem Brethren: the agreement was rejected by Egyptian opinion in its fixed determination to regain 'southern Egypt' and to eliminate all trace of the occupation of 1882. Nokrashy Pasha, who succeeded Sidky, decided on 25 January 1947 to submit the dispute to the United Nations, i.e. to the U.S.A. Eisenhower sympathetically depreciated the potential value of the Canal in wartime to the Secretary-General of the Arab League and reportedly said 'I can destroy it from Chicago.'[5] Attlee's challenge in January 1947 to the classification by the Chiefs of Staff of the Middle East as a vital 'main support area' produced their private threat of a joint resignation inspired by Montgomery.[6]

The British evacuation of Alexandria on 14 February 1947 raised the garrison of Palestine to 100,000. The evacuation of Cairo on 31 March ended the occupation begun in 1882 and encouraged Britain to push the Sudan towards independence. It withdrew British troops from their dangerously exposed location in the Delta to the more defensible position of the Canal Zone and restricted them to the limits laid down in the Treaty of 1936. It transferred the H.Q. of Middle East Command to Fayid, caused no strategic reappraisal of the Canal[7] but provoked a sarcastic enquiry in the Commons for some

---

[1] Hansard, *Commons Debates*, 6 May 1946, 873, I. Fraser.

[2] Lord Altrincham, 'The Nation of the Nile', *National Review* (June 1946), 461. C. Falls, 'The British Commonwealth and the Middle East', *Illustrated London News*, 18 May 1946, 538. *The Times*, 16 May 1946, 5 vii, 'Planning Empire Defence'.

[3] B. L. Montgomery, *The Memoirs of Field-Marshal The Viscount Montgomery of Alamein* (London, Collins, 1958), 421-2.

[4] Hansard, *Commons Debates*, 1 August 1946, 1256, Churchill.

[5] *The Times*, 3 January 1952, 4 iii.   [6] Montgomery, *Memoirs*, 435-6.

[7] R. la Bruyère, 'Le Canal de Suez dans la Stratégie Planétaire', *Revue Hommes et Mondes* (Décembre 1947), 544-52.

assurance that the Government's Canal shares would not be offered to the Russian Government.[1] It also identified the Canal Company more than ever before with the occupying power. The Egyptian Companies Law of 20 January 1947 required 40 per cent or thirteen of the Company's directors to be Egyptian within three months from 29 July 1947 and 75 per cent of its personnel to be Egyptian within three years. Thus the Government combined its attack on the British occupation with one on the Company, which deemed the law inapplicable to itself and won the support of Levantine opinion in Egypt. An Egyptian pupil of C. K. Webster popularized in Arabic and English the hostile tradition developed by Sabry, emphasized the economic disadvantages of the Canal to Egypt and blamed it for the loss of her independence.[2] In France a hostile study of the Company as a monopoly[3] was largely submerged beneath the traditional emphasis on the benefits of the Canal to the world.[4] The Company won a favourable judgment on 17 May from the Mixed Court of Appeal at Alexandria, which recognized the useful function of an international money of account of fixed value, invalidated the judgment of the Cairo Court in 1946 and ruled that the gold franc was to be converted into Egyptian currency through the intermediary of the dollar, so enabling the Company to pay the accumulated balances of twelve years to the bondholders from 15 June 1947.

Egypt's Note of 28 May to the diplomatic missions in Cairo requested ten days' notice from any power proposing to send warships through the Canal. That Note produced no protest against the end of the era of unrestricted transit inaugurated by Ismail: it prevented Britain from converting the Canal Zone into a naval as well as a military base. Egypt also requested in the financial negotiations opened in London on 6 June the transfer of the British shares in the Canal Company in part payment of her war credits. Egypt's withdrawal from the sterling area on 15 July took place under the agreement of 30 June and destroyed the bond established in 1885 between the Egyptian pound and the pound sterling. It compelled the Canal Company to decide that its tariff would be shown only in Egyptian pounds and piastres from 2 September 1947 in order to secure exemption from Egyptian foreign exchange regulations.[5] Egypt then appealed to the Security Council on 8 July to end the British occupation. Britain claimed that the Treaty of 1936 would remain in force until 1956 and that the presence of British troops in Egypt was no threat to peace but was necessary to guard the Canal. Egypt failed on 28 August to gain the necessary two-thirds majority vote and was thus forced to choose between unilateral denunciation and the resumption of direct negotiations. England announced

[1] Hansard, *Commons Debates*, 24 April 1947, 1258–9, Waldron Smithers.

[2] M. Rifaat, *The Awakening of Modern Egypt* (London, Longmans, 1947), 125, 130, 136.

[3] R. and J. Nousbaum and G. Hutchings, *Compagnie Universelle du Canal de Suez* (Paris, Clermont, 1947).

[4] J. Dautry, *Le Percement de l'Isthme de Suez* (Paris, Bourrelier, 1947), 66–7. A. Siegfried, *Suez, Panama et les Routes Maritimes Mondiales* (Paris, Colin, 1940, 1948; London, Cape, 1940, 1948), 21, 194.

[5] R. R. Baxter, *The Law of International Waterways* (Harvard University Press, 1964), 58–9.

on 13 September the decision to transfer the main military stores depot for the Middle East from the Canal Zone to a supplementary base in Kenya and withdrew its military mission from Egypt in December. Thus growing insecurity in Egypt and Palestine forced Britain out to the periphery of the Arab world.

On 1 March 1948 Vogüé died in office at the age of eighty and was succeeded by François Charles-Roux (1879–1961). The new President was the son of Jules Charles-Roux who had become a director of the Canal Company in 1889, a vice-president in 1896 and its historian in 1900 as well as the Chairman from 1904 to 1918 of the Compagnie Générale Transatlantique. François had gained diplomatic experience in Petersburg (1902–4), and in Constantinople (1905–7). In Cairo between 1907 and 1912 he found the agency of the Canal Company ranked as a second French Embassy and made it his second home.[1] He served in London from 1912 to 1914 under Paul Cambon and in Rome from 1916 to 1925 under Camille Barrère. He began to publish studies of Franco-Egyptian history from 1908.[2] Therein he related the prehistory of the Suez Canal as a French design[3] and emphasized the independence of the isthmus of Egypt and its association with the Indies rather than with the Nile.[4] After service on the International Commission of the Danube in 1925–6 he became Minister Plenipotentiary to Prague from 1926 to 1932 and Ambassador to the Holy See from 1932 to 1940, when he became head of the French Foreign Office for the first five months of the Vichy regime. He became a member of the Institut d'Égypte and was elected to the Academy of Moral and Political Sciences of the Institut de France in 1934. His illustrated diplomatic history of the Suez Canal as a Franco-Egyptian achievement[5] was written with the aid of the works of Douin and Sabry as well as of the research he had done for his father's history.[6] Charles-Roux was elected a director of the Canal Company in 1944 at the age of sixty-five and President on 6 April 1948 at the age of sixty-nine, the oldest President-elect in the history of the Company. As President he pursued his labours as an historian of the French era in the Levant[7] and stressed the instrumental function of the Company which enabled it to fulfil Egypt's predestined role as a link between the continents.[8]

[1] F. Charles-Roux, *Souvenirs Diplomatiques d'un Âge Révolu* (Paris, Fayard, 1956), 185, 199.

[2] Idem, *La Production du Coton en Égypte* (Paris, Colin, 1908). Idem, *Les Origines de l'Expédition d'Égypte* (Paris, Plon, 1910). Idem, 'Le Capital Français en Égypte', *Égypte Contemporaine*, ii (1911), 465–502.

[3] Idem, *Autour d'une Route. L'Angleterre, l'Isthme de Suez et l'Égypte au XVIIIe siècle* (Paris, Plon, 1922).

[4] Idem, 'L'Isthme de Suez et les Rivalités Européennes au XVIe siècle, *Revue de l'histoire des colonies françaises* (Avril–Juin 1924), 153–92. Idem, 'Le projet français de commerce avec l'Inde par Suez sous le règne de Louis XVI', *Revue de l'histoire des colonies françaises* (Juillet–Décembre 1925), 411–49, 551–618. Idem, *L'Angleterre et l'Expédition Française en Égypte* (Paris, Plon, 1925).

[5] G. Hanotaux (ed.), *Histoire de la Nation Égyptienne* (Paris, Plon, 1936), VI, *L'Égypte de 1801 à 1882*, 229–332, 'Le Canal de Suez—L'Œuvre de Mohamed Said et d'Ismail Pacha'.

[6] J. Charles-Roux, *L'Isthme et le Canal de Suez* (1901).

[7] F. Charles-Roux, 'France, Égypte et Mer Rouge, de 1715 à 1798', *Cahiers d'Histoire Égyptienne* (Janvier 1951), 117–95. Idem, *Thiers et Méhémet-Ali* (Paris, Plon, 1951).

[8] *Le Canal de Suez*, 15 Juin 1948, 9229.

PART V

THE ARAB RENAISSANCE, 1948–1956

34

THE RISE OF THE ARABIAN OIL TRADE OF AMERICA, 1945-1951

THE traffic of the Canal was transformed more rapidly after the end of the war than at any previous time by the growth of the oil exports of Saudi Arabia and Kuwait, which increased the trade of the Canal faster than that of the world as a whole but concealed the slow recovery of trade in almost all commodities other than oil. The volume of northbound cargo surpassed that of 1937 in 1947 while that of southbound cargo recovered only slowly and did not surpass the peak pre-war levels of 1929 and 1937 until 1949. The slow recovery of northbound cargo was masked partly by the spate of oil and partly by the two-way flow of sugar, cereals, coal, cotton and manufactured metals. The volume of northbound cargo other than oil surpassed that of 1937 only in 1951. Thus the traffic of the Canal reflected the destruction inflicted on the export-economies of Indo-China and the Dutch East Indies by the war, the occupation and the liberation. The war had cut Asia off from its markets in Europe, reduced agricultural production and encouraged local consumption. It had thereby depressed the export of primary produce, especially of cereals, sugar, oil-seeds and textile fibres, and reduced the importance of the old export-colonies in the traffic of the Canal.[1] The growing pressure of population of the food supplies of Asia also reduced the northbound flow of cereals and left Australia as the great source of northbound wheat: it even produced a southbound flow of cereals and encouraged Egypt to export rice through the Canal to Japan from 1948.

Traffic was reduced most of all by the renaissance of Asia and by the resurgence of its peasantry against the master-races of the West and the civilization of Europe under the stimulus of the meteoric war-time career of Japan. The fountain-lands of millennial culture, India, China, Iran and Egypt, served as the focus of that revival. Their liberation from colonial rule entailed an attack on the economic activity of the West in Asia and a reduction in trade during the period of revolt. The successor-states to the European empires made the old colonial ports into the new national capitals of independent Asia. Those cities survived attempts to transfer the capital to an indigenous inland location and grew even faster after the establishment of independence than before. They remained centres of economic Westernization, concealed beneath a growing verbal onslaught on 'colonialism' and 'imperialism'. The new states sought to develop manufacturing industry so as to make good the

---

[1] M. Homolle, 'Les répercussions de la guerre sur le trafic du Canal de Suez', *Bulletin de la Société Belge d'Études et d'Expansion* (1948), 239-45.

destruction of the war and to achieve economic independence as the complement to political independence. They revered the factory as the great source
of armaments and the symbol of modern civilization. The stimulus given to
industry in Asia by the war was thus reinforced by the postwar upsurge of
nationalism. The resulting increase in the local demand for raw materials
shifted the centre of economic gravity from the ports to the hinterland as well
as from the foreign to the domestic market, decreased the surplus available
for export to the West and reduced northbound shipments of raw materials
such as cotton and of agricultural produce such as oil-seeds. The growth of
industry in Asia also led to the stabilization and even to the decline in southbound shipments of manufactures, first of woven cotton goods and then of
manufactured metals, railway materials, refined oil products and paper. The
Canal however benefited by a growing southbound flow of capital goods such
as machinery, cement, fertilizer and agricultural machinery and by a growing
northbound flow of woven jute bags, cotton textiles, cast-iron and such pro-
cessed raw materials as vegetable oils.

The establishment of the independence of India in 1947 ended the enterprise which had begun at Plassey and had transformed the subcontinent as
had no other revenue-collecting empire in history.[1] Partition restored the
natural division of the Indo-Gangetic plain but divided a united economy
between two states and diverted the energy of both India and Pakistan inwards
into economic reconstruction on a basis of self-sufficiency and in a spirit of
mutual antagonism. India gained most of the industries, the shipping tonnage,
the shipping lines, the shipyards and the ports. Karachi was the only port lost
by India, secured its long-sought independence from Bombay and began an
unprecedented period of growth as the first capital of a new state, despite the
restriction of its hinterland to West Pakistan. As a primary producer agricultural Pakistan became dependent on its exports of raw jute and raw cotton.
Its shipments of raw jute through the Canal were exceeded in 1946–8 by the
shipments of jute sacks from Calcutta. From 1948 however jute importers
turned increasingly from India to Pakistan for their supplies. India became
increasingly industrial and replaced its export surpluses from 1949 by import
surpluses. It became a net importer of cotton through the Canal from 1949,
so creating a southbound flow of the raw material which had provided the
Canal's first northbound cargo in 1870. It lost a market of 70,000,000 for its
cotton textile industry, was compelled to develop the export market to maintain capacity production in its mills and began to ship cotton textiles through
the Canal from 1950. It imposed export quotas on raw jute, because its jute
mills had been cut off from their supply of raw jute from East Pakistan, and
sharply reduced its exports of jute after 1951. It became a net importer of
wheat, creating a southbound flow of cereals through the Canal, especially
from the U.S.A. and the U.S.S.R. from 1948, to replace the lost supplies of

[1] N. V. Sovani, 'British Impact on India after 1850–1857', *Cahiers d'Histoire Mondiale*
(1955), 83.

the Punjab. Even Pakistan became a net importer of wheat in 1948–9. India introduced its first Five-Year Plan in 1950 and concluded barter agreements with the U.S.S.R.: it exchanged its jute and tea for Russian wheat and maize, shipped tobacco to Odessa from 1950 and began the export of iron ore to Russia from 1951.

The shipping lines between England and India were deprived of their security but not of their function. The P. & O. under William Currie, its chairman since 1938 and a director of the Canal Company since 1945, resumed its passenger sailings in May 1947 but without any mail contracts. It launched its last ships with Indian names in 1947 but could not readjust itself rapidly to the loss of the Indian Empire, the leave-traffic and the trooping service as well as to encroachment by competitors from both Europe and Asia on its preserves. The flags of India and Burma appeared in the Canal in 1948, followed by the flags of Pakistan in 1949 and Ceylon in 1953. The establishment of India's independence encouraged the development of substitute sources of supply of the commodities thitherto drawn from the subcontinent. The decline in India's exports of ground-nuts after 1946 stimulated the production of oil-seeds in South-East Asia and Tanganyika. Ceylon suffered by the encouragement given to the production of rubber in Malaya, of coffee in Ethiopia, Uganda and Madagascar and of tea in Turkey and Kenya. India had been displaced by the Persian Gulf in the traffic of the Canal during the war and never recovered its primacy as it increasingly manufactured its own raw materials. Its share in the shipping tonnage of the Canal declined from 20·2 per cent in 1947 to 13·2 per cent in 1948 and to 9 per cent in 1950. The loss of India shattered a whole structure of imperial power but left Britain still in control of the Indian Ocean and increased the importance of East Africa. It undermined the British position in the Middle East, eliminating the original purpose for the British presence and converting that sphere of influence into 'a last barbican of Empire'.[1] The loss of the Indian Army deprived Britain of a central strategic reserve which could operate to either east or west and therefore formed the keystone in the arch of imperial defence. Britain lost its common frontier with Iran and the effective basis of its policy in Iran. The emerging arc of danger centred as in 1902 around the Persian Gulf rather than around the Suez Canal and provoked the first suggestion for the establishment of a northern screen against Russia on the model of N.A.T.O. which would embrace the non-Arab Moslem powers from Turkey to Pakistan.[2] The Canal Company also gained by the election to its board in 1948 of Sir Francis Verner Wylie, who after thirty-four years in the I.C.S. became the first ex-Indian Governor to serve as an official director.

The decline in the exports of edible fats from the two leading producers of India and China was only partly offset by the increase in their export from the Philippines and Ceylon, creating a severe shortage of raw materials for

[1] A. P. Thornton, *The Imperial Idea and its Enemies* (1959), 330.
[2] O. Caroe, 'The Persian Gulf—A Romance', *The Round Table*, March 1949, 131–7.

both the English margarine industry and the French oil-seed industry. Marseilles was compelled to draw its oil-seeds from Senegal rather than from India and to rely less on the Canal than formerly. In England the Ministry of Food sought to obtain cheap food through the Kongwa ground-nut scheme developed in cooperation with Unilever from 1947 as a military operation and conducted first by a managing agency on the Indian model and then by the Overseas Food Corporation created in 1948. That scheme sought to produce short-term returns from a million empty and waterless acres through large-scale mechanization and the cooperation of African labour. The last great effort made by Europeans in Africa independent of African participation was integrated not with the general economic development of East Africa[1] but with an apparent attempt to build up a new India in Africa supported by a strategic base in Kenya, an economic base in Tanganyika and an immense Nile Dam at the Great Lakes. Cement was shipped southwards through the Canal in 1947–9 to Mtwara, 248 miles south of Dar-es-Salaam, to build the new port of Mikindani for the exports which never developed. East Africa's supply of ground-nuts to the traffic of the Canal rose from 3,000 tons in 1947 to 6,000 tons in 1948 and 8,000 tons in 1951 instead of the promised minimum of 600,000 tons. The revival of shipments from India and China, however, reduced their share in the total ground-nut shipments from 8 per cent in 1947 to 4 per cent in 1951.[2] In place of the promised ground-nuts Tanganyika exported sunflower seeds through the Canal in 1948–9 at a cost of £35,000,000 to the British tax-payer. The failure of the scheme saved Tanganyika from complete dependence on the British economy, Unilever and the Suez Canal.

The rise of oil production brought into the traffic of the Canal the two lands of Arabia and the U.S.A which thitherto had always remained marginal to it. The traffic of the U.S.A. through the Canal increased after the United States Navy, merchant marine and tanker fleet rose to world supremacy between 1942 and 1944 and maintained the U.S. flag as second only to the British in Canal traffic from 1943 to 1949. The U.S.A. possessed a huge domestic oil industry and controlled the world price of oil as the largest single producer and consumer. The war had, however, created a tremendous drain on its domestic reserves and increased its interest in the oil reserves of the Middle East, especially since English influence had grown at the expense of American as production closed down in Bahrein and Qatar in 1940, in Saudi Arabia in 1940–1 and in Kuwait in 1942. Standard Oil of California, which had formed the Californian Arabian Standard Oil Company (or C.A.S.O.C.) in 1933 and admitted the Texas Company to partnership therein in 1936, successfully opposed attempts by the U.S. Government to acquire oil reserves in Arabia and to build a pipeline to the Mediterranean to avoid Canal tolls.[3] C.A.S.O.C.

---

[1] K. M. Stahl, *Tanganyika: Sail in the Wilderness* (The Hague, Mouton, 1961), 96–102.

[2] *Supplément au Bulletin Le Canal de Suez*, 15 Juillet 1952, 'Oléagineux et Dérivés dans le Trafic Sud–Nord au Canal de Suez'.

[3] H. Feis, *Seen From E.A. Three International Episodes* (New York, Knopf, 1947), 93–190, 'The Government Gives Attention to the Oil of the Middle East'.

became the great private beneficiary by the estimate of 1944 which revised the possible reserves of Arabia upwards to equal those of the U.S.A., and those of the Middle East from 17 to 37 per cent of the world's total reserves. It renamed itself from 1944 the Arabian American Oil Company (or Aramco). The end of the war made possible the resumption of production on a large scale throughout the Middle East. The increase of production in the Persian Gulf was facilitated by the equalization from 1945 of Persian Gulf prices with U.S. Gulf prices for the U.S. Navy, so removing the plus from the 'Gulf-Plus' formula of 1928. Aramco adopted the idea of a cost-cutting Trans-Arabian Pipeline (or Tapline) to the Mediterranean and began full operation at its Ras Tanura refinery from December 1945 in order to supply the continuing needs of the U.S. Navy.

The eruption of nationalism in Iran in 1946 after three years of competition for oil concessions by Russian interests, Royal Dutch-Shell and Jersey Standard compelled Anglo-Iranian to build up its production from Kuwait and Iraq. On 30 June 1946 the British Tanker Company's *British Fusilier* loaded the first commercial shipment of Burgan crude oil at the new oil-port of Mina al Ahmadi for the British Petroleum Company's Refinery at Grangemouth. Thus Kuwait began to export the oil which it had discovered in 1938. It supplied the British market with sterling oil and expanded its shipments through the Canal even faster than Saudi Arabia. During 1946 British Canal tonnage first surpassed the levels of 1938 and 1929, shipments of crude oil first surpassed the record volume of 1927 and oil first exceeded half of the volume of northbound cargo. The election of Sir Hubert Heath Eves (1883–1961) brought to the board of the Canal Company in 1946 the representative of its largest client. Eves had been General Manager in India of the Burmah Oil Company and Representative in India of Anglo-Iranian before he joined Anglo-Iranian in London in 1921. He served as its Managing Director from 1924 to 1941, as its Deputy Chairman from 1941 to 1950 and as the chairman of the Tanker Tonnage Committee of the Petroleum Board from 1940 to 1946.

The Iraq Petroleum Company began the construction of a second parallel pipeline to Haifa and Tripoli in October 1946 in order to supplement the pipelines built in 1932–4 and to anticipate the construction of a Trans-Arabian pipeline. Thereupon the two American member companies of the Iraq Petroleum Company declared the anglocentric Red Line Agreement of 1928 dissolved so that they might be free to enter the oil industry of Saudi Arabia. The sharp rise in Saudi production and reserves required wide markets and enormous capital which could not be readily supplied by the alliance of California Standard and Texaco. Jersey Standard desired access to Saudi supplies of low-cost crude free from output regulation so as to strengthen its position in the home market against the war-swollen independent producers and began discussions for the purchase of an interest in Aramco on 4 September 1946. The completion of the contracts signed in 1947 to give Jersey

Standard and Socony an interest in Aramco and Tapline was, however, held up by the objections of the Compagnie Française des Pétroles which unlike the Canal Company had been declared an enemy alien corporation by Britain in 1941. The proposal by the U.S. Secretary of State Marshall in 1947 that the U.S.A. should help to revive a working economy in the world was intended to solve Europe's postwar dollar-shortage, to end the British drain on the Caribbean sources of oil-supply and to preserve them as a strategic reserve for future use by the U.S.A. The Marshall Plan enabled the American oil companies to supply Western Europe with oil from the Middle East and began a new era in the extension of American influence in Europe as well as in the Middle East. Jersey Standard thereby sought to gain a share of Middle East oil proportionate to its dominant position in the oil industry of the world.[1] The independent producers secured in self-defence the suspension of the export licences necessary for the steel pipe for Tapline. Eight independents also founded the American Independent Oil Company (or Aminoil) in August 1947 for the particular purpose of foreign oil operations, especially in the Middle East. The regular shipment of oil from the Middle East to the U.S.A. began with the shipment of fuel oil from Bahrein through the Canal in June 1947 to Norfolk, Virginia, and with the first shipment of oil direct from Saudi Arabia in September 1947. During 1947 U.S. imports and exports of oil balanced as internal consumption grew and the U.S.A. imported 4·7 per cent of the volume of oil carried through the Canal while France imported 10·8 per cent and Britain 21·6 per cent. Some of those imports were carried under the flag of Panama, which increased its Canal tonnage tenfold and rose from the tenth to the fifth client-flag of the Company.

The Labour Government increased the British demand for oil as a deliberate policy to solve the social problem of the coal-mining areas and to offset the shortage of fuel felt acutely in the cold winter of 1946–7: it authorized in 1948 the construction of new refineries at the ports to process imported crude. The Economic Cooperation Law of 3 April 1948 stipulated for the purchase from the dollar aid granted to Europe of oil and oil-products from sources outside the U.S.A. as well as for their transportation by American shipping. The European Recovery Programme assumed that Western Europe would import half the oil produced by the Middle East at falling prices. The production of oil responded to the new American-financed demand of Western Europe and made its largest single increase since the birth of the oil industry in the Middle East. The daily average of oil-tanker transits through the Canal first exceeded the number of transits by other ships in March and April 1948. For the year as a whole tankers supplied fourteen out of the daily average of twenty-five transits. During 1948 total transits first exceeded their 1929 level while tanker tonnage rose by 101 per cent, northbound oil cargo by 109 per cent and net register tonnage by 50·6 per cent in a rate of increase which first

[1] J. A. Loftus, 'Middle East Oil: the Pattern of Control', *Middle East Journal* (January 1948), 20–1.

surpassed the records of 1880–1. Crude oil shipments through the Canal which had risen by 125 per cent during 1947 increased by 197·5 per cent during 1948 while oil production in the Middle East rose by 36 per cent. Thus crude oil nearly trebled in volume, assuming the first place in Canal shipments in October 1947, December 1947 and from March 1948 for the first time in thirty years. Northbound shipments of oil, which had been dominated successively by petrol (1907–21), crude oil (1922–5), petrol (1929–36) and fuel oil (1937–47), reflected the gathering momentum of the largest flow of crude in the history of the industry. Oil first supplied more than half of the volume of the total Canal cargo and 73 per cent of that of northbound cargo. From 1948 oil dominated the shipping, cargo and revenue of the waterway and therefore also its operation and improvement. The Persian Gulf, which had risen from the third client-region of the Canal in 1939 to the first during the war and supplied more than half of the Canal's cargo from 1946, became the focus of more than half of the Canal's shipping tonnage from 1948. The rate of expansion of exports from Kuwait and Saudi Arabia was treble that from Iran, despite the allocation of dollars to Britain for the purchase of oil from Iran and Iraq. Iran supplied for the first time less than half of the Canal's oil shipments and lost its primacy as Saudi Arabia rose to second place and even surpassed Iran in its volume of Canal shipments during December 1948. From 1947–8 the oil of the Middle East was thus diverted from the markets of Asia to those of Europe, and its trade from the orbit of Russia into that of Western Europe. The full significance of that fundamental change was not recognized until 1956. The oil shipped through the Canal became of far greater military than economic importance because it fuelled the forces of N.A.T.O. by land, sea and air. The beginning of the Cold War thus gave the U.S.A. a strategic interest in the Middle East and halted the British movement out to the periphery of the Arab world, making the air-bases of the Canal Zone more important than the Canal itself. The Marshall Plan encouraged the reactive consolidation of Soviet influence in Eastern Europe, which was symbolized by the liquidation in 1948 of the Danube Commission, the last vestige of the Crimean policy of the West.

The Middle East was a low-cost producer, like Baku, with a high ratio of fields discovered to the area explored, a high proportion of producing wells to wells drilled, a very high yield per well from huge reservoirs of thick beds at low depths as well as under high pressure and a long life-cycle of primary production per well.[1] Export was facilitated by the proximity of the fields to the seaboard and by the ease of access to the sea offered by the Gulf. The prices of Middle East oil which had risen more slowly and more gently than U.S. Gulf prices since 1946 began to decline from May 1948, partly under the pressure of the Economic Cooperation Administration.[2] Prices at Ras

[1] R. C. Julien, ' Le Pétrole dans l'Économie du Moyen-Orient', *Revue de Droit International pour le Moyen-Orient* (Mai 1951), 54–5.
[2] W. A. Leeman, *The Price of Middle East Oil: an Essay in Political Economy* (1962), 143–4.

Tanura became the new basis from June 1948 for the computation of all Persian Gulf f.o.b. prices for crude.[1] Between June 1948 and September 1949 prices declined by 21·2 per cent and were equalized for Western Europe in 1948 between the Persian Gulf and the Gulf of Mexico. The price of Middle East and Venezuelan crude was however equalized on the basis of delivery in New York through the allotment of a theoretical freight rate between New York and London for tanker companies delivering Middle East oil in Western Europe, so as to protect the domestic oil industry of the U.S.A. at the Persian Gulf rather than at the U.S. border. During 1948 the U.S.A. reduced its share in world production below 60 per cent for the first time in forty years and became a net importer of oil. It increased its share of the oil carried through the Canal from 5 per cent in 1947 to 16 per cent in 1948, raised Panama from the fifth to the third largest client of the Canal with 9·4 per cent of the total tonnage and helped to reduce the British share therein from 63 per cent in 1946 to 47 per cent in 1947 and 37 per cent in 1948. Canada also began to import oil via Suez from 1948 so that the East–West flow of oil began to exceed the West–East flow in volume. The heavy American traffic encouraged the American purchase of Suez shares from 1948 and led the Canal Company to elect its first American director, with more readiness than it had shown to elect an Italian director in 1937–8. Somerville Pinckney Tuck had been Deputy Consul in Alexandria between 1913 and 1920, Envoy Extraordinary and Minister Plenipotentiary to Egypt from April 1944, and the first American Ambassador to Egypt from 1946 to 1948. His unanimous election to the board in place of a Frenchman disturbed the New Zealand-born Labour back-bencher Platts-Mills, who would have preferred a British citizen to an American and asked ' Is this part of the price we have to pay for the Americans giving us a little charity?'[2] The oil shortage in the U.S.A. made North America for the first time the largest single destination for oil shipped through the Canal in November and December 1948, its imports exceeding those of Britain and France. As home production caught up with demand during the mild winter of 1948–9 the U.S.A. reduced its imports of oil. World oil consumption was also slightly reduced during 1949, while oil shipments through the Canal continued to soar so that the total shipping and cargo tonnages of the Canal both exceeded the record levels of 1929. Shipments of oil from America to Europe sank by nearly a quarter as the oil-shed between the two Gulfs crossed the Atlantic.

Control of the oil of the Middle East was redistributed so that each member of the cartel of seven gained access to its vast reserves. Jersey Standard and Socony were finally freed in 1948 to complete their acquisition of an interest in Aramco in return for higher quotas of Iraqi crude to the Compagnie Française des Pétroles.[3] Their acquisition of shares in Aramco on 2 December 1948

---

[1] H. J. Frank, *Crude Oil Prices in the Middle East* (New York, Praeger, 1966), 33–4.
[2] Hansard, *Commons Debates*, 21 June 1948, 934, Platts-Mills.
[3] J. Rondot, *La Compagnie Française des Pétroles* (Paris, Plon, 1962), 91–100.

gave that company the greatest distributing organizations in the world while it opened to California Standard and Texaco the markets to the west of Suez without the uneconomic ordeal of competing for them.[1] The construction of the Trans-Arabian pipeline was facilitated by the entry of Jersey Standard into Aramco and by the resumption of the export of steel pipe from the U.S.A on 26 February 1949 after $20\frac{1}{2}$ months. American influence was further extended into the oil industry of Arabia by the grant to Aminoil in 1948 of the Kuwaiti concession in the barren and uninhabitable Neutral Zone between Kuwait and Saudi Arabia and by the grant to J. P. Getty in 1949 of the Saudi concession therein. The quest for those concessions had been stimulated by the expansion of Kuwait's production. Kuwait was estimated on 6 January 1949 to have 14 per cent of the world's reserves against the 11·4 per cent of Saudi Arabia and assumed first place in Canal oil shipments in March, May, July and August 1949. By the end of the year Mina al Ahmadi was in full operation, with the largest tanker-loading pier in the world and a refinery completed in November 1949 to supply furnace-oil and marine diesel-oil to tankers loading there with crude.

The rise of American oil production in the Middle East disturbed the balance of production in the U.S.A. and the balance of payments of Britain. Oil imports into the U.S.A. aroused the opposition of the independents, the coal interests and the railroads. Texas served as the balance-wheel for home production and Texas interests proposed from May 1949 a quota on foreign imports. That quota almost became mandatory under the Simpson bill which failed to become law by a single vote in 1951. In the sixteen states united under the Marshall Plan in the Organization for European Economic Cooperation (or O.E.E.C.) oil captured the largest single market of the coal industry as industry replaced transport as the fastest growing market for oil and the consumption of fuel oil first exceeded that of petrol from 1949. In England American oil increased to form 30 per cent of the oil marketed as Esso and Mobil petrol spread in competition with that of Shell and B.P. The dollar-content of 75–80 per cent of its price made it the largest single drain on the dollar reserves of the sterling area and exacted a heavy price for the increasing use of oil as the rise of American power diverted investment from the pound to the dollar. The Exchange Control Board could not stop that diversion of investment but began from the end of June 1949 to curtail the import of American oil together with all other dollar imports[2] while the Organization for European Economic Cooperation decided in July 1949 to co-ordinate refinery expansion in its member-countries. After the devaluation of the pound sterling on 18 September 1949 the domestic price of fuel in Britain rose by 34 per cent and the Government took steps to replace U.S. oil by British oil

---

[1] B. Shwadran, *The Middle East, Oil and the Great Powers* (New York, Praeger, 1955), 349–52.

[2] H. Mendershausen, *Dollar Shortage and Oil Surplus in 1949–1950* (Princeton University Essays in International Finance No. 11, November 1950), 15.

throughout the sterling area, raising the shipment of oil through the Canal from September 1949 and provoking strong protests from the American oil companies affected in their exports. As sterling oil replaced dollar oil in British imports, Kuwait assumed the lead from Saudi Arabia as well as from Iran in oil shipments through the Canal in January, April, May and July–December 1950. Qatar supplied another source of sterling oil from the Dukhan field which had been discovered in 1939 but was only brought into production between 1947 and 1949 by a subsidiary of the Iraq Petroleum Company, the Qatar Petroleum Company, to which Anglo-Iranian had transferred its concession under the Red Line Agreement. Its oil was first exported on the last day of 1949 across the peninsula to the deep-water anchorage of Umm Said. Qatar shipped the bulk of its production through the Canal from January 1950, its exports exceeding in volume those from Bahrein from 1951. The five Anglo-American oil agreements concluded between 23 May and 18 July 1950[1] effected substantial reductions in the dollar-content of imported oil. Jersey Standard agreed on 26 May to expand the capacity of its Esso Refinery at Fawley fivefold while Aramco agreed on 7 July to pay up to 25 per cent of its royalties in sterling. Thus Britain gained the largest refinery in Europe in that opened at Fawley on 14 September 1951, an economic interest in its protectorates in the sheikhdoms of Kuwait, Qatar and Bahrein, a potential interest in all the other sheikhdoms of the Gulf and a new stake in the Canal despite the withdrawal of British troops in 1946 from Iran and Iraq and in 1947 from India.

The rise of Arabian and Kuwaiti production transformed the oil trade of the Canal with unprecedented speed. Wealth shifted within the Middle East from the fertile crescent to the infertile crescent of the Gulf, placing the inland fields of Iraq at a growing disadvantage. The Gulf became the major region in the traffic of the Canal. Its massive export surplus was balanced by the import surplus via the Canal of India, the Far East and East Africa while its demand was stimulated for building materials, machinery and cement as well as for the traditional sugar. The extension of oil production along its geosyncline shifted its trade more than ever from the southern coast of Iran to the eastern shores of Arabia. It thereby shattered Iran's monopoly of the oil production of the Gulf and diverted the bulk of the foreign trade of Saudi Arabia and Kuwait through the Canal in addition to that of Iran. Of the three great centres of production Kuwait became most dependent on the Canal through which it never shipped less than 90 per cent of its production. Iran ranked first in the volume of its oil shipped through the waterway until 1949 when it was first surpassed by Kuwait as well as by Saudi Arabia and ranked third. Its share in the Canal shipments of oil was reduced from 53 per cent in 1947 to 30 per cent in 1950 while the share of Saudi Arabia rose from 17 to 29 per cent and that of Kuwait from 15 to 33 per cent.

Within Arabia the centre of gravity began to shift from the Hejaz towards

[1] H. Mendershausen, 30–1.

the Gulf, which formed the peninsula's main outlet to the sea because of the mountains restricting access from the west. The Saudi fields of the province of Hasa were developed faster than any other fields in the recorded history of the oil industry. Saudi Arabia's entry into the modern world was symbolized by the foundation of the Mecca Chamber of Commerce in 1948, the establishment in 1948 of direct radio-cable communication between New York and Jedda, the introduction of both an income-tax and a national anthem in 1950 and the completion between 1947 and 1951 of the railway from the capital of Riyadh to the oil-port of Dammam. The Saudi flag even increased its transits of the Canal from four in 1947 to fourteen in 1950. The survey parties of Aramco began to penetrate from 1948 into the sheikhdoms of the Trucial coast east of Qatar in competition with those of the Iraq Petroleum Company. In 1949 Saudi Arabia proclaimed its right to the subsoil and sea-bed adjacent to its coasts as the U.S.A. had done in 1945 and Iran a fortnight beforehand. It thereby anticipated the discovery in 1951 of the first submarine oilfield in the Persian Gulf, which it began to transform into the Arabian Gulf. Thus the U.S.A. began a new phase in its imperial expansion at the expense of Britain.

Along the seaboard of the Gulf the commercial civilization of the West was planted through a new series of oil-ports which developed as tanker terminals from Umm Said and Ras Tanura to Mina al Ahmadi, Fao and Abadan, with long jetties reaching out to deep water through the shallows of the western shores. The oil industry brought to the most undeveloped country of the Middle East the most advanced capitalism of the West and the mysteries of an uncomprehended technology. The oil companies undertook an immense investment of capital and developed the export trade to serve the market of distant Europe in utter isolation from the economic life of the locality and region. Their activity created very few jobs for the local population, inhibited rather than fostered Arab entrepreneurship and failed to diffuse the secondary benefits of manufacturing industry. They became closely associated with the kings, the sheikhs and the pashas rather than with the Arab people to whom their industry appeared as the very type of alien exploitation by a parasitic alliance of Western producer and consumer. They made gross profits estimated at 75 per cent of the total Persian Gulf price for oil,[1] paid niggardly royalties and rapidly depreciated the ledger-value of their investments.

The Middle East increased its share in the world production of oil from 5·9 per cent in 1938 to 12 per cent in 1948 and 16·5 per cent in 1950 when it displaced the Caribbean as the leading exporter of oil. The Canal's share in the world production of crude oil rose from 0·6 per cent in 1946 to 6·7 per cent in 1950. The Middle East which had supplied 19 per cent of Western Europe's needs of oil in 1938 and 25 per cent in 1946 increased its share to supply 67 per cent in 1950 and 69 per cent in 1951 as it approached the proportion of 80 per cent desired by the Economic Cooperation Administration. Oil from

[1] J. E. Hartshorn, *Oil Companies and Governments* (London, Faber, 1962), 99–100.

the Middle East replaced coal from Europe in the imports of Mediterranean ports, increasing their dependence on the Canal. England became the largest single market for the oil of the Middle East and raised its imports of crude from 5 per cent of the volume of its total oil imports in 1945 to 47 per cent in 1950. The British Tanker Company doubled its tonnage between 1945 and 1949 and maintained its primacy as the leading client of the Canal. Anglo-Iranian became the largest single overseas investment in British commerce and the most profitable of all British foreign investments. The import of oil increased as the mining, consumption and export of coal declined under the influence of the full employment and rising wages of postwar Europe. The decline of the coal industry encouraged Schuman's proposal in 1950 for a European Coal and Steel Alliance. The U.S.A. protected its own high-cost oil industry from the competition of oil produced at one-third of its cost while Britain failed to protect its own high-cost coal industry. The U.S.A. reduced its exports of oil to Europe and increased its share of Middle East oil production from 12 per cent in 1945 to 44 per cent by the end of 1950 but retarded the full expansion of oil production in the Middle East. Thus the centre of oil production was not displaced from America. The Middle East became less important for its production than for its reserves which rose from 37 per cent of the world's total reserves in 1944 to 45 per cent in 1950.[1] The high proportion of reserves to production limited the need for expensive exploration by the oil companies. The rise of the oil trade nevertheless doubled the share of the Canal in the volume of world trade in general from 6·8 per cent in 1947 to 13·2 per cent in 1950.

Oil was highly suitable to transportation by tanker and to international trade as a cheap bulk commodity which was highly portable but could not be stored for long because of the cost of containers and the risk of deterioration. The expansion of the oil trade and the rise of tanker traffic established the supremacy of tramp over liner shipping in the traffic of the Canal. It increased the number of transits in ballast, especially on the southbound voyage, from which tankers returned northwards fully laden. It also increased the number of motor-vessels using the waterway, oil-burners reaching their maximum number of transits in 1950. It helped steadily to increase the average size of vessels, especially of tankers, using the Canal. By 1950 the average Canal tanker exceeded the average tonnage of transiting vessels by 9 per cent, although it remained below the tonnage of the average tanker of the world fleet. The tanker cargo of 47,637,000 tons carried through the waterway in 1950 represented the peak proportion of 21·2 per cent of the total tanker-cargo carried by the world fleet in external trade.[2] Tankers thus established a discontinuous pipeline by sea from the Persian Gulf to Europe. From 1948 tanker revenues became the major source of the receipts of the Canal Company, which itself became a large shareholder in oil companies, especially in

[1] B. Shwadran, *The Middle East Oil and the Great Powers* (1955), 352–3, 435.
[2] *Le Canal de Suez*, 15 Novembre 1952, 'Les navires-citernes au Canal de Suez',

Fig. 2 *The Share of the Oil Trade in the Traffic of the Canal, 1939–1955*

	1939	1946	1950	1951*	1955
Shipping tonnage of the Persian Gulf as a proportion of total Canal tonnage	18·1	30·0	63·9	57·3	64·1
Tanker tonnage as proportion of total Canal tonnage	19·8	30·3	63·7	58·2	65·5
Tonnage of crude oil as a proportion of world production of crude	0·06	0·6	6·7	6·06	8·0
Tonnage of crude oil as a proportion of northbound oil	3·2	26·8	73·7	84·0	92·7
Tonnage of northbound oil as a proportion of northbound cargo	29·1	52·6	78·6	72·3	76·5
Tonnage of northbound cargo as a proportion of total cargo	69·5	72·7	83·3	77·3	81·3

* Abadan crisis

Source: Suez Canal Company, *Le Canal de Suez* (*Documents Statistiques*) (1950, 1956).

Royal Dutch-Shell. The rise of Norwegian tanker tonnage made Norway the second client-state of the Canal from 1950. Flags of convenience developed strongly in the tanker traffic such as that of Panama from 1947 and those of Liberia, Honduras and Costa Rica from 1949.

The oil traffic more than compensated for the comparative decline in post-war shipments of non-oil traffic. Oil became the dominant commodity in northbound cargo from 1946 and in total cargo from 1948 while high-priced raw materials maintained the value of the total trade of the Canal. Its growing volume confirmed the dominance of primary produce in northbound cargo and accentuated the disproportion between the volumes of northbound and southbound cargo. The regularity of oil shipments throughout the year reduced seasonal and cyclical fluctuations in traffic, although transits continued to decline between March and May. The sensitivity of the Canal's traffic to the world economic conjuncture was diminished as was the value of that traffic as an index to the trade-cycle. The greater importance of short-haul traffic made the Suez route far more economic than the Cape route but increased pressure for the reduction of tolls on a cheap bulk commodity. The growth of the oil trade enabled the Canal Company to make concessions to shipping in general. The United Kingdom Chamber of Shipping had begun direct consultation over tolls with the Canal Company in 1947, with the support of the American Merchant Marine Institute and the National Federation of American Shipping. The Company agreed to increase from 1 April 1948 the maximum allowance for crew and navigation spaces from 5 to 10 per cent of the gross tonnage under the Constantinople rules of 1873. That concession was achieved by direct negotiations which by-passed the London Committee. After renewed requests in 1949 to allow stewards' accommodation as deductible for tonnage-measurement the Company decided on 10 January 1950 to abolish passenger-dues as an alternative, on condition that the shipping interests did not again raise the question of stewards' accommodation before the end of the concession or before a revision of the rules of 1873. More passengers used the Canal than before the war despite the increase in air-travel and a decline from the postwar record figure of over 900,000 in both 1945 and 1946. Passenger-dues never supplied a revenue comparable to that earned from passenger traffic by railway companies or by mail shipping lines. Their share in total receipts declined from 3 per cent in 1946 to 0·91 per cent in 1948 and to 0·98 per cent in 1949. Their abolition from 15 April 1950 coincided with a large increase in the dividends distributed for 1949 and was followed by a gradual decline in the number of passengers from the 660,000 of 1950. The concession of 1949 especially benefited mail-boats and enabled the Company to postpone a toll-reduction proper for a year.

The Company was compelled to improve the waterway and to extend its facilities so as to cope with the rapid expansion of traffic. It allowed tankers to use floating searchlights from 1947 so as to eliminate their stopping at Port Said on the homeward voyage. It introduced mirror-buoys to reflect the beam of the searchlight and to demarcate the fairway like a main road on land. Above all, it drew up its seventh improvement programme in 1948 as the daily number of ships surpassed twenty-five, the tonnage continued to rise faster than transits as ships became deeper and the maximum permissible draught became exclusive to tankers from 1947. That £5,000,000 five-year programme was the first since the Company's Panama programme of 1921 and planned a general deepening together with the construction of a by-pass canal at Ballah. Such a by-pass would permit a maximum capacity of forty vessels per day and enable convoys to cross in the north at the by-pass as well as in the south in the Bitter Lakes. It would thus eliminate the one-way bottleneck of the first 45-mile section south of Port Said and avoid the passing of tankers with the associated danger of collision and fire. To relieve congestion the Company introduced the convoy system from 24 May 1948, although Port Said had not been designed as a convoy port. From 19 January 1949 it introduced two daily convoys in each direction, increasing the capacity of the waterway and reducing the disturbance to dredgers. The general deepening by 20 in. to 42 ft. 10 in. and to 46 feet in the northern half was completed by 23 July 1951 when the Farouk Canal was opened as a 7½-mile by-pass on the east side of the Canal at Ballah. The dream of 1883 was partly realized for the first time by creating two independent canals. Laden tankers from Suez were given the right of way through the by-pass so that they might proceed northwards non-stop and without deviation while the southbound convoy anchored in the western branch. The Company also sought to facilitate traffic by increasing the permissible speed from $7\frac{1}{2}$ to 8 knots, an increase which proved too damaging to the banks to be maintained above a year from November 1951 to November 1952. It made its first speed tests of water turbulence and bank erosion in 1951 in the Neyrpic hydraulic laboratory at Grenoble on a scale-model of the Canal, sixty-six years after the first scale-model of a tidal river had been built by Osborne Reynolds in Manchester in 1885.

The greatest challenge to the Canal came with the completion of the Trans-Arabian Pipeline in 1951 after the establishment of Israel diverted all Arab oil and pipelines from Haifa. Tapline was intended to replace by a 1,068-mile transit by pipe the 7,200-mile eighteen-day round trip around 'the Island of the Arabs' which was the largest peninsula in the world and half the size of India itself. It was also intended to avoid the Canal dues which were equivalent to a further 1,000 miles of sea-voyage. It was all the more feasible because the oilfields of Arabia were on the east coast rather than on the west coast. It was favoured by the Lebanon but was at first opposed by Syria until the shock of defeat by Israel brought about the first military coup in the modern Arab world. General Zaim seized power in Damascus, was recognized by the U.S. Government and signed the Tapline Agreement on 16 May 1949, six weeks after his coup. Tapline became the world's largest crude-oil pipeline and the first great pipeline to compete directly with ocean tankers and the Canal route. President Charles-Roux recognized it on 13 June 1950 as a serious competitor of the Canal but hoped that its reduction of the Canal's oil traffic would prove only temporary. After the final weld on 25 September 1950 the first oil was carried on 10 November to Sidon, where the first tanker was loaded on 3 December. The shares of the Canal Company thereupon declined in price by 8·3 per cent between 11 and 18 December. The use of the pipeline halved the length of a tanker-voyage, doubling the number of round trips possible per tanker per annum and the tonnage delivered per ton of capacity per annum. Thus it eliminated the employment of 70–80 tankers with 5 per cent of world tanker-capacity,[1] reduced the costs of transport by as much as 63 per cent[2] and created a large differential between prices in the Persian Gulf and prices at Sidon. It reduced single-voyage freights sharply from their 1950 peak and stimulated the development of the competitive capacity of tankers, especially through the creation of the economical super-tanker for the supply of the new refineries under construction in the ports of Western Europe.

The effects of Tapline on the traffic of the Canal were first felt during December 1950 and increased to a maximum by April 1951 as the pipeline reached capacity. Saudi Arabia had ranked first in the oil shipments of the Canal in June 1950 and retained second place to Kuwait from July, but was relegated in December to the third place after Kuwait and Iran. The total

[1] R. C. Julien, 'Le Pétrole dans l'Économie du Moyen-Orient', 57.
[2] W. A. Leeman, *The Price of Middle East Oil* (1962), 109.

volume of oil shipped through the Canal was reduced by 14 per cent in December, but the tonnage of crude oil was reduced by only 10 per cent as Kuwait expanded its shipments. Arabia's shipments via the pipeline first exceeded the volume of its shipments via the Canal in January 1951 and first reached the maximum capacity of the pipeline in April 1951,[1] when its shipments via the Canal sank to one-quarter of their level in April 1950. For 1951 as a whole Arabia reduced its shipments via the Canal by 7,221,000 tons or by 52·3 per cent and its share in northbound oil cargo from 29 per cent of the total in 1950 to 15 per cent in 1951. Shipments from Bahrein also declined by 30 per cent during 1951 because the Bahrein Petroleum Company was a subsidiary of California Standard and had drawn most of the oil for its refinery from Saudi Arabia. Thus Tapline enabled Qatar to replace Bahrein as the fourth largest source of Canal oil shipments. The imports of oil by the U.S.A. via Suez declined for the first time. Their reduction in volume by 49 per cent reduced the U.S. share in northbound oil from 16·4 per cent in 1950 to 7·8 per cent in 1951 and increased the share of Europe in proportion. The U.S. flag was relegated from the third to the fifth place for the first time since the war. The completion of Tapline stimulated a competitive reaction by the Canal Company as well as by the Iraq Petroleum Company, which undertook to complete a new pipeline to the Mediterranean of comparable capacity to Tapline. The Canal Company decided on 12 June 1951 to make from 15 September its first reduction of toll since the increase in 1941. It granted therein a more than proportionate reduction on ships in ballast and thus departed from the principle in effect between 1930 and 1950 whereby ships in ballast had paid half dues. Thus it sought to encourage the tanker companies whose vessels had been diverted from the Canal by the pipeline.

Tapline removed a bridle on production in Saudi Arabia, especially in the Abqaiq field located in 1940. It permitted the largest single increase in Saudi production in 1951 by 10,400,000 tons or 40 per cent, or by two-thirds of the capacity of the pipeline. The pipeline was however burdened by high capital costs and by fixed operating costs which did not fall with distance as in the case of tankers. Above all, its capacity was limited in contrast to the more flexible capacity of the Canal. Thus the pipeline carried only 39 per cent of the total volume of Saudi production in 1951 and 69 per cent of its volume of exports while the Canal carried the remaining 31 per cent. The loss to the Canal was thus limited by the continuing expansion of Saudi production, especially from the vast Ghawar field located in 1948, extended by further discoveries in 1949 and 1951 and recognized in 1952 as a unity over 140 miles in length, or the largest oil-field in the world by area. As the limited capacity of the pipeline imposed a new bridle on production Saudi shipments via the Canal rose, especially from November 1951, and enabled Aramco to replace Creole, the Venezuelan subsidiary of Jersey Standard, as the world's leading producer of oil in 1952. The completion of Tapline coincided with the con-

[1] *Le Canal de Suez*, 15 Août 1951, 'Revue du Trafic: Premier Semestre 1951'.

clusion of the first profit-sharing agreement in the oil industry of the Middle East. The Jedda Agreement of 30 December 1950 allotted the Government of Saudi Arabia a total share of one-half in Aramco's net operating revenues on the model of the agreement reached by Creole in Venezuela in 1943. Saudi Arabia was thus able to pursue its dynastic feud with the Hashemites, to reply to Iraq's establishment of a Development Board in 1950 and to frustrate Iraqi ambitions to absorb Syria by extending a dollar development-loan to Syria in 1951. Aramco became the great competitor of the Iraq Petroleum Company as well as of Anglo-Iranian. It supplied the evidence to justify Saudi expansion eastwards, at the expense of the British-protected sheikhs of the Trucial Coast, into the Empty Quarter and the oil-rich oasis of Buraimi on 31 August 1952. Saudi Arabia also supported Egypt in opposition to Iraq although the interest in the Canal of Aramco was far smaller than that of Anglo-Iranian. It was able to use its new-found wealth to abolish the pilgrim-dues from 1952, so increasing the traffic to Mecca and the associated slave-trade. In 1952 it also established the Saudi Arabian Monetary Agency as a modified central bank under an American chairman and first issued gold sovereigns as a standard currency in place of its dual currency of British gold sovereigns and Saudi Arabian silver. Aramco became the most remunerative of all oil investments and the greatest single overseas investment of the U.S.A., embodying one-quarter of the total capital invested in the whole Middle East oil industry in 1951.[1] Inevitably it served its Saudi hosts with as much diligence and zeal as the English East India Company had served the Mogul Empire during the seventeenth century.

[1] M. Yeganeh, 'Investment in the Petroleum Industry of the Middle East', *Middle East Journal* (Spring 1952), 244.

35

THE ARAB CAMPAIGN AGAINST ISRAEL, 1948–1951

THE year 1948 was a seed-plot of history in Western Asia as the year 1848 had been in Western Europe. The deepest aspirations of the Jews for a home of their own were then fulfilled at the expense of the Moslem Arabs. The conversion of Arab Palestine into Jewish Israel exported Europe's Jewish problem to Asia and outraged the whole community of Islam as the preceding war had never done. Thereby it frustrated Balfour's intention to buttress the Empire through a Jewish National Home and sapped the foundations of Britain's dominion throughout the Middle East. It also ruined Bevin's project for the consolidation of the British bases in the Canal Zone and Palestine. Bevin recognized the Jews only as citizens of an Arab Palestine and favoured British management for at least four more years, with a British base in Gaza. Thus he maintained the Arab policy of his Conservative predecessors as MacDonald had the Egyptian policy of his Conservative predecessors. His policy was rejected by both Arab and Jew so that work on the Gaza base was suspended and Zionist terrorism culminated in the murders of 1 August 1947. The announcement on 26 September that Britain intended to quit Palestine marked the failure of Bevin's grand design. It halted the transfer of military stores from the Canal Zone to Palestine and made Haifa and Rafa the two great centres for the evacuation of Palestine by sea and land.

Suez shares fell by 8·1 per cent between 9 March and 28 April 1948 as the mandate dissolved. On 14 May the State of Israel was proclaimed by Ben Gurion at Tel Aviv, which had been founded in 1909 as the first Jewish town in Arab Palestine. The conversion of a national home into a nation-state fulfilled the Biltmore Programme of 1942 rather than the Balfour Declaration of 1917. The new state was created by the world-policy of the U.S.A. and the U.S.S.R. in defiance of Britain. It survived the onslaught of five Arab armies, which were backed by British money, equipment, training and officers and were expected, by every British general except Wavell, to enter Haifa within ten days. Its Jewish citizens were severed from their roots in Europe by massacre and inspired by a fear of the utter destruction of their new-born state as well as by a determination to create a Zion for the oppressed. They fought with their backs to the sea with a centralized command, a military discipline and a religious ardour that the Arabs could not equal. The first campaign ensured the survival of their state. Their first offensive followed the evacuation of the last British troops on 30 June, quadrupled the area under their occupation and ensured the failure of an 'Indian' solution of the Palestine problem through partition. Their second offensive was directed against the

Egyptian troops in South Palestine and captured the southern desert of the Negev: it forced the bulk of the Egyptians back across the frontier but left one Egyptian brigade isolated for three months at Falluja as the sole defender of the honour of the Egyptian Army. Jewish troops crossed the Egyptian frontier on 22 December, captured El Auja on 27 December and Abu Ageila on 28–29 December and might have covered the remaining eighty miles to the Canal within forty-eight hours if a British ultimatum on 31 December had not compelled their immediate withdrawal. That ultimatum was a threat by Britain to invoke the 1936 Treaty of Alliance and to intervene on the side of Egypt which even in its deepest humiliation explicitly refused to invoke British aid. After Israel shot down four British Spitfires from the Canal Zone over its battlefield with Egypt on 7 January 1949, British troops landed at Akaba on 8 January. The British Government granted grudging de facto recognition to Israel on 29 January, eight months after the U.S.A. and the U.S.S.R. The final achievement of the Jews was to drive south to the Gulf of Akaba on 10 March at a point five miles west of Akaba, so gaining access to the Red Sea. That acquisition prevented the creation of an Anglo-Arab military base in Southern Palestine between the Canal Zone and Jordan. It deprived Egypt of the territory won by Cromer in 1906 and cut the land-bridge between the Delta and Arab Asia. The first war involving Egypt since 1877 made Egypt more Arab as its material links with the Arab world were severed. It also made the Canal into a barrier to the movement of Egyptian forces into Sinai and the British forces in the Canal Zone into an unwanted buffer. The Canal Company had been under pressure from Egypt to accept a bridge across the Canal since June 1947 and could no longer resist after the Dutch mail-boat *Volendam* struck the bridge at El Firdan on 16 November 1947 and put it out of action. A new bridge was authorized by the Government in May 1948 after the transfer to Egyptian control of the Kantara–Palestine railway but was opened at El Firdan on 10 January 1949 only at the very end of the third campaign.

The establishment of Israel crowned the labours of the World Zionist Organization and made possible the ceremonial transfer in August 1949 of the coffin of Herzl from Vienna to the renamed Mount Herzl in Jerusalem in fulfilment of Herzl's last wish. That Semitic renaissance, like the Arab awakening, reflected a triumph for Asia over Europe[1] and its traditional Kiplingite attitudes of superiority, gently ridiculed in the recollection that the Ten Commandments had been issued just east of Suez.[2] The descendants of the Russian Khazars converted to Judaism since the seventh century A.D. may well have provided the bulk of the Jewish population of the new state.[3] Their Jewish culture, however, reached far back beyond the Talmud in their

[1] D. Reed, *Somewhere South of Suez* (London, Cape, 1950), 309–11.
[2] M. Samuel, *The Gentleman and the Jew* (New York, Knopf, 1952), 37.
[3] D. M. Dunlop, *The History of the Jewish Khazars* (Princeton University Press, 1954), 262–3.

claims to the Holy Land and transformed the Christian year 1948 into the Jewish year 5708. The uprooting of 930,000 Arab peasants confirmed Arab fears that a nation of peasants and soldiers might seek under the pressure of an ingathering of exiles to expand to the full limits of historic Palestine and so become the Assyria or the Carthage of the Middle East. The Jewish diaspora was replaced by an Arab diaspora of refugees deprived of their home, their land and their nation. The expulsion of the Arab peasantry from 'occupied Palestine' also removed the greatest single obstacle to economic growth and made possible Israel's transformation from a socialist commonwealth into an outpost of private capitalism, the America of the Middle East and the Japan of Western Asia. The rootless mass democracy of Eastern Europe triumphed over the Jewish oligarchy of wealth with its shallow roots in the alien soil of Western Europe and its assimilationist ideology. The triumph of nationalism over liberalism in Europe in 1848 was thus re-enacted in Asia in 1948.

Britain was compelled to reorganize its strategy and to shift its forces from the heartland of the Arab world to its periphery, encouraging speculation throughout 1949 about a possible evacuation of the Canal Zone. Emanuel Shinwell, the first Jew to become a Labour M.P., declared as Minister of War during an inspection of the Canal Zone that he knew nothing of an early evacuation of British troops and so incurred general disapproval in Egypt.[1] The Canal Zone became increasingly important as the strategic fulcrum of the Middle East, although Egypt became correspondingly reluctant to recognize British rights to use the base. Military opinion could not believe that the Canal might be more of a liability than an asset nor grasp the limitations of the Suez route.[2] Cyprus regained some of the strategic significance which it had lost in 1882 and became the pioneer island-base of Western Asia comparable to the island-bases of Eastern Asia. England failed to secure a renewal of its treaty of alliance with Iraq and had to extend its treaty with Jordan, which became a twin Hashemite kingdom to Iraq as well as a strategic substitute for Palestine. The whole Arab basis of British policy was however undermined by the belief of the Arabs in their inassuageable bitterness that their most vital interests had been betrayed by Britain. The ignominious military defeat at the hands of those whom Sombart had classed as 'the most perfect type of a trading people' and the successful plantation in Asia of a client-state of the West spread a sense of shock, disaster, humiliation and betrayal throughout the Arab world. In vain Professor Koebner of the Hebrew University of Jerusalem studied the history of the concept of imperialism and contributed largely to its semantic devaluation in the West. To Asia Israel became an outpost of Western imperialism rather than a reconciler of East and West or a model of progress to a backward Arab world. Israel provided Arab Asia with a standing obstacle to its self-fulfilment and replaced France and Britain as

---

[1] *Manchester Guardian*, 30 November 1949, 5iv; 3 December, 8iv.
[2] H. W. Weigert, *New Compass of the World. A Symposium on Political Geography* (London, Harrap, 1949), 244–5, C. B. Fawcett, 'Life Lines of the British Empire'.

the great foe of Arab nationalism. It provided the Arab world with a common enemy and a common rallying-point, united it in negative repulsion as never before since the time of Saladin and revived the deep-embedded memory of the Crusades. The Moslem revival extended outside the Arab heartland to Turkey, the Lebanon, Persia and Egypt where the Moslem Brethren increased rapidly in numbers and influence. Farouk felt compelled to dissolve the order which thereupon assassinated the Prime Minister, Nokrashy Pasha. In reply 'unknown assailants' of the political police assassinated Hasan al-Banna on 12 February 1949, leaving his order to grow beneath the ban of the state. The Egyptian officers who had suffered the humiliation of betrayal, isolation and defeat at Falluja, as their predecessors had in the expedition of 1875–6 to Ethiopia, formed the first Committee of Free Officers in 1949. They canalized their fury, their disgust and their suspicion of treason against Farouk and the Wafd as royalist nationalism began to ebb before the rising tide of radical Arab nationalism and Moslem fervour. The strategic crust of the Middle East began to crumble under the volcanic pressure from the shattered pride of the peasant underworld. Israel had been established by military force and could be maintained only by military force so that its creation stimulated the reactive militarization of the whole Arab world. The first military coup occurred in Syria as a direct result of the Palestine disaster and produced the overthrow of constitutional government by the anti-British General Zaim in 1949. Western Asia thus became polarized between a single small satisfied community and its profoundly dissatisfied foes.

The failure to eliminate Israel on the battlefield encouraged the transfer of Arab hostility to the economic sphere, the consolidation of the Arab boycott of Israel and the closing of the oil-pipelines as well as the Canal to Israel. The pumping of oil from Iraq to Haifa stopped on 17 April 1948 and Haifa Refinery closed down on 15 May, the day after the departure of the last British High Commissioner for Palestine. The Jewish seizure of Haifa ended the construction of the second Kirkuk–Haifa pipeline which had been begun in 1946 and was within forty-two miles of completion. The investment therein of the Iraq Petroleum Company was devalued while the oil of Kirkuk was diverted to Tripoli, to which a second pipeline was completed in July 1949. The diversion of output from Haifa to Tripoli reduced the production of Kirkuk by 25 per cent and its exports by 50 per cent, imposing a restraint on Iraqi production which could only be removed by the construction of another major pipeline comparable to the Trans-Arabian Pipeline. The Palestine war delayed work on the Trans-Arabian Pipeline for a year, diverted all pipelines carrying Arab oil from the route through Palestine and established Syrian control over every pipeline. Israel was cut off from the supply of Arab oil by pipeline, reduced to dependence on oil imported by tanker and compelled to search for oil in its newly conquered territory. The Iraq Petroleum Company abandoned its exploration for oil in occupied Palestine and transferred its H.Q. from Haifa to Tripoli. The seven major oil companies took no share in the search for oil in Palestine. Haifa Refinery was closed from 22 December 1949 for the export of refined products and was kept in operation only on a quarter-capacity to supply the needs of Israel. Thus the conflict between Western interests in Arab oil and in Israel was resolved at the expense of Israel.

Iraq's oil blockade was supplemented by Egypt's restrictions on the shipment of contraband of war through the Canal to Israel.[1] Such restrictions had been expected by Weizmann only after the expiry of the concession in 1968, although he had contemplated an Akaba Canal via the Dead Sea to Tel Aviv. Egypt's first independent act of sovereignty over the Canal opened a new phase in its history by excluding from it the ships and cargo of one state. The day after the Egyptian invasion of Palestine on 14 May 1948 a military proclamation introduced the inspection and search of ships in the ports of Alexandria, Port Said and Suez on the pattern of the procedure in the 1939–45 war. The Customs administration was empowered on 18 May to confiscate contraband munitions and cargo destined for Palestine. All cargo exported from Palestine was declared contraband on 6 June, so excluding exports as well as imports from the Canal route. The resulting protests from Britain on 8 June and from the U.S.A. on 12 June compelled Egypt to claim on 23 June the rights of inspection and search and on 28 June the right to deny provisions and cargo to ships which carried goods to or from Israel. A proclamation of 29 June divided contraband into the four categories of arms, fuel, means of communication, and gold. On the beginning of the second campaign in Palestine the proclamation of 8 July created a Prize Court at Alexandria, with inquiry commissions at Alexandria, Port Said and Suez, and ordered the confiscation of Zionist warships in defiance of the rule that 'every prize must be judged'. A British protest on 9 July was countered by the Egyptian reply on 15 July that Port Said and Suez remained Egyptian ports, although they were also ports of access to the Canal. A decree of 23 July compelled all ships save tankers to submit their log-books to the Customs authorities and enabled Egypt to refuse supplies or repairs to ships which had been black-listed for touching at an Israeli port since the beginning of the war. Another decree on 31 August subordinated entry into the Canal to authorization by the Customs authorities and so added a customs inspection to the health and narcotics inspection of all northbound ships. Thus an almost complete structure of regulation of shipping was erected through the sympathy of the British Government for Egypt.[2] All those measures were extended on 22 October 1948 to tankers, the most important of all cargo-carriers to Israel since the closing of the pipelines.

Egypt undertook an extensive revision of its system of inspection after Israel's three successful campaigns for survival. On 10 January 1949 cargo shipped 'to order' which had thitherto been of suspect destination was

---

[1] M. El-Hefnaoui, *Les Problèmes Contemporains posés par le Canal de Suez* (Paris, Guillemot, 1951), 193–251. B. Avram, *The Evolution of the Suez Canal Status from 1869 up to 1956* (Geneva, Droz, 1958), 97–117.   [2] *The Times*, 31 May 1949, 4iv.

exempted from confiscation on presumptive grounds alone. On 29 June inspection was restricted to notoriously suspect ships after British protests on 6 and 16 June. At the same time the list of contraband articles was reduced to four categories while the proof of hostile destination was made more rigorous. On 21 July the abolition of military inspection freed the Egyptian Army from the onus of action which might be deemed a breach of the Armistice of Rhodes, leaving only a customs inspection. Despite those successive relaxations of control, Israel gained judgments in its favour from the Security Council on 11 August and from the Mixed Armistice Commission on 28 August. The list of contraband articles was then reduced on 14 September to a new minimum. Further protests were made to Egypt by France on 18 September, by Britain on 19 September and by Norway on 8 October. Israel established from 1949 the port of Eilat on the Gulf of Akaba to valorize its claim to a second coastline more than to create a competitive route to the Canal. Thereupon Saudi Arabia leased the islands of Tiran and Sanafir at the mouth of the Gulf to Egypt which occupied them and established shore batteries in December 1950 at Sharm el Sheikh and Ras Nasrani on the southern tip of Sinai, in order to close the Gulf to Israeli shipping and prevent Eilat from becoming a new Haifa.

The restrictions imposed by the royalist government of Egypt were maintained by the Wafd Ministry of Nahas Pasha, who refused Bevin's personal request for their abolition on 28 January 1950. In its decree of 6 February the Government listed six classes of contraband including oil, chemicals, airplanes and ships. The codification of the restrictions provoked the first question in the Commons on the subject by Somerset de Chair, Conservative M.P. for Paddington, on 20 March and encouraged a rumour that Britain and the U.S.A. might cut a new canal to replace the Suez Canal and carry Iranian oil to Haifa.[1] The Egyptian decree of 1 April made no mention of Zionist merchant ships as liable to confiscation on capture. The Tripartite Declaration by Britain, France and the U.S.A. on 25 May guaranteed Israel's frontiers and committed the U.S.A. to maintain an impartial balance between the interests of one million Zionists and those of seventy million Arabs. Thereafter Egypt introduced on 18 June a certificate of destination for oil-tankers using the Canal and so created an oil embargo, enforced from 13 July by the inspection of tankers' log-books on land instead of on board ship. British opposition to such an embargo became a defence of British shipping, British trade, British oil and the freedom of the seas even more than a defence of Israel. Only six of the twenty-three questions asked in the Commons on the subject during 1950 came from Jewish M.P.s.[2] Conservative M.P.s in Opposition suggested an appeal against Egyptian recalcitrance to the Convention of Constantinople,[3]

---

[1] D. Reed, *Somewhere South of Suez* (1950), 425.

[2] Hansard, *Commons Debates*, 19 April 1950, M. Lipton, B. Janner; 14 June, S. Silverman, B. Janner; 19 July, I. Mikardo; 26 July, B. Janner.

[3] Hansard, *Commons Debates*, 28 March 1950, A. Eden.

to the International Court at The Hague[1] or even to the United Nations.[2] British sentiment resented Egypt's apparent magnification of her conflict with Israel as well as her simultaneous attempt to remain neutral in a divided world and was infuriated by her refusal on 11 July to support the U.N. joint resolution calling for support in Korea. 'Is not the position that we are still supplying arms, that Egypt still does not adhere to this joint resolution, and that she still stops our tankers going through the Suez Canal, which really seems that she is getting away with too much?'[3]

The new restrictions on oil-tankers using the Canal were reinforced by Saudi Arabia's denial of its oil to Haifa from 1950 and cut Israel off from supplies of cheap fuel, compelling it to import its oil from Venezuela or Mexico. They provoked a protest to Egypt on 12 August by Britain which was supported by the U.S.A., Norway, France and Holland so that Suez share prices fell by 8·1 per cent between 12 and 16 August. Egypt's response was to require the captains of tankers from September to furnish guarantees that they would not unload their cargo in Palestine and so to create a new black-list of tankers visiting Israel after promising not to do so. Israel thereupon expelled the Beduin from the demilitarized zone of El Auja from 20 August and forced them across the Egyptian frontier on 2 September: she thereby secured control of the intersection of all the routes leading into Sinai and the indispensable basis for any offensive directed against the peninsula. In the Security Council the Israeli representative on 30 October assessed the direct cost of the Suez restrictions at tens of millions of pounds and their indirect cost at hundreds of millions of pounds. After further protests by the International Chamber of Shipping in October 1950, by the British Government and by the governments of five other maritime states Egypt announced the removal from 20 December of the restrictions which denied repair facilities at Egyptian ports to black-listed ships but prohibited their loading with cargo at Port Said. A fifth British note of protest to Egypt on 9 December was accompanied by others from the U.S.A., France, Denmark and Norway. Egypt's reply was to extend its territorial waters from 15 January 1951 to six miles in the Gulf of Suez, so cutting the Canal off from the high seas by a continuous stretch of Egyptian waters and reasserting the principle of the closed sea at the expense of that of the open sea.

Israel accused Egypt of maintaining a blockade in defiance of international law, the Convention of Constantinople and the Armistice of Rhodes. It denied that the armistice had left Egypt's belligerent rights intact and pleaded for strict justice in accordance with the letter of the law rather than for equitable treatment. It claimed an absolute freedom of transit under the Convention of Constantinople as a non-signatory power, assumed such freedom was a primary right of merchant-vessels and restricted Egypt's powers to the right to regulate but not to prohibit transit. It invariably used the term 'blockade' to

---

[1] Hansard, *Commons Debates*, 14 June 1950, Q. Hogg.   [2] Ibid., 14 June 1950, A. Eden.
[3] Ibid., 19 July 1950, 2253, A. Eden.

condemn the Egyptian restrictions[1] which it represented as the high-handed measures of an oppressor. It consistently isolated the Canal question from the Palestine question as a whole, with all its claims and counter-claims, as the issue with the widest potential support from the West.[2]

The Egyptian boycott was in fact a confession of weakness and impotence. Lacking a navy to use against Israel on the high seas Egypt was compelled to use the Canal ports to exercise her belligerent rights against a state which she did not recognize. Thereby she created a conflict for the first time in history between the local and the general use of the Canal, which had been created for the long-distance trade between Europe and Asia and had never carried much local trade. Egypt did not hesitate to exalt her supreme sovereign rights over the interests of world trade, so deterring the shipowners and shippers of the world from trade with Israel and imposing a derisory penalty on the maritime powers for their recognition of Israel. She claimed that her actions violated neither the Convention of Constantinople nor the Armistice of Rhodes nor international law in general,[3] but were modelled on the British measures taken during the wars of 1914–18 and 1939–45. In her war against Israel Egypt certainly acted in the spirit of a blockading power but did not in fact or in law maintain a blockade. She made no attempt to seal off the coastline of Israel, claimed only the rights of visit, search and seizure or the bare minimum of rights under the Armistice but exercised them in the Canal ports in order to eliminate the delay inseparable from the use of any other port. She entrusted the execution of her decrees from 1949 to civilian rather than to military officials and followed the precedents of international law rather than of national law in her Prize Court.[4] No appeal was raised against her actions to the International Court at The Hague which had checked German restrictions on the use of the Kiel Canal in 1923.

Egypt placed the Convention of Constantinople under its greatest and most enduring strain.[5] That Convention enshrined the principle of freedom of transit for all vessels without distinction of flag, forbade the exercise of any right of war or hostility in the Canal or its ports and specifically excluded the waterway from the exercise of the right of blockade in a clause intended to prohibit any Power other than Egypt from blockading the Canal from the sea-approaches. Egypt justified its restrictions as measures taken in self-defence under Article X of the Convention, which had been directed against any immediate and direct threat to the Canal or to Egypt from its use but had not been concerned with the ultimate use of any cargo in transit. Egypt had no fear of any attack via the Canal, although it lay 125 miles nearer the Delta

---

[1] A. Eban, *Voice of Israel* (London, Faber, 1958), 202–18, 'The Story of a Blockade'.

[2] A. H. Hourani, 'The Middle East and the Crisis of 1956', *St. Antony's Papers Number 4* (London, Chatto, 1958), 11.

[3] M. El-Hefnaoui, 198–227.

[4] J. Trappe, 'On the Jurisdiction of the Egyptian Prize Court, 1948–1960', *Revue Égyptienne de Droit International* (1960), 62.

[5] M. El-Hefnaoui, 220–7, 245–51.

than the military frontier of Israel. Nor did she fear damage to the Canal itself. She sought only to prevent Israel from building up its war-potential and so to preserve her leadership of the Arab world in the struggle against its mortal foe. For that policy she could find justification only in the ambiguities of Articles X and XI of the Convention of which she became the guardian and interpreter. Article XI specifically precluded interference with the free use of the Canal even in self-defence. The Egyptian Prize Court however denied non-signatories such as Israel any rights under the Convention. Egypt increasingly favoured a new Canal Statute placed under an international guarantee which would add the Red Sea to the maritime zone of the Canal and prohibit its use by the enemies of Egypt as well as by ships in their service.[1]

The boycott seems to have inflicted little material damage on Israel despite its exclusion from any normal use of the Canal. It denied Israel the use of the Canal for any future navy and prevented the creation of a strategic link between its two coastlines like that afforded to the U.S.A. at Panama. It prevented Israel from importing Arab oil and handicapped the refining and petrochemical industry of Haifa. It also restricted maritime communications with South Africa whose Jews ranked second only to those of America in their prosperity and their Zionist fervour. In fact it affected cargo more than shipping because Palestine had not been a maritime state nor Haifa a port on the main Suez route. In 1947 the Canal had been used by seventeen vessels under the flag of Palestine with a total tonnage of 21,608, or 0·06 per cent of the total tonnage, while Palestinian cargo using the Canal excluding oil had amounted to 176,000–200,000 tons, or to 1 per cent of the total non-oil cargo. In 1948 the last vessel under the flag of Palestine used the Canal. The list of contraband articles was not unduly extensive. Only thirty-eight British ships of 11,444 British transits between 1948 and 1950 were delayed or turned back by Egypt.[2] Israel nevertheless concluded that the very small proportion of ships searched proved that its cargo had been effectively diverted from the Suez route. The boycott however seems to have produced no reduction in traffic, no interference with international trade and little inconvenience to shipping. It called forth no League of Armed Neutrality in defence of Israel and simply prohibited any direct Israeli trade with Asia by the shortest route, confining its trade to its patrons in the West.

The boycott was deeply resented not merely by the commercial élites of Haifa and Eilat but by the whole Jewish population of Israel. It was rightly deemed a symbolic act expressing the Arab determination to refuse all recognition to the Zionist state as firmly as Jewish merchants had maintained from 1934 a boycott of German goods. It inflicted far more psychic than economic damage upon the status-conscious Israelis and therefore aroused a deep-seated feeling of insecurity and an inassuageable fear for the future. Israel's demand for the opening of the Canal thus became in effect a demand for

[1] M. El-Hefnaoui, 190–1, 303–7.
[2] Hansard, *Commons Debates*, 25 January 1954, 1446, S. Lloyd to E. Shinwell.

implicit recognition by the Arab world. Egypt increased her control over the Canal in the Arab cause and proclaimed herself the heir-apparent to the Canal Company,[1] which cooperated with the territorial authority to withhold facilities of transit from Israel while operating the waterway for the benefit of all other users. The Company thereby suffered greater moral than financial loss because it was as much as Israel a standard-bearer of Western civilization in Asia. The Egyptian Police, Coastguards and Customs officials increased their power in the Canal ports, which lost their special status under the Convention of Constantinople and were increasingly assimilated to Alexandria.

Egypt's unexpected assertion of sovereignty over the Canal was made while British troops remained in full occupation of the Canal Zone and only provoked attack when the Abadan crisis aroused a British hope to replace Abadan by Haifa Refinery and to resume the shipment of oil from Iraq to Haifa.[2] Thus Labour, Liberal and Conservative M.P.s condemned Egypt in the heated debate of 20 March 1951 when ex-R.N.V.R. Lieutenant and right-wing Labour M.P. R. T. Paget first publicly suggested that the Navy should be ordered to prevent interference with British ships on their lawful occasions at sea. Gaitskell as Chancellor of the Exchequer revealed that Britain intended only to claim demurrage losses from Egypt. Britain's reluctance to adopt a gunboat-policy necessitated a further diplomatic protest to Cairo on 29 May and encouraged a suggestion for the establishment of a free international port at Haifa inclusive of its oil refineries.[3] Lieutenant-General Riley of the U.N. Truce Supervision Organization reported on 12 June that the Egyptian embargo was in breach of the spirit if not the letter of the Armistice as an aggressive and hostile act. Egypt in reply tightened her restrictions and required from 18 June a certificate that oil cargoes had been unloaded in neutral ports for local consumption and had not ended up in Israeli hands, a stipulation directed at the entrepôt trade of Genoa with Haifa. The first ship to dock at Eilat had been a Greek vessel from Mombasa on 26 April. The British tanker *Empire Roach*, carrying a cargo of arms to Jordan, was however arrested on 1 July at the entrance to the Gulf of Akaba by an Egyptian corvette, provoking a British protest on 10 July and demands in the Commons for an appeal to the Security Council.[4] Israel itself seized the opportunity to protest to the Security Council on 11 July against the aggressive and hostile acts of Egypt in relation to the Canal and was joined by England on 18 July. Egypt and England then agreed on 29–30 July that British merchant ships bound for Akaba should first be cleared by the Egyptian authorities at Suez. In the Security Council a resolution calling on Egypt to end its restrictions was moved on 16 August by France, Britain and the U.S.A. and was passed on 1 September by nine votes with China,

---

[1] H. L. Hoskins, 'The Guardianship of the Suez Canal. A View of Anglo-Egyptian Relations', *Middle East Journal* (April 1950), 152.

[2] M. El-Hefnaoui, 232–45. A. Comstock, 'Nationalism Threatens the Canal', *Current History* (July 1951), 24–7.

[3] Hansard, *Commons Debates*, 6 June 1951, Dodds Parker.

[4] Ibid., 11 July 1951, Vosper, Fisher, Janner, Paget.

India and Russia abstaining. That resolution was fact-finding in character rather than juridically binding. It rejected categorically the Egyptian theory of active belligerent rights and self-defence under the Convention of 1888. It presumed the Armistice to be a permanent rather than a temporary cessation of hostilities. That judgment was one made by the interested parties because France had protested twenty-two times against Egypt's restrictions, the U.S.A. twelve times and Britain ten times. It was not based on law[1] or even on legal opinion and made no mention of the Convention of Constantinople but sought to replace law by authority. Egypt ignored it as India had ignored the successive resolutions on Kashmir passed between 1948 and 1951. Britain made no suggestion that the resolution should be enforced, did not offer to enforce it herself and was content to leave it as a political judgment. The failure of the maritime powers to take effective action encouraged Israel to declare Eilat a harbour on 25 June 1952 and to revive the idea of an Akaba Canal.[2]

The extension of Arab nationalism to the economic sphere undermined the basis of Jewish and Western commercial enterprise throughout Western Asia[3] and reinforced Arab interest in economic life. Thus the central banks were nationalized in Iraq and Iran in 1949, when the Government also affirmed its intention to secure a higher share in the profits of the Anglo-Iranian Oil Company. In Bagdad all Jewish commercial and banking firms were closed in 1950–51. In Syria the foreign electricity, water and tram companies were nationalized in 1951. In the Sudan the Gezira Board established in 1950 replaced the Sudan Plantations Syndicate, which was wound up in 1951. In Egypt Western enterprise suffered erosion through the expiration of the fifty-year concession granted in 1899 to the Port Said Salt Association, the nationalization of the National Bank of Egypt in 1950 and the sale of the Wagons-Lits and Pullman cars to the Egyptian Railways in 1950. Above all the abolition of the Mixed Courts on 15 October 1949 removed the last external legal protection from foreign enterprise in Egypt. Official pressure on the Canal Company increased steadily after the passage of the Companies Law of 1947. The Labour Conciliation Court at Port Said awarded pensions to its Egyptian workmen on 27 March 1948. Such pensions had been introduced in 1919 but suppressed in 1938 for workmen engaged thereafter so that from 1948 the Company was compelled to begin building up large pension funds twenty years before the expiry of its concession. The refusal of visas for pilots left the Company in need of 18 pilots to complete its staff of 130 and compelled it to introduce convoys from 28 May 1948. The Department of Commerce informed the Company in September 1948 that the Council of State had given its opinion on 5 May 1948 that the Companies Law of 1947 was

---

[1] *International and Comparative Law Quarterly* (January 1952), 91–2, 'The Security Council and the Suez Canal'.

[2] Lord Strabolgi, 'A Trans-Israel Canal as Alternative to Suez', *New Commonwealth*, 23 July 1952, 601–2.

[3] P. G. Franck, 'Economic Nationalism in the Middle East', *Middle East Journal* (Autumn 1952), 429–54.

applicable to it. The Company then admitted the first Egyptian engineer to its International Advisory Works Commission on 4 November 1948. Hussein Sirry Pasha was a non-party civil engineer who had followed his father's example and worked in the Ministry of Public Works from 1916 to 1939, serving his last three years as Minister. Thereafter he became Minister of Defence, Minister of Finance and, finally, as one of the king's friends and relatives, Prime Minister in 1940–1 and 1941–2. He was appointed to the Works Commission as a politician more than as an engineer. Thus the Company made a token concession to Egyptian nationalism whilst more than doubling its reserves during 1948.

Suez shares reached their all-time peak of 115,000 francs on 25 November 1948, an increase of 67 per cent above their level on 28 April 1948. They fell in price by 13 per cent between 7 and 23 March 1949 on the news of the Agreement of 7 March 1949 between the Company and the Government. That agreement followed three months of negotiation in Cairo and achieved a triumph for the Egyptian Minister of Commerce and Industry. François Charles-Roux yielded to Egypt's demands in the hope of preserving the Company's function in some form beyond 1968,[1] and the shareholders' meeting on 21 June adopted the new President's Report unanimously, despite several abstentions.[2] By that agreement[3] the Company undertook to allot Egypt immediately two further seats on the board of directors, increasing the Egyptian seats to four at the expense of the French directors, and to add three more seats gradually (in 1954, in 1959 and in 1964) so as to increase those seats to seven at the expense of the British shipowners. The Company also agreed to pay the Government 7 per cent of its gross profits per annum, which would equal 11 per cent of its net profits and £E805,000 for the year 1948, with a guaranteed minimum of £E350,000. It undertook to increase its Egyptian staff from 27 per cent to 90 per cent of the administrative posts as well as to 80 per cent of the technical posts, to appoint an Egyptian officer to its selection committee, to employ immediately twenty new Egyptian pilots and to recruit an Egyptian pilot for one of each two future vacancies. It agreed to transfer the municipal services at Ismailia, except for the water supply and the gardens, to a new municipality including two representatives of the Company, to create a fishing harbour at Port Said, to cede the Abbassieh Canal to the Government and to exempt all ships under 300 tons of all nationalities from Canal dues, which were estimated at £E95,000 (including £E50,000 for Egyptian vessels) but were partly offset by the high administrative costs involved. In return the Government agreed to grant and renew visas at the request of the Company and to extend the Company's rights to exploit the Attaqa quarries, rights which had expired in 1944.

[1] A. Siegfried, 'Les Canaux Internationaux', *Recueil des Cours-Académie de Droit International de la Haye* (1949-I), 45–6, 67.

[2] *Le Canal de Suez*, 15/25 Juin 1949, 9281–5, 9290–1.

[3] *Cahiers de l'Orient Contemporain*, (1949), 79–86 (full text); *Le Canal de Suez*, 15 Mars 1949, 9268 (summary text). M. El-Hefnaoui, 251–77.

The Agreement of 1949 was the necessary prelude to the execution of the works programme approved in November 1948 and stipulated that 95 per cent of the labour employed thereon should be Egyptian so that the new Farouk Canal was dug by fellahin with spades. The replacement of the fixed royalty conceded in 1937 by a percentage share in profits marked a return to the pre-1880 position in relations between the Company and the Government and made Egypt a privileged partner.[1] The addition of an 11 per cent share in the net profits to the 12 per cent paid in Egyptian taxes raised Egypt's share in the net profits to 23 per cent. The first levy of a general income tax in Egypt in 1949 raised the Company's payments of tax to the Government of Egypt by 1950 above those to the Government of France. The Company gave minimal publicity to the important pilot-clause, ceded the Ismailia Museum to the Government in November 1949 and published its first bilingual French and Arabic brochure on the Canal in 1950. Thenceforward it pursued a very conservative dividend policy so as to build up anew the reserves which had been exhausted during the war. It was compelled by the Egyptian labour courts in 1949 to grant the Egyptian 'agents' of the Company travel allowances and was then burdened by the Pensions Law of 1950 which enacted a comprehensive non-contributory scheme of social security. The Agreement made numerous concessions to Egypt but still exempted the Company from the Egyptian Companies Law and maintained the tradition established in 1866 of special conventions as the basis of its relations with the State. It granted Egypt only two instead of the thirteen directors on the board which it would have secured under the Law of 1947. It was violently opposed by the Wafd in the Senate because no financial gain was deemed adequate compensation for the restriction of the State's legislative sovereignty. It was ratified by the Chamber of Deputies on 8 August 1949 only after Farouk had dismissed his Saadist Ministry and made Hussein Sirry Pasha his Prime Minister for a third time with a Cabinet including some Wafdists. The general election of 1950 was freer from administrative pressure than any previous election, returned the Wafd to power by an overwhelming majority and enabled Nahas Pasha to replace Hussein Sirry at the head of a full Wafdist Cabinet.

As the moral basis of the Company was undermined in Egypt its position in the Western mind was strengthened by its contribution to the Egypt-France Exhibition at Paris (7 October–21 November 1949), by the public celebration of the centenary of Waghorn's death by the French colony at Port Tewfik on 7 January 1950 and by the publication of the first study of the Canal by the Historical Society of the Isthmus.[2] Although the Misr Maritime Navigation Company launched the 6,440-ton *Port Said* in 1951, the Government

---

[1] *The Times*, 14 September 1949, 5 VI–VII, 'Control of the Suez Canal. Status of Egypt as a Privileged Partner'. M. Perrett, 'Future of the Suez Canal. Egypt's Claims and Aspirations', *Commonwealth and Empire Review* (January 1950), 40–6. I. B. Makdour, 'Le Canal de Suez et l'économie égyptienne', *Bulletin de la Société Belge d'Études et d'Expansion* (Novembre 1949), 763–6.

[2] P. Reymond, *Le Port de Port Said* (Le Caire, Le Scribe Égyptien, 1950).

continued to oppose the development of Port Said and neglected to develop the new fishing harbour built by the Company. It prevented the Company from introducing a code for traffic control in Suez Bay drawn up in 1950 by the United Kingdom Chamber of Shipping. The new Wafd Government nominated as directors Wacyf Boutros Ghali Pasha and, to the consternation of the Company, Ahmed Mohamed Abboud Pasha. The Copt Boutros Ghali was an unobjectionable candidate as the Foreign Minister in the first ministry of Zaglul in 1924 as well as in the first, second and third ministries of Nahas in 1928, 1930 and 1936–8. Abboud Pasha was a close associate of Hussein Sirry Pasha and a known supporter of the Wafd but the first businessman to be nominated by Egypt to the board. A Palestinian, he had developed his interests in the fertilizer and sugar industry of the Aswan district from 1930 and had branched out into transportation, cotton, chemicals and engineering. He had built up a combine like that of the Misr Group and had become Egypt's greatest businessman and tax-evader. He had been a director of the English Coaling Company since 1934 and became Chairman of Thornycroft (Egypt) Ltd., Chairman of the Khedivial Mail Line and a member of the Higher Advisory Economic Council created in 1950. He extended his economic empire to include a great fertilizer factory which he opened at Suez in 1951, the first in the Middle East to use waste gas from the oil refineries in the manufacture of calcium nitrate as well as to encroach on the isthmian kingdom of the Company. His nomination to the board of the Canal Company was only accepted after Nahas undertook a special trip to Paris in 1950 and maintained in prolonged discussions the right of the Government to appoint directors rather than merely to propose their names. Thus the Wafd gained a victory for Egypt and frustrated the hope of the Company that the Agreement of 1949 would make the concessionary power its passive associate as it had been in 1854.

36

THE ABADAN CRISIS AND THE OIL
BOOM IN KUWAIT, 1951-1956

THE small sheikhdom of Kuwait became the main source of oil shipped through the Canal during 1950 but only established a decisive supremacy when shipments were reduced from Arabia and Iran during 1951. It expanded its production during the Abadan crisis so as to fill the gap left by Iran and then revealed its overpowering comparative advantages. In Kuwait oil was easier to extract and nearer to the coast than it was in Saudi Arabia. Its oil-producing sands were over 1,000 feet in thickness or more than fivefold the thickness of those in Saudi Arabia. They were more porous and permeable than any other in the whole Middle East. Their oil was raised to the surface by a natural water-drive, pumped to the 400-feet high Ahmadi Ridge and then allowed to flow by gravity for another six miles to the tanker terminal at Mina al Ahmadi. Such advantages made possible the extraordinarily rapid development of its production when the Anglo-Iranian Oil Company was nationalized ten years after the Anglo-Russian invasion of Iran in 1941. The publication of the new profit-sharing agreement of 30 December 1950 between Saudi Arabia and Aramco increased Iranian discontent with Anglo-Iranian, which had paid Iran £122,000,000 in royalties for the 333,000,000 tons of oil worth £1,200,000,000 which it had extracted since 1913. On 19 February 1951 the nationalization of Anglo-Iranian was proposed by the deputy Mossadek, who was an elderly conservative landowner, the son of a Qajar princess and an uncompromising opponent of Reza Shah. Nationalization was voted by the Chamber amidst general exultation which stimulated demands for nationalization in Iraq, Egypt and Syria and reduced Suez shares by 8 per cent between 16 and 19 March. It produced a strike at Abadan lasting from 26 March to 26 April and necessitated the despatch of a British cruiser from Malta to the Gulf because Indian forces were no longer available as they had been in 1946. Oil shipments from Iran through the Canal remained stationary from January to March but fell by 5 per cent during April from the level of April 1950 and by nearly 20 per cent during May.

The appointment of Mossadek as Prime Minister on 27 April inspired the British Foreign Secretary to announce in the Commons on 1 May that the monthly oil royalties of £2,000,000 for May would be withheld. On the next day the Shah decreed the nationalization of the oil industry of Iran, 'for the happiness and prosperity of the Iranian nation and for the purpose of securing world peace'.[1] Thereby the revised concession of 1933 which was due to

[1] A. W. Ford, *The Anglo-Iranian Oil Dispute of 1951–1952* (University of California Press, Berkeley, 1954), 268, Appendix IV.

expire in 1993 was revoked and control over the largest supply of crude in the Middle East as well as over the largest refinery in the world was transferred from Anglo-Iranian to the new National Iranian Oil Company. Anglo-Iranian supplied 10 per cent of the national income of Iran, 32 per cent of the Government's income directly as well as another 18 per cent indirectly and 80 per cent of the foreign exchange earned by Iran. The British Government expected a popular revolt to overthrow Mossadek but was disappointed, because the great mass of the population had gained nothing from the oil revenues and did not feel their loss. For Iran the triumph was pre-eminently symbolic rather than material, in Mossadek's addition on 15 May of the prefix 'former' to the title of Anglo-Iranian and in the hoisting on 11 June of the Iranian flag over the head office of the Company at Khurramshahr, so completing the achievement of Reza Khan in 1925 and compelling Charles-Roux to deny on 12 June Cairo rumours of the nationalization of the Canal Company. After Iran demanded on 14 June 75 per cent of the Company's receipts from its sales, the output of the Abadan Refinery began to slow down from 16 June and all the tankers of the major oil companies were diverted from Abadan. During June the Canal lost 150,000 net register tons of tankers in ballast en route to Iran but gained 270,000 tons of tankers in ballast en route to Kuwait, which increased its oil shipments through the Canal by 36 per cent in April and by 61 per cent during June to become the main beneficiary by the demand for oil induced by the Korean War.

Iran's demand on 28 June for receipts from the captains of tankers ended all exports of oil from the sixteen jetties at Abadan by 1 July although fifty-four tankers lay in Iraqi waters in the Shatt el Arab. The Refinery worked at half capacity from the end of June and stopped production completely on 31 July, three weeks after Iranian officials took possession of British communications in Abadan. 'The greatest single overseas enterprise in British commerce had ground to a standstill.'[1] Eighteen empty tankers with an aggregate tonnage of 114,000 returned through the Canal, so reversing the trend of southbound tankers in ballast which had characterized the oil traffic of the waterway since 1913. Tanker transits through the Canal fell below the number of other ships for the first time since October 1949. Oil shipments from Iran through the Canal declined by 75 per cent from the level of June while shipments from Kuwait rose by 71 per cent. Kuwait could not, however, expand its shipments rapidly enough to replace Iran immediately so that total oil shipments declined during July by 15 per cent from their level in July 1950, reducing their share in northbound cargo from 83 to 72 per cent.[2] The closing of the most versatile refinery in the world also cut off the supply of petroleum products to the oiling stations along the Suez route and ended the northward shipment of refined oil. It disrupted the pattern of oil bunkering for all ships within the vast area between Cape Town, Port Said, Yokohama and Wellington

[1] H. Longhurst, *Adventure in Oil. The Story of B.P.* (London, Sidgwick, 1959), 144.
[2] *Le Canal de Suez*, 15 Septembre 1951, 9426.

and set in motion from July an increasing flow southwards of refined oil from the U.S.A. as well as from Europe. In August oil shipments from Iran disappeared from the Canal for the first time since 1913 so that Canal shipments remained 15 per cent below their level for August 1950. In September Canal shipments of oil reached their low-point of 27 per cent below the level of September 1950, although crude oil shipments were only 7 per cent less.[1]

After the final break-down of negotiations Anglo-Iranian ordered on 23 August the evacuation of the oil-fields and announced on 4 September that it would sue anyone who attempted to buy Iranian oil. The British Government forbade on 10 September the export to Iran of such scarce goods as sugar, iron, steel, non-ferrous metals, alloys, railway trucks and material. Thus the Government joined the Company in its economic boycott of Iran and reduced the volume of exports, especially of sugar, through the Canal to the Gulf. After Mossadek notified the Company on 25 September of its definitive expulsion Iranian troops occupied the refinery on 27 September and the British Government announced its decision on 1 October to withdraw the remaining staff of Anglo-Iranian. The exodus of 268 Britons on the cruiser *Mauritius* on 4 October marked the end of the Anglo-Persian saga begun in 1907. During October the shipments of refined products northwards through the Canal reached their lowest level since October 1927 and raised the share of crude oil to 98 per cent of the total volume of northbound oil. From October however crude shipments began to expand from their low-point of September, maintained their rate of increase during November,[2] when tanker transits regained their primacy, and doubled their rate of increase during December. Only in January 1952 did the volume of total oil shipments end their six-months' depression and rise above the level for January 1951. The crisis thus made its main impact on the traffic of the Canal between May and December 1951, immediately after the impact of Tapline between December 1950 and April 1951.

During 1951 Iran's oil shipments through the Canal declined by 50 per cent while its share in those shipments sank from 30 to 17 per cent. The Persian Gulf became the sole region served by the Canal to record a decrease in its shipping tonnage and in its cargo tonnage, which declined respectively by 11·95 and 8·75 per cent. Northbound oil shipments fell by 9·8 per cent, tanker tonnage by 10·3 per cent and southbound tanker tonnage in ballast by 20 per cent while northbound tanker tonnage in ballast rose by 465 per cent. That reduction in tanker tonnage was the first since the war and affected especially the flags of Panama, the U.S.A. and Britain. The passage of the first three vessels under the Iranian flag during 1951 supplied no significant compensation to the Canal Company. The Canal's proportion of the total tanker-cargo carried by the world fleet in external trade declined from the peak of 21·2 per cent in 1950 to 17·6 per cent in 1951. The 1,144 different tankers which made

[1] *Le Canal de Suez*, 15 Octobre 1951, 9430.
[2] Ibid., 15 Novembre 1951, 9434; 15 Décembre 1951, 1938.

5,913 transits through the waterway, or 5·2 each, nevertheless represented a gross tonnage of 11,000,000 or 60·5 per cent of the world tanker fleet of 18,210,000 gross tons. The oil trade of the Persian Gulf was so influential in the genera ltraffic of the Canal that the oil crisis of 1951 produced an absolute reduction in British tonnage using the Canal by 1·3 per cent, in total shipping tonnage by 1·8, in northbound cargo tonnage by 1·9 and in receipts by 1·4 per cent. The severity of the first postwar recession in traffic was largely mitigated by the Korean War boom and by the expansion of non-oil cargo by 28 per cent and of southbound cargo by 44 per cent. The volume of non-tanker shipping tonnage rose by 13·2 per cent and exceeded its 1937 level for the first time in 1951. The Canal Company was able to avoid a reduction in its dividends for 1951 and even to increase them by 3 per cent.

The nationalization of Anglo-Iranian was the greatest blow ever inflicted on the British economic empire in the Middle East. At a single stroke it reduced the British share of the capital invested in the Middle East oil industry from 49 to 14 per cent[1] and the British share of Middle East oil production from 53 to 24 per cent. It increased the U.S. share of Middle East oil production from 44 to 58 per cent, left the American oil companies in control of 42 per cent of the capital invested in the industry and encouraged them to aspire to extend their interests even further. It ruptured diplomatic relations between Britain and Iran, and ended the era of British hegemony in the Persian Gulf, making Iraq under Nuri es Said more important than ever as a British base: the British embassy left Tehran on 1 November 1952 for Bagdad along the road built in 1942 by British military engineers. The shock of nationalization to the other oil companies secured the speedy extension of the 50–50 profit-sharing agreement to Kuwait from 1951 as well as to Bahrein, Qatar and Iraq from 1952. Thus Aramco won implicit recognition as the pioneer in making concessions to the Arab oil-states, which acquired a vested interest in the high crude oil prices from which their profits were thenceforward calculated. The increased interest in Arab oil led the Arab League to establish its Oil Experts Committee in September 1951 and two leading oil companies to pay homage to Arab pride by transferring their headquarters to Arab cities. The example of Anglo-Egyptian Oilfields Ltd. which had decided in 1950 to transfer its seat to Cairo was followed in 1952 by Aramco, which transferred its H.Q. from New York to Dhahran, and by the Iraq Petroleum Company, which transferred its H.Q. from Tripoli to Bagdad. Aramco also enforced a total prohibition of alcoholic drinks on its employees from the end of 1952 in deference to Wahhabi susceptibilities. Thus American civilization on the subtropical fringe of the heartland of Islam reverted to the older Puritan tradition of New England in order to maintain the security of American investments in the oil of the free world. The Iraq Petroleum Company also sought to integrate itself into the life of Iraq on the

---

[1] M. Yeganeh, 'Investment in the Petroleum Industry of the Middle East', *Middle East Journal* (Spring 1952), 243.

pattern of partnership pursued by Aramco. It began the construction of refineries from 1952 and ceased to be wholly an export company. Lebanon was encouraged in 1952 to repudiate a new agreement on transit fees and to demand that the 50–50 principle should be extended to the transport of oil through the Lebanon. The Iraq Petroleum Company in reply diverted its new pipeline from Tripoli in Lebanon to Banias in Syria.

Anglo-Iranian suffered the nationalization of its assets in Iran without compensation other than its past profits. Cut off from its original base it was forced back into reliance upon its sixty-five subsidiary companies, and especially upon its half-share in the Kuwait Oil Company established in 1934. Galvanized into a new phase of expansion, it sought to enforce a boycott of Iranian oil in all the markets of the world and used the oil of Kuwait to make that boycott effective with the support of the cartel of the seven. It rerouted the tankers of the British Tanker Company, especially to Kuwait, and bought oil from Russia until Kuwait had expanded its production to replace Iran.[1] It intensified the search for oil in Kuwait and Iraq, decided to build a refinery at Aden to replace Abadan and undertook the construction of monster-tankers to ferry crude oil over long distances. Thus the refined oil and the crude oil of Iran could both be excluded from foreign markets. During 1951 Kuwait increased the volume of its production by 63 per cent, and the volume of its exports through the Canal by 61 per cent while the tankers loading at Kuwait rose in number by 74·5 per cent. Kuwait increased its share in the oil shipments of the Canal from 32·6 per cent in 1950 to 59 per cent in 1951, reaching the proportion of 65 per cent by July 1951. Thenceforward it dominated the Persian Gulf tonnage of the waterway. Although it could not immediately fill the gap left by Iran the expansion of its production raised aggregate oil shipments through the waterway in July–December 1951 above their level in January–June 1951 when the competition of Tapline had depressed their volume. During the oil crisis of 1951 crude imports into Britain first exceeded refined imports in volume, British oil imports via the Canal rose by 21 per cent and the British proportion of the Canal's oil shipments rose from 20 per cent in 1950 to 32 per cent in 1951 so that Britain became more dependent than ever on the waterway. The rapid expansion of production in Kuwait was encouraged by the extension of the concession of the Kuwait Oil Company by seventeen years until 2026, making it the longest concession on record, in return for the grant on 30 November 1951 of 50 per cent of the profits to Kuwait. At the same time the Anglo-American alliance of Anglo-Iranian and Gulf Oil in the Kuwait Oil Company was modified by the cancellation on 30 November 1951 of their agreement of 1933 which restricted the marketing of Kuwaiti oil by either partner to the disturbance or injury of the other's trade and had been undermined by a Gulf-Shell contract of 1947 for the marketing of Gulf's Kuwaiti oil by Shell.[2] The profits of the Kuwait Oil Company

[1] *The Times*, 30 October 1951, 5vi, 'Closing the Oil Gap'.
[2] W. A. Leeman, *The Price of Middle East Oil* (1962), 26, 161.

were even greater than those of Aramco[1] because Kuwait had absorbed only 7 per cent of the total capital of the Middle East oil industry but produced 36 per cent of its total oil in 1952 and did not produce by its expansion any reduction in the price of Middle East oil in general. Anglo-Iranian maintained its share of Middle East oil production unchanged and remained the price-leader in the Middle East oil market by the forbearance of Jersey Standard and Royal Dutch-Shell. Its British Tanker Company remained the largest single client of the Canal.

The closing of Abadan Refinery ushered in a new phase in the southbound oil traffic and ended the northbound shipment of petroleum products, which had supplied 26·2 per cent of total northbound cargo during 1950. Crude oil which had increased in volume by 45 per cent during 1950 rose by only 2·7 per cent during 1951, but the share of crude in the total volume of northbound oil shipments rose from 74 to 84 per cent. Kuwait as a simple exporter of crude thus displaced Iran as an exporter of both crude and refined oil. The closing of Abadan Refinery ushered in a new phase of refinery-construction east of Suez. It enabled India to insist on the construction of three refineries by Burmah-Shell, Stanvac and Caltex in return for the modification of its restrictions on foreign capital in 1952. It inspired Anglo-Iranian to undertake the construction of new major refineries on the periphery of the new Asia at Aden from September 1952 and at Kwinana near Fremantle from January 1953, in order to avoid giving new hostages to Asian nationalism. It also encouraged the large-scale extension of refinery-capacity in Western Europe, with the aid of subsidies from the U.S.A. through the Organization for European Economic Cooperation. To supply the local markets thitherto supplied from Abadan, refined oil products were shipped southwards through the Canal in increasing volume from July 1951. Such shipments came from Britain, the U.S.A., France and the Caribbean to supply fuel oil to Aden and petrol to India, increasing the loaded tankers in southbound tonnage twenty-fold and the shipments of southbound oil seventeen-fold from 111,000 tons in 1950 to 1,931,000 tons during 1951. During 1952 the volume of southbound cargo rose by 26·3 per cent but the tonnage of loaded southbound tankers rose by 220 per cent and the volume of southbound refined oil by 232 per cent. The Canal Company virtually received double dues thereon since the southbound oil was refined from Persian Gulf crude. That large revival of the southbound oil trade coincided with the decline of southbound coal shipments, from their postwar peak of 549,000 tons in 1950, by 40 per cent in 1951 and with their collapse during 1953 after their revival between 1948 and 1952. In 1952 the volume of bunker shipments of coal from Britain was first exceeded by those of fuel oil while the total value of coal exports was exceeded by that of exports of fuel oil. The number of Suez transits by motor-vessels exceeded those by steamships from 1953 and the tonnage of motor vessels outweighed steamer tonnage from 1955. Thus oil displaced coal in the fuel

---

[1] Leeman, 74–5.

of transiting vessels as well as in the cargo of the Canal. The decline of the coal-export trade compelled ships to leave in ballast and weakened the balance of payments of Britain. It reduced her carrying trade and entrepôt trade and removed one of her greatest advantages in the use of the Suez route.

During 1952 northbound oil cargo which had fallen by 10 per cent in 1951 rose by 7·2 per cent. During January–June 1952 Kuwait's shipments through the Canal rose by almost enough to balance the deficit left by Iran from January–June 1951. The rise of Kuwait stimulated competition by all other producers east of Suez. Iraq made its first shipment through the Canal in January 1952 from the Zubair field which had been located in 1948 to the west of Basra. The Basrah Petroleum Company, established in 1938 as a subsidiary of the Iraq Petroleum Company, began production in 1951 and shipped its oil for export by a 75-mile pipeline to the oil terminal built at Fao between 1948 and 1951. Thus Iraq's complete dependence on the Syrian pipeline for its export of oil ended. During 1952 Iraq shipped 11 per cent of its total oil production through the Canal, ranked fourth after Kuwait, Arabia and Qatar and opened another source of sterling oil to Britain. Kuwait continued to expand its production and export and raised its share of the northbound oil cargo from 73 per cent in 1952 to the peak proportion of 81 per cent in 1953 when it became the leading producer of oil in the Middle East, the fourth largest in the world and the second greatest exporter after Venezuela. Kuwait raised its proved reserves above those of Saudi Arabia with the discovery of the fields at Magwa in 1951 and Ahmadi in 1952. It remained essentially a producer and exporter of crude oil. It supplied Britain with sterling oil, with American dollars for oil sold outside the sterling area and with an expanding market for British exports and British oil equipment. Thus it was linked increasingly in economic interest to Britain which had been distrusted by Sheikh Ahmad (1921–50) since the British-imposed Treaty of Uqair in 1922 had given two-thirds of Kuwait's territory to Ibn Saud of Nejd. Britain preserved the independence of the sheikhdom against the dynastic expansion of Saudi Arabia which aimed to complete the work of 1922. The rapid expansion of oil royalties from £4,000,000 in 1949 to £20,000,000 in 1952 and £60,000,000 in 1953 freed the Sabah Sheikh, however, from financial dependence on Britain and on the local merchant families. The Sheikh became one of the richest men in the world and the absolute ruler of a state with a very limited territory, an increasingly cosmopolitan population of unnaturalized foreigners and an Anglo-American town in Ahmadi. The growth of the oil industry took place in a State without any agricultural base and diverted the local population increasingly from shipbuilding, sailing and pearl-fishing. Kuwait established a Development and Welfare Board in 1952 to supervise a six-year development plan, so following the example of Iraq rather than that of Saudi Arabia. The Kuwait Investment Board established in 1953 with its H.Q. in London became the largest single investor on the London Stock Exchange. It made Kuwait an invaluable support of the sterling area and of the function of sterling as a reserve currency, which thereby became dependent on the maintenance of confidence by the Arab world in British foreign policy. The Sheikh extended the sudden wealth earned through the boycott of the oil of Iran to his subjects in the blessings of distilled water as well as of technical education. The adoption of modern technology was symbolized in 1953 by the establishment of Kuwait Airways in association with B.O.A.C. and by the first three transits of the Canal under the Kuwaiti flag.

Kuwait was never linked to the Mediterranean by pipeline and became more dependent on the Canal than any other producer apart from the minor producer of Qatar. Iraq remained more dependent on pipelines than any other producer while Saudi Arabia enjoyed the advantage of choice between pipeline and Canal. The Iraq Petroleum Company, which had built each of its two pipelines to Tripoli in three years in 1932–4 and 1948–51, completed the large-diameter pipeline from Kirkuk to Banias in seventeen months, or six months ahead of schedule. The line was completed on 10 April and officially inaugurated on 18 November 1952. With an annual capacity of 40,000,000 tons or 175 per cent more than that of Tapline it lifted the restriction on the output of Kirkuk imposed by the closure of the line to Haifa in 1948 and trebled the oil production of Iraq between 1951 and 1953 when it reached the daily level of production reached by Kuwait in 1951. Because the Iraq Petroleum Company refined none of its export oil it ushered in a new phase in the competition for crude between the Canal and the pipelines, halting the steady rise in crude shipments via the Canal after May 1952. It also stabilized the production of crude in Saudi Arabia, which rose from the third to the second exporter of oil through the Canal in 1952 only because of the boycott of Iran. It had been estimated in 1949 that the completion of the three pipelines to Sidon, Tripoli and Banias would reduce oil traffic through the Canal by 50 per cent. Despite the completion of the third pipeline and the almost complete absence of Iranian oil, northbound oil cargo declined only in March 1953, recovered in April and surpassed the record volume of July 1950 in May. For the year 1953 Middle East oil production rose by 14·4 per cent while the volume of northbound oil rose by 7·6 per cent, surpassed the record shipments of 1950 and employed 55·4 per cent of the world's gross tanker tonnage on the Suez route. During 1953 the three pipelines carried 38,800,000 tons of oil while the Canal carried 49,400,000 tons or 27 per cent more than the pipelines. France reduced its imports via the Canal for the first time since 1947 and increased its imports from the Mediterranean terminals because the Compagnie Française des Pétroles could take full advantage of its Iraqi quotas, which rose tenfold between 1949 and 1953.[1] Those pipelines deprived the Canal of any monopoly in the transport of oil to Western Europe and extended a small share in the profits of the oil industry to the transit-states. All remained under the control of Syria and reached capacity in 1953–5. Thus during 1954 shipments by pipeline rose by 4·2 per cent while shipments by the Canal rose by 15·3 per

[1] J. Rondot, *La Compagnie Française des Pétroles* (1962), 114.

cent although world trade rose only by 7 per cent and industrial production in Europe only by 9 per cent. Saudi Arabia had reduced its shipments via the Canal by 52 per cent in 1951, by 10·5 per cent in 1952 and by 28·2 per cent in 1953 but increased its shipments via the Canal from 1954.

The development of the large tanker from 1951 was stimulated by the increased shipment of low-cost crude oil to distant refineries and enhanced the competitive capacity of the Canal but revealed the sharp limits imposed by the waterway on the size of ships in its maximum permissible draught of 34 feet. Tanker transits of that maximum draught rose from eleven in 1950 to thirty-two in 1951, forty-eight in 1952 and sixty-seven in 1953. The first large 30,000 deadweight-ton tankers to use the Canal were all newly built, the *British Adventure* of the British Tanker Company in September 1951 with a net register tonnage of 18,950 compared to the average tanker tonnage of 10,470 and the *Bérénice* of the Compagnie Auxiliaire de Navigation which passed southwards in March 1952 en route from Le Havre to Ras Tanura. The *World Unity* of Stavros Niarchos returned northwards in 1952 with a record cargo of 31,000 tons of crude. The *Tina Onassis* of Aristotle Onassis passed through in December 1953 with a cargo of 34,500 tons of crude from Kuwait for London and a net register tonnage of 23,000 when the average tanker tonnage was 11,420. Such great tankers used only a small amount of oil fuel en route to Suez and were compelled by the limited depth of the waterway to use the Cape route for the return voyage in order to earn maximum freight. Their alternative course was to pass through the Canal with a load below their capacity and then to fill up at the pipeline terminals 200 miles further north on the Mediterranean coast. Aristotle Onassis sought to eliminate that additional voyage and began in 1953 engineering studies for a by-pass pipeline along the side of the Canal, comprising three parallel 32 in. lines with a roadway and pumping facilities. Such a line would have been most unwelcome to the Canal Company as a competitor and a standing reproof. Onassis also demonstrated the limitations of the Canal when after the death of Ibn Saud he established the Saudi Arabian Maritime Tankers Company on 20 January 1954 against the violent objections of Aramco and launched in Hamburg on 15 June the world's largest tanker, the *Al-Malik Saud Al-Awal*, whose draught of 38 ft. 11 in. and deadweight tonnage of 47,000 precluded its economic use of the Canal, through which it could carry only 40,000 tons, and confined it to the Banias–Le Havre route. He was compelled by Aramco's objections to charter it in 1955 to Socony.

The increase in the size of tankers raised the share of tankers in the tonnage of the Canal faster than it increased their share in the number of transits. It increased steadily the average tonnage of vessels in transit and made depth far more important than width to the biggest tankers. The Canal Company could not afford to lag behind the adaptation of tanker terminals to large tankers and was compelled to improve the facilities of the Canal anew as it approached the last fifteen years of its concession. It completed the enlargement of Port Said harbour on 17 June 1953 and maintained thenceforward a 437-yard-wide channel for big ships in the Great Bitter Lake. It reached agreement with Egypt on new rules for the lighting and buoying of Suez Bay and introduced them from 1 December 1953 so as to facilitate the marshalling of convoys. It organized the convoys more tightly from 16 June 1954 further to speed up traffic. After the daily average number of ships reached the waterway's capacity of 39·2 in April 1954 the Company increased the maximum permissible draught for the first time since 1936 from 34 feet to 34 ft 6 in. from 10 May and to 35 feet from 16 December so as to facilitate passage by large tankers up to a deadweight tonnage of 38,000. On 7 December 1954 the board of directors decided to undertake the first section of an eighth works programme so as to create additional by-passes at Port Said and Kabrit, to increase capacity to forty-eight transits daily and to permit the passage of ships with a draught of 36 feet, or tankers of 45,000 deadweight tons. The board had already decided on 16 April to yield to the request of the Chamber of Shipping of the United Kingdom to reduce tolls from 15 July and to reduce the tolls on ships in ballast from 46·5 to 45·6 per cent of the full tariff, mainly for the benefit of tankers. To facilitate the control of convoys it brought into operation in 1955 the radio-telephone and the teleprinter between the Company offices and pilots as well as between ship and ship. The International Chamber of Shipping nevertheless requested a further reduction in dues in April 1955.

Tanker owners reduced their costs by registering their vessels under the flags of states with beneficial maritime codes such as the Liberian Maritime Code of December 1948, the first ship registered under which was the *World Peace* of Niarchos in March 1949. Similar legislation had been passed by Costa Rica in 1941 and Honduras in 1943. The flags of Liberia and Costa Rica first appeared in the waterway in 1949 while the flag of Honduras expanded its tonnage in 1949–50. Such 'flags of convenience' as the Organization for European Economic Cooperation called them in 1954 increased their share in the tanker traffic of the Canal after the Abadan crisis. Liberia rose from the eighth largest client of the Canal in 1950 to the fifth in 1953 and the third in 1954 when it surpassed Panama as the leading tanker-flag and contributed 9 per cent of the total tonnage. It increased its tanker tonnage using the Canal nearly sixfold and its share in the total tanker tonnage from 5 per cent in 1951 to 17 per cent in 1955. Its tonnage was mainly employed by the oil companies of the U.S.A. and increased as that of the U.S.A. declined, although not in exact correlation. The U.S. share of the tanker tonnage declined from 10·3 per cent in 1951 to 3·6 per cent in 1953 and 1·6 per cent in 1955 as that of the Greek shipowners increased.[1]

The first attempt to break the Anglo-Iranian blockade of Iranian oil failed when the Supreme Court of Aden helpfully ruled on 9 January 1953 that the 900-ton oil cargo of the Italian tanker *Rose Marie* was the property of Anglo-

[1] H. Solow, 'Those Resourceful Greek Shipping Men', *Fortune* (October 1953), 244.

Iranian, despite the nationalization of the oil-fields. The second attempt succeeded and brought Iranian oil through the Canal in February 1953 for the first time in nineteen months. The exclusion of Italy from direct access to the cheap oil of the Middle East for its developing refining industry had led the Ente Petrolifero Italia-Medio-Oriente to conclude a contract with the National Iranian Oil Company in 1952. In fulfilment of that contract the Italian tanker *Miriella* brought 4,600 tons of fuel from Abadan (20 January–14 February 1953) to Venice where the Court rejected on 11 March Anglo-Iranian's demands for the judicial seizure of the cargo. In March a further 10,000 tons passed through the Canal en route from Bandar Mashur to Leghorn. Iran had been forced to reduce its production to less than 5 per cent of the volume of 1950 but became able to contribute 83,000 tons or 6 per cent of its production to the Canal shipments of 1953. The cartel of the seven maintained their unity against the challenge from Iran. They first extended their collective operations to the field of production after the Shah took advantage of the rise of royalist nationalism thirteen years after his exile. He dismissed Mossadek on 12 August 1953 and appointed a new military government which reopened diplomatic relations with Britain on 5 December. The international oil companies formed the new consortium of Iranian Oil Participants on 9 April 1954 with its seat in Holland in order to undertake the production of oil in Iran. In that consortium Anglo-Iranian secured a share of 40 per cent, the five big American companies 35 per cent, Royal Dutch-Shell 14 per cent, the Compagnie Française des Pétroles 6 per cent and nine U.S. independents, including Getty and Aminoil, 5 per cent. The consortium allotted Iran 50 per cent of the profits and upheld the principle of nationalization but avoided direct control in practice. The National Iranian Oil Company, reduced to an ancillary role in production, sought to rescue as much as possible from the wreck of Mossadek's policy and became a great innovator in the discovery, loading and transport of oil as well as in the formation of oil policy. The redistribution of control of the Middle East oil industry left Anglo-Iranian wholly dependent on the Middle East for its supplies of oil and Royal Dutch the least dependent of all the big seven companies. Socony, California Standard and Texaco relied on the region for one-third of their supplies and Gulf for 60 per cent but Jersey Standard for only 18 per cent. Royal Dutch remained rather short of supplies of cheap crude and drew 15 per cent of its supplies from the region but marketed Gulf's Kuwaiti oil under the contract of 1947.

Abadan still shipped the bulk of its exports to Asia but failed to regain its former monopoly of refining for the ports of the Indian Ocean. The imports of southbound fuel oil to Aden reached their peak in 1952 and declined during 1953 as the refineries at Ras Tanura and Bahrein increased their output. Anglo-Iranian imported on 19 July 1954 its first cargo of Kuwaiti crude to Little Aden, where it opened its new refinery on 1 August. It thereby gave Aden a new oil-port and its largest industry so that it could end its imports of fuel oil from October and become again one of the cheapest bunkering ports in the world. After the Final Agreement of 19 September with the Consortium was ratified by the Chamber on 21 October and approved by the Shah on 29 October tankers from eight companies led by the *British Advocate* of the British Tanker Company began loading again at Abadan on 30 October.[1] Iran raised its oil shipments through the Canal from 43,000 tons in September to 127,000 tons in November, when it surpassed Bahrein, and to 185,000 tons in December, when it surpassed Iraq to rank fourth. Anglo-Iranian received £25,000,000 from Iran in settlement of all its claims as well as an estimated £214,000,000 from the seven other members of the consortium.[2] It announced on 3 November the distribution to its shareholders of a bonus of £80,550,000 from its general reserve and the change of its name from 17 December to the British Petroleum Company. Thus it responded to the Iranian challenge by achieving the greatest expansion in its history. It reduced its Persian history to a mere episode in a continuing career of development which enabled its net income for 1955 to surpass that for 1950. The resumption of economic relations between Iran and the West was crowned by the conclusion of the Bagdad Pact in 1955. The British Government was encouraged to decide in 1955 on the rapid expansion of the use of oil in power-stations, the reinforcement of the garrison in Aden and the eviction of Saudi forces from the Buraimi oasis, which was accomplished on 26 October 1955 at the price of ending diplomatic relations with Saudi Arabia. British interests became committed to the defence of the Sabah Sheikhs of Kuwait and of the al Thani Sheikhs of Qatar against Saudi Arabia, of the al Khalifah Sheikhs of Bahrein against Iran and of Aden against the tribes of the Hadhramaut.

The first commercial strike of oil in the Kuwait-Nejd Neutral Zone was made at Wafra in 1953 after U.S. oil imports via Suez began to rise again in 1952 and U.S. oil production first sank below 50 per cent of the world total in 1953. The first shipment of Wafra crude was shipped by Aminoil on a Norwegian tanker at Mina al Ahmadi and carried through the Canal to Houston, Texas, in February 1954.[3] Getty developed the new port of Mina Saud in 1955 because Saudi Arabia refused to allow him to pipe his share of oil from the Neutral Zone to Kuwait, whose Sheikh retaliated by forcing Aminoil to separate its crude from Getty's and to build another terminal at Mina Abdullah, so creating three separate tanker terminals along twenty miles of coast. The first shipment of oil from Mina Saud passed through the Canal in April 1955. The expansion of production from the Neutral Zone was wholly the work of American enterprise and supplied Kuwait with dollars from Aminoil but facilitated the drain of dollars from the central reserves of the sterling area through Kuwait. The U.S.A. however adopted voluntary import quotas during the recession of 1954 to limit imports from 1955 to

---

[1] *Financial Times*, 1 November 1954, 1 iv.
[2] *The Times*, 6 August 1954, 6 i; 31 August, 10 ii.
[3] *New York Times*, 28 February 1954, III, 1 viii.

10 per cent of the total U.S. demand, so preventing the oil-shed moving inland into the U.S.A., forcing the excluded oil into other markets and intensifying the competition between coal and oil in Western Europe. The Canal dues were heavier on oil than on wheat, wool or rubber and helped to protect the industry of the U.S.A. from the competition of the Middle East but made the Cape route competitive for tankers to the U.S.A. as it could not be for tankers to Europe.

The southbound flow of bunker oil began to decline from July 1954 and reached its pre-Abadan level in October 1954 when Aden made its first shipment of refined oil northwards to the Mediterranean and Abadan followed with a similar shipment. Bahrein's shipments of refined oil via Suez also revived in 1954 for the first time since 1948. India reduced its imports of southbound refined oil from October 1954 when the Standard Vacuum refinery was opened on 19 November at Trombay Island, Bombay, where the Burmah-Shell refinery was also opened on 17 March 1955. Southbound oil tonnage thus declined from its peak of 7,231,000 tons in 1953 by 16 per cent in 1954 and by 69 per cent in 1955 when northbound shipments of refined oil rose to their highest level since 1951 to form 7 per cent of northbound oil tonnage. In April 1956 the first shipment of gas oil from British Petroleum's Kwinana refinery, which had been opened in 1955, passed through the Canal en route to Genoa. The rise of the oil trade of the Persian Gulf and the Gulf of Suez enabled the value of the trade of Suez to exceed that of Port Said from 1954 and stimulated Egypt to begin a dynamic search for oil from 1954. Suez gained a State refinery with a pipeline to Cairo inaugurated on 24 July 1956 and began its long-delayed expansion as the oil port of the metropolis.

The continued expansion of the oil trade reinforced the domination of the Persian Gulf in the traffic of the Canal and restored its pre-Abadan proportion of total tonnage in 1955. Iran seems to have expanded its exports at the expense of those from Qatar, which declined in 1955 after five successive years of increase. Iran surpassed Qatar in January 1955 to rank third in shipments of oil through the Canal: it surpassed Saudi Arabia in July 1955 and January 1956 to rank second after Kuwait. The Consortium maintained Iran as a producer of crude rather than of refined oil and did not permit its shipments to exceed those of Kuwait, which remained the leading producer in the Middle East from 1953 until 1965. Kuwait became a pure exporter whose exports were treble its National Income. In 1955 it supplied 39 per cent of the crude exports of the Middle East and 63 per cent of the crude shipments through the Canal while Saudi Arabia supplied 10 per cent, Iran 7·4, Iraq 6 and Qatar 6 per cent. It remained a pure producer of crude until the Kuwait Oil Company decided early in 1956 on a sixfold expansion of the capacity of its refinery at Mina al Ahmadi. Its counterpart were the refineries in Western Europe, which trebled their capacity between 1950 and 1955 and made the leading producers of refined oil, Britain, France, the U.S.A., Italy and the Netherlands, into the leading importers of crude via the Canal. The concentration of the most profitable of the processes of the oil industry in Europe reduced the strain on reserves of foreign exchange but reduced the value of crude imports from the Middle East below the value of refined imports from North America and ranked the share by value of Canal oil shipments at one-quarter of their share by volume in northbound cargo. Oil formed 76·5 per cent of the volume of northbound cargo in 1955 but less than 20 per cent of its value.

The Canal benefited by the fall in tanker freights and by the growing demands of transit-states to compete so effectively with the pipelines that it carried off the bulk of the annual increment in the oil production of the Middle East from 1954. Thus the oil production of the region rose by 18 per cent during 1955 but pipeline shipments declined by 1·2 per cent while northbound shipments of crude via the Canal rose by 14 per cent. The Canal raised its proportion of world tanker cargo from 18·4 per cent in 1952 to 19·1 per cent in 1955 but did not regain its peak proportion of 1950. Tankers which formed 18 per cent of the gross tonnage of the world fleet and 58·5 per cent of that of the world tanker fleet provided 65·5 per cent of the tonnage of the Canal in 1955. The 1,370 tankers made 5·75 transits each on the average while 2,310 other vessels made three transits each on the average in 1955. Tanker tonnage developed its own autonomy through the vast expansion in the trade in the most portable of fuels. Six flags supplied 81 per cent of the Canal's tanker tonnage in 1955: Britain supplied 20·6 per cent, Liberia and Norway 17 per cent each, Panama and France 9 per cent each and Italy 8 per cent. Norway employed more than a third of its tanker tonnage in the transport of oil through the Canal to Europe and the U.S.A.: it maintained its position as the second client of the Canal from 1950. The construction of more economical tankers increased the tonnage of the average tanker by 20 per cent between 1951 and 1955 and the tonnage of the average transiting vessel by 12·5 per cent: the average tanker was 9 per cent larger than the average vessel in 1950 but 20 per cent larger in 1955. The expansion in tanker traffic strained the capacity of the waterway to its limits and made the bridge built in 1952–4 across the Canal for Egyptian military traffic to the Palestine front a grave hindrance. The bridge was opened on 1 November and restricted the fairway in width to 315 feet. It was struck two months later by Niarchos' tanker *World Peace*, holding up 150 ships for four full days from 31 December 1954 to 3 January 1955.

The oil boom established the dominance of cargo over passenger traffic more decisively than ever before. It ranked Port Said from 1953 above all the ports of Europe and Asia in its transits and its tonnage. It raised the tonnage of the Canal above that of the Sault Ste. Marie Canals in 1954 for the first time since 1889[1] and to a level almost treble that of the Panama Canal by 1955. By 1955 the Canal carried 12·8 per cent of the volume of world trade but

---

[1] A. G. Ballert, 'The Soo and the Suez', *Science*, 28 October 1955, 822–3. A. G. Ballert, 'The Soo versus the Suez', *Canadian Geographical Journal* (November 1956), 160–7.

13·3 per cent of its value. It carried 9 per cent of the volume of world dry cargo but 19 per cent of the volume of world tanker cargo. It was hardly used by such important bulk commodities as coal, iron ore and wheat but by cheap bulk oil, expensive raw materials and manufactures. Textile fibres supplied 2 per cent of the volume of northbound cargo but 60 per cent of its value, of which wool formed 20 per cent, silk 20 per cent and cotton 20 per cent while rubber added another 10 per cent and tea 5 per cent. The Canal carried 43 per cent of the volume of coconut oil and ground-nut oil entering into world trade, 45 per cent of the copra, 54 per cent of the tea, 58 per cent of the tin and 69 per cent of the rubber. It increased its share in the volume of world production of oil from 6 per cent in 1950 to 8 per cent in 1955. In 1955 it carried 43 per cent of the oil production of the Middle East, 46 per cent of its oil exports and 64 per cent of its oil exports to the West. It carried 45 per cent of the crude oil imports of Western Europe, 44 per cent of those of Italy, 47 per cent of those of France and 75 per cent of those of Britain which however imported through the Canal only 46 per cent of the value of its imports of oil because its refined imports from America were expensive while its crude imports from the Persian Gulf were cheap. Thus the Middle East supplied only 18·2 per cent of the value of the cargo of the Canal but 66 per cent of its volume.[1] The Canal remained far more important in the foreign trade of the lands east of Suez than in that of those west of Suez.[2] It nevertheless remained dominated by Western shipping which supplied 97·6 per cent of its tonnage under twenty-eight flags, including 88 per cent under the seven flags of Britain, Norway, Liberia, France, Italy, Panama and the Netherlands.

The seven great oil companies supplied the ultimate demand for the tankers dominating the traffic of the Canal. They cooperated in production, transportation, and, above all, in marketing, where their high-cost distribution organizations formed the real basis of their power. Their administered prices remained wholly uninfluenced by the consumer and restricted competition to the field of service. The companies benefited greatly by the inelastic demand for petrol, whose monopoly was one never attained by lamp-oil nor threatened by the commercial development of alternative engines for cars.[3] They competed not so much with each other as with other producers of energy, especially of coal, and so provoked the defensive formation of the European Coal and Steel Community in 1952. They encouraged the spread of oil fuel and discouraged the development of alternative fuels or sources of energy.[3] They used up the by-products of refining in their new petrochemical industry to manufacture rubber, plastics, artificial fibres, detergents, pesticides and fertilizers. Technocrats revered oil more than any other fuel and identified economic growth

[1] United Nations Department of Economic and Social Affairs, *Economic Developments in the Middle East 1955–1956. Supplement to World Economic Survey, 1956* (New York, 1957), 99–101.
[2] *United Nations Monthly Bulletin of Statistics* (December 1956), xii, 'The Importance of the Suez Canal in World Trade'.
[3] Pierre Fontaine, *Les Secrèts du Pétrole* (Paris, Les Sept Couleurs, 1963), 49–75, 103–30.

with the expansion of the power industries in the past as well as in the present.[1] They fostered the myth that oil was the life-blood of modern industry, agriculture and transport as well as the very basis of civilization. Thus the oil companies were able to maximize their share of the expanding markets for oil products in Europe and also to minimize their share of the heavy social costs.

Those great companies found in the cheap oil of the Middle East a vital interest which they inevitably inclined to identify with the general interest of the West. Thus they encouraged the diffusion of the interrelated myths that oil-resources were highly localized, that Europe was utterly dependent on the oil of the Middle East and that the Suez Canal was the oil lifeline of the West. In fact oil resources were by no means as limited in extent as the concessions of the oil companies, which wished to maximize the value of their investment therein as well as in refineries in Europe. Their policies therefore encouraged the use of low-cost foreign oil rather than of high-cost domestic oil but sterilized the oil resources of Europe, Africa and Asia Minor and created a structural strain on the reserves of foreign exchange necessary to pay $2,000,000,000 per annum for oil imports into Europe.[2] Their high prices for Middle East oil were essential in order to protect the high-cost oil industry of the U.S.A.[3] but could not prevent a growing shift from oil to natural gas in the U.S.A. Their high profits freed them from dependence on the world capital market, financed their continued expansion and enabled them to use their fields in the Arab world as cost-free reservoirs. The Middle East had increased its share of world production from 16·7 per cent in 1950 to 21·2 per cent in 1955 but its share of world reserves from 45 per cent in 1950 to 65 per cent in 1955 and 75 per cent in 1956[4] so that its potential importance for the future outweighed its current importance almost fourfold. In fact the sixteen countries of the O.E.E.C. still found in coal the mainstay of their energy economy and used oil in 1955 for only 18 per cent of their total requirements of energy.[5] The coal-producing countries of Belgium, France, Germany, the Netherlands and England depended least on oil while the coal-importing countries of Portugal, Switzerland, Sweden, Norway, Iceland and Ireland consumed a much greater proportion of oil. Only the small states of Denmark, Ireland, Sweden, Portugal, Iceland and Greece depended on oil for more than one-third of their total supplies of energy. By contrast the U.S.A. derived 67 per cent of its total needs of energy from oil while the Communist world clung to coal and hydro-electricity. As Europe replaced the U.S.A. as the

[1] P. Bairoch, 'Le mythe de la croissance économique rapide au XIXe siècle', *Revue de l'Institut de Sociologie* (1962), 321–3.

[2] O.E.E.C., *Oil the Outlook for Europe* (Paris, O.E.E.C., 1956), 67.

[3] United Nations Economic and Social Council, Economic Commission for Europe, *The Price of Oil in Western Europe* (Geneva, 1955), 2–3, 10–23.

[4] *New York Times*, 3 February 1956, 1 vii, Wallace E. Pratt's revision of proved reserves at the end of 1954 from 126,300 million barrels to 230,000 million barrels out of 306,000 million barrels in the Free World.

[5] O.E.E.C., *Oil the Outlook for Europe* (1956), 13, 25–7.

fastest growing market for oil, the O.E.E.C. estimated that the contribution of oil to the total supplies of energy would rise from 18 per cent in 1955 to 21–4 per cent in 1960 and to 24–36 per cent in 1975.[1] Thus the oil companies aspired to subdue the 'oil-less' lands of Europe more fully to the hegemony of their alien enterprise and to valorize their hard-won concessions in the Middle East. They became partners of the State in the Middle East as well as in the West but could never protect their wells by more than barbed-wire fences. Their efficiency as true international organizations was limited in the Middle East by their private ownership, their commercial basis and the profit-motivation of their Western managements. Thus they became inevitably suspect of exploiting a gift of Allah in the interests of the infidel, especially in the transit-states of Egypt and Syria, whose Arab nationalism burned the fiercest. They supplied from the Middle East 79 per cent of the total volume of Europe's oil imports in 1955. The Canal carried only 45 per cent of those imports while the Syrian pipelines carried 33 per cent and the Cape route 4 per cent. The real importance of the Canal like that of the Middle East lay in the ensuing twenty years. The Canal Company found the burden of improvement of the waterway increasingly heavy as tanker tonnage grew at a consistent rate of 15 per cent per annum during 1954, 1955 and 1956. It was therefore inspired from 1955 to hope that the oil companies might help it to secure either an extension of its concession or a new concession linking the Company and Egypt as partners. Thus it might become like them a standard-bearer of the new mercantilism in the interests of world trade as well as of its shareholders.

[1] O.E.E.C., *Oil the Outlook for Europe* (1956), 30.

37

EGYPT'S BATTLE FOR THE CANAL, 1951–1954

THE dissolution of the world-empires of the European Powers ushered in a time of troubles for the West as the familiar landmarks of the preceding century in Asia disappeared amidst confusion and alarm. The disintegration of the British Empire began with the surrender of India and the Nile Delta in 1947, the Afrikaner victory in the South African general election of 1948 and the establishment of Israel in Arab Asia. Thus the Cape–Cairo–Calcutta axis of the greatest empire in world history was shattered, imperilling the security of the Suez route more than that of the Cape route. In Eastern Asia an era of Chinese history ended with the Communist revolution, which was carried to victory by the peasantry and culminated in the capture of Manchuria, sixteen years after its establishment as a Japanese puppet-state. Communist troops from the north crossed the Yangtze on 20 April 1949 and disabled the sloop *Amethyst*, the last British gunboat on the 'Son of the Ocean'.[1] The reunion of China under Communist rule ended the longest civil war in modern history together with the era of the unequal treaties, the treaty ports and gunboat-diplomacy. China's revolt against social hierarchy, family, religion, property, Christianity and Europe created the greatest single breach in the structure of world capitalism since 1917. The occupation of Shanghai on 27 May 1949 ended the great era of the international settlement and made Hong Kong once more a refugee camp and a rock of exile as it had been during the Tai-Ping Rebellion. The island became an asylum for Kuomintang capital, capitalists and workmen, the last survivor of the unequal treaties and the new terminus of China-going P. & O. vessels. Thus the West migrated from the fringe of the treaty-ports to its island-bases on the rimland of the new Asia. The trade of the Canal was not adversely affected because China remained an autarchic state and had even been exceeded in soya production by the U.S.A. in 1949. Formosa, which had been made by Japan into a major producer and exporter of sugar from the 1900s, became the last base of the Kuomintang and exported sugar through the Canal from 1949 to 1953. Mainland China began its industrialization on a large scale, restricted its foreign trade to a State-to-State basis and shifted the balance of its industry and population from the coast to the hinterland. China replaced India as the great patron of revolution in Asia which was swept by its seventh wave of unrest since 1913. That unrest united the great cultures of the East, the Sinic, the Hindu-Buddhist and the Islamic, in a common hostility to the

[1] D. Reed, *Somewhere South of Suez* (London, Cape, 1950), 7, Dedication 'To H.M.S. *Amethyst*, July 1949'.

44-2

West and in a common sense of an Asian unity which had thitherto been lacking. The Canal became thenceforward the route by which the new Asia could threaten Europe and so reverse the pattern of the nineteenth century.[1]

The establishment of the independence of India in 1947 and of China in 1949 was followed by that of Indonesia, the greatest island-power in the world, where Java had made its first postwar shipments to the Netherlands of sugar in March 1948, of molasses in January 1949 and of bauxite in February 1949. The Netherlands sank from the fourth to the seventh largest client of the Canal during 1948 and reduced its trade via the Canal even more after the establishment in 1949 of independent Indonesia. The Canal lost one of its oldest and greatest clients, although Indonesia remained the largest single producer of pepper, quinine, kapok and, from 1951, of rubber. The Netherlands reoriented its trade from East to West and drew its oil from the West Indies more than from the Persian Gulf. Islam gained by the establishment of Indonesia and even more by the growth of Arab nationalism which revolutionized Western Asia as the Communist victory revolutionized Eastern Asia. Arab nationalism was religious rather than ethnic in origin and nearly always favoured Islam against any other creed. It spread within the sphere of the Arabic language which was the tongue of a world religion, a world empire and a culture without music or painting to weaken the power of the spoken word. It found its greatest support in the historic capitals of Arab empire, Cairo, Damascus and Bagdad. Its standard-bearers became the hidden generation born between 1910 and 1920 who grew up under the European successors to the Ottoman Turks after 1918 and found locust-control a poor substitute for independence. Those radical nationalists aspired to achieve unity, freedom and dignity for their people in opposition to the divide-and-conquer policy of the new Turks. Their influence became the greater because so few Arabs thought in terms of territorial nationality or of loyalty to the State. The intrusion of Israel strengthened the Arab-Moslem community which overshadowed the deep divisions within the societies of Western Asia and reinforced the moral unity extending from the Maghrib to the Arabian Gulf. Even the traffic of the Canal reflected the Arab revival when the first vessels appeared under the flag of Lebanon in 1946, Morocco in 1948, Tunis and Syria in 1951 and Yemen in 1952. The Arab culture of Nilotic Egypt was reinvigorated in response to the Iraqi and Saudi bids for the leadership of the Arab world as well as to the British attempt to maintain the Sudan in separation from Egypt. The West recognized the strategic unity of the Middle East but not the emerging moral unity of the Arab-Moslem world. The British in particular still believed in an unconditional harmony of interests between themselves and the Arabs, as the Americans believed with as much basis in the special affection of the Chinese for themselves.

Anglo-Egyptian friction reached new heights over the Treaty of 1936 after

[1] Moustapha El-Hefnaoui, *Les Problèmes Contemporains Posés par le Canal de Suez* (1951), 73.

Farouk became reconciled in 1949 to Nahas as the sole alternative to rule by martial law. British interests were simultaneously consolidated in the Canal Zone through the conversion in 1949–50 of their temporary barracks and camps into permanent constructions to house over 20,000 troops. Those interests were strategic rather than economic since trade could be diverted to the Cape route whereas British troops could not be transferred to any other base because no Arab oil-state was eager to replace Egypt as a bastion of defence for the West. Those troops remained therefore in the Canal Zone without the continuing consent of Egypt. The Wafd sought once more to fulfil its historic function and to end the British occupation as well as the Treaty of 1936 by negotiation. It spent almost two years in repeated efforts at negotiation because Farouk wished to keep the British garrison as an additional support to his throne and feared the social consequences of an abrogation of the Treaty. The recurrent fluctuations in Suez shares in 1950–1 reflected the varying temperature of Anglo-Egyptian relations as share-values slumped far more than dividends. The first discussions on the Suez base were undertaken on 5 June 1950 between the C.I.G.S. General Slim, Nahas and Salah El-Din, who requested immediate and total evacuation.[1] Slim asked for an alliance to maintain troops in Egypt for common defence in peacetime because Russian troops could reach Egypt in four months: he rejected Nahas' offer on 6 June of the right of re-entry to the base in an emergency. Egypt could recognize no other enemy than England save for Israel and could tolerate no foreign occupation masked beneath a defence treaty. She had no interest in the defence of the West against Russia and regarded the Cold War as a civil war between rival exploiters, seeing Stalin as no more of a threat than Hitler. She did not want to become a pawn in the Great Game of the Great Powers or to be defended against her own wishes.[2] The British ambassador suggested on 8 July a compromise by distinguishing between the fighting forces which would be evacuated and the technicians who would remain. Salah El-Din thought however that the technicians irreplaceable by Egyptians numbered some hundreds rather than thousands and that G.H.Q. might well be on board a ship.

The Foreign Office rejected Egypt's demand for evacuation on 8 September.[3] The failure of renewed talks between Nahas and the British ambassador in October was followed by the deterioration of Anglo-Egyptian relations and a decline in royal support for the Wafd. Nahas' threatened abrogation of the Treaty of 1936 in the Speech from the Throne on 16 November earned unanimous applause in the press of Damascus and Bagdad and precipitated attacks in Jordan on Glubb Pasha as well as on its treaty of alliance with Britain. Bevin's refusal to consider the unilateral abrogation of the Treaty

[1] Farag Moussa, *Les Négociations Anglo-Égyptiennes de 1950–1951 sur Suez et le Soudan* (Geneva, Droz, 1955), 21–4.

[2] A. P. Thornton, *The Imperial Idea and its Enemies* (1959), 347.

[3] *The Times*, 29 September 1950, 5 vi, 'Britain and Egypt. Defence of the Canal Zone as Crucial Issue'.

because of the international importance of the Canal produced the first open rift between the Cairo students and the Wafd in the demonstrations on 22 November. In renewed conversations in London Salah El-Din demanded from Bevin on 9 December the unity of Egypt and the Sudan as well as the evacuation of British troops within a year.[1] Egypt benefited by the tension between England and the U.S.A. in 1950–1 and by the building-up of the U.S. Sixth Fleet in the Mediterranean to more than double the strength of the British Fleet. British efforts to secure transit-rights through Syria to link up her forces in the Canal Zone with those in Iraq were frustrated.[2] The impassioned debate of 20 March 1951 on the Anglo-Egyptian Financial Agreement providing for the release of £150,000,000 of Egypt's sterling balances during the following ten years revealed the sharp opposition between English and Egyptian nationalism and reduced the majority of the Labour Government to three. The British Notes of 11 April offered the evacuation of its fighting forces by 1956 but were categorically rejected by Egypt on 24 April because opinion had hardened against alignment with the West after the revolt of Iran. On 1 May a Wafdist deputy tore up a copy of the 1936 Treaty in the Chamber amid sustained and unanimous applause and invited the Government to declare traitors any Egyptians who collaborated with the British forces.

Moustapha El-Hefnaoui, the Director of the Egyptian Press Office in Paris and a personal friend of Salah El-Din, mooted the possibility of unilateral denunciation with an international mandate[3] so as to regain in the Canal Zone 'the nerve centre of Egyptian territory... on which the life and death of the land depends'.[4] He was inspired by Mossadek's example to recommend the conclusion of a new Convention with the Canal Company to replace that of 1949. He recognized that the remaining seventeen years of the Company's concession was a short time in the life of a nation and therefore suggested a procedure for the transfer of administration from the Company to Egypt through the early appointment of a joint technical commission of valuation and the creation of a duplicate Egyptian technical and administrative personnel.[5] On 16 March 1951 he recommended to Nahas the creation of a new portfolio, a Minister of Suez Canal Affairs for the period from 1952 to 1968, so encouraging the introduction of a private member's bill of nationalization,[6] which profoundly disturbed the Canal Company. Hefnaoui's thesis was the most elaborate product of the first predominantly Arabic literature on the Canal called forth by the crisis in Anglo-Egyptian relations. The crisis stimulated the interest of Levantine intellectuals in the occupation of 1882 and in the barbarization of the West in the East, reviving Flaubert's idea of the

[1] F. Moussa, 31–5.

[2] P. Seale, *The Struggle for Syria. A Study of Post-War Arab Politics* (London, Oxford University Press, 1965), 104.

[3] M. El-Hefnaoui, *Les Problèmes Contemporains posés par le Canal de Suez* (1951), 125–6.

[4] Ibid., 190, 250.   [5] Ibid., 287–93.

[6] *The Times*, 20 March 1951, 4iii. *Manchester Guardian*, 29 March 1951, 5i, 7ii.

isthmus-of-Suez Orient in a study which won the Prix France-Égypte in
1953.[1] Zionist fears for the security of the Canal[2] were diffused through the
mass-media of communication[3] and the first documentary film about the
Canal.[4] The Egyptian cause was supported not only by Americans but also
by Russians who were disturbed by the passage of the 'greatest hydrotechnic
creation of the nineteenth century'[5] from the control of the monopoly-
capitalism of England to that of the U.S.A. France blamed Britain's difficulties on its consistently anti-French policy in the Levant and on its refusal ever
since 1864[6] to accept the internationalization of the Canal. In the disenchant-
ment with private capitalism inherited by the 1950s[7] from the 1930s the cause
of the Company was publicly identified in France with the heroic figure of
'the greatest entrepreneur in the world in the second half of the nineteenth
century'[8] in the first biography based on the private papers of Lesseps[9] and
in the first vessel named after him since 1880, the *Ferdinand de Lesseps* built
for the Messageries in 1951.

The Korean War was produced by China's attempt to recover the first of
its tributary-states. The resistance of the West marked the beginning of a
sustained attempt to seal China off from the outer world after a century of
effort since the Opium War to open it up.[10] The establishment of the independence of India and of China had ended an era in the internal history of those
countries. The resurgence of China in the world marked the true end of the
Vasco da Gama epoch of Asian history[11] and ushered in a new era of world
history comparable only to the decline of the ancient world or to the waning
of the Middle Ages. Charles-Roux's pessimistic reminder on 13 June 1950
that the Company's dividend must include an element of capital-repayment

[1] Hassan el Nouty, *Le Proche-Orient dans la Littérature Française de Nerval à Barrès*
(Paris, Nizet, 1958).
[2] S. J. Weinberger, 'The Suez Canal in Anglo-Egyptian Relations', *Middle Eastern Affairs*
(December 1950), 347–56.
[3] W. R. Moore, 'The Spotlight Swings to Suez', *National Geographic Magazine* (January
1952), 105–15. H. J. Schonfield, *The Suez Canal in World Affairs* (London, Constellation,
1952), reviewed by H. L. Hoskins in *Middle East Journal* (Summer 1953), 393.
[4] *The Suez Canal* (1952), based on articles in *Life*, 5 November 1951, 32–8; 3 December
1951, 21.
[5] I. A. Dementjew, *Der Sueskanal* (Leipzig, VEB Bibliographisches Institut, 1954, from
the Russian edition of 1952), 13, 19, 22.
[6] C. M. Bellet, 'A Propos de Suez. L'Arbitrage de Napoleon III (1864)'. *Revue Politique
et Parliamentaire* (Décembre 1951), 373–82.
[7] G. Schwarzenberger, *Power Politics* (London, Cape, 1951, second edition), 129.
[8] L. H. Dupriez and D. C. Hague (ed.). *Economic Progress. Papers and Proceedings of a
Round Table held by the International Economic Association* (Louvain, Institut de Recherches
Économiques, 1955), 525.
[9] G. E. Bonnet, 'Ferdinand de Lesseps—Le Canal de Suez 1854–1866', *Revue des Deux
Mondes*, 15 Mars 1950. Idem, *Ferdinand de Lesseps. Le Diplomate. Le Créateur de Suez* (Paris,
Plon, 1951).
[10] O. Lattimore, *From China Looking Outward. An Inaugural Lecture* (Leeds University
Press, 1964), 1.
[11] K. M. Panikkar, *Asia and Western Dominance. A Survey of the Vasco da Gama Epoch of
Asian History, 1498–1945* (London, Allen, 1953).

because the value of the share could not be reconstituted on the Bourse in eighteen years[1] reduced share-prices by 8 per cent (12–16 June): the outbreak of war on 25 June reduced prices by 15 per cent (23 June–18 July). The traffic of the Canal was, however, increased by the war which ended the recession of June 1950 and revived the shipment of oil after a decline in world demand had produced an oil surplus in 1949–50. The war increased the military consumption of oil and ended the clash between Britain and the U.S.A. over dollar-sterling oil. It enlarged the markets of the primary producers of jute, cotton, rubber, manganese, copper, tin, zinc, lead and bauxite. It increased the shipments through the Canal to the U.S.A. of rubber, especially in the form of latex, and manganese, the volume of which doubled between 1949 and 1952. China and Manchuria were eliminated from the international market in oil-seeds in which they had just reappeared in 1950 to supply the immense demand for soya meal generated by the expansion of the broiler chicken industry in the West. The resulting rise in the price of oils and fats increased shipments of oil-seeds through the Canal in 1950 and 1951. The war coincided with shortages of coal and grain in Europe and Asia in the winter of 1950–1, peak shipments of American wheat via Suez in 1951–2 to India and Pakistan, an increase in India's share in the cargo tonnage of the Canal, the reduction of India's purchases of Australian wheat to nil and an expansion in Australia's wheat shipments via Suez by 124 per cent in 1951.[2] Thus it raised freights and ushered in a great boom in shipping.

The war led to the extension of large-scale military aid by Russia to China, diverted China's foreign trade from the capitalist to the communist bloc and united Communist China and Russia in common opposition to the West. The war thus stimulated a large-scale increase in Polish shipping using the Canal from 1951 when Poland quadrupled its tonnage and rose from the twenty-third to the sixteenth client of the Canal. It also brought the flags of Hungary in 1951 and of Bulgaria in 1952 through the Canal for the first time. Ships with strategic materials for Communist China used the Canal despite the embargo-resolution of the United Nations of 18 May 1951. The war ended the activity of British merchants and missionaries in China, making Hong Kong the home for another of the lost causes of Asia. The announcement by Eden as Foreign Secretary on 20 May 1952 that the majority of British enterprises still operating in China had decided to withdraw from that country ended the era of Western dominance. The European firms in Asia began to redeploy their interests into Malaya, Australia, Canada, the U.S.A. and Europe. The war transformed the economy of Hong Kong which was debarred from its entrepôt trade with China and completely cut off from its traditional hinterland. Forced to develop new seaward hinterlands in Japan, Indo-China, Borneo, the Philippines

[1] R. Thery, 'La Position du Canal de Suez Dix-Huit Ans avant l'Expiration de sa Concession', *L'Économiste Européen*, 23 Juillet 1950, 39–41.

[2] *Supplément au Bulletin Le Canal de Suez*, 15 Mai 1953, 'Mouvement Maritime et Commercial avec l'Australie'. Ibid., 15 Octobre 1953, 'Trafic du Blé au Canal: son Évolution de 1909 à 1952'.

and Malaya,[1] the island experienced prodigious industrial and financial development and became the Beirut of Eastern Asia. The revived fear of the
yellow peril in Australia encouraged large-scale immigration via the Canal
particularly from Germany and Italy in special emigrant vessels in 1951–2.
The war also stimulated the economic expansion of Japan and brought the
first shipment of Japanese steel through the Canal in 1951 to Britain and
Sweden. The Nippon Yusen Kaisha reintroduced the flag of Japan to the
waterway in October 1951 on the *Eiroka Maru* en route from Yokohama to
Hamburg while the Osaka Shoshen Kaisha built the *Suez Maru* in 1953. The
war was far more instrumental in expanding traffic through the Panama Canal
whose transits rose by 19 per cent between 1950 and 1952 while those via Suez
rose by only 3·5 per cent. It maintained the number of troops using the Canal
at a high level up to 1953 but proved to be the last conflict east of Suez in
which the West enjoyed the unrestricted use of 'freedom's Suez'.[2] It was
followed by the first appearance in the Canal of two new flags in 1953, that of
South Korea and that of Ethiopia, which had gained a seaboard in 1952 for
the first time since 1890 in return for its yeoman services during the war to the
United Nations and the U.S.A. The conflict also encouraged the West to
project a Middle East Command on the model of N.A.T.O. after the repeated
despatch of reinforcements to Korea from the Canal Zone.

A secret conference of Defence Ministers of the white states of the Commonwealth considered between 21 and 26 June 1951 the despatch of Australian, New Zealand and South African troops to the Canal Zone under such a
new Middle East Command. In the Commons the Foreign Secretary Morrison insisted on British rights under the Treaty of 1936 to use the base until
1956 and called on American support for the defence of Suez. Salah El-Din
replied on 6 August that the British Government had thereby closed the door
to further discussion. For two more months the Wafd Government hesitated,
despite mass demonstrations on the fifteenth anniversary of the Treaty on
26 August against the Treaty, imperialism and the English.[3] Nahas, encouraged by Mossadek's resolute action against Anglo-Iranian, finally capitulated on 4 October to the pressure of public opinion.[4] On 8 October he
introduced legislation to end the Treaty, which he had himself concluded,
amid thunders of applause in the Assembly and further mass demonstrations
in the streets. He cited eighteen precedents for unilateral denunciation, beginning with Russia's denunciation of the Black Sea clauses of the Treaty of
Paris in 1870. The capitulation of the Wafd to the national cause reduced
Suez shares by 6·8 per cent (8–10 October) and unleashed a great wave of
popular enthusiasm. Egypt's claims were asserted by the despatch of auxiliary
police to the Canal towns. Nahas won the support of every Arab state except

---

[1] B. Boxer, *Ocean Shipping in the Evolution of Hong Kong* (University of Chicago, Department of Geography Research Paper 72, 1961), 3–8.

[2] P. Viereck, *Shame and Glory of the Intellectuals. Babbit Jr. vs. the Rediscovery of Values*
(Boston, Beacon, 1953), 239.

[3] F. Moussa, 236. [4] Ibid., 241.

the Sudan and rejected on 15 October the offer by N.A.T.O. of the occupation of Egyptian soil by four powers in place of one under a Middle East Defence Organization, which had been projected in Ottawa on 18 September. Britain refused to surrender its position as the chief guardian of the Middle East[1] and clung to its rights under the Treaty, compelling Egypt to reveal the complete dependence of the Canal Zone on the Delta and the dependence of British rights on Egyptian acquiescence.

After the Treaty was abrogated by the unanimous vote of Parliament on 15 October large parties of students from Cairo arrived on 16 October by road and rail in Ismailia, where riots began with the burning of six British buses in the Place Champollion and looters of a N.A.A.F.I. canteen were aided by the Egyptian police. At Abu Sueir contractor's labour left the R.A.F. station as non-cooperation began on the Indian pattern. Throughout the zone military traffic was refused by civilian telephone exchanges and the State railways.[2] The total damage to British property mounted to £500,000.[3] General Erskine, the commander of the British garrison, suppressed the riots and, on his own initiative, seized control of the bridge at El Firdan, so cutting off the Egyptian Army in the Gaza strip from the Delta and compelling the Labour Government to take resolute action in his support.[4] Britain sent immediate reinforcements of troops and warships to the Canal Zone and prohibited the export of arms to Egypt on 22 October. The Egyptian Customs ceased to clear British Army goods from 17 October, compelling the British Army to take over Adabiya Port on 18 October. Egypt then black-listed from 18 October all ships violating its decree on the treatment of the British forces in the Canal Zone and subjected them to the same disadvantages as those that had touched at Israeli ports. A boycott of British goods was launched on 19 October throughout Egypt and was extended in the Canal Zone to a boycott of English shoppers. The Egyptian labour-force working for the British forces continued to shrink, especially after the Moslem Brethren established road-blocks for the confiscation of passes to military camps. The British Army was compelled to isolate the Canal Zone as far as possible from the rest of Egypt and to rely increasingly upon its own resources to handle its own rail traffic, shipping communications, supplies and oil. The Canal Company was placed in a dilemma, being forced to choose between Britain and Egypt when asked by the Egyptian Customs on 23 October to deny pilots to ships working for the British forces in the Canal Zone. The Company recognized that the zone had virtually passed under British martial law and accepted the use of the Canal by British ships without pilots, although they were refused clearance from 24 October. Thus it provoked attacks in the Egyptian press and a suggestion in *El Ahram* on 27 October that it should be nationalized.[5] The Free Officers under Nasser,

[1] *The Times*, 10 October 1951, 5 iii.
[2] Ibid., 17 October, 6 vi.   [3] Ibid., 20 October, 6 ii.
[4] Ibid., 17 October, 7 ii, 'Time for Firmness'. K. Martin, 'The Gambit in Egypt', *New Statesman*, 20 October 1951, 423.
[5] *The Times*, 29 October 1951, 4 vi.

the president of their executive committee since 1950, and Sirag ud Din, the Minister of the Interior, even planned for the Canal to be permanently blocked by the mining of a British ship in transit.[1] The labour force at the British depot at Tel el Kebir declined from a 75 per cent turn-out on 22 October to one of 40 per cent on 25 October after Sirag ud Din organized the return to Cairo of 18,000 Egyptian workers and their families.

The general election of 25 October 1951 converted the Conservative minority of six into a majority of seventeen and opposed the electoral democracies of England and Egypt as never before. The new Churchill–Eden Government poured more reinforcements into the Canal Zone and imported labour from Mauritius and Cyprus, which also supplied the fresh produce denied by the Delta. A strike by the Egyptian searchlight operators and mooring-boat workers then compelled the Company to end night convoys through the Canal after 29 October and to restrict night-time navigation to vessels operating their own searchlights.[2] General Erskine told his troops on 30 October that 'we are standing on our rights and have no intention of being starved out, forced out or knocked out'.[3] A guerrilla was then launched on 31 October by 'liberation battalions' of nationalists and 'Young Brethren' of the Moslem Brethren, producing bloody clashes at Port Said, Ismailia and Suez. The landing of reinforcements at Port Said on 6 November raised Suez shares by 6 per cent (5–7 November). The guerrilla was directed not against a State but against an army of occupation. Its operations of sniping, cable-cutting and night attack avoided the concentrated forces of the British Army in favour of their outposts, detachments, families, individual members and communications. The guerrilla fighters lacked the shelter of mountain or forest but enjoyed the protection of the villages of the isthmus and the support of their fellow-Moslems against the infidel. They compelled the British to protect every movement made by their troops, sharply increasing the cost of the occupation. Egypt made no attempt however to dam the Sweet Water Canal while Erskine in return did not interfere with the free flow of oil from Suez to Cairo.

Ismailia as the great centre of communications became the main focus of conflict, like Alexandria in 1882. Erskine was compelled to recognize on 12 November that the town was no longer safe for its 1,100 service families, which were evacuated between 20 and 23 November. The auxiliary police first opened fire on the British at Ismailia on 17–18 November and at Suez on 3 December, when the total number of Egyptians killed since 16 October rose to 117. After attacks on the water-reservoir at Kafr Abdu the British Army demolished on 8–9 December a whole Arab village of fifty brick houses, despite the objection of the British ambassador, in order to create a new and safer road to the waterworks.[4] The Wafd Government, which had vainly

[1] *The Times*, 14 December 1953, 8iv; 15 December 1953, 6vii.
[2] Ibid., 30 October 1951, 4v.
[3] Ibid., 31 October 1951, 6vi; 30 October, 4v.   [4] Ibid., 10 December, 4i.

ordered the Governor of Suez with his 800 police to give battle to 8,000 British troops,[1] decided on 9 December to dismiss all the 500 British subjects in its service and to authorize all citizens to bear arms. It protested to the United Nations on 11 December as well as to Britain on 14 December and recalled its ambassador from London on 13 December. Egypt ceased to send her officers to England for training and recruited a German military mission.[2] Guerrillas derailed a military train in the Canal Zone for the first time on 16 December and forced Erskine to forbid movement by night throughout the zone from 20 December. Cypriot and Greek labour in British employment was intimidated from serving the British without protection. The despatch of the first batch of Cairo University students as youth commandos to the zone provoked Erskine's warning on 26 December that he would be obliged to crush them with the powerful forces he had not yet used.[3] The Government newspaper *Gumhour al Misri* then reported on 31 December plans for a general attack from the Canal Zone by the Western Powers on Russia and offered £E1,000 to the Egyptian who killed 'the red-faced thief Erskine'[4] as well as £E100 for each British officer.

British opinion failed to recognize that pressure from the police, the army officers, the students and the Moslem Brethren was shifting Egyptian resistance from the Indian to the Zionist pattern.[5] On 4 January Centurion tanks fired 20-pounder shells into buildings at Suez used by guerrillas and so brought out all the 1,500 Egyptian employees of the Canal Company on strike from 7 January,[6] leaving no Egyptians engaged in maintaining the flow of traffic. The workers of Port Said assumed their traditional place in the vanguard of the battle for independence while civilians in Ismailia marched about openly with tommy-guns.[7] The Canal Company feared a general strike by all its workmen for three days (8–10 January) until it accepted a token stoppage of one hour per day.[8] The Navy took over control of traffic at Port Said.[9] The Company was forced to condone British action and became the object of attack, its communications between Ismailia and Cairo being cut by skirmishes. Pilots secured police protection when returning along the Canal road after duty. The Residency and the Company offices at Ismailia were damaged on 10 January by automatic fire which nearly killed President Charles-Roux.[10] One hundred guerrillas of the National Liberation Army fought their first major action on 12 January against a military train near Tel el Kebir. The British used tanks in order to win the second battle of Tel el Kebir but created the first student-martyrs and precipitated a general exodus from the village to the

---

[1] *The Times*, 15 December 1953, 6 vii.

[2] Y. Famchon and M. Leruth, *L'Allemagne et le Moyen-Orient. Analyse d'une Pénétration Économique Contemporaine* (Paris, Éditions des Relations Internationales, 1957), 33.

[3] *The Times*, 27 December 1951, 6i.   [4] Ibid., 1 January 1952, 6 vi.

[5] Ibid., 28 December 1951, 5 vi–vii, 'British Task on the Suez Canal Zone. A Vital Holding Operation'; ibid., 10 January 1952, 5 iii, 'Disorders in Egypt'; ibid., 17 January 1952, 6 v.

[6] *The Times*, 8 January 1952, 6 vi.   [7] Ibid., 9 January, 5 iii.

[8] Ibid., 10 January, 4 v.   [9] Ibid., 10 January, 3 ii.

[10] Ibid., 11 January, 4 v.

Delta.[1] The road from Moascar to Tel el Kebir had become so exposed to attack from the villages through which it passed that the Army was forced to construct an alternative by-pass road, to use 25-pounder field guns against snipers on 15 January[2] and to arrest 170 armed Egyptian police on 16 January in the two villages of El Hamada and Tel el Kebir South.

The escalation of the conflict increased the strain on the Army, despite the reinforcement of the 43,000 troops by another 40,000. Churchill was compelled to appeal on 10 January for the despatch of a brigade or battalion of U.S. Marines to the Canal Zone[3] and on 12 January for the despatch of naval help by Norway and the Netherlands.[4] In his address to a joint session of Congress on 17 January he asked for the despatch of token forces by the U.S.A., France and Turkey. 'We do not seek to be masters of Egypt. We are there only as servants and guardians of the commerce of the world.'[5] His suggestion was received in stony silence by Congress and emphatically rejected by the State Department, while Egypt sent Notes on 19 January to the U.S.A., France, Norway, Holland and Sweden declaring that the despatch of warships to the Canal Zone would be a clearly hostile act. The climax to hostilities was reached in Ismailia after Erskine evicted 8,000 Egyptians from the south-west quarter, one of the main guerrilla centres, and then found it necessary to disarm the auxiliary police, who had been ordered to resist arrest by Sirag ud Din. In the battle of Ismailia on 25 January Erskine's forces captured the Police H.Q., killing 41, taking 790 into custody[6] and raising Suez shares by 7·8 per cent (23–28 January). That military action was far more important than the demolitions at Kafr Abdu. It finally destroyed any possibility of agreement between Egypt and England on the presence in peacetime of British troops in the Canal Zone:[7] it saved Ismailia and lost the Canal Zone. It deeply impressed the British General Staff with the fighting capacity of the Egyptians: it provoked suggestions for a transfer to the Gaza strip[8] and for the construction of a Gaza–Akaba Canal,[9] which was thus revived for the seventh time since its original proposal in 1855. Above all, it transformed the fellahin-police from petty tyrants into popular heroes and precipitated the riots of Black Saturday, 26 January, when the Moslem Brethren, the Socialists and the students attacked the European quarter of Cairo to the cry of 'Allah akbar' and 'We want arms to fight for the Canal'. The rioters were joined by the police in revolt against the sacrifice of their comrades at Ismailia by the Government. Their systematic onslaught on the shrines of European civilization,

[1] *The Times*, 14 January, 4i–ii.
[2] *Manchester Guardian*, 16 January 1952, 5 vii.
[3] Lord Moran, *Winston Churchill. The Struggle for Survival 1940–1965* (London, Constable, 1966), 362.
[4] *The Times*, 14 January 1952, 4 ii.
[5] *Manchester Guardian*, 18 January, 7 ii.
[6] *The Times*, 26 January, 4i–ii. *Manchester Guardian*, 26 January, 5 ii.
[7] Hansard, *Commons Debates*, 5 February 1952, 860, John Freeman.
[8] *Manchester Guardian*, 26 January, 4i. *The Times*, 28 January, 5 ii.
[9] Hansard, *Commons Debates*, 5 February 1952, 911–12, G. Wigg.

including the symbols of the three successive stages of the occupation in Shepheard's Hotel, Thomas Cook's and B.O.A.C., destroyed 400 buildings at a cost of £10,000,000 and killed 17 British subjects. Farouk used the demonstration to dismiss the Wafd Ministry and replaced Nahas by Aly Maher. The new government ordered the National Liberation Army to evacuate its positions in the Canal Zone, reopening communications between Cairo and Suez and ushering in a détente in Anglo-Egyptian relations.

At Port Said the searchlight electricians began to resume work on 1 February[1] and so restored the night-time use of the waterway. They were followed by some of the mooring men, by the Customs officials on 4 February and by the stevedores on 12 February when the first ship worked by Egyptian labour passed through the port. The Company paid its employees a special bonus in recognition of their achievement in facilitating the passage of a record number of ships, of which 37 per cent had been British, during the four months of the crisis. Its shares rose by 22·6 per cent between 29 January and 27 February but declined by 6 per cent (21–26 March) after the British occupation of Ismailia ended. It contributed to the cost of a new Mosque at Ismailia after Farouk ordered the street signs to be changed from French to Arabic. British opinion still could not recognize that direct foreign control of the Canal Zone was only possible through the direct foreign control of Egypt itself.[2] The Cairo riots inspired the Free Officers to advance their date for the seizure of power from 1954–5 to 1952.[3] Those riots shattered the foundations of the monarchical State which foundered in a welter of Byzantine intrigue. Abboud Pasha, a director of the Canal Company since 1951, bribed Elias Andraos Pasha, who was the fifth pasha since 1913 to be appointed as the Government's Special Commissioner with the Canal Company, to use his influence as a royal councillor to overthrow Hilali Pasha, the successor of Aly Maher.[4] Abboud thereby averted a claim for millions of unpaid taxes and brought back to power Hussein Sirry Pasha. The new government was the third of four palace-led Cabinets and was disapproved by the whole country: it lasted for barely three weeks, the monarchy for three days longer. On 23 July 1952 ninety Free Officers with small-arms took the fate of Egypt into Egyptian hands for the first time in twenty-seven centuries.[5] They were borne to power on the seventh and greatest wave of Egyptian unrest since 1882 and sought to fulfil the hopes of the previous national movements of 1892, 1908, 1919, 1926, 1935 and 1946, because the Army had become increasingly more representative of the inarticulate peasantry than either the Assembly or the Wafd. Farouk relied upon intervention in his favour by the British troops from the Canal Zone which was forbidden by Eden and precluded by Nasser's

[1] *The Times*, 4 February 1952, 4 iii.

[2] Ibid., 13 February, 5 v, A. H. Hourani, 'Control of Suez'; ibid., 3 March, 5 vii, 'Middle East Defence: Strategic Importance of the Canal Zone'.

[3] T. Little, *Modern Egypt* (London, Benn, 1967), 137.

[4] A. Eden, *Full Circle* (London, Cassell, 1960), 236–7.

[5] J. and S. Lacouture, *Egypt in Transition* (London, Methuen, 1956), 277–9.

troops across the road to Ismailia. Thus Farouk paid the price for the humiliation of Egypt at Abdin, Falluja and Ismailia. On 27 July he sailed into exile from a deserted quayside at Alexandria[1] on the same yacht which had carried his grandfather into exile in 1879. The Macedonian dynasty of Mehemet Ali came to an end with its tenth ruler, having lasted for ninety-three years longer than the ten years after his death foretold by its founder.

The revolution of 1952 neither enlarged the political nation nor affected the material condition of the Egyptian people but wholly transformed their moral environment. The establishment of a government of Egyptians by Egyptians for Egyptians stirred new life within the most fertile of river valleys, ended the identification of the abundance of the Delta with resignation of the spirit and began the sustained shift of the civilization of the Nile to a new level. The Army's function as the great vehicle of modernization, frustrated and shattered in 1882, was restored in 1952 so as to open new channels of social mobility and create a drive for the modernization of society as a whole. The resulting militarization of society, economy and bureaucracy inspired the people of the Nile to look increasingly to the Government as an army to its leader rather than as a bird at the hunter. To prevent the capture of society by the Moslem Brethren the new regime placed less emphasis on the Moslem past of Egypt than on her Pharaonic past, developing a mass interest therein comparable to that engendered among European intellectuals in the 1840s and Levantine intellectuals in the 1920s. The tise of an Arabic-speaking intelligentsia began to weaken the predominance of French culture in Egypt. The Municipal Council of Port Said renamed the most northerly street of the port the Rue du 23 Juillet in order to commemorate the dawn of a new era which promised to extend to all citizens the luxury of self-respect. The symbolic achievement of self-determination by one-third of the population of the Arab world created an Arab rival to progressive Israel and revolutionized the aspirations of the younger generation in Amman, Beirut and Bagdad. The new regime sent Egypt's greatest landowner into exile and triumphed over the Parliament of the pashas, which had overwhelmingly defeated the three agrarian bills of 1945 and 1950. The abolition on 30 July of the civil titles of the Ottoman regime was intended to end the reign of the hundred families and set an example followed in Jordan, Lebanon and Libya. The Law of Agrarian Reform of 8 September compelled the resignation of Aly Maher and encouraged the first proposals for an Aswan High Dam which would give Egypt control of her own water-supply.

The Canal Company had experienced a crisis on almost every change of ruler in Egypt but was more seriously weakened by the Egyptian renaissance than by the battle for the Canal. It lost the services of Elias Andraos Pasha, who resigned as royal councillor at the demand of Neguib and was then arrested.[2] Its shares declined by only 2·2 per cent between 25 and 30 July, rising thereafter by 9 per cent by 6 August. The new Government, however,

---

[1] *The Times*, 28 July 1952, 6 ii.   [2] Ibid., 26 July 1952, 4 iii.

raised the Egyptian tax on the Company's revenue from 16 to 17 per cent on 13 August. It resumed control of the bridge at El Firdan from 9 October and began building a new military bridge across the Canal. It fulfilled Hefnaoui's recommendation of 1951 and created on 15 October a new Suez Canal Department attached to the Ministry of Commerce and Industry in order to prepare for the end of the concession in 1968 and to acquaint itself with the operations of the Company, reducing the price of Suez shares by only 3·8 per cent (14–16 October). It also began to refuse entry visas for foreign pilots so as to accelerate the appointment of qualified Egyptians. The Company's response followed its traditional pattern: it decided not to erect the statue of Fuad for which a pedestal had been built at Port Fuad and it renamed the Farouk Canal the Ballah By-Pass. It also published its first brochure on the Canal in Arabic for local consumption, expanded its medical services and built a Medical Centre at Ismailia in 1952–3. Although the Company repaid its 75-year loan of 1887 by 1952 ten years before its due date and opened a New York office in 1952[1] to handle its American investments its investment policy was attacked at the shareholders' meeting in 1953 because it brought in only 3 per cent on £28,600,000 and made no provision to free the Company's reserves from Egyptian control through the establishment of a separate French investment trust.[2] Thenceforward the Company accelerated the amortization of its shares.

 The boycott of Israeli shipping which had been established by a Palace ministry in 1948 and strengthened by the Wafd Ministry was maintained by the military regime of General Neguib. Under the Conservative Government Labour M.P.s pleaded for forceful action, as Conservative M.P.s had under the Labour Government. Thus George Jeger asked Selwyn Lloyd to force a passage through the Canal for Haifa-bound tankers, adding that the Foreign Secretary 'when he was in opposition, roared like a rabbit for resolute action'.[3] The need of the military regime for arms and the revival of a scheme for a Middle East Defence Organization brought the Minister of War to Cairo. Head reaffirmed that Egypt was the logical place for a Middle East base[4] and that the Canal Zone was 'absolutely vital strategically' because Cyprus could be only a station but not a base.[5] Neguib denounced his 'hateful and horrible' statement, concluded on 30 September that 'at need the British troops would evacuate the United Kingdom but not the Canal Zone of Egypt'[6] and emphasized on 28 December that Egyptians could defend their own fatherland better than others to the last man.[7] By January 1953 G.H.Q., Middle East, had recognized that the Canal Zone base with its £700,000,000 of equipment was useless without active Egyptian cooperation. The number of troops had

[1] *New York Times*, 27 October 1953, 55i.
[2] *Le Canal de Suez*, 15 Juin 1953, 9524.
[3] Hansard, *Commons Debates*, 26 May 1952, 912, G. Jeger.
[4] *The Times*, 22 September 1952, 4iv.
[5] *Manchester Guardian*, 25 September, 7vi.
[6] *The Times*, 1 October, 6iii.
[7] Ibid., 29 December, 6v; 30 December, 5vii.

been raised to 80,000, of whom 50,000 were employed in defending the 30,000 in the base against the Egyptian Army, aided and trained by German instructors and staff officers, while 12,000 Mauritian and East African pioneers had been imported to perform the services thitherto performed by Egyptian labour. The defence of the Canal Zone had increased its costs to over £50,000,000 per annum while it had also increased friction with Jordan and Iraq and retarded recruiting to the Regular Army. The Army's reappraisal of its needs was encouraged by the entry into N.A.T.O. of Turkey, dominating Cyprus, and by the Egyptian General Staff's Note of 9 January 1953 on the strategic importance of the Canal. That Note emphasized Egypt's capacity to defend the Canal herself, the incapacity of England and France to defend their possessions in the Far East and the dependence of the security of the Canal on the security of the Mediterranean route. Its message was reinforced by Nasser's threat of a resumption of the guerrilla if England did not evacuate the Canal Zone and by American pressure upon Britain. The Anglo-Egyptian agreement of 12 February 1953 on the Sudan was concluded by the British Government in the hope to secure better terms of agreement on the Canal Zone[1] but brought together a number of rebellious Conservative M.P.s led by Julian Amery in opposition to the idea of evacuation. Israel also became alarmed at the prospect of the disappearance of the British buffer between Egypt and Palestine: she vainly demanded on 14 April to be consulted by Britain and the U.S.A. in any negotiations over the Canal and then sought to reach an entente with France.

Talks began in Cairo on 27 April after Nasser agreed to accept British technicians, but were suspended on 6 May after six meetings because Egypt insisted on assent to the principle of evacuation and on the transmission of orders to base personnel through the Egyptian authorities, while Britain refused to accept less than an agreement for twenty-five years. A new crisis in Anglo-Egyptian relations began after Dulles visited Neguib, and Churchill affirmed in the Commons[2] that Britain intended to stay in the Canal Zone, even if it necessitated a rapprochement with Russia at the expense of the special relationship with the U.S.A. Egypt forbade on 13 May the supply of provisions to the British Army without special authority and commandos began to land from Cyprus at Port Said from 14 May while the youth of Suez welcomed two officers of the Revolutionary Council on 15 May with a plea to reopen the guerrilla in their cry 'We want to be the Mau-Mau of the Canal! We want to liberate the Canal!' Official British opinion doubted whether the Egyptians could achieve in the Canal Zone what the Greeks had failed to achieve in the Piraeus or the French in Bordeaux[3] and did not shirk the comparison between the anti-German resistance movements and the anti-

---

[1] *The Spectator*, 20 February 1953, 204–5, 'East of Suez'. Major-General L. O. Lyne, 'Strategy and the Suez Canal', *The Listener*, 19 March 1953.
[2] Hansard, *Commons Debates*, 11 May 1953, 888–95.
[3] *The Round Table* (June 1953), 226, 'The Future of the Suez Canal Zone'.

British movement in the Canal Zone in its wish to retain control of 'the Clap-ham Junction of the British Commonwealth'.[1] In Anglo-American talks on the Canal in Washington Dulles, however, persuaded the British to surrender their insistence on the permanent maintenance of technicians to service the base[2] and proposed on 11 July evacuation within eighteen months and the retention of 4,000 technicians for five years at the utmost. Under heavy American pressure England accepted the principle of evacuation within eighteen months while Egypt accepted the presence of 4,000 technicians for three years[3] and so secured her first promise of arms aid from Eisenhower on 15 July. Nasser made a 'death or victory' speech on 2 August at Ismailia 'this dearest part of our sacred country'[4] and proposed to the Arab League that an Arab Army of 150,000 should be raised and based in the Canal Zone.[5] The readiness of the Government to capitulate to American pressure and Egyptian threats aroused growing opposition among its own supporters. At the Conservative Party Conference Julian Amery warned the Government on 8 October that the nation which had already endured 'the scuttle from Pales-tine and the shame of Abadan' would not tolerate the evacuation of 'the hinge of our imperial strength'.[6] Salisbury's readiness to accept a permanent com-mitment of 70,000 troops to the Canal Zone[6] provoked a fierce retort on 9 October from Nasser, who threatened 'a popular organised struggle by millions of Egyptians'.[7] Negotiations then broke down on 21 October over the question of the uniform of the technicians because Churchill was deter-mined to retain military control of the base. Raids on British troops became however rarer and weaker than in the past.

Early in December the Conservative Government decided to transfer H.Q., Middle East Forces, from the Canal Zone to Cyprus.[8] On 15 December thirty-nine Conservative M.P.s tabled a motion of protest against the re-sumption of negotiations with Egypt and were joined on 16 December by two more.[9] Those forty-one members of the Suez Group did not originally

[1] *The Round Table* (June 1953), 222.
[2] *The Times*, 13 July 1953, 6iii; 14 July, 6i–ii; 20 July, 7vi–vii.
[3] T. R. Little, 'Britain, Egypt and the Canal Zone since July 1952', *The World Today* (May 1954), 194–5.
[4] *The Times*, 3 August 1953, 6iii.
[5] Ibid., 26 August 1953, 5i.
[6] Ibid., 9 October, 1953, 2v.
[7] Ibid., 10 October, 5iv; 22 October, 8iii.
[8] Eden, *Full Circle*, 244.
[9] House of Commons, *Notices of Motion Given on Tuesday 15th December 1953, No. 31.* 839, The six sponsors were Julian Amery, R. Assheton, C. J. Holland-Martin, John Morrison, Captain C. Waterhouse and Charles Williams. The other signatories were P. A. D. Baker, P. Bell, W. H. Bromley-Davenport, F. F. A. Burden, T. Clarke, R. F. Crouch, P. Donner, J. A. L. Duncan, A. Fell, F. Graham, R. Grimston, J. Hall, Frederic Harris, Reader Harris, W. W. Hicks-Beach, Viscount Hinchingbrooke, I. M. Horobin, H. M. Hyde, H. W. Kerr, E. A. H. Legge-Bourke, G. Lloyd, F. Maclean, P. Maitland, D. Marshall, A. Maude, J. Mellor, G. D. N. Nabarro, J. E. Powell, W. R. Rees-Davies, D. Savory, W. Teeling, Herbert Williams and Paul Williams, joined on the following day by I. J. Pitman and Brigadier Rayner.

personify extremist opinion so much as the broad groundswell of traditional national sentiment. They had been born in the 1900s and educated in the Edwardian ethos of empire as befitted the middle class from which they mostly came, although they did include one viscount, three baronets, four knights and two Privy Councillors and they did rally earnest support in the House of Lords.[1] They certainly drew inspiration from romantic Zionists such as Amery but they attracted neither of the two Jewish members of their Parliamentary Party. Many were soldiers or ex-soldiers but none were sailors. They represented mainly constituencies in England either in the industrial areas or in the counties, together with the imperial outposts in Ulster, the Scottish Lowlands and South Wales but excluding the Highlands and Welsh Wales. Their opponents concluded that they comprised embittered ex-Ministers and young ambitious newly elected back-benchers.[2] In fact they were held together by a coherent and positive belief in England and in the Empire which transcended the mere hunger for office. They recognized that the Government had lost touch, under American and Egyptian pressure, with national opinion and they wished to renew its waning faith in Britain's mission. Their leader Captain Waterhouse cherished a religious belief in the Empire[3] and was determined to call a halt to the long succession of retreats and withdrawals made by the British Government since VE-day. He objected strongly to the pursuit of a Labour policy of evacuation by a Conservative Government. He was not concerned primarily with the security of shipping or of oil supplies but with the role of the Suez base as an outpost of Empire, so winning the emotional if not the intellectual approval of Churchill.[4] He thought that it would be possible to hold Port Said or Suez with one or two brigades whilst evacuating the rest of the Canal Zone,[5] a policy which would have maintained 'Suez as a sore in the side of Africa'.[6] The Suez Group spoke for England and gave the press a national cause. They won strong support in the constituency associations, the party organization and the committees of the House. They would have exerted even greater influence upon the party leadership if the Labour Left led by Bevan had not in opposition to Shinwell offered its support to the Government and so produced a convulsive closure of the Conservative ranks.

The Suez Rebels focused attention upon the isthmus and so encouraged some exaggeration of the past importance of the Canal and of the Desert War,

[1] Hansard, *Lords Debates*, 17 December 1953, 190–8, 206–15, 238–40, 240–6, Lords Rennell, Hankey, Vansittart and Killearn.

[2] A. Nutting, *No End of the Lesson. The Story of Suez* (London, Constable, 1967), 22. Grimston and Kerr had been Parliamentary Secretaries in 1945, Assheton Financial Secretary to the Treasury in 1943–4 and Waterhouse Parliamentary Secretary to the Board of Trade from 1941 to 1945. The average age of the group in 1954 was 50 but three of its members were in their thirties—Amery, Baker and Paul Williams.

[3] Hansard, *Commons Debates*, 17 December 1953, 592, 623, C. Waterhouse and Viscount Lambton.

[4] Ibid., 662, R. Crossman. [5] Ibid., 599, Waterhouse.

[6] Ibid., 622, Viscount Lambton.

as was manifest in the first attendance of royalty at the Alamein Dinner in 1953, the unveiling of the Alamein Memorial in 1954 and the publication of the first volume of General Playfair's military history.[1] Egypt's increasing influence over the Canal, however, strengthened its own tradition of the Canal's history at the expense of the nationalist traditions of Europe.[2] The Egyptian revolution of 1952 reawakened interest in the military revolution of 1882[3] and in 'the third British occupation of Egypt'.[4] It also alarmed the economic élites of the West[5] and encouraged the Zionist Kimche to urge the British to defend the Canal as 'the base of the Commonwealth'.[6] It brought the British Government however to the very brink of evacuation, compelled a reappraisal of imperial strategy and diverted interest to the alternative routes via Canada and the Cape.[7] London was linked to Johannesburg by a regular service of Comets from 1952 as well as to Cape Town by the Union-Castle Line, whose *Edinburgh Castle* first broke the Cape record of 1938 by arriving in January 1954 in 11 days and 21 hours. Thus the new strategy of empire enhanced the value of the Cape route, which Sukarno in 1955 called 'the lifeline of imperialism': it also encouraged the creation in 1952 of a self-governing Sudan and in 1953 of an Aden Municipality as well as a South Arabian Federation.

In the Canal Zone twenty-one attacks during January 1954 inaugurated a resumption of the guerrilla, which encouraged a suggestion for the transfer of the British base to Israeli territory south of the Beersheba–Gaza line[8] and revived complaints against Egyptian restrictions on Israeli cargo, especially by members of the Suez Group.[9] Egypt had placed foodstuffs on the contraband list on 30 November 1953 during Israel's trade-negotiations with India and Pakistan. Her right to deny passage in self-defence to Israeli ships was maintained by Eden in January 1954 against his own Minister of State.[10] The Israeli representative at the Security Council claimed on 12 March that Egypt's restrictions had throttled 95 per cent of the shipping to Israel and

[1] I. S. O. Playfair, *The Mediterranean and Middle East* (London, H.M.S.O. 1954), xxvi.

[2] P. Herrmann, *Conquest by Man* (London, Hamilton, 1954), 359.

[3] A. Greiss, 'La Crise de 1882 et le Mouvement Orabi', *Cahiers d'Histoire Égyptienne* (Mars 1953), 47–74.

[4] M. M. Safwat, 'The Background of the British Occupation of the Suez Canal and Egypt in 1882', *Islamic Review* (December 1953), 24–8.

[5] A. Siegfried, 'The Suez: International Roadway', *Foreign Affairs* (July 1953), 616–17, 631–2. H. L. Hoskins, 'Some Aspects of the Security Problem in the Middle East', *American Political Science Review* (March 1953), 188–98.

[6] J. Kimche, *Seven Fallen Pillars. The Middle East, 1945–1952* (London, Secker, 1953, second edition), 395. H. J. Schonfield, *Egypt, Cross Road on a World Highway* (Peace News Pamphlet, 1953, 16 pp.).

[7] W. G. East, 'The Mediterranean: Pivot of Peace and War', *Foreign Affairs* (July 1953), 623.

[8] R. H. Crossman, 'Breakdown of the Suez Talks', *New Statesman*, 30 January 1954, 121.

[9] Hansard, *Commons Debates*, 25 January 1954, P. Maitland, H. Williams; 3 February, P. Williams; 10 February, P. Maitland; 17 February, P. Maitland; 11 March, F. Harris; 17 May, H. Williams.

[10] A. Nutting, *No End of a Lesson*, 22.

100 per cent of its crude oil imports, to facilitate which an Akaba–Haifa pipeline was proposed[1] as a new version of the Akaba Canal. A resolution in condemnation of Egypt was moved by New Zealand and secured eight votes, but was vetoed on 29 March by Lebanon and Russia, while Nationalist China abstained, preventing Israel from repeating its diplomatic triumph of 1951. Within Egypt Nasser, supported by the Army, established his supremacy over Neguib, supported by the Moslem Brethren, and was appointed Prime Minister on 17 April. Nasser achieved a great triumph by ending the guerrilla after five months and compelling a resumption of talks. He reached agreement with Nutting and Head on the principle of evacuation which official British opinion had come reluctantly to accept.[2] Eden recognized that the base could not usefully be maintained against the hostility of Egypt,[3] and persuaded Churchill with the support of all the Cabinet[4] to abandon his demand to maintain uniformed workers at the base. The Chiefs of Staff had already considered Captain Waterhouse's proposal for a Fayid airfield-base. They were not however prepared either to guard its extended lines of communication as far as Port Said or Suez or to launch a Fayid air-lift.[5] The Ministry of Defence therefore announced on 23 June its intention to transfer the H.Q. of Middle East Forces to Cyprus.[6] The resumption of Anglo-Egyptian talks on 11 July encouraged vain proposals by Zionist sympathizers for the transfer of the base to the Negev desert[7] and by one of the Suez Rebels for the establishment of a neutral zone in the Canal area on the Panama model of 1903 as a separate and 'neutral nation, probably with an Arab prince as ruler'.[8] An agreement was initialled on 27 July, while Suez shares rose by 23·6 per cent (5–27 July) to the benefit of the Treasury as well as of the French shareholders.

The Anglo-Egyptian Agreement of 1954 was not called a treaty because of the odium attached in Egypt to the Treaty of 1936, which Britain thereby agreed to terminate. It was to last for seven years and it provided for the withdrawal of British troops within twenty months of its signature, for the maintenance of the base by 1,200 civilian technicians, of whom 800 might be from outside Egypt, and for its remilitarization in the limited emergency of an attack by a foreign power excluding Israel. Thus Egypt secured acceptance of the principle of evacuation by 1956 which Britain had offered in 1951,

---

[1] Hansard, *Lords Debates*, 16 March 1954, 400–1, Hore Belisha. *The Times*, 20 March 1954, 5 ii.

[2] *The Round Table* (June 1954), 223–35, 'Cross Purposes in Egypt. Two Years of the Revolution'.

[3] Eden, *Full Circle*, 256, 260.

[4] Lord Moran, *Winston Churchill* (1966), 478, 580, 'The Prime Minister and the Suez Rebels'.

[5] Hansard, *Commons Debates*, 29 July 1954, 730, A. Head.

[6] *The Times*, 24 June 1954, 6 iv.

[7] *Manchester Guardian*, 12 July 1954, 6 vi, E. L. Mallalieu, 'Suez or the Negev? A Possible Alternative'.

[8] Hansard, *Commons Debates*, 26 July 1954, 21, W. Teeling.

while Britain could only secure the right of re-entry which Nahas had offered in 1950. Egypt accepted twenty in place of fifteen months as the period for evacuation but secured the substance of her demands. England gained only the shadow, a right of re-entry in the event of an actual war but not in the event of an emergency nor even in the event of an attack upon Iran or Israel. England also had to accept an agreement for only seven years instead of for ten years. She had to reduce the number of technicians from 4,000 to 800. The Agreement also recognized the Canal as an integral part of Egypt but not as vital to the British Empire as it had been described in the Treaty of 1936 and in the Commons by Head in 1946. Thus it ended the era in which the Canal had been regarded as the corner-stone of imperial strategy.[1] It reduced England to the same status as other users of the waterway by depriving her of the right to defend it under any pretext whatsoever. It therefore recognized the international importance of the Canal, both Governments expressing their determination to uphold the Convention of Constantinople, which had been devised against Britain in 1888 but became from 1954 a protection for British interests.

The Agreement ended the siege of the Canal Zone and embodied the capitulation of the garrison.[2] The sole positive gain was to liberate 2⅓ divisions to form a strategic reserve. In England it was attacked by peers of the realm[3] including Lord Hankey, a director of the Canal Company since 1938. In the Commons it was discussed in sorrow, anguish and anger by M.P.s who 'were born in the days when Suez meant something in the history books that we read'.[4] The Suez Group upheld the concept of empire enunciated by Churchill in 1929 and 1946 against the Churchill of 1954 who appeared to be emulating Peel repealing the Corn Laws or Wellington trying to pass the Reform Bill.[5] They emphasized that 60 per cent of the Canal's traffic passed to or from Commonwealth ports,[6] that the evacuation of 'the linch-pin of the British Commonwealth'[7] was bound to be a permanent surrender with no real hope of a re-entry, and that the loss of such a 'hinge of fate'[8] was the inevitable prelude to the creation of an Egyptian Empire.[9] Major Legge-Bourke resigned the party whip on 14 July[10] in protest against an agreement which comprised 'all that is left of eighty years of British endeavour, thought and forethought . . . This is not a sell-out. It is a give-away.'[11] The normal 317 votes marshalled

[1] *The Times*, 24 June 1954, 6iv.
[2] Hansard, *Commons Debates*, 29 July 1934, 772, J. Amery. *The Times*, 10 July 1954, 7v, Lords Hankey, Killearn, Rennell and Vansittart.
[3] Hansard, *Lords Debates*, 28 July 1954, 217–20, 253–60, 266–74, Lords Hankey and Killearn; 29 July 1954, 338–9, 362, 391–2, Lord Killearn.
[4] Hansard, *Commons Debates*, 29 July 1954, 803, F. Lee.
[5] *Illustrated London News*, 14 August 1954, 242, A. Bryant, 'Our Note Book'.
[6] *Time and Tide*, 24 July 1954, 981, J. Amery, 'Hold on to Suez'.
[7] Ibid., 31 July 1954, 1011, 'Abandoning Suez'.
[8] *Daily Telegraph*, 17 July 1954, 6vi, P. Maitland.
[9] Ibid., 5 July 1954, 6iii–vi, C. Waterhouse, 'Suez and Why We Should Stay'.
[10] *The Times*, 14 July 1954, 8vi; 15 July, 8ii.
[11] Hansard, *Commons Debates*, 29 July 1954, 738, 739, C. Waterhouse.

by the Government Whips were substantially reduced when the Agreement was approved in the Commons on 29 July by 257 votes including those of six Labour M.P.s[1] and four of the original 41 rebels[2] against the 26 votes cast by the stalwarts of the Suez Group.[3]

The evacuation of material from the Canal Zone began on 4 August and that of troops on 11 August, ending the English era in Egypt[4] and beginning a rapid decline in effective British power in the Middle East.[5] It marked the greatest change in the balance of power in the region since the Turkish renaissance of 1923.[6] British hegemony was not destroyed but was transformed through the building-up of bases in Iraq, Jordan, Libya, Cyprus and Aden. Cyprus became the first great island-base of Western Asia on the pattern of Eastern Asia and was publicly denied for ever the right of self-determination,[7] although the local population was as hostile as in Egypt and revolted openly from the night of 31 March 1955. In Egypt the agreement was welcomed by the workmen and employees of the Canal Company but aroused the opposition of Neguib, the Wafd, the Communists and the Moslem Brethren, whose Supreme Guide denounced it on 2 August as treasonable because it provided for re-entry by the hated British troops and recognized the Canal as an international passage to the benefit of Israel. Egypt had nevertheless emerged as the victor in her defence of 'the Egyptian Stalingrad', having acquired her own liberators, heroes and martyrs of the Canal. She benefited by the lifting of the British embargo on the shipment of arms on 30 August and remained thenceforward the sole power responsible for the maintenance of the liberty of navigation enshrined in the Convention of Constantinople.

Israel had built up its own merchant marine after its Reparations Agreement of 1952 with Germany but had become more hostile to the Arab boycott as its isolation increased. It had been alarmed by England's negotiations for evacuation and had sought to obtain firm support for its claim to use the Canal from the Security Council before the evacuation took place. Egypt therefore allowed shipping to and from Israel to pass unhindered through the Canal between February and September 1954 so as to avoid antagonizing either the

---

[1] Emrys Hughes, J. McGovern, D. Donnelly, F. Brockway, J. Carmichael and J. C. Forman.

[2] P. Bell, W. H. Bromley-Davenport, F. Maclean and D. Marshall.

[3] J. Amery, R. Assheton, R. F. Crouch, J. A. L. Duncan, A. Fell, F. Graham, Viscount Hinchingbrooke, C. J. Holland-Martin, I. M. Horobin, H. M. Hyde, H. W. Kerr, E. A. H. Legge-Bourke, G. Lloyd, P. Maitland, A. Maude, J. Mellor, G. D. N. Nabarro, I. J. Pitman, J. E. Powell, W. R. Rees-Davies, W. Teeling, C. Waterhouse, C. Williams, P. Williams joined by W. Darling and H. B. Kerby, for whom R. Grimston and P. Donner acted as tellers. T. Clarke paired. Burden, R. Harris, F. Harris and Savory were absent. Seven abstainers included Hall, Hicks-Beach, Morrison and Rayner. Sir Herbert Williams had just died. *Daily Telegraph*, 30 July 1954, 1 iii. *The Times*, 28 July, 8 ii; 29 July, 6 v; 30 July, 8 iii.

[4] *New York Times*, 18 July 1954, 9 i, H. W. Baldwin, 'Suez marks the end of an era'.

[5] *Daily Telegraph*, 28 July 1954, 6 i.

[6] A. H. Hourani, 'The Anglo-Egyptian Agreement: Some Causes and Implications', *Middle East Journal* (Summer 1955), 239.

[7] Hansard, *Commons Debates*, 28 July 1954, 508, H. Hopkinson.

U.S.A. or Britain. Israel then established an entente with France after Mendès-France became Prime Minister,[1] while American Zionists sought in August 1954 to prevent the evacuation of the Canal Zone as well as to secure the free use of the Canal to Israel.[2] Israel engaged in the bitterest fighting since 1949 on the Gaza border between 22 August and 3 September. It then determined to test the new Egyptian regime by sending the first Israeli-owned vessel since 1949 to attempt the passage of the Canal. The *Bat Galim* carried meat, plywood and hides from Massawa for Haifa but was seized at Port Tewfik on 28 September after allegedly firing on Egyptian fishermen in the Gulf of Suez.[3] Its seizure frustrated the intended creation of a test-case and confirmed the Egyptian boycott. The incident encouraged the Canal Company to ask the Harvard Law School in October 1954 to undertake a study of the law of international waterways,[4] and Israel to pursue its successful negotiations with France for the supply of Mystère jet-fighters.[5] The opening of the new military bridge across the Canal on 1 November 1954 paid homage to Egypt's new popular slogan 'After Suez, Palestine' but reduced Suez shares by 4·8 per cent (31 October–4 November). Nasser's foreign policy however moved towards the U.S.A. and Britain in order to prevent the capture of the revolution by Communism. Egypt asked on 24 September for a loan from the World Bank to finance the Aswan High Dam and accepted on 2 November a new and cheaper plan for the dam, together with a grant made by the United States on 6 November for a survey.

The decline of the British Empire was followed by that of its great rival, the French Empire, after the end of the Korean War in 1953 diverted Russian and Chinese interest to the war against France in Indo-China. The fall of Dien Bien Phu on 7 May 1954 ended an eight-year war, an empire established in 1860 and a medieval dream of the regeneration of the East by France. It followed the first transits under the Thai and Vietnamese flags in 1953 and reduced the tonnage of French military transports using the Canal en route to Indo-China by 37 per cent during 1954 as well as the number of troops using the Canal markedly during 1954 and 1955. The Oriental phase of French history ended amid the laments of the remaining enclaves of French culture at the prospect that nothing more might remain in the East of the Western revolution than remained of Nestorian Christianity.[6] France became thenceforward increasingly sensitive to threats to its surviving power and influence,[7] especially after the peasantry of its African Ireland revolted openly on 31 October 1954 with the encouragement of Nasser. France nevertheless

[1] M. Bar-Zohar, *Suez Ultra-Secret* (Paris, Fayard, 1964), 65.
[2] A. M. Lilienthal, *There Goes the Middle East* (New York, Bookmailer, 1957, 1961), 102–3.
[3] E. Ereli, 'The *Bat Galim* Case before the Security Council', *Middle Eastern Affairs* (April 1955), 108–17.
[4] R. R. Baxter, *The Law of International Waterways* (Harvard University Press, 1964), v.
[5] M. Bar-Zohar, *Suez Ultra-Secret*, 66–7, 76, 79.
[6] F. Léger, *Les Influences Occidentales dans la Révolution de l'Orient 1850–1950* (Paris, Plon, 1955), ii. 242.
[7] *Supplément au Canal de Suez*, 15 Juin 1954.

retained its Polynesian island-empire, based on New Caledonia and Tahiti, protected from the mainland by the Anglo-American island bases and supplemented by Jibuti, a free port since 1949. Its shipping tonnage using the Canal rose by 15 per cent during 1955 as the oil traffic offset the decline of imperial trade.

The traffic of the Canal reflected the changing balance of power in the postwar world especially in the rapid recovery of the defeated powers of 1945. Thus the Italian flag rose from the rank of seventh in 1946–7 to that of sixth in 1949 and then to that of fifth in 1955. Germany reappeared in the traffic of the Canal in 1949 and continued to benefit by its non-imperial status. It resumed its services to East Africa and India in 1950, to the Persian Gulf in 1951 and to the Far East in 1953.[1] It rose from the position of twentieth to that of fourteenth in 1951 and to that of eleventh in 1954, shipping about 12 per cent of its exports through the Canal in 1956.[2] Above all, the Japanese flag rose steadily from the rank of twenty-seventh in 1951 to that of seventeenth in 1953 and to that of thirteenth in 1955. The resurgence of Asia was also manifest in the cargo as well as in the flags of the Canal. Iron ore was shipped from China to Eastern Europe from 1951 and first exceeded the tonnage of manganese from 1954, dominating the mineral traffic thenceforward. A flood of duty-free textiles also began to pour through the Canal from 1954–5 into the English market, benefiting the Manchester merchants, destroying the Lancashire cotton industry and restoring the pre-1813 balance of the textile trade between East and West. The re-entry of Russia into the world oil market was marked by its first southbound shipments of refined oil from Batum to Siberia in August 1954 and of lamp-oil from Russia to Egypt in November 1954. The shipment of aviation fuel from Constanza to China in a Finnish tanker alarmed the U.S.A.[3] and was followed by the first shipment of Russian oil to North Viet-Nam in 1955 as well as to Siberia and China. The first shipment of Russian crude to Egypt in July 1955 was made together with the shipment of Soviet arms: it created the first southbound passage of crude oil in the history of the Canal and marked a new phase in the traffic which had begun in 1877. Russia had declined from the eleventh largest client of the Canal in 1946 to the nineteenth in 1953 but increased its Suez tonnage by 47 per cent during 1954 and by 81 per cent in 1955 so that it rose to the position of fourteenth, immediately after Japan.

The victory of the Viet-Minh threatened to expose Asia to a new expansion of Communist power. The U.S.A. sought in reply to defend the free world by extending military aid to Iraq and Pakistan, by refusing to supply arms to Egypt unless she adhered to a military pact and by encouraging the formation of new regional pacts on the model of N.A.T.O. in South-East Asia in 1954 and in the Middle East in 1955. The Bagdad Pact made possible the large-scale

[1] *The Times*, 13 July 1953, 6 iii.
[2] J. J. Malone, 'Germany and the Suez Crisis', *Middle East Journal* (Winter 1966), 21.
[3] *New York Times*, 5 March 1955, 2 vi.

flow of American arms to Iraq and destroyed the balance of power in the Middle East precariously maintained since 1950:[1] it aroused the violent antagonism of France, Russia and Egypt. Nuri thus cloaked his bid for supremacy in the Arab world behind a rival to the Arab Collective Security Pact of 1950. His conflict with Nasser became more bitter, especially for the control of Jordan and Syria, because the creation of a northern tier of defence filled the void left by the evacuation of the Canal Zone but left the way open to build a southern tier based upon Egypt. The Pact failed to revive the old dream of Anglo-Moslem solidarity. It destroyed England's good relations with the Arab states as well as with Egypt. Above all it reduced Russia's security in the only area where she lacked buffer-states and so facilitated instead of hindering her penetration of the Arab world.

Nasser appointed in October 1954 a Suez Canal Committee under Dr. Helmy Bahgat Badaoui (1904–57), a former Professor of Law, who had been the Minister of Commerce from 1952 to 1954 under whom the Suez Canal Department had been created. Badaoui had become first for some months the Special Commissioner of the Government with the Canal Company and then a director in 1955. After Mahmud Yunus, a Colonel of Engineers and director of the State Refinery at Suez, undertook a secret survey of the Company Nasser announced on 17 November 1954 the preparation of an agenda for discussions with the Company. The continued refusal of visas for foreign pilots increased the pressure on the Company, whose function was defended in the customary internationalist terms[2] against the rising tide of Egyptian nationalism. The Company completed the amortization of over half its shares for the first time by 31 December 1954 and created on 8 September 1955 the Société d'Investissements Mobiliers as a French investment trust under French law to manage its long-term investments. France suspended the shipment of arms to Egypt in September in retaliation for the anti-French propaganda diffused by Cairo. Egypt thereupon informed the Canal Company that it no longer recognized the agreement of 1947 exempting the Company from currency-control regulations and declared itself ready to negotiate a new agreement, demanding the construction of a harbour in Lake Timsah as well as the doubling of the number of Egyptian pilots and so reducing the value of Suez shares by 9·5 per cent (5–25 October). In December 1955 Egypt demanded the investment of the Company's entire reserves in Egyptian undertakings, the appointment by the Government of half of the board of directors and the appointment of the Government's own representatives to the executive committee,[3] so sharply increasing the pressure on the Company.

The Anglo-Egyptian Agreement was signed in Cairo on 19 October 1954, ratified on 6 December and followed by the first massive departure of troops

[1] M. Bar-Zohar, *Suez Ultra-Secret*, 82.

[2] P. Bineau, *Le Canal de Suez* (Paris, Minuit, 1954), 190–1. H. Poydenot, *Le Canal de Suez* (Paris, Presses Universitaires de France, 1955), 116.

[3] T. Robertson, *Crisis. The Inside Story of the Suez Conspiracy* (London, Hutchinson, 1965), 29.

from the Canal Zone on 10 December. By 18 February 1955 the first phase of the evacuation had withdrawn 21,000 out of the 80,000 troops. The Canal had been built from the north to the south: the evacuation of the Canal Zone proceeded from south to north, making possible the hoisting of the Egyptian flag over the former British barracks at Chalouf by Nasser on 22 March and leaving no British troops south of Geneifa thereafter. In the second phase of the operation the British Government enlisted the cooperation of several large business firms with Middle East interests in order to undertake the conversion of the base from military to civilian operation. Five main contracts were signed,[1] with Vickers-Armstrongs for armaments and tanks, with Associated Commercial Vehicles, Austin Motors and Rootes Motors for tracked and wheeled vehicles, with Imperial Chemical Industries for the ammunition depot, with Balfour, Beatty & Co. for power-supply and water-filtration, with George Wimpey & Co., Holloway Brothers (London), and John Laing & Son for civil engineering and water-distribution, while the Shell Company of Egypt continued to operate the oil storage installations and International Aeradio was invited to maintain aviation services. The Suez Consortium of those firms formed six operating companies[2] with a co-ordinating management company[3] under an independent chairman. Thus the Canal Zone base was transformed into a great neo-mercantilist enterprise wherein limited companies combined private and public interest in the same spirit as the chartered companies had under the Tudor and Stuart monarchs. By 18 October 1955 the third phase of evacuation had been completed: 49,000 troops had left Egypt while 31,000 remained for the two final stages. The disappearance of the market provided by British troops damaged the trade of Ismailia much more than that of Suez or Port Said. The evacuation prevented the complete Egyptianization of British policy but left Egypt with a lower standard of living than in 1882[4] and was followed by no literature of justification comparable to that which blossomed in the wake of the British withdrawal from India.

The end of England's mission in Egypt removed the protection of military power which had overshadowed the Canal Company since 1882. Egypt remained the defender of the waterway and the ruler of Sinai. Her frontier with Israel became thenceforward the main field of Arab-Israeli conflict. The crew of the *Bat Galim* were released through Gaza on 1 January 1955 but its cargo was confiscated in defiance of a promise made to return it to Israel. Ben

---

[1] *Financial Times*, 21 October 1954, 7 vi.

[2] Suez Contractors (Engineers) Ltd., registered on 13 January 1955. Suez Contractors (Vehicles) Ltd., registered on 7 February 1955. Suez Contractors (Ammunition) Ltd., registered on 9 February 1955. Suez Contractors (Electricity) Ltd., registered on 24 February 1955. Suez Contractors (Maintenance) Ltd., registered on 21 March 1955. Suez Contractors (Aviation Services) Ltd., registered on 30 April 1955.

[3] Suez Contractors Management Company Ltd., registered on 1 March 1955 and renamed on 26 January 1956 Suez Contractors (Services) Ltd.

[4] P. O'Brien, *The Revolution in Egypt's Economic System. From Private Enterprise to Socialism, 1952–1965* (London, Oxford University Press, 1966), 1–2.

Gurion thereupon became Minister of Defence on 17 February and sent paratroops to raid Gaza on 28 February. That massive reprisal converted Egypt from the least into the most belligerent of Arab states and encouraged Nasser to turn for arms from the U.S.A. to Russia, after conversations with Tito on board the *Galeb* in the Canal on 5 February, so as to offset the supply of arms by France to Israel.

The first Israeli tanker came into service in December 1954, carried 14 per cent of Israel's imports of crude during 1955 and increased the pressure to make the Gulf of Akaba an Israeli oil route. The Governor of the Canal area asked the Canal Company on 9 September to send to the Customs a daily list of ships expected at the ports of the Canal before their arrival, so extending inspection outside the Canal ports and keeping all unannounced vessels outside the limits of the Canal. New regulations were also introduced on 11 September restricting El Al planes from using the Gulf of Akaba en route to South Africa, and ships from entering the Gulf without the prior permission of Egypt.[1] In reply Ben Gurion as Premier-designate sent troops to occupy the El Auja triangle on 21 September in preparation for an invasion of Sinai. He also declared on 25 September that the Gulf would be opened to Israeli shipping in one year or less.[2] He thereby created the atmosphere of crisis heightened by Nasser's announcement on 27 September that Egypt had ordered £150,000,000 of arms from Russia. Russia thus by-passed the precarious northern defensive tier established at Bagdad and shattered America's strategic plan for the Middle East. The dispatch of Soviet arms ended the Western monopoly of the supply of arms to the region and destroyed the balance of arms maintained therein since 1950. It portended a virtual Russian fortress on the Canal and a counterpoise to American air-power and naval power in the Mediterranean. It alarmed England for her rights of readmission to the Canal Zone base and inspired her to divert her purchases of cotton from Egypt to the Sudan. The announcement was however greeted with an ecstasy of rejoicing throughout the Arab world as a defiance of the West. The arms deal isolated Iraq and restored Egypt's control of the Arab League. It made Nasser the leader of the Arab world and his armies the foremost therein. It was regarded by Israel as its death-sentence because it implied the establishment of a decisive military superiority in the Arab world. It therefore committed Israel to undertake a preventive war before Egypt had learnt how to use her new arms, i.e. within three years.

Egypt's comprehensive law of 19 October on the economic boycott of Israel was accepted on practical grounds by the U.S. Navy and by the British Government.[3] The U.S.A. took up the Russian challenge and so made the Middle East a new theatre of conflict between the two world-powers with Egypt in precarious imbalance between them. It offered from November 1955

---

[1] *The Times*, 12 September 1955, 8 iii; 14 September, 7 vii.
[2] *New York Times*, 27 September 1955, 5 i.
[3] Hansard, *Commons Debates*, 30 November 1955, 2287, H. Macmillan.

to finance the construction of the Aswan High Dam[1] in order to persuade Nasser to cancel the arms deal before arms arrived on any large scale,[2] to return as the prodigal son to the embrace of the West and to concentrate on internal social and economic reform. That offer was made for political rather than for economic reasons and was endorsed at the N.A.T.O. Conference in December 1955. The announcement on 17 December of British and American aid for the High Dam involved the West once more in the Nile Valley and entailed incalculable political risks. Ben Gurion had already concluded that the acquisition of Sinai was necessary in order permanently to open the Gulf of Akaba and to reinspire the disparate populations of his state with faith in their mission as a Chosen People. He became Prime Minister on 2 November[3] and concluded the secret agreement of 12 November by which France agreed to supply tanks and Mystère 4 jet-fighters.[4] Thus France armed Israel for battle against the guardian of the Straits of Tiran in order to preserve its Algerian empire.

[1] N. Deney, 'Les États-Unis et le Financement du Barrage d'Assouan', *Revue Française de Science Politique* (Juin 1962), 366–7.

[2] S. Adams, *Firsthand Report. The Story of the Eisenhower Administration* (New York, Harper, 1961), 249.

[3] M. Dayan, *Diary of the Sinai Campaign* (London, Weidenfeld, 1966), 13. R. Meinertzhagen, *Middle East Diary 1917–1956* (London, Cresset, 1959), 275–8, 2 November 1955.

[4] M. Bar-Zohar, *Suez Ultra-Secret* (1964), 110.

38

THE SUEZ CRISIS OF 1956

IN 1956 two successive crises were created by the nationalization of the Canal Company and by the invasion of Egypt. The act of nationalization completed the destruction of the balance of power in the Middle East: the Anglo-French invasion sought to restore that balance in Western interests. The decisions which led Israel, France and Britain into their combined assault on Egypt were taken separately between January and May of 1956, several months before the nationalization of the Canal Company. The Suez crisis thus had no fundamental connexion with Suez, with the Canal or with the Canal Company.[1] That crisis emerged rather from the conflict between the West and Arab nationalism, from the aspiration of the Arabs to liquidate the empire of the infidel within the realm of Islam and from the determination of the West to maintain its Arab empire.[2] France needed Algeria and England needed Iraq to retain their status as Great Powers. The postwar empire of Britain in the Middle East had relied increasingly upon conservative dynastic nationalism for support against revolutionary Arab nationalism. It found its last buttress in the Bagdad Pact, which created a bitter conflict between Nuri and Nasser for supremacy in the Arab world and especially for the control of Jordan. The accession of Jordan to the Bagdad Pact of its sister-monarchy was suggested by the British Colonial Secretary and Foreign Secretary but was frustrated in December 1955 by the opposition of its Palestinian population. The use of the Arab Legion to maintain order in the subsequent riots of 7 January 1956 cost Glubb Pasha his position as its commander.

The brusque dismissal of Glubb on 1 March dealt a serious blow to England's military position in the whole region and even more to its dream of Arab empire. That blow impressed the British Government as one inspired by Nasser. The Prime Minister yielded to the pressure of the Suez Group,[3] held an emergency Cabinet and deported Archbishop Makarios to the Seychelles on 7 March amid a surge of Conservative approval. He also ended all important contacts with the Government of Egypt,[4] concluding that a change of ruler in Egypt was essential to prevent Nasserite revolutions by young officers in Jordan, Syria, Iraq and Saudi Arabia and the total subversion of the British position throughout the Middle East.[5] Israel simultaneously began

---

[1] H. Azeau, Le Piège de Suez (5 Novembre 1956) (Paris, Laffont, 1964), 110.
[2] E. B. Childers, The Road to Suez (London, MacGibbon, 1962), 171–92.
[3] R. Churchill, The Rise and Fall of Sir Anthony Eden (London, MacGibbon, 1959), 225.
[4] T. Little, Egypt (London, Benn, 1958), 281.
[5] A. Eden, Full Circle (London, Cassell, 1960), 465.

to plan a preventive war against Egypt,[1] while France passed the point of no return in its Algerian war as Tunis and Morocco regained their full independence. England's suggestion to Russia that the supply of arms to the Middle East should be controlled[2] provoked Nasser's diplomatic recognition of Communist China on 16 May, so opening up to Egypt an alternative source of arms to Russia. Dulles then decided to profit by Russia's declaration of neutrality in the Middle East on 17 April and to withdraw the aid promised to finance the Aswan High Dam,[3] an offer which he had begun to reconsider from March under British pressure.[4] He thereby intended to force Nasser to choose between the Dam and Russian arms.[5] Nasser realized that Dulles would no longer sanction the loan[6] but nevertheless hastened to accept it after a Russian 'offer' of aid was first mooted and then denied on 30 June. Dulles thereupon publicly withdrew on 19 July the offer which Egypt had publicly accepted, taking the final decision by himself[7] after two months of leisurely consideration and one week of intensive study.[8]

Nasser objected not to the withdrawal of aid but to the insulting manner in which the refusal was conveyed and especially to the explanatory slur upon Egypt's economic reputation. He was the more sensitive since Egypt's political independence had been complete since 13 June when the last British troops had left Port Said five days before the agreed date without any ceremony. On 'Independence Day', 18 June, Nasser raised the Egyptian flag over Navy House amid jubilation at the final liberation of Egypt's sacred soil. England followed the American example in withdrawing her promise of support for the Dam. The Dam was intended to insure Egypt against the independence of the Sudan and the division of control over the Nile. It would also expand her cultivated area by 30 per cent, provide a partial substitute for land redistribution and supply power for the manufacture of high-grade steel. Thus it would help to shift the basis of the economy from agriculture to heavy industry, make Egypt ultimately independent of all foreign sources of arms-supply and become a source of wealth rather than a 'second Suez Canal'.[9] Nasser abandoned any hope of a counter-offer from Russia and decided to finance the Dam from the profits of the Suez Canal because he could strike at America

---

[1] E. Berger, *Covenant and the Sword. Arab-Israeli Relations 1948–56* (London, Routledge, 1965), 206, 208. M. Bar-Zohar, *The Armed Prophet. A Biography of Ben Gurion* (London, Barker, 1967), 209.

[2] *The Observer*, 5 July 1964, 6iv, Nasser quoting minutes of Eden–Khruschev talks.

[3] T. Little, 282.

[4] N. Deney, 'Les États-Unis et le Financement du Barrage d'Assouan', *Revue Française de Science Politique* (Juin 1962), 384–5.

[5] H. Finer, *Dulles over Suez* (Chicago, Quadrangle, 1964), 48–54.

[6] A. Moncrieff and P. Calvocoressi, *Suez Ten Years After* (London, B.B.C., 1967), 41–2.

[7] Deney, 390–1. R. Murphy, *Diplomat among Warriors* (London, Collins, 1964), 459–60. D. D. Eisenhower, *The White House Years. Waging Peace 1956–1961* (London, Heinemann, 1965), 33–4.

[8] *New York Times*, 21 July 1956, 3ii–iii.

[9] J. E. Dougherty, 'The Aswan Decision in Perspective', *Political Science Quarterly* (March 1959), 22, quoting *Al Kahira* of 22 June 1956.

only through her allies in Europe. He calculated that Britain would not be able to invade Egypt for four months because the bulk of her military equipment in the Middle East was locked up in the Canal Zone base under Egyptian guards. He knew that France had its army tied down in Algeria and assumed that Russia would have to support Egypt in order to preserve its newly-won prestige in the Arab world.

The decision taken by Nasser on 21 July[1] was ratified by the Revolutionary Council on 23 July and announced to a crowd of 200,000 at Alexandria on 26 July, the fourth anniversary of the abdication of Farouk. At the close of his 2½-hour speech Nasser denounced the Canal as 'an edifice of oppression' and the Canal Company as 'a state within the state' as well as 'a source of exploitation and extortion'. He attacked the World Bank for seeking a virtual veto over Egypt's programme of investment and called Eugene Black a modern Ferdinand de Lesseps. At the repetition of the code-word 'Lesseps' the Egyptian troops, who were listening by their radios to his speech made in the vernacular, began the occupation of the Canal Company's offices in Port Said, Ismailia, Suez and Cairo. The operation which Ismail had aspired to undertake in 1874 was completed with military precision before Nasser ended his address with the triumphant announcement of the nationalization of the Company and of the intention to form a new Suez Canal Company. 'And it will be run by Egyptians! Egyptians! Egyptians!'[2] His reprisal against America aroused a tidal wave of popular enthusiasm in Alexandria, Egypt and the Arab world, where the conversion of the Suez Canal into 'the Arabs' Canal'[3] strengthened his position against Nuri. In Cairo Nasser was acclaimed as 'Hero of Suez',[4] while in Port Said an angry crowd sought to overturn the statue of Lesseps, whom they regarded as a symbol of European imperialism in the East.[5] The act of nationalization did not surprise the world of Asia, Africa or Latin America which regarded American investment as a right and bitterly resented its denial. It was indeed acclaimed by thirty-two governments extending from China to Spain and representing two-thirds of the world's population.[6] Its audacity encouraged Indonesia in emulation to repudiate on 4 August its debts of £200,000,000 to the Netherlands, Spain to agitate for the cession of Gibraltar, Iran to claim Bahrein, Lebanon to threaten the Tripoli Refinery of the Iraq Petroleum Company, and Panama to aspire to nationalize the Panama Canal.

The Canal Company had not been well served by the concession of a monopoly nor by its limited tenure. It had never widened the Canal to the

---

[1] *New York Times*, 9 October 1966, 21i, 'Nasser's '56 Plan on Suez Revealed'.

[2] Ibid., 27 July 1956, 2iv, not quoted in the official text in M. Khalil, *The Arab States and the Arab League* (Beirut, Khayats, 1962), ii. 742–71.

[3] Eden, 443. [4] *Le Monde*, 28 Juillet 1956, 3v.

[5] A. Nouseir and H. Moonis, *The Suez Canal. Facts and Documents* (Cairo, 1956), 40.

[6] G. S. Nikitina, *Der Suezkanal: nationales Eigentum des aegyptischen Volkes* (Berlin, Deutscher Verlag der Wissenschaften, 1957), 51–5, 'Die ganze fortschrittliche Menschheit auf der Seite Aegyptens'.

proportions desired in 1856 so as to allow two vessels to pass in transit. Nor had it deepened the waterway as fast as the newer Panama Canal was deepened. It had never been able since the 1900s to keep pace with the demands of traffic, except during the depression of 1929–32. It was slow to recognize the Canal as 'a continuous creation'[1] and began to number its improvement programmes only from 1948. By July 1956 it had half-finished the construction of the new by-passes at Port Fuad and Kabrit and had begun to consider the conversion of the Canal into a double waterway for the whole of its length in a ninth programme projected for 1956–60. It did not adopt new equipment before it had been thoroughly tested and only acquired in 1950 its first suction-dredger, which had been invented in the 1860s. The Company had nevertheless carefully shepherded 397,434 toll-paying transits through the waterway since the passage of the *Sin-Nanzing* in 1869 and within its self-imposed limits operated the Canal with superb efficiency. Such success doomed the Company because its monopoly was what Egypt most desired.

The Company had increased the proportion of Egyptians from 24 per cent of its total staff in 1949 to 42 per cent in July 1956. In self-defence it had however sought to delay the Egyptianization of its higher staff, especially of its pilots, of whom only 17 per cent were Egyptian. It insisted that pilots should on recruitment be of a maximum age of thirty-five, should have had ten years' experience on the high seas including two as a master mariner, and should then train for two years as a Canal pilot to qualify for their highly paid and responsible posts. It had however agreed in March 1956 to engage thirty-two Egyptian pilots within a year. In its isthmian principality the Company preserved the essential dualism of Western economic enterprise in Asia. It promulgated its own rules for navigation as a quasi-public legislator and maintained its independence of general Egyptian legislation to the very end. It paid the highest wages in the land and developed a mission of social service to its dependent community but never won the hearts of the people or eliminated the hostility of the State. Its precarious position had been undermined by its support of Britain during the battle for the Canal in 1951–2 and by the subsequent national renaissance. The unrenamed towns of the isthmus served as standing witnesses in republican Egypt to the Company's past identification with the exiled Turkish dynasty. The sustained opposition of the Government prevented the development of the ports of the Canal as ports of export. The introduction of convoys made Port Said into more of a marshalling harbour than a port while their more elaborate organization restricted the commercial opportunities of the port's shopkeepers. Its free port suffered from the post-war competition of the rival free zones of Beirut and Genoa and never developed like the Colon Free Zone created by Panama in 1948.

---

[1] F. Charles-Roux, 'Le Coup de Suez', *Revue de Paris* (Octobre 1956), 19. Idem, 'Le coup de force du Gouvernement Égyptien contre la Compagnie Universelle du Canal Maritime de Suez', *Revue des travaux de l'Académie des Sciences Morales et Politiques*, 19 Novembre 1956, 144–5.

The Company's revenues had grown in proportion to the expansion of international trade. The postwar oil boom had eclipsed the memory of the depressions of the 1930s and the 1940s and had established its prosperity on a firmer basis than ever before. Between 1869 and 1942 the tonnage of the Canal and the receipts of the Company rose in every year above the level of the preceding year except in twenty-four years out of the seventy-four. In the thirteen years from 1943 to 1955, however, traffic receded only in 1951. Thus the Company quickly reconstituted its reserves, which were protected by its inscrutable accounting procedures and supplemented by the undervaluation of its Paris offices, which had a book-value of £500,000 but a market-value of £15,000,000 to £20,000,000.[1] Its shareholders continued to reap a rich harvest despite the reduction of tolls to 54 per cent of their permitted maximum and the depression of share-prices by the increasing political pressure from Egypt. Its payments to Egypt had doubled from £E3,000,000 in 1951 to £E6,000,000 in 1955 but provided a constant 2 per cent of the Government's receipts. Its long-term investments held in Egyptian pounds had risen by 14·5 per cent from £464,000 in 1952 to £532,500 in 1955 but their share in its total portfolio had fallen from 4·7 to 3·2 per cent. The Company therefore agreed on 30 May 1956 to increase its reserves in Egypt by £E16,000,000 between 1956 and 1963 by investing in development projects.

The law of nationalization was drawn up by Hefnaoui while the legal justification was provided by Badaoui, who discovered that the Company had failed to create in Lake Timsah an inland harbour for vessels of the highest tonnage as it had agreed to do under its concession. The Company had been nominally Egyptian since 1866 but had remained effectively French in its seat, capital, administration, personnel, technology, ethos and language. It had never acquired an international status, despite its title and its international function, as Charles-Roux admitted at the shareholders' meeting on 12 June 1956.[2] Nationalization removed the basis of existence of the Company in Egyptian law[3] and provoked ingenious attempts to prove that the Company

---

[1] *Investor's Chronicle*, 1 September 1956, 712, 'Suez Canal Share Values'.

[2] *Le Canal de Suez*, 15 Juin 1956, Supplement, fifteenth page.

[3] D. Rauschning, *Der Streit um den Suezkanal* (Forschungsstelle für Völkerrecht der Universität Hamburg, 1956), xx, xxvi. E. Brüel, 'Die völkerrechtliche Stellung des Suezkanals und die Nationalisierung der Kanalgesellschaft', *Archiv des Völkerrechts* (Juli 1958), 48, 55. *Harvard Law Review* (January 1957), 480–90, 'Nationalization of the Suez Canal Company'. R. Slovenko, 'Nationalization and Nasser', *Tulane Studies in Political Science*, iv (1957), 86–92. R. Delson, 'Nationalization of the Suez Canal Company', *Columbia Law Review* (June 1957), 784–5. M. D. Generales, 'Suez-National Sovereignty and International Waterways', *World Affairs Quarterly* (July 1958), 177–8. H. Calvert, 'The Nationalization of the Suez Canal Company in International Law', *Annual Law Review* (December 1957), 30–57. B. Broms, *The Legal Status of the Suez Canal* (Vammala, 1961), 188. J. A. Obieta, *The International Status of the Suez Canal* (The Hague, Nijhoff, 1960), 102. Y. S. Arias, *El Canal de Suez. Aspecto Historico, Juridico, Politico y Economico* (Universidad de Concepción, 1958), 78, 80. J. Alejandrino y Medina, *Suez y el Derecho International* (Madrid, 1959), 130. G. Vaucher, *Gamal Abdel Nasser et son équipe* (Paris, Julliard, 1960), ii. 222–4. Y. van der Mensbrugghe, *Les Garanties de la Liberté de Navigation dans le Canal de Suez* (1964), 218.

was really international.[1] The Company had endured for ninety-eight years in a land where the Transit Service had existed for only twelve years (1835–46) before it had been Egyptianized. Its successful survival for so long in a land with an unrivalled capacity for assimilating the foreigner must have been due to its operation on the territorial fringe of Egypt as well as to the protection of British troops from 1882 until 1956. Its nationalization took place forty-four days after the evacuation of the last British troops left it as the last surviving symbol of foreign domination.

The Egyptian Law of 26 July in effect equated nationalization with confiscation.[2] It purported to nationalize all the assets of the Company but did not nationalize all the shares of the Company, which would have been a more subtle method of securing all the foreign assets than the dissolution of the Company.[3] Two-thirds of the reserves of £65,000,000 remained outside Egypt so that ordinary shares fell in value only by 26 per cent between 27 and 31 July while founders' shares sank by 44 per cent and Civil Society shares by 53 per cent,[4] since both lacked a vote. The nationalization of the Company destroyed the last buffer between the Canal and Egypt. It established a fully sovereign Power in control of the waterway, achieving a great diplomatic triumph for Nasser and giving him an important weapon for future use against Europe.[5] Europe abandoned with indecent haste the cause of the Company,[6] whose moral basis had been undermined by its financial success and by the anti-capitalist crusade of the 1930s as well as by its neutralist policy in 1935 and 1940–4. No capitalist organization had ever been sacrificed with such speed or unanimity. No Power or people responded to the Company's repeated pleas for its restoration. The Powers made no attempt to appeal to the International Court of Justice, accepted the fact of nationalization and proved reluctant even to request compensation for the Company.[7]

The dramatic assertion of Egypt's sovereignty threatened the future security of the Suez route and wounded the imperial pride of both France and England. The nationalism of both Powers reached a peak sixteen years after their

---

[1] R. Pinto, 'En Quoi l'Égypte a violé ses Obligations Internationales', *Le Monde*, 3 Octobre 1956, 3 iii–v. B. Goldman, 'La Compagnie de Suez Société Internationale', *Le Monde*, 4 Octobre 1956, 3 iv–v. G. Scelle, 'La Nationalisation du Canal de Suez et le Droit International', *Annuaire Français de Droit International* (1956), 3–19. T. T. F. Huang, 'Some International and Legal Aspects of the Suez Canal Question', *American Journal of International Law* (April 1957), 277–307. E. Rubin, *The Suez Canal. The Great Internationale* (London, De Vero, 1956).

[2] M. Bronfenbrenner, 'The Appeal of Confiscation in Economic Development', *Economic Development and Cultural Change* (April 1955), 201–18. M. Domke, 'American Protection against Foreign Expropriation in the Light of the Suez Canal Crisis', *University of Pennsylvania Law Review* (June 1957), 1033–4. H. J. Abs, *Der Schutz wohlerworbener Rechte im internationalen Verkehr als europäische Aufgabe* (Heidelberg, 1956), 16–17.

[3] Delson, 780–1.

[4] A. Vène, 'Le Canal de Suez et le Portefeuille Français', *Le Monde Économique et Financier*, 5 Août 1956, iii:i; 19 Août 1956, iii:ii.

[5] G. Cansacchi, 'I Termini Giuridici e Politici della Controversià di Suez', *Oriente Moderno* (Febbraio 1957), 92. *The Economist*, 4 August 1956, 31, 'Europe's Achilles Heel'.

[6] Azeau, 121–2. [7] Eisenhower, 47.

humiliating defeats by Germany in 1940 and focused on Egypt, whose threat to the Canal appeared as only one aspect of a bid to establish a new hegemony over all the Arab world. The imperial tradition of France was older than that of England and the wound to its pride was the greater. For France the Canal was not only a proud heritage from its imperial past but also an increasingly important route for the import of Arab oil. France had rapidly expanded its use of the Suez route, raising its flag from the position of sixth in the traffic in 1947–8 and fifth in 1949–50 to that of third in 1952–3 and fourth in 1954–5, i.e. to the same relative rank which it had held from 1910 until 1934. Its share in the total tonnage had risen from 7·7 per cent in 1950 to 9·4 per cent in 1955, which was a greater proportionate share than it had held since the 1870s. The Canal was not an export route for France as it was for England but an import route, primarily for oil, although it also carried 38·6 per cent of its imports of manganese, 72 per cent of its imports of rubber and all of its imports of jute. In 1955 it carried 15 per cent of its foreign trade by value but 22·5 per cent of the volume of its imports and 47 per cent of its oil imports. Those imports came increasingly from the Persian Gulf after Victor de Metz, Manager of the Compagnie Française des Pétroles since 1937 and its President since 1945, secured a 6 per cent share in the Iranian oil consortium of 1954. The Canal route employed 90 per cent of French tanker tonnage, which formed 70 per cent of the total French Suez tonnage. Thus France became the second greatest consumer of oil in Europe and increasingly dependent upon Arab oil as well as on the Canal. Metz became a director of the Canal Company in 1955 and began to explore for oil in the Sahara so as to fulfil the original aim of his company and secure control of a French oil supply. Such a supply was discovered in June 1956 400 miles south of Algiers, making France more determined than before to preserve its remaining empire in Africa and therefore more hostile than ever to Nasser, Pan-Arabism and the U.S.A.[1] The French policy of repression in Algeria provoked a boycott of French ships by the dockers of Port Said for two weeks from 8 June 1956. The act of nationalization then dealt a rude blow to France's dream of empire in the East and to its greatest imperial corporation. The Canal Company remained the creation of a national hero and the agent of a national cause as well as a source of foreign exchange and rich dividends. The isthmus of Suez remained the home of 1,600 Frenchmen and an outpost of Latin civilization in the Levant as well as the theatre of a great imperial epic. France was not prepared to sacrifice it so soon after the loss of Indo-China or while it was still fighting to keep Algeria French. It immediately decided to overthrow Nasser and so to conquer Algeria in Egypt.

England remained the main client of the Canal and in 1955 supplied 21 per cent of the total tanker tonnage, 45 per cent of the non-tanker tonnage and 28 per cent of the total net register tonnage, paying £9,000,000 to £10,000,000

---

[1] H. Lüthy and D. Rodnick, *French Motivations in the Suez Crisis* (Princeton, Institute for International Social Research, 1956), 87.

out of the total of £32,500,000 received in tolls. The Canal was used by 60 per cent of Britain's foreign-going merchant fleet and by nearly 50 per cent of her tanker fleet, carrying 31 per cent of the total volume of northbound oil and supplying England with 75 per cent of her imports of crude. It remained more important in the trade of England than of Europe but was used by only 25 per cent of the total value of British trade, by only 20·6 per cent of the total shipping tonnage reaching British ports and by only 15·4 per cent of the total shipping tonnage leaving British ports.[1] Thus the Treasury did not expect any serious consequences to follow even if the Canal were blocked.[2] England however still provided most of the warships using the Canal and held a proprietary interest of 44 per cent in the ordinary shares of the Canal Company. Her deep-rooted memory of the Canal as an imperial highway and of the Canal Zone as an imperial base[3] survived the evacuation and was made more evocative by the Suez Group. That Group seemed justified in its prophecies of disaster and became thenceforward as influential in the Government as it was in the constituencies.[4]

The Prime Minister apparently decided 'to knock Nasser off his perch'[5] so as to leave Nuri in command of the Arab world and able to lead it into the desired defensive alliance with the West. He therefore established a Committee of 'Suez Ministers' as a War Cabinet on 27 July[6] but was restrained from launching an immediate preventive war against Egypt by the refusal of the U.S.A. to participate.[7] Dulles thenceforward undermined each successive British attempt to use force against Nasser and authorized American ships on 5 August to pay their dues to the new Suez Canal Authority while American interests aspired to form an American-Egyptian company to operate the Canal.[8] The Prime Minister adopted the demand for internationalization as a war-cry more than as a peace-parley, recalled 25,000 reservists on 2 August and so committed his considerable prestige to the overthrow of Nasser. Joint Anglo-French military planning began on 5 August after the refusal of U.S. help compelled England to grant France a major role in the projected operation against Egypt.[9] France cooperated with both England and Israel against their common enemy in Egypt and accepted a subordinate military role in return for diplomatic primacy. Israel aspired to create a new buffer in Sinai to fill the void left between itself and Egypt by the withdrawal of the British garrison,

[1] D. C. Watt, *Britain and the Suez Canal. The Background* (London, Royal Institute of International Affairs, 1956), 10, 12.

[2] H. Thomas, *The Suez Affair* (London, Weidenfeld, 1967), 75.

[3] W. F. Longgood, *Suez Story. Key to the Middle East* (New York, Greenberg, 1957), 122.

[4] N. Nicolson, *People and Parliament* (London, Weidenfeld, 1958), 114, 117.

[5] Hansard, *Lords Debates*, 28 March 1962, 1002–3, Lord Montgomery. *The Times*, 30 March 1962, 14 v, Sir Anthony Eden.

[6] H. Thomas, *The Suez Affair*, 40–1. Churchill, 242–3. A. Hüsler, *Contribution à l'Étude de l'Élaboration de la Politique Étrangère Britannique (1945–1956)* (Geneva, Droz, 1961), 156–8.

[7] Azeau, 132. Murphy, 463. M. Bar-Zohar, *Suez Ultra-Secret* (1964), 131. *The Times*, 30 July 1956, 9 v, J. Amery.

[8] E. Sablier, 'L'Égypte devant l'Orage', *Le Monde*, 25 Août 1956, 3 v.

[9] Azeau, 132.

to open the Gulf of Akaba to its shipping and to extend its frontier to the Canal. Its interests benefited by the revival of the project for an Akaba Canal,[1] by the Franco-Israeli agreement of 7 August to begin an emergency programme of arms deliveries to Israel,[2] by the admission to the Canal of two vessels under charter to the Israel Navigation Company with cement for East Africa[3] and by the insistence of the eighteen Powers in the London Conference on the operation of the Canal 'without political motivation in favour of, or in prejudice against, any user' (i.e. Israel).[4] Thus Egypt was to be forced formally to accept the use of the Canal by Israeli shipping as well as its international operation. International control would have been even more restrictive of Egyptian sovereignty than the Canal Company and lacked any analogy since the abolition of the Danube Commission in 1948. The Arab world accordingly observed 'Suez Canal Day' when the London Conference opened on 16 August and a general strike closed all the shops even in pro-Western Karachi and Beirut, where banners proclaimed 'After the Canal, Palestine'.[5]

The Canal Company persuaded the Governments of France and England though not of the U.S.A. that Egypt could not operate the waterway without the Company's pilots. On 3 September it arranged their withdrawal for 15 September[6] in the expectation that the resulting paralysis of traffic would compel Egypt to appeal for their return.[7] That calculation of risks revealed little consideration for the clientele of the waterway and implied its comparative unimportance to Europe. The European pilots steered their last convoys on 14 September and left at midnight, ending an era in the history of the waterway and throwing down the supreme challenge to the new Canal Authority. Out of 205 pilots Egypt was left with 7 Greeks and 26 Egyptians.[8] There were also nine 'newly trained' Egyptians recruited under the 1956 Agreement from veteran shipmasters who had made thousands of trips through the Canal on their own Arab vessels and knew it like a book.[9] Those forty-two pilots successfully escorted forty-one ships through the Canal on 15 September and thirty-six more on 16 September, although they had to work overtime up to seventeen hours a day. On 17 September the daily convoys were raised from two to three of thirty-five ships and the shipping agents of Port Said recognized that Egypt had won through without the aid of foreign pilots, old or new.[10] The Egyptians had come to accept the Western view of

[1] *The Times*, 30 July 1956, 9v; 3 August, 9v, Hore-Belisha.

[2] Bar-Zohar, 141.

[3] *The Times*, 8 August 1956, 8iii.

[4] A. Nutting, *No End of a Lesson. The Story of Suez*, 54. D. Ben Gurion, *Israel: Years of Challenge* (London, Blond, 1964), 106–7.

[5] M. Adams, *Suez and After. Year of Crisis* (Boston, Beacon, 1958), 24.

[6] Azeau, 208.

[7] *The Times*, 13 September 1956, 11vi–vii, 'The Pilot's Point of View'.

[8] *The Observer*, 16 September 1956, 1i.

[9] *New York Times*, 16 September 1956, 2v.

[10] Ibid., 18 September 1956, 4i; 24 September, 1vii. M. Adams, 58–64. *The Times*, 8 October 1956, 6i.

their own technical inferiority and were more surprised than anyone else by the unexpected success of their pilots. The task of pilotage was facilitated by the relative ease of navigation through a lockless sea-level canal and by the diversion of traffic around the Cape which reduced it temporarily by 25 per cent. The effective operation of the Canal from 15 September enabled Nasser to succeed where Mossadek had failed and completed the subjugation of the isthmus. It enabled the weekly holiday of Canal personnel to be changed from the Christian Sunday to the Moslem Friday from 1 October. It encouraged the Italian Government to decide on 27 September to pay dues to the new Canal Authority, which was receiving 42 per cent of the dues while the Company continued to receive 58 per cent thereof, through Nasser's forbearance. Users regained their confidence and increased the tonnage of the Canal by 11 per cent during October after two months of declining traffic. Dulles' proposed Suez Canal Users' Association was deprived of both function and credit after Nasser denounced it as a war-users' association. France however regarded Egypt's success as an intolerable provocation and decided on 15 September that Israel should be encouraged to launch an invasion. Ben Gurion then agreed to attack Egypt in conjunction with France and England on dates fixed by them.[1]

Mollet informed Eden on 26 September of Israel's projected Sinai offensive[2] and so inspired the British Government to press as never before Israel's right to use the Canal.[3] Dulles' repudiation of force as a weapon of the User's Association reduced it to what Gaitskell called a Cape-users' association and encouraged the projection of an American shipping consortium for the development of the Canal.[4] It aroused a deep distrust in Europe of American policy and seemed to degrade Britain to the level of 'just an island in the Atlantic, a recipient of charity and a convenient outpost'.[5] In its anti-American mood the British Cabinet sanctioned on 3 October the invasion of Egypt in association with an Israeli attack.[6] The Israeli battle-orders of 5 October accordingly provided for the establishment of an Israeli defence line on the east bank of the Canal[7] while the Franco-Israeli agreement of 10 October provided for the complete coordination of the Israeli and Anglo-French attacks.[8] France thus ensured that the separate strategic plans of its two allies interlocked. Egypt then succumbed to economic pressure from her foes and to diplomatic pressure from her friends.[9] She conceded the principle of user-

---

[1] Bar-Zohar, *Ben Gurion*, 220.

[2] Azeau, 225. T. Robertson, *Crisis. The Inside Story of the Suez Conspiracy* (London, Hutchinson, 1964), 136. A. Fontaine, *Histoire de la Guerre Froide, ii, 1950–1967* (Paris, Fayard, 1967), 267–8.

[3] Finer, 322.

[4] *New York Times*, 4 October 1956, 1viii; 5 October, 2iii.

[5] R. M. Meinertzhagen, *Middle East Diary 1917–1956*, 294, 296, 8 and 9 October. *The Times*, 12 October 1956, 5i, J. Amery.

[6] Thomas, 96. Robertson, 139–40.

[7] M. Dayan, *Diary of the Sinai Campaign* (London, Weidenfeld, 1966), 209.

[8] Bar-Zohar, *Suez Ultra-Secret*, 149.   [9] Nutting, 74–5.

participation in the operation of the Canal but not the admission of Israeli ships on which France insisted.[1] Israel understood the Six Principles adopted by the Security Council on 13 October to protect the rights of its ships.[2] Egypt however refused to agree to automatic sanctions for discrimination against Canal users (i.e. Israel).[3] England thus became the agent first of French and then of Israeli policy in her mounting resentment of America's Fabian technique of constantly postponing action 'from pretext to pretext, from device to device, and from contrivance to contrivance'.[4] The plan for Anglo-French intervention in an Israeli-Egyptian war was outlined at Chequers by the French on 14 October[5] and accepted in Paris by the English on 16 October. The aim was to seize the Canal in the name of separating the combatants, to supervise the movement of shipping and to break the Egyptian blockade of Israel. Israel hoped as much as France or England to overthrow Nasser[6] but sought primarily to make the Gulf of Akaba a national highway which would become in effect a substitute for the Suez Canal.[7] 'Eilath is our Suez.'[8] The Protocol of Sèvres was signed on 24 October by British, French and Israeli representatives:[9] it apparently arranged for the war to begin on 29 October, for the first Israeli communiqué to create a 'threat' to the Canal and for the English bombardment of Egypt's airfields so as to relieve the fears of Israel.[10] General Dayan was accordingly instructed to subordinate the basic purpose of Israel's campaign, the capture of the Straits of Tiran, to the creation of a threat to the Canal.[11] In his revised battle-orders of 25 October he therefore used his knowledge that Anglo-French operations would be launched on 31 October and ordered a paratroop drop on the Mitla Pass[12] which was expressly designed to justify Anglo-French intervention. The Suez operation thus became the inevitable outcome of the previous co-ordination, 'complete understanding and joint preparation' by England, France and Israel.[13] England however disdained tactical cooperation with Israel in order to preserve her reputation in Arab eyes. Thereby she denied herself the military benefits but incurred all the political odium of such cooperation.

[1] *Le Monde*, 4 Novembre 1966, 4ii, Pineau.
[2] Finer, 309, 320. [3] Eden, 504.
[4] Eden, 505. [5] Nutting, 91–3.
[6] Finer, 392.
[7] M. P. Price, 'The Suez Crisis in Perspective', *Contemporary Review* (October 1956), 197. R. Lepotier, 'La Guerre des Isthmes dans la Bataille d'Afrique', *Revue de Défense Nationale* (Octobre 1956), 1178–9.
[8] M. M. El-Behairy, 'The Suez Canal in World Politics, 1945–1961' (Ph.D. Thesis, Ohio State University, 1961), 269, quoting Galili's speech in the Knesset from *The Jerusalem Post*, 17 October 1956.
[9] T. Robertson, *Crisis. The Inside Story of the Suez Conspiracy*, 161–2. Bar-Zohar, *Suez Ultra-Secret*, 165–8. Azeau, 248–9. Fontaine, 269. Thomas, 113–15. Nutting, 101–2. *Le Monde*, 4 Novembre 1966, 4iv, Pineau. Moncrieff and Calvocoressi, 83–107. Bar-Zohar, *Ben Gurion*, 226–38.
[10] Bar-Zohar, 168. [11] Dayan, 60–7.
[12] Dayan, 210–11.
[13] Nutting, 126. *The Observer*, 11 November 1956, 9vii. *Manchester Guardian*, 23 November 1956, 9i–ii. H. Nicolson, Diaries and Letters 1945–1962 (London, Collins, 1968), 314.

Israel's invasion of Sinai enjoyed all the advantages of a surprise attack. Its first war-bulletin asserted at 21.00 hours on 29 October that its forces were 'on the approaches to the Suez Canal' although its paratroops were forty miles away and its ground-forces were over 130 miles away. The Anglo-French ultimatum which had been decided upon at Sèvres then faced Egypt with the threat of war from the north, south and east. Air attacks were scheduled to begin at dawn on 31 October but began only after dusk from 19.00 hours and from the discreet height of 40,000 feet[1] on eight airfields in the Canal Zone and on four outside Cairo. Those raids inflicted little damage in proportion to their size[1] but began to turn world opinion against Britain. They also forced Nasser half an hour after they began to order the evacuation of Sinai, giving Israel a free hand in the peninsula but depriving it of a true military victory.[2] Nasser also ordered the blocking of the Canal, which was undertaken on 1 November by the Suez Canal Authority and the Egyptian Army. England was aware of Egypt's plans but failed to carry out her intended precision-bombing of the block-vessels before they could be towed into position and sunk.[3] The blocking of the Canal was accomplished much more extensively and effectively than the English had expected. It restored the barrier between the Mediterranean and the Red Sea, diverted traffic around the Cape and sharply reduced the annual carrying-capacity of world shipping. It finally ended the payment of Canal dues to the Suez Canal Company. It also made Britain and France dependent upon American oil, American tankers and American dollars at the very time when the tripartite onslaught on Egypt had aroused America's overwhelming wrath against the disturbers of the peace.

Sir Anthony Eden seems to have been taken by surprise by the speed, the strength and the unanimity with which the world condemned British policy. Nasser gauged the power of the rising tide of world opinion in his favour and realized with incredulity that his foes in uniting to overthrow him had delivered themselves into his hands. He therefore ordered Syria and Jordan not to intervene, preserved the bulk of his army intact, distributed arms to the civilian population on 3 November and prepared for a guerrilla while waiting for world opinion to save Egypt. In the interim Port Said became what Alexandria had been in 1882 and Ismailia in 1952 when it was attacked by aircraft on 3-4 November, invaded from the air on 5 November and hailed in the Cairo press from 6 November as the 'new Stalingrad'. The paratroopers who had been intended for use against Suez and Ismailia found the Egyptians better armed than themselves and suffered immediate and heavy casualties.[4] They proved unable to capture and clear the city so as to make

[1] V. Flintham, 'Suez 1956: a lesson in air power', *Air Pictorial* (August 1965), 271.
[2] E. B. Childers, 'The Sinai War, 1956', *Middle East Forum* (February 1961), 20-8. Azeau, 256, 275, 281, 301.
[3] Eden, 534. Dayan, 129. Nutting, 132-3. *Manchester Guardian*, 2 November 1956, 1 iii.
[4] A. J. Barker, *Suez. The Seven Day War* (London, Faber, 1964), 136. S. Cavenagh, *Airborne to Suez* (London, Kimber, 1965), 123, 131.

possible an unopposed advance along the Canal.[1] On 6 November the invading commandos discovered that the civilian population had taken over the task of defence and were immediately drawn into a guerrilla for which they were unprepared. The Egyptians rallied even boys of 11–12 to defend the European city and 'our Canal'. They fought without any orders, organization, discipline or code of war. They proved far readier to die than the Europeans[2] and inflicted far greater losses than had been expected. Thereby they held up a vast combined operation modelled on the invasion of Normandy and delayed any southward advance until 19.00 hours on 6 November.[3] Five hours later the invading forces halted in a tactically defenceless position at El Cap, 23 miles south of their landing-point. The resistance of Port Said thus prevented the capture of the Canal Zone in the estimated six days. It preserved the independence of Egypt which had been lost, also at Pelusium, 2,500 years earlier, to Cambyses of Persia. The British Government agreed to a cease-fire in its undeclared war under tremendous pressure from the U.S.A. which on 5 November despatched virtual ultimatums to both Paris and London,[4] sanctioned massive sales of sterling by the Federal Reserve Bank,[5] prevented the withdrawal of British deposits with the International Monetary Fund and declined to grant emergency financial credits to England. In yielding to American pressure England placed her armed forces in a humiliating position, shattered her entente with France and exposed herself to even harsher pressure from the U.S.A.[6] Within England the Government also came under pressure from such traditionally Conservative institutions as the oil companies, *The Times*, the Foreign Office,[7] the Treasury, the B.B.C.,[8] the Law Officers of the Crown,[9] the Service chiefs[10] and the Church of England,[11] which made it clear that it could no longer be considered as the Tory Party at prayer. Most important of all would have been the opposition of the highest person in the realm if it be true that the Prime Minister went to war 'against the wishes of his Sovereign'.[12]

The crisis divided England as sorely as it did the Commonwealth. It became as much a cultural as a political crisis, deriving its special intensity from the internal tensions which had emerged on the dissolution of England's war-forged unity in the minds of the first postwar generation. The transformation of English culture seems to have begun during 1955 with the

[1] C. Keightley, 'Despatch. Operations in Egypt—November to December 1956', *Supplement to the London Gazette*, 10 September 1957, 5331–3.
[2] B. Laforesse, *Le Bilan de l'Équipée de l'Égypte* (Paris, Ethéel, 1957), 108–9.
[3] Barker, 163.   [4] Azeau, 321.   [5] Churchill, 287–9. Finer, 428–9.
[6] Eden, 561.   [7] Nutting, 137–8. Churchill, 283.
[8] G. Waterfield, 'Suez and the Role of Broadcasting', *The Listener*, 29 December 1966, 947–9. H. Grisewood, *One Thing at a Time. An Autobiography* (London, Hutchinson, 1968), 194–204.   [9] Thomas, 127.
[10] D. C. Watt, *Personalities and Policies* (London, Longmans, 1965), 50.
[11] A. Sampson, *Anatomy of Britain* (London, Hodder, 1962), 164.
[12] Sir Charles Petrie, 'Biggest Backfire of the Century', in *The Illustrated London News*, 6 May 1967, 28iii. J. R. Tournoux, *Secrèts d'État* (Paris, Plon, 1960), 169. Bar-Zohar, *Suez Ultra-Secret*, 204–5. *Le Monde*, 1 Novembre 1966, 5ii, A. Fontaine.

realization of the relative failure of the wartime dream of a classless Welfare State[1] and the reopening of an abyss in society which was widened by the articulation of a divorce between the U and the non-U modes of life,[2] between the 'Establishment' and 'the Outsider'[3], between the great tradition of national unity and the counter-tradition of dissent,[4] between the national classes who had suffered a progressive narrowing of their outlets for aggression[5] and the angry young men[6] of unofficial England who lamented the disappearance of all the good, brave causes of the past.[6] That cultural transformation was manifested in the rising tide of humanitarian opinion which was powerful enough to force the Government to restrict its warlike operations to the absolute minimum. It engendered an internal crisis quite unconnected with the Canal and far transcending any question of personalities, parties or politics. That sub-political reaction alienated the younger generation below the age of twenty-five from their elders more acutely than ever before, but was largely ignored by the political nation because it took place amongst the voteless non-political nation.

The political nation was itself sharply divided by the crisis. Critics of the operation inveighed against what they regarded as the immorality and hypocrisy of a police-action, of a partisan foreign policy and of an apparent collusion with Israel[7] with the associated repudiation of the Whig constitution, the Liberal tradition and the progress-ethic. The supporters of the Government proved less articulate than its critics and were compelled to devise a series of transparent excuses in order to pacify Arab opinion. They nevertheless saw the central issue as primarily one of national unity, national tradition, national identity and national self-preservation against a threat from within as well as from without. The Government seems to have rallied almost unanimous support among the upper and lower orders of society, in the ranks of the rural aristocracy and the urbanized peasantry.[8] The middle class was, however, deeply divided, producing the most vehement advocates[9] as well as the most indignant critics of the operation and of 'the hard crude lumpish chauvinism of the English upper classes and their supporters'.[10] The extent

[1] R. M. Titmuss, *The Social Division of Welfare* (Eleanor Rathbone Memorial Lecture, 1 December 1955) (Liverpool University Press, 1956), 4, 20.

[2] N. Mitford (ed.), *Noblesse Oblige: an enquiry into the identifiable characteristics of the English aristocracy* (London, Hamilton, 1956).

[3] *The Spectator*, 29 July 1955, 156; 23 September 1955, 380, Henry Fairlie, 'Political Commentary'. Colin Wilson, *The Outsider* (London, Gollancz, 26 May 1956).

[4] A. J. P. Taylor, *The Trouble Makers. Dissent over Foreign Policy 1792–1939. The Ford Lectures Delivered in the University of Oxford in Hilary Term 1956* (London, Hamilton, 1957).

[5] G. Gorer, *Exploring English Character* (London, Cresset, 1955), 287.

[6] John Osborne, *Look Back in Anger* (The Royal Court Theatre, 8 May 1956, reviewed in *The Observer*, 13 May 1956, 11 and published by Faber in 1957).

[7] T. Callander, *The Athenian Empire and the British* (London, Weidenfeld, 1961), 162, 'From Sarajevo to Suez'.

[8] P. Worsthorne, 'Class and Conflict in British Foreign Policy', *Foreign Affairs* (April 1959), 422. *Journal of Economic History* (March 1960), 99, S. B. Saul.

[9] Wayland Young, 'Psychopolitics', *Socialist Commentary* (January 1957), 8–9.

[10] R. B. McCallum, 'The Flight to Liberalism', *Contemporary Review* (October 1958), 247.

and the intensity of the dissent from official policy was indicated by the stream of letters of protest to *The Times* as well as to the liberal press, the efflorescence of pamphlets, the studied efforts to instigate a mutiny or a general strike[1] and the proposals to revive impeachment[2] or even a war-crimes tribunal.[3] In the Commons the spectre of class-war reared its head[4] and the sitting was suspended on 1 November for the first time since 1936. Outside Parliament demonstrations were held in twenty cities and the mass-rally by 40,000 in Trafalgar Square on 'Suez Sunday', 4 November, was followed by the first London riots since 1926. Above all, petitions of protest were signed by some 2,100 university teachers[5] including 377 Oxford dons[6] in an almost unprecedented action by senior members of the University and by twelve Fellows of Christ Church. In general the educated and the intelligent classes refused to commit what Benda had taught them was the treason of the intellectuals. They condemned the immorality and inexpediency of the operation much more strongly than the general population.[7] They opposed Sir Anthony in 1956 for the same reasons that they had supported him in 1938 whereas 'it is broadly true that the supporters of Munich were the supporters of Suez'.[8] Sir Edward Boyle, the most prominent intellectual in the Cabinet, felt compelled to resign from the Government. The unprecedented dissidence of the intellectuals[9] seemed to threaten the whole aristocratic mould of English life,[10] profoundly influenced the media of communication and made the opposition to the Government appear far more extensive than it really seems to have been. In fact the Government enjoyed the support of possibly 75 per cent of the whole population, in the opinion of one of its independent critics.[11] Support for the Government was greatest among people above the age of forty and was almost overwhelming among the Edwardian generation

[1] *Manchester Guardian*, 1 November 1956, 8 iii, 'Conscience'; 3 November, 6 iv; 5 November, 9 iii; 7 November, 4 iii, 14 iii.

[2] Ibid., 6 November 1956, 8 v, V. Mayes.

[3] Ibid., 9 November 1956, 8 v, H. J. Perkin.

[4] Hansard, *Commons Debates*, 1 November 1956, 1745–6, Mrs E. M. Braddock. 'At a time when people on the other side of the House are voting away the lives of the ordinary working-class people, every one of them can be branded as a murderer of every working-class boy who dies... They are a lot of slayers and murderers.'

[5] Including 377 in Oxford, 245 in London, 242 in Cambridge, 176 in Manchester, 160 in Liverpool, 145 in Leeds, 116 in Bristol, 103 in Newcastle and 90 in Durham.

[6] *The Oxford Magazine*, 8 November 1956, 81, 88–9, 114, 140. *The Observer*, 11 November 1956, 9 v. M. Beloff, 'Suez and the British Conscience. A Personal Report', *Commentary* (April 1957), 310–12. S. E. Finer, *Backbench Opinion in the House of Commons 1955–1959* (Oxford, Pergamon, 1961), 92.

[7] *The Mensa Proceedings* (February 1957), 3. V. Serebriakoff, *I.Q. A Mensa Analysis and History* (London, Hutchinson, 1966), 144.

[8] M. Wight, 'Brutus in Foreign Policy', *International Affairs* (July 1960), 303.

[9] C. Brogan, *Suez. Who was Right?* (London, Coram, 1957), 6. K. Amis, *Socialism and the Intellectuals* (London, Fabian Tract 304, 1957), 11–12. A. Hartley, *A State of England* (London, Hutchinson, 1963), 67–78, 'Frustration of the Intellectuals'.

[10] M. Muggeridge, 'Eden Agonistes', *New Statesman*, 8 December 1956, 736–7. J. H. Huizinga, *Confessions of a European in England* (London, Heinemann, 1958), 246–76.

[11] Stephen King-Hall, *King-Hall News Letter*, 2 January 1957, 622; 15 May 1957, 770.

above the age of fifty-five,[1] while opposition was strongest in the age-group between twenty-five and thirty-five. That support was revealed in the increase in circulation of all the organs of the press supporting official policy and in the decrease in circulation of all the opposing organs of the liberal press. It increased markedly during the first week of November[2] as world opinion turned against England. The full extent of democratic support seems to have been largely concealed by the subsequent failure of the operation, which seems to have produced a much sterner condemnation than any on account of its improbity.

The Suez Crisis has been variously interpreted as a supreme conflict between Eden and Nasser, between English and Egyptian nationalism, between capitalism and Communism,[3] between democracy and dictatorship[4] or between world trade and Egyptian nationalism.[5] The crisis seems to have been above all a decisive confrontation between the old Europe and the new Asia.[6] The colonial world shook off its inherited subservience to imperial Europe and revealed a growing disposition to discard Europe's principles of international law, especially its respect for the sanctity of contract and for the rights of private property. The strength of Europe's reaction stemmed from the threat to its imperial pride as much as to its investments. Nevertheless it delayed the nationalization of other Western enterprises in Asia for over a decade, but discouraged investment in the underdeveloped lands most in need of capital. Europe declined to abandon its inherited assumptions of superiority and proved most reluctant to recognize in Asia either the principle of territorial sovereignty which it had accepted for its own states since 1648 or the responsibility of the State for social and economic welfare which its own states had assumed since 1945. The East thus united during the crisis in defence of the aspirations inherited from the West. Those wish-dreams had revolutionized its life during 'the Asian century'[7] as much as the Romantic revelation of the East had stabilized the life of Europe after 1815.

The cause of Europe was abandoned in 1956 by Asia, including those states which depended most upon the Canal for their foreign trade as well as the traditional allies and clients of the West. Thus at the first London Conference

---

[1] H. Cole, 'Public Opinion and the Suez Crisis. A Retrospect', *Fabian Journal* (March 1957), 12.

[2] *Manchester Guardian*, 6 November 1956, 6vii; 8 November, 8vii. *The Observer*, 11 November 1956, 2v; 18 November, 8v. S. King-Hall, *King-Hall News Letter*, 14 November 1956, 508. L. D. Epstein, *British Politics in the Suez Crisis* (London, Pall Mall, 1964), 142–3.

[3] M. Djilas, *The New Class* (New York, Praeger, 1957), 200.

[4] Eden, *Full Circle*, 584.

[5] B. Lavergne, *Problèmes Africains. Afrique noire–Algérie–Affaire de Suez* (Paris, Larose, 1957), 93–5.

[6] H. Lüthy, 'Ruhm und Ende der Kolonisation', *Der Monat* (Juli 1957), 34–7, reprinted in *Nach dem Untergang des Abendlandes* (Köln, Kiepenheuer, 1964), 377–80. F. Wartenweiler, *Suez. Asien. Afrika* (Zürich, Rotapfel, 1957), 40. F. Fanon, *The Wretched of the Earth* (London, MacGibbon, 1965), 62.

[7] J. Romein, *The Asian Century, A History of Modern Nationalism in Asia* (London, Allen, 1962), 389.

Ethiopia, Iran, Pakistan, Turkey and Japan accepted the Dulles Plan together with thirteen Western states. At the second London Conference only Iran and Turkey joined the Suez Canal Users' Association while Iran alone from Asia was appointed to its Executive Group of six. After the outbreak of hostilities Turkey condemned on 1 November the 'arbitrary and impulsive' policy of certain unnamed Powers in the Middle East. The delegate of the senior Asian member of the Commonwealth organized the condemnation of England and France on 2 November by the largest majority in the history of the General Assembly of the United Nations. Finally, Iran voted with Russia in the Security Council on 6 November against England, France and Israel. Thus the invasion of Egypt united Asia and Africa in sharp opposition to Europe and brought a 'Third World' into existence as a participator in the World's Debate.

The Arab world was convulsed by rage and anger at the attack on the leader of the Arab revolution against the West.[1] By associating herself with the two mortal foes of the Arab world Britain destroyed the influence which she had sought to preserve. The 'tripartite aggression' shattered England's treaties of alliance with Jordan, Libya, Egypt and Iraq. It destroyed all British rights in the Canal Zone base and precluded any possibility of a future re-entry. It undermined the Bagdad Pact and increased Arab hostility towards the member-states of Turkey and Iraq. It almost overthrew the dictator Nuri while making Nasser more powerful than ever before. It tilted the delicate balance of sentiment in the Lebanon against its Christian élite. The Arabs believed that the war was not supported by the British people[2] and decided that the war-machine of their foes would not be fuelled by Arab oil. Their determination was manifested in the sabotage of the pipelines from Iraq in Syria on 3 November, in the general strike in Bahrein on 4 November, in the end of oil exports from Saudi Arabia to Britain and France on 9 November and in the embargo placed by the Lebanon on tankers loading for Britain and France. The Arab states then met in conference at Beirut (13–15 November) and resolved that no repair of the pipeline or clearance of the Canal should take place until the evacuation of Egypt was complete. The production of oil fell least in Iran but most in Iraq. It sank more in Kuwait than in Saudi Arabia because Tapline remained open, unlike its rival in the Canal, to the benefit of Aramco at the expense of British Petroleum. The oil companies sought to conceal from the West the full extent of Arab hostility and earnestly affirmed that the shortage was one of tankers rather than of oil.

[1] *Cahiers de l'Orient Contemporain* (1956), 36–185. *Orient* (Janvier 1957), 288–314; (Avril 1957), 153–203. B. Lewis, 'The Middle East and North Africa', *Chambers's Encyclopaedia World Survey 1957*, 284–92. G. Kirk and F. Stoakes, 'The Arab World', *Annual Register: 1956*, 273–310. M. M. El-Behairy, 'The Suez Canal in World Politics, 1945–1961' (1961), 318–49. J. B. Glubb, *Britain and the Arabs. A Study of Fifty Years 1908 to 1958* (London, Hodder, 1959), 329–47. A. H. Hourani, 'The Middle East and the Crisis of 1956', *St. Antony's Papers Number 4* (London, Chatto, 1958), 9–42.
[2] E. B. Childers, *The Road to Suez* (London, MacGibbon, 1962), 393–4.

Suez shares which had risen with the invasion declined by 28 November to a level 16 per cent below that of 30 October. The U.S.A. reinforced its sterling sanctions by oil sanctions[1] and suspended an oil-lift to Europe planned since 13 August. It drained England's dollar-reserves by 30 November below their safety-level for the first time since 1952 and brought near the spectre of devaluation. It also forbade all contacts between the U.S. and the U.K. Delegations to the United Nations[2] and declined to allow the Prime Ministers of England or France to visit Washington before they had announced their intention to withdraw their troops.[3] The resulting increase in anti-American sentiment in Britain imposed a great strain upon all American-supported institutions, and agencies, despite their diligent concentration upon the iniquities of Hungary rather than upon those of Suez.[4] That resentment was reflected in the motion tabled by the Suez Group on 27 November[5] and in Lord Hinchingbrooke's declaration on 30 November: 'The Suez Canal and the area surrounding it are in some essential sense part of the United Kingdom. I refuse to allow the Government of my country to throw it away.'[6] The official announcement of the decision to withdraw on 3 December provoked bitter comments from the Suez Group and fifteen Conservative abstentions from the vote of 6 December. The evacuation from Port Said was completed on 22 December, being followed by the triumphant re-entry of Egyptian troops on 23 December and the retaliatory destruction of the statue of Lesseps on 25 December.[7] Lesseps was elevated to immortality in the history of France[8] but relegated thenceforward to oblivion in the history of Egypt. The prophecy made in 1899 was denied fulfilment, that the statue would stand at the entrance of the Canal for ever as a symbol of the new century of peace about to dawn.

The resignation of Sir Anthony Eden, broken in heart and in health, ended the career of a perfect English gentleman who had personified the noblest ideals of a whole generation. Whether his resignation took place under American pressure, as has been alleged,[9] has not been established. Nevertheless it seemed to mark the end of an era which had been dominated by

---

[1] C. L. Robertson, *The Emergency Oil Lift to Europe in the Suez Crisis* (Indianapolis, Bobbs-Merrill, 1965), 21. Sherman Adams, *Firsthand Report. The Story of the Eisenhower Administration* (New York, Harper, 1961), 261–70.

[2] P. Dixon, *Double Diploma. The Life of Sir Pierson Dixon Don and Diplomat* (London, Hutchinson, 1968), 276–7.

[3] Sherman Adams, 259–60. Eden, 567. Finer, 445–6.

[4] R. Miliband and J. Saville (ed.), *The Socialist Register 1964* (London, Merlin Press, 1964), 197–8, J. Saville, 'The Politics of *Encounter*'. The concentration on Hungary at the expense of Suez was characteristic also of at least three of the twelve periodicals related to *Encounter*, namely *Preuves* (Paris), *Forum* (Vienna), and *Der Monat* (Berlin).

[5] L. D. Epstein, *British Politics in the Suez Crisis*, 57, 123.

[6] *The Times*, 1 December 1956, 4iv.

[7] *Le Canal de Suez*, 15 Janvier 1957, 9704, 'La Statue de Ferdinand de Lesseps'.

[8] G. E. Bonnet, *Ferdinand de Lesseps* (Paris, Plon, 1951, 1959).

[9] R. Lacoste, 'La crise de Suez et le déclin de l'Europe', *Revue générale belge* (Janvier 1957), 62. A. Schoenenberg, *Der Nahe Osten rückt näher* (München, Isar, 1957), 190.

Churchill and by Churchill's political heir. England faced the traumatic experience of defeat which France had known in 1940, the U.S.A. in 1941 and Germany in 1945. 'Never did Britain stand so low since the death of Gordon in Khartoum. One feels it every,where; despair and hopelessness... What we want at the moment is a Cromwell.'[1] 'The dream of moral leadership, with which we had fleetingly comforted ourselves, ended on the banks of the Sweetwater Canal.'[2] Sir Anthony's successor however presided over the rapid recovery of his country and of his party.[3] He made no immediate change in foreign policy but renewed the special relationship with the U.S.A.[4] and sanctioned the reorganization of the armed forces on the basis of the shortest war in history. When he formally recognized the winds of change he recognized those to the south of Suez but not those to the east of Suez. The new leader of the Opposition possessed a comparable belief in England's great role 'east of Suez'[5] and so restored the unity of foreign policy towards Asia,[6] preserving as Prime Minister his belief in England's special responsibility for the Indian Ocean until the Arab-Israeli War of 1967. The maintenance of such continuity in foreign policy was aided by the academic reduction of the collision of two worlds to the minor proportions of 'the Suez Incident'.[7] The older generation wrote off the operation as an ephemeral episode but could not prevent the word 'Suez' from becoming thenceforth a synonym for dissension, defeat and disaster. The younger 'Suez generation' diverted its interest into an a-political renaissance which may have been strengthened by the failure during the Suez crisis of the administrative process, political remedies and constitutional conventions.[8] Its members helped to transform English culture in its superficies even more perhaps than in its foundations. They certainly reinvigorated the progress-ethic and revived the tradition of the dissidence of dissent in such strength as thitherto only Matthew Arnold had known it. Such was the legacy inherited by Young England from the Year of the Comet,[9] which may well have marked a turning-point in the cultural if not in the political history of England.

The concentration of an unprecedented military force of 80,000 men, 500 aircraft and 140 warships against Port Said helped to diffuse a whole complex of myths, which assumed the tactical importance of the Canal in 1956 to have been a measure of its commercial value and exaggerated its economic function

[1] R. M. Meinertzhagen, *Middle East Diary 1917–1956*, 319, 328, 10 January and 1 March 1957.

[2] A. Hartley, *A State of England*, 20.

[3] Earl of Kilmuir, *Political Adventure. The Memoirs of the Earl of Kilmuir* (London, Weidenfeld, 1964), 308–9.

[4] Eisenhower, 122. Sherman Adams, 288.

[5] Hansard, *Commons Debates*, 17 June 1964, 1403, H. Wilson.

[6] K. H. Wocker, 'Suez—das englische Trauma. Zehn Jahre danach—Wilson hat aus den Fehlern Edens wenig gelernt', *Die Zeit*, 29 Juli 1966, 6.

[7] P. W. Thayer (ed.), *Tensions in the Middle East* (Baltimore, Johns Hopkins Press, 1958), 53, B. Lewis, 'The Middle East in World Affairs'.

[8] J. B. Priestley, *Topside: or the Future of England* (London, Heinemann, 1958), 26–8.

[9] Osbert Lancaster, *The Year of the Comet* (London, Gryphon, 1957).

at the expense of its military utility. Those myths reproduced in effect the official explanation that the expedition had been directed against Suez instead of Cairo, that it had originated from a threat to the freedom of navigation through the Canal and that it had been intended to ensure the free flow of oil to Europe. Such myths diffused through the mass-media of the film and the textbook[1] were inevitably projected backwards in strategic guise into the past. Thus it was suggested that the road to India had been the key to British foreign policy as well as to the history of the Mediterranean between 1830 and 1870,[2] that concern for the Suez route to India had caused the occupation of Egypt in 'the Suez Crisis, 1882',[3] the scramble for Africa and the perpetuation of the British occupation until 1956[4] and that the opening of the Canal had ushered in a new era in the history of shipping[5] and in the history of all the neighbouring lands and seas such as Palestine, the Sudan, East Africa, the Mediterranean, the Red Sea and the Indian Ocean.[6] Such judgments overvalued the Canal in the past just as it had been overvalued in 1956. They culminated in the dating of the transition from modern to contemporary history between the Suez crisis of 1882 and the Suez crisis of 1956.[7]

The closing of the Suez route reduced the trade of all the ports of call from Gibraltar to Colombo and inflicted most damage upon the ports of the Adriatic. It increased the traffic of the Panama Canal and of the Cape route, of which South Africa proved itself a parochial guardian.[8] It gave a temporary advantage over Europe to Japan, Australia and the U.S.A. in their trade with Asia. It raised shipping freights, enhanced the profits of shipowners and stimulated shipbuilding, especially in Japan. The expected pressure on shipping tonnage and on commodity prices proved however to be as much an overestimate as the menace of an oil shortage. The oil companies rerouted their ships via the Cape and imposed compensatory surcharges but did not

[1] A. Sondergaard, *My First Geography of the Suez Canal* (New York, Little, 1960; London, Dobson, 1962).

[2] *The New Cambridge Modern History* (Cambridge University Press, 1960), x. 416, C. W. Crawley, 'The Mediterranean'.

[3] R. Robinson, J. Gallagher and A. Denny, *Africa and the Victorians. The Official Mind of Imperialism* (London, Macmillan, 1961), 76, 159. A. A. H. Knightbridge, 'Gladstone and the Invasion of Egypt in 1882' (B.Litt. Thesis, University of Oxford, 1960), 257–61.

[4] *The New Cambridge Modern History* (Cambridge University Press, 1962), xi. 589, A. P. Thornton, 'Imperial Frontiers in the Levant, 1870–1900', reprinted in *For the File on Empire. Essays and Reviews* (London, Macmillan, 1968), 246.

[5] C. R. V. Gibbs, *British Passenger Liners of the Five Oceans* (London, Putnam, 1963), 147, 239, 249.

[6] A. L. Tibawi, *British Interests in Palestine 1800–1901* (London, Oxford University Press, 1961), 180. R. Gray, *A History of the Southern Sudan, 1839–1889* (London, Oxford University Press, 1961), 171. N. R. Bennett, *Studies in East African History* (Boston University Press, 1963), 38. F. Ponteil, *La Méditerranée et les Puissances depuis l'Ouverture jusqu'à la Nationalisation du Canal de Suez* (Paris, Payot, 1964). T. E. Marston, *Britain's Imperial Role in the Red Sea Area 1800–1878* (Hamden, 1961), 385, 486, 499. A. Toussaint, *Histoire de l'Océan Indien* (Paris, Presses Universitaires de Erance, 1960), 2.

[7] G. Barraclough, *An Introduction to Contemporary History* (London, Watts, 1964), 62.

[8] *New York Times*, 18 September 1956, 3v; *The Times*, 7 January 1957, 9v, E. H. Louw. J. Mohan, 'South Africa and the Suez Crisis', *International Journal* (Autumn 1961), 352–3.

eliminate wasteful cross-hauls to the U.S.A. in their fear of the independent producers.[1] The anticipated shortfall of 40 per cent in supplies of oil was reduced to one of 15 per cent during the five months' emergency from November 1956 to March 1957 while the total shipments to Europe declined by only 8 per cent,[2] cutting total energy supplies by a mere 2 per cent. Thus no major crisis followed in France, England or in Europe[3] despite a reduction in the rate of economic growth, implying that Nasser's real challenge had been political more than economic. The crisis in oil supply from the Middle East nevertheless encouraged a rise in the price of oil in America by 25 per cent from 3 January 1957,[4] a search for oil and gas to the west of the Canal, an expansion in the production of high-cost atomic energy and a proliferation of suggested alternative routes to the Canal including an 'anti-Nasser' pipeline to the Mediterranean coast of Turkey as well as an even more chimerical Eilat–Haifa pipeline. It also revived the schemes of the 1850s for the construction of Cape leviathans in the form of super-tankers of 65,000 tons, with a draught of 46 feet, or 10 feet more than the maximum permissible for the Canal, and even of 'super-super tankers' of 80,000 tons.[5]

The Canal remained closed for longer than ever before in its history although Egypt had only sunk vessels and had not demolished the banks. Nasser frustrated the plan for a separate United Nations 'Canal Force' to protect the clearing of the Canal[6] and delayed the final salvage-work until Israel had been forced on 7 March 1957 to evacuate the Gaza strip. Thus Egypt used her sovereignty over the Canal for the first time as a diplomatic weapon. The cost of clearance was only half of what had been anticipated and was met through a 3 per cent surcharge paid by the users of the Canal rather than by Egypt, as England and France demanded, or by Israel, England and France, as Egypt demanded. England and France proposed on 18 February the payment of dues to the U.N. or to the World Bank as an international neutral custodian and the retention of half for development as well as for compensation to the Canal Company.[7] Nasser insisted, however, on the payment of dues in full to Egypt[8] and re-opened the Canal on 9 April on his own terms. The Memorandum of 24 April was Egypt's first Canal Regulation since 1854; it allotted the unprecedented proportion of 25 per cent of gross

[1] P. H. Frankel, 'Oil Supplies during the Suez Crisis', *Journal of Industrial Economics* (February 1958), 95.

[2] H. Lubell, *Middle East Oil Crises and Western Europe's Energy Supplies* (Baltimore, Johns Hopkins Press, 1963), 15.

[3] J. Gascuel, 'L'Économie Française au Lendemain de la Crise de Suez', *Politique Étrangère* (1957), 94–5.

[4] H. J. Frank, *Crude Oil Prices in the Middle East* (New York, Praeger, 1966), 82–7.

[5] C. J. V. Murphy, 'Oil East of Suez', *Fortune* (October 1956), 260.

[6] H. L. Mason, 'The United Nations Emergency Force', *Tulane Studies in Political Science*, iv (1957), 46.

[7] Suez Canal Company, *The Suez Canal Company and the Decision Taken by the Egyptian Government on 26th July 1956. Second Part* (August 1956–May 1957), 58, 67.

[8] *New York Times*, 24 March 1957, 1vii. *The Economist*, 23 March 1957, 982, 'For Whom the Canal Tolls'.

receipts to capital-development and precluded the raising of tolls by more than
1 per cent in any one year but made no provision for consultation with users
or for the insulation of the Canal from politics. Thus it established the un-
fettered control of Egypt over the waterway.[1] The British Government then
publicly recognized that the Canal was not as essential to the British economy
as had been thought[2] and announced on 13 May that British ships might use
the Canal on Egypt's terms[3] in 'the greatest spectacular retreat from Egypt
since the time of Moses. (Laughter.)'[4] Immediately eight M.P.s led by Lord
Hinchingbrooke, the honourable remnant of 'the gallant forty-one' of the
Suez Group formed in 1953, resigned from the Conservative Party.[5] Traffic
was nevertheless diverted from the Cape route to the Canal because the saving
of distance amounted to 48 per cent of the freight and Canal dues only to
4·8 per cent thereof.[6] The waterway became once more the oil artery of Europe,
in whose markets the oil of the Middle East regained its competitive position
to such an extent that British Petroleum raised its prices to profit by the
advance made by Jersey Standard. The Canal traffic reached its pre-crisis
level by the end of June while oil tonnage rose during July by 10 per cent
above the level for July 1956.[7] Petrol rationing ended in France and England
and freight surcharges were abolished. A severe depression afflicted first the
world tanker market and then the oil market, benefiting the Canal at the
expense of Tapline. Shipping experienced its first great slump since the 1930s
but the Canal continued to absorb a rising proportion of world trade until
1961.

Warships, troopships and mail-boats returned to the Canal route from
mid-July. Egypt professed her respect for the Convention of 1888, although
she extended her territorial waters to twelve miles from 17 February 1958 and
so embraced the three-mile limit off the Canal wholly within Egyptian waters.
She continued to exclude Israeli ships from the Canal but allowed Israeli
goods in non-Israeli shipping to pass usually without hindrance during 1957
and 1958. From February 1959 she once more confiscated such commodities
and thereby blocked the export even of non-strategic goods from Haifa to
Asia.[8] Israel's military successes did but build higher the walls around its
ghetto-State. It failed to retain control of Sinai,[9] to preserve the eastern bank
of the Canal in the hands of the United Nations or to gain unrestricted use

[1] Y. van der Mensbrugghe, *Les Garanties de la Liberté de Navigation dans le Canal de Suez*
(1964), 288–304.
[2] *The Times*, 7 May 1957, 7 v, H. Watkinson.
[3] Ibid., 13 May, 10 iii; 14 May, 10 i.   [4] Ibid., 14 May, 4 vi, Emrys Hughes.
[5] A. Fell, Viscount Hinchingbrooke, P. Maitland, A. Maude, V. Raikes and P. Williams,
joined by J. Biggs-Davison and L. Turner.
[6] S. Helander, 'Der Suezkanal in seiner gegenwärtigen weltwirtschaftlichen und weltpolitischen Bedeutung', *Wirtschaftsdienst* (Juni 1957), 332.
[7] *Manchester Guardian*, 17 December 1957, 6 vi, M. Adams, 'Suez Back to Normal'.
The Times, 17 April 1958, 13, 'Suez Canal Back to Normal'.
[8] *Middle East Record* (1960), i. 39–45, 'Freedom of Navigation in the Suez Canal'.
[9] L. N. Bloomfield, *Egypt, Israel and the Gulf of Aqaba in International Law* (Toronto,
Carswell, 1957), 138–43.

of the waterway.[1] It opened the Gulf of Akaba to its shipping under the protection of the United Nations force stationed at Sharm el Sheikh and of the naval base opened at Eilat on 27 December 1956 on the arrival of an Israeli frigate after a voyage around the Cape of six weeks.[2] Israel remained burdened with the most irrational economy in the world, based upon faith, hope and charity,[3] and more debarred than ever by Arab hostility from commerce with its neighbours as well as from the construction of a 32-inch Eilat–Haifa oil pipeline. It therefore began to use the Gulf for long-distance foreign trade in order to import oil from Iran as well as ground-nuts from East Africa and to export potash to Ceylon as well as copper and phosphates to Japan. Israel's increasing use of the Gulf took place under alien protection and rested on the acquiescence of the Arab states, all of whom protested against what they considered to be the defilement of the maritime highway to Mecca.

The Suez Crisis marked a turning-point in the history of Europe, Asia, Africa and Egypt if not in that of England or of the Middle East. It gave as great a stimulus to the Asian renaissance as the victory of Japan in 1905 so that the evacuation from Port Said was hailed as the equivalent of Salamis.[4] It also stimulated African endeavours to secure full independence from Europe, diverted American attention from the invasion of Cuba by Fidel Castro on 2 December 1956 and so helped to bring new centres of world-revolution into existence. In Egypt the Anglo-French-Israeli assault failed to overthrow Nasser but strengthened his position immensely and unexpectedly, making the revolution popular as never before and rallying to his support the richer classes impoverished by his policies. The war destroyed British influence in Egypt as completely as the 1840 crisis had done. It revealed the bankruptcy of the legend of French civilization in Egypt, ending the role of the Levantine communities as intermediaries between East and West, the history of the Jewish community after 2,200 years and the Alexandrian period of cosmopolitan and semi-colonial Egypt.[5] It undermined the private sector of the economy and extended the public sector through the nationalization or Egyptianization of fifty-five French and British firms. Thereby it carried much further the work begun on 26 July, ushered in a new era of economic planning and reinforced an immemorial tradition of State-control.

In the Middle East as a whole the crisis only accentuated existing tensions,

[1] *The Times*, 14 May 1957, 9iii. Bar-Zohar, *Ben Gurion*, 220.

[2] *New York Times*, 28 December 1956, 3i; 4 January 1957, 3vii; 17 January 1957, 7i. B. Boxer, *Israeli Shipping and Foreign Trade* (University of Chicago, Department of Geography Research Paper no. 48, April 1957), 139–40.

[3] N. Bentwich, 'Israel after Suez', *Journal of the Royal Central Asian Society* (April 1961), 163.

[4] G. Mann, *Propyläen Weltgeschichte* (Berlin, Propyläen Verlag, 1961), x. 151, K. M. Panikkar, 'Neue Staaten in Asien und Afrika'.

[5] G. Ketman, 'Du papier et des fèves. Portrait de l'intelligentsia égyptienne', *Preuves* (Janvier 1957), 16–18. J. J. Faust, 'L'Égypte d'une Révolution à l'Autre', *Études Méditerranéenes* (Été 1957), 45, 65.

although it seemed to mark the end of an era to American observers.[1] In particular it made apparent to all the decline of British power during the 1940s[2] and made Nasser the prisoner of Arab nationalism,[3] precipitating a series of interlocking crises in Jordan, Syria, Iraq and Lebanon as the U.S.A. and the U.S.S.R. manoeuvred in defence of their new clients. The creation of the United Arab Republic established a unified control over the flow of oil to the West through the pipelines and the Canal. The subsequent revolution in Iraq took place three weeks after the pipelines had regained their full capacity on 25 June 1958. It was far more important than the Suez Crisis because it destroyed the last British base in the Arab heartland and deprived the Bagdad Pact of its sole Arab member. It finally shattered the Arab dream of England and exiled her to the strategic infertile crescent which flanked Arabia from Aden to Kuwait. England was even compelled in 1961 to demonstrate its power to defend Kuwait against Iraq[4] while Kuwait was compelled to appease Egypt by the investment of some of its oil royalties in Arab economic projects.[5]

In Europe the crisis benefited Germany and Italy at the expense of France and England but destroyed the moral foundations of the North Atlantic Treaty Organization.[6] France felt betrayed by both England and the U.S.A. She suffered the profound humiliation of her armed forces, the annihilation of her cultural empire in Egypt and the destruction of her isthmian kingdom. 'The only French survival in the isthmus is the cemeteries.'[7] France was forced to undertake the devaluation which England avoided, but remained determined to retain Algeria. She concluded that N.A.T.O. was 'the wrong alliance in the wrong place, against the wrong enemy'[8] and undertook the agonizing reappraisal of policy with which Dulles had threatened her in 1954. She decided to turn towards her 'national and hereditary foe' of Germany, to make the new Common Market into an extension of French empire, to create a nuclear weapon industry in order to eliminate any future atomic blackmail, and to regain full control over all her armed forces in order to make possible her withdrawal from N.A.T.O. Thus she declined to follow England's example in reconciling herself to American hegemony[9] but strove thenceforward

[1] J. C. Hurewitz, *Diplomacy in the Near and Middle East. A Documentary Record: 1535–1956* (Princeton, Van Nostrand, 1956).

[2] A. H. Hourani, 'The Middle East and the Crisis of 1956', *St. Antony's Papers Number 4*, 20–2.

[3] W. Range, 'An Interpretation of Nasserism', *Western Political Quarterly* (December 1959), 1010–13.

[4] *New York Times*, 5 July 1961, ıvii; 6 July, 31 v. R. Hewins, *A Golden Dream: the Miracle of Kuwait* (London, Allen, 1963), 280–305.

[5] B. Shwadran, 'The Kuwait Incident', *Middle East Affairs* (February 1962), 51.

[6] R. Lacoste, 'La crise de Suez et le déclin de l'Europe', *Revue générale belge* (Janvier 1957), 61.

[7] F. Charles-Roux, 'Ce qui disparaît d'Égypte avec la Compagnie Universelle du Canal Maritime de Suez', *Revue des travaux de l'Académie des Sciences Morales et Politiques*, 1 Juillet 1957, 5.

[8] H. Lüthy and D. Rodnick, *French Motivations in the Suez Crisis*, 55.

[9] G. Schwarzenberger, 'Hegemonial Intervention', *Year Book of World Affairs* (1959), 263–4.

to unite Europe into an independent world-force under French leadership transformed by a Gaullist-military renaissance.

For the Canal Company the crisis marked the end of its Egyptian era but not the end of its existence. The Company had survived successive crises ever since its foundation and revealed an unexpected resilience in 1956. It never contemplated dissolution and declined to disappear from history, even at the fiat of a State. It began a new career as an investment trust and formed the Channel Tunnel Study Group on the model of the Suez Canal Study Society of 1846 at its Paris offices on 26 July 1957. On 25 June 1957 its shareholders approved thirteen resolutions[1] which extended the life of the Company to 31 December 2050, reduced its board of directors from thirty-two to twelve and replaced the executive committee by a President-Managing Director. Jacques Georges-Picot, a former Inspector of Finances as well as a Professor of Politics and General Manager since 1953, succeeded Charles-Roux from 23 December 1957. He reunited the powers of President and Managing-Director which had remained divorced since 1893 and, at the age of 57, became the youngest president in the history of the Company except for Lesseps himself. The six shipowner-directors resigned but the British Government retained its shareholding and its official directors, although without the control which its shares would have given it in any other company.[2] On 24 December 1957 the Company was gazetted French under the law of 1 June 1957 and so became subject to French law as never before in its history. The shareholders approved on 21 April 1958 the reorganization of its four classes of shares into a single class of 10,000-franc share so as to establish beyond doubt the right of the holders of founders' shares and Civil Society shares to participate in any compensation.[3] The general meeting of 4 July changed the name of the Company to the Suez Finance Company and approved a preliminary agreement of 29 April with the Egyptian Government, despite a few dissenting shouts of 'Munich!'.[4] The Final Agreement signed at Geneva on 13 July 1958 was achieved through the mediation of the World Bank and not of the Governments of France or England. That agreement embodied the principle of the territoriality of nationalization by dividing debts and assets on a territorial basis. The Company abandoned its claim to compensation for the loss of twelve years' future revenue and accepted £E28,300,000 in settlement of its original claim of £204,000,000. Egypt abandoned her claim to the assets of the Company outside Egypt and recognized the survival of the Company outside Egypt after 26 July 1956.[5] Thus the Company avoided a decade

[1] *Le Canal de Suez* (Juin 1957), 9734–47. *The Economist*, 29 June 1957, 1180, 'The Boys without the Jobs'.

[2] *The Economist*, 5 October 1957, 57–9, 'Something from Suez?'

[3] *The Suez Canal* (May 1958), 25.

[4] *The Economist*, 12 July 1958, 152, 'Suez ex Canal'. Compagnie Financière de Suez, *Bulletin No. 1* (July 1958), 11.

[5] L. Focsaneanu, 'L'Accord ayant pour objet l'Indemnisation de la Compagnie de Suez Nationalisée par l'Egypte', *Annuaire Français de Droit International* (1959), 203–4.

of further conflict with Egypt and reorganized itself as successfully as Anglo-Iranian had done after Abadan. It registered the Banque de la Compagnie Financière de Suez in Paris on 1 April 1959 and the Suez Finance Company (London) Ltd. on 24 June 1959. It became the leading financial holding company in France.[1] It continued to date its formation from 1858 and benefited from the reaffirmation of its own tradition of the history of the Canal.[2]

The Canal was not neglected by its Egyptian administration despite the gloomy prophecies made by technocrats in the West. The Suez Canal Authority maintained the standards of management set by the Company to which it proved a worthy successor.[3] By the decree of 16 July 1957 the Authority was granted administrative autonomy and was empowered to run the Canal as a private commercial enterprise. Yunus became President in succession to Badaoui as well as Managing-Director from 1957 to 1966, so uniting the same powers as those of Georges-Picot. The Authority retained the Canal Company's hierarchical organization, its centralized control of transit, its elaborate code of navigation, its unique measurement-gauge, its metric system, its use of French as an office-language, its compilation of traffic-statistics and its paternal guardianship of 'the Suez Canal Family'. It was freed, however, from the restrictions imposed on the Company by the concessions of 1854–6 as well as from the influence of the Stock Exchange so that its engineer-directors could elaborate much more fully the inherent logic of an engineering enterprise. It established a hydrographic research unit at Ismailia in 1960, a pilotage scheme for Suez Bay in 1960, shipyards at Port Said in 1960 as well as at Suez in 1962 and a Measurement Institute at Ismailia in 1961. Thus it extended its activity to dominate the isthmus as the Company had never done whilst adopting the company form of organization for its subsidiary activities. Above all, it linked the Canal to the Delta through the deep quays built at Port Said between 1961 and 1965. Port Said ended its era as a European city, developed a new Arab city, and became Bur Said from 1959.[4] It lost its tourist traffic to Aden and suffered a decline in its bunkering and provisioning services,[5] but acquired a Cenotaph to commemorate its 974 dead and a Victory Museum from 1959.[6] Throughout the isthmus the minds and hearts of the population were united every year on the new festival-

---

[1] *New York Times*, 6 November 1966, III, 1 iv.

[2] C. E. Boillot, 'Suez Canal', *Encyclopedia Americana*, vol. 25 (1965), 799–801. S. C. Burchell and C. Issawi, *Building the Suez Canal* (New York, Harper, 1966). S. C. Burchell and A. Chassigneux, *Le Canal de Suez* (Paris, Éditions R.S.T., 1967).

[3] *Financial Times*, 25 September 1962, 7, 'The Suez Canal Six Years after Nationalisation'. *The Times*, 3 April 1963, 13, 'Suez Canal Fears Confounded'; Ibid., 26 July 1966, 13 i, 'Suez Ten Years After'. *Financial Times*, 27 July 1966, 7 vi, 'The Suez Canal. How the Sceptics Were Confounded'.

[4] U.S. Board on Geographic Names, *Gazetteer No. 45. Egypt and the Gaza Strip* (Washington, Department of the Interior, June 1959), 90, 292.

[5] *New York Times*, 6 November 1966, III, 13 ii.

[6] P. D. Smith, 'The Black Museum', *New Statesman*, 16 November 1962, 701–2.

days of 26 July, 15 September and 23 December, which marked the successive stages in the triumph of Egypt over Europe in 1956. The Authority survived for ten years without a strike until 9 October 1966.[1]

Oil continued to provide the staple cargo of the Canal and the tanker its representative client. England remained the leading user of the waterway until its tonnage was surpassed by that of Liberia in December 1964 and by that of Norway in October 1965, so ending the British dominance established in 1869. The Canal Authority was granted an improvement-loan by the World Bank in 1959, despite the opposition of Israel. Thus it was able to improve the waterway by means of foreign loans and to reduce its proportion of revenue reinvested from the intended 25 to 14 per cent. Its revenues became a growing source of foreign exchange in competition with cotton exports which were increasingly bartered. They helped the National Income to grow at the rate desired in the first Five-Year Plan introduced in 1960. They helped to finance Egypt's war in the Yemen as well as the Aswan High Dam.[2] The Authority's greatest achievement was to raise the maximum permissible draught from 35 feet to 37 feet from 19 September 1960 and then to 38 feet for tankers of 60,000 tons d.w. from 29 February 1964,[3] so compelling a competitive increase in the size of the super-tankers using the Cape route.

In 1964 the Authority secured an improvement loan from Kuwait and imposed improvement-dues on vessels over 37 feet in draught, so first securing from the heaviest users of the Canal's facilities a proportionate contribution to the high cost of its deepening. At the same time it made its first general increase in dues after the completion of the first phase of the Aswan High Dam had precluded the possibility of any complaints about the diversion of its profits to the service of the Nile. It then revealed how fully it had absorbed the spirit of commercial enterprise from the Suez Canal Company and began to charge as much as the traffic would bear, making further annual increases in 1965 and 1966.[4] Thus it provoked the oil companies to consider in 1965 tankers of 170,000 tons d.w. of 57-feet draught, and in 1966 tankers of 200,000 tons d.w. of 62-feet draught and even tankers of 300,000 tons d.w.[5] The Authority replied by proposing on 4 March 1966 to lay an oil pipeline parallel to the Canal to provide immediate relief and to raise the maximum permissible draught by 1971 to 41 feet for ships of 110,000 tons d.w.[6] but could not prevent the diversion of a growing number of giant tankers to the Cape route even before the war of 1967. The Authority remained a model of Western technology for diffusion to Egypt as well as for display to admiring visitors from the Third World. It served as a great spearhead of Westernization in Egypt as well as a pattern for

[1] *New York Times*, 27 October 1966, 9i.
[2] *The Economist*, 2 April 1966, 66, 'Suez: Ten Years After'.
[3] United Arab Republic, Suez Canal Authority, *Annual Bulletin, 1957*; *Suez Canal Report, 1958–1965*.
[4] *The Scotsman*, 3 June 1966, 9i–iv, I. Beeston, 'Suez Canal faces uncertain future'.
[5] *Financial Times*, 29 June 1966, 10i.
[6] Ibid., 27 July 1966, 7vii.

the Aswan High Dam Authority. Such public utilities paid continuing homage to the cultural victory of the West which was veiled beneath its political defeat in the Suez Crisis of 1956. Under the 'Caesars of Asia'[1] the East asserted its independence but adopted the civilization of Europe more rapidly than ever before. Thus the unity of mankind was restored and Suez ceased to mark the dividing-point between the worlds of East and West.[2]

[1] J. Cheverny, *Éloge du Colonialisme. Essai sur les Révolutions d'Asie* (Paris, Julliard, 1961), 15.

[2] A. J. Toynbee, *Between Niger and Nile* (London, Oxford University Press, 1965), 61.

GRAPHS, STATISTICAL TABLES, BIBLIOGRAPHY AND MAPS

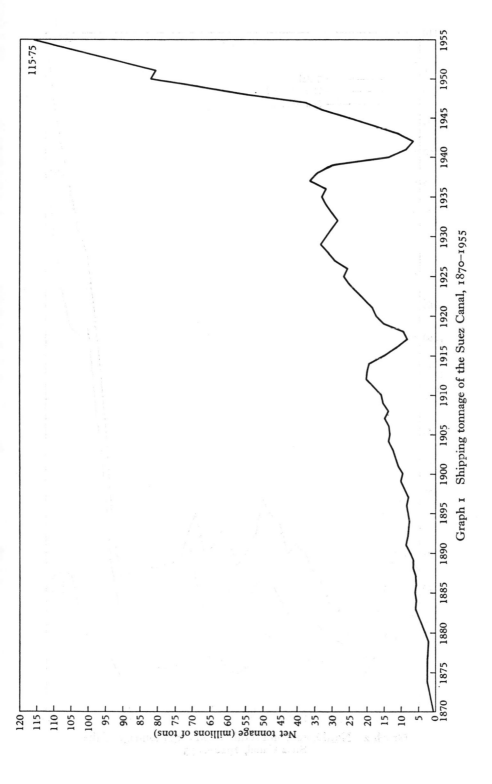

Graph 1 Shipping tonnage of the Suez Canal, 1870–1955

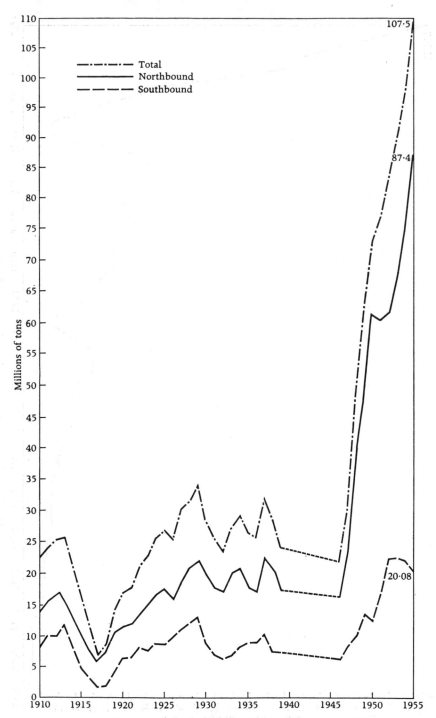

Graph 2 Northbound and southbound cargo tonnage of the
Suez Canal, 1910–1955

Table 1 751

The Shipping Tonnage of the Suez Canal 1869–1955

Year	Suez tonnage	Annual % increase	British tonnage	Annual % increase	British % of total tonnage
1869	11,280		10,850		
1870	436,609	3770·65	289,234	2,500·0	66·25
1871	761,467	74·41	546,453	89·0	71·76
1872	1,160,744	52·44	1,059,926	30·0	73·65
1873	1,367,768	17·84	1,499,792	41·5	71·93
1874	1,631,650	19·29	1,797,495	19·8	74·16
1875	2,009,984	23·19	2,181,387	21·4	74·18
1876	2,096,772	4·32	2,343,523	7·44	76·28
1877	2,355,448	12·34	2,698,878	15·1	78·94
1878	2,269,678	−3·64	2,630,285	−2·52	79·91
1879	2,263,332	−0·28	2,508,525	−4·63	77·50
1880	3,057,422	35·08	3,446,431	37·4	79·33
1881	4,136,780	35·30	4,792,118	39·0	82·70
1882	5,074,809	22·68	4,126,253	21·0	81·31
1883	5,775,862	13·81	4,406,088	6·77	76·29
1884	5,871,501	1·66	4,466,930	1·38	76·08
1885	6,335,753	7·91	4,864,049	8·9	76·77
1886	5,767,656	−8·97	4,436,688	−8·79	76·92
1887	5,903,024	2·35	4,516,773	1·8	76·52
1888	6,640,834	12·50	5,223,255	15·65	78·65
1889	6,783,187	2·14	5,352,886	2·48	78·91
1890	6,890,094	1·58	5,331,095	−0·46	77·37
1891	8,698,777	26·25	6,837,665	28·2	78·61
1892	7,712,029	−11·34	5,826,862	−14·9	75·56
1893	7,659,060	−0·69	5,752,934	−1·27	75·11
1894	8,039,175	4·96	5,996,796	4·24	74·60
1895	8,448,383	5·09	6,062,587	1·1	71·76
1896	8,560,284	1·32	5,817,769	−4·4	67·96
1897	7,899,374	−7·72	5,319,136	−8·57	67·34
1898	9,238,603	16·95	6,297,743	18·4	68·17
1899	9,895,630	7·11	6,586,311	4·59	66·56
1900	9,738,152	−1·59	5,605,421	−14·9	57·56
1901	10,823,840	11·15	6,252,819	11·53	57·77
1902	11,248,413	3·92	6,772,911	8·15	60·21
1903	11,907,288	5·86	7,403,553	9·3	62·18
1904	13,401,835	12·55	8,833,929	19·35	65·92
1905	13,134,105	−2·00	8,356,940	−5·4	63·63
1906	13,445,504	2·37	8,299,931	−0·68	61·73
1907	14,728,434	9·54	9,495,868	14·4	64·47
1908	13,633,283	−7·44	8,302,802	−12·6	60·90
1909	15,407,527	13·01	9,592,387	15·5	62·26
1910	16,581,898	7·62	10,423,610	8·66	62·86
1911	18,324,794	10·51	11,715,947	12·4	63·94
1912	20,275,120	10·64	12,847,621	9·65	63·37
1913	20,033,884	−1·19	12,052,484	−6·19	60·16
1914	19,409,495	−3·12	12,910,278	7·11	66·52
1915	15,266,155	−21·35	11,656,038	−9·7	76·35
1916	12,325,347	−19·26	9,788,190	−16·00	79·42

Year	Suez tonnage	Annual % increase	British tonnage	Annual % increase	British % of total tonnage
1917	8,368,918	−32·10	6,164,201	−37·00	73·66
1918	9,251,601	10·55	7,356,371	19·35	79·51
1919	16,013,802	73·09	11,355,067	54·3	70·91
1920	17,574,657	9·75	10,838,842	−4·55	61·67
1921	18,118,999	3·10	11,397,019	5·15	62·90
1922	20,743,245	14·48	13,382,710	17·42	64·52
1923	22,730,162	9·58	14,264,214	6·6	62·76
1924	25,109,882	10·47	14,994,681	5·13	59·72
1925	26,761,935	6·58	16,016,439	6·81	59·85
1926	26,060,377	−2·62	14,968,938	−6·54	57·44
1927	28,962,048	11·13	16,534,445	10·47	57·09
1928	31,905,902	10·16	18,124,074	9·6	56·80
1929	33,466,014	4·89	19,114,282	5·45	57·12
1930	31,668,759	−5·37	17,600,483	−7·93	55·58
1931	30,027,966	−5·18	16,624,352	−5·54	55·36
1932	28,340,290	−5·62	15,721,294	−5·43	55·47
1933	30,676,672	8·24	16,733,484	6·4	54·55
1934	31,750,802	3·50	17,238,128	3·0	54·29
1935	32,810,968	3·34	15,734,818	−8·72	47·96
1936	32,378,883	−1·32	15,052,138	−4·34	46·49
1937	36,491,332	12·70	17,254,182	14·63	47·28
1938	34,418,187	−5·68	17,357,743	0·6	50·43
1939	29,573,394	−14·08	15,208,712	−12·4	51·43
1940	13,535,712	−54·23	7,449,913	−50·8	55·04
1941	8,262,841	−38·96	5,632,544	−24·4	68·17
1942	7,027,763	−14·95	4,578,441	−18·72	65·15
1943	11,273,802	60·42	6,711,511	46·5	59·53
1944	18,124,952	60·77	10,344,856	54·1	57·08
1945	25,064,966	38·29	15,149,927	46·5	60·44
1946	32,731,631	30·59	20,485,786	35·2	62·59
1947	36,576,581	11·75	17,276,262	−15·15	47·23
1948	55,081,056	50·59	20,726,246	20·0	37·63
1949	68,861,548	25·02	24,883,987	20·5	36·14
1950	81,795,523	18·78	26,557,386	6·72	32·47
1951	80,356,338	−1·76	26,900,063	1·29	33·48
1952	86,137,037	7·19	28,496,661	5·93	33·08
1953	92,905,439	7·86	31,262,257	9·7	33·65
1954	102,493,851	10·32	32,909,191	5·26	32·11
1955	115,756,398	12·94	32,789,874	−0·364	28·33

Source: *Le Canal de Suez*, 1870–1957.

N.B. Suez tonnage was net official tonnage from 1 February 1870 and net register tonnage, under the rules of the Conference of Constantinople of 18 December 1873, from 29 April 1874. Net register tonnage remained a unique Suez tonnage and the lowest in the whole series of measurement-tonnages, equalling 66 per cent of gross tonnage in 1873, 72 per cent thereof in 1900 and 75 per cent thereof in 1955. British tonnage was net tonnage from 1869 to 1871, gross tonnage from 1872 to 1881 and net Suez tonnage from 1882. (P. Parfond, 'La Jauge du Canal de Suez et les Droits de Transit', *La Revue Maritime* (Janvier 1957), 84–109.)

Table 2
Northbound and Southbound Cargo Tonnage, 1906–1955

Year	Northbound tonnage	Annual % increase	Southbound tonnage	Annual % increase
1906	9,821,000		8,246,000	
1907	11,618,000	18·30	8,497,000	3·04
1908	10,314,000	−11·22	8,129,000	−4·34
1909	11,935,000	15·72	7,986,000	−1·76
1910	14,006,000	17·35	8,429,000	5·55
1911	15,052,000	7·47	9,496,000	12·63
1912	15,662,000	4·05	9,782,000	2·98
1913	14,455,000	−7·71	11,320,000	15·7
1914	12,296,000	−14·94	9,039,000	−20·1
1915	9,774,000	−20·51	5,365,000	−40·6
1916	7,178,000	−26·56	3,415,000	−36·3
1917	5,436,000	−24·27	1,339,000	−60·8
1918	6,222,000	14·46	1,610,000	20·2
1919	10,211,000	64·11	3,762,000	134·0
1920	10,729,000	5·07	6,318,000	67·8
1921	10,933,000	1·90	6,576,000	4·08
1922	13,168,000	20·44	8,192,000	24·6
1923	15,073,000	14·47	7,704,000	−5·96
1924	16,711,000	10·87	8,818,000	14·45
1925	17,777,000	6·38	8,801,000	−0·193
1926	15,605,000	−12·22	9,804,000	11·4
1927	18,442,000	18·18	11,082,000	13·0
1928	20,659,000	12·02	11,963,000	7·96
1929	21,620,000	4·65	12,896,000	7·8
1930	19,077,000	−11·76	9,434,000	−26·9
1931	17,955,000	−5·88	7,377,000	−22·0
1932	17,318,000	−3·55	6,314,000	−14·4
1933	19,712,000	13·82	7,203,000	14·1
1934	20,464,000	3·81	7,984,000	10·8
1935	17,404,000	−14·95	8,924,000	11·8
1936	16,727,000	−3·89	8,829,000	−1·06
1937	22,619,000	35·22	10,157,000	15·0
1938	21,011,000	−7·11	7,768,000	−23·6
1939	17,161,000	−18·32	7,517,000	−3·23
1946	15,931,000		5,995,000	
1947	22,767,000	42·91	7,821,000	30·4
1948	39,653,000	74·17	9,716,000	24·2
1949	48,027,000	21·12	13,028,000	34
1950	60,468,000	25·90	12,141,000	−6·8
1951	59,333,000	−1·88	17,420,000	43·5
1952	61,447,000	3·56	22,001,000	26·28
1953	67,881,000	10·47	22,518,000	2·32
1954	74,511,000	9·77	22,370,000	−0·66
1955	87,426,000	17·33	20,082,000	−10·24

Source: *Le Can al de Suez*, 1908–1956.

Table 3
The Share of Canal Cargo in World Trade, 1920–1966

Year	Canal cargo tonnage (million metric tons)	Volume of external world trade (million metric tons)	Canal share of world trade (%)
1875	1·382	88	1·57
1878	2·155	103	2·08
1880	2·387	113	2·11
1899	13·628	182	7·5
1913	25·775	348	7·4
1920	17·047	288	5·92
1921	17·509	285	6·14
1922	21·360	320	6·67
1923	22·777	327	6·95
1924	25·529	369	6·92
1925	26·578	397	6·68
1926	25·409	400	6·36
1927	29·524	442	6·68
1928	32·622	453	7·20
1929	34·516	470	7·35
1930	28·511	440	6·48
1931	25·332	380	6·67
1932	23·632	350	6·75
1933	26·915	360	7·48
1934	28·448	390	7·29
1935	26·328	410	6·42
1936	25·556	430	5·94
1937	32·776	490	6·69
1938	28·779	470	6·12
1947	30·588	450	6·80
1948	49·369	490	10·08
1949	61·055	510	11·97
1950	72·609	550	13·20
1951	76·753	640	11·99
1952	83·448	660	12·64
1953	90·399	690	13·10
1954	96·881	740	13·09
1955	107·508	840	12·80
1956	100·983	920	10·98
1957	81·323	960	11·70
1958	139·373	930	15·00
1959	148·254	990	15·00
1960	168·883	1,100	15·33
1961	172·394	1,170	14·73
1962	182·397	1,260	14·5
1963	193·532	1,360	14·2
1964	210·981	1,550	13·6
1965	225·442	1,670	13·5
1966	241·893	1,790	13·5

Source: *Le Canal de Suez*, 12 Mai 1872, 2 ii; 2 Décembre 1877, 4; 12 Mars 1881, 3. *Le Canal de Suez* (*Documents Statistiques*) (1956). Suez Canal Authority, *Annual Report*, 1957–66. *United Nations Statistical Year Book*, 1966, 77. *United Nations Monthly Bulletin of Statistics*, January 1968, xv.

Table 4
Receipts and Dividends of the Canal Company, *1870–1955*

Year	Annual receipts fr c	% increase	Dividends fr c	% increase	Share of dividends in total receipts (%)
1870	9,274,328 87				
1871	13,276,074 50	43·15			
1872	18,325,024 46	38·03			
1873	24,831,126	35·50			
1874	26,726,144 71	7·63			
1875	30,844,635 91	15·41	1,061,709 35		3·44
1876	31,174,694 35	1·07	2,002,913 51	88·65	6·43
1877	33,975,648 15	8·98	4,500,080 26	124·68	13·25
1878	32,496,335 33	−4·35	3,627,109 76	−19·40	11·16
1879	30,949,148 85	−4·76	2,744,880 98	−24·32	8·87
1880	41,820,899 96	35·13	12,330,142 07	349·20	29·48
1881	54,676,189 26	30·74	24,678,046 38	100·14	45·13
1882	63,409,593 44	15·97	31,674,313 22	28·35	49·95
1883	68,523,344 73	8·06	35,863,541 26	13·23	52·34
1884	65,408,294 56	−4·55	35,071,850 93	−2·21	53·62
1885	65,049,945 21	−0·55	34,028,767 02	−2·97	52·31
1886	59,022,626 28	−9·27	28,358,166 14	−16·67	48·05
1887	60,510,328 60	2·52	29,988,495 52	5·75	49·56
1888	67,705,348 16	11·89	36,271,477 11	20·95	53·57
1889	69,765,492 40	3·04	37,212,821 03	2·60	53·33
1890	70,460,910 30	1·00	38,133,384 13	2·47	54·12
1891	86,866,913 55	23·28	49,091,892 53	28·74	56·51
1892	77,809,780 77	−10·43	41,728,543 28	−15·00	53·63
1893	76,579,992 02	−1·58	40,615,536 74	−2·67	53·04
1894	76,951,153 91	0·48	40,367,323 94	−0·61	52·46
1895	80,702,787 35	4·88	41,969,014 08	3·97	52·00
1896	82,222,855 26	1·88	42,283,380 28	0·75	51·43
1897	75,607,029 40	−8·05	40,913,802 81	−3·24	54·11
1898	87,906,254 99	16·27	46,618,028 17	13·94	53·03
1899	94,317,505 30	7·29	51,538,028 16	10·55	54·64
1900	93,451,403 12	−0·92	51,568,450 70	0·06	55·18
1901	103,121,726 38	10·35	61,330,704 22	18·93	59·47
1902	106,849,760 29	3·62	61,497,464 78	0·27	57·56
1903	106,875,865 95	0·02	64,565,633 80	4·99	60·41
1904	119,176,398 45	11·51	70,926,197 18	9·85	59·51
1905	117,308,196 82	−1·57	71,173,521 12	0·35	60·67
1906	111,989,122 98	−4·54	71,377,464 78	0·29	63·74
1907	120,118,521 06	7·26	71,385,915 49	0·01	59·43
1908	111,490,959 54	−7·18	71,451,830 98	0·09	64·09
1909	123,477,833 88	10·75	77,483,380 28	8·44	62·75
1910	133,704,212 09	8·28	82,427,042 25	6·38	61·65
1911	138,038,224 74	3·24	87,075,492 95	5·64	63·08
1912	139,922,639 23	1·37	87,292,957 74	0·25	62·39

Year	Annual receipts fr c	% increase	Dividends fr c	% increase	Share of dividends in total receipts (%)
1913	129,925,949	−7·14	87,862,535 21	0·65	67·63
1914	125,121,237 54	−3·70	61,656,338 02	−29·83	49·28
1915	98,228,098 87	−21·49	61,567,887 33	−0·14	62·68
1916	89,044,276 83	−9·35	43,707,042 26	−29·01	49·08
1917	72,019,026 97	−19·12	29,356,619 71	−32·83	40·76
1918	92,969,910 09	29·09	49,920,563 38	70·05	53·70
1919	184,708,395 03	98·68	104,225,352 11	108·78	56·43
1920	267,460,679 06	44·80	143,661,971 83	37·84	53·71
1921	260,135,996 61	−2·74	149,261,971 83	3·90	57·38
1922	305,455,608 72	17·42	192,641,126 76	29·06	63·07
1923	419,250,419 65	37·25	264,061,971 83	37·07	62·98
1924	508,584,356 42	21·31	354,573,521 12	34·28	69·72
1925	608,677,855 31	19·68	464,770,704 22	31·08	76·36
1926	746,547,805 80	22·65	598,892,394 36	28·86	80·22
1927	784,595,099 54	5·10	636,642,253 52	6·30	81·14
1928	1,167,112,088 03	48·75	712,192,676 05	11·87	61·02
1929	1,189,958,441 03	1·96	737,478,309 86	3·55	61·98
1930	1,098,547,518 64	−7·68	718,309,859 15	−2·60	65·39
1931	979,877,486 54	−10·80	612,326,760 56	−14·75	62·49
1932	834,158,270 93	−14·87	505,284,507 04	−17·48	60·57
1933	886,983,266 76	6·33	522,185,915 49	3·34	58·87
1934	895,130,847 47	0·92	522,185,915 49		58·34
1935	927,746,902 82	3·64	552,878,873 23	5·88	59·59
1936	986,213,234 43	6·30	625,791,549 29	13·19	63·45
1937	1,448,484,829 90	46·87	852,236,619 71	36·19	58·84
1938	1,784,278,090 60	23·18	914,861,971 83	7·35	51·27
1940	713,813,965				
1941	627,120,908	−12·2			
1942	640,312,917	2·1			
1943	922,791,162 30	44·00			
1944	1,477,980,393 47	60·03			
1945	2,687,510,074 65	82·00			
1946	6,253,785,799 02	132·80	4,394,366,197 18		70·27
1947	6,754,467,862 27	8·01	3,605,633,802 80	−17·95	53·38
1948	19,935,442,100 93	195·14	7,887,323,943 65	118·75	39·56
1949	25,936,945,898 22	30·10	8,450,704,225 35	7·14	32·58
1950	28,020,286,230	8·03	9,859,154,930	16·67	35·18
1951	27,633,623,806	−1·38	10,140,845,070	2·86	36·70
1952	28,379,481,562	2·70	10,140,845,070		35·73
1953	30,853,530,514	8·72	10,422,535,211	2·78	33·78
1954	32,455,700,791	5·19	10,422,535,211		32·11
1955	34,538,854,701	6·42	10,704,225,352	2·70	30·99

Source: *Le Canal de Suez*, 1870–1957.

N.B. The francs were gold francs up to 1927 and thereafter French francs according to the laws of 25 June 1928 and 1 October 1936.

Table 5
Dividends Paid to the British Government, 1895–1960

Year ending 31 March	Annual dividend £ s. d.	Market value of Government's shares on 31 March (£)	Annual % increase in market value
1895*	279,011 8 5	23,892,955	
1896	673,417 19 3	22,627,000	−5·30
1897	694,075 8 6	22,299,000	−1·45
1898	698,684 0 8	24,435,000	9·58
1899	678,856 9 8	26,451,000	8·25
1900	801,818 2 4	24,312,000	−8·09
1901	814,766 17 4	25,806,000	6·15
1902	847,570 9 7	27,935,000	8·25
1903	933,778 1 4	26,485,000	−5·19
1904	936,151 0 0	28,910,000	9·16
1905	990,198 17 1	30,857,000	6·73
1906	1,053,323 2 3	31,080,000	0·72
1907	1,054,027 17 1	31,796,000	2·30
1908	1,127,821 7 4	31,055,000	−2·33
1909	1,058,374 0 2	32,667,000	5·19
1910	1,056,207 5 5	35,295,000	8·04
1911	1,129,260 0 0	37,608,000	6·55
1912	1,187,934 9 4	44,046,000	17·12
1913	1,318,685 11 6	39,015,000	−11·42
1914	1,246,370 8 0	34,929,000	−10·47
1915	1,154,275 17 5	29,993,000	−14·13
1916	858,151 16 8	24,858,000	−17·12
1917	773,486 7 1	27,464,000	10·48
1918	524,318 11 11	29,628,000	7·88
1919	617,214 6 8	32,818,000	10·77
1920	682,497 8 7	23,192,000	−29·33
1921	798,566 9 0	19,364,000	−16·51
1922	1,094,303 8 10	19,740,125	1·94
1923	919,753 10 4	19,206,335	−2·70
1924	878,202 11 7	22,416,737	16·72
1925	1,090,263 10 9	35,022,750	56·23
1926	1,115,161 2 8	32,121,885	−8·28
1927	1,099,750 14 11	36,194,585	12·68
1928	1,546,272 5 3	51,343,115	41·85
1929	1,696,932 8 2	72,258,844	40·74
1930	1,834,139 10 10	54,574,331	−24·47
1931	1,870,696 12 2	42,690,310	−21·78
1932	2,238,879 4 11	52,947,640	24·03
1933	2,254,979 12 9	65,588,792	23·87
1934	2,078,590 4 8	88,694,717	35·23
1935	2,394,827 17 5	93,199,777	5·08
1936	2,449,072 15 10	88,345,135	−5·20
1937	2,248,436 10 11	78,622,059	−11·01
1938	1,975,657 11 0	46,396,999	−40·99

* Half-year ending 1 January.

Year ending 31 March	Annual dividend £ s. d.	Market value of Government's shares on 31 March (£)	Annual % increase in Market value
1939	1,699,269 6 1	27,683,263	−40·33
1940	1,410,957 16 8	32,035,239	15·72
1941		32,035,239	
1942	606,605 15 9	32,035,239	
1943	Nil	32,035,239	
1944	Nil	32,035,239	
1945	Nil	32,035,239	
1946	Nil	44,250,000	38·13
1.1.41 to 1.1.47	755,729 15 2	31,855,000	−28·01
1948	4,683,003 16 5	24,592,310	−22·80
1949	1,580,680 16 11	27,988,440	13·81
1950	2,453,404 7 0	43,683,420	56·08
1951	2,650,688 0 0	24,585,808	−43·72
1952	2,875,799 0 0	32,627,954	32·71
1953	2,861,495 0 0	26,986,068	−17·29
1954	2,852,796 0 0	27,301,130	1·17
1955	2,925,414 0 0	36,542,450	33·85
1956	2,916,500 0 0	29,285,478	−19·86
1957	2,145,336 0 0	15,023,764	−48·70
1958	196,199 0 0	13,608,499	−9·42
1959	728,571 0 0	14,730,772	8·25
1960	3,662,623 0 0	15,342,579	4·15
1961	1,802,707 0 0		

Source: *Finance Accounts of the United Kingdom*, 1895–1962.

BIBLIOGRAPHY

BIBLIOGRAPHIES OF THE CANAL

BENHAWY, M. A. EL-, 'The Suez Canal: a Descriptive Bibliography', Ph.D. Thesis, University of Michigan, 1964.

CHARLES-ROUX, J., *L'Isthme et le Canal de Suez. Historique-État Actuel*, ii. 465–540. Paris, Hachette, 1901.

FONTAINE, A. L., *Monographie Cartographique de l'Isthme de Suez*, Le Caire, Le Scribe Egyptien, 1955, Mémoires de la *SEHGIS, ii.

GOBY, J. E., 'Matériaux pour servir à l'Établissement d'une Bibliographie de l'Isthme et du Canal de Suez. Ouvrages et Articles antérieurs à 1902 non cités

* SEHGIS = Société des Études Historiques et Géographiques de l'Isthme de Suez.

par J. Charles-Roux', *SEHGIS, Note d'Information No. 12–14*, Février 1948, 17–19; Mars 1948, 26–34, Avril 1948, 44–51.

GOBY. J. E., 'Bibliographie Critique du Canal de Suez', *Bulletin de la *SEHGIS*, v, 237–56, Le Caire, Imprimerie de l'Institut Français d'Archéologie Orientale, 1954.

LORIN, H., *Bibliographie Géographique de l'Égypte*, Le Caire, Imprimerie de l'Institut Français d'Archéologie Orientale, 1928, i. 379–421.

MAUNIER, R., *Bibliographie Économique, Juridique et Sociale de l'Égypte Moderne (1798–1916)*, Le Caire, Imprimerie de l'Institut Français d'Archéologie Orientale, 1918, 177–212.

MORRISON, H. A., JR., *List of Books and of Articles in Periodicals Relating to Interoceanic Canal and Railway Routes*, Washington, Government Printing Office, 1900, 95–131.

HISTORIES OF EGYPT

BLUNT, W. S., *Secret History of the English Occupation of Egypt*, London, Unwin, 1909.
—— *Gordon at Khartoum. Being a Personal Narrative of Events*, London, Swift, 1911.
—— *My Diaries, Being a Personal Narrative of Events, 1888–1914*, 2 vols., London, Secker, 1919.

CAMERON, D. A., *Egypt in the Nineteenth Century or Mehemet Ali and his Successors until the British Occupation in 1882*, London, Smith, 1898.

COCHERIS, J., *Situation Internationale de l'Égypte et du Soudan (Juridique et Politique)*, Paris, Plon, 1903.

CROUCHLEY, A. E., *The Economic Development of Modern Egypt*, London, Longmans, 1938.

DICEY, E., *England and Egypt*, London, Chapman, 1881.
—— *The Story of the Khedivate*, London, Rivington, 1902.

DOUIN, G., *Histoire du Règne du Khédive Ismail*, 3 vols., Roma, Istituto Poligrafico dello Stato, 1933–6.

HAMZA, A. M., *The Public Debt of Egypt 1854–1876*, Cairo, Government Press, 1944.

JERROLD, W. B., *Egypt under Ismail-Pacha*, London, Tinsley, 1879.

LANDES, D. S., *Bankers and Pashas. International Finance and Economic Imperialism in Egypt*, London, Heinemann, 1958.

LÉON, E. DE, *The Khedive's Egypt; or, The Old House of Bondage under New Masters*, London, Low, 1877, 1882.

LORING, W. W., *A Confederate Soldier in Egypt*, New York, Dodd, 1884.

McCOAN, J. C., *Egypt As It Is*, London, Cassell, 1887.
—— *Egypt Under Ismail. A Romance of History*, London, Chapman, 1889.

MERRUAU, P., *L'Égypte Contemporaine de Méhémet Ali à Said Pasha (1840–1857)*, Paris, Didier, 1857.

MILNER, A., *England in Egypt*, London, Arnold, 1892.

ROTHSTEIN, T., *Egypt's Ruin: a Financial and Administrative Record*, London, Fifield, 1910.

SABRY, M., *Épisode de la Question d'Afrique. L'Empire Égyptien sous Ismail et l'Ingérence Anglo-Française (1863–1879)*, Paris, Geuthner, 1933.

SAFRAN, N., *Egypt in Search of Political Community. An Analysis of the Intellectual and Political Evolution of Egypt, 1804–1952*, Harvard University Press, 1961.

SAINT-HILAIRE, J. B., *Lettres sur l'Égypte*, Paris, Lévy, 1856.

* SEHGIS = Société des Études Historiques et Géographiques de l'Isthme de Suez.

SAINT-HILAIRE, J. B., *Egypt and the Great Suez Canal. A Narrative of Travels*, London, Bentley, 1857, a translation of the preceding work with an additional appendix.

SAMMARCO, A., 'Les Règnes de Abbas, de Said et d'Ismail (1848–1879) avec un aperçu de l'histoire du Canal de Suez', *Précis de l'Histoire d'Égypte par divers Historiens et Archéologues*, tome 4, Roma, Istituto Poligrafico dello Stato, 1935.

—— 'Le Règne du Khédive Ismail de 1863 à 1875', *Histoire de l'Égypte Moderne depuis Mohammed Ali jusqu'à l'occupation britannique (1801–1882) d'après les documents originaux égyptiens et étrangers*, tome III, Le Caire, Imprimerie de l'Institut Français d'Archéologie Orientale, 1937.

SENIOR, N. W., *Conversations and Journals in Egypt and Malta*, 2 vols., London, Low, 1882.

ZINCKE, F. B., *Egypt of the Pharaohs and of the Kedivé*, London, Smith, 1871.

THE P. & O. AND THE OVERLAND ROUTE 1835–1855

ANDERSON, A., *Steam Communication with India. A Letter to the Directors of the Projected East Indian Steam Navigation Company*, London, Smith, 1840.

—— *Communications with India, China & C. via Egypt. The Political Position of their Transit through Egypt Considered*, London, Unwin, 1843.

—— *Communications with India, China & C. Observations on the Practicability & Utility of Opening a Communication Between the Red Sea and the Mediterranean, by a Ship Canal through the Isthmus of Suez*, London, Smith, 1843.

BARBER, J., *A Letter to the Right Hon. Sir John Cam Hobhouse, Bart, M.P. President of the India Board, etc, etc, etc. On Steam Navigation with India, and suggesting the Best Mode of Carrying it into Effect via the Red Sea*, London, Richardson, 1837.

CABLE, BOYD, *A Hundred Year History of the P. & O. Peninsular & Oriental Steam Navigation Company, 1837–1937*, London, Nicholson, 1937.

CLARKSON, E., 'The Suez Navigable Canal, for Accelerated Communication with India, *The Foreign & Colonial Quarterly Review*, October 1843, reprinted by the British and Foreign Agency Office, London, in 1843.

CLUNN, P. E., *Lieutenant Waghorn, R.N., Pioneer of the Overland Route to India*, London, Wheatley, 1893.

DASSI, G. F., *Notes on Sueis and its Trade with the Ports of the Red Sea, with Tables of Equivalents and Imports etc. for the First 6 Months of 1859*, Constantinople, 1859; Naples, 1860, abridged in *Journal of the Statistical Society*, December 1860, 465–74.

DIVINE, A. D., *These Splendid Ships. The Story of the Peninsular and Oriental Line*, London, Muller, 1960.

GALLOWAY, J. A., M.I.C.E., *Observations on the Proposed Improvements in the Overland Route via Egypt, with Remarks on the Ship Canal, the Boulac Canal, and the Suez Railroad*, London, Weal, 1844.

GRAVESON, S., 'The Overland Mail to India. Chronological Data', *Postal History Society, Bulletin No. 15*, September 1940.

GRINDLAY, R. M., *A View of the Present State of the Question as to Steam Communication with India*, London, Smith, 1837.

GRIFFITH, G. D., *A Journey, Across the Desert, from Ceylon to Marseilles*, 2 vols., London, Colburn, 1845.

HOLMES, W. D., *Report on Steam Communication with India, via the Red Sea*, London, Weal, 1838.

KELLY, J. B., *Britain and the Persian Gulf, 1795–1880*, Oxford, Clarendon Press, 1968, 260–342.

LARDNER, D., *Steam Communication with India by the Red Sea; in a Letter to the Right Honourable Lord Viscount Melbourne illustrated by Plans of the Route, and Charts of the Principal Stations*, London, Allen, 1837.

LINDSAY, W. S., *History of Merchant Shipping*, iv. 336–415, 'Steam to India', London, Low, 1876.

LOW, C. R., *History of the Indian Navy (1613–1863)*, London, Bentley, 1877.

MARSTON, T. E., *Britain's Imperial Role in the Red Sea Area 1800–1878*, Hamden, Connecticut, Shoe String Press, 1961.

PARBURY, G., *Hand Book for India and Egypt, comprising the Narrative of a Journey from Calcutta to England*, London, Allen, 1841.

PEACOCK, T. L., 'On Steam Navigation to India', *Edinburgh Review*, January 1835.

PURYEAR, V. J., *France & the Levant. From the Bourbon Restoration to the Peace of Kutiah*, Berkeley, University of California Press, 1941.

RODKEY, F. S., *The Turco-Egyptian Question in the Relations of England, France and Russia, 1832–1841*, University of Illinois Press, 1921.

SCHEER, F., *The Cape of Good Hope versus Egypt; or Political and Commercial Considerations on the Proper Line of Steam Communication with the East Indies*, London, Steill, 1839.

SIDEBOTTOM, J. K., *The Overland Mail. A Postal Historical Study of the Mail Route to India*, London, Allen for the Postal Historical Society, 1948.

STOCQUELER, J. H., 'Overland Trips in General, and a Trip in Particular', *The Asiatic Journal and Monthly Miscellany*, October 1843.

TAGHER, J., 'Mohammed Ali et les Anglais à Suez, dans la Mer Rouge et en Abyssinie', *Cahiers d'Histoire Égyptienne*, 1950.

THORNER, D., *Investment in Empire: British Railway and Steam Shipping Enterprise in India 1825–1849*, Philadelphia, University of Pennsylvania Press, 1950.

VETCH, J., *Inquiry into the Means of Establishing a Ship Navigation between the Mediterranean and Red Sea*, London, Richardson, 1843.

WAGHORN, T., *Egypt as it is in 1837*, London, Smith, 1837.

—— *The Acceleration of Mails (Once a Fortnight) between England and the East Indies and Vice Versa*, London, Smith, 1843.

WIENER, L., *L'Égypte et ses Chemins de Fer*, Bruxelles, Weissenbruch, 1932, 47–82.

WILSON, J. H., *On Steam Communication between Bombay and Suez, with an Account of the Hugh Lindsay's Four Voyages*, Bombay, American Mission Press, 1833.

—— *Facts connected with the Origin and Progress of Steam Communication between India and England*, London, Johnson, 1850.

HISTORIES OF THE CANAL

CHARLES-ROUX, J., *L'Isthme et le Canal de Suez. Historique-État Actuel*, 2 vols., Paris, Hachette, 1901.

GEORGI, R. and DUFOUR-FERONCE, A., *Urkunden zur Geschichte des Suezkanals*, Leipzig, Weicher, 1913.

HALLBERG, C. W., *The Suez Canal, its History and Diplomatic Importance*, New York, Columbia University Press, 1931.

HOSKINS, H. L., *British Routes to India*, New York, Longmans, 1928.

Sammarco, A., *Suez Storia e Problemi secondo documenti inediti egiziani ed europei*, Milano, Garzanti, 1943.

Siegfried, A., *Suez and Panama*, London, Cape, 1940.

Voisin, F. P., *Le Canal de Suez*, 7 vols., Paris, Dunod, 1902–6.

Wilson, A. T., *The Suez Canal. Its Past, Present and Future*, London, Oxford University Press, 1933, 1939.

FERDINAND DE LESSEPS

Batbedat, T., *De Lesseps Intime*, Paris, Juven, 1901.

Bertrand, A. and Ferrier, E., *Ferdinand de Lesseps, Sa Vie Son Œuvre*, Paris, Charpentier, 1887.

Bridier, L., *Une Famille Française. Les De Lesseps*, Paris, Fontemoing, 1900.

Edgar-Bonnet, G., *Ferdinand de Lesseps. Le Diplomate. Le Créateur de Suez*, Paris, Plon, 1951.

—— *Ferdinand de Lesseps. Après Suez. Le Pionnier de Panama*, Paris, Plon, 1959.

Lesseps, F. de, *The History of the Suez Canal. A Personal Narrative*, Edinburgh, Blackwood, 1876.

—— *Lettres, Journal et Documents pour servir à l'Histoire du Canal de Suez*, 5 vols., Paris, Didier, 1875–81.

—— *Percement de l'Isthme de Suez*, 6 vols., Paris, Plon, 1855–60.

—— *Souvenirs de quarante ans*, Paris, Nouvelle Revue, 1887.

PUBLICATIONS OF THE COMPAGNIE UNIVERSELLE DU CANAL MARITIME DE SUEZ

Le Canal de Suez. Journal Maritime et Commercial, 1870–1.

Le Canal de Suez. Bulletin Décadaire de la Compagnie Universelle du Canal Maritime de Suez, 1872–1939.

Le Canal de Suez. Bulletin de la Compagnie Universelle du Canal Maritime de Suez, 1947–58.

Le Canal Maritime de Suez. Note, Tableaux et Planches, Paris, 1937, 1952.

Le Canal de Suez (Documents statistiques), Paris, 'La Typographique', 1950, 1956.

Exposition Franco-Britannique Londres 1908. Le Canal Maritime de Suez. Note, Tableau et Planches, Paris, Publications Périodiques, 1908.

Recueil Chronologique et Annoté des Actes Constitutifs de la Compagnie Universelle du Canal Maritime de Suez et des Conventions conclues avec le Gouvernement Égyptien, Cairo, 1911, 1930; Paris, Desfossés, 1950.

THE CANAL ROUTE, 1855–1858

Allemagne, H. R. d', *Prosper Enfantin et les Grandes Entreprises du XIXe Siècle*, Paris, Gründ, 1935.

Andrew, W. P., *Memoir on the Euphrates Valley Route to India*, London, Allen, 1857.

—— *The Scinde Railway and its Relations to the Euphrates Valley and other Routes to India*, London, Allen, 1856.

BARRAULT, A. and E., 'Le Canal de Suez et la Question du Trace, les Divers Projets en Présence', *Revue des Deux Mondes*, 1 Janvier 1856.

BAUDE, J. J., 'De l'Isthme de Suez et du Canal Maritime à Ouvrir de la Méditerranée à la Mer Rouge', *Revue des Deux Mondes*, 15 Mars 1855.

CONINCK, F. DE, *Lettres sur le Percement de l'Isthme de Suez, Avis aux Petites Bourses*, Le Havre, Lemale, 1858.

—— *Réponse de Frédéric de Coninck au Journal de la Compagnie Universelle de l'Isthme de Suez du 1 Janvier 1859*, Le Havre, Lemale, 1859.

—— *Seconde et dernière Réponse de Frédéric de Coninck au Journal de la Compagnie Universelle de l'Isthme de Suez*, Le Havre, Lemale, 1859.

—— *Du Percement de l'Isthme de Suez. Nouvelles Considérations*, Le Havre, Lemale, 1859.

DESPLACES, E. E., *Le Canal de Suez. Épisode de l'Histoire du XIXe Siècle*, Paris, 1858.

HOSKINS, H. L., *British Routes to India*, New York, Longmans, 1928.

KENNEY, C. L., *The Gates of the East: Ten Chapters on the Isthmus of Suez Canal*, London, Ward, 1857.

LAYARD, A. H., 'Communication with India. The Suez and Euphrates Routes', *Quarterly Review*, October 1857.

PATTERSON, R. H., 'The Syrian Route to the East', *Blackwood's Edinburgh Magazine*, October 1857.

PIM, B., 'Remarks on the Isthmus of Suez with Special Reference to the Proposed Canal', *Proceedings of the Royal Geographical Society*, 11 April 1859.

REEVE, H., 'The Suez Canal', *Edinburgh Review*, January 1856.

'Rival Routes from England to India', *Bombay Quarterly Review*, April 1857.

TALABOT, P., 'Le Canal des Deux Mers d'Alexandrie à Suez. Moyens d'Exécution', *Revue des Deux Mondes*, 15 Mai 1855.

THOMPSON, J. P., 'Three New Routes to India', *North American Review*, July 1856.

WEISS, E., 'Der Suez-Canal und der französische Einfluss in Aegypten', *Das Ausland*, 16 Julius 1858.

THE CONSTRUCTION OF THE CANAL, 1859–1869

BADGER, G. P., *A Visit to the Isthmus of Suez Canal Works*, London, Smith, 1862.

BELL, K., 'British Policy Towards the Construction of the Suez Canal, 1859–1865', *Transactions of the Royal Historical Society*, 1965.

BERCHÈRE, N., *Le Désert de Suez. Cinq Mois dans l'Isthme*, Paris, Hetzel, 1863.

BLAKESLEY, J. W., 'M. De Lesseps & the Suez Canal', *Macmillan's Magazine*, March 1860.

BROOKS, W. A., 'The Isthmus of Suez Navigation Project, Considered in Reference to the Physical Impediments to its Realization', *The Civil Engineer & Architect's Journal*, 1 June and 1 July 1860.

BRÜLL, A., FLACHAT, E. & SCIAMA, J., 'The Suez Canal Works', *The Engineer*, 11 and 18 November 1864.

CERVANI, G., *Il 'Voyage en Egypte' (1861–1862) di Pasquale Revoltella*, Trieste, ALUT., 1962.

CHABAUD, E. P. DE, *La Vérité sur le Canal de Suez par le Journal des Travaux Publics*, Paris, Dentu, 1865.

CLERK, J., 'The Suez Canal', *Fortnightly Review*, 1 January 1869.

CONINCK, F. DE, *Le Canal de Suez et le Gouvernement Ottoman*, Le Havre, Lemale, 1863.

—— *Les Actions et obligations de la Compagnie du Canal Maritime de Suez*, Le Havre, Lemale, 1868.

CONRAD, F. W., *Reizen naar de Landengte van Suez, Egypte, het Heilige Land*, 'S Gravenhage, Nijhoff, 1859.

DENISON, W. T., 'The Suez Canal', *Proceedings of the Institution of Civil Engineers*, 16 April 1867.

DUFF-GORDON, A., 'A Trip to the Isthmus of Suez', *Macmillan's Magazine*, May 1865.

FITZGERALD, W. F. V., *The Suez Canal, The Eastern Question and Abyssinia*, London, Longmans, 1867.

FLACHAT, E., BRÜLL, ACHILLE & BADOIS, E., 'Mémoire sur les Travaux de l'Isthme de Suez', *Mémoires et Compte Rendu des Travaux de la Société des Ingenieurs Civils*, 7 Octobre et 16 Decembre 1864.

FOUQUIER, A., *Hors de Paris. Canal de Suez*, Paris, Legras, 1869.

FOWLER, J., 'The Suez Canal', *The Times*, 18 February 1869, 4i–iii and 9iv–v; *Engineering*, 19 February 1869, 118–19.

GUILLEMIN, A., *L'Égypte Actuelle. Son Agriculture et le percement de l'Isthme de Suez*, Paris, Challamel, 1867.

HAWKSHAW, J., 'The Suez Canal', *The Engineer*, 31 July and 7 August 1863.

KNIGHTON, W., 'The Isthmus of Suez Canal', *Bentley's Miscellany*, September 1867.

LANGE, D. A., 'A Narrative of the Suez Canal Works', *Journal of the Society of Arts*, 29 April 1870.

LAVALLEY, A., 'Travaux d'Exécution du Canal Maritime de l'Isthme de Suez', *Mémoires et Compte Rendu des Travaux de la Société des Ingénieurs Civils*, 26 Juillet 1867.

LAYRLE, J., 'Une Visite aux Travaux de Percement de l'Isthme de Suez', *Revue Contemporaine*, Avril 1863.

LECONTE, C., *Promenade dans l'Isthme de Suez*, Paris, Chaix, 1864.

LÉON, E. DE, 'Ferdinand de Lesseps and the Suez Canal', *Putnam's Magazine*, June 1869.

LYNCH, T. K., *A Visit to the Suez Canal*, London, Day, 1866.

MARLOWE, J., *The Making of the Suez Canal*, London, Cresset, 1964.

MITCHELL, H., 'The Coast of Egypt and the Suez Canal', *North American Review*, October 1869.

OLIVEIRA, B., *A Few Observations upon the Works of the Isthmus of Suez Canal made during a Visit in April 1863*, London, Harrison, 1863.

OLIVO, U., and CANALI, G., *Sui Lavori del Taglio dell'Istmo di Suez*, Venezia, Antonelli, 1869.

RITT, O., *Histoire de l'Isthme de Suez*, Paris, Hachette, 1869.

ROUSSIN, A., 'L'Isthme de Suez et les Travaux du Canal Maritime', *Revue des Deux Mondes*, 15 Juillet 1867.

RUSSELL, W. H., *A Diary in the East during the Tour of the Prince and Princess of Wales*, London, Routledge, 1869.

SIMENCOURT, A. DE, *L'Isthme de Suez. Son Percement. Examen au point de vue des Intérêts Commerciaux de la France et de l'Europe Occidentale*, Paris, Dentu, 1859.

TEGETHOFF, W. VON, 'Der Canal über den Isthmus von Suez', *Oesterreichische Revue*, März 1866.

THOMASSY, J., *De la Puissance Maritime*, Paris, Douniol, 1866, 69–110, 'Les Routes Commerciales et la Révolution Maritime au XIXe Siècle'.

TORELLI, L., *Descrizione di Porto Said, del Canale Marittimo e di Suez*, Venezia, Antonelli, 1869.

VIERNE, H., 'Les Intérêts de la Compagnie du Canal de Suez et ceux du Gouvernement Égyptien', *Revue Contemporaine*, Janvier 1864.

VOISIN, F. P., *Le Canal de Suez. II. Description des Travaux de Premier Établissement*, iv–vi Paris, Dunod, 1906.

THE INAUGURATION OF THE CANAL, 1869

ARLÈS-DUFOUR, J. B., *Le Percement de l'Isthme de Suez. Enfantin (1833–1855), M. de Lesseps (1855–1869) (Résumé Historique)*, Paris, Dentu, 1869.

ARROW, F., *A Fortnight in Egypt at the Opening of the Suez Canal*, London, Smith, 1869.

BALATRI, L., *L'Istmo di Suez. Descrizione Storica*, Firenze, Ducci, 1869.

BARDON Y GOMEZ, L., *Viaje a Egypto con motivo de la Apertura del Canal de Suez*, Madrid, Labajos, 1870.

BATEMAN, J. F., 'Some Account of the Suez Canal, in a Letter to the President', *Proceedings of the Royal Society of London*, 6 January 1870.

BIAN, L., *Rapport sur l'Inauguration du Canal de Suez présenté à la Chambre de Commerce de Mulhouse par son Délégué Louis Bian*, Mulhouse, Bader, 1870.

BLANC, C., *Voyage de la Haute Egypt*, Paris, Renouard, 1876.

BOZOLI, G. M., *L'Istmo di Suez. Lavori storici e statistici*, Ferrara, Taddei, 1870.

BRUGSCH, K. H., *Mein Leben und mein Wandern*, 283–98, Berlin, Allgemeiner Verein für Deutscher Litteratur, 1894.

CARRÉ, J. M., *Voyageurs et Écrivains Français en Égypte*, ii. 289–360, Le Caire, Imprimerie de l'Institut Français d'Archéologie Orientale, 1932.

CESANA, G. A., *Da Firenze a Suez. E Viceversa. Impressioni di Viaggio*, Firenze, Fodratti, 1870.

CHARLES-ROUX, J., *L'Isthme et le Canal de Suez. Historique. État Actuel*, i. 379–407. Paris, Hachette, 1901.

—— *Vingt Ans de Vie Publique*, 410–24, Paris, Guillaumin, 1892.

CORA, G., *Da Brindisi a Bombay. Sguardo Fisico, Politico, Etnografico, Storico, Economico sulla linea di navigazione da Brindisi a Bombay attraverso il Canale di Suez*, Casale, Corrado, 1869.

COVINO, A., *L'Istmo di Suez ossia il Passaggio alle Indie a traverso l'Egitto*, Torino, Negro, 1870.

DALENG, C., *L'Europe et l'Isthme de Suez*, Paris, Lachaud, 1869.

DES GARETS, COMTESSE, 'Souvenirs sur l'Impératrice Eugénie. III', *Revue de Paris*, 15 Novembre 1928.

DICEY, E., *The Morning Land*, ii. 85–209. London, Macmillan, 1870.

DODD, G., 'The Great Suez Canal', *The British Almanac of the Society for the Diffusion of Useful Knowledge. Companion to the Almanac; or Year-Book of General Information for 1870*, London, 1870, 105–27.

DORI, L., 'Esquisse Historique de Port-Said', *Cahiers d'Histoire Égyptienne* Octobre 1954, 220–8.

DOUIN, G., *Histoire du Règne du Khédive Ismail*, ii. 431–75, Roma, 1934.

DROHOJOWSKA, A. J. F. A., *L'Égypte et le Canal de Suez*, Paris, Laporte, 1870.

EATON, F. A., 'The Suez Canal', *Macmillan's Magazine*, November 1869.

EÇA DE QUEIROZ, J. M., '"Von Port Said nach Suez" Brief über die Einweihung des Suez-Kanals'. *Aufbau. Kulturpolitische Monatsschrift*, Januar 1957.

FENN, G. M., *George Alfred Henty, The Story of an Active Life*, 165–73, London, Blackie, 1907.

FLORENZANO, G., *Suez ed il Nilo. Ricordi*, Napoli, Trani, 1870.

FONTANE, M. & RIOU, E., *Le Canal Maritime de Suez Illustré. Histoire du Canal et des Travaux par M. Fontane. Itinéraire de l'Isthme par M. Riou*, Paris, Marc, 1869.

—— *Voyage Pittoresque à travers l'Isthme de Suez. 25 Grandes Aquarelles d'après Nature par Riou*, Paris, Dupont, 1869.

FROMENTIN, E., 'Notes d'un voyage en Égypte (Octobre, Novembre et Décembre 1869)', in Louis Gonse, *Eugène Fromentin, Peintre et Écrivain*, 257–339, Paris, Quantin, 1881.

HAMLEY, W. G., *A New Sea and An Old Land, being Papers Suggested by a Visit to Egypt at the end of 1869*, Edinburgh, Blackwood, 1871.

—— 'The Opening of the Suez Canal: as Communicated to Bullion Bales, Esq. of Manchester, by his Friend Mr. Scamper', *Blackwood's Edinburgh Magazine*, January–June 1870.

LANG, A., *Life, Letters and Diaries of Sir Stafford Northcote First Earl of Iddesleigh*, i. 354–68, Edinburgh, Blackwood, 1891.

LECORDIER, L., *Une Goutte d'Eau dans le Canal de Suez*, 15 pp. Paris, Dentu, 1869.

LOGIN, T., 'Report on the Suez Canal', *The Artizan*, 1 October and 1 November 1870.

MILNES, R. M., 'The Opening of the Suez Canal', *Proceedings of the Royal Geographical Society*, 10 January 1870.

NICOLE, G., *Inauguration du Canal de Suez. Voyage des Souverains*, Paris, Didier, 1869.

NOURSE, J. E., *The Maritime Canal of Suez: Brief Memoir of the Enterprize from its Earliest Date*, 40–9, Washington, Philp & Solomons, 1869.

PIETSCH, L., 'Meine Erlebnisse bei der Eröffnung des Suezkanals', *Aus der Heimat und der Fremde. Erlebtes und Gesehenes*, 291–324, Berlin, Allgemeiner Verein für Deutscher Litteratur, 1903.

REID, T. W., *The Life, Letters and Friendships of Richard Monckton Milnes, First Lord Houghton*, ii. 205–18, London, Cassell, 1890.

RUSSEL, A., *Egypt: The Opening of the Great Canal*, Edinburgh, *The Scotsman*, 1869.

RUSSELL, W. H., 'The Inauguration of the Suez Canal', *The Times*, 30 November 1869, 7; 7 December, 7–8; 11 December, 5.

STANLEY, H. M., *My Early Travels and Adventures in Africa and Asia*, ii. 1–73, London, Low, 1895.

STEPHAN, H., 'Der Suezkanal und seine Eröffnung', *Unsere Zeit*, 1870, 1–21 and 97–128.

TAGLIONI, C., *Deux Mois en Égypte. Journal d'un Invité du Khédive*, Paris, Amyot, 1870.

TEX, N. J. DEN, *Egypte en het Suez-Kanaal. Voorlezing gehouden in Felix Meritis*, Amsterdam, Van Kampen, 1870.
—— 'Journal de mon voyage en Égypte, 1869', *Cahiers d'Histoire Égyptienne*, Février 1952, 111–43.

THE ECONOMIC EFFECTS OF THE OPENING OF THE CANAL

ARROW, F., 'On the Influence of the Suez Canal on Trade with India', *Journal of the Society of Arts*, 11 March 1870.
BARZELLOTTI, P. L., *La Questione Commercial d'Oriente. L'Italia e il Canale di Suez. Cenni Storici e Considerazioni*, Firenze, Botta, 1869.
BATE, J., 'On the Opening of the Suez Canal Route to India, China & Australia, and its Prospective Results', *Proceedings of the Royal Colonial Institute*, 1870.
BILBAUT, T., *L'Isthme de Suez et les Intérêts Internationaux*, Douai, Crépin, 1869.
BOCCARDO, G., *Il Bosforo di Suez in Relazione col Commercio del Mondo e segnatamente col Commercio dell'Italia. Cenni ed Osservazioni*, Forli, Gherardi, 1869.
BOELEN, G. J., BUNGE, J. G., and BOISSEVAIN, J., *Directe Stoomvaart op Java door het Suez-Kanaal*, Amsterdam, Munster, 1870.
BOGAARS, G., 'The Effect of the Opening of the Suez Canal on the Trade and Development of Singapore', *Journal of the Malayan Branch, Royal Asiatic Society*, March 1955.
CANTONI, G., *Il Canale di Suez e l'Agricoltura Italiano*, Milano, Il Sole, 1876.
CONINCK, F. DE, *Le Canal de Suez après l'Inauguration*, Le Havre, Lemale, 1869.
CORRENTI, C., 'Sull'Istmo di Suez e sul Commercio Orientale', *Bollettino della Società Geografica Italiana*, Settembre 1869, 489–98.
DUNCAN & CO., WALTER, 'Produce Shipments from Calcutta to Great Britain for Thirteen Years, 1870 to 1882—Since Opening of Suez Canal', *Supplement to the British Trade Journal*, 1 August 1883.
FAIRLIE, J. A., 'The Economic Effects of Ship Canals', *Annals of the American Academy of Political and Social Science*, January 1898.
FLETCHER, M. E., 'Suez and Britain: an Historical Study', Ph.D. Thesis, University of Wisconsin, 1957.
—— 'The Suez Canal and World Shipping, 1869–1914', *Journal of Economic History*, December 1958.
GÖDEL-LANNOY, R. O. VON, *Notizen zur Orentirung in den durch den Suës-Kanal erschlossenen westasiatischen und ostafrikanischen Handelsgebieten*, Triest, Ohswaldt, 1869.
KALCHBERG, V. VON, *Der Suez-Canal und die Zukunft des Directen Oesterreichisch-Ostindischen Handels*, Wien, Gerold, 1870.
MAGNIAC, C., 'On the Commercial Aspects of the Suez Canal', *Journal of the Society of Arts*, 18 February 1876.
MERCHANT, J., 'Le Canal Maritime de Suez. Première Année d'Exploitation (1870)', *Journal des Économistes*, Juillet 1871.
PIERREIN, J., 'Marseille et le Canal de Suez', *Annales de la Faculté des Lettres d'Aix*, 1956.
SAMUDA, J. D'A., 'The Influence of the Suez Canal on Ocean Navigation', *Transactions of the Institution of Naval Architects*, 6 April 1870.

STEELE, J., *The Suez Canal: its Present and Future. A Round-About Paper*, London, Simpkin, 1872.

STREFFLEUR, V. VON, *Österreich und der Suez-Canal*, Wien, Waldheim, 1870.

THE SALE OF THE KHEDIVE'S SHARES 1875

AMOS, S., *The Purchase of the Suez Canal Shares; and International Law*, London, Ridgway, 1876.

BLOCH, C., *Les Relations entre la France et la Grande-Bretagne (1871–1878)*, 249–65, Paris, Éditions Internationales, 1955.

BLOWITZ, H. S. DE, 'Reminiscences of a Journalist', *Contemporary Review*, February 1893.

—— *My Memoirs*, London, Arnold, 1904, 343–50, 'Diplomacy and Journalism'.

BUCKLE, G. E., *Life of Disraeli*, v. 439–62. London, Murray, 1920.

CAMPBELL, G., 'Our Dealings with Egypt, and the Possible Results', *Fortnightly Review*, 1 February 1876.

COWELL, H., 'Public Affairs', *Blackwood's Edinburgh Magazine*, January 1876.

COX, F. J., 'The Suez Canal Incident of 1874', *Cahiers d'Histoire Égyptienne*, Octobre 1952.

CRABITÈS, P., *The Spoliation of Suez*, London, Routledge, 1940, 166–203, 'Was Disraeli Outmanoeuvred?'

DIXON, W. H., 'The False Move on Egypt', *The Gentleman's Magazine*, January 1876.

—— 'The Way to Egypt', *The Gentleman's Magazine*, February 1876.

FARR, W., 'On the Valuation of Railways, Telegraphs, Water Companies, Canals & Other Commercial Concerns, with Prospective, Deferred, Increasing, Decreasing or Terminating Profits... VIII Suez Canal', *Journal of the Statistical Society*, 16 May 1876, 497–504.

FITZGERALD, P., *The Great Canal at Suez: its Political, Engineering and Financial History. With an Account of the Struggles of its Projector, Ferdinand de Lesseps*, ii. 269–303, London, Tinsley, 1876.

GAVARD, C., *Un Diplomate à Londres. Lettres et Notes 1871–1877*, Paris, Plon, 1895.

HELANDER, S., 'Disraelis Erwerb der Suezkanal-Aktien. Kritik einer Legende', *Orient-Nachrichten*, April 1939.

HERON, R. M., *The Suez Canal Question (The Substance of a Letter addressed to the First Lord of the Treasury)*, London, Hatchards, 1875.

HYNDMAN, H. M., *The Record of an Adventurous Life*, 163–4, London, Macmillan, 1911.

JEFFERIES, J. R., *Suez-Cide!! Or, How Miss Britannia Bought a Dirty Puddle and Lost Her Sugar-Plums*, 20 pp., London, Snow, 1876.

LESAGE, C., 'L'Achat des Actions de Suez 1875', *Revue de Paris*, 15 Novembre 1905.

—— *L'Invasion Anglaise en Égypte. L'Achat des Actions de Suez*, Paris, Plon, 1906.

LEVADÉ, L., *Question Européenne. Le Suez en Décembre 1875*, Paris, Garnier, 1875.

LOFTUS, A., *The Diplomatic Reminiscences of Lord Augustus Loftus*, London, Cassell. 1894.

MAGNIAC, C., 'On the Commercial Aspects of the Suez Canal, with especial reference to the trade with India', *Journal of the Society of Arts*, 18 February 1876.

MAZADE, C. DE, 'Chronique de la Quinzaine' 30 Novembre 1875 & 14 Décembre 1875, *Revue des Deux Mondes*, Novembre–Décembre 1875.

MIÉVILLE, W. F., 'Side-Lights on the Story of the Suez Canal', *Nineteenth Century*, July 1910.

MORLEY, J., 'Home & Foreign Affairs', *Fortnightly Review*, 1 January 1876.

NEWTON, A., *Lord Lyons. A Record of British Diplomacy*, ii. 85–94, London, Arnold, 1913.

NEYMARCK, A., *Finances Contemporaines*, Paris, Guillaumin, 1905, tome iii, 80–6, 'Le Canal de Suez. Achat par l'Angleterre des Actions du Khédive'.

POLLOCK, W., 'The Suez Canal Purchase', *Saturday Review*, 4 December 1875.

REEVE, H., 'The Suez Canal', *Edinburgh Review*, January 1876.

ROBERTS, L. E., 'Egypt as a Factor in European Power Politics, 1875–1878', in L. P. Wallace & W. C. Askew, *Power, Public Opinion & Diplomacy. Essays in Honor of E. M. Carroll*, Duke University Press, 1959.

SABRY, M., *L'Empire Égyptien sous Ismail (1863–1879)*, Paris, Geuthner, 1933, 159–80.

SCOTT, J. W. R., *The Story of the Pall Mall Gazette, of its first editor Frederick Greenwood and of its founder George Murray Smith*, London, Oxford University Press, 1950.

—— 'Who Secured the Suez Canal Shares?', *Quarterly Review*, July 1949.

TAGHER, J., 'La première intervention britannique dans les affaires intérieures de l'Égypte ou les dessous de la mission Cave', *Cahiers d'Histoire Égyptienne*, Octobre 1952.

THOMPSON, G. C., *Public Opinion and Lord Beaconsfield 1875–1880*, i. 237–52 London, Macmillan, 1886.

TWISS, T., 'The Neutralization of the Suez Canal', *The Hour*, 29 November 1875, 5v; 2 December, 5v; 6 December, 5v; 9 December, 6i.

—— 'La Neutralisation du Canal de Suez', *Revue de Droit International*, 1875.

VALBERT, G., 'L'Angleterre et le Canal de Suez', *Revue des Deux Mondes*, 1 Janvier 1876.

WILSON, A. T., *The Suez Canal. Its Past, Present and Future*, 44–58, London, Oxford University Press, 1933.

WOLF, L., 'The Story of the Khedive's Shares', *The Times*, 26 December 1905, 11, reprinted in *Essays in Jewish History*, 287–308, London, Jewish Historical Society of England, 1934.

WOLFF, H. D., 'The Suez Canal an International Highway', *Quarterly Review*, October 1876.

THE RUSSO–TURKISH WAR, 1877–1878

ANDREW, W. P., 'Euphrates Valley Route to India', *Journal of the Society of Arts*, 20 February 1880.

BAMFORTH, W., 'British Interests in the Tigris–Euphrates Valley: 1856–1888', M.A. Thesis, University of London, May 1948.

BLUNT, W. S., 'On Proposed Indo-Mediterranean Railways', *Report of the Forty-Ninth Meeting of the British Association*, 1879, 440–2, London, Murray, 1879.

—— 'An Indo-Mediterranean Railway: Fiction and Fact', *Fortnightly Review*, 1 November 1879.

BUNSEN, G. VON, 'Germany and Egypt', *Nineteenth Century*, September 1877.

CAMERON, V. L., 'The Indo-Mediterranean Railway', *Macmillan's Magazine*, September and November 1879.

—— 'My Travels in Mesopotamia, especially with reference to a Proposed Indo-Mediterranean Railway', *Journal of the Royal United Service Institution*, 20, February 1880.

—— *Our Future Highway*, 2 vols., London, Macmillan, 1880.

CLARK, B. L., 'On the Employment of Clark and Standfield's Floating Docks at Naval Stations, and the Means they afford of Transporting Large Ironclads through the Suez Canal', *Journal of the Royal United Service Institution*, 11 June 1877.

CLARKE, H., 'On Railways to India and Turkey', *Journal of the Society of Arts*, 13 December 1878.

CURRIE, D., 'Maritime Warfare; the Importance to the British Empire of a Complete System of Telegraphs, Coaling Stations and Graving Docks', *Journal of the Royal United Service Institution*, 2 March 1877.

DALRYMPLE, G. E., *The Syrian Great Eastern Railway to India*, 26 pp., London, Skeffington, 1878.

The Dardanelles for England. The True Solution of the Eastern Question, London, Chapman, 1876.

DICEY, E., 'Our Route to India', *Nineteenth Century*, June 1877.

—— 'The Future of Egypt', *Nineteenth Century*, August 1877.

—— 'Mr. Gladstone and our Empire', *Nineteenth Century*, September 1877.

—— 'Egypt and the Khedive', *Nineteenth Century*, December 1877.

—— 'England's Policy at the Congress', *Nineteenth Century*, April 1878.

An Englishman, *England in Egypt. The Highway to India. A Proposal submitted to the People of England by an Englishman*, London, King, 1877.

GLADSTONE, W. E., 'Aggression on Egypt and Freedom in the East', *Nineteenth Century*, August 1877, reprinted in *Gleanings of Past Years, 1851–1877*, Murray, 1879, iv.

—— 'The Paths of Honour and of Shame', *Nineteenth Century*, March 1878.

—— 'Liberty in the East and West', *Nineteenth Century*, June 1878.

GOLDSMID, F. J., 'On Communications with British India under Possible Contingencies', *Journal of the Royal United Service Institution*, 14 June 1878.

GRANT DUFF, M. E., 'Russia II', *Nineteenth Century*, April 1877.

GREG, W. R., 'Employment of our Asiatic Forces in European Wars', *Fortnightly Review*, 1 June 1878.

HAUGHTON, B., *A Railway to India*, 10 pp., London, Gaskill, 1879.

—— 'The Best Route for a Line of Railway to India', *Journal of the Society of Arts*, 9 April 1880.

HAVELOCK, H. M., 'Constantinople and our Road to India', *Fortnightly Review*, 1 January 1877.

LAING, S., 'A Plain View of British Interests', *Fortnightly Review*, 1 March 1878.

LAVALEYE, E. DE, 'British Interests in the Present Crisis', *Fortnightly Review*, 1 July 1877.

LEE, D. E., *Great Britain and the Cyprus Convention Policy of 1878*, Harvard University Press, 1934.

MacCoan, J. C., *Our New Protectorate. Turkey in Asia. Its Geography, Races, Resources and Government*, 2 vols., London, Chapman, 1879.

Macdonell, J., 'The Legal Position of the Dardanelles and Suez Canal', *Fraser's Magazine*, May 1878.

Patterson, R. H., 'The New Routes to India', *Blackwood's Edinburgh Magazine*, October 1878.

Smith, G., 'The Policy of Aggrandizement', *Fortnightly Review*, September 1877.

—— 'The Eastern Crisis', *Fortnightly Review*, 1 May 1878.

Townsend, M., 'The Summons to the Sepoys', *The Spectator*, 4, 11, 18 and 25 May 1878.

Twiss, T., 'The Protectorate of the Suez Canal', *Nautical Magazine*, October 1878.

—— *The Place of the Suez Canal in the System of International Law*, 10 pp., London, Clowes, 1878.

THE OCCUPATION OF EGYPT, 1882

Ahmed, J. M., *The Intellectual Origins of Egyptian Nationalism*, London, Oxford University Press, 1960.

Baker, S. W., *The Egyptian Question, being letters to 'The Times' and 'Pall Mall Gazette'*, 94 pp., London, Macmillan, 1884.

Bell, C. F. M., *Khedives and Pashas. Sketches of Contemporary Egyptian Rulers and Statesmen. By One Who Knows Them Well*, London, Low, 1884.

Blunt, W. S., *Secret History of the English Occupation of Egypt, being a personal Narrative of Events*, London, Unwin, 1907.

Cameron, D. A., *Egypt in the Nineteenth Century or Mehemet Ali and his Successors until the British Occupation in 1882*, London, Smith, 1898.

Cox, F. J., 'Arabi and Stone: Egypt's First Military Rebellion, 1882', *Cahiers d'Histoire Égyptienne*, Avril 1956.

Cromer, Lord, *Modern Egypt*, London, Macmillan, 1908.

Daniel, N., *Islam, Europe and Empire*, 384–415, Edinburgh University Press, 1966.

Egerton, F., Rathbone, W., and Norwood, C. M., *Great Britain, Egypt and the Suez Canal*, 32 pp., London, Chapman, 1884.

Greiss, A., 'La Crise de 1882 et le Mouvement Orabi', *Cahiers d'Histoire Égyptienne*, Mars 1953, 47–74.

Hennebert, E., *Les Anglais en Égypte. L'Angleterre et le Mahdi, Arabi et le Canal de Suez*, Paris, Corbeil, 1884.

Keay, S., *Spoiling the Egyptians. A Tale of Shame*, London, Paul, 1882.

Knightbridge, A. A. H., 'Gladstone and the Invasion of Egypt in 1882', B.Litt. Thesis, University of Oxford, 1960.

Léon, E. de, *Egypt under its Khedives*, London, Low, 1882.

Malortie, C. de, *Egypt: Native Rulers and Foreign Interference*, London, Ridgway, 1882.

Maurice, J. F., *Military History of the Campaign of 1882 in Egypt. Prepared in the Intelligence Branch of the War Office*, London, H.M.S.O., 1887.

Mulhall, M. G., 'Egyptian Finance', *Contemporary Review*, October 1882.

NEWCOME, F. N., 'The Suez Canal and the Euphrates Valley Railway', *Nautical Magazine*, September 1882.

NINET, J., 'Origin of the National Party in Egypt', *Nineteenth Century*, January 1883.

RAMM, A. (ed.), *The Political Correspondence of Mr. Gladstone and Lord Granville, 1876–1886*, Oxford, Clarendon Press, 1962.

RATHBONE, W., 'Great Britain and the Suez Canal', *Fortnightly Review*, 1 August 1882.

ROBINSON, R., GALLAGHER, J. and DENNY, A., *Africa and the Victorians. The Official Mind of Imperialism*, London, Macmillan, 1961.

ROYLE, C., *The Egyptian Campaigns, 1882 to 1885*, London, Hurst, 1886, 1900.

SANDES, E. W. C., *The Royal Engineers in Egypt and the Sudan*, Chatham, Institute of Royal Engineers, 1937.

STUART, H. W. V., *Egypt after the War*, London, Murray, 1883.

THIBAULT, P., 'La Question d'Égypte et la presse française en 1882', *Cahiers d'Histoire Égyptienne*, Octobre 1951, 1–78; Juin 1953, 97–138.

VOGT, H., *The Egyptian War of 1882*, London, Paul, 1883.

VYSE, G. W., *Egypt: Political, Financial and Strategical*, London, Allen, 1882.

WALLACE, D. M., *Egypt and the Egyptian Question*, London, Macmillan, 1883.

THE AGITATION FOR A BRITISH CANAL 1883

APPLETON, L., *The Maritime Canal of Suez*, London, British and Foreign Arbitration Association, 1888.

BECK, W., *New Waterway to the East by a Valley of Passengers*, London, West, 1882.

B., H., *The Suez Canal and the Liberal Government; or, the 'Policy' of Deceit*, London, Wilson, 1884.

CAMPBELL, W., 'Postal Communication with the East; India in Six and Australia in Sixteen Days', *Proceedings of the Royal Colonial Institute*, 8 May 1883.

CONDER, C. R., 'The Canal Dilemma. Our True Route to India', *Blackwood's Edinburgh Magazine*, September 1883.

DICEY, E., 'Why Not Purchase the Suez Canal?', *Nineteenth Century*, August 1883.

DUNSANY, LORD, 'England and the Suez Canal', *Nineteenth Century*, October 1882.

FELL, J. B., 'The Euphrates Valley Railway as an Alternative Route to India', *Journal of the Society of Arts*, 28 September 1883.

—— 'On the Necessity of Improved Means of Communication with India by the Euphrates Valley Route', *Journal of the Royal United Service Institution*, 28 March 1884.

FLAIX, M. E. F. DE, *L'Indépendance de l'Égypte et le Régime International du Canal de Suez*, Paris, Guillaumin, 1883.

FLEURY, J., 'De l'Élargissement du Canal de Suez', *Le Génie Civil*, 3 Mai 1884.

FOWLER, J., and BAKER, B., 'A Sweet-Water Ship Canal through Egypt' *Nineteenth Century*, January 1883.

GALLUT, A., 'Le Canal Maritime de Suez', *Le Génie Civil*, 15 Juin 1883.

HAUGHTON, B., *The Block on the Suez Canal. A Paper Read before the Civil and Mechanical Engineers' Society on the 5th December 1883*, London, The Society, 1884.

Hull, E. C. P., *England and the Suez Canal: the Situation Reviewed. A Brief Statement showing that a Parallel British Canal has now become an absolute necessity*, London, Spottiswoode, 1883.

Ladame, J., *Canal de Suez. Étude sur les Diverses Questions à l'ordre du Jour*, Paris, Chez l'Auteur, 1884.

Magniac, C., 'The Pretensions of M. de Lesseps', *Nineteenth Century*, January 1884.

Malortie, C. de, 'The Road to the East and its Protection', *National Review*, September 1883.

Mills, A., 'The Suez Canal', *National Review*, July 1883.

Mongrédien, A., *The Suez Canal Question*, London, Cassell, 1883.

Nourse, J. E., *The Maritime Canal of Suez, from its Inauguration, November 17, 1869, to the Year 1884*, Washington, 1884.

Price, J. S., *The Early History of the Suez Canal*, London, Hazell, 1883.

Reid, R. T., 'The Suez Canal Question', *Contemporary Review*, August 1883.

Rundall, F. H., 'The Suez Canal: its Engineering, Civil and Political Aspects', *Journal of the Society of Arts*, 26 January 1883.

—— *The Highway of Egypt, is it the Suez Canal or any other Route between the Mediterranean and Red Sea?*, London, King, 1882.

Salis, F. von, 'Der Suez-Kanal', *Allgemeine Bauzeitung*, 1883.

Say, L., 'France & England in Egypt', *Fortnightly Review*, August 1883.

'A Second Suez Canal', *Nautical Magazine*, July 1883.

Thomassy, J., *La Question de Suez et la Politique de l'Angleterre*, Paris, Dentu, 1883.

Voisin, F. P., *Le Canal de Suez*, Paris, Dunod, 1902, iii. 1–103.

Waring, C., 'The Trusteeship of the Suez Canal', *Fortnightly Review*, November 1883.

Waterfield, O. C., 'The Negotiations with M. de Lesseps', *Fortnightly Review*, August 1883.

—— *The New Suez Canal. Considerations addressed to the Committee of Shipowners appointed at the Meeting held on Thursday, May 10th, at the Cannon Street Hotel*, London, Matchin, 28 May 1883.

THE CONVENTION OF CONSTANTINOPLE, 1888

Asser, T. M. C., 'La Convention de Constantinople pour le Libre Usage du Canal de Suez', *Revue de Droit International et de Législation Comparée*, Bruxelles, 1888.

Avram, B., *The Evolution of the Suez Canal Status from 1869 up to 1956. A Historico-Juridical Study*, Geneva, Droz, 1958.

Avril, A. d', 'Négociations Relatives au Canal de Suez', *Revue d'Histoire Diplomatique*, Janvier et Mars 1888.

Borelli, O., 'Le Régime des eaux du Canal du Suez au Point de Vue du Droit Public International Maritime', *Choses Politiques d'Égypte, 1883–1895*, note iv, 547–72, Paris, Flammarion, 1895.

Camand, M. L., *Étude sur le Régime Juridique du Canal de Suez*, Grenoble, Allier, 1899.

Dedreux, R., *Der Suezkanal im internationalen Rechte*, Tübingen, Mohr, 1913.

HOLLAND, T. E., 'The International Position of the Suez Canal', *Fortnightly Review*, July 1883, reprinted in *Studies in International Law*, Oxford, Clarendon Press, 1898.

LAWRENCE, T. J., 'The Suez Canal in International Law', *Law Magazine and Review*, February 1884, reprinted in *Essays on Some Disputed Questions in Modern International Law*, Cambridge, Deighton, 1884.

MOSTOFI, K., 'The Suez Dispute: a Case Study of a Treaty', *Western Political Quarterly*, March 1957.

RHEINSTROM, H., *Die völkerrechtliche Stellung der internationalen Kanäle*, Revai, Budapest, 1937.

ROSSIGNOL, L. M., *Le Canal de Suez (Étude Historique et Juridique)*, Paris, Giard, 1898.

SCHIARABATI, A., *De la Condition Juridique du Canal de Suez avant et après la Grande Guerre*, Lyon, Bascou, 1930.

SWINDEREN, R. DE M. VAN, *Het Suez-Kanaal*, Groningen, Huber, 1886.

TWISS, T., 'De la Sécurité de la Navigation dans le Canal de Suez', *Revue de Droit International*, 1882.

—— 'The Freedom of the Navigation of the Suez Canal', *Law Magazine and Review*, February 1883.

—— 'Le Canal Maritime de Suez et la Commission Internationale de Paris', *Revue de Droit International*, 1885.

—— 'On International Conventions for the Neutralisation of Territory and their Applicability to the Suez Canal', *Law Magazine and Review*, November 1887, reprinted separately, London, Clowes, 1887.

WESTLAKE, J., 'Interoceanic Ship Canals', *International Law. Part I, Peace*, i. 321–31, Cambridge University Press, 1904.

WHITTUCK, E. A., *International Canals*, Peace Handbooks no. 150, London, H.M.S.O., 1920.

WOLFF, H. D., 'The Suez Canal and the Egyptian Question', *Quarterly Review*, October 1887.

THE CAPE–MEDITERRANEAN DEBATE, 1892–1895

CLARKE, G. S., 'England and the Mediterranean. A Reply to Mr. Laird Clowes', *Nineteenth Century*, April 1895.

CLOWES, W. L., ('Nauticus'), 'Sea Power, its Past and its Future', *Fortnightly Review*, December 1893.

—— 'Toulon and the French Navy', *Nineteenth Century*, December 1893.

—— 'The Naval Manoeuvres', *Fortnightly Review*, September 1894.

—— 'Our Warning from the Naval Manoeuvres', *Nineteenth Century*, September 1894.

—— 'The Millstone Round the Neck of England', *Nineteenth Century*, March 1895.

—— 'Braggadocio about the Mediterranean. A Rejoinder', *Nineteenth Century*, May 1895.

COLOMB, P. H., 'England in the Mediterranean', *North American Review*, May 1894.

CRAIGIE, R. W., 'Maritime Supremacy being Essential for the General Protection of the British Empire and its Commerce, to what extent, if any, should our Naval Force be Supplemented by Fixed Defences at Home and Abroad, and to whom should they be confided?', *Journal of the Royal United Service Institution*, 1892.

ELSDALE, A., 'Should We Hold on to the Mediterranean in War?', *Nineteenth Century*, February 1895.

GAMBIER, J. W., 'An Exchange for Gibraltar', *Fortnightly Review*, May 1893.

HOOD, A., 'The British Navy', *Quarterly Review*, April 1894.

HOOPER, G., 'How the Political and Military Power of England is Affected by the Suez Canal', *United Service Magazine*, September 1890.

LANGER, W. L., *The Franco-Russian Alliance 1890–1894*, Harvard University Press, 1929.

LAUGHTON, J. K., 'Naval Armaments', *Edinburgh Review*, April 1894.

LOWE, C. J., *Salisbury and the Mediterranean 1886–1896*, London, Routledge, 1965.

MARDER, A. J., *British Naval Policy 1880–1905. The anatomy of British sea power*, London, Putnam, 1940.

ROBINSON, R., GALLAGHER, J. and DENNY, A., *Africa and the Victorians. The official mind of imperialism*, Macmillan, 1961.

SANDERSON, G. N., *England, Europe and the Upper Nile 1882–1899*, Edinburgh University Press, 1965.

SYMONDS, T., 'The Needs of the Navy', *Fortnightly Review*, 1 August 1893.

WILSON, H. W., 'Our Position in the Mediterranean', *United Service Magazine*, October 1894.

THE PANAMA CRISIS

BOND, E., 'The Gates of the Pacific', *Nautical Magazine*, February 1893.

BOWES, I., *Rails and Waterways, George Stephenson and M. Ferdinand de Lesseps*, Manchester, Heywood, 1893.

BUNAU-VARILLA, P., *Panama. The Creation, Destruction and Resurrection*, London, Constable, 1913.

COURAU, R., *Ferdinand de Lesseps de l'Apothéose de Suez au Scandale de Panama*, Paris, Grasset, 1932.

DANSETTE, A., *Les Affaires de Panama*, Paris, Perrin, 1934.

DEMACHY, E., *Le Scandale de Panama. Les Juifs Allemands et le Parlement Français. Le Rôle de Charles de Lesseps*, Paris, Demachy, 1892.

DRUMONT, E., *La Dernière Bataille. Nouvelle Étude Psychologique et Sociale*, 323–360, 'Une Entreprise au XIXe Siècle. Panama', Paris, Dentu, 1890.

DU VAL, M. P., *And the Mountains Will Move; the Story of the Building of the Panama Canal*, Stanford University Press, 1947.

EDGAR-BONNET, G., *Ferdinand de Lesseps. Après Suez. Le Pionnier de Panama*, Paris, Plon, 1959.

FERRIS, G. T., 'The Romance of the Great Canal', *Cosmopolitan*, April 1894.

FLORIDIAN, L. M., *Les Coulisses du Panama*, Paris, Savine, 1891.

LAHAYE, R., *Les Dividendes Prochaines de l'Action Suez et l'Avenir du Canal*, Paris, Chaix, 1892.

MACK, G., *The Land Divided. A History of the Panama Canal and Other Isthmian Canal Projects*, New York, Knopf, 1944.

MICARD, E., *Le Canal de Suez et le Génie Française*, Paris, Roger, 1930.

NELSON, W., *Five Years at Panama. The Trans-Isthmian Canal*, London, Low, 1891.

'The Panama Canal', *Nautical Magazine*, March 1889.

PAPONOT, F., *Suez et Panama. Une Solution*, Paris, Baudry, 1889.

PAPONOT, F., *Le Canal de Panama. A M. Ferdinand de Lesseps. Solution de la Question Financière. Fin de la Liquidation*, Paris, Baudry, 1891.

—— *Canal de Panama. Son relèvement par le Suez. Appel aux Armateurs de toutes les Nations*, Paris, Baudry, 1892.

REYMOND, P., 'Panama. L'Œuvre des Français et des Américains. Projets d'avenir', *Bulletin de la Société des Études Historiques et Géographiques de l'Isthme de Suez*, iii, 1948.

ROUANET, G., *Les Complicités du Panama. Pages d'histoire sociale contemporaine* Paris, Savine, 1893.

SEYMOUR, E. H., 'The Present State of the Panama Canal', *Nineteenth Century*, February 1892.

SHERARD, R. H., 'The Count de Lesseps of Today', *McClure's Magazine*, June 1893.

SMITH, G. B., *The Life and Enterprises of Ferdinand de Lesseps*, London, Allen, 1893.

WHEELER, W. H., 'Ferdinand de Lesseps and the Suez and Panama Canals', *Longman's Magazine*, February 1895.

WHYMPER, E., 'The Panama Canal', *Contemporary Review*, March 1889.

THE WAR OF 1914–1918

ARTHUR, G., *General Sir John Maxwell*, London, Murray, 1932.

BRIGGS, M. S., *Through Egypt in War-Time*, London, Unwin, 1918.

CHACK, P., 'L'Attaque et la défense du Canal de Suez. (Février 1915)', *Revue des Deux Mondes*, 15 Décembre 1925, 1 et 15 Janvier 1926, reprinted in *On se bat sur Mer*, 141–257, 'La France sauve le Canal de Suez (Février 1915)', Paris, Les Éditions de France, 1926.

DOUIN, G., *Un Épisode de la Guerre Mondiale. L'Attaque du Canal de Suez (3 Février 1915)*, Paris, Delagrave, 1922.

DUMAS, A., 'Le Canal de Suez. État actuel et résultats d'exploitation', *Le Génie Civil*, 19 Juin 1915.

ELGOOD, P. G., *Egypt and the Army*, London, Oxford University Press, 1924.

GARNER, J. W., *Prize Law during the World War*, New York, Macmillan 1927.

GULLETT, H. S., *The Australian Imperial Forces in Sinai and Palestine 1914–1918. Official History of Australia in the War of 1914–18*, vol. vii, Sydney, Angus, 1923.

JARVIS, C. S., *Yesterday and Today in Sinai*, 144–57, 'Sinai and the War of 1914–1918', Edinburgh, Blackwood, 1931.

KEDOURIE, E., *England and the Middle East. The Destruction of the Ottoman Empire 1914–1921*, London, Bowes, 1956.

KRESS VON KRESSENSTEIN, F., 'Die Kriegführung in der Wüste', in T. Wiegand, *Sinai* 1–35, Berlin, Gruyter, 1920.

—— *Mit den Türken zum Suez Kanal*, Berlin, Schlegel, 1938.

LARCHER, M., 'La Première Offensive contre le Canal de Suez (3 Février 1915; Relation Turque)', *La Revue Maritime*, Octobre 1924.

LLOYD, E. H., 'Work in Connection with the Suez Canal Defences in 1916, which was undertaken by the Egyptian Ministry of Public Works officials for and in conjunction with the Royal Engineers', *Proceedings of the Institution of Civil Engineers*, ccvii, 11 February 1919.

MACMUNN, G. and FALLS, C., *Military Operations. Egypt and Palestine from the*

Outbreak of the War with Germany to June 1917. Official History of the War, 3 vols., H.M.S.O., 1928, 1930.

MASSEY, W. T., *The Desert Campaigns*, London, Constable, 1918.

MURRAY, A., *Despatches (June 1916–June 1917)*, London, Dent, 1920.

Naval and Military Despatches relating to Operations in the War, Part VI. Published in the 'London Gazette', May to December 1916, H.M.S.O., 1917.

POWLES, G. C., *The New Zealanders in Sinai and Palestine. Official History New Zealand's Effort in the Great War*, vol. iii, *Sinai and Palestine*, Auckland, Whitcombe, 1922.

RAIMONDI, J., 'Bac-Transbordeur et Pont Tournant pour la traversée du canal maritime de Suez à Kantara', *Le Génie Civil*, 15 Mars 1919.

SANDES, E. W. C., *The Royal Engineers in Egypt and the Sudan*, Institute of Royal Engineers, Chatham, 1937.

THIERRY, G. DE, 'Der Suezkanal während des Weltkrieges', *Weltwirtschaft*, 1920.

THORNTON, A. P., *The Imperial Idea and Its Enemies. A Study in British Power*, 153–85, London, Macmillan, 1959.

The Times History of the War, vol. iv (London, 'The Times', 1915), 321–60, 'The First "Invasion of Egypt"'; vol. x (1917), 365–404, 'The Campaign in Eastern Egypt'.

TOWNROE, B. S., 'Tunnel and Canal', *Cornhill Magazine*, May 1929.

WAVELL, A. P., *The Palestine Campaigns*, 23–51, 'The Defence of the Suez Canal', London, Constable, 1928.

YATE, A. C., 'Turkish Arabia as a Link of Empire', *Journal of the Royal United Service Institution*, November 1915.

THE GERMAN AGITATION OF 1915–1916

DEMIANI, A., 'Deutschlands Anrecht an den Suezkanal', *Süddeutsche Monatshefte*, September 1916.

DIX, A., 'Die verkehrspolitische Bedeutung des Suezkanals', *Geographishe Zeitschrift*, 18 Februar 1916.

FELDMANN, W., *Reise zur Suesfront*, Weimar, Kiepenheuer, 1917.

GOTTLOB, A., 'Das Eindringen Englands in Ägypten', *Die Grenzboten*, April 1915.

HENNIG, R., 'Die Bedeutung des Suezkanals für das englische Wirtschaftsleben', *Deutsche Kolonialzeitung*, 1916.

—— 'Der verkehrsgeographische Wert des Suez- und des Bagdad-Weges. Ein Vergleich', *Geographische Zeitschrift*, 19 Dezember 1916.

—— 'Die wirtschaftliche Bedeutung des Suezkanals', *Jahrbücher für Nationalökonomie und Statistik*, 1917.

JANELL, W., 'Deutschlands Anteil am Suezkanal', *Die Grenzboten*, Mai 1915.

MARGULIES, H., *Der Kampf zwischen Suez und Bagdad im Altertum*, Weimar, Kiepenheuer, 1916.

OBERHUMMER, E., 'Ägypten und der Suezkanal. Eine politische Betrachtung', *Deutsche Revue*, Januar 1915.

SERMAN, E., *Mit den Türken an der Front*, Berlin, Scherl, 1915.

SMITH, T. F. A., 'German War Literature on the Near and Middle East', *Quarterly Review*, January 1917.

STEINDORFF, G., 'Die Ostgrenze Ägyptens und der Suezkanal', *Zeitschrift für Politik*, 1917.

THIERRY, G. DE, 'England und der Suezkanal', *Weltwirtschaft. Zeitschrift für Weltwirtschaft und Weltverkehr*, Februar 1916.

WANNISCH, D. VON, 'Der Suezkanal und dessen Beziehungen zur europäischen Mächtegruppierung', *Deutsche Revue*, März 1916.

THE ETHIOPIAN WAR, 1935–1936

AGLIETTI, B., *Il Canale di Suez ed i Rapporti Anglo-Egiziani*, Firenze, Carlo, 27 June 1939.

AMBROSINI, G., 'Il Canale di Suez', *Annali dell'Africa Italiana*, Marzo 1939.

ANCHIERI, E., *Il Canale di Suez*, Milano, Lombarda, 1937.

BAER, G. W., *The Coming of the Italo-Ethiopian War*, Harvard University Press, 1967.

BAHON, M., *Le Libre Usage du Canal de Suez et sa 'Neutralité'*, Paris, Communication faite à l'Académie de Marine, 23 Avril 1936.

BARATTA, M., 'L'Italia e il Canale di Suez', *La Geografia*, Maggio–Dicembre 1929.

BERKOL, F. N., *Le Statut Juridique Actuel des Portes Maritimes Orientales de la Méditerranée (Les Détroits—le Canal de Suez)*, 419–76, 'La Convention de Constantinople et le Pacte de la Société des Nations', Paris, Sirey, 1940.

BONO, E. DE, *Anno XIIII. The Conquest of an Empire*, London, Cresset, 1937.

BUELL, R. L., *The Suez Canal and League Sanctions*, Geneva Research Center, 1935, translated in *Revue Générale de Droit International Public*, 1936, 50–76.

BUISKOOL, J. A. E., *De Internationalisatie van het Suez-Kanaal*, Zwolle, Willink, 1938.

Il Canale di Suez nella Storia, nell'Economia, nel Diritto, Milano, Istituto per Gli Studi di Politica Internazionale, 1935.

CITO DE BITETTO, C., *Méditerranée, Mer Rouge, Routes Imperiales*, Paris, Grasset, 1937.

CRABITÈS, P., 'Guarding Suez', *Asia*, January 1937.

DEMORGNY, G., 'Suez (Le Canal de)', in A. F. Frangulis (ed.), *Dictionnaire Diplomatique*, Paris, Académie Diplomatique Internationale, 1937, 'Fermeture Eventuelle du Canal de Suez'.

DIENA, G., *Il Canale di Suez e il Patto della Società delle Nazioni*, Venezia, Ferrari, 1937.

GIANNINI, A., 'Il Regime Giuridico del Canale di Suez', *Oriente Moderno*, Luglio 1935.

GUIBAL, R., *De l'influence du Pacte de la Société des Nations sur le Statut International du Canal de Suez*, Paris, Les Presses Modernes, 1937.

—— *Peut-On fermer le Canal de Suez?*, Paris, Pedone, 1937, a reprint of the preceding work.

HOSKINS, H. L., 'The Suez Canal in Time of War', *Foreign Affairs*, October 1935.

LANDECKER, W., 'Suezkanal und Italienisch-Abessinischer Konflikt', *Revue de Droit International*, Juli 1935.

LE GOFF, M., 'Le Statut Aérien du Canal de Suez d'après le Traité Anglo-Egyptien du 26 août 1936', *Revue Générale de Droit International Public*, Mars 1939.

MOLFINO, G., *Il Canale di Suez e il suo regime internazionale*, Genova, Orfini, 15 March 1936.

POIAGA, A., *Suez, Aspetti del Problema*, Milano, XX Annuale dei Fasci Italiani di Combattimento, 1939.

RHEINSTROM, H., *Die völkerrechtliche Stellung der internationalen Kanäle*, Budapest, Revai, 1937.

RICHTHOFEN, H. VON, *Der Suez-Kanal im Weltkrieg und in der Nachkriegzeit: Eine völkerrechtliche Studie*, Berlin, Siegismund, 1939.

SALVEMINI, G., *Prelude to World War II*, London, Gollancz, 1951.

SANDIFORD, R., 'Il Canale di Suez e il suo regime internazionale'. *Rivista Marittima*, Novembre 1935.

TRITONJ, R., 'A Chi appartiene il Canale di Suez?', *Nuova Antologia*, 1 Maggio 1936.

VILLARI, L., *Storia Diplomatica del Conflitto Italo-Etiopico*, 111–18, Bologna, Zanichelli, 1943.

VITON, A., 'The Suez Canal and Italy', *Asia*, June 1939.

THE WAR OF 1939–1945

CUNNINGHAM, A. B., *A Sailor's Odyssey. The Autobiography of Admiral of the Fleet Viscount Cunningham of Hyndhope*, London, Hutchinson, 1951.

DEWHURST, C., *Limelight for Suez*, Cairo, Schindler, 1946.

HIRSZOWICZ, L., *The Third Reich and the Arab East*, London, Routledge, 1966.

KIRK, G., *The Middle East in the War. Survey of International Affairs 1939–1946*, Oxford University Press, 1952.

LAFFAILLE, E., 'Conférence sur le Canal de Suez', *Note d'information, Société des Études Historiques et Géographiques de l'Isthme de Suez*, 24 Novembre 1950, 114–27.

PLAYFAIR, I. S. O., *The Mediterranean and Middle East. History of the Second World War*, H.M.S.O. 1954, 1956, 1960, 1966.

STRABOLGI, LORD, *From Gibraltar to Suez. The Battle of the Middle Sea*, London, Hutchinson, 1941.

THE BOYCOTT OF ISRAEL

AVRAM, B., *The Evolution of the Suez Canal Status from 1869 up to 1956. A Historico-Juridical Study*, 97–154, Geneva, Droz, 1958.

BADR, G. M., 'Israel and the Suez Canal. A New Approach', *Revue Égyptienne de Droit International*, 1961.

BAXTER, R. R., 'Passage of Ships through International Waterways in Time of War', *British Yearbook of International Law*, 1954.

—— *The Law of International Waterways with particular reference to Interoceanic Canals*, Harvard University Press, 1964, 221–36.

BLOOMFIELD, L. M., *Egypt, Israel and the Gulf of Aqaba in International Law*, Toronto, Carswell, 1957.

BROMS, B., *The Legal Status of the Suez Canal*, 121–66, Vammala, Vammalan Kirjapaino Oy, 1961.

COMSTOCK, A., 'Nationalism threatens the Canal', *Current History*, July 1951.

DINITZ, S., 'The Legal Aspects of the Egyptian Blockade of the Suez Canal', *Georgetown Law Journal*, Winter 1956–7.

EBAN, A. S., 'The Story of a Blockade', *Voice of Israel*, London, Faber, 1958.

'Freedom of Navigation through the Suez Canal. The Israelo-Egyptian Dispute discussed by a Legal Correspondent', *Petroleum Times*, 2 September 1955, 911–15.

GHOBASHY, O. Z., 'Egypt's Attitude Towards International Law as expressed in the United Nations. The Egyptian-Israeli Dispute on the Freedom of Navigation in the Suez Canal', *Revue Égyptienne de Droit International*, 1955.

GROSS, L., 'Passage through the Suez Canal of Israel-bound Cargo and Israel Ships', *American Journal of International Law*, July 1957.

HEFNAOUI, M. EL-, *Les Problèmes Contemporains posés par le Canal de Suez*, 193–251, Paris, Guillemot, 1951.

KIRK, G., *The Middle East 1945–1950. Survey of International Affairs*, Oxford University Press, 1954.

MENSBRUGGHE, Y. VAN DER, *Les Garanties de la Liberté de Navigation dans le Canal de Suez*, Paris, Pichon, 1964.

'La Question Palestinienne et la Liberté de Passage du Canal de Suez', *Revue Égyptienne de Droit International*, 1951.

ROUSSOS, G., 'Le Principe de la Liberté de Passage du Canal de Suez et l'Application des Règles du Droit de la Guerre Maritime', *Revue de Droit International pour le Moyen-Orient*, Décembre 1951.

TRAPPE, J., 'On the Jurisdiction of the Egyptian Prize Court, 1948–1960', *Revue Égyptienne de Droit International*, 1960.

EGYPT'S BATTLE FOR THE CANAL, 1951–1954

ABEGG, L., 'Der Umstrittene Kanal. Zur Geschichte der englisch-ägyptischen Verhandlungen', *Aussenpolitik*, April 1954.

—— *Neue Herren in Mittelost. Arabische Politik Heute*, 393–413, Stuttgart, Deutsche Verlags-Anstalt, 1954.

ALEXANDER, M., 'North and West of Suez', *Twentieth Century*, December 1954.

HANNA, P. L., 'The Anglo-Egyptian Negotiations, 1950–1952', *Middle Eastern Affairs*, August 1952.

HOSKINS, H. L., 'The Guardianship of the Suez Canal. A View of Anglo-Egyptian Relations', *Middle East Journal*, April 1950.

—— 'Some Aspects of the Security Problem in the Middle East', *American Political Science Review*, March 1953.

—— *The Middle East: Problem Area in World Politics*, New York, Macmillan, 1954.

HOURANI, A. H., 'The Anglo-Egyptian Agreement: Some Causes and Implications', *Middle East Journal*, Summer 1955.

LITTLE, T. R., 'Britain, Egypt and the Canal Zone since July 1952', *World Today*, May 1954.

MOORE, W. R., 'The Spotlight Swings to Suez', *National Geographic Magazine*, January 1952.

MOUSSA, F., *Les Négociations Anglo Égyptiennes de 1950–1951 sur Suez et le Soudan*, Geneva, Droz, 1955.

MURPHY, J. J. W., 'The First Round on the Suez Canal, 1951–1952', *Studies. An Irish Quarterly Review*, Winter 1956.

ROWLATT, M., 'Thoughts on the Anglo-Egyptian Agreement', *Contemporary Review*, December 1954.

Savory, D. L., 'The Abandonment of the Suez Canal', *Contemporary Review*, May 1960.
Selak, C. B., 'The Suez Canal Base Agreement of 1954. Its Background and Implications', *American Journal of International Law*, October 1955.
Siegfried, A., 'The Suez: International Roadway', *Foreign Affairs*, July 1953.
Studnitz, H. G. von, 'Die Zukunft des Suezkanals', *Aussenpolitik*, Juni 1954.
Weinberger, S. J., 'The Suez Canal in Anglo-Egyptian Relations', *Middle Eastern Affairs*, December 1950.

THE MAINTENANCE OF THE WATERWAY

Conrad, J. F. W., 'Het Suez-Kanaal', *Tijdschrift van het Koninklijk Instituut van Ingenieurs*, 1902–3.
Goby, J. E., 'Problèmes Techniques de la Conservation et de l'Amélioration du Canal de Suez', *L'Universitaire Science et Techniques*, Avril 1956.
Hartley, C., 'A Short History of the Engineering Works of the Suez Canal', *Proceedings of the Institution of Civil Engineers*, 13 March 1900.
Mennessier, P., 'Les Dragues et le Canal de Suez', *Bulletin de la Société des Études Historiques et Géographiques de l'Isthme de Suez*, 1948.
Quellennec, E., 'Dredging Rock in the Suez Canal', *Engineering*, 28 June 1907.
Tillier, L., 'La Navigation dans le Canal de Suez', *La Revue du Mois*, 10 Novembre, 10 Décembre 1907.
'La Durée du Transit des Navires', *Le Canal de Suez*, 12 Juillet 1908.
'La Navigation de Nuit', *Le Canal de Suez*, 22 Septembre 1909.
'L'Extraction du Rocher Sous-Marin au Canal de Suez', *Le Canal de Suez*, 2 Avril 1910.
'Le Matériel de Dragage de la Compagnie', *Le Canal de Suez*, nos. 1395, 1396, 1398, 1399 and 1423, 22 Septembre 1910–2 Juillet 1911.
'Le Pilotage dans le Canal de Suez', *Le Canal de Suez*, 22 Mars 1911.

THE TOWNS OF THE ISTHMUS OF SUEZ

Couvidou, H., *Itinéraire du Canal de Suez. Voyage à travers l'Isthme*, Port Said, Mourès, 1875.
Girard, B., *Souvenirs Maritimes 1881–1883*, Paris, Chamuel, 1895, 222–30, 285–90.

ISMAILIA

Boysson, G. de, 'Histoire de la Ville d'Ismailia de sa Fondation à l'Inauguration du Canal', *Notes d'information, Société d'Études Historiques et Géographiques de l'Isthme de Suez*, Mars–Août 1950, 19–22.

SUEZ

Girard, B., 'L'Égypte en 1882. Suez, Ismaïlia', *La Revue Maritime*, Octobre 1883, 149–52.
Jondet, G., *Le Port de Suez*, Le Caire, Imprimerie de l'Institut Français d'Archéologie Orientale, 1919.
—— 'Les Travaux d'Extension du Port de Suez', *Le Génie Civil*, 28 Juin 1919.

WEST, G., 'The Trade and Commerce of the Port of Suez for 1872. Report by Consul George West for the Year 1872', *Reports from H.M. Consuls on the Manufactures, Commerce & C. of their Consular Districts*, March 1873. Reprinted in *The Practical Magazine*, 1873, 447–63.

PORT SAID

DORI, L., 'Esquisse historique de Port-Said', *Cahiers d'Histoire Égyptienne*, Octobre 1954, Janvier 1956, Juillet 1956.
GIRARD, B., 'L'Égypte en 1882. Port Saïd', *La Revue Maritime*, Septembre 1883, 551–558.
REYMOND, P., *Le Port de Port-Said*, Cairo, Le Scribe Égyptien, 1950.
SOLLETTY, A., 'Port-Said', *Annales de Géographie*, 15 Septembre 1934.

THE PORTS OF ASIA

ADEN

HUNTER, F. M., *An Account of the British Settlement of Aden in Arabia*, London, Trübner, 1877.

BOMBAY

SULIVAN, R. F. J., *One Hundred Years of Bombay. History of the Bombay Chamber of Commerce 1836–1936*, Bombay, Times of India Press, 1937.

HONG KONG

EITEL, E. J., *Europe in China. The History of Hongkong from the Beginning to the Year 1882*, London, Luzac, 1895.

KARACHI

BAILLIE, A. F., *Kurrachee: (Karachi) Past: Present: and Future*, Calcutta, Thacker, 1890.

MADRAS

SRINIVASACHARI, C. S., *History of the City of Madras. Written for the Tercentenary Celebration Committee, 1939*, Madras, Varadachary, 1939.

SHANGHAI

DYCE, C. M., *Personal Reminiscences of Thirty Years' Residence in the Model Settlement Shanghai, 1870–1900*, London, Chapman, 1906.
MURPHEY, W. R., *Shanghai, Key to Modern China*, Harvard University Press, 1953.

SINGAPORE

MAKEPEACE, W., BROOKE, G. E. and BRADDELL, R. St. J., *One Hundred Years of Singapore*, 2 vols., London, Murray, 1921.
BOGAARS, G., 'The Effect of the Opening of the Suez Canal on the Trade and Development of Singapore', *Journal of the Malayan Branch, Royal Asiatic Society*, March 1955.

TIENTSIN

RASMUSSEN, O. D., *Tientsin. An Illustrated Outline History*, Tientsin Press, 1925.

784 *Bibliography*

THE SHIPPING LINES OF THE SUEZ ROUTE

ANDERSON, R., *White Star*, Prescot, Stephenson, 1964.

BLAKE, G., *The Ben Line. The History of William Thomson & Co. of Leith and Edinburgh, and of the Ships owned and managed by them, 1825–1955*, London, Nelson, 1956.

—— *B.I. Centenary 1856–1956*, London, Collins, 1956.

—— *Gellatly's 1862–1962. A Short History of the Firm*, London, Blackie, 1962.

BOER, M. G. DE, *Gedenkboek der Stoomvaart Maatschappij Nederland 1870–1920*, Amsterdam, Van Leer, 1920.

—— *Geschiedenis der Amsterdamsche Stoomvaart*, 3 vols., Amsterdam, Scheltema, 1921.

BOWEN, F. C., *History of the Canadian Pacific Line*, London, Low, 1928.

—— *The Flag of the Southern Cross. The History of Shaw Savill and Albion Co. Limited 1858–1939*, London, Shaw Savill, 1948.

BRACKMANN, K., *Fünfzig Jahre deutscher Afrikaschiffahrt. Die Geschichte der Woermann-Linie und der Deutschen Ost-Afrika Linie*, Berlin, Reimer, 1935.

BRUGMANS, I. J., *Tachtig Jaren Varen met de Nederland. 1870–1950*, Amsterdam, 'Nederland', 1950.

CABLE, B., *A Hundred Year History of the P. & O., 1837–1937*, London, Nicholson, 1937.

CODIGNOLA, A., *Rubattino*, Bologna, Cappelli, 1938.

HIMER, K., *Die Hamburg-Amerika Linie im sechsten Jahrzehnt ihrer Entwicklung 1897–1907*, Berlin, Eckstein, 1907.

HYDE, F. E., 'The Expansion of Liverpool's Carrying Trade with the Far East and Australia, 1860–1914', *Transactions of the Royal Historical Society*, 1956.

—— 'British Shipping Companies and East and South-East Asia, 1860–1939', in C. D. Cowan (ed.), *The Economic Development of South-East Asia*, London, Allen, 1964.

—— *Shipping Enterprise and Management 1830–1939. Harrisons of Liverpool*, Liverpool University Press, 1967.

HYDE, F. E. and HARRIS, J. R., *Blue Funnel: a History of Alfred Holt and Company of Liverpool from 1865 to 1914*, Liverpool University Press, 1956.

LOFTIE, W. J., *Illustrated Guide of the Orient Line of Steamers between England and Australia*, London, Orient Steam Navigation Company Ltd., 1880.

MABER, J. M., *North Star to Southern Cross, The Story of the Australasian Seaways*, Prescot, Stephenson, 1967.

MACGREGOR, D. R., *The China Bird. The History of Captain Killick and One Hundred Years of Sail and Steam*, London, Chatto, 1961.

McLELLAN, R. S., *Anchor Line 1856–1956*, Glasgow, Anchor Line, 1956.

MARRINER, S., *Rathbones of Liverpool 1845–73*, Liverpool University Press, 1961.

MARRINER, S. and HYDE, F. E., *The Senior, John Samuel Swire 1825–98. Management in Far Eastern Shipping Trades*, Liverpool University Press, 1967.

MATHIES, O., *Hamburgs Reederei 1814–1914*, Hamburg, Friedrichsen, 1924.

MILNE, T. E., 'British Shipping in the Nineteenth Century: a Study of the Ben Line Papers', in P. L. Payne (ed.), *Studies in Scottish Business History*, 345–66, London, Cass, 1967.

MURRAY, M., *Ships and South Africa. A Maritime Chronicle of the Cape*, London, Oxford University Press, 1933.

MURRAY, M., *Union-Castle Chronicle 1853–1953*, London, Longmans, 1953.

NEUBAUR, P., *Der Norddeutsche Lloyd. 50 Jahre der Entwicklung, 1857–1907*, Leipzig, Grunow, 1907.

PAPENDRECHT, A. H. VAN, *De Zeilvloot van Willem Ruys Jan Danielszoon en de Rotterdamsche Lloyd*, Rotterdam, Wyt, 1933.

WARDLE, A. C., *Steam Conquers the Pacific. A Record of Maritime Achievement 1840–1940*, London, Hodder, 1940.

WATERS, S. D., *Clipper Ship to Motor Liner. The Story of the New Zealand Shipping Company 1873–1939*, London, New Zealand Shipping Company, 1939.

—— *Shaw Savill Line. One Hundred Years of Trading*, Christchurch, Whitcombe, 1961.

—— *Union Line. A Short History of the Union Steam Ship Company of New Zealand Ltd. 1875–1951*, Wellington, Union Steam Ship Company, 1951.

THE TRAFFIC OF THE CANAL

CÉPÈDE, M., and LENGELLÉ, M., *Économie alimentaire du Globe. Essai d'interprétation*, 434–61, Paris, Médicis, 1953.

'L'Évolution du Trafic du Canal de Suez et son Rôle dans la Conjoncture Mondiale', *Institut National de la Statistique et des Études Économiques. Études et Conjonctures. Économie Mondiale*, Janvier–Février 1949.

FLETCHER, M. E., 'Suez and Britain: An Historical Study of the Effects of the Suez Canal on the British Economy', Ph.D. Thesis, University of Wisconsin, 1957.

GLÜCKS, W., *Die Handels- und Verkehrsbedeutung des Suezkanals für die deutsche Volkswirtschaft nach dem Weltkriege*, München Gladbach, Rixen, 1929.

HEYMANN, E., 'Der Verkehr im Suezkanal 1912–1914 und 1919–1926', *Weltwirtschaftliches Archiv*, Januar 1927.

ISSA, H. H., *Les Courants économiques comparés du Canal de Suez et du Canal de Panama*, Genève, Jullien, 1938.

JULIEN, H. C., *Le Trafic du Canal de Suez. Conjoncture économique et prévisions*, Paris, Sirey, 1933.

KELLER, W., *Darstellung der Wege der heutigen Dampferrouten im Mittelmeer unter Würdigung der wirtschaftlichen und politisch-geographischen Bedeutung der Hauptrouten*, Wurzburg, Triltsch, 1934.

LENGELLÉ, M., 'Le Trafic des Arachides par le Canal de Suez', *Cahiers Coloniaux*, Janvier 1950, Avril 1950.

—— 'Le Trafic du Canal de Suez', *Cahiers Économiques*, Novembre 1952, Décembre 1952.

MEHRLIN, G., *Der Suezkanal als Konjunkturanzeiger der Weltwirtschaft*, Zürich, Girsberger, 1945.

POSSAT, H., 'Der Suezkanal in der Weltwirtschaft. Seine Vorteile und seine Entwicklung', Wien, Dissertation, 1947.

REYMOND, P., *Histoire de la Navigation dans le Canal de Suez*, Le Caire, Imprimerie de l'Institut Français d'Archéologie Orientale, 1956.

SAINT-VICTOR, G. DE, *Le Canal de Suez*, Paris, Sirey, 1934.

SCHICK, WILHELM, *Die Bedeutung des Suez- und Panamakanals, ein Vergleich*, Köln, Zimmerman, 1936.

SCHOENWALDT, M., 'Die Konjunkturschwankungen im Verkehr der grossen See-schiffahrtskanäle: ein Beitrag zur Erkenntnis internationaler Konjunkturen: Der Suezkanal', *Weltwirtschaftliches Archiv*, April 1927.

SPANGENBERG, J., *Die Veränderungen des Seeverkehrs im Indischen Ozean seit dem Weltkriege*, Stuttgart, Fink, 1930.

VOSS, M., *Der Suezkanal und seine Stellung im Weltverkehr*, Wien, Lechner, 1904.

THE OIL TRADE OF THE MIDDLE EAST

ARABIAN AMERICAN OIL COMPANY, *Middle East Oil Development*, 4th edition, Aramco, March 1956.

BLONDEL, F., 'Le Pétrole au Moyen-Orient', *Comptes Rendus, Académie des Sciences Coloniales*, 554–70, 9 Novembre 1956.

CAROE, O. K., *Wells of Power, The Oilfields of Southern Asia. A Regional and Global Study*, London, Macmillan, 1951.

ELWELL-SUTTON, L. P., *Persian Oil. A Study in Power Politics*, London, Lawrence, 1955.

FINNIE, D. H., *Desert Enterprise. The Middle East Oil Industry in its Local Environment*, Harvard University Press, 1958.

FONTAINE, P., *Le Pétrole du Moyen-Orient et les Trusts*, Paris, Les Sept Couleurs, 1960.

FRANK, H. J., *Crude Oil Prices in the Middle East. A Study in Oligopolistic Price Behavior*, New York, Praeger, 1966.

HANS, J., *Homo Œconomicus Islamicus. Wirtschaftswandel und sozialer Aufbruch im Islam*, Wien, Leon, 1952.

HAY, R., 'The Impact of the Oil Industry on the Persian Gulf Shaykhdoms', *Middle East Journal*, Autumn 1955.

ISSAWI, C., and YEGANEH, M., *The Economics of Middle Eastern Oil*, London, Faber, 1962.

JULIEN, R. C., 'Le Pétrole dans l'économie du Moyen-Orient', *Revue de Droit International pour le Moyen-Orient*, Mai 1951.

LEBKICHER, R., *Aramco and World Oil*, Aramco, 1950, 1952.

LEEMAN, W. A., *The Price of Middle East Oil: an Essay in Political Economy*, Ithaca, Cornell University Press, 1962.

LENCZOWSKI, G., *Oil and the State in the Middle East*, Ithaca, Cornell University Press, 1960.

LONGHURST, H., *Adventure in Oil. The Story of British Petroleum*, London, Sidgwick, 1959.

LONGRIGG, S. H., *Oil in the Middle East: its Discovery and Development*, London, Oxford University Press, 1954, 1961, 1968.

MARLOWE, J., *The Persian Gulf in the Twentieth Century*, London, Cresset, 1962.

MIKDASHI, Z., *A Financial Analysis of Middle Eastern Oil Concessions: 1901–65*, New York, Praeger, 1966.

MIKESELL, R. F., and CHENERY, H. B., *Arabian Oil, America's Stake in the Middle East*, Chapel Hill, University of North Carolina Press, 1949.

NORMAND, S. and ACKER, J., *La Route du Pétrole au Moyen-Orient*, Paris, Horizons de France, 1956.

RONDOT, J., *La Compagnie Française des Pétroles*, Paris, Plon, 1962.

SHWADRAN, B., *The Middle East, Oil and the Great Powers*, New York, Praeger, 1955, 1959.

SIMPSON, D. J., 'Impact of the Oil Industry on the Middle East', *World Affairs Quarterly*, April 1957.

'Le Trafic des huiles minérales par le Canal de Suez', *Le Canal de Suez*, 6300, 25 Novembre et 5 Décembre 1921.

'Les Bateaux-Citernes sur la Route de Suez', *Le Canal de Suez*, 6515, 15 Avril 1923.

'Les Relations avec le Golfe Persique par le Canal de Suez', *Le Canal de Suez*, 6219, 25 Mai 1921.

'Les Relations maritimes avec le Golfe Persique. Rôle des huiles minérales', *Le Canal de Suez*, 25 Juillet 1923, 6566–6567.

'Les Flottes de Bateaux-Citernes', *Le Canal de Suez*, 6674–5, 25 Avril 1924.

'Les Pétroles de la Perse', *Le Canal de Suez*, 7181–3, 25 Juin 1927.

'Le Commerce de l'essence', *Le Canal de Suez*, 7888–9, 25 Décembre 1931.

'Les Bateaux-Citernes dans le trafic du Canal en 1931', *Le Canal de Suez*, 7931–3, 15 Avril 1932.

'Le Trafic nord–sud des pétroles via Suez (1913–1933)', *Le Canal de Suez*, 8316–17, 15 Juillet 1934.

'Le Trafic nord–sud des pétroles', *Le Canal de Suez*, 8504–5, 15 Septembre 1935.

'Le Trafic sud–nord du mazout', *Le Canal de Suez*, 8552–3, 15 Janvier 1936.

'Les Pétroles de Russie', *Le Canal de Suez*, 8671–3, 25 Septembre 1936.

'Les Navires-Citernes sur la Route du Canal en 1934 et en 1935', *Le Canal de Suez*, 8683–5, 25 Octobre 1936.

'Les Envois de pétroles des Iles Bahrein', *Le Canal de Suez*, 8852, 5 Novembre 1937.

'Les Bateaux-Citernes dans le mouvement maritime du Canal', *Le Canal de Suez*, 9084–5, 25 Avril 1939.

'Les Navires-Citernes au Canal de Suez', *Supplément au Bulletin Le Canal de Suez*, 15 Novembre 1952.

THE NATIONALIZATION OF THE CANAL COMPANY

ABS, H. J., *Der Schutz wohlerworbener Rechte im internationalen Verkehr als europäische Aufgabe. Betrachtungen zur Entwicklung der Suezkrise*, Heidelberg, 'Recht und Wirtschaft', 1956.

ALEJANDRO Y MEDINA, J., *Suez y el Derecho Internacional*, 88–131, Madrid, Instituto 'Francisco de Vitoria', 1959.

ARIAS, Y. S., *El Canal de Suez. Aspecto Historico, Juridico, Politico y Economico*, 71–124, Universidad de Concepción, 1958.

'L'Aspect Juridique de la Question de Suez', *Les Cahiers de l'Europe Naissante*, II, Modena, Società Tipografica Editrice Modenese, 1956.

ATIYAH, E. S., 'Die Suezkanal-Krise in arabischer Sicht', *Europa-Archiv*, 9409–14, 20 Dezember 1956.

BOUTROS-GHALI, B., 'Aspects du Problème du Canal de Suez', *Revue Égyptienne de Droit International*, 1957.

BOUTROS-GHALI, B. and CHLALA, Y., 'Le Problème du Canal de Suez. Chronologie et documents, 1854–1956'. *Revue Égyptienne de Droit International*, 1956.

BOUTROS-GHALI, B. and CHLALA, Y., *Le Canal de Suez 1854–1957. Chronologie. Documents*, Alexandrie, Société Égyptienne de Droit International, 1958.

BROMS, B., *The Legal Status of the Suez Canal*, 167–212, Vammala, Vammalan Kirjapaino Oy, 1961.

BRÜEL, E., 'Die völkerrechtliche Stellung des Suezkanals und die Nationalisierung der Kanalgesellschaft', *Archiv des Völkerrechts*, Juli 1958.

CALVERT, H., 'The Nationalization of the Suez Canal Company in International Law', *Annual Law Review*, December 1957.

CANSACCHI, G., 'I Termini giuridici e politici della Controversià di Suez', *Oriente Moderno*, Febbraio 1957.

'A Challenge to Law. Colonel Nasser and the Suez Canal', *The Round Table*, August 1956.

CHARLES-ROUX, F., 'Ce que la France perd avec le Canal de Suez', *La Nouvelle Revue Française d'Outre-Mer*, Mars 1957, 121–7, summarized in *Le Canal de Suez*, 9721–2, 15 Mai 1957.

—— 'Ce qui disparaît d'Égypte avec la Compagnie Universelle du Canal Maritime de Suez', *Revue des Travaux de l'Académie des Sciences Morales et Politiques*, 1 Juillet 1957.

—— 'Le coup de force du Gouvernement Égyptien contre la Compagnie Universelle du Canal Maritime de Suez', *Revue des Travaux de l'Académie des Sciences Morales et Politiques*, 19 Novembre 1956.

—— 'Le Coup de Suez', *Revue de Paris*, Octobre 1956.

'Company and Canal. Egypt's Action in Perspective of International Law', *The Times*, 2 August 1956, 9vi.

DELSON, R., 'Nationalization of the Suez Canal Company: Issues of Public and Private International Law', *Columbia Law Review*, June 1957.

DENEY, N., 'Les États-Unis et le financement du Barrage d'Assouan', *Revue Française de Science Politique*, Juin 1962.

DOMKE, M., 'American Protection against Foreign Expropriation in the Light of the Suez Canal Crisis', *University of Pennsylvania Law Review*, June 1957.

DOUGHERTY, J. E., 'The Aswan Decision in Perspective', *Political Science Quarterly*, March 1959.

FAHMY-ABDOU, A., *La Nazionalizzazione della Società del Canale di Suez*, Cairo, 'Mondiale', 1962.

FEINER, L., 'The Aswan Dam Development Project', *Middle East Journal*, Autumn 1952.

FINCH, G. A., 'Navigation and Use of the Suez Canal', *Proceedings of the American Society of International Law*, 25 April 1957.

FOCSANEANU, L., 'L'Accord ayant pour objet l'indemnisation de la Compagnie de Suez nationalisée par l'Égypte', *Annuaire Français de Droit International*, 1959.

GENERALES, M. D., 'Suez. National Sovereignty and International Waterways', *World Affairs Quarterly*, July 1958.

HOSTIE, J. F., 'Notes on the International Statute of the Suez Canal', *Tulane Law Review*, April 1957.

HUANG, T. T. F., 'Some International and Legal Aspects of the Suez Canal Question', *American Journal of International Law*, April 1957.

LACOUTURE, J. and S., *Egypt in Transition*, 453–504, 'The Great Test', London, Methuen, 1958.

LITTLE, T., *High Dam at Aswan. The Subjugation of the Nile*, London, Methuen, 1965.

MAITY, A., *The Problem of the Suez Canal*, Calcutta, World Press, 1956.

MENSBRUGGHE, Y. VAN DER, *Les Garanties de la Liberté de Navigation dans le Canal de Suez*, 187–256, Paris, Pichon, 1964.

MEYER, G., 'Le Problème de Suez', *Revue Politique et Parlementaire*, Octobre 1956.

'Nationalization of the Suez Canal Company', *Harvard Law Review*, January 1957.

NOUSEIR, A., MOONIS, H., *et alia*, *The Suez Canal. Facts and Documents*, Cairo, Selected Studies No. 5, 1956.

OBIETA, J. A., *The International Status of the Suez Canal*, 90–111, The Hague, Nijhoff, 1960.

OLMSTEAD, C. J., 'International Law: Nationalization of the Suez Canal', *Annual Survey of American Law*, 1956.

—— 'International Law: Nationalization of the Suez Canal', *New York University Law Review*, January 1957.

PADELFORD, N. J., 'The Panama Canal and the Suez Crisis', *Proceedings of the American Society of International Law*, 25 April 1957.

PINTO, R., 'En Quoi l'Égypte a violé ses Obligations Internationales', *Le Monde*, 3 Octobre 1956, 3 iii–v.

—— 'L'Affaire de Suez. Problèmes Juridiques', *Annuaire Français de Droit International*, 1956.

—— 'Der Suezkrise', *Jahrbuch für Internationales Recht*, 1957.

PRADELLE, G. DE LA, 'L'Égypte a-t-elle violé le Droit International?', *Le Monde*, 26 Septembre 1956, 3 i; 6 Octobre 1956, 6 i.

RAUSCHNING, D., *Der Streit um den Suezkanal. Analyse-Materialen-Bibliographie*, Hektographierte Veröffentlichungen der Forschungsstelle für Völkerrecht der Universität Hamburg Nr. 27, 1956.

—— 'Der Widerstreit von nationalen und internationalen Interessen im Suez-konflikt', *Wirtschaftsdienst*, August 1956.

Republic of Egypt, Ministry for Foreign Affairs, *White Paper on the Nationalisation of the Suez Maritime Canal Company*, Cairo, Government Press, 12 August 1956.

ROSSBACH, A., 'Der britische Standpunkt im Suezkonflikt 1956', Doctoral Dissertation in Law, Ludwig-Maximilians-Universität, Munich, 1959.

RUBIN, E., *The Suez Canal. The Great Internationale*, London, De Vero, 1956.

SCELLE, G., 'La Nationalisation du Canal de Suez et le Droit International', *Annuaire Français de Droit International*, 1956, reprinted in *Le Canal de Suez*, Octobre 1957, 9762–7.

SLOVENKO, R., 'Nationalization and Nasser', *Tulane Studies in Political Science IV. International Law and the Middle East Crisis. A Symposium*, 79–93, New Orleans, Tulane University, 1957.

SOTTILÉ, A., 'La Compétence de l'O.N.U. concernant la question de Suez', *Revue de Droit International*, Septembre 1956.

SUEZ CANAL COMPANY, *The Suez Canal Company and the Decision Taken by the Egyptian Government on 26th July 1956* (26 July–15 September 1956), Paris, S.E.F., 1956.

—— *The Suez Canal Company and the Decision Taken by the Egyptian Government on 26th July 1956. Second Part* (August 1956–May 1957), Paris, S.E.F., 1957.

VISSCHER, P. DE, 'Les Aspects juridiques fondamentaux de la Question de Suez', *Revue Générale de Droit International Public*, Juillet 1958.

WATT, D. C., *Britain and the Suez Canal. The Background*, London, Royal Institute of International Affairs, 1956.

—— *Documents on the Suez Crisis 26 July to 6 November 1956*, London, Royal Institute of International Affairs, 1957.

WEINBERGER, S. J., 'The Suez Canal Issue 1956', *Middle East Affairs*, February 1957.

THE SUEZ CRISIS OF 1956

N.B. The best guides through the labyrinth of crisis-literature seem at the time of writing to be those provided by Azeau, Childers, Hourani, Nutting and Thomas. Childers pioneered the historical analysis of the issue of collusion and emphasized the absence of any real 'secrets of Suez' five years before the tabu on the subject was broken outside England in 1964 by Bar-Zohar, Finer, Robertson and Azeau, the author of the most brilliant of syntheses.

ADAMS, M., *Suez and After. Year of Crisis*, Boston, Beacon, 1958.

—— 'Middle East after Suez', *Manchester Guardian*, 26 July 1957, 8 vi–vii; 29 July, 6 vi–vii.

—— 'In a Limbo of Humiliation... Suez Ten Years Ago', *The Guardian*, 25 October 1966, 8 iii–v.

—— 'Only Fringe Benefits for Britain: Problems and Prejudices in the Middle East', *The Guardian*, 26 October 1966, 10 iii–v.

ADAMS, S., *Firsthand Report. The Story of the Eisenhower Administration*, 245–70, 'Showdown at Suez', New York, Harper, 1961.

AFIFI, M. H., *The Arabs and the United Nations*, 83–102, London, Longmans, 1964.

AITCHISON, J. H., 'Canadian Foreign Policy in the House and on the Hustings', *International Journal*, Autumn 1957.

ALLAUN, F., *The Cost of Suez*, London, Union of Democratic Control, 1957.

ANTHON, C. G., 'Das Suezkanalproblem in Geschichte und neuester Entwicklung', *Zeitschrift für Politik*, 1957.

ATYEO, H. C., 'Egypt since the Suez Crisis', *Middle Eastern Affairs*, June 1958.

AUSPEX, 'L'Italia di fronte alla Crisi di Suez', *Nuova Antologia*, Dicembre 1956.

AZEAU, H., *Le Piège de Suez (5 Novembre 1956)*, Paris, Laffont, 1964.

BALL, W. M., 'Problems of Australian Foreign Policy, July–December 1956: The Australian Reaction to the Suez Crisis', *Australian Journal of Politics and History*, May 1957.

BAR-ZOHAR, M., *The Armed Prophet. A Biography of Ben Gurion*, 217–54, London, Barker, 1967.

—— *Suez Ultra-Secret*, Paris, Fayard, 1964.

BARCLAY, C. N., 'Anglo-French Operations against Port Said, 1956 (Operation 'Musketeer')', *Army Quarterly*, April 1957.

BARKER, A. J., *Suez. The Seven Day War*, London, Faber, 1964.

BARRACLOUGH, G., *Survey of International Affairs 1955–1956*, London, Oxford University Press, 1960.

—— *Survey of International Affairs 1956–1958*, Oxford University Press, 1962.

BEAL, J. R., *John Foster Dulles. A Biography*, 246–88, New York, Harper, 1957.

BELOFF, M., 'Suez and the British Conscience. A Personal Report', *Commentary*, April 1957.

—— 'The Predicament of American Foreign Policy', *University of Toronto Quarterly*, July 1957, reprinted in *The Great Powers. Essays in Twentieth-Century Politics*, 188–201, London, Allen, 1959.

BENTWICH, N., 'Israel after Suez', *Journal of the Royal Central Asian Society*, April 1961.

BERGER, E., *Covenant and the Sword. Arab-Israeli Relations 1948–56*, London, Routledge, 1965.

BIRKENHEAD, LORD, *Walter Monckton. The Life of Viscount Monckton of Brenchley*, 303–10, London, Weidenfeld, 1969.

BLAXLAND, G., *Objective Egypt*, London, Muller, 1966.

BLECHMAN, B. M., 'The Quantitative Evaluation of Foreign Policy Alternatives: Sinai, 1956', *Journal of Conflict Resolution*, December 1966.

BRECHER, M., *India and World Politics. Krishna Menon's View of the World*, 62–84, London, Oxford University Press, 1968.

BROGAN, C., *Suez. Who Was Right?*, London, Coram, 1957.

BROGAN, D. W., 'Egypt, Great Britain and the American People', *Cambridge Review*, 10 November 1956.

—— 'America and the British Right', *The Listener*, 21 February 1957.

BROMBERGER, M. and S., *Secrets of Suez*, London, Pan, 1957.

BURNS, E. M. L., *Between Arab and Israeli*, London, Harrap, 1962.

BYFORD-JONES, W., *Oil on Troubled Waters*, London, Hale, 1957.

CALVOCORESSI, P., *World Politics since 1945*, 172–99, London, Longmans, 1968.

CAMILLE, P., *Suez ou la haute farce du vaincu triomphant*, Paris, Debresse, 1957.

CAMPBELL, J. C., *Defense of the Middle East. Problems of American Policy*, 99–119, New York, Harper, 1958.

CASTANEDA, J., 'Certain Legal Consequences of the Suez Crisis', *Revue Égyptienne de Droit International*, 1963.

CAVENAGH, S., *Airborne to Suez*, London, Kimber, 1965.

CHARLES-ROUX, F., 'Le Blocage du Canal de Suez', *Comptes Rendus, Académie des Sciences Coloniales*, 23 Novembre 1956.

CHATEAUVIEUX, P., 'L'Opinion Américaine et Anglaise devant la Crise de Suez', *Revue de Défense Nationale*, Octobre 1956.

CHILDERS, E. B., *The Road to Suez. A Study of Western–Arab Relations*, London, MacGibbon, 1962.

—— 'The Sinai War, 1956', *Middle East Forum*, February 1961.

—— 'The Ultimatum', *The Spectator*, 30 October 1959, 579–91, 703.

CHURCHILL, R., *The Rise and Fall of Sir Anthony Eden*, London, MacGibbon, 1959.

CLARK, D. M. J., *Suez Touchdown. A Soldier's Tale*, London, Davies, 1964.

COHEN, M., 'The United Nations Emergency Force: a Preliminary View', *International Journal*, Spring 1957.

COLE, H., 'Public Opinion and the Suez Crisis. A Retrospect', *Fabian Journal*, March 1957.

CONNELL, J., *The Most Important Country: the True Story of the Suez Crisis and the events leading to it* (London, Cassell, 1957), reviewed in *The Spectator*, 19 July 1957, 84–5, by Lord Altrincham, 'The Canal and Mr. Connell'.

CORBETT, P. E., 'Power and Law at Suez', *International Journal*, Winter 1956–7.

DALLIN, D. J., *Soviet Foreign Policy after Stalin*, 385–421, London, Methuen, 1962.

DAYAN, M., *Diary of the Sinai Campaign*, London, Weidenfeld, 1966.

DIXON, P., *Double Diploma. The Life of Sir Pierson Dixon Don and Diplomat*, London, Hutchinson, 1968.

DUMONT, C. and LE PLEUX, P., 'L'Affaire de Suez', *Cahiers de l'Orient Contemporain*, 1956, 36–101.

EAGLETON, C., 'The United Nations and the Suez Crisis', in P. W. Thayer (ed.), *Tensions in the Middle East*, 273–96, Baltimore, Johns Hopkins Press, 1958.

EAYRS, J., 'Canadian Policy and Opinion during the Suez Crisis', *International Journal*, Spring 1957.

—— *The Commonwealth and Suez. A Documentary Survey*, London, Oxford University Press, 1964.

—— 'Suez, Britain, and the Canadian Conscience', in *Canada in World Affairs October 1955 to June 1957*, 182–93, Toronto, Oxford University Press, 1959.

EBAN, A., 'Sinai and Suez—A Retrospect', in *Voice of Israel*, 236–48, London, Faber, 1958.

EDEN, A., *The Memoirs of the Rt. Hon. Sir Anthony Eden, K.G., P.C., M.C. Full Circle*, 419–584, London, Cassell, 1960. Reviewed in *The Spectator*, 5 February 1960, 167–8 by I. Gilmour, 'Eden, Dulles and Collusion'; *The Spectator*, 4 March 1960, 311–15 by I. Gilmour, 'Half-Circle'; *The Times Literary Supplement*, 4 March 1960, 138, 'Anglo-Saxon Attitudes'; *The Twentieth Century*, March 1960, 235–40 by A. Buchan, 'Le chevalier mal fet'; *International Affairs*, July 1960, 299–309, by M. Wight, 'Brutus in Foreign Policy'; *Observer*, 28 February 1960, 16, by W. Hayter, 'The Cost of Force'; *Sunday Times*, 28 February 1960, 21–2, by the Marquess of Salisbury, 'No Cause for Shame', by Hugh Gaitskell 'Errors and Omissions', by Robert Menzies, 'History will uphold the Eden Decision' and by Robert Murphy, 'The Difficulty of Dealing with Friends'; E. Monroe, *Britain's Moment in the Middle East 1914–1956*, 203–6, London, Chatto, 1963.

EISENHOWER, D. D., *The White House Years. Waging Peace 1956–1961*, 20–99, London, Heinemann, 1965.

EPSTEIN, L. D., 'British M.P.s and their Local Parties: the Suez Cases', *American Political Science Review*, June 1960.

—— *British Politics in the Suez Crisis*, London, Pall Mall, 1964, reviewed by Lord Henderson and D. Walker-Smith in *Political Science Quarterly*, September 1965, 415–26.

—— 'Partisan Foreign Policy: Britain in the Suez Crisis', *World Politics*, January 1960.

FALLS, C., 'Operation Musketeer', *Brassey's Annual*, 1957.

FAUST, J. J., 'L'Égypte d'une Révolution à l'Autre...' *Études Méditerrannéenes*, Été 1957.

FEIS, H., 'Suez Scenario: a Lamentable Tale', *Foreign Affairs*, July 1960.

FINER, H., *Dulles over Suez. The Theory and Practice of his Diplomacy*, Chicago, Quadrangle, 1964.

FITZSIMONS, M. A., 'The Suez Crisis and the Containment Policy', *Review of Politics*, October 1957.

—— *Empire by Treaty. Britain and the Middle East in the Twentieth Century*, 161–225, University of Notre Dame Press, 1964.

FLANDIN, P. E., 'L'Affaire de Suez', *Revue des Deux Mondes*, 1 Novembre 1956.
—— 'Les Suites de l'Affaire de Suez', *Revue des Deux Mondes*, 1 Avril 1957.
FLINTHAM, V., 'Suez 1956: a Lesson in Air Power', *Air Pictorial*, August 1965, September 1965.
FONTAINE, A., 'Il y a dix ans, La Guerre de Suez', *Le Monde*, 30–1 Octobre 1966 1, 8; 1 Novembre 1966, 5.
—— *Histoire de la Guerre Froide ii, 1950–1967*, 183–208, 263–311, Paris, Fayard, 1967.
FOOT, M. and JONES, M., *Guilty Men, 1957*, London, Gollancz, 1957.
FRANGULIS, A. F. (ed.), *Dictionnaire Diplomatique*, Paris, Académie Diplomatique Internationale, 1957, 1054–94 'Suez (la question du canal de)'.
GALLÉAN, G., *Des Deux Cotés du Canal. Égypte–Israël*, Paris, Calmann-Lévy, 1958.
GLUBB, J. B., 'Britain and the Middle East', *Journal of the Royal Central Asian Society*, July 1957.
GOODHART, A. L., 'Grounds for Action at Suez', *Optima*, March 1957.
—— 'Some Legal Aspects of the Suez Situation', in P. W. Thayer (ed.), *Tensions in the Middle East*, 243–72, Baltimore, Johns Hopkins Press, 1958.
GOOLD-ADAMS, R., *John Foster Dulles. A Reappraisal*, 191–262, New York, Appleton, 1962.
GREENWOOD, G., 'Australia's Triangular Foreign Policy', *Foreign Affairs*, July 1957.
GRISEWOOD, H., *One Thing at a Time. An Autobiography*, London, Hutchinson, 1968.
HARPER, N., 'Australia and Suez', in G. Greenwood and N. Harper, *Australia in World Affairs 1950–55*, 341–56, Melbourne, Cheshire, 1957.
HART, B. H. L., 'Operation Musketeer', *The Observer*, 24 February 1957, 8.
HASSON, J. M., *Suez. Représailles et Menottes*, Paris, Debresse, 1959.
HAYTER, W., *The Kremlin and the Embassy*, 140–54, 'Hungary and Suez', London, Hodder, 1966.
HENEIN, G., 'Inventaire contre le Désespoir', *Études Méditerrannéenes*, Été 1957.
HENRIQUES, R. D. Q., *One Hundred Hours to Suez. An Account of Israel's Campaign in the Sinai Peninsula*, London, Collins, 1957.
—— 'The Ultimatum: a Dissenting View', *The Spectator*, 6 November 1959, 623–5.
HERBERT, E. S., *Damage and Casualties in Port Said. Report by Sir Edwin Herbert on his investigation into the effects of the Military Action in October and November, 1956*, Cmnd. 47 of 1956, H.M.S.O., London.
HONIG, F., 'Legal Aspects of the Suez Crisis', *World Today*, May 1957.
HOSKINS, H. L., 'The Suez Canal', *Current History*, November 1957.
HOURANI, A. H., 'The Middle East and the Crisis of 1956', *St. Antony's Papers, Number 4. Middle Eastern Affairs Number 1*, London, Chatto, 1958.
—— '*A Moment of Change: the Crisis of 1956*', in *A Vision of History. Near Eastern and Other Essays*, London, Constable, 1961.
HUDSON, G. F., 'The Great Catastrophe', in W. Z. Laqueur (ed.), *The Middle East in Transition: Studies in Contemporary History*, 112–20, London, Routledge, 1958.
HUGHES, E., *Macmillan. Portrait of a Politician*, 116–25, London, Allen, 1962.
—— *The Suez Skeleton*, Labour's Voice Newspapers, Suez Special Edition, 4 pp., Manchester, 1959.
HUIZINGA, J. H., *Confessions of a European in England*, 246–96, London, Heinemann, 1958.
HUMBARACI, A., *Middle East Indictment*, London, Hale, 1958.

HÜSLER, A., *Contribution à l'étude de l'élaboration de la Politique Étrangère Britannique (1945–1956)*, 129–215, '*La Crise de Suez*', Genève, Droz, 1961.

IONIDES, M., *Divide and Lose. The Arab Revolt of 1955–58*, London, Bles, 1960.

JOHNSON, P., *The Suez War*, London, MacGibbon, 1957.

—— *Journey into Chaos*, London, MacGibbon, 1958.

KAYSER, J., 'La Presse Française et la Crise de Suez', *Politique Étrangère*, Mars 1957.

KEIGHTLEY, C., 'Despatch. Operations in Egypt—November to December 1956'. *Supplement to the London Gazette*, 10 September 1957, 5327–37, reviewed in *The Times*, 13 September 1957, 11 ii, 'Soldier's Story'.

KILMUIR, EARL OF, *Political Adventure. The Memoirs of the Earl of Kilmuir*, 255–97, London, Weidenfeld, 1964.

KIRK, G. E., *Contemporary Arab Politics. A Concise History*, 45–90, 'The Great Divorce', London, Methuen, 1961.

LABOUR PARTY, *The Truth About Suez*, London, Labour Party, 1956.

LACOSTE, R., 'La Crise de Suez et le déclin de l'Europe', *Revue générale belge*, Janvier 1957.

LAFORESSE, B., *Le Bilan de l'équipée de l'Égypte*, Paris, Ethéel, 1957.

LANCASTER, O., *The Year of the Comet*, London, Gryphon, 1957.

LAQUEUR, W. Z., *The Soviet Union and the Middle East*, 229–46, 'The Year of Suez', London, Routledge, 1959.

LASH, J. P., *Dag Hammarskjold*, 66–111, London, Cassell, 1962.

LAVERGNE, B., 'L'Affaire de Suez ou la dernière infidélité des États-Unis. La Fin du Pacte Atlantique', *L'Année Politique et Économique*, Octobre 1956, reprinted in *Problèmes Africains*, 82–118, Paris, Larose, 1957.

LENGYEL, E., *Egypt's Role in World Affairs*, Washington, Public Affairs, 1957.

LEPOTIER, R., 'La Guerre des Isthmes dans la Bataille d'Afrique', *Revue de Défense Nationale*, Octobre 1956.

LEWINSON, G., 'Suez and its Consequences: The Israel View', *World Today*, April 1957.

LITTLE, T., *Egypt*, 280–306, London, Benn, 1958.

—— *Modern Egypt*, 151–76, London, Benn, 1967.

LÜTHY, H., and RODNICK, D., *French Motivations in the Suez Crisis*, Princeton, Institute for International Social Research, 1956.

McCALLUM, R. B., 'The Flight to Liberalism', *Contemporary Review*, 242–8, October 1958.

McCLURE, JR., J. F., 'The Law of International Waterways. An Approach to a Suez Canal Solution', *University of Pennsylvania Law Review*, March 1957.

McDERMOTT, G., *The Eden Legacy*, 127–66, London, Frewin, 1969.

McKENZIE, R. T., *British Political Parties. The Distribution of Power within the Conservative and Labour Parties*, 2nd ed., 582–92, London, Heinemann, 1963.

MALONE, J. J. 'Germany and the Suez Crisis,' *Middle East Journal*, Winter 1966.

MARTIN, L. W., 'The Bournemouth Affair: Britain's First Primary Election', *Journal of Politics*, November 1960.

MASON, H. L., 'The United Nations Emergency Force', *Tulane Studies in Political Science*, *IV*, 25–48, New Orleans, Tulane University, 1957.

MATTHEWS, R. O., 'The Suez Canal Dispute: A Case Study in Peaceful Settlement', *International Organization*, Winter 1967.

MEINERTZHAGEN, R. M., *Middle East Diary 1917–1956*, 275–369, London, Cresset‘ 1959.

MEINERTZHAGEN, R. M., *Middle East Muddle*, 7 pp., London, Author, 1957.

MENZIES, R. G., *Afternoon Light. Some Memories of Men and Events*, 149–85. 'My Suez Story', London, Cassell, 1967.

MILLAR, T. B., *The Commonwealth and the United Nations*, 62–75, Sydney University Press, 1967.

MILLER, J. D. B., *Britain and the Old Dominions*, 246–54, London, Chatto, 1966.

MILLIOT, L., 'La Crise Égyptienne de Suez', *Comptes Rendus, Académie des Science Coloniales*, 23 Novembre 1956.

MOHAN, J., 'India, Pakistan, Suez and the Commonwealth', *International Journal*, Summer 1960.

—— 'Parliamentary Opinions on the Suez Crisis in Australia and New Zealand', *International Studies*, July 1960, 60–79.

—— 'South Africa and the Suez Crisis', *International Journal*, Autumn 1961.

MONCRIEFF, A. and CALVOCORESSI, P., *Suez Ten Years After. Broadcasts from the B.B.C. Third Programme*, London, B.B.C., 1967.

MONROE, E., *Britain's Moment in the Middle East 1914–1956*, London, Chatto, 1963.

—— 'Suez Secrets: the Jigsaw Completed', *The Observer*, 24 July 1966, 9.

MORRIS, J., *The Market of Seleukia*, London, Faber, 1957.

MUGGERIDGE, M., 'Eden Agonistes', *New Statesman*, 8 December 1956, 736–7.

MURPHY, R., *Diplomat Among Warriors*, 457–79, London, Collins, 1964.

NASSER, G. A., 'My Revolutionary Life. My Side of Suez', *Sunday Times*, 24 June 1962, 21–2.

NICOLSON, N., *People and Parliament*, 106–65, London, Weidenfeld, 1958.

NIMER, B., 'Dulles, Suez and Democratic Diplomacy', *Western Political Quarterly*, September 1959.

NOLTE, R. H., 'Year of Decision in the Middle East', *Yale Review*, December 1956.

NUTTING, A., *I Saw for Myself. The Aftermath of Suez*, London, Hollis, 1958.

—— *No End of a Lesson. The Story of Suez*, London, Constable, 1967, reviewed by Nigel Nicolson, 'The Sneak' in *The New Statesman*, 30 June 1967, 908.

OWEN, J., 'The Polls and Newspaper Opinion of the Suez Crisis', *Public Opinion Quarterly*, Fall 1957.

PINEAU, C., 'Dix ans après. Si j'avais à refaire l'opération de Suez', *Le Monde*, 4 Novembre 1966, 4.

POLK, W. R., 'A Decade of Discovery: America in the Middle East, 1947–1958', *St. Antony's Papers, Number 11. Middle Eastern Affairs, Number 2*, London, Chatto, 1961, reprinted in *The United States and the Arab World*, Harvard University Press, 1965, 261–84.

QUILICI, F., *Le Pétrole et la Haine. Choses vues en terres d'Islam*, Paris, Fayard, 1957.

RAUSCHNING, D., 'Die Abwicklung des Suezkanalkonfliktes', *Jahrbuch für Internationales Recht*, Mai 1959.

ROBERTSON, T., *Crisis. The Inside Story of the Suez Conspiracy*, London, Hutchinson, 1964.

ROUGEMONT, D. DE, 'Sur Suez et ses environs historiques', *Preuves*, Octobre 1956.

SALMON, J., 'Les Opérations internationales de dégagement du Canal de Suez, *Annuaire Français de Droit International*, 1957.

SAMPSON, A., *Macmillan. A Study in Ambiguity*, 115–26, London, Lane, 1967.

SAVORY, D., 'Sequel to the Suez Crisis', *Contemporary Review*, February, May, August 1961.

SAWER, G., 'Problems of Australian Foreign Policy, June 1956–June 1957', *Australian Journal of Politics and History*, November 1957.

SCHRAMM, W., *One Day in the World's Press. Fourteen Great Newspapers on a Day of Crisis, November 2 1956*, Stanford University Press, 1959.

SEALE, P., *The Struggle for Syria. A Study of Post-War Arab Politics 1945–1958*, 247–82, 'Syria's Road to Suez', London, Oxford University Press, 1965.

SMITH, C. J., 'Suez and the Commando Carrier Concept', *Journal of the Royal United Service Institution*, February 1963.

SMOLANSKY, O. M., 'Moscow and the Suez Crisis, 1956: a Reappraisal', *Political Science Quarterly*, December 1965.

SPARROW, G., '*R.A.B.*' *Study of a Statesman*, 123–40, London, Odhams, 1965.

STANLEY, G. F. G., 'Failure at Suez', *International Journal*, Spring 1957.

STOCK, E., *Israel on the Road to Sinai 1949–1956*, Cornell University Press, 1967.

STOCKWELL, H., 'Suez from the Inside', *Sunday Telegraph*, 30 October, 6 and 13 November 1966.

STRANGE, S., 'Suez and After', *Yearbook of World Affairs*, 1957.

SWEET-ESCOTT, B., 'The Middle East since Suez', *World Today*, December 1957.

THOMAS, H., *The Suez Affair*, London, Weidenfeld, 1967.

TOURNOUX, J. R., *Secrets d'État*, 147–79, Paris, Plon, 1960.

TRIBE, D., 'Suez: could it happen again?', *Twentieth Century*, Autumn 1966, 16–19.

UTLEY, T. E., *Not Guilty. The Conservative Reply*, London, MacGibbon, 1957.

VAUCHER, G., *Gamal Abdel Nasser et son équipe*, ii. 184–251, Paris, Julliard, 1960.

VENKATARAMANI, M. S., 'Oil and U.S. Foreign Policy during the Suez Crisis, 1956–7', *International Studies*, October 1960.

VERITY, F., *Guilty Men of Suez*, London, Truth, 1957.

VERNANT, J., 'Frankreichs Haltung in der Suez-Krise', *Europa-Archiv*, 9429–32, 20 Dezember 1956.

WATERFIELD, G., 'Suez and the Role of Broadcasting', *The Listener*, 29 December 1966, 947–9.

WATT, D. C., 'Was Eden Right About Nasser?', *The Spectator*, 28 October 1966, 538.

WEBSTER, C. K., 'After the Suez Crisis: Problems Before Us', *The Listener*, 13 December 1956, 971–2.

WINT, G. and CALVOCORESSI, P., *Middle East Crisis*, London, Penguin, 1957.

WRIGHT, Q., 'Intervention, 1956', *American Journal of International Law*, April 1957.

YOUNG, WAYLAND, 'Psychopolitics', *Socialist Commentary*, January 1957.

—— 'London Letter', *Kenyon Review*, Spring 1957, reprinted with the preceding article in *Thirty-Four Articles*, 35–44, London, Weidenfeld, 1965.

THE ECONOMIC ASPECTS OF THE SUEZ CRISIS

'Aftermath of Suez', *Far Eastern Economic Review*, 14 February 1957.

BARJOT, P., 'Suez, Complexe Orient-Occident', *Revue Maritime*, Décembre 1956.

BES, J., 'De betekenis van het Suezkanaal voor de Tankvaart', *De Blauwe Wimpel*, no. 11, 328–32, 1956.

'The Canal and the Cape. Costs of Diversion', *Manchester Guardian*, 19 September 1956, 6–7.

CARFORA, G., 'Le consequenze economiche della crisi del Canale di Suez', *Rivista di Politica Economica*, Agosto 1956.

'The Cost of Suez. Economic Background of the Canal Dispute', *The Round Table*, December 1956.

'Economics of Super-tankers', *The Economist*, 4 August 1956.

FAMCHON, Y. and LERUTH, M., *L'Allemagne et le Moyen-Orient. Analyse d'une pénétration économique contemporaine*, Paris, Éditions des Relations Internationales, 1957.

FRANKEL, P. H., 'Oil Supplies during the Suez Crisis—On Meeting a Political Emergency', *Journal of Industrial Economics*, February 1958.

GASCUEL, J., 'L'Économie Française au lendemain de la Crise de Suez', *Politique Étrangère*, 1957.

HELANDER, S., 'Der Suezkanal in seiner gegenwärtigen weltwirtschaftlichen und weltpolitischen Bedeutung', *Wirtschaftsdienst*, Juni 1957.

LEMAIRE, M., 'Les Routes du Pétrole', *Revue des Deux Mondes*, 15 Janvier 1957.

LENCZOWSKI, G., *Oil and State in the Middle East*, 319–50, 'Repercussions of the Suez Crisis', Cornell University Press, 1960.

LEVY, W. J., 'Issues in International Oil Policy', *Foreign Affairs*, April 1957.

LUBELL, H., 'Middle East Crises and World Petroleum Movements', *Middle East Affairs*, November 1958.

—— *Middle East Oil Crises and Western Europe's Energy Supplies*, Baltimore, Johns Hopkins Press, 1963.

MALLAKH, R. El, and McGUIRE, C., 'The Economics of the Suez Canal under U.A.R. Management', *Middle East Journal*, Spring 1960.

'Middle East Oil. Europe's Lifeblood?', *The Banker*, November 1956.

MOUNTJOY, A. B., 'The Suez Canal at Mid-Century', *Economic Geography*, April 1958.

MURPHY, C. J. V., 'Oil East of Suez', *Fortune*, October 1956.

MUSSET, R., 'La Crise de Suez et la Pétrole. Ses Enseignements', *Annales de Géographie*, Mars 1959.

Organisation for European Economic Cooperation, *Eighth Report. Europe Today and in 1960*, Paris, O.E.E.C., 1957, I, *Europe To-Day*, 55–63, 'The Economic Impact of the Suez Crisis'.

Organisation for European Economic Cooperation, *Europe's Need for Oil. Implications and Lessons of the Suez Crisis*, Paris, O.E.E.C., 1958.

PIERREIN, L., 'Marseille et le Canal de Suez', *Annales de la Faculté des Lettres d'Aix*, 1956.

'Répercussions de l'affaire de Suez sur l'Économie Française', *Le Canal de Suez*, 9705–6, 15 Janvier 1957.

ROBERTSON, C. L., *The Emergency Oil Lift to Europe in the Suez Crisis*, Inter-University Case Series, No. 86, Indianapolis, Bobbs-Merrill, 1965.

SABBAN, G. EL, 'The Aswan High Dam', *Middle Eastern Affairs*, December 1955.

SHWADRAN, B., 'Oil in the Middle East Crisis', *International Journal*, Winter 1956–7, reprinted in *The Middle East, Oil and the Great Powers 1959*, 450–61, New York Council for Middle Eastern Affairs Press, 1959 revised edition.

SOUBEYROL, J., 'La Condition Juridique des Pipe-Lines en Droit International', *Annuaire Français de Droit International*, 1958.

United Nations Monthly Bulletin of Statistics, December 1956, 'The Importance of the Suez Canal in World Trade'.

United Nations Department of Economic and Social Affairs, *Economic Survey of Europe in 1956*, iii. 33–7, 'The Impact of the Suez Crisis', Geneva, 1957.

United Nations Department of Economic and Social Affairs, *Economic Developments in the Middle East 1955–1956. Supplement to World Economic Survey, 1956*, 99–112, 'Preliminary Review of the Economic Impact of the Suez Canal Crisis on the Middle East', New York, 1957.

'Via Suez', *The Economist*, 4 August 1956.

WOODRUFF, W. and MCGREGOR, L., *The Suez Canal and the Australian Economy*, Melbourne University Press, 1957.

WORSWICK, G. D. N. and ADY, P. H., *The British Economy in the Nineteen-Fifties*, 38–41, Oxford, Clarendon Press, 1962.

WOUTERS, H. E., 'The Suez Canal Crisis—and its Consequences', Supplement to *Capital*, 20 December 1956.

Burlo

oute pro

Tanta

xandria Cairo

Railway

Nile

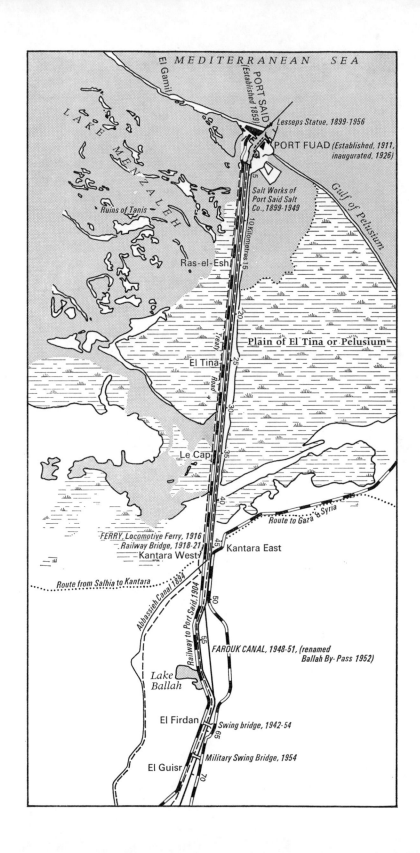

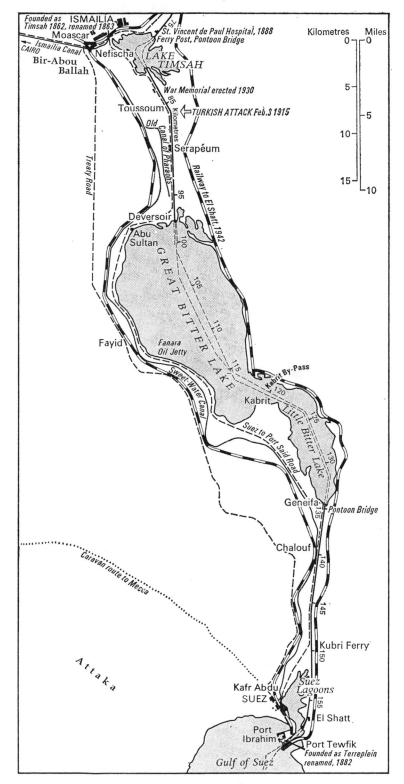

Map 2 The Suez Canal

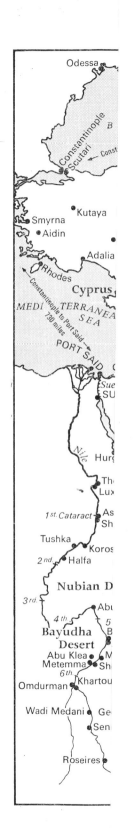

INDEX

Abadan crisis (1951), 669, 674–9, 683–6, 743
Abadan Refinery, 520–1, 532, 535, 566–72, 614, 630, 653, 675–6, 679, 684
Abbas Bazaar, 402
Abbas Hilmi, 435, 438, 469–70, 503, 508, 518, 532, 533, 590
Abbas Hilmi Basin, 404, 504
Abbas Pasha, 28, 33, 66, 425
Abbassieh Canal, 403–4, 671
Abboud Pasha, Ahmed Mohamed, 673, 702
Abd el Kadr, 42, 59, 67, 69
Abdul Aziz, Sultan, 60, 81, 84, 88, 243
Abdul Hamid II, Sultan, 274, 296
Abegg, L., 781
Abel, F., 445, 446
Aberdeen, 348
Aberdeen White Star Line, 343
Abqaiq, 658
Abs, H. J., 723, 787
Absolom, J., 28
Abu Ageila, 661
Abu Ballah, Bir, 67
Abu Simbel, 5
Abu Sueir, 566, 622, 698
Abu Sultan, 622
Abu Zenima, 515, 567, 579, 583, 586, 614, 626
Achilles, 182
Achin, 142, 176
Achinese War, 176, 276, 446
Achmet Jemal Pasha, 534–5, 537, 543, 544
Achnacarry Agreement, (1928), 571
Acker, J., 786
Aconcagua, 347
Acre, 16, 270, 401, 517
Acre–Kuwait railway, 151, 270
Acton, Lord, 483
Adabiya Bay, 626, 698
Adams, F., 388
Adams, H., 405
Adams, M., 726, 739, 790
Adams, R. E. C., 548
Adams, S., 717, 790
Adams, V., 597
Addis Ababa, 432, 603
Adelaide, 10, 34, 186, 345, 346, 347, 436, 525
Aden, 99
Aden:
a coaling station, 8; occupied, 13; supplied via the Cape, 18; used by French, 1845–83, 23, 326; becomes a base of Parsi merchants, 38, and of P. & O., 36; rediscovers water-tanks, 37; acquires branch line to Mauritius, 63; transformed by opening of Canal, 131, 136–7, 201; threatened by rivals, 103–4, 110–11, and by Turkey, 136; becomes an entrepôt, 136, 401, and a cable station, 159–60, 186; linked to Zanzibar and Cape, 204–10; deepens harbour, 251; recognized as boundary of Indian Empire, 251–2; fortified, 24, 131, 268, 301, 333, 432; acquires cable to Cape, 272; extends

influence, 300; increases rivals, 326; acquires oil bunkers, 522, 569, and ferry service to Bombay, 523, 581; threatened by Turkey, 532, 536; enjoys wartime boom in 1935, 601; transferred to Foreign Office, 606, 609; captures tourist traffic of Port Said, 743
Aden, Gulf of, 136, 621
  Little, 684
  Municipality, 708
  Port Trust, 382
  Protectorate, 432, 532, 607
  Refinery, 678, 684–5, 686
  Supreme Court, 683–4
Adonis, 103
Adowa, 454, 594, 599
Adria, 141
Adriatic & Oriental Steam Navigation Company, 75, 139
Adriatic route, 19, 23, 117, 140, 538, 737. *See also* Austrian Lloyd, Trieste, Venice
Adriatica Line, 595
Adye, J. M., 286
Afghan Wars, (1839–42), 17; (1878–9), 268, 328
Afghanistan, 13, 627
Afifi, M. el H., 790
Africa, 196, 264–5, 432–3, 740
Africa, (1865), 100, 104
Africa, (1870), 186
Africa, (1871), 119, 207
Africa, Committee of French, 427, 529
Africa, partition of, 273, 433
African Committee, French National, 256
Africana, 107
Afrique, 104, 111
Agadir crisis (1911), 518
Agamemnon, 181, 183
Agar-Hamilton, J. A. I., 628
Agnes, 186
Ahmad, Sheikh, of Kuwait, 680
Ahmadi, 680
Ahmed, J. M., 772
Aida, 87, 134–5, 240, 415
Aigle, 85, 86, 179
air transport:
  air attacks on Canal, 537, 540; 621–4, 625–7, 629; 729; air fields in isthmus, 553, 661, 729; air mail, 553, 558, 581; air power, Italian, 595, 602, 606, 616, 625; air travel, 656
Aitchison, C. U., 134
Aitchison, J. H., 790
Aitken, Lilburn & Co., 203
Aiton, W., 70
Aix, 399
Ajax, 76
Akaba, 22, 532, 534, 558, 624, 661, 669
Akaba–Ascalon canal, 56
Akaba–Beirut railway, 499

Red Sea:
studied by Marston, 737; unbearable heat, 20, 590; peculiarities of navigation, 7, 195; leads to Holy Places of Islam, 41; lacks lighthouses until 1862, 38, 63, 400; coveted by France, 4; navigated by steam, 8, by P. & O., 18, and by Messageries, 63; first coaling-station, 13; exit secured by England, 42; attracts French interest, 56, 62; acquires indigenous steam navigation company, 57, and first cable, 58; made an English lake by P. & O., 73; enjoys wartime boom in 1868, 78; acquires second cable, 78; extends tidal influence to Bitter Lakes, 81–2, 105, 398; attracts Greek traders, 93, and Continental ironclads, 97; facilitates southward extension of Anglo-French rivalry, 111; arouses interest of Italy, 103–4, Turkey, Netherlands, 104 and Austria, 207; main sphere of the trade of Suez, 129; becomes a through-way, 130–7, 468, and a zone of Turco-Egyptian expansion, 134–5,

854 *Index*